BRIEF CONTENTS

MANAGEMENT INFORMATION SYSTEMS

Strategy and Action

SECOND EDITION

Charles Parker
Thomas Case

Mitchell McGRAW-HILL

New York St. Louis San Francisco Auckland Bogotá Caracas
Lisbon London Madrid Mexico Milan Montreal New Delhi Paris
San Juan Singapore Sydney Tokyo Toronto Watsonville

Mitchell **McGRAW-HILL**
Watsonville, CA 95076

MANAGEMENT INFORMATION SYSTEMS, Second Edition
International Editions 1993

1 2 3 4 5 6 7 8 9 0 KKP UPE 9 8 7 6 5 4 3

ISBN 0-07-048573-9

Sponsoring editor: Erika Berg
Editorial assistant: Jennifer Gilliland
Director of production: Jane Somers
Project managers: Jonathan Peck and Joan Keyes,
                 Jonathan Peck Typographers
Copyeditor: Karen Richardson, Convert-It!
Interior designer: Susan Vaughan
Cover designer: John Edeen
Cover photo: Ed Honowitz, Tony Stone Worldwide
Composition: Jonathan Peck Typographers
Illustrator: Carl Yoshihara
Technical reviewers: Anne McClanahan
                     Ken Kozar

Library of Congress Card Catalog No. 92-64185

When ordering this title, use ISBN 0-07-113581-2

Printed in Singapore

DETAILED CONTENTS

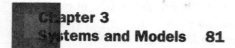

Chapter 8
Telecommunications   335

Chapter 11
Knowledge-Based Systems   477

Chapter 12
Office Information Systems   511

Chapter 19
Selected Issues in MIS Management 805

PREFACE TO THE INSTRUCTOR

Advances in information technology (IT) continue to accelerate. To be competitive in such a dynamic environment, today's graduates can expect to be challenged daily to keep pace with the technical and managerial issues and opportunities surrounding the development and use of information systems. This book is designed for business students and information systems majors who need to understand the emerging role of information systems in business.

Information is the lifeblood of an organization. As managers, graduates will depend on accurate, accessible and useful information. They will depend on information systems to be responsive to their unique information needs, to empower them to think and act strategically, develop effective plans, and make decisions that increase their own and their organization's competitiveness.

Management Information Systems: Strategy and Action, Second Edition, recognizes that access to the right information at the right time is pivotal to developing a strategic posture that exploits opportunities and thwarts threats posed by the dynamic business environment of the 1990s.

MAJOR THEMES OF THIS TEXT

To prepare graduates to meet the challenges of the 1990s, the following themes guided the development of this text:

Corporate Strategy

Most organizations are guided by a corporate strategy. Increasingly, IT plays a crucial role in the development and implementation of such strategies. The importance of strategy, critical success factors, and competitive applications of IT is a theme of this text, and demonstrates IT's potential to enhance management's productivity, operational efficiency, and the overall effectiveness of organizations.

Bias Toward Action

Ultimately, people - managers, users, and IS specialists working together are responsible for the success or failure of an information system. Therefore this text balances technical issues with managerial issues. This theme is punctuated by:

- the integrated use of real-world examples throughout the text

- boxed feature articles highlighting the issues surrounding IT in a broad spectrum of organizations

- case studies illustrating how actual businesses have applied IT to enhance their competitive advantage

Networking and International Issues

As international competition increases, organizations have become increasingly alert to opportunities to integrate computing and communication technologies in new and innovative ways. As a result, organizations have managed to increase their productivity and market share, improve and expand product lines, and leverage existing services on both domestic and international fronts. While the focus of Chapter 8, the pervasive nature of networking, the emergence of global information systems, and associated management issues are addressed throughout this book.

CURRENT COVERAGE

All of the topics of concern to tomorrow's managers are covered in this text. The following figure summarizes many of them.

Topic	Primary Coverage
Backbone networks	Chapter 8
CASE technology	Chapters 6, 14, 15, and 16
CISC versus RISC processors	Chapter 5
Client-server systems	Chapter 8
Computer security	Chapters 16 and 19
Critical success factors	Chapters 3 and 18
Data administration	Chapter 7
Database management	Chapter 7
Distributed systems	Chapter 8, and throughout the text
Distributed databases	Chapter 7
Downsizing	Chapter 18, and throughout the text
EDI	Chapters 8, 9, 13, and throughout the text
End-user development	Chapter 17
Ethical issues	Chapters 6 and 19
Expert systems/AI	Chapter 11
Ergonomics	Chapters 2 and 15
Executive information systems	Chapter 10
External databases	Chapters 7, 8, and 10
Fourth generation languages	Chapters 6, 10, 15, 16, and 17
Fuzzy logic systems	Chapter 11
Global networks	Chapters 8, 18, and 19
Graphical user interfaces	Chapter 6
GDSSs	Chapter 10
Groupware	Chapters 10 and 12
Imaging systems	Chapters 5 and 12

Topic	Primary Coverage
Information centers	Chapter 17
Intelligent copiers	Chapter 12
International issues	Chapters 8, 18, 19, and throughout the text
Interorganizational MISs	Chapters 1, 3, 7, 8, 12, 18, and 19
ISDN	Chapter 8
JAD	Chapter 15
Local area networks	Chapters 5 and 8
Management of quality	Chapters 3, 4, and 12
MRP II	Chapter 13
Multimedia systems	Chapter 7
Natural language systems	Chapters 6, 11, and 12
Network management	Chapters 8, and 19
Network operating systems	Chapters 5 and 8
Neural networks	Chapter 11
Object-oriented programming	Chapters 6, 15, and 16
Optical disk technologies	Chapters 5 and 12
Outsourcing	Chapters 6 and 18
Parallel processing	Chapters 5 and 6
Personal digital assistants	Chapter 12
Pen-based computers	Chapter 5
Prototyping	Chapters 14, 15, 16, and 17
RAD	Chapter 15
RAID systems	Chapter 5
Robotics	Chapters 11 and 14
Smart-card systems	Chapter 5
Strategic MISs	Chapter 1, 18, and throughout the text
Strategic planning	Chapters 3 and 18
SQL	Chapter 7
Telecommunications	Chapter 8
Telecommuting	Chapter 12
Teleconferencing	Chapter 12
Voice-based systems	Chapters 5, 11, and 12
Wide area networks	Chapters 8 and 19
Wireless networks	Chapter 8

PRIMARY CHANGES

The reception to the First Edition of **Management Information Systems: Strategy & Action** was overwhemingly positive. Adopters and reviewers have helped us keep pace with their students' needs and course objectives. Below is a summary of their primary suggestions and how we've responded in the Second Edition.

Suggested Change	**Our Response**
Increase emphasis on managerial issues	Increased emphasis throughout the text, especially in chapters 14-17
Reduce coverage of hardware details	Consolidated and updated previous chapters 5 and 8 into new Chapter 5
Integrate coverage of distributed systems and networking	Coverage integrated throughout the text, especially in chapters 8, 18, 19
Increase coverage of EDI and inter-organizational systems	Expanded coverage in chapters 8, 9, 18, and 19 demonstrates strategic importance of electronic links between firms
Highlight international issues where most relevant	Examples of international issues added to each chapter; expanded coverage in chapters 8, 18, and 19 illustrates the role of global networking in multinational firms
Alert students to the ethical issues raised by the use of information technology	Expanded coverage of ethics in chapters 6 and 19; examples interspersed throughout the text
Include coverage of GDSS, groupware, and workgroup computing	New coverage added to chapters 10 and 12 illustrate the types of systems available to support work-group activities
Increase coverage of downsizing and outsourcing	New coverage added to Chapter 18 illustrates why these are key managerial issues for the 1990s
Increase emphasis on the use of information systems in small business	Several new end-of-chapter cases stress small business issues; more small business examples integrated throughout the text
Improve text design	New design of figures makes the subject easier and more interesting to understand

FLEXIBLE, MODULAR ORGANIZATION

The modular approach of this book provides maximum instructional flexibility. The text is divided into six parts:

Part One: Introduction covers the major roles played by information systems and how they have emerged as strategic weapons in the corporate arsenal. MIS fundamentals along with examples illustrating the goals and potential benefits of information systems are included.

Part Two: People, Organizations, Systems, and Management covers the role of people and human factors in information systems, how information systems vary across different types of organizations, how organizational systems can help develop and implement long-range plans to compete in our dynamic business environment, and how information systems can help managers make effective decisions and fulfill the many roles they are asked to play.

Part Three: Information Technology Concepts overviews fundamental hardware, software, database management, and telecommunications concepts that are important for the manager of the 1990s to understand.

Part Four: MIS in Practice addresses transaction processing systems, management reporting systems, decision support systems, workgroup support systems, executive information systems, knowledge-based systems, and office information systems. Information technology related to the functional areas of business are also discussed.

Part Five: Building MISs examines both traditional and emerging systems development practices. The roles of managers and users in systems development are emphasized as well as the importance of user training and the utilization of newer approaches that often enable organizations to implement new systems quickly and effectively.

Part Six: Information Systems Management covers several management-related topics including linking MIS plans with corporate strategic plans, international issues, downsizing, outsourcing, computer ethics, computer security, and future information technology developments.

This modular organization recognizes that various approaches are used to teach MIS, and enables instructors to customize the text to meet their specific course objectives.

INSTRUCTOR'S SUPPORTING MATERIALS

Management Information Systems: Strategy & Action, Second Edition, is accompanied by the following support materials:

Instructor's Manual The author-written Instructor's Manual contains lecture outlines, teaching tips and strategies, and answers to all review, discussion, and in-text case study questions for each chapter.

Transparency Masters A set of more than 100 ready-to-use transparency masters supports this text. The set includes figures in the text and original figures. The masters are keyed to the lecture outlines in the Instructor's Manual.

Computerized Test Bank The author-developed Test Bank, available in hardcopy and computerized formats, contains approximately 3000 true/false, multiple choice, fill-in, and matching questions.

Ethical Decision Making and Information Technology: An Introduction with Cases, by Kallman and Grillo is designed for use as a case study supplement in any MIS course. Chapter 1 defines ethics. Chapter 2 relates ethics to the use of IT. And by applying a 4-step analysis process to an ethical dilemma, Chapter 3 illustrates how to reach a defensible decision. The 18 cases that follow challenge students to apply the knowledge they've gained in chapters 1-3 to recognize, evaluate, and react responsibly to ethical dilemmas. Mitchell McGraw-Hill, 1993, ISBN: 0-07-033884-1.

ACKNOWLEDGMENTS

The efforts of countless people went into the creation of this book. Some of these people shared their experiences teaching and learning about management information systems. Others reviewed drafts of the current edition and offered helpful suggestions for improving the discussion and presenting the material. And, of course, still others were responsible for transforming the physical manuscript into this text.

We would particularly like to thank Efrem Mallach from University of Massachusetts, Lowell, for his extremely helpful and detailed reviews, and Anne McClannahan of Ohio University and Ken Kozar of University of Colorado, Boulder, for their technical reviews. Their ideas and suggestions played a key role shaping this second edition. We would also like to thank the following reviewers for their many helpful suggestions during the development of the second edition:

Dennis Adams,
University of Houston

Gary Armstrong,
Shippensburg University

Brent Bandy,
University of Wisconsin, Oshkosh

Glen Boyer,
Brigham Young University

Barbara Denison,
Wright State University

Carroll Frenzel,
University of Colorado, Boulder

Jane MacKay,
Texas Christian University

Betty Kleen,
Nicholls State University

Fred Kohun,
Robert Morris College

Ken Kozar,
University of Colorado, Boulder

Charles Lutz,
Utah State University

Efrem Mallach,
University of Massachusetts, Lowell

Anne McClannahan,
Ohio University

Ken McFarland,
Pepperdine University

William McHenry,
Georgetown University

Jamal Munshi,
Sonoma State University

Ryan Nelson,
University of Virginia

Peter Newson,
University of Western Ontario

Tom Philpott,
The University of Texas at Austin

William Shrode,
Florida State University

Hal Smith,
Brigham Young University

Jeff Smith,
Georgetown University

Jill Smith,
University of Denver

Robert Spillman,
Radford University

Collectively, these reviewers and their valuable comments strengthened the overall quality of this text.

We would like to thank Judy Shugart and the College of Business Office of Publications at Georgia Southern University for their efforts in different phases of preparing the manuscript. Kathy Ausherman, Barbara Focht, and Sandy Crutchfield from the Department of Management at Georgia Southern helped ensure that critical deadlines were met. At Mitchell Publishing, we are especially grateful for the efforts of Erika Berg, Jennifer Gilliland, Jane Somers, and John Ambrose. We are also indebted to copyeditor Karen Richardson from Convert-It!, and to Joan Keyes, Michael MacFall, Susan Vaughan and the staff of Jonathan Peck Typographers for the production of this book.

Charles Parker
Thomas Case

Part ONE
Introduction

Chapter 1
Introduction to Management
Information Systems

Chapter

Introduction to Management Information Systems

After completing this chapter, you will be able to:

Define management information system (MIS) and describe several types of information systems

Discuss specific purposes served by information systems

Name and describe the elements of a computer-based information system (CBIS)

Explain briefly how a computer system works

Discuss how the strategic use of information technology can help a company gain a competitive advantage

Identify the challenges facing the people who design, use, or approve information systems

Today, largely through advances in computer and communications technologies, we are living at a time that many people call the *information age*. One major reason our era is so named is because most working people today have jobs that are information-intensive. For example, jobs such as teacher, accountant, lawyer, and manager are all predominantly based on the handling of information. This emphasis differs from that of earlier decades, in which most jobs involved some type of physical labor applied on farms or in factories.

Since the late 1950s, the majority of the U.S. labor force has been employed in information-related jobs. By the late 1960s, nearly half of the Gross National Product (GNP) and over half of the labor income in the U.S. came from information-related activities. This shift from industrial and agricultural-related jobs to information-related jobs is by no means unique to the United States. Indeed, research investigations have observed parallel changes for other advanced nations around the globe, especially those in Europe and the Pacific Rim.

In his book *Powershift,* Alvin Toffler suggests that we are coming to the end of the information age and are beginning a new age of information processing and communications capabilities that is best described as the *knowledge age*. According to Toffler, *knowledge* is further refined information. Advanced computing approaches such as "intelligent" database management systems, multimedia systems, and knowledge-based systems (such as expert systems and artificial intelligence, neural networks, and other "fifth-generation" systems) are making it possible to manipulate and refine information into knowledge more easily than ever before. In their book *The Rise of the Expert Company*, Edward Feigenbaum, Pamela McCorduck, and H. Penny Nii predict that during the 1990s, the majority of the new computer applications developed for Fortune 1,000 companies will be knowledge-based systems. If they are right, Toffler's contentions will be supported.

As you will see from reading this text, information technologies continue to shape not only the way people perform work, but also the products that many businesses turn out and the manner in which many businesses compete. Once considered only a routine cost item for most companies in their paperwork handling, information processing has become a matter of strategic importance for most of today's organizations. In many industries—such as banking, insurance, and travel—it is virtually impossible for an organization to compete unless its customers are given the level of service that is possible only with high-technology systems. In addition, businesses in a variety of industries are using information technologies to both "lock in" their customers and "lock out" competitors.

In the area of communications, many medium- and large-sized organizations now recognize that they are competing in a global environment; aggressive market players must be connected to virtually everyone with whom they need to do business, no matter where they are located. Organizations that make the decision to develop multinational operations should do so with the knowledge that they will have to build global telecommunication networks to tie together information systems at the different locations.

The movement toward a global economy—or what some have called the "global village"—is evident in many unfolding trends:

- Global financing, in which deals involving the currencies and securities of several nations can be pulled together quickly.

- Global sourcing, wherein firms shop worldwide for low-priced raw materials or labor.

- Joint ventures plus research and development (R&D) efforts that cross both organizational and international boundaries.

Further evidence is provided in the number of organizations, both domestic and foreign, that are developing multinational operations. For example, according to James Budney, Dr. Paul Stern—president, CEO, and chairman of the board at Northern Telecom (a Canadian telecommunications equipment company)—states, "It is a major corporate objective to gain business at a greater rate internationally [outside of North America]." Today, even businesses that do not sell their products or services abroad are finding that they still must contend with foreign competitors. This requires the timely monitoring of such statistics as relative wage rates, exchange rates, interest rates, and public policies.

The primary purposes of this text are to encourage you to appreciate information as a key organizational resource and to help you understand the technologies and other forces that influence both how we obtain information and why we need it. Chances are that the profession you choose in life will depend heavily on the skillful use of information and knowledge—and that a sizable portion of this information will be computer-generated. You may (and, in fact, are likely to) have a desktop computer in your office that you will routinely use to retrieve, manipulate, or disseminate information. You may be a traveling salesperson with a laptop or notebook computer equipped with a modem for transmitting daily sales information back to the office. Or you may be an executive in a corporation whose very future hinges on strategically applying information technology in new and innovative ways. Any of these roles requires a working knowledge of information technology and its uses.

But learning about information systems is much more than merely learning about technology. In this text, we will also cover:

- The science and art of management and decision making.

- Psychological and behavioral issues that often determine the success or failure of an information system.

- Environmental and technological forces that create the opportunity to use information as a competitive weapon.
- How to build information systems in a sensible and manageable way.

Chapter 1 begins by defining what an information system is and describing its components. Information management, and the role computer technology plays in it, are discussed next. Finally, in the section entitled "Learning About Management Information Systems," we will look at critical information systems issues confronting organizations in the coming decade and some of the challenges associated with studying these systems. We will also examine why the study of information systems is not a tidy, easily mastered pursuit.

INTRODUCTION TO MANAGEMENT INFORMATION SYSTEMS

Management information systems (MIS) became a serious field of study largely because of the development of computers and computer-related technologies. MIS, like many other computer terms, represents an evolving concept. To fully appreciate what people might mean when they refer to the term *information system*, we need to first turn the calendar back a few years, to the early 1950s.

The Emergence of Management Information Systems

In June 1951, a memorable event took place in the history of modern computing. The U.S. Bureau of the Census purchased a computer called Univac I. This machine was the first electronic computer produced by a business machine company (Remington Rand) specifically for business purposes. Until that time, computers had been found only in laboratories, where they were used for scientific and defense work.

The predominant business applications of the 1950s were payroll, billing, and various other types of routine clerical and accounting operations. These *transaction processing* applications (so named because they involve the processing of financial accounting transactions and similar functions) were relatively easy to structure using the limited number of and typically hard-to-use computer languages of the 1950s. Also, these computer applications were relatively easy to cost justify to upper management. If, for example, a computer system could do the work of a hundred bookkeepers, each of whom earned $6,000 annually, a company would recover a cost of $600,000 within a year. The terms *electronic data processing (EDP)* and *automatic data processing (ADP)* were frequently used to describe business computing environments of the 1950s. As computers became more common, the "electronic" and "automated" adjectives were looked upon as redundant, and the term *data processing (DP)* evolved to describe both types of applications.

The first computers were failure-prone, difficult to operate, and—by today's standards—crawled along at a snail's pace. Computer professionals often had their hands full just in getting accurate paychecks and billing statements out on time. By the mid-1960s, however, the atmosphere was starting to change. Advances in disk technology made it possible to get to data faster and to access data in different ways. Programming languages improved dramatically, making it much easier to develop and code new applications. The development and refinement of **operating systems**—the programs that manage and control the operations of computer equipment—enabled computers to run with less manual intervention. Also, entering jobs from terminals at remote sites became commonplace. In general, people began to accept computers and to rely on the outputs that they produced.

Each of these developments—and others—contributed to the rise of the so-called management information system (MIS). During the 1960s and 1970s, this term was used in a very limited way to apply to the set of programs that generated periodic printed reports. The primary purpose of these reports was to help managers with decision making.

For example, one of the main jobs of the receivables component of the transaction processing system is to correctly calculate customer account balances and to produce customer statements reflecting those balances. However, receivables data can also be used to create reports and supply information to a variety of managers for decision-making purposes. A credit manager, for instance, could receive a monthly report showing the payment history of each customer. This report might help the credit manager decide which customers should be denied credit, which customers should receive credit-limit increases, which customers should be sent payment-reminder notices, and which customers should be handed over to a collection agency. From this same receivables data, a report might be generated for a marketing manager that provides both past and projected sales on each product; such information might lead the marketing manager to make better product promotion, selling, or performance-evaluation decisions. Several other managers in the organization might be on a distribution list to receive this same report, since sales trends are often of general interest because they are viewed as a barometer of the health of the organization. Other types of managers might benefit from reports derived from other data captured by the receivables system.

All of these early information systems were by-products of the transaction processing systems then in effect. The transaction processing component of the system provided the operational data needed to run the company efficiently on a day-to-day basis, and the management information systems component provided reports and information that enabled managers to make decisions more effectively. Unfortunately, these early information systems often had limited impact: They often possessed limited flexibility or were constrained to manipulating transaction processing data. Also, they frequently were not responsive to the information needs of particular individuals.

As management information systems became commonplace in industry during the late 1960s, many overzealous MIS professionals began pushing the concept of a "total information system"—that is, an enterprise-wide megasystem that could meet all of the firm's decision-making and transaction processing needs. These created grandiose expectations within organizations. When MIS professionals were unable to deliver on their promises, many line managers felt that the information systems concept was being oversold. Consequently, as failures began to occur and disappointments started to mount, the term "management information systems" came to take on a negative connotation. In fact, Russell Ackoff (a leading scholar) dourly referred to the MIS concept as "management misinformation systems."

Major developments in the 1970s included microcomputers, interactive display devices, bargain-basement price tags on computing equipment, "user-friendly" software, and improvements in database technology. These and other forces combined to pave the way for the decision support system (DSS). The management information systems of the 1960s had supplied a wide audience of decision makers with preplanned information in the form of periodically printed reports. In the 1970s and 1980s, decision support systems provided many of those same decision makers with easy-to-use computing and communications capabilities that could meet their individual information needs.

For instance, decision support systems enabled managers to sit at interactive display terminals or microcomputer workstations and search through databases for useful information relating to the decisions they must make. Easy-to-use modeling and analysis tools made it possible to graph data or perform computations. With a DSS, customized queries and reports can be generated at a manager's workstation—without the assistance of a computer professional. A current example is the popular spreadsheet package; a common component of many decision support systems.

Another development of the 1970s and 1980s—the increasing appearance of assorted computer and communications technologies in offices—also expanded the role of information systems. These **office automation (OA)** technologies include word processing, desktop publishing, electronic mail, facsimile, and several other computer- and communications-based processes. The integration of these technologies within a single office setting is now commonly called an office information system (OIS), which will be explained in more detail later.

The development of an OIS and a DSS has often been driven by the needs of users in the various departments and subunits of an organization. In many organizations, this has resulted in the creation of systems that meet local information and decision-making needs quite well. However, in some instances, such user-driven development has resulted in the creation of disparate "islands of technology." Today, one of the biggest challenges facing both MIS professionals and users is the integration of these systems with those used for mainstream information processing activities. Major initiatives are underway in many organizations in response to this challenge.

In the 1980s, information technologies took on a new role in organizations—that of a strategic weapon. One early reported case of the strategic use of information technology is that of McKesson, a large drug distributor. In the early 1980s, McKesson provided its drugstore clients with communications terminals, thereby making it convenient for them to place orders on McKesson's host computer. This move not only enabled McKesson to tie in its customer base more closely, but it also served to streamline the company's order processing operations and to temporarily lock out competitors. Although some of McKesson's key competitors did catch up, the heavy investment in technology was too much for many firms to bear. Consequently, when the wholesale drug market later quadrupled, McKesson's sales volume increased dramatically. As Robert Kelley, a management professor at Carnegie-Mellon University, commented regarding the lesson learned in the McKesson case, "What [many companies] overlook is that the technology can create larger markets."

Michael Parker and Victor Millar saw the information technology revolution as affecting competition in three important ways:

1. It changes industry structures, thereby altering the rules of competition.
2. It creates the opportunity for competitive advantage by providing new ways to outperform rivals.
3. It spawns whole new businesses, often from within a company's existing operations.

Throughout this text, we will explore the reasons why information technology has made such impacts on organizations and interorganizational competition. Many of the book's examples, boxed features, and cases are purposely included to illustrate these impacts and to help you understand how information technology has changed and will continue to change. We will also discuss how organizations can successfully operate and compete by using up-to-date information technology methods.

What is a Management Information System?

The preceding historical developments are noteworthy because they lay the groundwork for the definition of management information systems that we will use in this text. These historical perspectives will also help you to appreciate the basis for alternative definitions that are frequently found in the professional literature devoted to this subject.

In this text, we consider a **management information system (MIS)** to be any system that provides people with either data or information relating to an organization's operations. Management information systems support the activities of employees, owners, customers, and other key people in the organization's environment—either by efficiently processing data to assist with the transaction work load or by effectively supplying information to authorized people in a timely manner. For example, the transaction processing (data processing) systems that perform accounting and clerical functions are information systems. So, too, are the systems that generated the periodic, preplanned reports characterizing the 1960s (which we will call **management reporting systems (MRS)** from now on). Decision support systems, office information systems, and knowledge-based systems should also be viewed as facets of an organization's information system, along with interorganizational *electronic data interchange (EDI)* systems that strategically link a firm to its customers or suppliers.

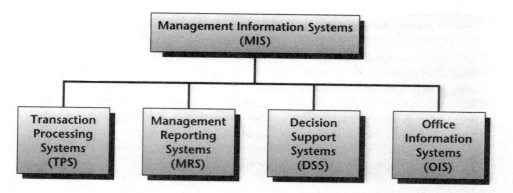

Figure 1.1 MIS subsystems. Knowledge-based systems such as artificial intelligence (AI) and expert systems (ES) are also information systems, but are not depicted as separate subsystems because they may be used in conjunction with a TPS, MRS, DSS, and OIS.

MIS Subsystems

In order to implement this definition, we can think of the MIS effort in an organization as composed of the following four subsystems (see Figure 1.1):

- *Transaction processing systems* A firm's **transaction processing systems (TPS)** comprise the routine, day-to-day accounting operations that have been an important part of most firms' computer processing since the early 1950s. These "paperwork processing" operations—many of which provide linkages among the customer, organization, warehouse, and factory—include accounts receivable, accounts payable, inventory control, and many other operations. Activities comprising the transaction processing function, and the relationship of these activities to each other, will be covered in detail in Chapter 9.

- *Management reporting systems* A management reporting system (MRS) generates the preplanned printed reports that began to evolve in the 1960s for decision-making purposes. As mentioned earlier, reports produced through an MRS are commonly by-products of the extensive and detailed databases assembled by transaction processing systems. Typically, the facts contained in these reports consist of routine summary and exception information about organizational operations. Another term that has been used quite commonly for this type of system is *information reporting system (IRS)*; this term is often attributed to Robert Zmud. During the 1960s, an organization's MIS largely consisted of its transaction processing and management reporting systems. As noted previously, MIS took on a negative connotation in many organizations during the 1960s due to limitations of the MRS and the overcommitments of zealous MIS professionals. In order to distinguish between our umbrella concept of MIS (as depicted in Figure 1.1) and the more restrictive definition of MIS prevalent in the 1960s and 1970s, we will use the term "management reporting system" to refer to the MIS subcomponents that generate preplanned reports for managers. Like the TPS, the MRS will be covered in more detail in Chapter 9.

■ **Decision support systems** A **decision support system (DSS)** provides a set of easy-to-use modeling, retrieving, and reporting capabilities so that people can generate the information they feel will be useful to them when making decisions. For instance, a DSS might allow a manager to sit at an interactive terminal and browse through data, analyze them, and create specially tailored reports. Rather than consisting of a semi-frozen set of data or information outputs, as the TPS and MRS do, the DSS provides tools for enhancing user decision making. Further development of the DSS, coupled with the trend toward networking personal computers, have resulted in *group decision support systems (GDSS)* that support the activities and decision making of entire work teams, rather than just individuals. Group decision support systems and decision support systems are covered further in Chapter 10, along with the related topic of *executive information systems (EIS)*, which assist top-level managers in carrying out their responsibilities.

■ **Office information systems** Office information systems (OIS) include the use of such computer-based, office-oriented technologies as word processing, desktop publishing, electronic mail, video teleconferencing, and so on. Of all the components that fall under the MIS umbrella, the OIS area is the least uniform, overlapping to a great extent with TPS, MRS, and especially DSS. The OIS and its associated technologies will be covered more extensively in Chapter 12.

Because knowledge-based systems have become key parts of an organization's subsystems, they are not considered to be in a separate subset of MIS. Both *expert systems (ES)* and *artificial intelligence (AI)* are knowledge-based systems that mimic human decision-making processes. An ES is typically a rule-based system that solves problems in a manner similar to a human expert's methods. AI includes robotics and applications such as vision inspection systems for spotting defects as products roll off manufacturing assembly lines. These technologies are expected to blossom as business applications during the rest of this century. ES and AI applications will be covered more fully in Chapter 11, along with other knowledge-based systems such as *neural networks*.

As you read through MIS literature, you will uncover other definitions for the systems just mentioned and a much broader range of implementations. Some individuals who recall the inflexible management reporting systems of the 1960s think only of management information systems in terms of fixed-format reports and fail to include DSS, OA, ES, and AI under the MIS umbrella. However, in this text, the terms "information systems" and "management information systems" usually are interchangeable. While subtle differences between them do exist, virtually all information systems used in organizational environments are somehow connected with some form of management activity.

Strictly speaking, an MIS need not be computerized. However, especially in large organizations, they almost always are. Even in small firms, the low cost of microcomputers has made computer-based information systems an increasingly widespread reality. This growing pervasiveness of computer-based information systems has been spurred by continual declines in information processing costs. Joanne Yates and Robert Benjamin estimate that the cost of information technology decreases by about 30 percent a year. Also, according to Michael Porter and Victor Millar, the cost of computer information processing relative to manual information processing has become at least 8,000 times less expensive over the last 30 years. Therefore, because of the ever-increasing use of computers in organizational settings, the terms "management information system" and "information system" refer to computer-based processes in this text—unless we specifically state otherwise.

INFORMATION RESOURCE MANAGEMENT: AN INTRODUCTION

Most large organizations recognize information as a corporate resource of considerable value. Throughout this text, we will also consider information as a precious resource and look at a number of ways in which this resource can be effectively used by organizations.

Data Versus Information

Many people use the terms **data** and **information** synonymously. To technology professionals, however, there is a distinct and important difference. Data refer to facts. (Note that data is the plural form of datum; many people mistakenly treat data as a singular noun.) When data are filtered through one or more processors so that they take on both meaning and value to a person, they become information. Information, rather than data, is what people use to make decisions. Figure 1.2 helps illustrate these differences, but let's look at a few additional examples to clarify this distinction.

Virtually any fact is an example of data. For instance, the names and phone numbers of all students at Colorado State University and the details regarding flights departing and arriving daily at New York City's JFK airport are each examples of data. When a person calls a local airline agent about flying from JFK to Phoenix, both the agent and the client are interested in extracting information from the large bank of airline data available. They want to know, for instance, the price and availability of specific seats on specific dates for specific times be-

Data Versus Information	
Data are . . .	Information is . . .
▨ stored facts	▨ presented facts
▨ inactive (they exist)	▨ active (it enables doing)
▨ technology-based	▨ business-based
▨ gathered from various sources	▨ transformed from data

Figure 1.2 Some of the differences between data and information. (Adapted from Christoff)

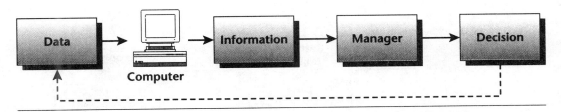

Figure 1.3 The processing of data into information. Both computers and human minds can transform data into useful information. As information is used to make decisions, it too eventually becomes part of the data pool for future decision making (shown by the dashed line).

tween two specific cities. Knowing how to find the right types of information for clients quickly is vital to the airline agency business.

In the examples just provided, both the computer and the human mind act as processors that select data and transform them into meaningful information. As information is generated from data, it too eventually becomes part of the data store. This data processing–information cycle is shown in Figure 1.3. Some of the types of information that may be provided to decision makers after data are transformed into information by computers is depicted in Figure 1.4. The format of the information received is often dictated by the needs and preferences of decision makers.

What is Information Resource Management?

Because so many of an organization's key operations and decision-making processes depend on the use of information, many firms perceive it as a key resource. One example is the travel agent just discussed, whose skillful handling of information can gain or lose bookings. Thus—along with such ordinary tangible assets as property, plant, equipment, personnel, and financial resources—information and knowledge have substantial value to organizations.

The term used to describe this view of information is **information resource management (IRM)**: a concept that recognizes information as a key resource that should (as should any vital resource) be properly managed. Other fields also think of their assets in this way. For example, the business fields of organizational behavior and human resource management are based on the recognition of an organization's employees as key assets.

In IRM-oriented firms, information is seen as a desirable investment that can be used strategically to provide a competitive edge, rather than only as a necessary expense that must be controlled. Within such firms, MIS is perceived as an area that can generate opportunities or value for the organization, not merely as a source of problems.

Because MIS is seen as playing a pivotal role in the future successes of IRM-oriented firms, the person in charge of the MIS area is often found at the vice-presidential level. This person—who may hold the title of **chief informa-**

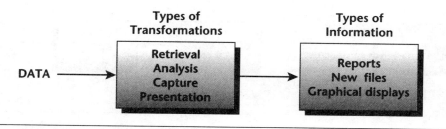

Figure 1.4 Some of the types of information that may be provided to managers and users as a result of the data processing–information cycle shown in Figure 1.3. (Adapted from Christoff)

tion officer (CIO)—usually reports to the firm's **chief executive officer (CEO)** or company head. In this position, the MIS department head participates in strategic planning and other key decisions that are made by the organization's top-level managers.

Goals of Information Systems

Now that we have defined information, explored its potential value to an organization, and enumerated the components of an MIS, let's examine the specific purposes served by information systems. The following are some ways in which information systems can help an organization; they are summarized in Figure 1.5.

Operational Efficiency

Operational efficiency refers to doing routine tasks better, faster, or cheaper. The oldest MIS subsystem, transaction processing, has served this purpose admirably for many years. For instance, large organizations would have to staff a prohibitive number of clerks, at an astronomical cost, if documents such as bills and paychecks had to be prepared manually instead of by using computerized a TPS. Also, even using all these additional people probably would not match the speed at which such tasks could be completed by using computer technology.

Inventory control personnel use the computer to help cut the costs of carrying inventory. A method that companies traditionally have used to reduce inventory holding costs is to apply computer-driven mathematical models that find optimum inventory levels for their stock. A more recent method, however, is for companies to pass inventory holding costs back to suppliers by connecting those suppliers to their own private communications networks; the company can then order inventory as needed. One large automobile manufacturer, for example, requires its suppliers to carry certain minimum levels of inventory—or else risk being dropped from its supplier list.

Another prime area for operational efficiency is the office. For instance, word processors greatly increase typing efficiency, especially if the documents being typed sometimes need to be revised. Also, many firms claim that office

Benefits of Information Systems
▓ Operational efficiency
▓ Functional effectiveness
▓ Spotting and taking advantage of opportunities
▓ Better service
▓ Product creation and improvement
▓ Altering the basis of competition
▓ Client lock-in
▓ Competitor lock-out

Figure 1.5 Benefits of information systems. Any (or all) of these benefits can be gained through the effective use of information systems.

technologies such as desktop publishing and computerized presentation graphics have substantially saved both time and money by facilitating in-house document preparation.

Functional Effectiveness

Whereas a TPS is predominantly oriented toward satisfying efficiency objectives, a DSS is often oriented toward *functional effectiveness*—for example, toward helping managers make better decisions or helping salespeople close sales with clients.

American Express, for instance, chose to use artificial intelligence to improve the effectiveness of the credit-authorization function that's used when merchants call for approval. The system, dubbed Authorizer's Assistant, pulls together the skills of the company's best credit managers and embeds these skills in software. Authorizer's Assistant is specifically tailored to flag situations that human authorizers are likely to miss. One internal study performed soon after the system was installed indicated that the system had reduced the number of approved transactions ending up as bad debts by 50 percent.

Information available to salespeople at the point of sale can also improve effectiveness. A large hospital, for example, considered switching from a Merck & Co. antibiotic to a competitive product that was half the price. While at the client site, the Merck salesperson—armed with a laptop computer that tied into a central database—searched clinical and lab studies from the Food & Drug Administration and found that the competing drug had not been consistently effective in treating gynecological infections. Because of literally having this research data at their fingertips, the salesperson and Merck kept the account.

In the public sector, decision support systems were developed that use models to predict how forest fires will spread and how various fire-fighting tactics will work. These systems have increased fire-fighting effectiveness. One Idaho blaze, for example, cost the U.S. Forest Service $400,000 to extinguish versus an estimated $3.7 million it would have cost if conventional, manual decision-making tools were used.

Using Information Technology to Improve Customer Service

As markets grow tighter and more competitive, and as product life cycles shorten, an increasing number of businesses are counting on superior customer service to help them compete.

". . . USING INFORMATION TECHNOLOGY TO PROVIDE BETTER CUSTOMER SERVICE CAN BE AN EXCELLENT INVESTMENT."

Customer service used to mean getting the customer the right product at the right time and giving refunds with a smile to disgruntled buyers. Now, it means pleasing buyers in many ways. For example, customers may want to choose from a wide variety of products and options; some may want to order electronically, pay by charge card, and have goods delivered immediately.

Information technology can provide the flexibility and service that customers are increasingly demanding and can ensure that key accounts are not lost. Because gaining a new customer can cost up to five times more than retaining an existing one, using information technology to provide better customer service can be an excellent investment.

Information systems can be used in numerous ways to provide better customer service. Whirlpool Corporation, for example, integrated imaging, artificial intelligence, and other technologies to provide speedy customer response. Publisher Simon and Schuster developed an automated 24-hour touch-tone order-entry system that handles routine price and availability inquiries. Such service-oriented systems should become increasingly common.

Adapted from Slater (1992).

Quality Customer Service

Few examples better illustrate the importance of information technologies in providing improved service to customers than the automatic teller machines (ATMs) used by most banks and the reservations systems used by travel agents.

ATMs enable bank depositors to withdraw money 24 hours a day, 7 days a week. Also, they promote operational efficiency by cutting personnel costs. ATM-like services abound in other industries as well: kiosks are used at ski slopes and subway stations to dispense tickets, at convenience stores to rent videotapes, and at gas stations to sell gas.

Currently, two systems—United Airlines' Apollo and American Airlines' Sabre—control more than two-thirds of the U.S. airlines reservations market. These and other reservations systems not only provide travel agents with the types of information they need to best support their customers, but they also offer other types of services to adopting agencies, such as the ability to make a customer's car rental and hotel reservations. American Airlines' Sabre system has been so successful that *Computerworld* quoted company chairman Robert Crandall as remarking, "If you told me I had to sell either the airline or the system, I'd probably sell the airline."

Product Creation and Enhancement

In some industries—notably banking, insurance, financial services, and travel—information is often a major force in creating the product being sold. For instance, it is typically the effective use of information that distinguishes a good investment portfolio from a bad one, or that separates a well-designed travel itinerary from one with long airport layovers.

Products that can be differentiated largely on the basis of the information inherent in them are called information-intensive products. In industries characterized by information-intensive products (such as those mentioned in the previous paragraph), it is quite possible to create new products or improve old ones with information technology.

In the insurance industry, computers are widely used to customize insurance packages for particular groups or clients. In the brokerage industry, analyst brokers use computers to design portfolios targeted to the specific investment objectives of key market segments. Merrill Lynch, for instance, scored a major coup in 1977 when it created its Cash Management Account (CMA), a financial package consisting of a charge card, checking account, money-market fund, and brokerage service. The CMA, which brought close to a half million new brokerage accounts and an estimated $60 million in annual fees to Merrill Lynch, shattered the traditional boundary between the banking and securities industries. It is a product that is only possible with information-age technology that can integrate and manage data from a variety of sources. The introduction of the CMA temporarily left Merrill Lynch's competitors far behind.

The development, manufacturing, and distribution of non-information–intensive products has also been assisted by advances in information technology. Engineering and drafting tasks were simplified by *computer-aided design (CAD)*, *computer-aided engineering (CAE)*, and the development of powerful engineering workstations. According to Thomas Case and John Pickett, many companies have recognized the potential of investing in information technology to support research and development (R&D) activities and have reported that productivity gains and faster product development rates typically result from such investments. Robotics and artificial intelligence, MRP II (manufacturing resource planning) systems, *computer-aided manufacturing (CAM)*, and development of on-line information linkages among purchasing, manufacturing, and distribution are making it possible to implement *flexible manufacturing systems (FMS)* and *computer-integrated manufacturing (CIM)* applications.

Altering the Basis of Competition

By creating new products through information technology, some businesses may also change the very basis of competition within their industries. For instance, F. Warren McFarlan states that in the late 1970s, a major distributor of magazines to newsstands and stores used its records of weekly shipments and returns from each of its customers to alter the current basis of competition within its industry: cost. With these customer data, it created programs to determine profit per square foot for every magazine, newsstand, and store. The distributor then compared the results obtained across economically and ethnically similar neighborhoods. Consequently, the distributor was able to tell each of its customers how to improve its product mix. This management feature enabled the distributor to substantially increase its profit.

Identifying and Exploiting Business Opportunities

In the popular book *Thriving on Chaos*, Tom Peters depicts a present and future world characterized by a fast pace and often random changes (that is, chaos). Adapting quickly to change, taking advantage of shorter product life cycles, and exploiting niche markets are keys to success in this environment. Under these circumstances, the computer is an ideal tool for spotting subtle changes or trends in market data that are not visible to the human eye, and helping an organization to move rapidly forward once a change in the environment is identified. Likewise, communications technology is well-suited for quickly bringing together the geographically dispersed pieces of information that are needed to make these decisions in large organizations. By using information and communications technology in this way, new opportunities may be quickly identified and exploited.

For instance, when looking for good buying and selling opportunities, many stockbrokers and financial officers use computers to track stocks and issue buy or sell orders automatically. The October 1987 U.S. stock market crash was attributed not only to traditional crises such as the national deficit, but also to the so-called "program traders" who had accounted for an estimated 30 percent of the New York Stock Exchange volume during the previous bull market. Program traders rely on computers and communications technology to quickly identify changes in stock prices so that they can issue buy and sell orders in a way that will minimize losses and maximize returns—many of these systems automatically issue such orders when certain price levels are reached. During the 1987 crash, the speed of program trading systems caused a flood of sell orders, which helped to push a declining market into a crash.

As mentioned previously, the airline industry is well-known for its innovative use of technology to take advantage of opportunities. American Airlines, for instance, gained a major competitive advantage soon after the airlines were deregulated by using a detailed database of their customer travel information to restructure their air fares.

Client Lock-In/Competitor Lock-Out

The McKesson drug distribution case noted earlier is a prime illustration of using technology to lock in customers and lock out competitors. Both the firm and its customers benefited from the cooperative arrangement, while competitors found themselves left out. In similar situations, competitors have faced an uphill battle when trying to put an unwanted second terminal on a customer's desk. Also, the firm with the terminal already there can pull its customers closer to it by improving services and establishing levels of convenience that make it hard for those customers to even consider using a second system. Singer, for example, has built an interorganizational transaction processing system that allows customers to access Singer's computer to place orders, check the status of their orders, and check prices and product availabilities.

American Hospital Supply and a major international bank have applied the same formula as McKesson and Singer. In the late 1970s, American Hospital Supply (a subsidiary of Baxter Health Care Corporation) created a customer support system that electronically links AHS-provided terminals in thousands of hospitals to computers in its supply centers. The system maintains hospital inventories and enables supplies to be ordered electronically, with most of the supplies coming directly from AHS. The international bank placed terminals on the desks of the chief financial officers of its big European clients to allow them to transfer funds directly to their U.S. accounts at the bank.

As a further incentive, some companies have also enabled customers using their systems to access certain software for their own use. American Airlines and American Express, for instance, have established services on their computer systems that let client firms automate their travel and expense reports. Several other airlines have systems that help agents determine the lowest fares.

Leveraging Your Investment in Information Technology

Many public accounting firms and many other organizations in various non-computer–related industries have recently started to leverage their substantial technology investments through "outsourcing" or selling MIS products on the side. For instance, many banks leverage—or spread out—their huge investments in technology by offering their services to smaller banks. Also, the "Big Six" accounting firms today are competing vigorously in the software business, selling such items as auditing, tax assistance, and analysis software to clients (many of whom are not even clients of their mainstream auditing operations). Arthur Andersen—a large accounting firm that sells both software and systems-building expertise—employs about 8,500 computer experts alone. This company has also become one of the major outsourcing service providers over the last few years and has made a substantial profit from selling information services to other companies.

Firms in many other industries—Travelers Insurance (insurance), Celanese (chemicals), Citicorp (banking), Boeing (aircraft manufacturing), and JC Penney (retailing), to name just a few—are also competing vigorously in the software business. For example, JC Penney markets credit card authorization and verification systems to outside organizations; one of its major clients is Gulf Oil. Donald Siebert, chairman of JC Penney, has said that the leading retailers of the 1990s will not necessarily be the best merchandisers; instead, they will be the ones who best exploit technology.

These MIS goals indicate that organizations are now using computer systems for much more than just supporting day-to-day transaction processing operations. They also indicate that information technology can provide competitive advantages in a variety of ways. Many organizations now realize the strategic importance of information systems and the importance of having a computer-literate work force. We will explore these issues and applications throughout the text.

INFORMATION TECHNOLOGY FUNDAMENTALS

Computers are an essential part of modern information systems, and it is virtually impossible to study information systems today without knowing something about them and how they operate. In fact, without computers, it is unlikely that information systems would even be considered a serious field of study. In this section, we will look at some of the basic components of a computer-based information system.

Components of Computer-Based Information Systems

A **computer-based information system (CBIS)** is an information system in which the computer plays a major role. Such a system consists of the following elements:

- *Hardware*   The term **hardware** refers to machinery. This category includes the computer itself, which is often referred to as the **central processing unit (CPU)**, and all of its support equipment. Among the support equipment are input and output devices, storage devices, and communications devices. These are depicted in Figure 1.6.

- *Software*   The term **software** refers to computer programs and the manuals (if any) that support them. Computer programs are machine-readable instructions that direct the circuitry within the hardware parts of the CBIS to function in ways that produce useful information from data. Programs are generally stored on some input/output medium—often a disk or tape—for use by the computer.

- *Data*   As we defined earlier, data are facts that are used by programs to produce useful information. Like programs, data are generally stored in machine-readable form on disk or tape until the computer needs them.

- *Procedures*   Procedures are the policies that govern the operation of a computer system. "Procedures are to people what software is to hardware" is a common analogy that is used to illustrate the role of procedures in a CBIS. For instance, the steps that must be taken to enter a password and log on to a computer terminal are a procedure. The actions needed to restore the computer system to its operational state after a major power failure are another example of a procedure. Procedures often specify the actions that people should take in a step-by-step manner.

- *People*   Every CBIS needs people if it is to be useful. Often the most overlooked element of the CBIS, people are probably the components that most influence the success or failure of information systems. Users, programmers, systems analysts, and database administrators are just some of the people associated with computer-based information systems.

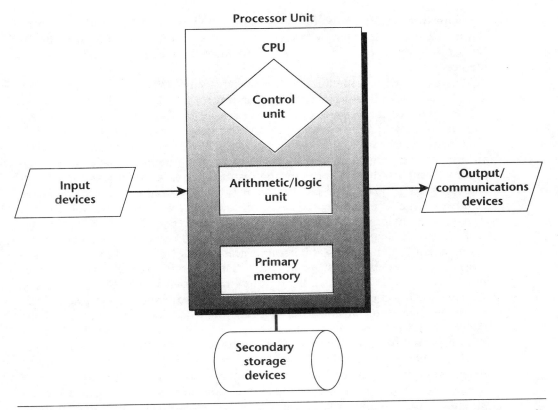

Figure 1.6 The hardware components of a computer-based information system (CBIS) consist, at minimum, of input, processing, output, and storage devices. Communications hardware may also be included to make it possible for the CBIS to communicate with other computer-based information systems.

Programmers, Users, and Systems Analysts

Traditionally, a person who writes a computer program is called a **programmer** and the person who uses the results of a computer program is called a **user** (or *end-user*). Today, with so many users writing instructions for their own personal computer systems, the programmer-user distinction is often blurred. In this text, we will reserve the word "programmer" to refer to a computer professional whose specific job function is to write computer programs.

Another key computer professional is mentioned in this text: the **systems analyst**. One of the main duties of the systems analyst is to assess the computer-related needs of users and to design systems that meet these needs.

Technical Operation of a CBIS

The technical operation of a CBIS consists of four parts: input, processing, output, and storage. An **input device** is a hardware device (such as a keyboard) that supplies data to the CBIS. The data are then processed by the CPU under software instructions. Subsequently, information is produced and sent to an **output device**—for example, to a printer or a monitor. As the computer is working, it retrieves, uses, and stores data in an electronic space called its memory.

There are two types of memory—that which the computer accesses directly as it is working (called **primary** or **main memory**) and that which consists of the entire library of machine-readable resources at its disposal (called **secondary storage** or *auxiliary memory*). Primary memory serves the function of a scratchpad—in order to make changes to data in secondary storage, the data are transferred from secondary storage to primary memory, where the computer works with them before sending results back to secondary storage. Disks and tapes are probably the most familiar types of secondary storage. Primary memory, which commonly consists of rapid-access semiconductor storage chips, is usually located inside the "box" that houses the CPU.

Let's look at an example of how data may be processed into information. An airline agent in Omaha sits at a communications terminal—a hardware device consisting of a keyboard for input and a display device for output—and types in a command that requests a listing of all flights between New York and Los Angeles for this afternoon. Communications hardware and software sends this input message to an airline reservations system in Chicago, where both the computer and the disk devices containing all flight data are located. The computer retrieves from secondary storage both the program that contains the machine instructions to display flights between two cities and the data that the program needs. These are loaded into primary memory and the data are then processed. When the computer is finished, other hardware and software components of the CBIS see that the information produced is transmitted back to Omaha and output on the agent's terminal. All of this takes place within a few seconds. Should the agent need further information—perhaps confirmation on a hotel or rental car—other programs and other sets of data would be summoned from remote computer systems and processed in a similar way.

The programs available on a CBIS consist of two types: applications software and systems software. **Application software** refers to programs that enable computers to do the types of work that people most directly need to get their jobs done: processing checks, listing flight information, keeping track of orders, making out budgets, and so on. **Systems software**, on the other hand, consists of background programs that ensure that this work gets done efficiently and correctly. For instance, systems programs are necessary to see that communications are sent properly from Omaha to Chicago and, also, that the computer system interfaces properly with users. Probably the most important piece of systems software is the computer's operating system—the main set of control programs that ensure that a given set of software will work with a given set of hardware.

Both application software and systems software are written in programming languages. We will cover a number of such languages in Chapter 6. Realistically, every CBIS has access to a limited number of languages with which both users and programmers can work.

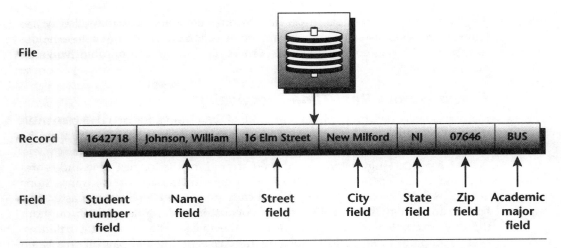

File

Record

| 1642718 | Johnson, William | 16 Elm Street | New Milford | NJ | 07646 | BUS |

Field

| Student number field | Name field | Street field | City field | State field | Zip field | Academic major field |

Figure 1.7 A student file. The disk file represented here contains student records for a university. If 30,000 students are enrolled for classes, the file will contain 30,000 records. Each record of the file shown here contains seven fields: student number, name, street, city, state, zip code, and major.

Organizing Data on Computer-Based Information Systems

To be processed by a CBIS, data must be systematically organized. The most common method is to arrange data into fields, records, files, and databases.

A **field** is a collection of related characters—for example, JOHN SMITH, 222 Sunset Boulevard, or $55.33. A **record** is a collection of related fields, and a **file** is a collection of related records. The relationships among fields, records, and a file is shown in Figure 1.7. Depicted in the figure is a disk file consisting of 30,000 student records, each of which represents one of the 30,000 students enrolled at a university. Each record in the file contains seven data fields: student number, name, street, city, state, zip code, and major.

A file containing semipermanent data, such as the one in Figure 1.7, is often called a *master file*. A university would probably have other master files containing faculty and course data. On the other hand, files that contain records representing transactions—business-related events that take place on each of the entities represented in a master file—are called *transaction files*. Some transaction file data that a university might keep on its students would be grades earned in courses and tuition payments made during a particular semester or quarter.

Many organizations use *file management* software or *database management systems (DBMS)* to manage their data. These software products take data that would normally exist as separate files and integrate them into a larger unit called a **database**. So, for instance, a student database would likely contain all data relating to students—both data that exist in student master files and data that exist in transaction files. As in the files example, a university using database software would probably also have faculty and course databases. In many database systems, the data appearing in different databases may also be related. Some database systems use an organization scheme similar to a fields-records-files arrangement, whereas others use more complicated ways to organize data.

Batch Versus Real-Time Processing

Many modern operating systems can update data from a file or a database in either the batch or real-time mode. The way that a system updates data can be critical to MIS performance.

Batch processing systems have been around for the longest time and represent one of the least expensive ways to update. In these systems, transactions are collected, or batched, and periodically processed against a master file. For instance, many banks collect records of customer deposits made throughout the day and batch these nightly against the master file of account balances. Many companies also perform such operations as billing and payroll on a batch basis.

With **real-time processing**, updates are made to files or databases as soon as they take place. Perhaps the most familiar example of real-time updating is the airlines' passenger reservations systems. As soon as a seat is sold on a flight, for instance, the flight's remaining seat count is updated immediately so that all agents using the system will know exactly how many seats are left on the flight. Batching transactions and processing them periodically against seat counts would not work in reservations systems; too many flights would be oversold. Bank withdrawals are also processed in the real-time mode. If withdrawals were batched nightly (as deposits typically are), criminals would not have to use guns to rob banks. Instead, people could withdraw any amount of money because the withdrawal amount would not be checked against the bank balance until it was too late to refuse an excessive withdrawal.

If you keep these fundamentals in mind, it should be easier for you to comprehend and assimilate some of the more technical sections of this text, such as Part 3.

LEARNING ABOUT MANAGEMENT INFORMATION SYSTEMS

In this section, we will cover some of the topics that are most important to learning about information systems. First, to establish priorities, we will look at the MIS issues that are seen as being most important to both MIS and non-MIS managers. Then, we will turn to the numerous challenges faced in the study of MIS and how this text is organized to facilitate understanding of this important field.

Key Issues in Management Information Systems

Surveys frequently appear in MIS literature that report on information systems issues perceived by management to be most critical (for instance, see Ball and Harris; Dickson et al.; Hartog and Herbert; Brancheau and Wetherbe; and Niederman, Brancheau, and Wetherbe). These surveys tend to indicate that as both organizations and MISs have shifted over the years to meet changing condi-

KEY MIS ISSUES

Issue Description	Issue Rank by Year of Publication			
	1982	1984	1987	1991
Information architecture	NR	NR	8	1
Data resource	4	9	7	2
Strategic planning	1	1	1	3
MIS human resources	7	8	12	4
Organizational learning	8	6	3	5
Technology infrastructure	NR	NR	NR	6
MIS organization alignment	9	7	5	7
Competitive advantage	NR	NR	2	8
Software development	13	4	13	9
Telecommunication systems	3	13	11	10
MIS role and contribution	NR	15	4	11
Electronic data interchange	NR	NR	14	12
Distributed systems	NR	NR	NR	12
CASE technology	NR	NR	NR	12
Applications portfolio	NR	10	16	15
MIS effectiveness measurement	2	5	9	16
Executive/decision support	5	10	NR	17
End-user computing	11	2	6	18
Security and control	12	14	18	19
Disaster recovery	NR	NR	NR	20
Organizational structure	18	NR	NR	21
Technology islands	NR	3	10	22
Global systems	NR	NR	NR	22
Image technology	NR	NR	NR	24
MIS asset accounting	NR	NR	NR	25

Note: NR indicates item was not ranked as a key issue.

Figure 1.8 Key MIS issues identified by information systems professionals. The survey results indicate that strategic planning for MIS continues to be one of the most important issues; however, developing an appropriate information architecture and data resource management have also emerged as key issues. (Adapted from Neiderman, Brancheau, and Wetherbe)

tions, so too have priorities shifted. Some of these priority shifts are illustrated in Figure 1.8. Each of the issues will be addressed at one or more junctures in this text.

As this figure shows, these studies have consistently found strategic planning to be a top priority. **Strategic planning** is the long-range planning process that is undertaken by organizations to see that broad goals are established and the mechanisms for achieving such goals are put into place.

Strategic planning for MIS, incidentally, is not the same thing as the strategic use of information systems technology. The strategic use of an information system refers to using information technology to gain a competitive advantage. Theoretically, a firm is realizing a **competitive advantage** when information technology is used either to alter the basis of competition within an industry—to alter, for example, price, cost, quality, or service—or, more commonly, to substantially help the firm get ahead of its competitors. Setting up communications terminals at customer sites to lock in customers and lock out competitors and using computers to create new investment vehicles for clients are both cases in which information systems are used for competitive advantage.

Challenges in the Study of MIS

If you have read this chapter carefully, you have probably discovered that MIS is not a tidy discipline filled with easy-to-articulate problems and easy-to-find answers. MIS proficiency is attained through:

- An understanding of people and their behaviors.
- An intuitive feel for what management will accept.
- A current knowledge of technology-based disciplines such as computers and communications.
- An understanding of planning and control matters.
- A solid grounding in accounting (because information systems are rich in accounting data and terminology).
- A sense of perspective that enables you to see how all of these things fit together and which are most important.

Even after defining a problem, finding a solution, and implementing it, you may still never be sure that the best course of action was taken. These facts lead us to a consideration of some of the distinctive challenges that face the people who design, use, or approve management information systems:

- *MIS incorporates a wide variety of knowledge areas* Functional areas of business that rely heavily on information systems include accounting, finance, marketing, and manufacturing. Many management information systems, in fact, span several such areas. For an information system to be successful in any of these functional business areas, the systems designer must become familiar with the unique problems encountered in that particular area or areas. Having both technical knowledge and practical experience is very useful. Among the other fields that heavily influence the study of MIS are organizational behavior, computers, communications, and strategic planning.
- *Both technology and technology-related products are evolving at an extremely fast and unpredictable pace* Each week, new technological devel-

opments and products are announced. These announcements, coming from different sources, are often presented to the world chaotically. Thus, it is difficult for people who must be up-to-date about information technology to keep up. As Darrel Owen writes, this situation was summed up by a manager in the energy industry: "The blitz of new technology is often more than the IS organization can deal with effectively. . . . If there were a single phrase to describe the state of the IS organization in dealing with this new technology, 'semi-ordered technologically induced chaos' would be a telling choice." Since no one can possibly be proficient in all new technologies, a sense of perspective about how to assimilate important trends, problems, and opportunities must be developed.

■ *Many of the terms used in MIS environments are imprecise and controversial* Because information technologies are evolving at such a rapid pace, many terms have definitions that are ambiguous or still rapidly evolving. The unrelenting release of new hardware, software, and communications technologies mentioned previously only fuels this problem and delays a consensus about what constitutes an MIS, DSS, or "fifth-generation system."

■ *MIS problems often are not easy to define or structure* It is not unusual to find MIS-related problems difficult to articulate. For instance, poor service may be seen as a problem when, in fact, it is only a symptom; the real culprit could be raw material delays in the factory. Also, once defined, many MIS-related problems are often solved through an indescribable (and sometimes uncomfortable) combination of subjective judgment and objective fact. Further, because computer technology and businesses are evolving so rapidly, many problems are dynamic in nature; key elements of the environment may change while the problem is being defined or solved.

■ *The body of knowledge in MIS is relatively recent and scarce* Unlike disciplines such as mathematics and physics, which have existed for centuries and have spurred volumes of research, MIS has only been recognized as a serious field of study since the 1960s. Furthermore, a large amount of MIS knowledge—like knowledge in the social sciences—is hampered by lack of experimental control; small samples (a great deal of MIS research is case-based); narrow conclusions (MIS is heavily contingency-based—meaning that conclusions depend on a particular set of circumstances and may not be valid under another set); changes in the environment that diminish the significance of earlier studies; and conflict among research results. A number of professionals would also argue that many important areas of MIS are still largely unaddressed.

■ *A lack of rapport often exists between MIS personnel and management and also between MIS personnel and users* A number of researchers have shown that MIS personnel tend to be more loyal to their profession than to the needs of the organization. Consequently, many of them have over-pushed technological solutions to problems. Also, a number of computer people have alienated both users and managers with "technobabble" (also known as "computerspeak" or "computerese")—the overuse of specialized computer terms. According to David Freedman, one former Harvard Business School professor states that a major goal at that institution is to "turn [students] into people who can't be snowed by IS managers, to teach them to get what they want from technical managers."

■ *Spending money on information systems is still somewhat of a mystery* No universal standards have been established regarding how much to spend on information technologies or how much to spend in each applications area. The problem of what to spend has become more severe in recent years, with general increases in the level of resource commitment to MIS. This problem has also been complicated because many of the newer technologies and systems result in benefits—such as better and faster information with which to make decisions—that are difficult to quantify in dollar terms. Unfortunately, many of these information systems, which are potentially the most valuable to the firm, are shunned by efficiency-conscious, cost-justify-everything–minded executives.

The fact that MIS is a relatively complex area of study raises some interesting points. First, because so many areas of study are involved, you might think that a genius-level IQ is required to become proficient in MIS. Fortunately, this is not true. Today's MIS professionals and MIS-savvy managers need to be good problem solvers, the type of people who can walk into an unfamiliar environment and instinctively know how to establish priorities. For companies in which MIS is a strategic priority, the people dealing with MIS issues should also be creative enough to identify opportunities in which new technology can solve old problems.

Second, again because so many areas of study are involved in MIS, there's the question of which areas are most critical to the MIS professional. You may be tempted to answer "computers" or "technology." However, the consensus among most business and MIS leaders today is "management." Many people believe that it is better to teach a seasoned manager enough computer principles to basically understand the process than to teach a seasoned computer professional some principles of management. This business emphasis is strongest in IRM-minded organizations, where information systems management must be concerned with such issues as corporate strategy and repositioning of the firm.

Third is the issue of professional opportunity. Areas of knowledge that are relatively easy to structure and to learn generally offer little opportunity for financial reward and advancement. MIS, on the other hand, often requires a person to create a workable structure out of chaos. The skills required of an MIS professional are often the same skills required of the organization's top person, the CEO.

The Organization of This Text

The challenges to be faced in the study of information systems bring us to the issue of how and why this text is organized the way it is. Basically, the book is organized around the five-component model of a CBIS that was described earlier in this chapter. The components represented in that model are hardware, software, data, procedures, and people. Each of these dimensions is represented in one or more parts, or sets of chapters. You've just read Part 1, a general introduction to the information systems field.

Part 2 is composed predominantly of background topics that are useful to the study of information systems. Most of these topics concern people, organizations, and systems. Here, we will look at such topics as human behavior and how it affects MIS development, types and levels of decision making, and how corporate cultures affect both the business organization and the development of information systems. In this part, we will also formally define a "system" and look at several models of systems that can be effectively used to design or analyze an information system. Many of the models introduced here are referenced in subsequent chapters of the book.

Part 3, "Information Technology Concepts," covers many of the hardware, software, and data technologies that are vital when dealing with computer- and communications-based management information systems. Chapters 5 and 6, which cover hardware and software, introduce various types of computing equipment and computer programming tools. In Chapters 7 and 8, we cover the "hot" hardware and software topics—those that are becoming most critical to effective MIS management, such as database and telecommunication systems.

Part 4 examines the procedures component of MIS. It covers in detail the four primary MIS subsystems: transaction processing, information reporting systems, decision support systems, and office information systems. Here, we formally define each of these subsystems and explore the information needs satisfied by them. In doing this, we draw from earlier chapters. From the perspective established in Part 3, we look at the data, hardware, and software technologies that have gravitated into each of these subsystems. From our Part 2 perspective, we examine how human behavior, decision-making practices, and organizational policy have an important impact on MIS. Part 4 closes with a survey of the role of MIS in several of the major functional areas of business.

Part 5 addresses how information systems are built in organizations. Here, we will consider both traditional and non-traditional approaches to information systems development. Among the non-traditional approaches considered are prototyping philosophies and end-user approaches.

In Part 6, we cover issues relating to the management of MIS. Among the topics addressed are strategic MIS planning, choosing among MIS projects, pricing MIS services, budgeting, evaluating the MIS function, security and ethical issues, MIS training, and multinational aspects of MIS.

SUMMARY

Today's information technologies not only impact the processing of data, but also influence the way people do their jobs, the products that many businesses turn out, and the manner in which many businesses compete. Information processing has become, for many organizations, a matter of strategic importance. Many of them will be unable to compete unless customers are given the level of service that is possible only with high technology-based systems. Information, in many organizations, is a key resource; both technology professionals and regular managers must understand what it is capable of doing and how to best exploit it.

The predominant business applications of computers in the 1950s were transaction processing systems such as payroll and billing. During the 1960s, technology advances within organizations led to the rise of management information systems (MIS). Early management information systems—called management reporting systems (MRS)—consisted of periodic printed reports whose primary purpose was to help managers with decision making. Despite original high expectations, many of these systems were not overwhelming successes. In the 1970s, with the advent of microcomputers, user-friendly software, and other developments came decision support systems (DSS). These provided decision makers with the capability to meet their own information needs. About the same time, office automation (OA) technologies appeared. In the 1980s, the concept of information technology as a strategic weapon developed and the DSS concept evolved into executive information systems (EIS) and group decision support systems (GDSS). Networking, electronic data interchange (EDI), and effective data communications also became important issues. The 1990s promise continued advancements in information and communication technology and considerable development is expected in expert systems (ES), artificial intelligence (AI), and neural networks.

An MIS is a system that provides authorized people with timely data or information relating to an organization's operations. The MIS effort in an organization is composed of five subsystems: (1) transaction processing systems (TPS), (2) management reporting systems (MRS), (3) decision support systems (DSS), (4) knowledge-based systems including expert systems and artificial intelligence, and (5) office systems, commonly referred to as office information systems (OIS).

Data are facts that, when filtered through one or more processors so that they take on both meaning and value to a person or organization, become information. Information, rather than data, is what people use to make decisions. Information resource management (IRM) is a concept recognizing that information is a key resource and investment that should be managed strategically. The person in charge of MIS in IRM-oriented firms is often called the chief information officer (CIO), who usually reports to the organization's chief executive officer (CEO).

Information systems serve a number of specific purposes in organizations. For instance, they can lead to operational efficiency: doing things better, faster, or cheaper. Or they can result in functional effectiveness—for example, by helping managers in a particular subunit make better decisions. Information systems can also help organizations provide better service to customers and clients and, in many instances, can help companies create or improve products. Information systems can alter the basis of competition by changing key ingredients such as price, quality, and so on. Further, they may allow users to spot and take advantage of opportunities and can allow companies to lock in customers and lock out competitors. Finally, companies may be able to leverage technology investments by selling MIS products and services in addition to their main business function.

A computer-based information system (CBIS) consists of five elements: hardware including the central processing unit (CPU), software, data, procedures, and people. The technical operation of a CBIS consists of four items: input, processing, output, and storage. Input consists of getting data into the computer. Processing deals with performing operations on these data. Output involves retrieving data from the computer. Data are stored in memory: primary (main) memory and secondary storage or auxiliary memory. Primary memory is used to store data and programs as they are being processed by the computer, whereas secondary storage is used to store all data and programs on a semipermanent basis, often for repeated use.

Programs available on a CBIS are either applications software or systems software. Traditionally, programmers write computer programs; users (or end-users) work with the results. A systems analyst assesses the computer-related needs of users and designs systems to meet those needs.

To be processed by a CBIS, data must be systematically organized. Usually, they are arranged into fields, records, files, and databases. Data can be updated either through batch processing or real-time processing.

Surveys show that management views strategic planning for MIS to be one of its top priorities. Strategic planning (which refers to a long-range planning process) is not the same as the strategic use of information technology (which refers to employing computer and communication technology to gain material competitive advantage).

A number of challenges face those who design, use, and approve information systems. These challenges include the wide range of knowledge required; the fast and unpredictable pace at which technology and related products are evolving; the imprecise and controversial terms used in MIS environments; the difficulty of defining or structuring MIS problems; the relative newness and scarcity of MIS knowledge; the general lack of rapport between MIS personnel and management (and also between MIS personnel and users); and the lack of standards regarding costs.

MIS professionals and others who work with these systems must be good problem solvers, have a solid grounding in management, and be able to create workable structures from often chaotic situations.

KEY TERMS

Applications software

Batch processing

Central processing unit (CPU)

Chief executive officer (CEO)

Chief information officer (CIO)

Competitive advantage

Computer-based information system (CBIS)

Data

Database

Decision support system (DSS)

Field

File

Hardware

Information

Information resource management (IRM)

Input device

Management information system (MIS)

Management reporting system (MRS)

Office automation (OA)

Office information system (OIS)

Operating system

Output device

Primary (main) memory

Programmer

Real-time processing

Record

Secondary storage

Software

Strategic planning

Systems analyst

Systems software

Transaction processing system (TPS)

User

REVIEW QUESTIONS

1. What are some of the trends that have caused information systems to assume a key role in modern organizations?

2. How can an economy be based on information? How is a knowledge-based economy different from an information-based economy?

3. In what ways can a business leverage a large investment in CBIS resources? Provide at least two example of MIS "outsourcing."

4. Describe the evolution of information systems from the 1950s to the present. What were the characteristics of the information systems during each of these evolutionary phases?

5. What is an information system? What are the characteristics of each of the different MIS subsystems?

6. What is IRM? What are the characteristics of IRM-oriented firms? Why may IRM be critical to a firm?

7. Describe the difference between data and information.

8. What are the goals of information systems? How may each of these goals be achieved?

9. Provide several examples showing how information itself can be used to create or enhance both information-intensive and conventional products.

10. Provide at least two examples that show how businesses can use information technology to lock in customers and lock out competitors.

11. How may information technology alter the basis of competition? Provide examples to support your response.

12. Describe the differences among each of the elements of a computer-based information system. Provide examples to clarify your responses.

13. How does applications software differ systems software? Provide examples of each type of software to reinforce your responses.

14. How are data organized and managed in a CBIS?

15. What is the difference between batch processing and real-time processing? Provide at least one example of each type of processing to reinforce your response.

16. What are the key issues facing MIS managers? Why are these issues so important?

17. Why are strategic planning and competitive advantage two of the most critical MIS management issues? How do these differ?

18. What special challenges are faced by MIS students and managers? Why do these challenges exist?

DISCUSSION QUESTIONS

1. Why is it difficult to define, without controversy, what an information system is?

2. Some people claim that the term "competitive advantage" is overused. For instance, it might be argued that many of the examples mentioned in this chapter represent creative, rather than strategic, uses of computers. What do you think?

3. The "total information system" envisioned in the 1960s never became a reality. Was this just an idea ahead of its time, or are there other reasons why this concept failed?

CASE STUDY

Using Information Technology for Competitive Advantage

There are few better examples of the use of information technology for competitive advantage than airline reservation systems. Today, most airlines make more money from their reservation systems than they do from actually flying passengers. For example, American Airlines' reservation system consistently accounts for more than 50 percent of the company's total revenues.

Sabre, American's reservation system, was the first its kind. It was expensive to develop and when it came on-line, competitors filed lawsuits claiming that it gave American an unfair advantage; it also sent them scrambling to develop their own systems. The initial competitive edge that Sabre provided has continued into the 1990s—roughly three out of five tickets issued to air travelers are booked through Sabre. The lawsuits against American spawned by Sabre have also continued. Once, while talking about legislation that would force American to divest itself of Sabre, Robert Crandall, chairman and CEO of American Airlines, commented: "If you told me I had to sell either the airline or the system, I'd probably sell the airline."

Sabre, like most of the reservation systems used today, was developed in response to the deregulation of the airline industry that started in the late 1970s and continued through the 1980s. Deregulation made it possible for airlines to establish their own fares, routes, and services. Fare wars, deeply discounted fares, special packages for frequent flyers and business travelers, and other changes resulting from deregulation have made airlines a preferred mode of business travel.

Here's how it all works. Each of the major airlines has its own reservation system. For example, American Airlines has Sabre, United Airlines' system is dubbed Apollo, TWA's system is called PARS, and Delta has DATAS. More than 90 percent of the over 40,000 travel agencies in the U.S. hook directly into these systems. As a general rule, each agency is connected to only one system. From there, it can access and book flights on other carriers. Studies show, however, that the airline providing an agency's reservation system is up to 30 percent more likely to receive bookings on its flights. Understandably, each airline wants to increase the number of agencies hooked to its system.

The systems communicate with one another in real time. This makes it possible, for instance, to book a seat on a Delta Flight through Sabre, or to book an American flight through PARS. However, each time that a reservation is made for a competing airline, the airline that owns the reservation system receives a fee. Hence, to avoid paying fees to competitors, each airline wants to book as many seats as possible through its own system.

An airline can use its reservation system for competitive advantage in many ways. Tactics employed include:

- Controlling the information displayed on travel agents' screens. For instance, the airline that owns the reservation system often display its flights first (or in a preferential manner) before showing those of competitors.

- Having travel agencies sign contracts that make it difficult for them to switch to a competitor's system.
- Charging fees for airlines that want to have their flights listed in the reservation system.
- Offering information processing and office automation services for free (or for a nominal fee) for travel agents choosing to hook into the system.
- Offering free microcomputer workstation terminals to travel agencies. These terminals can also be used for local processing tasks when not needed for booking airline tickets.
- Expanding the services offered through the reservation systems so that travel agents can easily reserve rental cars, hotel rooms, and so on for travelers.

The major airlines have spun off their reservation systems into separate subsidiaries that are expected to be profitable in their own right. These subsidiaries often sell computer services and excess computing resources both to smaller airlines and to companies in other industries.

Competition among the airlines shows no signs of slowing down during the 1990s. Fare wars, special packages for frequent flyers, and new travel services continue to make the airlines industry dynamic and volatile. Some companies, such as Eastern and Pan Am, have folded as the result of the competitive pressures. With each bankruptcy, the remaining competitors practically trip over one another to obtain gates and lucrative routes at major airports . Information technology has already played a critical role in shaping how the major airlines compete with one another and will undoubtedly continue to do so in the years ahead.

Adapted from Hopper (1990), Copeland (1991), Winkler (1990), Betts (1992), and Lawrence (1992).

DISCUSSION

1. Discuss how airline reservation systems help the airline operate more efficiently and assist them in providing good levels of customer service.

2. How have airline reservation systems altered the manner in which the major airlines compete against one another? How have these systems made it more difficult for newer, smaller airlines to compete against the major carriers?

3. How are the airline reservation systems used to lock-in travel agents and lock-out competitors?

4. How do you think the airline reservation systems should be changed to provide new levels of customer service and efficiency? What additional services do you think they should offer? Why do you think airline passengers would be interested in these?

Part TWO

People, Organizations, Systems, and Management

Chapter 2
People and Organizations

Chapter 3
Systems and Models

Chapter 4
Management and Decision Making

Chapter 2.

People and Organizations

After completing this chapter, you will be able to:

Describe some characteristics of people that often impact the design and performance of information systems

Name some of the ways in which differences among organizations can affect the role played by information systems

Identify the principal responsibility areas in the MIS infrastructure

Describe how the roles that people and groups assume in organizations can impact information systems

Information systems are often referred to as sociotechnical systems. That is, they are composed of technology-related products and concepts that can only be fully understood within the context of the people and organizations that use those products. Systems developers should make sure that people and organization factors are carefully considered when designing and implementing information systems. Many systems have failed because implementers overlooked the importance of human and organizational factors. In this chapter, we will examine some of the reasons why these dimensions should not be ignored.

Chapter 2 is about the behavioral and organizational components of a management information system (MIS). It has often been noted that people are the most important part of any organization and, consequently, of any MIS. After all, if it has superior people, an organization can be successful and may even overcome deficiencies in hardware, software, data, and procedures. However, an organization with superior hardware, software, data, and procedures may never become profitable if the people in charge are not capable. After all, it is people who "manage" management information systems.

We will first look at some of the physical and psychological characteristics of people that are relevant to an MIS environment. Then, we will turn to the properties of organizations: collections of people and groups. Finally, we will examine some of the results that are encountered when people interact in organizational settings. Before turning to these important issues, please note that this chapter's purpose is not to provide an exhaustive overview of people and organizational factors. Instead, we will concentrate on the issues that are most relevant to MIS design and operation.

PEOPLE

The people component of a management information system is often overlooked or underconsidered. A long list of cases exist in which, on the drawing board, it appeared that proposed information systems would work successfully. However, when implemented, these systems failed miserably. Why? In some cases, the systems exceeded the mental and emotional capabilities of the people who had to use them. Others failed because designers incorrectly assumed that work groups that historically competed against each other would suddenly—magically—cooperate in order to make the system work. Still more information systems failed because they never fully received backing from the top executives in the companies.

In this section, we will look at some of the characteristics of people that often impact on the design and performance of information systems. Later in the chapter, we will see how the organizational environment affects the way that people behave.

Physiological Factors

Most jobs in an information systems environment do not, at first, seem physically demanding. After all, not many heavy objects have to be lifted and no one is forced into hazardous assignments in which death is a very real possibility. But MIS jobs can be physically demanding in other ways. For example, clerks who spend continuous hours entering data into a display terminal may, at the end of a day, suffer from eyestrain, headaches, neck and back problems, and general exhaustion. These physical problems can emanate from a number of sources, such as the equipment, the workspace, or the social environment.

Even in the 1980s, many display workstations were built with glare-producing screens and attached keyboards that often forced users into awkward positions in order to both input data and see computer output on the screen. Today, fortunately, most display devices are designed with such features as tinted or tiltable screens (to cut down on glare) and detachable keyboards. Even so, display devices do give off low levels of radiation, that may be harmful if used over a long period of time. The Swedish government was among the first to develop conservative standards for monitor emissions. These monitors are now available worldwide; some vendors are using conformance to these standards as a selling point. Although display devices that comply with the Swedish standards typically cost more than those that don't, many companies and individual users feel that the additional cost is justified.

A worker's physical workspace can also be a problem. For example, the furniture might be poorly designed, forcing workers into uncomfortable postures. Or the lighting may impart a stress-producing glare on the display screen. Poorly conceived office acoustics may also contribute to distressing noise levels. Even the work environment can contribute to problems if workers are forced into long hours, or if the incentives keep workers moving at a grueling pace.

Ergonomics

The field that studies computer workspaces and their effects on users is known as **ergonomics**. This field attempts to overcome the problems associated with poorly designed computer workspaces that cause unnecessary physical and mental stress or strain. Research in this field has also made it for possible vision-impaired, hearing-impaired, and developmentally disabled individuals to make productive use of information technology. The Americans with Disabilities Act (ADA) enacted in 1990 has also resulted in increased attention on developing ways to make information technology more accessible and usable by disabled workers.

Ergonomics research has prompted manufacturers of display devices to incorporate improvements such tiltable, flicker-free screens; eye-soothing display colors; and contoured, detachable keyboards. Research in this area has resulted in special input and output interfaces for disabled workers—such as voice or eye-movement activated input devices—as well as Braille keyboards and printers. Besides hardware, ergonomic researchers have focused on lighting, acoustics, and furniture design. Minimizing problems in these areas is both humanly desirable and can, in the long run, be productive for the organization.

Ergonomics is likely to increase in importance in the years ahead if predicted worker shortages do, in fact, occur. Demographics indicate that the number of available workers is declining and will continue to do so in the foreseeable future. For this reason, increasing worker productivity and well-being through ergonomics may play a key role in the competitiveness of organizations.

Worker Skills and Abilities

Organization behavior researchers—who study the factors that influence the work behaviors of individuals and groups—have recognized that many on-the-job behaviors are affected by the skills and abilities that workers possess. These skills and abilities are usually described as being relatively stable physical and intellectual characteristics that determine an employee's capability to perform job tasks. Lack of appropriate abilities and skills can limit a worker's productivity. For example, if a clerk-typist does not have the manual dexterity to master the fundamentals of typing or keyboard entry, his or her performance is likely to suffer.

Two categories of skills and abilities are commonly identified: physical abilities and mental abilities. *Physical abilities* include both basic physical capabilities (for example, strength, flexibility, and stamina) and psychomotor abilities (such as manual dexterity, eye-hand coordination, and reaction time). *Mental abilities* are more concerned with the intellectual capabilities of workers and are closely linked to how a person makes decisions and processes information. Included in this category are factors such as verbal comprehension, memory processes, and mathematical aptitude. While both factors must be considered when designing information systems, the mental abilities of users are likely to play the primary role.

Intelligence and Sophistication

Information systems must be tailored to both the level of intelligence and the level of sophistication of the people using them. Intelligence refers basically to a person's ability to reason, whereas sophistication refers largely to factors such as age and experience. Together, they make a large contribution to the user's ability to perform on the job.

You should note that a relationship does not necessarily exist between a worker's professional sophistication and his or her computer sophistication. For example, executives or senior professionals may be very knowledgeable and effective in jobs they perform for their organizations, but still be quite unsophisticated when using computers. Typically, executives and senior executives do not rise to such positions unless they are competent in their functional areas; however, many started climbing to the top before computers, especially microcomputers, became commonplace. Managers and professionals who are new to computers should benefit from the user-friendly interfaces described in the following section of this chapter.

User Interfaces

Many of the user interfaces for workers who enter transaction processing data are intended for individuals who are relatively unsophisticated when it comes to computers. For example, the point-of-sale (POS) systems designed to collect sales data at fast-food restaurants are typically designed for the lowest capability workers that are expected to use them. If you have ever eaten at a McDonald's or Kentucky Fried Chicken franchise, you may have noticed that their terminals have special keyboards, or keyboard templates, to facilitate fast and accurate data entry. If, for example, a customer buys a double cheeseburger at $1.57, all the clerk may have to do is press a key that has a picture of the item that the customer wants to order. Some systems even have different keys for different sized items (such as "large" versus "regular" sized fries).

The benefits of such easy-to-use systems include quick training for new workers and the organization's ability to hire semi-skilled or unskilled workers. In many instances, this can be a cost-effective business strategy, especially for organizations that experience high turnover rates. It is usually much easier for an organization to handle high turnover rates when replacements can be quickly trained to be productive employees.

As a general rule, the more rigorous the demands made on operators, the more vulnerable the system is to failure. However, users with sophisticated computer knowledge often want features in an MIS that low-sophistication users may find undesirable. For example, high-sophistication users may want shortcuts (for example, they don't want to be slowed down by having to select from computer menus) and the ability to manipulate all the options. Less sophisticated users, on the other hand, often don't want their options to become complex; they want the initiative to come from the computer. These users typically want menus with limited or clear choices, extensive on-line help features, and confirmation for all operations. In general, when the system will be used by unskilled or unsophisticated users, it should be as user-friendly as possible—well-documented, easy to use, easy to learn, and easy to understand. It should try not to make the user feel stupid or abandoned. Even very experienced computer users are likely to appreciate such features—especially those who recall struggling with user-hostile systems in the past.

Frequency of use is another important consideration when designing a user interface. Infrequent users may learn a system more quickly and work best when there are graphical interfaces (such as icons that a person can point to when using a mouse), good help features, and on-screen reminders showing where they are and what they can do next. Frequent users, in contrast, often work at a more reflexive level and usually prefer interfaces with minimal keystrokes, fast response, and short messages so that the interactive dialogue doesn't slow down. To satisfy both types of users, many systems provide alter-

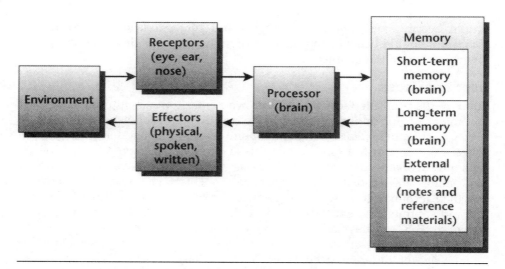

Figure 2.1 A human information processing model. (Adapted from Newell and Simon)

native interfaces for both novices and experienced users. For example, Word-Perfect, a popular word-processing package, now has a menu-driven interface for novices and users who prefer menus, in addition to its regular user interface.

Memory Processes

People differ in both their ability to memorize and in the speed with which they recall the facts that are committed to memory. Thus, information systems often must be built to incorporate memory principles.

Allen Newell and Herbert Simon's theory of human information processing—depicted in Figure 2.1—suggests that human memory (like that of the computer) is made up of three components: short-term memory, long-term memory, and external memory. In short-term memory, people hold data in chunks—that is, in units that consist of such items as words or pictures. Research, such as that performed by George Miller, indicates that humans are typically able to keep anywhere from five to nine (7 ± 2) chunks active in short-term memory at any one time. Long-term memory is like the computer's on-line secondary storage; it contains data that can be easily accessed, but that are not being actively processed. A person's external memory is like a computer's off-line secondary storage. Facts that exist in books, file folders, written documents, and computer disks are stored here.

Because short-term memory is easily accessible, most people are more likely to use data from short-term memory rather than rely on data from either long-term or external memory. Thus, a basic principle of good information system design is to keep vital decision-making facts as close as possible to users. If the user has to search or work hard for necessary information, he or she may decide not to do so.

Bob Stahl, a human-factors expert, said about the relationship between memory and the design of software interfaces:

> [Short-term] memory decays in about 15 seconds. If a menu presents [too many] choices, the users will have to read the choices each time, slowing them down and confusing them, until the options are eventually converted to long-term memory. . . . Similarly, recognition memory is much easier than re-call memory. Asking the user to recognize a file name from a displayed list and to highlight it with the cursor is a vast improvement over requiring the user to recall the correct file. . . .

When designing user screens and menu systems for users, human memory processes should be considered. Research on memory processes suggests that a terminal operator should be able to backtrack easily to an earlier point in an interactive session, thereby limiting the number of facts that he or she needs to commit to memory. This research also suggests that interactive response rates for the computer should be fast enough for vital data to remain in the user's active, short-term memory. The liberal use of menus is also recommended by this research because menus often spare users the tedium of memorizing commands.

Other memory-process research suggests that people differ in their preferred mode of encoding (memorizing) long-term memories. For example, some individuals are "visualizers" who encode memories pictorially and have very vivid, colorful, even "photographic" memories. Other individuals are auditorially oriented and are more likely to remember things that they hear. Still other individuals are kinesthetically oriented and tend to remember things that they have experienced; they can remember exactly how they felt when an important event took place. Because of these encoding process differences, providing users with alternative computer interfaces should be considered. For example, an icon-based or graphical user interface could be provided for visualizers, an audio input and output interface for audi-torially oriented users, and a touchscreen system for kinesthetically oriented users.

Learning

How people learn is an important consideration when building or upgrading computer systems. Many organizations have found that training people on how to use new technologies is gobbling up an increasing share of the computing dollar; for this reason, training may become a high priority.

As we approach the year 2000, non-traditional learning devices such as *computer-aided instruction (CAI)*, videotapes, and *interactive video* disks are play-ing larger roles in user training. The availability of such learning tools has had a positive effect on how rapidly users can learn and become proficient with new systems. Many of these high-tech learning approaches are also used for non-MIS training; for instance, many firms are using video disk technology to train their sales forces, factory workers, and repair people.

Psychological Factors

Basically, people think and act within the confines of what they are able and willing to do. Many of these abilities and behaviors are either innate (possessed at birth) or environmental (learned from the person's surroundings). The country and society that people grow up in, their families, the groups they belong to, and other life experiences help to mold people's personalities. Because many abilities and behaviors are complex, most psychologists conclude that they result from a combination of innate and environmental factors.

A large number of psychological factors may contribute to the success or failure of information systems. In this section, we will look at some of these factors: perception, biases, attitudes, values, cultural factors, risk-taking tendencies, adaptability to change, stress, and motivation.

Perception

Two people often see the same thing in different ways. Perceptual processes can have a significant impact on how people, events, information, and systems are viewed. Two managers, for instance, may read the same performance report and obtain radically different impressions.

Because people differ in the ways that they perceive data and systems, additional steps may be needed to ensure that everyone using them perceives certain things in the same desired way. For example, in software packages, clear on-screen menus and effectively written system procedures can help users perceive exactly what they should do. Ideally, the instructions should tell the user where he or she is, how to move back to the previous step, and what to do next. Systems that include such features are likely to be perceived positively—as useful, well-designed, and user-friendly.

Perception may also play a significant role during the development of information systems. Numerous studies show that users are generally more receptive to a new system if they have participated somehow in its development. Frequently, studies find that participation is an effective way to reduce resistance to change and to ensure the success of the change efforts.

Bias

Almost everyone has biases of some sort that affect his or her perception and behavior. For example, many people are heavily biased by first impressions. Research investigations show that first impressions can bias subsequent perceptions, even if the information on which they are based is later found to be false. Because of the powerful impact of first impressions or *primacy effects*, it is important that information systems make a good first impression on managers and users.

Timing may be a critical factor in the biases that managers and users develop toward new or proposed information systems. For example, if a proposed information system is first presented to management at a bad time (perhaps when costs must be drastically cut), management may be forever biased against it. Because the system was rejected once for being too costly, management may be more likely to reject it again in the future. Even when business conditions improve, the first impression that the system was too expensive or non-critical may linger and make it difficult for management to appreciate the system's merits.

Another bias-related issue is *stereotyping*—the generalization of a trait or behavior to all members of a given group. For example, many users and managers have preconceived notions of computer people; they often stereotype them as "technology pushers." At the same time, MIS personnel often have preconceived notions of users and managers as technological illiterates who need "hand holding." Once a stereotype is developed, it may be self-perpetuating because stereotypes cause perceivers to process only information that is consistent with the stereotype and to ignore inconsistent information. Because of these characteristics, stereotyping can be dangerous and overwhelm otherwise healthy interactions between people. Since high-quality interpersonal relationships between MIS staff members and users are needed—especially during the systems development process—it is important for both managers and MIS personnel to be aware of the stereotypes that may undermine their relationships.

Attitudes

An attitude is an expression of feelings about people, objects, activities, and events. Job attitudes, especially *job satisfaction*, reflect one's overall predisposition toward work and the organization.

People with positive attitudes are often productive workers. Poor attitudes can cause people to work less effectively and, in extreme cases, can lead them to sabotage or undermine systems. For instance, disgruntled employees (such as workers who have been passed over for promotion or recently fired) have often been the perpetrators of computer crimes. Such employees have illegally diverted electronic funds or have stolen information resources such as software or data. Some have succeeded in sabotaging the main computer system and even entire networks. Computer viruses, logic bombs, and several of the other methods (discussed in Chapter 19) are also used to sabotage computer systems.

Job attitudes and job satisfaction levels can be important barometers of morale levels and organizational success. Hence, it is important for managers to monitor these. Decreasing morale and job satisfaction levels may be indications of more serious problems and deserve managerial attention.

Risk-Taking Tendencies

Risk is a measure of how people perceive and deal with uncertain outcomes. Individuals can be classified along a continuum with respect to risk. At one end of the continuum is the "risk seeker"; at the other end, the "risk avoider." Besides personal inclinations to accept or reject risk, the outcomes and likelihoods involved in a specific situation will also determine the perceived level of risk.

Risk factors can affect information systems in a variety of ways. For example, some conservative MIS managers have been accused of selecting IBM computing systems for their firms even when systems offered by other vendors appeared to be more appropriate to their needs. As one computer adage goes, "No one ever got fired for buying IBM." The behavior of these managers may be interpreted as a form of risk avoidance.

At the other end of the spectrum are companies that have installed large transaction processing systems without adequate backup and security systems. Even if it reduces expenses, this is a risk-laden decision. After all, the result could be absolute disaster for organizations whose success is dependent on the continual operation of their transaction processing systems.

Studies also suggest a possible connection between risk and knowledge about technology. For example, many senior executives in large companies are not comfortable with their knowledge of information technology. In many instances, they feel that their subordinates are more knowledgeable about information technology than they are. Since people are more likely to take risks in familiar areas, non-knowledgeable executives may view computer and other technologically oriented acquisitions as more troublesome than acquisitions in the areas that they know. When upper management is not very knowledgeable about information technology, an organization's MIS executives may have difficulty getting it to see the merits of particular technological solutions. In these situations, information systems proposals may have to be stated in terms that executives can understand and in ways that help them fully understand the proposed technology and its potential impacts.

Willingness to Change

Some people, no matter what is done to encourage or coax them, are reluctant to change or may outright refuse to do so. This type of behavior may be seen, for example, in high-level managers and executives who are absolutely unwilling to work interactively with computer systems. Sometimes this is because they feel that this type of work is beneath them and should be done by subordinates. In other cases, ego problems may be involved, such as the fear of being exposed as a computer-illiterate. In some instances, the manager really just does not have the time or patience to learn how to use a computer. Whatever the reason, as the adage goes: "You can bring a horse to water, but you can't make it drink." We would add: "Especially if the horse has a title and clout!"

Because of rapid technological advancements, change—sometimes disruptive change—is a fact of life for computer professionals, users, and managers. In many organizations, users are asked to adapt to new systems, hardware, and software on a regular basis. If these changes are poorly managed, people might use changes to the information system as a focal point around which to cluster other grievances. Some of the reasons why people may be resistant to change are summarized in Figure 2.2.

Many researchers note that users are more likely to adopt new technologies when there is a "felt need" for the new systems. If they don't feel that a new system is necessary, users are more likely to resist it. MIS personnel and managers may have to work together to educate users about the features and benefits of a new system. In some instances, just learning why the new system

Why People Resist Change

- People don't see a reason for the change

- People fear a loss of status, power, authority, freedom, responsibility, money, or employment

- People worry that their loss will be greater than their gain

- People may have had a history of negative experiences with change

- People fear lack of competency or an inability to perform the new task or function

- People fear the unknown

- People suspect the change will result in a new social structure, altering who works with whom and in what way

- People feel that they are not ready for a change

Figure 2.2 Some of the reasons why people resist change. Change is a particularly important variable in managing MIS environments because both technology and business conditions often change at a rapid pace. Anticipating and addressing resistance to change is an important aspect of systems developers' jobs. (Adapted from French and Bell)

is superior to the current one creates a felt need for the change and gets users excited about the implementation of the new system.

Stress

Change—whether it involves downsizing from an IBM mainframe to a local area network; moving from a small town to a large urban area; or being monitored, fired, or reassigned—almost always introduces emotional stress. Researchers have found that extreme stress can impair a person's ability to make good decisions. It often forces people into coping patterns, where they just "put up" with situations rather than trying to change them. In addition, prolonged exposure to stressful situations may result in the undesirable psychological states known as "learned helplessness" or "burnout." Such long-term exposure also increases the likelihood of serious physical ailments such as heart disease and high blood pressure.

Stress-related problems cost companies hundreds of billions of dollars annually. One survey indicated that three-quarters of the workers in the U.S. labor force feel that their jobs are stressful. Other studies have found that a significant number of American managers suffer from too much stress; as a result, some become abusive, intolerant, and dictatorial.

Although excessive amounts of stress are harmful to a person's well-being, moderate amounts of stress may actually produce some good results. For example, many studies have revealed that modest amounts of stress can lead to higher worker performance levels. Also, although some managers complain about on-the-job stress, few actually want less-pressured jobs!

In spite of the fact that moderate levels of stress may enhance worker productivity, an organization's information system should not be a major source of stress. Ideally, users should not experience high levels of anxiety or frustration when working with the computer system. In most instances, it is desirable for the system to make work easier—not more difficult—for users. Dysfunctional levels of stress are likely to be experienced when users feel that the computer system inhibits their productivity.

Computer monitoring of job performance may also be a source of added stress for workers. Such systems can cause resentment and negative user behaviors, including reduced levels of customer service. Organizations considering the implementation of these productivity monitoring systems should anticipate how workers are likely to react and carefully weigh whether the added stress is worth it.

Culture

The way in which people think and behave is strongly influenced by the social environment, or culture, to which they are accustomed. Thus, an information system that worked successfully in New York or Toronto may not be as effective in Mexico City or Tokyo.

Much has been written about the Japanese and their success with both technology and manufacturing techniques. Cultural factors are frequently identified as being important determinants of this success. Some evidence also exists that cultural differences may even be reflected in MIS design. Robert Cole, an expert on competitive performance, observed that:

> The Japanese operate with more selective and simpler information systems . . . [they] focus less on measuring the costs of quality, however, than on information geared to upgrading quality . . . many U.S. companies [in comparison] have overly elaborate measurement systems that are in effect powerful control mechanisms for distributing punishment and rewards.

Cultural factors and values should not be overlooked in MIS design and development. Later in the chapter, we will also look at corporate culture, which refers to the cultural environment present in an organization or an organizational subunit.

Motivation

So far, we have discussed a number of factors that contribute to the way people behave at work and how they react to information technology. All of these factors are important, but often they merely provide background facts about people. Such factors may need a mechanism to transform them into some type of action. In many cases, that mechanism is motivation. Motivation is a major reason why a person does certain things, and many behavioral psychologists feel that a lot of behavior can be explained in terms of motivational factors.

Motivation is often defined as the force that energizes and sustains goal-directed behavior. This force may originate from outside the individual (such as the opportunity to earn a bonus or other significant reward), from internal processes, or from a combination of these. No matter what its source, the force is channeled into goal-directed behavior.

Many psychologists have noted a connection between motivation and frustration. Numerous studies have shown that highly motivated individuals are

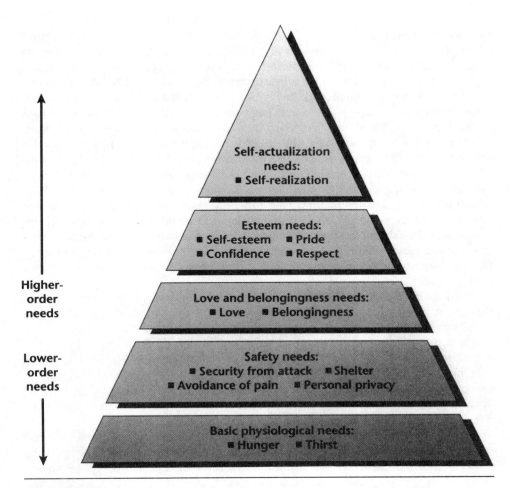

Figure 2.3 Maslow's hierarchy of needs is one of the most widely known theories of motivation. According to this theory, individuals become motivated to satisfy higher-order needs only after they have successfully satisfied lower-order needs. (Adapted from Maslow)

not easily thwarted from achieving their goals and are more likely to get around barriers that stand between them and their goals. Less motivated individuals, on the other hand, are more likely to give up when they encounter frustrating barriers. Because of the negative reactions that less motivated workers may have, systems developers should do what they can to minimize user frustration. Whenever possible, an organization's information system should be a source of motivation, not a source of frustration.

Many respected theories of motivation have been developed. One of the most widely known was proposed by psychologist Abraham Maslow during the 1940s. Maslow believed that people are motivated by five basic categories of needs that can be grouped into a hierarchy (see Figure 2.3). According to this hierarchy, people are motivated to satisfy their lower-order needs (for example, physiological and safety) before they become concerned with satisfying their higher-order ones (such as esteem and self-actualization). The Maslow hierarchy, of course, is only a general model to explain how people are motivated. It cannot explain everything about why specific people behave the way they do.

Frederick Herzberg's Motivator-Hygiene Theory is another well-known motivation theory. Herzberg's research suggests that job dissatisfaction is caused by inadequate levels of what he called hygiene factors—including salary levels, relationships with co-workers, the quality of supervision, company policies, and other job context factors. His theory states that even when adequate levels of hygiene factors exist, workers still may not be satisfied or motivated. This is because motivation and job satisfaction are caused by another set of factors, which he calls motivator factors. These include such items as opportunities for advancement, recognition, challenging tasks, and professional growth and development. Herzberg cautions managers that it is important to make sure that the hygiene factors remain at adequate levels. Furthermore, employee jobs may have to be redesigned in order to ensure that adequate levels of the motivator factors exist.

Because he recognized that the content of the jobs that workers perform may determine motivation, Herzberg became known as the "father of the job enrichment movement." Combining specialized tasks into meaningful units, asking workers to perform a wider range of tasks, and assigning duties to workers that were previously carried out by supervisors are some of the ways in which jobs may be enriched. Managers, systems analysts, and designers should keep these job enrichment principles in mind when developing new information systems or upgrading old ones. If they do, the new system may have a more positive impact on the motivation levels of users.

Numerous other motivation theories present various perspectives on what motivates people in the workplace. A lengthy discussion of these is beyond the scope of this text. Just remember that the more managers and MIS professionals know about people's motives, the better the chances of designing an information system that will help them become productive and achieve their goals.

Motivational theories and approaches play other important roles in organizations. For example, many businesses have developed elaborate performance evaluation and incentive plans to motivate employees into greater productivity. Money has been a prime motivational force in most companies. But money works as an incentive only to a certain extent. As people meet the needs that can be satisfied by money, they start needing different motivations; for example, challenging work, responsibility, and recognition.

MIS professionals are motivated by many of the same incentives that influence other employees. However, since rapid technology changes impact MIS professionals more than other employees, such factors as technological obsolescence and job stability often assume greater motivational importance. To remain productive and retain their jobs, it is often necessary for MIS professionals to keep current on the changes taking place in information technology. MIS executives should look for approaches that can be used to motivate their staff to stay up-to-date and maintain high levels of productivity. If MIS personnel are unable or unwilling to stay current on new software or systems that enhance productivity, their own job security may be threatened.

Other Psychological Factors

Several other psychological factors have important implications for information systems design and development. These include flexibility, information overload, and optimism/pessimism.

Flexibility

People aren't always sure what information they really need. Moreover, since business conditions are always changing, new information needs surface almost continuously. Whatever the case, users generally like to be able to change their minds. Because people are seldom sure of their needs, and because needs are not static, flexibility should be designed into systems whenever possible. As you will see later in the text, flexibility has been a driving force in the development of decision support systems and flexible manufacturing systems.

Information Overload

The rate at which people can process the facts with which they are presented is limited; in addition, this rate differs among individuals because some people can handle more facts than others. Many information systems, however, have been correctly accused of overloading users with information or a preponderance of data. Advances in information technology have made it easy to flood users with information. Although some people are very capable of sifting through this information, other users may feel that they are drowning in a sea of data. When confronted with waves of data and ambiguity about which are most important, users and managers are likely to experience stress or frustration, causing them to be less effective when making decisions. Hence, as a general rule, an information system should be designed to only present decision makers with the relevant information that they need; it should not overwhelm them with an overabundance of unnecessary or unimportant information.

Optimism/Pessimism

People are often overly optimistic about what they think can be accomplished. Consequently, it is wise to take what people say they can do with the proverbial grain of salt. If a system designer says, "This system will cost $500,000," it's likely that the system will cost more than that amount, rather than less. Research by A. Tversky and D. Kahneman suggests that people are more sensitive to negative outcomes than to positive ones. Consequently, they are more inclined to flavor reality with a dose of optimism than to give it straight. Managers and users should be aware of these tendencies when listening to estimates provided by MIS professionals; by the same token, MIS professionals should be wary of estimates provided by users and managers.

While some people always seem to look on the bright side, others always seem to take a skeptical, if not completely pessimistic, view of proposals for new systems. Sometimes this stems from past information systems failures. For example, if a major information system is implemented and fails to live up to its expectations, pessimism may spread among managers when new information systems are proposed. After having been "burned" in the past, managers may feel that new information systems are unlikely to ever solve organizational problems. In general, MIS personnel should anticipate that some managers are likely to be pessimistic about the merits of new systems and they should be prepared to counter these reactions.

ORGANIZATIONS

Among the thousands of organizations that exist throughout the world, no two are exactly alike. Yet most have a number of features in common. In this section, we will consider some general ways to characterize organizations, some of the job types found in many organizations, and some of the ways in which organizations structure their MIS functions.

Organizational Characteristics

An **organization**, as we will define it here, is a relatively long-term, output-producing entity that consists of one or more people, has one or more underlying goals, and conducts itself in ways to achieve these goals. Thus, General Motors, the National Wildlife Foundation, the Canadian government, the Committee to Re-elect the President, and even writers such as Stephen King and Danielle Steel are all organizations under this broad definition. Each of these types of output-producing entities can benefit from some aspect of an information system. In the following section, we discuss some of the dimensions that organization theorists use to classify organizations. While there are many other dimensions that could be considered, we will briefly discuss only those dimensions of greatest importance to information systems design and development.

Product Line

Organizations exist to provide outputs, or "products," to consumers. These products are generally classified into either tangible goods or services.

Tangible goods are those products that you can touch or hold in your hand—for example, television sets, shoes, cars, furniture, and vegetables. Organizations in the tangible-goods business are often classified as either manufacturers or merchandisers. *Manufacturers*, such as Chrysler, Panasonic, and Seagram's, make tangible products. *Merchandisers*, such as Wal-Mart, Safeway, Kroger, and Franklin's Chevrolet in Statesboro, Georgia, sell tangible products made or raised by someone else.

Information systems generally play a key role in both manufacturing and merchandising firms. As we noted in Chapter 1, a widespread trend in both types of companies is to use information technology to tie in suppliers more closely. For many manufacturing firms, an additional key to survival in the 1990s and beyond is flexibility—the ability to take advantage of the shorter product development and product life cycles made possible by information technology.

Organizations in the *services* business do such tasks as disseminate information, give advice, manage assets, and provide financing. Included in the service segment are banks, insurance companies, law and accounting firms, and educational institutions. Many types of services tend to be information-intensive. Banks and financial service companies, for example, are among the heaviest users of information-processing technology. Through the use of computers and communications, these firms can create completely new products, such as personally tailored portfolios, programmed trading systems, and financing packages. The creation of such products may give an organization a competitive advantage and are often cited as examples of the strategic use of information technology. Generally, the more sophisticated and complicated an organization's services are, the more sophisticated its information system must be.

For companies with diverse product lines that have evolved through mergers and acquisitions, a major problem concerns differences between the information systems of the firms involved in the merger or acquisition. Because the information systems in the two (or more) firms were developed independently, they can be difficult to integrate. For example, with the consolidation taking place in the banking industry, many of the emerging megabanks are facing major system-integration problems. A related—and often more serious—problem associated with mergers and acquisitions is that the management styles and philosophies of the different businesses that are forced together are often incompatible. Hence, many organizations involved in mergers and acquisitions must deal with organizational behavior problems at the same time that they are trying to rectify systems integration problems.

Expansion Strategies and Systems Integration

The term *integration* is often used to refer to the way a firm's product line fits together as that product line expands. Firms may pursue a variety of growth strategies. For example, some firms expand by acquiring or merging with highly similar businesses. Others expand by acquiring or merging with businesses who serve as suppliers or consumers of their products. To see the difference between these two expansion strategies, let's look at an example.

Suppose that XYZ Books, a single-site bookstore, decides to grow by acquiring another bookstore. This is an example of geographic expansion through the acquisition of a similar business. If, however, XYZ Books decides instead to expand its operations by acquiring a publishing company, XYZ would then be pursuing an expansion strategy called vertical integration. With *vertical integration*, a firm expands by acquiring other businesses or by creating new facilities that supply its inputs or serve as a customer for its outputs. In this case, XYZ would be acquiring a supplier of the products on its shelves.

Firms that expand by acquiring similar businesses often have an easier time integrating their information systems with those of the businesses they acquire. Two bookstores, for example, often possess information systems that can carry out the same types of functions. Because of these functional similarities, integrating their existing information systems may not be too difficult. However, when a vertical integration strategy is followed, there may be significant differences between the functions performed by the systems; getting them to effectively communicate and exchange data may present a real challenge. Because the information systems being merged were designed to support different types of operations, there may not be a clear way to seamlessly link them.

Size

Organizations are found in a variety of sizes. Large organizations include the U.S. government, Chrysler, AT&T, and IBM; such organizations may employ hundreds of thousands (or even millions) workers. Small organizations may consist of only one or two people. Most organizations, of course, are somewhere between these extremes.

In large firms, we often find organizations within organizations. For example, the U.S. Department of Defense, the Federal Reserve, and the U.S. Department of Labor are all branches of the U.S. government. Although these departments are large enough to function somewhat autonomously—and many of their information systems are set up that way—they are still under control of the U.S. government. Within General Motors, major product-line divisions include Buick, Oldsmobile, Chevrolet, and GMC Trucks. Like the various departments of the U.S. government, these GM divisions are mostly independent, but their information systems must be integrated with the one at GM headquarters so that the information requirements of the larger organization can be met.

A major problem facing most large firms in this fast-paced information age is that, since the activities of more people must be coordinated, it may take a long time to react to external changes in the environment. Because of their size and bureaucratic characteristics, larger firms often lack the flexibility and entrepreneurial structure that make it easier to survive in a world of rapid change. This is not to imply, however, that they are helpless. Some large firms have avoided this dilemma by setting up special structures for special projects. In 1980, for instance, IBM established a special task force to develop its Personal Computer (PC). The task force was separated from headquarters and insulated from the usual bureaucratic entanglements. The IBM PC's subsequent success has caused IBM to use task forces and special structures more extensively for other key projects.

Organizational Structure

The way in which an organization formally groups work activities is called organizational structure. Often, the way in which a firm is structured goes a long way toward explaining the workings of its information systems. The following are four fundamental structures that organizations have found useful for creating departments, divisions, and other subunits:

- **Functi⬢** One of the most common ways to departmentalize is by work function—for instance, finance, marketing, operations, personnel, and research and development (R&D). Firms that use this approach often have a separate MIS department.

  Not all firms that organize by work function use the same functional categories. For example, manufacturing firms often use the term *production* (or manufacturing) instead of or in addition to operations. Some firms are structured by technical function; firms in the construction industry often organize by such categories as "carpenter," "plumber," and similar functions. One of this approach's advantages is that all of an organization's specialists in a particular area are grouped together. Less experienced workers are likely to benefit from working on a day-to-day basis with senior employees. Another advantage is that employees in each of these subunits are likely to be more aware of their information needs and will know which needs are not being met by the organization's information system.

- **Product** A number of organizations, especially large ones with diverse product lines such as Proctor & Gamble, are organized along product lines or product families. GM's car and truck divisions are another example. Also, banks usually have separate departments for commercial transactions, trust accounts, and personal loans. Organizations that follow this organizational approach, especially the larger ones, may have an MIS subunit within each of the major departments or divisions.

- **Customer** Companies in some industries find it useful to organize by customer type. For instance, firms in the publishing industry are typically structured by fiction works, nonfiction works, children's books, textbooks, and similar customer categories. In addition, some textbook publishers have one division responsible for textbooks aimed at college and university customers and another division responsible for the books intended for high school and elementary school audiences. Many organizations are divided along similar industrial and consumer lines.

- **Geography** Organizing by geographic area, or place, is a common method for structuring firms that are physically dispersed. For example, multinational firms often organize by country; a large police force, by precinct. United Airlines, Sears, and the Federal Reserve Board are other examples of organizations that have adopted some form of geographic structuring.

The advantages of departmentalizing along product, customer, and geographic lines are similar. All three structural approaches, when supported by a well-designed information system, make it possible for the organization to be responsive to particular markets or market segments. In general, organizations that can detect and react to market changes quickly are likely to be remain competitive.

Usually, a combination of these structural approaches is found in large organizations. In corporate headquarters, administrative and corporate strategic

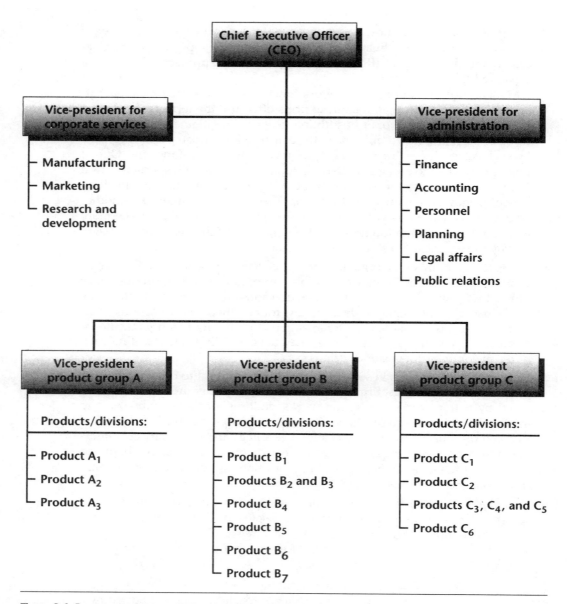

Figure 2.4 Departmental structuring in a large organization.

planning activities often have a functional orientation, such as marketing, finance, or manufacturing (see Figure 2.4). The next level of structuring may be by product or product group, geography, or customer group. At General Foods, for instance, product groups (breakfast foods, beverages, desserts, main meal products, and pet foods) are referred to as *strategic business units (SBU)*. An SBU often operates as an independent profit center within the parent organization and is responsible for its own development and survival. Within each group or SBU, many firms have further product, customer, geographic, or functional divisions. The point is that *hybrid structures* (combinations of functional, product, customer, and geographic divisions) are often found in larger firms.

The way that an organization departmentalizes will have a significant impact on how the organization's information system is designed and evolves. In general, the organization chart displays how information must move vertically (up and down) within the firm. Such information linkages should be built into the organization's information system. Information linkages across departmental boundaries must also be built or developed. Any changes to an organization's structure, such as adding a new product line, will necessarily result in modifications of the firm's MIS.

Centralized Versus Decentralized

The terms "centralized" and "decentralized" are important management concepts. Often, they are used to refer to the distribution of authority and decision making within an organization. Some people, however, use these terms when referring to the distribution of information-technology resources throughout the firm. Here, we will use these terms in their distribution of authority and decision-making context. Differences between centralized and distributed information processing will be explained more fully later in the text.

Centralized organizations are firms in which all the major decisions are made at the top of the organizational hierarchy. In such organizations, people at the top are in control of day-to-day operations. In the years when founder Henry Ford was running the Ford Motor Company, the auto manufacturer was a very centralized organization. Every key decision—and many less important ones—was made directly by Mr. Ford. For example, he insisted on approving all purchase orders within the firm, a task that most CEOs of his stature delegated to subordinates. Today, Ford Motor Company is run quite differently than it was during its early years when Henry Ford was there, but many businesses (especially smaller ones) are still run in a highly centralized manner.

In **decentralized organizations**, responsibility for key decisions is distributed as far down in the management hierarchy as is prudently possible. One of the advantages of decentralization is that it gives lower-level managers substantial practice at making decisions in preparation for moving up the management hierarchy. Examples of the advantages of both centralized and decentralized organizational structures are shown in Figure 2.5.

Many degrees of decentralization are found among organizations (see Figure 2.6). For example, many companies today operate under the umbrella of a "holding company" that, aside from setting certain profitability objectives, lets each member company make decisions on its own. Or, as stated earlier, many large firms are broken up into several strategic business units. In practice, the terms "centralized" and "decentralized" are used in a relative way; few pure forms of these authority structures exist. The degree to which an organization is decentralized may be dependent on a number of environmental and internal

Centralized	Decentralized
■ Higher degree of standardization	■ Quicker response to unique problems
■ Less pressure on subordinates	■ Ideas can come from many sources
■ Most jobs are well-defined	■ Employees have more control over environment
■ Well-defined line of command	■ More conducive to a mixed product line

Figure 2.5 Some of the advantages and disadvantages of both centralized and decentralized organizational structures.

factors. Some of the factors that may affect the degree to which a firm chooses to centralize or decentralize decision-making authority are given in Figure 2.7.

Of course, the extent to which a firm is centralized or decentralized will have a significant influence on the design and development of its information systems. In highly centralized organizations, the information system should make it possible for fairly detailed information about business operations to flow to the upper-level managers who are responsible for the day-to-day functioning of the firm. In highly decentralized organizations, such detailed information is likely to be routed to lower-levels managers in particular departments or divisions, rather than to top-level decision-makers.

Profit Versus Nonprofit

All organizations fall into either the profit or nonprofit category.

Profit-making organizations are in business to make money. Many of these firms have secondary objectives as well, such as becoming the leaders of their industries or providing products of extraordinary quality to consumers. But the bottom line for these organizations is turning a profit. If this goal is not satisfactorily achieved, management may be replaced and the organization may not survive.

Nonprofit (or not-for-profit) organizations often have more service-oriented objectives, such as helping people in need, protecting the environment, advancing knowledge, or promoting a particular cause. Although profit making is not

Structure	Characteristics	Discussion
Totally centralized	All policy determined by higher management	Best in static environment with similar products
Centralized with independent units	Most policy set by higher management, but independent units set own policy	Allows for innovative development in centralized environment
Decentralized with broad central policy making	Autonomous operation under higher-level guidelines	Allows independent units with higher-level coordination
Totally decentralized	All decisions made by independent business units	Faster response to problems and more innovation possible

Figure 2.6 A summary of how organizations may differ in the degree to which they are decentralized.

Contingencies Affecting Centralization/Decentralization

Decision magnitude	The greater the financial ramification of the decision, the more likely the decision will be made at the top of the hierarchy
Consistency	In firms where it is important to maintain a consistency with respect to price, quality, delivery, and service, it is best to have a policy established and controlled at the top of the hierarchy
Availability	For decentralization to work properly, it is imperative that capable managers be available to shoulder decision-making authority
Control	For decentralization to work properly, it is important that control systems be set up to ensure that key tasks at the lower levels are being carried out satisfactorily
Corporate culture	Some firms are strongly committed to centralized or decentralized management style, and will probably remain that way for some time, even though logic may suggest otherwise
Environmental constraints	Such bodies external to the organization as government and labor unions may constrain certain types of decisions from being decentralized. For instance, where national unions bargain with the entire company, certain decision-making prerogatives are no longer available to local management

Figure 2.7 Contingencies affecting the degree of centralizaton and decentralization in a firm. Over time, many large firms and their business units vary in the degree to which they are decentralized, depending on the presence, absence, and strength of factors such as those shown here.

the driving force, these organizations typically have many of the same management and decision-making concerns of profit-making businesses. For example, each of these organizations has "products" and "consumers." Also, each must generally determine how effectively their products or services are being disseminated to consumers. To an organization such as the Colorado Division of Wildlife, protecting "wildlife" and "providing hunting and fishing benefits for residents and non-residents" are considered to be products. The Division closely monitors wildlife populations and measures the effectiveness of hunting and fishing programs in order to assess whether or not it is successfully delivering these products.

Even though nonprofit organizations do not have a profit-making objective, most of them have budgets or are self-supporting (their financial resources often come from fund raising, donations, and support from foundations or government agencies). Maximizing return on resources and controlling costs are often of paramount importance. Like those for profit-making organizations, the information systems for nonprofit organizations should be designed to assist them in effectively managing these resources and in determining whether their objectives are being met. When nonprofit organizations have information systems that are efficient, cost-effective, and equipped with appropriate software, their information systems can play a key role in the achievement of their objectives (see related box, page 74).

Public Sector Versus Private Sector

Federal, state, and local government agencies are called public sector organizations. Virtually all other organizations fall into the private sector. Public sector organizations are generally nonprofit.

Free-spirited employees in the public sector often must face layers of bureaucracy when they attempt to make changes. Often, public sector organizations can pursue only legislated objectives. In contrast to the way the private sector works, in the public sector, the legislatures that initiate edicts are usually not responsible for implementing them.

According to Timothy Matherly and Lee Stepina, the public sector often has older technology-related equipment than the private sector and has traditionally found it more difficult to attract and train high-quality computer professionals. These drawbacks present special challenges to MIS executives of public sector organizations. However, a growing number of public sector organizations realize that information systems can play a critical role in their effectiveness and are taking steps to upgrade their systems and salary structures.

Jobs in Organizations

Many organizations (or divisions of organizations) follow a hierarchical, functional-departmentation structure such as the one shown in Figure 2.8. For simplicity, only a portion of the entire chart is shown.

At the top of the hierarchy in Figure 2.8 is the board of directors. Publicly held corporations—organizations that are financed largely by issuing stock—are typically controlled by a *board of directors*. The board members are selected by stockholders, each of whom generally carries voting clout proportionate to the number of stock shares that he or she holds. The board, in turn, selects key corporate officers, such as the leader or president (usually known as the chief executive officer, or CEO). In the hierarchy, everything below the level of the board represents the firm's management, which is responsible for running the organization. In Chapter 4, we will look at how these management positions can be subdivided into top-level, middle-level, and lower-level slots.

Line Versus Staff Positions

Most positions within an organization can be classified as being either line or staff. A *line position* is one that involves direct authority (that is, direct decision-making responsibility) over people or products in the organization. A person in a *staff position* often has no such authority. Usually, the main role of the staff person is to offer decision support or advice to line managers.

In Figure 2.8, line positions are connected by vertical lines; staff positions by horizontal lines. The only staff positions shown in the figure are for production planning (which involves such responsibilities as finding the best way to schedule production runs and determining a cost-effective number of units to produce on any given run) and quality assurance (which ensures that the products being manufactured meet certain specifications and quality standards).

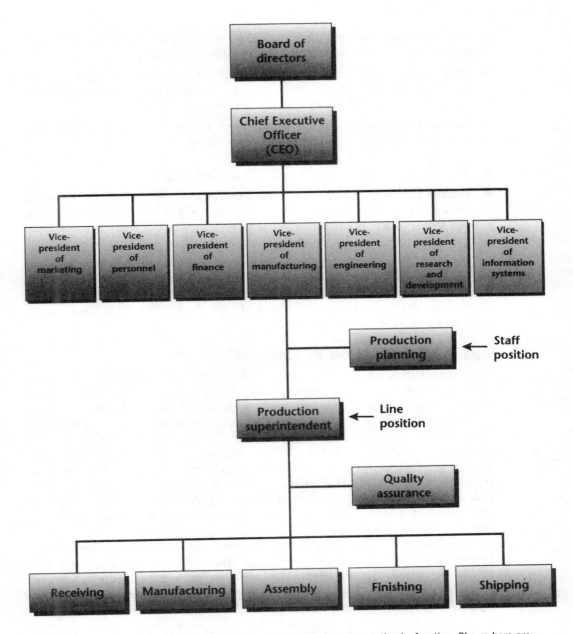

Figure 2.8 A partial organization chart for an organization with departmentation by function. Shown here are vice-presidential positions and some of the key jobs in the manufacturing area. For most organizations, so many jobs exist that it is impossible to show them all in a single diagram.

Many possible advice-authority relationships exist between line and staff. Four of the most common of these are the following:

- **Pure advice**   Staff personnel provide advice, but line personnel have the final decision. Line personnel have the option of taking the advice of staff or ignoring it.
- **Compulsory advice**   Line personnel must at least listen to staff. If staff advice is not followed, line personnel must be able to justify their decision to management.
- **Concurrence**   Line and staff must agree on the action to be taken.
- **Limited authority**   Staff recommendations on certain items must be implemented by line management. For example, in Figure 2.8, if too many defective products are being produced, the quality assurance manager may order a halt in production until appropriate adjustments or corrections are made.

Because of these roles and certain characteristics that typify people in line and staff positions, line and staff personnel are frequently in conflict. We will touch on this point again later in the chapter; however, at this point it is important to note that in many organizations, MIS personnel often find themselves in staff, rather than line, positions.

THE MIS FUNCTION IN ORGANIZATIONS

The MIS function may be organized in several different ways. In many firms—especially those that departmentalize along functional lines—the MIS area is organized in a centralized manner, similar to that shown in Figure 2.9. When centralized structures are used, key areas are often broken out as separate subunits. In Figure 2.9, five principal areas are identified: information center, office automation, systems development, programming, and computer operations. This figure also shows two staff functions that often cut across the line areas: data administration and telecommunications. In this section, we will briefly discuss these line areas and the duties of the MIS personnel with whom managers and users are most likely to interact. Discussion of the other roles depicted in Figure 2.9 will be delayed until Chapters 17, 18, and 19.

Before turning to some of the key MIS personnel found in organizations, it is important to reiterate that the centralized structure illustrated in Figure 2.9 is just one of many ways to organize the MIS area. Some firms, such as Manufacturers Hanover, have found a combination of centralized corporate structures and decentralized business functions to be very effective. In general, the MIS area should be organized in a manner that helps it achieve its (and the larger organization's) objectives. As Alfred Chandler noted, "structure follows strategy," and the MIS area should not be allowed to ignore this principle. If the existing structure for the MIS area does not assist the organization in achieving its strategic goals, it should be reorganized.

In some cases, entire organizations may be reorganized in order to adopt structures that are more in line with new strategic initiatives. For example, in 1991 IBM underwent a major reorganization in order to shift its focus to inde-

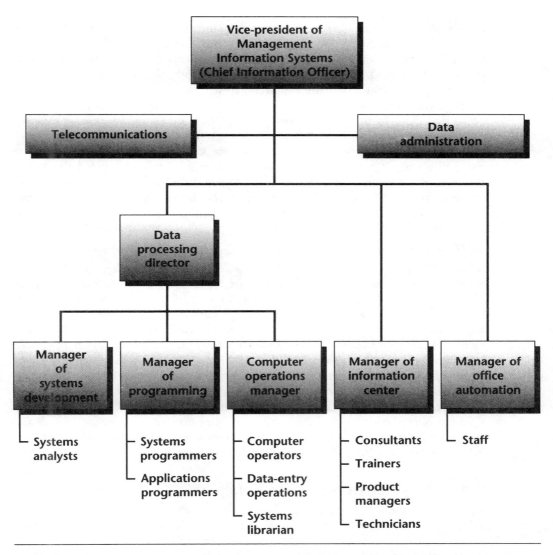

Figure 2.9 An organization chart showing common MIS jobs and typical relationships among them in a centralized MIS structure. While many of the reporting relationships depicted here are common, the structure of MIS departments can vary considerably between organizations. The growing importance of MIS in most organizations has led to an increasing variety of MIS structures.

pendent business units that could be more responsive to particular types of customers. In 1992, Apple Computer, Inc. replaced its traditional organization by geographic area with more functionally oriented groups—purportedly to prepare it for markets other than computers, especially the telecommunications, consumer electronics, media, and publishing markets.

In many organizations, the MIS infrastructure is in the midst of what Richard Nolan has described as a period of "technological discontinuity"—that is, a transition period from a centralized, mainframe-oriented, transaction processing environment to one in which end-user concerns are playing an ever-increasing role. Such transitions often have an impact on the distribution of power within the MIS area. Traditionally, MIS line managers, especially data processing managers, had the limelight all to themselves—now, they have to share it with the information center, the office automation group, and other areas that cater to the needs of users. The migration of transaction processing and other key applications from mainframes to local area networks (LAN) and distributed processing environments (information systems that are designed to meet the computing needs of particular subunits) has also eroded the traditional power base of data processing managers. In the meantime, the increased importance of networking has enhanced the power and clout of business telecommunications managers in many organizations.

MIS Personnel

In the following section, we will briefly identify the titles, roles, and major responsibilities of the MIS personnel who are most likely to interact directly with managers and users. This is not an exhaustive set of job titles and job descriptions—many other job titles may be found within the MIS areas of organizations. An abbreviated discussion of the typical duties of each is provided to help you understand what they do and how they are likely to interact with users. We will discuss some of the roles of MIS personnel at this point because most managers find it easier to interact with someone from another part of the organization when they know that person's duties and responsibilities. Another reason for discussing these roles now is because they are mentioned frequently throughout the text. We feel that you will better appreciate later sections of the book by giving you a brief overview of who these people are, what they do, and how they are likely to interact with users and managers.

Computer Operations Personnel

Computer operations personnel are the people responsible for the day-to-day operation of transaction processing systems, management reporting systems, and all other shared multiuser computers. Some of the job titles for the people in this category are the following:

- ■ **Computer operations manager** The **computer operations manager** is the person in charge of the entire operations activity. Generally, the computer operations manager will be responsible for hiring and assigning the other operations personnel, establishing operations center policies, planning the installation and removal of equipment, and generally, doing all other tasks to ensure that data get processed as efficiently as possible.

- ■ **Computer operators** **Computer operators** are the people in charge of running the equipment at the computer center. It is their job to load tapes and disks, monitor system performance, initiate solutions to equipment malfunctions, and similar functions.

- **Data-entry personnel** **Data-entry personnel** are the people who enter data into the main computer system. Although most large organizations still employ a sizable number of people for data entry, the trend today is to move away from centralized data entry, whenever possible, and to have users capture data in machine-readable form at its source.

- **Systems librarians** **Systems librarians** are responsible for managing data stored off-line on such media as tapes and disks. Included among the resources catalogued by systems librarians are backup copies of important programs and data, and records kept for archival purposes.

Systems Analysts

Systems analysts are the technology professionals charged with analyzing, designing, and implementing large computer-based information systems. Because they are the crucial interface among users, upper management, and programmers, they must be skilled in business, computers, and other technology-based areas. They must also possess good interpersonal communication skills.

Systems analysts must be able to talk to users to determine their information processing needs. They must be able to translate user needs and information requirements into terms and formats that computer programmers and telecommunications personnel can understand and use. Because systems analysts are such crucial communication links between users and technically oriented computer professionals, it is crucial that they possess exceptional communication and people skills.

Programmers

The computer professionals who are specifically charged with writing computer programs are called programmers. Some of the types of programmers that may be found in organizations are applications programmers, maintenance programmers, and systems programmers.

Applications programmers code applications programs—the software that serves the direct needs of end-users. Generally, it is the systems analyst who initially specifies what needed programs must do. Armed with a set of formal—often technical—specifications from the analyst, the applications programmer then writes programs from them. Applications programmers may also be charged with the responsibility of maintaining, updating, and keeping applications programs running for years after they were initially written. Programmers who specialize in these activities are called **maintenance programmers.**

Systems programmers code the systems software that controls the operation of computer hardware and makes it possible to run applications programs. Managers and users are much more likely to encounter and interact with applications and maintenance programmers than with systems programmers. However, it may be necessary for them to consult with systems programmers when technical problems are encountered.

Information Center Personnel

The **information center (IC)** is one of the newer MIS areas in many organizations. It is usually established to help end-users choose the decision-support resources they need in order to better perform their jobs. Other activities executed by the IC are training users in how to use specific software packages, supporting users on a continuing basis—which often includes a "hotline"—and setting standards that promote the sensible growth of personal computing resources within the firm. Because of these roles, managers and users may interact very frequently with IC staff members. In many organizations, IC personnel have more contact with users and managers than any of the other types of MIS personnel.

OA Personnel

In some firms, an office automation (OA) group is responsible for providing the firm with a cost-efficient, integrated approach to exploiting such office technologies as electronic document processing and electronic mail. Typical duties of the OA staff are setting up a long-range plan for OA, arranging for product demonstrations, and helping end-users with system choices.

MIS Management

At the top of the computer hierarchy are MIS executives. In some organizations, the person at the top may hold the title of vice-president (or director) of information systems or data processing director. The precise titles used to describe these jobs vary among organizations. In some organizations, the vice-president (director) of information systems is the chief information officer (CIO). These MIS executives oversee the full range of MIS-related activities, including transaction processing—which traditionally accounts for the largest share of the information processing dollar—as well as telecommunications, data administration, and end-user support.

In many organizations, a **data processing (DP) director** is responsible for all personnel involved with the company's major transaction processing applications, especially when these are mainframe-based. In these environments, programmers, systems analysts, and operations personnel may be under the DP director's control (refer back to Figure 2.9, page 65).

Database Administrators

Database administrators are often found in organizations that have an integrated database. Database administrators are responsible for ensuring that users and programmers have access to the data that they need in order to make decisions or run applications. They are also responsible for ensuring both the integrity (accuracy and currency) and security (safety from unauthorized access or system failures) of the data in the database. Database administrators are often found in mainframe-based relational database environments. Managers and users are likely to have to contact and work with database administrators in order to gain access to the data they need.

Telecommunications and Network Management

Telecommunications managers and **network managers** are responsible for meeting the data communications needs of users in the organization. The increasing trend toward networking and distributed processing has increased the importance and prevalence of these positions. Many individuals in these jobs are responsible for all business telecommunications systems, including those for voice and video communications (for example, video teleconferencing). **Local area network (LAN) managers** are also becoming more common in organizations.

ORGANIZATIONAL BEHAVIOR

So far, we have discussed some general principles of human behavior and a number of organizational properties that have an impact on information systems design and development. Organizational behavior—the way people behave in organizations—is both a function of what people bring into the organizational environment and the environment itself. People bring their abilities, expectations, past experiences, values, attitudes, personal beliefs, and other personal factors to the organizational settings in which they work. The organization has its own set of characteristics; these are often reflected in its structures, jobs, management hierarchy, reward system, and so forth. The interaction of personal and organizational factors often shapes organizational culture, power structures, and intergroup dynamics. Each of these can have a significant impact on the role that MIS plays in an organization.

Corporate Culture

The term *culture* has traditionally pertained to general differences among people that exist across geographical boundaries. However, culture is not a concept confined entirely to countries or to geographical areas. Culture is a general concept that relates to the shared philosophies, ideologies, values, assumptions, beliefs, expectations, and norms that knit any type of community together.

In the same way, we have corporate cultures, since organizations form their own social systems. Just as there are many different cultures and subcultures around the world, many different corporate cultures also exist. Corporate culture provides the social energy that drives an organization. Much of what takes place in an organization is influenced by its cultural qualities of shared meaning, norms, assumptions, rituals, heroes, and unwritten rules.

The formality or informality of an organization's work climate is often strongly influenced by its culture. For example, in some organizations, the atmosphere is very formal; in others, it is informal. *Formality* refers to the degree of specification given to such matters as responsibility, authority, and discretion. Organizations that are small and that deal with relatively innovative products are often more informal than larger, more bureaucratic organizations. People at all levels of informal organizations may be on a first-name basis, and the office of the leader may not be much classier than the office of the person running the mailroom. Informal organizations also tend to place less weight on rigid planning procedures, rank, and tradition—decision making and even the information systems that are in place may reflect a spontaneous, "shoot-from-the-hip" style. In the computer industry, IBM has the reputation of having a formal culture, Tandem, however, is widely known for having an informal culture.

The formality or informality of an organization often reflects the ideas of the leader or the patterns established by industry. In established industries, large corporations with mature product lines are often more formal and deliberate in decision making. Corporate culture can influence a number of important attitudes within an organization, such as its orientation toward superior customer service or product quality or its desire to develop a reputation for being a "cutting edge" company or an "innovator." These attitudes may be manifested in the strategic goals pursued by the organization and the manner in which it implements its strategies. IBM, for instance, has established customer service as a priority and has consciously worked to maintain the reputation for outstanding customer service. The Helpware "hotline" it established in 1992 is a recent example of this. Companies may build their culture around other strategic goals; for example, a company may strive to develop a reputation for turning out high-quality "clone" products or for being one of the best "low-cost/high-volume" producers in its industry.

Power

Power refers to the ability to summon resources to accomplish objectives. Power issues frequently show up in both the development and use of information systems. Five leading issues concerning power and the MIS area of an organization are listed in Figure 2.10:

- *Traditional redistribution* Information systems have frequently had the effect of redistributing power within an organization. For example, rapid and reliable computer processing has enabled some decision-related processes, once solely performed by human beings, to be usurped by machines. People who make credit authorization decisions, for instance, now find computers supplying some of the "expert knowledge" that once only humans were capable of imparting. Furthermore, if the system is programmed to not violate certain policies, the human credit authorizer might be locked out of taking certain courses of action. Computer and communications technologies have also often had the effect of distributing decision-making power that was once centralized at one location to other locations throughout the firm.

- *Monitoring* Since performance data in a variety of occupations are now easily recordable through information technology and often instantly avail-

Power Issues in MIS

- Traditional redistribution of user power caused by new systems
- Loss of power due to information systems monitoring
- Overall power of the MIS department
- Erosion in MIS department power caused by end-user-developed systems
- Importance of users beyond that suggested by their organizatonal positions

Figure 2.10 Five important areas concerning the role of power in information systems.

able to interested parties, this is another example of how high-tech can affect power balances. For instance, information systems often monitor the key-stroke speed and the break periods of data-entry clerks. Many firms also use systems to monitor long-distance calls of employees. These and similar systems can give managers more power over subordinates. However, as noted previously, they are also likely to increase the stress levels of the employees who are being monitored.

■ *Power of MIS department* The overall power of the MIS department is usually directly proportional to the perceived strategic relevance of MIS to key executives. If, for example, the CEO does not consider information to be one of the organization's most critical assets, the MIS department is unlikely to have considerable clout within the organization. If MIS executives wield little power, the organization's information system may be inadequate or much less sophisticated than it should be.

■ *End-user development* In many organizations, the balance of power has also been tipped by the introduction and diffusion of microcomputers. As noted earlier in the chapter, MIS personnel—managers, programmers, systems analysts, and operations people—used to be the "only game in town." The power to compute or not was largely in the hands of the computer professionals—if users wanted to get their computing done, they were forced to depend on the MIS staff. However, as microcomputers spread throughout organizations and users began to develop their own systems, computer professionals began to see their power base erode. Many of their services became expendable. Even worse, MIS budgets were often cut to allow for outside purchases of microcomputer systems by other departments. Companies that created information centers to encourage and support end-user development have often observed a power shift toward IC staff and away from traditional MIS roles.

Many industry observers feel that what we have seen of the microcomputer revolution is only the tip of the iceberg and that, at some future point, user departments with their own internal sources of MIS expertise—business systems analysts—will be commonplace. Should this happen, the MIS department may turn full circle back to its role of the 1950s: being the "keepers of the keys" to any remaining large mainframes and centralized transaction processing systems.

■ *Importance beyond organizational position* The importance of individuals beyond that suggested by their organizational positions is sometimes loosely referred to as "political clout." The information systems designer should identify such individuals and take special care when dealing with them. For example, if the firm's chief financial officer (CFO)—the vice-president of finance—really has more power in determining the strategic destiny of the firm than the CEO, then more effort should be expended on selling the CFO, rather than the CEO, on MIS development. Also, when developing new systems for users, more time should be allotted to users who have both the power and the inclination to effectively influence or train other users. The ultimate success of the system may be largely determined by these users and their opinions.

The power issues and power shifts associated with MIS cannot be ignored when attempting to understand how MIS staff members relate and interact with users and managers within their organizations. It may even have a significant impact on the relationships among members of the MIS staff.

Intergroup Conflict

It is a sad fact that people do not get along as well as they should. Conflicts among people are inevitably going to flare up now and then, and managers should keep aware of likely trouble spots.

For example, the relationship between computer professionals and users—and also between computer professionals and management—has often been stormy. Computer professionals have frequently been perceived by both users and management as being more concerned about technology than about practical consequences. Furthermore, as J. Daniel Couger and Robert Zawacki's research suggests, many computer professionals are more loyal to their professions than to the organizations for which they work. The technical language spoken by computer professionals has also been known to alienate users and to make communication between MIS staff and users more difficult.

In many organizations, the positions held by MIS professionals are considered to be staff, rather than line. As described earlier, squabbles between line and staff personnel are not uncommon in organizations. Line managers and MIS staff members may have different points of view regarding a particular situation, but often only one of these groups (usually the line managers) makes the final decision about what is going to happen. This may leave MIS managers with only one way to influence the decisions of line managers—the power of persuasion. To add to these problems, research has shown that staff personnel are often younger and better educated than the line managers they advise. So, imagine the arguments that could take place when a 22-year-old, fresh-out-of-college inventory control expert tries to sell a 42-year-old school-of-hard-knocks warehouse manager on the use of sophisticated mathematical modeling approaches—none of which the veteran understands.

Differences among the goals of two or more groups can also be a source of intergroup conflict. For example, an inventory manager may be most effective when he or she maintains relatively low inventories in order to minimize total inventory costs. A sales manager, on the other hand, often prefers to have excessively high inventories in order to avoid being out-of-stock because a lack of merchandise can drive customers into the eager clutches of competitors. MIS personnel should be familiar with the goals of the subunits that comprise the organization and should be sensitive to goal differences among them. If they are aware of the competing goal orientations among groups, MIS personnel should be better able to provide the different subunits with the specific information that they need. Appropriate information exchanges among subunits often helps to minimize the potential for major intergroup flare-ups; it may be up to MIS professionals to ensure that these communication bridges are built and maintained.

Intragroup Dynamics

A tremendous amount of research has taken place over the past 60–70 years concerning the behavior of people in groups. With respect to the development of information systems, some of the key research has focused on group size, roles, participation, leadership, norms, and status.

Group Size

One of the first principles learned by a juggler is that it is possible to have only so many balls in the air at the same time. So, too, does performance diminish when too many people are being coordinated at once. Numerous research investigations have revealed that performance often declines when the number of people being supervised surpasses seven. These studies also indicate that the practical limit on the size of a group is influenced by factors such as the task being performed and the skill or ability levels of the members of the group.

The number of individuals that can be supervised effectively at any one time is commonly referred to as span of control. In many organizations, information technology is making it possible for supervisors to have a larger span of control. Electronic mail is one of the information technologies that has the potential to increase a manager's span of control—and his or her ability to stay in touch with subordinates who are out of the office most of the time (such as traveling salespersons) or at remote office locations. Computerized performance monitoring systems—mentioned earlier in the chapter—also have the potential to increase a manager's effective span of control.

Norms

Norms are (usually unwritten) rules or behavioral standards that govern what group members should do. Norms regulate the behaviors of group members. Ignoring or departing from norms may result in an individual's being labeled a "social deviant" or outcast. Research indicates that cohesive or close-knit groups are more likely to enforce their norms than are less cohesive groups.

The degree to which people in a group conform to norms may influence how they react to information systems. For example, in some groups, the

IT Helps Wilderness Society Track Delicate Ecosystems

The environment has emerged as one of the major business issues of the 1990s. Environmental advocacy groups are increasingly turning to information technology to educate business managers about the fragile nature of forest ecosystems.

The Wilderness Society has developed an information system that produces what many scientists claim to be the best evidence available about the impacts of humans on forest

"THE HEART OF THE SYSTEM IS A MAPPING SYSTEM CAPABLE OF COMPARING OLD PHOTOGRAPHS WITH NEW IMAGES . . . ."

ecosystems. Its system combines expert system and graphics software to visually display how forest ecosystems—including water systems and endangered species habitats—

have changed over the years. The system's outputs have been used in court cases, which resulted in injunctions halting timber cutting in some areas.

The heart of the system is a mapping system capable of comparing old photographs with new images generated from satellite imaging and aerial photographs. This allows foresters to see how "old growth" has been replaced by "new growth" or bare ground (resulting from human encroachment).

The Wilderness Society's computer-based ecology mapping system is a constructive addition to our understanding of how human actions affect the environment. The system received a *Computerworld* Smithsonian Award honoring it as an IT application that improves the world in which we live.

Adapted from Horwitt (1992).

---

so-called "bandwagon effect" may be observed, meaning that once an attitude or perception develops among several members of a group, virtually everyone in the group will conform to this belief. Thus, if an analyst approaches a user group in which there is a great deal of skepticism toward the MIS area, he or she should be extremely careful, especially if the potential for bandwagoning is high. The slightest mishap in this type of situation could bring a flood of "we knew this system was going to be no good" criticisms and subsequent group closed-mindedness.

A norm that many organizations—especially large, formal ones—possess is a tendency to make changes incrementally, which means in small steps, rather than all at once. In such a situation, an analyst attempting to make too many changes at the same time may encounter strong resistance.

Status

Status refers to the relative ranking of an individual in a group or organization. People can achieve status in a group in a number of ways: through the position they hold in the organizational hierarchy, through the type of work they perform, through their personalities, and through their competencies.

Often, because of their status within the organization, executives have a strong ego to protect. This is especially likely in formal organizations, where workers at lower levels rarely make contact with executives, and where executives frequently take on an aura of unapproachability. In organizations with entrenched status differences, it may be unsatisfactory to have high-level personnel take part in the same computer training sessions as personnel ranked at significantly lower levels. The high-level people may be afraid to expose any computer illiteracy to lower-level personnel. If this fact is overlooked, the training sessions may be counterproductive for both high- and low-status personnel.

Roles

A *role* is an expected behavior. In many firms, a person's job is the initial basis for determining his or her role.

Among the most common and most serious role-related problems is *role ambiguity,* which occurs when job duties are unclear. This may result from either a poor job description or poor management. Historically, MIS personnel have complained that their job priorities are vague and that continual restructuring seems to take place within their departments. Many of these complaints are because MIS is a rapidly evolving discipline and many lower-level MIS managers have either a limited management background or little appreciation of management priorities.

Computer professionals such as systems analysts sometimes also suffer from *role conflict* in the course of performing their jobs. Role conflict refers to clashing job demands. For instance, analysts are evaluated by superiors in the MIS department under one set of priorities, but their jobs often involve satisfying users who have other sets of priorities.

Participation

Since the 1920s, studies have indicated that people can be more productive if they actively participate in the management of their own work environments. Over the years, many successful managers have used *participative management* and *empowerment* approaches to get workers more involved; for instance, by soliciting ideas from them, including them in decision making, and giving them credit for suggestions. A number of studies reveal that such approaches can be effectively used to develop and implement new information systems. These investigations indicate that an MIS project is more likely to succeed when there are high levels of user participation. Through such participation, users are likely to better understand new systems and to appreciate their benefits.

Leadership

The history of the world is rich with examples showing how individual leaders have made a difference. Leadership is important to the study of MIS for a variety of reasons. The changing role of MIS in many organizations is requiring different types of leadership from MIS executives than what was expected in the past. Moreover, since leaders are the people who usually "make a difference" in an organization, it is important for the systems designer to identify leaders among users; also, the CIO should identify who is truly running the firm.

MIS executives who are strong leaders are often able to have a significant impact on their organization's strategic plans and the overall corporate perception of the MIS area. Strong MIS leaders can ensure that MIS concerns are reflected in these strategic plans and that the MIS area will be able to help the organization achieve its long-term objectives. MIS executives with obvious leadership qualities, especially those with a vision for the role that the MIS area should play in the future, are likely to help develop and maintain a positive image for MIS throughout the organization.

SUMMARY

People are the most important part of any organization, and thus, of any MIS. An MIS often succeeds or fails on the basis of the people involved. A number of human characteristics can have an impact on the design and performance of information systems. Among such characteristics are physical and psychological limitations; behavior, including the effects of intelligence, willingness to change, stress, perception, bias, risk, flexibility, memory, information overload, learning ability, culture, optimism, and values; and motivation. These individual differences must be taken into account by systems designers.

Although no two organizations are alike, most have a number of features in common. As with human characteristics, these features often impact the design and performance of management information systems. Organizations can be characterized in a number of ways. For example, they can be classified according to their product line or their size. They can also be classified according to structure—that is, the way that they formally group work activities. Furthermore, they can be classified as profit versus nonprofit, public versus private, and by their corporate cultures, which is the social energy that drives them. Organizations can also be either centralized or decentralized, and may choose from different types of expansion strategies.

Jobs in organizations are either line positions (those with direct decision-making authority) or staff positions (those that usually provide support or advice). The top line job in an organization is president or chief executive officer (CEO). In general, management positions are broken down into top-level, middle-level, and lower-level slots. A major role of the MIS department is to provide key managers at all levels with the kind of information they regularly need to do their jobs.

In many organizations, the MIS function is organized into five principal line areas: operations, systems development, programming, the information center, and office automation. Computer operations personnel—which include the computer operations manager, computer operators, data-entry operators, and systems librarians—are responsible for the day-to-day operation of multiuser systems, including transaction processing and formal reporting systems. Systems analysts investigate, design, and implement large computer-based information systems. Applications programmers write applications programs, whereas systems programmers are responsible for writing systems programs. Information center (IC) personnel help users choose decision support resources. Office automation (OA) personnel provide the firm with an integrated approach to exploiting office technologies. Database administrators and network managers, including LAN managers, play important roles in many organizations. At the top of the MIS hierarchy is the chief information officer (CIO) or another MIS executive, who oversees all MIS-related activities. In organizations with centralized transaction processing systems, a data processing (DP) director may oversee a large number of MIS personnel.

Organizational behavior is a function both of what people bring to the organizational environment and of that environment itself. A number of organizational behavioral issues have an impact on MIS. These include corporate culture (the shared values, assumptions, and norms of the organization), power (the influence people have to accomplish objectives), the degree and type of intergroup conflict present, and several characteristics of intragroup dynamics, such as span of control, norms and status, roles, participation, and leadership

KEY TERMS

Applications programmer

Centralized organization

Computer operations manager

Computer operations personnel

Computer operator

Data-entry personnel

Data processing (DP) director

Decentralized organization

Ergonomics

Information center (IC)

Local area network (LAN) managers

Maintenance programmers

Network managers

Norm

Organization

Systems librarians

Systems programmer

Telecommunications managers

REVIEW

REVIEW QUESTIONS

1. What are some of the people factors that must be considered when developing information systems?

2. Why may information technologies cause stress in the workplace?

3. How are first impressions important in the systems development process?

4. In what ways can a CEO's risk-taking tendencies be important to a company and the company's MIS?

5. Explain why worker skill, ability, intelligence, and sophistication levels should be taken into account when designing user interfaces.

6. In what ways do centralized organizations differ from decentralized organizations? How is the degree of the centralization or decentralization likely to affect MIS design and development?

7. Identify several types of organizational structures and explain how MIS design and development is likely to be affected by each.

8. How do the roles and responsibilities of the various types of MIS personnel differ?

9. What expansion strategies may be followed by organizations? How may these be related to systems integration?

10. How do systems programmers differ from applications and maintenance programmers?

11. In what ways may power influence what happens in an MIS environment? Why is leadership important in this environment?

12. What are some of the organizational behavior issues that must be confronted by MIS developers? Why are these important?

DISCUSSION QUESTIONS

1. Support or criticize the following:

> Information overload is an inevitable consequence of the modern information age. Chaotic conditions imparted by changing technology and world markets are forcing managers to open their eyes wider and take in more potentially irrelevant data than ever before in their search for new opportunities and potential problems. The MIS department may actually be wasting time or doing a disservice to management by filtering carefully the information it provides.

2. In what ways does the inclusion of people in CBIS environments make MIS a more difficult area to study?

3. Developing systems that span across different departments has long been a problem in building information systems. Why do you think this is the case?

Auto Dealership Uses a Variety of Information Systems to Compete

Franklin Chevrolet/Toyota is an automobile dealership in Statesboro, Georgia. It sells and services both new and used cars and helps its customers arrange financing. It is a typical car dealership in many respects and, like so many others, it relies heavily on information technology to help it compete.

Videotext is one of the main systems in the parts and service departments. The videotext system is essentially an on-line parts catalog. Terminals sit on top of the service counter and their screens swivel for viewing from both sides. The search for a part begins when a walk-in customer or one of Franklin's mechanics tells the parts attendant the year and model of the vehicle that needs a part. Instantly, a visual image of the vehicle appears on the screen. The system make it possible to zoom in on any component of the vehicle—even the tiniest—and the swivel screen makes it possible for the customer or mechanic to visually verify that what is showing on the screen is what is needed. After verification, the parts attendant can obtain the part number for each needed piece from the videotext system. Each part number is then entered into another computer terminal to determine if the part is in stock or must be ordered. Parts that are not in stock are ordered electronically.

The system also allows the parts attendant to first search the parts inventory of other dealerships in the area. If none of the other dealerships has the needed part, an electronic order is submitted to the company that supplies the part. The electronic order receipt returned by the supplier indicates when the part will be delivered to the dealership.

The sales function is supported by several systems. Clerical workers use desktop publishing software to design newspaper ads aimed at attracting buyers to the showrooms and lots. If salespeople are unable to interest potential buyers in vehicles they have on the lot, they will use a system that allows them to see if a vehicle with the appropriate set of options is available at another dealership in the region. If an appropriate match cannot be found, an order can be electronically placed with the factory for a vehicle that includes everything the customer wants.

The finance area of the dealership is equipped with systems that allow buyers to know exactly what their monthly payments will be if they finance through the dealership, local banks, or the General Motors Acceptance Corporation (GMAC). The system can also be used to perform instant credit checks and to set up automatic checking account deduction payments for customers with accounts at local banks.

Franklin recently set up a special room for a new microcomputer-based multimedia training system. The system—produced and distributed by General Motors—combines video, audio, text, and data elements. Beginning, intermediate, advanced, and refresher training modules are available for mechanics, parts attendants, and salespeople.

The dealership anticipates that its IT support will become even more sophisticated in the years ahead. It expects the text-based systems in the sales offices to be replaced by sophisticated graphics systems so that customers can see what their custom orders will actually look like. Franklin also expects each service bay to have a computer terminal that runs expert system software to assist mechanics in diagnosing problems and identifying the most efficient set of service options. On-line videoconferencing systems are also expected; these will put mechanics in touch with human experts who will guide them through tricky repair procedures.

Adapted primarily from interviews with Franklin Chevrolet/Toyota managers and employees by T. Case (1992). Also adapted from Eckerson (1992).

DISCUSSION

1. Describe how the systems in place at this car dealership help each of its functional areas to be more effective and efficient.

2. What types of interorganizational systems are being used by the car dealership? How do these help the dealership compete and provide high levels of quality service?

3. How are the multimedia training system and other anticipated IT changes likely to benefit the dealership in the long run?

4. Identify three other types of systems that you feel would help car dealerships such as Franklin Chevrolet/Toyota be more effective, efficient, or competitive. What benefits are they likely to receive if they implement your recommendations?

Chapter 3

Systems and Models

After completing this chapter, you will be able to:

Define a system

Explain the role of models in studying systems

Describe common types of systems and models encountered in the field of MIS

Enumerate and discuss the components of several important models of organizations, including the strategic-planning model, the critical success factor model, and the management control model

So far in this text, the term "system" has been used rather loosely. A management information system has been defined and several examples have been provided. However, we have not yet formally identified those general properties that systems possess. In this chapter, we will look more closely at systems—what comprises them, how we can best represent them on paper or in words, how they differ, and so on.

The chapter opens by defining a system. Next, we explore several models that represent systems. The role of models is extremely important in studying systems because through models, we can understand how systems are developed and work. Then we will look at some important models of organizations and organizational processes, including a strategic planning model, a critical success factors model, and a management control model.

Although one objective of this chapter is to present the rudiments of systems theory, another is to promote the importance of thinking systematically. So, for example, as you study the models in this chapter—which cover useful ways in which to structure your thinking about organizations, organizational processes, and the MIS function—try to apply these models to the other organizational and MIS concepts throughout the text.

WHAT IS A SYSTEM?

A **system** is a set of interrelated elements that collectively work together to achieve some common purpose or goal. A football game, for instance, is played according to a system that is composed of such elements as teams, stadiums, equipment, referees, and rules. Another system is a computer-based information system (CBIS). A CBIS is a collection of people, hardware, software, data, and procedures that interact to provide timely data and information, both internally and externally, to authorized people who need it.

Components of a System

A **system element** can be a tangible object (such as a car or a person), an abstract concept (such as data or information), or an event (such as March 23 or "groundbreaking ceremony"). Tangible objects, of course, are those objects that we can touch or measure. Abstract concepts and events are intangible.

When classifying systems, we frequently differentiate between a system's logical description and physical description. The **logical description** of a system is a representation that specifies essential system elements in broad, often abstract terms. A **physical description** of the same system would be much more precise about how it is actually implemented. For example, if we want to describe a computer system, we might use the terms "input," "processing," and "output"—which are broad, imprecise concepts. Such terms are useful in describing logically, in general terms, how systems work. However, if we were to state that a *keyboard* is to be used as an input device on a *microcomputer* system, which uses both a *printer* and *monitor* as output devices, we are describing a system in physical terms.

System Environment

All systems function within some sort of **environment**. The environment, like the system, is a collection of elements. These elements surround the system and often interact with it.

For any given problem, there are many types of systems and many types of environments. Thus, it is important for be clear about what constitutes the system and the environment of interest. For instance, a physician looking at human systems may be interested in studying the entire human body as a system, not just a part of it (such as the central nervous system only). If the entire human body is the system of interest, the physician is likely to define the environment more broadly than he or she might if the focus was on just the central nervous system.

Systems are normally delimited by a **boundary**, which separates them from their environment. Anything within the boundary is part of the system; anything outside is part of the environment. What is included in the system and what is included in the environment depend on the particular problem being studied.

Let's consider another example to make this distinction clear. Suppose a systems analyst is studying a computer installation in order to determine how to reduce the time it takes to get batch jobs completed. For this type of problem, the system description will probably include people. Batch turnaround may be impacted by a number of people-related factors—for example, current user practices in submitting data, the speed of data-entry operators, and the schedule established by the computer operator. On the other hand, if the problem being studied is how to make a particular computer program execute more efficiently on a given computer, people would probably not be considered as part of the system's environment. In this instance, system elements would include purely technical concerns such as the program itself, system software routines, the data used by the program, and the hardware on which the program is being run.

Describing a system and its environment is often not as simple as suggested by the preceding examples. The systems analyst may spend many hours deciding what to include or leave out as system elements. On the one hand, the analyst should be thorough and include as many elements as possible. On the other hand, the analyst must weigh the thoroughness objective against the need for simplicity and comprehension.

Figure 3.1 shows one way of depicting a system and its environment. Each of the geometrical icons in the figure represents a system element. The arrows

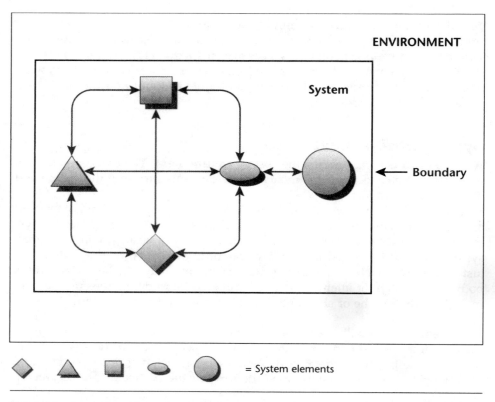

Figure 3.1 A system and its environment. A boundary separates a system from its environment.

indicate the relationships among these elements. In some cases, the elements themselves may represent entire systems. When this occurs, we commonly refer to such elements as *subsystems*. A *suprasystem* refers to the entity formed by a system and the other equivalent systems with which it interacts. A suprasystem is the next larger enclosing system that consists of the given system and the others at its level.

To further illustrate what we mean by subsystems and suprasystems, please skip ahead to Figure 3.3. As you can observe in this figure, an organization may be subdivided into numerous functional areas, such as marketing, finance, manufacturing, research and development, and so on. Each of these functional areas can be viewed as a subsystem of the larger organizational system because each could be considered to be a system in and of itself. For example, marketing may be viewed as a system that consists of elements such as market research, advertising, sales, and so on. Collectively, these elements in the marketing area may be viewed as making up the marketing suprasystem. Similarly, the various functional areas (subsystems) of an organization are elements in the same suprasystem within the organization.

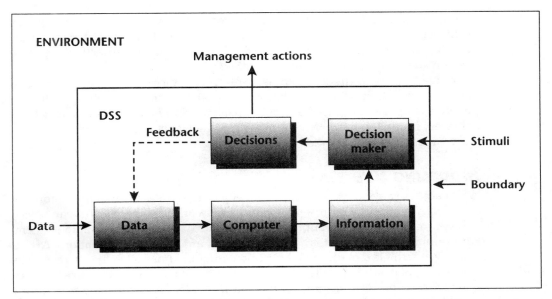

Figure 3.2 A model of an open system. Most of the systems that occur naturally in business are open systems, and they interact with such environmental elements as consumers, suppliers, competitors, government, and foreign countries.

Open Versus Closed Systems

Systems are often classified as open or closed. A **closed system** is self-contained and does not interact or make exchanges across its boundaries with its environment. In other words, a closed system is one that has no interaction with any element not contained in it. An **open system** is one that interacts and makes exchanges with its environment. In figures and graphs illustrating open systems, such exchanges are typically shown because it is important for people perceiving the system model to understand that such exchanges affect the system and its performance.

An open system representation of a decision support system (DSS) is depicted in Figure 3.2. Here we see data entering the system from the environment and being processed into information by a computer. A decision maker, in turn, takes that information and uses it to make decisions. The management actions resulting from the decisions—perhaps a change in an item's price or the acquisition of a new company—are passed back as data into the environment, where such elements as customers or competitors react in some way, thereby generating even more data. Because it is important to show that decision making does not take place in a vacuum, the open system representation is appropriate here.

The dotted line shown in the figure is often called a *feedback loop*. In the feedback loop depicted, the results of decisions are "fed back" within the system to affect its future performance. Here, the dotted line represents management actions not passed into the environment. For instance, the decision maker may decide that a new pricing formula should be applied to the data before a final decision can be reached. Or the decision maker may use an action resulting from one decision as data for another decision.

Virtually all systems in business are technically open systems, whether or not we choose to model them that way. In other words, decisions made in a particular business are based at least in part on what is happening in that business's environment. Furthermore, many critical events in the environment happen as a result of actions taken by the business.

MODELING SYSTEMS

When studying systems, it is often convenient to represent them in the form of a model. A **model** is a representation of a real-world element (such as an object, concept, or event) or a group of elements and the relationships among them. For example, a toy Lear Jet is a physical model of a plane. The equation "Area = length × width" is a math model for calculating the internal area of a rectangle. A drawing of a human skeleton is a graphical model of the bone structures of humans and the relationships among these structures. Models help us frame our thinking about items in the world. The toy plane enables a child to visualize what it is like to fly. The equation for the area of a rectangle enables a mathematician to describe a shape. The drawing of the skeleton enables a medical student to understand both anatomy and the possible causes of human disorders.

The field of MIS also uses many models. Because management information systems are often complex, it helps to have a few models that simplify and clarify them. Wherever possible, this text will emphasize simple models. Although complex models can be both useful and appropriate in many situations, they are often limited because they can be very difficult for anyone except the model's original designer to understand. We will emphasize this design and presentation theme throughout the book: KEEP THINGS SIMPLE!

General Versus Specific Models

Models may be classified in many ways. One way concerns how general or specific the models are. *General models* are models that can be applied to a wide variety of settings, whereas *specific models* are those that apply to a specific situation.

For example, many of the graphical models presented in this chapter are general models that can represent virtually any type of organization: large or small, profit or nonprofit, and so on. However, by modeling a general element such as "consumers" more specifically—for example, "moviegoers" or "non-moviegoers"—we may be able to create models that would be of particular interest to certain sectors of the entertainment industry.

In this book, most of the models presented are general. This is intentional because a textbook should be targeted to a wide audience and not to a particu-

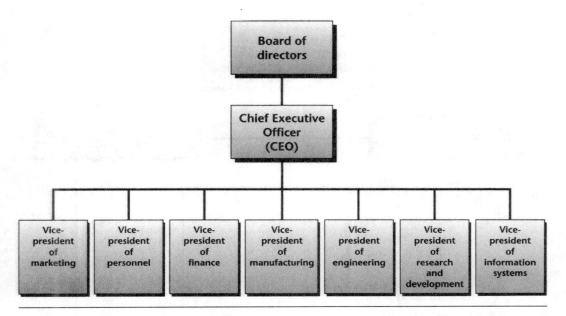

Figure 3.3 Topmost-level organization chart.

lar company or industry. However, remember that a specific model is often more useful when attempting to understand a specific situation.

Levels of Models

Some models are so complex that it is impossible to represent them adequately without breaking them down into simpler models. For example, consider the organization chart in Figure 3.3.

In large firms, it is usually both impossible and impractical to represent all of the firm's jobs on a single organization chart. Consequently, there will often be a hierarchy of these charts. The top chart in this hierarchy shows positions at the highest level of the organization, as does the one shown in Figure 3.3. More detail is presented in the lower levels of the hierarchy (see, for example, Figures 3.4 and 3.5).

Figure 3.4 represents an intermediate level of detail for the organization depicted in Figure 3.3. Shown in Figure 3.4 are the top-level line management and staff positions in the MIS department. Figure 3.5, on the other hand, represents a section of the organization at the finest level of detail; it shows all the operations personnel in the MIS department. These employees include the operations manager, data-entry supervisor, three data-entry operators (DO), head computer operator, two senior-level (SO) and three junior-level (JO) computer operators, the head systems librarian, and two assistant librarians (AL). Throughout the book, you will encounter other examples of models specified at varying levels of detail.

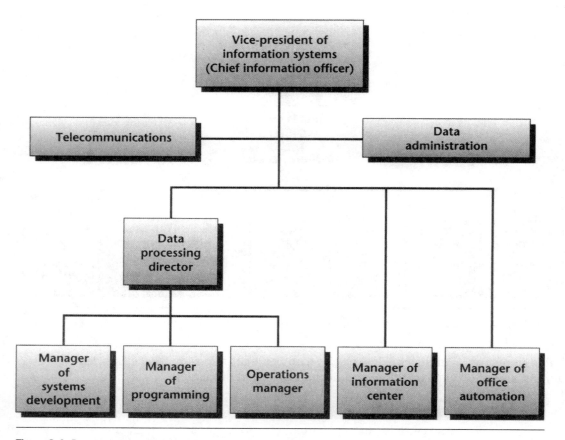

Figure 3.4 Department-level organization chart (MIS department).

Types of Models

Models may be classified in several other ways. One widely used method looks at models as being primarily one of the following four types:

- Graphical models
- Mathematical models
- Narrative models
- Physical models

In the field of MIS, all of these model types are used to represent systems and their component parts.

Graphical Models

Graphical models generally use such symbols as icons, boxes, and lines to represent real-world elements and the relationships among them. An example of a graphical model is the structure chart shown in Figure 3.6. *Structure charts* are

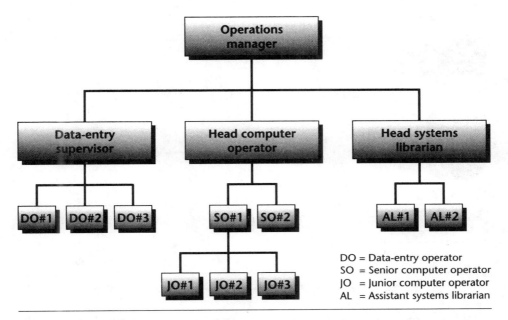

Figure 3.5 Area-level organization chart (computer operations area of the information systems department).

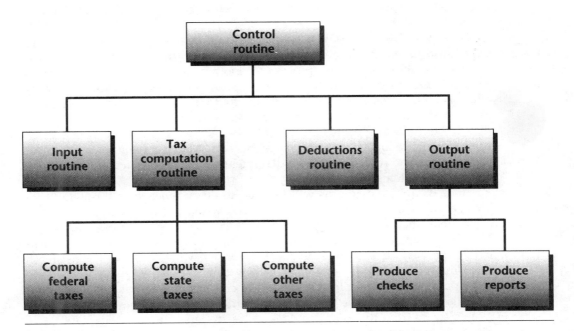

Figure 3.6 A structure chart for a computer program. This type of graphical model shows how a computer program is organized hierarchically to do work. The structure chart shown here depicts the processing tasks that must be performed in a payroll application.

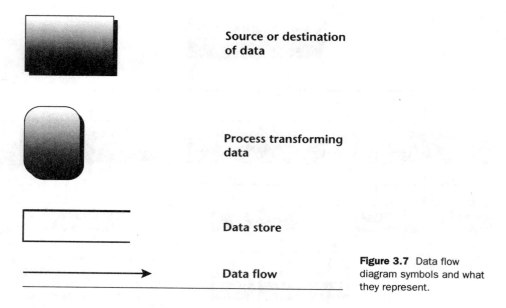

Source or destination of data

Process transforming data

Data store

Data flow

Figure 3.7 Data flow diagram symbols and what they represent.

commonly used to show how computer programs are organized. Each of the rectangles shown in the chart represents a well-defined processing task or program module. The modules are then arranged hierarchically to show their relationship to one another. This particular structure chart has been used to model a payroll application.

Data flow diagrams (DFD) are widely used by systems analysts to graphically illustrate information systems. These graphical models show how data or information move from one process to another in an organizational system. They are useful for showing how systems work and are often used by systems analysts both to design systems and to clarify to users, programmers, and other systems analysts how components of a system fit together. Data flow diagrams that do not refer to specific hardware devices, software products, or people are used to provide logical descriptions of systems. Managers and users are likely to encounter and review data flow diagrams and other graphical flowcharts developed by systems analysts.

Since data flow diagrams will be used to describe systems throughout the book, at this point we will examine how they work. The complete set of graphical symbols that we will use is shown in Figure 3.7. Note that more than one set of symbols can be used in data flow diagrams; however, once any set is learned, it is quite easy to learn the others. Hence, we will use this set consistently throughout the text.

A data flow diagram for the payroll operations of a firm is given in Figure 3.8. It is common practice to number the process boxes, as shown in the figure. Note also that the diagram provides a description of the various data flows. This, too, is standard practice. In reviewing the diagram carefully, note the difference between a data flow and a data store. A *data flow* relates to data or information in motion; a *data store* refers strictly to data at rest (such as data on disk or in a filing cabinet).

Usually, a number of simplifying assumptions are made when a data flow diagram is constructed. For example, matters such as the opening and closing of files, error processing, and the handling of unusual (exception) conditions are ignored. In Figure 3.8, for instance, we have purposely left out the procedures that might be followed if a check were made out for an amount that appeared unusual. Such exception handling procedures are commonly considered to be "housekeeping" chores that are much less important than other essential business operations. Because of this, they are usually not depicted in data flow diagrams.

Data flow diagrams can also be used to reflect various levels of detail. Later, in Part 5 of the text, we will look at how both high- and low-level-of-detail data flow diagrams are constructed.

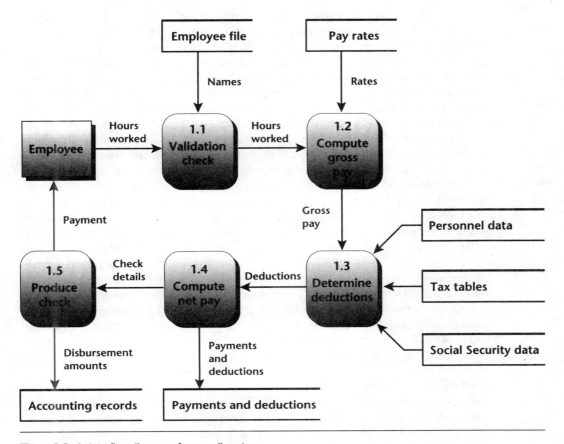

Figure 3.8 A data flow diagram of a payroll system.

Mathematical Models

A *mathematical model* is used to express quantifiable phenomena, or the relationship among several such phenomena, in mathematical terms. For example, the mathematical model or equation:

$$Q = \sqrt{\frac{2DC}{PH}}$$

is used to calculate the economic order quantity (Q) of a specific product. This is the quantity of the product that is most cost-effective to order when the stock of the product is getting low. This model shows that economic order quantity is a function of four variables: the annual usage of the product (D), the cost of placing an individual order (C), the price for the product (P), and the unit cost of carrying items in inventory (H). We will not go into specifics here concerning how each of these variables is derived. However, many firms rely on such models for computing order quantities.

The mathematical model just described was relatively simple. It involved a single, independent formula. Many computer programs can also be seen as mathematical models—especially when their program statements contain formulas that require mathematical computations. In many computer programs, the results of calculations performed in one program statement are used as input to subsequent statements. In some computer programs, more complex types of mathematical models are used—for example, models involving interdependent formulas. In models with interdependent formulas, values for variables must be solved simultaneously. Some of these models, such as the econometric models used to predict trends in the U.S. economy, involve thousands of simultaneous equations. Using anything but a computer to solve such a system of equations would be impossible.

Some of the mathematical models that are commonly incorporated in management reporting systems (MRS) and decision support systems (DSS) are summarized in Figure 3.9. These techniques are considered to be management science or operations research models. Numerous other approaches, including financial models and statistical techniques, are often found in DSS and MRS environments. Such mathematical models of business systems are useful sources of decision-making information—for both MRS and DSS systems. In MRS systems, modeling tools deliver a fixed set of outputs; if users need new types of information, programmers or analysts usually must change the models to provide that information. With interactive DSS systems, users can typically make model changes directly and get immediate results; also, users can often select dynamically from a variety of modeling tools.

Narrative Models

Narrative models describe a system without trying to illustrate it in a formula or graph. Some examples of narrative models are the spoken words describing an object or event, a written description of a procedure, and a photograph or

Problem Type	Example
Linear programming	Finding the least-cost way to produce a gasoline from specific crude oils, while meeting limitations on crude supplies and certain blending restrictions
Scheduling	Finding the best way to schedule tasks on an assembly line or a communications network in order to maximize throughput
Transportation	Finding the least-cost routes to ship goods from several sources to several destinations
Assignment	Finding the best way to assign specific people (on a team) to specific jobs in order to maximize the effectiveness of the team
Dynamic programming	Finding the least-cost way to optimize the sum of manufacturing and inventory carrying costs so that parts manufactured in one month become inventory available for shipment next month
Goal programming	Determining the mixture of policies or actions that best meets a certain set of goals
Regression	Finding patterns and trends that best fit a particular set of data, such as predicting sales levels from store location, store size, and disposable income of store customers
Inventory	Finding the optimal levels of products held in storage areas, which will minimize total inventory costs
Queuing	Determining how many check-out counters to have open during peak sales periods, which will minimize the amount of time that customers have to wait
Project management	Determining which project tasks must be done sequentially and which can be done simultaneously in order to complete the project in the shortest amount of time
Simulation	Examining various production and cost scenarios to assess the risk inherent in meeting profitability and delivery-date targets for a new product

Figure 3.9 Some of the mathematical programming models commonly found in management reporting and decision support systems.

videotape of an object or event. For example, a written description of a worker's job duties is a narrative model.

Physical Models

A *physical model* is usually a three-dimensional representation that can be held or touched. In such fields as architecture, physical models of buildings are widely used to show clients what new facilities will look like before they are built. In automobile design, physical models of cars are helpful to see if a certain design will work. Also, physical models of humans (crash dummies) are used when testing safety features. In MIS, the most common type of physical model is the system prototype. A *prototype* is a small "pilot" model of a hardware or software system that is used to guide the systems analyst in building a larger system.

Who is Responsible for Developing Models?

In large, formal systems, developing models is usually the responsibility of professionals trained in the use of modeling. Graphical and narrative models of a CBIS are usually constructed by systems analysts, whereas mathematical models are commonly created by the operations research or management science staff, who are specially trained in building mathematical models. In either case, the professionals responsible for creating the models will work with users to ensure that the models are representative. For smaller systems, modeling (often of a less formal and sophisticated nature) may be performed by ordinary users.

MODELS OF ORGANIZATIONAL SYSTEMS

So far, we have covered some ways to model systems and some terminology associated with systems theory. Now we will use a few examples in order to put both the models and the terminology into perspective. Here, we will look at some of the models that are helpful when depicting various aspects of organizations, information systems, and their environments.

A General Model of the Organization and Its External Environment

Figure 3.10 shows a model of an open system that is used to characterize many organizations. It is a model that you will encounter frequently throughout the text, in one form or another. In most organizations, the major points of management's attention are consumers, suppliers, competitors, the labor supply, and the economic and social environment in which the organization operates. We should remember these elements as we consider the current and potential uses of MIS in the organization.

- **Consumers** Consumers include both present and potential customers (or clients) for the product or service that the organization provides. Consumers are important because they represent the revenue (or funding) that the organization needs to stay alive. Most organizations require a steady stream of information about consumers in order to operate effectively. For example, which products or services are consumers purchasing? What are consumers' tastes? What percentage of consumers is being reached by promotional schemes?

- **Suppliers** Suppliers include the sources that make available the goods and services the organization requires to keep operating. For manufacturing firms, such as Chrysler and General Foods, the supply of goods consists mainly of raw materials. For merchandising firms, such as Wal-Mart and Sears, supplies consist of finished goods that are sold directly to consumers. All manufacturing and merchandising organizations need information concerning any changes in the availability and pricing of major supplies.

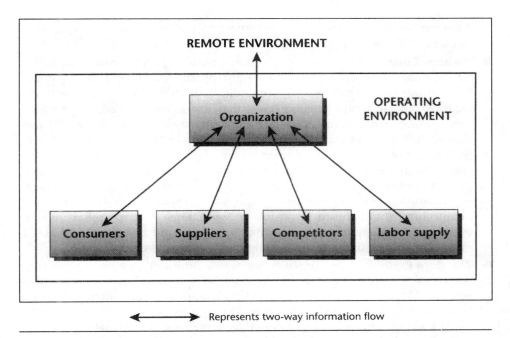

REMOTE ENVIRONMENT

Organization

OPERATING ENVIRONMENT

Consumers   Suppliers   Competitors   Labor supply

←————→ Represents two-way information flow

Figure 3.10 The organization and its external environments. The operating environment consists of forces closest to the organization: consumers, suppliers, competitors, and the labor supply. The remote environment represents factors originating beyond the operating environment, such as economic, political, technological, and government forces. The operating and remote environments form the external environment.

- *Competitors* Most firms have to be keenly aware of the strengths, weaknesses, and strategic tactics of the competition. This means getting a steady supply of information about competitive products and strategies, determining the market share enjoyed by competitors, and so forth. Naturally, such information is not easy to obtain.

- *Labor Supply* The performance of both manufacturing and merchandising firms also depends on an adequate supply of both operational and managerial labor. Service organizations—such as Arthur Andersen, Indiana University, and the U.S. Immigration Department—do not produce tangible goods for sale, and labor is the main supply-side problem. Virtually every organization needs information about changes in the availability and cost of labor.

- *External Environment* In management literature, the model shown in Figure 3.10 is often depicted as consisting of two components: the organization (or the system) and its external environment. The **external environment** consists of all relevant forces outside the organization and is composed of an operating environment and a remote environment.

- *Operating Environment* An organization's **operating environment** consists of the forces that are most closely associated with the organization's specific competitive situation. Typically, the operating environment will include the elements we just discussed: the organization's consumers, suppliers, competitors, and labor supply.

- **Remote Environment** An organization's **remote environment** consists of all the relevant outside forces and conditions that are beyond the organization's direct control and specific competitive situation. The government, for example, is constantly passing laws that determine competitive practices among all organizations. Also, developments anywhere in the world can sharply influence what the organization is doing or how consumers behave. Such factors are often lumped together and defined as the organization's remote environment. Each organization has its own remote environment and, in each of these environments, some factors are more significant than others. For example, a firm in the airlines industry constantly needs information about current and future government regulations. A corporation making electronic products that are also made in Japan needs information about events in Japan and the relative strength of the Japanese yen.

- **The Organization** Every organization needs information about its own internal effectiveness. For example, are tasks being done in the most cost-effective way? What income was generated last month and how much did it vary from what was predicted? How well did each salesperson do last month? All of these questions can be answered by some type of information system.

The arrows shown in Figure 3.10 represent information flow. The two-way nature of the arrows indicates that information flows to and from the organization. For example, the consumer-to-organization arrow depicts that an action by the organization (such as coming out with new products, advertising products in the media, or developing a new price structure) will ordinarily result in information being passed to the consumer. When the consumer takes an action (such as buying or not buying a product at a given price level or registering a complaint), that action will ordinarily result in information being passed back to the organization. Both the action taken by the organization and consumer response to it are relevant to the organization.

In order to keep Figure 3.10 simple, we have shown arrows only to and from the organization. Of course, information flows frequently exist between each of the external environment components in the diagram, any or none of which may be relevant to modeling a particular decision situation.

Although each of the components in Figure 3.10 has rich information systems potential, information systems have traditionally been more successful in some areas than in others. For example, many formal corporate information systems focus primarily on internal efficiency. Data available related to internal efficiency are easily obtainable within the organization, and the decision environments that can be modeled from these data are more capable of being structured than other components. Data on competitors, however, are probably the least available of all the components modeled in Figure 3.10—yet competitor information is extremely valuable to any organization.

By observing the model in Figure 3.10, you can begin to appreciate the importance of strategy in the development of information systems. The person in charge of an organization's information systems needs a solid knowledge of the organizational environment—and of the direction the organization must take in the future. We will look at models used specifically for strategic planning purposes in the following subsection and also in Chapter 18.

Strategic-Planning Models

One of the most important tasks in managing any organization is strategic planning, the act of plotting the general long-term direction of the firm. Strategic plans often determine the context or backdrop for other managerial decisions—that is, they are one of the factors that influence daily decisions that managers must make. In general, managerial decisions should be consistent with and supportive of the organization's strategic plans. Thus, while strategic planning is most identified with top-level executives, knowledge of the strategic plan and the strategic-planning process can be useful to managers and workers at any level.

Strategic planning can be beneficial to the organization in a number of ways (see Figure 3.11). It forces management to anticipate the future and the direction that it wants the organization to take. Since strategic plans have an impact on the entire organization, managers throughout the company are often involved in the development of strategic plans. Once formulated, strategic plans provide benchmarks that help the organization assess its progress and effectiveness in reaching long-term goals.

However, as indicated in Figure 3.11, strategic planning can be time-consuming, influenced by organizational politics, and viewed as a disruptive bureaucratic exercise. In spite of these potential shortcomings, organizational strategic-planning processes often have a significant impact on the activities and long-range objectives of MIS. In addition, the strategic use of information technology is one of mechanisms in which strategic plans are implemented in organizations.

Figure 3.12 shows a representative strategic-planning model for organizations. The elements found in this model are discussed in the following subsections.

Mission

Every firm has a reason for existing. The **mission** of any firm is a broad, enduring statement of intent. It should convey the business in which the firm sees itself in a way that reflects both the values and priorities of owners and management. Figure 3.13 (page 100) provides several examples of corporate mission statements.

The mission of a firm is an important piece of information to management on all levels. For example, an organization that sees itself as an "information technologies supplier" is one that has a much wider scope of activities available to it than one that sees itself strictly as a "keyboard manufacturer" or a "word-processing software supplier." More than 30 years ago, Theodore Leavitt criticized managers for having overly narrow perceptions of their businesses'

BENEFITS AND DRAWBACKS OF STRATEGIC PLANNING

Benefits	Drawbacks
■ Provides organization with common sense of direction and purpose	■ Can be a time- and resource-consuming process
■ Facilitates the coordination of subunit activities	■ Often promotes political maneuvering among major subunits
■ Promotes long-term thinking among managers and employees	■ The planning process may be nothing more than a bureaucratic ritual
■ Provides a forum for proposing and critically evaluating alternative goals, objectives, and plans	■ May be viewed as a burden — as a supplemental management task that must be performed in addition to day-to-day duties
■ Forces organization to identify environmental threats and opportunities	■ After being formulated, strategic plans may not be implemented
■ Provides organizations with benchmarks and targets against which performance can be evaluated	■ May compromise future flexibility and responsiveness to unanticipated environmental changes
■ Often makes it possible for managers at all levels and from all areas to provide input	
■ Is often supplemented by contingency planning, which reduces the planning which reduces the need for crisis management	
■ Helps subunits understand each other's goals, objectives, and activities	
■ Provides MIS with the framework needed to formulate long-term plans for integrating information technology and business operations	

Figure 3.11 The benefits and drawbacks associated with strategic-planning processes in organizations. While significant benefits may be derived form strategic planning, the process can be time-consuming and is not immune from organizational politics.

missions. He cited the example of the railroads, who saw themselves in the railroad business, rather than in the more broadly based transportation business. Perhaps that is why we do not fly the Union Pacific or Atcheson, Topeka, and Santa Fe airlines today.

Changing technologies and world events constantly force organizations to rethink their business. Television, for example, forced Hollywood to see itself in the entertainment business, rather than just the movie business. Recent advances in information technology have forced many firms to think of themselves in more creative ways. For example, a newswire service reconceptualized its business as being essentially a bit-moving operation (getting data from one point to another), with news being only one of the types of bits that it was capable of moving. According to Eric Clemons and F. Warren McFarlan, this broadened vision led the company to develop and offer new services and information, such as up-to-the-second foreign exchange.

Deregulation of certain industries—for example, the airlines and financial-services industries—has also caused some companies to rethink their mission.

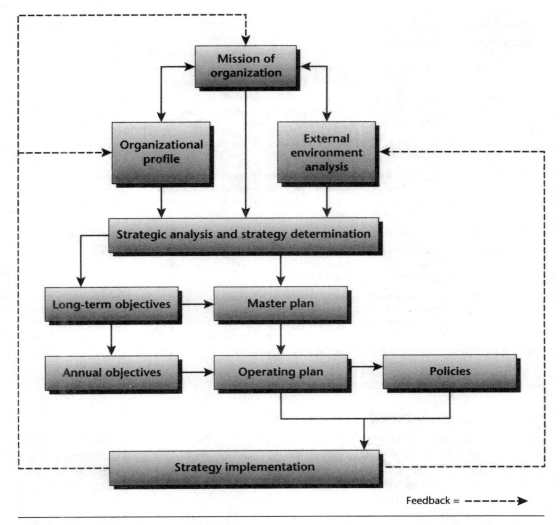

Figure 3.12 A graphical model of strategic-planning processes in organizations. The process starts with a definition of broad goals and purposes (the mission statement) and ends with the implementation of a specific plan. The results of the implementation provide feedback that guides future strategic-planning activities.

For instance, Merrill Lynch moved from the stock-brokerage business to financial services when it created its Cash Management Account. With new opportunities created almost daily by information technologies, the mission issue has moved to center stage for many top level managers.

The mission of an organization is often related to the prevailing corporate culture. For example, a company that sees itself as a "technology leader" is likely to attract people whose attitudes reflect an active interest in producing cutting-edge products. As James Quinn points out, culture often provides direction for creative and entrepreneurial forces within the firm.

Component Addressed	Excerpt
▪ Customer	To anticipate and meet market needs of farmers, ranchers, and rural communities within North America (CENEX)
▪ Product	AMAX's principal products are molybdenum, coal, iron ore, copper, lead, zinc, petroleum and natural gas, potash, phosphates, nickel, tungsten, silver, gold, and magnesium (AMAX)
▪ Geographic domain	We are dedicated to the total success of Corning Glass Works as a worldwide competitor (Corning Glass)
▪ Technology	Control Data is in the business of applying microelectronics and computer technology in two general areas: computer-related hardware; and computing-enhancing services, which include computation, information, education, and finance (Control Data)
▪ Philosophy	We are committed to improve health care throughout the world (Baxter Travenol)
▪ Self-concept	Hoover Universal is a diversified, multi-industry corporation with strong manufacturing capabilities, entrepreneurial policies, and individual business unit autonomy (Hoover Universal)
▪ Concern for public image	We must be responsive to the broader concerns of the public including especially the general desire for improvement in the quality of life, equal opportunity for all, and the constructive use of natural resources (Sun Company)

Figure 3.13 Excerpts from corporate mission statements. (Adapted from Pearce and David)

Company Profile

The profile of a firm is, basically, what a firm would see if it could look at itself objectively in a mirror. What are its particular strengths? What are its weaknesses? The answers to these questions should include a self-analysis of all the important functional areas of the business—for example, finance, marketing, engineering, research and development, manufacturing, personnel, and information systems. Formal reviews or *management audits* may be used to establish or update a company's profile.

The profile reflects that the planning alternatives open to the firm are completely contingent on the firm's current status. For example, it would be foolhardy for a firm to consider building a global information network and opening new plants in Europe and the Pacific Rim if it is clearly underfinanced or if it possesses outdated information technology.

Considerations of the strengths and weaknesses of the firm may even cause planners to rethink its mission statement. For example, is the firm really in the right business? Does the organization have the appropriate information technology to help it survive and prosper? If not, company executives should reconsider the feasibility of their goals.

External Environment Analysis

An analysis of the external environment looks at factors in both the operating and remote environments. Here, planners must consider the firm's actual and potential customers, competitors, material suppliers and labor pool, trends in consumer tastes and in the industry in which the firm operates, governmental factors that might influence the firm, and even such possible "acts of God" as earthquakes (which may influence disaster recovery planning). Any force external to the firm that could realistically impact the firm's future performance is considered in an analysis of the external environment. Scenarios or forecasts of what may transpire in any of these key areas should also be considered.

In this part of the strategic-planning process, it is useful to make lists for each important external component, showing key pieces of decision-making information. An analysis of the firm's external environment may also cause planners to rethink the appropriateness of the company's mission.

Strategic Analysis and Choice of Strategy

Analyses of the mission, the profile of the firm, and the external environment should tell the planner where the firm is now and what the future might bring. For example, the planner should know whether the company is figuratively sailing smoothly on an impregnable ship or drifting toward the high seas in a leaky rowboat. Incidentally, this type of information is valuable for anyone to know, whether or not they are in a strategic-planning capacity. If they are the captain of the leaky rowboat, for instance, they must change course. If they are a passenger, they may want to bail out and swim toward another boat.

At this point in the planning effort, a list of long-term strategies should be considered, and either one strategy or a number of complementary strategies should be picked from several alternatives. A **strategy** is a general statement of what the firm should be doing. For example, if the firm involved in the planning effort is the XYZ bookstore we discussed in Chapter 2, some alternative strategies might be to do nothing and maintain the status quo (sometimes this alternative evolves from a "don't-fix-it-unless-it's-broken" management philosophy), sell out to competing bookstore, alter the mix of books sold, expand the product line to include non-book products, expand the business by acquiring another bookstore, or move to another site. If the bookstore is located in St. Paul, Minnesota, and the mission statement includes such a clause as "to continually serve the residents of St. Paul. . . ," then any moving or expansion options might be restricted to the confines of St. Paul. However, if management feels that expansion to Minneapolis is feasible, the restrictive language of the mission statement might be changed to allow it to serve not only the residents of St. Paul, but also the region around St. Paul.

Generally speaking, the feasibility or appropriateness of each strategic option should be carefully considered. The use of "devil's advocates" or "dialectical inquiry" often serve to scrutinize strategic options. Both of these approaches force planners to identify the arguments against an option—its weaknesses, drawbacks, risks, and so on.

Objectives

Objectives are specific targets or milestones that must be reached in order to execute a strategy. For example, if the strategy chosen by our bookstore is to sell non-book items, the objectives would state the percentage of shelfspace in the store that will be allocated to these items, the specific mix of product types involved, timetables for getting the new items onto the shelves, and the projected profitability contributions from these non-book items.

Whenever possible, objectives should be articulated in a specific, quantifiable way: How much? When? Which ones? The objectives that the firm seeks over a multiyear period are called *long-term objectives*; ones that the organization hopes to achieve during the current year are called *annual objectives*.

Plans

A **plan** is a comprehensive, dynamic statement showing how the strategy and objectives will be implemented. For example, in the bookstore example, the plan might call for an additional person to be hired by June 1 who will be in charge of selecting and stocking non-book items. The *master plan* is long range, whereas the *operating plan* is usually formulated for a shorter time span, often on an annual basis.

Policies

Policies are directives that guide employees after a strategy is implemented. Policies limit employee discretion and decision-making authority on certain matters, and are formulated to ensure that the actions taken are in the firm's best interests. The following policies might be appropriate for the XYZ bookstore:

■ If a book is not in stock, it will be immediately located and made available to the customer within seven days.

■ Any book may be returned within thirty days of purchase for a full refund, no questions asked.

■ All employees will be paid on the first day of the month.

In many firms, procedures are developed to assist in the implementation of policies. They provide even more detailed guidance on how workers should behave in particular situations. These detailed guidelines are sometimes referred to as standard operating procedures (SOP). For example, the bookstore may develop a procedure specifying that when a customer returns a book within 30 days, the cashier must complete a form noting the return and indicating the refund amount taken from the cash drawer.

The Automated Salesperson

Many companies are getting excited about sales automation technology. The reason for the excitement is understandable: when properly implemented, sales force automation systems can substantially boost individual sales productivity and morale. Equipped with a laptop and appropriate software, a sales representative in the field can, with a few keystrokes, place orders, check product availability, or confirm shipping dates from a customer's office. These systems have the potential to reduce paperwork, streamline administrative chores, improve presentation and selling aids, and help salespeople better target sales prospects.

Texaco Lubricants Company in Houston is a good example of a company that has embraced emerging sales automation systems. Its 200-person sales force is outfitted with laptops and communications technology that allow salespeople to review marketing reports and customer information from the field, place orders, handle sales-call reporting, and perform various messaging functions.

". . . SALES FORCE AUTOMATION SYSTEMS CAN SUBSTANTIALLY BOOST INDIVIDUAL SALES PRODUCTIVITY AND MORALE."

During the 1990s, a steady stream of products and technologies aimed at automating the activities of professional salespeople is expected to flood the market. New sales automation software are being designed for laptops, notebooks, and pen-based computers. For the 1990s, industry experts predict annual average increases of 35 percent for sales automation products.

Adapted from Radding and Maglita (1992).

Strategy Implementation

Strategy implementation is the physical act of putting a strategy into practice. Implementation is absolutely critical; often, strategies fail not because they are poorly conceived, but because they are poorly implemented. The strategic plan, since it's a tool, is only as good as the people who use it. If preparation or implementation is faulty, the planning process breaks down.

For all its merits, strategic planning is often criticized for locking people who live in a changing world into a fixed plan. It is true that many important events cannot be anticipated and therefore cannot be incorporated into the strategic-planning process. How many executives, for instance, could have forecast Suddam Hussein's invasion of Kuwait in 1991? Or how many company presidents could have correctly predicted, as few as five years ago, the impact that imaging systems and electronic data interchange are expected to have on their organizations during the 1990s?

The strategic plan should not be so tightly formulated that management is unable to react to unusual, critical events that take place. What is needed instead, in the words of Daniel J. Isenberg, is *strategic opportunism*, or "the ability

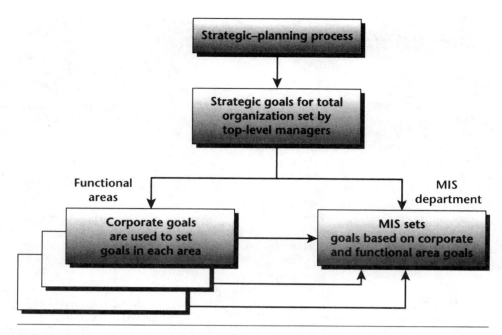

Figure 3.14 The relationships among strategic goals, functional department goals, and MIS goals.

to remain focused on long-term objectives while staying flexible enough to solve day-to-day problems and recognize new opportunities." Isenberg observes that many experienced managers leave strategic gaps in their plans—scheduled time-outs they use to reassess situations—and avoid formulating long-term goals in excessive detail. This enables them to respond to the chaos imparted by short-term problems.

Referring back to Figure 3.12 (page 99), note the feedback loops to the mission and profile boxes. These loops indicate that the results observed from implementing the strategy will affect the future mission and company profile. The manner in which the organization conducts future external environment analysis is also likely to be affected by the strategy it selects and implements. This shows that strategic planning and implementation is an ongoing process.

Information Technology and Corporate Strategic Planning

Management information systems assist strategic planners by making both internal and external data more accessible. Transaction processing systems create extensive internal databases that are useful when developing company profiles. Networking and data communications technology—along with the increasing availability of external databases—have made it easier to monitor and assemble valuable information about the external environment. The data and information generated by these systems can assist in making forecasts and in assembling the data and information that planners need during later stages of the process. Management information systems can also capture the data needed to assess

STRATEGIC GOALS AND BENEFITS OF INFORMATION SYSTEMS

Possible Goals	Examples of Potential Benefits		
Increasing operational efficiency	Streamlined work processes	Increased worker productivity	Enhanced product/service quality
Improving functional effectiveness	Increased efficiency and productivity	Improved subunit planning and decision making	Better coordination among subunits
Enhancing service quality	Increased retention of existing clients	Increased demand for products/services	Reduced customer complaints
Improving product creation and improvement processes	Increased numbers of new products and services	Increased number of markets and industries in which organization competes	Expanded variety of production and distribution channels
Client lock-in/customer lock-out	Closer coordination of organization's activities with those of customers and suppliers	Increased difficulty for new competitors who want to enter the market	Reduced operational costs for both organization and suppliers/customers

Figure 3.15 Examples of the strategic potential of information systems.

whether strategic plans are being effectively implemented. Decision support systems (DSS) that incorporate the mathematical models summarized earlier in the chapter and executive information systems (EIS) will especially help managers involved in these important planning functions.

Strategic MIS Planning

An organization's strategic plans usually have a major impact on MIS plans. As we just noted, strategic plans are the starting point for the plans that are made in various functional areas of the organization (see Figure 3.14). This figure also illustrates that both the organization's overall strategic plans and the long-term goals developed by the functional areas of the organization serve as key inputs to the planning processes that take place within the MIS area.

Because Chapter 18 fully addresses the connection between overall organizational strategies and strategic management of MIS, this topic will not be discussed in depth here. However, please note that information systems planning follows the same general process as that used to develop corporate plans. Also note that the organization's strategic plans provide the framework in which MIS plans are developed and carried out, perhaps resulting in the development of MIS mission statements, objectives, and strategies.

The strategic potential of information systems should not be overlooked in either corporate or MIS planning activities. These were introduced in Chapter 1 and some of these are summarized in Figure 3.15. Any strategy must be operationalized and applied in order to realize its benefits to the organization. Strategy should lead to action; if it does not, the time and energy devoted to

Application Area	Potential Competitive Advantages
Customer service	Improved loyalty, retention, and relationships may result from letting customers tap into your database in order to track their orders and shipments.
Financial management	Financial float times can be reduced or eliminated through electronic funds transfers. On-line access to stock market and financial databases can improve investment decisions.
Customer lock-in	Direct communication links with customers through electronic data interchange or other means can streamline order entry and coordinate the exchange of products or services.
Product creation and improvement	Appropriate electronic links between customer service, market intelligence, and research and development can be used to translate customer needs, complaints, and suggestions into product/service improvements and new products/services.
Direct marketing	Using appropriate consumer databases and search routines can help ferret out the best new customer prospects. This increases the probability of a sale and reduces costs associated with "shotgun" sales efforts.
Sales productivity	Equipping your sales force with portable computers, pen-based computers, and so on makes it possible to enter orders from customer premises, access the most recent pricing and product availability data, and prepare sales presentations without having to return to the home office. This can translate into increased sales, quicker customer deliveries, better cash flow, and less paperwork for salespeople.
Selling excess computing capacity	Allowing outsiders to use your information system's excess capacity to run their own applications can be a new revenue source for the organization and can help cover your investment in sophisticated information technology. This may also be used to lock in customers and as a component in your customer service program.

Figure 3.16 Examples of ways in which companies can gain a competitive edge through the strategic application of information technology.

developing the strategy have been wasted. Figure 3.16 illustrates some of the ways in which the strategic potential of information technology might be realized; that is, it depicts how information technology might be applied in pursuit of the strategic targets outlined in Figure 3.15.

Critical Success Factors

Another commonly used approach for connecting MIS plans with corporate plans involves the determination of crucial organizational activities and information requirements. This approach allows the organization and its managers to "zero in" on what is truly important to the long-term prosperity and survival of the organization. Once these are known at the corporate level, they can be used to analyze MIS requirements and, subsequently, for evaluating MIS.

Every organization must perform a number of tasks. In many organizations, these include strategic planning, obtaining financing, manufacturing some type of salable product, marketing the products, hiring and retaining personnel, and

Organization-Wide Critical Success Factors (CSF)

- Consistently produce high-quality products

- Maintain inventories to satisfy customer demand

- Continually innovate purchasing, production, and distribution processes

- Continually develop successful new products

- Handle special orders and customized products

- Increase employee productivity

- Project a positive image in community, market, and industry

- Expand operations and distribution channels in all parts of the world

- Provide high levels of customer service

Figure 3.17 A general set of critical success factors (CSF) for a major company.

so on. Certain tasks (or factors) will contribute most heavily to the success of the organization. These are often called **critical success factors (CSF)**. A general set of critical success factors for a major company is provided in Figure 3.17.

Critical success factors are often closely associated with the long-term goals of an organization—that is, if they are effectively addressed, the organization should be in a better position to attain its goals. For example, to be successful in the car industry, such factors as attractive styling, an effective dealer organization, tight control of manufacturing, and quality are frequently deemed most critical to success. A supermarket, on the other hand, may consider product mix, inventory management, promotion, and price as its critical success factors. And to a company in the overnight delivery business, reliability and cost efficiency are keys to survival and success.

For every critical success factor found, there are a number of key information needs that, if identified, will help managers make crucial decisions. For example, to correctly assess consumer styling tastes, information must be obtained about what consumers are currently purchasing and about possible trends that might influence future tastes. Once these information needs are known, the role of MIS in satisfying these needs becomes clearer; in many instances, this means that critical success factors for MIS can be identified (see Figure 3.18, page 108). Figure 3.19 (page 109) provides some examples of the MIS critical success factors that should help fulfill the factors found in Figure 3.17.

An ultimate goal of the MIS function, then, is to equip the organization with information systems that make it possible to do the things specified in the firm's list of critical success factors. How well it meets this goal is one of the principal ways in which it should be evaluated. Unfortunately, many systems miss the mark in this regard. A surprising number of companies have little information to disseminate among managers beyond that available from transaction processing systems—and transaction processing is more geared to satisfying the day-to-day needs than long-term decision making. In Chapter 18,

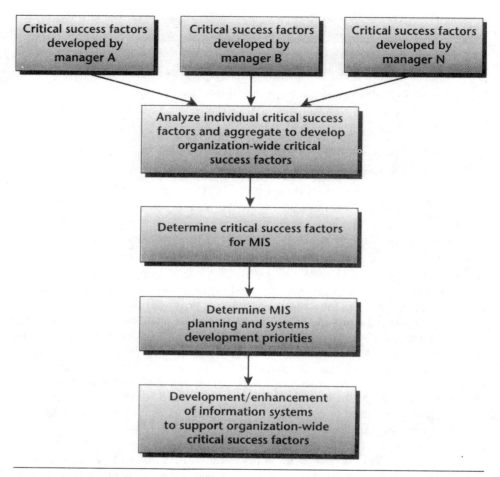

Figure 3.18 A critical success factor (CSF) model for MIS planning. After critical success factors for the entire organization have been identified, critical success factors for the MIS area can be determined.

we will consider the identification of critical success factors more fully, along with other tools used to manage and evaluate the MIS function.

Management Control

The two models we just reviewed—the strategic planning model and the critical success factors model—are geared to analysis and planning tasks. Another important management activity is control. **Control** refers to the process in which steps are taken to recognize, assess, and (possibly) correct deviations from plan. A diagram illustrating the general nature of the control process is shown in Figure 3.20.

In this figure, the rectangle labeled "Plan" refers to activities that previously were planned—for example, first-quarter production levels. These target

Critical Success Factors for MIS

- Provide high-quality service and system documentation to all end-users
- Develop bar code and memory button inventory management systems that enhance the integrity of inventory databases
- Improve scope and ease of use of supplier, work-in-progress, and shipping databases
- Improve information sharing among marketing, production, and research and development in order to promote product development and enhancement
- Install integrated expert systems, computer-aided design, and robotics that make it economically feasible to manufacture special and custom orders
- Improve user interfaces and user training programs in order to enhance end-user productivity
- Assist in the development of multimedia systems and applications that project a "state-of-the-art" corporate image
- Develop a cost-effective, expandable global information system that integrates worldwide operations and product distribution channels
- Improve the marketing information system to better service customers

Figure 3.19 Example of critical success factors for the MIS area of an organization.

amounts (or standards) would probably be in the organization's operating plan. Such resources as time, personnel, plant, and capital are allocated to achieve the planned level of performance. As the production process ensues, certain disturbances may take place—either within the firm or in the external environment—to cause production to slip off plan. For instance, there may be a shortage of key parts, a strike, or a failure of some critical equipment. In any case, actual pro-

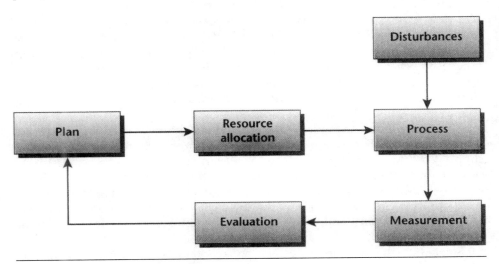

Figure 3.20 A management control model. Represented in the model are all important tasks associated with the planning control cycle—from establishing process requirements to measuring and evaluating the process.

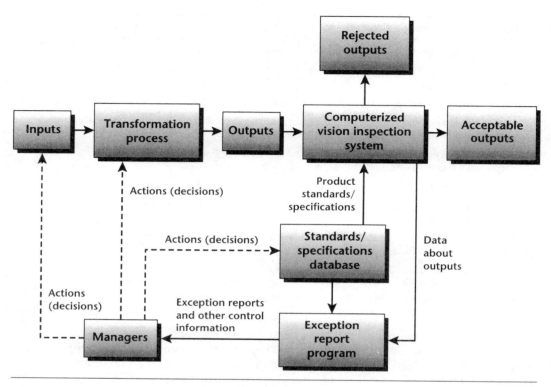

Figure 3.21 The role of information technology in the control process.

duction is measured on a regular basis, so that management has an ongoing idea of whether planned levels are being achieved. If planned levels are much greater than actual levels for, perhaps, several days, management may decide to take some type of action. For instance, it may adjust planned levels of production to reflect new conditions or, possibly, change the resource allocation to bring actual levels up to planned levels (for example, by adding an overtime shift). Then, the plan-allocate-process-measure-evaluate control cycle begins anew.

The model shown in Figure 3.20 is general enough to be used for a variety of control purposes. For example, a manager might observe that an employee is slipping below some expected level of performance (plan). As a measure of control, the manager might decide to reprimand the employee in a constructive way (an allocation of the manager's time resource). The employee then resumes work (process); in the meantime, the manager continues to observe the employee (measurement) and assess whether the employee's work is improving (evaluation).

Related to the control process is **management by exception**. In this approach, activities are allowed to continue unless a significant deviation from plans or standards occurs. Only when activities get seriously "out of whack" do managers step in and make corrections or adjustments. *Exception reports* are

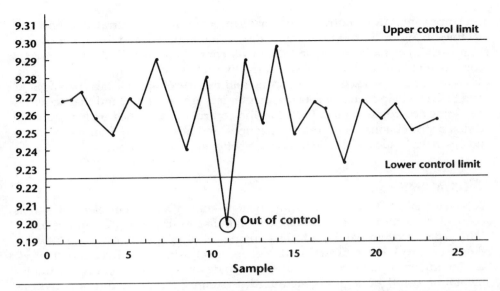

Figure 3.22 An example of a control chart used in statistical quality control (SQC) and statistical process control (SPC).

usually produced on a periodic basis by an organization's management reporting system. They provide managers with information about organizational activities that are not going according to plan or are out of control. The exception reporting process and the role of information systems in the control process are illustrated in Figure 3.21. Data about outputs are fed into the information system and are compared against preset standards or targets. If significant deviations from standards occur, these will be highlighted in exception reports in order to signal managers that corrective action should be taken.

In manufacturing settings, *statistical quality control (SQC)* and *statistical process control (SPC)* are two commonly used approaches that stem directly from the fundamental concept of management by exception. Originating in the United States, these approaches were first widely used in Japan and are among the primary reasons why the Japanese have had such tremendous manufacturing success in the last two decades.

Both approaches allow workers to determine the extent to which operations are staying within acceptable ranges. As long as they do, operations continue as normal. When significant deviations (exceptions) from the standards occur, appropriate adjustments are made. Sampling and sample statistics are commonly used in SQC and SPC to determine whether standards are being met. For example, samples of the outputs of the production process can be taken at regular intervals and appropriate measures made on each item in each sample. Sample means (averages) and/or standard deviations (a summary measure of how far from the average individual items tend to be) are often calculated and compared to "control limits" (see Figure 3.22). Computer support is provided for these calculations in most organizations.

Upper and lower control limits for a sample mean are illustrated as horizontal lines in Figure 3.22. If the sample mean is too high (beyond the upper control limit—UCL) or too low (beyond the lower control limit—LCL), the situation is considered to be out of control and corrective action is needed.

As you can see, exception reporting and the use of approaches such as SQC and SPC can help managers ensure that targets are being met and that activities are going according to plan. Planning and controlling activities are key managerial and professional tasks in organizations and advances in information technology have made it possible to provide better support for them.

SUMMARY

A system is a set of related components—known as system elements—that collectively form a unified whole. One familiar example is a computer-based information system (CBIS), which is composed of people, hardware, software, data, and procedures. Systems are frequently classified as physical or logical, depending on whether the elements used to describe them are primarily implementation-based or highly generalized. Systems function within an environment and open systems interact with their environments across their system boundaries. Virtually all business systems are open systems.

Models are often used to depict and study systems. Models are representations of a real-world element, or of several elements and the relationships among them. In the field of MIS, models are classified as graphical (using symbols to represent elements), mathematical (using formulas to represent quantifiable phenomena and the relationships among them), narrative (explaining systems through words, text, or tables), and physical (using three-dimensional tangible representations).

Graphical models are useful for depicting various aspects of organizations and their environments. One commonly used model of the firm shows the organization interacting with various elements in its environment. The organization's operating environment includes consumers, suppliers, the labor supply, and competitors—that is, those forces with which the organization interacts most closely. All other relevant forces are part of the organization's remote environment. Together, the operating and remote environments form the external environment of the organization.

Data flow diagrams are graphical models that show how data or information move from one process or store to another within an organizational system. These are used extensively by systems analysts. Users and managers involved in systems development efforts are also likely to encounter them.

Another process that can be depicted graphically is strategic-planning, which is used to plot the long-term direction of a firm. The elements of this model include the mission statement, company profile, analysis of the external environment, analysis and choice of strategy, objectives (specific targets that must be reached to execute a strategy), plans (programs that show how the objectives will be carried out), and policies (procedures for guiding employees after a strategy is implemented). Information technology plays an increasingly important role in the strategic planning process.

Other modeling approaches covered in this chapter include the critical success factors (CSF) technique and the management control model. The critical success factors model is based on the fact that certain key tasks (factors) contribute heavily to, for example, organizational or job success. Management control models represent the process in which steps are taken to recognize, assess, and correct deviation from a plan. Exception reporting, statistical quality control (SQC), and statistical process control (SPC) are all types of management control activities that can be supported by information technology.

KEY TERMS

Boundary	Objective
Closed system	Open system
Control	Operating environment
Critical success factor (CSF)	Physical description
Data flow diagram (DFD)	Plan
Environment	Policies
External environment	Remote environment
Logical description	Strategy
Management by exception	System
Mission	System element
Model	

REVIEW

REVIEW QUESTIONS

1. Identify and describe the components and elements typically found in systems models.

2. Distinguish between a closed system and an open system.

3. What is the difference between a logical and physical description of a system? Provide an example of a system and describe it both logically and physically to make your point.

4. How are models related to systems?

5. What are the differences among graphical, mathematical, narrative, and physical models? Provide at least one MIS example for each of these.

6. What purpose is served by data flow diagrams? Why is it important for users and managers to know about data flow diagrams?

7. What are the differences among an organization's operating, remote, and external environments? Describe how MIS may be related to each of the key components of an organization's operating environment.

8. What is an organization's mission? How is a mission statement formulated and what factors may cause it to be reconsidered or reformulated?

9. Provide an overview of the strategic planning process in organizations. Also, discuss how information technology may be used to support the strategic planning activities of managers.

10. What are the differences among strategies, objectives, plans, and policies?

11. What are critical success factors? What role do they play in developing and evaluating information systems?

12. Describe the management control process. What is the role of information technology in this process?

13. What is management by exception? How are exception reporting, statistical process control, and statistical quality control related to management by exception? How is information technology related to these control activities?

DISCUSSION QUESTIONS

1. How does a person decide which elements belong in a system and which elements belong in the system's environment? Why is this a crucial decision in modeling and systems development activities?

2. Theoretically, a closed organizational system does not exist. Why is this so and why bother to study closed systems in organizations if they do not really exist?

3. Sophisticated mathematical modeling tools are now available to ordinary end-users of microcomputer systems in organizations. What advantages and drawbacks do these tools present to the organization?

4. What types of problems might arise that will cause a strategic-planning model such as that shown in Figure 3.10 (page 95) not to work?

CASE STUDY

Gulfstream Aerospace Reshuffles MIS to Support Corporate Strategy

Gulfstream Aerospace Corporation is headquartered in Savannah, Georgia. It manufactures executive jets and outfits them to customer specifications. Its jets, powered by fuel-efficient Rolls Royce engines, hold many of the world's air speed records. Not long ago, it set the air speed record for flights between California and Japan; one of Gulfstream's MIS executives, Harry Butler, piloted the aircraft.

Gulfstream jets are expensive—in the past, the average price has been $15 million. Arab oil sheiks are among their regular customers. The U.S. government has also bought several jets for high-speed radar surveillance and for ferrying high-ranking military officials to hot spots. Gulfstream jets earned official praise during Desert Storm.

Because of the expense, Gulfstream historically has not produced very many planes per year. However, the company has remained profitable and has made its 3,500 person payroll—even in years when it produced fewer than 50 jets. Its planes are highly reliable and Gulfstream has a reputation for outstanding service. When a customer experiences a problem, Gulfstream flies a maintenance crew to wherever in the world the plane is located. Normally, the plane is back in the air in less than 24 hours.

Besides providing outstanding service, Gulfstream customizes the interior of a plane with whatever equipment and finishing touches the customer desires or can afford. For example, one plane was ordered by the king of Jordan's family as a surprise birthday present. It contained a mural of the town in which the king grew up (valued at $500,000) and solid gold fittings throughout.

Gulfstream manufactures the basic aircraft (which is airworthy when finished) in one building and then sends it to another building, where the custom outfitting is completed. The custom work puts a lot of pressure on the company's engineering staff; the purchasing department, understandably, has to handle many one-time special orders.

Gulfstream was founded by Allen E. Paulson, a Horatio Alger Award recipient and self-made man. Paulson purchased the small aircraft division of Grumman and used it to build Gulfstream. One clause of the purchase agreement mandated that Gulfstream would continue to provide parts and service to all small Grumman planes, including some models that dated back to the 1950s. Gulfstream continues to honor this clause; most of the service for Grumman products is provided by sites in Oklahoma and California.

In 1991, when nearing retirement, Paulson hired William Lowe to be Gulfstream's CEO. Prior to joining Gulfstream, Lowe had previously made his mark at IBM and Xerox. At IBM, he led the project team that developed the first IBM PC. As vice president at Xerox, he helped the company weather some turbulent times.

Within a year, Lowe announced his intention to transform Gulfstream from a $1 billion a year to a $4 billion a year company. He implemented a strategic-planning process, which the company lacked prior to his arrival. He also launched an aggressive marketing program that included prime-time commercials during the 1992 Olympics.

To support his ambitious goals, Lowe created organization development and research and development subunits. He also reshuffled the MIS department. Upon his arrival, the MIS department was centralized (similar to the arrangement depicted in Figure 2.9, page 65) with a large IBM mainframe as focal point for almost all of the processing. Most systems analysts and programmers were moved to the various functional areas within the organization, including the purchasing, marketing, production, inventory management, custom finishing, and service/maintenance areas. Only a small core staff remains from the once-powerful, centralized MIS department. Their job primary goals are to provide seamless interfaces between Gulfstream's major subunits and to develop strategic applications.

Lowe has challenged the organization to design several new Gulfstream models that would be affordable by smaller corporations. Gulfstream and Russian engineers are also teaming up to develop the world's first supersonic executive jet.

William Lowe has made it clear that he wants to see tremendous growth and expansion in Gulfstream business operations in the next few years. He also expects that IT will play a significant role in supporting these changes.

Adapted primarily from interviews with Gulfstream managers by T. Case (1992). Also adapted from Kolcum (1990), and Baldo (1989).

DISCUSSION

1. Insiders at Gulfstream have commented that in the past, Gulfstream was an effective organization (because it achieved its major goals), but was inefficient. What kinds of systems should Gulfstream have to make its purchasing, custom finishing, and service/maintenance areas more efficient and functionally effective?

2. What is the value of hiring a CEO such as William Lowe, who is knowledgeable about information technology? In the long run, how is this likely to be beneficial for Gulfstream?

3. What long-term benefits is Gulfstream likely to reap from moving most of its systems analysts and programmers to the company's functional departments?

4. What types of organizational structures seem to be most consistent with the changes that the new CEO has outlined? If a shift from a functional orientation occurs, what do you think will replace it? Why? Do you expect the organization to become more decentralized? Why?

5. What power issues is Gulfstream likely to encounter as a result of changes that have taken place in the MIS department? How are intergroup and intragroup dynamics likely to change?

Chapter 4

Management and Decision Making

After completing this chapter, you will be able to:

Explain what is meant by contingency-based management

Identify some major contingency-based factors that must be handled in a management situation

List a variety of activities that are part of the management process

Contrast several different types of decisions and styles of management

Discuss the stages of the decision-making process

Describe the difference between efficiency and effectiveness

In Chapter 2, we looked at the people component of MIS from a behavioral perspective. We considered the various problems and challenges that occur when people are brought into an organizational environment. In this chapter, we will examine two of the most vital tasks that people perform in an organization: management and decision making.

We start by looking at management: What it is, how it is practiced, and how the process of management might be improved. Next, we turn to decision making. Here we will consider types of decisions, sources of decision-making information, and choosing a course of action.

MANAGEMENT

Every organization requires some form of **management**—processes ensuring that basic functions are performed. Although management is studied as a science, practicing it effectively is more like an art. That is, we can study management by breaking it down into definable tasks, but putting everything together in the right proportions requires some intuitive skill. To a certain extent, good management is similar to the description of a good piece of art: It is what you have left over after everything else has been explained.

This is not to imply that management cannot be studied effectively. A sound educational base can help to prevent managers from overlooking factors that should be considered in decision-making situations. However, good management—like most new skills—is usually a blend of knowledge and experience. And, in the end, a large part of management comes down to people skills—understanding people, creating good impressions so that people are more receptive to ideas and requests, using appropriate timing and discretion, and so on.

What managers do and how they do it effectively have long been debated. Here, we will consider both the science and the art of management.

Levels of Management

Management positions in a firm are often broken down into three levels: upper management (the president and vice-presidents), middle management (the people responsible for anything between upper and lower management), and lower management (the people directly responsible for managing those who produce the firm's outputs). The roles of these levels of management are summarized in the pyramid in Figure 4.1. We will cover the roles played by managers at these different levels in greater detail later in the chapter.

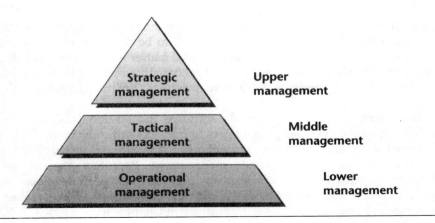

Strategic
management

Upper
management

Tactical
management

Middle
management

Operational
management

Lower
management

Figure 4.1 The three levels of management. The fact that each level of management is governed by a different set of information needs has contributed to the wide variety of information systems in use today.

Upper-Level Management

Upper-level managers are primarily responsible for plotting the company's future moves. Perhaps the most important task of upper-level management is strategic planning—determining the goals, objectives, and plans that chart the organization's long-range course. As we indicated in Chapter 3, to establish such plans, upper-level managers need broad-based information about trends—for both their companies as well as for the external environment. Strategic-planning decisions and the information required to make them are usually seen as being of a relatively "unstructured" nature—that is, no specific formula determines what is needed to make successful decisions in this area.

Generally, upper-level managers must be able to tolerate a very high amount of ambiguity in their decision-making environments. In fact, a great deal of their decision making has been described as "seat of the pants"—combining a small amount of "hard data" with a lot of "soft data." Weston Agor, an executive behavior researcher, claims, "without exception, top managers in every organization differ from middle- and lower-level managers in their ability to use intuition to make decisions on the job. . . . These managers have a sense or vision of what is coming—and how to move their organizations in response to that vision."

Before the 1980s, computer and communications technologies had little impact on the decision-making processes of upper-level management. Today, however, as MIS is expanding beyond its traditional transaction processing roots into use as a competitive tool, upper-level management is becoming more directly involved with using technology and with confronting technology-based issues. In addition, many members of the new generation of managers who are working their way up the corporate ladder have used computers in school or in lower-level positions. As they rise into top management positions, they are more likely than their predecessors to be aware of how information technology can help the organization. Still, no matter what technical skills managers possess, when technology has the potential to alter the basis of competition or provide a company with new products, top management will take notice.

The recent boom in user-friendly software and on-line databases has also made it easier for upper-level managers to interact with computers. These have facilitated the acquisition and integration of the information needed for strategic planning and enterprise-wide management. Executive support systems (ESS) and executive information systems (EIS) have also been developed to satisfy the special information needs of top-level managers. These systems and their uses will be discussed more extensively in Chapter 10.

Middle-Level Management

The information requirements of middle management are slightly different from those of upper management. Middle management mostly involves **tactical planning** (determining the best ways to get the job done) and control. Middle-level managers are seldom told how to perform their jobs in specific terms. More than anyone else, they must figure out what concrete actions should be taken to translate strategic financial, sales, and production goals into results.

Because middle managers are caught between the pressure to produce results for their superiors and the need to obtain cooperation from their subordinates, they are often caught in a "political vise." To get ahead, they need top-level endorsement. (Often, this endorsement is obtainable only when superiors are made to "look good," although achieving this may not help the organization.) But to be effective, they also need to maintain the loyalty of subordinates, and that might mean standing up for subordinates at critical times, even if upper management disagrees.

The information requirements of middle managers have been partially satisfied by reports generated by management reporting systems (MRS). Decision support systems (DSS) have also assisted middle managers who are called upon to make a combination of structured and non-structured decisions.

Lower-Level Management

Lower-level managers are directly responsible for planning and controlling the activities of workers so that higher-level targets are met. Generally, such managers need detailed reports that describe what needs to be done by each work unit and how well each unit is progressing toward production targets. Generally, the information needs of lower-level management tend to be very short term and are most easily structured into formal systems. Historically, information systems support for management has been most visible at the lower levels. The planning activity of lower-level managers is frequently called **operational planning**.

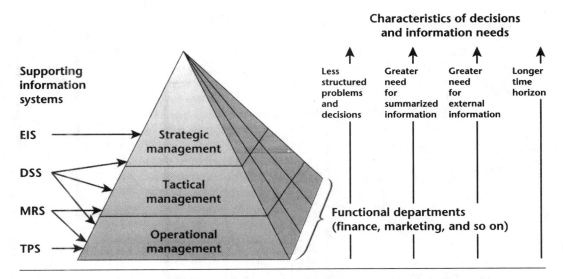

Figure 4.2 Examples of some of the ways in which the characteristics of decisions and information needs vary across levels. This figure also shows the types of informaton systems likely to provide managers at different levels with the information they need to make decisions.

Many of the transaction processing tasks mentioned earlier (accounts receivable, accounts payable, and so on) generate data that are most directly useful to lower-level management and their subordinates. When these data are summarized and consolidated by management reporting systems, they become the information that non-managers, lower-level managers, and many middle-level managers need to perform their jobs.

A summary of some of the major differences between the decision attributes and information requirements of upper- and lower-level managers is provided in Figure 4.2. The types of information systems that are most likely to satisfy the information needs of managers at the three levels are also illustrated in this figure.

A Contingency Approach to Management

Most books written about management today recognize that it is largely **contingency-based**. That is, there is no "best" way to manage that is applicable to every manager, of every organization, in every circumstance, at every point in time. Instead, management action is contingent (depends) on the situation involved. Effective management thus requires that managers be able to adapt to situational factors and constraints.

Contingency-attuned managers· neither wholeheartedly embrace nor reject traditional management theory. Rather, they feel that theory is useful to varying degrees, depending on major situational factors. Thus, to be effective, the manager must have a knowledge of management theory; an attitude reflecting that both theory and situational factors are useful under certain conditions; and

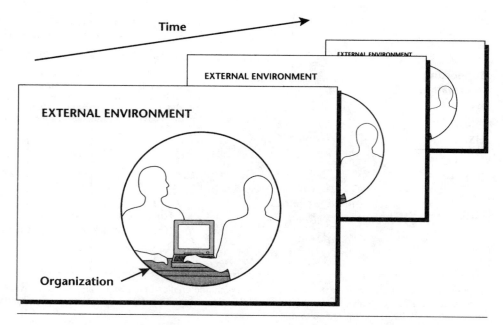

Figure 4.3 Managerial contingencies. Almost every management problem boils down to certain decision makers, in a specific organization, operating in a specialized external environment, at a specific point in time.

a skill for identifying, analyzing, and correcting complex situations. It is the fact that every situation is different that makes both management and MIS so difficult and inexact, yet so fascinating and challenging to study.

Management knowledge can be gained through a variety of sources including experience as a manager and textbooks. Textbooks are useful for helping us structure our ideas about management theory. They provide an overall view of the important issues in the field. Texts are also useful for teaching some "universal truths" about management—that is, principles of management that are largely contingency-independent.

The major contingency factors that must be understood in any management situation are the external environment, the internal organization, time, and the decision makers. Stated another way, management condenses to decision makers in an organization, operating in a specific environment, at a particular point in time. These contingency factors are described in the following subsections and depicted in Figure 4.3.

External Environment

The external environment of an organization involves both a general culture (technological, sociological, economic, political, and so on) and a particular set of groups with which the organization must interact. As mentioned in Chapter 3, these groups usually include customers, suppliers, competitors, labor supply, labor unions, and governments.

The external environment is a major contingency variable for many reasons. In order to survive and evolve, an organization must adapt effectively to changes that take place in its environment. The inability to adjust to environmental changes can erode the effectiveness of an organization and threaten its continued existence.

Internal Organization

Internally, the organization consists of all the owners, employees, cultures, tangible assets, structures, jobs, histories, policies, plans, procedures, and so forth, that are identified as belonging to or being a part of the organization. Within the complex chemistry formed by various levels of each of these elements, work takes place. Moreover, any of these items may become an important contingency factor in a given situation.

For example, a new MIS executive in an organization may have a vision of what the MIS department could become and may want to replace all outdated systems and staff members who are considered incompetent. Although this action may be theoretically possible, certain contingency factors could preclude it from happening. Employees of all levels of competencies may be protected by law, union contract, or company policy. Funds may not be available to replace the outdated systems. People might find the current systems useful, even though they are outdated. Or, being new, the MIS executive may have a weak base of power or political support and would risk alienating upper management if employees were fired.

Also, regarding the internal organization, note that many decisions take place within a certain set of higher-level goals and objectives. If the company decides it should move in a certain strategic direction, that direction should be considered by managers to be a major contingency factor. An example is when a company has undergone a series of financial setbacks that have put it into a retrenchment mode—a circumstance that usually requires cost-cutting ideas, not new ways to spend money. Of course, there are no strict rules; if management, for instance, sees an important investment opportunity unfolding in its external environment while it is retrenching, it should carefully consider the importance of that opportunity. Some opportunities may appear only once in a lifetime.

Stages of Growth and Time Factors

Time is an important contingency factor in management in two major ways.

First, the world is constantly changing: existing competitors are getting stronger or weaker, new competitors will inevitably enter the market, consumer tastes are changing, and the government will eventually alter the way in which business is conducted. Thus, decisions that are appropriate today may not be appropriate tomorrow.

The so-called **stages-of-growth (SOG) curve** in Figure 4.4 is especially useful for considering why certain MIS decisions made at one point may be inappropriate at another time. MIS executives find the stages of growth models useful as a general framework for planning. SOG curves are also more useful

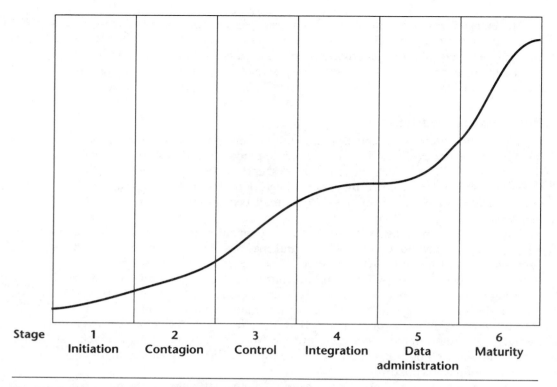

| Stage | 1
Initiation | 2
Contagion | 3
Control | 4
Integration | 5
Data
administration | 6
Maturity |

Figure 4.4 The six stages of data processing growth and some of the major characteristics of each.

for understanding changes in decision-making perspectives that occur after the introduction of new systems and throughout the system maturation process. Figure 4.5 summarizes the major characteristics and management issues associated with the stages of growth of information technology.

According to the SOG model, in stage 1 (when a system is new) a lot of discovery, experimentation, and error processes occur. If the system survives, it begins to achieve more widespread acceptance. Thus, stage 2—contagion—takes place.

Stage 3 is typified by fine-tuning and control: setting standards, managing costs, developing plans for further growth, and so on. Stage 4 is characterized by system refinements, especially those centering around database technologies; planning and control systems for MIS also become more systematic, better integrated, and formal during this stage. During stage 5, the database systems introduced during stage 4 give managers an appreciation for the value of data and information, causing data administration functions to be introduced. At some point, the system matures and enters stage 6; at this time, the technology and management functions form an integrated entity. However, new technologies may prevent a system from reaching stage 6 and full maturity—in fact, the

SIX STAGES OF GROWTH

Stage	Characteristics/Issues
1. Initiation	The new technology is introduced into the organization and some users start applying it. Its use gradually increases as users become comfortable with the technology and how it can be used.
2. Contagion	More users and subunits become familiar with the technology and its applications. Its use proliferates and demand for it among users increases. Enthusiasm for the new technology grows rapidly.
3. Control	During this stage, management becomes increasingly concerned about the economics of the technology. The benefits and costs of the technology become important concerns. Planning and control issues are introduced. Users are made accountable for utilizing the technology in a cost-effective manner.
4. Integration	Systems continue to proliferate and existing applications are upgraded, using database technology. Planning and control systems are formalized and the notion of systems integration becomes dominant. Management becomes interested in leveraging existing systems and databases.
5. Data administration	During this stage, management becomes increasingly concerned with the value of data and information. Data administration functions are created to manage and control databases to ensure that they are effectively utilized and appropriately shared across applications.
6. Maturity	In organizations that reach this stage, the technology and the management process are integrated into an effective functional entity. Strategic data planning and data resource management become the joint responsibilities of MIS and users.

Figure 4.5 A summary of the characteristics and major issues associated with the stages-of-growth model. The stage that an organization or new system is in will impact the types of decisions that are made.

introduction of new technologies may result in partial or complete system overhauls, causing the life cycle to begin anew.

The stages-of-growth model is especially important in the study of business and MIS because the appropriateness of certain decisions relates to what growth stage the organization, system, or product is in. For example, start-up companies in fast-paced industries often find that they are too busy serving clients to think about such measures as control or information systems development. Often, in the very early stages of an organization's growth cycle, it is hard even to imagine what types of systems would be most effective. People are still in the process of discovering what their business really involves at this point.

Also, the type of leadership required for companies at the beginning of their growth cycles is often totally different from what is desirable when the company is in the latter stages of development. For example, while an entrepreneur is likely to be running a company at the beginning—Steve Jobs at Apple Computer and Kenneth G. Fisher at Prime Computer are good illustrations—they are often replaced by professional managers oriented toward refinement objectives such as marketing, control, or consolidation. As one type of leader is replaced by another, the entire corporate culture of the organization often changes and its organization structures are also likely to change.

Regarding information technology, the microcomputer revolution in many organizations is now well entrenched and moving into the control and integration stages of management. As organizations spend large portions of their information systems budgets on microcomputers, such issues as establishing buying standards, data-integrity procedures, local area network controls, and security measures for these systems are receiving increasing attention. When most firms experienced the first big wave of microcomputer buying in the mid-1980s, few made such control issues a high priority.

New developments such as expert systems and neural networks are still in the initiation stage. In addition, many people would claim that transaction processing systems, which have been around since the 1950s, are at the mature stage of development.

The stage at which systems or applications are in their growth often dictates the appropriate management approach. For example, control procedures are often seen as undesirable during the early stages of growth because they can be a deterrent to further growth. An example is the cost of using large systems. To encourage users to experiment when a system is new, use of the system is usually free. In this manner, users begin gaining confidence in the system and systems developers learn more about the system's potential through this process. One company, for example, equipped its field sales staff with pen-based computers soon after they started to appear on the market. A year later, they did a formal assessment of how they were being used. The results of this assessment were subsequently used to formulate systems development plans for this new technology.

Another important contingency is *timing*; that is, instinctively knowing when it is appropriate to take certain actions. For instance, people are often more receptive to changes when they are in a good mood (and less receptive when they are in a bad one); thus, it is important to time certain announcements carefully. Since the MIS effort often depends heavily on the success of a handful of key systems—and these systems must obtain top-level management approval before being developed extensively—timing can be crucial to MIS executives. Good managers often have an innate sense of timing.

Personal Factors

Organizations don't manage; people do. Thus, an important contingency factor in any management situation is the manager or managers charged with authority.

A management style that works for one manager may not be effective for another. For example, some managers are more sensitive and people-oriented than others. If the solution to a problem demands that a people-oriented manager take a harsh action against subordinates, it is possible that he or she will not be able to accomplish the task. It is also often the case that, as situations change, a management style that worked in one situation will not work in another. As a company grows, for instance, some managers find that the interpersonal style that worked well for them when the company was small is no longer suitable in the larger company. As the roles of decision makers change, so too may the desire of decision makers to work in the firm.

Two other important contingencies are *conflicts of interest* and *power shifts* that might result from decisions. For instance, as implied earlier, middle managers are often in a role-conflict position, trying to please upper management while also trying to do well for the employees reporting to them. Systems analysts, who must meet the conflicting interests of the MIS department, users, and upper management, are another example of a role-conflict position. The concern about power is especially relevant in an MIS environment because information systems often have the effect of shifting and redistributing power, putting the people who will gain or lose it in a conflict-of-interest position. For example, many data processing managers attempted to undermine microcomputers when they first made inroads to organizations, seeing them as a threat to their mainframe-based power. Thomas Gerrity and John Rockhart cite a case in which one MIS department successfully pushed a complex programming language as a company standard in order to thwart threats to their power base from end-user computing.

The *values* of decision makers represent another important contingency factor. For instance, firing people would probably be last on the list of possibilities for most employee-sensitive managers. Also, whereas some people value most of the results they achieve professionally, other people look upon the quality of life as being more important. Thus, the decision maker who values the interpersonal contact of a small firm may dismiss any decision alternatives that would increase the size of the firm. Also, a decision maker who values risk-taking and a fast pace may not be receptive to decision alternatives that require "playing a waiting game."

To sum up the importance of the decision maker as a key contingency factor: No matter how rational an alternative looks to an impartial observer, that alternative may not be the one chosen by the person making the decision. One of the main purposes of Chapter 2 was to illustrate that, because people are a major component in any CBIS and they behave in unpredictable ways, the analyst should not discount their importance.

Managerial Roles

In 1916, Henri Fayol proposed one of the earliest theories describing what managers do. Fayol suggested that management consisted of five functions: planning, controlling, organizing, commanding, and coordinating. In the mid-1970s, Henry Mintzberg argued that Fayol's list was incomplete because it failed to explicitly recognize certain tasks—for instance, the manager's role as negotiator or fire-fighter. Mintzberg devised an alternate, refined list (see Figure 4.6). Mintzberg's list is organized into ten managerial subfunctions that, in turn, are aggregated into three major functions. Mintzberg refers to the functions and subfunctions as roles. A description of each role and several examples are given in the following subsections.

Interpersonal	Informational	Decisional
▪ Figurehead	▪ Monitor	▪ Entrepreneur
▪ Leadership	▪ Disseminator	▪ Disturbance handler
▪ Liaison	▪ Spokesperson	▪ Resource allocator
		▪ Negotiator

Figure 4.6 Mintzberg's managerial roles. Managers often perform several hundred activities each day, any of which can be classified into one or more of the ten roles shown here.

Interpersonal Roles

The **interpersonal roles** of management—which center upon interaction with people—have traditionally been underplayed. However, many successful managers claim that the most critical dimension of their job is dealing with people. Mark McCormack, a CEO in a multinational company, states, "I can't imagine anyone being effective in business without having some insight into people. . . . Every aspect of [business] comes back to people—managing them, selling to them, working with them, simply getting them to do what you want them to do." Mintzberg cites three interpersonal roles of management: figurehead, leader, and liaison.

The manager's *figurehead role* relates largely to the ceremonial duties performed by a manager as a result of his or her position. For example, a manager of an oil refinery in Port Arthur, Texas, might oversee visits made by high-level executives from other parts of the organization or from outside the organization. Managers are often expected, as figureheads, to also make themselves "visible" to subordinates. For instance, Chrysler president Lee Iacocca recalls in his autobiography a time when he felt it was necessary, as CEO, to personally address workers in order to pull them together: "During 1980, I went to every single Chrysler plant in order to speak directly to the workers. At a series of mass meetings, I thanked them for sticking with us during these bad times. I told them that when things got better, we'd try to get them back to parity with Ford and GM workers but that it wouldn't happen overnight. I gave them my pitch, and they hooted and hollered, and some of them applauded and some of them booed."

Leadership—the ability to successfully influence people in order to translate intention into reality—has become a popular management issue in recent years. *Business Week*, *The Wall Street Journal*, and other business publications frequently run articles on the impacts that leaders have had on their firms. Lee Iacocca's leadership at Chrysler and Ross Perot's leadership at Electronic Data Systems (EDS) verge on being legendary and have helped make both men into public figures. Leadership is so vital to the success of both a company and its information systems effort that we will consider it in more detail later in this chapter.

Whereas the leadership role concerns intragroup relations, the *liaison role* involves contact with people outside of the manager's particular work unit. A refinery manager in Port Arthur, Texas, for example, may have superiors in New York that must be regularly dealt with on an interpersonal level. Also, this refinery manager may want to cultivate interpersonal relationships with key customers or with community leaders. All of these activities call for the manager to interact with others across system boundaries; boundary-spanning skills are essential to effectively fulfill the liaison role.

In the past, information technologies often had little to offer managers in the fulfillment of their interpersonal roles. Today, this is no longer the case. The combination of computer and communication technologies has provided managers with new ways to communicate and to stay in touch with others. Electronic mail, voice mail, and video teleconferencing may be effectively used by managers to demonstrate their ongoing attention to important situations. Such systems allow managers to have an electronic presence with others, even when a physical, interpersonal presence is not possible. In Chapter 12, we will discuss these types of systems in more detail.

Informational Roles

Informational roles relate to the manager as a receiver or sender of information. Included among the informational roles are the role of the manager as a monitor, disseminator, and spokesperson.

In the *monitor role*, the manager collects information. This information then either remains the property of the manager or it is disseminated (widely distributed). Information that is disseminated either stays within the manager's work unit or is distributed outside (see Figure 4.7). Generally, different standards are applied to both the quality and the appearance of information disseminated to outside parties than to information that stays within the work group. For instance, the manager may establish very high standards to ensure the accuracy and reliability of information disseminated externally because outsiders might be less understanding of incorrect information. Information sent to outsiders is often packaged more carefully; it may be output on high-quality paper with a letter-quality or laser printer; it may be accompanied by attention-grabbing presentation graphics or be bound in an attractive folder. When distributing information within the work unit, the manager is fulfilling the *disseminator role*; when distributing information outside the work unit, the *spokesperson role* is being fulfilled.

Many of the information technologies covered in this text can help managers fulfill their informational roles. Management reporting systems (MRS) and executive information systems (EIS) can be used to acquire and summarize the information that they need. The technologies associated with decision support systems (DSS) and office information systems (OIS) may be used to help managers appropriately analyze and format information for dissemination and presentation. The general support that information systems provide in fulfilling Mintzberg's roles is illustrated in Figure 4.8.

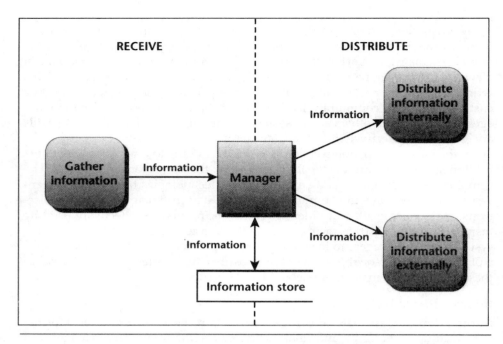

RECEIVE | DISTRIBUTE

Gather information → Information → Manager → Information → Distribute information internally

Manager → Information → Distribute information externally

Information ↕ Information store

Figure 4.7 The manager as a receiver and sender of information. Usually, different standards apply to information disseminated outside the work unit than to information staying inside. Of course, some information gathered by the manager will not be disseminated.

Decisional Roles

A large part of management and information systems theory covers planning and control issues. The planning and control functions of management are reflected most heavily in **decisional roles**, which include entrepreneurism, disturbance handling, resource allocation, and negotiation. Planning and control functions are so critical to management that we will cover them in detail later in this section.

An entrepreneur is a person who initiates a venture and cultivates it into a reality, assuming a considerable amount of risk in doing so. The *entrepreneurial role* of the manager involves the vision the manager has regarding what must be done in order to successfully perform his or her job. Having a general vision of what needs to be done, and having the initiative to see it through, is the starting point for all other planning and control activities.

The *disturbance-handler role* of the manager relates to control. Managers must devise a system for identifying and handling disturbances as they arise. In order to know if a disturbance constitutes a problem, the manager must have a firm idea of what needs to be accomplished. When something stands in the way of accomplishment, it automatically becomes a problem. Often, control and containment measures need to be taken to solve the problem; most problems, unfortunately, do not disappear on their own.

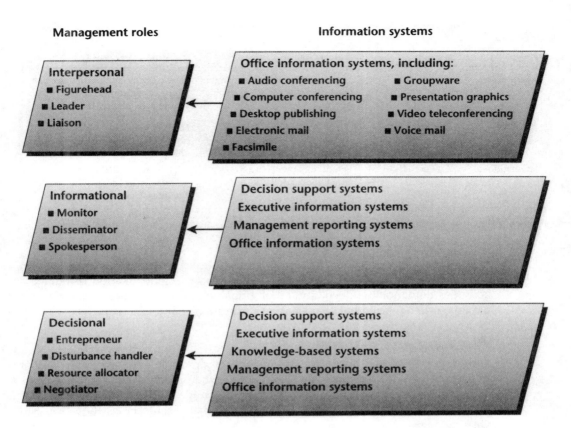

Management roles

Interpersonal
- Figurehead
- Leader
- Liaison

Informational
- Monitor
- Disseminator
- Spokesperson

Decisional
- Entrepreneur
- Disturbance handler
- Resource allocator
- Negotiator

Information systems

Office information systems, including:
- Audio conferencing
- Computer conferencing
- Desktop publishing
- Electronic mail
- Facsimile
- Groupware
- Presentation graphics
- Video teleconferencing
- Voice mail

Decision support systems
Executive information systems
Management reporting systems
Office information systems

Decision support systems
Executive information systems
Knowledge-based systems
Management reporting systems
Office information systems

Figure 4.8 Examples of the information systems and information technologies that may help managers fulfill the various roles described by Mintzberg.

The *resource allocation role* is related to planning. After the entrepreneurial vision is established, the manager must plan for it to happen. Virtually every planning problem can be seen as one of allocating resources. Planning your future, for example, involves allocating time to doing specific things. Planning the building of a house involves allocating people to construction tasks, money to building supplies, and construction activities to a schedule.

The *negotiation role* requires the manager to fight for his or her vision. A manufacturing manager who wants to increase production by 30 percent, for example, may have to negotiate with superiors for funds to buy a new factory or production system. A manager who wants to increase the quality of staff often has to negotiate with upper management for better worker salaries and benefits.

As shown in Figure 4.8, types of information systems that support managers in fulfilling their decisional roles are often the same ones that support them in their informational roles. Over time, advances in information and communication technologies should make it easier for managers to effectively fulfill all of their roles. Some experts even predict that the effective use of information

Type of Planning	Management Level	Description	Example Decision
Strategic	Upper	Planning the most important tasks to be done	The executive committee decides that a company should move into a new product area
Tactical	Middle	Planning how strategic tasks are to be carried out	Managers decide which specific types of products in the new area will result in the highest profits
Operational	Lower	Planning how tactical tasks are to be carried out	Managers decide how to produce the chosen products with certain facilities, labor, and supplies

Figure 4.9 Types of planning and the management levels at which each type of planning is most likely to occur.

technology will be essential for fulfilling these roles in the future, especially in companies that want to expand internationally. The globalization of business activities demands the development of global telecommunication networks and a managerial "reach" that spans national boundaries and time zones.

Planning and Control

Although Mintzberg does an excellent job of describing the various roles of managers, he does not particularly emphasize the planning and control aspects of management. In fact, the words "planning" and "control" do not appear at all in any of the ten Mintzberg roles (although they cut across these roles to varying degrees).

Earlier in the chapter, we introduced the importance of these activities and how they relate to the various levels of management. However, because managerial planning and control activities are particularly prevalent in the information systems literature, we will discuss them separately here.

Planning

R. N. Anthony was one of the first people to formally recognize three different types of planning: strategic planning, tactical planning, and operational planning. These are explained here and shown in Figure 4.9.

- **Strategic planning** As mentioned earlier in this chapter and in Chapter 3, strategic planning generally refers to long-range, organization-wide planning activities that take place at the highest levels of the organization. Strategic planners look at the "big-picture" view of what is currently happening both within their organizations and outside of them. Then the planners chart a course representing what should be done.

    Strategic planning can also take place at other levels of the organization. Many of the functional areas—finance, marketing, and MIS—have their own strategic plans that key off those of the enterprise. The result is often a hierarchy of goals and objectives within the organization. If the strategic objectives of the organization's subunits are fulfilled, those for the entire organization are more likely to be accomplished.

In virtually every organization, upper management is responsible for formulating the organization-wide strategic plan. This master plan then becomes the basis for other strategic planning within the firm and for tactical planning efforts, both of which are typically the responsibility of middle- and lower-level managers. Chief executive officers, chief financial officers, MIS executives, vice-presidents, and planning staff members may be involved in the development of the strategic plan for the entire organization. As noted in Chapter 3, after the organization-wide strategic plan is developed, the top-level MIS managers would be responsible for developing an MIS strategic plan that is consistent with the organization's overall plan. The processes that may be used to formulate MIS strategic plans will be discussed in Chapter 18.

■ *Tactical planning* As mentioned earlier, tactical planning is the technique of determining how strategic objectives will be accomplished. For instance, if the strategic plan identifies a 30 percent increase in the value or the growth of the firm by 1999, a tactical plan must be devised regarding how to accomplish such an objective. A tactical marketing plan might call for a 10 percent annual increase in prices, for example, plus the creation of certain new products and the elimination of products that do not meet profitability objectives. As noted earlier, tactical planning is usually the job of middle-level management.

■ *Operational planning* Operational planning, also discussed previously, involves planning at the finest level of detail. It involves the translation of tactical plans into short-term plans, such as work and production schedules. Operational planning is typically the job of lower-level management.

The operational plan begins where the tactical plan ends. For example, if the tactical plan calls for a 10 percent increase in prices, lower-level management must decide such matters as which prices will be raised (and on what products), how long prices will remain at current levels, and which distribution channels will be affected. Or, if middle-level management comes up with a production plan showing that certain product quantities must be available for shipment by the beginning of each month, then lower-level management has to devise an appropriate production schedule to meet these predefined targets.

Role of Information Systems in Planning

Information systems have historically provided greater support for the planning activities of lower-level managers because much of the information that lower management needs is available from transaction processing systems (TPS). The management reporting systems (MRS) that first appeared in the 1960s were mostly targeted to middle levels of management. Only recently, with the rise of decision support systems, executive support systems, and executive information systems, have information systems begun to satisfy the strategic planning information needs of upper-level management.

Control and Contingency Planning

Plans of any type are difficult to accomplish unless people are regularly apprised as to whether everything is going according to plan. If, for example, a plan is to produce 10,000 units of product in a given month, and workers are behind schedule two days into the plan, management should be able to find this out. Or if a person who was expected to fill a critical slot is making a lot of mistakes, management should have an adequate warning system so that appropriate actions can be taken.

Good management typically means having control systems in place to monitor, audit, or otherwise track activities. If something goes wrong or appears unusual, management should find out before it is too late. Rarely do formulated plans unfold without a hitch. Therefore, designing appropriate control measures should be a critical part of every planning effort. When certain events may be anticipated to go off course, many managers find it useful to set up contingency plans. A *contingency plan* goes into effect if something seriously wrong happens with the master plan. Usually a contingency plan deals with specific and explicit departures from the master plan. For example, a contingency plan might be devised for dealing with the situation in which actual sales volume falls 5 percent or more below sales forecasts. Having a well-thought-out contingency plan enables managers to react immediately when something unusual happens, without having to waste time, fumble around for a solution, or enter a crisis management mode.

Today, a lot of attention is spent on control activities in businesses. Some critics charge that too much attention is spent on control in the United States. Several observers, for instance, in comparing U.S. and Japanese information systems, imply that U.S. firms spend too much time seeing if people are performing their jobs correctly; computerized performance monitoring systems are often cited as a manifestation of this tendency. Whether these allegations are true or not, one concept is clear: Some balance must be struck between planning and control activities in each organization.

Managerial Styles

Many books have been written about managerial style. Some—such as Mark McCormack's *What They Don't Teach You in Harvard Business School* and Thomas Peters and Robert Waterman's *In Search of Excellence*—were best sellers when they were first published and are management classics. Peters' book *Liberation Management: Necessary Disorganization for the Nanosecond Nineties* is likely to be one of the 1990s classics. Here we look at several issues that are the part of management style.

Leaders

- Are opportunity finders (as opposed to routine problem solvers)

- Are people who do the right things (in addition to doing things the right way)

- Know how to make other people feel good and to inspire other people

- Accept people as they are, not as they would necessarily like them to be

- Focus on the present rather than the past

- Have the ability to trust others and to take risks based on that trust

- Do not need constant approval or recognition

- Have a vision of the future that directs their actions

- Think in terms of success; failure is a concept that doesn't exist

- Do not waste time by worrying

Figure 4.10 Qualities found in many leaders. Through the years, recognition of leadership qualities has remained relatively constant, wheras comprehensive theories about what leadership really is and who can exercise it have changed dramatically.

Leadership

Effective management often means good leadership. There is no consensus, however, on what makes an effective leader. In fact, organizational theorists Warren Bennis and Burt Nanus claim that over 350 definitions of leadership exist in the professional literature, making leadership "the most studied and least understood topic of any in the social sciences."

According to R. J. House, leadership qualities include adherence to a set of goals that potential followers will see as worthwhile; also, leaders are perceived by followers as capable of providing a path that leads to the achievement of worthwhile goals. People tend to follow another person when they perceive that person as having a good chance of succeeding. They perceive that, by following a successful person, they will also reach a desirable outcome. Leadership is widely seen today in terms of contingency or situational theories; that is, leadership qualities and approaches that may be effective in one set of circumstances might not work in another. Some key leadership qualities are shown in Figure 4.10.

Theory X Versus Theory Y

The *Theory X and Theory Y* views of management were proposed by Douglas McGregor in the 1950s. According to McGregor, Theory X (autocratic) managers believe that people have an inherent dislike for work and will shirk it whenever possible. Regarding management style, adherence to this belief results in carefully directing worker efforts and in having strong systems to motivate and control workers. Theory Y managers, on the other hand, believe that people like their work and receive satisfaction from it. Regarding management style, this belief holds that, for certain types of activities, people can motivate and manage themselves reasonably well; hence, strong motivation and control systems may not be needed. Often, Theory Y managers will ask subordinates to participate in decision-making activities.

Today, most management scholars recognize that few situations fall strictly within either the Theory X or Theory Y realm. Certain types of jobs—such as those involving highly repetitive, assembly-line tasks—will tend to attract people who consider work to be a chore. Likewise, certain other types of jobs—such as that of creative director at an advertising agency—will tend to attract people who love their work. However, since no two people are alike, many highly motivated blue-collar workers love coming to work and many well-educated, highly paid professionals hate what they do for a living.

Delegation of Authority

The best managers are often the ones who know how to skillfully delegate authority. Delegating authority involves knowing what tasks to do yourself and what tasks to pass on to subordinates. Knowing what jobs to do yourself and what to delegate depends on a number of interrelated factors—your own strengths and weaknesses, the strengths and weaknesses of subordinates, the time available to perform the work that must be done, the importance of the task, the risk level associated with task success, and so on. Delegation of authority and autocratic (Theory X) management approaches are often incompatible.

Management by Exception

The term "management by exception" was introduced in Chapter 3. It refers to a management control style in which the majority of managerial attention is focused on deviations from standard. Thus, the manager will be mostly concerned with either exceptionally bad performance (which might trigger a decision to replace people or to change a method of doing work) or exceptionally good performance (which might trigger a decision to promote someone or to try a new idea in a new area). Of course, this style of management cannot be applied without considering other factors. A manager should always be on the lookout for potential problems and new opportunities, even when everything seems to be running smoothly. Exploiting new opportunities is a key to effective planning, which we will discuss shortly.

Management by Objectives

An approach known as **management by objectives (MBO)** is sometimes used to direct and evaluate the performance of workers. It involves setting goals for individual workers (or groups) to achieve and reviews of goals accomplished (or progress toward doing so). For example, a salesperson may set a goal of 30 new clients and $2 million in sales for next year. Such goals, of course, are subject to final approval by management. Research suggests that worker participation in goal-setting translates into greater efforts to achieve the goals; if goals are set by management without worker involvement, worker efforts and the commitment to accomplishing them may be lacking.

H. Edward Wrapp, among others, suggests that management by objectives is often "unworkable" at the upper levels of management. This observation is not surprising because upper-level managers must make decisions that are not as well-defined as those made at lower levels; also, they must be able to make decisions quickly if needed. In such circumstances, whether or not they are accomplishing previously set objectives becomes superfluous.

MANAGERIAL DECISION MAKING

Decision making has been called the essence of management because it is the most basic function that managers are paid to do. In the next few sections, we will look at several important issues regarding managerial decision making—notably, types of decisions, sources of information for making decisions, choosing among alternatives, and evaluating decisions. However, before we cover these things, let's first turn to both the theoretical and practical perspectives of one of the main ingredients of decisions—information.

Characteristics of Effective Information

Since the start of this book, we have covered a number of important concepts that relate to human information processing. Some general patterns or principles of human information processing may be derived from research literature and four of these are summarized here.

- **Information is something that is perceived**   Stated another way, information refers to data that have been processed by the human mind and therefore have been given some type of meaning. Perceptual and personality factors influence the manner in which data are encoded, processed, and stored. Thus, two people looking at the same set of data often focus on and perceive different things, perhaps reaching different conclusions. Sometimes, it is almost as if the two individuals have been provided with different pieces of information.

- **Information reduces uncertainty about a situation**   People tend to seek out information because certain facts may help to minimize the risk of making a wrong decision and increase the likelihood of making the right one.

- **The human mind processes information in chunks, taken from short-term memory**   Because people usually find it easier to draw from short-term rather than long-term or external memory when they are initiating an action, information is likely to have the greatest influence when key data are readily accessible in a person's short-term memory.

- **The rate at which people can process data into information is finite**   If too many data are presented within a certain time frame, the result is information overload. Since individuals can typically only process 7 ± 2 chunks of

The Practicality Of Virtual Reality

Virtual reality is a concept that leaps beyond both graphical user interfaces and multimedia systems to actually put users "inside" a database so that they can select or organize information with hand and body movements. Users wear a helmet-like device that completely covers both eyes and ears to create a computer-simulated reality that changes as the users move.

"VIRTUAL REALITY APPLICATIONS ARE NOT LIMITED TO VISUALIZATION TASKS."

Several companies are developing business applications for this new technology. An application for a major Japanese electronics firm will allow consumers to browse for products in a "virtual showroom." Another virtual reality application allows aircraft wing designers to use hand motions to simulate the flow of air across wing surfaces.

Virtual reality applications are not limited to visualization tasks. With acoustic modeling—the duplication of human hearing in a virtual environment—sound changes "direction" as users manipulate their way through the simulated environment. Architects can use acoustic modeling to test how different structural configurations, building materials, and partition positions will affect the acoustics of yet-to-be-built rooms or open spaces.

Scott Fisher, co-founder and manager of Telepresence, sees applications in jobs in which workers must react to vast amounts of data. Says Fisher, "The challenge is, how can you display that to make better decisions?. . . Navigating through data is not a fun experience."

Adapted from Wilder (1992).

---

data at one time, materials such as reports, graphs, and tables should be formatted so that they do not overwhelm decision makers with more information than can be easily understood.

In practice, these principles have been widely used in MIS design to affect both the content and presentation of information system outputs.

Content

The most important quality of any MIS output is that it contain the types of information that people really need. As simple as this sounds, in many cases it has not been practiced. For example, some managers play the "numbers game," asking for reports that produce numbers so that upper-level management can see evidence of how well they did their jobs. When lower-level managers transmit information to superiors, they often highlight data to imply that things are going well and to submerge any negative data. Thus, a production manager may favor information showing that a production line had little downtime or that shop floor absenteeism was minimal, and to forego information suggesting that the product was not being produced the right way or that workers were not being optimally used.

DESIRABLE QUALITIES OF INFORMATION	
Quality	**Description**
▨ Availability	Is accessible to those who need it
▨ Comprehensibility	Is understandable to those who need it
▨ Relevance	Has a bearing on matters pertaining to the performance of the organization
▨ Usefulness	Is in a form that makes it capable of being used
▨ Timeliness	Is available at the right time
▨ Reliability	Can be counted on to be trustworthy
▨ Accuracy	Is correct
▨ Consistency	Is not self-contradictory

Figure 4.11 Desirable information qualities. The importance of each of the qualities shown here depends on the application and a number of situational variables.

People are also more inclined to gather information that is easy to measure or obtain over information that is more difficult to quantify or that is less accessible. For instance, many management reporting systems have been criticized for providing more easily assembled financial accounting data to managers who really need cost accounting data (which is often more difficult to derive). To minimize the potential problems that may result from these tendencies, it is important for systems analysts and designers to consider what types of information managers really need to do a better job. The report formats and screens should supply decision makers with relevant information—even if it is difficult to integrate the data needed to produce the necessary decision-making information.

To be valuable to decision makers, information should have as many of the following properties as possible: availability, comprehensibility, relevance, usefulness, timeliness, reliability, accuracy, and consistency. Figure 4.11 provides a brief definition of each of these properties. Systems developers should regard these properties as providing guidance for designing all systems outputs delivered by the system to decision makers. Managers and users should use these properties as criteria for evaluating the effectiveness of their system outputs.

Presentation

Presentation refers to the methods of increasing the likelihood that report or screen information will be both comprehensible and useful. Increasingly, presentation has also been used to maximize the impact that outputs have on users and decision makers. Output presentation is important in the same way that a person's outside appearance is important. Although the way a person dresses may have little to do with their worth, it often creates an impression that has significant consequences. A variety of techniques to present data more effectively may be used, including:

- **Eliminating unnecessary information** Some people feel that the more information that is stuffed into a report, display screen, or briefcase, the better. However, the reverse is usually true. The presence of unnecessary information detracts from the impact of key information. Information overload is usually the end result.

- **Carefully formatting critical information** The physical placement of information on a page or display screen can be important. If critical information is relegated to places where decision makers are not apt to look, it may go unnoticed. Also, on printed reports, it is often helpful to leave ample "white space" (such as wide margins or other unprinted areas) so managers can annotate the report with written comments.

- **Putting information into its most useful form** Some information has greater impact if it is converted from absolute form into relative form. For example, numbers often have more informational value if they are computed as percentages or presented as deviations (to show, for example, the discrepancy between planned and actual expenses). Although it may be possible for managers to compute such information from other values contained in the report, managers are usually too busy to do extra work to obtain the information they need. A good MIS puts information into the form that managers find most useful.

- **Using color** The availability of color monitors, plotters, and printers makes it possible to use color to highlight important information. For example, in reports comparing the quarterly earnings of a number of divisions, losses can be shown in red and profits in blue. Color make it possible for key information to be immediately noticeable to the decision maker (unless, of course, the decision maker is colorblind). The use of color should be deliberate and meaningful, however. Using too many colors can contribute to information overload, and colors used in inconsistent or inappropriate ways may create unnecessary confusion.

- **Using graphics** You've probably heard the saying that "One picture is worth a thousand words." In many cases, a quick glance at pictures (or presentation graphics), such as those shown in Figure 4.12, can provide a person with the same amount of information that might otherwise take a few minutes to explain orally. This difference might sound trivial, but managers can waste a lot of time and energy—and miss the full value of the information in front of them—unless the enormous amount of information they have to learn is presented in an easily understood way. As spreadsheet and graphics packages and laser printers become more widely used in offices, a greater number of reports will include presentation graphics.

Appropriate formatting of screens and reports can have a tremendous impact on the extent to which users and managers perceive an organization's MIS as being useful and user-friendly. Systems developers should pay close attention to not only what the content of systems output should be, but also to how it can be most effectively presented. The development and refinement of

(a) Tabular data

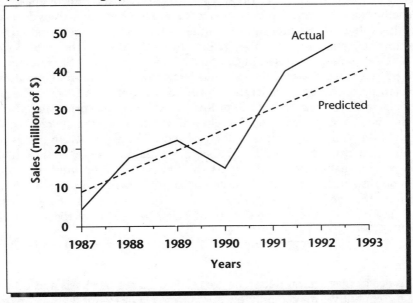

| | Sales (millions of $) | |
Year	Actual	Predicted
1987	4	7
1988	18	13
1989	22	19
1990	15	25
1991	37	31
1992	43	36
1993	—	42

(b) Presentation graphic

Figure 4.12 If the purpose of information is to convey a trend quickly, presentation graphics such as the one in Figure 4.12(b) are generally more effective than the tabular form of data in Figure 4.12(a). The same data are being depicted in both instances.

desktop publishing packages such as Ventura and Aldus PageMaker have made it easier to generate and modify page formats in order to maximize appearance and impact. Many word-processing packages—such as Microsoft Word, WordPerfect, and Ami Pro—also have a number of desktop publishing features.

Types of Decisions

Managerial decisions may be classified in many ways. Common classification schemes categorize decisions with respect to their degree of importance, frequency, and degree of structure.

Importance

Important decisions obviously warrant close management attention. Although it may seem unnecessary to point out that managers should spend most of their decision-making time improving the quality of the decisions that really count, often managers spend too much time focusing on unimportant issues or trying to solve the wrong problems. In their book, *The Bigness Complex*, Walter Adams and James Brock point out that many managers and organizations have been so preoccupied with economy-of-scale measures (that is, efficiently producing more goods in cheaper ways) that they have ignored such new market realities as manufacturing flexibility and speed in meeting demand—which, in the long run, may be more important to organizational survival and effectiveness.

Whether or not management seems to be making right or wrong decisions is not at issue here. It is important to understand that managers should spend some time reflecting on what they really should be doing. The critical success factors (CSF) model discussed in Chapter 3 is one approach that managers can use to pinpoint areas where they should focus their decision-making attention. For instance, for managers of a retail store such as K-Mart or Macy's, the critical success factors are likely to include product mix, inventory, price, and sales promotion. The CSF approach would suggest that a retail store manager's greatest amount of decision-making time and effort should be expended in these areas.

In his autobiography, Lee Iacocca suggests another set of factors that may dictate where managers should focus their efforts: "When you're in a crisis, there's no time to run a study. You've got to put down on a piece of paper the ten things that you absolutely have to do. That's what you concentrate on. Everything else—forget it. The specter of dying has a way of focusing your attention in a big hurry."

Frequency

Some types of managerial decisions are made on a regular basis and others are made infrequently—maybe only once in a career. For example, most managers must evaluate the performance of subordinates on a regular basis, often annually. To facilitate this process, some type of formal system for doing this should be provided, rather than making managers "reinvent the wheel" every time they perform performance appraisals. Besides saving time, having a dependable system ensures a certain amount of decision-making consistency—something that, at least in the case of performance appraisal, is usually important. On the other hand, a company may go through a merger or acquisition only once or twice over the course of its existence, if at all. Because mergers and acquisitions are so infrequent, and because each is likely to be different, a formal system for dealing with them is usually not necessary.

Level of Decision	Type of Decision		
	Structured	**Semistructured**	**Unstructured**
▪ Strategic	Enterprise performance analysis	Production facility location	New product decisions
▪ Tactical	Budget analysis	Short-term forecasting	Advertising
▪ Operational	Accounts receivable	Inventory control	Project scheduling

Figure 4.13 Examples of structured, semistructured, and unstructured decisions found at the three levels of management. While the problems facing top-level managers are often more ustructured than those of low-level managers, all three degrees of structure may occur at each of the three levels.

Frequently made decisions are most commonly candidates for automation. Generally, as a decision maker becomes familiar with a decision scenario and the options available for dealing with the situation, he or she often finds it relatively easy to tell a programmer or an analyst how to automate the decision. Frequent, routine decisions with a finite set of known options are sometimes called **programmable decisions**. While once-in-a-lifetime decisions are often critical to organizational success, the unique set of circumstances that surround them make them much less programmable. However, general-purpose decision-support tools—such as spreadsheets and modeling packages—can often assist managers in making such critical, but infrequent, decisions.

Structured Versus Unstructured Decisions

A **structured decision** is one that is made according to specified procedures or rules. For example, deciding to send a reminder notice to a customer for an overdue balance is generally considered to be a structured decision. In other words, it is relatively easy to develop a procedure for handling such a situation.

Decisions such as how to advertise a new product or how much to spend on MIS, on the other hand, are harder to specify or to program. These types of decisions are called **unstructured decisions**. That is, these types of decisions often involve a high degree of freedom and no precedent. They may require a lot of creativity and intuition from the decision maker and they may defy formulation into a standard set of rules. It is difficult to tell what factors will come into play in an unstructured decision. Even if a set of factors is identified, assigning priorities to them may be impossible. In such a decision environment, the manager is faced with piecing together bits of a puzzle; never really quite sure if the right puzzle is being solved, never having all the necessary pieces, but usually being under pressure to make the decision anyway. Strategic decisions are often described as being unstructured decisions.

Most decisions made in organizations can be classified as structured, unstructured, or semistructured. Examples of each type are shown in Figure 4.13. For example, deciding what levels of inventory to carry for a particular product is often a relatively structured decision that may be determined by using the EOQ models mentioned in Chapter 3 or other inventory management models.

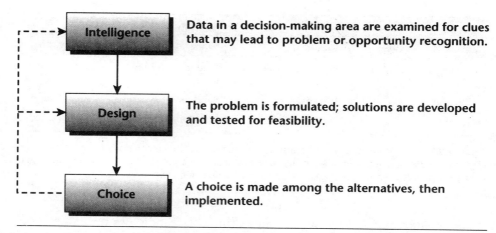

Intelligence — Data in a decision-making area are examined for clues that may lead to problem or opportunity recognition.

Design — The problem is formulated; solutions are developed and tested for feasibility.

Choice — A choice is made among the alternatives, then implemented.

Figure 4.14 Simon's model of the decision-making process. The feedback loops indicate that activities carried out at later stages may cause decision makers to return to activities associated with previous stages.

However, inventory decisions will probably become less structured than the reminder-notice example given previously, especially when dynamic changes are taking place in customer demand forthe product or if a new warehouse must be built to take advantage of a supplier's best quantity discount price. Often, the term **semistructured decision** is used to refer to a decision that has both structured and unstructured components.

THE DECISION-MAKING PROCESS

One view of the decision-making process was originally proposed by Herbert A. Simon in 1960 and is still widely accepted.

In the first stage of Simon's model (see Figure 4.14), the intelligence phase, there is recognition that a problem must be solved or that an opportunity exists that can be exploited. In this stage, data are typically gathered about the problem or opportunity. Many of these data are raw facts and some of these facts may be analyzed by mathematical models and other processes, which will produce more data.

In the second stage, design, the decision maker sifts through the data that have been assembled about the problem or opportunity and tries to understand the problem or opportunity and the decision-making situation. During this stage, solutions are generated and screened for feasibility, using the criteria or standards that have been specified.

In the third stage of Simon's model, a choice is made and implemented. The wisdom of the chosen solution is often evaluated in terms of its efficiency or effectiveness after it has been implemented.

Some of the various types of information and tools that may be used at each stage of the decision-making process are shown in Figure 4.15.

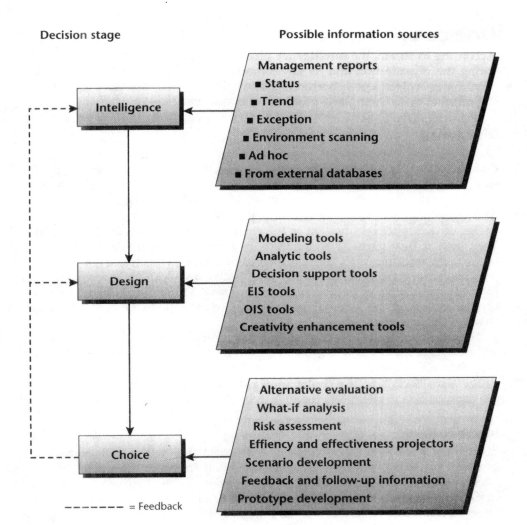

Decision stage

Possible information sources

Intelligence

Management reports
- Status
- Trend
- Exception
- Environment scanning
- Ad hoc
- From external databases

Design

Modeling tools
Analytic tools
Decision support tools
EIS tools
OIS tools
Creativity enhancement tools

Choice

Alternative evaluation
What-if analysis
Risk assessment
Effiency and effectiveness projectors
Scenario development
Feedback and follow-up information
Prototype development

- - - - - - - = Feedback

Figure 4.15 Examples of types of information that may be used at each of the stages of the decision-making process.

The decision-making process illustrated in Figures 4.14 and 4.15 may, on several occasions, involve backtracking to earlier stages. For example, some data are gathered; then, an attempt is made to define the problem. To do this sufficiently, more data may have to be gathered before there is a second attempt to define the problem. Similar backtracking and refinement may occur during each of the other stages.

The steps in Simon's model, and the issues related to each step, are discussed more fully in the text that follows.

Intelligence

According to Simon, the **intelligence** phase of decision making involves monitoring the organization and its environment for problems and opportunities, identifying problems or opportunities, and gathering data that have some bearing on what to do about these problems or opportunities.

Monitoring

Many decision environments require systems that regularly monitor sets of data, in order to quickly identify shifts or trends that signal a problem or opportunity. For example, many Wall Street brokers use computers to closely monitor (in real-time) movements in individual stocks and whole markets. As soon as a discernible shift occurs, buy or sell orders can be electronically made. The availability of such packages has led to the emergence of program trading and has been held at least partially accountable for some of the daily dramatic downturns in the stock market. Other decision environments — such as a lamp retailer deciding what types of lamps to buy for a lamp store — call for less regular and less structured types of environmental monitoring. Monitoring both the internal organization and the external environment is the key to keeping aware of changes that are taking place.

Systems capable of monitoring and detecting changes in the organization and environment can also help managers in determining whether or not existing plans and standard operating procedures should be replaced by contingency plans. Switching to a contingency plan at the right time can greatly assist the organization in effectively reacting to the detected change.

Identification

Identifying a problem or opportunity is the next step in the decision-making process. Successful problem identification often involves differentiating between problems and symptoms of problems. For example, "excessive inventory costs" is generally considered a problem, but having "high inventory levels" is often merely a symptom that may or may not indicate the existence of a problem. Although high inventory levels can often lead to an excessive cost problem, they sometimes do not — such as when high inventories are carried because the supplier offers outstanding discounts on quantity purchases or because important customers require goods to always be in stock. In both of these cases, it would be unwise to consider high inventory levels a problem; in fact, in these instances, reducing inventory levels are more likely to create, rather than alleviate, problems.

Opportunities are usually much harder to spot than problems because it is difficult to anticipate when opportunities will materialize. For example, if a major competitor goes out of business or declares bankruptcy, an opportunity is created to capture a larger share of the market. While some companies have contingency plans in place to take advantage of such events, most do not because the chances of their occurring are remote or difficult to anticipate. Consequently, when they crop up, managers have a hard time deciding how best to

	Sources	
Information Type	Internal	External
▓ Formal	Exception reports Periodic management reports Predictive reports (forecasts) Management audits Scheduled meetings	Public databases Information services Industry reports Trade publications Industry forums Consultants
▓ Informal	Casual conversations Organizational grapevine Management-by-walking-around	Personal contacts Trade shows Networking

Figure 4.16 Some formal and informal sources of both internal and external information that may be useful during the decision-making process.

handle them. Also, some opportunities go unrecognized due to lack of interest or understanding. For instance, many managers are not aware of how new information technology can be a potential investment opportunity that may provide their organization with a competitive advantage; often, they see it only as a source of potential cost problems.

Gathering Data

Many potential sources of decision-making information exist. Two such sources are internal data and external data. Each of these types of data may consist of raw fact or opinion.

- **Internal versus external data**   *Internal data* are data available within the organization. Many of these data come from formal sources such as the transaction processing or cost accounting systems. Informal internal sources include word-of-mouth "facts," gossip, opinions, and personal observations. The latter sources may reveal interesting information that is hidden or absent in formal data. Figure 4.16 summarizes some of the formal and informal sources of both internal and external data on which decisions may be based.

   External data are those that come from the external environment—for example, news that a competitor has just introduced a new product, results of a survey discussed in a trade journal, or an opinion of an industry expert about a new trend in consumer tastes. External data are especially useful to executives in decision making and strategic planning. Like internal data, external data can come from both formal and informal sources.

- **Raw fact versus opinion**   Data showing that a certain group of consumers spent $33 million last year or that a particular organization had a sales revenue of $60 million are examples of raw facts. Raw facts represent events that have actually happened or that most people regard as true without verifying them. On the other hand, data projecting that consumers will spend $51 million this year, or that consumers would have spent $40 million last year if inflation had not increased, are opinions. Opinions represent what

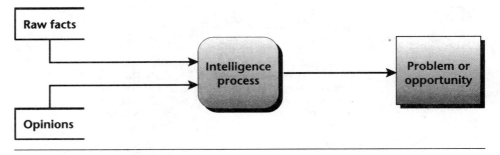

Figure 4.17 The human intelligence process. Raw facts and opinions are typically combined to recognize a problem or opportunity.

might happen in the future or what could have happened in the past. Opinions—some of the most sophisticated and compelling of which are based on some type of mathematical modeling—involve assumptions. Assumptions, of course, are often subject to debate, but an adage among management scientists states: "If you accept my premises, you have to accept my conclusions." Because opinions can be stated in a way that makes them appear to be facts, it is important for managers to be able to distinguish opinions from raw facts.

A model showing the intelligence process is given in Figure 4.17. Raw facts and opinions are considered by the decision maker. These data are then used to generate other opinions. For example, an executive trying to decide whether to build a new facility may look at last quarter's earnings (raw fact), this quarter's forecasted earnings (opinion), and a comprehensive industry outlook (opinion). If the company did poorly last quarter, the industry outlook is bleak, and if an executive hears of about a newly released technology (more raw fact), the executive may consider how the new technology in a new facility could be exploited to markedly increase sales (opportunity recognition).

Style

As noted earlier, two people who are given the same set of data may reach different conclusions. Not everyone draws the same conclusions from the same set of facts. Also, many of us use different intelligence data-gathering approaches when making a decision. Some people think intuitively about problems, while others think systematically. Some people prefer to have combined data or summaries, while others prefer more detailed data. Former U.S. President Ronald Reagan, for example, preferred highly summarized information for decision making, whereas General Arnold Schwartzkoph (the person in charge of Desert Storm) looked at very detailed sets of data before drawing conclusions. That people make decisions based on different inputs is a flexibility consideration that should be designed, wherever possible, into information systems—especially into information reporting and decision support systems.

Design

The design stage of Simon's model includes the activities associated with formulating a problem or an opportunity, developing alternative solutions to resolve the problem or exploit the opportunity, and testing solutions for feasibility.

Formulation

Formulation involves rigorously defining a problem or an opportunity. This might include modeling the problem mathematically or drawing various graphical models and submodels of the underlying system. Some of the mathematical models that may be used at this point in the decision-making process were discussed in Chapter 3.

Determining Decision Criteria

It is usually a good idea to develop the criteria or standards that will be used to compare alternative solutions prior to generating them. Specifying the dimensions on which alternatives will be compared in advance can help managers develop a short list of feasible alternatives from a much larger set of potential solutions to the problem. While deciding on decision criteria and the weights that should be placed on them are not immune to political influences, approaches such as the Kepner-Tregoe technique can help managers separate conditions that absolutely must be met by an acceptable solution (called "must criteria") from desirable, but non-essential, conditions (called "want criteria"). A must criterion could be "Solution must not cost more than $10,000," while a want criterion might be "Solution will have a positive impact on employee morale." If both must and want criteria are carefully selected in advance, it becomes easier to identify and select from the feasible solutions to the problem; the best alternative is the one that satisfies all of the must criteria and also satisfies the want criteria more fully than the others.

Developing Alternatives

Developing a wide variety of alternative solutions to a problem is one of the keys to successful decision making. The more alternatives that are available, the greater the likelihood of identifying a good solution to the problem. In order to view important problems from a number of perspectives and to increase the chances that a diverse set of alternatives will be developed, organizations often use group decision-making approaches. Committees, project teams, and task forces may be formed to deal with specific problems. The following are some other group approaches.

The *Delphi technique* is sometimes used to fuse the ideas of several people into a realistic list of options. Usually, a panel of experts is put together to work on a problem. A facilitator serves as the communications link among the members of the group who typically never meet face-to-face. The facilitator presents the problem to group members, summarizes their solutions, and gives them back to the group members. Over several repetitions of this presentation-solution-feedback cycle, a group consensus about the short list of potential solutions emerges.

The *nominal group technique* is a structured, face-to-face, group activity with separate solution generation and solution evaluation phases. Each group member takes a turn at making solution suggestions, each alternative is discussed for the same period of time, and then group members rank the alternatives; solutions with the most positive average ranks are identified as the better ones.

Brainstorming is a freewheeling group activity for generating ideas or solutions to a problem. The ground rule of brainstorming groups is that "no ideas are too crazy." These and other group approaches can be used to identify a diverse set of possible solutions to the problem.

Groupware, work group computer systems, and group decision support systems (GDSS) have been developed to assist workers in the completion of group tasks. Many of these systems incorporate brainstorming, nominal group, or Delphi processes.

Creativity Stimulation Software

Over the past decade, commercially available software packages have been developed to assist managers in developing creative or innovative solutions to problems. International and technological forces are making it especially important to develop new solutions. Enhanced creativity and innovation are the strategic goals of many organizations because of the competitive advantages that may result. While research on the impact of creativity-enhancing software has been sparse, the potential for using this computer technology is considerable.

Solution Evaluation and Choice

Forecasting tools are often used to assist in identifying feasible solutions to a problem. *Scenario approaches,* for example, can be useful for developing alternatives and recognizing the potential fallout from those alternatives. Scenario approaches are often used to help develop contingency plans, especially for best and worst case scenarios. Both the Delphi and scenario techniques test decision alternatives, to some degree, as they are being developed. The Delphi approach tests the feasibility of alternatives by subjecting them to the scrutiny of fellow "experts"; scenario procedures require alternatives to be tested by directly considering how people might react to a given choice. These and other mechanisms for screening alternatives and for identifying their strengths and weaknesses are commonly used in organizations, especially when strategic decisions are being made.

Another method that is popular today in the design of computer systems, and one that will be considered at length later in the book, is prototyping. Prototyping involves the following process: quickly formulating a working model of a solution, testing the model to see how it works, improving the model based on feedback, testing it again, and so on—until a workable solution is found. In effect, prototype development suggests that the user can perform intelligence functions and create the design in a relatively incomplete manner, proceed to the choice stage with a relatively low investment in time and capital, and then go back to earlier stages to refine the prototype, and so on, until the prototype is satisfactory. Prototyping is especially useful when development is seen as a process that can be enhanced by feedback and learning. Ultimately, the prototype can be expanded and become the final system or it can be discarded (which is a "throw-away prototype") and replaced by a full-scale final system.

The **choice** of an action depends on a variety of factors. These include the external environment, the internal organization, time, and the decision maker. Two others that we will discuss at length later in the text are the costs and benefits associated with certain actions. The level of risk that decision makers are willing to accept is another important factor.

How Risk Affects Decision Making

Virtually all types of choices, because they involve some uncertainty with respect to outcomes, involve some risk. **Risk** is introduced into a decision-making environment when the possible outcomes of a decision and the probabilities of those outcomes are either known or capable of being estimated. Fortunately, risk can usually be modeled and measured. After risk in a specific situation is assessed, management must decide the amount of risk that it is willing to accept.

Figure 4.18 shows how risk might be modeled and used in decision making. Option A considers an initial investment of $80,000 which is expected to return a total of $210,000. Here, expected values have been calculated by multiplying the probabilities associated with outcomes (.2, .7, and .1) by outcome values (in this case, payoffs of $300,000, $200,000, or $100,000) in order to arrive at an overall expected value ($210,000). The probabilities used in this example serve as substitutes for risk. After analyzing past and projected data, we may also be able to determine that there is a 20 percent chance that a $300,000 return or more is achievable with this investment. We will also assume that the downside risk—that is, the probability of achieving a less-than-typical return—is modest at 10 percent.

Now consider investment option B. For this option, an initial investment of $80,000, has a higher expected return ($230,000) than option A. However, it has a higher downside risk (40 percent). Looking at this option more closely, there is a 40 percent chance that it will result in total disaster and only a 10 percent chance that its return will exceed the lowest return possible with option A. Still, that one in ten chance for a really big payoff ($1,800,000) may appeal to some investors.

At this point, in order to determine which of these options is most attractive, managers must assess how much risk they can handle. A company choosing

Investment Option A: $80,000

Probability	Return on investment
20%	$300,000
70%	$200,000
10%	$100,000

Expected return:
20% × $300,000 +
70% × $200,000 +
10% × $100,000 = $210,000

Investment Option B: $80,000

Probability	Return on investment
10%	$1,800,000
50%	$ 100,000
40%	$ 0

Expected return:
10% × $1,800,000 +
50% × $100,000 +
40% × $0 = $230,000

Figure 4.18 Assessing risk by using expected values.

option B, because it has the higher expected return, would be *risk-seeking*. A company choosing option A, because it has less downside risk, would be either *risk-averse* or *neutral* toward risk. Measuring the riskiness of an option both helps the decision maker limit the number of available alternatives (for example, overly risky options may not be given further consideration) and, as just described, make choices. Just how much risk a decision maker is willing to accept depends largely on his or her risk-taking tendencies and on certain situational variables. Risk measures can also be used by managers and MIS executives to screen options when developing a portfolio of systems development projects. Similarly, investment brokers may put together investment portfolios for clients by identifying high-and low-risk investment options.

EVALUATING DECISION MAKING

Once a decision is made, it must be implemented. Like plans, decisions may be effectively or ineffectively implemented. No matter how they are implemented, only through implementation can the appropriateness of a solution be judged. An appropriate solution is one that at least partially alleviates a problem (that is, narrows the gap between actual and desired performance levels).

Often, the appropriateness of a chosen solution can only be evaluated by obtaining feedback on the results of a decision. Feedback helps decision makers learn whether the solution works, and possibly, to adjust when bad choices are made. Decision results also provide the organization with an opportunity to evaluate decision makers. If the feedback indicates that the problem was helped after the implementation of the selected solution, then the chosen course of action—and the decision maker(s) involved—are likely to be evaluated positively. However, if the problem is not helped by the chosen solution, then the decision-making process and the decision makers involved may be open to criticism. Unfortunately, it is often impossible for both decision makers and the organization to determine if better results would have been obtained by choosing another course of action. Indeed, it is possible that the chosen solution didn't work because the problem was not adequately defined or properly implemented, or because of political and other factors that limited the number of feasible solutions. No matter what causes a solution to fail, the lack of problem resolution often reflects negatively on the managers involved in making the decision.

Although both decision makers and the organization are concerned with the results of decisions, and stunning results are usually the fastest route to professional success, the evaluation focus is usually on how well the decision-making process was implemented. Did decision makers focus on the "right" things? Was the decision executed in the "right" way?

Effectiveness Versus Efficiency

Virtually all decisions made by managers are designed to improve either effectiveness or efficiency. **Effectiveness** addresses system outputs; an effective organization is typically considered to be one that achieves its goals and objectives. **Efficiency**, on the other hand, addresses the use of resources to produce results. An efficient organization produces its outputs in a cost-effective manner. Looked at another way, being effective means having done the right thing, whereas being efficient means that something was done the right way. To see the difference between the two terms, consider writing a novel. If the novel sold a lot of copies and the author achieved the success that was sought, the author would be effective. If the author produced the novel quickly on his or her word processor, the author was efficient at writing it.

Organizations tend to measure and control efficiency much more than they do effectiveness. However, considerable evidence suggests that success and competitive advantage are likely to be associated with organizations that are more concerned with long-run effectiveness than with short-term efficiency.

Efficiency measures are often easier to produce than effectiveness measures. Consequently, it may be simpler to justify to superiors a $200,000 computer system that will save $100,000 annually in out-of-pocket transaction processing costs than it is to justify a $200,000 decision support system that might help a key manager make better decisions—decisions that might add $1 million in annual profits to the bottom line. As an example, Lee Gremillion and Philip Pyburn relate the frustration of a firm's controller lamenting the justification of a proposed sales support system: "How much of an impact is the system really going to have? If the salesmen have better information, can analyze sales trends, and can assess the results of in-store promotions, will they sell more product? Unless you can justify the development cost with a reduced sales force or an increased sales volume, then we're better off investing in new automation equipment for the plant."

Conflict often arises within an organization to do whatever is measurable, rather than do whatever may actually be more effective. Reward systems are often more prone to honor a manager who kept costs below the year's annual plan than a manager who strayed from the plan in order to divert resources into equipment that would translate into superior organizational performance over the next five years.

Warren Bennis and Burt Nanus feel that the overefficiency problem in organizations is a leadership issue:

> The problem with many organizations, and especially the ones that are failing, is that they tend to be overmanaged and underled. . . . They may excel in the ability to handle the routine, yet never question whether the routine should be done at all. There is a profound difference between management and leadership, and both are important. . . . The distinction is crucial. Managers are people who do things right and leaders are people who do the right thing. The difference may be summarized as activities of vision and judgment—effectiveness—versus the activities of mastering routines—efficiency.

SUMMARY

Every organization requires some form of management. In most organizations there are three levels of management: upper, middle, and lower. The planning and decision-making activities performed vary from level to level.

Most theoretical treatments consider management to be contingency-based. Thus, to be effective, managers must know the key contingencies and have the requisite skills for identifying, analyzing, and correcting complex problems. The major contingency factors that must be handled in management situations include the external environment, the internal organization, time, and the characteristics of the decision makers.

According to the model of management proposed by Henry Mintzberg, managers assume three general roles. Interpersonal roles are those that involve interaction with people. Informational roles relate to the manager as a receiver or sender of information. Decisional roles are those that mostly involve planning and control. Each of these general roles is subdivided into several subfunctions. Interpersonal roles include the roles of figurehead, leader, and liaison. Informational roles include the roles of monitor, disseminator, and spokesperson. The roles of entrepreneur, disturbance handler, resource allocator, and negotiator are included under the decisional role.

There are three types of planning: strategic, tactical, and operational. Each is most closely associated with a management level: upper, middle, and lower, respectively. Control systems that monitor or audit activities are also important to good management. Control is a logical follow-up to planning.

Management style involves several issues. Particularly important is leadership ability, which refers to the power to influence others to take actions. The Theory X and Theory Y dichotomy, which refers to managers having either tight or loose control over workers, was one of the first management theories. Today, most scholars agree that most management situations fall somewhere between the two extremes that Theory X and Theory Y represent. The ability to delegate authority is another issue in management style. Other management approaches related to planning and control include management by exception and management by objectives (MBO).

Decisions are at the heart of management. Decisions can be classified with respect to their degree of importance, frequency, and degree of structure. Structured decisions are those made according to specified rules. Unstructured decisions involve little precedent and require creativity and intuition. Semistructured decisions combine components of both structured and unstructured decisions.

The decision-making process may involve three basic stages: intelligence, design, and choice. In the intelligence stage, data are gathered and analyzed. In the design stage, the problem is studied, and solutions are generated and tested. In the choice stage, a solution is selected and implemented.

Almost all types of choices, because they involve some uncertainty with respect to outcomes, will entail some risk. Risk is introduced into a decision-making environment when the possible outcomes of a decision are known and the probabilities of those outcomes are either known or capable of being estimated.

Virtually all decisions made by managers are designed to improve either effectiveness or efficiency. Effectiveness addresses system outputs. Efficiency, on the other hand, involves the use of resources to produce results.

REVIEW

KEY TERMS

Choice	Management by objectives (MBO)
Contigency-based management	Operational planning
Decisional roles	Programmable decisions
Effectiveness	Risk
Efficiency	Semistructured decision
Informational roles	Stages of growth (SOG) curve
Intelligence	Structured decision
Interpersonal roles	Tactical planning
Leadership	Unstructured decision
Management	

REVIEW QUESTIONS

1. How do the activities performed by upper-level, middle-level, and lower-level managers differ?

2. Why is management usually considered to be contingency-based? What major types of contingency factors are likely to affect managerial decision-making and what are the implications of these for MIS design?

3. Why is the stages-of-growth curve useful in studying information systems and the managerial decisions associated with information systems?

4. What are the differences among the interpersonal, informational, and decisional roles of managers? What information systems are likely to be most useful in carrying out these roles?

5. What are the differences among strategic, tactical, and operational planning? What types of information systems are best suited for each type of planning? Why?

6. Why is it difficult to define leadership?

7. How does management by exception differ from management by objectives? What roles may computers play in each of these approaches?

8. What are the differences among structured, unstructured, and semi-structured decisions? Provide at least one example of each. What types of information systems are most useful for each type of decision?

9. What types of activities are performed during the intelligence phase of decision making? What types of information systems are needed to support these activities?

10. What approaches may be used to ensure that decision makers have a wide range of alternative solutions? What role may computers play in the generation of alternative solutions?

11. How can the element of risk be handled when making decisions?

12. How is effectiveness different from efficiency?

DISCUSSION QUESTIONS

1. A manager claims to need a new microcomputer system in order to prepare departmental budgets. What type of contingencies will determine whether this is a good course of action or a bad one?

2. How do Mintzberg's ten managerial roles relate to the planning and control functions of management? What types of information systems are likely to help managers fulfill each of these roles?

3. It has been said that the chaotic nature of business today, caused by new international pressures and the rapid introduction of new technologies, has made the subject of risk much more important. Do you agree? Why or why not?

CASE STUDY

Using CAD for Competitive Advantage

For most of this century, few companies in the world could claim to have produced more fabric than Burlington Industries. Past success notwithstanding, this industry leader is now playing catch-up. Many U.S. textile mills are technologically outdated. And American labor is expensive compared to that of Asia. Many of the companies are working as hard as they can just to make sure that they don't lose any more ground.

So how do companies caught in the middle of such unfavorable odds compete? One way, and a strategy chosen by Burlington, is cutting down on the time it takes to design fabric and get it into the hands of the customer.

Before converting to computer-aided design (CAD), Burlington designers used to draw patterns for fabric by hand. Each time a designer styles a pattern, thousands of possible combinations of color and thread come into play. Using manual methods, sketching and weaving fabric samples could easily take a month. Even for experienced designers, the finished samples could produce unpleasant surprises.

Today—using microcomputers, proprietary software, and various graphics tools (such as high-resolution color monitors)—designers can access on-screen menus to create an intuitively appealing fabric design and watch the computer system draw it in a few minutes. If the designer likes what he or she sees, a hardcopy of the design can be printed on a high-quality printer and presented to a customer for inspection.

There are several features that textile manufacturers, including Burlington, would like to add to their systems. For example, they would like customers to be able to see true renditions of fabric colors and textures—both on-screen and in hardcopy form. Ideally, both designers and customers should be able to compare two or more fabric designs on the same screen, using some type of windowing facility. Several companies are implementing systems that will allow them to store designs created for customers in digital form and in image databases. These will make it easy to access previous designs and then to use the CAD facilities to modify them. Almost all major textile manufacturers are moving toward true CAD/CAM (computer-aided design and computer-aided manufacturing) systems that make it possible to transmit a design created on-screen or stored in a database to the weaving machines. Such CAD/CAM systems automate weaving machine setup and represent a significant step toward creating the computer-integrated manufacturing (CIM) systems that the industry feels it must have to be globally competitive during the next century.

Burlington and other textile manufacturers are considering providing software so that their bigger, regular customers can develop their own designs and subsequently transmit them to factories for manufacturing. This would, in essence, create interorganizational CAD/CAM systems and may, in the long run, reduce the number of designers carried on the manufacturers' payrolls. Most companies in this industry are also setting up electronic data interchange (EDI) systems between themselves and their customers and suppliers. An EDI system that links a fabric supplier with a retail customer such as Wal-Mart can provide suppliers with virtually instant knowledge of the movement of its goods on the retailer's floor, thus enabling it to more closely meet that retailer's stock needs. Similar links between textile manufacturers and their suppliers are helping the fabric makers reduce their raw material inventory costs. In most instances, these systems are being created to facilitate the creation of just-in-time (JIT) inventory management systems.

Whether such efforts are enough to bail out domestic firms struggling in the U.S. textile industry is still unknown. Because it is hard to imagine labor costs in the United States falling below those of most Asian countries within the next decade, firms in the U.S. textile industry are going to have to make clever use of technology if they want to survive.

Adapted from Fox (1991), Stasiowski (1989), Stovicek (1991), and interviews with Burlington managers by T. Case (1992).

DISCUSSION

1. Describe how the CAD, CAD/CAM, and interorganizational systems used and developed by textile manufacturers are helping to reduce the time it takes them to design and get fabric to customers.

2. When suppliers are electronically linked to manufacturers and when manufacturers are linked to their customers, what operational benefits are likely to be realized by each type of firm (suppliers, manufacturers, and customers)?

3. Describe three other ways (ways not described in this case study) in which information technology could be used by textile manufacturers to be more competitive.

Part THREE

Information Technology Concepts

Chapter 5

Hardware Fundamentals

After completing this chapter, you will be able to:

Describe several approaches used to deploy computer hardware in organizations

Describe several types of input devices used with personal computers

Explain the importance of source data automation and identify some of the ways in which source data automation are implemented

Describe the components of the CPU and how they work together during the machine cycle to process program instructions

Identify some of the emerging CPU architectures and ways of making a CPU run faster

Describe the differences among microcomputers, midrange computers, mainframes, and supercomputers and how they are used by businesses

Identify the major secondary storage devices used for both personal computers and larger systems

Identify some of the specialized output devices that are used in business settings

Name several common types of display devices

Describe ways in which printers may be differentiated

Hardware refers to the equipment in a computer-based information system (CBIS). As you will see after reading this chapter, a wide variety of computer hardware is available in today's technology marketplace; hundreds of different general-purpose computers, printers, and display devices exist. A large number of lesser used devices such as plotters, voice systems, scanners, and digitizers are also available. And many specialized types of hardware are tailored to a variety of areas: medicine, manufacturing, publishing, banking, graphic arts, photography, and so on.

This chapter opens with a brief discussion of organizational approaches to computing so that you will appreciate the contexts in which hardware devices are used. Next, we turn to specific types of equipment, starting with input devices. Then we consider processing devices before turning to secondary storage and output hardware. In each section, we first consider the devices that managers and users are most likely to use in today's businesses—those associated with microcomputers—before providing an overview of more specialized equipment and hardware.

Collectively, the hardware devices presented in this chapter cover the full spectrum of equipment used in the input-processing-output-storage process. We will postpone a discussion of communications devices—which perform ancillary input, processing, output, and storage functions in computer networks— until Chapter 8. While the information provided in these chapters is somewhat technical in nature, all are items that managers should know in order to make good decisions about computer systems.

ORGANIZATIONAL COMPUTING: PERSPECTIVES

In Part 2 of this book, we stressed the importance of designing a CBIS in ways that make it easier for managers and users to perform their jobs. If this is done, users should be more productive; also, managers at all levels should be better able to carry out their planning and control functions.

In general, the computer systems found in organizations should be designed to support user work practices. If people work independently and rarely need to share their work with others, the focus should be on providing systems that effectively support their individual endeavors. However, if individuals work as part of a group or team, the systems that they use should make it easy for them to share their work, data, and information.

Figure 5.1 shows three common ways in which computer systems are configured in organizations: large-system computing, stand-alone personal computing, and network computing. Large-system computing makes it possible for

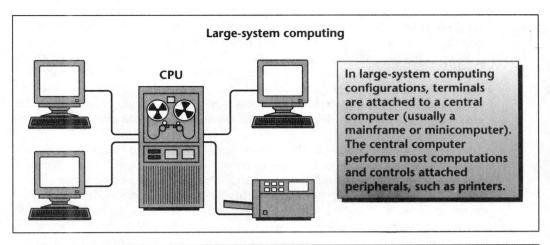

Large-system computing

CPU

In large-system computing configurations, terminals are attached to a central computer (usually a mainframe or minicomputer). The central computer performs most computations and controls attached peripherals, such as printers.

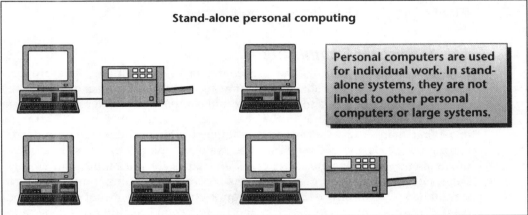

Stand-alone personal computing

Personal computers are used for individual work. In stand-alone systems, they are not linked to other personal computers or large systems.

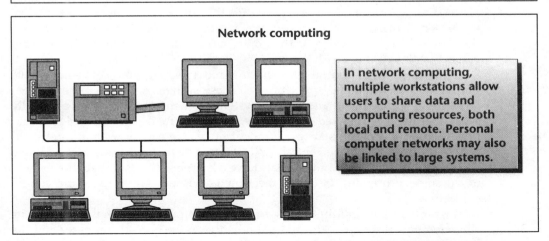

Network computing

In network computing, multiple workstations allow users to share data and computing resources, both local and remote. Personal computer networks may also be linked to large systems.

Figure 5.1 Three commonly used ways to deploy computer systems in organizations. A CBIS should be organized in ways that mirror the work practices and information needs of users and managers.

multiple users to simultaneously share a large central computer. This system is commonly used in organizations that rely on central databases for order processing, inventory management, and other transaction processing operations. In stand-alone personal computing arrangements, users have their own machines—usually microcomputers—and rarely share their data or resources. In network computing, users have their own computers—but, because they are connected to a network, it is possible for them to share data and computer resources.

We will briefly discuss each of these approaches in the following sections. However, before doing so, be sure to note that elements of all three types of arrangements may be found in an organization. That is, some users may be tied into a large central computer, while others may work independently on personal computers that lack the hardware and/or software to enable them to share their work with others. In some subunits, workers' personal computers may be networked, while in others they are not. In larger organizations, it is not uncommon to find all three types of arrangements in use.

Large-System Computing

In large-system computing, the processing tasks of multiple users are performed on a single centralized computer. In most business organizations, the central computer will be a mainframe or minicomputer; the differences between these will be described later in the chapter. Historically, this was the arrangement that many organizations first employed after deciding to computerize. During the 1950s and early 1960s, these systems typically operated in a batch-processing mode using punched cards and tapes for data input and storage. Later, on-line transaction processing was possible, permitting multiple users to simultaneously perform transactions from terminals. This meant that all input went directly from the terminal to the central computer for processing; after processing, all outputs to users came directly from the central computer. Most of the terminals used in these systems were called **dumb terminals** because they could do no processing on their own, serving only as input/output mechanisms that linked users with the central CPU.

Over time, large centralized systems and their support equipment have grown more efficient and sophisticated. These systems continue to be the centerpieces of management information systems in many organizations, especially those that need centralized order entry, inventory management, and distribution systems. In many instances, dumb terminals have given way to **intelligent terminals** that relieve the central CPU of some of its processing tasks. Unlike dumb terminals, intelligent terminals have a built-in processor that allows them to do some processing tasks on their own—without the help of the central computer.

Trying to serve multiple users via large centralized systems can have its shortcomings. It requires almost total reliance on the central computer and the lines between it and the terminals; if either are damaged or malfunction, work

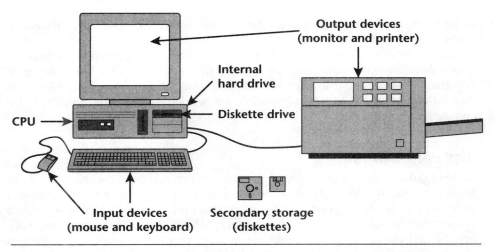

Output devices
(monitor and printer)

Internal
hard drive

CPU

Diskette drive

Input devices
(mouse and keyboard)

Secondary storage
(diskettes)

Figure 5.2 Hardware components associated with personal computer systems. The affordable prices of these systems have made them common fixtures in many organizations and homes.

cannot be performed. Also, the central computer may function very slowly when too many users access it simultaneously during peak business periods. Such shortcomings are among the reasons why many organizations have supplemented or replaced their centralized systems with personal computing and network computing arrangements.

Personal Computing

In the business world, personal computing systems—first introduced in the late 1970s—proliferated during the 1980s. An example of a personal computing system found in many organizations is depicted in Figure 5.2. Since the late 1980s, worldwide shipments of personal computers have exceeded those for the larger systems that had previously dominated the computer industry.

The philosophy behind personal computing is that a computer should be readily available to help an individual perform his or her work at any time. Many tasks are individual by nature; for example, word processing, developing graphics for presentations, working with spreadsheets, and keeping personal calendars. Over time, the range of tasks that a personal computer can accomplish has steadily increased—largely because of the increasing availability of high-quality software. Some smaller businesses rely only on a personal computer for all of their accounting, inventory management, customer database, and transaction processing operations.

Personal computers can be connected to each other or to larger computers to form networks; they can also be used as *stand-alone systems*. In this text, a stand-alone system is one that is not connected to or does not communicate with another computer system (or network). The personal computing systems discussed in this section are stand-alone systems. In the next section, we will describe how personal computers can be networked with central processing units.

As you will see throughout this book, advances in information technology have taken personal computing capabilities in many directions. These systems, and the software they use, have become increasingly user-friendly. Today's organizations continue to find new ways for workers to use these systems for competitive advantage.

Network Computing

Most organizations expect their employees to work together. As noted in Chapter 2, workers are grouped into subunits, departments, and other organizational structures in order to facilitate their interaction and to coordinate their efforts toward the achievement of strategic goals. Most types of organizations, both private and public sector, are looking for easier and better ways for workers to share information and computing resources.

In network computing arrangements, individuals do their own work on personal computers (or workstations), but are linked to a telecommunication network that allows them to share information and resources with others. Users in these environments may share databases, memos and other messages, and work in progress (such as drafts of documents). They are also likely to share printers, fax machines, and links to external data sources. Providing duplicates of these resources for each of the members of the work group is too costly for many organizations.

Personal computers can be networked in numerous ways. For example, by using modems and communications software, personal computers may be linked to a large central computer via telephone lines. Alternatively, multiple personal computers (as well as such devices as printers and fax machines) may be connected to form a **local area network** or **LAN**. In some instances, the development of local area networks and other networks has made it possible for organizations to move applications that were traditionally run only on large central computers to less expensive networks.

Networking is a hot topic in many organizations and is important when developing supportive information systems infrastructures. Many organizations are in the process of connecting existing local area networks to one another and to their large centralized systems. Others are in the process of building global networks to support expanded operations in Europe, the Pacific Rim, and other parts of the world. Still others are developing *interorganizational systems (IOS)* that tie their computer systems to those of their key suppliers and/or customers. Because of the importance of networking in today's organizations, we will devote an entire chapter (Chapter 8) to the subject.

In the next section, we will discuss some of the CBIS hardware devices commonly used by managers and users. Because personal computers—either stand-alone or networked—are the computers that managers use most often, we will devote most of this discussion to the hardware devices associated with these systems.

INPUT TECHNOLOGIES

Input devices are used to enter data into computer systems. Most people use a keyboard and monitor to input data. While a monitor could be an output device (because its display screen is used to verify data entered through the keyboard), it may also be considered input hardware. **Terminals**—including both the dumb and intelligent varieties described in the previous section—frequently employ a keyboard-display screen combination for data input, sometimes in a self-contained unit.

End-User Input Devices

In most of the personal computer systems found in organizations today, keyboard entry is supplemented by a device called a **mouse**. A mouse is a device, about the size of a deck of playing cards, that moves the cursor around the screen quickly. (The **cursor** is a screen element, such as a blinking underline character or a small arrow, that points to a particular position on the screen.) The mouse unit rests on a roller ball platform. As a person moves it across a flat surface, the motion of the ball is translated into the movement of a pointer on the monitor screen. The mouse is not designed to replace the keyboard; it merely enhances the user's cursor-moving ability.

The mouse became popular with the introduction of the Apple Macintosh and its icon-based screens. **Icons** are special symbols that represent commands or program options. When a user points to an icon and depresses a button on the mouse unit, the computer system carries out the task that the icon represents. The introduction of Windows and OS/2—icon-based operating systems for IBM and IBM-compatible personal computers—has made the mouse a standard feature in these systems as well.

A **trackball** consists of a sphere resting on rollers with only the top of the sphere exposed outside its case. Like the mouse, a trackball makes it easy to move the cursor across the display screen. The cursor moves in whatever direction the user spins the sphere. Many users prefer a trackball to a mouse because it requires less desk space when in operation. Some manufacturers are building a trackball into the keyboard sections of portable personal computer systems. For example, trackballs are standard features in Apple's Powerbook family of portable computers.

A **joystick** is another cursor-control device. Joysticks look like a car's stick shift and are often used for computer games and for on-screen drawing and design tasks such as computer-aided design (CAD) applications.

The **light pen** is sometimes used with a display device. The pen contains a light-sensitive cell at its tip; when this tip is placed near the screen, the computer system can determine its position. Light pens are often used in graphics applications in order to draw lines and shapes on the screen.

The **touch screen**, which is sensitive to human fingers, is similar to a light pen in that the computer system can sense where the finger is pointing on the screen. Touch screens are useful for such applications as factory work; a laborer, who may be wearing gloves, can easily point to a selection on the screen instead of trying to press keys. Also, the touch screen can be useful in applications in which the operator may be untrained or unsophisticated. For instance, if the user is a bank customer who does not have time to read computer instructions, a clearly labeled touch screen will quickly get the user involved.

Pen-Based Technologies

One of the newest innovations for businesses and consumers are pen-based computers. **Pen-based computers** are hand-held, tablet-sized computers with advanced handwriting-recognition technologies; they are also called *notepad computers* or *tablet computers*. Using a special stylus, users print, draw, or calculate directly on the screen. The CPU translates each pen stroke into digitized characters. While these systems are full-fledged computer systems in their own right, they are included in this section because their display screen data-entry approaches are their most distinctive features.

Pen-based computers are already being used by insurance agents and claims adjusters, police, pollsters, market researchers, health care workers, appraisers, route and truck drivers, salespeople, and service personnel. In some instances, the electronic forms that they fill in are transmitted directly back to mainframes by using cellular phone services or radio frequencies.

Imaging and Digitizing Devices

An imaging device is hardware that transforms such graphical images as drawings, photographs, and maps into machine-readable form.

One type of imaging device is a **digitizing tablet**. This device is particularly useful for creating and modifying drawings. A pen-like stylus is used by the operator to trace an image on a flat tablet. As the stylus passes over the tablet, the traced image is stored in the computer system's memory and sent to the display device.

A **crosshair cursor** is an imaging device used to input such graphically intensive objects as maps, surveys, and floor plan designs. It operates similarly to the stylus of the digitizing tablet: An image is digitized and stored as the crosshair on the cursor mechanism passes over it. A keypad on the cursor allows other information to be entered. For instance, if a person is using the crosshair cursor to digitize a map, such information as the names of cities and the identities of roads, rivers, or bridges can be entered from the keypad.

Another type of imaging device is the **image scanner**. This device is particularly useful for digitizing images such as photographs, invoice forms, and important documents into computer memory. Some of today's low-speed printers have removable print heads that can be replaced with a scanning head, enabling the printer to double as an image scanner.

Hand-held scanners are another type of imaging device that transforms text or graphical images into machine-readable data. Organizations that frequently receive typed documents, such as law firms and publishers, may use such scanners to convert the typed pages to word-processing files. They can also be used for entering logos and other graphics for desktop publishing applications.

A number of other creative applications for imaging technology exist. For instance, digitizing copiers are now available that can reproduce photographs and images from television sets or video cassette recorders. Also available are digitizing cameras (which can take pictures and immediately store them into digital memory) and three-dimensional digitizers (which can trace over a physical object and record its exact physical shape within computer memory).

Document imaging uses facsimile-based technology to replace paper documents with electronic images. These images are then stored, retrieved, displayed, printed, and distributed as needed. These and other imaging devices are moving us closer to the "paperless office."

Voice-Input Devices

Voice-input devices consist of equipment that is designed to recognize the human voice, which is not as simple as it seems. People often pronounce words in different ways, slur words together so that they are difficult to separate, garble their speech, and use unique combinations of words.

Although machines that react flawlessly to the human voice are not prevalent yet, progress in voice input systems continues daily. Today, many systems have to be trained to recognize particular words (done by converting voice sounds into digital patterns), most of them have very limited vocabularies (often about 1,000 words or less), and virtually none will work unless each spoken word is clearly enunciated by the operator.

Most of the commercial applications of voice input have been relatively simple. For instance, one company uses voice-input equipment to sort the thousands of pieces of mail it receives daily by having operators speak the first initial and first four letters of the recipient's last name into a headset. Other companies use voice input on loading docks and in warehouses for entering identification numbers on the boxes they are moving. Voice input is particularly useful in work areas that are not conducive to keyboard and other display-screen-oriented input. Voice-input hardware is also sold as an enhancement to spreadsheet packages so that users can enter numbers more quickly.

But the biggest challenge for voice input is to minimize the need for keyboard data entry in word processing. Although some pilot systems are operating and show great promise, commercial voice-input word processing—which requires a minimum recognition of 10,000 words—is still not a reality.

Special-Purpose Input Devices

Until now, the discussion of input hardware has primarily focused on devices used with personal computers and found in office settings. Now, we will briefly consider some of the more specialized types of data-entry devices. Many of these are used in conjunction with transaction processing systems, especially those utilizing a centralized large system to process transactions. Virtually all of the systems covered in this section are implemented by organizations to enhance terminal operator productivity, reduce errors, and otherwise improve the organization's operating efficiency. In the following subsections, we will look at source data automation such as special terminal keyboard interfaces, optical character recognition (OCR), magnetic ink character recognition (MICR), and smart cards.

Source Data Automation

One of the most pressing technical issues with regard to competitive advantage is **source data automation**—capturing data electronically at the point where it is generated. For example, when a sale is made, source data automation implies that the transaction is recorded immediately in machine-readable form, rather than in a handwritten form that later needs to be transcribed to machine. This means that data are available quickly to the people who need them. Also, generally fewer errors are made when data are captured electronically at the source. In addition, the high cost of transcription is bypassed. Data integrity and accuracy can be enhanced through source data automation in two ways: (1) by providing system controls that reject faulty transaction data and (2) by having the person responsible for data entry make any necessary corrections immediately.

All of the technologies discussed here facilitate source data automation. After capturing data by electronic means, it may also be possible to make those data available on a real-time basis or on a fast-turnaround basis to other interested parties, either locally or remotely. In some industries, such as the information-intensive financial services and retailing sectors of the economy, deciding which data are to be captured at the source is an important issue. For example, if consumer profile data and comprehensive product data are collected at the point of sale, it may be possible to discover "who" is most likely to buy "what," thus enabling firms to more quickly tailor inventory and selling strategies to key markets. Collecting the right information at the point of sale may give an organization a competitive edge.

Specialized Keyboards

A variety of specialized keyboards are available for niche applications. For instance, many of the keyboards used in the fast-food industry have a membrane panel rather than conventional, sculpted keys. A customized template can be placed over this panel with such entries as "regular cheeseburger," "jumbo cheeseburger," and so forth. Such keyboards make it easy to enter transaction data quickly and efficiently.

In Chapter 2, we noted that organizations choose special keyboard layouts based on the characteristics of the people who use them. If relatively unskilled operators will use them, the keyboards should be relatively simple to understand. Special modifications may also be needed so that disabled workers can utilize a keyboard.

Optical Character Recognition

Optical character recognition (OCR) refers to a variety of technologies that use special characters and codes that are recognized by optical means. Recognition

ABCDEFGHIJKLMN
OPQRSTUVWXYZ
1234567890

Figure 5.3 Commonly used fonts in optical character recognition (OCR) systems. In order for OCR symbols to be read by light wands and other special scanning devices, it is important that they conform to industry OCR font standards, such as the OCR-B standard.

means that the OCR system is designed to identify the text characters it reads—as opposed to a machine such as a copier, which transfers text but does not understand it. Sometimes, characters or codes must conform to an industry standard (see Figure 5.3). Special-purpose scanning hardware must be acquired that is equipped both to recognize the standard and to accommodate the size of the document or the type of package on which the character or code appears. OCR equipment is widely used in the retail and grocery industries.

In many areas, OCR is giving way to **intelligent character recognition (ICR)**. With ICR, the scanner is "teachable"; that is, it can learn that the same letter or number can look differently when fonts are changed. Unlike an OCR scanner, after it knows what fonts are acceptable, it will not reject a character.

- *Optical characters* Optical characters, such as those in Figure 5.3, are designed so that they are identifiable to both humans and optical-scanning equipment. The characters must conform to a particular font, and only if the scanner is familiar with the font can it read the characters. Optical characters are often read by a **wand scanner** (or **light wand**) that is attached to another device, such as an electronic cash register.

- *Optical codes* Although many optical codes (commonly known as bar codes) are in existence, perhaps the most familiar is the bar code—called the *universal product code (UPC)*—found on supermarket goods and many other retail products (see Figure 5.4, page 174). These codes are often read by passing them in front of an optical-scanning station, such as the familiar optical window built into the laser check-out counter in most large supermarkets. Currently, more than 80 percent of the products sold in supermarkets carry UPC codes. Bar codes can also be read by wands.

  Bar codes are being used for an increasing variety of applications. For example, the U.S. Postal Service uses bar codes (such as those found on business reply envelopes) to sort mail and to track express mail packages. Overnight delivery services have also developed and implemented their own bar-code systems in order to increase the efficiency of their package handling and tracking services. Railroad companies, such as CSX, have placed bar codes on the sides of box cars, and scanners alongside tracks, in order to keep up with box car locations—both en route to their destinations or when parked on sidings. Bar codes are also being used in warehouses and retail stores to assist in inventory management, in the health care industry, and even in direct-mail operations.

0   4800126568

Figure 5.4   An example of a UPC code used on supermarket products. The digit to the left of the bars indicates the product category and the two sets of numbers below the bars identify the manufacturer and the product.

Until recently, most bar codes have been one-dimensional. One-dimensional bar codes encode all information along a single line. The thickness of the bars and spaces carry information, while the height of the symbol makes manual scanning easier. Two-dimensional bar codes enable users to pack a lot more data in the same small space by stacking a series of independently scannable bar-code lines into a rectangular symbol. One code alone allows more than 1,100 bytes of data to be placed in a symbol that is less than 2 inches on each side. These new codes, along with advancements in scanning technologies, mean that bar codes will be used in even more applications in the future.

The term **point-of-sale (POS)** applies to situations in which optical-scanning equipment records purchases—such as in the retail and grocery industries. At the hub of any POS system is the so-called electronic cash register, which is itself a microcomputer system or terminal. POS equipment is one of the main vehicles for source data entry in transaction processing systems that interface with the consumer. In addition to the savings gained in labor costs and to the fewer errors that are made, POS environments can make key information available faster to the managers who need it.

Magnetic Ink Character Recognition

Magnetic ink character recognition (MICR) is used by the banking industry for the processing of checks. The entire banking community follows a single font standard, consisting of 14 characters, which is shown in Figure 5.5. Specialized equipment is used in the industry to encode, decode, sort, and process checks.

Smart Card Systems

Smart cards resemble credit cards in size and shape; however, they contain a microprocessor chip and memory, and some include a keypad as well. These were pioneered in France and many organizations are still just experimenting with them. In many instances, smart cards make it possible for organizations to provide new or enhanced services for customers.

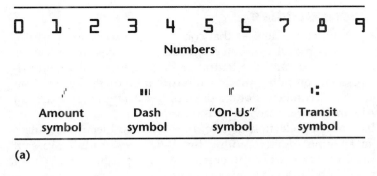

Numbers

Amount symbol	Dash symbol	"On-Us" symbol	Transit symbol

(a)

(b)

Figure 5.5 Magnetic ink character recognition (MICR) characters are printed in magnetic ink at the bottom of checks. Special readers and sorters are used in the banking industry to automate check processing. The 14 characters that make up the MICR code are shown in (a). The check in (b) shows where MICR characters are found on checks.

So far, smart cards are used most frequently to make electronic purchases and to electronically transfer funds between accounts. However, the potential applications for these abound. For example, in the health care industry, smart cards could be used to store the holder's identity, address, insurance data, relatives, allergies, and even a brief medical history. If the card holder was disabled by an accident or illness, the card could be used immediately to assist with treatment. Smart cards could also be used for security applications. For example, a card could contain the digitized fingerprint of the cardholder, which could be compared at a security checkpoint to fingerprints of people who are authorized to enter a secured area.

PROCESSING TECHNOLOGIES

Processing hardware includes the devices that compute, compare, and perform special instructions. In a personal computer system, the processing device is called the *system unit*, which contains the central processing unit (CPU) and primary storage. In a personal computer, the actual box that holds the system unit is also likely to house the secondary storage devices (for example, disk drives) as well as other hardware devices (such as add-in cards).

Every CPU is basically a collection of electronic circuits. Electronic pulses enter the CPU from an input device. Within the CPU, these pulses are sent under program control through circuits to create new pulses. Eventually, a set of pulses leaves the CPU and heads for an output or storage device. What happens in the CPU's circuitry? The process that takes place is known as the machine cycle. To understand this process, it's helpful to be familiar with how the CPU is organized, what its parts are, and how electronic impulses move from one component to another to process data.

Central Processing Unit

The central processing unit is made up of two key components: the **control unit** and the **arithmetic-logic unit (ALU)**. During the processing of a program, these two components work in harmony with primary memory. The CPU in most personal computers today is found on a single chip called a **microprocessor**, which contains the circuitry for both the control unit and the ALU.

The main function of the control unit is to coordinate the activities of the other parts of the computer system when program statements are being executed. It directs the flow of data between peripheral devices and primary memory, and between primary memory and the ALU. In a sense, it is the "executive" component in the computer because it causes all of the other components to carry out their assigned tasks. The control unit is responsible for decoding program instructions, getting the rest of the system set up to execute program instructions, and signaling the other components when it is time for them to carry out their functions. This is analogous to the tasks of an orchestra conductor who must read the music and ensure that the musicians in the various parts of the orchestra play their parts at just the right moments.

The main functions of the ALU are to carry out all of the mathematical (addition, subtraction, multiplication, and division) and logical operations (comparing two data values to determine if they are equal, if one is greater than another one, and so on) required by the program. It is this component that does the rapid number-crunching made famous by computers. As we will see, all data coming into the CPU, including nonnumeric data (such as letters of the alphabet) are stored in digital (binary numeric code) form. This makes it possible to perform logical operations on letters or words, as well as on numbers.

To enhance the computer's performance, the control unit and the ALU contain special storage locations called **registers** that act as high-speed staging areas. Program instructions and data are usually loaded into the registers from primary memory just before processing. The registers in the control unit decode program instructions. Registers in the ALU are where the arithmetic and logical operations needed to transform data into information are performed.

Other important components of the CPU are buses. **Buses** are the circuits that connect the CPU to primary memory and to input/output/storage devices; some vendors refer to these circuits as "channels" or "processor channels." Bits (binary digits) move from one part of the computer system to others through the buses. For example, buses make it possible to move program instructions and data from primary memory to the CPU for processing.

Today, a number of microcomputer bus standards exist. One of these is IBM's Micro Channel Architecture (found on the high end of the IBM PS/2 line of microcomputers). Nubus is used on most of the recent Apple Macintoshes, and EISA (Enhanced Industry Standard Architecture) is found on the micro-computers made by Compaq and many other IBM-compatible vendors. Each of these standards takes better advantage of the capabilities of the personal computer operating systems that are now available. These operating systems will be discussed more fully in the next chapter.

Primary Memory

Primary memory—sometimes also referred to as main memory or internal memory—can be directly addressed by the CPU. Primary memory contains the programs and data that were read from an input device or a secondary storage device, intermediate results of programs being processed, and output that is ready to be sent to an output device or to a secondary storage device. Primary memory is like a scratchpad—that is, data are temporarily placed there, computations are performed on these data, and certain results become worthy of preservation and are transferred elsewhere.

On virtually all computer systems, primary memory is temporary (or *volatile*)—that is, it loses its contents when the computer's power is shut off. Also, relative to other forms of storage, primary memory is expensive. Thus, in multiuser systems, when the computer is finished processing a job for one user, that same portion of primary memory will be overwritten with other data or programs that need to be processed for other users. The sizes and access speeds of primary memories differ among systems.

When programs are being processed, the main roles of primary memory are to hold:

- The program statements for the programs currently being processed, as well as the data needed by the programs.

- The resident portions of the operating system that remain in main memory after the system is booted up (turned on).

- The intermediate processing results.

- Output that is ready to be transmitted to secondary storage or to an output device.

Once programs, data, intermediate results, and output are stored in primary memory, the CPU must be able to find them again. To make this possible, every location in primary memory has an *address*. In many computer systems, a table is automatically set up and maintained that provides the address where the first character in each stored program or data block can be found. Whenever a block of data, an instruction, a program, or the result of a calculation is stored in memory, it is assigned an address so that the CPU can locate it again when needed.

Random access memory (RAM) is commonly used to refer to primary memory. The term "random access" implies that the computer can go directly to any given address within the memory and read or write data there. The amount of RAM in primary memory is usually measured in kilobytes (thousands of bytes) or megabytes (millions of bytes). For example, a microcomputer with 640 kilobytes of RAM possesses approximately 640,000 random access memory locations, while a machine with two megabytes of RAM has a little more than 2,000,000 random access addresses.

In microcomputers, RAM is usually implemented as memory chips—often 64 or 256 kilobytes each—which are mounted on the main circuit board (sometimes called the "motherboard") in the system unit. The main memory of most microcomputers on the market today ranges from 640 kilobytes to 32 megabytes; machines with one or four megabytes of RAM are typical of the microcomputers found in businesses.

Closely associated with RAM is the concept of **read-only memory (ROM).** With ROM, programs are etched directly on a semiconductor chip where they can be read (and run), but not written upon; this etching process is done when the chip is manufactured. The resulting chips (sometimes called *firmware* to distinguish these permanent, non-changeable programs from modifiable "software") are then mounted on circuit boards within the computer unit itself, where they can be accessed more quickly by the computer than if they were on disk or tape.

Generally, the programs on ROM are placed on the chips by chip manufacturers. Equipment is also available so that users can write their own ROM programs and reuse ROM chips. Chips on which users can install their own programs, but not reuse, are called *PROM* for Programmable Read Only Memory. Reusable ROM chips can be erased by special processes and then reprogrammed; these are known by many names, including EPROM (for Erasable, Programmable Read Only Memory), EEPROM (for Electronically Erasable, Programmable Read Only Memory), and EAPROM (for Electronically Alterable, Programmable Read Only Memory).

Many manufacturers place portions of their operating systems into ROM to make them more rapidly accessible. In personal computers, ROM is often used to store the parts of the operating system that are involved with start-up or "booting" procedures. (These are the routines that bring the resident portions of the operating system into RAM and make it possible for the system to run the application programs that managers and users need to do their jobs). On many machines, the amount of ROM is small, often about 40 to 128 kilobytes.

The Machine Cycle

Now that we have described the components of the CPU, let's see how these elements work together to process program instructions.

Every instruction that is issued to a computer (whether it is part of a lengthy application program, typed in by a user in the form of a command, or the result of using a mouse to click on an icon) is broken down into machine-level instructions that can be decoded and executed by the CPU.

The computer has a built-in **system clock** that synchronizes its operations. It is analogous to using a metronome to synchronize work for an orchestra. During each clock tick, a single task is carried out; for example, a single piece of data could be moved from primary memory to a register in the ALU. A clock tick is roughly equivalent to one of the steps in the machine cycle.

Clock speed is typically measured in *megahertz (Mhz)* or millions of cycles per second. For personal computers, clock speeds of 12, 16, 20, 25, and 33 Mhz are common. Even 66 Mhz systems are available and some experts predict that 100 Mhz systems will be common in a few years. With higher clock speeds, the computer can "tick" through the steps needed to process program instructions more rapidly, making it possible to execute more program instructions in the same time period.

The processing of a single, machine-level instruction is performed during a **machine cycle**. A machine cycle has two parts: an **instruction cycle (I-cycle)** and an **execution cycle (E-cycle)**. During the I-cycle, the control unit retrieves a program instruction from primary memory, decodes it, and prepares the system for subsequent processing. During the E-cycle, data needed for processing are retrieved from primary memory and processed. The steps in the I-cycle and E-cycle are illustrated in Figure 5.6.

A computer may have to go through thousands, millions, or even billions of machine cycles to fully process a single program. However, computers can perform a lot of work in a very short period of time. In the slowest computers, cycle times are measured in milliseconds (thousandths of a second). Today, most cycle times are measured in microseconds (millionths of a second) or nanoseconds (billionths of a second); the fastest of today's computers have cycle times measured in picoseconds (trillionths of a second).

"Sizing" a CBIS

During systems development activities, decisions have to be made about how powerful computers must be to satisfy current and future information processing requirements. Advances in information technology have made it more difficult for managers to rely solely on classifications such as microcomputer, minicomputer, and mainframes when deciding how large a system is needed. Because of the fuzzy areas that exist in these traditional classification schemes, it is vital for managers and users to be aware of the other dimensions or criteria that may be used to judge the power and potential workload of computers.

Five common standards of measurement that have evolved are bits, bytes, hertz, MIPS, and FLOPS. Bits and bytes relate to the capacity of primary

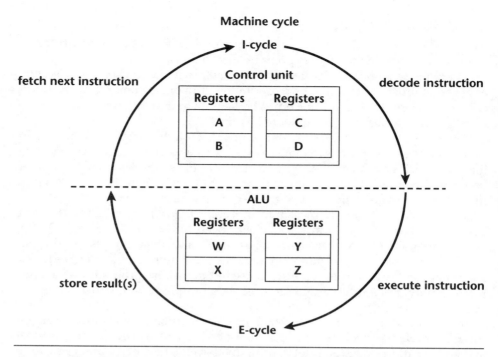

Machine cycle

I-cycle

fetch next instruction

Control unit

Registers	Registers
A	C
B	D

decode instruction

ALU

Registers	Registers
W	Y
X	Z

store result(s)

execute instruction

E-cycle

Figure 5.6 Program instructions are decoded and executed by the CPU during the machine cycle. During the instruction cycle (I-cycle), program instructions are loaded into registers in the control unit and decoded. During the execution cycle (E-cycle), data are moved from primary memory to registers in the the arithmetic-logic unit (ALU) and processed.

storage, register capacity, and the width of buses and channels. Hertz, MIPS, and FLOPS refer to processor speed and throughput (the amount of work that the processor can perform in a given time period).

Bits

The term **bit** is a contraction of the two words "binary digit". Digital computers use processing patterns derived from the binary numbers scheme in which all data are represented as a string of binary digits—0s and 1s. (Virtually all computers found in modern computer-based information systems are digital computers.) Each alphabetic character, digit, and special symbol manipulated by these computer systems is translated into a unique configuration of 0 and 1 bits. Generally, the more bits a computer can process or move around at a time, the faster and more powerful it is. The number of bits that can be manipulated at one time is often referred to as the computer's *word size*. Word size usually indicates the size of the buses and registers within the CPU. For instance, a 16-bit computer can manipulate 16 bits at a time within the CPU; a 32-bit computer, 32 bits. Larger systems often have larger word sizes than personal computers. For example, mainframes typically manipulate 64 bits—some supercomputers have processors that manipulate 128 bits at a time.

Managers should be aware that not all 16-bit or 32-bit computers are equivalent in processing power. In some instances, a machine that is marketed as having a 32-bit processor may not be a "true" 32-bit machine. Such machines may have 32-bit registers in the CPU, but only have 16-bit buses to move data from one part of the system to another. Since registers are not processed until they are filled, a machine with 32-bit registers and 16-bit buses would need extra retrieval steps during the machine cycle. Such machines could be slower (given the same model microprocessor and clock speed) than true 32-bit machines (those with 32-bit registers and 32-bit buses), where extra retrievals may not be necessary.

Why do some vendors manufacture machines with smaller buses than registers? The answer is that both larger registers and larger buses typically translate into greater manufacturing expense. Building processors with smaller buses than registers often means cheaper prices for consumers.

It is important to remember that both registers and buses are measured in terms of the number of bits that they can handle at one time and that no two computers marketed as being 32-bit (or 16-bit) machines are alike. Both register size and bus size should be taken into account when determining what is needed. Also note that a 32-bit standard is emerging, not only for register and bus sizes, but also for the circuits that connect the CPU to input, output, storage, and communications devices.

Bytes

Most digital computer systems translate each alphabetic character, digit, or special symbol it manipulates into a unique configuration of bits. Such a configuration of bits is called a **byte**. For example, in one coding scheme, the letter A is represented by the byte 11000001. Within the CPU, all programs and data are in either byte form or some other binary-based form. When processing is finished, output results are typically translated back into a natural-language form the user can understand (for example, the byte 11000001 would be translated to the letter A for display on a screen or in a report).

The primary memory of a computer system is typically measured in 1024-byte multiples. A multiple of approximately a thousand bytes is called a *kilobyte* (commonly abbreviated *KB*). A multiple of approximately a million bytes is called a *megabyte (MB)* and a multiple of approximately a billion bytes is called a *gigabyte (GB)*. Today, for instance, many of the 16-bit personal computers used in organizations are limited by a main memory of 640KB (unless this has been extended by adding additional memory chips). True 32-bit microcomputers often have at least a megabyte of primary memory; on some high-end machines, this may be extended to several gigabytes.

Character	EBCDIC	ASCII	Character	EBCDIC	ASCII
0	11110000	0110000	I	11001001	1001001
1	11110001	0110001	J	11010001	1001010
2	11110010	0110010	K	11010010	1001011
3	11110011	0110011	L	11010011	1001100
4	11110100	0110100	M	11010100	1001101
5	11110101	0110101	N	11010101	1001110
6	11110110	0110110	O	11010110	1001111
7	11110111	0110111	P	11010111	1010000
8	11111000	0111000	Q	11011000	1010001
9	11111001	0111001	R	11011001	1010010
A	11000001	1000001	S	11100010	1010011
B	11000010	1000010	T	11100011	1010100
C	11000011	1000011	U	11100100	1010101
D	11000100	1000100	V	11100101	1010110
E	11000101	1000101	W	11100110	1010111
F	11000110	1000110	X	11100111	1011000
G	11000111	1000111	Y	11101000	1011001
H	11001000	1001000	Z	11101001	1011010

Figure 5.7 Examples of the EBCDIC and ASCII codes. Each string of bits (1s and 0s) represents a single character or byte. Both 7-bit and 8-bit versions of ASCII are used—the 7-bit version is illustrated here.

The primary memories of larger systems (such as those for minicomputers and mainframes) are commonly measured in megabytes, while those in supercomputers are frequently measured in gigabytes. Terabyte (trillion byte) systems are also being developed. As we will see later in this chapter, the storage capacities of storage media are also commonly measured in kilobytes, megabytes, and gigabytes.

EBCDIC and ASCII

Two binary-based codes commonly used to represent characters in byte form on a computer system are EBCDIC (Extended Binary-Coded Decimal Interchange Code) and ASCII (American Standard Code for Information Interchange). These codes are shown in Figure 5.7.

EBCDIC employs 8 bits to a character, whereas ASCII uses 7 or 8. Thus, EBCDIC permits a total of 256 characters to be represented (2 to the eighth power = 256); ASCII, 128 or 256 characters. With both systems, there is plenty of room to represent all the printable text characters needed in the English language, plus some specialized codes. EBCDIC and 7-bit ASCII can be used on the same computer system by appending an eighth bit (a zero) to each ASCII byte. Many application software packages seized this eighth ASCII bit and used it to create an extended set of 128 characters; while ASCII-8 is used commonly today, the 7-bit version is still used in some networking configurations.

IBM originally developed EBCDIC for its larger systems, especially its mainframes. Today, it is still the code most commonly used on these machines. ASCII was developed through the cooperative efforts of the American National Standards Institute and several other computer manufacturers. ASCII is typically the code of choice for data communications and for character manipulation performed outside the IBM-mainframe world.

Hertz, MIPS, and FLOPS

Hertz, MIPS, and FLOPS are three measures that relate to computer speed and throughput.

As noted during our discussion of the machine cycle, *hertz* is commonly used to rate the clock speed of microprocessors. Many of the personal computers produced by IBM models and the manufacturers of IBM-compatible machines have processors that run at 20 Mhz (megahertz)—or faster. In a 20-Mhz machine, the microprocessor clock used to synchronize computer operations runs at 20 million cycles per second (or 20 million ticks of the clock). In general, personal computer clock speeds range from less than 10 to 50 Mhz; machines with 16 Mhz, 20 Mhz, 25 Mhz, 33 Mhz, 50 Mhz and 66 Mhz are the most common.

MIPS is an acronym that stands for **millions of instructions per second**. MIPS is often used as a measure of how much work (or throughput) a computer can do in one second; machines with higher MIPS generally have greater processing power than machines with lower MIPS. Figure 5.8 compares the MIPS ranges (past, present, and predicted) for personal computers with those for the larger systems discussed in the next section of the chapter.

The term **FLOPS** means **floating-point operations per second**. Floating-point operations are the addition, subtraction, multiplication, division, and other numeric operations performed on decimal numbers. Since floating-point operations are more commonly associated with scientific and engineering applications, FLOPS is often used as a criterion when comparing systems to support such activities. Because supercomputers are more likely to be used for scientific than business applications, it is common to see FLOPS used to compare supercomputer speeds. Many supercomputers operate in the megaflops (MFLOPS) and gigaflops (GFLOPS) range.

Types of Computer Systems

Computers are often broadly classified into one of four size categories. From smallest to largest, these categories are microcomputers, minicomputers, mainframe computers, and supercomputers. Because microcomputers, minicomputers (mid-range systems), and mainframes are used more commonly than

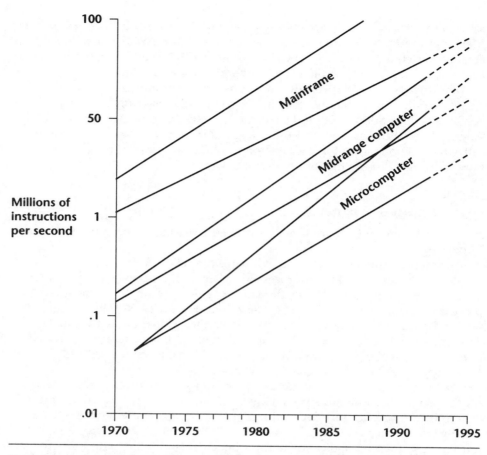

100

50

**Millions of
instructions
per second**

1

.1

.01

1970   1975   1980   1985   1990   1995

Mainframe

Midrange computer

Microcomputer

Figure 5.8 A comparison of the performance ranges of microcomputers, midrange systems, and mainframes in millions of instructions per second (MIPS). (Adapted from Peled)

supercomputers for business applications, we will focus on these. A table of how these differ is found in Figure 5.9.

These categories generally relate to how powerful the computer is, as established by such items as processing speed or volume, primary memory capacity, the number of peripherals that can be simultaneously supported, and the capabilities of those peripheral devices. At best, the categories are approximate. It is not unusual, for instance, to discover microcomputers that are more powerful than some minicomputers, and minicomputers that are more powerful than some mainframes. Over the years, the distinctions among these categories has gotten blurry. However, managers and users are likely to encounter these terms for many years to come and it is important for them to know how these are likely to differ.

Type of Computer	Common Characteristics
▦ Mainframe	A large system designed to serve many simultaneous users, sometimes more than 100. New low-end systems typically cost more than $200,000; high-end systems may cost millions of dollars.
▦ Midrange computer	A medium-sized computer that can serve many simultaneous users, but usually not as many as a mainframe. Typically, these cost between $20,000 and $200,000, but high-end midrange systems may exceed $1 million.
▦ Microcomputer	A small computer that is generally designed to serve a single user. Low-end systems may cost less than $1,000. High-end systems rarely exceed $20,000.

Figure 5.9 A summary of some of the major differences among microcomputers, minicomputers (midrange systems), and mainframes. Over the years, the distinction among these classifications has gotten fuzzier, rather than clearer. In general, the costs of each of these systems continues to decrease—many powerful microcomputers cost less than $2,000.

Microcomputer Systems

A **microcomputer system** is a full-fledged computer system that uses a microprocessor as its CPU; these are also called *personal computer systems*. Microcomputers first were available for widespread use in the 1970s, when it became possible to put the entire circuitry of a computer (CPU) onto a small silicon chip.

The earliest microcomputers were capable of supporting only a single user at a time. While many of the microcomputers found in organizations today are designed to support a single user, multiuser microcomputer systems are also available and are becoming more prevalent. In multiuser systems, a powerful microcomputer may be used to substitute for mainframe or minicomputers in a configuration that is similar to the large-system approach depicted in Figure 5.1 (page 165). Single-user personal computers are also being connected to one another to form networks. Multiuser microcomputers play key roles in some of the networks that are developed.

Most of the early microcomputers were limited in terms of primary memory and processing capabilities. Today, many high-end microcomputers rival some mainframes in processing power (see Figure 5.8) and primary memory.

Currently, IBM and Apple are the two most prominent manufacturers of microcomputer system units, which are the "boxes" that enclose the microcomputer chip and its associated circuitry (see Figure 5.2, page 167). Companies such as Compaq, Dell, Gateway, Leading Edge, Packard Bell, and Tandy are contenders in this market. Most microcomputer systems are either of the desktop or laptop (portable) variety.

■ *Portable system* **Portable computer systems** are designed compactly so they can fold shut like a briefcase or fit in a traveling case. Many of these are also called *laptop computer systems* because they are capable of fitting in a person's lap. However, most users would argue that these machines are best

Microcomputer Type	1991	1992	1993
Desktop	10.3 million	9.5 million	9 million
Laptop/notebook	1.6 million	2.3 million	2.2 million
Pentop*	30,000	210,000	1 million
Pen-based tablet	45,000	267,000	423,000

*Pen-based desktop systems

Figure 5.10 Industry experts expect sales of desktop and laptop systems to stabilize during the early 1990s. However, demand for pen-based computers, both desktop and portable, is expected to rise dramatically during this time frame. (Adapted from *The Computerworld IS Pocket Guide for Success*)

utilized when placed on a flat, stable surface. *Notebook computers* are smaller, lighter, and usually more expensive than laptops. Generally, notebooks and laptops are useful in almost all situations in which a computer has to be carried from place to place. Typical applications for portable computers include: when a field salesperson interacts on the road with clients, when a computer system is checked out by employees who are taking it off-premises, and when a computer system is shifted from room to room to make presentations during meetings. Toshiba, Compaq, Zeos, Apple, and Dell are some of the leading vendors, but the number of companies manufacturing portables is increasing.

Portable microcomputers are becoming more numerous and smaller varieties are being designed, including pocket and palmtop micros; most of the pen-based computers mentioned earlier in the chapter are also considered to be portable computers. Some of the market projections for portable systems are summarized in Figure 5.10.

Even "wearable" micros have been introduced. For example, CompCap (from Park Engineering Associates) is a one-pound, belt-mounted IBM-compatible computer. The user wears a soft headband that holds a microphone for voice input and a small eyepiece in front of one eye; the wearer sees a monitor display when looking into the eyepiece. In one company, shipping clerks read purchase order numbers into the microphone. The speech processor in the units process the information; the locations of the ordered items appear on the eyepiece display.

Portable computers are making an impact in many environments as a competitive tool. Many companies have equipped their salespeople with portables so that they can call in orders and stay in touch with the organization while on the road. For instance, in one case that was mentioned in Chapter 1, a large hospital almost switched from a Merck & Co. drug to a cheaper, competitive product. Armed with a portable computer, the Merck salesman searched through Food & Drug Administration clinical studies

Smart Cards: The World's New Way to Pay

More than 20,000 riders on vehicles owned by the Regional Transportation Authority of Northeastern Illinois (RTANI) are using smart cards to pay their fares. RTANI vehicles are equipped with smart-card readers that note the passenger's identity, as well as the date and time of the ride. The fare is automatically deducted from the card's "electronic purse." At the end of the day, the captured data are uploaded to a local area network and aggregated.

"SMART CARDS ARE USUALLY MORE SECURE THAN CONVEN-TIONAL CREDIT CARDS . . . ."

This is just one of the pilot smart card programs underway in the U.S. Smart cards are even more popular in other parts of the world. Several million smart cards are used in Europe and Japan—and the variety of ways in which they are being used is increasing.

A smart card is about the same size as a credit card and often has the same embossed lettering on the front and a magnetic strip on the back. However, embedded in the card are a memory chip, microprocessor, and other circuitry. Smart cards are usually more secure than conventional credit cards, whose magnetic strip can be copied quite easily; copying the circuitry in a smart card is much more difficult.

A new generation of smart cards may be under development. Optical cards—which do not rely on electronics—are, in some ways, more intelligent than smart cards. Some available optical cards have a capacity of 2.86MB—the equivalent of 1,200 typewritten pages. This is five times greater than the memory possessed by the most sophisticated smart cards.

Adapted from Alexander (1992).

---

that were available on a remote database. He found that the competitor's product had not been effective in treating gynecological infections. Because the salesman used his personal computer so quickly and effectively, Merck kept the account.

- **Desktop systems** Desktop computer systems are those with which most people are familiar. These machines are so named because they fit on a desktop. Most desktop machines available in the marketplace are IBM-compatible. Also, most desktop systems are designed to accommodate only one user at a time. Because of this, these machines are often called single-user desktop systems.

Multiuser desktop computer systems—sometimes called supermicrocomputers (or supermicros)—use operating systems such as UNIX or OS/2, which allow two or more users to be logged into the system concurrently. These systems have evolved with the more powerful microprocessor chips that have become available in recent years, most notably the Intel 80386 and 80486 chips and the Motorola 68020, 68030, and 68040 chips. Intel has also released its 80586 chips and is working on even more advanced models.

These are likely to launch new, even more powerful microcomputer systems during the next few years.

Two of the leading contenders in the multiuser desktop market are the high-end machines in the IBM PS/2 and the Apple Macintosh "families." A "family" consists of computers that differ in speed, power, and performance. For example, the lower-end PS/2s—such as the Model 25—are designed to be single-user systems; their primary storage capacities and clock speeds are usually lower than that found in the high-end machines such as the Model 90.

Many of the desktop systems with multiuser capabilities are employed as single-user systems because of the extra power they offer. In some instances, this makes them much more useful for such tasks as medium-scale database management and desktop publishing.

Enhancing Microcomputer Systems: Add-In Boards

The functions that many desktop and portable microcomputers are able to carry out can be extended by installing add-in boards. **Add-in boards** are card-like pieces of hardware that plug into expansion slots found in the system unit. These contain the circuitry for interfacing with specific types of peripheral devices (such as an OCR scanner) and/or to enable the user to carry out one or more specific functions. For example, if you want to add a more sophisticated display screen to your system, you may need to install a new display adaptor board. Similarly, if you want to make it possible for your system to communicate with fax machines, you will need to install a fax board.

Many types of add-in boards are available for both desktop and portable micros. Most of these boards provide new functions that were unavailable with the standard system or provide a value-added capability that enhances existing functions. The variety of add-in boards continues to increase. Figure 5.11 lists some popular add-in boards and the functions they perform.

Midrange Systems

Minicomputers (or minis), which first became available in the 1960s, were also a product of the trend in shrinking CPU circuitry. Most of the earliest minicomputers were used for engineering and scientific applications, and minicomputers are still a common fixture in those areas. Later, minis were applied to the solution of small business problems. With small businesses and smaller business units (such as offices or departments) being able to afford their own minicomputers, the first serious movement toward distributing computing power throughout the organization began. Until the first minis were developed, it was very difficult for most users to actually get their hands directly on a computer system, so this was a significant and welcome event.

The very smallest minicomputers, such as some models in Digital Equipment Corporation's MicroVAX line, are virtually indistinguishable in processing power from some high-end microcomputers, whereas the largest minis (sometimes called superminis) can pack more power than a small mainframe.

Board Type	Purpose
Cache card	Provides the logic for "disk caching," an operation that reduces the number of disk accesses.
Coprocessor board	Contains either a numeric coprocessor, which speeds up arithmetic, or a graphics coprocessor, which enhances graphics capabilities.
Disk controller card	Interfaces a disk unit of a certain type with a computer system.
Display adapter board	Interfaces a monochrome or color display with a given system unit. Such a board is not necessary in many newer, 32-bit microcomputers, which have interfacing circuitry built in.
Emulator board	Enables a microcomputer system to function as a communications terminal to a mainframe or minicomputer.
Fax board	Provides the functionality of a facsimile machine.
LAN board	Enables the microcomputer system to function as a workstation in a local area network (LAN).
Memory expansion board	Provides a system unit with more RAM.
Modem board	Provides a modem on a board.
Multifunction board	Packages a variety of independent functions into a single board.
Upgrade board	Turns a computer system of one type into a computer system of another type—for example, an IBM PC AT into an IBM PS/2. Alternatively, the board may enable the computer system to run concurrent central processing units so that applications can run on dedicated processors at about the same time. Also referred to as an accelerator board, turbo board, or concurrent processor.

Figure 5.11 A summary of some popular add-in boards for microcomputers. These make it possible for users to carry out additional functions and generally extend the functionality of microcomputer systems.

Minicomputers are often used to drive a number of terminals, printers, and other peripheral devices. Usually, mainframes can simultaneously support more peripheral devices than minis, but for many moderately sized organizations, minicomputers may be all that is needed.

The electronic cash registers associated with point-of-sale (POS) systems—discussed earlier in the chapter—are often on-line to minicomputers. Systems that support a particular functional area of a business—such as marketing or research and development (R&D)—are also often minicomputer-based. Minicomputers are typically priced anywhere from about $10,000 to $300,000; most fall in the $20,000 to $200,000 range.

Minis may be selected by an organization for a variety of reasons. For instance, processing that could take place on a large (mainframe) computer can often be distributed among several minis—sometimes at a much lower cost. Some small companies that find their processing needs too substantial for a microcomputer-based system, but not nearly substantial enough to require a mainframe, often find minicomputers to be exactly what they need. Additionally, minicomputer-like technical workstations may help engineers design products or structures.

Vendor	Approximate Number of Systems in U.S. in 1992
DEC	170,000
IBM	150,000
NCR	55,000
Hewlett-Packard	39,000
Data General	23,000
Wang	19,000
Prime	10,000

Figure 5.12 The leading vendors of midrange systems and the approximate number of systems at U.S. installations in 1992 are shown in this figure. (Adapted from *The Computerworld IS Pocket Guide for Success*)

Among the well-known vendors of minicomputers are Digital Equipment Corporation (DEC), Data General, Hewlett-Packard, IBM, Prime, and Wang (see Figure 5.12). The IBM AS/400 family of midrange computers (a new term for minicomputers) is now a dominating force in the minicomputer market. The DEC MicroVAX family is IBM's leading contender. IBM's AS/400 line is so successful that if this division left the main company, it would be the second largest computer company in the world—second only to IBM itself.

Mainframes

In most large organizations, **mainframes** are the workhorses for transaction processing applications. In many firms, several mainframes are located in a processing center—or operations center—that runs 24 hours a day, 7 days a week. Such centers often serve users on terminals during the working hours and, during off hours, process large jobs that might otherwise slow terminal response time—batch updating, payroll, and billing, to name a few.

Of all the sizes of computers discussed here, mainframes are the most technologically mature. In fact, from the early 1950s until the late 1960s, virtually all computer processing in business was mainframe-based. Since the mid-1950s, IBM has been the dominant world manufacturer of mainframes, and still claims a majority of the market. However, Fujitsu and NEC, Japan's leading computer companies, have made significant inroads in the world's mainframe market. In the U.S., IBM continues to be the dominant force (see Figure 5.13), with Unisys

Year	Total U.S. Mainframe Installation	Percent IBM
1988	27,274	93%
1990	26,886	95%
1992	23,920*	95%

*estimated

Figure 5.13 IBM mainframes have been the dominant force in large-system installations in the U.S. The decline in the total number of mainframes in use is a reflection of the general trend toward downsizing large systems and shifting applications to smaller hardware platforms.

(a company formed in 1986 by the merger of the Burroughs and Sperry corporations) vying for a distant second place.

Mainframes typically support more peripheral devices and simultaneous users than minicomputers and are likely to be the primary host processors in computer networks. Prices for mainframes are usually $500,000–$10,000,000. In 1992, the cost per MIPS of processing power was approximately $100,000. By 1996, the cost per MIPS on mainframe systems is expected to drop to $15,000.

Supercomputers

Some organizations need computers that can work at extraordinarily fast speeds or that are exceptionally accurate. Computer-generated movies and commercials, for instance, demand enormous amounts of high-speed computation. A single frame in such a video clip can involve 70 billion computations. To provide animation at a rate of 24 frames a second, an incredible amount of computation is needed in a very short period of time. Weather forecasting and structural modeling are two other applications that have unusually high computational or accuracy demands.

To meet such special needs, machines called **supercomputers** are usually required. Generally, these machines are very expensive, costing from $2 million to about $20 million. Cray and Fujitsu are two of the leading supercomputer vendors.

Recently, some companies have tried to bring supercomputer-level power down to ordinary business applications. For example, Goldman Sachs, the New York-based investment firm, recently purchased a minisupercomputer—a machine with about 25 percent of the power of a regular supercomputer, but costing less than $1 million—for certain types of traditionally mainframe-based work. Supercomputers are also being used, although not widely yet, for such tasks as economic and financial forecasting. Some people speculate that such machines may eventually replace the mainframe for certain transaction processing tasks. However, most experts predict that mainframe-based transaction-processing applications will be moved to midrange and local area network systems instead.

Emerging Processing Technologies

Two important changes are taking place in CPU architectures that may change the nature of computer processors. The first is the development of reduced instruction set computing (RISC) and the second involves parallel processing.

Reduced Instruction Set Computing (RISC)

Most of today's computers use chips manufactured by Intel Corporation. In 1991, 20.4 million microcomputers with Intel microprocessors were sold. Intel's chips are based on a technology called **complex instruction set computing (CISC)**; this approach has been used since the first digital computers appeared. In this approach, the microprocessors contain circuitry for executing a wide range of computer instructions—many have several hundred operations hardwired (built) into their circuitry. Circuitry is available for commonly used instructions (such as adding two numbers together), as well as circuitry for less frequently needed instructions (such as dividing one large fractional number by another in a manner that produces highly precise results). For many applications, only 20 percent of the built-in operations are needed to perform 80 percent of the processing tasks. The presence of seldom used specialized instructions adds complexity to the CPU and often reduces its performance.

Reduced instruction set computers (RISC) were first introduced in the 1970s and studies have shown that these may work up to ten times faster than conventional CISC-based computers that have larger instruction sets. Despite their name, RISC doesn't always mean reducing the number of hard-wired instructions. More commonly, this approach imposes limits on the number of tasks contained in each instruction. With RISC instructions, everything gets done in one tick of the microprocessor's clock. Having simple instructions also means that simpler circuits are needed, and this frees up space on the chip for special speed-enhancing circuits. In some types of computing applications—especially those in science and research, where computations are abundant and processor speed is extremely important—RISC machines can deliver impressive results, often performing computations 5 to 15 times faster than a CISC-based CPU.

Many vendors—such as IBM, Compaq, Hewlett-Packard, and DEC—have developed RISC-based machines. Sun Microsystems is one of the leading vendors of RISC-based machines, especially in developing multiuser systems for engineering and scientific applications.

Today, many experts predict that RISC-based machines will become the standard in engineering environments and communications systems. However, the emergence of RISC-based computers for general-purpose applications has been slowed because conventional software often needs to be modified before work can be done on them. While more than 20,000 commercially available software packages could be run on Intel-based CISC machines in 1992, less than 4,000 programs were available for RISC-based machines. The lack of available software has inhibited many CISC machine owners from switching to RISC-based machines—and may be why less than 310,000 RISC-based machines were sold in 1991.

Parallel Processing

Despite the astounding evolution of computer systems over the past 50 years, most are still driven by a single CPU. This is known as *von Neumann architecture*—named after mathematician and computer pioneer John von Neumann. In this approach, a single CPU can perform instructions only in serial (one step at a time), whether working exclusively on one program or juggling several concurrently.

In recent years, promising research has been done on an alternative to von Neumann architecture. Scientists are experimenting with ways to have two or more central processing units and memories perform tasks in parallel. Therefore, instead of having to rely on a single processor to solve a lengthy calcula-

Processor Models	Number of Transistors	MIPS*	Year**
486	1.2 million	20	1990
586	3 million	100	1993
686	7 million	175	1994
786	20 million	250	1996

Figure 5.14 Microprocessor chips continue to become more powerful. Much of this is due to being able to pack more transistors in the same space. This figure shows how microprocessor chips manufactured by Intel are expected to change during the 1990s. (Adapted from Hof)

* Millions of instructions per second

** Year when volume shipments should begin; public unveiling of the processor should occur about 12 months earlier than start of volume shipments

tion, a computer system using **parallel processing** assigns different portions of the problem to different central processing units to work on simultaneously. The problem can thus be solved more quickly with this approach. While this type of architecture creates a whole new set of challenges, such as how the activities of the different processors be most efficiently coordinated, most industry insiders see parallel processing as an unstoppable future reality for all types of systems from supercomputers to microcomputers.

Increasing Processor Speeds

Over the years, a number of strategies were used to make computers faster. In addition to reduced instruction set and parallel computing, processor speed can be enhanced by moving circuits closer together and by utilizing new semiconductor materials.

- ■ *Moving circuits closer together* As complex as computers seem to be, one natural law of physics cannot be ignored: the shorter the length of the circuit paths, the less time it takes to move programs and data along them. Advances in the field of *microelectronics* have made it possible for chip and computer manufacturers to pack circuitry increasingly close together. Each new generation of chips typically means that twice as many circuits can be packed into the same sized space. In the last two decades, chip circuitry has progressed from LSI (large scale integration) through VSLI (very large scale integration) to ULSI (ultra large scale integration). Today, it is possible to pack more than a million circuits on a single fingernail-sized chip; in the near future, this is likely to double or quadruple (see Figure 5.14 regarding Intel's plans).

- ■ *New material* Most CPU chips consist of metallic circuitry that is etched onto a silicon base. Silicon-based chips have been popular since the 1970s, when manufacturing techniques for microminiaturizing circuitry became widely available.

   Today, several alternatives to silicon-backed chips are being developed. Among these are gallium arsenide chips, superconductors, optical processing, biotechnology, and vacuum electronics (see related box, page 205):

SECONDARY STORAGE TECHNOLOGIES

Whereas primary (internal) memory temporarily stores the inputs, computations, and outputs that the computer is currently processing, secondary storage saves programs and data for repeated use. Although it is slower than primary memory, secondary memory is significantly less expensive and its storage capabilities are much more extensive. Also, unlike primary memory, secondary storage is *nonvolatile*—that is, its contents are retained when the computer's power is shut off.

Secondary storage involves both a medium and a peripheral storage device. The *medium* is the actual recording surface that is used to store programs and data, whereas the *storage device*—on which the medium is mounted—is used to read from and write to the medium. For instance, if the medium of choice is a 3½-inch floppy disk, a floppy disk drive device that reads this size of disk must be included as part of the system. If, on the other hand, the medium used is a 12-inch tape reel, a tape drive unit is needed to write and read the data or programs stored on the tape. Every medium has a particular storage device that must be used with it.

Some storage media are removable, while others are not. When using *removable-media* devices, the medium has to be loaded and unloaded from its affiliated hardware device, just as a person places or removes a CD from its player. Some secondary storage devices, as discussed later, use *nonremovable media*.

Accessing Data

Often, business data that reside in secondary storage are composed of records— employee records, records of customer transactions, records of scheduled flights, and so on. After records are processed, they need to be accessed.

There are two basic types of access methods: sequential and direct. With *sequential access*, the records in a file are retrieved one after another in the same sequence in which they are physically stored on the media. With *direct access* (also known as *random access*), records can be retrieved in any sequence, independent of the specific physical locations of the records on the medium.

Magnetic tape is an example of a secondary storage medium that allows only sequential access. If the user wants a data record in the middle of the tape, he or she has to pass through all physically prior records to get to it. **Magnetic disks**, on the other hand, can be used for both sequential and direct access. For instance, a user can access data or programs on the disk by asking for them in the order in which they are physically stored, or the user can access specific data or records via the addresses assigned to them.

Some applications rely on sequential access while in others, only direct access is feasible. Payroll files, for example, are often processed sequentially. The system will typically read through the employee records on disk (or tape) in sequence and process a check corresponding to each record in the file. Airlines reservations databases represent a system in which direct access is needed. Since reservations databases contain data on thousands of flights, it is too time-consuming to search sequentially for the ones of interest every time a passenger buys a ticket. Thus, these systems use direct-access procedures to retrieve specific flight data.

Virtually all secondary storage media and their associated hardware units can be classified as sequential- or direct-access devices. Any device with direct or random access capabilities can be categorized as a **direct access storage device (DASD)**. Most direct access storage devices can also be used for sequential access.

Disk Access Speeds

One of the most common methods of comparing disk technologies is in terms of their access speeds—the time it takes to locate the data or file on the disk, read it, and transfer it to primary memory so that the user can work with it. Read and write times are sometimes also used to measure the speed of a DASD. Access speed for microcomputer systems is usually measured in milliseconds (ms).

Once data are written to a disk (or other direct access medium), the time it takes to read and send them to the CPU for processing is known as *access time*. Access time can be broken down into three parts:

- *Seek time* is the time it takes to position the read/write head over the track on which the requested data are stored.
- *Search time* (or *rotational delay*) is the time it takes the disk to spin until its read/write head is positioned at the beginning of the requested data.
- *Data transfer time* is the time it takes to activate the read/write head, read the requested data, and transmit them to primary memory for processing.

Access time varies considerably among direct access storage devices. For hard disks found in the system units of microcomputers on the market today, access times may be less than 20 milliseconds.

Seek and search time comprise the bulk of a device's access time because they both involve mechanical movement of disk drive components. When faster access times are needed, putting multiple read/write heads on the same access arm can significantly reduce seek time. In fact, some disk systems have a read/write head for each track on each recording surface; this virtually eliminates seek time. Of course, disk drives that rotate disks at faster rates are also likely to have better access times.

Because faster access may translate into better customer service and greater user productivity, it should be considered carefully when determining what type of disk system to install.

Disk Devices and Media

Today, disks are the most common storage medium in the information systems industry. In this section, we will cover some of the most commercially significant disk products for microcomputers. Later, we will look at the disk technologies found in midrange and mainframe systems.

Diskettes

Diskettes or **floppy disks** are the most common secondary storage medium found on microcomputer systems. Diskettes are mylar platters that are coated with a magnetizable substance, typically iron oxide. As with other types of magnetic disks, the concentric tracks on them contain the binary representations of data and programs. Each diskette is contained in a square-shaped plastic or paper jacket that protects the disk surfaces from dust and damage.

To be used, a diskette must be inserted into the proper type and size of diskette drive. The diskette will fit into the drive only one way. Read/write heads contained in the drive access the data stored on the diskette through a recording window in the outer jacket.

Diskettes are commonly available in diameters of 5¼ inches and 3½ inches, although other sizes may be used. The 5¼-inch floppies flourished with the introduction of the IBM PC in the early 1980s and they are still common. However, 5¼-inch floppy disks have been eclipsed by the newer 3½-inch diskettes, which have greater storage capacity and a more durable storage casing.

A number of other characteristics differentiate diskettes, as follows:

- ■ *Sectoring requirements* During formatting (a disk preparation program performed by the operating system), sectors are created in order to divide a diskette into addressable areas. Most diskettes available for microcomputer systems are "soft-sectored," meaning they can be formatted by whatever operating system is in use on the microcomputer. Different operating systems use different sectoring schemes. Therefore, a disk that has been formatted for an Apple Macintosh will be unreadable by a standard IBM-compatible machine that uses MS-DOS.

- ■ *Density* Density refers to the number of bits or tracks packed onto the recording surface of a diskette. The three most common grades of density—from least to most dense—are *single-density (SD)*, *double-density (DD)*, and *high-density (HD)*. Diskette drives vary in their capacity to read such disks. High-density drives usually can read both high- and low-density disks. However, low-density drives often cannot read disks with densities higher than that for which they were designed. High-density 3½-inch diskettes hold 1.44MB of data; however, some of the latest ones store 2.88MB. 5¼-inch diskettes that hold 720KB are double-density while those that hold 1.2MB are high-density.

- ■ *Single- versus double-sided* Diskettes and their drives are either single- or double-sided. Just as it sounds, *double-sided (DS)* diskettes can store twice as much data as *single-sided (SS)* diskettes. Single-sided drives can read only single-sided diskettes, whereas double-sided drives can read both single-sided and double-sided diskettes. Double-sided drives are used most frequently in today's microcomputers.

Winchester Disks

Winchester disk units—or Winchesters—consist of one or more hard disks, an access mechanism, and read/write heads, all of which are hermetically sealed in a case. Because the Winchester unit is protected and free from air contamination, it can be rotated at higher rates of speed than other types of hard magnetic disks; also, its tracks can be closer together. Although they involve nonremovable media, Winchester disks work according to many of the same principles as removable-pack disks.

Although frequently used on larger computer systems, probably the most common application of Winchesters today is on microcomputer systems. Most microcomputer users refer to Winchesters simply as **hard disks**. Winchester disks are especially appropriate for microcomputer users in commercial environments, which typically need on-line access to greater stores of data and faster access speeds.

Winchesters are found in a variety of capacities and diameters. Capacities commonly range from 10MB to 200MB, although capacities exceeding 200MB are increasingly available for microcomputers. Diameters range from 2½ inches (for portable microcomputer systems) to about 14 inches (for mainframes).

Most Winchester disk systems on microcomputers are internal. Thus, the Winchester unit fits within the computer's system unit—the box that houses the computer, RAM, and associated circuitry. External Winchester systems, popular on larger computers, house the Winchester mechanism in a separate hardware device, detached from the system unit. External hard disks are also available for both desktop and portable microcomputers.

Cartridge Disks

Cartridge disks consist of a removable hard disk packaged into a plastic cartridge. In order to access the data and programs on the cartridge, the user must insert it into a secondary storage unit that accepts such media. A *Bernoulli box* is probably the best known example of this type of storage technology for microcomputers. As with other magnetic disk forms, cartridge disks vary with respect to diameter and capacity—ranging from about 3½ inches to 14 inches in diameter, and from a few megabytes to several hundred megabytes in capacity. Access times to data stored on cartridge disks rivals that of microcomputer hard disks.

Cartridge disks have an advantage over Winchesters regarding capacity and security. With respect to capacity, the more cartridges a person has, the more bytes of secondary storage are available. Thus, cartridge capacity is limited only by cost considerations. Unlike a microcomputer hard disk, when a cartridge disk is filled up, it can easily be replaced with a new one; hard disk capacity problems may be avoided with these systems. Furthermore, cartridges offer better security than Winchesters because they can be removed from the disk storage unit and placed in a safe location. Because they can be removed, disk cartridges are also an alternative to tape as backup media for data stored on Winchesters.

Optical Disk Technologies

A secondary storage technology that is becoming increasingly popular is the **optical disk** (also called laser disks and video disks). Optical disks use technol-

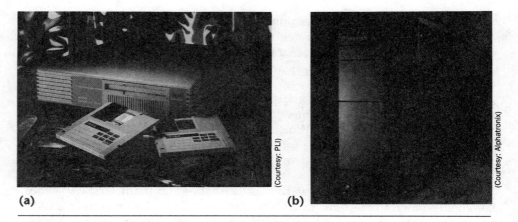

(a)   (b)

(Courtesy: PLI)

(Courtesy: Alphatronix)

Figure 5.15 Examples of optical disk technologies: (a) disk drive and (b) jukebox. Such technologies are growing in popularity and are expected to be increasingly common during the 1990s.

ogy that is similar to the compact disk (CD) found in many music systems (see Figure 5.15). The most compelling feature of optical disks is their capacity. A single optical disk, which is slightly larger than a floppy, is capable of storing over 250,000 pages or more of text—more storage than is necessary to store the entire contents of the *Encyclopedia Brittanica*! Another important feature is their ability to store text, data, graphics, audio, and video images on the same disk surface. No other secondary storage medium is so versatile. Because of large capacity and versatile storage capabilities, optical systems are central components in multimedia and imaging systems; both will be described later in the book.

The two most common forms of optical disks are CD-ROM and WORM. Most optical disks today use **CD-ROM** (compact disk, read-only memory) technology. The user buys a prerecorded disk and reads it on an optical disk unit. The disk is permanently etched and cannot be altered. Furthermore, the optical disk unit onto which the CD-ROM disk is mounted is only capable of reading (not writing) data. A single 3½-inch CD-ROM disk typically holds 640MB of data; the 8-inch and 12-inch CD-ROM disks for mainframes may hold more than a gigabyte of data.

WORM ("write once, read many" times) are another type of optical disk system. WORM disks cost more but enable the user to write to them. Once data or programs are written to the disk, however, they cannot be erased. WORM disk capacity is typically measured in gigabytes. Many organizations that previously used microfilm-based systems for document management have turned to WORM systems.

Erasable optical disk systems that permit data to be recorded and later updated have recently become available. *Magneto-optical disks* are a well-known example of these. Like WORM disks, magneto-optical disks typically hold more than a gigabyte of data. Unlike WORM or CD-ROM, these disks can be erased and written over; some vendors claim that their disks can be rewritten one million times.

Optical disks work through laser technology. Laser beams of high intensity are used to write to the disk. During recording, microscopic pits, holes, or bubbles are created by the laser beam along tracks in the disk's surface; the size and shape of the pit, hole, or bubble determines whether it represents a 1 or a 0 bit. Beams of a lower intensity enable the disk to be read. High-data densities are possible because laser beams have been perfected that can be directed with extreme precision. With magnetic media, if bits are placed too close to each other, their magnetic fields can mix and become garbled.

Optical disk systems are often slower than magnetic disk systems and, because they are still new to the computing environment, software written for these systems is just becoming plentiful. Today, optical disks are used mostly for mass and archival storage, but eventually, they may completely replace magnetic disks or emerge as a major competitive business weapon. For instance, since an entire, voluminous database can be written on a single optical disk that costs only a few dollars, companies can easily send disks to key sites or to clients. This saves communications costs and, possibly, may result in a competitive advantage.

A pharmaceutical company in Delaware uses optical disks for records management. The firm uses a *jukebox storage* system capable of accessing 64 optical disks—a total storage capacity equivalent to 8,500 five-drawer file cabinets. To get a drug approved by the Federal Drug Administration (FDA), a lot of paperwork is generated; much of it is prepared by different word-processing packages, using different file formats. By scanning the documents and storing them in an optical disk system, cases can be efficiently consolidated and archived at a central location, while automated retrieval is achieved. Writer Susan Janus quotes the director of research at the pharmaceutical company as saying, "We found we were spending a heck of a lot of time chasing paper. These systems reduce document retrieval time by 25 percent. You can get to any one page in the system in about 25 seconds."

Video Disks

A **video disk** can store text, video, and audio data. Video disks can be accessed a frame at a time (to provide still information) or played like a phonograph record (to supply up to an hour of moving action). Any of the 54,000 tracks on the surface of typical video disk can be accessed in about three seconds.

Video disks were first introduced in 1983, as a video game product. Today, however, they can provide companies with a competitive advantage, as indicated by the following examples:

- At the Florsheim shoe outlet in Chicago's Water Tower Palace, video disks help shoppers select from among several hundred styles of shoes. If customers cannot find the pair they want, Florsheim promises to locate and deliver the shoes to their homes within a week.

- To such retailers as Sears, which offers thousands of types and sizes of household products, video disk technology offers an attractive solution to the problem of large inventories. Interactive video disk systems at some Sears locations have expert-system software that also provides shoppers with an extra bonus: decorating tips. Sears intends to expand these systems storewide.

- At some Dayton-Hudson department stores, customers can use an interactive video disk system to buy furniture. By selecting options presented at a touch screen, customers can see the furniture that interests them and put it in a variety of room settings.

- Video disk systems were developed to help real estate agents conduct better searches for homes and properties for their clients. For example, the client describes the type of home desired—perhaps three bedrooms, a garage, and priced below $200,000. When these data are entered into the video disk system, photographs and even "video tours" of existing homes meeting the description can be summoned to the display screen.

- Video disks are widely used for training applications. At a growing number of companies—Ford, Chrysler, Xerox, Pfizer, and Massachusetts Mutual Life Insurance, to name just a few—video disk systems take on such training tasks as showing how to boost factory performance, helping service technicians do a faster and better job, and training clerks to analyze insurance applications. The U.S. Army has also made extensive use of video disks for training purposes.

Video disks are also used by automobile manufacturers to show their lines and by travel agents to interest clients in resorts. In the future, some industry observers predict that many businesses will develop automatic customer service centers equipped with video disk components so that consumers do not have to depend only on clerks and showrooms. When a desired item flashes on the display screen, the customer can insert a credit card in a device that resembles a bank's automatic teller machine and order that item immediately. Sears introduced systems like this in many of its department stores. Even the U.S. Postal Service is spending close to $5 million to develop an automated video disk system that will allow its patrons to do many of the activities that human postal clerks now perform.

Tape Devices and Media

Cartridge tapes represent the leading edge of tape technology. Tape cartridges are available for both large and small computer systems.

Tape cartridges for microcomputer systems, which resemble cassette tapes in appearance, are frequently used to back up hard disks. These tapes, which are not designed for processing purposes, are sometimes called *streaming tapes*. The capacities of these tapes vary, but several megabytes of storage are typical. Streaming tapes can usually back up the contents of a hard disk in a few minutes. Among the leading tape cartridge system vendors are Colorado Memory Systems, Everex Systems, Micro Solutions, Summit Memory Systems, and Tallgrass Technologies Corporation.

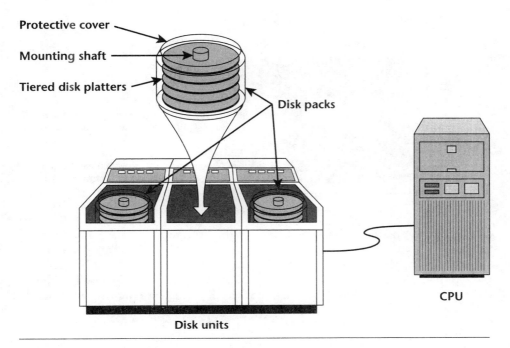

Figure 5.16 An example of a removable disk pack system.

Storage Technologies for Larger Systems

So far, the discussion of secondary storage technologies has focused primarily on the storage media and devices that are used in conjunction with microcomputer systems. While these are the technologies that most people will use on the job, some workers will rely on larger midrange or mainframe-based systems to carry out their tasks. For that reason, we will briefly describe the characteristics of the storage technologies that are found in larger systems.

Removable-Pack Disks

Removable-pack disk systems, such as that depicted in Figure 5.16, have been used since the 1960s. These systems, which are most commonly found on mainframes and other large computer systems, consist of several rigid disk platters stacked into a single unit called a **disk pack**. These high-storage-capacity packs are mounted or removed from the associated disk drive unit in much the same way that diskettes are inserted and removed from smaller disk units. When a pack is on-line (that is, mounted onto a drive contained in the unit, which spins the disk) data can be read from or written to any portion of it.

Many removable-pack disk systems use disks that are 14 inches in diameter. Data are stored as binary bits on the top and bottom surfaces of the disks in concentric tracks (see Figure 5.17). It is common to find several hundred tracks of data on each surface and 12 or more disks per pack. Each pack is protected by its own dust cover. As further protection against data loss, the top surface

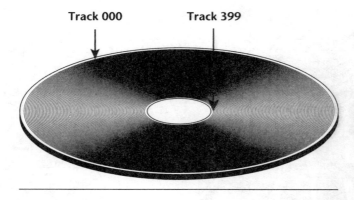

Figure 5.17 A disk surface. Each disk surface consists of concentric tracks on which data are physically stored. Microcomputer hard disks often contain hundreds of tracks; diskettes usually hold 80 tracks.

of the topmost disk and bottom surface of the bottommost disk generally stay unused.

Data on a disk are read or written through the read/write heads, which are moved in and out among the tracks by an access mechanism. Generally, a head corresponds to each recordable disk surface. Reading and writing commonly

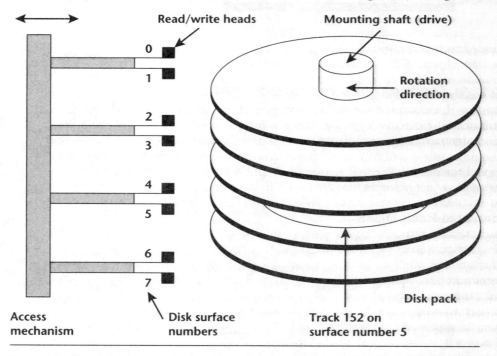

Figure 5.18 Movable access mechanism. The access mechanism moves in and out between the disk platters to access data stored in tracks on the disk surface. For example, to read data on surface number 5, track 152, the access mechanism moves to track 152 and the read/write head for disk surface number 5 is activated for reading.

**Disk surface
numbers**

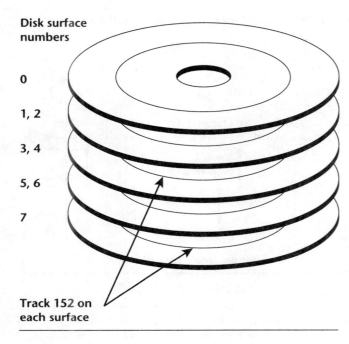

0

1, 2

3, 4

5, 6

7

**Track 152 on
each surface**

Figure 5.19 Disk cylinders. The imaginary surface formed by the same relative track on each surface is called a disk cylinder. So, for instance, cylinder 152 on an eight-surface pack is the imaginary cylinder formed by all eight-track 152s.

take place as shown in Figure 5.18. As the rotating shaft spins, the access mechanism moves the heads in and out between the disk surfaces in order to access particular disk addresses. When one of the heads is above a track that must be read from or written to, it is activated by the disk unit. None of the heads, incidentally, ever touches a disk. To do so would cause massive damage—commonly known as a "head crash." Instead, the heads glide just millionths of an inch above the disk surface, electronically reading or writing data.

While studying multi-platter disk-pack systems, it is helpful to understand the concept of a disk cylinder. A *cylinder* refers to corresponding tracks on different surfaces. So, for instance, cylinder 152 would include all track 152s on surfaces 0 through 7 in an eight-surface pack (see Figure 5.19). Generally, related data are stored on the same cylinder—rather than on the same surface—by the disk system because it is faster to access data in this manner.

Redundant Arrays of Inexpensive Disks

As discussed later, in large systems, files and databases are frequently stored on one or more disk packs. While the access times to data stored this way are often quite fast, developers tried to find alternative systems with faster access times. One such development that shows considerable promise are **RAID (redundant arrays of inexpensive disks)** systems. The differences between these and traditional disk pack systems are illustrated in Figure 5.20. RAID places data on multiple small disks instead of on one large disk-pack. In theory, this should result in improved access time and greater data availability at a reasonable cost.

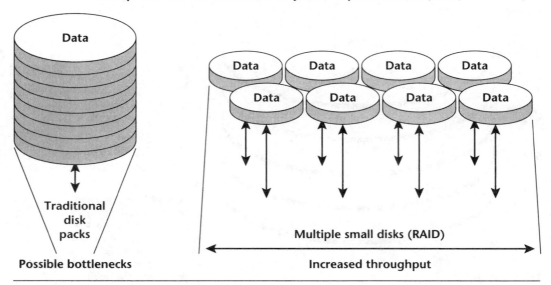

Conceptual View of Redundant Arrays of Inexpensive Disks (RAID)

Figure 5.20 RAID systems. Redundant arrays of inexpensive disks (RAID) have emerged as a popular secondary storage technology during the 1990s, especially in local area networks and larger systems. Most of these provide disk mirroring—a backup approach that automatically duplicates data on two or more disks—and faster access to data than is typically possible with disk packs.

RAID systems are currently available for organizations that have mainframes. RAID systems were also developed for PC and local area networks. Their performance and storage capacities motivate organizations to move transaction processing and database applications from large computers to networks. Some experts predict that RAID will be as important to storage technology as RISC has been to central processing units.

Tape Devices

Magnetic tape is probably the oldest secondary storage technology still in wide use. As noted previously, its biggest drawback is that it can only access data sequentially. However, many data processing operations are sequential or batch-oriented in nature, and tape is still economical. Here, we will look at the two most popular forms of magnetic tape for large-system MIS applications: detachable-reel magnetic tapes and tape cartridges.

Detachable-Reel Magnetic Tapes

Many of the tapes used with mainframes and minicomputers are stored on *detachable reels.* These plastic tapes are, like disks, coated with a magnetizable surface (often iron oxide) that can be encoded with 0 and 1 bits. Tapes come in various widths, lengths, and data densities. A common specification is a 2400-foot reel of ½-inch diameter tape that packs data at 6250 bytes per inch.

New Substances, Smaller Circuits Mean More Speed and Power

To meet future business computing needs, alternatives to silicon-based chips are under development. These include:

- **Gallium arsenide chips** Gallium arsenide chips are capable of moving electrons ten times faster than silicon chips. Because they emit less heat, it is possible to pack circuits closer together—allowing the processor to perform more tasks per sec -ond.

- **Superconductors** Researchers are searching for "superconductor" substances (materials that conduct electricity with extremely little resistance) to replace silicon. Such substances may result in circuitry that is 100 times faster than today's chips.

- **Optical processing** Optical processing uses light waves instead of electrons to do processing tasks. Those already developed can move data ten times faster than sil-

icon-based processors; they have the potential to be hundreds of times faster.

- **Biotechnology** Scientists have "grown" tiny molecules shaped to act like circuits that pass electrons from molecule to molecule. With such technology, circuits could be 500 times smaller than they are today.

". . . CIRCUITS COULD BE 500 TIMES SMALLER THAN THEY ARE TODAY."

- **Tubes on a chips** Scientists believe it is possible to place 10 billion microscopic vacuum tubes on a five-inch wafer. Since electrons travel much faster in a vacuum, tubes on a chip may be 1,000 times more powerful than today's silicon-based chips.

Adapted from Freedman (1992).

Recording densities of tapes are often cited as bytes per inch (bpi) because in most instances, a character (byte) is represented as a vertical slice of bits across the tracks of tape surfaces.

Tapes are read on a hardware device called a *tape unit* (Figure 5.21). Basically, this unit works the same way as the reel-to-reel tape units that were once popular on home stereo systems. An empty take-up reel, running at the same speed as the supply reel on which the tape is initially wound, accepts the tape as it is being processed. The tape is processed by passing it by read/write heads located between the two reels. Depending on the instructions given to the computer system, data can then either be read from the tape or written to it.

Tape Cartridge Systems

In 1986, IBM introduced a tape cartridge system, the IBM 3480, for its 3090 line of mainframes. Each of these cartridges has a capacity of 200MB and a data-transfer rate of 3MB/sec. Unlike conventional detachable-reel tapes, which use 9 parallel tracks, these ½-inch tapes store data in 18 tracks. In 1992, IBM released 36-track tape cartridges for use in its mainframes and AS/400 family of midrange computers.

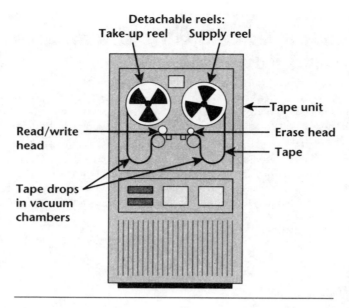

Detachable reels:
Take-up reel   Supply reel

Tape unit

Read/write head

Erase head

Tape

Tape drops in vacuum chambers

Figure 5.21 Magnetic tape units are still widely used in larger systems.

OUTPUT TECHNOLOGY

Display Devices

Virtually everyone who interacts with a computer system today uses some type of **display device**. These peripheral hardware units consist of a television-like viewing screen, to which computer output is sent. The two most common types of display devices found today are monitors and terminals.

Monitors are the devices found most commonly with microcomputer systems. As mentioned previously, a monitor is just a "box with a viewing screen." On the screen, the user is able to see not only what was entered into the computer, but the computer output as well.

A terminal, or video display terminal (VDT), is basically a monitor with a keyboard attached to it. Thus, it becomes an input/output workstation. Terminals are most commonly found in settings that are remote from the main computer and they interact with the computer through communications lines or networks. Airline agents are familiar examples of people who use communications terminals. Tellers in banks and cashiers in many retail settings also use terminals to perform their work duties.

Display devices are particularly useful because they allow people to analyze or extract data from the computer system without creating a lot of paper. Nonetheless, many of the results produced by the computer eventually need to be put into hardcopy (printed) form. Thus, most people using display devices also have a printer available so that they can keep their results in a permanent form.

Figure 5.22 The character R formed from a 5-by-7 dot matrix of pixels.

Hundreds of different display devices are now available. Although a number of important features distinguish one display device from another, the four that follow are among the most significant.

Screen Resolution

One of the most important features used to differentiate display devices is the clarity, or *resolution*, of the images that are formed on-screen. Most display devices form images from tiny dots—called *pixels* (a contraction of the two words "picture elements")—that are arranged in a rectangular pattern. Figure 5.22, for instance, shows how the letter R would be formed by a system that displays standard text characters in a 5-by-7 matrix of dots. The more dots that are available to display any image on-screen, the sharper the image (the greater the resolution) is.

Some of the newer and most advanced standards for screen resolution are *VGA* (video graphics array), *EVGA* (enhanced video graphics array), and *SVGA* (super video graphics array). These are available for many of the IBM-compatible microcomputers on the market, including laptop and notebook personal computers. Basic VGA provides a text mode that partitions the screen into 640-by-480 pixels. Other display modes available with VGA, EVGA, and SVGA are 800-by-600, 1024-by-768, and 1280-by-1024.

As expected, high-resolution monitors usually carry heftier price tags. However, for some engineering, scientific, and desktop publishing applications in which television-like graphics are needed, investments in high-end monitors are often justifiable. Lower monitor resolution standards will not provide the necessary clarity. For instance, the graphics mode of the CGA (color graphics adapter) standard, which was popular prior to the availability of VGA, only has a resolution of 320-by-200 pixels.

Of course, not everyone needs a display device with the highest resolution possible. For word processing, a text resolution of 720-by-350 pixels—available with many inexpensive, stand-alone word processor systems—is usually sufficient. When using desktop publishing applications, however—where extra clarity and many shades of gray are useful in discerning such images as photographs—high-end VGA-class resolution is strongly recommended.

Managers and users should know that the monitor itself is only part of the cost associated with having high-resolution output. To take full advantage of the capabilities of high-end monitors, microcomputers must be equipped with appropriate *video cards* that plug into the system boards. As might be expected, the video cards necessary for high-resolution VGA output are more expensive than those available for low-end VGA.

Text and Graphics

Many display devices made today (principal exceptions are inexpensive terminals such as those used in dedicated transaction processing applications) can produce both text and graphics output. Text output is composed entirely of alphabetic characters, digits, and special characters. Graphics output includes such images as drawings, charts, photographs, and maps.

Display devices that are capable of producing graphics output commonly employ a method called bit-mapping. *Bit-mapped devices* allow each individual pixel on the screen to be controlled by the computer. Thus, any type of image that can be formed from the rectangular grid of dots on the screen (for example, a 640-by-480 grid) is possible. *Character-addressable devices* are not bit-mapped and partition the screen into standard character widths—for example, a series of 5-by-7 dot widths—to display text.

Perhaps the most important business-related use for graphics is presentation graphics, which will be discussed more extensively in Chapter 6. Presentation graphics enable managers to easily construct such information-intensive images as bar charts, pie charts, and line charts on their display devices and have these images sent to a printer, plotter, or slide-making machine so they can be used later for presentations in meetings. Because these types of graphical images are relatively simple, a super-high-resolution workstation that can display photographs and sophisticated artwork is not needed.

Graphics display devices have been widely used for many years in the engineering and scientific disciplines. The display devices used for applications in these areas are extremely sophisticated and expensive, costing several thousand dollars. These display devices—often attached to RISC-based microcomputers called *workstations*—provide resolutions that are typically much higher than those needed by most microcomputer users. Recently, however, workstations have become popular in the marketing area, where they help some companies create three-dimensional package designs or fabric textures on-screen before the companies become committed to a design strategy. Such applications as these collectively fall under the heading of computer-aided design (CAD).

Some examples of workstations found at the low end of the market are the IBM RISCsystem/6000, DEC's VAXstation, and most products sold by Sun Microsystems. With the introduction of 32-bit microcomputer systems and their accompanying high-resolution monitors, many graphics applications that were once possible only on workstations have migrated to micros. At the high end of the technical workstation market are such devices as the $80,000 Pixar Image Computer system, which claims to be 200 times faster than a typical minicomputer and, for some graphics applications, faster than a low-end supercomputer. An interesting note: Pixar is a spinoff of Lucasfilm, Ltd.—the company that produces popular computer-graphics-intensive films.

Monochrome Versus Color

When selecting a display device, the user must decide whether it should output monochrome or color images.

Monochrome display devices output images in a single foreground color. The most common choices are amber on a black background, green on a black background, and black on a white background. A reverse-video feature is also available on most systems to reverse the foreground/background designations; for instance, to produce black on an amber background. *Color display devices* are available that produce anywhere from four to an infinite number of colors. For applications such as word processing, transaction processing, and many types of management analysis, a monochrome monitor—which is much cheaper than a color monitor—may be sufficient.

Although color monitors are not absolutely necessary for most business applications, they have become very popular. By highlighting some types of information on the screen in color, for instance, managers are able to more quickly separate the important information from standard material. Also, color is superior for communicating certain types of graphics information quickly; for example, information in color-coded sectors of a pie chart (as long as the user is not color-blind).

CRT Versus Flat-Panel

Most of the display devices used today are of the **cathode ray tube (CRT)** type. These devices use a large tube-type element that looks like the picture tube in a standard TV set. Inside the tube is a gun that lights up the phosphorescent pixels on the screen surface. Although CRT technology is relatively inexpensive and reliable, CRT-type display devices are rather bulky and limited in the resolution that they provide.

Currently challenging the CRT in the display device marketplace is the **flat-panel display**. The most common of these devices use either a liquid crystal display (LCD) or gas-plasma technology. To form images, LCD devices use crystalline materials sandwiched between two panes of glass. When heat or voltage is applied, the crystals line up. This prevents light from passing through certain areas and produces the display. Gas-plasma displays, which provide better resolution but are more expensive than liquid crystal displays, use gas trapped between glass to form images.

The biggest advantage of flat-panel displays is that they are lightweight and compact. This makes them especially useful for laptop, notebook, and pocket personal computers, which can be valuable competitive weapons when used by a company's sales forces while out in the field. Flat-panel displays are also capable of providing a much higher resolution than the CRT and they consume less power; many of them follow VGA standards.

Most of the flat-panel displays for portable microcomputers are monochrome. However, since 1992, color flat-panel displays for portables have been available from most vendors. A disadvantage is that color flat-panel displays are still in the fledgling stages of development and are relatively expensive.

Printers

Display devices are useful because they allow easy access to vast amounts of data and also, because they do not waste paper. However, they have several major limitations:

- Output cannot be removed from the display screen.

- The amount of output that can be handled at any time is limited by the size of the display screen and by the rate at which a person can flip through screen-sized pages.

- The user cannot inscribe helpful annotations on display device output with a pencil or pen (unless it is designed to be a pen-based system).

- The user must be physically present at the display device to see the output that it provides.

To overcome any or all of these disadvantages, a device that supplies output in portable form is needed. The most important of these devices is the printer.

Just as several important ways exist to differentiate among display devices, there are several important ways to differentiate among printers. Besides price, two of the most important of these are the quality of the output produced and the speed of the device.

Print Quality

Quality is largely a function of the speed at which the printer is run and the technology that is in use.

Regarding speed, usually the faster the printer is operated, the lower the output quality will be. Many printers can work in more than one speed mode. For instance, most dot-matrix printers used with microcomputer systems can operate at a fast (draft-quality) speed or at a slower (near-letter-quality or NLQ) pace. In many of these printers, the slower speed enables more elements of the printing mechanism to act upon the paper in a given amount of time. This makes it possible to produce more fully formed and visually appealing characters.

Many types of printing technologies are used today. One way to classify these technologies is whether they are impact or nonimpact printers. *Impact printers* work by having wires or embossed characters strike a piece of paper or a ribbon so that a character is formed on a page. This is the principle that operates conventional typewriter keys. *Nonimpact printers,* on the other hand, use some quieter method, such as heating, spraying, or electrostatically forming characters onto a page.

In addition to being either impact or nonimpact, most microcomputer printers fall into one of the following classes: solid-font printers, dot-matrix printers, ink-jet printers, thermal-transfer printers, or laser printers.

Solid-Font Printers

Solid-font printers represent one of the older printing technologies used with microcomputers. These have a printing element with fully formed characters—similar to those found on conventional typewriters. The two most common printers that fall into this category are the daisywheel printer and the print-thimble printer. Solid-font printers are targeted to text applications; they provide very limited graphics support. The good news about daisywheel and print-thimble printers is that their output quality is exceptionally high. The bad news is that they operate at very slow speeds: 15 to 80 characters per second. The popularity and use of solid-font printers has dropped substantially since the introduction of low-cost laser printers that rival the quality of their output.

Dot-Matrix Printers

The type of printer that is most commonly used in microcomputer systems is the dot-matrix printer. **Dot-matrix printers** are impact printers that form dot-matrix characters on paper. At one time, dot-matrix characters were considered too "boxy-looking" for distribution outside an organization. Today, however, the print heads on impact dot-matrix printers have improved so much that it is often difficult to differentiate between a dot-matrix-produced character and one produced on a solid-font printer. While many early print heads contained only 7 pins, state-of-the-art models now have about 30.

Dot-matrix printers typically can work at speeds between 100 and 200 characters per second. Usually, they work in near-letter-quality or draft-quality modes. They are also capable of producing bit-mapped graphics.

Ink-Jet Printers

Some **ink-jet printers** are used for color output, but black-and-white ink-jet printers are more widely found. With this type of printer, images are produced by spraying the paper with electrically charged ink through small apertures in a print head. Many current ink-jet printers hold several color cartridges simultaneously, enabling multicolor output to be produced. These printers can also be used in place of plotters (described later in the chapter) for producing overhead transparencies as output. Recently, ink-jet technology has become popular in small, portable printers that accompany portable microcomputers.

Thermal-Transfer Printers

Thermal-transfer printers create images by melting a wax-based ink off a ribbon onto the paper. These printers can be used to produce letter-quality text, color, and graphics. In speed, they rival dot-matrix printers and even some small laser printers. Unfortunately, they are relatively expensive. Both ribbons and the print head have to be replaced more often on thermal-transfer printers than on printers using other technologies.

Laser Printers

Laser printers work in a manner that is similar to photocopiers. Images are formed by charging hundreds of thousands of dots on a platen with a laser beam. Toner is then affixed to the platen and, when paper comes into contact with it, an image is formed from the toner that adheres to the charged dots. Laser printers are popular for all sizes of computer systems. On microcomputer systems, they are widely used for letter-quality output and for desktop publishing applications. On larger computer systems, they produce fast, high-quality output. More than any other printing technology, laser printers represent the wave of the future.

Most laser printers contain their own microprocessors and can process computer programs without using a microcomputer. This characteristic has produced printer languages such as *PostScript* and *Page Composition Language (PCL)*. An advantage of printer languages is printing flexibility—making multiple fonts, multiple print sizes, and outstanding graphics possible. Another advantage of printer languages is the ability to off-load the process of building the printed display from the microcomputer to the printer's microprocessor. This makes it possible for users to work on other tasks while the printer works independently.

Printing Technologies for Larger Systems

In large systems (where minicomputers and mainframes are found), a high volume of printed output may be needed. Several types of printers are commonly used for large output volumes. These include chain and band printers, line printers, and page printers.

- ■ *Chain and band printers*   Chain and band printers are impact printers that operate at relatively high speeds. They are most commonly found on mainframe and minicomputer systems. In a *chain printer*, a chain is formed of slugs that have fully formed characters embossed on them. The chain revolves at a high speed past the printing positions on the page. As characters pass in front of their correct page positions, hammers located at each position are activated to strike the character images onto the paper. *Band printers* work under a similar principle, except that the characters are located on a scalloped steel band instead of a chain.

- ■ *Line printers*   Line printers are the workhorses of mainframe and minicomputer systems. The most common types of line printers are band printers and chain printers (discussed previously). Line printers work mostly by impact printing methods and produce 300–3,000 lines per minute. Some observers speculate that line printers will be inched out of the market by low-cost laser printers.

■ **Page printers** Page printers exist for all sizes of computer systems. Many of these printers work by laser technology, as discussed earlier. Mainframe-level page printers can produce over 300 pages per minute, whereas many of those targeted to microcomputer systems produce about 6–15 pages per minute.

Special-Purpose Output Devices

Although display devices and printers are the most popular types of output devices, a large variety of other output devices are used for specialized purposes. Four that we will cover here are plotters, voice-output devices, film recorders, and computer output microfilm (COM).

Plotters

A **plotter** is a peripheral device that is primarily used to produce graphical output. Plotters can be classified in a variety of ways. One of the most important of these is by whether they work with drawing pens or by electrostatic means.

Pen plotters use drawing pens, sometimes in different colors, to draw graphical images—such as charts, drawings, and maps—on paper. Electrostatic plotters are relatively new. These plotters are faster than pen plotters, although the output quality produced by them is not usually as high. Electrostatic plotters work by imparting electrostatic charges, to which toner adheres, onto paper.

Plotters vary from hand-held models (costing hundreds of dollars) to models costing thousands of dollars that are larger than a king-sized bed. Plotters are generally used for engineering and scientific applications, as well as business presentation graphics.

Voice-Output

Anyone who dials the phone number of someone who moved probably encounters a **voice-output device**. To save operators from the tedium of repeating information, these devices use either prerecorded messages or messages that are extemporaneously packaged together from short, synthesized voice segments. Voice-output systems are especially appropriate for applications in which a request (input) to a system is made in machine-readable form and requires a predictable type of voice response.

In the previous example, when someone dials a phone number that was changed, a computer system on the phone network notes the digits that are dialed. Prerecorded voice segments of each of the ten digits are available to this system, as well as other prerecorded voice information. If the number dialed is no longer in service, the system retrieves its "no-longer-in-service" routine and packages that together with the voice clips corresponding to the number that was just dialed. On the other hand, if someone moved and left a forwarding number, the computer system looks up the new number and packages it together with a "the-number-you-dialed-has-been-changed" routine and the voice clips corresponding to the new number. When all the information segments are put together, it sounds almost as though a real voice is delivering the message. Many voice systems have a vocabulary of a few hundred words or phrases, but are limited in the way in which this vocabulary can be put together.

Voice-output technology is also frequently used to quote the price of securities over the phone and by banks and the airlines to provide automated information to their customers. Many universities allow students to register for classes by using touch-tone phones that hook into a voice system. Some grocery chains have voice-output devices that inform shoppers of what is being purchased as bar codes are read by the embedded laser scanner. Any type of application in which people can input requests in machine-readable form—and the responses to those requests are relatively limited—is a good candidate for voice-output technology.

Film Recorders

Film recorders are camera-like devices that place computer output onto such media as 35mm film, 4-by-5-inch transparencies, and overhead transparencies. Virtually any image that is capable of being captured on a display device can be captured by a film recorder. About 20 percent of all film slides are now computer-generated.

Once slides are prepared, they can be shown through a standard manual presentation or by using a presentation ("storyboard") package such as General Parametrics Corporation's Video Show system. Using Video Show, image files can be created on a microcomputer system—and stored on disk—using any of about 35 presentation graphics software packages. The Video Show system can access these image files, both producing the images for display on a large monitor and creating transition effects, such as dissolves, between images. The user can display the images at various speeds as well.

Computer Output Microfilm

Computer output microfilm (COM) is a way of placing computer output on microfilm media, typically either a microfilm reel or microfiche card. A 4-by-6-inch microfiche card can contain the equivalent of 270 printed pages. Putting images of documents on microfilm can result in tremendous savings in paper costs, storage space, mailing costs, and document handling. COM is particularly useful for organizations that must keep massive files of information that do not need to be updated. It is also useful for organizations that need to manipulate large amounts of data, but cannot afford fast methods of on-line storage.

The process of producing microfilm or microfiche output generally takes place off-line on a special COM unit. This device displays an image of each page on a screen and produces microfilmed photographs from these images. To read the microfilm or microfiche that COM units produce, users either manually select and mount the reels or cards onto appropriate reading devices or use an auxiliary retrieval system driven by a micro- or minicomputer that automatically locates and mounts the desired frames.

Some people speculate that COM will be gradually replaced by optical disk systems and image-processing systems. However, COM should continue to be a popular component in document management systems for quite awhile.

Summary

Hardware refers to the equipment in a CBIS. It is important for managers to have a working understanding of information technology because they must frequently make knowledgeable decisions about the computer hardware used in their work areas. The main types of CBIS hardware are the central processing unit (CPU)—and its support devices, including input, secondary storage, and output devices.

Generally, organizations deploy computer equipment in ways that help them achieve their strategic goals and make it easier for managers and users to do their jobs. Three types of hardware deployment approaches may be found in organizations. In the large-system computing approach, multiple users interact with powerful centralized computers through terminals. This was the most widely used approach before personal computers became common and is still found in most large organizations, especially those that need centralized transaction processing systems. In the personal computing approach, personal computers help individual users perform their jobs. This approach became popular during the early 1980s. However, in the personal computing approach, users cannot electronically share their work with others because the personal computers are not linked together to form a network. In network computing, multiple personal computers are connected in a manner that allows them to share data and computing resources. The data and resources may either be at the worksite or somewhere else. Network computing is rapidly becoming the most common type of organizational computing. Many organizations are moving applications that traditionally ran on large centralized computers to network platforms.

Of the many input devices available, the keyboard is the most common. The keyboard is almost always used with a display device (monitor). The mouse, which quickly moves the cursor around, is another widely used input device in personal computer systems. Trackballs provide very good cursor control capabilities. The light pen, which has a light-sensitive tip, is often used in graphics applications to draw on the screen. The touch screen is sensitive to human fingers; that is, the computer can sense where a finger is touching the screen. Pen-based computers, with advanced handwriting recognition capabilities, allow users to write on the display screen with a special stylus; these will grow in popularity during the 1990s. Imaging and digitizing devices—such as digitizing tablets, crosshair cursors, and image scanners—transform graphical images such as drawings and maps into machine-readable form. Imaging processing systems using optical storage media are increasingly used for document management.

Regarding input, one of the most pressing technical issues in MIS is source data automation; that is, capturing data electronically at the point where they are generated. With source data entry, business transactions can be recorded immediately and data made available quickly to the people who need them. Optical character recognition (OCR) refers to a variety of technologies that use special characters or codes that can be recognized by optical means. One of the most familiar OCR applications is a bar code called the Universal Product Code, which is imprinted on the packaging of supermarket goods and is read by scanners at supermarket check-out counters. The term "point-of-sale (POS)" often refers to situations in which OCR equipment records purchases. Bar codes are being used in an increasing variety of business applications. Magnetic ink character recognition (MICR) is a technology used by the banking industry to process checks. Voice-input devices refer to systems that recognize the human voice and make it possible to process spoken commands.

The CPU is made up of three primary components: the control unit, the arithmetic-logic unit (ALU), and primary memory. During the machine cycle, the control unit decodes program instructions and coordinates the execution of those instructions by the rest of the system. All mathematical and logical operations are performed by the ALU. Primary memory temporarily contains programs and data that have been input, intermediate results, and output that is ready to send to an output device. Primary memory is alternatively called main memory, internal memory, or random access memory (RAM). Primary memory is directly addressable by the computer. Closely associated with RAM is ROM (read-only memory), which contains software functions that can be read, but not written over.

Regarding size, computers are broadly divided into four groups: microcomputers, minicomputers, mainframes, and supercomputers. Microcomputers—commonly known as micros or personal computers (PC)—are generally the smallest and least expensive. Many different types of microcomputers exist, including desktop, laptop, notebook, palmtop, and pen-based. Most are designed for only one user, but some powerful desktop systems may be the primary processor in a multiuser system. Minicomputers, which are larger and more powerful than micros, are often aimed at small businesses. Mainframes are the most technologically mature type of computer and traditionally are the workhorses for transaction processing. They are generally more powerful, more expensive, and can support more users than minis. Supercomputers are the most powerful and most expensive type of computer, costing as much as $20 million. These computers are more likely to be used for scientific and engineering applications than for business applications.

Five standards of measurement for computer systems are bits, bytes, hertz, MIPS, and FLOPS. Bits and bytes relate to the size of storage or the width of a data path. On each computer system, each alphabetic character, digit, and special symbol is configured from two bits: 0 and 1. Each 8-bit configuration is called a byte. Approximately a thousand bytes is a kilobyte (KB or K-byte), about a million is called a megabyte (MB or M-byte), and approximately a billion is called a gigabyte (GB or G-byte). EBCDIC and ASCII are two binary-based codes used to represent data in byte form. Hertz, MIPS, and FLOPS are measures of speed. Hertz is commonly used to measure the speed of microcomputer systems, MIPS (millions of instructions per second) to compare mainframe and/or minicomputer speeds, and FLOPS (floating-point operations per second) to compare supercomputer speeds.

Two of the major emerging technologies for computer processors are reduced instruction set computing (RISC) and parallel processing. In contrast to the more common and more traditional complex instruction set computers (CISC), RISC-based computers use simplified instructions that can be performed in a single tick of the system's internal clock. These may also contain a smaller number of hardwired instructions than conventional CISC machines. While RISC-based machines are becoming popular as engineering workstations, the limited availability of software to run on these machines has inhibited widespread use. In parallel processing, programs are divided into segments and the different segments are processed simultaneously by different central processing units. Many experts feel that parallel processing is the wave of the future.

Both RISC-based machines and parallel processing can increase a computer system's speed and throughput. Other approaches used to make computers faster include packing more circuits on chips and using new substances and superconductors.

Secondary (external) storage saves programs and data for repeated use. Two methods of accessing programs or data in secondary storage are sequential access (records are retrieved one after the other in the same sequence in which they are physically stored) and direct or random access (records can be retrieved in any order, independent of the way they are stored). Magnetic tape is a secondary storage medium that allows only sequential access, whereas magnetic disk allows both types of access.

Many types of disk products currently exist, including magnetic disks—for example, Winchester disks and floppy diskettes—and optical disks. With Winchester disk systems, the access mechanism and read/write heads are hermetically sealed in a case, enabling the disks to rotate faster and the disk tracks to be placed closer together. Diskettes, which are made of a plastic that is coated with a magnetic material, are the most common type of disk found on microcomputer systems. Disk cartridge systems, such as Bernoulli systems, are also used in microcomputer systems. Optical disks, which work through laser technology, have enormous storage capacity, but are slower than magnetic disks. Video disks are a type of optical disk that can store text, video, and audio data. They are widely used for training applications and are helpful in an increasing variety of other business applications. Tape cartridges, which resemble cassette tapes, are often used to back up the contents of the hard disks found in microcomputers.

Some of the popular storage technologies found in larger systems include removable disk packs, detachable-reel magnetic tapes, and cartridge tapes. Removable-pack hard disks consist of rigid disks that are tiered and packaged into a removable disk pack. Redundant arrays of inexpensive disks (RAID) are one of the newest disk-oriented technologies, used in both larger systems and networks. Cartridge tapes have large storage capacities, are easier to handle than the detachable-reel tapes, and represent the leading edge of tape technology.

Output devices that consist of a television-like viewing screen to which computer output is sent are called display devices. Two common types of display devices are monitors (usually found with microcomputers) and communications terminals (workstations connected to large, remote computers). Display devices are distinguished by screen resolution, text and/or graphics modes, monochrome or color, and CRT or flat-panel displays. Displays that produce graphics output commonly use a method called bit mapping. Bit-mapped devices allow each pixel on the screen to be controlled by the operator. Character-addressable devices, on the other hand, partition the screen into standard character widths. Most display devices are cathode ray tube (CRT) devices, which use a tube-type element similar to a television tube. Flat-panel displays commonly use either liquid crystal displays (LCD) or gas-plasma displays to form images; these are common in portable microcomputer systems.

Printers are important because they supply output in a portable form. Printers can be differentiated by (1) quality of output and (2) speed. Solid-font printers produce very-high-quality text output; two common types are daisywheel and print-thimble printers. Impact dot-matrix printers form dot-matrix characters on paper by striking it through inked ribbon. They are generally faster than solid-font printers, but do not have a high output quality. Ink-jet printers, which are popular for color output, produce images by spraying electrically charged ink through small openings in a print head. Thermal-transfer printers create images by melting wax-based ink from a ribbon onto paper. Laser printers work by charging dots on a platen with a laser beam. Toner is affixed to the platen and images are formed from the toner that adheres to the charged dots. More than any other type of printer, laser printers represent the wave of the future.

Chain printers and band printers are relatively fast impact printers that are most commonly found on mainframes and minicomputers. High-speed laser printers are used more commonly in conjunction with mainframes and midrange systems. Detachable-reel tape systems are also widely used in larger systems.

Other output devices include plotters, voice-output devices, film recorders, and computer output microfilm (COM). Plotters are designed to produce graphical output. Voice-output devices provide synthesized voice segments as output. Film recorders are camera-like devices that place computer output onto such film media as 35mm film and overhead transparencies. COM can put images of documents and photographs on microfilm; it is widely used by organizations that otherwise would have to store large volumes of paper documents.

KEY TERMS

Add-in boards

Arithmetic-logic unit (ALU)

Bit

Bus

Byte

Cathode ray tube (CRT)

CD-ROM (compact disk read-only memory)

Complex instruction set computing (CISC)

Computer output microfilm (COM)

Control unit

Crosshair cursor

Cursor

Digitizing tablet

Direct access storage device (DASD)

Disk pack

Diskette (floppy disk)

Display device

Dot-matrix printer

Dumb terminals

Execution cycles

Flat-panel display

Floating-point operations per second (FLOPS)

Hand-held scanner

Hard disk

Icon

Image scanner

Ink-jet printer

Instruction cycle (I-cycle)

Intelligent character recognition (ICR)

Intelligent terminals

Joystick

Laser printer

Light pen

Local area network (LAN)

Machine cycle

Magnetic disk

Magnetic ink character recognition (MICR)

Magnetic tape

Mainframe

Microcomputer system

Microprocessor

Millions of instructions per second (MIPS)

Minicomputer

Mouse

Optical character recognition (OCR)

Optical disk

Parallel processing

Pen-based computer

Plotter

Point-of-sale (POS)

Portable computer system

Random access memory (RAM)

Read-only memory (ROM)

Reduced instruction set computing (RISC)

Redundant arrays of inexpensive disks (RAID)

Registers

Source data automation

Supercomputer

System clock

Terminal

Thermal-transfer printer

Touch screen

Trackball

Video disk

Voice-input devices

Voice-output devices

Wand scanner (light wand)

Winchester disk

WORM (write once, read many)

REVIEW QUESTIONS

1. What are the characteristics of each of the organizational approaches to computing? What are the advantages and disadvantages of each?

2. Describe the characteristics of the various types of input devices likely to be used in personal computer systems.

3. What is source data automation? What are the characteristics and advantages of the various source data automation approaches commonly used in organizations?

4. What are the functions of each of the components of a CPU? How do these components interact during the machine cycle?

5. How do microcomputers differ from minicomputers and mainframes? What are the different types of microcomputers? How do these differ? How are supercomputers used?

6. What is reduced instruction set computing (RISC)? What is parallel processing? Why are these important?

7. What are some of the ways in which to speed up computers?

8. How do diskettes differ? For what purposes would a microcomputer user need a hard disk?

9. What advantages and disadvantages do optical disks have relative to magnetic disks? How are video disks being used by businesses?

10. What are the benefits and drawbacks of tape-storage devices?

11. How does bit mapping differ from character mapping? In what other ways do display devices differ?

12. How do laser printers work differently from other types of printers used in microcomputer systems? Why have laser printers become so popular?

13. What are the characteristics and uses of plotters, film recorders, voice-output systems, and computer output microfilm?

14. What are the differences between image-processing technology and pen-based computers? Why are these becoming more popular?

DISCUSSION QUESTIONS

1. Suppose your manager tells you, "We want people to focus on using technology for their jobs rather than knowing how to use technology." Comment on the advantages and disadvantages to this approach. Also, what contingencies, with respect to either the organization or its external environment, might make this approach more or less attractive?

2. What do you suppose is the greatest advantage to source data automation: lower data-entry costs, fewer errors, or faster information to those who need it? Describe the reasoning behind your answer.

3. Many organizations quickly gain competitive advantage by acquiring new, pioneering technology systems—and then their competition buys the same system and the advantage is lost. How can competitive advantage through new technology systems be sustained?

CASE STUDY

Will the Banks Meet the MIS Challenge?

"**F**or thirty years, bankers lived by the 3-4-3 rule," claims consultant David Gilbert. "Borrow at 3 percent, loan at 4 percent, and go home at 3 o'clock." In today's global-oriented, consumer-conscious, computer-and-communications-driven, deregulated business environment, however, the whole concept of banking is being redefined. As the traditionally conservative banking community awakens to the competitive realities imposed by the new environment, MIS moves further into the forefront as the tool that the banking community needs to strategically position its members.

Many of the top banks—for example, CitiBank, Nations Bank, and Mellon—have responded to the call for change by investing heavily in state-of-the-art banking systems. But many industry observers feel that most banks are still in the technological Dark Ages and are not prepared to deal with today's marketplace. Some of the other major concerns expressed by industry observers include:

- Many banks are disproportionately invested in back-end technologies such as automated check processing and accounting systems. While necessary, these cost-minimizing transaction processing systems are unable to perform the front-end, customer-oriented, analysis tasks necessary to gain competitive advantage.

- Deregulation has removed most of the barriers to regional and interstate banking, and has also altered the invesment

alternatives open to banks; these changes favor entirely new banking systems. For instance, deregulation is moving many banks to build distributed systems and networks that provide better support for branch banking. Deregulation and the increasingly large investment needed in computer and communications technology has also led to consolidation. Larger banks are growing even bigger, often by acquiring and swallowing up their smaller competitors.

- Global banking, financial services companies, and national financial databases are encroaching on markets once taken for granted by most U.S. banks. Local banks that once bragged about having the best rate in town for a certificate of deposit (C.D.) now have to contend either with larger banks in larger cities or such large, national investment houses as Fidelity Investments and Value Line. Furthermore, commercial accounts are increasingly being courted by foreign banks, many of which are trying to gain competitive advantage in the United States by setting up global telecommunication links that make investing as painless as possible.

- Despite widespread predictions of "the checkless society"—where most banking transactions are made electronically by consumers with debit or smart cards from terminals in retail stores and from home computers—we are still very far away from that realization.

While electronic funds transfer (EFT) increases each year, banking in the 1990s will probably remain primarily check-based. However, check-processing systems are likely to change. Many banks are migrating toward imaging systems that scan customer checks into an image database as they are processed. Rather than receiving bulky envelopes containing canceled checks, an increasing number of bank customers are receiving a page or two of reduced check images with their bank statements.

- In the new banking environment, computers themselves can be effective selling devices. A bank officer who uses a desktop computer or a laptop to instantly demonstrate to a customer how much money an IRA or Keogh account strategy will produce in 20 years is going a long way toward selling that customer on both the product and the bank. To maintain their sophisticated corporate customers, banks will increasingly need quick-thinking, computer-literate, marketing-oriented managers to survive the next decade.

Adapted from Brown (1989), Arend (1992), O'Heney (1991), Nash (1992), Wilder and Ambrosio (1991).

DISCUSSION

1. In what ways does information technology impact the banking industry? Describe at least three ways in which it contributes to increased operating efficiency and improved customer service.

2. In addition to check processing, what are some other ways in which banks are likely to use imaging systems?

3. Why do you think that EFT has not had a greater impact on banking?

4. If you were in charge, how would you use information technology to make your bank globally competitive?

Chapter 6

Software Fundamentals

After completing this chapter, you will be able to:

Describe the differences between systems software and application software

Appreciate the variety of tasks performed by operating systems and systems software

Identify the major operating systems used on both microcomputers and larger systems

Identify several important types of systems software

Describe the general uses of the major types of application software packages used on microcomputers

Describe the significance of each generation of programming languages

Explain the properties and uses of several high-level languages found in MIS environments

Appreciate the diversity and uses of fourth-generation languages

Chapter 5 introduced you to various types of hardware associated with computer-based information systems (CBIS): the computer, primary memory, secondary storage, and input and output devices. Here, we will consider another major component of a CBIS: software.

Software often includes both computer programs and their accompanying *documentation*—that is, the complete set of instructions that enables people involved with the CBIS to use the computer system to perform work. In this chapter, we will mostly be concerned with types of computer programs. We will discuss the importance of program documentation more completely in Chapter 14.

All programs on a computer system can be broken down into two main categories: application software and systems software. Application software includes user-oriented programs written in programming languages. Application software includes the programs, software packages, and tools needed for such specific, end-user-oriented tasks as billing, accounts receivable, word processing, payroll, database management, and executive support.

As seen in Figure 6.1, two main categories of application software exist. *General-purpose application software* includes programs and packages that may be used by workers in most organizational subunits—such as word processing, spreadsheets, database or file management, and presentation graphics. These are more likely to be purchased externally than developed internally by the organization. *Special-purpose application software* includes programs and packages that support the activities of workers in a particular subunit. Accounting, payroll, inventory management, and production scheduling are usually classified as special-purpose application software because they are used by a more limited number of users or subunits than are general-purpose applications. Although a growing number of commercially available packages and systems (hardware/software combinations) can be purchased to support these activities, many organizations still employ application programmers to write and maintain the special-purpose application software that they need; increasingly, application programmers are also used to customize commercially available special-purpose software for their employers.

Systems software consists of "background" programs that enable application software to run smoothly on a specific set of hardware. Different categories of systems software are displayed in Figure 6.1. Since managers need a working knowledge of operating systems, language translators, and utility programs, we will discuss these more fully than the other types of systems software shown.

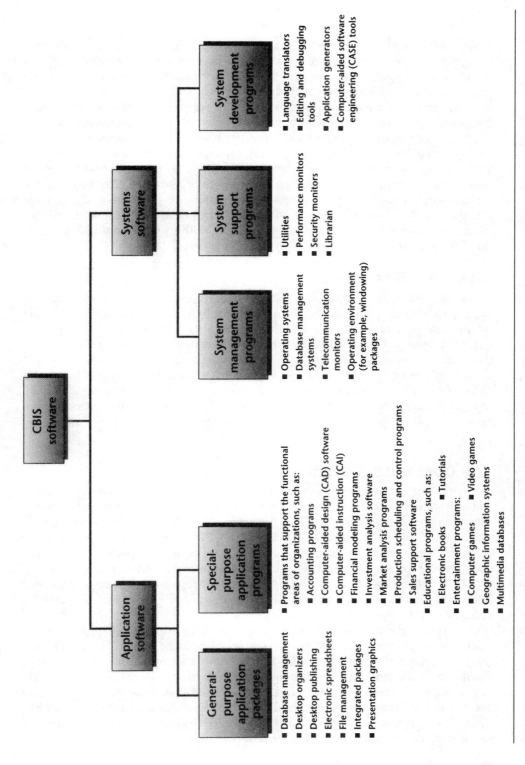

Figure 6.1 Types of software found in a CBIS. Application software includes both the general- and special-purpose programs that users need to do their jobs. Systems software includes the management, support, and development programs that make it possible to run application programs on CBIS hardware.

As mentioned in Chapter 2, systems software is written and maintained by *systems programmers;* systems programmers often have a computer science or electrical engineering background. Companies that develop operating systems—such as Microsoft—or that manufacture and distribute multiuser systems for minicomputers, mainframes, and networks may employ many systems programmers; smaller organizations may employ none. In most organizations, application programmers substantially outnumber systems programmers.

Now that we've covered the basics of application and systems software, we will discuss the first software that a user is likely to encounter when sitting down at a microcomputer or terminal—the operating system. After this, we will look at some other types of systems software, including utilities and language translators. Next, we will turn to the major types of application software that businesses use. Finally, we will discuss some of the programming languages that both systems and application programmers use.

SYSTEMS SOFTWARE

To many people, any mention of software means application software, such as word processing, spreadsheets, and payroll programs. But application software is only one part of the software story. Forming the interface between application programs and the hardware of the CBIS is systems software, which enables the CBIS to run in an efficient manner, smoothing over any rough spots that users might encounter. Many types of systems software exist and it is beyond the scope of this text to provide a comprehensive, in-depth discussion. Instead, we will focus on the types of systems software that managers and users will encounter most frequently: operating systems, language translators, and utility programs.

The Operating System

An operating system is the main collection of programs that manage a computer system's operations. The primary function of the operating system is the management and control of CBIS resources. This involves the allocation of hardware, programs, and data resources to CBIS users in the wisest manner possible. Some activities included in this role are providing pathways for users to access the hardware, software, and data authorized for them to use; ensuring that CBIS resources are not unwittingly wasted through poor management; and allowing users to declare any special processing needs as they interact with the computer to do their work.

Operating systems come in many varieties. Like application software, each operating system is designed to meet a specific set of needs. For instance, a large computer at a university will typically need an operating system that is flexible because students, faculty, and administration collectively have a wide range of processing needs; in fact, several operating systems may be available for use on a university's main computer. The airlines industry typically requires operating systems that provide both fast response and real-time control of tasks. In addition, some operating systems can accommodate only a single user at a time, while other operating systems can accommodate many users at the same time.

Components of the Operating System

Although what manufacturers call an operating system differs widely, most operating systems have many similar elements. These generally include a supervisor, a command-language translator, an input/output control system (IOCS), and a librarian.

At the heart of every operating system is a program called the *supervisor*. The overall coordination and management of the operating system is performed by this program. Located in primary memory when the computer system is on, the supervisor initiates the call to other parts of the operating system for resources and places any programs that are retrieved during this process into main memory.

The *command-language translator* transforms the needs of users into actions that the operating system takes. Like other software packages, the operating system has its own language—called a *command language*—with which users and programmers issue commands. In many mainframe environments—especially IBM—the command language is known as a *job-control language (JCL)*. Some typical commands include: getting a listing of files, formatting disks, copying programs, and erasing files. It is the command-language translator that converts such commands into the machine language of the computer.

The *input/output control system (IOCS)* interacts with input and output hardware devices. Thus, if the supervisor determines that a program should be retrieved from disk for a user, it hands the task over to the IOCS.

The *librarian* is the software element that catalogs and manages data, programs, file space, and users. Managers and users are most likely to encounter librarian software in multiuser systems in which users share computer resources. For instance, when users log on to a computer system with an identification number, the task of determining if access should be authorized is performed by the librarian.

Microcomputer Operating Systems

The most important type of systems software for microcomputers is the operating system. For users, the operating system is the gateway to application programs, data, and other CBIS resources. A variety of popular operating systems are available for today's microcomputers (see Figure 6.2). The following are basic characteristics of some of the most popular microcomputer operating systems.

MS-DOS

The most widely used microcomputer operating system (OS) is *MS-DOS* (for *MicroSoft-Disk Operating System*). This OS is a licensed product of Microsoft, Inc. and about 70 percent of today's microcomputers use it. In 1992, more than 75 million microcomputers worldwide used MS-DOS.

OPERATING SYSTEMS FOR MICROCOMPUTERS

Operating System	Description
Macintosh system software	Icon-oriented operating system used on Apple Macintosh microcomputers
MS-DOS	The most widely used operating system on IBM-compatible microcomputers
NetWare	The most widely used operating system on local area networks (LAN) composed of microcomputers
OS/2	An operating system designed for use on higher-end IBM and IBM-compatible microcomputers
PenPoint	An operating system designed for use on pen-based computers
PC-DOS	The operating systems used most widely on IBM microcomputers
UNIX	A multiuser, multitasking operating system used on small computers—popular on RISC-based microcomputers
Windows	A multitasking operating environment with a graphical user interface used on IBM and IBM-compatible microcomputers

Figure 6.2 Some of the popular operating systems for microcomputers.

MS-DOS and *PC-DOS* are essentially the same operating system. PC-DOS was initially developed by Microsoft for the IBM PC, while MS-DOS was devised for use on IBM-compatible microcomputers—systems that look and work like the IBM PC. Except for some minor differences, MS-DOS and PC-DOS are virtually identical.

Both MS-DOS and PC-DOS have been revised several times since they were first released. Each major revision is referred to as a *version* (sometimes called a *release*). The current version of MS-DOS is MS-DOS 5.0. The term "version" is also used in reference to revisions of application software packages (such as updating from WordPerfect 5.0 to WordPerfect 5.1).

Macintosh System 7

In 1984, Apple Computer, Inc. released one of the first microcomputer operating systems with a graphical user interface (GUI). This was designed for use with Apple's Macintosh family of microcomputers, each of which included a mouse. The mouse and Macintosh's operating system made it possible for users to manipulate programs and files by using on-screen graphical symbols called icons. For example, to delete a file, the user could first move the mouse and point to the icon representing the file. Then, by holding down a button on the mouse, the user could drag the file's icon to a trash can icon for disposal.

The Macintosh's GUI continues to provide users with a rich and interesting visual environment; this makes the Mac an exceptionally user-friendly machine. Like MS-DOS, Macintosh's operating system was revised on numerous occasions; the current version is 7. Several other microcomputer operating systems popular during the early 1990s followed Apple's lead by providing GUI environments, plus mouse-based point-and-click user interfaces. However, Apple should receive credit for popularizing graphical user interfaces.

OS/2

In 1987, when IBM unveiled its new PS/2 family of microcomputers, it also announced a new OS that had been co-developed with Microsoft. *OS/2* (for *Operating System/2*) was intended to be a successor to MS-DOS and was designed to take advantage of Intel's 80286 (and later) microprocessors. It allowed users to run several application programs simultaneously. For example, a user could sort a database table at the same time that he or she printed out a word-processing document and updated a spreadsheet. We will describe how this is possible in a later section on interleaving techniques.

OS/2 also was the first operating system for IBM and IBM-compatible microcomputers that provided users with a graphical user interface: Presentation Manager.

OS/2 Version 1.0 never really caught on, in spite of its GUI and advanced features. In terms of bytes, it was a large OS that required substantial disk and memory space. Many users felt it was cumbersome to install and use—and, when released, there were few general-purpose application packages (such as word processing, database, and spreadsheets) available for it. The lukewarm public reaction it received discouraged software vendors from developing OS/2 versions of their products.

The release of Windows 3.0 (discussed next) was another reason why OS/2 1.0 was never a commercial success. Like OS/2, Windows 3.0 provided users with a GUI, but was designed to work with, not replace, MS-DOS. This meant that the massive set of application software packages that were designed to run under MS-DOS could still be run under Windows.

In 1992, IBM and Microsoft released OS/2 Version 2.0. The initial advertising claimed that it would provide "better DOS than DOS and better windows than Windows." The market reaction to OS/2 2.0 is more positive than it was to OS/2 1.0 and more software vendors will release OS/2 2.0 versions of their products.

Windows

Perhaps the most significant recent development in microcomputer operating systems was the release of *Windows Version 3.0* by Microsoft. Windows made the mouse standard equipment on IBM and IBM-compatible microcomputers. Like OS/2, it provides users with a GUI (called Program Manager) and the ability to run two or more application programs simultaneously. Unlike OS/2, Windows runs "on top" of MS-DOS, which means that MS-DOS applications can be run before, after, and even within a Windows session. As noted previously, this also means that the massive set of commercially available application programs designed for MS-DOS can still be run under Windows. However, users and organizations that switched to Windows didn't have long to wait for Windows versions of most of their favorite application packages. Virtually all the major software vendors released Windows versions of their products soon after Windows 3.0 hit the market—and most still see a Windows version of their packages as having a higher priority than an OS/2 2.0 version.

In 1992, Microsoft released *Windows Version 3.1*, which works in conjunction with MS-DOS 5.0 (and higher). In the first month after its release, it set all-time sales records for new software packages. Software vendors rushed to release new versions of their products, which also produced some big commercial and critical successes.

Also in 1992, Microsoft announced its intention to release *Windows NT* (for *New Technology*), which will operate in conjunction with future versions of MS-DOS, OS/2, and UNIX (discussed next). Windows NT is designed to take advantage of RISC-based processors, as well as machines built around Intel's more advanced CISC-based processors, such as the 80386 and 80486. (The differences between RISC-based and CISC-based machines were discussed in Chapter 5.) Because Windows NT will run on both types of machines, as well as in conjunction with several other operating systems, software developers may only have to develop one version of their product (instead of multiple versions as they do now). This should be a boon for RISC-based processor sales, which lagged during the early 1990s due to a lack of available general-purpose software.

UNIX

UNIX is another operating system used in some microcomputing environments. It was initially developed by AT&T at Bell Labs during the 1970s and is really a family of operating systems that runs on a variety of different types and sizes of computers. Its flexible design makes this possible. Unlike MS-DOS and OS/2 (used on machines with Intel chips or their clones) or Macintosh System 7 (based on Motorola chips), UNIX is not built to be run on a single family of processors. Computers from micros to mainframes can run UNIX, and UNIX can interconnect devices manufactured by different vendors to form networks. This flexibility gives UNIX a big advantage over competing operating systems for some applications.

UNIX is more popular among scientific and engineering users than among business users. It has developed a large and loyal following with these types of users. UNIX is often used on RISC-based workstations, especially those that are part of multiuser systems.

In spite of its popularity with technical users, many business users feel that UNIX has a relatively complicated and unfriendly user interface. Recently, graphical user interfaces for UNIX, such as Open-View and X-Windows, have become popular. These may enhance UNIX's acceptance by a larger segment of business users.

Operating Systems for Pen-Based Computers

In Chapter 5, we discussed a hot new microcomputer product—pen-based computers. These systems, which convert a user's handwriting to text and data, need operating systems to run application programs and to bring out their full business potential. Two early leaders in operating systems for pen-based systems are Microsoft's Windows for Pen Computing and PenPoint from Go Corporation. Grid Systems, one of the first companies to release a pen-based computer, ships PenRight and PenDOS with its systems. PenPoint and Windows for Pen Computing require at least an Intel 80386-based pen machine to run efficiently; in the early 1990s, these were relatively rare. However, some indications suggest that Windows for Pen Computing and PenPoint will emerge as the standard operating systems for pen-based machines, largely because software vendors plan to release more applications that run under them than on any others.

Trends in Microcomputer Operating Systems

The most important trends in microcomputer operating systems are to provide users with windowing capabilities and graphical user interfaces (GUI).

- **Windowing capabilities** Software with *windowing capabilities* allows users to create one or more windows on the screen of the display device. Windowing capabilities are probably most useful for multitasking environments where, for example, a user can work on two programs or spreadsheets concurrently (one shown in the main part of the display and the other shown in the window). Windowing capabilities are commonly found in non-multitasking environments as well. For instance, users can buy utilities that allow a clock, calculator, memo, or appointment calendar to appear in an on-screen window.

  Many windowing packages are shells that fit over an operating system. Sometimes the term "operating environment" is used to describe packages in which windowing is an essential, integrated ingredient of the systems environment. Macintosh System 7, Microsoft Windows, OS/2, and Open-View for UNIX are some operating systems that provide users with windowing capabilities. Most industry observers feel that such windowing interfaces are now a standard feature in operating systems.

- **Graphical user interfaces (GUI)** Since learning, remembering, and using many different keyboard commands can be intimidating to users, many operating systems vendors developed operating environments that provide an easier-to-use **graphical user interface (GUI)**. Several examples are depicted in Figure 6.3. A GUI typically uses dialogue boxes, drop-down menus, icons, scroll bars, and pointers instead of commands to interface with the operating system. Most are mouse-based point-and-click systems for activating programs, data files, and other features.

- **Common user access (CUA)** To make it easier for users working with operating systems that provide windowing capabilities and a graphical user interface, IBM promotes the concept of a common user access (CUA) among software vendors. CUA helps users quickly learn the mechanics of software packages that run on windowing and GUI operating systems. For example, in Windows 3.1, the File menu always appears in the upper lefthand corner of the screen, the Help menu is the last menu option on the right, and other

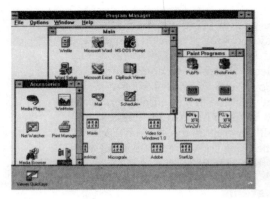

(a) Windows 3.1

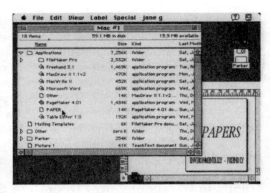

(b) Macintosh System 7

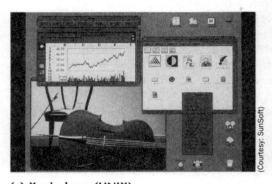

(c) X windows (UNIX)

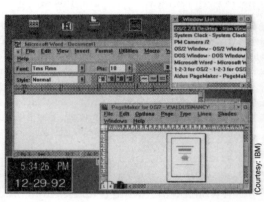

(d) OS/2 2.0

Figure 6.3 Examples of operating systems with graphical user interfaces (GUI).

options appear between the File and Help menus. Software vendors who conform to CUA provide users with the same visual environment in the Windows versions of their products: File on the left, Help on the right, and other options in the middle (see Figure 6.4 for an example). Because of this commonality, users always know where to go for file options (such as opening and saving) and for help, no matter what package they are using. This makes it easier for them to concentrate on the middle options when learning a new package. Most users—both new and sophisticated—agree that this is a desirable feature.

Network Operating Systems

As noted in Chapter 5, connecting microcomputers to one another to form local area networks (LAN) became popular during the late 1980s and local area net-

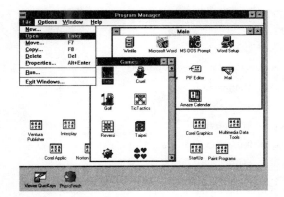

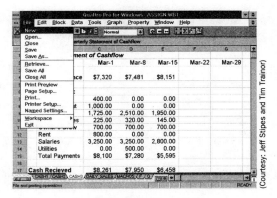

(a) Windows screen

(b) Screen from Quattro Pro 4.0 for Windows

(Courtesy: Jeff Stipes and Tim Trainor)

Figure 6.4 An example of common user access (CUA). Note how the menu bars in both the operating system and application package start with "File" and end with "Help."

works are increasingly prevalent in the 1990s. This makes it necessary for managers and users to be familiar with network operating systems, in addition to the other microcomputer operating systems discussed previously.

NetWare—a network operating system developed by Novell, Inc.—is the most widely used operating system found in microcomputer-based networks. Like other network operating systems, users interact with NetWare when they are logging on to the network or when they are dealing with a printer or hard disk that is not part of their microcomputer. Because NetWare runs on top of their microcomputer operating system (such as MS-DOS), users can retrieve or save files on a shared hard disk and can print files on a shared printer. Other network operating systems also make it possible to share computing resources.

Operating Systems for Larger Systems

As you might expect, operating systems for midrange and mainframe systems are often more complex than those for microcomputers. Some of the more popular operating systems for large systems are described in Figure 6.5. MVS is the most common operating system used on IBM mainframes. OS/400, an operating system for the IBM AS/400 line of midrange computers, is used at most of the sites where the AS/400 is installed (over 47,000 in 1992). VMS is the operating system used most frequently on DEC midrange and mainframe systems.

Interleaving Techniques

As indicated in Chapter 5, large centralized systems often support multiple simultaneous users. The users' terminals may have limited processing capabili-

LARGE-SYSTEM OPERATING SYSTEMS

AIX	IBM's proprietary version of UNIX
AOS, DG	Operating systems used on Data General minicomputers
COS, UNICOS	Operating systems used on Cray supercomputers
MCP/AS, OS/1100	Operating systems used on Unisys mainframes
MVS, VM	Operating systems used on IBM mainframes
OS/400	The operating system used most commonly on the IBM AS/400 line of midrange computers
PICK	A highly portable multiuser, multitasking operating system used on minicomputers and some microcomputers.
UNIX	A family of portable multiuser, multitasking operating systems used on minicomputers, microcomputers, and some mainframes
VMS	An operating system available for DEC's VAX series of minicomputers

Figure 6.5 Some common operating systems for larger computing platforms.

ties and actual processing may be done entirely on the large computer that is connected to the terminals. Hence, this computing configuration requires an operating system that enables many users to concurrently share the central processor. To do this, the operating systems on large computer systems often combine (interleave) the processing work of multiple simultaneous users or applications in a manner that achieves the highest possible resource efficiency. Among the interleaving techniques commonly used are multiprogramming, multitasking, time-sharing, foreground/background processing, virtual memory, and multiprocessing.

■ *Multiprogramming* Multiprogramming is often used in multiuser operating systems. **Multiprogramming** is a process in which the computer works on two or more programs concurrently, or side by side. Since a single computer can do only a single operation at one time, it will work on one program for awhile, then start processing another program, and then possibly go to a third program, and so on. For instance, the computer might be doing some computations on the first of several programs when it encounters a READ statement. While it is waiting for data to be retrieved from memory, it can begin working on a second program. When it encounters an input or output operation in the second program that might cause it to interrupt processing, it goes back to the first program or even on to another program. Thus, with multiprogramming, the operating system keeps the CPU busy working on two or more programs simultaneously. Multiprogramming is often used as an umbrella term that includes multitasking, time-sharing, and foreground/background processing.

Hi, I'm Victor; I'm Here to Help You

When traffic law violators walk up to the two royal blue kiosks stationed outside the Long Beach, California Municipal Court House, they are greeted by Victor, a computer-simulated human face on a computer screen. Victor helps the city process traffic and parking ticket citations. For fines, Victor accepts credit cards, bank debit cards, and personal checks. For drivers who want to challenge their tickets, Victor helps schedule court appearances.

"VICTOR IS PROGRAMMED TO ANSWER THE QUESTIONS THAT DRIVERS ARE LIKELY TO ASK ABOUT THEIR TRAFFIC TICKETS."

Victor was created to help Los Angeles County streamline how it processes traffic tickets. The county issued more than 125,000 traffic and parking tickets each year and needed a system to make the traffic court more efficient.

Victor is programmed to answer the questions that drivers are likely to ask about their traffic tickets. Victor helps users to access the county's traffic and parking violation database, which holds information from each of the county's 24 municipal courts. Victor can even explain how the fine amount was set.

Victor also provides assistance to other court systems in L.A. County. Victor is used to explain the rationale behind bail amounts, and to tutor people on the ins and outs of small-claims court. Soon, Victor may be selling birth certificates and marriage licenses; not long after that, Victor should be helping users file small-claims suits at his kiosks.

Adapted from Nash (1992).

- *Multitasking* **Multitasking** refers to the operating system's ability to execute two or more of a single user's tasks concurrently. *Multitasking operating systems* are often contrasted with *single-user operating systems.* Single-user operating systems have traditionally been the most common type of operating system for microcomputers. These only allow the user to work on one task at a time. For example, with many single-user operating systems for microcomputer systems, a word-processing user cannot effectively type in a document while another document is being printed out on an attached printer. For microcomputers, multitasking operating systems provide single users with multiprogramming capabilities. This is often accomplished through foreground/background processing (discussed later). Multitasking operating systems for microcomputers—such as Windows, OS/2, UNIX, Xenix, and Macintosh System 7—only run on the more powerful microprocessors that were developed; older machines with less powerful microprocessors typically have single-user operating systems.

- *Time-sharing* **Time-sharing** is a very popular technique that allows a CPU to simultaneously support the activities of several terminal users. Time-sharing allocates small, fixed time slots to terminal users as their jobs are being processed. For instance, the computer might allocate 100 milliseconds to user 1, then 100 milliseconds to user 2, and then 100 milliseconds to user 3, and so on. If 100 users are on the system, it will allocate 100 milliseconds to each one before it returns to the top of the job queue and then gives each user another 100 milliseconds. The computer moves so rapidly from one user's work to another that each user feels as though he or she has exclusive use of the computer system. Because this approach involves the systematic allocation of time slots to system users, it is also commonly known as *time-slicing*.

- *Foreground/background processing* Usually, it is possible to partition main memory into logically separate areas. This enables, for instance, two different operating systems to work on the same machine because each will have its own memory to manage in its own way. Partitioning also allows separate "job streams" to be set up. A common procedure is to set up a partition for high-priority tasks (called a foreground partition) and one for low-priority tasks (called a background partition). With **foreground/background processing**, foreground jobs are usually handled first. When no foreground task awaits processing, the computer goes to the background partition and starts processing tasks there. As other foreground tasks come into the job queue, the computer leaves the background partition and resumes working in the foreground.

- *Virtual memory* **Virtual memory** systems, sometimes called *virtual storage* systems, extend primary memory by treating disk storage as a logical extension of RAM. The technique works by dividing a program on disk into fixed-length pages or into logical, variable-length segments.

  Virtual memory is typically implemented as follows. Programs stored on disk are broken up into fixed-length pages. When a program needs to be processed, the first few pages of it are brought into primary memory. Then, the computer system starts processing the program. If the computer needs a page it does not have, it brings that page in from secondary storage and overwrites it onto the memory locations occupied by a page it no longer needs. Processing continues in this manner until the program finishes.

  By allowing programs to be broken up into smaller parts, and by allowing only certain parts to be in main memory at any one time, virtual memory enables computers to get by with less main memory than usual. Of course, during page swapping in multiprogramming environments, the system may switch to other programs and tasks.

  Virtual memory is tricky because writing software that determines which pages or segments are to be swapped in and out of real storage is a systems programming art. A disadvantage of virtual memory systems is that time is lost when page swapping occurs. In some cases, the same pages will be brought in and out of primary memory an unusually large number of times, which is an undesirable condition known as *thrashing*. Machines that do not offer a virtual memory feature usually compensate for this by having larger primary memories.

■ **_Multiprocessing_** As noted in previous chapters, multiprocessing (or parallel processing) refers to the use of two or more central processing units, linked together, to perform coordinated work simultaneously. The difference between multiprogramming and multiprocessing is that multiprogramming involves processing several programs concurrently on a single CPU, whereas multiprocessing means handling several parts of the same program simultaneously on several central processing units.

Although parallel processing is not widespread yet, multiprocessing should be the wave of the future. Because of the availability of cheaper but more powerful processors, many computer manufacturers are now designing hardware and software systems to do multiprocessing. Since several machines can work as a team and operate in parallel, jobs can be processed much more rapidly than on a single machine. The parallel processing architectures discussed in today's computer literature involve anywhere from a few supercomputers working in parallel to tens of thousands of microprocessors.

Other Important Types of Systems Software

While operating systems are by far the most important type of systems software that managers and users should understand, they should also understand two other types of systems software: language translators and utility programs.

Language Translators

Whether a person is running a special-purpose application program written in a programming language (such as COBOL or BASIC) or using a general-purpose application program (such as Lotus 1-2-3), all instructions and data must be translated into machine language—strings of 0s and 1s—before any processing can occur. The software products that do this are collectively called **language translators**. Some software products come with built-in language translators; in other cases, the translator comes as a separate package. In any event, without a translator, no processing can occur. The three most widely used types of language translators are compilers, interpreters, and assemblers.

■ **_Compilers_** A **compiler** translates an entire program into machine language before the program is executed. Compilers are most commonly used to translate high-level languages such as COBOL, FORTRAN, and Pascal. As explained shortly, compilers typically result in programs that can be executed much more swiftly than those handled by interpreters. Since either a

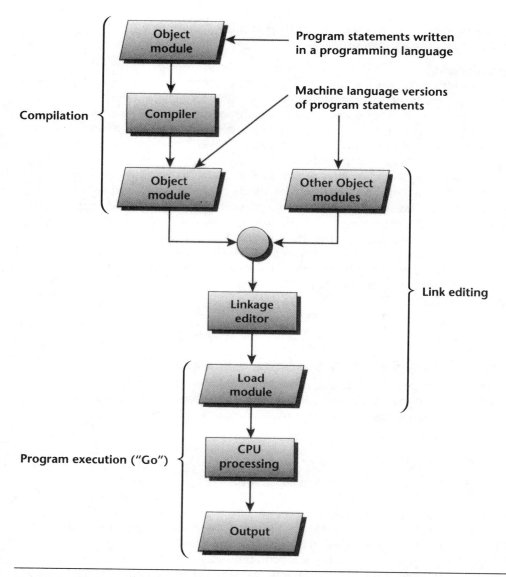

Figure 6.6 The program translation process. In order for application programs to be executed on a computer, their program statements must be translated (by language translation software) into machine language. This figure illustrates the process used to translate programs written in higher-level languages into machine language.

compiler or an interpreter can be developed to translate most languages, compilers would be preferred in environments where execution speed is important.

Compilers work in the manner illustrated in Figure 6.6. A program is entered into the computer system and submitted to the appropriate compiler. For instance, a COBOL program is input to a COBOL compiler; a Pascal program, to a Pascal compiler. The program submitted for compilation is called a *source program* (or source module). The compiler then translates the program into machine language, producing an *object program* (or object module). Then, another software program called a *linkage editor* binds the object module of this program to object modules of any subprograms that must be used to complete processing. The resultant program, which is ready for computer execution, is called a *load program* (or load module). It is the load program that the computer actually executes.

The entire process is sometimes referred to as "compile/link-edit/go," corresponding to the compilation, link-editing, and execution stages that the user must go through to get a program processed. Programs can be saved on disk for processing in either source-, object-, or load-module form. Frequently run applications will often be saved in load-module form to avoid repeated compilation and link-editing.

■ *Interpreters* Whereas compilers translate programs into machine language all at once before programs are run, **interpreters** translate programs a line at a time as they are being run. For instance, if a user has a program in which a single statement is executed a thousand times during the course of the program's run, the interpreter would translate that statement a thousand different times into machine language. With an interpreter, each statement is translated into machine language just before it is executed. No object module or storable load module is ever produced.

Although interpreters have the glaring weakness of inefficiency because they translate statements over and over, they do have some compelling advantages over compilers. First, they are usually easier and faster to use, since the user is not bothered with distinct and time-consuming compile, link-edit, and execution stages. Second, they typically provide users with superior error messages. When a program contains an error and "blows up," the interpreter knows exactly which statement triggered the error—the one it last translated. Because interpreters stop when errors are encountered, they help programmers debug their programs; this boosts programmer productivity and reduces program development time. Syntax errors encountered by compilers during the program translation process are counted, but the diagnostic routines and error messages associated with most compilers do not help programmers locate errors as readily as interpreters. Third, an interpreter for a 3GL typically requires less storage space in primary memory than a compiler for that language. So they may be ideal for programming environments in which main memory is limited, such as on low-end microcomputers. Fourth, interpreters are usually less expensive than compilers.

Programs written in simple languages such as BASIC are more likely to be interpreted than compiled because these programs are often developed on microcomputers. Although most microcomputer systems come equipped with a BASIC interpreter, few include a compiler. When BASIC is used in a commercial production environment, however, it is often advantageous to acquire a BASIC compiler. Ideally, program development is first performed using interpreters; then, using a compiler and linkage editor, the final version of the program is compiled and link-edited into directly executable code.

- **Assemblers** Assemblers are used exclusively with assembly languages (described later in this chapter). They work similarly to compilers, translating an assembly-language program into object code.

    Because assembly-language programs are usually more machine efficient than those written in high-level languages, a two-step translation process may take place. First, the high-level language is translated to assembly language; then, using an assembler, it is converted to machine language.

Utility Programs

Utility programs are systems programs that perform general system-support tasks. For instance, a utility program might be used to format or copy a disk, transfer the contents of a tape to disk, or convert a program from ASCII to EBCDIC.

In many instances, it is unclear what differentiates an operating system routine from a utility program. Some programs that one vendor bundles into an operating system might be offered by another vendor as separately priced and packaged utility programs.

A wide variety of utilities are available to carry out special tasks. A number of these are listed in Figure 6.7.

Next, we will look at three types of utility programs found in most computer systems: sort utilities, spooling software, and text editors. These examples will give you an idea of some of the roles played by utilities.

- **Sort utilities** *Sort utility* programs are those that sort data. For example, suppose we have a file of student records, such as those described in Chapter 1's Figure 1.7 (see page 23). We could declare "name" the *primary sort key* and arrange the file alphabetically on the name field. This would be useful for, perhaps, producing a student directory. Alternatively, we could sort the file by major, and then within major, by name. Here, we would declare major as the primary sort key and name as the *secondary sort key*. Although the examples described here use only one or two sort keys, many sorting packages enable the user to identify 12 or more sort keys and to arrange outputted records in either ascending or descending order on each declared key.

    Sort utilities are often found in mainframe and minicomputer environments. In the microcomputing world, it is typical for sort routines to be bundled into application packages; for example, sort routines are commonly found in spreadsheet and database management software.

- **Spooling software** The purpose of *spooling software* is to compensate for the speed differences between the computer and its peripheral devices. Spooling software is usually encountered in large-system and network com-

Type of Utility	Purpose
Backup utilities	Back up the contents of a hard disk
Cosmetic utilities	Customize the user environment—for example, by changing menu formats or monitor display colors
Data compression utilities	Compress (and decompress) files so that they take up less space in secondary storage
Device drivers	Make it possible for application software to run on specific hardware configurations
Diagnostic software	Detect bugs and other software problems that can affect performance
Disk organizers	Maximize space utilization on disks
Disk toolkits	Recover and repair lost or damaged files on disks
Extenders	Add programs, commands, or fonts to operating system menus
File transfer utilities	Facilitate the transfer of files between different programs or computer systems
Keyboard utilities	Reconfigure keyboard or construct keyboard macros—programs that execute when certain keys are pressed
Performance monitors	Determine how efficiently the computer system is working
Screen capture programs	Print out or store any image on the screen
Screen savers	Turn off display (or run a display program) when not being used
Sort utilities	Sort a file or database in a user-defined manner
Spooling programs	Control outputs sent to printers and free up computer while printing a file
Text editors	Allow text in a non-document file to be manipulated
Text retrieval utilities	Help users find misplaced files by typing in short character or text strings
Virus toolkits	Scan systems and disks for the presence of viruses and help the user contain and eliminate them
Work group utilities	Enable networked computer users to send messages to one another

Figure 6.7 Some of the utility programs found in computing environments and the tasks that they execute.

puting environments. For instance, during the time it takes to type in or print out all the words on this page, the computer could begin and finish processing dozens of programs. The computer would be horribly bottlenecked if it had to wait for slow input and output devices before it could resume processing. It just does not make sense for a large computer, which may be worth millions of dollars, to spend any time sitting idle because main memory is full of processed-but-unprinted jobs and the printer attached to the system cannot move fast enough.

To preclude the computer from being slowed down by input and output devices, many computer systems employ spooling software. These programs take the results of completed programs and move them from primary memory to disk. The area on the disk where the program results are sent is commonly called the output spooling area. Thus, the output device can be left to interact primarily with the disk unit, not the CPU. Spooling utilities can also be used on the input side, so that programs and data to be processed are temporarily stored in an input spooling area on disk.

- **Text editors** *Text editors* are programs that allow text in a file to be created and modified. These utilities are probably most useful to professional programmers, who constantly face the problems of cutting and pasting programs together, changing data files by eliminating certain data fields, changing the order of certain data fields, adding new data fields, and changing the format of data. Although text editors closely resemble word processors, they are not the same. Word processors are specifically designed to prepare such "document" materials as letters and reports, whereas text editors are specifically designed to manipulate "non-document" instructions in computer programs or data in files. Text editors lack the extensive text-formatting and document-printing capabilities found on most word processors.

APPLICATION SOFTWARE

Application programs perform specific processing tasks for users. Programming languages and other program development software (such as language translators) are used by application programmers to develop application programs.

As noted in Chapter 2, in many organizations, the application programs they use were developed in-house by application programmers employed within the MIS departments of those organizations. In some cases, the software was written specifically for the organization by external consultants or programmers. While custom-written software is often expensive, it may be the only long-term, cost-effective way that organizations can acquire the application programs that they need to perform necessary tasks.

Over time, organizations have increasingly turned to professional software development companies for the application programs that they need. Commercially developed software programs can be purchased off-the-shelf by organizations. Many of the "canned," general-purpose application programs used by organizations (such as word processing and spreadsheet packages) are the same ones that are sold to home users in microcomputer and software stores. Other commercially available packages that satisfy the special needs of particular organizations (for example, dentist offices, law firms, and video stores) are marketed only to those types of clients.

Since many of the commercial software packages lack features that users want, third-party software companies often develop add-on programs designed to work with the packages. Several companies, for example, have developed add-on packages for Lotus 1-2-3, one of the leading commercially available spreadsheet programs. Among other features, these add-on applications make it possible to display more of a Lotus 1-2-3 spreadsheet on-screen, develop customized graphics, and print out long spreadsheets sideways instead of vertically. The availability of these add-ons makes it easier for organizations to standardize on Lotus 1-2-3, even if it does not fully meet their needs. By purchasing appropriate add-on programs, the standard package can often be extended in ways that are needed by the organization. Hence, the decision about which software package to purchase is not always based solely on its standard features; the availability of third-party add-on programs or additional modules directly from software vendors may also be a consideration.

Some organizational software needs may be met by *public domain software* and *shareware*. Both of these are often distributed via electronic bulletin boards (which will be covered in Chapter 8) and typically have been developed by individuals or small software development companies. Users who obtain copies of shareware programs from bulletin boards are expected to pay a small fee to the developers—generally less than $50 per copy. The diversity of shareware programs is enormous, but graphics, communication, disk utilities, and computer games are among the more common applications. Public domain software gets its name from its widespread accessibility at no cost—its public-access nature. Like books at a public library, copies can be obtained at no cost. Because there is no charge for acquiring a copy, public domain software is sometimes called "freeware." Shareware and public domain software can satisfy a wide variety of organizational needs and should not be overlooked as an application software sources. However, programs acquired from electronic bulletin boards may be carriers of computer viruses and should be scanned by a virus checker before being used.

Note that application programs are always written for use with a particular operating system. For example, a word-processing program that is designed for Apple Macintosh machines (using Macintosh System 7 as their operating system) will not run on an MS-DOS machine. However, in many instances, a commercially available package initially developed for one operating system will be reworked by the software development company so that it can be used with other operating systems. For example, WordPerfect—one of the most widely used word-processing packages—has one version available for IBM-compatible machines that run MS-DOS and a second version available for use on the Apple Macintosh. Therefore, the quantity and variety of readily available application programs are important features to consider when selecting an operating system.

Application software packages are discussed throughout this book; in many cases, major vendors are identified. Many types of application programs are used in organizations and their diversity is increasing. Some of these—such as commercially available word-processing, spreadsheet, and database management programs—can be used by virtually any organization. Others are classified as *industry-specific software* packages that are tailored to the needs of a particular industry. For example, in the construction industry, many job cost estimation programs exist that help contractors develop bids and determine a project's construction costs. Still others are *functionally specific software* packages because they address the needs of a major functional area of business, such as accounting, marketing, finance, manufacturing, or human resources management. Software appropriate for each of these major organizational functions will be discussed in more detail in Chapters 9 and 13.

General-Purpose Microcomputer Application Software

The variety of application software products now available for microcomputer systems is astoundingly large and still growing rapidly. In addition to the software developed exclusively for microcomputer systems, a number of packages once available only to mainframes and minicomputers have now been implemented in microcomputer versions. In fact, many computer professionals like working with "friendly" microcomputer software so much that microcomputer software has noticeably impacted the current development of application software for mainframes and minicomputers.

The three most important types of application software products targeted to end-users of microcomputer systems are word processors, spreadsheets, and file/database management programs. These products often rely heavily on the use of fourth-generation languages.

- **Word processors** *Word processors* are software packages that turn a computer system into a powerful typewriting tool—and much more. Some word processors are the hub of integrated office systems that have facilities for desktop publishing, electronic calendaring, and electronic mail. We will look at both word processors and sophisticated office systems in Chapter 12. Some of the leading microcomputer word-processing packages are listed in Figure 6.8.

- **Spreadsheets** *Spreadsheets* are software packages that essentially turn a computer system into a sophisticated electronic calculator. Many spreadsheet packages also have presentation graphics generators that take data and easily convert them into several types of charts for management presentations at meetings. Some of the leading spreadsheet products in the microcomputer marketplace are listed in Figure 6.9.

Product	Vendor
Ami Pro	Lotus Development Corporation
DeScribe	DeScribe, Inc.
JustWrite	Symantec Corporation
MacWrite	Claris Corporation
MultiMate	Borland International
PC-Write	Quicksoft, Inc.
Professional Write	Software Publishing Corporation
Word	Microsoft Corporation
WordPerfect	WordPerfect Corporation
WordStar	WordStar International, Inc.
XyWrite	XyQuest, Inc.
Volkswriter	Lifetree Software, Inc.

Figure 6.8 Leading word-processing packages. Word-processing packages are standard features in most office environments and are used more extensively than any other type of general-purpose application software.

Product	Vendor
Excel	Microsoft Corporation
Lotus 1-2-3	Lotus Development Corporation
Lucid 3-D	Dac Easy Inc.
MultiPlan	Microsoft Corporation
PlanPerfect	WordPerfect Corporation
Pro Plan	Software Publishing Corporation
Quattro Pro	Borland International
Smart Spreadsheet	Informix Software, Inc.
SuperCalc	Computer Associates International, Inc.

Figure 6.9 Leading spreadsheet packages. Spreadsheet packages are among the most widely used application packages by managers. They are especially useful for performing "what-if" analyses and are often found in decision support systems.

■ ***File managers and database management systems*** *File managers* and database management systems store large amounts of data, provide rapid access to these data, and prepare reports from them. Some of the leading database management packages are listed in Figure 6.10. File and database management systems are covered more extensively in Chapter 7.

It is common for vendors to include more than one of these software functions, and perhaps others as well, into a single package. When this is done, the resulting product is called an *integrated software package*. Integrated software packages have the advantage of providing users with a single command syntax and interface, as well as a lower aggregate price than if they bought the individual components separately. On the negative side, integrated software may offer the user much more functionality than he or she really needs, with greater learning and processing overhead. Plus, the combined quality of the software may not be as high as if the user had purchased software components separately from several vendors. Two of today's major integrated software products are the Software Group's Enable and Microsoft's Works.

Product	Vendor
Dataease	Software Solutions, Inc.
dBASE	Borland International/Ashton Tate
FoxBase, FoxPro	Microsoft/Fox Software
Knowledgeman	Micro Data Base Systems, Inc.
Oracle	Oracle Corporation
Paradox	Borland International
R:Base	Microrim, Inc.
Team-up	Unlimited Processing, Inc.

Figure 6.10 Leading database management packages. Database management systems provide managers with flexible access to stored data and easy-to-use report generation features.

Special-Purpose Microcomputer Application Software

While most readers are familiar with the general-purpose application programs for microcomputers just described, they may not be aware of the wide variety of ways in which microcomputer systems perform other business tasks.

- **Transaction processing** In businesses of all sizes, computer systems are commonly used for entering, processing, and managing transactions. Among these tasks are accounts receivable, accounts payable, payroll, general ledger, and the other activities associated with an accounting information system. Increasingly, microcomputer workstations are replacing standard terminals as data-entry devices in large computer networks. Image-processing systems and pen-based computers, discussed in the last chapter, are changing the way in which some types of transactions are processed. Transaction processing systems will be discussed more fully in Chapter 9.

- **Analysis and decision making** Such business data as consumer buying patterns, cost and profitability trends, and variances from budgeted amounts are often analyzed using application software. A wide variety of macros, functions, and templates are also commercially available to build decision support systems that help users perform financial and statistical analyses. Many decision support systems incorporate *statistical software* and *management science software* to utilize the mathematical models that were discussed in Chapter 3. *Expert systems software* is increasingly used to assist in analysis and decision making. *Groupware* programs, which provide electronics links among people who work together, are becoming standard in group decision support systems. *Executive information system software*, specialized programs that support the decision making of top-level managers, are also commercially available. DSS, GDSS, and executive information systems are discussed more extensively in Chapter 10; expert systems and other knowledge-based systems are discussed in Chapter 11.

- **Planning, coordinating, scheduling, and organizing** Such tasks as financial planning, budgeting, preparing expense and sales reports, preparing meeting agendas, preparing and monitoring project schedules, and managing appointments are often done with the assistance of application software. Software for maintaining personal calendars and appointments, as well as Rolodex-type organizers, are also widely available; these are commonly known as *desktop organizer software*. Chapter 12 discusses some of these managerial support activities more fully. *Project management software* makes it easy for managers to use Gantt charts, PERT, CPM, and the other project management tools mentioned in Chapter 3.

- **Retrieving and updating** An abundance of software products exists to search through data files for specific records or through correspondence files for specific documents. When retrieval capabilities are present, so too are those for updates. The file and database processing systems used to perform these tasks will be discussed in the next chapter. *Multimedia software*—software packages that link data, text, audio, and video images during the development of multimedia database systems—is also more commonly used.

- **Reporting** Retrieved data can be sorted, classified, summarized, and ultimately printed as neatly formatted management reports. Also, ordinary reports can be significantly enhanced by using a variety of *desktop publishing* packages. Fourth-generation query languages and report generators make it easy to develop customized reports; some of these will be discussed later in this chapter.

- **Writing** Microcomputers are commonly used as word processors to prepare letters, memos, manuscripts, and other documents. The support software available to writers includes on-line spelling checkers, thesaurus lookups, and readability analysis, plus automatic outline, table of contents, and index preparation. Desktop publishing and commercial art systems are also used frequently by writers and corporate publishing staffs.

- **Presenting** Packages are widely available to prepare "canned" proposals to upper management, 35-mm slide and plotter-produced presentation graphics for meetings, and typeset-quality report and presentation materials. *Presentation graphics software* packages that assist with these activities include Harvard Graphics and Freelance Graphics. The graphics components of an increasing number of spreadsheet and database management packages produce presentation-quality graphs and reports. Desktop publishing software packages and laser printers have also made it easier to develop high-quality presentation materials; desktop publishing will be covered more extensively in Chapter 12.

- **Communicating** Computer networks are becoming more prevalent in businesses. Among these are electronic mail networks, local area networking, networking corporate mainframes, and networking with suppliers or customers through electronic data interchange (EDI) systems. *Communications software* and network software make it possible for these systems to operate and carry out important business activities. These systems will be discussed more fully in Chapter 8.

- **Training** Computer systems are playing an increasing role in worker training. For example, many commercially available software packages are accompanied by training disks or *tutorial software* that enables users to learn the package at their own paces. Additionally, many computer-aided instruction (CAI) and interactive video disk systems train workers for a wide variety of jobs. *Training software* helps individuals develop skills or knowledge in a wide variety of fields.

These are just some of the wide range of business activities supported by microcomputer application software. Of course, other application software is available to assist virtually all of the functional business areas described in Chapter 13, including software for manufacturing, finance, and marketing.

PROGRAMMING LANGUAGES

The general- and special-purpose application software programs needed to carry out business activities are written in programming languages. Many experienced programmers are proficient in more than one programming language, but an organization often standardizes on a certain language (or languages) for the application programs written in-house.

A **programming language** is a set of rules that enables instructions to be written for a computer. These languages consist of programming commands that combine to form programming statements that tell the computer system what to do and when to do it. The process of writing program statements is often called *coding,* while the resulting programming statements are often called *program code.*

People can use a computer system to do specific types of work only if the work is described to the computer system with instructions written in a programming language. To accomplish this, some people become proficient in one or more specific programming languages and write their own programs. Most people, however, use programs that were written by someone else to perform the work they need to do.

Programming languages were created over time to meet a variety of needs. For instance, every person is at a different level of technological sophistication. Thus, some languages were designed for people who know computers very well and would like to manipulate data on a bit level; other languages were designed for inexperienced users, even those who profess to hate computers.

Also, the needs of applications are often different. In business data processing, for instance, lots of records need to be quickly processed and the computations required on each record are relatively simple. In scientific work, on the other hand, computations can be extensive. Thus, different languages have evolved for data processing and for scientific purposes. Although they are hard to count, hundreds of programming languages exist in the world today, serving a variety of purposes.

Evolution of Programming Languages

To understand the direction and role of software in today's computing environment, it is useful to have some knowledge about the evolution of language-based products. Here, we will briefly consider how software evolved, from the time the first programming languages were introduced to the present (see Figure 6.11).

Low-Level Languages

In the early days of computers, using the computer meant having a special knowledge of how the computer actually worked. The only languages available for use were machine language and assembly language, which were very difficult to use.

Machine language was the first language available to programmers and constitutes the first generation of programming languages. All machine-language instructions consist of strings of 0s and 1s (see Figure 6.12). Every instruction is specified at the finest level of detail to the computer and is coded using the binary numbering system. Machine language is considered a

GENERATIONS OF PROGRAMMING LANGUAGES		
Generation	**Language**	**Period**
1	Machine language	1940s–1950s
2	Assembly language	1950s–1960s
3	High-level programming languages	1960s–1970s
4	Very-high-level programming languages	1970s–1980s
5	AI-based languages, natural languages, object-oriented languages, and parallel processing languages	1980s–1990s

Figure 6.11 Programming language generations. Programming languages have evolved considerably since computers became common in organizations. At first, all programs were written in machine language. Today, most of the languages are written in third generation (or later) languages.

low-level language because every instruction written for it corresponds to base-level tasks of the computer on which it operates. Although few people still write programs in machine language, every program instruction written in a higher-level programming language must be translated (by language translator software) into machine language before it can be executed. Each type of computer has its own distinct machine language; a machine-language program that works on one type of computer will not necessarily work on another.

Assembly languages, pioneered by Grace Hopper in the early 1950s, constitute the second generation of programming languages. Assembly languages allow machine-language instructions to be written in a shorthand way through mnemonics (memory aids). An assembly-language counterpart for the machine-language instruction in Figure 6.12, for instance, might be

    S   P,B

Here, each field of binary digits is replaced by symbols that are more easily remembered and understood. In this example, S means subtract the contents

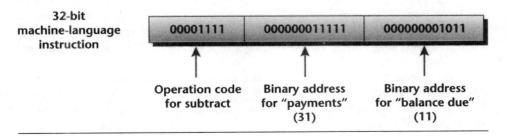

Figure 6.12 An example of a machine-language instruction. This particular instruction tells the computer to take the amount in main-memory location number 31 (11111 is the binary equivalent of the decimal number 31) and subtract it from the amount in main-memory location number 11. Because machine-language programs consist of strings of bits (1s and 0s), they are difficult to follow and debug. These difficulties stimulated the development of assembly and higher-level languages.

Processing Task	Assembly-Language Mnemonic	Machine-Language Equivalent
Add memory to register	A	01011010
Add register to register	AR	00011010
Branch on condition	BC	01000111
Compare memory locations	CLC	11010101
Compare registers	CR	00011001
Divide register by memory	D	01011101
Divide register by register	DR	00011101
Load from memory into register	L	01011000
Move data (copy)	MVC	11010010
Multiply register by memory	M	01011100
Multiply register by register	MR	00011100
Store register in memory	ST	01010000
Subtract memory from register	S	01011011
Subtract register from register	SR	00011011

Figure 6.13 Examples of assembly-language mnemonics and their machine-language translation. While still somewhat cryptic, assembly-language mnemonics make it easier to develop and debug application programs. Although the oldest of the languages that must be translated into machine language, assembly language is still widely used.

of memory location P (holding customer payment) from register B (holding customer current balance). As you can see, assembly languages make it easier for programmers to code instructions. A listing of some frequently used assembly-language mnemonics, and what they mean, is shown in Figure 6.13.

Actually, although considered a low-level language just one step up from machine language, assembly languages are still widely used by programmers today. Because they are very close to machine language, they can write application programs that take special advantage of the way particular computers are built. Many professional program developers—who may be writing word processing, spreadsheet, or communications software for the commercial marketplace—often choose to write certain parts of their software in assembly language. As a result, these programs will generally run faster and use storage more conservatively than if they had been written in a higher-level language such as BASIC or Pascal. However, writing assembly-language programs is tedious and time-consuming. With computers continually becoming faster and programmmers becoming more expensive, assembly languages are losing their appeal.

Are Personal Computers Keeping Workers from Being Productive?

Changes in microcomputers and other forms of information technology that have the potential to improve worker productivity are likely to be approved by managers. However, many of the potential productivity gains made possible by more sophisticated processors and peripherals; more user-friendly software and operating systems; and faster, more flexible access to databases are often unrealized. Why? Workers may be driven to distraction by the new technology. Some of the major sources of lost productivity are the following:

- **Fiddling with fonts** Workers often spend too much time preening documents to get them to look exactly the way that they want. The inclusion of desktop publishing features in word-processing packages contributes to this problem.
- **The networking nemesis** Too often, workers try to build their own local area networks or to install new network operat

ing systems and software without the assistance of MIS professionals. System crashes, lost data, and oodles of lost productivity are frequent outcomes of such bootstrap networking efforts.

"WORKERS MAY BE DRIVEN TO DISTRACTION BY THE NEW TECHNOLOGY."

- **Super spreadsheets** Some workers, after they are familiar with spreadsheets, tend to go overboard. They create spreadsheets that are too large or too complex. This can bog down updating and reporting activities. According to some estimates, resulting productivity losses annually equal about 2 percent of the gross national product. Awareness of these potential time wasters can help managers develop appropriate and enforceable rules.

High-Level Languages

Following the assembly-language era came the third generation of programming languages, characterized by the development of **high-level languages** (or **third-generation languages**). This category includes COBOL, BASIC, FORTRAN, Pascal, PL/I, and Ada.

High-level languages differ from their low-level counterparts in that they contain less coding detail. For instance, a relatively straightforward operation such as adding five numbers can be done in a single program instruction in a high-level language:

```
X = A + B + C + D + E
```

This simple computation would require several instructions in a low-level language. Remember, a single computer can perform only one step at a time. To add five numbers, it must add the first number to the second, then add the third number to this sum, and so on. In machine language, the programmer has to specifically tell the computer to take all of these steps. However, because high-level languages take the programmer above the mechanics of the machine, the programmer is unable to optimize machine performance, as is possible with a lower-level language. Thus, the cost paid by moving to a high-level language is that programs will not run as efficiently.

Because of third-generation languages, programming became easier, faster, and more accessible to greater numbers of people. In fact, BASIC, developed by John Kemeny and Thomas Kurtz in the 1960s, can be learned by people who do not consider themselves to be programmers. Nonetheless, BASIC is still beyond the reach of many potential computer users. It requires learning and adhering to a fastidious programming-language syntax and it often takes a lot of time to write a BASIC program that will do even a small amount of useful work.

Very-High-Level Languages

Very-high-level languages evolved to make programming even easier. Today, these are also called fourth-generation languages, which we will describe more fully in the next section.

The principle behind a **very-high-level language** is to enable users to tell the computer what should be done rather than how something should be done. For instance, when sorting numbers, many high-level languages require over 20 programming statements and some tricky logic. Even in languages that have their own sort statement, the file handling involved can be burdensome. In a very-high-level language, however, the user might only need to point on the screen to the area to be sorted, then point to the column on which the sort is to take place, and finally, tell the language package whether to sort from high to low or from low to high. Then, without complicated instructions, the sort takes place. Because very-high-level languages spare the user from describing procedures in order to do work, they are often called **non-procedural languages**. High-level languages are predominantly **procedural languages**.

One of the first very-high-level languages was RPG (Report Program Generator), introduced in the mid-1960s. The concept behind RPG was to make it easier for programmers to code routine business reports. With RPG, a programmer describes to the computer system what a report should look like—but not how to produce it. Thus, the programmer instructs the computer system regarding what titles to put into the report, which data go into which columns, where totals and subtotals should be taken, and so on. The RPG package then decides how this can best be done and generates its own machine-language program to write the report. Although RPG represented a new philosophy in writing computer programs, it is not the type of language that ordinary, non-sophisticated people can use. Nonetheless, it was a hint of things to come.

Today, a variety of programming languages are being used by application programmers including third- (high-level languages), fourth- (very-high-level languages), and some fifth-generation languages. Some of the more widely used application programming languages are summarized in Figure 6.14. Fourth-generation languages are described more fully in the next section.

Language	Type*	Description
Ada	H	Powerful, highly structured language adopted by the U.S. Defense Department
ALGOL	H	Language similar to FORTRAN, but more comprehensive and flexible
APL	H	Highly compact, scientific language
BASIC	H	Language most widely used by beginning programmers
C	H	Versatile, mid-range language used widely to develop application software packages
C++	VH	Popular object-oriented programming language
COBOL	H	Most widely used language for transaction processing applications
FORTH	L/H	Stack-oriented language that is midway between an assembly language and a high-level language
FORTRAN	H	Oldest surviving high-level language; used mostly for scientific applications
KL1	VH	One of the first parallel processing languages (developed in Japan)
LISP	H	Language used widely for artificial intelligence applications
Logo	H	Of the languages on this list, the easiest to learn, even by children
Modula-2	H	Pascal look-alike with special capabilities for developing systems software
Pascal	H	Highly structured language useful for developing large programs
PL/I	H	Language supporting both business data processing and scientific processing
Prolog	H	Language widely used for artificial intelligence applications
RPG	VH	Report generation language
Smalltalk	VH	Language designed to manipulate graphical objects
SQL	VH	Structured Query Language (SQL) is the most widely used language with relational databases

* L = low level, H = high level, VH = very-high level

Figure 6.14 Some widely used high-level and very-high-level languages and their properties. Hundreds of languages were developed through the years, with many no longer in use. Those that survive undergo periodic revisions to reflect changing user needs, programming styles, and hardware approaches.

Fourth-Generation Languages

Fourth-generation languages (4GL), which appeared about ten years after RPG, make such tasks as report generation and data retrieval even easier. In fact, some fourth-generation languages simplify the job of obtaining computer information so much that ordinary end-users, who normally do not want to program, find them easy to use. Whether the act of generating reports or retrieving information with some of these software products actually constitutes programming, however, is debatable.

The age of microcomputer systems, which began in the mid-1970s, promoted the widespread use of other types of very-high-level languages—for example, those that accompany spreadsheets, file managers, and database

DIFFERENCES BETWEEN THIRD- AND FOURTH-GENERATION LANGUAGES

Third-generation languages (3GL)	Fourth-generation languages (4GL)
▪ May be difficult to learn and use	▪ Many are easy to learn and use
▪ Many were developed for use by professional programmers	▪ Most have been developed for use by end-users, as well as MIS professionals
▪ Many were designed for use in file-oriented environments—must be modified for use with databases	▪ Most were designed for use in database environments
▪ Often require a large number of program statements to perform a task—take longer to write program	▪ Usually require far fewer instructions to perform the same task—programming time is usually shorter
▪ Program statements may be difficult to read and understand	▪ Commands are very English-like and easier for end-users and MIS professionals to understand
▪ May be difficult to debug and maintain	▪ Shorter programs and English-like commands usually make it easier to debug and maintain 4GL programs
▪ Procedural nature and length of program contribute to application backlogs	▪ Improvements in programmer productivity often help reduce application backlogs
▪ When appropriately structured, 3GL programs usually execute efficiently on processing hardware	▪ Often consume many more machine cycles than 3GL programs carrying out the same task

Figure 6.15 Differences between third- and fourth-generation programming languages. While most of the programs used today are written in third-generation languages, fourth-generation languages are becoming more popular.

management systems. These program packages are particularly targeted to the on-the-job needs of non-computer professionals.

Very-high-level languages, as well as advances in microcomputer-based systems and sophisticated communications networks, bring more people into contact with computers than ever before. These software tools do have certain drawbacks, however, which we will discuss later. When they are suitable, though, they offer compelling advantages to both programmers and users. Some of the major differences between third- and fourth-generation languages are summarized in Figure 6.15.

Because fourth-generation languages are still evolving, many scholars disagree on about how they should be defined. One property that most fourth-generation languages share, however, is an emphasis on improving the on-the-job productivity of users and programmers. James Martin, a respected MIS trainer and author, feels that a language should not be considered a 4GL unless it enables programmers to achieve significant productivity gains over those possible with a 3GL. Thus, 4GL products are often collectively referred to as "productivity software."

In this text, we will consider a 4GL to be an easy-to-learn, easy-to-use, high-productivity language product that competes primarily in the applications domain once monopolized by third-generation languages. To be a legitimate

Type of Tool	Description
▨ Application generators	Used to develop application programs
▨ Application packages	Prewritten programs (often commercially available) for applications such as word processing, spreadsheets, and various accounting tasks
▨ Decision support system tools	Used to create financial schedules, budgets, models of decision environments, and so on
▨ Graphics generators	Used to quickly prepare presentation graphics
▨ Report generators	Used to quickly develop management reports
▨ Retrieval and update languages	Used to retrieve information from files or databases and to update (add, delete, or modify) the data they contain

Figure 6.16 The major types of 4GL programs and their characteristics. The evolution of 4GL programs has made it possible for both users and programmers to be more productive.

4GL, the product should be capable of being learned in a few days and capable of being put into code much more rapidly than a comparative 3GL.

Fourth-generation languages can help increase programmer productivity and make it easier to maintain programs after they are created. While 4GL programs can often be created quickly, they are not faultless. Indeed, many are not designed to optimize the use of primary memory and computer resources; large programs that support many simultaneous on-line users are typically better handled by a 3GL or assembly language. When being executed, 4GL programs often consume significantly more machine cycles than 3GL programs that perform the same task. This may result in slow response times. Faster and more powerful processors, along with 4GL product refinement, are likely to compensate for these deficiencies over time. However, managers should carefully consider both the advantages and disadvantages of 4GL programs before deciding whether the organization should adopt them on a wide scale.

Fourth-Generation Languages in the MIS Marketplace

The 4GL products found in the marketplace are diverse and serve a wide variety of application areas. Some are designed especially for users, some are targeted for programmers, and some try to satisfy the needs of both users and programmers. In addition, some are chiefly procedural in nature, others are primarily non-procedural, and still others combine procedural and non-procedural elements. Whatever the circumstances, all of these are designed to expedite the program-coding process.

Six types of 4GL programs typically found in software products are report generators, retrieval and update languages, decision support software tools, graphics generators, application packages, and application generators (see Figure 6.16). In some instances, several of these functions are integrated in a single package. For example, Focus, a 4GL product from Information Builders International, is often classified as being a decision support package because it can perform report generation, database query and update, and graphics generation. It could also be considered an application generator because of some of the other functions that are built into this package.

Report Generators

A **report generator** is a software product that enables the user to produce customized reports quickly. Such a package usually contains facilities that allow data to be extracted from files or databases and used to create reports in a variety of formats. Report generators typically provide users and programmers with a lot of control over how data is formatted, organized, and displayed. Extracted data can often be mathematically or logically manipulated to create additional information for display in the final report. Figure 6.17 shows a report generated by Focus.

Retrieval and Update Languages

Two tasks performed by many 4GL products are retrieval and update; the languages that make it possible to perform these tasks are often called *query languages*. *Retrieval* capabilities enable users to fetch information from files or databases, whereas *update* capabilities allow information to be added, deleted, or modified. Query languages are often used in an interactive, on-line environment to search a database or file to find (and extract) the records that satisfy specific selection criteria. For example, 4GL query commands such as:

```
SELECT CLASS = 2, STATE = 'CA'
DISPLAY ALL STUDENT-ID, NAME
```

might be used to retrieve and display the ID numbers and names of all Californian sophomores from a file or database. Updating the contents of one or more records is often facilitated by these languages. For example, commands such as:

```
EDIT STUDENT-ID = '9214667'
CHANGE CLASS TO 3
```

can be used to change the classification of student number 9214667 from sophomore to junior.

Available retrieval and update languages have different kinds of syntax and structure; however, many are moving closer to "natural language" interfaces. The following example, a query using INTELLECT, illustrates this:

```
REPORT THE BASE SALARY, COMMISSIONS, AND YEARS OF SERVICE, BROKEN DOWN
BY STATE AND CITY, FOR MANAGERS IN OREGON AND WASHINGTON
```

Fourth-generation languages that are frequently updated will be accompanied by a certain level of security in order to provide protection against unauthorized retrieval or changes. Since query languages are especially well-suited to relational database environments, they will also be discussed in the next chapter, which covers database management.

```
TABLE FILE SALES
PRINT NAME AND AMOUNT AND DATE
BY REGION BY SITE
IF AMOUNT GT 1000
ON REGION SKIP-LINE
END
```

(a) This short Focus program produces . . .

```
PAGE 1
REGION      SITE     NAME                        AMOUNT        DATE

MA          NEWK     ELIZABETH GAS              $2,877.30      93 AUG
            NEWY     KOCH RECONSTRUCTION        $6,086.23      93 APR
            PHIL     ROSS INC.                  $3,890.22      93 JUL
                     LASSITER CONSTRUCTION      $1,120.22      93 SEP

MW          CHIC     BAKESHORE INC.             $5,678.23      93 OCT
                     ROPERS BROTHERS            $2,789.20      93 AUG
            CLEV     BOVEY PARTS                $6,769.22      93 MAY
                     ERIE INC.                  $1,556.78      93 JAN

NE          ALBN     ROCK CITY BUILDER          $1,722.30      93 JUL
            BOST     HANCOCK RESTORERS          $8,246.20      93 FEB
                     WANKEL CONSTRUCTION        $2,345.25      93 JUN
                     WARNER INDUSTRIES          $3,155.25      93 OCT
            STAM     ACORN INC.                 $2,006.20      93 MAR
                     KANGERS CONSTRUCTION       $2,790.50      93 JUN
                     DART INDUSTRIES            $7,780.22      93 MAY
                     ARISTA MANUFACTURING       $4,295.90      93 FEB

SE          ATL      RICHS STORES               $1,345.17      93 AUG
            WASH     CAPITOL WHOLESALE          $3,789.00      93 JUN
                     FEDERAL DEPOT              $2,195.25      93 MAR
```

(b) . . . this complete report.

Figure 6.17 Report generation with Focus. The short, six-line program in (a) is used on a file called SALES to generate the report in (b). A program written in a 3GL such as COBOL may need 100 lines of code to produce a similar report.

Decision Support Tools

End-user-oriented *decision support tools* include spreadsheets, statistical software, and modeling packages, which Chapter 10 covers fully. These language products are specifically designed to provide capabilities to users, to help them build decision support systems, and to assist in making decisions. They enable users to create their own banks of data, to build models that crank through calculations, and to perform analyses upon results. One of the most useful types of analysis facilitated by these packages is *what-if analysis*, in which users investigate contingencies that have a bearing on the decisions they are making. Figure 6.18 shows how a what-if analysis might be performed with Lotus 1-2-3.

Graphics Generators

Presentation-graphics-oriented fourth-generation languages quickly construct such graphs as line charts, bar charts, pie charts, and scattergrams (see Figure 6.19). Some stand-alone **graphics generators**, such as Harvard Graphics and Freelance Graphics, are available. However, most graphics-oriented 4GL programs are bundled as component spreadsheets, modeling packages, reporting packages, and so on. Whatever the situation, it is generally easy for users to ask for data and specify how they are charted.

Application Packages

Off-the-shelf **application packages** are canned programs designed for common types of business applications such as payroll processing, accounts receivable, invoicing, or word processing. These are often marketed commercially and are available for mainframes, minicomputers, and microcomputers. Basically, the person who buys or leases such a program sets a few parameters within the package to tailor it to a specific organizational environment and then runs it.

In the past, application packages were relatively inflexible in meeting the needs of a wide range of organizations. If the package did not fit the organization exactly, modifications were often a nightmare. However, these packages have improved substantially throughout the last few years, with a richer set of parameters to widen their usefulness. Although most application packages are specifically designed for computer professionals, a number of recent products are targeted directly to end-users. For example, for accounting applications, packages like DacEasy and Quicken can be mastered quite easily by users with little computer sophistication.

Application Generators

An **application generator** is a 4GL package that enables a user or programmer to quickly develop a set of programs that comprise an entire application. Basically, a user specifies what needs to be done and the application generator produces the appropriate code. Most full-function application generators produce code for input, validation, update, and processing; some of these are interactive (on-line) and allow users sitting at a terminal to define inputs, files, processing, processing requirements, and report formats by responding to questions.

```
              A               B          C          D          E
  1                    Profit and Loss Statement
  2                        January, 1993
  3
  4      000's omitted       Prod. A    Prod. B    Prod. C    Total
  5      -------------       -------    -------    -------    -----
  6      Gross Sales          $100       $200       $200      $500
  7        Sales Returns       $20        $80        $60      $160
  8      Net Sales             $80       $120       $140      $340
  9        Cost of Goods Sold  $30        $60        $70      $160
 10      Gross Margin          $50        $60        $70      $180
 11        Administrative Expenses  $35    $30        $30       $95
 12      Gross Income          $15        $30        $40       $85
 13        Interest             $1         $2         $2        $5
 14        Taxes                $7        $14        $19       $40
 15      Net Income            $7        $14        $19       $40
```

(a) Cells B6, C6, and D6 are multiplied by 10 percent.

```
              A               B          C          D          E
  1                    Profit and Loss Statement
  2                        January, 1993
  3
  4      000's omitted       Prod. A    Prod. B    Prod. C    Total
  5      -------------       -------    -------    -------    -----
  6      Gross Sales          $110       $220       $220      $550
  7        Sales Returns       $20        $80        $60      $160
  8      Net Sales             $90       $140       $160      $390
  9        Cost of Goods Sold  $30        $60        $70      $160
 10      Gross Margin          $60        $80        $90      $230
 11        Administrative Expenses  $35    $30        $30       $95
 12      Gross Income          $25        $50        $60      $135
 13        Interest             $1         $2         $2        $5
 14        Taxes               $12        $25        $30       $67
 15      Net Income           $12        $23        $28       $63
```

(b) Within seconds, the spreadsheet is updated.

Figure 6.18 What-if analysis using Lotus 1-2-3. With most spreadsheet packages, to find an answer to such questions as "What if sales increased 10 percent?" a formula is applied to the affected values and the spreadsheet package recalculates the entire worksheet. In this example, cells B6, C6, and D6 in the worksheet in (a) are multiplied by 10 percent and—within seconds—the spreadsheet package produces the worksheet in (b). Notice that many other fields also changed as a result of these edits.

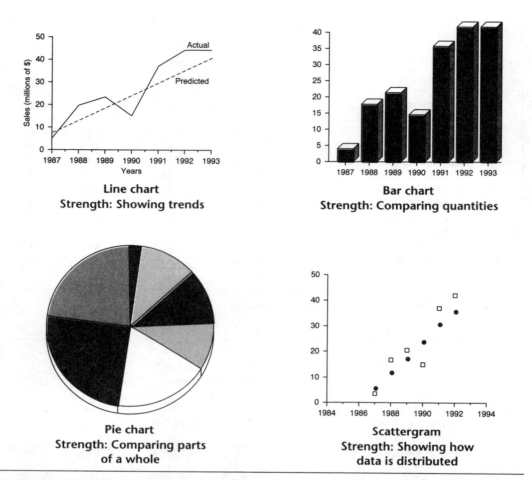

Line chart
Strength: Showing trends

Bar chart
Strength: Comparing quantities

Pie chart
**Strength: Comparing parts
of a whole**

Scattergram
**Strength: Showing how
data is distributed**

Figure 6.19 Common types of presentation graphics. Presentation graphics play an increasingly greater role in decision support applications because they provide a professional look to business presentations.

Application generators targeted to programmers are predominantly mainframe-based and generally include tools for file (or database) creation and maintenance; routines for queries and reports; a screen-painting feature to create input and output layouts; a reusable-code library (a library that allows the storage of widely used program segments, which can be "cut and pasted" into new programs); a code generator to produce error-free COBOL (or other 3GL) code from 4GL statements; and a data dictionary facility to coordinate the building of applications systematically.

The following example illustrates how a **code generator** may be used. A programmer simulates portions of a COBOL application program in Pacbase, which is a proprietary application generator from CGI Systems, Inc. Usually this is accomplished by answering a series of fill-in-the-blank screens on pro-

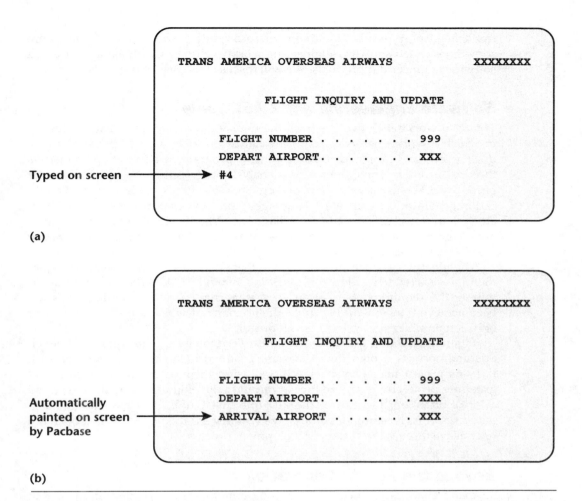

Typed on screen ⟶

```
        TRANS AMERICA OVERSEAS AIRWAYS              XXXXXXXX


                      FLIGHT INQUIRY AND UPDATE


              FLIGHT NUMBER . . . . . . . 999
              DEPART AIRPORT. . . . . . . XXX
              #4
```

(a)

Automatically painted on screen by Pacbase ⟶

```
        TRANS AMERICA OVERSEAS AIRWAYS              XXXXXXXX


                      FLIGHT INQUIRY AND UPDATE


              FLIGHT NUMBER . . . . . . . 999
              DEPART AIRPORT. . . . . . . XXX
              ARRIVAL AIRPORT . . . . . . XXX
```

(b)

Figure 6.20 Interactive screen-painting feature available with Pacbase. To design screens automatically, the programmmer or analyst enters preassigned numeric screen descriptors for the data elements that will appear on the screen. Here, the "#4" typed onto the screen in (a) refers to the element "Arrival Airport," which is automatically "painted" on to the screen in (b).

gram parameters and using a "paint feature" to quickly create input and output layouts (see Figure 6.20). These segments are then fed to the Pacbase generator, which contains a precompiler to translate the requirements suggested by the filled-in data into COBOL code. The COBOL segments may consist of 70 percent of the final COBOL program. The programmer then codes the other 30 percent—which consists of critical portions of the program, as well as control segments that tie everything together—in a shorthand version of COBOL that is available with Pacbase or, alternatively, in standard COBOL.

Some application generators can also generate code from a set of system diagrams showing user and system requirements. The products that fall into this category—typically found on microcomputers and minicomputers—are sometimes called software engineering workbenches or CASE (computer-aided software engineering) products. We will discuss this class of products next.

Software Engineering and CASE Tools

The term **workbench** evolves from the fields of carpentry and manufacturing, in which a workbench consists of the hardware tools used to physically produce a product. Similarly, in computing, a program or application represents the final product. Thus, the systems analyst, programmer, or project manager needs a workbench environment of software tools; for example, code and application generators, specification languages, and tools that can be used to generate system flowcharts or data flow diagrams. When a variety of such 4GL tools are integrated, the resulting product is called a *software engineering workbench* or *CASE (computer-aided software engineering) tool.*

The ideal workbench product is one that spans the entire systems development process (which will be discussed in Chapters 14, 15, and 16)—from determining the requirements of users to system maintenance. This ideal has not been achieved; most workbench products (many of which are PC-based) cover only certain phases of systems development.

Figure 6.21 shows a CASE tool, Cadre Technology's Teamwork, as it develops and corrects a data flow diagram. Teamwork can also be used for such tasks as project management. CASE tools and their potential to increase programmer productivity and reduce application development time have received a lot of attention. Because of the key role that CASE tools have assumed in many systems development efforts, we will discuss the use of these tools more fully as we discuss the systems development process.

Beyond the Fourth Generation

So many changes are occurring in programming-language development that some people have dubbed them the fifth generation of programming languages. Four important areas of development are expert systems, natural languages, object-oriented languages, and parallel processing languages. Most of the gains realized so far in these areas are small relative to their forecasted potential.

Expert Systems

Expert systems refer to software with the type of intelligence and reasoning processes normally attributed to human experts. Their role in language development is with respect to improving the human/machine interface. Such software may someday result in the elimination from computer systems of both human input errors and programming-logic errors. Such software might also allow computer systems to come up with better answers than humans in many critical decision-making areas. Other roles of expert systems will be discussed in Chapter 11.

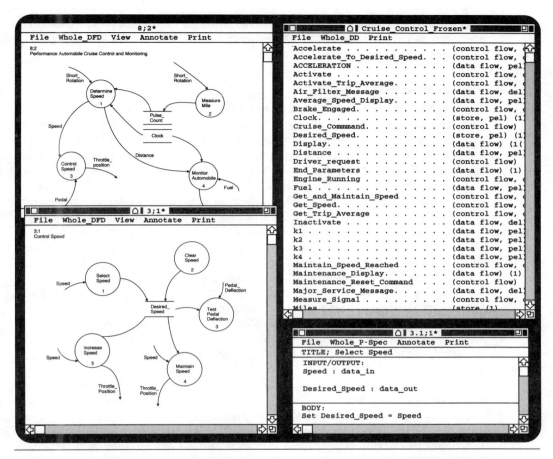

Figure 6.21 An example of a software engineering workbench package—Cadre Technology's Teamwork—one of the many products in the computer-aided software engineering (CASE) marketplace. As data flow diagrams are developed, windows can be summoned to check for syntax errors and inconsistencies.

Natural Languages

One of the biggest limitations of computer processing involves the user interface. In many instances, both users and computer professionals could do much more with machines if it were not necessary to learn programming languages. One solution, of course, is for humans to relate their needs directly to the machine in a natural language such as English.

Many experts predict that the next generation of programming languages will be dominated by natural languages that will enable users to interact with computer systems in their native tongues. This will make it unnecessary for users to learn to use the rules or syntax of a particular programming language. Instead, requests to the computer would be written similar to a memo and the natural language system would translate the instructions into machine language.

Natural language processing systems are still in their infancy. Currently, they are most often found as a front-end for file and database management packages when retrieving information for simple reports.

Object-Oriented Languages

Object-oriented languages use objects (packets of information and instructions on how to manipulate these packets) and messages (communications among objects). Instead of applying functions to data as conventional programming languages do, object-oriented languages have the messages tell objects what to do and the objects decide how to do it. For instance, an object might be a cursor on the screen and a message to it might consist of instructions to move to another position, drawing a line as it proceeds. Object-oriented languages are especially useful for graphical-oriented user interfaces. These have given rise to *object-oriented programming (OOP)*, an approach that makes extensive use of reusable code and that can speed up program development time and decrease the backlog of application program needs. *Smalltalk* is perhaps the archetype of the object-oriented programming systems (OOPS). It was pioneered by Alan Kay in the late 1960s, when he was a graduate student at the University of Utah. *Reusable code* refers to logically connected program code that has been written into small modules that can be "cut and pasted" together to write programs. Thus, an object-oriented program can consist of several off-the-shelf modules that are "glued together" through a custom-written shell program.

Many people feel that object-oriented languages have the potential to increase productivity and some industry experts predict that most software will eventually be written as reusable-code programs—with standards guiding the creation of commercial reusable-code modules. Several recent revisions of other languages, such as C++ and Object COBOL, reflect the interest in OOP. Many industry leaders consider OOP to be an unstoppable movement because of its potential to shorten application program development time and to significantly reduce the application backlogs common in most organizations.

Parallel Processing Languages

As noted in Chapter 5, parallel processing refers to dividing work so that it can be performed on several central processing units operating simultaneously. With hardware prices shrinking, this approach is now a practical way to speed up information processing. Also, it should dramatically change the way computer programs are written.

To date, very few parallel programming languages have been developed. KL1—developed by Japan's Institute for New Generation Computer Technology (ICOT)—is one of the first parallel programming languages to be widely used. Still, very few parallel programming languages are in use, and most of these are in prototype form.

MANAGEMENT ISSUES

A number of management issues are associated with software and application development. These include reducing the application backlogs that have accumulated to massive proportions in many organizations and ensuring that software copyright laws are not intentionally or inadvertently violated by users.

Application Backlogs

Most of the application programs used in organizations today were written in a high-level language. Different languages have different strengths and weaknesses—for example, some are better suited for business processing activities, while others are better for scientific and engineering applications. Still others were designed as general-purpose languages that can be used for both business and scientific applications.

COBOL (COmmon Business-Oriented Language) is arguably the most important language used in business today. More programs currently utilized in business organizations were written in COBOL than in any other language. An estimated three trillion lines of COBOL code are now being used worldwide.

Probably the biggest disadvantage of COBOL programs, and those written in other high-level languages, is that they take a long time to write. High-level languages often require programmers to specify computational procedures and data formats in fine detail; because of this, they tend to be lengthy. Both the time it takes to write working high-level language programs and the shortage of competent programmers have contributed to an application backlog in most companies.

Studies indicate that organizations often have application development backlogs of between 2–4 years. This means that after making a request for a new system, users may wait several long years before the MIS staff even starts work on the project. In many companies, the "visible" backlog has led to an "invisible" backlog: applications that are not even submitted because users are frustrated by the wait. The invisible backlog is sizable, often 1–2 times the size of the visible backlog.

Approaches for Reducing Application Backlogs

Users in many organizations, frustrated by the inability of MIS personnel to respond to their needs, sometimes take matters into their own hands by developing their own applications. The extent to which such end-user development should be controlled is an important management issue; the potential benefits and problems associated with end-user development will be explored more extensively in Chapter 17.

Allowing end-users to develop their own applications is only one of several approaches that may reduce application backlogs. Other approaches were mentioned in previous sections of this chapter. These include the use of a compact programming language such as C in place of verbose languages such as COBOL, the use of object-oriented programming and OOP languages such as C++, and the use of application generators and other 4GL products (all of which can significantly boost programmer productivity).

On the surface, it may seem that the wisest and most expedient business decision is to switch to languages, packages, and programming practices that promote more rapid development of applications. However, this is not always as easy as it sounds. Many seasoned programmers resist these new languages and packages because they make the programmer's skills, which were learned over a number of years, obsolete. Retraining is often necessary and the transition period may be an organizational nightmare. Some programmers view fourth-generation languages and their products as technologically unsophisticated and suitable only for end-users; if they express these opinions often and loudly, they can inhibit the organizational adoption of these new approaches.

It is important for managers to ensure that programmers are using languages that are appropriate for the applications they are responsible for developing. For example, COBOL should not be used in place of a scientifically oriented language, such as FORTRAN, to develop engineering applications. Similarly, scientifically oriented languages should not be used by programmers charged with developing business applications.

In many instances, a wise organization adopts policies that standardize it on a few languages (rather than allowing programmers to use whatever they want). Such standardization encourages programmers to help each other out and to become increasingly proficient in a few languages, rather than marginally proficient in numerous languages. Such policies are especially important in organizations that encourage team programming. However, even though an organization may have policies specifying which languages to use, these policies should not be so restrictive that they force programmers to use languages that are inappropriate for the types of applications they are developing.

Since application packages are readily available for an increasing variety of business uses, many organizations are faced with "build versus buy" decisions. In an increasing number of cases, it is more cost-effective to acquire commercially available products than to have programmers develop them in-house. Many industry experts expect the role of programmers to change over the next decade to one in which they are asked to evaluate and customize commercially available packages, rather than writing programs from scratch. Purchasing application programs can be a quick way to reduce application backlogs, particularly for organizations that can afford the expense.

Another decision facing many organizations is whether or not to "outsource," which is contracting with another organization to do some (or all) of their application development or information processing. If a substantial part of their information processing tasks are outsourced, an organization may use their in-house programmers and MIS professionals to concentrate on developing "mission-critical" applications instead.

An alternative to outsourcing is subcontracting. Not all programs must be developed by programmers employed by the firm. In many instances, it is wiser and more cost-effective to off-load application development to firms that specialize in developing the needed programs.

The global opportunities for outsourcing and subcontracting are increasing. Because the costs of talented programmers vary considerably around the world, these are often attractive options for cost-conscious managers and MIS executives. When five programmers can be hired in India for what it costs to hire one programmer in the United States, managers are understandably viewing application development in more global terms than in the past.

Site Licensing and Copy Protection

If the organization intends to use commercially available application software on more than one machine, managers should be aware of the copyright agreements that the software vendor provides. Some companies require that a copy of the package must be purchased for each computer on which it will be used. Others allow customers to pay a single fee for use of the software on all or a specified number of computers in the organization; these companies require management to sign a *site licensing agreement* to use the software on the specified quantity of computers. To prevent users from making illegal copies of their software, some software vendors market *copy-protected software*—packages that are written so that they cannot be copied easily.

Site licensing and copy protection are just two of the management issues that should be considered when purchasing commercially available software packages. Managers should also ensure that the software will run on the hardware platforms that are available within the organization. For example, do available microcomputers have sufficient primary memory? Will the software work easily with the peripheral devices that are commonly used within the organization?

Since application packages are written to work with a particular operating system, it is important to ensure that the package can be utilized on the organization's computers. Of course, cost and the currentness of the package should also be considered; if the software will be updated in the future, the software vendor's update policy should be reviewed carefully.

These are just some of the management issues associated with programming languages and application development. Others will be explored and developed throughout the rest of the text, especially in Chapters 14–16.

SUMMARY

Software refers to the complete set of instructions that enables people working with the CBIS to perform their work. Two categories of software exist: application software (programs written to perform the processing tasks that users need to do their jobs) and systems software ("background" programs that enable application programs to run smoothly on a specific set of hardware).

Systems software enables users to develop and execute application programs. The most important piece of systems software is the operating system, a collection of programs that manages CBIS resources. Popular operating systems for microcomputers include MS-DOS, Macintosh System 7, Windows, and UNIX. Recently, most operating systems have incorporated windowing capabilities and a graphical user interface. Network operating systems are also encountered more widely by managers and users. NetWare, a network operating system developed by Novell, Inc., is the most widely used operating system found in local area networks.

Operating systems for larger systems often interleave work processing in order to achieve resource efficiency. Several common techniques for doing this include multiprogramming, whereby two or more programs execute concurrently; multitasking, whereby two or more tasks execute concurrently; time-sharing, a process that allocates slices of time to terminal users one at a time; virtual memory, whereby programs are divided on disk into segments that fit more easily into main memory; foreground/background processing, whereby jobs are handled according to highest priority; and multiprocessing, whereby two or more central processing units are linked together to perform coordinated work.

Another form of systems software is the language translator, a program that translates other programs into machine language for the computer to process. Three types of language translators are compilers, which translate an entire program before it is executed; interpreters, which translate programs one line at a time; and assemblers, which translate assembly languages into object code.

Utility programs perform general systems support tasks, such as formatting or copying a disk. Three commonly used utilities are sort utilities, spooling software, and text editors.

Application software is available to support a wide range of organizational activities. It may be developed in-house by application programmers, purchased from software vendors, or taken from electronic bulletin boards in the form of public domain software or shareware. Word processing, spreadsheet, and file/database management software are the most common types of packages utilized on microcomputers. However, microcomputers are increasingly used in a number of other areas, including transaction processing, analysis and decision making, data/file retrieval and updating, desktop organizing, writing, creating presentation-quality graphics, desktop publishing, and training.

A programming language is a set of rules that enables instructions to be written for a computer. Programming languages are created and changed over time to meet a variety of needs. Machine language was the first language available to programmers. It alone represents the first of five generations of languages. Machine language is considered a low-level language because each instruction corresponds to base-level tasks of the computer on which it operates. Assembly languages belong to the second generation of languages. In assembly languages, the binary digits of machine language are replaced by more easily remembered symbols. High-level languages—which include COBOL, BASIC, and FORTRAN—are the third generation of computer languages. With high-level languages, less coding detail is required than with machine and assembly languages. Very-high-level languages—which comprise the fourth generation—have evolved to make programming even easier. They are often called nonprocedural languages because the user does not have to describe step-by-step procedures that tell the computer how to work. The fifth generation will see developments in the areas of expert systems, natural languages, object-oriented languages, and parallel processing languages.

Fourth-generation languages (4GL) are easy to learn and, consequently, they can make both users and programmers highly productive. Fourth-generation languages are currently divided into several functional categories. Among these are report generators, which help prepare reports; retrieval and update languages, which respectively assist users in making queries or modifications to data in files or databases; decision support tools, which help users analyze data; graphics generators, which assist with graph preparation; application packages, which are prewritten solutions to applications; application generators, which enable a programmer to develop a set of programs that comprise an entire application; code generators, an application generator that produces error-free 3GL code from 4GL statements; and software engineering workbenches (or CASE), which integrate a variety of 4GL tools that are of specific interest to the systems analyst or programmer. It is not uncommon for a 4GL product to fall into more than one of these functional categories.

Numerous management issues are associated with the use of programming languages. The most important issue is reducing the extensive application backlogs found in many organizations. Increasing programmer productivity and reducing application development time help reduce such backlogs. The use of fourth-generation languages, object-oriented programming, and CASE tools have grown in popularity because of their potential to enhance programmer productivity and reduce application development time. In addition, managers should take steps to ensure that application programmers use appropriate languages to develop programs needed by the organization. Managers must also wrestle with decisions about whether it is more cost-effective to develop applications in-house, subcontract with software development firms, or enter into outsourcing agreements with organizations that provide information processing services.

KEY TERMS

Application generator	Low-level language
Application package	Machine language
Assembler	Multiprogramming
Assembly language	Multitasking
COBOL	Nonprocedural language
Code generator	Procedural language
Compiler	Programming language
Foreground/background processing	Report generator
Fourth-generation language (4GL)	Third-generation language (3GL)
Graphical user interface (GUI)	Time-sharing
Graphics generator	Utility program
High-level language	Very-high-level language
Interpreter	Virtual memory
Language translator	Workbench

REVIEW QUESTIONS

1. What is the difference between application and systems software? How does general-purpose application software differ from special-purpose application software?

2. What functions are carried out by an operating system?

3. Why are operating systems that provide a graphical user interface growing in popularity? Identify several examples.

4. What are the differences among multiprogramming, multitasking, and multiprocessing?

5. What are the differences among compilers, interpreters, and assemblers?

6. What functions are performed by utility programs?

7. What types of business applications are likely to be carried out by using microcomputers?

8. What are the differences among the various generations of programming languages? Identify examples of the languages associated with each generation.

9. What are the characteristics of each of the following languages: COBOL, BASIC, FORTRAN, Pascal, C, Smalltalk, LISP?

10. What is the significance of reusable code and object-oriented programming?

11. What are the characteristics of the different types of fourth-generation languages?

12. What are the major advantages and disadvantages of fourth-generation languages?

13. What are software engineering workbenches? How may CASE tools help an organization fulfill strategic MIS objectives?

14. What are application backlogs? What approaches may be used to reduce application backlogs?

DISCUSSION QUESTIONS

1. In the near future, computer systems should evolve in which users will not need any special programming or computer in order to work with them at a fairly sophisticated level. Describe the types of user interfaces that these systems would need in order for this to happen.

2. What types of standards are necessary to develop useful reusable-code modules?

3. Do you think COBOL will be replaced entirely within the next decade? Within the next two decades? What is likely to take its place? Provide reasons for your answer.

4. Some industry analysts suggest that delaying a standardized version of UNIX will help some companies. What types of companies will benefit from such a delay and why?

CASE STUDY

Are U.S. Programmers a Dying Breed?

American programmers are under siege. Edward Yourdon's book, *The Decline and Fall of the American Programmer,* depicts programmers in the U.S. as arrogant mavericks who are reluctant to embrace more efficient programming languages, CASE tools, fourth-generation languages, and other approaches (such as object-oriented programming) that can make them competitive in the world marketplace. Yourdon points out that programmers in India and Philippines may be up to five times less expensive (in terms of salaries and benefits), but are comparable in competence. Such labor cost differences are causing many American firms to outsource programming tasks to contract programming companies in other parts of the world.

Downsizing—that is, the movement of applications that were traditionally run on mainframes to smaller hardware platforms such as local area networks—is another source of stress for American programmers. During the 1990s, the number of mainframes used in the U.S. has steadily declined, and the number of computer programmers employed in the U.S. has also fallen.

The disintegration of the Soviet Union means that programmers from Russia and the other members of the Commonwealth of Independent States (CIS), who were formerly employed by the military or heavy industry, are now available to help with commercial software ventures. And, they are becoming very competitive.

Generally, the software produced by CIS programmers is theory-rich; that is, they are programs that encapsulate and integrate concepts from diverse intellectual fields. Many of the programmers are physicists, mathematicians, or geologists first and software developers second.

The average CIS programmer makes less than half the salary of his or her American counterpart. Largely due to a dearth of mainframes and minicomputers and no market for large computer systems—because of the controlled Soviet economy—most CIS programmers have PC experience. Among the software companies that have sprung up in the post-Soviet economy, C and C++ are the two most commonly used languages. Assembly language and Pascal are also widely used. The percentage of CIS software development firms using object-oriented design and object-oriented programming exceeds that found in the U.S.

Entrepreneur Lev Weinstein assembled a collection of former Soviet programmers and formed a contract programming firm that specializes in large systems development and integration. Companies from Europe and the United States have reduced labor costs by more than 30 percent by using Weinstein's employees.

In addition to contract programming, former Soviet programmers have developed PC board design software (software that assists electrical engineers in designing PC circuitboards), expert system development toolkits (to facilitate the development and refinement of expert systems), health diagnostic systems, and a variety of educational software for children.

While U.S. programmers are feeling some pressure from CIS counterparts who are low in cost but not in talent, U.S. corporations are recognizing some tremendous opportunities. Strategic planners see the opportunity to work together with the new CIS software companies to develop the advertising, sales, billing, shipping, and customer support systems needed for other companies that are emerging in the former communist states.

Adapted from Yourdon (1992) and Morrison (1992).

DISCUSSION

1. Describe how the use of object-oriented programming, CASE tools, and fourth-generation languages could help American programmers be more efficient and competitive in the world marketplace.

2. What challenges will be faced by companies who want to use CIS programmers to develop business software (for example, billing, shipping, and customer support) for emerging CIS companies? What steps could be taken to meet these challenges?

3. What opportunities do the new CIS software development firms offer to companies from other parts of the world?

4. Is it right for an American company to contract with foreign programmers to develop applications? Why or why not? What long-terms affects may such actions have?

Chapter

7

Database Management

After completing this chapter, you will be able to:

Explain how files and database systems can enhance managerial decision making

Describe how managers and users typically interface with file and database systems

Describe the limitations of file processing

Name several ways that data can be organized

Identify the advantages and disadvantages of database management systems (DBMS)

Identify the fundamental data structures associated with database management systems

Identify some of the features found in large and small database management systems

Describe some of the new developments in file and database systems and their importance

Data management is one of the key strategic issues facing organizations in the 1990s. With information assuming an ever-important role in the future of businesses, and with data being the primary raw material from which information is derived, such a situation was perhaps inevitable.

At one time, the data in most organizations were managed manually by using file folders and notes on the backs of envelopes. Today, with high-speed computers and communications making quality merchandise and good service necessary in a competitive environment, data management is much more sophisticated. In this chapter, we will primarily look at the types of software tools that assume a principal role in data management—both tools that organize the mass of data a business handles and tools that access these data in useful ways.

The issue of how to manage data receives a great deal of attention from information systems professionals. The next section, "Data Management," explains why. There, we cover some of the concerns that make data management such an important area of study. Next, we turn to the file management software and strategies used to organize and access data stored in files. The last several sections of this chapter cover database management systems: what they are, how they work, why they are gaining in popularity, and how they differ from one another.

DATA MANAGEMENT

Managerial decision making is likely to be most effective when managers are able to quickly access the information they need on demand. Since ready access to relevant data and information is essential for effective decision making, managers need to know what information is available and how to access it, as well as how it can be used to make decisions.

Today, most of the data and information needed for managerial decision making is stored in computer-based files and databases. Lower-level managers are the most likely to use computer-based files and databases to help them perform day-to-day operational tasks and to develop operational plans. Top-level managers are likely to use information stored in both organizational and external databases to develop strategic plans. Since managers at all levels of an organization will probably need data and information stored in computer files and databases to fulfill their responsibilities, it is important for them to understand basic file and database concepts. Such knowledge may help managers locate, access, and effectively utilize the information that they need to make decisions.

In Chapter 1, we defined each of the levels in the data hierarchy; these definitions are briefly summarized in Figure 7.1. In Chapter 5, we discussed sec-

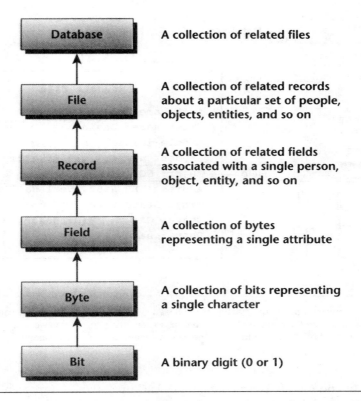

Database	A collection of related files
File	A collection of related records about a particular set of people, objects, entities, and so on
Record	A collection of related fields associated with a single person, object, entity, and so on
Field	A collection of bytes representing a single attribute
Byte	A collection of bits representing a single character
Bit	A binary digit (0 or 1)

Figure 7.1 The data hierarchy. Data stored in computer-based files and databases are physically put on storage media as binary digits (bits). Bits are organized into characters (bytes), bytes into fields, and fields into records. A set of related records is considered a file and a collection of related files is called a database.

ondary storage and noted that data may be physically stored on a variety of media, including magnetic disks, magnetic tapes, optical disks, microfilm, and even paper (such as business forms, memos, and reports). In paper-based systems, data are often organized as illustrated in Figure 7.2. For example, a filing cabinet in the Department of Management at Georgia Southern University contains file folders for students pursuing two majors: management and information systems. Folders for management majors are contained in one drawer of the filing cabinet and collectively constitute a file. Folders for information systems majors are stored in another drawer and collectively make up a second file. The filing cabinet itself can be considered a database because it is made up of two administratively related sets of files (related by the fact that the administrative functions for both majors are carried out by the Department of Management). Since most of the information found in the student file folders is also stored in computer-based files and databases, administrators and faculty members at Georgia Southern University have more than one way to access student data.

Computer-based storage offers several advantages over paper-based storage, including the abilities to capture and store data compactly and efficiently,

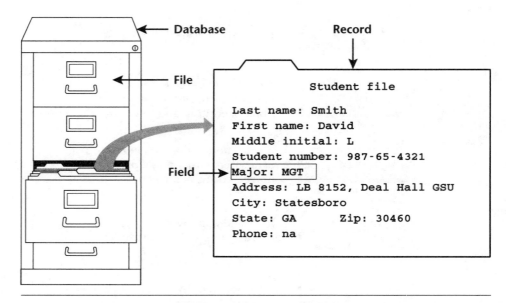

Figure 7.2 Data organization in a manual, paper-based system. In this example, the contents of an individual file folder are the equivalent of a record, all folders in a particular drawer are the equivalent to a file, and the set of all files contained in the filing cabinet represents a database.

quickly edit and modify stored data, make backup copies of important data and information, and rapidly access data stored in large files. However, it is the speed with which records stored in computer-based files and databases can be accessed that is, arguably, the most important advantage of these systems over paper-based systems. For example, in a computer-based system, it may take just a few seconds for a business manager to find and list the records of all account holders who have not made a purchase in the last 60 days—even if the firm has over 200,000 accounts. In a paper-based system (where account records are stored in file folders), this same search could take days or weeks. Because computer-based systems provide more data and information to decision makers in a more timely manner, they have dramatically changed the decision-making environment for managers.

Of course, other organizational advantages are also associated with computer-based file and database systems. For example, customer transactions and inquiries can be processed more quickly and efficiently, customer orders can be tracked more effectively, and new levels of customer service can be attained. In addition, like managerial decision making, user productivity may be enhanced—especially for users involved with processing customer transactions.

Major Issues in Data Management

Today, data and information are extremely valuable resources in almost all organizations. Since data generally exist in abundance, how to manage them effectively is of paramount concern to MIS professionals. Virtually all issues regarding the effective management of data fall into at least one of the following categories:

- **Content** What data should the organization collect in the future? What data is it currently collecting?

- **Access** In what ways must authorized users access data in order to effectively perform their jobs? This question involves the timing required to get data to users when they need it, and also the issue of which users have a right to which data.

- **Organization** In what ways should data be logically and physically organized to achieve the types of data accesses required by users?

- **Accuracy** Which validation, editing, and auditing procedures are necessary in every stage of the input-processing-output cycle to ensure that data—and information generated from the data—are correct?

- **Integrity** What controls are necessary in each stage of the input-processing-output-storage cycle to ensure that data are up-to-date and that changes to specific occurrences of data are made everywhere in the system?

- **Security** How will data be protected from such possible events as unauthorized access, unauthorized modification, outright theft, and malicious or unintentional destruction?

- **Privacy** How will data be safeguarded to protect the rights of individuals to privacy?

- **Cost** How should data-related costs be controlled? To which sets of data and information needs should scarce resources be allocated?

The challenge of effectively addressing these issues is complicated by the fact that we are living in a dynamic, seemingly chaotic world. The environment will inevitably change in the future; thus, some of these changes are unpredictable. The data management systems designed today are often created under conflicting criteria in order to provide immediate access to data needed to satisfy current decision-making requirements—and to supply the flexibility to handle the data and information needs of tomorrow.

Unfortunately, it is impossible to adequately cover all of these important issues in a single chapter on data management. In fact, it is even a heroic task to cover all of them in a single book on database systems. To try to do some justice to this important set of concepts, database systems and data management will be covered at several points in this textbook:

- This chapter is primarily devoted to the major managerial and technical matters concerning the organization and access of data. Here, we cover the principal types of software used to access data and explain how data must be organized on secondary storage devices so that these software products can access them in the most effective way.

- Chapter 19 discusses some of the controls used to ensure the accuracy, integrity, and privacy of data, along with other control and security issues.

```
                         Student file

        Last name:
        First name:
        Middle initial:
        Student number:
        Major:
        Address:
        City:
        State:              Zip:
        Phone:
```

Figure 7.3 An on–screen form (template) for entering a student record in a file or database. Data management software for microcomputers provides the capabilities to develop (and customize) templates—often as part of the file or database creation process. Most data management software packages also make it possible to modify templates in order to adapt to changing needs.

■ Chapters 18 and 19, on the management of MIS, consider decisions pertaining to strategically allocating resources to data-related activities. Also covered in these chapters are the security-related issues of computer crime and disaster recovery.

User Interfaces

Users and managers are most likely to directly interface with computer-based files and databases at terminals or microcomputers by using data management software. There are two major types of data management software: file managers and database management systems (DBMS). Similar to other popular types of software products, numerous data management software packages are available for both small and large computer systems. In many cases, users work with an on-screen form or **template** (see Figure 7.3) when entering data into computer files or databases. When personal databases (those designed for use by a single user) are being created on microcomputer systems, the data management software makes it possible to create a template for data entry. The development of a template is often part of the process of creating a file or database table.

Creating a file or database table also involves defining the fields displayed in data-entry templates. Five of the common types of field definitions found in commercially available file and database management systems for microcomputers are described in Figure 7.4. Readers who have worked with file and database packages are probably already familiar with those field types.

Most data management software packages for microcomputers also provide menus that make it possible to carry out a variety of tasks. Some of the typical menu options included in such packages are depicted in Figure 7.5. Besides

Field Type	Description
▪ Numeric	Store integer numbers or numbers containing decimal points. These can be mathematically manipulated (added, subtracted, multiplied, divided, and so on).
▪ Character	Store data that cannot be mathematically manipulated (such as letters of the alphabet). Data in these fields can, however, be compared, sorted, or indexed.
▪ Date	Store dates in particular formats such as MM/DD/YY. These fields can be sorted or indexed; some mathematical manipulation is possible (such as subtracting one date from another to determine the number of days between them).
▪ Memo	Store text information such as a narrative description of an attribute of a person, object, or entity. These fields cannot be mathematically manipulated or compared, but can be edited and output (as can any other field).
▪ Logical	Store a single character of data such as a "Y" (for"yes") or an "N" (for "no"). Can be used to select records from a file. (Character, number, and date fields can also be used to select records meeting certain conditions from a file.)

Figure 7.4 Types of field definitions found in data management software packages. Many business applications require a variety of field definitions. Character, numeric, logical, date, and memo field definitions are found in most of the data management software packages on the market. Defining fields properly is important because the operations that can be performed on a field are often determined by how it is defined.

making it possible to create new files and database tables, most systems make it easy to update files. In a fundamental sense, *updating* (or *maintaining*) a file or database means adding new records, modifying the contents of existing records (for example, to reflect a change in an employee's address or phone number), and deleting existing records. Such updating facilities are also available with the data management software used in network and large-computing environments.

Most data management software packages provide mechanisms for developing reports, both on-screen and printed. It is usually possible to specify which fields to include in a report and whether or not particular data conditions have to be met before data from a record will be listed in the report (for example, if employee salary must be greater than or equal to $10,000). Figure 7.6 provides an example of a printed report that might be generated from a student file or database table. This same report could be sent to a display screen if a hard-copy (printed) version of it was not needed.

In network and large-system computing environments, managers and users may have less personal control over the templates they can use, the updating tasks they can perform, and the types of reports they are allowed to generate or access. In many instances, managers may have to submit a formal request to the MIS department if they want changes made in data-entry templates or report formats. This is primarily because in these environments, important files and databases are shared by multiple users. Because of this, multiuser environments typically have more formal and stringent controls over file creation, access, and retrieval. The reasons for this will be explored more fully in subsequent sections of this chapter.

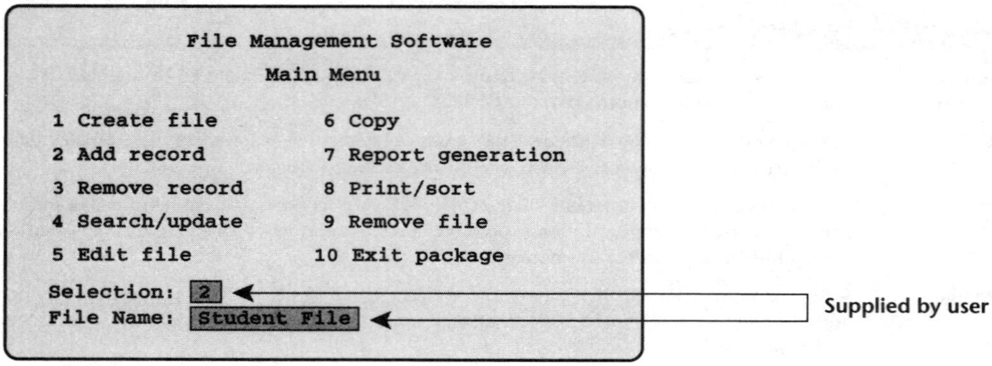

```
                File Management Software
                      Main Menu

   1 Create file            6 Copy

   2 Add record             7 Report generation

   3 Remove record          8 Print/sort

   4 Search/update          9 Remove file

   5 Edit file             10 Exit package

   Selection:  2       ◄──────────────────────────────  Supplied by user
   File Name: Student File  ◄
```

Key:

Menu Option	Allows User To:
▪ Create	Create a template, specify field types, and define field lengths for a new file
▪ Add record	Add new records to the file
▪ Remove record	Delete records from the file
▪ Search/update	Retrieve and modify (update) specific records from the file
▪ Edit file	Add, delete, or modify fields in file records
▪ Copy	Make a copy of a file or portions of a file
▪ Report generation	Specify report format and contents
▪ Print/sort	Print a report or sort a file on one or more keys
▪ Remove file	Delete entire file from secondary storage
▪ Exit package	Leave file management package and return to operating system

Figure 7.5 Menu options commonly found in data management software packages. Most data management systems for microcomputers make it possible to create new files or database tables, add and delete records, edit the contents of existing records, change the structure of existing files (for example, by adding or deleting fields), and delete files or tables. Other options may also be available, depending on the sophistication of the package.

FILE MANAGEMENT

Most types of business data are best understood by users when they are logically organized into fields, records, and files. **File processing** refers to an environment in which data are physically organized into files (collections of related records). In many instances, a file in a file-processing environment "belongs" (is linked) to a specific application program. In database management environments, the data and files (tables) may be shared by many application programs.

Many of the file management software programs used in organizations today are either written in-house (often in COBOL) or developed by software vendors (often using fourth-generation languages).

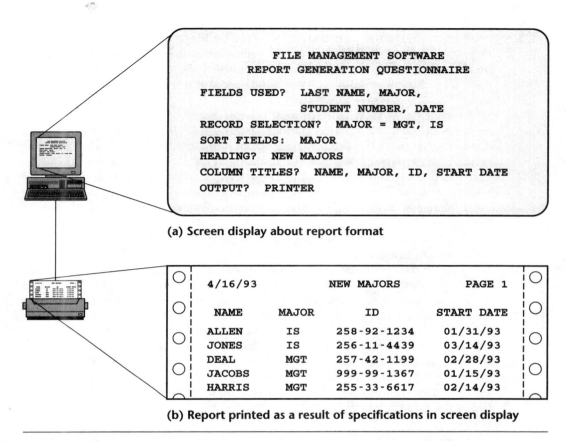

(a) Screen display about report format

(b) Report printed as a result of specifications in screen display

Figure 7.6 An example of a report developed using a data management software package. The report generation features associated with most microcomputer data management systems enable users to retrieve information from files and databases easily and in the format that they need.

Evolution and Limitations

For the first 20 years of commercial computer processing, computing was limited to punched-card input and printed output. Display terminals did not come into widespread use until the mid-1970s. The organization of data into files fit well with this environment. A punched card could be used to hold a record; a stack of punched cards could hold a file.

During these first two decades, both the data files and the application programs that used them were developed interdependently. This is called **program-data dependence**. For instance, when a COBOL program was developed to satisfy certain data processing or information needs, a COBOL-compatible data file had to be created to use with it. BASIC programs required their own BASIC-compatible files, and so on. Each programming language had its own particular method for formatting data, so a data file created under the rules of one language often could not be used with programs written in another language. Processing flexibility was not common in the 1950s and 1960s. During this time frame, there was no particular concern about sharing data across applications; this contributed to the redundancy and integrity problems described later.

Eventually, as data management became more of a problem, many businesses adopted COBOL as the standard language for their applications. But this did not solve every file-processing problem. For instance, even if every applications program was coded in COBOL, the way in which a data file was organized might make it unsuitable for new needs. As you will learn later in the chapter, if a file is organized only for sequential access, for example, it will not meet the needs of applications that require direct access to individual records in the file.

One solution to the file-organization problem that many firms adopted was to create duplicate versions of the data files or portions of files—for instance, one version that could be used for one type of processing, and another version that could be used for another type of processing. Unfortunately, this led to two additional problems: data redundancy and lack of data integrity. **Data redundancy** concerns the problems of inefficient data storage and wasted storage space. That is, data that seemingly should be stored in only one storage location now occupy two or more storage locations. The lack of **data integrity** results from the fact that updates to data stored in one file may not be made to the other files containing the same data. Ideally, organizational data should be current—even if duplicates of the data are stored in more than one location. When the contents of files conflict, confusion may reign.

An Example of File Processing

Figure 7.7(a) shows the master customer file for Mad About Cameras, a mail-order catalog firm that sells photographic equipment and supplies. For purposes of illustration, only 12 customers and a limited amount of data about them are shown. In a real-life firm, of course, there may be several thousand customers and many other pieces of data about each one, such as phone number, credit limit, charge card status, and so on. Collectively, the customer records constitute a file, called CUSTOMER-MASTER.

Also consider the files in (b), (c), and (d). These are other files used by Mad About Cameras in its order-processing operations. Shown in these figures are a product file in (b), PRODUCT-MASTER, which contains product descriptions and product prices; an order file in (c), ORDER-TRANSACTION, which shows when specific orders were placed by specific customers; and an order details file in (d), ORDER-DETAILS, which shows the merchandise that was shipped for each order. The two order files reference data that are also stored in other files; for instance, the ORDER-TRANSACTION file references the customer numbers that are found in the CUSTOMER-MASTER file.

Some of the files provided in Figure 7.7 can be used on their own to produce useful information, without relating them to data in other files. For instance, we

```
CUST     CUSTOMER                                                         ZIP
#        NAME                STREET              CITY        STATE CODE
-----------------------------------------------------------------------------
101      Foulkes, Chester    22 Strawbridge      Venice       CA   90291
102      Finney, Bill        41 Dreary Rd.       Ocean Park   WA   98640
104      Billings, Ellen     P.O. Box 437        Smoke Tree   CA   92262
109      Tipp, F.            1500 Sky Mesa Rd.   Beaumont     CA   92223
110      Mona, Lisa          Star Route, Box 9   Mojave       CA   93501
115      Carson, Susan       P.O. Box 2778       Roslyn       WA   98941
116      Massey, Ken         14 Elm St.          Venice       CA   90291
120      Topps, Helen        4468 Redwood Dr.    Moses Lake   WA   98837
121      Winston, Howard     70 Lincoln St.      Medford      OR   97501
123      Evans, Bertha       P.O. Box 398        Spokane      WA   99254
124      Smith, H.M.         33 Sunset Blvd.     Seattle      WA   98197
127      Province, Al        Jones Rd.           Beaverton    OR   97075
```

(a) CUSTOMER-MASTER file

```
PROD    PRODUCT
#       DESCRIPTION      PRICE
-------------------------------
001     Tripod          $120.00
002     T-100 Lens      $100.00
003     T-200 Lens      $200.00
004     F-3 Camera      $350.00
005     Binoculars      $ 80.00
```

(b) PRODUCT-MASTER file

```
ORDER    CUSTOMER
#        #                    DATE
------------------------------------
001      101                  1/3/93
002      110                  1/6/93
003      115                  1/6/93
004      116                  1/7/93
```

(c) ORDER-TRANSACTION file

```
ORDER                PRODUCT
#        QUANTITY     #
-----------------------------
001         2         002
001         1         004
002         2         001
003         2         001
003         1         002
003         1         003
004         1         002
004         1         005
```

(d) ORDER-DETAILS file

Figure 7.7 An example of file processing: Mad About Cameras' four data files.

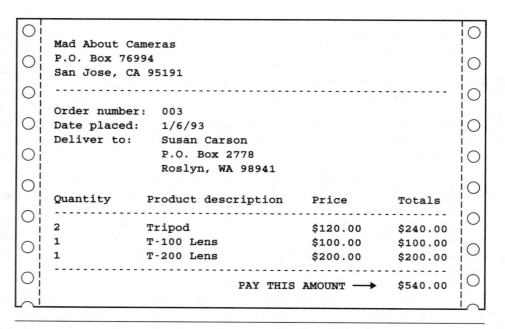

```
  Mad About Cameras
  P.O. Box 76994
  San Jose, CA 95191
  ---------------------------------------------------------------

  Order number:   003
  Date placed:    1/6/93
  Deliver to:     Susan Carson
                  P.O. Box 2778
                  Roslyn, WA 98941


  Quantity        Product description    Price        Totals
  ---------------------------------------------------------------
  2               Tripod                 $120.00      $240.00
  1               T-100 Lens             $100.00      $100.00
  1               T-200 Lens             $200.00      $200.00
  ---------------------------------------------------------------
                          PAY THIS AMOUNT ────▶       $540.00
```

Figure 7.8 An invoice prepared from four data files shown in Figure 7.7.

can use the CUSTOMER-MASTER file to get a breakdown of customers by state or to prepare mailing labels that are sorted by zip code. Similarly, the PRODUCT-MASTER file can be used to compile a list of products in various price categories. The ORDER-TRANSACTION file can help prepare a report showing in which months of the year most orders are placed.

A wealth of information can also be produced by combining data from several files. For instance, by combining the data of all four files, we can prepare invoices, such as the one shown in Figure 7.8. Or, by combining data from the PRODUCT-MASTER and ORDER-DETAILS files, we can prepare sales reports showing which products have accounted for the most sales. Also, by combining data from the CUSTOMER-MASTER and ORDER-DETAILS files, we can find out which customers or geographical areas accounted for the greatest dollar volume of sales.

However, interrelating data from two or more files may be problematic in many file-processing environments. Special programs may have to be written to interrelate the data and this can be especially challenging if the files are structured for different languages. Of course, it is possible to create new files to expedite application processing; for instance, in Figure 7.8, creating a fifth file that consists of selected data from the original four files, just to process invoices. Unfortunately, this can exacerbate the redundancy, integrity, and program-data dependence problems cited earlier.

As will be explained later in this chapter, database processing makes it relatively easy to interrelate data from two or more files. Also, database processing can reduce the program-data dependence, redundancy, and lack-of-integrity problems inherent in file-processing systems.

However, despite its drawbacks, file processing remains very popular today, especially in mainframe and large-system environments. Why? (1) File processing is relatively simple to understand; (2) file processing is relatively inexpensive; (3) numerous organizations already possess a large bank of existing programs that were created for file-processing environments, and many of these companies consider it either too expensive, too time-consuming, or just too much trouble to convert them for use in a database environment; (4) as you will learn later, file-processing systems are sometimes less vulnerable to failure than are database management systems; and (5) database processing is not the solution to every application problem. In many areas, file management works just fine.

File Management Software

A file manager is a software package that lets users and programmers organize data into files and then process those files. File managers perform such important processing tasks as information retrieval and report preparation; they are available for both large and small computers.

File managers designed for microcomputers are normally targeted to end-users, allowing them to create files by following easy-to-use, menu-driven routines that accompany the package. As previously illustrated in Figure 7.3 (page 282), the user will generally be involved with designing a template—or on-screen form—for each file. Later, that same user can summon fresh copies of the template to the screen so that records can be typed into them. Packages targeted to mainframes, however, are generally aimed at the programmer's level of sophistication. They usually have routines that allow interfacing with already existing data files, as well as sophisticated facilities for the creation of new files and templates. The subsequent data entry, using templates created by MIS professionals, is typically performed by data-entry personnel.

The file manager can be used to create and store as many files as necessary. Besides creating reports and allowing users to search for records having specific characteristics, most packages permit users to sort records and create *filter* environments, which temporarily establish subfiles composed of only certain types of records or fields. For instance, from a national file representing people of all sexes and ages, a subfile of California males under 30 could be created.

Internally Developed File Management Programs

File managers developed in-house (by the organization's programmers) are often designed to process data in batches and output preplanned documents and reports. When managers or users desire report formats different from existing ones, a formal request may be required. A systems analyst might interview the users making the request in order to determine what the contents and format of the new report should be. A new program may have to be designed, coded, and debugged. And, because of the application backlog problems discussed in Chapter 6, the completion of this process may take months.

The time it takes to get a new report programmed and delivered means that getting specially developed, one-time reports to managers attempting to deal with immediate problems may be difficult. The way the system is set up may inhibit managers from getting answers to customized questions about data in files in a timely manner. Managers may be limited to only those report formats that are anticipated when the program is designed—and many of these may provide only routine information.

Commercial File Management Software

An increasing number of organizations are using file management packages developed by software vendors, especially on microcomputers. As noted previously, these packages make it possible for users to create record formats and enter data into records, then sort, search, and develop reports from these files. In many instances, such software can also be used to analyze mainframe data on microcomputers.

Commercial file management software is available for all types of computing platforms, from microcomputers to mainframes, and from stand-alone to networked machines. In addition to those that manage files containing only text and numbers, specialized file managers are available. For example, some packages allow images (such as photographs) in addition to text and data. Multimedia systems (discussed later in the chapter) may also include audio and video clips.

DATA ACCESS AND ORGANIZATION METHODS

Organizing and accessing data are two of the driving forces behind data management. *Organizing* data involves arranging data in storage so that they may be easily accessed. *Accessing* data refers to retrieving data from storage. Data organization and access are important determinants of how easily managers and users can obtain the information they need to do their jobs. Since some organization and access schemes provide faster or more flexible ways to locate individual records than others, it is important for managers to anticipate what data they—and their subordinates—will need when designing files and databases.

Organizing and accessing data are, of course, related—just as organization and access are related in non-computer environments. For instance, the way a student chooses to organize notes for a class influences how accessible those notes are. And the way a videotape, compact disk, or cassette tape collection is organized impacts how easy it is to locate a movie or musical performance later. Basically, the managerial challenge in data organization and access is deciding how the data are likely to be accessed by users and then deciding the best way to organize them to facilitate these types of accesses.

In the next section, we will look first at access methods, and then at strategies for organizing data. Later, we will discuss the topic of secondary keys, which represent a way to access data in multiple ways, even though we can only physically organize them one way.

Access Methods

As mentioned in Chapter 5, there are two principal ways to access data: sequentially or directly. Sequential access refers to accessing records in the sequence in which they are physically stored. Direct access refers to accessing data in a manner that is relatively independent of the way the data are physically stored. Direct access is any type of access that does not require scanning all the records that precede a desired one. With direct access, individual records in a file can be accessed at random, in no particular order or sequence.

Much of the data being processed will either be on magnetic tape or disk. Tape is capable only of sequential access, whereas disks can be used for both sequential and direct access.

Organization Methods

Although there are two principal types of access, many more ways to organize data exist. The way a person decides to organize data is important since some methods of organization may preclude certain types of access. Consider a book library, for instance. If books were organized on shelves in the order in which they were acquired by the library, a reader would have a difficult time trying to find a specific title. Trying to acquire all of the books on a particular subject would be even more complex because these would be scattered throughout the library.

Five of the common ways for organizing data are serial, sequential, indexed, indexed-sequential, and direct organization. For simplicity, throughout the discussion of these methods (and in the later discussion of secondary keys), we will assume a file-processing environment which is organized in accord with the program(s) used to update it. However, any of these methods may also be used in database environments in which a file (table) may be shared by numerous programs or users.

Before starting, we should mention that most records are organized, and later accessed, with respect to one or more fields within the individual records. These fields are usually called **key fields**. For example, the Internal Revenue Service primarily organizes and accesses taxpayers through one important key field: Social Security number. Many large mail-order catalog firms access their customer records during order entry by using a combination of two key fields: zip code and last name.

Serial

The simplest organization scheme is serial. With **serial organization**, records are arranged one after another, in no particular order—other than, perhaps, the chronological order in which records are added to the file. Serial organization is

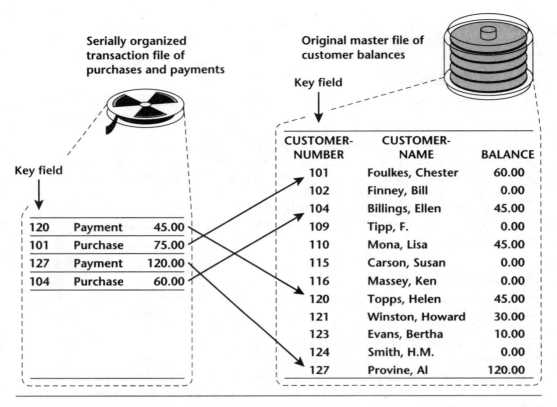

Figure 7.9 Updating a master file, using data from a serially organized file. In this example, the individual records of the master file are updated randomly, depending on the order of the records in the serially ordered transaction file.

commonly found with transaction data, where records are created in a file in the order in which transactions take place.

Records in a serially organized file are sometimes processed in the order in which they occur. For example, when such a file consists of daily purchase and payment transaction data, it is often used nightly to update records in a master account file. Since transactions are in random order by key field, in order to perform this update, records must be accessed randomly from the master file. This process is illustrated in Figure 7.9.

Transaction data is not the only type of data found in serially organized files. In many businesses, customer account numbers are issued in a serial manner. In this scheme, a new customer is given the next highest account number that has not been issued and the data about the new customer (such as name, address, and phone number) are placed at the end of the existing customer account file. When this approach is used, it is easy to distinguish the long-time customers from the new ones; the long-time customers have lower account numbers.

```
          CUSTOMER-NUMBER              CUSTOMER-NAME
          ------------------------------------------
               101                     Foulkes, Chester
               102                     Finney, Bill
               104                     Billings, Ellen
               109                     Tipp, F.
               110                     Mona, Lisa
               115                     Carson, Susan
               116                     Massey, Ken
               120                     Topps, Helen
               121                     Winston, Howard
               123                     Evans, Bertha
               124                     Smith, H.M.
               127                     Provine, Al
                ↑
             Key field
```

Figure 7.10 A sequential file. This file is ordered by its primary key—CUSTOMER NUMBER. The number of records is small, to serve only illustrative purposes.

Sequential

In files that follow a **sequential organization**, records are arranged one after another, in a predetermined order. For instance, the file in Figure 7.10 is organized sequentially by customer number. If this file were stored on a disk or tape, record 101 would physically be the first record in the file, followed by record 102, and so on.

The field on which records are sequentially organized is often called the **primary key**. In many sequential organization schemes, the primary key will have a unique value. For instance, no two customers will be assigned the same customer number. When the primary keys have a unique value, they can be used to access individual records in the file.

Although uniqueness for the primary key is not mandatory in all types of processing, such a property often simplifies processing. For example, to reorganize records from a serial file into a sequential file, the records are usually sorted on the primary key. By reorganizing a serial transaction file into a sequential file, it is often possible to update related files faster and more efficiently than is possible by using the procedures illustrated in Figure 7.9. This means that the individuals responsible for updating files may be able to perform more processing tasks on their work shifts, which has obvious economic benefits for their employers.

A common operation performed in MIS shops is a sequential batch update, in which the transaction file is organized sequentially and the master file is accessed sequentially. As described in Chapter 1, the master file typically contains semipermanent data—data that will not change quickly or often (such as a customer's name, address, and phone number). The transaction file, on the other hand, contains records that represent business transactions involving the entities (for example, customers) represented in the master file. Each transaction is considered to be a unique business event. Prior to processing, the records in the transaction file are sorted so that all transactions associated with a particular master file record are grouped together. The order of the sorted transaction records correspond to the order of the records in the master file. A sequential batch update is depicted in Figure 7.11. As modifications, deletions, and additions are made to master file records, and as records are read from the original master file that are not in the transaction file, all are transferred to an updated master file, as shown in the figure.

To process the files in Figure 7.11, the computer starts at the beginning of each file and reads the first records. If the key fields in these records match, the update program checks to see that the operation being performed is authorized or permitted. Unauthorized operations usually include trying to modify a record that is not in the master file, trying to add a record that is already in the master file, and trying to delete a record that is not in the master file. If the operation is permissible, it is performed; otherwise, an error condition is noted in a separate error file. After one of these actions happens, the files roll forward to their respective next records. If the key field in the transaction file is greater than the key field in the master file, the master file rolls forward until it either locates a record that matches the key field in the transaction or locates a key field that is greater than the key field in the transaction. If it can match the key field in the transaction record, then a modification (update) or a deletion of the record in the master file can take place. If it cannot match the key field in the transaction record, a new record can be added to the master file.

Indexed

Records in an indexed file may be physically stored sequentially, serially, or even randomly. A second file—known as an *index*—makes it possible to access individual records directly, no matter how the records are physically stored. To directly access individual records, users consult an index to select the records of interest. The file or database management software then retrieves the records from storage for on-screen display or hardcopy output. This process is analogous to a library patron's consulting a card catalog in order to determine the location of a particular book; however, in the library, the patron is usually responsible for retrieving the book.

Access to individual records in a file may be possible through multiple indexes. Just as the location of a book in a library may be found through author, title, or subject indexes, in computer-based files, multiple indexes provide users with several ways to locate individual records. For example, access to records in a bank's customer master file may be possible through Social Security number, address, phone number, and customer account number indexes. Multiple indexes often provide users with greater flexibility in locating records and this may translate into better customer service and enhanced user productivity.

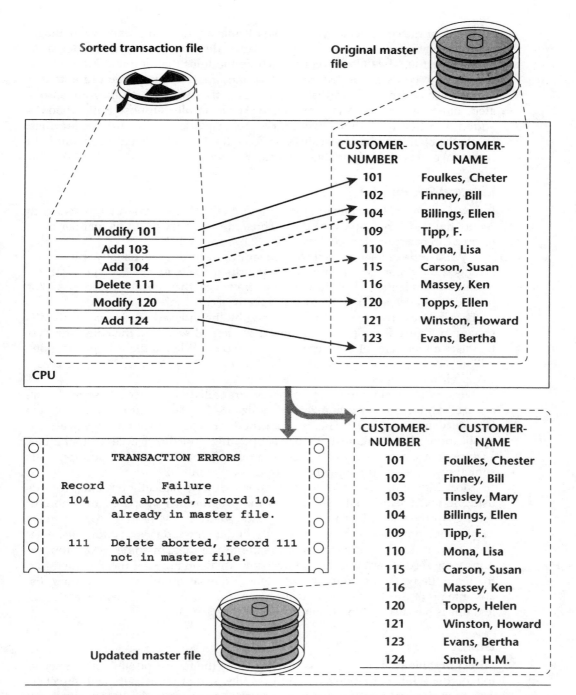

Figure 7.11 A sequential batch update. As each record is read from the transaction file, the sequential batch update program check to see if the transaction is consistent with the information in the master file. If it is, an updated master-file record is produced; otherwise, an entry is made into an error file.

Many of the commercially available file management and database management software packages make it quite easy to develop one or more indexes for an existing file. They also typically include modules that automatically update indexes as records are added, deleted, or modified. It is important to note that indexes are additional files that, like the data files with which they are associated, must be updated and maintained. For example, suppose a new book is added to a library without new entries being made in the card catalog files. While the book may be physically stored on the shelf, library patrons would not be aware of its existence or able to locate it easily.

Indexed-Sequential

Indexed-sequential organization is a file organization scheme that allows both sequential and direct access to data. Thus, files organized in this manner must be on a direct access storage device (DASD), such as disk.

With **indexed-sequential organization**, records are usually physically arranged on a storage medium by their primary key, just as they are with sequential organization. The difference is, however, that an index also exists for the file; it can be used to look up and directly access individual records.

Direct access to a file that is organized by the indexed-sequential method is shown in Figure 7.12. In many indexed-sequential schemes, the computer system uses a hierarchy of indexes to locate a record. When a file is large, its index will also be large. Using several levels of indexing helps to speed up user access to individual records.

Files set up to allow this type of access are called *ISAM* (*indexed-sequential access method*) files. Many organizations utilize ISAM files because of their relative flexibility and simplicity. This is often the best type of files for organizational applications that demand both batch updating and direct access capabilities. *Virtual storage access method* (*VSAM*)—an extension of the ISAM approach—is sometimes used in large-system computing environments.

Most MIS shops have utility programs that automatically organize records using indexed-sequential methods, so the programmer is spared the chore of setting up the individual indexes. Luckily, many ISAM (and VSAM) systems have utility programs that automatically update the indexes as additions, deletions, and other critical changes are made to the files. In some ISAM applications, new records are put into an overflow area and are later incorporated into the main file when it is reorganized. Hence, in most situations, the primary disadvantages of this type of organization concern file and index maintenance (unless this is handled automatically by utility programs).

Direct

Direct organization is a scheme that provides the fastest possible direct access to records. While both indexed and ISAM files also provide users with direct access to individual records, direct organization is typically the best when access time is critical and when updating all the records in the file in a batch is not needed.

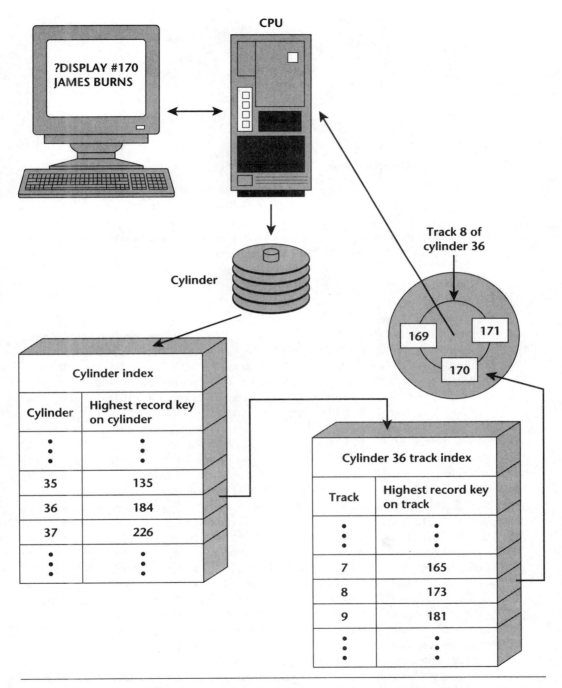

Figure 7.12 Indexed-sequential file organization. To locate a record in secondary storage, the computer system uses both a cylinder and track index to find the disk surface and track on which the record is stored. Cylinders and tracks were discussed in Chapter 5.

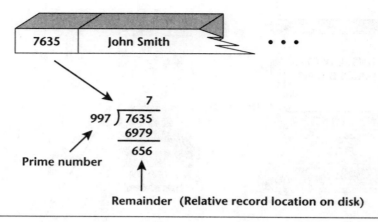

Figure 7.13 In this example of hashing, the key field is divided by the prime number closet to—but less than—the number of records in the file. The remainder is subsequently used to determine the relative address of the record in the file.

Access to an individual record in a direct file works by taking the primary key of the record and using a formula—called a *hashing algorithm*—to mathematically transform that key field directly to a record location in the file. Later, when the record has to be accessed, that same formula is used to calculate its location. Files that provide such rapid access to individual records are sometimes called *random* files; random access is a direct access method that derives a storage location from a record key without using an index.

Many hashing algorithms have been developed. One popular procedure is to use prime numbers somewhere in the formula process, which Figure 7.13 illustrates. (If you want to duplicate these results, be sure to manually divide the numbers. Using a calculator will not produce the same answers.) Here, the key field is divided by a prime number that corresponds to the maximum number of storage locations allocated for the records of this file. The remainder obtained in this division is then used as the relative address of the record, but relative addresses can be directly translated into physical locations on the storage medium. For example, if the relative address of a particular record computes to 656 and, perhaps, the records in this file are to be stored in the second cylinder of a disk pack, this record is stored in the 656th physical position on that cylinder. If 100 records could be stored on each track, this record would be in the 56th record position of the seventh surface of the second cylinder. Because relative addresses are created during this process, these files are sometimes referred to as *relative files*.

Hashing algorithms sometimes produce results indicating that two or more different records should be stored at the same relative disk address. This type of situation is called a *collision*; the record keys that collide are called *synonyms*. When this type of situation results, a second storage location must be found for one of the records. Good hashing algorithms are those that result in a minimum

Beyond Post-It Notes: Stick-On Memory Buttons

Move over bar codes—memory buttons are on the way. The buttons are stainless steel canisters that resemble a watch battery and contain a microchip with 512 characters of information. Their adhesive backing allows users to attach them to virtually anything—from employee security badges to expensive equipment that must be tracked or monitored in the field. Most are powered by a battery that lasts ten years and can withstand temperature swings from −4 to 158° F.

Potential applications are the same as for bar codes. Vendors foresee using them on employee ID tags, hospital ID bracelets, hazardous waste drums, fire extinguishers, factory work-in-progress, medical samples, cargo containers, fleet vehicles, storage tanks, and even on ID tags for livestock. Buttons could also be attached to appliances and consumer products in order to record warranty information and service call records.

"THE BUTTONS ARE STAINLESS STEEL CANISTERS THAT RESEMBLE A WATCH BATTERY AND CONTAIN A MICROCHIP WITH 512 CHARACTERS OF INFORMATION."

Experts say that the contents of a button can be changed in the field (such as when a service call is made) and for virtually no charge. With a cost ranging from $2–$7, they are affordable by many businesses.

Memory buttons will challenge MIS professionals to find ways to keep up with the widely distributed data that can result from their use. Integrating memory buttons with mainstream computer systems is also likely to be challenging.

Adapted from Betts (1992).

of collisions, while at the same time, compacting the records of a file into the smallest amount of total disk space. Of course, good hashing algorithms also provide users and managers with quick, reliable access to the data and information they need.

Secondary Keys

Physically, if data are to be purposefully sequenced on disk, they can only be ordered on one key field. For example, it is physically impossible to place the customer file in Figure 7.7(a) (page 287) onto disk so that it is sequentially ordered on both the CUSTOMER-NUMBER and ZIP-CODE fields. Nonetheless, often we would like to have access to data through a number of keys, not just the ones on which they are physically ordered. This need led to the development of **secondary keys**.

To see how secondary keys work, refer again to the customer file in Figure 7.7(a). Suppose that this is an indexed-sequential file, so it can be accessed randomly, and its records are arranged with respect to a key field. In the figure, it is organized in ascending order on the CUSTOMER-NUMBER field. And, CUSTOMER-NUMBER is the primary key for this file.

Many organizations find it useful to sequence customer records on a customer number primary key, as Mad About Cameras did. The organization controls the value of this key and, generally, the value assigned to it can and should be unique. Thus, no two customers are assigned the same customer number. Values of the other keys (which are beyond the control of the firm) are often not unique. For example, two or more people sometimes have the same name, or two or more customers can live in the same state or city. If users wish to access records through any of these fields, they must declare them to be secondary keys.

To see where a secondary key might be useful, consider a problem that Mad About Cameras encounters frequently. Customers, when they phone in orders, usually have no idea what their customer number is. If the customer file were accessible only in the manner shown in Figure 7.7(a), company employees would have to perform a full-fledged file search—which is time-consuming—in order to uniquely identify virtually every calling customer who doesn't remember his or her number. In lieu of a full-fledged file search, secondary keys are often used in such a situation to find the customer number.

To handle this problem, the file shown in Figure 7.7(a) can be broken down into several lists, each one representing a particular zip code and containing customers who fall within that zip code. Furthermore, for each resulting list, the customers are accessible in sequential order by last name. So, for example, the 90291 zip code list would make available, in the order shown:

```
Foulkes, Chester 101
Massey, Ken 116
```

To help clarify what we are saying, let's consider what would happen if Ken Massey calls to place an order but can't recall his customer number. To obtain Mr. Massey's customer record, the order clerk would ask for his zip code. The clerk would then type the zip code into the computer terminal. The software managing the application would locate the specified zip code list and list all customers and customer numbers associated with the zip code—including Ken Massey's. The clerk could then type Mr. Massey's customer record into the terminal in order to retrieve his record.

Let's look at another example in which a secondary key would be useful. Assume that Mad About Cameras is headquartered in San Jose, California, where it operates a sizable outlet store to supplement its catalog business. Frequently, Mad About Cameras runs sales specials at its store and sends out special mailings to all California customers. Thus, the firm will probably want to establish the state field as a secondary-key field so personnel can locate California customers quickly, without having to search through the entire file for them.

What these examples suggest is that an organization may need access to data in a multitude of ways. Having many paths to locate the same data can enhance customer service and potentially provide the organization with a competitive advantage. This concern—rapid data access to all data about a customer—was, in fact, one of the driving forces behind the development of database management systems in many organizations. Before turning to the characteristics of these systems, let's briefly consider the types of file structures that are typically found in batch and interactive processing environments.

Batch Processing File Structures

If the records in a file do not have to be updated immediately, serial or sequential file organizations may be appropriate. When it is possible to accumulate a batch of requests for additions, deletions, and modifications to records in a file, the updating processes illustrated in Figures 7.9 (page 292) or 7.11 (page 295) may be possible. When records are stored on a medium (such as a tape) that only allows sequential access, batch updating is typically the only cost-effective approach; any other processing involving such media are, usually, too inefficient. Batch updating is also possible when an indexed-sequential file organization is used. Sequential batch updating is a fast, efficient way to update sequential files.

Payroll files are often updated in batches. Many customer account files are also updated in batches, particularly those that result in the issuance of customer billing statements. The frequency with which files are updated (and customer statements issued) can vary within an organization. For example, within a bank, the programs that produce checking account statements are often run just once a month; those for loan accounts or individual retirement accounts (IRA) may be run just 2–4 times a year.

Interactive Processing File Structures

In interactive (real-time) processing environments, the records in a file are usually updated one at a time in a random order. In such environments, users need to be able to access individual records for viewing or modification. They may also need to add or delete records from the file. To meet these user needs, the files in interactive processing environments typically use direct, indexed, or indexed-sequential organization schemes.

DATABASE MANAGEMENT

What we covered so far shows that users often need to access data quickly and in a variety of ways. Also, you have seen that many business applications require interrelating data that might conceivably exist in several independent files. These types of concerns—as well as those regarding program-data dependence, data redundancy, and data integrity—led to the development of database management systems. Basically, a database management system (DBMS) is a collection of software that is designed to provide a systematic, integrated, and flexible approach to organizing and accessing organizational data.

Database management systems differ from file management software primarily in that they enable flexible access to data that could possibly exist as separate files. They make it easy to access and integrate data from separate files in order to develop new report formats—even one-time ad hoc reports. This capability has tremendous potential for enhancing managerial decision making.

However, as a rule, since database management systems are more technically complex than file-oriented software packages, they are also more expensive and more difficult to master.

An Example of Database Processing

Now, we will turn to a simple example that illustrates why organizations might use database processing as an alternative to file processing. Imagine that a bank uses a file processing system with three different customer files: checking, savings, and loans. Often, customers call the bank with questions on several of their accounts.

Suppose a customer calls in with questions about his or her savings, checking, and loan accounts. The service representative might have to go through the following procedures: enter the checking-account-balance program, get the required checking information, and leave program; then, enter the savings-account-balance program, get the required savings information, and leave program; and so on. These procedures could be cumbersome, especially if each program has its own access rules.

The situation is especially frustrating for the representative when the customer needs other information from these files and requests it in random order. For instance, after getting balances in the three accounts, the customer might ask if a certain check was processed, thus requiring the representative to re-enter the checking account file.

Using database technology, it would be possible to put all of the information into a central database so that only one program or file entry is required. When the database pulls up the customer account, all of the checking, savings, and loan data are instantly available. After representatives learn how to use such a system, the time it takes to process customer requests would decrease and better, faster service would be provided to the customer. Today, when firms are striving for competitive advantage, database processing has become a particularly critical activity.

The Database

In a DBMS, data that could conceivably be put into several files are integrated into a single database. A database is simply an integrated collection of data. The database is created in such a way as to balance the data management objectives of speed, multiple access paths, minimum storage, program-data independence, and preservation of data integrity. Some of the ways that database management systems allow access to data are similar to the file access procedures described previously. Other DBMS properties will be discussed soon.

Different database systems have different ways of representing data physically on disk. These *physical* representations can be complex and generally do not concern the user. Basically, the DBMS tries to store data in ways that facilitate rapid access while economizing on storage. Of greater interest to the user is the *logical view* of the data; that is, how the user sees the relationships among data. For instance, a bank service representative should know that the database

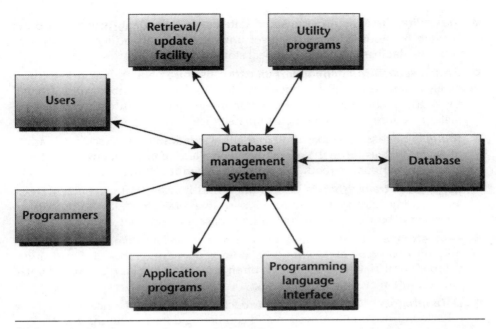

Figure 7.14 A database environment. The database management system provides users with a software interface to the data and data management resources that they need.

contains the names, addresses, and phone numbers of customers—as well as recent savings, checking, and loan histories. Exactly how these data elements are physically stored is not particularly important to the representative. Physical data descriptions are of concern, however, to the MIS department, which must select a database system that meets the needs of users at a reasonable cost.

Access Tools

Users access database data either with a relatively friendly database language (often a nonprocedural 4GL) that is bundled with the DBMS, or with an application program written in a programming language (usually coded by an application programmer). Most often, the DBMS will support COBOL, the principal data processing language in business; frequently, such languages as FORTRAN, BASIC, C, and PL/1 are also supported.

The DBMS provides an interface between users and programmers and the data and data management resources they must access. Users and programmers state their particular needs to the DBMS, which translates those needs so that data can be accessed from the database. Figure 7.14 illustrates this process.

Advantages and Disadvantages of Database Management

A true DBMS offers several advantages over file processing. The principal advantages of a DBMS are the following:

- **Flexibility** Because programs and data are independent, programs do not have to be modified when types of unrelated data are added to or deleted from the database, or when physical storage changes.

- **Fast response to information requests** Because data are integrated into a single database, complex requests can be handled much more rapidly than if the data were located in separate, non-integrated files. In many businesses, faster response means better customer service.

- **Multiple access** Database software allows data to be accessed in a variety of ways (such as through various key fields) and often, by using several programming languages (both 3GL and nonprocedural 4GL programs).

- **Lower user training costs** Users often find it easier to learn such systems and training costs may be reduced. Also, the total time taken to process requests may be shorter, which would increase user productivity.

- **Less storage** Theoretically, all occurrences of data items need be stored only once, thereby eliminating the storage of redundant data. Systems developers and database designers often use *data normalization* to minimize data redundancy.

- **Data integrity** Because data occurrences are stored only once, updates are reflected throughout the system and conflicting data are eliminated.

- **Better data management** Because data are stored in a central place, the organization knows where to find its data. Thus, efforts at establishing security, setting data standards, and applying other management procedures can be concentrated at a single location, rather than spread out over several.

Not every database system incorporates every one of these properties, and sometimes even true database systems relax one or more properties. For instance, many microcomputer database management systems physically store data in files. Although these files are interrelated in a way that makes their physical storage transparent to the database user, they result in redundant storage. For example, three different files may store the home addresses of employees. Because using less storage compacts data and makes them more difficult to access, some database systems relax the less-storage objective a bit, and duplicate certain data to speed up certain types of processing.

Perhaps the most significant disadvantage to database systems is their cost. For instance, database software can cost several hundred thousand dollars for large-computer systems. Because these systems are big, they can force an organization to upgrade to a larger, more expensive hardware platform. Just converting data from files to a database can be expensive—although it is a one-time expense. In addition, more sophisticated (and expensive) MIS personnel may be needed to operate and maintain the database system. Programmers may have to learn new languages and data-access techniques before they can write applications for the database systems. Data administrators and/or database administrators may have to be hired. Because database systems also increase vulnerability (a failure in one part of the system can make the entire system inactive and subsequent recovery more difficult), costly backup systems may be

ADVANTAGES AND DISADVANTAGES OF A DBMS	
Advantages	**Disadvantages**
▨ Fast response to information requests	▨ High costs:
▨ Multiple access	— Conversion
▨ Lower personnel costs	— More sophisticated hardware and software may be needed
▨ Flexibility	— Higher operating costs
▨ Reduced data redundancy	— Higher personnel costs
▨ Data integrity	▨ Greater complexity
▨ Better data management	▨ Higher vulnerability to failure
	▨ Recovery may be more difficult

Figure 7.15 A DBMS in many organizations go far beyond the personal productivity gains provided by other software packages. It often reaches across the entire organization, forming an infrastructure that is used to manage and control the organization's most important data and applications.

needed. Hence, many organizations have found that moving into a database environment ultimately costs millions of dollars.

Despite these disadvantages, many organizations cannot compete without database systems; moving to a database environment it is not a matter of "if," but "when." A summary of the major advantages and disadvantages associated with a DBMS appears in Figure 7.15.

Database Models

Every database system logically organizes data with respect to some model, called a **data model**, which describes how various pieces of data in the database are logically related to each other. Each type of data model has advantages and disadvantages relative to the processing of different types of applications. The three principal data models used by DBMS packages are

- Hierarchical (or tree) models
- Network models
- Relational models

These models differ in the manner in which data elements (fields) can be logically related and accessed. Hierarchical models are often considered to be the most restrictive; relational, the most flexible. An example of each model is provided in Figure 7.16. In the figure are some of the logical relationships that can be constructed among the types of data existing in a typical business college.

Hierarchical Data Models

Hierarchical data models organize data in the form of a tree. In a tree, the relationship among data elements is always one-to-many. For instance, each professor in Figure 7.16(a) is assigned to one and only one department. If, perhaps, Professor Shirley Lu taught both accounting and MIS courses, she would have to be represented twice in the database—once under accounting and once under MIS—in order to maintain the hierarchical model. The database system would not automatically know that the two occurrences of Professor Lu relate to the same person.

Network Data Models

In a **network data model**, the relationship among data elements can be one-to-many or many-to-many. The solid lines in the network of Figure 7.16(b) illustrate a one-to-many situation, in which many courses can be assigned to the same professor or the same grader. This type of network is commonly called a *simple network* design. If we allow such relationships as those suggested by the dotted lines in Figure 7.16(b)—in which two professors can co-teach a course and a class can have two graders—we have a *complex network* design. Not all commercial database packages that are capable of representing data as simple networks can represent them as complex networks. Nonetheless, a complex network can be broken down into functionally equivalent simple networks.

The earliest database systems, designed to meet the needs of transaction processing, were hierarchical and network systems. For transaction processing applications, which form the backbone of computing for most organizations, hierarchical and network products are still quite widely used. IBM's hierarchical IMS (Integrated Management Store), used in the 1960s, is still one of the most common database management systems found in mainframe environments.

As shown in Figure 7.16, hierarchical and network database management systems require access paths to be built into the database. For example, as you can see from the network structure of Figure 7.16(b), graders are subordinate to professors and classes. Thus, graders must be accessed through some professor-class combination. If a path does not exist in a database to get to data, it usually cannot be created by users. Although this restriction may appear to be without advantage, having preexisting paths into the database results in increased processing speed and greater security. Also, since accesses to transaction processing data are relatively predictable, building fixed access paths is usually not a problem.

Relational Data Models

Figure 7.16(c) shows data represented as a **relational data model**. In this model, data are placed into tables that are logically equivalent to files, where rows represent records and columns represent fields. One of the most important facts to note about relational data models is that data elements are not prerelated at all. For instance, no connection exists between a student table and a professor table. This would allow the student table in Figure 7.16(c) to be sorted by major without manipulating the professor table. As opposed to the hierarchical and network models, data can be related dynamically, by users, as an application is being developed. For example, when tables share a common field (such as the

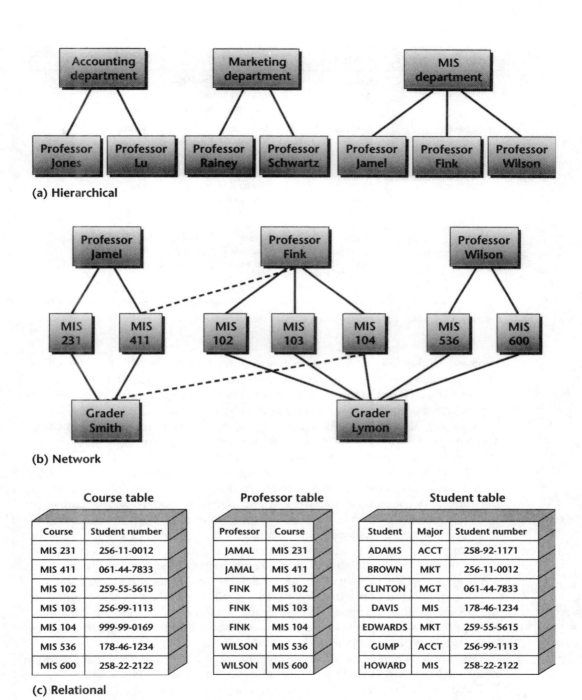

(a) Hierarchical

(b) Network

Course table

Course	Student number
MIS 231	256-11-0012
MIS 411	061-44-7833
MIS 102	259-55-5615
MIS 103	256-99-1113
MIS 104	999-99-0169
MIS 536	178-46-1234
MIS 600	258-22-2122

Professor table

Professor	Course
JAMAL	MIS 231
JAMAL	MIS 411
FINK	MIS 102
FINK	MIS 103
FINK	MIS 104
WILSON	MIS 536
WILSON	MIS 600

Student table

Student	Major	Student number
ADAMS	ACCT	258-92-1171
BROWN	MKT	256-11-0012
CLINTON	MGT	061-44-7833
DAVIS	MIS	178-46-1234
EDWARDS	MKT	259-55-5615
GUMP	ACCT	256-99-1113
HOWARD	MIS	258-22-2122

(c) Relational

Figure 7.16 Database data structures. Depicted are (a) hierarchical, (b) network, and (c) relational database structures.

Data Structure	Product	Vendor
Hierarchical	Focus	Information Builders International
	IMS, DL/1	IBM
	Ramis	On-Line Software International
Network	ADABAS	Software AG of North America
	IDMS	Computer Associates
	Image	Hewlett-Packard
	Total	Cincom
Relational	dBASE IV	Borland International/Ashton-Tate
	FoxPro	Microsoft/Fox Software
	Guru	Micro Data Base Systems
	Ingres	RTI
	Oracle	Oracle
	Paradox	Borland International
	RBase, System V	Microrim
	SQL/DS, DB2	IBM
	Supra	Cincom

Figure 7.17 Commercial implementions of major data structures.

professor and course tables, which share course fields), the tables can be joined and their data can be related. In fact, the three tables in Figure 7.16(c) could be joined through the course and student number fields to generate a class roll that lists course, instructor, student number , student, and major.

Virtually all database management systems targeted for microcomputers, and a majority of those now being implemented on larger computers, follow the relational data model. In mainframe environments, DB2 (an IBM product), INGRES, Oracle, and SAS are some of the leading relational database products. This model is usually much easier for non-computer professionals to understand and use. Unlike hierarchical and network models, access paths are not built into the database; users can relate data as they wish (within parameters set by the organization) while they query the database or prepare reports. They can also prepare programs that perform repetitive types of accesses. The flexibility afforded by relational database products is ideal for decision support applications, where it is generally unpredictable how users will access data.

This should not imply that organizations will allow users to access any data they want in an enterprise-level relational database. Although the capability may be there, security procedures will usually be set up to prevent certain users from certain types of accesses.

The implementation of hierarchical, network, and relational database models in a variety of widely used commercial database packages is shown in Figure 7.17. Although the trend today is toward relational products, some people argue that hierarchical products such as IMS and network products such as Computer Associates' IDMS (Integrated Data Management System) will hang onto a large share of the transaction processing market for awhile. The user bases for such products appears to have leveled off, yet they, like COBOL, have a loyal following and a strong base in industry. Moreover, IMS and IDMS have nearly three times the maturity of relational systems and, in areas where such features as security and data integrity rate high, they are still hard to beat.

DATABASE MANAGEMENT FOR LARGE SYSTEMS

Most of the database management systems used on large computers are designed for transaction processing environments and many follow the hierarchical or network data models. Database systems used in these environments must meet a number of specialized needs:

- Because these database products are relatively sophisticated, professional help is often required to set up the database and facilitate interaction with it.

- Several users may attempt to access the same parts of the database concurrently and their uses may be in conflict. Special controls are therefore needed to handle the conflicts.

- Transaction processing environments are dominated by a heavy investment in programs written in third-generation languages; thus, database management systems competing in this arena must interface with these languages.

- Because transaction processing systems represent the handling of critical business records, they require a number of tight controls.

Database Administration

The process of setting up and maintaining the database is the duty of the database administrator. Another important role found in large-system database environments is that of the data administrator.

As illustrated in Figure 7.18, the **data administrator (DA)** is the person with the central responsibility for the organization's data. Data administration is typically a policy-making function; because of this, the DA should have access to the organization's top-level managers. The data administrator decides what data will be stored in the database (that is, he or she plans the database) and establishes policies for accessing and maintaining the database (for example, policies for collecting, validating, sharing, and monitoring data to be stored in the database, especially shared data that supports many users). The DA is the key person involved in the strategic planning of data resources, which involves the determination of the principal business processes the database should support and the identification of the data needed to carry out these processes. In sum, the role played by the DA is more business—than technically—oriented.

The **database administrator (DBA)** is a database professional who actually creates and maintains the database, and also carries out the policies developed by the data administrator. The role of the DBA is more technical than that of the DA. The DBA is responsible for defining the internal layout of the database, and for ensuring that the internal layout optimizes system performance — especially in the principal business processing areas.

To design the database, the database administrator must get together with users and determine their data requirements. This involves establishing

IMPORTANT DATA RESOURCE MANAGEMENT FUNCTIONS	
Data Administrator (DA)	**Database Administrator (DBA)**
▪ Establish data and information policies	▪ Serve as liaison between users and programmers
▪ Perform strategic data planning	▪ Create and maintain database; plan hardware and software
▪ Develop policies for database integrity, privacy, and security	▪ Establish specific procedures for ensuring database integrity, privacy, and security
▪ Determine interorganizational data flows	▪ Ensure operational performance of DBMS
▪ Develop logical design for database	▪ Determine physical database design

Figure 7.18 Some of the major responsibilities of data administrators (DA) and database administrators (DBA).

schedule and accuracy requirements, needed access paths, frequency of access estimates, search strategies, physical storage requirements, response-time requirements, and security needs. Determining the source of the data and who will be in charge of origination and updates is also part of the design. The database administrator develops these requirements into a physical design that specifies hardware resources.

Defining the contents of the database is an important part of database creation and maintenance. **Data definition** is the process of describing formats and relationships among data elements, as well as how those data elements should be used. In large, transaction-processing-oriented database systems, a special language—called the **data definition language (DDL)**—is typically dedicated to the data definition function. Whereas the DDL describes in detail what formats will be followed by data going into the database, the database administrator has no knowledge of the individual data values that will subsequently be put there. These values are controlled by users.

Maintaining standards and controlling access are two other functions that the DBA handles. The DBA uses the DDL to carry out these functions. For instance, the DBA may make a rule specifying that data must be described in a certain way to the database system. Data descriptions not meeting the rules imposed through the DDL should be rejected and not placed in the data dictionary (described later). Also, invalid data values entered by users should also be rejected. Access controls are used to allow only specified users to access certain paths into the database, thereby preventing unauthorized accesses. For instance, in airline reservations systems, an airline agent should be prevented from giving a passenger an expired rate. However, a high-level supervisor might have the proper authorization code to make exceptions if doing so is in the best interest of the airline.

The DBA is responsible for preparing documentation, including recording the procedures, standards, guidelines, and data descriptions necessary for the efficient and continuing use of the database environment. Documentation should include materials to help end-users, database application programmers, the operations staff, and all personnel connected with the data administration function. Closely related to the process of preparing documentation for various database personnel is educating these personnel about their duties.

The database administrator is also responsible for seeing that the computer operations staff performs its database-processing-related responsibilities properly. Some of these operations details are loading the database, maintenance and security procedures, backup, scheduling the database for use, and restart and recovery procedures (which restore the database to its proper state after a hardware or software failure).

Monitoring the database environment includes such tasks as seeing that the database is meeting performance standards; making sure the accuracy, integrity, and security of data are maintained; setting up procedures for identifying and correcting violations of standards and guidelines; and documenting and correcting errors. Some of these tasks can be accomplished by conducting a periodic audit of the database environment.

The database administrator is also responsible for incorporating any enhancements into the database environment. Enhancements may include new utility programs or new system releases, changes in internal procedures for using the database, and new staff-developed features.

As you can see, both the DBA and the DA have important duties and responsibilities that must be carried out effectively. The strategic role of the DA—coupled with the more technical role of the DBA—should ensure that the database system meets the needs of users and managers, providing the organization with the support that it needs to achieve its strategic goals.

Setting Up Relational Databases

Creating relational databases is similar to the previously described process used to create files. However, with relational databases, data are structured into tables such as those shown in Figure 7.7 (page 287) and Figure 7.16(c) (page 307). These tables have rows and columns similar, respectively, to the records and fields of conventional files.

To establish each table, the user must name it (such as CUSTOMER-MASTER or PRODUCT-MASTER) and describe the data going into each column. This, in effect, is the data definition stage of developing the database. For a table such as PRODUCT-MASTER, in Figure 7.7(b), data may be defined in the following way:

Column Name	Data Type	Column Width	Decimal
PRODUCT-NUMBER	Character	3	—
PRODUCT-DESCRIPTION	Character	30	—
PRICE	Numeric	7	2

Here, the first two fields—PRODUCT-NUMBER and PRODUCT-DESCRIPTION—are defined as *character* fields, having a length of 3 and 30 characters, respectively. Character fields consist of string data that cannot be manipulated arithmetically, although they can be used for sorting. Price is defined as a *numeric* field (that is, one that can be manipulated mathematically) that can contain data having a maximum length of 7 characters and having two digits to the right of the decimal point. Thus, as long as the price of an item is 9999.99 dollars or less, it will be acceptable to the database system. Prices larger than this are rejected if the operator tries to enter them. Character and numeric fields are just two of the various field types available with a microcomputer-based DBMS.

Database Processing

The processing of database data is called **data manipulation**. There are generally two ways to manipulate data in a DBMS: (1) using a proprietary (4GL) database query language or (2) using a programming language (such as COBOL). A DBMS targeted to transaction processing on large computer systems usually contains separate language packages to handle these tasks. Ordinary users—such as executives, line managers, and clerical personnel—typically utilize a more user-oriented 4GL to pose retrieval queries, make authorized updates, and generate simple reports. The 4GL generally consists of easy-to-use nonprocedural commands that enable non-computer professionals to use the database without having to learn a high-level, procedural programming language. This type of 4GL is sometimes called a query language.

Programmers use programming languages extensively to write application programs for the database environment. Languages such as COBOL are usually capable of being enhanced through the DBMS with a set of database-specific commands. These commands are interspersed (embedded) with the regular commands of the language to develop applications. On the other hand, in the case of fast, specialized requests or when a prototype is desired, the programmer will likely use the database's 4GL or query language.

Structured Query Language (SQL)

SQL, which stands for Structured Query Language, is a data definition and data manipulation language found in relational database environments. In non-relational systems, separate data definition and data manipulation languages are common. SQL is now an international standard and is provided with most database management packages on the market today, as well as with some non-relational products. In end-user environments, SQL is usually hidden by more user-friendly interfaces, but is still the underlying DBMS language.

To create tables in SQL, the CREATE statement is used. A new database table can be created at any time with a CREATE TABLE statement. Using this statement makes it possible to define the characteristics of the fields to include in the table. For example, to create the ORDER-DETAILS table for Mad About Cameras (used in Figure 7.7(d) on page 287, the following SQL commands would be used:

```
CREATE TABLE ORDER-DETAILS
        (ORDER-NUMBER INTEGER NOT NULL.
        QUANTITY INTEGER NOT NULL.
```

```
PRODUCT-NUMBER NOT NULL.
PRIMARY KEY (ORDER-NUMBER));
```

In this example, the table attributes (fields) are defined as consisting of integers, and all attribute values must be specified when data are entered into the table (which is what the NOT NULL clause does). The other tables shown in Figure 7.7 (page 287) would be created in a similar way, but would include a wider range of field attributes, such as CHAR (for character) and DATE.

New columns (fields) could be added to the table by using an ALTER TABLE command (this would be used to delete columns as well). An entire table could be deleted using a DROP TABLE statement. CREATE, ALTER, and DROP are SQL's principal data definition statements. User views can be created in SQL with a CREATE VIEW statement. Such file and database changes are much easier to do in relational environments than in hierarchical and network systems.

As we have already noted, the strength of processing data with relational database systems lies in the ability of these systems to process data dynamically, without users being limited to preexisting access paths that were built into the database. Tables can be related by the data fields (columns) that they share. Although relational databases differ with respect to the properties and command sets they offer, three common ways that data are manipulated in a relational DBMS are through select, project, and join operations. The following operations are modeled after SQL's select command:

- **Select** The select operation is used to select records from a table with specific characteristics. For example, in Figure 7.7(a), the user may want to select all customers that reside in Venice, California. Thus, the user issues a command such as:

  ```
  SELECT CUSTOMER-NAME FROM CUSTOMER-MASTER
      WHERE CITY = "VENICE"
      AND STATE = "CA"
  ```

- **Project** The project operation is used to select specified fields or attributes from a table. For example, referring again to Figure 7.7(a), if the user wants to prepare a list that consists of names, cities, and states of all records in CUSTOMER-MASTER, the user issues a command such as:

  ```
  SELECT NAME, CITY, STATE FROM CUSTOMER-MASTER
  ```

- **Join** The examples shown so far manipulate data in a single table. The join operation enables two or more tables to be "cut and pasted" together. Suppose, for example, the user wants to create a table similar to the one in Figure 7.8 (page 288). This table consists of data taken from the CUSTOMER-MASTER and ORDER-TRANSACTION tables of Figure 7.7(a) and (c). The user would invoke a command such as:

  ```
  SELECT ORDER-NUMBER, CUSTOMER-NAME, DATE
      FROM CUSTOMER-MASTER, ORDER-TRANSACTION
      WHERE CUSTOMER-MASTER.CUSTOMER-NUMBER =
      ORDER-TRANSACTION.CUSTOMER-NUMBER
  ```

The system would then locate the desired tables and "cut and paste" them together in the manner described. The resultant table could also be named and saved, if desired.

Commands such as the ones described here can be used dynamically to query the database and to prepare custom reports, or they can be used in combination to produce a saveable program that can be recalled later. In addition to the data manipulation commands shown here, a variety of other commands are available with SQL—commands (such as INSERT, DELETE, and UPDATE) that can be used to update tables, perform mathematical computations, sort records, and perform looping logic.

Concurrent Access

Users on large transaction processing systems often need to access the same data at the same time. For instance, two travel agents, working independently, may want to sell the last seat on a flight. Naturally, the DBMS cannot allow this. Thus, many DBMS packages contain a **concurrent access** feature, which allows one user to temporarily seize control of certain data so that they can be processed without interference from other users.

Interfacing with Preexisting Applications

Another characteristic of database management systems used with large transaction processing systems relates to the fact a DBMS must tie into preexisting application programs. Many of these programs were originally coded in a 3GL, such as COBOL, several years before database systems were put into use. An interfacing feature known as a *host-language interface* is used to bridge this gap.

The host-language interface is a set of commands, functions, and other language elements that enhance a particular 3GL so that it can work in a specific database environment. For instance, the interface might allow use of a particular access method that is authorized by the DBMS—one that is not contained in the 3GL—or allow the programmer to point to specific database records. The third-generation languages that can be enhanced by such features are called **host languages**. Many database management systems will allow several languages to function as hosts.

To run a program that consists of host-language statements and data processing statements, the program is submitted to a *precompiler* that is available with the database package. The precompiler translates the entire program into standard host code so that it can run on standard host-language facilities. For instance, a COBOL precompiler translates a program consisting of standard COBOL and COBOL host-language statements into a program consisting entirely of standard COBOL statements. This program can then be used by the regular COBOL compiler, linkage editor, and loader available with the computer system.

Database Security

Because large, transaction-processing-oriented database management systems are used by several people, their databases are particularly vulnerable to security problems. For example, some people may attempt to illegally alter payroll data. Other people may try to inspect sensitive salary or bank deposit data that they are not authorized to see. Data may even be stolen or erased. In later chapters, we will explore some general solutions to these problems.

In large database environments, security is often handled by giving authorized users only "local views" of the full database. For example, users working on a mailing list application that accesses an employee database would be locked out of access to such sensitive employee data as salaries. In network-oriented database systems, the logical description of the entire database is often called a *schema* and the logical description of a restricted local view of the database is called a *subschema*. Subschemas are sometimes called *external views*. Subschemas only encompass a subset of the data elements in the entire database. For example, an application program's external view is composed of those elements needed to run the application program; hence, each application program has its own external view of the database. Figure 7.19 summarizes the different types of views found in database environments. Please note that users and application programmers need only be concerned with restricted logical descriptions of the data in the database and do not have to be concerned with

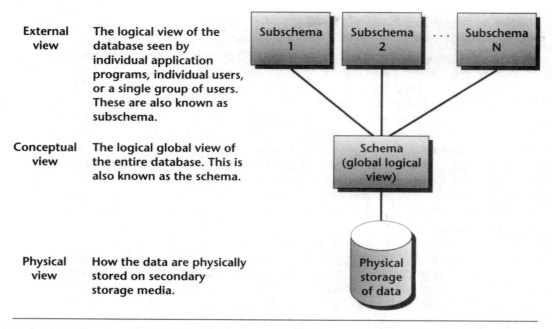

External view	The logical view of the database seen by individual application programs, individual users, or a single group of users. These are also known as subschema.	Subschema 1 Subschema 2 ... Subschema N
Conceptual view	The logical global view of the entire database. This is also known as the schema.	Schema (global logical view)
Physical view	How the data are physically stored on secondary storage media.	Physical storage of data

Figure 7.19 A summary of the different views of the data stored in a database. All of these views are likely to be found in large database management systems.

how the data are physically stored. This contributes to program-data independence in such environments.

Another common security strategy is to create a *shadow copy* of the entire database for users to access in a retrieval mode. Although this requires duplicating the entire database and not providing users with real-time access, it does eliminate the possibility of a retrieval-only user's somehow messing up the original database or slowing down processing. Virtually every computer program contains mistakes of some kind and many users have inadvertently tripped a code that caused unplanned and unpleasant actions to happen to a database.

Although we discussed security with respect to large database systems, security is also an issue in smaller environments. Certainly, if a microcomputer-oriented database package is used by a small company to run its business, security is important. So, too, is security important if a microcomputer DBMS employed by an executive for personal (decision support) use contains sensitive data. These facts notwithstanding, most microcomputer-oriented database management systems are still not as sophisticated about handling security as are the large packages. An even bigger problem, and one we discuss in Chapter 19, is the lack of user education with respect to security matters. Ultimately, no matter how sophisticated the security software is, systems are only as safe as the people guarding them.

Data Dictionaries/Directories

Another problem faced in large system environments concerns the enormous number of data that must be coordinated among several applications. To solve this problem, a mechanism must be available to keep track of data elements—for example, where they are used, where they originated, what names different applications call them, who is responsible for keeping them current, and so on. To provide such coordination, many large database management systems have a data dictionary/directory (DD/D) facility.

The **data dictionary** is similar to a regular dictionary in that it contains definitions and proper uses of entities that are stored in the database. Among the entities found in the dictionary are the identities of database programs; names of all of the data fields found in the database, along with the names of the programs that use them, descriptions of the data, and who is responsible for the data; and authorization (access) tables that specify users and the data and programs authorized for their use. Maintenance of the data dictionary is typically the responsibility of the database administrator.

The data dictionary is useful in many ways. For instance, if a data field is to be altered in any way or eliminated from the database, the dictionary can identify all programs that might require some modification. The data dictionary is also useful for protecting the integrity of database data (since the data element names are cross-referenced), helping programmers to quickly locate blocks of code (such as DATA DIVISION entries in a COBOL program) that can be reused in new applications, and ensuring that all design or coding actions performed by an analyst or a programmer are internally consistent with the application. For instance, if a programmer wishes to create a data name that is already in use, the dictionary facility can inform the programmer of this conflict.

Data dictionaries can be classified as either active or passive. *Active data dictionaries* are those that can influence on-line program development with a specific DBMS package, whereas *passive data dictionaries* are those that cannot. For instance, if a programmer is violating a rule in a system with an active data dictionary, the dictionary will be working alongside the application—in an on-line mode—to immediately notify the programmer of a problem. A passive data dictionary, on the other hand, is generally just an off-line repository of facts that does not directly interact with the application. Usually, active data dictionaries are designed to work with specific DBMS packages; passive data dictionaries may be used in conjunction with a variety of database management packages.

Whereas the data dictionary informs users or programmers of what data are available in the database and how they are used, the **data directory** keeps track of where these data are stored on disk. Thus, the data directory addresses the physical data description and, where hierarchical or network systems are used, the data directory keeps track of the paths to be followed for access.

Many DD/D facilities are acquired independently of their database management systems and they are also available for non-database processing environments. Most DD/D facilities are actually, themselves, full-fledged data management systems because they contain both software and data (the dictionary and the directory).

DD/D facilities, once confined almost exclusively to large database systems, are widespread in several other, smaller application areas. For instance, now that many 4GL programs are packaged with their own database systems, many of these products—such as application packages, application generators, and CASE workbenches—usually come equipped with their own DD/D facilities.

Distributed Databases

Many commercial-level processing environments require a large amount of similar facts to be distributed among several geographically dispersed sites. For instance, a state bank with several branches in several towns will have a lot of customer records. Many of these customers deal almost exclusively with a single branch, or perhaps with two or more branches in the same town. Thus, a sizable processing and communications savings is gained if each branch or region locally manages a database of its own customers. The bank should also find it economical to mail customer statements from a single office. Thus, some standardization and coordination are required to see that this is done effectively.

A database may be distributed in many ways. Two common methods are partitioning and duplicating the database. The method just discussed in the bank example involves *partitioning* the aggregate database so that each local site has the data needed to serve its own area.

Depending on the type of organization and application environment involved, a central site may also want a master file that shows the identity and whereabouts of every record distributed throughout the system. This database distribution method involves *duplicating (replicating)* the database so that a copy of the entire database is available at each local site. Although this method makes more data available at each location, it does entail the additional expense of each site's handling a potentially large number of records that it may never use. This can also create a big updating problem.

Figure 7.20 illustrates the differences between partitioned and duplicated databases. Chapter 8 will cover the technical details concerning communication networks that can be used by distributed databases.

DATABASE MANAGEMENT ON MICROCOMPUTERS

Most single-user database management systems that are available on minicomputers follow the relational data model, and most new database management systems implemented on mainframes are relational. However, many products used on microcomputers are hierarchical (for example, dBASE III PLUS), even though they give users the look and feel of a relational model. Despite this, true relational database systems for microcomputers are increasing in popularity—for example, Paradox, dBASE IV, and R:Base follow the relational model. In general, when compared to hierarchical and network DBMS products, relational database systems are much easier to learn and use.

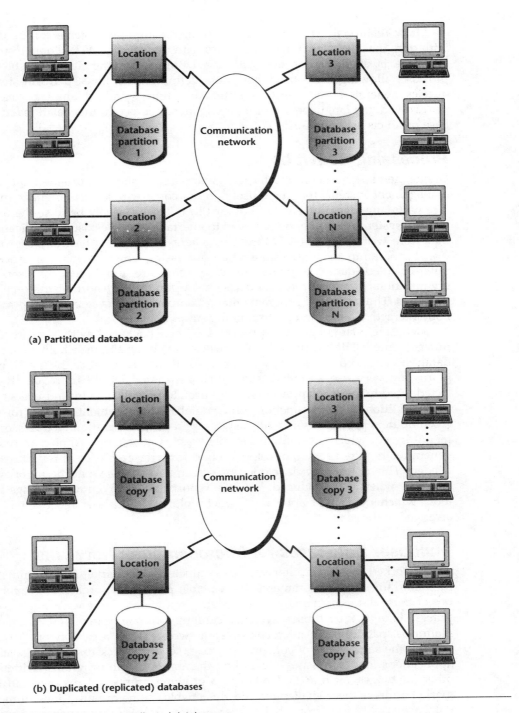

(a) Partitioned databases

(b) Duplicated (replicated) databases

Figure 7.20 Partitioned and replicated databases.

Many relational products targeted to microcomputer systems can be used with only the single language that comes with the package. When only a single language is available for use with the DBMS, that language must be all-purpose, allowing users to execute data definition functions, perform simple queries, generate reports, and program. Although a standard language has not yet evolved, the languages accompanying most microcomputer relational database products are based on SQL.

Processing Activities

Unlike their large-system counterparts, many microcomputer-oriented database management systems for single users do not come with a host-language interface with languages such as COBOL or PL/1. This is largely because the users of these systems generally do not need to interface with preexisting applications that were written in a 3GL. Moreover, whereas COBOL is basically a professional programmer-oriented transaction processing language, many microcomputer-oriented database management systems are purchased by users in organizations that want them for decision support or office administration (OA) purposes. Thus, the 4GL programs that accompany such systems must provide both interactive query and programming support.

Such single-language 4GL programs—when packaged with a microcomputer-oriented DBMS—must be all-purpose, enabling the user both to set up databases and to process data with them. Furthermore, most of these 4GL programs are very user-oriented, since their associated DBMS is frequently selected, used to develop applications, and used to process data by end-users.

In addition to query functions, most database management systems for microcomputers provide users with easy-to-use report preparation modules, often menu-driven, which are sometimes called report generators. Almost all report generators require users to develop a report form for each type of report that is needed. This is typically developed on-screen and shows what the report will look like when it is produced: how the report title and column headings will look, which fields will appear in which columns, and how records will be arranged in the report.

Multiuser Databases for Microcomputer Networks

As networked microcomputer systems compete in the market once dominated by mainframes, many commercially available products approach the capabilities of those database management systems that are available with larger computers. Like the multiuser systems running on mainframe and midrange platforms, packages for microcomputer networks (local area networks) must address the same types of concurrent access, security, backup, and preexisting applications interface issues—including the ability to run programs written in other languages, such as C. However, a growing number of packages on the market address these challenges and this enables some organizations to move database applications from their larger systems to LAN-based microcomputer environments. Such migration options have opened up because powerful,

EXAMPLES OF MULTIUSER DATABASES USED IN MICROCOMPUTER NETWORKS	
Product	**Vendor**
Advanced Revelation	Revelation Technologies, Inc.
DataEase	DataEase International, Inc.
DataFlex	Data Access Corporation
dBASE IV/Server Edition	Borland International
FoxPro/LAN	Microsoft/Fox Software
KnowledgeMan	Micro Data Base Systems, Inc.
Paradox	Borland International
R:Base	Microrim
Superbase 4	Software Publishing Corporation

Figure 7.21 Multiuser database management software for local area networks. The database management software available for these networks is often sophisticated enough to run the kinds of applications that previously required a minicomputer or mainframe.

LAN-based database management systems in existence today have facilities for controlling database access privileges. Some of the leading products (and their vendors) competing in this market are listed in Figure 7.21. Such software is typically found either on the main file-servers or on dedicated database servers, depending on the configuration of the LAN. Chapter 8 discusses LAN configurations more fully.

BEYOND TRADITIONAL DATABASE SYSTEMS

A number of current trends affect file and database management systems in organizations. As already noted, an increasing number of organizations have downsized their database processing applications—moving them from centralized mainframe-based processing environments to more cost-effective mid-range systems or LAN-based platforms. SQL is more widely used, primarily because of the current migration to relational database structures. In addition, new types of databases are cropping up in organizations, including object-oriented databases, multimedia systems, and image-based databases.

Object-Oriented Databases

File and database structures evolved in order to be suitable to changing application needs. Figure 7.22 illustrates this evolution of file and database structures. When applications were developed independently, simple file structures were sufficient. However, when organizations recognized the need for integrated databases, hierarchical, network, and subsequently relational data structures emerged. Today, databases with relational qualities that are capable of manipulating text, data, objects, images, and even video and sound clips are needed by many organizations.

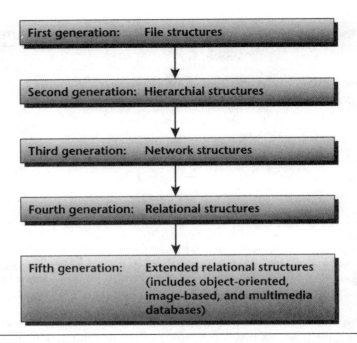

First generation: File structures

Second generation: Hierarchial structures

Third generation: Network structures

Fourth generation: Relational structures

Fifth generation: Extended relational structures
                      (includes object-oriented,
                      image-based, and multimedia
                      databases)

Figure 7.22   The evolution of file and database management systems. Over time, file organization and access schemes have undergone significant changes. Recently, object-oriented, image-based, and multimedia databases have made it possible to capture,store, and update new types of data and information.

While more flexible than their predecessors, relational databases are still based on data elements that describe the entities they store and hence, are best suited to handle character and numeric data. The results of many engineering applications, such as computer-aided design (CAD) and computer-aided engineering (CAE), are not handled easily by relational systems. Expert systems, image-processing systems, multimedia systems, computer-aided software engineering (CASE), project management software, and presentation graphics packages produce information that is important to the organization—information that often defies traditional file and database structures. The drawings, charts, multimedia documents, video clips, programs, and other objects generated by these systems can vary tremendously in type, length, content, and form. New structures are needed to handle such organizationally important information.

Object-oriented programming (OOP) was described in Chapter 6. **Object-oriented databases (OODB)** are a natural extension of OOP. Like other database management systems or DD/D facilities, OODB systems can be either active or passive—we will focus on active systems.

In an active OODB, every object is described by a set of attributes describing what the object is (for example, a set of program code for an expert system, a data flow diagram, or a CAD design for a new product). The behaviors of the object are also included; for example, the object for a CAD design of a new product could include instructions for on-screen display, shrinking, exploding, and rotation. Objects with similar attributes and behaviors can be grouped into classes and the attributes and behaviors of one object within a class can be inherited by other objects within the same class, which can speed up application development.

Object-oriented databases are still evolving, but the goal of each is to provide application developers with a repository of *reusable objects* that only need to be created once. This allows new applications to be put together by appropriately arranging the objects stored in the OODB. This can greatly accelerate application development time and reduce the application backlogs described previously.

Multimedia Data Management

Another evolving set of technologies for systematically managing graphics, drawings, and photographs—in addition to text and data—are multimedia data management systems. Some of these are called hypermedia systems. Such systems use computers and information technology to incorporate text, data, graphics, video, and audio within a single application. Optical and video disks are the predominant storage technologies for these systems.

Hypertext systems are used for the construction and interactive use of text databases. Apple's Hypercard for Macintosh microcomputers is one of the most widely used hypertext systems. Extensive development of hypertext and multimedia systems is expected through the 1990s and industry experts predict that a multibillion-dollar market for these products will exist in the next decade.

Once a multimedia application is developed, users can press a key on the keyboard or a button on a mouse (if touchscreen or light pen technology is not being employed) to retrieve screenfuls of text information. By pressing another key or button, video clips can be run; other buttons or keys activate related narration or music via an attached sound system. In brief, a plethora of interesting information in the form of text, graphics, video, or sound is at the user's disposal. An example of a multimedia database screen is shown in Figure 7.23.

Multimedia applications are being increasingly used in a number of areas:

■ **Merchandising** The potential of using multimedia systems to sell merchandise is almost unlimited. For example, multimedia systems are currently used in the real estate industry. After providing the system with basic preference information (such as area, number of bedrooms, and cost), the system provides images and basic information about homes fitting the description. Video tours, narrated by home owners or realtors, provide room-by-room presentations of particularly interesting offerings. These systems may also include important data about the area, such as weather, local schools, maps, and nearby sights.

Of course, real estate is only one of the many industries with an active interest in multimedia systems. In fact, multimedia systems are even being used to market themselves.

Figure 7.23 An example of a database screen from the St. Louis Zoo's "Teacher's Living World" multimedia kiosk. In multimedia databases, users can obtain data and information about an entry in a variety of formats, including text, data, still photos, and audio and video clips. Multimedia databases and applications are rapidly gaining in popularity.

(Courtesy: Arnowitz Production, Inc.)

- **Training** Companies are using multimedia to train employees at all levels in their organizations. For example, one telecommunication firm developed a multimedia system to teach workers how to fix phone cables.

- **Education** Multimedia systems are increasingly used as educational tools. For example, students learning French can pull up an on-screen video of someone speaking French and see the spoken words spelled out on another part of the screen. Some people predict that multimedia systems will completely change the way in which students are educated.

Image Processing and Document Management Systems

Image processing and document management systems, which were introduced in Chapter 5 (and discussed fully in Chapter 12), represent a final way in which companies are working with photographs, graphs, and document images that cannot be handled easily by a traditional database. While incapable of providing users with information in the variety of formats possible with multimedia systems, image-based databases are sufficient in many applications. Advances in optical storage and document scanning technologies have made these (and multimedia systems) attractive options for many organizations.

Such systems make it possible to create and store records that contain an image or photograph of a source document (see Figure 7.24). For example, these may be used to store the documents and pictures needed to process auto insurance claims. Such a system could also include the picture of an employee in an employee file or assist inventory clerks (especially newly hired ones) in identifying stock items.

In many instances, source documents—such as paper order invoices—that are scanned into such systems can be shredded and recycled. The document and other images stored in these systems might otherwise fill innumerable file cabinets. Hence, these systems represent a significant step toward paperless offices.

EXTERNAL DATABASES AND INFORMATION SERVICES

Most of the preceding discussion concerned databases that were developed and maintained within organizations. While managers must be familiar with their organization's internal databases, they should also be aware of the valuable information available through information utilities. **Information utilities** are companies that provide a variety of information services—including on-line access to external databases—to organizations or individuals that subscribe to their services. Figure 7.25 shows some of the leading information utilities and a brief summary of their services. Most often, access is gained to these services over telephone lines via a microcomputer and modem.

Examples of firms offering information about the business environment (stored in large computer data banks) are CompuServe, Dow Jones News, and Mead Data Central. Subscribers to services like these have access to such data as business publications, up-to-date financial statistics for thousands of companies, business and economic news, and domestic and foreign exchange data.

Also, information-retrieval firms specialize in certain types of market data for specific industries. A corporation may subscribe to one or more of these services so that employees such as marketing managers and sales forecasters can obtain up-to-date industry information. Managers with access to such services often claim that they can obtain needed information in a fraction of the time required before they used such services. Also, information obtained from the information utility is often more current than information gleaned from such off-line sources as newsletters and printed reports.

All of the databases discussed in this section have the potential to enhance user access to needed information and to improve managerial decision making. They also reflect how file and database technologies have dramatically changed the managerial decision-making environment. The ability to have the data and information that a manager needs to make better decisions, provide better customer service, rapidly develop new applications, and outduel competitors is greater today than it has ever been in the past; it will be even better tomorrow.

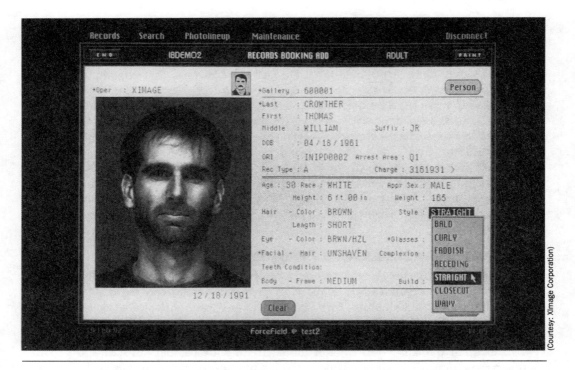

Figure 7.24 Example of a record in a mug-shot database used by police in San Jose, California. Image-based databases, such as this one, make it possible to capture and store records that contain document images or photos.

These new developments should help you appreciate the various ways in which file and database management systems can be configured and utilized to facilitate the achievement of strategic goals. As with many other management decisions, the selection of an appropriate file and database system should be based on numerous factors. When selecting or designing a file or database management system, managers must consider both how the data and information will be used and how it should be formatted for maximum effectiveness. This chapter's overview of what the file and database options are and its discussion of how they work should help you make these important decisions.

SUMMARY

Data are one of an organization's most valuable resources. Ready access to data and information can enhance managerial decision making and user productivity. Managers and users typically access computer-based data and information at microcomputers or terminals, using file and database management software. These software packages allow users to create files, enter data, update data, retrieve data, and generate reports.

SOME MAJOR ON-LINE INFORMATION SERVICES AND EXTERNAL DATABASES

Information Service	Description
▪ CompuServe and The Source	Provide personal computer users with access to statistical databases (such as business and financial market statistics), bibliographic databases (such as news, sports, electronic encyclopedias, and reference materials) and other services, including airline reservations, buying services, bulletin boards, and so on.
▪ Data Resources, Inc.	Furnishes statistical databases for the agricultural, banking, commodities, energies, financial services, insurance, steel, and transportation industries. Also includes demographics and economic databases.
▪ Dow Jones Information Service	Gives statistical databases for the stock market, financial markets, and so on, and detailed financial statistics for corporations on the major stock exchange in the U.S. Also provides general news services from The Associated Press, *Barron's*, the Dow Jones News Service, *The Wall Street Journal*, and Wall Street Week. An on-line electronic encyclopedia is also available.
▪ Interactive Data Corporation	Supplies statistical databases from Chase Econometric Associates, Standard & Poor's, and Value Line covering agriculture, the automobile industry, banking, commodities, economics, the energy industry, financial markets, insurance, and international business.
▪ Lockheed Information Systems	Provides the DIALOG system, which includes over 75 different databases for agriculture, business, economics, education, energy, engineering, environment, foundations, government, international business, patents, pharmaceuticals, news publications, science, and social sciences.
▪ Mead Data Central	Lexis and Nexis are its two best-known services. Lexis provides legal research information; including case law, court decisions, and federal regulations. Nexis provides full text versions of articles appearing in over 100 newspapers magazines, newsletters, government publications, and so on. Also provides the Advertising & Marketing Intelligence (AMI) databank, the National Automated Accounting Research System, and on-line electronic encyclopedia.

Figure 7.25 Examples of popular on-line databases. Over 4,000 on-line database services were accessible by organizations in 1993. Most provide specialized information to assist many of the functional areas of a business organization. During the 1990s, these services will be a growth industry.

One of the earliest and still most common ways to store data is in files. With file processing, data are physically organized into files and a program can process only one file at a time. Although file processing is effective for some types of applications, it often leads to such problems as program-data dependence, data redundancy, and lack of data integrity. Database management systems can reduce or eliminate these problems.

Data can be accessed in two principal ways: sequential access and direct access. With sequential access, data are accessed in the order in which they are physically stored. Direct access, or random access, refers to accessing data independently of the order in which they are stored.

Data can also be organized in several ways. Most records are organized and later accessed with respect to one or more fields of data, which are called key fields. With serial organization, records are arranged one after the other, often in chronological order. Files that follow a sequential organization, on the other hand, have records arranged one after the other, but in predetermined order—according to a field called the primary key. With indexed-sequential organization, records are also organized by a primary key; however, an index exists for the file, through which record locations can be found and records accessed directly. Direct organization gives the fastest direct access to records by finding locations through the use of a hashing algorithm.

Secondary keys may be used to build indexed files and to provide users with alternative access paths to stored data. Multiple indexes provide users with greater flexibility in locating records stored in a file or database.

A database management system (DBMS) is a collection of software products designed to provide a systematic, integrated, and flexible approach to organizing and accessing organizational data. In a DBMS, data that could conceivably span several files are integrated into a single database. Database management systems have numerous advantages, including fast response time to requests, multiple access, lower user training costs, flexibility, less storage, data integrity, and better data management. Their main disadvantage is cost.

Every database system logically organizes data with respect to some data model. A hierarchical data model organizes data in the form of a tree. In such a model, the relationship among data elements is one-to-many. A network data model relates elements in both one-to-many and many-to-many configurations. Relational data structures place data into tables, in rows (records), and in columns (fields). This allows the greatest flexibility in access and manipulation of data. Relational data structures are increasing in popularity.

On large systems, strategic planning for an organization's data resources is carried out by a data administrator. A database administrator is responsible for the implementation of the plans developed by the data administrator and the day-to-day operations of databases. One important duty of the database administrator is data definition, the process of describing formats and relationships among data elements. A data definition language (DDL) is typically dedicated to this function in many large systems.

The processing of database data is called data manipulation. This is usually done by using a 4GL or a 3GL host processing language such as COBOL. SQL is also being increasingly used in database processing.

Multiuser database management systems often contain a concurrent access feature, which allows one user to seize control of certain data during processing. A DBMS also must interface with programs coded in a 3GL. It often does this via a host-language interface. Languages that can be enhanced in this manner are called host languages. Security is a problem with database management systems. Managing and coordinating the enormous amount of data in a database is handled by a data dictionary, which defines and notes the proper uses of database entities in a manner similar to a conventional dictionary, and a data directory, which keep track of where data are stored on disk.

Many database management systems are now available for microcomputers. Most vendors of relational database products base their accompanying languages on SQL (Structured Query Language). Multiuser database systems for LAN-based systems are also becoming more popular.

Like hierarchical and network databases, relational databases are designed for character and numeric data. They cannot easily accommodate graphs, photographs, document images, video, audio, and other "objects" containing data and information that are important to the organization. Several systems assist in managing these types of data and information, including object-oriented databases (OODB), multimedia data management systems, and image-processing systems. Significant development is expected in each of these systems over the next few years.

By using a communications software package and modem, managers and other microcomputer users can have on-line access to various information utilities and external databases. Having access to the data and information contained in such on-line databases can improve strategic—as well as operational—planning and decision making.

KEY TERMS

Concurrent access
Data administrator (DA)
Data definition
Data definition language (DDL)
Data dictionary
Data directory
Data integrity
Data manipulation
Data model
Data redundancy
Database administrator (DBA)
Direct organization
File processing
Hierarchical data model

Host language
Indexed-sequential organization
Information utility
Key field
Network data model
Object-oriented database (OODB)
Primary key
Program-data dependence
Relational data model
Secondary key
Sequential organization
Serial organization
Structured Query Language (SQL)
Template

REVIEW QUESTIONS

1. Explain how computer-based file and database processing systems have changed managerial decision-making environments.
2. Discuss the major issues related to the management of data.
3. What is meant by "data integrity"?
4. What are the characteristics and drawbacks of file processing?
5. What are the differences between a file manager and a database management system?
6. Identify and describe the different approaches that may be used for organizing data.
7. What are the differences between primary and secondary keys? What is the importance of each in file and database management systems?
8. What are the advantages and disadvantages of indexed-sequential files?
9. What is the purpose of a hashing algorithm? What are collisions and synonyms and how may these be handled?
10. Describe the functions carried out by a database management system (DBMS).
11. What are the advantages and disadvantages of database management systems?
12. Identify and describe the data structures used in database systems.
13. How do the roles of data administrators and database administrators differ?

14. What are the differences among data definition, data manipulation, and query languages?
15. What is SQL? Why is it important?
16. What is the purpose of a data dictionary?
17. Describe the data management roles played by object-oriented databases, multimedia systems, and image database systems.
18. What are information utilities? What are some examples of information utilities and what are some of the services they provide?

Discussion Questions

1. Why might an organization prefer a distributed database architecture, rather than a centralized database that allows users access from remote locations?
2. In what ways might database technology benefit a mail-order catalog firm such as L.L. Bean, Eddie Bauer, or Land's End?
3. What types of controls are necessary to ensure that the database is both protected from harm and not misused?
4. What types of factors should be considered when selecting an appropriate file organization and data structure for a particular application? For what types of applications are each of the different file and data structures best suited?

Image Databases: A Brewer Taste-Tests New Technology

Anheuser-Busch, like many companies that have been around for awhile, has a rich and interesting history that it is trying to preserve. Among its memorabilia are thousands of artifacts—such as old beer bottles, cans, coasters, tokens, signs, and the like—as well as reams of old business and personal correspondence, much of it generated by its first president, Adolphus Busch.

About 24,000 pages of Adolphus Busch's personal correspondence are owned by the firm. These have been bound into 42 volumes that are called "the letter-press books." Keeping track of all these items is no easy task. Increasingly, many organizations are turning to computerized photo databases, image databases, or multimedia databases to identify and manage data on items that are convenient to store as complex visual images. At Busch, the motivation to apply computers evolved from a request made by president August Busch III to find information on selected subjects from the letter-press books. Just a page-by-page perusal of the 12 dozen volumes of the bound set took 6 people almost 14 months.

The firm's response was to buy a packaged solution from a turnkey vendor that specializes in photo database systems. Turnkey vendors buy general-purpose software and hardware from various firms and configure them into specialized niche products or customized systems. With the system Busch acquired, each artifact is first photographed. The photos are then read by an image scanner and stored on WORM (Write Once/Read Many) optical disk. Historical documents are also scanned into the system; however, because Adolphus Busch's written records were too delicate for scanning, they had to be typed into the system. Other hardware elements include a microcomputer, a color monitor, and a laser printer.

Each artifact or written record stored in the system is assigned a descriptive code (such as bottle, can, or coaster) and a unique identification number. Also, a number of important characteristics about each item can be stored—for instance, the date of the artifact, a notation that the artifact contains the phrase "America's Largest and Favorite Brewery," or a picture of Busch's famous Clydesdale team of horses. So, for instance, if an archivist wanted to locate all serving trays that contained pictures of the Clydesdales, he or she might enter the keyword "tray," followed by the search string "Clydesdale."

Busch is not alone in its desire to use photo databases and other technologies for storing images. Other popular applications include security and personnel systems, real estate, parts ordering, and inventory control. For instance, McDonnell-Douglas has field-tested a picture database for manufacturing airplanes. When a worker needs to perform a complicated assembly operation, he or she can call up relevant photos of the operation in order to better understand how to do the job. In the security and personnel areas, numerous companies are using systems that allow "picture identification cards" of each employee to be stored in a computerized database. Image databases make it possible for fire departments to store maps of streets, as well as blueprints of the interiors of buildings (showing fire exits and escape points). While a firefighting unit is being dispatched to a fire, analysts at headquarters can start retrieving images in the database and designing a firefighting strategy. Claims one user in the electric power industry, "The possibilities for this technology are endless."

Relatively speaking, image and multimedia databases are still in the early stages of development. Standards are just starting to emerge and many of the systems already in use are not compatible with one another. Some of them interface with popular text database products such as Ashton-Tate's dBASE, but most of them are compatible with a very limited range of mainstream information technology applications. Part of the problem is because devices as cameras, video cassette recorders (VCR), and video compact disk (CD) players—which are used to input these image-capable technologies—work much differently than the digital computers that eventually manipulate the images, creating another problem. After all, photography, television, and computers were developed independently of one another. However, during the 1990s, advances in digital video processors and related technologies are likely to overcome these incompatibility problems and make photo, image, and multimedia databases attractive to a wider variety of firms.

Adapted from Stoll (1988) and Lunin (1990).

DISCUSSION

1. What are the advantages of photo databases and other image-capable databases over the text- and numbers-oriented databases described in the chapter? What problems may organizations encounter in developing and using such systems?

2. In what ways are multimedia databases superior to photo databases such as the one used by Anheuser-Busch? Provide examples of several other types of corporate artifacts—which cannot be stored in its photo database—that Anheuser-Busch could store in a multimedia database .

3. Describe at least five ways in which organizations could use photo, image, or multmedia databases that are not mentioned in this Case Study.

4. Demonstrate through examples how photo and other image-based database technologies can help workers be more effective (not just more efficient).

Chapter

8

Telecommunications

After completing this chapter, you will be able to:

Identify situations in which telecommunication technology is useful

Place telecommunication applications into a systematic framework

Identify the advantages and disadvantages of distributed processing

Name several types of communications media and their properties

Identify and describe several types of computer networks

Describe the characteristics of wide area and local area networks

Describe some of the executive challenges associated with managing telecommunications

Telecommunication is a term that refers to any system in which data or information is sent over some type of transmission medium—for instance, over a phone wire or cable, or through the air (as are microwave signals). Telecommunication is taking place when students at a university communicate with a central mainframe through terminals or microcomputers located in dorm rooms, or when a retail store in Orono, Maine, sends data at night to a regional processing center in Waltham, Massachusetts.

Telecommunication is not new to many organizations, although its importance has increased tremendously in recent years. Today, many businesses at home and abroad are rapidly moving toward a worldwide economic base, which shifts the relevance of telecommunication from being merely the necessary means to move data to being both a competitive weapon and a survival tool. For example, through telecommunication technology, many companies are establishing electronic links (both domestically and worldwide) with customers or suppliers. Such interorganizational networking allows companies to realize such competitive advantages as lower inventory costs, lower material prices, a shorter time frame to get work done, locked-in customers, locked-out competitors, and an ability to react more quickly to problems or opportunities. Some companies took a reactive role to telecommunication technologies—as many banks did in response to automatic teller machines—while others (such as McKesson, American Hospital Supply, and Singer) were proactively involved.

In this chapter, we explore both fundamentals of telecommunication and the strategic importance of telecommunication in MIS. Covered first are several examples of telecommunication and a framework relating these examples. Then, we look at a few technical issues associated with telecommunication, beginning with a discussion of the media used to transmit data and the nature of the signals used to encode data. Next, we cover the networking services and facilities available for telecommunications. Numerous issues concerning the management of teleprocessing systems—including the way communications networks are set up and managed—are then explored. The chapter concludes with a discussion of the challenges facing executives in assessing the impact of communications technologies.

TELECOMMUNICATION: STRATEGIC CONSIDERATIONS

Before the mid-1970s, the computer systems of most organizations were *centralized*. This meant that the processing power for a company (or major subunit)

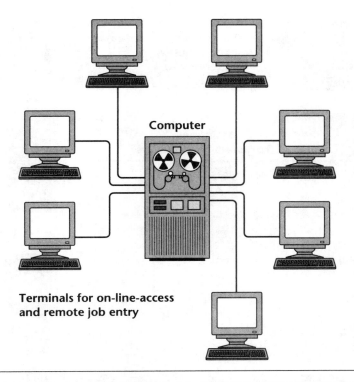

Computer

**Terminals for on-line-access
and remote job entry**

Figure 8.1 An example of a centralized computer network. Centralized computer networks were among the first types of data communications systems used by organizations.

was concentrated in a single large processor, usually a mainframe (see Figure 8.1). However, centralized information systems gave way to distributed processing and the networking of multiple computers (see Figure 8.2). This change started when it became possible to have on-line access to the central computer and remote job entry from distant terminals.

Some of the earliest telecommunication applications in business, instituted in the 1960s and 1970s, were the airlines passenger-reservations systems, the intracompany networks that provided display-workstation access to centralized mainframes, and the wide area time-sharing networks that sold remote computer processing services to companies equipped with teletypewriters.

When microcomputers were first introduced, they were typically used as stand-alone systems. However, during the 1980s, local area networks (LAN), developed by connecting microcomputers, became popular. Electronic mail systems also became popular during the 1980s, as did digital private branch exchanges, which we will discuss later, and the use of remote, external data banks maintained by information utilities. These changes presented organizations with newer, faster types of communication and information flows. They made it easier for managers to communicate and share information with one

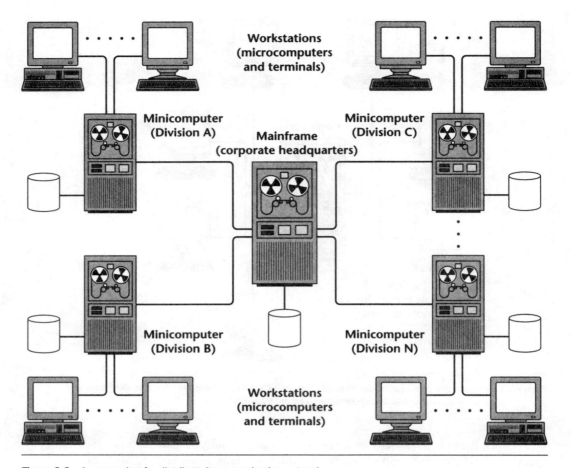

Figure 8.2 An example of a distributed communication network.

another, even when located at remote sites. These changes also made it easier to obtain data and information (from both internal and external sources) needed to make strategic decisions.

As telecommunication technologies increase in sophistication and decrease in cost, they are cast in yet a new light: as competitive weapons. One such weapon is the interorganizational system (IOS), a telecommunication system that two or more companies share. This represents a break with the tradition of building information systems solely for internal use. Other telecommunication systems that may be used as competitive weapons are the private networks (on both national and global levels) that some companies have developed. Some of the companies maintaining these systems are leveraging their network investments by selling their excess capacity or telecommunication expertise to other firms.

On a day-to-day level, telecommunication applications are pervading many organizational activities. Several of these are introduced here, but are covered

	VALUE		
Impact	**Efficiency**	**Effectiveness**	**Innovation**
▪ Time	Accelerate business process	Reduce information float	Create better service
▪ Geography	Recapture scale	Ensure global management control	Penetrate new markets
▪ Relationships	Bypass intermediaries	Replicate scarce knowledge	Build umbilical cords

Figure 8.3 Some of the ways in which telecommunications can benefit organizations. Telecommunication technologies can help an organization achieve many strategic and operational goals. This figure summarizes some of the ways that these can impact organizations.

more extensively in the material on office information systems (Chapter 12). *Electronic mail (e-mail)* systems, computer-age equivalents of traditional mailboxes, are used in a growing number of organizations. *Voice mail* systems are increasingly used to digitize and store voice messages; these are the high-tech equivalent of stand-alone answering machines. *Facsimile (fax) machines* are a standard fixture in most offices for sending hardcopy document images from one location to another over ordinary phone lines. *Videoconferencing (video teleconferencing)* systems are also more commonly used in large organizations. These allow organizations to hold electronic committee meetings in real time; participants never even have to leave their offices. In addition, *electronic bulletin boards* are used to distribute information to workers and people outside the organization. Each person with access to the bulletin board can post new information, or see what others were posted. Many hardware and software vendors established bulletins to provide users with help and a way to exchange tips and advice. *Cellular phone systems* are also used for both voice and data communications. Portable computers—in conjunction with cellular phone systems—allow users to gain access to organizational computing resources from remote locations and while traveling between locations.

An Applications Framework

According to Michael Hammer and Glenn Mangurian, a framework for viewing telecommunication applications might identify three principal areas of impact: compression of time, overcoming geographical restrictions, and restructuring relationships. It also would characterize the business value of an information system with regard to increased operating efficiency, improved functional effectiveness, and a basic transformation of a firm's business functions (innovation). According to the framework, telecommunications can benefit the organization in the following ways (see Figure 8.3).

Compressing Time

Through sophisticated communications links, organizations can transmit data almost instantaneously. One benefit of this is that work can be done faster; for instance, brokers can execute many more stock trades over computer networks in a given span of time than they ever could through traditional communications networks. The trades are executed more accurately, too. Telecommunication systems also benefit users by managing *information float*, the time it takes to get information from the source into the hands of decision makers. For example, electronic mail technology enables documents to be transmitted around the globe almost immediately, and the timely receipt of such information facilitates rapid decision making. Better service is yet another benefit. The interorganizational systems that some companies have set up with their suppliers (or suppliers with their customers) so that materials are always available when needed are important to note. For example, Wal-Mart wins special treatment from its suppliers because it first gives them special treatment. According to Peter Coy, about 3,800 vendors receive daily sales data directly from Wal-Mart stores and 1,500 of these have the same decision and analysis software that Wal-Mart's own buyers use to check product performance in various markets. This helps Wal-Mart's suppliers know "what's hot and what's not" so that they can adjust their operations accordingly.

The Gannett Corporation edits and composes each issue of *USA Today* at its Arlington, Virginia, headquarters. Once composed, the images are transmitted via satellite to 36 printing plants on three continents. Its use of computing and communication technology enables *USA Today* to live up to its claim of being "America's only daily newspaper."

The time compression made possible by combining computing and communications technology is also seen in the systems that support overnight package delivery companies such as Federal Express and United Parcel Service. Both companies are known for service, quality, and reliability.

Overcoming Geographical Restrictions

Communications technologies enable geographically dispersed organizations to function, to some degree, as if they were all located at a single site. Thus, dispersed organizations can still realize some of the economies of scale enjoyed by single-site firms. For example, by linking inventory databases together among sites, firms can maintain less combined inventory. Returning to Peter Coy's example, Wal-Mart collects and analyzes sales data from its stores on a daily basis, which helps it learn what merchandise is moving slowly. This also helps the corporation avoid the overstocking and deep price discounting techniques that other chains must use to clear out slow-moving stock (such as Kmart's "blue-light specials"). Purportedly, Wal-Mart's corporate management can get up-to-date sales data in 15 minutes, while it takes Kmart three days and Sears three weeks to get the same data.

Another drawback of geographical dispersion is ensuring quality and leadership consistency among business units. Through teleprocessing, organizations can better control dispersed units, ensuring that they are following enterprise-level goals. Teleprocessing can also help firms penetrate new markets faster. Several organizations have adopted an "electronic presence" in geographical areas where they have no significant physical presence. For example, a financial services organization could provide its full range of products via telecommunication links to remote field offices staffed by skeleton crews. Thus, a larger geographic area could be served without significantly increasing staffing costs. In some cases, the electronic presence has the effect of extending business hours across time zones. The high-tech term used for electronic presence is *logical office*.

Restructuring Business Relationships

Teleprocessing technologies provide certain benefits by restructuring the way people interact when working. For example, many companies developed telemarketing systems that directly provide customers with service from a central staff that has good access to information, thereby eliminating the need for field salespeople to physically attend to all orders and service calls. Also, several companies have comprehensive transaction processing systems that operate with real-time databases; these systems eliminate the need for hand-carrying paperwork from desk to desk and making a plethora of phone calls.

A second major restructuring of relationships involves the ability to capture and disseminate expert knowledge electronically. For example, a large manufacturer of industrial machinery has an expert maintenance processor as part of its main computer system. If this machine crashes for any reason, it can be immediately connected by phone to the vendor's computer, which performs a fault analysis and relays repair instructions back to the operator.

The framework just outlined helps us to see how computer networks can have strategic value for the organization. The following examples cover other ways in which telecommunications benefits organizations or somehow forces their hand in strategy considerations.

Strategic Alliances

Recently, many organizations have gone beyond distributed transaction processing systems by creating interorganizational systems (IOS) that link their computers with those of key customers and/or suppliers. These systems are examples of electronic data interchange (EDI), which Figure 8.4 illustrates. EDI allows standard business documents, such as purchase orders and invoices, to be electronically exchanged among companies. EDI saves time and money; transaction documents can be exchanged instantly and can minimize printing and paper-handling costs, as well as postage costs. EDI is also a means of "locking in" customers and/or suppliers by making it easier to do business with the company. However, as more and more companies adopt EDI, this competitive advantage is likely to diminish.

EDI has been adopted by most large U.S. manufacturers, merchandisers, and financial institutions, including Chase Manhattan Bank, Citicorp, General Electric, General Foods, General Mills, General Motors, KMart, J.C. Penney, Procter & Gamble, and Sears. In addition, nearly 80 percent of all orders placed

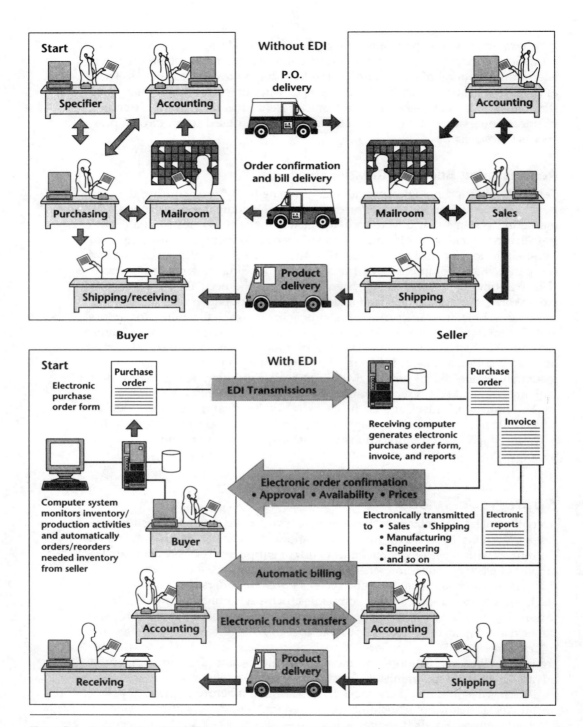

Figure 8.4 An illustration of how EDI can restructure business relationships among organizations.

by pharmacies are done via EDI. By 1995, more than 400,000 firms worldwide are expected to be using EDI, including nearly all of the Fortune 1000 companies. All segments of business, industry, and government are expected to be users.

EDI Examples

General Motors is one of the long-time users of EDI. PPG Industries, one of GM's suppliers, started using EDI during the 1960s to monitor inventory orders and shipments to GM. PPG recently linked its billing functions to GM via EDI as well.

Pillsbury has improved its ability to supply its customers by using EDI services for invoicing, order processing, and payment processing. The performance of its Burger King fast-food chain was improved through the integration of ordering and payment functions via EDI. Burger King is also able to track inventory needs and point-of-sale activity through EDI.

General Mills, a major U.S. cereal manufacturer, set up an IOS with its suppliers. This system was motivated by the manufacturer in order to develop close, long-term relationships with fewer suppliers. It also enables the cereal manufacturer to pressure suppliers into meeting its availability standards, and to drop those suppliers who cannot meet them.

DISTRIBUTED PROCESSING SYSTEMS

At one time, transaction processing operations such as accounts receivable and order entry were totally centralized. Today, advances in computer networking technologies allow many organizations to distribute transaction processing operations to multiple sites.

Distributed processing implies that an organization's computer resources and information processing activities are located at more than one location. Today, it also implies that computer resources are connected or networked in some manner.

Distributed Processing Examples

Many current organizations have distributed transaction processing systems in place. Some examples follow.

- **A mail-order catalog firm**   In the Midwest, a telecommunication configuration links a mail-order catalog firm's headquarters with its warehouse. Each day, the firm processes hundreds of phone and mail orders from its customers. At headquarters, several I/O devices (display terminals and printers) are connected to a local mainframe. The computer's storage facilities contain real-time data about product prices, stock levels, and customers. Authorized salespeople and warehouse personnel may draw on any of these data as they process an order.

  Orders received at headquarters are entered into communications terminals and transmitted to the warehouse, which is located at another site.

Communications terminals with bar-code readers are used at the warehouse to update inventory whenever products are either received from vendors or sent to customers. Warehouse printers produce shipping labels and invoices. The communications link between the headquarters site and the warehouse is the regular national phone network.

Before this order-entry system was installed, order clerks had to work from computer-generated, hardcopy reports that showed stock levels and prices. These reports were distributed to the clerks every morning. A clerk, therefore, did not have completely up-to-date information on product availabilities and items ordered by customers were often out of stock. Also, frequent shipping delays and numerous operator-induced errors frustrated both in-house personnel and customers.

- **Distributed banking** A large, intrastate bank distributed its customer accounts among three regional databases. This move resulted in lower overall communications costs and better local service. However, customer statements are still processed and mailed from a central office.

  Automatic teller machines (ATM) at most banks in the U.S. are part of regional, national, and international ATM networks. Electronic funds transfer (EFT) between banks over communications lines also changed banking operations. In 1992, over eight billion dollars changed hands daily via EFT.

- **Overnight delivery service** John Camillus and Albert Lederer use the example of an overnight, small-package shipper that considered distributing management of the real-time routing of its vans. Its first alternative was to set up dispatchers in local offices or airports, in order to coordinate pickups and deliveries by radio and microcomputer. The shipper finally chose a centralized approach, using mainframes, satellite-based communications, and dumb terminals in vans (so that messages could be accepted while the driver was away). A major factor in the decision was that the routing of the company's aircraft and vans were best accomplished through complex mathematical algorithms that were most easily administered from a central facility. Applying these algorithms in dozens or hundreds of decentralized computing facilities, where different standards might be used, was not feasible for a company so heavily dependent on its reputation for reliability.

  The first two examples illustrate some of the wide variety of ways in which distributed processing systems can be implemented. Many compelling reasons exist as to why managers should be interested in distributed processing systems for their organizations. However, as illustrated by the overnight delivery service example, valid reasons also exist for proceeding cautiously with the implementation of these systems. A summary of the potential advantages and drawbacks associated with distributed processing systems is provided in Figure 8.5 and in the following sections.

Advantages of Distributed Processing

Managers and organizations have become interested in distributed processing for many reasons:

ADVANTAGES/DISADVANTAGES OF DISTRIBUTED INFORMATION PROCESSING

Advantages	Disadvantages
▪ Better satisfaction of local needs	▪ Some loss of control with respect to managing computing expenses, buying discounts, and seeing that standards are managed (for example, standards ensuring system compatibility, data security, and data integrity)
▪ Faster response time	
▪ More flexibility in reacting to changes	
▪ Better tailoring of facilities to specific applications	▪ More sophisticated applications are possible on a larger computer system than on several smaller ones
▪ Lower communications-related costs	
▪ Avoidance of problems associated with intersite data flow (for instance, between foreign affiliates)	▪ Less staff specialization possible with distribution
	▪ Easier integration of applications possible with centralization

Figure 8.5 A summary of the advantages and disadvantages of distributed processing systems. These issues are being confronted by an increasing number of organizations that are interested in building enterprise-wide and global telecommunication networks.

- **Quicker response time** By locating processing power close to users, response time is typically improved. This means that the system responds rapidly to commands entered by users, which can translate into improved customer service, especially in transaction processing environments. Centralized systems are more likely to slow down when many users simultaneously make demands on the host computer; this can degrade response time, as well as customer service. However, some distributed systems are also prone to this problem.

- **Lower costs** Long-distance communication costs are declining at a slower rate than the cost of computer power. Distributed processing can reduce the volume of data that must be transmitted over long-distances and thereby reduce long-distance costs. When much of the data is input, edited, and processed locally, long-distance communication costs are minimized. The maturation of microcomputer networks provides organizations with additional distributed processing options and the opportunity to move applications from centralized hosts to microcomputer-based platforms.

- **Improved data integrity** High degrees of accuracy and currentness may be achieved by giving users control over data entry and storage. Users at local levels are more likely to know local data and spot errors quickly. Misspelled customer names and incorrect order quantities invariably are detected by the people who work most closely with specific customers. Hence, when distributed databases are part of a distributed processing system, improved data integrity may result.

- **Reduced host processor costs** Distributed processing reduces the burden on a centralized host and may make it unnecessary to upgrade to a larger, more expensive central processor as the organization and its information processing volumes expand. The productive life of a costly mainframe can be extended by off-loading some its processing tasks to other, less expensive machines (whose total costs are usually a fraction of the cost needed to upgrade the central processor). Also, by off-loading some of the work, the response time for users who remain connected to the central host should improve.

- **Increased reliability** When the host fails in a centralized system, the entire system is disrupted. In distributed systems, only part of the system should be seriously affected by the failure of a processor. Often, other computers in distributed system serve as backups in case a processor fails. This means that little disruption in processing operations and customer service should occur, even at the site of the processor failure.

- **Resource sharing** As noted in Chapter 5, one of the main advantages of developing microcomputer networks is because they make it possible to share expensive resources such as high-speed, color laser printers, fast data storage devices, and high-priced software packages. Distributed systems may also enable users to take advantage of computer resources at other sites.

These are just some of the reasons why organizations are interested in distributed processing. Of course, many of their advantages concern increased user and customer satisfaction. Reduced response times, increased reliability, and improved data integrity all enable users to more effectively carry out their duties; these can also directly contribute to better customer service. Resource sharing, reduced mainframe wear and tear, and reduced long-distance communications costs are all important to managers and contribute to the organization's profits.

Areas of Managerial Concern

Although distributed processing systems are helpful in many organizations, managers should also be aware of the following drawbacks:

- **Shortage of MIS professionals** Business telecommunication specialists are in short supply and it is often difficult to find the experienced MIS professionals that are needed to operate and maintain distributed systems.

- **Standardization** Distributed processing often forces organizations to adopt some type of standards concerning the acquisition of computing resources. Incompatibility and connectivity problems are likely if remote sites have few limitations regarding the acquisition of hardware and software. Solving incompatibility problems is usually difficult and expensive. System reliability and maintenance is likely to be enhanced if hardware and software acquisition standards are developed during the early stages of the transition to a distributed system.

- **Data integrity** Archiving or backing up files and databases, which are essential operations in centralized systems, become even more vital in distrib-

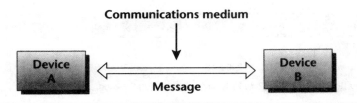

Figure 8.6 A basic model of a telecommunication system. Essentially, a telecommunication network is created whenever two or more devices are linked by way of a communications medium.

uted systems. It is important to ensure that data are not lost or altered during their transmission from one location to another. *Message logging* and *transaction logging* operations typically must be built into distributed systems. In each, a copy of the data to be transmitted is made before transmission. If a system or line failure occurs during data transmission, then a copy of the original data still exists. Transaction logging is mandatory in distributed transaction processing environments in order for audit trails to be established. In some systems, a copy is made by each computer that receives the data—not just by the original sender and final receiver. Database and system recovery procedures must also developed and are often more complex than recovery operations for centralized systems.

■ *Security* Networking and distributed processing introduce additional security problems. More opportunities exist for people to break into the system to steal or alter data, insert a computer virus, and engage in fraud or embezzlement. Sophisticated security measures may be needed to combat these potential problems. *Encryption* of data and messages (analogous to scrambling a television signal) may be necessary. Virus detection and eradication programs are a standard feature in many distributed systems, as are sophisticated password and log-in procedures.

Organizations entering the distributed processing arena must be willing to address these concerns. Work is underway in most of these areas to ensure that systems operate as reliably and securely as possible.

COMMUNICATIONS MEDIA

Most telecommunication systems consist, in part, of some combination of input, output, processing, and storage devices that are linked together through some sort of communications media. However, in telecommunication networks, the input, processing, output, and storage devices are likely to be classified as sending and receiving equipment. This is illustrated for two devices, linked by a single medium, in Figure 8.6. As a message is transmitted from one device to another, the first device functions as a sender and the second device as a receiver. When a response is sent back the other way, these roles are reversed.

It is important for managers in the 1990s to have a fundamental understanding of telecommunication technologies so that they will be in a better position to make knowledgeable decisions about the types of networks they and

Medium	Common Transfer Rates (Bits Per Second)
Physical Wires	
Private line	300; 1200; 2400; 4800; 9600; 19,200; 38,400; 56,000; 64,000; 80,000
Switched line	300; 1200; 2400; 4800; 9600; 19,200; 38,400
Leased line	2400; 4800; 9600; 19,200; 56,000; 64,000
Coaxial cable	1M, 2M, 10M, 50M, 100M
T-1, T-2, T-3, T-4	1.5M, 6.3M, 46M, 281M
Fiber optics	Over 2 Gigabits
Wireless	
Microwave	To 45M
Radio waves	9600
Satellite	To 50M

Figure 8.7 Types of communications media commonly found in computer networks and their characteristics.

subordinates need. Some of the most essential telecommunication technologies and concepts are described in the following sections.

Media Speed and Capacity

The speed at which data moves along a communications medium is often measured in *bits per second (bps)*. Transmission speeds for sending most types of data in a CBIS vary from about 300 bps (when modems are used with some phone lines) to over a billion bits per second (when using fiber optic cable). Figure 8.7 shows the speeds of numerous communications media and services.

Types of Media

A variety of media link devices in a communications network. The communications channels that these provide can carry either analog or digital signals. All **communications media** fall into one of two broad classes: physical lines or wireless media. These media are shown in Figure 8.7 and are described next.

Physical Lines

The three principal types of physical lines that dominate today's telecommunication systems are twisted-wire pairs, coaxial cable, and fiber optic cable. While both twisted-pair and coaxial cable are still commonly used, fiber optic cable is the wave of the future.

Twisted-wire pairs are the least expensive type of communications medium. For years, they have been used by the telephone companies to develop telephone networks. Small wires are twisted together in pairs, each of which can handle a single phone conversation, and the pairs are bound together into large cables. Twisted-wire pairs were developed primarily as a voice-oriented, telephone communications medium; their capacity is typically lower than the others discussed next. However, the capacity of twisted-wire pairs can be expanded by proper shielding and communications equipment. Because of this, local area network developers are seeing new interest in twisted-wire pairs. Many of the private, switched, and leased options in Figure 8.7 are based on twisted-wire pairs.

Coaxial cable (coax) is primarily a phenomenon of the cable television industry. Its development was largely motivated by the desire to bring interference-free television to rural areas. Coaxial cable comes in all types of sizes and characteristics, some of which can support impressive data-transmission speeds and capacities. Coax is widely used to establish local area networks, which we will cover later in the chapter.

Fiber optic cable, which is relatively new among the media technologies, consists of thousands of hair-thin strands of glass that are bound together as a cable. Data are sent along the cable as light waves, from a high-powered, laser beam source. Compared to coaxial cable, fiber optic cable has greater channel capacity and is lighter, faster, and compacter. Transmission speeds in excess of 5 gigabits (5 billion bits) per second are reported. Such rates would make it possible to transmit the entire contents of a 30-volume encyclopedia from coast-to-coast in less than a second. Also, because it is virtually impossible to cut the cable to send data to unauthorized points, these cables are highly resistant to being tapped. Fiber optic cable will be the primary media of future communications systems.

Wireless Media

Telecommunications that do not involve physical wires are becoming more widely used. This category includes microwave transmissions (both terrestrial and satellite), cellular radio, and wireless local area networks based on radio waves.

■ *Microwave and satellite communications* An alternative to physically stringing up communications lines to connect devices is to send signals through the air. This can be done through microwaves, which are high-frequency radio signals. Microwaving works only if an obstacle-free communications path exists between transmitting devices. Two principal ways to implement microwave technology are terrestrial microwave stations and satellites.

Terrestrial microwave stations are ground-based communications stations that are designed to communicate with each other or with satellites. Ground stations that communicate with each other must be within line of sight. Even in flat terrains, the curvature of the earth limits the distance between stations to 30 miles. Sometimes, they must be placed on top of tall buildings or mountains in order to ensure an obstacle-free communications path. As with any telecommunication media, the transmitted signal weakens (attenuates) as it travels from sender to receiver. To compensate for signal attenuation, a receiving microwave station amplifies the signal before passing it along to another station. Unike other media, heavy rain can affect microwave transmission.

Since it is impractical to dot the entire surface of the earth with microwave stations, especially over the ocean, communications satellites are important. **Communications satellites** are extraterrestrial communications devices that pass messages between microwave stations on earth. Satellites hover at a distance of 22,300 miles above the earth's surface, moving synchronously with the rotation of the earth so that they appear stationary to a ground observer.

Very small aperture terminals (VSAT) are popular, relatively inexpensive, and unobtrusive satellite dishes. Numerous organizations replaced leased line systems with VSAT satellite systems. These are often seen on the tops of buildings and make it possible to establish high-capacity satellite links between widely dispersed business locations. The utilization of VSAT systems is expected to grow during the 1990s.

Both communications satellites and terrestrial microwave stations are especially designed for sending large quantities of data one way at a time. Because of the long transmission distances involved, satellite systems may not be suitable for some applications that require fast-response, two-way interactive communication.

■ *Cellular radio* As noted previously, portable computers used in conjunction with cellular phone systems are being more commonly used by organizations. *Cellular radio* is a radio (telephone) communications—a wireless media—technology that divides a geographic area into "cells" in a honeycomb fashion. A central computer and special communications equipment controls and coordinates the transmissions of mobile phone and portable microcomputers as users move from one cell to another; cellular phone services typically provide an interface with the regular public phone network. Federal Express uses a cellular system for data communications, with terminals located in its thousands of delivery vans.

■ *Wireless local area networks* Another example of wireless media are wireless local area networks (LAN). The devices included in these networks—which are often called *personal communications networks (PCN)*—communicate via radio waves. These are typically best suited for communications within a single building or limited geographic area because the longer the distance between devices, the greater the chance of signal distortion.

Related to wireless local area networks are networks that rely on radio waves for data transmission over long distances. One of the earliest implementations of such a network was called ALOHANET, connecting the branch campuses of the University of Hawaii, located on several of the Hawaiian Islands. More recently, NCR released pen-based notepad computers that can transmit data over radio wave networks, using neither physical lines nor cellular modem connections.

■ *Infrared transmissions* Data transmission using infrared light rays has been implemented by some companies for short-distance communications.

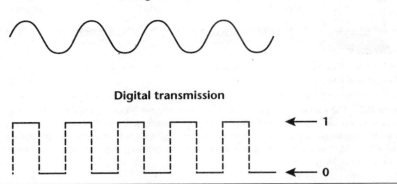

Figure 8.8 The difference between analog and digital signals. Telephone systems were originally designed to carry analog signals. The emergence of computers and information technologies created a high demand for digital transmission services. In response, telephone companies are rapidly replacing analog-based equipment with digital devices. In many areas, modems must be used to convert the digital signals generated by computers to analog signals that can be transmitted over existing communications lines.

These are relatively inexpensive, easy-to-install systems that are not subject to regulatory agency restrictions, as long as they are used within a single building or business operations site (can consist of two or more buildings). Similar to microwave systems, no obstructions can exist between sender and receiver; also, when using infrared transmissions between two buildings, significant smoke and fog levels may cause interference.

Media Signals

The signals that pass along physical wires and wireless media can be classified as either analog or digital.

Analog signals carry data as continuous waves. For instance, the human voice consists of numerous complex inflections that are combinations of sound waves. Much of the phone system still in place across the U.S.—which was implemented years ago to capture the richness of the human voice—is an example of an analog transmission medium. All signals that travel over these older telephone lines are in analog form.

Digital signals carry data as on/off or high/low electrical signals. Thus, the 1-bit of a data byte can be represented as an on (high) signal; the 0-bit, an off (low) signal. The new equipment being installed by phone companies is designed for digital transmission of both data and voice. The difference between analog and digital signals is shown in Figure 8.8.

Modems

Most of the phone lines used today are analog. However, computers and their support equipment are digital. Because of this, an interfacing device is necessary in order to transmit digital data over analog phone lines. The device devel-

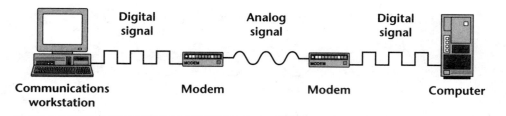

Digital signal   **Analog signal**   **Digital signal**

Communications workstation   **Modem**   **Modem**   **Computer**

Figure 8.9 The role of a modem in telecommunications. Modems take the digital signal transmitted by a computer (or another information technology device, such as a fax machine) and convert it to an analog signal for transmission over communications media. This conversion process is called modulation. Modems can also demodulate analog signals intended for the computer by converting them to digital form.

oped for such a purpose is called a **modem** (an abbreviation of modulator/demodulator). As Figure 8.9 illustrates, modems can translate (modulate) digital impulses generated by one device and convert them to an analog signal that is compatible with the phone lines. When the message reaches its destination at the receiving end, another modem is used to translate (demodulate) the analog signals back into digital form. When a message must be sent back the other way (to the originating device), this process is reversed.

Salespeople who are on the road often communicate with their home offices via modem. A communications software package (such as Crosstalk, ProComm, or Laplink) is typically used to establish the connection between the salesperson's portable computer and a computer in the home office. His or her sales data can then be transmitted over telephone lines. Some airlines are experimenting with in-flight services that allow passengers to plug their portables to telephone links at their seats so that they can send data over wireless networks while en route to their next destination (see related box, page 354).

Digital Lines

Today, there is a trend in telecommunications toward digital lines. Digital lines transmit data significantly faster and more accurately than analog lines. Also, with digital lines, several types of data (such as text, voice, graphics, and video) can be sent along the same channel. And, of course, no modem is required when sender, medium, and receiver are all using digital data. High-capacity digital services are already quite common. T-1 lines (discussed later in the chapter) are in wide use and provide channel capacities of 1.544 Mbps. T-2, T-3, and T-4 facilities provide even faster data transmission speeds.

ISDN

An ongoing effort to provide integrated, all-digital communication service to users is the Integrated Services Digital Network (ISDN), now being gradually introduced around the world. Although these services are already available in some areas (see Figure 8.10), global ISDN is not expected before the year 2000. ISDN, because of its built-in intelligence, will enable all types of data—

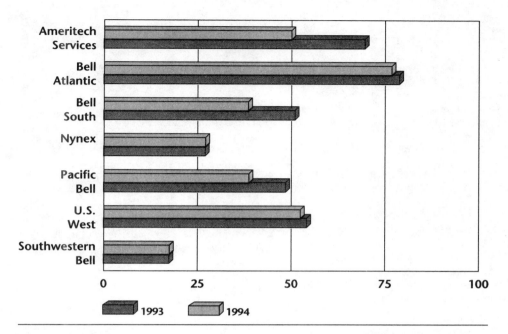

Percent of Lines in Wire Centers Planned to Have ISDN Presence

1993   1994

Figure 8.10 ISDN implementation goals for the Regional Bell Holding Companies (RBHC): the Baby Bells. As this figure illustrates, these companies plan to bring ISDN capabilities to many areas by 1994. All areas of the country should have ISDN capabilities by the turn of the century. ISDN implementation efforts are also underway in most parts of the world, especially Europe and the Pacific Rim. (Adapted from Kerr)

facsimile, video, voice, and data—to be sent over a single network. The basic ISDN channel will have a capacity of 64,000 bps, enough for many of the video-conferencing systems available today. Such speeds are faster than most modems. In Susan Kerr's article on the application wave behind ISDN, Virginia Haggerty, an IBM product marketing manager, sums up the difference this way: sending a 50-page document with a 2400 baud modem takes approximately 8 minutes. Using ISDN, the document can be sent in 15 seconds.

One study, conducted by the Business Research Group (a subsidiary of Cahners Publishing Company in Newton, Massachusetts) found that many user organizations plan to use ISDN to interconnect local area networks (LAN) and to connect these networks to other communications devices—such as packet-switched networks, private branch exchanges, workstations, and host computers (most of these are discussed more fully later in the chapter). In 1992, DEC released a RISC-based workstation that is "ISDN-ready." This development signals the coming importance of ISDN.

ISDN is already spurring the development of applications that can enhance user productivity or provide a competitive edge. According to Susan Kerr's

Datamation article, Edward Hodgson, manager of computing and communications for Schindler Elevator Corporation, is building a centralized imaging system using ISDN. Hodgson wants to enable elevator service people equipped with portables to use ISDN to call headquarters and retrieve images of the parts being serviced. Says Hodgson, "Without ISDN, we couldn't figure out how to access it [the centralized imaging system] without going broke." At Johns Hopkins Health System in Baltimore, clerks already audit supplies in storerooms with handheld devices and the collected data are transmitted via ISDN to a mainframe.

ISDN will be a major factor in business telecommunication throughout the 1990s. While not the only way to move data at high speeds, its availability from telephone companies should make ISDN an attractive option.

Serial Versus Parallel Transmission

Data are transmitted along a communications medium either in serial or in parallel. Most microcomputer owners know that their machines are equipped with serial and parallel ports. These enable the computer to transmit both serial and parallel digital signals. Figure 8.11 illustrates the difference between these two types of transmission.

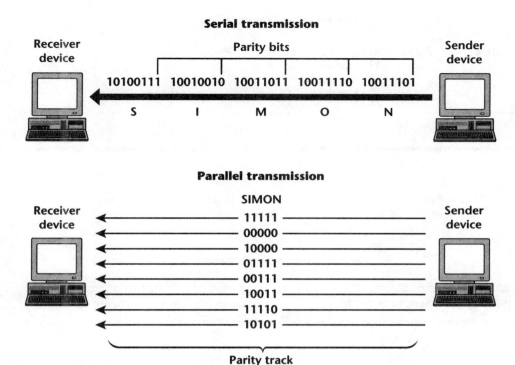

Figure 8.11 Serial and parallel transmission. In serial transmission, data are transmitted one bit after another. In parallel transmission, data are transmitted one byte (character) after another. Parallel transmission is typically used for only very short-distance communications. Serial is used for longer distance transmissions and is the status quo in most wide area and microcomputer networks.

In both serial and parallel transmission, the bytes corresponding to each message are sent along a medium, one after another. Thus, for the one-word message

`SIMON`

the byte representation of the "S" is sent first, then "I," then "M," and so on. Serial and parallel transmission differ in that, in **serial transmission**, the bits of each byte are sent along a single path one after another. In **parallel transmission**, separate, parallel paths correspond to each bit of a byte so that all the bits arrive at the destination simultaneously.

Because parallel transmission can get messages to its destinations sooner, it is faster than serial transmission. But, because more wiring is needed to set up the extra bit paths, parallel processing is much more expensive. Often, devices that are located within a few feet of each other will communicate in parallel, whereas devices that are further apart than this communicate in serial. For example, a microcomputer may use parallel transmission to send a word-processing document to a printer that is connected to it. However, this same

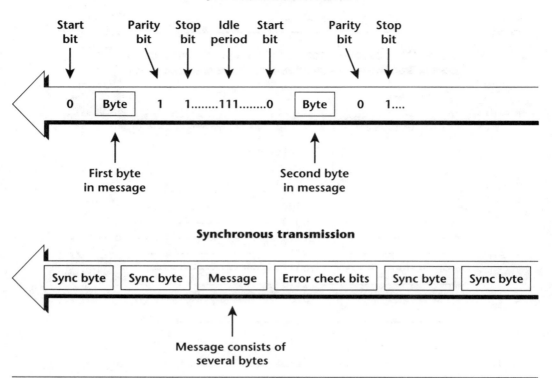

Figure 8.12 The difference between asynchronous and synchronous transmission. Asynchronous transmission transmits a byte (character or keystroke) at a time to a receiving computer, whereas synchronous transmission transmits multiple bytes in the form of packets or frames. Asychronous is widely used to connect dumb terminals to host computers, using cheap, low-speed lines. Synchronous is commonly used when large volumes of data or information must be transmitted from one device to another.

document could be transmitted to another printer much farther away by using serial transmission.

Asynchronous Versus Synchronous Transmission

Serial transmission can occur either asynchronously or synchronously. Both of these terms refer to the way that data are packaged as they are sent along a communications medium. Figure 8.12 shows the difference between asynchronous and synchronous transmission.

In **asynchronous transmission**, a data package consists of a single character, which is preceded by a "start bit" (a 0) and ends with a "stop bit" (a 1). Asynchronous transmission might occur, perhaps, when an operator at a keyboard types messages to a computer. As each key is struck, the byte representation of the keystroke is packaged and sent "up the line" to the computer. As soon as the computer senses a start bit, it prepares itself to read the character. When the sender device is on-line but idle, it is sending the computer a continuous stream of stop bits.

Asynchronous transmission usually involves less expensive equipment than synchronous transmission. Often, only low-speed communications lines are needed and the terminals located on the ends of the line may be dumb or severely restricted in processing capability; the important processing tasks are typically performed by the host. Asynchronous transmission is feasible when real cost is incurred by having a lot of idle time on the communications medium.

Synchronous transmission is used for fast transmission of large blocks of data at a single time. Each data package may consist of hundreds of characters. The package is sandwiched between one or two "sync bytes," which serve a function similar to the start and stop bits used for asynchronous transmission. Synchronous transmission is often used when transmission speeds of 2400 bps or higher are needed along the communications medium. For instance, a chain store might send all of its data to a central headquarters facility overnight, using synchronous transmission. Since all the data are ready to go at the start of transmission, and toll charges can be minimized if they are sent quickly, synchronous transmission is a good choice.

The primary means of checking errors in asynchronous transmissions involves the use of a *parity bit*. This extra bit is added to each byte as a check measure so that the sum of all the 1-bits of every byte come out to either an odd or even number. In odd-parity systems, the 1-bits always sum to an odd number; in even-parity systems, an even number. In Figure 8.11, an odd parity scheme is used with the 7-bit ASCII representation of each byte. When a receiving device receives a byte, it checks the parity bit against its own count of the number of 1-bits in the byte. If the parity bit is consistent with its count, the byte is concluded to have been received corrected. When the count is inconsistent with the received parity bit, an error is detected.

In Figure 8.12, error check bits are part of the entire message package. Message packages in many syncronous protocols begin and end with one or more "sync" bytes—the actual message and error check bits are sandwiched between those sync bytes. In most synchronous protocols, some type of *cyclical redundancy checking (CRC)* is used and the error check bits generated by this process are embedded in the message package by the sending device. CRC enables receiving devices to detect almost all of the errors found in the data bytes that are received. CRC is recognized as one of the best error detection schemes for data communications. While used most commonly with synchronous protocols, CRC can also be used with asynchronous transmissions.

NETWORKING ALTERNATIVES

When communications media are used to link together various computer hardware devices, the resulting product is called a *network*. A telecommunication network is one in which input, output, and storage devices are put into communication with one or more computers. When a centralized computer is used to perform the bulk of the processing on the network, that device is commonly called a **host computer**, or host. When there are multiple machines in the network at which significant processing is done, each location is typically called a *node*.

Networks vary considerably in scope. As discussed previously, those that extend no farther than within a room, building, or campus are called local area networks (LAN). Networks that cover large geographic areas—such as a country or the entire globe—are called **wide area networks (WAN).** A WAN that covers a metropolitan area is sometimes put in a separate subcategory called a MAN *(metropolitan area network)*.

Data transmission rates are typically faster in a LAN than in a WAN. In a LAN, transmission rates between 1 and 10 million bits per second are most common, but local area networks with speeds over 100 Mbps are available. Wide area networks—especially those employing common carrier phone lines—may not be able to surpass 9600 bps without leasing higher speed lines. However, long distance telephone companies—such as AT&T, U.S. Sprint, and MCI—have an increasing variety of higher speed options available for businesses.

Network Topologies

The term *topology* refers to the physical pattern to which a network conforms; that is, the physical layout of the network's computers, terminals, and links. The four topologies observed most often are the hierarchical, star, bus, and ring networks. While most industrial-strength networks incorporate complex interconnections that don't conform neatly to any of these four simple topologies, they are the fundamental structures on which most networks are built.

Hierarchical Networks

Hierarchical networks are the most traditional type. They may consist of a host computer—either a mainframe, minicomputer, or supermicro—at the top of the hierarchy and terminals or workstations at the bottom. In the middle of the hierarchy are hardware devices such as communications controllers, each of which manages the communications exchange among a cluster of workstations and the host computer. One of the advantages of this type of network is that failure of the host does not disable processing at the major nodes—particularly if the devices at the middle (controller) levels of the hierarchy are powerful enough to allow processing to continue within the subunits until the host (or the links to the host) are operational.

A good example of a hierarchical network arrangement was depicted in Figure 8.2 (page 338). Since hierarchical networks can be implemented in a manner that closely resembles a firm's organizational chart, they are frequently used for wide area networks.

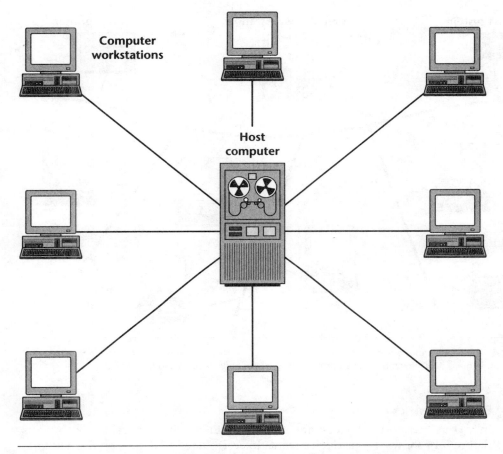

Figure 8.13 An example of a star topology. In star topologies, all devices in the network are connected to a central host. If the host fails, the network fails.

Star Networks

In a **star network**, several devices are connected to a central device, as Figure 8.13 shows. Thus, a network in which several terminals or workstations are serviced by a host computer is an example of a star network. Yet another example is the PBX, which will be discussed later. Micro-to-mainframe linkages also form star networks in most instances.

For devices to communicate with one another in a star network, their messages have to be routed through the central "hub" device. The processor located at the hub does most of the processing and is usually the site where the database is located. All terminal-to-terminal communications must go through the hub. If the hub fails, the entire network is disabled.

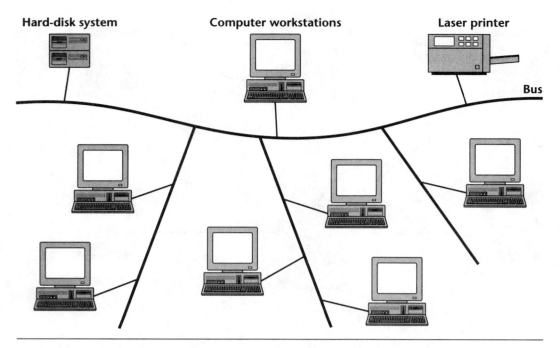

Hard-disk system **Computer workstations** **Laser printer**

Bus

Figure 8.14 An example of a bus network. In bus networks, all devices are connected to a common cable, called a bus. In many new implementations of this topology, fiber optic cable is used as the bus.

Bus Networks

In a **bus network**, devices are connected to a common cable, or bus, as Figure 8.14 shows. If one device wants to access another device on the network, it puts a message addressed to that device on the bus. If one of the devices attached to the bus fails, the rest of the network is not affected. The network fails only when the bus fails. Bus failures are rare because the bus is simply a wire with no active components; it almost has to be sliced in two before it will fail.

Ring Networks

In a **ring network**, illustrated in Figure 8.15, each device is serially connected in a closed ring pattern. If one device wants to send a message to another device on the network, the message has to pass through all the devices that lie between the two.

Switching Alternatives

Many users can be simultaneously connected to a network of communications channels. The means for establishing interconnections between two nodes—so that communication can take place—is called *switching*. For example, the public

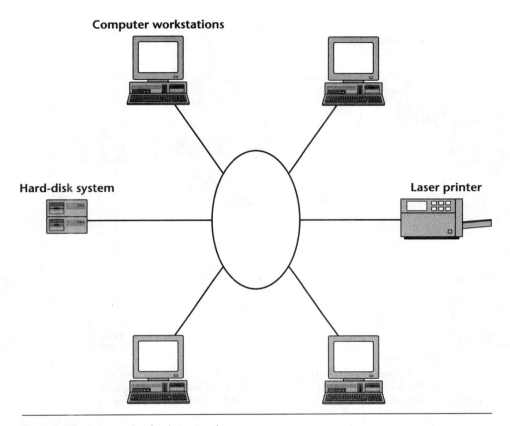

Computer workstations

Hard-disk system

Laser printer

Figure 8.15 An example of a ring network.

telephone network is designed to provide access between any two points in the network. In order to achieve this flexibility, the circuitry of the phone system is set up so that paths along the network can be switched. As a call is made into the system from a sender device, it is switched to the proper receiving device.

Three methods are commonly used to switch data in communications networks: circuit switching, message switching, and packet switching.

- ■ *Circuit switching* Circuit switching is what most of us encounter on our home phones. We place a call and either get our destination party or encounter a busy signal. If we get a busy signal, we cannot transmit any message. A single circuit is used for the duration of the call.

- ■ *Message switching* With message switching, an entire message is moved through the network—from its source to its destination. In sophisticated computer systems, nodes in a network often have a "store and forward" capability. This enables them to accept a message as a unit and, if necessary, to pass it on to another node at a later time. A message is likely to be stored at

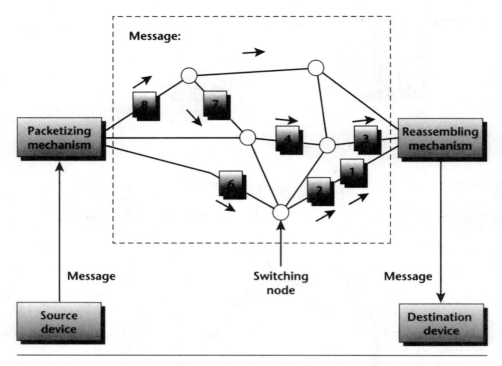

Message:

Packetizing mechanism

Reassembling mechanism

Message

Switching node

Message

Source device

Destination device

Figure 8.16   An example of a packet–switching network. Public packet-switching networks provide organizations with cost-effective ways to transmit data from one point to another. Messages are broken into packets by special devices and reassembled into their original form at the receiving end.

a node when either the link or the next node is busy or temporarily out of service.

- **Packet switching**   Packet switching is a procedure that breaks up a message into fixed-length packets, generally 80 to 150 characters in length, at the message source (see Figure 8.16). Each of the packets may take a different route through the network to reach the destination. At the destination, the packets are reassembled into a meaningful message. In some packet-switching networks, the route taken by each of the packets is dynamically determined as it moves through the network. Special networking software optimizes the flow of traffic through the network.

Wide Area Networks

Organizations have many options with respect to network services and facilities. Among these options are the common carriers, such as the firms that develop and maintain the public phone system; the value-added network (VAN) vendors, who provide additional services using the facilities provided by common carriers; and the communications media vendors, who provide facilities that may be acquired for private use.

Common Carriers

Common carriers are firms that are licensed by the government to provide wide area communications services to the general public. These companies offer the use of wide area telecommunication infrastructures. Probably the most familiar common carriers are the Bell-system phone companies (such as NYNEX and Bell South), which provide in-state and regional service; long distance carriers such as MCI, Sprint, and AT&T; and locally owned telephone companies. Still another group of common carriers are the specialized carrier companies that operate their own satellites and sell capacity on them.

Common carriers offer many types of channels. The most widely used are dial-up lines and leased lines. *Dial-up telephone lines* are rented from local telephone companies; most people have this telephone service in their homes. After installation, a monthly fee keeps the line in service and additional charges accrue for long-distance usage. Dial-up telephone lines are typically switched lines that frequently use analog signaling. Typical data communications speeds range from 300 bps to 9600 bps. The Bell-system companies—and their competitors—are making other high-speed, digital switching services available in many areas. Among these are "384" (38.4 thousand bits per second) and "switched 56" (56 thousand bits per second) services. As digital lines and communications equipment become more pervasive, additional high-speed services are expected.

Leased telephone lines are high-speed circuits that can be leased from common carriers. Because of line "conditioning" (available for a small additional monthly charge), leased lines typically provide more accurate communications and higher data transmission lines than do dial-up lines. Speeds on leased digital lines are also high. For example, speeds on T-1 lines range from 9600 bps to 1.544 mbs. Even higher speeds are available on T-2, T-3, and T-4 lines (see Figure 8.7, page 348). Lines are usually leased by organizations because with higher usage levels, leasing is cheaper than paying long-distance toll charges by the minute.

Dedicated lines can be leased or purchased from either common carriers or other vendors that sell communications media for private use. These are "private" lines because they do not have to be shared with others; in many instances, an organization may share a non-dedicated leased line with one or more other organizations. Dedicated lines are economical when a person needs speed above that offered on switched lines and when large quantities of data must be sent between devices.

Closely associated with dedicated lines are private networks. A firm has exclusive use of a *private network*. It normally consists of computers and terminals owned by that firm, as well as media links owned or leased from a common carrier.

Value-Added Networks

Value-added network (VAN) vendors are organizations that provide a service to the public over common carrier facilities. These networks often lease

Wireless Nets Snare Both Big and Small Fish

Wireless data networks are expected to show tremendous growth during the 1990s. Wireless networks use radio frequencies and cellular phone channels to move data through the air. They untether workers from the need to be physically connected to some type of cabling (for example, telephone lines, coaxial cable, or fiber optics) in order to interact with company computers.

"WIRELESS NETWORKS USE RADIO FREQUENCIES AND CELLULAR PHONE CHANNELS TO MOVE DATA THROUGH THE AIR."

Federal Express Corporation relies on a radio-based data communications network to tie all of its offices, planes, and ground vehicles to corporate computers in Memphis. This network makes it possible for FedEx to trace any customer's package from the time it is picked up to the time it is delivered. It also helps the company maintain its dominant place in the industry.

In the past, wireless nets were do-it-yourself projects affordable only by large companies. Now, numerous wireless options are within reach of the masses. For example, Ardis and Ram are two public wireless data networks that are only slightly more expensive than cellular phone service. Some companies are also having their wireless data transmission needs met by the cellular phone networks and by paging systems, whose advanced pagers can handle both numbers and text. For more localized coverage, fleet dispatch systems are used to transmit data over the same networks that dispatch taxis, vans, and other vehicles. Wireless local area networks are also becoming popular in office settings. These services and technologies are expected to expand fivefold during the 1990s.

Adapted from Therrien and Hawkins (1992).

---

channels from common carriers and then re-lease the channels to others. They "add-value" to these channels by providing special features to their customers, such as packet-switching services, electronic mail, store and forward capabilities, and data code and protocol conversion.

Value-added carriers offer their customers high-quality, relatively inexpensive service in return for a membership fee and usage charges. Unlike long-distance dial-up charges that are based on connect time—how long the circuit is used—value-added usage charges are often based on the amount of data that is actually transmitted over the network. This makes it possible for VAN vendors to offer subscribers enticing prices and still be profitable.

Within the United States, numerous networks using packet switching are available. These include GTE's Telenet, General Electric's Mark*Net, and Tymeshare's Tymnet. These are so popular that common carriers, Western Union, and large corporations (such as IBM, Boeing, and RCA) now provide VAN services. Packet-switched networks are also available in most countries around the world. Some examples of these are Canada's Datapac, Australia's Austpac, and Europe's Euronet. Global packet-switching and VAN services are also available.

The variety of VAN services constantly grows. Some of these are designed to serve a wide range of organizations, while others serve only particular industries or organizations interested in special types of telecommunication services. For example, in response to widespread (and growing) interest, AT&T and US Sprint introduced public videoconferencing services. Also, many of the information utilities described in the last chapter (including CompuServe, Dialog, Dow-Jones News Retrieval Service, and The Source) connect their computers to public packet-switching networks. ISDN, described earlier in this chapter, provides organizations with another set of generally available value-added services. One of the best known industry-specific value-added networks is the cooperatively owned SWIFT network, which connects over 2,000 banks around the world for funds transfers and other financial clearing purposes.

WAN Protocols and Network Architectures

Dissimilar devices cannot communicate with each other unless a strict set of communications standards is followed. Such standards are commonly referred to as protocols. A **protocol** is a set of rules required to initiate and maintain communication between a sender and receiver device.

Both national and international organizations have attempted to establish suitable protocols. Among the most widely known of these are X.25 (established for packet switching by ISO, the International Standards Organization).

However, many of the protocols developed are incompatible with one another. For example, several protocols exist for electronic data interchange (EDI), which was described earlier in the chapter. The lack of a single EDI protocol confuses organizations anticipating the implementation of EDI. At last, a single protocol for EDI—known as X.12—is starting to take hold in many organizations worldwide, but EDIFACT, another EDI protocol is still popular in Europe.

Protocols specify whether asynchronous or synchronous transmission will be used, how data will be packaged and recognized, and what error-handling procedures will be used. When networks are designed and built, a collection of standard protocols are generally chosen and packaged with hardware and software. This protocol/hardware/software combination (that is, the physical implementation of a collection of protocols) is often called a **network architecture**. One of the most widely known architectures is **System Network Architecture (SNA)**, developed by IBM.

SNA gained its greatest acceptance in the United States, where it has most successfully been implemented on private networks. SNA utilizes a *closed* network design; that is, SNA is designed around IBM hardware and software products only. Other architectures, on the other hand, utilize an *open* network design, which permits products from several vendors to be interconnected. Numerous other vendors developed architectures that feature their products. Digital Equipment's DECnet is one of the best known alternatives to SNA.

Figure 8.17 illustrates the **Open System Interconnection (OSI)**, developed by ISO. This protocol reference model is composed of seven layers. The figure

Layer	Description
1. Physical	Handles voltages, electrical pulses, connectors, and switches so that data can be transmitted over network media.
2. Data link	Controls grouping data into blocks (message packets) and transferring blocks from one point in the network to another.
3. Network	Controls the routing of data and messages through the channels of a network.
4. Transport	Controls data transfer for the complete transmission path, from sending point to receiving point.
5. Session	Establishes and terminates communications links between computers.
6. Presentation	Formats data for transfer between different systems.
7. Application	Provides network services to users and user applications, including file transfer. Provides user interfaces with the systems.

Figure 8.17 The Open Systems Interconnection (OSI) model. Developed by the International Standards Organization (ISO), this model consists of seven layers. This figure summarizes data communications tasks carried out by each of the seven layers.

describes the functions that protocols and networks must handle at each of the seven levels in order for data to be transmitted from one user to another.

TCP/IP (Transmission Control Protocol/Internet Protocol) is one of the oldest networking standards. It was developed for the U.S. Department of Defense's Advanced Research Project Agency network (ARPANET). ARPANET evolved into Internet, and Internet will probably evolve into NREN (the National Research and Education Network)—a fiber optic-based data highway capable of gigabit transmission rates. TCP/IP is a reasonably efficient and error-free protocol that is surging in popularity because of its ability to transfer large files. It deals with only layers 3 and 4 of the OSI model, enabling it to work with virtually any type of link at layers 1 and 2. Layers 5 through 7 are left up to the user organization.

WAN Hardware

Devices on a communications network cannot all work independently of the others. Methods must be established so that common network goals are met and communications take place smoothly. Coordinating communications traffic on a network is done by both hardware and software elements. In this subsection, we look at some of the hardware devices and their associated software-resident functions. These devices include controllers, multiplexers, concentrators, and front-end processors. Specifically, we consider how each of these devices works in a hierarchical network. In the next section, we consider such software elements as teleprocessing (TP) monitors and telecommunication access programs. Figure 8.18 depicts the major hardware devices that support wide-area networks.

- **Hosts** In a WAN, hosts are usually large mainframe computers. In very large wide area networks, several mainframes or minicomputers serve as

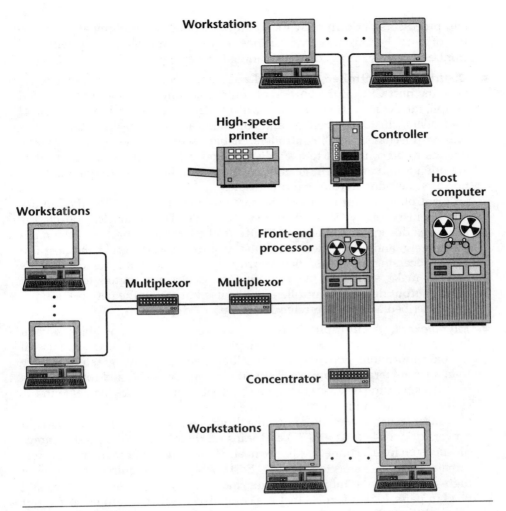

Workstations

High-speed printer

Controller

Host computer

Workstations

Front-end processor

Multiplexor   **Multiplexor**

Concentrator

Workstations

Figure 8.18 A graphical illustration of some of the major types of hardware found in wide area networks (WAN).

hosts. Hosts typically provide WAN users with access to application programs and database management systems.

■ *Front-end processors* Input/output (I/O) tasks are some of the most time-consuming chores that computers perform; these include accepting data from terminals and providing output to terminals, printers, and other output devices. These tasks must be done constantly in data communications networks. In some instances, a second computer, the **front-end processor (FEP)**, is placed between terminals and the host, in order to perform most of the I/O operations for the host. This enables the host to work almost exclusively on data processing tasks. Front-end processors vary in sophistication and in the variety of communications activities they perform. Some front-end processors perform network control functions and preliminary processing of data. For instance, the airlines' passenger reservations systems use front-end processors to edit data coming in from agents.

- **Controllers** Controllers are specialized computers whose purpose is to relieve the host CPU of the burden of communicating with a lot of low-speed peripheral devices. These are known by many names, including terminal controllers, cluster controllers, and communications controllers. Like multiplexers (discussed next), controllers enable several terminals or peripheral devices to be connected to a single high-speed line to the host. Controllers are often found at the remote ends of high-speed lines, and frequently function as scaled-down front-end processors.

    Controllers perform almost the same role for the host CPU that an appointment secretary does for a busy executive. The controller collects the messages destined for the host CPU from the terminals, packages them appropriately, and sends them on to the host for processing. As the host finishes processing messages, they return to the controller; it is the controller's task to make sure that the returning messages are routed to the right input/output devices. Controllers can be used in any of the network topologies described earlier: hierarchical, star, bus, or ring.

- **Multiplexers** A **multiplexer** is a hardware device that enables several low-speed devices to share the same high-speed line. Multiplexers are useful in communications networks because lines generally have greater capacity than a single terminal can use. Thus, if a company is charged for time on a line, it's smart to pack as much data as possible in the space available in the channels and to minimize any idle time.

    Multiplexers accept data streams from several terminals (typically in powers of two: 4, 8, 16, and 32) and transmit them over high-speed communications channels connected to the host. The result is that many remote terminals can be connected to the host, while the required number of high-speed lines is minimized. Like modems, multiplexers are typically used in pairs so that signals that are combined at one end can be sorted out (de-multiplexed) at the other.

    Recently, T-1 multiplexers were used on high-capacity digital lines, which can carry as much voice and data traffic as 24 conventional (analog) phone lines. T-1 multiplexers can result in significant cost savings to firms with sizable telecommunication traffic.

- **Concentrators** A **concentrator** is a hardware device that combines the functions of a controller and a multiplexer. Most concentrators use a store-and-forward messaging approach: storing messages from many low-speed devices until the quantity of data is sufficient to make it worthwhile to send over a high-speed line.

    In the airlines' passenger reservations systems, concentrators are commonly used at key sites to gather messages sent in from airline agents. When enough messages are collected to make forwarding worthwhile, the messages are sent to the centralized reservations system for processing. All of this happens so fast that most agents are not even aware that their messages are being held up by the concentrator.

■ ***Protocol converters, gateways, and bridges*** Because an organization's wide area network typically evolved over numerous years, it is often composed of a mixture of many types of computers, transmission channels, transmission modes, and data codes. To enable diverse systems components to communicate with one another and to operate as a functional unit, protocol conversion may be needed. For example, it may be necessary to convert asynchronous transmissions to a synchronous message packet, or to convert from ASCII to EBCDIC. Protocol conversion can be accomplished via hardware, software, or a combination of hardware and software.

Workstations in one network often need access to computer resources in another network or another part of a WAN. For example, an office manager using a local area network might want to access an information service that is offered by a VAN over the public phone system. In order to accommodate this type of need, gateways and bridges are often necessary. A **gateway** is a collection of hardware and software facilities that enables devices on one network to communicate with devices on another, dissimilar network.

Bridges have the same general characteristics as gateways, but connect networks that employ similar protocols and topologies. *Routers* are similar to bridges in that they connect two similar networks. However, unlike bridges, this connection is done at level 3 of the OSI model—the network level (refer back to Figure 8.17, page 366). Bridges establish connections at levels 1 and 2 and are less complex than routers.

WAN Software

Many types of communications devices require software to function. For example, software enables controllers to poll (communicate in a round-robin fashion) terminals. And most modems are used in conjunction with communications software (such as Crosstalk and Procomm), which enables users to carry out functions such as developing personal phone directories for accessing various computers and automatically logging in to on-line databases. In any large communications system, a variety of communications software programs make it possible for users to carry out their tasks and for managers to access the data and information that they need in order to make decisions. While many types of WAN software exist—such as teleprocessing monitors and network control programs—an in-depth discussion of them is beyond the scope of this book.

Local Area Networks

Common carriers and value-added networks are closely associated with wide area network service, which can cover a geographical area as small as a city or as big as the world. However, many organizations need networks that connect nearby facilities—perhaps computers and terminals that are located in the same

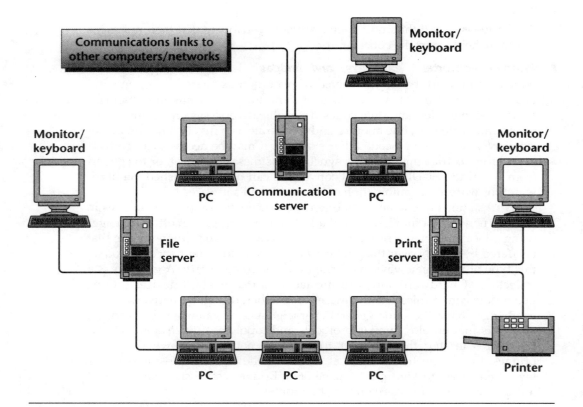

Figure 8.19 An example of a client/server LAN.

building or several microcomputer stations located on the same university campus. Such networks are usually local area networks (LAN). The three most common types of local networks are cable-based local area networks, private branch exchanges (PBX), and hierarchical networks.

LAN Hardware Configurations

As we discussed in Chapter 5, local area networks are often used to share computer resources. For instance, as Figure 8.19 shows, microcomputer workstations consisting of system units, diskette units, keyboards, and monitors are linked together in a LAN and allowed to share both an expensive laser printer and a large, mass-storage area. In many local area networks, twisted-pair wires are used as the transmission medium; however, other cabling or wireless media may be used.

Local networks do not use host computers; processors within the network itself manage the devices. In many local area networks, the processor used to manage the large mass-storage area (which stores application software such as word processing, spreadsheets, and so on) for general LAN use is called a *file server*. The file server is often a high-end microcomputer that controls access to shared disk space, programs, and data—generally controlling the network. Similarly, a device that manages printing operations, such as spooling and the print queue, is called a *print server*.

Both file servers and print servers are examples of devices that are found in *client/server* LAN designs such as the one in Figure 8.19. Within client/server systems, shared resources are placed at dedicated servers that manage the resources on behalf of the client workstations that share them. Hence, a variety of different servers could be in these systems, including database servers, document scanner servers, and communications servers. The latter manages communications devices such as modems, gateways, bridges, and access to other external computing resources such as the organization's host processor.

While client/server local area networks are the most widely used type of configuration, other LAN alternatives exist. For example, a *peer-to-peer* LAN features distributed, rather than centrally managed, systems. In effect, any workstation in a peer-to-peer LAN functions as a server by making the data on its hard drive or peripherals available to the other workstations on the LAN. Peer-to-peer local area networks are typically limited to less than 20 workstations.

The *multiuser DOS* LAN is centrally managed like the client/server LAN. However, like the peer-to-peer LAN, they are typically limited to under 20 workstations. The most common operating system used in this type of LAN is Multiuser DOS, an operating system that runs MS-DOS software, uses MS-DOS commands, and follows MS-DOS conventions. Because Multiuser DOS provides the power of the central 386 or 486 PC to linked workstations, the workstations do not have to be full stand-alone personal computers. Less expensive, dumb terminals and older 8088 personal computers can be used instead; users will still have the processing capability of a 386 or 486 machine.

The *zero-slot* LAN links personal computers and printers with cables connected to the computers' standard serial or parallel ports—the software that controls the transfer of data between the networked machines. A zero-slot LAN is the least expensive, but most limited, means of networking microcomputers. Most analysts agree that no more than three or four personal computers should be the networked in this manner.

LAN hardware may be laid out in any of the topologies identified in the section on wide area networks. However, star, ring, and bus topologies are the most common.

While twisted-pair wires are the most frequently used communications medium in local area networks, coaxial cables, fiber optic cables, and wireless transmissions using radio waves and infrared signals are also quite common. *FDDI* (Fiber Distributed Data Interface) is a relatively new standard for high-speed local area networks that uses the token-passing technique (discussed later) and fiber optic cable to achieve speeds of up to 100 Mbps.

Network interface cards, one of the microcomputer add-in boards described in Chapter 2, make it possible to connect microcomputers to local area networks. These cards provide whatever signal translation is needed between the computer and the network. Different LAN protocols, discussed next, usually demand different interface cards or a single-card cable of handling more than one protocol.

LAN Protocols

The three most common types of protocols found in local area networks are polling, contention, and token passing. While each of these protocols may be used with any of the topologies, each is usually associated with a particular hardware layout.

Polling is often used with star topologies, such as the one illustrated in Figure 8.13 (page 359). Each controller polls the terminals in its cluster in a round-robin fashion, asking each one if it has a message to send. If a terminal has a message, it passes it to the controller. The controller polls the terminals from a prespecified polling list—perhaps 1, 2, 3, 4, 1, 2, 3, 4, 1, and so on (if each terminal is to get the same amount of attention).

Contention is often used with bus configurations, such as the one illustrated in Figure 8.14 (page 360). Contention is so named because terminals must contend for the use the bus that connects them.

Carrier sense multiple access with collision detection (CSMA/CD) is one of the best known contention protocols. Unlike polling or token passing, where they must wait for a poll or for the token, with a CSMA/CD approach, devices can access the network whenever they want. The collision-detection feature ensures that when two devices transmit messages at the same time, causing the messages to collide and interfere with each other, receivers will ignore the garbled message; senders will retransmit their messages when the line is clear. Ethernet and Ungermann-Bass's Net/One are well-known local network designs that use CSMA/CD.

Token passing is often used with ring and star networks. With token passing, a small packet called a token is passed from one device to the next. Messages and their addresses can be stored on the token. As the token is passed from one device to the next, the receivers check to see if the token is addressed to them. When it is, the terminal removes the message and sends the token to the next device. With token passing, there is no chance of devices colliding as they vie for service.

LAN Software

The primary software associated with local area networks is the network operating system (NOS). This set of programs usually resides on the file server and provides services for adding new devices to the network, installing application software, diagnosing network problems, assembling network usage statistics, and routing messages. It may also include programs for managing each of the dedicated servers in the network, providing electronic mail services, and allowing remote users to access LAN resources via dial-up lines.

Figure 8.20 identifies some of the most commonly used LAN network operating systems. Novell controls the lion's share of the LAN operating system market (nearly 60%). None of the competing products commands as much as 10 percent of the business.

LEADING LAN OPERATING SYSTEMS VENDORS	
Vendor	**Leading Product**
Novell	NetWare
Microsoft	LAN Manager
IBM	LAN Server
Apple	AppleShare
DEC	Pathworks
Banyan Systems	Vines

Figure 8.20   Some of the leading vendors of LAN operating systems and their products.

Private Branch Exchanges (PBX)

Most organizations have their own telephone switchboards, or private branch exchanges (PBX) (see Figure 8.21). The earliest PBX—which can still be observed in many 1930s and 1940s movies—consisted of an array of telephone operators stationed at board devices, switching plugs in and out of the board to connect callers. Today, of course, these connections are made by computer. Sometimes, these computer-based private branch exchanges are called *CBX* (for *computerized branch exchange)* or *PABX* (for *private automatic branch exchange).*

Besides phones, a PBX can connect into a variety of other devices, such as communications terminals, computers, printers, facsimile machines, and printers. Many of the newer private branch exchanges use digital technology and not only connect voice and information equipment within the organization, but also provide access to value-added networks and long-distance carriers. Some new private branch exchanges also include ISDN connections.

Centrex Services

For companies that want PBX-like capabilities, but cannot bear the equipment and operational costs associated with a PBX, Centrex may help. *Centrex* services can often be leased from local telephone companies. They provide subscribing organizations with functions and services similar to those of a PBX. The primary difference between Centrex and PBX is that with Centrex, switching is done at a local telephone company's central office, rather than at the customer's premises. The telephone company, not the subscribing organization, is responsible for managing and operating the switch.

Centrex often gives users lower cost voice and data communications services than are possible with a PBX. However, acquiring a PBX gives a company greater control over the usage of its telephone system and often provides purchasers with additional features and services not available with Centrex. Also, since the line costs associated with a PBX can be spread out over its service life (rather than being a recurring monthly lease charge), the long-term costs of a

Conceptual Diagram of a PBX

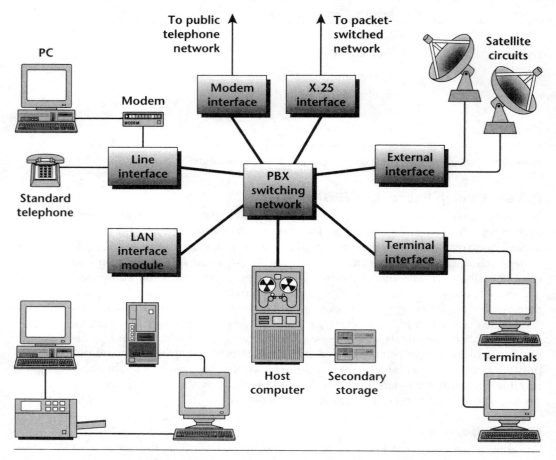

Figure 8.21 An example of how a private branch exchange (PBX) can be used to establish a local area network capable of handling both voice and data communications. Many of the digital private branch exchanges installed today provide gateways to packet-switching networks and other long-distance services; many are also ISDN-ready.

PBX may be lower than that for Centrex services. These are a few of the trade-offs that an organization must consider when choosing between a PBX and Centrex services.

Backbone Networks

One of the biggest challenges facing many organizations concerns interconnecting local area networks and other computing resources. As you have seen, local area networks may be configured quite differently and may use different protocols. These differences must be addressed by organizations that want to enable users in one LAN to share data, information, and computer resources with users in another LAN. Many organizations use backbone networks to meet these challenges. Figure 8.22 gives an example of a backbone network.

In many instances, fiber optic cable is used for the physical cabling of the backbone network. A standard protocol (for example, Ethernet or TCP/IP) is chosen and local area networks (plus other computing/communications devices) are connected to the backbone through bridges, gateways, and protocol converters. The backbone typically provides users in a LAN with access to the organization's larger computers (such as mainframes and supercomputers) and may provide mechanisms for linking with packet-switching services, ISDN, Internet, and other external networks.

Interconnecting local area networks and establishing LAN to WAN interfaces are just some of the telecommunication challenges facing organizations. The following sections discuss other major challenges in today's business environments.

MANAGEMENT ISSUES

Not long ago, corporate telecommunication management consisted primarily of monitoring and controlling telephone-related costs. The necessary acquisition of resources such as distributed processing networks and digital private branch exchanges demanded more expertise than could be supplied by some telecommunication groups, thus requiring computer expertise. Today, telecommunication technologies are changing faster than computing technologies and are entering into corporate-level strategy decisions, requiring still another level of talent.

As communications technologies continue to become even more widespread and powerful (as well as cheaper), managers must continue to monitor telecommunication-related developments and assess their potential impact. Authors Eric Clemons and F. Warren McFarlan, among others, raise some important questions that managers must address:

- What value does the firm provide to customers and how might telecommunication technologies change this?
- Whom is the firm competing against and how might telecommunication technologies change the structure of the competitive environment?
- Do telecommunication technologies have the potential to change the mission of the firm, thus putting it into a new competitive environment?
- Can customers be locked into the firm's communications systems by being given faster, easier, and cheaper service, as well as incentives for staying with their current supplier?
- Can competitors be locked out through an aggressive use of technology?
- In what areas of the firm's internal or external environment will communications technologies help most?
- Will technology allow the firm to attain some desirable strategic position before its competitors, and then sustain a lead over them?

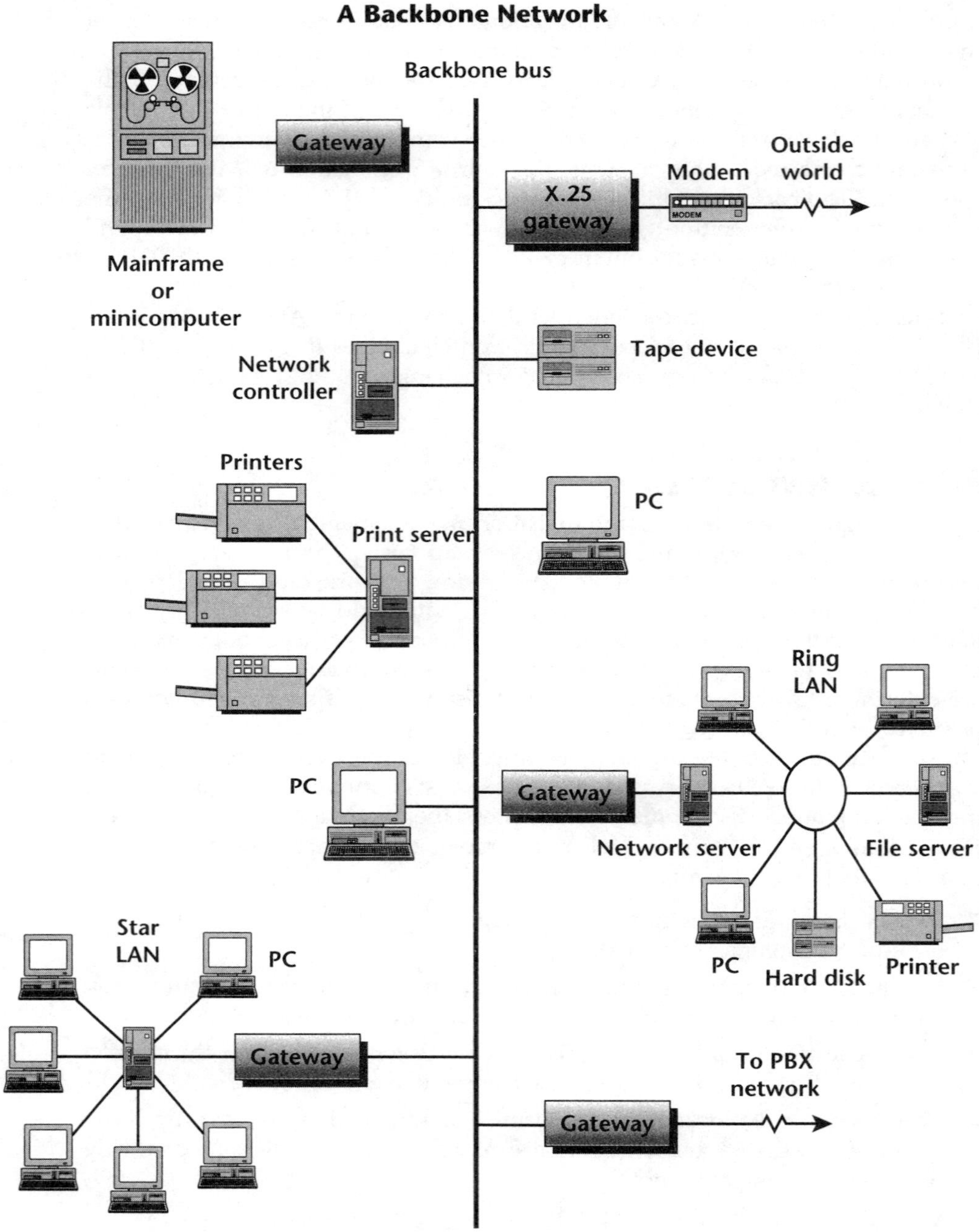

A Backbone Network

Backbone bus

Figure 8.22 Using a backbone network to interconnect local area networks and other computer resources.

- Should the firm take pioneering initiative with telecommunications, even though the cutting-edge technologies being applied have a short and inconclusive track record?

Executive management will need the help of technically oriented communications specialists to answer such questions. As you can appreciate after reading this chapter, deciding strategic uses of telecommunication technology and technically determining, how a telecommunication system will best work are two entirely distinct issues, requiring two distinctly different bases of expertise.

To take full advantage of communications technologies, business managers need some help from the technical specialists. Just as key specialists must appreciate the strategic significance of technology and the business priorities of the firm, so too must managers understand the capabilities and limitations of technology. Bridging this gap is difficult. The fusion of managers and specialists is necessary, however, to successfully handle multidimensional telecommunication problems and opportunities. This fusion is especially vital because telecommunication costs often constitute both a major MIS expense and a major opportunity for strategic positioning.

TRENDS AND FUTURE DEVELOPMENTS

Telecommunications and networking bring us closer to global information systems, both public and private. Advancing technology in this area contributes to the globalization of the business environment. This has generated a growing demand for high-speed communications links and international connectivity standards that make it easier to develop and expand wide area networks.

An ongoing migration of common carrier services is going toward digital equipment and away from analog-based systems. ISDN is expected to be one of the major services provided both by common carriers and value-added networks by the year 2000.

Fiber optic media should dominate terrestrial communications, while microwaves and satellite communications will be used even more widely than they are now. Wireless networks, most using radio or microwave frequencies, will increasingly be used; some experts predict that by 1995, 25 percent of workers in the U.S. will use some type of wireless communications on a day-to-day basis.

To ensure connectivity, telecommunication hardware and software vendors are expected to conform to the OSI reference model and ISO standards. Increased compliance with standards should promote the development of enterprise-wide information systems and standards that make it easier to establish effective LAN and WAN interfaces. Simple Network Management Protocol (SNMP) is often cited as a protocol that can be used to develop enterprise-wide networks; for this reason, it should become more popular.

IBM's network architecture, SNA, should continue to play a key role in the ongoing evolution of business telecommunications. SNA recently expanded to include AIX, IBM's proprietary version of UNIX—a move that shows IBM's commitment to open up its network architecture and allow it to evolve. Such evolutionary changes may be essential if IBM intends to hold on to its established base of over 50,000 SNA installations worldwide.

Electronic data interchange (EDI) systems are already changing the flow of documents between organizations and their suppliers and customers. These are likely to proliferate by the year 2000.

Many experts feel that the continuing development of sophisticated telecommunication infrastructures is essential for future competitiveness in numerous industries. A consortium of U.S. companies, universities, and government agencies are working on the blueprint for a fiber optic-based "data highway"— called NREN (the National Research and Education Network)—which will allow data transmission rates exceeding 1 billion bits per second. This should facilitate changes in a number of sectors, including research and development, education, medicine, and information services to the home.

It is important for managers and professionals to stay aware of developments in business telecommunications. These are just some of the trends that should be considered, especially when making systems development decisions. Several other trends that are direct offshoots of advances in telecommunications will be discussed later in the book.

SUMMARY

Telecommunications (or teleprocessing) refers to any system in which data or information are sent among two or more processors over some type of transmission medium. Telecommunications can benefit the organization by reducing information float (the time it takes to get information from one point to another), overcoming geographical restrictions, and restructuring the way people and organizations interact.

Distributed processing is generally defined as dividing a workload among two or more computer systems. It has numerous advantages and disadvantages. The trend of ever smaller computer systems has made distributed processing a relatively "hot" topic over the last several years.

Two broad classes of communications media exist: physical lines and wireless. The three principal types of physical lines today are twisted-pair wires, coaxial cable, and fiber optic cable. The main devices for microwave transmission are terrestrial (earth-bound) microwave stations and communications satellites. However, numerous other wireless systems are increasingly used, including cellular phone systems, radio-wave-based systems, and systems using infrared transmissions.

A communications medium's speed is rated in bits per second (bps). Communications lines pass along signals that are either analog or digital. Modems interface these two types of signals, allowing digital data to be sent over analog phone lines. The trend, however, is toward lines and communications equipment that are digital.

Data are also transmitted either in serial or parallel. Serial transmission has the bits of each byte sent along a single path, one after another. In parallel transmission, bits are sent along parallel paths, so they all arrive at the same time.

Serial transmission can occur either asynchronously or synchronously. In asynchronous transmission, a single character is transmitted at a time, preceded by a start bit and followed by a stop bit. Synchronous transmission is used for transmitting large blocks of data at once, at fast speeds. In asynchronous transmission, a parity bit sums the bits of each byte at the receiver location as a means of checking for transmission errors; in synchronous transmissions, cyclical redundancy checking is the primary error-detection and correction mechanism.

When communications media are used to link together various hardware devices, the result is a network. When a centralized computer exists that does most of the processing in a network, it is called a host computer. A network topology is the pattern to which a network conforms. The four most common network forms are hierarchical, star, bus, and ring.

Organizations have a number of options with respect to network services and facilities. They can use common carriers, which provide wide area network (WAN) services. They can use switched lines, for more calling flexibility. Or they can use dedicated lines, which provide private links among two or more locations. Three methods used to switch lines are circuit switching, message switching, and packet switching.

Value-added network (VAN) vendors provide services over common carrier facilities. Common carriers and value-added networks are usually associated with wide area network services.

Devices communicate with each other via standards called protocols. One example of a protocol is the X.12 standard for electronic data interchange (EDI), which involves transmitting specially formatted documents from one computer to another. A protocol/hardware/software combination is called a network architecture. One of the best-known network architectures is IBM's System Network Architecture (SNA).

Some hardware devices for coordinating communications traffic in wide area networks are front-end processors, controllers, multiplexers, and concentrators. Many types of software exist for coordinating communications traffic in wide area networks, including multiuser operating systems, communications software packages that allow microcomputers to connect to host computers over communications media, and specialized software such as teleprocessing monitors and network control programs.

In contrast to wide area networks are local networks. Two common types are cable-based local area networks (LAN) and private branch exchanges (PBX). Many types of LAN hardware and configurations exist; client/server local area networks are the most common. Twisted-pair wire is most often used to connect devices in a LAN, but coaxial cable and fiber optic cables may also be used. Many LAN protocols use polling or contention for terminal management. Token passing is another popular type of LAN protocol. Workstations on local networks often access wide area networks via gateways, which allow dissimilar networks to be connected. Bridges connect devices in similar networks.

Today's telecommunications are a matter of strategic importance to companies. As communications technologies continue to become even more widespread, powerful, and cheaper, top management must closely monitor telecommunication-related developments and assess their potential impacts on business.

REVIEW

KEY TERMS

Analog signal

Asynchronous transmission

Bridge

Bus network

Coaxial cable (coax)

Common carrier

Communications medium

Communications satellite

Concentrator

Contention

Controller

Digital signal

Distributed processing

Fiber optic cable

Front-end processor (FEP)

Gateway

Host computer

Modem

Multiplexer

Network architecture

Open System Interconnection (OSI)

Packet switching

Parallel transmission

Polling

Protocol

Ring network

Serial transmission

Star network

Synchronous transmission

System Network Architecture (SNA)

Telecommunication

Token passing

Twisted-wire pairs

Value-added network (VAN)

Wide area network (WAN)

REVIEW QUESTIONS

1. In what ways is it possible to use telecommunication methodologies to make the organization both more efficient and more effective?

2. What is meant by "information float"? How is the combination of information and telecommunication technologies reducing information float?

3. What are the characteristics, advantages, and disadvantages of distributed processing systems?

4. Identify the major types of communications media and the situations in which each might be appropriate.

5. When is a modem needed? What does a modem do?

6. What is the difference between serial transmission and parallel transmission? When is each likely to be used?

7. What are the differences among switched, leased, and dedicated lines?

8. How may data be switched in a network?

9. What types of services are offered by value-added network (VAN) vendors?

10. What are the major types of hardware devices found in wide area networks and what functions do they carry out?

11. What is meant by network topologies? What are the differences among the four fundamental types of network topologies?

12. What is SNA and why is it important?

13. What is the OSI reference model and why is it important?

14. How do local area networks differ from wide area networks?

15. What are the characteristics of client/server local area networks? What types of servers may be included?

16. What are the differences among client/server, peer-to-peer, multiuser DOS, and zero-slot local area networks?

17. What is the significance of a communications protocol?

18. What are the differences among polling, contention, and token passing?

19. What are the telecommunication challenges that face business managers as they head toward the year 2000?

DISCUSSION QUESTIONS

1. Recent MIS literature stresses the growing importance of global telecommunication networks in gaining competitive advantage. In what ways are global networks going to be a vital MIS strategy for organizations in certain industries in the near future?

2. Companies are finding telecommunication talent relatively hard to find. What types of problems and opportunities does this shortage create?

3. Suppose a firm has its world headquarters in North America and also has European and Pacific Rim headquarter sites. Approximately 300 worldwide offices must keep in relatively close contact with the headquarter site in their particular area, and headquarter sites need to exchange data occasionally. What alternatives exist for such a firm to acquire a network so that the sites may communicate with each other? Also state the advantages and disadvantages of each alternative.

CASE STUDY

Global Networking during the 1990s

American President Companies (APC), a worldwide shipper, is just one of the many firms that has responded to the call for setting up a worldwide communications network. Using a combination of satellite and terrestrially based communication links that connect from New York to Kuwait, it can keep track of cargo in transit throughout North America and Asia. Besides helping APC with daily operations, the network provides competitive advantage: a customer needing to know the status or location of a shipment can call an APC computer on an 800 area code number and receive a digitized-voice response within seconds.

Companies in the fast-paced financial-services sector—where successfully executing a buy or sell order in any corner of the world is often determined by a matter of seconds—look at global networking in terms of "when," not "if." For instance, Merrill Lynch has developed a network that allows a stockbroker in Atlanta or Detroit to buy shares of overseas stocks directly from foreign exchanges, instead of through a trader in New York. Merrill is no small player among firms that take telecommunication very seriously; the company runs up an annual communications tab of almost a half a billion dollars.

Reacting quickly to changing world conditions is yet another reason why many firms are rushing to set up global networks. For instance, when the dollar falls below a certain level on European exchanges, Westinghouse can reroute its European electronic mail operation from England to the United States. This helps the company avoid sudden, undesirable increases in its communications costs.

When setting up a global network, a firm has numerous choices. Many organizations (such as American President Companies) that want to establish their own private networks are likely to have to use various communications media and vendors. Part of an organization's private network may be implemented by "buying" lines from one or more networks offered by firms that already have global networks in place. Today, most of the global networks are operated by the so-called phone companies (such as AT&T, U.S. Sprint, Nippon, and British Telecomm) and by some of the large computer manufacturers (such as IBM, DEC, and Unisys). The IBM network, for instance, extends to more than 150 countries and hooks up its 400,000 employees. IBM sells excess capacity on the network to other companies. Some other large firms (such as Toyota and Sears) have also built networks and sell excess capacity to outsiders.

Firms that are trying to establish global networks may encounter many obstacles. First, the elements of the network—probably coming from a variety of vendors—must be able to communicate with each other. Second, the laws regarding international communications are diverse, sometimes very restrictive, and change constantly. For instance, private microwave networks are banned in many parts of Europe, and many European countries require equipment to be approved before it can be put into use—a process that can delay building a network by months or years. Many countries are now rethinking their communications strategies, however. While they want to protect their own domestic industries, they do not want to thwart the benefits enjoyed through foreign investment. Third, teleprocessing is one of the fastest-changing technology areas. Equipment put into place today will probably be obsolete in three or four years. Also, finding the right professional talent in this area is tough—and the knowledge base is moving so quickly that it is difficult to keep up without making it a full-time priority.

Adapted from Rymer (1992), Lusa (1992), Steinbart and Ravinder (1992).

DISCUSSION

1. Compile a list of opportunities and problems facing firms that want to put global networks into place. Briefly describe why each is an opportunity or problem.

2. Compile a list of opportunities and problems facing countries in reassessing their communications strategies. Briefly describe why each should be considered a problem or an opportunity.

3. Why do you think so many organizations that are expanding their operations to Europe have contracted with established telecommunication companies in the European countries they are expanding to? How may such companies help the expanding firms develop their telecommunication network?

4. For companies like IBM that have established global networks in place, what are the advantages of selling excess communications capacity? If you were an IBM executive, how might you restrict access to your network? What types of international communications would you provide for free?

Part FOUR

MIS in Practice

Transaction Processing and Management Reporting Systems

After completing this chapter, you will be able to:

Describe the characteristics of the major subsystems of computer-based information systems

Define transaction processing system (TPS) and describe some of the properties that distinguish a TPS from other types of information systems

Explain the impact that technology has had on transaction processing

Identify and describe several transaction processing subsystems

Define management reporting system (MRS) and describe some of the properties that distinguish an MRS from other types of information systems

List and describe the major types of reports output by management reporting systems

In this chapter, we look at two of the earliest types of management information systems (MIS): transaction processing systems (TPS), and management reporting systems (MRS). Both of these systems are primarily oriented toward predefined types of data or information.

Most companies must provide regular support to a number of data-oriented, transaction processing operations that involve a massive amount of record keeping. These operations—payroll, order entry, and inventory control, to name just a few—were the first business applications of computers in organizations and are still among the most important. Without their computer-based transaction processing systems, most businesses could not survive in today's fast-paced business environment. In fact, according to a study conducted at the University of Minnesota, banks would have to close after two days without computer-based transaction processing systems, distribution companies would bog down in four days, and factories would grind to a halt within a week.

In recent years, some computer-based transaction processing systems have produced a new competitive business weapon: the interorganizational system (IOS). In many organizations, electronic data interchange (EDI) and imaging systems impact the manner in which some transactions are processed. Another important trend is the downsizing of transaction processing—moving transaction processing applications from mainframes to minicomputers, microcomputers, and local area networks.

Historically, management reporting systems were the first types of management information systems whose main purpose was to supply information to managers for decision-making purposes. The earliest management reporting systems produced reports that were by-products of transaction processing systems. Some management reporting systems were eventually developed that used their own, independent data sources. Today, management reporting systems of both types are still widely used. However, these are not the only sources of data and information used by managers to make decisions. Advances in technology have made it possible to provide managers with decision support systems (DSS) that provide managers with a lot of flexibility in assembling the data they need for decision making.

We begin this chapter by reviewing the framework that we have used to classify information systems throughout this text. Keeping this classification system in mind is especially important as you read this chapter and the next three. Then, we will cover some general properties of transaction processing systems. From there, we cover specific transaction processing subsystems—payroll, order entry, inventory, accounts receivable, and several others. Finally, we turn to management reporting systems, discussing their nature and evolu-

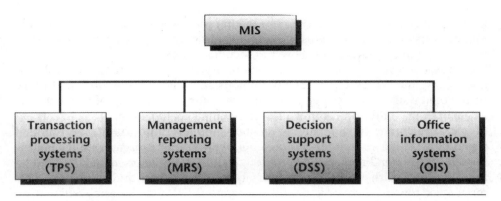

Figure 9.1 An MIS framework.

tion from by-products of transaction processing systems, and providing several examples.

A MANAGEMENT INFORMATION SYSTEMS FRAMEWORK

Many terms characterize the types of information systems found in organizations. We frequently hear about "data processing systems," "management information systems," "decision support systems," "executive information systems," "marketing information systems," and "expert systems," to cite just a few. Their meanings are often unclear because these terms are used loosely by people who are not computer professionals and because they are constantly being redefined by changes in technology.

In this section, we will review the framework first presented in Chapter 1 for studying these terms. It is this framework and the nature of the systems represented in it that form the core of our discussion in this part of the textbook.

In Chapter 1, we defined a management information system (MIS) to be any system that provides people with either data or information relating to an organization's operations. Management information systems support the activities of employees, owners, customers, and other key people in the organization's environment, either by efficiently processing data to assist with the transaction workload or by quickly and effectively supplying information to authorized people. As described in Chapter 1, computer-based management information systems may be composed of any or all of the following component subsystems (see Figure 9.1).

Transaction Processing Systems

A transaction processing system (TPS) supports the processing of a firm's business transactions. For example, the TPS of a department store can record customer purchases, prepare billings to customers, and order merchandise from suppliers—as well as interrelate these tasks and others into an overall accounting system. The TPS of a college or university, on the other hand, helps perform such tasks as enrolling students in courses, billing students for tuition, and issuing paychecks to faculty. The transaction processing system associated with a large pension fund may assist stockbrokers in executing buy and sell orders, then help with accounting for those transactions.

Transaction processing systems keep an organization running smoothly by automating the processing of the voluminous amounts of paperwork that must be handled daily. These systems include the accurate recording of transactions, as well as the control procedures used in issuing such documents as paychecks, invoices, customer statements, payment reminders, tuition bills, and student schedules. Unlike other MIS components, the TPS of an organization may be far-reaching, extending completely through and out of the organization, linking together the entire financial system, factory, customers, and suppliers. The movement toward electronic data interchange (EDI) and the establishment of electronic links with suppliers and customers is an example of an extension of an organization's TPS. EDI and other systems (for example, electronic funds transfer (EFT), image processing, and document management systems) could radically reduce the total amount of physical paperwork that organizations' transaction processing systems have traditionally had to handle.

In this chapter, we will cover the traditional types of transaction processing systems and subsystems that are found in most businesses. In addition, we will look at transaction processing-related EDI and interorganizational systems (IOS) that span two or more businesses.

Sometimes, the term *data processing system* is used synonymously with the term "transaction processing system" because the primary purpose of these systems is to effectively process the data that arise from transactions. Alternatively, the term "operations" is frequently used to describe the transaction processing component of an MIS.

Management Reporting Systems

A management reporting system (MRS) is an information system that provides predefined types of information to management for relatively structured types of decisions. As opposed to focusing purely on data and the efficient processing of data (which characterize transaction processing systems), management reporting systems focus on information and, occasionally, on effectiveness. Later in this chapter, we will look in depth at management reporting systems and how they provide decision-making information to managers.

Sometimes, the term "management information system" is used synonymously with the term "management reporting system." In fact, to most computer professionals in the late 1960s and early 1970s, management information systems referred specifically to the hardcopy, management-oriented reports that existed beyond transaction-oriented data processing. At that time, the taxonomy of business systems consisted only of TPS and MIS, which were considered two distinct components. Today, some people still regard MIS as being rigidly defined this way; they regard such newer developments as decision support systems (DSS) and office information systems (OIS) as concepts that are distinct from MIS.

As mentioned, the term "management information system" was used widely for many years—and it's not easy to overcome an old habit. However, many researchers today regard management information systems as an evolving, umbrella concept that covers a wide variety of systems—which is evident by the numerous books titled *Management Information Systems* or *Information Systems*. Also, it can be confusing to use MIS as both an umbrella concept and as a differently defined subset of that concept. So, management reporting system (MRS) will be used in this text to represent the MIS subsystem that issues preformatted reports to managers. MIS will be used as the umbrella concept that incorporates TPS, MRS, DSS, OIS, and knowledge-based systems. We hope that this will minimize confusion in this text.

Decision Support Systems

A *decision support system (DSS)* provides tools that enable managers to develop information in the manner that best suits the decisions they are currently trying to make. Unlike the MRS, which delivers specific types of information in a preplanned format, the DSS provides the manager with the computing and communications capabilities to develop his or her own decision models, databases, and report formats. Decision support systems often also focus on such areas as flexibility in meeting a variety of continually changing needs, heavy user/display device interactions, and trial-and-error modeling processes.

Over the years, a variety of decision support systems have evolved. For example, decision support systems targeted to executives are often called executive information systems (EIS) or *executive support systems (ESS)*. Group decision support systems (GDSS)—which support the work activities of work groups—are also quite common. The terms "sales support system" and "marketing information system" pop up occasionally, although it is often unclear whether they are referring to DSS, MRS, TPS, OIS, or knowledge-based systems (or all of these!) targeted to selling applications.

Knowledge-Based Systems

Chapter 11 will cover decision support systems and their characteristics. Chapter 12 will then discuss the closely related topic of *knowledge-based systems*, which include expert systems (ES), artificial intelligence (AI), and neural networks. Although these systems probably offer the greatest potential benefits to the DSS area, they could actually benefit any of the application areas under the MIS umbrella. In the future, knowledge-based systems are likely to be infused into virtually every type of organizational information system, including TPS, DSS, EIS, and office systems. Because of this, knowledge-based systems are not shown separately in the MIS framework presented in Figure 9.1.

Office Systems

Office automation (OA) has traditionally referred to a wide variety of computer-based technologies that make office workers more productive. The diverse set of OA tools that enhance office productivity, efficiency, and effectiveness are often collectively called office information systems (OIS). These will be discussed in Chapter 12.

The taxonomy (classification system) just described does not always provide distinct boundaries that allow a given system to be neatly put into only one category. For example, many office systems can also be classified as decision support systems or DSS tools (such as spreadsheets), which can make office workers more productive and also help managers make better decisions. The blurry line between decision support systems and office systems should be expected because most decision makers work in some type of office environment.

As another example of ambiguity, a database management system that manages transaction data for a firm might also offer some decision support. For instance, if a customer calls up L.L. Bean to order a down jacket and finds that none is currently in stock, but that some will arrive from the supplier in 11 days, that customer is encountering a transaction processing system that may help to keep the customer's business through effective data management and better decision support. This is the case of a traditional transaction processing system that, through advances in technology, has a DSS-like, value-added addition. And—also out of step with tradition—the decision maker (the customer) is outside the organization.

The main point of these last examples is to show that, although we can distinguish among TPS, MRS, DSS, and office systems to some extent, these once distinct "islands of technology" are today blending together in many different ways. Considering how to typologize the overall system is often more of an academic than a practical exercise.

TRANSACTION PROCESSING

Computer-based transaction processing systems are often considered the bread-and-butter MIS application. No matter how nervous upper management in a medium to large organization is about spending in the information systems area, it knows that it cannot pull the plug on its TPS and survive.

Many of these organizations have had computer-based transaction processing systems since the 1950s. Most of these systems more than paid for themselves and have justified a full-time support staff consisting of computer professionals. Most transaction processing systems have been—and still are—mainframe-oriented. IBM equipment and their compatibles currently claim the lion's share of the transaction processing marketplace and are expected to hold onto this lead throughout the 1990s.

Today, many firms consider transaction processing to be their most important computer application. A surprisingly large number of firms, however, have not carried computer-based information processing far beyond the transaction processing stage.

Because most firms of any size have transaction processing systems in place, this market is not growing as quickly as those for DSS products, knowledge-based systems, and office information systems. In another sense, transaction processing systems are relatively entrenched; many firms have millions of dollars invested in their transaction processing systems and think largely in terms of maintaining or modifying their current systems, rather than replacing them with entirely new systems.

However, the possibility of extending current transaction processing systems across traditional organizational boundaries, to tie in customers and suppliers more closely, has given many transaction processing systems a new slant. Transaction processing systems in many organizations today are used in this way as competitive weapons. Additionally, the move from dumb terminals to intelligent microcomputer-based workstations is expected to alter transaction processing in other ways, such as by distributing certain traditionally mainframe-based centralized transaction processing functions closer to their funtional areas.

The Nature of Transaction Processing

For many businesses, a transaction refers to an exchange of goods or services for money. For example, suppose a retailer buys 100 sleeping bags from a wholesaler. From the retailer's end, inventory is increased and a counterbalancing promise to pay the wholesaler is established. When payment is eventually made, the retailer loses cash—but this is counterbalanced by eliminating the payable charge on its records. Organizations such as academic institutions and hospitals have other ways of defining and dealing with transactions. In general, a **transaction** is a recorded business event, often reflecting a routine exchange that affects the financial well-being of an organization.

As noted previously, a transaction processing system (TPS) supports the processing of an organization's transactions. This includes accounting for the transactions on its records, as well as providing support activities such as sending out payment reminders (which, although not transactions themselves, are related to transactions). Recently, gaining competitive advantage has become a transaction processing concern in some firms, especially those that are working to tie customers and suppliers together more closely with the organization's traditional TPS via electronic linkages.

Transaction Processing Functions

Three functions performed by most transaction processing systems are bookkeeping, issuance, and control reporting.

- **Bookkeeping** Bookkeeping involves keeping accurate records of a firm's business transactions. Virtually every organization is involved with day-to-day business transactions between groups such as customers and vendors. For example, banks typically use both human tellers and automatic teller machines to record deposits and withdrawals of account holders. The airlines have reservation systems that keep track of all tickets purchased by passengers. Supermarkets and department stores capture customer item purchases with a variety of sophisticated input (for example, point-of-sale) equipment. Colleges and universities record student registrations and fees paid by students. All of these tasks involve keeping accurate records of the firm's business transactions.

In most organizations, bookkeeping involves generally accepted principles of financial accounting. However, financial accounting data are often not all the data that many managers need to help them make decisions. For example, the book value of an asset might not reflect the asset's true worth to the organization.

- **Issuance** Issuance refers to the production of such documents as paychecks, invoices, periodic statements (monthly telephone and credit card bills, for example), and payment reminders. The creation of these documents is absolutely necessary to the effective operation of the company; that is, these documents are not discretionary, as are many other types of MIS-related documents (such as interoffice memos and informational reports). The documents associated with transaction processing systems are discussed more fully in the section on the transaction processing cycle.

- **Control reporting** Reports that are produced as a by-product of transaction processing operations, and that also serve operations-control purposes, are called **control reports**. For example, as paychecks are prepared in batches, a *payroll edit report* is generally produced to show who was paid what amount. This report can be used to ensure that paycheck amounts are accurate before the paychecks are actually distributed. In transaction processing systems that handle large volumes of business transactions, an **error report** is often used to flag invalid transactions that were rejected by the system and must be reprocessed. In other situations, an exception report can be used to flag unusual transactions, such as a check for an exceptionally large amount. We will look at other types of reports associated with the transaction processing cycle in the next section of the chapter. Other types of transaction processing controls will be covered in Chapter 15.

Role of Information Technology in Transaction Processing

The earliest transaction processing systems were manual systems. Clerks would record transactions in a journal or on numbered, multipart forms. These transactions would later be transferred, manually, to a central system of handwritten records or file folders representing individual customers or suppliers. These records would be set up to trigger statements to customers or checks to suppliers. Many small businesses still operate with manual transaction processing systems; however, inexpensive and easy-to-use computer technology is finding its way into more small businesses.

To most businesses, manual systems present numerous problems that are solvable by computer and communications technologies:

- **Error level** With manual systems, an uncomfortable level of error often exists. Frequently, clerks look up the wrong prices, add prices incorrectly on invoices, or produce garbled journal entries or source documents. Sickness, worry, moodiness, and other inherently human variables can also contribute to high error rates in manual systems.

- **_Temporary or permanent loss of data_**   Source documents and file folders are easily lost or misplaced. This often results in lost customer payments and delayed purchases or payments.

- **_Labor intensity_**   Manual systems are labor intensive and, therefore, costly. For instance, data from a single transaction often have to be transcribed several times, and many types of low-volatility data (data that change infrequently, such as product descriptions and customer names or addresses) have to be re-recorded by clerks every time a new transaction takes place. Additionally, a lot of time is wasted coordinating data from departments; for instance, making phone calls to trace the status of a customer order.

- **_Poor level of service_**   As can be surmised from the last example, the level of service support in manual systems is often inferior. For instance, customers like to know immediately if goods are in stock, when goods not in stock will be arriving, when they can expect an order to arrive, what their current status is regarding payments, and so on. This level of information support is difficult to achieve with a manual system.

- **_Poor response_**   Virtually everything takes longer to do with a manual system. For example, when orders are taken, the order-entry department might have to contact the accounts receivable department for a credit check before an order can be validated. Today, many computerized order-entry operations are connected to a centralized database and, when a customer telephones, credit status can be verified immediately. As another example, if a manager wants to find out if a customer has ordered a specific type of product in the last month, the manager might have to search through mounds of documents to find the answer. Because such tasks take longer, important queries will go unanswered.

As technologies such as computers and communications became available to handle the transaction processing workload, MIS departments responded to it in different ways. Some organizations simply took their manual systems and coded them directly into the computer. Thus, all of the bugs in their manual systems were inherited by their computer systems. Other organizations realized that technology can change the way people work. Thus, they re-thought their transaction processing systems before automating them.

For example, an organization not taking full advantage of available technology may design its transaction processing system as a file-processing counterpart to handwritten, multipart source documents. In such a system, as each electronic document is originated, it is sent to several files; each file gets a page of the multipart form. As documents are processed by a department, they are sent along to other files. In other words, every paperwork operation resembles its counterpart in the manual system; the only difference is that the documents and the file folders are electronic.

Some of the problems associated with manual systems may still exist in these types of electronic systems. For example, if a copy of a document is corrected in one electronic file folder, the correction will not necessarily be reflected in other copies of the document in other electronic folders—thereby producing inconsistent data and data integrity problems such as those discussed in Chapter 7. In contrast, an organization concerned with taking full advantage of information technology is likely to migrate to a database management system. This can eliminate problems such as redundant data and poor data integrity, and may also integrate transaction data in a way that makes the system more useful and more responsive to queries.

Besides enabling transaction processing systems to be more efficient, technology has changed transaction processing in other ways. For example, information technology is one of the main reasons why credit cards proliferate in our society. Also, without computerized transaction processing systems, check processing would still be slow and clumsy. Many firms would not be able to handle anywhere near the number of customers that they do today, or to supply anything close to the level of service, or make available the multitude of products that their customers request.

Today, inexpensive computer and communications devices are setting up two new challenges to transaction processing: using the TPS as a competitive weapon and getting better information more quickly to the right people. The next section explores how these and other benefits of high technology are being specifically incorporated into transaction processing systems.

The Transaction Processing Cycle

Transaction processing systems capture and process transaction data. The data that are captured and processed are used to update organizational files and databases. Transaction databases are among the most extensive, richest, and most detailed sets of data created and stored by organizations. This data, or at least parts of this data, frequently serve as inputs for the other types of systems displayed in Figure 9.1 (page 389). Reports generated by the MRS typically assemble and summarize data that were initially captured by the TPS. TPS data also often "feed" DSS, EIS, and knowledge-based systems implemented within the organization.

Figure 9.2 depicts the transaction processing cycle. It consists of five basic parts: data entry, transaction processing, file and database processing, document and report generation, and inquiry processing. Each of these parts is summarized next.

Data Entry

The first step in the transaction processing cycle involves data entry. **Data entry** concerns collecting, recording, coding, and editing transaction data. In a CBIS, transaction data must be converted to a form that can be entered directly into the computer system for processing.

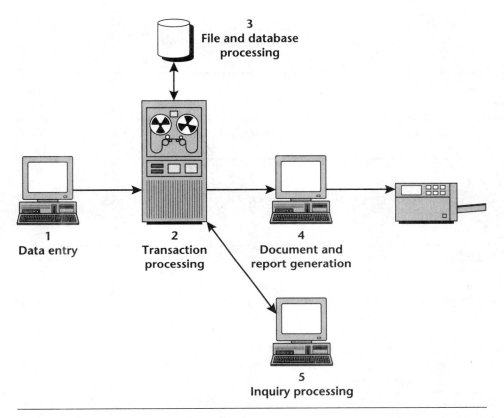

Figure 9.2 The transaction processing cycle. Most transaction processing systems use a five-step process. The process begins with capture and entry of transaction data, then continues with the actual processing of transaction data and updating of files and/or databases. After these processing and updating tasks conclude, document and report generation and inquiry processing activities can occur.

In traditional systems, data entry typically starts by capturing transaction data on *source documents* such as purchase orders, payroll time sheets, and order invoices. These documents are usually batched and transferred to data-entry specialists. After a manual audit, which is an editing process (often consisting of only a visual inspection of the source documents for omissions and obvious inaccuracies), data from acceptable source documents are converted to machine-readable form. Unacceptable source documents found by this process are often returned to their originators so that they can be corrected. The conversion to machine-readable form often means using a key-to-tape or key-to-disk system—data from the source documents are placed directly onto tape or disk for later processing. Prior to processing, the machine-readable transaction data are further edited (using the accuracy controls discussed in Chapter 15), then sorted. Figure 9.3 illustrates the traditional data-entry process.

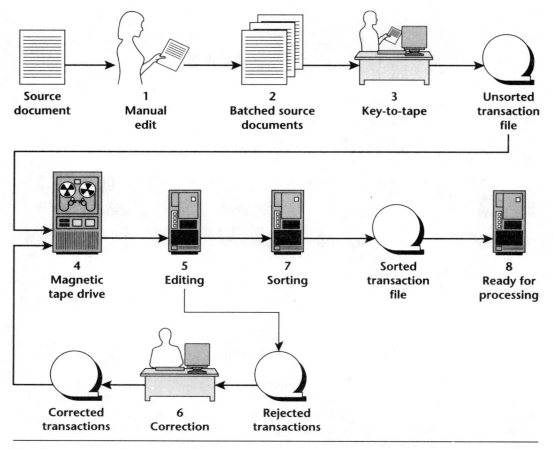

Figure 9.3 A traditional data-entry system. In such systems, prior to processing, source documents containing transaction data are manually edited, batched, and keyed onto tape or disk. Once entered into the computer system, the data are edited again, corrected as necessary, and sorted before they are used to update files and databases, generate reports, and so on.

Traditional data-entry systems are giving way to automated data-entry systems in a growing number of organizations. Many of these utilize the source data automation (SDA) approaches that were described in Chapter 5. Each of these methods reduces or eliminates many of the activities, people, and media required by traditional data-entry systems (see Figure 9.4 for examples of some of the major ways in which transaction data can be input). Figure 9.5 provides an example of an automated data-entry system. Electronic data interchange (EDI) systems and document management systems are also changing the ways in which transaction data and source documents are captured, stored, and handled by organizations.

Type of Transaction	Data-Entry Device	Direct Data-Entry Example
Airline reservation	CRT terminal	On-line terminal connected to airline's computerized reservation system used to enter customer data.
Checking account deposit	Automated teller machine (ATM)	Account holder uses ATM to enter the deposit amount; magnetic ink character recognition (MICR) unit will later read account identifications from deposit slip and checks.
Insurance claim entry	Pen-based computer	Working at a damage site, the adjuster fills in a form appearing on the screen with the electronic "pen." The data are transmitted to the office over the cellular telephone network.
Inventory taking in grocery wholesaler's warehouse	Bar-code reader	Bar-code reader scans the Universal Product Code (UPC) for the grocery product being stored.
Order entry by sales representative in field	Laptop computer	Salespeople transmit orders from customer locations to corporate computer over telephone lines.
Retail sale in department store	Touch screen	Sales clerk touches video display terminal (VDT) screen with finger or wand and identifies the desired product.
Retail sale in supermarket	Point-of-sale (POS) terminal	Point-of-sale (POS) terminal records the sale with an optical character recognition (OCR) device embedded in the check-out counter and transmits the data to a computer.
Spoken inventory query	Voice input device	Item is identified by numeric code spoken into microphone.
Unattended gasoline purchase	"Smart-card" reader	Smart-card reader accepts smart card. Funds are transferred automatically from customer's to vendor's account.

Figure 9.4 Some of the ways in which transaction data can be directly entered into a transaction processing system. Many of these approaches enhance user productivity, customer service, and operational efficiency.

Transaction Processing and File/Database Updating

After data are in machine-readable form, the transactions must be processed. This can be accomplished in two basic ways: (1) batch processing (or batch updating), in which transaction data are accumulated over a period of time and then processed periodically as a batch, and (2) real-time processing, in which each transaction is processed immediately after it occurs. Batch processing is still heavily used by organizations; however, the use of real-time processing is growing and should eventually become the primary means of processing transaction data, especially in medium and large businesses.

Figure 9.6 illustrates how a batch processing system works. The goal of most batch processing programs is to update organizational master files by

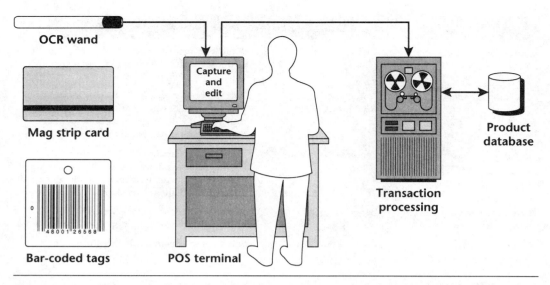

Figure 9.5 An example of an automated data-entry system for sales transactions, which illustrates some of the ways in which transaction data can be captured at the point of sale (POS). POS systems such as this are common in the retail industry.

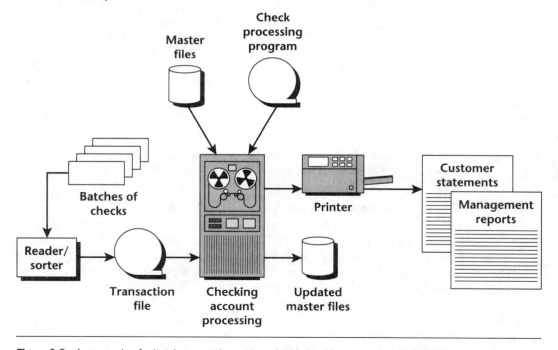

Figure 9.6 An example of a batch processing system. In this banking example, batches of checks are accumulated and processed. In most banks, this occurs on a daily basis.

incorporating data from transaction files. Such updating is done periodically (for example, daily, weekly, or monthly), depending on how current the information needs to be to make business decisions.

Real-time processing systems process transaction data (plus update files and databases) immediately as it is captured; batches are not accumulated for later processing. On-line terminals or source data automation equipment is used to input data directly into the computer; files and databases are stored on on-line direct access storage devices (DASD). Records and other data elements contained in these files and databases are updated immediately in real-time transaction processing systems. Figure 9.7 provides an example of a real-time transaction processing system.

Document and Report Generation

The final stages of the transaction processing cycle typically involve the generation of outputs such as documents and reports. Documents produced by a TPS are called *transaction documents*, which may be categorized as follows:

- **Information documents** These documents verify, confirm, or prove that transactions have occurred or were attempted. Sales receipts, order confirmations, customer invoices, and customer statements may be generated to document that a transaction took place. A credit rejection notice may serve to communicate that a transaction was attempted, but refused because of a problem in the customer's credit history.

- **Turnaround documents** Some invoices and customer statements contain a perforated tear-off portion that should be returned to the sender, along with the customer's payment. When this type of document is generated by the TPS, it is known as a turnaround document. Many turnaround documents used today can be read by magnetic (for example, if MICR is used) or OCR (optical character recognition) scanners after they return to the organization.

- **Action documents** Action documents initiate actions or transactions on the part of recipients. A paycheck, for example, authorizes a bank to cash or otherwise process an employee's check. A purchase order similarly authorizes a supplier to send needed items to the organization that submitted it.

As noted previously in this chapter, a TPS can also provide several types of reports or on-screen displays related to transaction data capturing and processing. These are not specifically tailored to management use, as are the types of reports mentioned in the MRS section of this chapter, but may still be reviewed by managers. The major types of these include:

- **Accounting statements** These must be generated for legal purposes and legally document the financial performance of a business. These may include general ledger summaries, cash flow statements, balance sheets, and income statements; all of these are directly related to transaction processing activities. The role of most of these will be clarified in the following section on TPS subsystems.

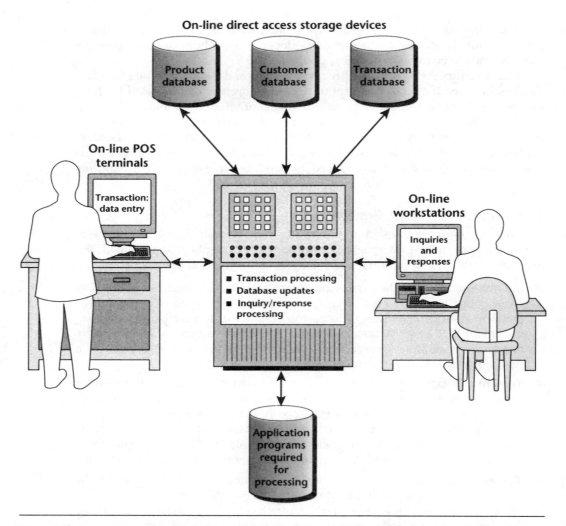

Figure 9.7 An example of a real-time sales processing system. In real-time systems, transaction processing, inquiries, and file/database updates are performed immediately, using on-line devices.

- **Control listings** Control listings are detailed reports that describe each transaction occurring during a specific time period. These are sometimes called transaction logs. A payroll register, for example, will list every check issued by the payroll system.

- **Edit reports** Reports that describe errors encountered during processing (or traditional data entry) are often called edit reports. Transactions involving invalid account numbers, incorrect totals, and missing data are usually listed in edit reports.

Inquiry Processing

An increasing number of transaction processing systems support the on-line interrogation of on-line files and databases by authorized users. For example, a customer may wish to check on the status of an order that was placed earlier. A checking account holder at a bank may call to inquire whether a certain check cleared. Inquiry processing capabilities enable customers to discover the answers to these questions. In general, inquiry processing enables authorized users to make inquiries and receive responses concerning the results of recent transaction activity. These responses are often displayed in a prespecified format on the user's workstation screen. It may also be possible to print out a copy of what appears on the screen by using a printer attached to the user's workstation.

Transaction Processing Subsystems

In this section, we will cover some of the major transaction processing subsystems found in most firms. In larger organizations, these operations are usually computerized. In smaller organizations, the scale of the operations may not justify even partial computerization. For example, clerks might manually handle payroll, sales orders, inventory control, accounts receivable and payable, and general ledger. However, because of the pace and complexity of business today, plus the low cost and relative ease of computing and communications technologies, virtually all but the smallest firms have technology-based transaction processing systems.

An example of how the transaction processing subsystems that we will cover in this chapter can be interrelated is shown in the data flow diagram in Figure 9.8. This diagram could provide an illustration of the interrelationships between data processing activities carried out by merchandising firms such as department stores, which sell products manufactured by other companies. It could also depict the transaction processing operations of a wholesale distribution firm. The traditional functions of the subsystems shown in Figure 9.8 are, briefly, as follows:

- **Payroll**   Pays employees.
- **Order entry**   Records customer purchases.
- **Inventory**   Manages the goods available for sale.
- **Invoicing**   Produces invoices.
- **Shipping**   Gets goods from the firm into the hands of customers.
- **Accounts receivable**   Manages customer accounts and sends statements to customers.
- **Purchasing**   Coordinates orders with vendors.

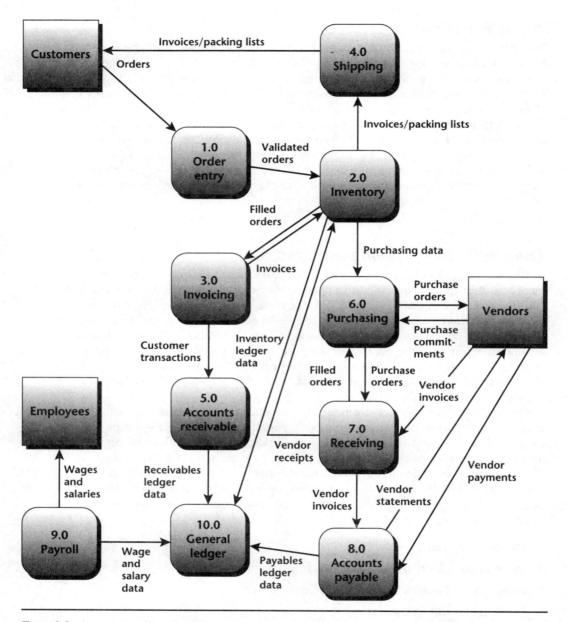

Figure 9.8 An example of how the various subsystems of an organization's transaction processing system may interrelate.

- **Receiving** Receives both shipments from vendors and returns from customers.
- **Accounts payable** Manages payments to vendors.
- **General ledger** Ties all of the transaction processing subsystems together.

Each subsystem serves a variety of purposes; we will cover each subsystem more extensively later. Because adequately representing an entire transaction processing system in a single data flow diagram is such a massive undertaking, three simplifying guidelines were followed in preparing Figure 9.8: (1) no data stores are shown, (2) report information normally provided to management for control purposes is omitted, and (3) exception procedures such as stockouts and complaints are omitted. The diagram does, however, effectively show how transaction processing subsystems may interrelate. For example, customer orders typically trigger demands on inventory. As products are sold, invoices are created and the receivables subsystem is notified that money is due. Also, goods have to be scheduled for shipment and, as stocks deplete, orders must be placed with suppliers.

The systems designed to support transaction processing operations are primarily data-oriented. Accurate data must be printed on paychecks, reflected in bills to customers, and used to update and maintain customer, supplier, employee, and asset records. Some of these data can be used for decision-making purposes as well, but supporting internal decision making is not the primary purpose for capturing them. In practice, it is often difficult to delineate where the TPS ends and other MIS subsystems, such as the MRS, begin.

Payroll

The transaction processing subsystems used to produce paychecks for employees are called **payroll processing systems**. These systems also must produce data for tax purposes, such as W-2 forms and reports to federal, state, county, and city tax offices. Additionally, payroll processing systems must keep track of such items as Social Security payments, union dues, and group insurance deductions.

In many organizations, payroll is the first transaction processing subsystem to be computerized because it is relatively straightforward and independent of other systems. Although a wide variety of additional requirements have made payroll processing systems more complex than they were in the 1950s, they are still among the simplest of the transaction processing subsystems to implement.

Payroll processing must interface with the general ledger system, which integrates transactions from a variety of other transaction processing subsystems. In addition, there may be a link between payroll and production control systems—for instance, a job-shop system in which the hours put in by employees on jobs are charged against those jobs. Payroll systems, of course, must also often interface with the transaction processing systems of those banks in which direct deposits are made for employees.

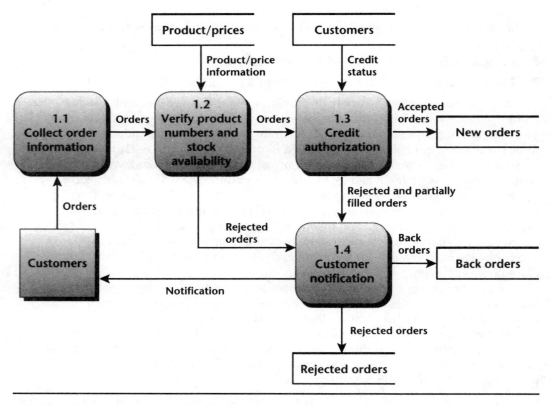

Figure 9.9 An example of a data flow diagram for an order-entry subsystem.

Payroll processing is usually a batch operation. Many organizations that pay employees once a month will prepare paychecks at the end or middle of the month. Other organizations prepare paychecks for all employees on a weekly or bi-weekly basis. Many organizations pay some types of workers on a weekly basis, others bi-weekly, and still others only once a month. Hence, the complexity of the payroll subsystem may vary considerably among organizations.

Order Entry

The **order-entry system** is the transaction processing subsystem that processes customer orders. Orders may come from a variety of sources—perhaps by mail, phone, and fax—from customers who are ordering on a demand basis. They can also be generated by "ticklers" within the order-entry system itself; for instance, if customers are scheduled to have goods delivered on a regular, periodic basis. An order-entry subsystem for the mail portion of a mail-order catalog firm is depicted in the data flow diagram of Figure 9.9.

In most instances, as each order is received by mail or by phone, the product numbers and product descriptions in the order are checked for accuracy. Also, stock levels in inventory are checked to determine what portion of the order can be filled immediately. At this point, the order is identified as either one that can be partially or completely filled, or one that cannot be filled at all. Orders that, for one reason or another, cannot be filled are deemed "rejected" and sent to the customer notification operation. In the case of a rejected order, a letter may be sent to the customer that explains the specific nature of the problem (such as a product being out of stock or the presence of conflicting information on the order). In some cases, the customer may be notified of such problems by phone. Orders that can be partially or completely filled are "costed out" with respect to item prices and subtotals, then sent on to the credit authorization step. Here, given such factors as the charge amount associated with the order, the method of payment, and the credit status of the customer, the part of the order that can be filled may be approved or disapproved. Approved orders are sent to the warehouse for filling; as noted above, rejected orders and orders that can only be partially filled result in some type of customer notification.

The earliest computer-based order-entry systems did little more than keep track of orders in a systematic way. Communications technologies facilitated distributed order-entry systems—for example, the airline reservations systems that allow worldwide computer-based bookings by thousands of travel agents. Database technology boosted further the power of many order-entry systems, enabling order-entry/sales personnel to interrelate data from various sources to help speed up or to close orders. For instance, personnel who are skilled at searching through databases of product information can rapidly provide customers with options from which to choose, closing a sale while the customer is still on the phone—and still in a buying mood.

Today, many firms are tying important customers more closely into their order-entry systems with electronic data interchange (EDI) and interorganizational information systems (IOS), using their order-entry systems as competitive weapons to lock in these customers and lock out competitors. One such example is American Hospital Supply (AHS) Corporation, one of the nation's largest distributors of hospital equipment and supplies. AHS was the first hospital supply company to provide their customers with terminals that hooked into AHS's order-entry system. Using an on-line catalog, customers can place orders electronically with AHS. The system also apprises the customer of the expected delivery date and generates invoicing, shipping, and inventory information for AHS. By making it convenient for customers to place orders and by offering incentives for customers to use their system, AHS makes it difficult for customers to leave them. Also, by realizing that once employees in customer-ordering departments learned how to use AHS's system, they would be more reluctant to learn a competitor's system, AHS had, in effect, locked out most competitors.

American Hospital Supply's order-entry system changed the way that organizations compete in the hospital supply business. When AHS first introduced their system, it was unique and provided them with an initial competitive advantage. Competitors soon followed with their own systems—including those that would work on the terminals supplied by AHS—and what was once a competitive advantage soon became a competitive necessity.

Similar competitive stories are told in other industries. American Airlines' reservations systems, SABRE, is another example of how an order-entry/transaction processing system can initially give a company a competitive advantage and force competitors to develop comparable systems. In the case of SABRE, that initial advantage has been sustained quite well over time. According to *Business Week*, in mid-1992, two of every five airline tickets were booked via SABRE. Numerous other examples of the strategic use of order-entry systems were presented in previous chapters.

Another novel way in which organizations are using telecommunications to extend their order-entry systems is by using laptops and pen-based computers to collect and transmit customer orders. By providing these types of computers to traveling salespeople, customer orders can be collected in electronic form. These can then be transmitted to the home office in batches—perhaps from the salesperson's hotel room at the end of the day (many hotel rooms now have modem jacks)—or even instantly via a cellular phone system. Expediting customer orders by using such systems often improves customer service and reduces the amount of paperwork that salespeople need to do, thereby giving them more time to contact potential customers and service existing accounts.

Fax systems provide customers with other ways to place orders. Today, the order forms inserted in most mail-order catalogs not only contain instructions about placing phone orders (usually through a no-cost-to-the-customer 800 number), but also provide another 24-hour 800 number for faxing the order form to the retailer. In many of these systems, faxed order forms may never be converted back to a paper document by the recipient; instead, these are captured by computer fax boards and routed to electronic files containing images of the faxed document, which can then be viewed on a display screen.

Inventory

The quantity of product that a merchandising firm has available to sell at any given time is called its *inventory*. An **inventory system** monitors the quantity of each product available for sale and helps ensure that proper stock levels are maintained.

Inventory does not necessarily refer exclusively to physical merchandise or to goods available for immediate delivery. In airline passenger reservation systems, for instance, inventory corresponds to the number of seats available on flights; in the registration system at a typical university or college, inventory corresponds to the openings available in each class. In the auto industry, where electronic information networks let dealers know what has been scheduled for production, inventory is often perceived as representing the total of current and projected vehicles for sale. By using such networks to "sell production," Volvo Cars of North America reduced the amount of time its Swedish imports had to wait at port in Newark, New Jersey, from 20 to 3 days.

In addition to helping managers maintain reasonable inventory levels, inventory systems generate a variety of useful information to management. For instance, management can find out which products are moving fastest or slowest from inventory, the rate of inventory turnover (the number of times

```
GROUP: GARDEN PRODUCTS                                           3/15/93


PRODUCT   PRODUCT              BEG   QTY  QTY   ON    ON    TOTAL      UNIT
          DESCRIPTION          QTY   REC  SOLD  HAND  ORDER AVAILABLE  PRICE

8410      GLOVES               100   50   40    110   10    120        16.50
8420      SPRINKLER SYSTEM     0     0    0     10    10    20         47.00
8425      PRUNING SAW          15    30   10    35    10    45         24.00
8426      HAND WEEDER          20    10   15    30    10    40         10.00
8442      SPRAY GUN            30    10   30    10    0     10         15.00
8444      WATER COMPUTER       0     0    0     0     50    50         65.00
8445      WATERING CAN         250   40   80    210   10    220        30.00
8451      SPADE                200   100  50    250   0     250        18.00


0: NEXT SCREEN     1: PREVIOUS SCREEN     2: GOTO MENU     3: EXIT
```

Figure 9.10 A display screen showing inventory data.

that the value of inventory is sold in a period), profitability per square foot of shelf space, facts about any active backorders, the average time it takes to fill backorders, and so on. Figure 9.10 provides a screen showing the types of inventory-status information commonly available in an inventory database. Some companies have this information available in on-line databases for interested and authorized management personnel. For example, a manager using a fourth-generation language (4GL) might issue a command such as

`DISPLAY PRODUCT-NUMBER FOR SALES < 100 UNITS`

to query an inventory database about slow-moving items (that is, those selling fewer than 100 units in the last week).

Figure 9.11 gives a data flow diagram for the inventory system of our mail-order firm. In this example, new orders are received regularly from the order-entry subsystem of Figure 9.9. These orders, as well as backorders, are filled from available stock. In our example, where stock is not available to completely fill a new order, part of that order is put on backorder. In some companies, however, the entire order may be put on backorder if part of it cannot be filled. A backorder notice is usually sent to the customer as part of the order-entry process.

In most organizations, as orders are filled, an invoice or packing slip is placed inside the box—except perhaps for customers on account. The box is sent to the shipping department with shipping orders, and the transaction data are sent to accounts receivable. When stock is low or insufficient, the purchasing department will be notified (possibly by electronic means) of the items out of stock and the reorder amount. Many companies have specific reorder-point

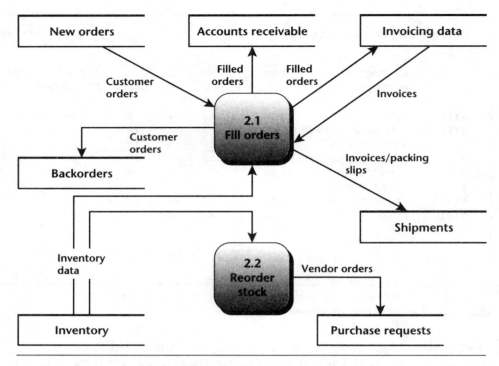

Figure 9.11 An example of a data flow diagram for an inventory subsystem.

and order-quantity policies; that is, when the stock of item X reaches a level of Y units, immediately reorder Z units. As stock is replenished, this is duly noted in the inventory records.

In the data flow diagram shown in Figure 9.11, we considered the inventory system of a merchandising firm, an organization that buys finished products and resells them in virtually the same form. The inventory systems of manufacturing firms, which make new products from raw materials, are a bit more complicated. We will discuss some of these types of integrated inventory management systems in Chapter 13.

A growing trend in both merchandising and manufacturing systems is for firms to tie their suppliers into their inventory systems. This results in shifting inventory handling costs to the supplier, facilitates shopping electronically among suppliers for the lowest prices (if several suppliers are tied in), and enables a firm to have greater control over the availability of goods from suppliers. Such interorganizational and EDI systems are buyer-initiated in some instances, and seller-initiated in others. The buyer might initiate a system like this to realize benefits such as those we described. In these instances, carrying higher inventories might be viewed by the seller as a strategy necessary for locking in the buyer and locking out competitors.

Often, the arrival of supplier inventories is timed so that goods arrive barely in time to be used at the retailer or factory destination. Consequently, these

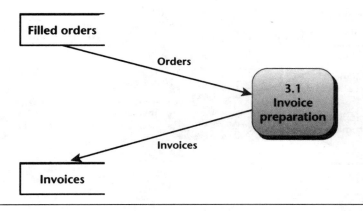

Figure 9.12   A data flow representation of an invoicing subsystem.

close-to-the-bone inventory-carrying systems are known as *just-in-time (JIT)* systems. JIT systems help the receiving organization reduce inventory-related costs, including overhead expenses, maintenance costs, and taxes. Such systems are used extensively in Japan and contribute to that nation's industrial success. JIT systems are becoming more widely used worldwide; advances in communications and information technology facilitate the spread of such systems.

Invoicing

The **invoicing system** is the transaction processing subsystem that creates invoices and sometimes, packing slips. A *packing slip* shows little more than what products are contained in a shipment; prices are either hidden or missing. The customer is also sent a bill—typically called an *invoice* or a *statement* from accounts receivable. Some companies use a combination invoice/packing slip that is both a listing of purchases and a bill.

Conceptually, an invoicing subsystem (see Figure 9.12) is relatively straightforward. As orders are filled, the system is notified that this task has been completed; a bill is then prepared. Here, information such as the items ordered, product descriptions and prices, and customer name and address—all of which are contained on the order—are combined to prepare the invoice. The utility of database technology in preparing invoices was described in Chapter 7.

Shipping

As Figure 9.13 indicates, the **shipping system** is conceptually simple. Sealed, addressed packages of goods are received from inventory, often with shipping instructions. Shipping instructions generally specify a particular shipping method (for example, C.O.D., Federal Express, or UPS), and may provide a warning to shippers (for example, "Fragile" or "Do Not Bend"). When no shipping method or warning is specified, the shipping department will attempt to ship the goods in the most cost-effective, reliable way to the customer. If the goods are valuable in any way, insurance is often another factor in shipping.

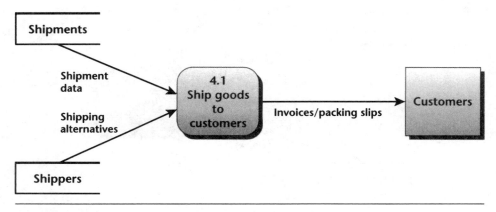

Figure 9.13 A data flow representation of a shipping subsystem.

Technology has affected the shipping operation in several ways. For instance, computer and communications systems make it much easier to succeed in the overnight package delivery business. Also, technology increased the number of shipping options enormously, especially when the product being shipped is information-intensive. Information technology has also materially affected the tracing of shipped goods—giving the shippers another "value-added service" to differentiate themselves from competitors. For example, one overnight delivery service advertises that, in 30 minutes or less, it can let a sender (or receiver) know the exact location of a package while it is en route. This is possible because the bar code on each package is read every time it is loaded onto the next shipping vehicle.

Accounts Receivable

In many firms, customers pay by credit card or have goods charged to their accounts. The **accounts receivable (A/R) system** (or receivables system) is the transaction processing subsystem that manages customer purchase records, payments, and account balances.

Figure 9.14 shows the accounts receivable subsystem for our mail-order firm. As goods are packaged for shipment in the inventory subsystem, either a packing slip or a combination invoice/packing slip is usually enclosed in the shipping carton. Customers who have established accounts may not be invoiced with each shipment. These customers are typically billed monthly through statements that are similar to those received from credit card or telephone companies. Whatever the method of billing, all customer purchase transactions are sent to the receivables department, where they are edited and made part of the regular receivables file. As payments are received from customers, these too are reflected in the receivables file. Other tasks performed from data in a receivables system include analyzing sales patterns and producing information on current and past due accounts. While the accounts receivable function may not be set up exactly like this in other organizations, substantial similarities will probably exist.

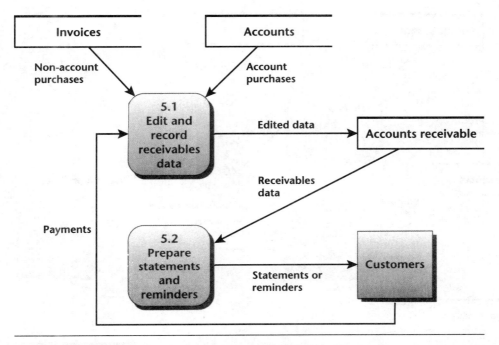

Figure 9.14 A data flow representation of an accounts receivable subsystem.

Because accounts receivable reflects such a large percentage of the revenue coming into a firm, it generally gets a great deal of attention. Computerized accounts receivable systems enable a firm to keep track of outstanding balances, and most firms know that the longer a bill is left unpaid, the smaller the chance that it will ever be collected. Also, the more money tied up in receivables, the less money the firm has to invest in financial markets or new opportunities.

Westinghouse's advanced industrial systems division provides just one of many examples in which technology has helped reduce the receivables burden. Receivables were lowered almost 50 percent over previous levels by having service technicians file job reports electronically. This change in procedure also cut ten days off the manual billing process.

Allied Stores—a big, New York-based, Canadian-owned retailer whose holdings include stores such as Stern's, Jordan Marsh, and Brooks Brothers—is one of many organizations that has streamlined its customer-payment-reminder operations. Before computerization, this task involved a lot of manual paperwork. Now, many reminder situations are handled by phone. When confronting a tardy consumer, the information the caller needs conveniently pops up on a display terminal.

Purchasing

Many companies use a central purchasing department to procure the goods they need. The advantages of a centralized purchasing department are cost

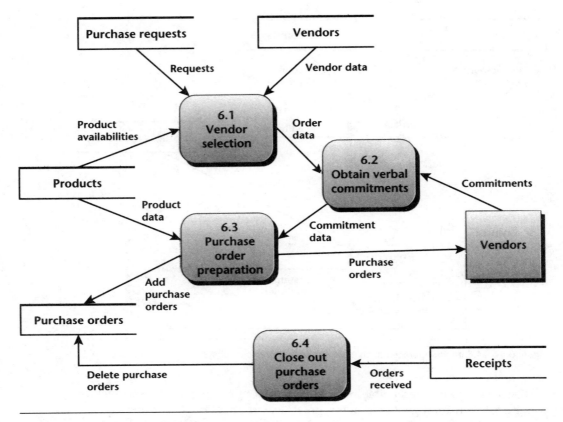

Figure 9.15 A data flow representation of a purchasing subsystem.

control, vendor control, and taking advantage of discounts realized by quantity buying. The major disadvantage is inconvenience to the other departments in the organization for whom the goods are being purchased.

As requests are made to the purchasing department by telephone, interoffice memos, computer, or other means, they are formally logged into a purchase request file that is part of a **purchasing system** (see Figure 9.15). At that point, buyers in the purchasing department begin the vendor-selection process.

In many cases, this decision is relatively routine. Generally, the buyer first contacts a salesperson in the vendor organization to get a satisfactory price and delivery commitment. Then, the buyer prepares a formal *purchase order.* In many companies, the standard operating procedure is to send one copy of the purchase order to the vendor and a second copy to the receiving department so its personnel can verify the contents of the shipment when it arrives; a third copy is kept on file in the purchasing department as an "open order." As soon as the receiving department accepts the goods, the purchasing department is notified so that it can close out the purchase order.

Connecticut Mutual Life Insurance Company Embraces Imaging

Connecticut Mutual Life Insurance Company is the sixth oldest insurer in the U.S., but no dust lies on its information systems. For example, paper mail—which used to take five to seven days to a manually sort and deliver—is scanned into an imaging system, indexed, and electronically dispatched along optimally (cost-effective) routes automatically determined by the software. The new image-based process has reduced mail-handling time to just a few hours.

"THIS VENERABLE INSURER . . . HAS BROKEN ITS DEPENDENCY ON PAPER."

Phoned-in customer questions that previously triggered manual searches through warehoused information files and took up to three days to resolve, can now be answered in several minutes—while the caller is still on the phone. Bringing imaging technology to check services—which automatically withdraws premium payments from customer checking accounts—also significantly reduces processing time.

This venerable insurer feels that its multimillion dollar investment in imaging technology has broken its dependency on paper. Productivity increased by more than 35 percent, staff morale is invigorated, and the ivy-covered company is now a vanguard of the imaging boom that analysts predict will hit, full force, about 1995. By then, Connecticut Mutual plans to be riding a "second wave" of imaging applications, which will include image-driven automated claims forms, letter generation, and client premium management systems.

Adapted from Margolis (1992).

In many companies, the purchasing operation is heavily computerized. Purchase requests are created electronically and sent by electronic mail (or other data communication) systems to the company's central purchasing department. If a request is approved, the resulting active purchase orders can be electronically prepared and stored in a database so that approval, purchase, shipment, receipt, and payment information is available in a central place. This saves time-consuming phone calls and shuffling through paperwork to find the current status of a request. Document management systems and image-processing systems may also help reduce paper shuffling by scanning all important documents and forms into accessible databases.

In firms that are electronically linked to suppliers, purchasing agents can often search through vendor databases to find the lowest prices. These types of interorganizational systems and/or EDI systems are increasingly common in many industries.

Technology is used in many new and creative ways to create electronic purchase orders. Levi Strauss, for instance, is one of the many apparel manufacturers that communicate electronically with retailers, who send them electronic purchase orders. They developed a system named LeviLink, which affixes bar

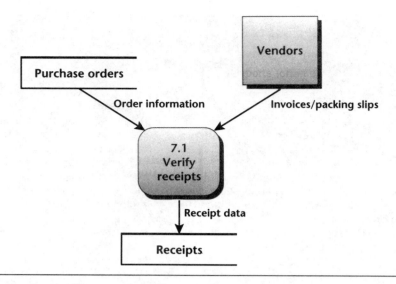

Figure 9.16 A data flow diagram representing a receiving subsystem.

codes on products at factories and traces goods through retail channels. For example, at Designs, Inc., a Massachusetts-based retailer with over 40 stores, data on sales of specific Levi Strauss products are collected in POS computer/cash registers. These data are sent nightly to Designs' mainframe computer, which sends Levi Strauss an electronic order each weekend. Such electronic purchase orders represent 25 percent of the total orders for Levis. Other electronic purchase order systems are common in the grocery and automotive supply industries.

Receiving

The function of a **receiving system** in a receiving department is to receive, inspect, and accept or reject goods that vendors ship. As goods are received, the shipping cartons are opened, the contents are checked against the information on the purchase order, the price of the shipment is verified, and the goods are inspected for possible damage. If the goods are satisfactory, they are typically routed either to inventory or to the department initiating the purchase request. The purchasing department is also notified so that it can close out the purchase order. Also, accounts payable must be apprised. Figure 9.16 depicts a typical receiving subsystem. Sophisticated bar-code systems are expected to automate many receiving functions during the 1990s.

Accounts Payable

Most firms have accounts with their major suppliers (vendors). The **accounts payable (A/P)**—or simply "payables"—**system** is the transaction processing subsystem that handles payments to suppliers. It keeps track of invoices from

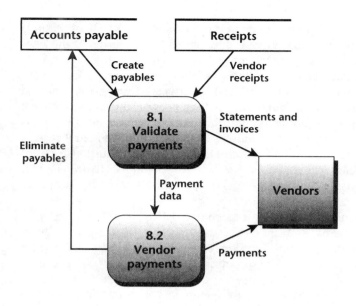

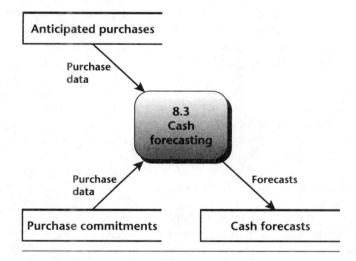

Figure 9.17 A data flow diagram representing a payables subsystem.

suppliers, determines the optimum time to pay invoices, produces checks to pay invoices, and performs cash management activities (thereby ensuring that cash is always available when bills must be paid).

Figure 9.17 shows a data flow representation of the payables system. A payable is a liability that is created as soon as goods (or services) are received from vendors. The invoices and statements are validated against the actual receipt of goods found in the receipt file and, if all of the information is in order, the payable is created on the books. At this point, as many as 30, 60, or 90 days may elapse before the bill is actually paid, depending on the terms of the vendor. As soon as the payment is made and recorded, the payable is closed out.

Also shown in the data flow diagram is another important part of many payables functions: cash forecasting. This task involves ensuring that enough cash is available to meet vendor obligations as they occur. To prepare the cash forecast, the payables group should be notified of all purchase obligations as soon as these obligations occur (which may be well ahead of the actual receipt of the goods). Any information about anticipated purchases should also be included in the cash forecast. An abundance of cash forecasting software is available commercially to assist with these tasks; we will discuss this software further in Chapter 13.

As one example of how technology has changed the payables function, a manufacturer of glass, paint, and chemicals used to pay "dozens, even hundreds" of invoices to some of their suppliers every month. Using a computer system to automate their payables, the organization consolidates bills and now writes one check per month to each supplier.

At Ford, the results of automating payables were just as dramatic. Before automation, when an invoice arrived from a supplier, a clerk called the plant to check on the satisfactory arrival of the parts. Then, purchasing was contacted to confirm the invoice prices. If everything was in order, payment was authorized; otherwise, discrepancies had to be analyzed. Ford had 500 people paying bills this way until it automated the process. Today, the receiving department inspects and approves the goods coming in, then enters data from the vendor packing slip into a terminal tied to a centralized computer. This main computer checks the packing slip with the purchase order and, if everything is in order, payment is automatically authorized and a check is produced. Under ordinary circumstances, suppliers no longer need to send Ford an invoice.

The Ford story has two interesting postscripts. At first, Ford anticipated that only 100 jobs would be cut; however, they eventually eliminated approximately 375 positions. This was because Ford originally considered computerizing the payables operation without first looking at how technology would change the way that work was done. Second, one of the most difficult implementation problems faced by Ford with the proposed new system was getting people from manufacturing, finance, purchasing, and data processing to change the way they performed work. For instance, purchasing personnel are now responsible for ensuring that prices in the computer are up-to-date, finance relinquished some of its check-writing power, and different personnel now ascertain the satisfactory arrival of goods. As Ford and numerous other companies have learned, using information technology to automate one part of its transaction processing system often leads to work flow modifications throughout the organization.

General Ledger

The **general ledger (G/L) system** (see Figure 9.18) integrates transaction data from the other major transaction processing subsystems—payroll, accounts

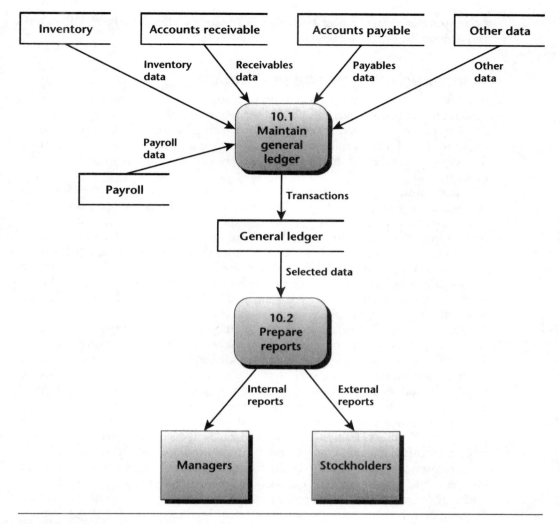

Figure 9.18 A data flow diagram representation of a general ledger system.

receivable, accounts payable, and so on. Besides ensuring that the records of the firm balance, the G/L system is used for budget planning, responsibility reporting, cost allocation, and profitability accounting. Among the major outputs of the G/L system are the balance sheet, which shows the firm's assets balanced against its equities, and the profit-and-loss (income) statement, which shows how revenues and expenses contribute to the firm's profit or loss.

General ledger programs can be very large, consisting of hundreds of integrated program modules and hundreds of thousands of lines of code. Some mainframe-based, general ledger application packages commonly used in industry are IBM's Interactive Financial System, MSA's General Ledger

Accounting System, Dun & Bradsteet Software's General Ledger: Millenium, and Cincom's Control: Financial.

Transaction Processing in Practice

In many firms, transaction processing operations similar to those described in this chapter are computerized. On the whole, transaction processing operations are very easily structured and ideal for processing by computer. Also, the benefits of transaction processing to the firm—carrying lower inventories or cutting unnecessary jobs, for example—are relatively easy to quantify and to justify to management.

Many companies have had their transaction processing applications computerized for years. COBOL has traditionally been the language of choice for these applications, and IBM mainframes the usual hardware choice. A lot of these applications were first coded years ago in COBOL, and then modified or rewritten to reflect both new processing environments and changing business conditions. While both COBOL and mainframes are deeply entrenched in the transaction processing world, many observers feel that they will give way to fourth-generation languages (4GL) and microcomputer-based local area networks (LAN) eventually. Such changes will evolve slowly.

Regarding the historical evolution of the transaction processing environment, programs had to be modified or overhauled as transaction processing systems moved from tape to disk and later, from file-oriented environments to database environments. For such applications as order entry, programs had to be overhauled as transaction processing systems evolved from card-oriented batch environments into terminal-oriented, real-time environments. Many transaction processing systems were modified over the years to reflect moves from centralized decision-making environments to decentralized ones (and possibly back again the other way), and to accommodate interorganizational links to customers and suppliers. The interorganizational links have caused some companies to look upon their transaction processing systems as potential competitive weapons, and not merely as efficiency-oriented paperwork processors. Fortunately, the accounting practices of most businesses do not change drastically, and this provides some stability to transaction processing.

When a firm is new or is overhauling one of its present transaction processing subsystems, it can either develop the application in-house or buy a prepackaged application package. Payroll processing is usually a logical choice for packaged programs because payroll processing is relatively uncomplicated, and keeping up with the complexities of tax accounting can be a chore—especially when taxes must be paid to a number of states or provinces. One popular commercial package, ALLTAX, maintains tax routines for every U.S. state and every Canadian province, as well as routines for federal taxes. Inventory control, in contrast, is probably the least likely choice for packaged software because it is the most complicated and inventory practices vary widely among companies. Many accounting application packages are available as an integrated system of accounting functions, any or all of which may be purchased.

Allied Stores, mentioned earlier in the chapter, is one of the many companies that uses packaged software. Allied has consolidated, integrating dozens of dissimilar systems developed to support its six divisions (each of which is a department store chain). According to Allied's CIO, most of its current systems were 8–20 years old, integrated either poorly or not at all, predominantly paper-based, hard to use, and developed with no thought of centralization. The centralization project involved shifting all of its major accounting systems to a single data center and running 33 new transaction processing and merchandising application packages. To accelerate the process of implementation, Allied chose packaged transaction processing software from Dun & Bradstreet and merchandising software from Peter R. Johnson and Associates.

MANAGEMENT REPORTING SYSTEMS

As noted earlier in the chapter, a management reporting system (MRS) is an information system that provides predefined types of information to management. Historically, the main output of the MRS was hardcopy summary and exception reports that were distributed by the MIS department to line departments at periodic intervals or on demand. Today, reports are still the mainstay of the MRS. With the infusion of display technology into today's business workplace, however, many of the information outputs traditionally available in hardcopy form with an MRS are now available in screen form. Also, the range of report types is much greater. For example, the continuously scrolled displays at airports showing arrivals and departures of planes (or those at brokerage houses showing changes in stock prices) provide predefined and structured types of information. The form of this information, however, would not traditionally be considered a report.

Management reporting systems are used for both management planning and management control functions. Earlier in the chapter, we covered a few other types of reports, such as edit reports and error reports, that primarily serve operational control functions. Edit and error reports are generally not included under MRS; instead, they are more closely identified with the transaction processing systems they serve. Because MRS reports are associated with managerial decision making and not with the operations functions of a TPS, their value is often hard to quantify. Figure 9.19 lists some of the properties typically found in an MRS.

Evolution of Management Reporting Systems

When management reporting systems were first introduced in the late 1950s, they were virtually all by-products of routine transaction processing operations. For example, when bills were batched at the end of a period, a variety of informative hardcopy reports could be produced by the computer—showing how customer purchases were distributed among various products, which sales regions or sales groups accounted for the greatest portion of sales, which customer accounts were overdue, and so on. Some of the types of information produced were new to managers. Other types of information had been avail-

PROPERTIES OF MANAGEMENT REPORTING SYSTEMS

- Support structured and semistructured decisions, primarily at the middle- and lower-management levels

- Provide fixed types of information, in an established format; the information requirements of users are normally known and stable

- Often implemented with voluminous, hardcopy reports, requiring each user to search specifically for key information

- Usually require a formal request to be submitted; formal systems development may be required to approve the request

- Often require a formal run schedule

- Usually consist of internal operational data, rather than data about the external environment

- Usually more concerned with data about the past than data relating to the future

- Often oriented to summary and exception reporting

Figure 9.19 Characteristic properties of management reporting systems. Many management reporting systems specialize in producing periodic reports from operational-level transaction processing data. These reports are used for a wide variety of planning, monitoring, and control activities.

able for years with manual systems; the computer merely improved their accuracy and sped up their availability to users. When a particular report request was desired by management, it was formally coded (usually in COBOL) and made available. Many management reporting systems were targeted to the information needs of middle-level managers—in contrast to transaction processing systems, which generally met the needs of lower levels of management.

By the mid-1960s, users and computer professionals felt comfortable with the outputs produced by computers, and many organizations became over-optimistic regarding what these systems could do. At this time, computers beat skilled masters at playing chess, and mathematical techniques were developed to demonstrate how adept computers were at finding optimum solutions to complex operational problems. Many computer professionals discussed the immediate viability of "total systems"—systems that integrated every part of the organization by computer. And some bewildered executives, who knew nothing about computers other than that they were amazing machines, made unwise business decisions. When many of these ambitious efforts failed, MIS was tagged with much of the blame. The failures notwithstanding, many less pretentious management reporting systems did well for companies and are still going strong. The following examples show how management reporting systems are used today in organizations:

- Every Tuesday morning, the CEO of a medium-sized company receives a computer report summarizing product sales of the previous week. The same report is also available to the sales department. The program producing the report was originally written in COBOL in 1975 and has since been modified several times to reflect new decision-making needs.

- The registrar of a university wanted a report that both identified minority students majoring in the social sciences and showed which of those students were receiving financial aid. Six months after a formal request was made for such a program to the MIS department, a computer services programmer produced the report, using a 4GL with strong report-generating capabilities.

In organizations where the MRS is developed by the MIS department, a formal proposal often must be submitted first. The proposal then competes with other MIS projects. If approved, the appropriate resources are scheduled for it. Many firms have a visible backlog of 2–4 years on proposals. This, in turn, has created an even greater invisible backlog—requests that are not submitted because users do not want to wait.

Types of Reports

An MRS can produce either hardcopy report output or display output. As mentioned earlier, hardcopy reports are the most common form of output produced by an MRS.

Reports produced by management reporting systems usually fall into one of three categories: scheduled reports, exception reports, and demand reports.

- *Scheduled reports* **Scheduled reports** (sometimes called periodic reports) are those that are issued periodically. Two examples of such reports are daily production reports and monthly performance reports. These types of reports can be used either for planning or control purposes.

- *Exception reports* **Exception reports** are issued when something unusual takes place that requires the attention of management. For instance, an expense overrun would likely trigger the generation of an exception report. Exception reports are used primarily for control purposes.

- *Demand reports* **Demand reports** are generated when someone with authority requests such a report. An example is an executive asking for a financial report on a merger candidate.

Most of the reports produced by an MRS are either scheduled reports or exception reports. With the heavy application backlog that is now typical of many large firms, and with easy-to-use spreadsheet and database software available, many managers are taking the do-it-yourself approach to demand reporting.

Structuring Report Content

The information contained in the reports generated by the MRS should provide decision makers in the organization with the information they need. Ideally, the informational content of each MRS report should be relevant, timely, accurate, and verifiable.

Relevance refers to the usefulness of the report contents. In general, the goal of an MRS is to provide report recipients with information that meets their

Telecommuting Helps Hewlett-Packard Retain Valued Executives

In an effort to discourage experienced sales executives from leaving, Hewlett-Packard is offering them the chance to work at home four days a week. This move to telecommuting should result in productivity gains and savings of hundreds of thousands of dollars. In some regions, as many as 50 percent of the company's telesales force could eventually participate in the project. According to one HP manager, "There isn't a person here who isn't excited about this."

Each telecommuting salesperson's home office is equipped with approximately $5,000 of information technology, including a 386-based microcomputer, sales software programs, two phone lines, and a fax modem. The software allows salespeople to maintain customer account profiles, plus send updates on accounts and new orders to an HP minicomputer at the regional office. By linking to the minicomputer, salespeople can exchange electronic mail, call up the latest prices and availability of products, and assemble quotations for customers.

"WITH LOWER TURNOVER, THERE WILL BE LESS NEED TO TRAIN NEW HIRES."

Currently, salespeople stay with HP an average of three years. With telecommuting, HP expects this average to become four or five years. With lower turnover, there will be less need to train new hires. This results in significant savings in training costs—which amount to between $60,000 and $80,000 per person during the first year of employment. With fewer inexperienced salespeople in the field, Hewlett-Packard also anticipates closing more sales.

Adapted from Horwitt (1992).

---

specific decision-making needs. Decision makers are unlikely to use reports containing minimal levels of relevant data. Designing reports that maximize useful information while minimizing irrelevant information usually involves taking the recipient's level in the management hierarchy into account. As noted in Chapter 4, managers at lower levels in the organization typically need more detailed information than top-level managers, who tend to prefer highly summarized, aggregated information. Managers at the top of the hierarchy are also more likely than low-level managers to need information that has an external focus. The report recipient's functional specialty should also be taken into account (for example, accounting personnel should be provided with information that is relevant to accounting decisions, while marketing managers should be provided with marketing-related information). Balancing completeness (providing all the information that the decision maker needs) with conciseness (providing only the information needed) is one of the challenges that report designers face when deciding on the relevance of report contents.

Timeliness refers to the extent to which the information is delivered to decision makers in time for them to use it. Ideally, timely reports should be provided to decision makers when needed—on demand, in some instances.

Accurate, relevant reports that reach the user prior to decision making are more likely to be incorporated into the decision-making process—and may lead to more effective decisions. When reports arrive too late, they are virtually useless—even if their contents are relevant to the decisions being made.

Accuracy, in the most basic sense, refers to the degree to which the information contained in the report is free of errors. This also implies that the information in the report is current and reliable. If the MRS regularly generates reports that contain inaccurate information, decision makers will soon ignore the reports and are likely to brand them (and in some cases, the entire MRS) as unreliable and not useful for decision making. Reports that consistently contain inaccurate data or information will be treated by decision makers as if they are unimportant.

Verifiability refers to what extent a report's accuracy can be substantiated by other business data that the organization has captured and stored. Reports about transaction processing activities, for example, should be traceable via *audit trails* to the actual transactions on which the reports are based. Reports that are easily verifiable are likely to be trusted by organizational decision makers and therefore used during the decision-making process.

Role of MRS Outputs in Management

MRS output can appear in a hardcopy report format or—like the examples of the airline arrival/departure and brokerage house screens presented earlier—in display format. In an MRS, display information is usually made available on either perpetually scrolled screens that are not turned off and are not user-controlled (such as those at airports or in brokerage houses) or on conventional display workstations, where fixed, predefined screens can be summoned by users on demand.

What distinguishes a display-oriented MRS from a DSS is flexibility. The format and types of information on MRS screens are predefined; the format and types of information on DSS screens are not. In a DSS, users are provided with the capabilities to generate their own information, usually in their own way.

No matter what type of output is used, the format should be clear (easy to read and understand), presented in a useful form (for example, narrative, numeric, or graphic), and sequenced in a logical matter (one that follows typical decision-making patterns). Decision making may also be enhanced by using formats that highlight important or exceptional information that should not be overlooked by the decision maker. These and several other approaches that may improve the format and content of reports issued to management were discussed in Chapter 4.

SUMMARY

A management information system (MIS) is any system supporting the timely use, management, and processing of data or information by authorized people in the organization's environment. Management information systems are composed of any or all of four component subsystems: transaction processing systems (TPS), management reporting systems (MRS), decision support systems (DSS), and office information systems (OIS). Expert systems and other knowledge-based systems are being increasingly used in conjunction with each of these subsystems.

A transaction may be defined as a routine business event—an exchange that affects the financial well-being of an organization. A TPS, then, is a system that supports the processing of an organization's transactions.

All transaction processing systems perform three functions: bookkeeping, issuance, and control reporting. Bookkeeping involves keeping accurate records of a firm's transactions. Issuance involves the production of business documents, such as paychecks and invoices. Control reports, such as edit reports and error reports, are by-products of a TPS that exist for control purposes.

Manual systems present a number of problems that are often solvable by computer technology. Manual systems are error-prone; they result in data getting easily lost or misplaced. They are labor intensive, their level of service is often low, and they provide poor response to information requests. Computer-based management information systems have both overcome the inefficiencies associated with manual transaction processing and have evolved so that transaction processing systems can be used as competitive weapons.

The transaction processing cycle consists of five major segments: data entry, transaction processing, file/database updating, report/document generation, and inquiry/response processing. Data entry may involve off-line key-to-media input and editing in batch processing systems. Alternatively, on-line input from source data automation terminals—along with immediate processing and file updating—is possible in real-time processing systems. After files and databases are updated, inquiries may be made by authorized users. A number of transaction processing subsystems are found in most firms. The payroll processing system, one of the oldest computerized systems in many firms, produces paychecks for employees and data for tax purposes. Payroll processing is usually a batch process.

Order-entry systems process customer orders. Today, many firms use these systems strategically; for instance, by developing interorganizational information systems (IOS) or electronic data interchange (EDI) systems that tie customers in more closely and keep competitors out.

An inventory system monitors the quantity of each product available for sale and helps ensure proper stock levels. IOS and EDI systems are also used with inventory systems in order to tie suppliers more closely to the firm. Just-in-time systems ensure that inventory supplies arrive just when needed, so that the organization avoids high inventory costs.

The invoicing system, which is a comparatively simple system, creates invoices and/or packing slips. The shipping system receives goods from inventory and ships them out according to instructions. Technology has increased the number of shipping options.

Accounts receivable (A/R) systems manage customer purchases payments and account balances. Because accounts receivable reflects a large percentage of the revenue coming into a firm, it receives a lot of attention.

The purchasing system assists with the acquisition of goods. Purchasing department personnel often select a vendor, prepare a purchase order, and send the order to the vendor (with copies to the other departments that need them). In many organizations, the purchasing operation is highly computerized so that no physical copies of the purchase order need to be sent; only one copy exists in a central database. The receiving system receives, inspects, and accepts or rejects goods that vendors have shipped.

The accounts payable (A/P) system handles payments to suppliers. It assists with managing vendors' invoices, helps determine the optimum time to pay invoices, produces checks, and assists with cash management activities.

The general ledger (G/L) system integrates transaction data from all the other transaction processing subsystems. It is used for budget planning, responsibility reporting, cost allocation, and profitability accounting. It is also used to prepare the firm's balance sheet and profit-and-loss (income) statement.

Management reporting systems (MRS) provide predefined types of information to management, which uses them for management planning and control functions. First introduced in the 1950s, management reporting systems are by-products of transaction processing systems. Today, many management reporting systems are still linked to transaction processing systems, although some have independent sources of data.

The most common type of output produced by an MRS is hardcopy reports—usually scheduled reports, exception reports, and demand reports. Ideally, the information contained in MRS reports is timely, relevant, accurate, and verifiable.

KEY TERMS

Accounts payable (A/P) system	Invoicing system
Accounts receivable (A/R) system	Order-entry system
Control report	Payroll processing system
Data entry	Purchasing system
Demand report	Receiving system
Error report	Scheduled report
Exception report	Shipping system
General ledger (G/L) system	Transaction
Inventory system	

REVIEW QUESTIONS

1. What are the differences among transaction processing systems, management reporting systems, and decision support systems?

2. What is a transaction? Provide several examples of different types of organizational transactions.

3. What are some of the major problems associated with manual transaction processing systems? What are the major benefits of computer-based transaction processing?

4. What are the characteristics of each of the steps in transaction processing cycle?

5. How do batch transaction processing systems differ from real-time transaction processing systems?

6. Provide several examples of different types of reports and documents associated with transaction processing systems.

7. How has technology changed transaction processing?

8. How may transaction processing be impacted by electronic data interchange (EDI) and interorganizational systems (IOS)?

9. Define the term "inventory."

10. What is the difference between accounts receivable and accounts payable?

11. Why is it more likely that an organization will acquire an application package for payroll than for other transaction processing functions?

12. In what ways has technology changed the purchasing function?

13. What are the characteristics of an MRS?

14. What types of reports are generated by an MRS? What should be the characteristics of the information contained in MRS reports?

DISCUSSION QUESTIONS

1. Why is it often difficult to classify a system distinctly as a transaction processing system, decision support system, or information reporting system? Provide some examples.

2. What types of implementation problems are likely to be encountered as transaction processing moves from mainframes to distributed minicomputers and microcomputer-based local area networks?

3. In what ways might information technology impact the decision to centralize or decentralize the purchasing operation?

4. What impacts may EDI and imaging systems have on the manner in which transactions are processed by an organization? What other new technologies are having an impact on transaction processing systems?

CASE STUDY

EDI: Changing the Way Businesses Do Business

General Motors, Cummins Engine, and Wal-Mart are three companies that have passed "the word" out to their suppliers. And that word is to get moving with EDI. "We don't give them ultimatums," says Cummins' manager of supply administration. "We just give them no reason not to get on with EDI." Wal-Mart is much tougher; most suppliers who refuse to link up are dropped.

EDI—electronic data interchange—is a communications method that enables direct computer-to-computer exchange of such transaction processing documents as purchase orders, invoices, and bills of lading. Lately, it has become an interorganizational pipeline between companies and their suppliers. Claims an IBM vice-president, "Doing business without EDI will soon be like doing business without the telephone." Says the Arthur D. Little (ADL) consultant whose 1980 study of the grocery industry kindled widespread interest in EDI, "In the last few years, people have found that EDI's going to happen, it's inevitable, and it's something they're going to have to learn to do"—if they haven't done so already.

Before 1980, only a handful of companies took EDI seriously. One of those was Kansas-based Yellow Freight Company. "We have had to try to sell the concept for the last ten years," says an MIS manager at Yellow Freight. "People saw EDI as a technical function that appeared to be significantly different from what they had done before. So they hesitated to spend money on what might be a pipe dream. But as EDI began to spread, the benefits were so great that everyone saw an opportunity for cost savings." Many industry observers feel it was the ADL study that got the ball rolling for EDI. When the study concluded that grocers would save a third of a billion dollars a year if only half of them implemented EDI, people listened.

Because of the substantial cost savings involved—in cutting down on paperwork, shortening handling time, and reducing data-entry errors—suppliers are getting the message that hooking into EDI means more orders coming their way; not hooking into EDI means fewer orders. Companies going the EDI route also gain competitive advantage through getting information more quickly—and moving products faster. "The threat of losing business is really convincing companies that are hesitating," says a manager in the industry. Says another, "EDI is no longer just 'nice to have.' It's a 'must have.' Companies are no longer running pilot projects where they're trying EDI to see if it works and being very cautious about spending money for its implementation. EDI is no longer an option in corporate America."

But for the companies that take the plunge, implementing EDI is no easy task. Integrating EDI software into a conventional transaction processing system, to enable it to communicate with a foreign system owned by a supplier, can easily take a year or more. And the conversion can also be expensive. According to one study, it costs nearly $100,000 to integrate a single application, such as order entry, into an EDI system; the job is likely to take more than 1,400 hours of custom programming.

Many companies, including Wal-Mart, are not scared by such investments and the challenge of integrating EDI with its everyday business operations. Wal-Mart has developed one of the most extensive EDI networks in the retail industry. In 1992, Wal-Mart issued ultimatums to reluctant suppliers: either link up or be dropped as a supplier. The ultimatums added to the "bully" reputation it had already developed from its dealings with suppliers and some claimed it was outright coercion. From Wal-Mart's point of view, the move was simply good business. It would further reduce the company's order-processing costs and help it maintain its competitive low product pricing strategy.

During the 1990s, EDI is expected to become even more commonplace. Standards are emerging, such as the X.12 standard—which is most popular in the U.S.—and EDIFACT, which is the most widely used in Europe. Such standards are making it easier for companies to develop EDI networks with suppliers. EDI is also expected to be used internally within organizations (such as between purchasing departments and the departments purchasing supplies) to reduce the paperwork exchanged between subunits. Many organizations are adding electronic funds transfer (EFT) modules to their EDI systems so that electronic payments may be made to suppliers.

Adapted from Anonymous (1991), Mehler (1992), and Tracy (1991).

DISCUSSION

1. What types of a company's transaction processing subsystems are likely candidates for EDI? Briefly discuss how each would be affected. What other transaction processing subsystems are likely to be affected as EFT components are added to EDI systems?

2. Provide several ways in which EDI helps organizations become more efficient. How may EDI be used to lock in suppliers? How may it alter the basis of competition within an industry?

3. Provide several examples of how EDI may be used within organizations. What are the advantages of using EDI internally?

4. Is it right for a company like Wal-Mart to force suppliers to link up to its EDI system? What are some of the other approaches that could be used to encourage suppliers to establish EDI links?

Chapter

10

Decision Support Systems

After completing this chapter, you will be able to:

Define decision support system (DSS) and describe some of the properties that distinguish a DSS from other types of information systems

Differentiate among structured, semistructured, and unstructured decisions

Identify the types of processing tasks commonly performed by a DSS

Differentiate among specific decision support systems, DSS generators, and DSS tools

Name several types of user interfaces commonly employed by decision support systems

Provide several examples of DSS applications

Describe the characteristics of group decision support systems (GDSS) and how they may be implemented

Describe the types of decisions made by executives and the properties that characterize those decisions

Define executive information system (EIS) and list the characteristics of executive information systems

During the 1970s, systems designed to help decision makers devise solutions to unstructured and partially structured problems evolved. These systems largely consist of tools that can be customized in a variety of ways to solve computationally or clerically intensive problems. Such systems are particularly useful to higher-level managers whose requirements for information are somewhat unpredictable. They are called decision support systems (DSS).

In this chapter, we begin by defining a DSS and describing the properties that differentiate it from other types of management information systems. A number of examples support this discussion. Next, we look at the types of processing needs for which a DSS is most useful and some of the software and hardware packages specifically designed for decision support. Then, we discuss the characteristics of group decision support systems (GDSS) and the software and hardware configurations associated with them. Finally, we turn to executive information systems (EIS) and explore their potential for improving the quality of strategic-level planning and control.

What Is a DSS?

The term "management information system" was first coined to distinguish the systems that merely process transaction data from systems whose primary purpose is to provide information. The first information-oriented MIS possessed the characteristics of the management reporting systems (MRS) described in Chapter 9; that is, they provided fixed, preformatted information in a standardized way. Typical outputs of this type were computer-produced, hardcopy summary and exception reports that a company's MIS department might circulate periodically to various middle managers.

As developments in interactive display technology, microcomputing, and easy-to-use software systems changed the way in which managers were provided with information—and led to a growing understanding of how technology could support difficult decisions—a new term was coined to distinguish this new system from a report-based MRS. This new term—"decision support system"—resulted from the fact that these systems were more flexible and adaptable to changing decision-making requirements than traditional management reporting systems.

In this text, we define a **decision support system (DSS)** as a system that provides tools to managers to assist them in solving semistructured and unstructured problems in their own, somewhat personalized, way. Often, some type of modeling environment—perhaps a very simple environment such as the one accompanying a spreadsheet package—is involved. A DSS is not intended to make decisions for managers, but rather to provide managers with a set of capabilities that enables them to generate the information they feel is needed to make decisions. In other words, a DSS supports the human decision-making process, rather than providing a means to replace it.

Systems that replace human decision making—rather than support it—are sometimes called *programmed decision systems*. These systems are used to make routine, structured decisions, such as approving loans or credit, reordering inventory, triggering reminder notices, and selecting audit samples. In programmed decision systems, the focus is on doing something more efficiently; in decision support systems, the focus is on helping decision makers become more effective.

Technically, a DSS does not need to involve high technology. For example, to a writer, a selected group of journal and text resources at a local library—and a strategy for using those resources—may serve as part of a decision support system. To a novice accountant in a large accounting firm, the advice offered by a senior tax partner may be part of that novice's decision support system. In this technology-oriented text, however, we will assume that all of the decision support systems discussed are computer-based information systems (CBIS).

DSS Goals and Applications

Few terms have been redefined as many times in technical literature, or defined in so many different ways at any single point in time, as the decision support system. Today, most researchers agree that decision support systems are characterized by at least three properties: (1) they support semistructured or unstructured decision making, (2) they are flexible enough to respond to the changing needs of decision makers, and (3) they are easy to use. Here, we will look at both of these properties and at other properties that—while not mandatory for a DSS—are common to most of them.

Semistructured and Unstructured Decisions

As we described in Chapter 4, structured decisions are those that are easily made from a given set of inputs. These types of decisions—such as deciding to issue a reminder notice if a bill is overdue or deciding to sell a stock under a given set of market conditions—can be programmed fairly easily. Unstructured decisions and semistructured decisions, however, are decisions for which information obtained from a computer system is only a portion of the total knowledge needed to make the decision.

The DSS is particularly well adapted to help with semistructured and unstructured decisions; however, it can be designed to support structured decision making as well. A manager, for instance, can browse through data at will (perhaps at a display terminal). When enough information is gleaned from this process to supplement other information (perhaps some of it noncomputer-based), a decision can be reached. In a well-designed DSS, the depth to which the available data can be tapped for useful information often is limited only by the time and patience of the manager.

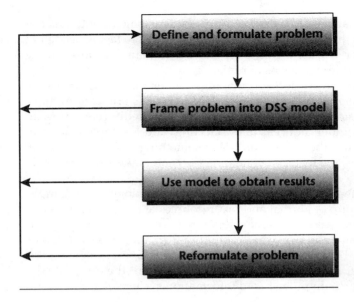

Figure 10.1 Steps in solving a problem with a DSS.

In Figure 10.1, we see how a semistructured problem might be solved by using a DSS. The problem is first defined and formulated. It is then modeled with DSS software. Next, the model is run on the computer to provide results. The modeler, in reviewing these results, might decide to completely reformulate the problem, refine the model, or use the model to obtain other results. For example, a user might define a problem that involves simulating cash flows under a variety of business conditions by using financial modeling software. The DSS model is then run, providing results. Depending on what the results of the model indicate about cash flow, the user might decide to completely re-model the problem, make small modifications to the current model, run the model under a number of new assumptions, or accept the results. For instance, if the model revealed inadequate cash flows to support organizational operations, model modifications should be developed and run. The modification process might continue for several iterations until an acceptable cash flow is identified.

Ability to Adapt to Changing Needs

Semistructured and unstructured decisions often do not conform to a pre-defined set of decision-making rules. Because of this, their decision support systems need to provide for enough flexibility to enable users to model their own information needs, and should be capable of adapting to changing information needs.

With a formal MRS, specific outputs—usually in the form of hardcopy reports or preformatted display screens—are established well ahead of the time that they are actually used. Often, the specification involves a lengthy, customized application program, supporting documentation, and a run schedule. For example, a production manager might make a formal request to the MIS department for a monthly report. The utility of such a report is usually then assessed by a committee and, possibly, scheduled for development. (As noted in previous chapters, many MIS departments are saddled with a 2- to 4-year application backlog and may be unable to fulfill the manager's request immediately.) After the report is designed and a program is written specifically to generate it, the types of information supplied to the manager by that report are "frozen." If information needs change substantially, another formal report request must be submitted to get the program rewritten.

The DSS designer understands that managers usually do not know what information they need in advance and, even if they did, those information needs constantly change. Thus, rather than lock the system into rigid information-producing requirements, capabilities and tools are provided to enable users to meet their own output needs.

Flexibility in a DSS is of paramount importance. Information requests made to a DSS will often be relatively unsystematic and idiosyncratic. For example, a sales manager at a display device might request the price of a specific product. A few seconds later, the manager might change her mind and ask for a listing of the vendors of several other products. The next request, a couple of minutes later, may be a ranking of the top salespeople in a particular sales region over the last two months. A report might even be requested at the end of the session, combining data from several of these inquiries.

Since the demands made by the user on the DSS are not fully predetermined, the user might request information in any of a variety of formats. In well-designed decision support systems, managers can ask spontaneous questions, as these questions occur to them, and receive almost immediate responses. The manager can make many requests without being sure at any point where the search for information will lead next. The manager often needs a variety of tools to satisfy such requests: formulas, functions, sorts, graphs, formal models, and so on. The output from a DSS may also be used to prepare customized outputs for examination by other people; for example, a manager preparing presentation graphics for a meeting.

Ease of Learning and Use

Since decision support systems are often built and operated by users rather than by computer professionals, the tools that accompany them should be relatively easy to learn and use. Software tools often employ user-oriented interfaces—grids, graphics, nonprocedural fourth-generation languages (4GL), natural English, and easily read documentation—to make it easier for users to conceptualize and perform the decision-making process. As is the case with most computer applications during the 1990s, graphical user interfaces (GUI) are becoming more common in decision support systems. Also, such tools often liberally employ a number of help aids—memory joggers, useful diagnostics, a help feature, and undo commands—because general users typically do not have the skills to interpret cryptic error messages.

Although interactive display devices are not considered a requirement for a DSS, many decision support systems employ them. First, display devices provide users with relatively fast, often real-time, responses, thus enabling the process depicted in Figure 10.1 to be conducted as rapidly as the user wants. Fast electronic responses facilitate maintaining a train of thought as the problem-solving process takes place; real-time responses assure the user that up-to-date (that is, really useful) data are being supplied to the decision-making process. In addition, interactive systems enable the user to base each new request on the system's responses to earlier requests. In non-interactive systems, if a decision must be made within a certain time frame and system turnaround time is slow, managers are often forced to batch together a large number of potentially useful requests; this can involve a lot of extra contingency planning. The point here is that although interactive display devices are not required for a DSS, they do help to make many decision support systems friendly and useful.

Other DSS Properties

By being focused on solving semistructured and unstructured problems, decision support systems are especially useful to the decision-making needs of higher-level managers. This is not to imply that decision support systems cannot benefit managers or non-managers at lower levels—in fact, they often do. But decision-making needs at lower levels can be anticipated better than at higher levels, so certain aspects of decision support systems, such as their calculator-type tools and modeling capabilities, may be unnecessary in decision support systems that support lower-level managers.

To increase the quality of the decisions made by managers, most decision support systems incorporate models tailored to the decision-making environment. In some cases, the models are developed by professionals who are skilled in model-building techniques. But, more often, the models are user-developed. Because of this, decision support systems require an interface that provides users with the tools to build their own models and an intuitive conceptual framework so that users can assess their own progress. Later in the chapter, we will look at executive information systems (EIS), which rely less on the use of user-constructed models than do traditional decision support systems.

Another general property of many (but not all) decision support systems is that they are harder to cost-justify to management than, for example, transaction processing systems. Often, it is difficult to assess whether a DSS will actually improve the quality of a decision. Even if most people agree that decision making will be improved, it is hard to quantify the benefits directly attributable to the DSS. For example, a manager might claim that use of a spreadsheet package enabled a budget to be prepared more quickly and with a higher level of quality than was previously possible. An observer, on the other hand, might argue that the manager got so carried away with what the spreadsheet software

PROPERTIES OF DECISION SUPPORT SYSTEMS

Decision Support Systems are Typically Characterized By:

- Support for semistructured and unstructured decision making

- Flexibility in specifying output requirements

- Ease of use and ease of development for non-professionals

- Fast response

- High degree of user control and interaction

In Addition, Many are Characterized By:

- Middle or top management focus

- Interactive capabilities

- Use of models

- Difficulty in cost justifying

- Evolutionary development

- Focus on managerial effectiveness, rather than efficiency

Figure 10.2 Properties of decision support systems. What specifically constitutes a DSS is a rapidly evolving issue.

could do that what should have taken five minutes to submit in handwritten form took an hour. These reservations notwithstanding, many DSS tools are so inexpensive and so easy to implement that many managers have installed them anyway—feeling, perhaps, that they really cannot afford to get bogged down in traditional cost justification. Figure 10.2 provides a summary of general properties found in some or all decision support systems.

COMPONENTS OF A DSS

The primary components of a DSS are illustrated in Figure 10.3. As this figure shows, a combination of hardware, software, and data is necessary to provide interactive decision support for managers and users (who are also part of the DSS). The major features of the hardware and software components of a DSS are summarized as follows:

- *Hardware* In order to provide interactive capabilities, microcomputers may be used on a stand-alone basis or may be connected to larger computer systems (by telecommunication links) that have DSS software, models, and data resources. Interactive display terminals may be used in place of microcomputers when DSS software, models, and data resources all reside on host computers. In stand-alone systems, DSS software, models, and data may be stored on a single microcomputer; communications software may be used to

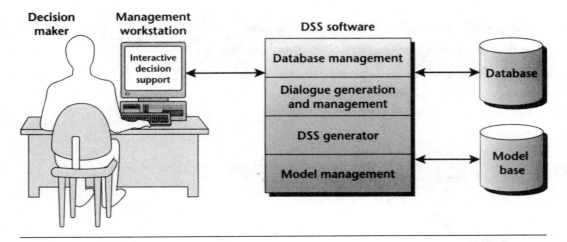

Figure 10.3 Components of a DSS. Decision support systems consist of hardware, software, data, and decision makers. The main categories of DSS software include the database management software, dialogue generation and management software, DSS generator, and model management software.

enable decision makers to access external databases such as those provided by the information utilities discussed in Chapter 7.

■ **Software** The software packages used to develop and maintain decision support systems are usually called **DSS generators**; these typically contain modules for database, model, and dialogue management.

The *database management* module makes it possible to create, maintain, and query DSS databases. As Figure 10.4 shows, the database management component allows for DSS databases to be created by extracting data from external and internal (both corporate and personal) sources. This module typically has many of the same capabilities for interrogation and maintenance found in the database management systems discussed in Chapter 7. As we pointed out in Chapter 7, a relational database management system is often better suited for such usage than are either hierarchical or network database management systems. The retrieval, data reconfiguration, selection, and projection tasks described in the following section are typically associated with the database management module of the DSS generator.

The *model management* component makes it possible to create, maintain, and apply quantitative, mathematical, and other models that manipulate DSS data. Figure 10.5 illustrates this DSS module. As you can observe in this figure, the model database may consist of a wide variety of models and data manipulation tools. The calculator activities, functions, and analysis tools (for example, statistical optimizing and sensitivity analysis tools) described in the next section may all be aspects of the model management module. Many of the software packages discussed in the "DSS Development" section of this chapter may also be included in the model management component. Note that the exact contents of the model base are built on the needs of individual decision makers.

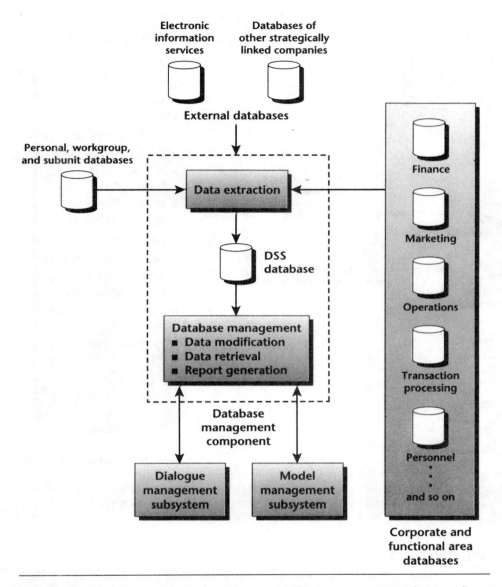

Figure 10.4 The data management subsystem of a DSS. The data management subsystem allows the user to create DSS databases by extracting data from other databases and, in some systems, databases that are external to the organization.

The *dialogue management* module provides the user with the easy-to-operate interfaces (such as screen formats) that support flexible, interactive input and output. It is illustrated more fully in Figure 10.6. The support interfaces, commands, and templates described in the "DSS Development" section of the chapter are aspects of the dialogue management component.

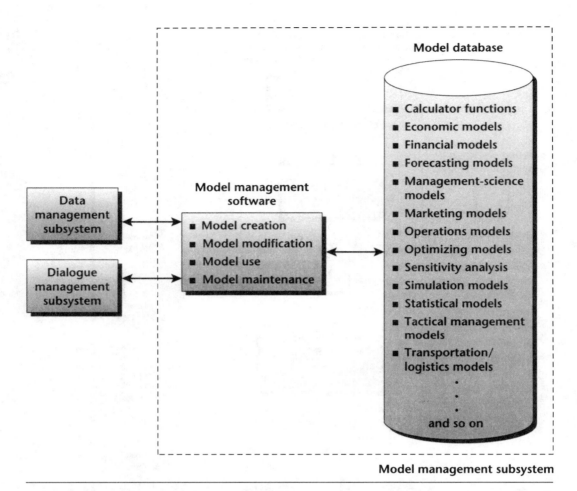

Figure 10.5 The model management subsystem of a DSS. The model management software makes it possible for users to create, maintain, and use models needed to make decisions. The model database may contain a wide variety of models, depending on the needs of decision makers.

PUTTING A DSS TO WORK

In this section, we will look at some of the tasks commonly performed by decision support systems. Four tasks that we address in this section are information retrieval, data reconfiguration, calculator activities, and analysis.

Information Retrieval

Information retrieval in a DSS environment refers to the act of extracting information from a database, or from data files, for the purpose of making decisions. As described earlier, the retrieval is often carried out at an interactive display station, where each new set of information obtained can be used to direct the search for other types of information.

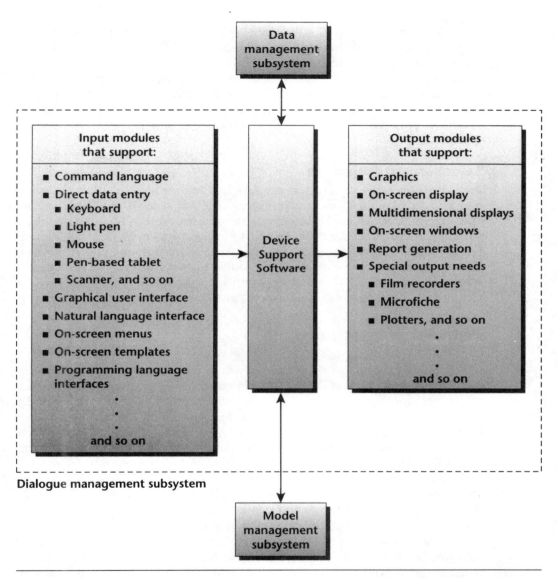

Figure 10.6 The dialogue management subsystem of a DSS. The dialogue management system provides users with a flexible, interactive interface for input, processing, and output.

The decision maker using the DSS might retrieve small bits of information at the display workstation. If the amount of information needed is extensive, or if the information must be put into permanent form so it can be studied later, the decision maker might ask the DSS to prepare a comprehensive printed report.

Usually, the sequence of retrievals made by the user is unanticipated. For example, the manager might see a few startling pieces of information on the display and, as a result of these, suddenly produce a report that provides more detail about the situation. Or the manager might continue to use the DSS in a display retrieval mode, looking for different types of information on different types of products, in random order.

At upper levels in the management hierarchy, the decision maker often wants access to internal and external databases. Many decision support systems designed for use by higher-level managers make it possible to access the on-line databases provided by information utilities; some of these were identified in Chapter 7.

Selection and Projection

Two common types of retrieval are selection and projection. With respect to logical data files, *selection* involves separating out records that have specific characteristics; for example, identifying all males over age 65 in an employee file or database. *Projection*, with respect to logical files, involves obtaining only certain fields of data; for example, extracting all names and phone numbers from an employee file or database. Of course, retrieval often involves a combination of both selection and projection—for example, determining only the names and phone numbers of all male employees over age 65.

Data Reconfiguration

Often, managers using a DSS want information in a form other than that in which the data are logically represented within the computer system. For example, a manager looking at several sets of comparative sales figures on products may want those figures represented in pie chart form. Or, if the number of different products in each set is too large to conveniently represent in such a graphical form, the manager may want a sorted listing of each set, arranged in descending order from the biggest sellers to the smallest. Both of these situations require the DSS to reconfigure the original data into some new form.

The ability to reconfigure data makes it possible for managers and other decision makers to look at existing data from alternative perspectives. Figure 10.7 shows an example that covers four common reconfiguration situations: sorting, exchanging fields, joining, and presentation graphics.

Sorting data involves rearranging records in a file or a subset of a file so that they appear in a specific order. Most sort routines with decision support systems enable several sort keys (fields that are sorted) to be activated, so that sorts within sorts can also be performed. In Figure 10.7(a), the file was sorted on the name field. If desired, the data could also be sorted first by state, then (alphabetically) by name.

Exchanging fields or columns is another method available for reconfiguring data. If data are arranged so that, for instance, the name field appears on a report or on a display screen before the city and state fields, the DSS user can specify that these fields be output in the reverse order. This is shown in Figure 10.7(b).

Joining enables users to cut and paste data from different existing logical files to form new logical files. An example of joining data is shown in Figure

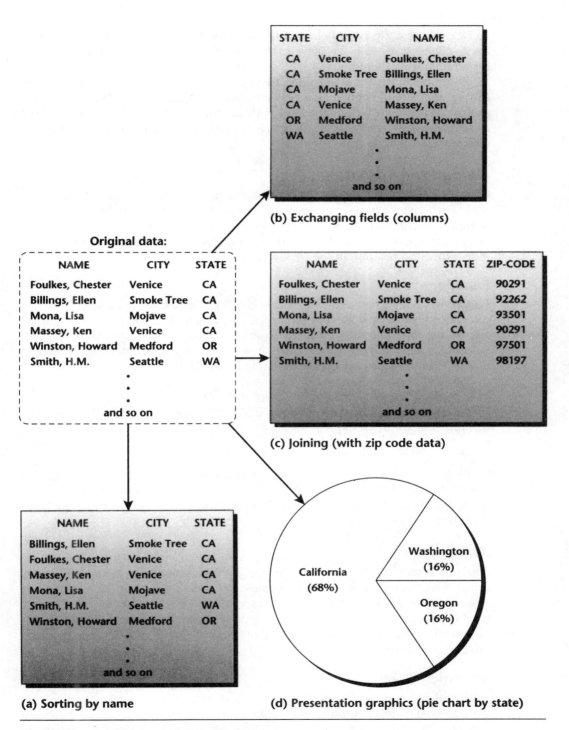

Original data:

NAME	CITY	STATE
Foulkes, Chester	Venice	CA
Billings, Ellen	Smoke Tree	CA
Mona, Lisa	Mojave	CA
Massey, Ken	Venice	CA
Winston, Howard	Medford	OR
Smith, H.M.	Seattle	WA

and so on

(b) Exchanging fields (columns)

STATE	CITY	NAME
CA	Venice	Foulkes, Chester
CA	Smoke Tree	Billings, Ellen
CA	Mojave	Mona, Lisa
CA	Venice	Massey, Ken
OR	Medford	Winston, Howard
WA	Seattle	Smith, H.M.

and so on

(c) Joining (with zip code data)

NAME	CITY	STATE	ZIP-CODE
Foulkes, Chester	Venice	CA	90291
Billings, Ellen	Smoke Tree	CA	92262
Mona, Lisa	Mojave	CA	93501
Massey, Ken	Venice	CA	90291
Winston, Howard	Medford	OR	97501
Smith, H.M.	Seattle	WA	98197

and so on

(a) Sorting by name

NAME	CITY	STATE
Billings, Ellen	Smoke Tree	CA
Foulkes, Chester	Venice	CA
Massey, Ken	Venice	CA
Mona, Lisa	Mojave	CA
Smith, H.M.	Seattle	WA
Winston, Howard	Medford	OR

and so on

(d) Presentation graphics (pie chart by state)

California (68%)
Washington (16%)
Oregon (16%)

Figure 10.7 Examples of reconfiguring data.

10.7(c), where a zip code field is appended to the original file. Data that have been joined can also be saved in that new form, while their original form remains unaltered.

Presentation graphics tools allow users to put data into a graphical form that can be easily understood. This is illustrated in Figure 10.7(d), where data are put into a pie chart. When working with graphics routines, users will typically have a choice of several types of graphs or charts, as well as coloring and pattern designs for each graphic element.

Calculator Activities

Calculator activities refer to the set of tasks that normally can be done with a calculator. These activities are generally implemented either by having the user write out a complete formula, specifying all the variables involved and how arithmetic operations should be performed on them, or by having the user summon a function resident in the DSS or DSS tool.

Functions

Functions are prestored formulas that enable a user to perform a calculator-type task as soon as the function is invoked. Using a function, for instance, the user can add numbers in a column or, perhaps, find the present value of a cash flow stream. A list of some widely used functions found in many DSS tools and packages is shown in Figure 10.8.

For instance, in Lotus's 1-2-3 spreadsheet package, a user can determine how much a ten-year benefit stream of $100,000 per year is worth today at a 15 percent discounting rate. Using 1-2-3's net present value (NPV) function, this function would be expressed as

```
@NPV (100000, .15, 10)
```

Lotus 1-2-3 recognizes this value as a function by the presence of the @ symbol before the name of the function. When it encounters this function in a worksheet, it automatically performs the computation and substitutes the result for the function expression.

Analysis

Analysis refers to using a DSS to review a set of facts and to assist in drawing conclusions based on those facts. Because the decision support environment is semistructured, both the user and machine interact in this process. Four widely used types of DSS analysis tools, or techniques brought by users to the DSS environment, are statistical tools, optimizing tools, what-if analysis, and artificial intelligence routines.

Statistical Tools

Statistical tools enable users to perform a variety of statistical operations on data, as well as to do a number of other data-handling tasks, such as distributing data into categories of the user's choosing. Statistical operations normally

Arithmetic and Statistical Functions

SUM	Calculates the sum of several numbers
MAX	Finds the highest value among several numbers
MIN	Finds the lowest value among several numbers
COUNT	Counts the number of filled spreadsheet cells in a contiguous block
AVG	Calculates the average of several numbers
STD	Calculates standard deviation of several numbers
SQRT	Calculates the square root of several numbers
ABS	Calculates the absolute value of a constant, variable, or expression
LN	Calculates the natural log of a constant, variable, or expression
LOG	Calculates the base-10 log of a constant, variable, or expression

Financial Functions

PV	Calculates the present value of an annuity
NPV	Calculates the present value of an uneven cash flow
FV	Calculates the future value of an annuity
PMT	Calculates an annuity from a present value

Conditional Functions

IF	Selects an alternative based on whether a condition is true or false
CHOOSE	Chooses a value from a list

Date Functions

TODAY	Supplies today's date
DATE	Calculates the number of days between two dates

Figure 10.8   Some commonly used calculator functions.

include regression analysis (procedures used to discern patterns in or make predictions from a set of data), correlation analysis (tools used to find the strength of association among data), and a variety of statistical inference methodologies (procedures such as analysis of variance, t-tests, Chi-square analysis, and confidence limits; they can be used to determine whether a conclusion drawn from data is statistically significant).

Statistical methods are usually descriptive or predictive in nature; that is, they describe patterns among data or forecast events based on present or past happenings. In addition to the standard statistical tools mentioned here, many packages offer a variety of specialized tools, such as factor analysis, discriminant analysis, and cluster analysis (see Figure 10.9). Some of the most widely used statistical tools in business are the variety of regression routines used for

Operation	Description
Test of hypothesis	Determines whether a hypothesis is statistically significant
Correlation analysis	Determines the strength of association among a number of variables
Regression analysis	Determines a mathematical relationship that shows how variables may be related
Analysis of variance (ANOVA)	Shows whether differences among groupings of observations are statistically significant
Nonparametric statistics	A collection of inference methods used for small samples or for cases where the underlying probability distribution is unknown
Discriminant analysis	A multivariate, regression-like technique used when the dependent variable (Y variable) is scaled into categories (such as users versus nonusers)
Cluster analysis	A method that classifies observations into groups in such a way that the similarities within groups are minimized and the differences between groups are maximized
Factor analysis	A method that reduces a large number of variables into a smaller number of factors, while retaining most of the information in the process
Forecasting techniques	A collection of methods—including regression analysis, exponential smoothing, the Box-Jenkins technique, input/output analysis, and econometric techniques—that is used to predict the future from a set of observations

Figure 10.9 Operations found in many statistical packages. Software packages that are heavily oriented toward forecasting techniques are often called forecasting packages. Many statistical packages also include routines for summarizing, sorting, and classifying data. Some also include graphics generation features.

forecasting purposes. These are particularly valuable when strategic plans are being formulated.

Optimizing Tools

A number of mathematical optimizing tools were mentioned in Chapter 3. Among these techniques are inventory control models, mathematical programming, Monte Carlo simulation, queuing theory, and network modeling. All of these mathematical modeling tools can be used to recommend certain choices to the decision maker, and many of them can generate a rich assortment of descriptive and predictive information as well. One of the most widely used optimizing techniques for business decision makers is the Monte Carlo simulation.

Typically, in decision support environments that feature one or more optimizing tools, the user can choose specific parameters (variables) for the models as well as determine, to a limited extent, how certain relationships are to be specified among those parameters. The specified model and its data are then input to the computer and the results noted. At that point, the user either accepts the information or reformulates the problem and again goes through the process suggested in Figure 10.1 (page 434).

Flexibility really sets a DSS apart from an MRS with respect to developing such models. With a DSS, the user can dynamically specify variables and values

```
                        IFPS/PLUS
                   OPTIMIZATION OPTIONS

        MODEL: FORECAST

                   VARIABLE              COLUMNS(S)      VALUE
                   --------              ----------      -----
    OBJECTIVE: MAXIMIZE NET INCOME          TOTAL
    DECISIONS: SALES GROWTH RATE             1993
  CONSTRAINTS: DEBT TO TOTAL CAPITAL     1988-1992 =      40%
               CURRENT RATIO             1988-1992 =    4.00X
               END OPTIMIZATION
               ENTER THE CONSTRAINT VALUES YOU WISH TO USE
```

Figure 10.10 Using Execucom's IFPS/Plus for what-if analysis. Each time the user solves the problem shown, the objective, decisions, or constraints can be changed. Here, the user could run the model again, changing the debt-to-capital ratio from 40 percent to some other value.

for models, and even build models without strict guidelines. With an MRS, the user is locked into a prespecified model.

What-If Analysis

What-if analysis is a non-probabilistic simulation technique that enables a user to reformulate a problem repeatedly until helpful information is obtained. For example, a manager might use a DSS generator (such as Execucom's IFPS/Plus, Figure 10.10) to build a DSS to maximize the net income for a new product in the coming year. IFPS/Plus is an updated version of IFPS (Interactive Financial Modeling System)—one of the best known and most widely used modeling packages.

Often, in the course of using a DSS generator to solve a problem, more than one set of estimates may be needed. What if the debt-to-capital ratio is 10 percent too high? What happens if sales projections are 10 percent too low? What if bank borrowing rates increase by 2 percent? Or what if product development is delayed by a year? DSS generators make it quite easy for users to develop multiple sets of estimates. However, DSS generators are not the only tools that can perform what-if analysis; spreadsheets are also well suited for this.

Refiguring calculations on the basis of all these what-ifs can take weeks to do by hand, but they are standard in the DSS world. For each what-if query, all the manager need do is change an underlying assumption or the value of a parameter and re-run the model. At the end of the interactive session, several of these runs can be used to make decisions and, perhaps, convince other management members of the appropriateness of the chosen action.

In certain contexts, what-if analysis is called *sensitivity analysis*. The goal of sensitivity analysis is to find out how sensitive a solution suggested by a model

Nordstrom's (Almost) Paperless Office

Not long ago, the paperless office was only a dream. However, some companies have made steady progress toward paperless operations. Many businesses found that they could cut printing costs by providing managers with on-line access to reports that were traditionally printed and distributed by data processing centers.

Nordstrom, Inc., a Seattle-based department store chain, started on-line access to management reports several years ago. The company estimates that it saves at least $2 million a year from this change. Before this move, the paper produced by the data center grew at an annual rate of 21 percent. Since providing on-line access, the number of printed pages is reduced by more than 50 percent.

Managers, who were initially resistant to the change, find that they now have faster access to fresher information. They also like the ability to customize the information con-

tained in the reports (often by eliminating irrelevant information) to best suit their needs.

"SINCE PROVIDING ON-LINE ACCESS, THE NUMBER OF PRINTED PAGES IS REDUCED BY MORE THAN 50 PERCENT."

The on-line access system is just one of the steps that Nordstrom is taking toward paperless operations. The company regularly sponsors contests to generate new paper reduction ideas. Through its newsletter, Nordstrom keeps everyone informed about progress toward paperless operations, including updates on how many trees are being saved and new employee ideas. The company also started planting trees for each new percentage point drop in paper use.

Adapted from Ambrosio (1992).

---

is to changes in the model parameters. For example, it might be useful for a bank manager to know how much change should be expected in the profitability of a project if mortgage rates were to change by a quarter of a percent in the next month. Or a chemical producer might want to know that $60,000 per month could be saved in production costs if only the availability of a raw material could be increased by 10 percent.

Artificial Intelligence

Artificial intelligence (AI) or expert system routines may dramatically improve the usefulness of the analysis function of a DSS. In the next chapter, we will look in depth at the role played by AI and other knowledge-based systems throughout MIS. Here, we will consider only one example of using AI to enhance a DSS: why analysis, the AI-based explanation feature that goes one step beyond the traditional what-if analysis that is available with most decision support systems.

Why analysis is a technique in which, after inspecting the results of DSS computations on-screen, the user can ask the DSS to explain why something happened. Figure 10.11 shows the use of why analysis with Execucom's

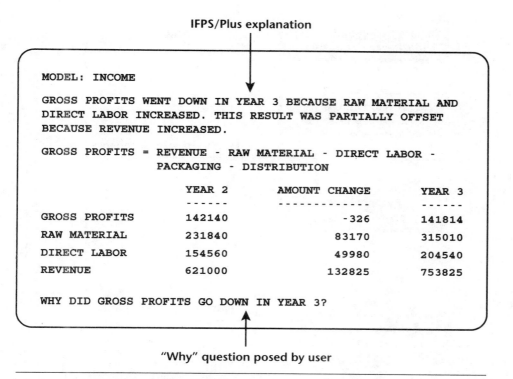

```
MODEL: INCOME

GROSS PROFITS WENT DOWN IN YEAR 3 BECAUSE RAW MATERIAL AND
DIRECT LABOR INCREASED. THIS RESULT WAS PARTIALLY OFFSET
BECAUSE REVENUE INCREASED.

GROSS PROFITS = REVENUE - RAW MATERIAL - DIRECT LABOR -
                PACKAGING - DISTRIBUTION

                        YEAR 2        AMOUNT CHANGE       YEAR 3
                        ------        -------------       ------
GROSS PROFITS           142140                 -326       141814
RAW MATERIAL            231840                83170       315010
DIRECT LABOR            154560                49980       204540
REVENUE                 621000               132825       753825


WHY DID GROSS PROFITS GO DOWN IN YEAR 3?
```

"Why" question posed by user

Figure 10.11   Using Execucom's IFPS/Plus for why analysis. At the bottom of the screen is a natural language query posed by the decision maker in response to the computations at the center of the screen. At top is the resulting IFPS/Plus explanation.

IFPS/Plus modeling package. The AI feature embedded in the package evaluates the significance of key indicators that influence the results of previous computations and responds with its "opinion" as to why the event happened. Both AI explanation facilities and natural-language interfaces will be more fully discussed in Chapter 12.

DSS DEVELOPMENT

Decision support systems are usually created in an evolutionary manner. Figure 10.12 illustrates the general nature of the DSS development process. Once user decision-making needs are identified, a preliminary model (or prototype) of the DSS is constructed. After the user has some initial experiences with the DSS prototype, it may be refined to provide better results. This process may continue for several iterations. Many decision support systems rely heavily on models and, theoretically, the building of models that have recurring utility is never complete. In this sense, the DSS is never finished; after the initial final product is built, the DSS continues to evolve.

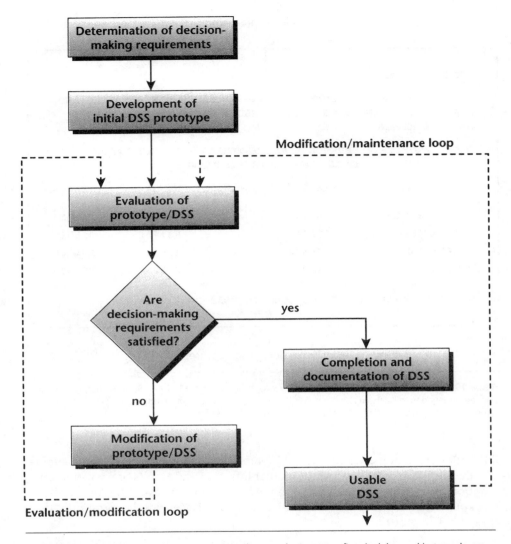

Figure 10.12 The DSS development process. In many instances, after decision-making needs are identified and an initial prototype developed, several evaluation/modification iterations may be needed before the DSS is ready for use.

DSS Products

Hardware and software products used to develop and implement decision support systems abound in the marketplace. Here, we will first consider how these products may be classified. Then, we will look at the variety of software tools that are often used to develop decision support systems and that may also be embedded in them. Finally, we will explore the types of user interfaces that may be found in decision support systems.

DSS technology may be classified in many ways. R. H. Sprague and E. D. Carlson proposed a well-known framework that classifies products falling under the DSS umbrella into three categories: specific decision support systems, DSS generators, and DSS tools.

A **specific DSS** allows one or more decision makers to deal with a specific problem or set of related problems. For example, a specific DSS is used by the city of San Jose, California. The DSS enables police officers planning patrol beats to call up maps of their areas and try various allocations of officers to these beats. For each proposed what-if allocation, the DSS provides a measure of effectiveness. A specific DSS might be programmed from scratch by an organization (an expensive alternative) or developed from a DSS generator.

A DSS generator is a package of related hardware and software (and, often, procedures and data) that allows the user to quickly and easily build a specific DSS. For instance, the police-beat DSS just described was built with a DSS generator called Geodata Analysis and Display System (GADS). GADS has also been used to build other decision support systems having nothing to do with police beats—for example, building a decision support system to assist in the routing of IBM copier repairpeople. The generator software is often an application package that enables the user to customize the generator to a specific application. An example of a DSS generator, IFPS/Plus, was used earlier. Figure 10.13 provides an overview of IFPS/Plus's capabilities.

A **DSS tool** is a hardware, software, procedure, or data element that enables the user to build either a specific DSS or a DSS generator. For instance, such spreadsheet products as Lotus's 1-2-3 and Computer Associates' SuperCalc—both general-purpose "calculators"—can be used as DSS tools. When Lotus 1-2-3 is combined with a microcomputer, a monitor, and a printer, and the operating systems software to build a system that allows a specific sales manager to review the performance of his or her salespeople, the resulting product is a specific DSS. Figure 10.14 lists numerous DSS tools, specific decision support systems, and DSS generators found in business settings.

DSS Development Tools

From our discussion, it should be apparent that many different types of software tools can be used to build decision support systems. While the variety of such software tools is large (and increasing), by far the most common are database management systems, spreadsheets, and modeling packages.

Database Management Systems

Many decision support systems are used in combination with some type of database. This is especially true for decision support systems that need strong support in the information-retrieval area. Often, the 4GL available with the database management system—the sophisticated software system that controls database-related activities—is used to build the DSS. The 4GL is also likely to be part of the dialogue management system of the resulting DSS.

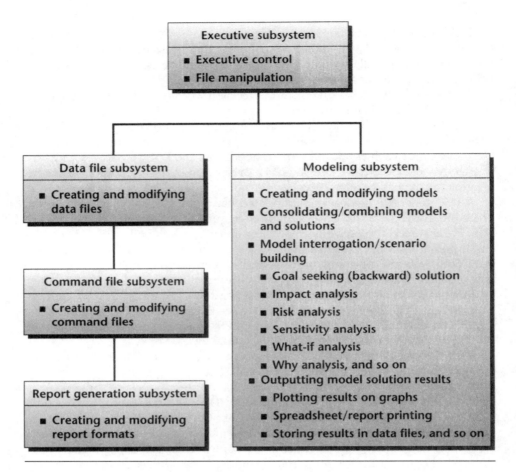

Figure 10.13 An example of the components of a DSS generator: Execucom's IFPS/Plus. The orientation of IFPS/Plus toward interactive decision support is shown in this depiction of the package's major components.

As mentioned in Chapter 7, relational database management systems are ideal for situations in which unanticipated types of accesses to a database are expected. This often happens in decision support environments, where information needs are semistructured or unstructured and the DSS is independent from the transaction processing system. Relational database data exist in the form of tables, and those tables can be related in any authorized manner chosen by the user. This design contrasts with hierarchical and network databases, where predictable types of accesses are normally encountered and predefined paths are built for those accesses by a data administrator. In the latter types of databases, the user cannot easily relate data in a way that does not correspond to a predefined path.

Although hierarchical and network database models are less suitable in terms of providing the flexibility needed by a DSS, and the transaction process-

SPECIFIC DECISION SUPPORT SYSTEMS	
Company	**Specific Decision Support Systems**
American Airlines	Pricing decisions and choosing air routes
First United Bank Corporation	Evaluating investments
Frito-Lay, Inc.	Pricing, advertising, and promotion decisions
IBM	Determining routing for repairpeople
National Gypsum	Corporate planning and forecasting
Southern Railway	Dispatching and routing trains
Texas Oil and Gas	Evaluating potential drill sites
LTV Corporation	Finding best sale terms of downtown office
Wells Fargo Bank	Planning postmerger operations
Zale Corporation	Evaluating potential retailing sites

DSS GENERATORS	
Product	**Vendor**
EMPIRE	Applied Data Research, Inc.
EXPRESS	Management Decision Systems, Inc.
GADS	IBM
Accent R	National Information Systems
MODEL	Lloyd Bush and Associates
SIMPLAN	Simplan Systems, Inc.
System W	Comshare, Inc.
IFPS/Plus	Execucom Systems Corporation

DSS TOOLS

Microcomputer systems

Database management systems

Display devices

General-purpose programming languages

Optimization tools

Statistical tools

Spreadsheet packages

Graphics generators

Figure 10.14 Examples of specific decision support systems, DSS generators, and DSS tools.

ing data typically managed with these models are less suitable for the decision-making needs of upper-level management, both of these traditional types of database models are commonly seen in DSS environments that support middle- and lower-level management. Two examples are a DSS that enables a salesperson to inspect levels of current inventory on a display terminal in order to find substitute products in an out-of-stock situation, and a DSS that allows a credit manager to decide whether to authorize certain customer purchases. In both cases, the DSS must access data managed by the TPS.

With the movement toward object-oriented programming, object-oriented databases (OODB) will probably become part of the data management component of decision support systems in the near future. Image-based databases (described in Chapter 7) are also likely to become facets of some decision support systems. Apple's HyperCard and similar products already enable users to develop graphically oriented databases. HyperCard allows the user to work on a graphical screen as if he or she were working naturally at a desk. Basically, HyperCard operates by allowing users to create a set of computerized index cards—and this set can be huge. These cards can be related to one another in a user-designated manner and accessed by selecting them with a mouse.

Spreadsheets

Spreadsheets are sophisticated electronic calculators—with special strengths in the areas of calculator activities, data reconfiguration, and what-if analysis. Many of them also have a number of advanced modeling functions (such as regression analysis). In spreadsheet packages, data are usually contained directly in worksheet cells that are arranged in a grid that looks similar to accounting paper.

Spreadsheets are useful over an extremely wide number of decision support applications. A list of some of the current top-selling spreadsheet packages was provided in Chapter 6 (Figure 6.9, page 247). Despite their popularity, spreadsheets also have several weaknesses, such limited report writing flexibility (in some products, what you see on your display screen is all you can get in print), program-data dependence, and some (especially those found in integrated packages) lack audit trail capabilities to trace edits or updates. For the most part, spreadsheets are used in personal types of applications, where data are manually input and the spreadsheet software becomes a "souped-up electronic calculator" that can do a lot of recalculating and displaying in a short span of time.

Although spreadsheet packages and applications have traditionally been two-dimensional, the trend today is toward multidimensionality. Many managers want to see their organizations in more than two dimensions. For instance, three dimensions would enable a manager to look at accounts for each division by month; five dimensions would allow the manager to also view these accounts by product line and by distribution channel. Today, only the full-fledged modeling packages provide superior multidimensional facilities.

Product	Vendor
Javelin	Javelin Software
IFPS/Plus	Execucom Systems Corporation
Encore!	Ferox Microsystems Inc.
Infotab	National CSS
Business Modeler	Business Model Systems, Inc.
EMS	Economic Sciences Corporation
Enterprise	Citishare, Inc.
Simplan	Simplan Systems, Inc.
XSIM	Chase Decision Systems
System W	Comshare Inc.
Express	Management Decisions, Inc.

Figure 10.15 Some of the commercially available modeling packages targeted to business applications. As spreadsheets provide an increased number of modeling functions, the distinction between spreadsheets and modeling packages is becoming blurry.

Modeling Packages

Modeling packages are specifically designed to enable the user to construct complex quantitative algorithms, such as financial simulations or sales forecasting models. Most modeling packages are equipped with several analysis tools, including sophisticated statistical and optimizing techniques.

Many of the most popular modeling packages, such as IFPS/Plus, began on mainframes. Modeling packages enable easy integration of data into several dimensions, the building of very sophisticated types of models, and sophisticated types of analysis. Also, there is a central repository for data, whose form is independent of the model being developed. Some modeling packages also have built-in artificial intelligence capabilities.

A financial model that integrates revenues, costs, and profits of products with time periods, geographic areas, organizational units, product lines, and customer types might help answer such questions as: What will happen to profits if the Western Region's sales of product X to consumer accounts increased by 20 percent? How much would labor costs for product Y, produced by Divisions A and B, have to be lowered to increase by 5 percent the overall return on sales by the enterprise? Why are profits lower in Division A than Division B? Such questions are so difficult to answer by conventional means that they would probably never be asked if modeling packages were not available.

In choosing a modeling package as opposed to a spreadsheet, the user basically trades an easy-to-follow grid for the power of the fully featured model. A variety of modeling packages are listed in Figure 10.15. As spreadsheets develop more mathematical modeling capabilities, the line that separates spreadsheets from traditional modeling packages is blurring.

User Interfaces

Users must interact with a DSS through some type of hardware/software interface, which is commonly called the **user interface**. The hardware part of the user interface often consists of either a display terminal or a personal computer workstation hooked up to a multiuser computer (for example, a mainframe) or a stand-alone personal computer. A keyboard and a mouse are used for operator input. The software part of the interface typically involves invoking commands, filling in templates, and/or making physical modifications. Graphical user interfaces (GUI) are becoming more common in decision support systems, just as they are in most other software packages and systems.

Major criteria for designing or choosing the interface are ease of learning and use for the DSS user. Thus, when designing interfaces such as those described here, developers should consider human memory capacity, the likelihood of errors (and the user's having to fix them), the sophistication of the operator, and so on. Many of these people-oriented concerns were discussed in Chapter 2.

Command Interfaces

Issuing commands is the traditional way that both users and computer professionals interact with computer systems. Commands should be issued in the easiest possible way. This often means employing either a fourth-generation language (4GL) to allow the user to write out simple commands, or using a pointing mechanism (such as a mouse) so that the user can point to commands or icons on a graphically oriented display-screen menu. In a well-designed DSS, users have the option of issuing commands (the method usually favored by sophisticated users) or pointing (the method often chosen by beginners).

Of the DSS approaches covered earlier, modeling tools require the heaviest use of written commands; spreadsheets, the heaviest use of pointing mechanisms. Users of a spreadsheet's macro facility (which enables users to write and store keystroke sequences as small programs called macros) will experience both writing certain commands and pointing to certain others—all in the course of working with the spreadsheet. Database environments use both fourth-generation languages and menus extensively to drive applications.

A growing trend in command language-based decision support systems is the use of a natural-language command interface. With such a facility, the user and machine communicate in a user-familiar language such as English. A good command language should enable the user to build a customized "front end" to the DSS (perhaps a sequence of prompts, menus, or self-loading batch files) and to develop his or her own functions or features (for example, a library of special routines).

Pointer mechanisms and graphics-oriented screens also represent a distinct trend in the evolution of decision support systems. They allow DSS users—any of whom are unsophisticated in the use of computer technology and are not proficient at keyboarding—to work quickly, without having to learn a complicated and fastidious language syntax. Many industry observers predict that graphical user interfaces, fueled by powerful 80386-, 80486-, 68030-, and 68040-based microcomputers in the business mainstream, will completely overhaul end-user computing efforts in the coming decade.

Templates

A template is a prelabeled screen that only needs to be filled in with data. Data are usually typed into specific locations on the screen, and each of these locations is controlled by an algorithm that instructs the DSS what to do with the data. An example of a template and its use was provided earlier in the book (Figure 7.3, page 282). Templates are widely used in database, modeling, and spreadsheet environments, and they are appropriate in any other application environment that must make a large amount of data entry as easy as possible for the user or operator.

Physical Modification

Physical modification refers to allowing the DSS user to physically alter a model represented on the screen. For example, a spreadsheet user who inserts or deletes a row or a column has physically modified the worksheet model. The user of a digitizing tablet can often alter a graphical model represented on a display screen by "painting" modifications with the tablet's stylus.

The newer graphically oriented operating systems—such as Windows, OS/2, and Macintosh System 7—are bringing fresh meaning to physical modification. For example, in these environments, it is quite easy to add a narrative explanation developed in a word-processing package to a spreadsheet (or add a graph generated from a database) in order to create a technical report. As new versions of the DSS tools and software described previously are released, physical modification should become even easier.

DSS Examples

Now that we have explored some of the characteristics, components, developments, and properties of decision support systems, let's turn to a few examples that show how they are used in a variety of application environments.

A Wall Street DSS

A growing number of brokerage firms and investment banks use decision support systems when making investment decisions concerning the assets they control. The strategies behind these decisions are based both on a trader's sense of the market's direction and on the DSS's ability to identify subtle trends or disturbances in the market prices of securities and options.

A National Forest DSS

The staff managing a U.S. national forest built a land management database with a commercial DBMS package. The database contained information on characteristics of lands within the forest, broken down by specific land areas. A

4GL that accompanied the DBMS allowed the staff to model the expected behavior of forest fires under specific combinations of terrain, natural barriers, forest vegetation, and weather.

A fire broke out in the forest one summer and the staff had to decide on a suppression or containment strategy. Using the DSS, the staff simulated various scenarios that showed how the fire would spread. They also determined how each fire-fighting strategy would fare under each scenario, and at what cost. All of this took two hours; at the end, an all-out suppression strategy was selected. One fire official estimates that using computer-based decision support systems to simulate the spreading and fighting of forest fires saves about $10 million in fire-fighting efforts in just one year.

A Contract Negotiation DSS

An executive, about to negotiate an important contract with a client, used an ordinary spreadsheet package to model anticipated profits. Before the meeting with the client, the executive also used the spreadsheet package to build a set of mathematical models that would evaluate his financial position if the client were to propose any one of several possible contractual arrangements. When the meeting took place, his preparation enabled the executive to make immediate decisions and push the meeting toward the outcome he wanted. The executive completed a quick deal that gave him a favorable contract.

An Oil Executive's DSS

An executive vice-president at a major oil company spends 30–40 minutes a day at his desktop terminal, looking at internal data, global trends, and competitive pricing. During that time, he accesses a company database for the internal data he needs and two commercial databases for external data. The executive claims that he has more information in less time than ever before.

An Environmental DSS

Traditionally, the Environmental Protection Agency (EPA) deals separately with air pollution, water pollution, and land pollution in a given area. With the aid of high technology, the department can now integrate data from each of these pollution sources. For example, one DSS can answer such questions as: "To what extent will greater emissions restrictions reduce risk to humans?" Or, "What percentage of the pollutants in an area are attributable to such general sources as cars, as opposed to large industrial facilities?" In developing the DSS, the EPA involved local officials in the decision-making process; the result is a system that is usable by some people who never interacted with a computer before.

GROUP DECISION SUPPORT SYSTEMS

Decision support systems have generally resulted in better support for individual decision making and have often resulted in better decisions. However, many DSS approaches and techniques are not suitable for group decision-making environments. In many organizations, managers spend 80 percent or more

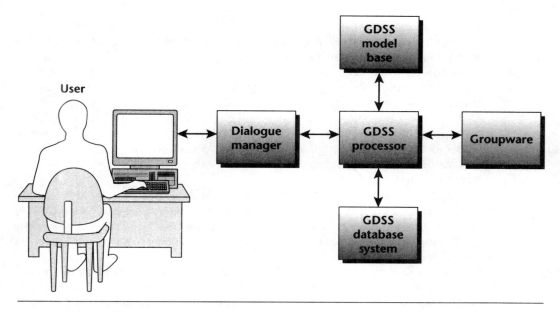

Figure 10.16 The components of a group decision support system (GDSS).

of their time in committee meetings and other group decision-making settings. While decision support systems are designed to enhance individual decision making, group decision support systems provide effective support in group decision-making settings.

Components of a GDSS

Group decision support systems (GDSS) consist of the hardware, software, data, and models that are needed to support the decision-making activities of particular groups. A GDSS possesses a number of features that distinguish it from a traditional DSS. Figure 10.16 illustrates how a GDSS is usually configured. The typical configuration consists of many of the elements found in a DSS: a model base, a database, and dialogue management systems. Groupware and the GDSS processor are unique features.

The *GDSS model base* consists of the mathematical, quantitative, and analytic models and tools that the group needs to make its decisions. As with an individual DSS, the models included in the model base will vary as a function of the needs of the decision-making group.

Many group decision support systems allow group members to have simultaneous access to common files and databases so that all members of the group can work on the same task at the same time. The *GDSS database system* makes this possible. Like traditional DSS database systems, the GDSS database system may extract data from personal, corporate, and external databases.

A GDSS may also include groupware—software that helps group members generate alternatives, analyze data, evaluate the choices, and reach decisions.

Groupware packages are designed to allow group members—whose workstations are connected by a telecommunication network (usually a local network)—to join together on a common project. Packages are available to support cooperative work and collaborative work. Besides group decision making, these packages support other work group activities—for example, electronic mail among group members, joint word processing of a document, and joint what-if analysis of an electronic spreadsheet. GDSS software may include word processing and text manipulation, database and file manipulation, spreadsheet or worksheet capabilities, graphics capabilities, decision-making aids (for example, mathematical, management science, and other analytical approaches), and communications facilities.

The *GDSS processor* consists of one or more computer systems that coordinate the processing activities of group members. This may be a dedicated server of one or more microcomputers in a LAN. In some cases, it may be a mainframe or minicomputer, especially when wide area group decision support systems are desired.

The *GDSS dialogue manager* helps group members communicate with each other and to interface with the other GDSS components. In many cases, one or more *group facilitators* or "chauffeurs"—individuals skilled in using GDSS technology—play a special role in coordinating group decision making. Chauffeurs facilitate the flow of information between group members and what appears on the "public screens"—the on-screen displays available to all group members—during a work session. Special software supports the facilitator running the meeting.

GDSS Configurations and Classifications

Group decision support systems can be configured in numerous ways. The actual configuration used is dependent on the needs of the group, the types of decisions that are supported, the frequency of GDSS use, and the geographic location of group members. Four alternative configurations follow:

- **Decision room** In the decision room approach, all the GDSS technology is in a single location, usually a single room. This may be feasible when decision makers are brought together to work on common projects; for example, when they all work in the same building or geographic area. Groups such as production management teams, market research groups, and financial analysis groups may all benefit from the decision room approach. Several universities and other organizations have developed GDSS decision rooms that serve as models for implementation in other organizations.

- **Local area network** In the LAN approach, GDSS technology is not concentrated in a single location, but is spread out among several locations within the same building or limited geographic area—usually in the offices of group members.

- **Teleconferencing** The teleconferencing approach ties together multiple widely dispersed decision rooms. Teleconferencing technology—which will

Dick Tracy Would Marvel at Personal Communicators of the 1990s

The communicator on the wrist of Dick Tracy, the fictional detective of comic strip and cinematic fame, is responsible for getting people excited about videophones and sophisticated portable communications devices. Experts predict that both will be realities by the year 2000 and will probably have features that surpass those of Tracy and his cohorts.

"THE PERSONAL COMMUNICATOR OF THE FUTURE WILL BE PART PHONE, PART PAGER, AND PART COMPUTER."

The personal communicator of the future will be part phone, part pager, and part computer. It will send and receive messages—including faxes—and will help you keep in touch with the office, no matter how far you roam. It will probably include both a pen pad and a keyboard and will be able to run a full range of business software. It will also include the communications technology needed to link to radio-based voice mail and electronic mail networks. Its voice-activated natural language interface will respond to your spoken commands.

If video-compression technologies continue to improve at the current rate, personal communicators are likely to have a videophone component by the year 2000. Motorola is one of the companies working diligently toward this end.

Personal communicators will be just one of the new types of technology to emerge from the blending fields of computers, consumer electronics, and telecommunications. Over time, this trend is likely to enable us to send and receive multimedia documents that combine text, sound, pictures, and video clips. What would Dick Tracy think of that?

Adapted from Schwartz (1992).

be described more fully in Chapter 12—electronically connects the widely distributed (even globally distributed) decision rooms.

- **Wide area decision network**   The wide area decision network is essentially a WAN version of the local area network GDSS approach. GDSS technology is distributed among group members (not concentrated in decision rooms) and connected by private or public WAN telecommunication links. The group facilitator and group members may all be at different, geographically dispersed locations. If several group members are found at each of the remote sites, several group facilitators may be involved in the coordination of GDSS work sessions.

Group decision support systems may also be classified by the level of support that they provide to group members. *Level-1 group decision support systems* provide technology that enables group members to electronically communicate with one another. All of the configurations just described have Level-1 capabilities. *Level-2 group decision support systems* provide support for group decision-making processes in addition to the communications capabilities provided by Level-1 group decision support systems. Level-2 group decision support systems typically furnish groupware that supports joint modeling and analytical approaches; they also provide the software support needed for determining group preferences through voting, ranking, rating, and other means. The Delphi Technique, the Nominal Group Technique (NGT), brainstorming, and other group creativity enhancement approaches may also be supported by a Level-2 GDSS. A *Level-3 group decision support system* provides all the capabilities of a Level-2 GDSS and also supplies facilities for formalizing group interaction patterns. For example, Robert's Rules of Order—the standard guide to parliamentary procedure—could be built into the system to ensure that proper steps were followed during group sessions. Or an "automated counselor" or expert system—which would give advice on available rules or procedures—could be designed into the system. Group members may also be able to write their own ground rules in a Level-3 GDSS.

GDSS Goals

Group decision support systems provide many unique features that go beyond those found in traditional decision support systems. When determining whether or not to implement a GDSS, managers should consider whether or not the proposed systems achieve the following goals:

- **Ease of use** Group decision support systems that are complex or hard to operate are not likely to be used. Groups often have less tolerance than individuals for systems that are difficult to learn. Hence, a GDSS should be easy to master and perceived as usable—and useful—by group members.

- **Provision of both general and specific support** The GDSS should provide support for both general and specific types of problems. It should support a wide range of group decision-making capabilities, as well as ensuring that specific groups can tailor the GDSS to support the decisions that they need to make. The provision of general and specific support should occur over the long run. It should be possible to expand and modify the model base as the needs of the group and the organization change over time.

- **Promotion of positive group behavior** A number of approaches may be used to promote positive behaviors among group members. Structured group decision-making activities—such as the Nominal Group Technique (NGT), the Delphi Technique, and brainstorming—can enhance group decision-making processes, as well as the group decisions that are reached. GDSS designers are now incorporating many of these features into commercially available GDSS packages; the availability of these options should be considered by potential adopters.

- **Suppression of negative group behavior** An effective GDSS will minimize counterproductive behavior among group members. For example, it will make it difficult for an individual to dominate the decision-making process and thereby inhibit input from other group members. A well-designed GDSS will also discourage one or more group members from sidetracking the group into non-productive areas. Procedures for effectively planning and managing GDSS meetings are incorporated into many GDSS packages.

It is wise for potential adopters to consider group decision support systems that possess these features.

Group decision support systems are becoming more widely used. Studies indicate that both private and public sector organizations are very interested in group decision support systems. They should be commonplace by the year 2000.

EXECUTIVE INFORMATION SYSTEMS (EIS)

An executive information system (EIS)—which is sometimes referred to as an executive support system (ESS)—is a DSS that is designed to meet the special needs of top-level managers. Some people use the terms "EIS" and "ESS" interchangeably, but others do not. Any distinction between the two usually is because executive support systems are likely to incorporate additional capabilities such as electronic mail. In this section, we first cover those people in organizations that are considered to be executives and examine the types of decisions they make. Then, we turn to the nature of executive decisions and the types of information that executives need most. Finally, some of the special characteristics of executive information systems—beyond those of other decision support systems—are discussed.

Executives

An **executive** can probably best be described as a manager at or near the top of the organizational hierarchy who exerts a strong influence on the course taken by the organization. The slots in a firm considered to be executive positions vary from company to company. For example, in IRM-oriented firms, the chief information officer (CIO) is usually an executive who participates in key strategic decisions. In other firms, the CIO is a middle manager (who often has a title other than CIO). And sometimes, the person in charge of an organization's CBIS is basically a data processing director.

Figure 10.17 shows the executive positions found in many corporations. A board of directors sits on top of most corporations. Board members are nominated for their positions by existing board members and by members of the organization's top corporate management; the final choices are ratified by stockholders. The board members, in turn, select the president. The president, or chief executive officer (CEO), is the person charged with the responsibility of operating the company effectively. In some cases, there are separate president and CEO positions, but most commonly, the president also holds the title of CEO.

The majority stockholders, in effect, own the company. Like the executives who run the company, they can exert a major influence on its mission, scope, and general direction. New vice-presidents in the functional areas are often selected by an *executive group*, which consists of the CEO and existing functional vice-presidents. In some organizations, the executive group acts in an advisory capacity to the president, who ultimately makes all the decisions; in others, the executive group can veto decisions made by the president and make decisions of their own.

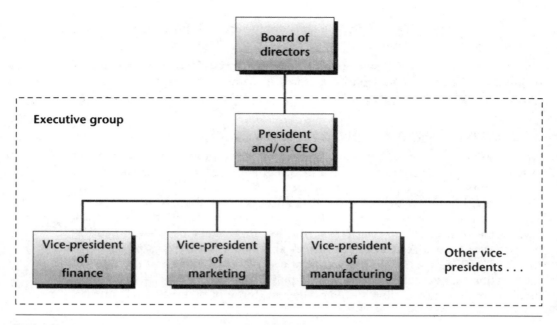

Figure 10.17 Examples of executive positions in organizations.

Executive Roles and Decision Making

Most executive decisions fall into one of three classes: strategic planning, tactical planning, and "fire-fighting" activities (see Figure 10.18). Also, executives need a certain degree of control to ensure that these activities are carried out properly.

Strategic Planning

Strategic planning involves determining the general, long-range direction of the organization. Typically, the CEO is ultimately responsible for the development of strategic plans. In firms with a participative style of management, members of the executive group help in formulating a strategic plan. In some cases, they can even veto the plan if, in their judgment, it seems likely to fail, or if it appears to violate the organization's mission statement. The strategic plan sets the stage for all other major forms of decision making within the company.

Tactical Planning

Whereas strategic planning addresses the general concerns of the firm, tactical planning refers to the how, when, where, and what issues involved with carrying out the strategic plan. Although executives will not normally be concerned with tactical details, they do need to worry about general tactics. For example, the vice-president of finance must address how the firm can best achieve a balance between debt and equity financing. And the marketing vice-president

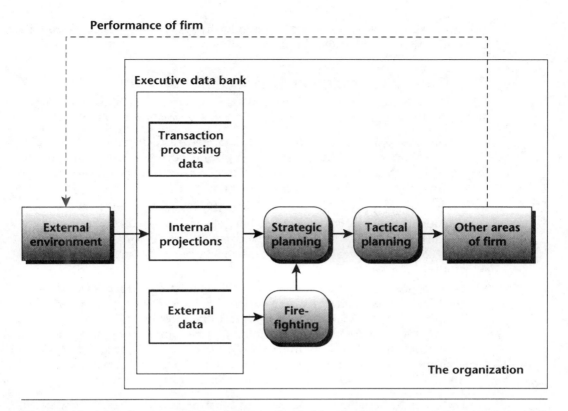

Figure 10.18 A data flow representation of the executive decision-planning environment. Corresponding control activities exist for each of the planning functions shown in this figure.

will need to consider which classes of products the company should produce to be successful in the marketplace.

Fire-Fighting

Major problems arise sometimes that must be resolved by someone at an executive level. For example, if a company is involved in a big lawsuit that threatens its financial solvency, an executive must get involved. Other possible fire-fighting activities include damage caused to a major facility, the announcement of an important product by a competitor, a strike, and a sharp reversal of the economy. Many of these events will call for key alterations in plans.

Control

In addition to planning and fire-fighting, executive management also needs to exert some general control over the organization. For example, if the strategic plan calls for a 20 percent increase in profitability, feedback is needed to ensure that certain actions taken within the organization are accomplishing that objective. Thus, executives will also periodically review key performance data to see how they compare against planned amounts.

The Executive Decision-Making Environment

Refer back to the executive decision-making environment shown in Figure 10.18. The three main data sources for executive information are as follows:

- **Transaction processing data** These data, generated from transaction processing systems, usually reflect the past and current performance of the firm. Thus, these data are most useful for normal control purposes and have relatively little value in long-range planning.

- **Internal projections** These data show the operating objectives for each functional area, expected revenues, budgets and planned expenses, and the overall financial plan for keeping the company afloat. Some of these projections cover a multiyear period and are most useful for assessing the current profile of the company.

- **External data** Although executives use internal data such as those supplied from transaction processing systems and internal forecasts, most of the data they use in decision making—in fact, the most critical data, and those used as the basis for strategic planning and handling fire-fighting efforts—come from the external environment. In many instances, it is only through environmental scanning and monitoring that strategic opportunities and competitive threats (both immediate and long term) can be identified.

The types of decisions that executives must make are broad. Often, executives make these decisions based on a vision they have regarding what it will take to make their companies successful. To a large extent, executives rely much more on their own intuition than on the sophisticated analytical skills that are required of specialists. Weston Agor claims that executives "have a sense or vision of what is coming—and how to move their organizations in response to that vision. They are particularly adept at generating new ideas and in providing ingenious solutions to old problems. They also function best in crises or situations of rapid change." The intuitive character of executive decision making is reflected strongly in the types of information found most useful to executives.

Five characteristics of the types of information used in executive decision making are lack of structure, high degree of uncertainty, future orientation, informal sources, and low level of detail. These are discussed next and are summarized in Figure 10.19.

- **Lack of structure** Many of the decisions made by executives are relatively unstructured. For instance, what general direction should the company take? Or what type of advertising campaign will best promote the new product line? These types of decisions are not as clear-cut as deciding how to debug a computer program or how to deal with an overdue account balance. Also, it is not always obvious which data are required or how to weigh

Properties of Executive Information

- Lack of structure
- High degree of uncertainty
- Future orientation
- Informal sources
- Low level of detail

Figure 10.19 Properties of information used in executive decision making. The strategic nature of executive decisions makes the information needs of executives different from those of ordinary managers.

available data when reaching a decision. For example, how does an executive assess the future direction of the economy if the six sources on which that person typically depends for information each forecast something different? Even the portfolio of decisions that need to be made by the executive is an open issue. Should time be spent, for instance, considering new businesses to enter—or should the company concentrate on looking for new markets for existing products?

- **High degree of uncertainty** Executives work in a decision space that is often characterized by a lack of precedent. For example, when the Arab oil embargo hit in the mid-1970s, no such previous event could be referenced for advice. When the stock market fell 508 points in October 1987, many people saw that event, too, as unprecedented, since the financial and economic world in 1929 (the date of the previous huge market crash) was not comparable in many respects to the 1980s. Executives also work in a decision space where results are not scientifically predictable from actions. If prices are lowered, for instance, product demand will not automatically increase.

- **Future orientation** Strategic-planning decisions are made in order to shape future events. As conditions change, organizations must change also. It is the executive's responsibility to make sure that the organization keeps pointed toward the future. Some key questions about the future include: "How will future technologies affect what the company is currently doing? What will the competition (or the government) do next? What products will consumers demand five years from now? Where will the economy move next, and how might that affect consumer buying patterns?" As you can see, the answers to all of these questions about the future external environment are vital.

- **Informal sources** Executives, more than other types of managers, rely heavily on informal sources for key information. For example, lunch with a colleague in another firm might reveal some important competitor strategies. Informal sources such as television might also feature news of momentous concern to the executive—news that he or she would probably never encounter in the company's database or in scheduled computer reports. Besides business meals and the media, some other important informal sources of information are meetings, tours around the company's facilities to chat with employees, brainstorming with a trusted colleague or two, and social events.

- **Low level of detail**   Most important executive decisions are made by observing broad trends. This requires the executive to be more aware of the large overview than the tiny items. Even so, many executives insist that the answers to some questions can only be found by mucking through details.

EIS Roles and Characteristics

Because executives deal primarily with data about the external environment and data that come from informal sources, they are usually less reliant on direct contact with information technology than other types of managers. When information from their company's computers is needed, many chief executive officers make their subordinates retrieve that information. Because executive information needs are more ambiguous than those of other levels of management, computers have historically been less useful to executives. Many executives have little hands-on experience with computers and don't fully appreciate how information technology can improve their personal productivity and decision-making skills.

Both business conditions and technology have changed dramatically in the last several years, however. Today, executives should turn directly to computers and other information technology for certain types of information in many important situations. According to Stephanie Wilkenson, a study at MIT's Sloan School of Management found that the use of computers by executives is a "steadily growing phenomenon, one that can have major impacts on the nature of executive work and the way organizations function."

Information technology and application software have become increasingly user-friendly. Operating systems with graphical user interfaces (GUI), such as Windows, have helped stimulate chief executive officers' interest in using computers. In addition, on-line computer services (such as the information utilities discussed in Chapter 7) that carry environmental information such as news, industry and economic reports, and worldwide and government data, are used more frequently by executives.

Stephanie Wilkenson writes that one executive, who uses a computer daily to check both external trends and internal data, claims, "I have more information than I would have normally received had I called the vice-president . . . and asked, 'How are we looking today?' " This same executive also relates, "Often, use of the computer leads to a tendency to look at more future-oriented marketing data and less traditional financial data." Claims another executive, "Because I'm a CEO, I have to focus on what's going on outside the company. In terms of my time at the computer, I probably spend two-thirds of it looking at Dow Jones News Service. I get a great deal of information about what's going on in the food industry this way. It is much easier than having my secretary watch newspapers and clip articles." Today, business is often conducted at such a fast pace that even executives find it increasingly difficult to survive without computers.

Common EIS Capabilities		
▪ Strategic-planning support capabilities	▪ Exceptional ease of learning and use	
▪ External environment focus	▪ Customization	
▪ Broad-based computing ability		

Figure 10.20 Common EIS capabilities. EIS are becoming more common in organizations as an increasing number of executives recognize them as a key to remaining competitive in today's dynamic business environment.

Computers can also lead to improving executive confidence. In Stephanie Wilkenson's article, one executive mentions, "I don't feel I work faster, just better . . . It's not really that I'm saving time, because now I'll dig deeper for more information. I'll do extra things to make the quality of my decisions better. When the quality is better, my decisions are more defensible. It makes me more confident." According to Sloan School research, in fact, increased confidence is an advantage of computers mentioned commonly by executives—confidence in the accuracy of the information obtained, in the decisions made on the basis of that information, and in having control of the enterprise. A research associate at Sloan's Center for Information System Research (CISR) claims that, "Better control leads to more focus on the future . . . The executive thinks, 'We're on track; I'll know if we go off track. Now I can think about the future.' "

All of these considerations bring us to some of the properties commonly found in executive support systems. Among these properties are those shown in Figure 10.20 and described in the following subsections.

Strategic-Planning Support

Since many executives consider strategic planning to be their top priority, it is essential that designers of executive information systems address this particular need. The designer should be familiar with strategic planning and critical success factor (CSF) models to determine how information technology might (such as those described in Chapter 3) enhance the organization's strategic-planning process. The greatest success in this area has been providing the executive with comprehensive retrieval capabilities so that he or she can quickly pull together the information needed to form a profile of an organization or organizational unit, a situation, or an important client.

External Environment Focus

Because events taking place in the environment are so important to executives, information about such events is usually among their most important needs. Thus, many executive information systems include links to commercial databases, such as those of Dow Jones News and Compustat, as well as to specialized databases that provide more specific types of consumer, industry, economic, and worldwide data (see Figure 7.25, page 327, for some of these databases). An adequate communications gateway is, of course, necessary so that the executive can access these data.

Broad-Based Computing Capabilities

Usually, executives do not have a strong need for modeling tools. Because executive decision making is less structured than that taking place at lower levels of the organization, their decision environments are more difficult to model. Also, since executives spend most of their time considering broad matters—for instance, pondering direction and dealing with competitors' strategies—they are generally less directly involved with quantitative detail and analysis, which is delegated to staff. Thus, most of their computing needs are relatively simple. Such tasks as information retrieval, spreadsheeting, and graph generation usually top the list of executive computing needs.

Exceptional Ease of Learning and Use

In most organizations, the time of executives is considered more valuable than that of any other worker. Hence, the support systems that cater to executives should reflect this. For instance, since presentation graphics can communicate information much more rapidly than can tabular data, a strong and easy-to-use graphics generator is a helpful tool in many executive information systems. Also, any issues dealing with the user interface become more worthy of close scrutiny; for instance, the ease of use of any command language, the availability of pointing devices and graphical user interfaces, fast response time, customized front-ends, non-cryptic error handling, and so on.

Customization

Because an executive's time is so precious relative to other employees, and the decisions made by executives are so critical to an organization's livelihood, special care must be given to the design of each EIS. Often, this means tailoring the basic model of an EIS to meet the special needs of each executive who wants to use it. For instance, if a million-dollar-a-year executive needs frequent, fast access to an internal financial database—data that might take the average employee ten instructions to access—it is usually worth assigning a programmer to write a special macro that enables the executive to access this data with only one or two keystrokes.

Commercially Available EIS Products

Many EIS generators—EIS development packages—are commercially available. Commander EIS (from Comshare, Inc.), Command Center (from Pilot Executive Software), Executive Edge (from Execucom Systems Corporation), and Express EIS (from Information Resources, Inc.) are among the market leaders in the U.S. RESOLVE is another leading product, especially in Europe.

Studies on EIS implementation show that thousands of companies have implemented executive information systems. Usually, the executive information systems provide executives with access to financial data, marketing and sales information, human resources information, manufacturing data, and competitive/strategic information. Electronic mail, access to external news and databases, word processing, spreadsheet, and automated filing capabilities are also common in business executive information systems. While it is often expensive to develop and maintain an EIS, many organizations feel that enhanced top-level decision making is a benefit that more than balances out any costs associated with the system.

SUMMARY

A decision support system (DSS) provides managers with the tools to assist them in making semistructured and unstructured decisions in their own way. In addition to focusing on semistructured and unstructured decisions, decision support systems facilitate outputs that are not predefined and that are easy to use.

Structured decisions are those that can be made easily from a given set of inputs. Semistructured and unstructured decisions, however, are those for which information obtained from a computer system is, at most, only a portion of the total needed for sound decision making.

DSS outputs are not predefined because managers do not always know in advance the types of information they will need. Besides, even if managers did know these types of information, their information needs constantly change. Thus, flexibility in a DSS is of paramount importance. Decision support systems must also be easy to learn because the users are not computer professionals. Other common properties found in decision support systems are fast response, a high degree of user control and interaction, interactive display technology, and the use of models.

The components of a DSS are the DSS generator, the model management system, the database management system, and the dialogue management system. The DSS generator is the software that is used to develop the DSS and coordinate its processing tasks. The model management system makes it possible to create, maintain, and apply the mathematical and analytical models that are used by the decision maker. The database management system enables users to create, maintain, and interrogate DSS databases and to extract data from both internal and external databases as necessary. The dialogue manager provides the interface between the user and the other DSS components; typically, the interface is interactive and flexible.

Four common tasks performed by decision support systems are information retrieval, data reconfiguration, calculator activities, and analysis. Information retrieval in a DSS environment usually refers to extracting information from a database or from data files in order to make a decision. Two types of retrieval are selection and projection.

Decision support systems also reconfigure data into forms other than the way they are logically represented in the computer system. They do this by enabling users to sort, exchange fields, join data, and use presentation graphics.

A DSS also enables users to perform calculator activities—a set of tasks that is normally done with a calculator. Such activities are implemented either by having the user write out a complete formula or by having him or her summon a function resident in the DSS. Functions are prestored formulas that perform calculator-type tasks.

A DSS is performing analysis when it allows users to review facts and draw conclusions based on those facts. Four types of DSS analysis tools or techniques are widely used. Statistical tools enable users to perform a variety of statistical operations on data, including regression analysis and correlation analysis. Optimizing tools are mathematical modeling tools that recommend certain choices to a decision maker. What-if analysis is a non-probabilistic technique that enables a user to reformulate a problem repeatedly, with different values for problem parameters, in the process of getting useful information. Artificial intelligence (AI) routines also improve the usefulness of the analysis function. One such routine is why analysis, a technique that enables the user to ask the DSS why something happened.

Under a framework proposed by R. H. Sprague and E. D. Carlson, DSS products are classified as specific decision support systems, DSS generators, or DSS tools. A specific DSS allows decision makers to handle a specific problem or set of related problems. A DSS generator is a package of related hardware and software that allows the user to quickly and easily build a specific DSS. A DSS tool refers to hardware, software, procedure, or data elements that enable decision makers to build either a specific DSS or a DSS generator.

Numerous software tools can be used to build decision support systems, including database management systems, spreadsheets, and modeling packages. Database management systems are most useful for information retrieval; spreadsheets, for simple types of analysis and reports. Modeling packages enable users to construct complex quantitative algorithms.

Users must interact with a DSS through a hardware/software interface called the user interface. The software part of the interface typically involves issuing commands, filling in templates, and/or making physical model modifications. Commands can be either typed in or pointed to. A template is a prelabeled screen that must be filled in with data.

Group decision support systems (GDSS) are decision support systems that support the decision-making activities of work groups. Many of the components of a GDSS resemble similar components in traditional decision support systems. A GDSS is composed of a model base, a GDSS processor, a dialogue manager, a database system, and special software known as groupware. Groupware enables group members to simultaneously work on the same word-processing document, do group what-if analysis on a spreadsheet, and perform other cooperative tasks such as generating and evaluating alternative solutions to a problem.

Group decision support systems may be configured in several ways. In decision room configurations, all GDSS technology in located in the same room; decision makers come to the room to use the GDSS. GDSS technology is distributed to group member offices or work areas in LAN GDSS configurations. When group member offices are geographically dispersed, a WAN GDSS configuration may be used. Numerous remotely distributed decision rooms can be electronically linked in the videoconferencing configuration.

Group decision support systems should be easy to use and should provide users with both general and specific decision support. A well-designed GDSS also facilitates productive behavior among group members and helps to suppress counterproductive behaviors.

An executive information system (EIS) is a DSS designed to meet the special needs of executives. Executives are people at or near the top of an organizational hierarchy who exert a strong influence on the course taken by the organization. These usually include the board of directors, the president or chief executive officer (CEO), and various vice-presidents.

Most executive decisions involve strategic planning, tactical planning, and fire-fighting activities. They also involve exerting some control over the organization in order to ensure that plans are implemented. Executive information comes from three main data sources: transaction processing data, internal projections, and external data.

Executive decisions are generally broad, and based to a large extent on intuition. These characteristics are reflected in the executive decision-making environment, which is itself characterized by a lack of structure, a high degree of uncertainty, a future orientation, use of informal sources, and a low level of detail.

To meet these challenges, executive information systems commonly have the following properties: an external environment focus, a strategic-planning capability, ease of learning and use, and custom tailoring to meet the unique needs of individual executives. A number of EIS software packages are commercially available. Executive information systems should become more prevalent during the 1990s.

KEY TERMS

Analysis

Decision support system (DSS)

DSS generator

DSS tool

Executive

Function

Group decision support system (GDSS)

Modeling package

Specific DSS

User interface

Why analysis

REVIEW

REVIEW QUESTIONS

1. How do decision support systems differ from management reporting systems?

2. How do structured, unstructured, and semistructured decisions differ?

3. How are the mathematical models mentioned in Chapter 3 related to decision support systems?

4. What are the characteristics of each component of a DSS? What functions are performed by each of these components?

5. What types of processing tasks are normally performed by decision support systems?

6. What is the role of presentation graphics in a DSS?

7. Identify several statistical tools that could be used in building or using a DSS.

8. What is what-if analysis and why is it particularly useful in decision support environments?

9. What are the differences among a specific DSS, a DSS generator, and a DSS tool? Provide several examples of each.

10. Why is it difficult in some cases to distinguish a modeling software package from a spreadsheet package?

11. What different types of interfaces might DSS users encounter?

12. What are the similarities and differences between decision support systems and group decision support systems? What are the goals of group decision support systems ?

13. How might a GDSS be configured?

14. How do executive information systems differ from decision support systems ?

15. Identify the types of executive information and the properties that characterize them.

16. Describe the capabilities of executive information systems.

DISCUSSION QUESTIONS

1. *Business Week* quotes the president of a large insurance company in Texas as saying of the decision support in his organization, "You can get so much [expletive deleted] information with them that you can get into the trees and forest stuff." The chief operating officer at an electronic components plant in Illinois, who tried three different decision support systems over a six-year period and got rid of them all, reports, "I found out you need a lot of familiarity with the machine to do things beyond the very simple. It is cheaper and more efficient to hire an expensive assistant who can do that." Please comment.

2. The term "decision support system" is commonly abused in practice, often being applied to virtually any type of system that provides some sort of decision-making data. Why do you think this is? Do you think the definition of a DSS will change in the future? Why or why not?

3. Many people feel that pointing mechanisms and graphical user interfaces are becoming standard items in most decision support systems. Why? Does this mean the end of written-command interfacing?

4. In what ways do executive information systems pose a threat to middle-level managers?

CASE STUDY

Fidelity Investment's EIS

Until recently, it took at least 10 employees to assemble the information needed to produce a critical 45-page report distributed each week to its senior financial staff. They had to gather the data, merge spreadsheets, and rely on "sneaker-net" to pull the information together. Now, most of the data are available on-line in the company's new Windows-based executive information system (EIS) and most of the legwork done by the 10 employees is history.

The EIS changed the way that Fidelity's executives access vital operational data. Instead of pasting together reports for general distribution from data stored in diverse databases, analysts and managers now use the EIS to access the information on-line via networked microcomputers. Now, there is no need to produce printed reports; each assembled report can be electronically transmitted to more than 100 EIS users.

Fidelity has prided itself on its commitment to investing in information technology to help it compete in volatile financial markets, both domestic and global. Fidelity Investments manages more than 60 mutual funds, including the Magellan—the largest American mutual fund. The company handles more than $165 billion in customer accounts and the investment decisions it makes have a major impact on both domestic and international stock exchanges.

Understandably, creating an EIS replete with the data access, modeling tools, and report generation facilities capable of assisting executive decision making was no small feat. The new system, called FAMIS (Financial Management and Management Information System) allows point-and-shoot access data. By clicking on an icon, the needed data are extracted. The data can then be manipulated by using a spreadsheet program (Excel) or the EIS modeling programs. The results can be saved in a variety of formats.

Reactions to the new system are positive. Analysts and financial managers indicate that they appreciate having access to data that are always fresh and relevant. They also have better faith in their projections and feel that they are able to adjust more rapidly to changes in the stock market—a critical advantage in the financial services area.

The MIS staff intends to continually add more features to Fidelity's EIS. Albert Niemi, Fidelity's director of distributed systems development and EIS project leader, is particularly interested in improving the ad hoc query capabilities. Says Niemi, "For example, the cash flow report might not have information right now about the number of new accounts sold for the Magellan fund, but we'd like to give the financial manager the ability to extract that data. In the past, it might have taken the IS department a week to produce that information, or it might not have been available at all."

Adapted from Amirrezvani (1992).

DISCUSSION

1. What are the advantages and disadvantages of executive information systems?
2. Why is it particularly difficult to design an EIS for an investment company like Fidelity?
3. What types of external data should Fidelity's EIS be able to access?
4. How is Fidelity's EIS likely to help it compete?

Chapter

Knowledge-Based Systems

After completing this chapter, you will be able to:

Define artificial intelligence

Discuss the main areas of AI research

Describe the components of an expert system

Provide examples of the use of expert systems in business

Describe the process used to develop expert systems

Describe some of the limitations of expert systems

Describe the characteristics of neural networks and how they are used by organizations

The term "artificial intelligence" connotes a futuristic world that is still over the horizon—a world populated by androids and computers such as HAL, the processor in the movie *2001: A Space Odyssey.* Although many researchers in the field of artificial intelligence do perceive such a world as an attainable reality, most successful efforts in artificial intelligence today are much less ambitious. This led some people to argue that the term "artificial intelligence" may be a poor one, since it connotes a capability that is today impossible to deliver.

In this chapter, we will explore the evolution of the artificial intelligence field and examine in depth the component of artificial intelligence with perhaps the greatest impact on MIS: expert systems. In doing this, we look at why expert systems and other knowledge-based systems are needed, how they work, how they differ from conventional computer-based applications, and what are some of their inherent limitations. We also examine some examples of knowledge-based systems found in practice.

Although knowledge-based systems are most closely associated with decision support functions, they are applicable to virtually any area under the MIS umbrella—including transaction processing systems, management reporting systems, and office systems.

ARTIFICIAL INTELLIGENCE

A computer is a device that, given some instructions, can perform work at extremely fast speeds by drawing upon a large memory. It can also be programmed to draw certain types of conclusions on the basis of the input it receives or the results of computations it performs. A good deal of human mental activity involves these same processes. For this reason, the abilities that can be imparted to computers to enable them to display intelligent, human-like behavior is commonly referred to as artificial intelligence (AI).

Evolution of AI

The term "artificial intelligence" was coined in the mid-1950s by John McCarthy at a conference at Dartmouth College. One of the features of that conference was a software processor that manipulated symbols instead of numbers (as such language processors as LISP and Prolog do today). Developers claimed that the processor, which proved several mathematical theorems, possessed a certain amount of "artificial intelligence."

As AI evolved, it was put to work solving a number of tasks. For instance, it continued to be used in the field of mathematics to prove theorems and to solve complex problems. In the field of gaming, researchers developed AI programs to play and win at tic-tac-toe, checkers, and chess. At the Massachusetts Institute of Technology (MIT), one researcher, Joseph Weizenbaum, created a psychiatry "expert" named Eliza, who would listen to the woes of human patients and diagnose their mental ills. Since the types of tasks performed by the programs involved in these applications required human intelligence, most people assumed that such programs possessed artificial intelligence.

This assumption was not always accurate, however. For instance, some of the early chess programs relied more on the brute force of the computer than they did on methods of intelligence. Many of these programs would calculate the effects of thousands of moves and countermoves and make their recommendations based on what appeared to be the best of these. But this is not usually the way that human chess players think. The chess experts instead rely on intuitive rules of thumb—called *heuristics*—to base their moves. One widely used heuristic, for instance, is to control the center of the chess board. As chess programs incorporated these heuristics, they truly embodied artificial intelligence techniques. Better yet, they improved dramatically, rivaling humans at the expert-level class in chess.

The exact definition of artificial intelligence is still hotly debated. Certainly, a lot of systems appear at first glance to fall under the general category of artificial intelligence—such as the early, brute force chess-playing programs that really display very little human-like intelligence. Two cornerstones of intelligent behavior are the ability to understand natural languages and the ability to reason. It follows, then, that computer systems providing capabilities in these areas, at a performance level that would be regarded as intelligent if observed in humans, should be considered AI-based systems. Thus, in this text we will consider **artificial intelligence (AI)** as a capability in computer systems to provide a level of performance that reflects human-like intelligence. Later, we will look at some technical characteristics that distinguish knowledge-based systems from conventional computer programs.

AI Applications

Today, the five main areas of AI research are expert systems, natural languages, vision systems, robotics, and neural networks, as Figure 11.1 illustrates.

Expert Systems

Expert systems are software systems that imitate the reasoning processes of human experts and provide decision makers with the type of advice they would normally receive from such human experts. For instance, an expert system in the area of investment portfolio management might ask its user a number of specific questions relating to investments for a particular client. How does the client feel about risk versus growth? How much can be invested? Does the client refuse to invest in any particular companies? Does the client have any preferences regarding specific types of securities? And so on. As each question is posed interactively to the user, and after each user responds, the expert system dynamically formulates the next question to be asked, until a suitable

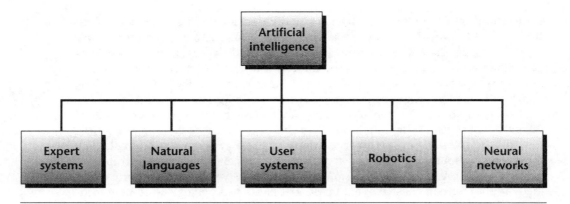

Figure 11.1 Areas of artificial intelligence (AI). While AI already influences the activities of some of today's managers, most industry observers feel that its effects will be more profound and widespread in the future.

portfolio is recommended. In reaching the decision, the system draws from an enormous database of stock descriptions and histories, research reports, and economic forecasts. The user involved here may be either a professional investment adviser or the actual client. The investment advisor may be using the expert system to uncover possibilities that he or she would never have imagined when advising the client.

A number of expert system application areas in business are listed in Figure 11.2. We will cover several current and proposed business-related application areas in depth later in the chapter. Most of the success in expert systems has been in rather narrow, specific areas; for instance, diagnostics in the medical field or advice in the tax-planning area. Less success has been achieved in developing highly generalized expert systems that are useful in all application areas.

Natural Languages

The area of **natural-language systems** involves using the computer to communicate with users in natural languages such as English, Spanish, French, or Chinese. Although it is relatively easy for the computer to provide natural-language output, input is much more difficult. For instance, although the definitions of words can be stored in a dictionary, the way in which combinations of words—or sentences—convey meaning is rather complex. Also, people often misuse words or use them in strange contexts. And even when humans finish communicating an idea or an intention, it is not always clear what they are trying to say.

Progress in natural-language interfaces has been somewhat slow, but nonetheless fruitful in some areas. The momentum for the development of such systems has increased in recent years. A few software products that allow users to issue natural-language commands are listed in Figure 11.3. As you can see, to

BUSINESS APPLICATIONS OF EXPERT SYSTEMS	
Accounting and Finance	
▪ Providing tax advice and assistance	▪ Selecting forecasting models
▪ Helping with credit-authorization decisions	▪ Providing investment advice
Marketing	
▪ Establishing sales quotas	▪ Assisting with marketing timing decisions
▪ Responding to customer inquiries	▪ Determining discount policies
▪ Referring problems to telemarketing centers	
Manufacturing	
▪ Determining whether a process is running correctly	▪ Scheduling job-shop tasks
▪ Analyzing quality and providing corrective measures	▪ Selecting transportation routes
	▪ Assisting with product design and facility layouts
▪ Maintaining facilities	
Personnel	
▪ Assessing applicant qualifications	▪ Giving employees assistance at filling out forms
General Business	
▪ Assisting with project proposals	▪ Educating trainees
▪ Recommending acquisition strategies	▪ Evaluating performance

Figure 11.2 Examples of business applications of expert systems. The number and variety of these and other knowledge-based systems increase every year.

date, many of the natural-language applications have concerned database queries and report generation.

Vision Systems

Vision systems are computer systems performing tasks that could, at one time, only be done through the use of the human eye. They often work through a technique called pattern recognition. For example, vision systems are commonly used today to inspect parts of subassemblies for defects. Such a system has a number of image patterns of defects stored in a database, and it consults these to determine whether the item being inspected is defective. This task is not as simple as it seems. Storing, accessing, and comparing a large number of images is difficult. Also, in some systems, if the item being inspected is tilted the wrong way, it has to be reoriented so that it is identifiable by the vision software.

NATURAL-LANGUAGE SYSTEMS AND APPLICATIONS

Product	Vendor	Description
Clout	Microrim, Inc.	Natural-language interface for Microrim's System V and R:Base 5000 database systems
Eliza	Artificial Intelligence Research	Natural-language interaction with a "psychotherapist"
EnQuery	Datamate Co.	Natural-language interface for COBOL report-writing applications
EQL (English Query Language)	Information Builders Inc.	Natural-language interface for PC/Focus
Guru	MDBS Inc.	Natural-language interface combined with database management, text processing, spreadsheet, graphics, 4GL, and communications capabilities
HAL	Lotus Development Corporation	Natural-language interface for Lotus 1-2-3
IA (Intelligent Assistant)	Symantec	Natural-language interface for Q&A integrated software package
K-Chat	MDBS Inc.	Natural-language interface for KnowledgeMan database system
Natural Language	DEC	Natural-language interface to direct marketing database
NLQ (Natural Language Query)	Battelle	Natural-language interface for Oracle and DB2
PC-IQ	Solutions, Inc.	Natural-language interface that converts natural-language commands to DOS
Prolog-86	Solution Systems	Programming language for creating natural-language interfaces
Ramis II English	On-Line Software	Natural-language interface for Ramis II application generator
SAS/English	SAS Institute	Natural-language interface for querying and reporting data from SAS data sets and external sources
Savvy	Excalibur Technologies Corp.	Natural-language-based database system
Voice Navigator	Articulate Systems Corporation	Natural-language interface that allows users to attach verbal notes to reports

Figure 11.3 Examples of natural-language systems and applications.

Robotics

Robotics is the field of artificial intelligence concerned with the design, manufacture, and implementation of robots. Robots are computer-controlled devices that mimic the motor activity of human beings.

Robots have been used in a wide variety of areas, with probably the greatest success in manufacturing. There, they perform jobs that are considered too dan-

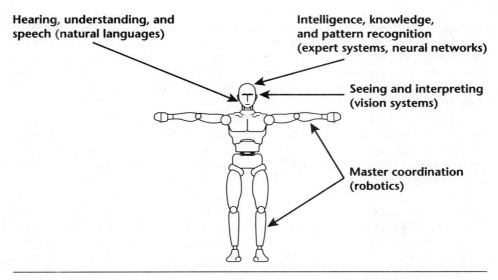

Hearing, understanding, and speech (natural languages)

Intelligence, knowledge, and pattern recognition (expert systems, neural networks)

Seeing and interpreting (vision systems)

Master coordination (robotics)

Figure 11.4 The ultimate AI product—an android. Such a product will be the beneficiary of the labors of all five AI areas—expert systems, natural languages, vision systems, robotics, and neural networks.

gerous, strenuous, monotonous, or expensive for humans to do. And often, robots can perform these jobs faster and better. For instance, IBM claims that the printer for its new line of PS/2 computers is more reliable due to robot manufacturing. Virtually no human hands touch these printers as they evolve from parts, to assembly, to testing, and finally to packaging. Robots are used in a variety of other settings: manufacturing cars, dipping parts into dangerous chemicals, spraying paints, mining coal, and so on. In Japan, they are even used to prepare sushi.

Although it may seem that many of these robots are "dumb," they are often aided by the other AI techniques—expert systems, natural languages, and vision systems—to identify objects and states in their environments so they can act accordingly. The ultimate AI product, of course, will be a robot that is virtually indistinguishable from a human being—the android of science fiction fame (see Figure 11.4). That, of course, is still far from realization. Even the androids popularized by the film industry (for example, 3CPO of *Star Wars*) and television (such as Commander Data on "Star Trek: The Next Generation") are roles filled by human actors.

Neural Networks

Perhaps the greatest amount of recent AI development is in the area of neural networks. **Neural networks** are knowledge-based computer systems that emulate the human brain's pattern recognition process. Neural-net systems aren't preprogrammed to provide predicable responses like conventional algorithms, even those found in expert systems; instead, they are designed to "learn" by observation and repetition. Some of the neural nets developed are software programs that work on conventional computers. Several organizations, however, developed hardware-based neural nets that often use parallel processing and interconnected nodes to simulate how the human nervous system works. Examples of business applications of neural networks can be found in the box on page 501— as well as in the more detailed discussion of neural networks later in this chapter.

This overview of AI's major categories should help you appreciate the variety of ways in which knowledge-based systems impact organizations and managers. Throughout the rest of this chapter, we will take a more thorough look at two of these AI categories: expert systems and neural networks. We will first examine why organizations and managers are so interested in expert systems. We then turn to some more technical issues, including the components of expert systems, how expertise is captured and represented, and how these systems are developed. Next, we will consider several specific examples of business applications of expert systems, how expert systems differ from conventional systems, and what some of their limitations are. In the final section of this chapter, we will look at neural networks and how these differ from expert systems. We will also discuss several specific examples of how organizations use neural networks.

THE NEED FOR EXPERT SYSTEMS

Expert labor is expensive and scarce. Knowledge workers—employees who routinely work with data and information to carry out their day-to-day duties— account for close to half of business's labor bill. The "stars"—the sharpest and most knowledgeable workers—are not easy to find and keep, and companies are often faced with a shortage of talent in key positions. Moreover, no matter how bright or knowledgeable certain people are, they often can handle only a few factors at a time. Both the limitations imposed by human information processing capability and the rushed pace at which business is conducted today put a practical limit on the quality of human decision making.

In order to maintain a competitive edge, companies need to hone the decision-making skills of the personnel they currently have. The following are a number of ways that expert systems might help in this (adapted from John F. Magee):

- You manage a firm that bids on numerous projects; most of them are unique. You have a lot of background data on competitors and their bidding strategies, potential sources of delays, and so forth. Experienced project managers could use these data to arrive at sound bidding strategies; however, you have no experienced managers in your firm. An expert system could capture the lines of thinking of a first-rate project manager, combining competitor data, data about the target project, and data about your firm's tendencies toward risk, pricing, and contracting. Thus, the expert system could provide decision support to inexperienced managers and guide them through the bidding process.

Benefits of Expert Systems

- Preserves knowledge that might be lost through retirement, resignation, or death of an acknowledged company expert

- Puts information into an active form so it can be summoned almost as a real-life expert might be summoned

- Assists novices in thinking the way experienced professionals do

- Is not subject to such human failings as fatigue, being too busy, or being emotional

- Can be effectively used as a strategic tool in the areas of marketing products, cutting costs, and improving products

Figure 11.5 Benefits of expert systems. The benefits cited above can help organizations lower costs, increase sales, increase productivity, and provide better service. Significant competitive advantage can also result from the appropriate application and use of expert systems.

- You are a life insurance agent. Your market has changed in recent years and you now compete with banks, brokerage houses, money-market fund managers, and a host of other new players, in addition to other life insurance agents. Your firm is pushing a variety of new products—universal life insurance and venture capital funds, for instance—with which you are not completely familiar. Also, your clients are becoming more inquisitive and sophisticated, and many of the questions you field seem to require a specialist in both tax and financial planning. An expert system could be used to great advantage here to build sophisticated, knowledge-based, tax- and financial-planning support systems to provide agents with a competitive edge when handling inquisitive clients.

- Your firm sells complex, custom-built products that are assembled mostly from standard components. Frequently, orders are changed as a product is being built. Because the products are complex, the changed specifications called in by a customer often do not agree with other specifications that are still in place. These discrepancies can be caught by a sharp engineer, but few engineers are knowledgeable enough about all phases of product assembly to notice subtle irregularities. Also, identifying an error and resolving it take time. An expert system could be used productively here to check new specifications to ensure that they are both internally consistent and fit with other product specifications.

Figure 11.5 gives a summary of the benefits that expert systems provide to the organization. As Figure 11.5 indicates, expert systems help to preserve expertise, make expertise available on demand, and help novices learn how experts tackle complex problems. They can also be used for strategic or competitive advantage.

Still, expert systems are not always the answer to managerial or organizational problems. They may not be appropriate in all situations. Some of the properties that potential applications should possess to qualify for expert system development are summarized in Figure 11.6. When the conditions specified

Expert System Suitability Criteria	
▪ Availability	One or more experts are capable of communicating how they go about solving the problems to which the expert system will be applied.
▪ Complexity	Solution of the problems for which the expert system will be used is a complex task that requires logical inference processing, which would not be easily handled by conventional information processing.
▪ Domain	The domain, or subject area, of the problem is relatively small and limited to a relatively well-defined problem area.
▪ Expertise	Solutions to the problem require the efforts of experts. That is, only a few people possess the knowledge, techniques, and intuition needed.
▪ Structure	The solution process must be able to cope with ill-structured, uncertain, missing, and conflicting data, and a dynamic problem-solving situation.

Figure 11.6 Factors to consider when determining if an expert system should be developed in a potential application area.

in Figure 11.6 are satisfied, a proposed expert system has the potential to positively contribute to organizational functioning. If these conditions are not satisfied, managerial caution about expert system development is warranted.

COMPONENTS OF AN EXPERT SYSTEM

Technically, knowledge can be represented in several ways in an expert system: through rule-based systems, frame-based systems, predicate-based systems, and other representation schemes. Rule-based systems are, by far, the most common in practice; those are the types of systems that we explore here.

The components of a **rule-based expert system** are shown in Figure 11.7. In the following subsections, we describe the purposes of each of these software and data components, as well as the roles of experts, knowledge engineers, and users in developing and working on these systems.

Knowledge Base

At the center of any rule-based expert system is its **knowledge base**, which contains specific facts about the expert area and rules that the expert system will use to make decisions based on those facts. The knowledge base represents the total available data bank for the expert system; it consists primarily of facts and rules (see Figure 11.8). The expert system's inference engine (discussed later) draws from the knowledge base to reach conclusions.

The **rules** in the knowledge base are usually coded in the form

    IF X THEN Y

where X is a condition and Y is an action to be taken if the condition is true. For example, if a company policy states that credit is to be automatically authorized only if a customer's total outstanding balance does not exceed $1,000 and the

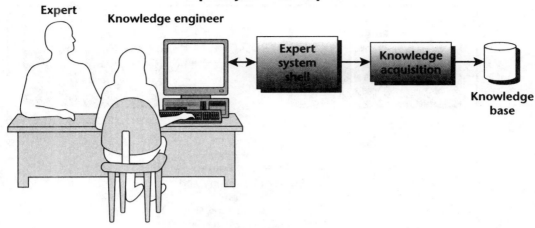

Expert System Development

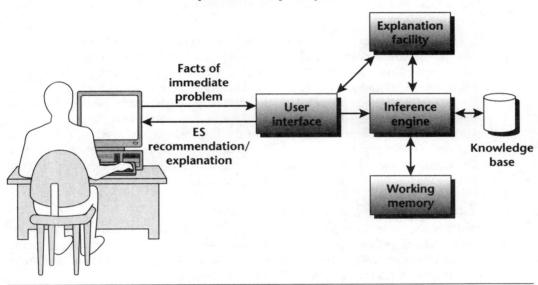

Operational Expert System

Figure 11.7 The main components of an expert system.

customer has made no more that two credit purchases already today, the policy can be coded into the following rules:

Rule 1: Authorize credit if total customer balance after transaction will be less than or equal to $1,000.

Rule 2: Authorize credit if customer has made not more than two credit purchases already today.

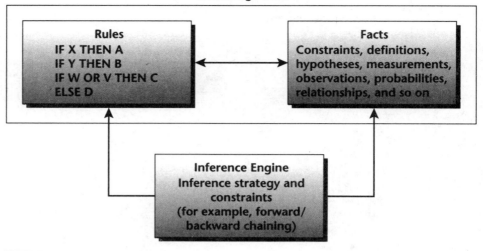

Figure 11.8 An illustration of the components of the knowledge base in a rule-based expert system.

Some of the facts in the knowledge base that are applied to these rules are the names and account numbers of current credit customers, the current outstanding balances and credit limits of each of these customers, proposed purchase amounts, and a list of lost or stolen cards.

One of the biggest frontiers in the knowledge-base area is the use of *multiple domains* of expertise—that is, the use of more than one knowledge base. For instance, the example provided earlier of the insurance agent needing both expert tax and financial advice is a good candidate for an expert system with two knowledge bases. With such a system, a set of rules must be developed to bridge the knowledge bases and resolve any conflicts.

Fuzzy Logic

Still another frontier is in the area of *fuzzy logic*. Most expert systems today are only capable of dealing with "binary logic"—yes or no, true or false. If expert systems are to truly incorporate human thinking patterns, they must handle such imprecise terms as "most," "many," or "some."

Fuzzy logic is the brainchild of Lofti A. Zedah, a retired computer science professor from the University of California at Berkeley. Larry Armstrong cites Zedah as saying, "Fuzzy logic accepts the fact that 99.9% of human reasoning is not precise, and it tries to conform to it." Organizations are finding that for some applications, fuzzy logic can provide better and higher quality results than traditional approaches. Fuzzy logic appliances and business applications have been popular among Japanese manufacturers for awhile, but have only recently become popular with U.S. companies. Ford Motor Company, for example, is developing a fuzzy logic system to keep a car's engine running smoothly under changing conditions. Whirlpool Corporation uses fuzzy logic to regulate

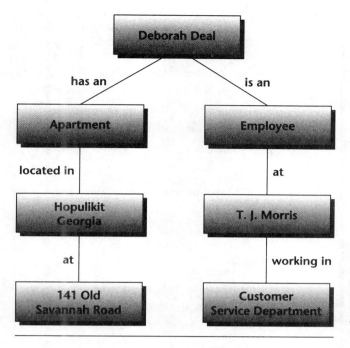

Figure 11.9 An example of a semantic network. This example demonstrates the relationship between items in a knowledge base that contains information on the individual Deborah Deal.

defrost cycles in its latest refrigerators. General Electric is pushing to use fuzzy logic to regulate jet-aircraft engines, save water in home appliances, and drive 200-ton rollers in steel mills. According to Larry Armstrong, Piero P. Bonissone, a computer scientist at GE's research and development center, says that appliance controls will be first because "it takes a shorter time to implement them, and there's a faster payoff."

Representing Knowledge and Expertise

One of the ways in which facts, knowledge, and relationships between facts can be stored in the knowledge base is by the development of *semantic networks*—a collection of linked facts, items, or nodes. Figure 11.9 shows an example of a semantic network.

Frames may also be used to capture and store knowledge in a knowledge base. *Frames* essentially develop relationships among facts about a specific object or entity. For all practical purposes, a frame is an "object" used in an expert system context—much of the current object-oriented technology is derived from earlier AI experiences with frames. However, since these are often discussed in the literature as being different knowledge-representation approaches, we will briefly discuss each of them.

Frames consist of "slots" in which facts about the entity are entered. Frames that share similar characteristics (for example, where the information in slots is identical for two or more entities) can be related to one another. Frames and relationships between frames are illustrated in Figure 11.10.

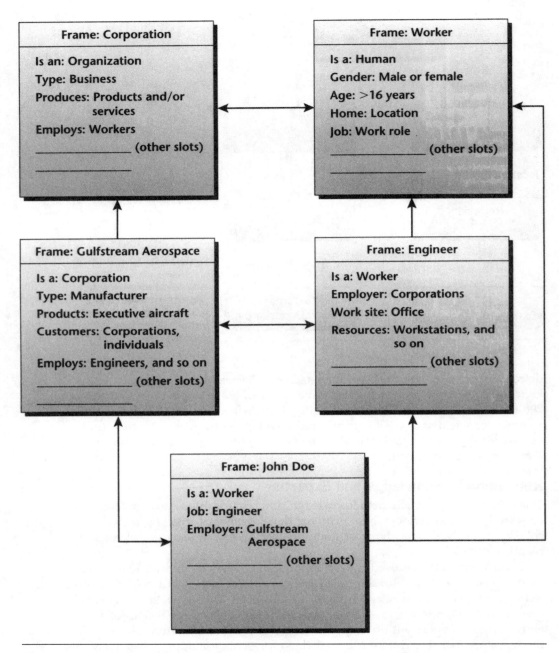

Figure 11.10 An example of a frame-based expert system knowledge base. The information in the "slots" in frames is used to interrelate frames.

Objects are a final, yet emerging, way of representing knowledge in the knowledge base of an expert system. Previously in the text, we described object-oriented programming (OOP) and object-oriented databases (OODB). Software is now available that enables programmers to develop *object-oriented expert systems*. In these systems, an *object* consists of data values used to describe the attributes of an entity, as well as the operations that can be performed upon the data. The development and use of object-oriented expert systems should expand dramatically during the remainder the 1990s.

Inference Engine

The **inference engine** is the system of programs that drives the expert system. The role of the inference engine in the overall expert system was depicted in Figures 11.7 and 11.8. These programs consult the knowledge base as they seek answers. In essence, the inference engine applies the facts and rules in the knowledge base(s) to the data about the problem supplied by users.

Inference engines operate with either a forward-chaining or backward-chaining mechanism; some operate with both. A **forward-chaining** mechanism first examines the knowledge base and the problem at hand; then, it attempts to discover a solution. For instance, a medical expert system may be used to examine a patient's symptoms and provide a diagnosis. Based on the symptomology, the expert system might locate several diseases that the patient may have. With **backward chaining**, on the other hand, the inference engine starts with a hypothesis or goal (such procedures are often called goal-driven inferential processes), which it then checks against the facts and rules in the knowledge base for consistency. So, for instance, the expert system might be given the goal to "find this patient's disease(s) and would work back from there, asking questions as necessary to confirm or refute candidate diagnoses."

Knowledge Acquisition Subsystem

The **knowledge acquisition subsystem** is the software component of an expert system that enables the **knowledge engineer**, a specialized systems analyst responsible for designing and maintaining the expert system, to build and refine an expert system's knowledge base. The knowledge engineer works with the knowledge acquisition subsystem to model decision logic, derive heuristics, and update the knowledge base.

In the past, when expert systems were written in traditional programming languages, one of the most difficult and time-consuming tasks associated with developing an expert system was creating and updating the knowledge base. Each fact, each relationship between facts, and each rule had to be programmed into the knowledge base; each change to the knowledge base also had to be programmed. Often, professional programmers were needed to perform these chores.

Now, knowledge base development and maintenance can be done using special, reasonably user-friendly software. This software provides a convenient and efficient means of capturing and storing the contents of the knowledge base. Users are often presented with easy-to-operate menus and templates for entering rules, facts, and relationships among facts. Once these are entered, the software correctly stores the information in the knowledge base. Such software makes it much easier and less expensive to develop, update, and refine the knowledge base.

User Interface

Users often interact with the expert system through a user interface. In most instances, the expert system prompts (asks) the user to supply information about the problem and the user types in the requested data. The data entered are examined by the inference engine and compared to the facts, rules, and relationships in the knowledge base. This examination and comparison process results in the system continuing to prompt the user for more information until the system has enough data about the current problem so that it can reach a conclusion. Thus the user interface for an expert system is highly interactive.

Another component of the user interface enables users and decision makers to design, create, and update an expert system. This component also is typically interactive and often provides users with menus and templates.

Ideally, the user interface should enable the user (decision maker) to communicate with the expert system in his or her own natural language—English, French, Japanese, or whatever—without needing to learn rigid, programming language syntax. However, as pointed out earlier in the text, **natural-language interfaces** are still in their infancy, but are expected to become more common in expert systems (and other information technology applications) in the years ahead.

Explanation Facility

After users supply information about the current problem-solving situation, the expert system reaches a conclusion and/or makes a recommendation (which can be output to a screen, printer, or storage device) about what should be done. In many instances, users are also interested in knowing the line of reasoning followed by the expert system in drawing conclusions. If this line of reasoning seems faulty to the user, the conclusions reached by the expert system may be considered invalid. The **explanation facility** communicates to a user the logic followed in reaching a decision and, in some cases, may also attempt to explain the importance of certain information inputs. Also, if the expert system cannot draw a conclusion, it should display what it has uncovered and let human experts use these facts to their advantage.

DEVELOPING EXPERT SYSTEMS

Like most computer systems, expert systems are developed by using a systematic development approach. Figure 11.11 provides a generic development process for expert systems. This approach starts with determining the requirements for the expert system (that is, what information it should provide to decision makers), then moves on to acquiring the knowledge to be put in the expert system's knowledge base from human experts. The third step involves constructing the components of the expert system; this results in an *expert system prototype*. The fourth step involves testing, debugging, and refining the system until the requirements determined during step one are met. The result of this fourth step is an *operational expert system*, which can make or assist in making decisions. To be useful over the long run, the expert system must be updated and maintained; this may involve adding new rules and facts to the knowledge base, making it possible to extract data or processing results from other parts of the organization's computer-based information system (CBIS), refining the inference engine, or improving the user interface or explanation facility.

One of the major challenges faced by knowledge engineers during the expert system development process is the acquisition of knowledge from human experts. Human expertise is developed over many years, and it is often difficult for experts to explain the reasoning processes that they used to attack and solve complex problems. Numerous research efforts are currently trying to determine effective ways of extracting human expertise in a form that can be used by knowledge engineers to develop expert systems.

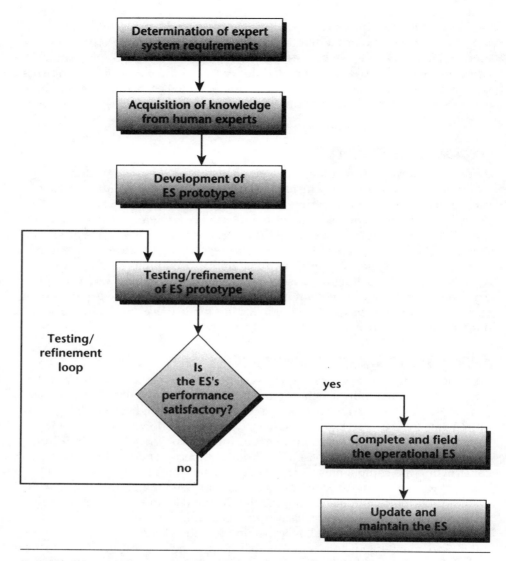

Figure 11.11 A summary of the steps in the expert system development and maintenance process. After the initial prototype is developed, several testing/refinement iterations may be performed before the operational expert system is put in the field and used.

In practice, three approaches are commonly used to develop the inference engine and other components of the expert system: the custom-built system, the expert system shell, and the expert system application package.

■ *Custom-built system* The first, and often the most expensive, approach is to write—from scratch—an inference engine that is specifically tailored and dedicated to an application. This is traditionally done using an AI develop-

EXPERT SYSTEM SHELLS	
Product	**Vendor**
Aion Execution System	Aion Corp.
EXSYS	EXSYS, Inc.
1st-Class Fusion	1st Class Expert Systems
Guru	MDBS, Inc.
KBMS	A1Corp.
Knowledge Engineering Environment (KEE)	Intellicorp
Level 5	Information Builders Int'l.
Nexpert Object	Neuron Data
Personal Consultant	Texas Instruments
VP-Expert	WordTech Systems, Inc.

Figure 11.12 Examples of expert system shells.

ment language such as LISP or Prolog. The knowledge base and other components of the expert system are also coded in this language.

- ■ **Expert system shell** The second approach, which is very popular (especially in today's microcomputer-based expert systems), is to acquire a prewritten **expert system shell** program. A shell is a generalized expert system product without a knowledge base. Most expert system shells available in the market are generic and not tailored to specific application areas or to specific industries.

   The shell product typically contains a 4GL that will enable the knowledge engineer to develop the knowledge base. Figure 11.12 provides examples of some of the expert system shells on the market today.

   Several factors should be considered when selecting an expert system shell, including the hardware platform (for example, microcomputer, minicomputer, or mainframe) that the system will be developed and utilized on; ease of use; availability of suitable knowledge representation structures (such as frames or objects); availability of appropriate reasoning structures (for example, backward versus forward chaining); the efficiency of the system's "run time" performance (some shell products result in notoriously slow systems); how easy it is to maintain and refine the system; and the compatibility of the product with other components of the organization's CBIS.

- ■ **Application package** The third alternative is to buy a prewritten, off-the-shelf expert system application package and fine-tune it to meet the particular needs of the organization. Application packages differ from shell programs in that users can interact right away with the application package, supplying values to key parameters through question-and-answer sessions. Application packages may ultimately be the most appealing for business

EXPERT SYSTEM APPLICATION PACKAGES		
Vendor	**Product**	**Application Area**
Applied Expert Systems, Inc.	Planpower	Financial planning
Sterling Wentworth Corp.	PlanMan	Financial planning
Palladian Software, Inc.	Financial Advisor	Financial planning
Persoft, Inc.	More	Mailing list name qualification

Figure 11.13 Examples of some expert system application packages and their application areas.

users since, beyond the purchase cost, very little development time is needed. Figure 11.13 lists some of the commercially available expert system applications packages for business.

Once the expert system is developed and implemented, it must be maintained and updated. To properly maintain and update an expert system, users should provide feedback to knowledge engineers on their experiences with the expert system and its explanation facility. If the facility is delivering insufficient or inappropriate conclusions—or if the explanations are based on faulty reasoning processes—the knowledge engineer may have to either modify or add to the rules or facts in the knowledge base—or make changes in the other components of the expert system. Over time, the number of rules in the knowledge base may expand dramatically. For example, the earliest versions of MYCIN—an expert system used to assist in medical diagnosis—contained about 5,000 rules. In its current version, the rule base is over 100,000 rules and the number of illnesses that can be diagnosed also increased (for example, new diseases such as AIDS and lyme disease were added to the knowledge base).

PUTTING EXPERT SYSTEMS TO WORK

The following are some representative examples of the growing use of expert systems in business. These systems are either currently in use or under development. In either case, they will give you a better understanding of both the use and potential of expert systems in business.

Production

An expert system was designed to analyze a manufacturer's production schedules, optimize the scheduling of resources, and identify opportunities to salvage materials in the rework pile for use in filling customer orders. Traditionally, it cost less for a company to discard unused materials than to spend time performing the necessary complex calculations to discover other uses for them. A typical process production factory can have anywhere from 5 to 10 percent of its inventory in a rework pile at any one time. Turning even half of that amount into salable finished goods has a significant impact on the company's bottom line.

Inspection

A parts manufacturer has a vision-aided expert system that compares X-ray images of a machined part with specification drawings. If a defect such as a crack is found, the system directs a carefully aimed laser beam at it to seal the crack and prevent it from spreading. Also, the system creates a report that goes to quality assurance concerning the nature of the defect and the remedy required to correct it.

Assembly

The XCON expert system created and used by Digital Equipment Corporation (DEC) helps to build and assemble computer systems ordered by clients. When a client order is input to the system, it is configured by the system into schedules and diagrams that show the components required by the order and the relationship among those components.

Field Service

A design engineer with Speed Queen uses an expert system to disseminate his expertise to service managers and repair people. The system asks repairpeople a carefully conceived sequence of diagnostic questions, such as: Is the machine turned on? Does the fault lie in the electronic controls or somewhere else? Does the tub fill? This has helped Speed Queen repairpeople to diagnose problems more quickly and to reduce the amount of time it takes to make most types of repairs.

Telephone Repair

NYNEX Corporation, the phone company for much of New York and New England, uses an expert system to assess whether a repair truck really needs to be dispatched when a customer reports a problem. Workers with no expertise in phone repair consult Max (Maintenance Administration Expert), which searches a knowledge base containing thousands of repair records to find one like the caller's problem. NYNEX claims that Max improves customer service and saves an estimated $6 million per year by reducing unnecessary service calls and by decreasing the amount of training needed by the staff that handles customer calls.

Auditing

An expert system helps auditors select auditing procedures with which to verify a firm's accounts receivable. Accounts receivable data such as internal control features and account collectability are input to the program and recommended auditing procedures are output.

Tax Accounting

A program called TAXADVISOR assists tax accountants with estate tax planning. The program helps clients arrange financial affairs so that income and death taxes are minimized, while maintaining sound investment decisions and adequate insurance coverage.

Additionally, one public accounting firm feels that its tax experts spend excessive amounts of time working through international tax problems. Coopers & Lybrand developed ExperTAX to assist clients with these and other tax problems.

Financial Planning

A program called FINANCIAL ADVISOR incorporates the financial advice of eight faculty members from MIT's Sloan School of Management and ten senior financial officers from major corporations. FINANCIAL ADVISOR provides advice on such topics as investment projects, products, and mergers and acquisitions. The system is used in businesses and is available commercially.

Investments

A Pennsylvania-based company is currently working on an expert system that combines probability theory, statistical analysis, pattern recognition, and simulation to help investors select stocks and manage portfolios. In tests performed with a prototype of the product, the gain realized was twice that of the Standard and Poor's 500 index.

Personnel

Traveler's Insurance uses an expert system to help employees fill out W-4 tax-withholding forms. The system alleviates the strain on Traveler's Insurance's personnel department, which was besieged with inquiries from employees having difficulty filling out the forms. The expert system's knowledge base contains both information from the W-4 form and suggestions from the personnel department. The microcomputer-based system asks employees questions about their filing status and produces a complete W-4 form based on their replies.

KnowledgePoint developed a product called Personnel Policy Expert, which assists companies in creating complete employee handbooks. It addresses approximately 60 policy issues and helps personnel managers make policy decisions that comply with current labor laws and prevailing personnel practices. The system prompts users for information about the importance of various policies and creates a draft version of the policy statement for inclusion in the handbook.

Marketing and Sales

Traveler's Mortgage Services, a subsidiary of Traveler's Insurance, has a loan prequalification expert system for its sales force. The client provides such facts as monthly payment objectives, data on whether or not it is desirable to minimize closing costs, and qualification data. The expert system output is an approval recommendation and, if the client is approved, a complete mortgage package. According to Janet Mason's article, an assistant vice-president of the firm claims that, "The expert system can work up to six combinations in two seconds, whereas it takes a salesperson 20 to 30 minutes to figure out a single combination."

Credit Authorization

Bad decisions in authorizing credit when merchants phoned for approval cost American Express hundreds of millions of dollars. To curb bad debts, American Express now has an expert system, called Authorizer's Assistant, that helps human authorizers decide whether a potential purchaser should be extended credit. The system gathers important information about a cardholder from 14 databases and compresses it down to two screens, which the human authorizers view to make their final decision as they are on-line with a merchant. In some cases, where the transaction raises absolutely no questions, the system is allowed to make decisions on its own.

Human Services Agency

The U.S. Human Services Agency in Merced County, California, developed an expert system called Magic that decides if applicants should receive welfare benefits. Magic consults a matrix of 6,000 government regulations to determine if an applicant qualifies. While it takes Magic an average of 72 hours to make a decision, it used to take trained clerks as long as three months to make the same decision and to calculate how much and what types of benefits the applicant could receive. Training time for new benefit clerks is dramatically reduced and the delivery of social services to eligible recipients is faster. Magic saves the county over $4 million per year in administrative and training costs.

Medical Prognosis

Medical prognosis concerns what is likely to happen to a patient once they are diagnosed as having a particular disease. Apache III is an expert system that predicts a patient's chances of living or dying. Its knowledge base contains the medical records of thousands of previously diagnosed patients and uses this information, along with the patient's own medical history and changes in the patient's condition, to determine the probability of survival. Studies show that the program can predict more accurately than top-notch doctors. Physicians who use Apache III claim that it helps them to respond the changes in patient conditions more quickly. Hospital administrators like Apache III because it helps the hospital staff control costs by focusing attention on the cases that are most likely to benefit.

EXPERT SYSTEMS VERSUS CONVENTIONAL APPLICATIONS

Many differences exist between the expert system approach and the conventional approach used to develop application software. Four of these differences are covered here:

- In conventional applications, the expert knowledge is buried in code located within the application program. In expert system applications, the expert knowledge and heuristics are in a distinct knowledge base that is located outside the software driving the application (the inference engine).

- Expert systems probe users interactively, in question-and-answer sessions. The answer to an attendant question is used by the expert system to pose the next question. In conventional applications, data are usually supplied all at once—perhaps from a filled-in template—to the application program for processing.

- In expert systems, a large amount of input (the knowledge base) is almost always used to create a small amount of output (such as a medical diagnosis for a specific patient, or the approval or disapproval of credit for a particular customer). Although this is also true today for some conventional applications, most often the reverse is true.

- In conventional applications, knowledge data are often highly structured and predefined. In expert systems, these same types of data are often semi-structured and, in many cases, some of them are created by the expert system from the experience it picks up. Many expert systems are capable of some degree of "learning," whereas most conventional programs are not.

Uses and Limitations of Expert Systems

Although both artificial intelligence and expert systems have great potential, they are sometimes heavily criticized by management as not living up to the fanfare that accompanied them. However, most computer professionals are still very positive about these problem-solving approaches. As Clyde Holsapple and Andrew Whinston predict:

> Although artificial intelligence (AI) has scarcely touched today's managers, it will begin to have dramatic and widespread impacts on their activities over the next few years. Looking farther out, to the end of the century, practical fruits from the past 30 years of AI research will be commonplace. The application of artificial intelligence techniques will play a major role in reshaping traditional notions of what organizations are, how they are managed, and how decisions are made. All of this presents a major challenge and an important opportunity to today's managers and organizations. Though the transition will not be without growing pains, it will lead to tremendous increases in the productivity of managers and organizations. Those organizations in the forefront of applying AI methods to aid in management will have distinct competitive advantages over those that lag.

Knowledgeable professionals generally agree with this point of view. Expert systems will indeed eventually infuse themselves deeply into almost all areas of computer processing. They do serve a clear need, and the future technical environment of faster processor chips, parallel processing architectures, and bigger memories that expert systems need to really show their potential power are on their way. AI is not a fad. AI routines will be built into many of today's conven-

Son of Terminator: Neural Nets for Business

Terminator, the fictional Arnold Schwarzenegger character, is powered by a neural network that enables him to create and adapt strategies. Neural networks are now used in conjunction with fuzzy logic and expert systems to enable business information systems to have Terminator-like qualities. Three major business application areas are

- **Financial applications** In the financial area, neural networks are used for fraud detection, risk analysis, and predictive modeling. Shearson Lehman Brothers, Inc. uses neural networks to predict changes in the stock market. The Chase Manhattan Bank NA uses them to detect credit card fraud.

- **Database exploration** Churchill Systems, a large hospital supply company, uses a neural net to search its database for inactive customers who are likely to make future purchases. After determining the key characteristics of the company's best customers, the neural network identifies the companies in the inactive customer file that most closely match the best customer profile.

> **"IN THE FINANCIAL AREA, NEURAL NETWORKS ARE USED FOR FRAUD DETECTION, RISK ANALYSIS, AND PREDICTIVE MODELING."**

- **Handwriting and speech recognition** Intel Corporation, the world's leading chip manufacturer, developed a neural network chip—the 80170NX—and is working to extend its capabilities to include image and speech processing. Products with limited abilities to read handwritten characters are already on the market. Elevators that respond to spoken commands and scanners capable of reading handwritten faxes should be available soon.

Adapted from Schwartz and Treece (1992).

tional computer software products, just as microprocessors are already built into hardware products. Within the next decade, look for typical spreadsheet packages, word-processing software, and database management systems to be equipped with artificial intelligence features.

Today, expert systems are used mostly to solve narrow problems such as medical diagnosis, aircraft engine analysis, credit approval, tax advice, and oil exploration. These problems involve a small volume of logically complex operations. Also, in each of these problem areas, a relatively universal pattern of logic can be identified (unlike, perhaps, determining the best way to create or to advertise a cereal product). These expert system applications are far removed from mainstream MIS tasks such as transaction processing, information retrieval, or budget preparation—many of which involve relatively simple operations. Mainframe-oriented MIS departments have not yet heavily invested in AI, preferring to wait until vendors build a suitable bridge between the artificial intelligence environment and standard, mainframe-based business applications.

However, many of these "narrow" problems are among the most critical to the firm: strategic planning and use of information for competitive advantage, for example. Also, many broad problems are composed of lots of narrow problems. Thus, saying that mainframe-based transaction processing is far removed from the world of expert systems is not the same as saying that certain transaction processing components could not benefit from expert systems. Expert systems that advise a company treasurer on the best way to pay for merchandise or that advise a travel agent on how to best put together a travel package are two of many significant examples.

Despite the promise of expert systems, they must overcome some tough opposition in order to serve beyond a decision support capacity. As Beau Sheil points out, "Consider the first patient who dies as a result of a bad diagnosis from a robotic doctor. Who will be held responsible?" Furthermore, Sheil cautions:

> It is quite possible that we will never see commercial airlines flown entirely under computer control even if that technology becomes clearly superior—statistically—to human pilots. The reason is that although human pilots crash the occasional plane when trying to land in poor weather, their failures are understandable and thus, though regrettable, can be tolerated. When the mechanical pilot fails, however, even though it might do so much less frequently, it is likely to be by flying a plane into the side of a mountain in broad daylight. And this kind of failure we are unlikely to tolerate, whatever the long-run statistics say.

NEURAL NETWORKS

Conventional computers, with all of their raw speed, are just not well equipped to handle some types of problems. This is where neural-net computers, or neural nets, can help. These systems, which are built to mimic the way the human brain works, are specially geared to solve pattern-recognition types of problems. For instance, when you recognize a person's face or signature—acts performed so quickly that usually you do not think much about how this is done—you are really performing pattern recognition. That is, you record and analyze a number of important patterns in an object, comparing them with patterns stored in memory, and then you draw a conclusion (that is, you make an observation).

Neural nets simulate the human pattern-recognition process by arranging processing elements, which often work in parallel, in layers. The connections between layers and between processing elements on the same level form a network. Figure 11.14 illustrates a generic neural network. The lowest layers look at general features of a pattern and pass them up to intermediate layers. For instance, take character recognition. The lower levels might recognize that a character has a few straight lines. The intermediate layers refine the perception of the character, but it is only at the highest layer that the character is recognized— for example, as the letter H.

One of the main reasons why organizations are interested in neural networks is the "learning" capabilities of these systems. The activation of a particular processing element in the neural net depends on which inputs to it were activated and the weights of the inputs activated by other processing units (see

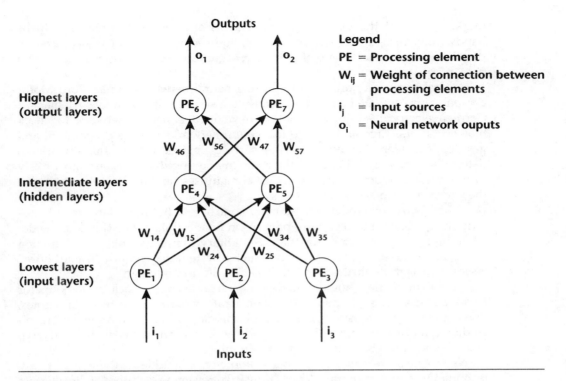

Outputs

Legend
PE = Processing element
W_{ij} = Weight of connection between processing elements
i_j = Input sources
o_i = Neural network ouputs

Highest layers (output layers)

Intermediate layers (hidden layers)

Lowest layers (input layers)

Inputs

Figure 11.14 The fundamental elements of a neural network.

Figure 11.14). "Knowledge" is represented by the pattern of connections and weights among the interconnected elements. Storing the pattern of weights and connections provides a baseline against which later inputs can be judged. During "training," the neural net "learns" by adjusting its weights in response to a collection of examples that users provide; each example contains values for both inputs and outputs. Once appropriate weights are determined, they are stored and used to evaluate the activation patterns associated with subsequent inputs. For example, a neural network trained to differentiate between customers who are good and bad credit risks would compare the activation pattern from a new customer's credit data with the patterns associated with known "poor" or "excellent" credit histories. If the new customer's activation pattern is similar to that for poor credit risk customers, the new customer's data could be flagged as a possible credit risk.

Ideally, as neural-net computers mature, they will utilize true parallel processing architectures throughout. Today, many so-called neural-net computers work with software emulation routines or through add-on boards, each of which work together with a conventional serial processor. Over 100 different neurocomputer designs have been implemented.

Neural-net computers have great potential in business, although it will be several more years before a wave of commercially viable products hits the market. Some of the major application areas appear, for the moment, to be handwriting recognition, quality control, and security. Each of these areas depends heavily on some type of pattern recognition: a character, a defect, and a person, respectively.

Several companies are already putting neural networks to use. Ford Motor company implemented a neural network that spots faulty paint jobs. Siemans, a German electrical equipment maker, developed a neural network to check blower motors. Arco and Texaco use neural networks to help pinpoint oil and gas deposits deep beneath the earth's surface. Speigel uses neural networks to determine which individuals in their vast marketing databases are most likely to buy their products. And Shearson Lehman uses neural networks to predict the performance of stocks and bonds.

Other neural networks assist quality control in a bottling plant, read handwritten zip codes, and recognize patterns in financial data. Westinghouse is developing a weapon system for the U.S. military that is capable of recognizing the image of a tank as ally or enemy—such a system may reduce "friendly fire" losses such as those incurred in 1991's Desert Storm campaign.

Neural networks should impact other areas as well, such as looking for trend patterns in sales data, analyzing strategy patterns within companies, looking for duplicate names in mailing lists, and making recommendations on credit or mortgage applications. Anywhere a pattern needs to be analyzed, neural nets should be considered as a solution.

Neural nets are still a fledgling technology, a sparkle in the eye of many technology entrepreneurs. When Edward Rosenfeld, editor of *Intelligence Newsletter*, looked into neural nets in 1984, he counted barely 24 companies doing some work in the field. In 1988, his count reached 175, with at least 125 of these involved in major projects. During the 1990s, neural nets should blossom as a technology and be woven into the MIS fabric of many organizations.

Summary

Artificial intelligence (AI) is the capability of computer systems to perform at a level that would be considered intelligent if observed in humans. Five main areas of AI research exist today: expert systems, natural languages, vision systems, robotics, and neural networks.

Expert systems are software systems that try to provide the type of advice that would normally come from human experts. To date, most successful expert systems have been in rather narrow, specific fields. However, expert systems have been developed for a rapidly growing number of fields.

Natural-language systems are those in which the computer communicates with users in a natural language, such as English or Chinese. The complexity of conveying meaning in a natural language has made progress in this area slow.

Vision systems are systems that perform tasks that could, at one time, only be done through use of the human eye. Image patterns are stored in a database and compared with the item being checked by a machine endowed with "sight."

Robotics is the field of AI concerned with the design, manufacture, and implementation of robots—computer-controlled devices that mimic the motor activity of humans. Robots have had their greatest success in manufacturing, where they perform jobs too dangerous, strenuous, monotonous, or expensive for humans to do.

Neural networks are computer systems that identify objects or patterns in a manner similar to the pattern recognition activities of the human brain. These networks are capable of "learning" input and data patterns and subsequently comparing new data and inputs to see how well they fit into learned patterns. Neural networks are implemented by using parallel processing and/or special software.

Expert systems are needed because human expert labor is expensive and scarce. In addition, the quality of human decision making is constrained by the limitations of human information processing and the fast pace of business today.

The most common type of expert system is a rule-based expert system, which consist of numerous components. At the center of such a system is its knowledge base, which contains all the specific facts about the expert area and the rules the system uses to make decisions based on those facts. The rules in a knowledge base are usually coded in the form:

`IF X THEN Y`

where X is a condition and Y is an action to be taken if the condition is true. Relationships between facts stored in the knowledge base may be represented as semantic networks, frames, or objects.

The inference engine is the system of the computer program that drives the expert system. It applies the rules, facts, and relationships between facts found in the knowledge base to data about the problem input by users. Three approaches are used to develop the inference engine: (1) custom build it; (2) acquire a prewritten, generic expert system shell, or (3) buy a prewritten, commercial application package and fine-tune it to fit the specific needs of the organization. Inference engines operate with either a forward-chaining mechanism, by which software routines first examine the knowledge base and then attempt to discover a solution—or a backward-chaining mechanism, by which software routines are first given a hypothesis, which they then check against the knowledge base—or by a combination of forward and backward chaining.

The knowledge acquisition subsystem of an expert system is the software component that enables the knowledge engineer to interact with the system. This subsystem makes it possible for the expertise of human experts to be placed in the knowledge base. The knowledge engineer is the MIS professional who designs and maintains the expert system.

Users can interact with the expert system through a user interface. Most of these are interactive; users key in responses to questions posed by the expert system. Natural-language interfaces for expert systems are still in their infancy.

The explanation facility communicates to the user the line of reasoning used in reaching a decision. It may also explain the importance of certain inputs, thus attempting to direct the user to a logical conclusion.

Expert systems are used in a variety of business areas, including production, inspection, assembly, auditing, tax accounting, finance, personnel, marketing and sales, field service, investments, and credit authorization.

Many differences exist between the expert system approach and the traditional approach to developing application software. First, in conventional application, the expert knowledge is buried in code within the application program; conversely, in expert systems, the knowledge is in a distinct knowledge base. Second, in conventional applications, data are usually supplied all at once to the computer system; in expert systems, users are probed interactively and new questions are posed in response to previous answers. Third, in conventional applications, a small amount of input often creates a large amount of output; in expert systems, the reverse is usually true. Finally, in conventional applications, knowledge data are often highly structured and predefined; in expert systems, they are often semistructured.

Although most professionals believe that expert systems will become very important in the future, the use of expert systems is still frequently criticized for not living up to expectations. As experience with expert systems matures, however, and as processor speeds and memories become more capable, expert systems will probably be infused into every important software product that could benefit by some type of expert advice.

Neural networks are also gaining in popularity, especially for pattern recognition tasks. Since these systems can be trained to recognize complex patterns and to compare new inputs against learned patterns, organizations find them useful for many applications, including handwriting recognition, quality control, and spotting patterns in financial information. Hundreds of neural networks have been implemented and many more should be developed in the years ahead.

KEY TERMS

Artificial intelligence (AI)

Backward chaining

Expert system

Expert system shell

Explanation facility

Forward chaining

Inference engine

Knowledge acquisition subsystem

Knowledge base

Knowledge engineer

Natural-language interface

Natural-language system

Neural network

Robotics

Rule

Rule-based expert system

Vision system

REVIEW QUESTIONS

1. What is artificial intelligence?

2. Provide several examples of expert systems.

3. How do AI applications such as expert systems, robotics, natural-language systems, vision systems, and neural networks demonstrate intelligence?

4. What are the characteristics and functions of each of the major components of an expert system?

5. What type of information is contained in an expert system's knowledge base? How may relationships between facts be represented?

6. How does a rule work in an expert system?

7. What is the difference between forward and backward chaining?

8. What is an expert system shell?

9. What types of alternatives are open to companies that want to acquire an expert system?

10. What is the purpose of a knowledge acquisition subsystem?

11. What is the difference between a computer program that uses expert systems and a conventional computer program?

12. What characteristics might an application possess to make it a candidate for solution by expert systems?

13. Identify several limitations of expert systems.

14. Describe the major characteristics of neural networks. How may these be implemented?

15. How do neural networks "learn" to recognize patterns?

16. Identify several applications of neural networks.

DISCUSSION QUESTIONS

1. Some people have called expert systems just "intelligent decision support systems." Do you agree with this assessment? Why or why not?

2. Identify some expert system applications that, to your knowledge, have not yet been commercially developed, but that hold tremendous potential for providing competitive advantage. Do you feel, in each of these situations, that the initial advantage is sustainable?

3. Many systems are reported in MIS literature as being expert systems when, in fact, they are not. What types of factors might lead to this confusion?

4. Many people see the so-called android, or close-to-human robot, as an ultimate application of artificial intelligence, computers, and technology. What types of resistance will be applied by humans to forestall this from happening?

CASE STUDY

Using an Expert System at American Express

In recent years, one of the best-known business applications of artificial intelligence has been Authorizer's Assistant—a knowledge-based system used by American Express to help credit authorizers make better credit decisions. Expert systems—and a completely revamped credit authorization system—were a logical choice for American Express for numerous reasons. Unlike the credit cards issued by many major banks, the American Express Card has no credit limit. Card holders are also expected to pay their balances in full each month.

Before implementing Authorizer's Assistant, both fraudulent use of charge cards and bad decisions in authorizing credit when merchants called for approval were costing the company hundreds of millions of dollars. Also, the system then in effect was slow and produced inconsistent results. Basically, it required human authorizers to first enter IBM's Transaction Processing Facility (TPF) and then use their own judgment to search independently through as many as a dozen IMS databases for specific cardholder information.

In late 1984, American Express executives decided to improve the authorization system. When expert systems were chosen as the route for new systems development, the company contracted with an outside expert system developer to create a preliminary working model of the system—a prototype—to be ready in about a year. The system created by the contractor is an expert system that runs on a microcomputer workstation that has a communications interface. This interface allows the expert system to tap data from the IMS cardholder databases hooked to an IBM mainframe.

When merchants call in for credit approval for a cardholder transaction, the expert system quickly pulls together any relevant database information, evaluates it, and makes either a decision or a recommendation as to whether or not credit should be granted. Usually taken into account are such factors as a cardholder's outstanding balance (the amount of cardholder transactions since the last statement was sent), payment history, buying habits, and the degree of risk involved. Should any warning signs appear, the system is even capable of asking merchants to obtain further information from the cardholder—such as information that would help to verify the identity of the cardholder.

About a quarter of all transactions processed by Authorizer's Assistant are straightforward enough to require no human intervention. In such cases, the system essentially makes a decision and transmits it to the merchant. The other transactions are referred by the system to human authorizers. Each is accompanied by an identification of the warning signs, an explanation regarding why the transaction is being referred, a recommendation for credit authorization or denial, and an encapsulation of relevant decision-making data culled from the databases. If the human authorizer disagrees with or questions a recommendation made by the expert system, he or she can override it.

When humans and the expert system work together on decisions, the system cuts processing time by about 20 percent. It has also slashed bad debts by 50 percent.

To develop the knowledge base, the expert system developer used a rule-based approach. In doing so, the developer's analysts interviewed American Express's five best authorizers in Fort Lauderdale, Florida, and constructed a knowledge base of 520 rules. After some refinement, the base was expanded to 800 rules. A credit authorization manager explains, "We began with a finite number of situations dealing with specific customer types or cases and from there broadened the scope."

Today, Authorizer's Assistant is still being used and supports the activities of more than 300 human authorizers scattered around the globe. Its knowledge base is gradually being refined and improved.

In addition to credit cards, the American Express Company provides a broad range of financial services, including mutual funds and insurance. In spite of such diversification, the 1990s have brought rocky financial times for American Express and its subsidiaries. One response to the financial stress is to improve its systems—including Authorizer's Assistant—and to integrate the systems that support its various divisions. American Express is very interested in using information technology to further streamline its operations and enhance its competitiveness.

Adapted from Alper (1987). Also adapted from Keyes (1991), Higgins (1992), and Stewart (1991).

DISCUSSION

1. How did Authorizer's Assistant improve the credit authorization process at American Express?

2. What good does it do to have Authorizer's Assistant evaluate cardholder buying habits when making credit authorization recommendations and decisions?

3. Do you think Authorizer's Assistant helps or hurts customer service? Explain your reasoning.

4. How could information assembled by Authorizer's Assistant be used by the investment and insurance divisions of American Express? How could information from the databases in the investment and insurance divisions help Authorizer's Assistant make recommendations?

5. How would a neural network improve American Express's credit authorization process? How could neural networks be used in the insurance and investment divisions of the company?

Chapter 12.

Office Information Systems

After completing this chapter, you will be able to:

Define office information systems (OIS) and office automation (OA)

Describe the types of workers found in an office

Describe the evolution that has taken place in office information systems

Describe the major types of office systems found in organizations

Identify several benefits derived from implementing office systems in organizations

Describe some of the challenges and issues associated with implementing office systems in organizations

Describe the characteristics of integrated office systems

During the past 25 years, computer technology has helped to dramatically increase productivity in the office. The movement toward automation in office tasks is often called office automation (OA). Office automation includes the new hardware and software technologies—word processors, spreadsheet packages, electronic mail, and so on—that make office workers more productive, plus the attendant situations created by OA technologies and the people that use these technologies. These combinations of information technologies that have a dramatic impact on day-to-day office operations are called office information systems (OIS). In this chapter, we explore office information systems and how they evolved.

The chapter begins by discussing the nature of office work and what specifically is covered under office information systems. Next, we look at the growing number of computer-related applications that typify office work today and how these technologies are implemented in practice. Finally, we explore integrated OIS packages, looking at the needs of OIS and where OIS is headed.

OFFICES AND OFFICE SYSTEMS

The basic nature of office work has changed drastically over the past 50 years. At one time, virtually the only role of equipment in the office was to help workers become more efficient. Until the mid-1960s, only the typewriter, phone, copying machine, and electronic adding machine were standard office equipment. Now, as computer technologies have a strong presence in offices, office workers have powerful tools that also make them more effective. For example, word processing and desktop publishing make information much easier to find and modify. Such DSS tools as spreadsheet packages help managers make decisions that are more informed than those they reached when using less powerful calculators.

Here, we will look at the types of workers found in the modern office environment and the types of tasks they perform. Then, we will explore the evolution of computing technologies into office work.

The Nature of the Office

Generally, an **office** is a place where staff and line professionals, secretaries, and clerks perform management and administrative tasks. The work performed by office workers is often called white collar work. In recent years, office workers have accounted for about 75 percent of the total business payroll costs in the United States.

Office Workers

Five types of workers can be found in the office: managers, staff professionals, line professionals, secretaries, and clerical personnel. Managers, staff professionals, and line professionals are often called **knowledge workers** because their work involves the greatest amount of knowledge of any people in the firm.

- *Managers* In general, managers spend a lot of time planning, coordinating, and controlling the activities of other people. Some examples are the firm's chief executive officer (CEO), the vice-president of operations, and the head of marketing research.

- *Staff professionals* Staff professionals support the activities of managers— for example, marketing or operations research analysts. Staff personnel have no direct line responsibility; that is, their role is mostly one of planning, analyzing, and informing management of their findings.

- *Line professionals* Line professionals include salespeople and purchasing agents. Line professionals typically interact daily with such outside groups as the firm's customers and suppliers.

- *Secretaries* Secretaries are normally assigned to one or more knowledge workers in an office. They perform such support tasks as typing, filing, answering phones, and keeping appointment calendars.

- *Clerical personnel* Clerical personnel are normally not assigned to anyone in particular; generally, they support the entire office. Typical types of clerical tasks are filing, typing, and assisting in report preparation.

OA Professionals

In many organizations, a separate support group is responsible for promoting and managing office system technologies. Some firms employ a full-time OA manager with a staff of several people. The OA personnel often perform a variety of representative office tasks on test or demonstration equipment and arrange for product demonstrations within the firm by OIS hardware and software vendors.

Office Work

The management and administrative tasks performed in the office can be divided into five general categories: decision-making, data manipulation, document-handling, communications, and storage activities. All of the office systems applications that we discuss in the next section of this chapter fall into at least one of these categories.

- *Decision making* The main job of the manager is to make decisions. The main job of the staff professional is to assist the manager in this activity. Thus, decision making is one of the most important tasks performed in the office. Virtually all knowledge workers are involved with key decisions of some type.

- **Data manipulation** A common office duty is preparing lists and numbers to present at meetings or to discuss with clients over the phone. This type of work involves the manipulation of data—either manually or by computer.

- **Document handling** A sizable portion of the work done by secretarial personnel, clerical personnel, and line professionals is document handling: creating and issuing documents, reviewing and responding to documents, and so on. For example, taking dictation and subsequently typing a letter from it or preparing a written budget both involve the handling of documents.

- **Communications** Office workers often spend a lot of time in meetings and on the telephone. Some managers spend almost 50 percent of their time on these communications activities.

- **Storage** An important office task is keeping accurate records. For example, the shipping office needs to keep records on products leaving the firm and the purchasing office must maintain records of open purchase orders. Also, in most firms, it is important to maintain storage of archival records and to locate those historical records when necessary.

The Evolution of Office Systems

As mentioned earlier, until the mid-1960s, virtually the only information technologies in the office were typewriters, phones, copying machines, and electric adding machines. Then, in 1964, a seemingly modest typing enhancement—called **word processing**—appeared. Since then, information processing in the office has never been the same.

Among the earliest word processors was the IBM magnetic tape selectric typewriter (MT/ST), which stored preprocessed text on a strip of magnetic tape. The tape unit on the MT/ST could be activated by a secretary at any time during the regular typing of a letter; it then automatically typed a prepared text segment onto a document. Obviously, a lot has changed since 1964. The tape units disappeared long ago, and computer workstations have replaced many standard typewriters.

The introduction of minicomputers and small business computers in the late 1960s and early 1970s also contributed to the alteration of the office's technology. Before then, virtually all computing was highly centralized, performed on mainframes that were located at a single (headquarters) site. Smaller computers made it possible to decentralize computing down to regional sites and individual offices. It was not unusual for large offices, in fact, to own their computers. This trend toward decentralization was called *distributed data processing (DDP)*. What the MT/ST was to the office in the 1960s, DDP was to the office in the 1970s.

Today, because of inexpensive microcomputer systems, quality microcomputer software, electronic mail, local area networking, and gateways to mainframe systems, office technology is changing yet again. The proliferation of computing technologies into office life has been so pervasive, in fact, that computer-illiterate knowledge workers have problems in most of today's offices. Two terms are associated with the computerization of offices in the 1980s and 1990s: office automation (OA) and departmental computing. In this text, office automation is preferred because it is more widely accepted.

Of all the areas currently under the MIS umbrella, the office information systems area is probably the hardest to define because it is composed of many different technologies and overlaps considerably with the end-user computing (EUC) and decision support system (DSS) areas. For example, a sales manager using a spreadsheet to model strategies falls under the areas of OIS, DSS, and EUC. If this person is a top-level manager, the spreadsheet may also be part of an executive information sytem (EIS). If the data are downloaded from a mainframe-based transaction processing system, then the resulting system is also part of a transaction processing system (TPS). Every office worker is a potential end-user, which, to some people, makes OIS a subset of EUC. However, because EUC also covers nonoffice workers, such as those in factories, the topics of end-user computing and development are addressed in more detail in Chapter 17.

The primary purpose of office information systems is to facilitate communication among members of an organization and between the organization and its external environment. Ideally, an office information system allows individuals and group members to create, store, and exchange messages through a variety of communications media, including data, documents, images, voice (audio), and video. OA is moving toward the realization of these ideals. The office of the future will probably have these features and even more. Integrated services digital network (ISDN) should facilitate such communication within and between offices. Advances in electronic data interchange (EDI), image processing, and document management systems should also enable organizations to move toward paperless office operations.

Types of OA Systems

Four major categories of office applications are document management systems, message-handling systems, teleconferencing systems, and office support systems. These, and some of the applications that fall under these headings, are summarized in Figure 12.1. Most of the remainder of this chapter will discuss these systems.

Document Management Systems

As Figure 12.1 indicates, document management systems include word processing, desktop publishing applications, and image-processing systems. Intelligent copier systems and other reprographic technologies (systems capable of making multiple copies of a document) are also facets of document management systems. The huge amount of paper documents generated currently makes this an extremely important OIS area. According to Janet Mann, in the early 1990s, U.S. businesses produced an average of nearly 100 billion original paper documents and 300–400 billion photocopies a year.

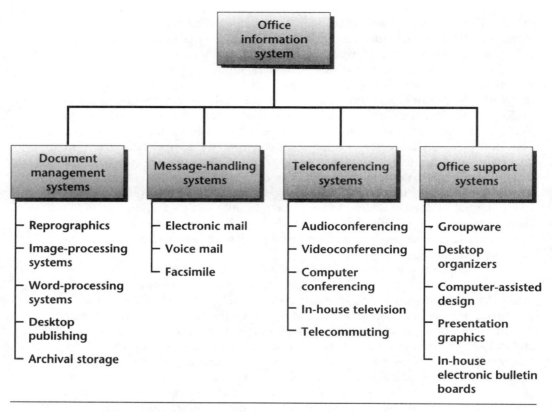

Figure 12.1 The major components of an office information system (OIS).

Word Processing

The most widely used and recognized office-system technology is word processing. Word processing involves hardware and software tools that allow the computer system to become more than a powerful typewriting device. Word processors enable documents to be created and edited electronically, with the assistance of the computer system's processor, memory, and display device. When the document is finished, it can be stored in secondary storage (typically on disk) or output on the system's printer in a variety of styles. Figure 12.2 lists a number of features commonly found on word processors.

Most of today's word processing uses word-processing software on a general-purpose computer system. These computer systems, of course, can be used for other purposes as well: preparing taxes, extracting records from files, or writing Pascal programs, to name just a few applications. Today, the biggest market for word-processing packages that run on general-purpose computers is in the microcomputing area, where such packages as WordPerfect, Microsoft Word, WordStar, and Ami Pro are among the current leaders (refer to Figure 6.8, page 246). WordPerfect and Microsoft Word alone captured over half of the

WORD-PROCESSING FEATURES

Standard Entering and Editing Operations

- Moving the cursor to various places on-screen
- Scrolling the document up and down
- Returning lines automatically
- Inserting and deleting characters and blocks of text
- Moving and copying blocks of text
- Searching for text strings
- Replacing text strings
- Spelling checker feature
- Thesaurus feature

Standard Print-Formatting Operations

- Adjusting line spacing
- Indenting blocks of text
- Reformatting blocks of text
- Centering text
- Proportionally spaced characters
- Automatic page numbering, headings, and footings
- Multiple columns per page
- Selection of fonts
- Orphan and widow elimination

Advanced Operations

- Mailing list preparation
- Form-letter boilerplating
- Math feature
- Sorting
- Redlining and edit tracing
- Cross-referencing
- Preparing indexes and tables of contents
- Integrating with spreadsheet programs
- Desktop publishing features
- Embedded typesetting codes

Figure 12.2 Word-processing features. Most word-processing packages perform the same types of operations. Recently, the market leaders have also incorporated several desktop publishing features.

word-processing market. Many of these packages recently released versions for the Windows operating environment. Newer versions of these packages incorporate numerous graphics and desktop publishing features that were not included in the earlier versions.

As computer networking is now popular, so are "shared" word-processing systems. Shared systems are specifically designed to share the resources of a communications network. Typically, these systems are implemented in one of two ways: (1) as several display terminal workstations that are connected to a host (a midrange or mainframe system) in a star (or hierarchical) configuration, or (2) as a local area network (LAN) consisting of several microcomputer workstations, a file server, a print server, and perhaps other servers as well. In a LAN, the software used may allow workers to concurrently prepare different parts of the same document, sharing their outputs over the network. As mentioned in Chapter 10, such multiuser word-processing software is a type of groupware; many group decision support systems (GDSS) enable group members to simultaneously create a single word-processing document.

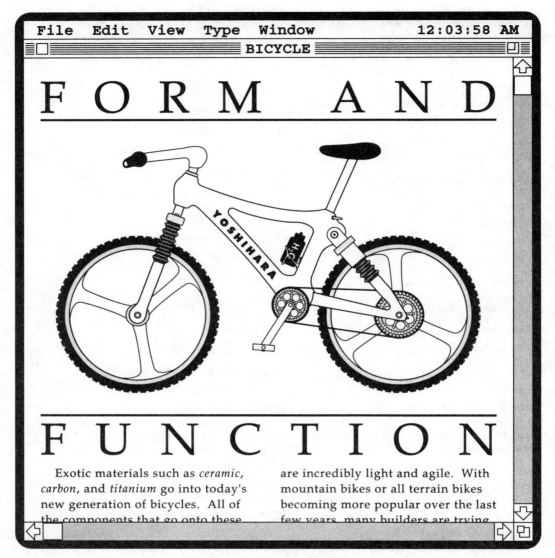

Figure 12.3 An example of desktop publishing output. Full-featured desktop publishing software packages enable users to create, edit, scale, and combine art, text, and photographic elements on the same page.

Desktop Publishing

An office technology that is currently very popular is desktop publishing. **Desktop publishing (DTP)** involves desktop microcomputer systems that are equipped with special hardware and software features to produce documents that look as though they were done by a professional print shop (see Figure 12.3). DTP users can combine word-processed text with such elements as artwork, photos, and a variety of magazine-style fonts. The overall effect can be stunningly attractive and very effective.

Configuring a Desktop Publishing System   Today, a wide variety of desktop publishing systems is found in the marketplace—at both the low end and the high end. As noted previously, many of the latest versions of the leading word-processing software packages have added desktop publishing features that enable them to be used as low-end desktop publishing systems.

Although a few very low-end packages can run on a regular IBM PS/2 or IBM compatible machine—configured with less than 1MB of RAM, a dot-matrix printer, and floppy-disk secondary storage—most of them require considerably more power if the user wants to take full advantage of the features they offer, especially the ability to create multicolor layouts and to perform photographic manipulation. Roughly translated, this means that a 32-bit computer, 2–8 megabytes of RAM, a laser printer, and a high-capacity hard disk are needed. Low-end systems typically allow users to combine a variety of graphical fonts onto a page, use prestored art images (called clip art) on pages, and draw lines and boxes to highlight text or art. Fonts and clip art software packages can also be purchased separately from third-party vendors to extend the options offered by the original package's vendor.

At the high end of the market, numerous additional options are possible. For instance, the user can digitize complex art images such as photos, which are composed of halftones that look good only at high levels of resolution. Also, a much greater variety of options is available with fonts and clip art. For example, both fonts and clip art can be scaled by users to various sizes; these can be created from scratch or edited, as well. Additionally, most high-end packages are designed to interface both laser printers and professional typesetting equipment.

Because graphics require high speeds and large memories, the greater the user's desktop publishing needs become, the more power is required of the desktop publishing system. A relatively unsophisticated desktop publishing application might require a system unit with at least 1MB of RAM and 20MB of hard disk storage; two to four times this amount is often needed for sophisticated applications. Sophisticated applications usually demand a laser printer that works at 300 dpi (dots per inch) resolution or better and can produce color separations, a full-page or two-page WYSIWYG (What You See Is What You Get) graphics monitor (that is, one that allows you to see one or two entire $8\frac{1}{2} \times$ 11" pages), an image scanner that can both digitize images and recognize text, a digitizing tablet (described in Chapter 5), software to interface with professional typesetting equipment, and several other specialized hardware and software elements.

The complexities of desktop publishing are often ignored or forgotten as users become seduced by the visually enticing images they see in the vendor literature. The extensive hardware and software requirements needed for truly dazzling desktop publishing applications can break some offices' budgets.

Challenges and Opportunities To the MIS organization, beyond the technology of desktop publishing lie many management-oriented challenges and several opportunities. Educating users and establishing standards for use are among these challenges. One of the biggest dangers of implementing desktop systems today is that some users carry DTP to its extreme, constantly reworking a document when they could be more effective doing other work. Another problem is the lack of general knowledge about desktop publishing—an application area that just started in the early 1980s.

Regarding opportunities, DTP systems are especially useful to the in-house publishing functions found in many organizations. Because numerous companies have acquired desktop publishing systems, DTP has completely restructured at least one entire industry—the typesetting business.

Desktop publishing also creates an opportunity to differentiate a product. For instance, a factor driving the spread of DTP is a change in people's aesthetic perceptions. A marketing manager in the medical field says, "I can type something up and put it on stationery, and it can be scientifically valid . . . and people don't look at it." But, claims the manager, when he produces the same document with desktop publishing tools, people will both read it and—because the two-column output looks like something from a scientific journal—give it greater credence.

Some of the leading desktop publishing systems are Aldus Corporation's PageMaker, Xerox Corporation's Ventura Publisher, Quark, Inc.'s Quark Express, Digital Research, Inc.'s, GEM Desktop Publisher, and Laser Friendly, Inc.'s The Office Publisher. Groupware versions of such systems are also used.

Reprographics

Reprographics is the process of reproducing multiple copies of a document. Office personnel are usually responsible for making more than one copy of a report, letter, and other documents. When documents are widely distributed, either internally or externally, reprographics often includes collating, folding, binding, and related tasks.

Multiple copies may be made in numerous ways. When only a few copies are needed, it may be cost effective to print out multiple copies using the printer(s) attached to the computer. Most of the time, however, a photocopier is used.

The most sophisticated type of copy equipment currently available is the **intelligent copier system** (or electronic printing system). As Figure 12.4 shows, documents created on microcomputer workstations or display terminals may be electronically transmitted to the intelligent copier. Previously created and stored documents may also be sent directly to the copier so that multiple copies can be made. Additionally, intelligent copiers can transmit documents to other systems. They are often used to merge the stored image of a business form with data supplied by workers at a microcomputer, display terminal, or another computer system—and then they electronically distribute the completed forms; of course, the completed forms can also be printed.

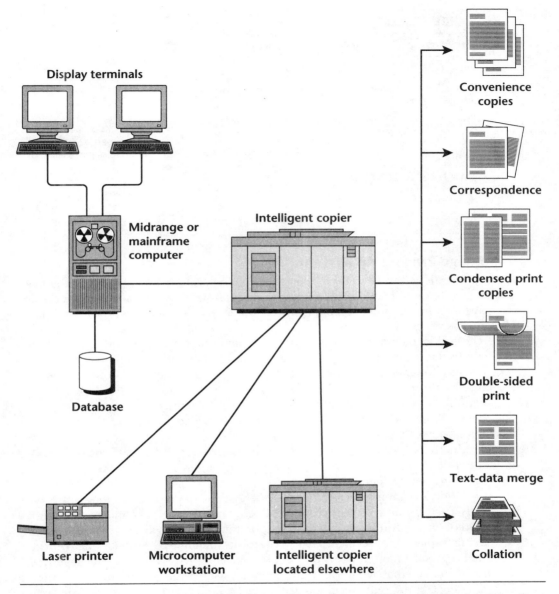

Display terminals

Midrange or mainframe computer

Database

Intelligent copier

Laser printer

Microcomputer workstation

Intelligent copier located elsewhere

Convenience copies

Correspondence

Condensed print copies

Double-sided print

Text-data merge

Collation

Figure 12.4 An example of an intelligent copier system. Over time, the capabilities of intelligent copier systems have increased. Most can communicate with other intelligent copiers, computers, and computer networks within the organization.

LARGE SYSTEMS	
Product	**Vendor**
ImagePlus	IBM
WIIS (Wang Integrated Image Systems)	Wang Laboratories, Inc.
AIMS (Advanced Image Management Systems)	Hewlett-Packard Co.
FileNet	FileNet Corporation
LAN-BASED SYSTEMS	
LaserView	LaserData, Inc.
ViewStar	ViewStar Corporation

Figure 12.5 Examples of commercially available image-processing software packages. Many of the vendors with packages designed for large systems also have versions for local area networks.

Image-Processing Systems

As mentioned in Chapter 5, image processing and document management systems are one of the fastest growing types of office systems. **Image-processing systems** (sometimes called electronic image management systems) allow users to electronically capture, store, process, and retrieve images of documents. These documents may include text, numeric data, handwriting, graphics, and photographs; in some cases, these may all be part of the same document. According to Janet Mann, the image-processing segment of the information industry should grow from $1.3 billion in 1990 to $8.9 billion in 1995. Most industry experts agree with Mann's assertion that "document imaging technology promises to reduce the problem of paper overload by providing information management with more efficient use of physical storage space and increased productivity." Of course, electronic data interchange (EDI) systems — discussed in earlier chapters — can also reduce an organization's paper document-handling requirements.

Optical scanning technologies — often called document scanners — are typically used in these systems to input documents. In the past, images were often stored on microfilm or microfiche, but microfilm-based systems are rapidly being replaced by optical disk storage technologies. Workstations outfitted with special image-processing circuit boards and software can retrieve document images that were input and stored. Laser printers are rapidly becoming the most commonly used output devices associated with image-processing systems.

As noted in Chapter 7, image database management systems are becoming more versatile as they are refined. LAN-based image-processing systems are also becoming more common. These often include several servers, each dedicated to a specific function such as database management, scanning, or printing. Figure 12.5 provides examples of some of the leading image-processing packages for large systems and local area networks. Figure 12.6 illustrates a generic LAN-based image-processing system.

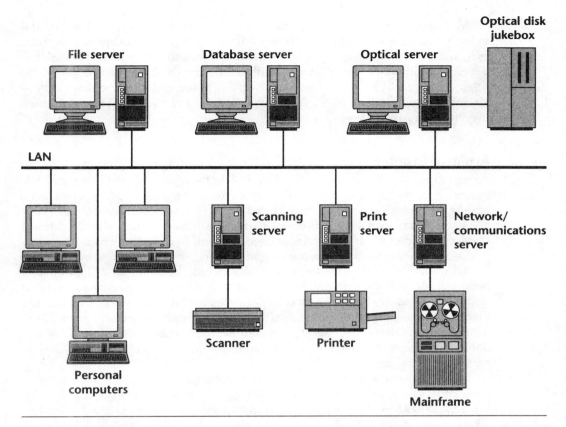

Figure 12.6 A generic LAN-based image-processing system. Most of these systems are found in client/server local area networks with dedicated servers for print, magnetic, and optical storage. Optical storage jukebox systems that hold multiple optical disks are becoming more common.

Electronic document management (EDM) systems are sophisticated image-processing systems. These systems typically allow digitized "voice notes" to be attached to specific document images and may have other special features as well, such as the ability to store multicolor documents and color photographs. EDM systems often interface with other office systems such as word processing, desktop publishing, electronic mail, and voice mail. These are increasingly used for processing documents associated with transaction processing systems. Documents such as invoices, statements issued to customers, customer correspondence, service requests, application forms, and contracts can be captured by EDM systems and electronically distributed and output whenever needed. Image processing and EDM systems have improved the productivity of office workers, resulting in some significant cost savings. As Jackyln Popuil notes, "Electronic document image-processing systems are becoming more productive, providing faster access at lower costs and enabling managers to make decisions more quickly." Also, these systems have the potential to greatly improve customer service.

Multimedia systems often integrate image processing with text, audio, and video processing technologies. These systems allow users to digitally capture, edit, and combine photographs, video, audio, text, and numeric data in order to develop multimedia presentations, multimedia databases, or interactive video sessions. Interactive video sessions allow users to see and hear prepared materials interactively, either in a prearranged order or randomly. These are often used for training purposes.

Archival Storage

As mentioned earlier, one of the key functions in an office is storage. The image-processing and electronic data management systems just discussed are among the hottest technologies for handling business documents. While these are used in an increasing number of organizations, several other traditional storage technologies are still widely used and will exist in some form for many years. For example, in numerous organizations, text and numeric data are stored on-line, on fast-access magnetic disk units. In addition, offices usually need archival storage to maintain historical data. To save the expense associated with storage space, handling, and paper costs, archival data was traditionally placed onto various media and stored off-line. Such media are also particularly useful to firms needing to keep large files available that do not have to be updated, or to firms that need to process large amounts of data but find on-line access too expensive.

Four common technologies used to store archival materials are magnetic tape, computer output microfilm (COM), optical disks, and diskettes (see Figure 12.7). These media are also useful for storing backup copies of documents, programs, or data.

- ■ *Magnetic tape* Magnetic tape is one of the oldest and most common ways of storing data for archival purposes. Tape is inexpensive, compact, and can store rather large text files.

- ■ *Computer output microfilm (COM)* Computer output microfilm (COM) refers to all technologies that either place data onto microfilm media—such as a reel of microfilm or a microfiche card—or that allow those media to be read by humans. Special computing hardware, usually operated off-line from the main computer system, is used to photograph page-sized images, reduce them, and place them onto microfilm media. While the images that are stored are not machine-readable (a drawback that limits the range of applications for these media), they can be read by using either a computer-operated retrieval device or through manually operated microfilm readers such as those available in most university libraries. Microfilming media are often superior to magnetic tape because they are better suited to graphic data, are easier to handle and use in many situations, and are more rugged. Figure 12.8 provides an example of a COM system.

- ■ *Optical disks* Optical disks are especially suited for archival storage because of their tremendous capacities. Optical disks for microcomputers store

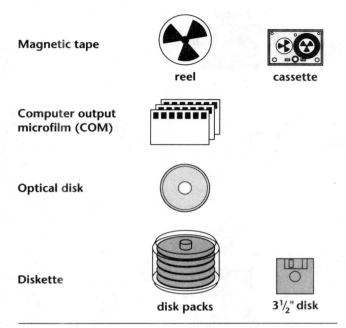

Archival Storage Media

Magnetic tape — reel | cassette

Computer output microfilm (COM)

Optical disk

Diskette — disk packs | 3½" disk

Figure 12.7 Commonly used archival storage media. The media listed here are useful for both archival purposes and many other applications.

650MB of data on a single 5¼" platter. Those for midrange and mainframe systems are usually larger in diameter and have storage capacities in the multigigabyte range. Jukebox storage and retrieval systems (such as the one depicted earlier in Figure 12.6) are more commonly used in LAN-based systems. Many industry experts feel that this medium will encroach seriously on the archival storage niche now occupied by COM.

■ ***Diskettes*** Diskettes are really only suitable in situations in which modest amounts of archival storage are necessary. For instance, many programmers use diskettes for personal archival purposes so that backup copies of data or programs can be quickly retrieved. Office personnel can also use diskettes to store electronic copies of important documents. As noted in Chapter 5's section on storage media and devices, RAID (redundant arrays of inexpensive disks) are now used more widely. RAID may represent a more effective and more secure approach for storing text and data in offices that have increasing archival storage requirements.

Message-Handling Systems

As previously illustrated in Figure 12.1 (page 516), several important OIS applications can be categorized as message-handling systems. These include facsimile systems, electronic mail, and voice mail systems.

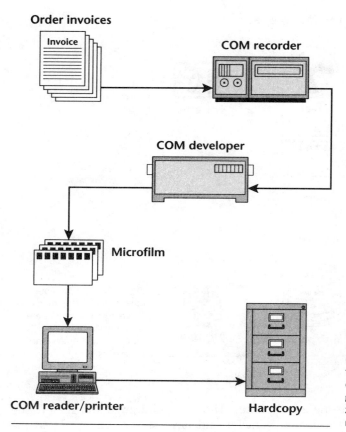

Order invoices

COM recorder

COM developer

Microfilm

COM reader/printer

Hardcopy

Figure 12.8 An example of a computer output microfilm (COM) system. COM systems take images and store them on microfilm, which can greatly reduce an organization's paper management requirements.

Facsimile (Fax)

Facsimile (fax) systems are commonplace in most organizations today. Fax machines enable hardcopy images of documents, graphics, and photographs to be transmitted from one location to another, either locally or around the world. Both the sending and receiving stations must have faxing equipment for this to happen; however, a relatively stable fax standard now exists that allows virtually any two fax machines to communicate with each other.

Fax machines are basically electronic document delivery systems that combine scanner and modem technology. An optical scanner reduces text or graphic images recorded on paper to electrical impulses that can be transmitted over telephone (or other) networks. Fax machines may be either analog or digital; the digital machines are typically faster. Sending faxed documents normally requires a relatively fast fax modem, about 9600 bps or greater. But even at these speeds, the clarity of some faxed documents may not measure up to the original or even to a photocopy of it. However, the quality of facsimile output is steadily increasing and the latest generation of fax machines utilize laser technology for both higher resolution and higher speed output.

What the Heck is Groupware?

Groupware is software designed to help members of a committee, project team, or work group coordinate work on common tasks. A wide range of groupware products is available.

- Information-sharing products help work group members exchange data through messaging and database functions. Products such as Notes from Lotus Development Corporation, Topic from Verity, Inc., and Cooperation from NCR Corporation fall into this category.

- Meetingwear or electronic meeting/conferencing products allow two or more users to simultaneously engage in electronic communication via their personal computers. Representative products are Aspects from Group Technologies, Inc., Instant Update from On Technology, Inc., and VisionQuest from Collaborative Technologies Corporation.

- Scheduling products make it easier to arrange meetings or coordinate conferences for a work group. Network

"IMPRESSIVE PRODUCTIVITY GAINS REPORTED BY SOME ORGANIZATIONS HAS FUELED INTEREST IN GROUPWARE . . ."

Scheduler from Powerscore and Action Plus from Action Plus Software are popular.

- Networked office automation software suites such as NewWave Office from Hewlett-Packard and WordPerfect Office from WordPerfect Corporation make it possible for workers to perform various tasks in sync with one another.

- E-mail packages with additional features such as project and task management are also classified as groupware. Higgins from Enable Software, Inc. is one of the best-known products.

Impressive productivity gains reported by some organizations has fueled interest in groupware; dramatic utilization increases are expected during the 1990s.

Adapted from LaPlante (1992).

Today, equipping microcomputers with fax boards, thus empowering them to communicate directly from RAM to a fax unit at another location, is becoming popular. Fax boards and their related software allow users to send documents stored on disk to other facsimile devices and to receive, store, display, and edit fax images transmitted from other fax devices. However, because the output received is a bit-mapped pattern, editing fax images is often difficult. Fax boards typically enable users to print out the documents that are received on dot-matrix or laser printers, which usually results in a better quality of output. However, as noted earlier, many of the new stand-alone fax systems can produce output of comparable quality.

Facsimile technologies often help organizations save money. Usually, the telephone line costs associated with sending a few pages of text are substantially less than sending those same pages by overnight mail. Many sophisticated fax systems can be programmed to send documents at times when phone rates are lowest; for example, between midnight and 6 A.M. Facsimile devices can also be merged with teleconferencing systems (discussed later in this chapter) to enable participants to share hardcopy materials.

Electronic Mail (E-Mail)

Electronic mail (E-mail) refers to technologies that send messages or documents from one electronic workstation to another. E-mail is the second most commonplace office systems application area (behind word processing).

A relatively common form of electronic mail in many organizations is the **electronic mailbox**. This type of system can be implemented in several ways. For instance, employees within a large organization may have electronic mailboxes that are managed by a mainframe, minicomputer, or local area network. When these employees use a workstation (which may be at their desks), they can call up their personal file—or mailbox—on the E-mail system to see if they have any messages. Or they can send a message to place in someone else's mailbox, as Figure 12.9 illustrates. These types of E-mail systems are typically standard components in integrated office packages, which will be discussed later in the chapter. A second way of implementing a mailbox system is through an outside vendor of such services; CompuServe and GE Information Services are just two of the information utilities that provide E-mail services to subscribers (see Figure 12.10). Here, all the user needs is a microcomputer, a modem, communications software, and an E-mailbox on the vendor's system. E-mailboxes may also be obtained on networks that numerous organizations can access. Bitnet and Internet, for example, provide global E-mail utilities.

Most types of E-mail can be implemented through non-integrated workstations that can be linked with mainframes through communications software; integrated local interoffice networks and local area networks; or private- or common carrier-based wide area networks. These networking alternatives were covered in Chapter 8. Wherever several devices can communicate with each other, the potential for E-mail exists.

A high degree of incompatibility usually exists among competing E-mail systems. Where dissimilar and public E-mail systems interface, some type of gateway is generally necessary to enable them to communicate. The International Standards Organization (ISO) promotes the X.400 and X.500 standards for E-mail systems. If vendors adhere to these standards, much of the existing incompatibility problems may be resolved. Managers considering adopting a new (or upgrading an existing) E-mail system should probably limit their choices to those that are consistent with the X.400 and X.500 standards.

Voice Mail

A **voice mail** system enables a regular voice message, sent over the phone, to be digitally stored at the receiving location. When accessed, the message is converted back into voice form. These are used by an increasing number of organizations and often employ software that runs on the organization's PBX equipment, rather than on the organization's host computers.

Voice mail systems require a computer, disk storage, and voice mailboxes that are similar to E-mailboxes. The sending and receiving instrument, however, is the telephone. Like E-mail messages, digitized voice messages can be

```
FRI 15 JAN 1993 8:30 A.M.

You have 3 memos awaiting
You have 8 ticklers
Master menu    1 Calendar
selections:    2 Memo processing
               3 Document
                 processing
               4 Utilities
               5 Exit to system


Enter choice: 2
```

(a) **Selecting a choice from the main E-mail menu. Here, the memo processing routine (submenu) is picked.**

```
MEMO PROCESSING

Memo processing    1 Create/edit
menu selections:   2 Read
                   3 File/memo
                     manager
                   4 Search
                   5 Directory
                   6 Exit to
                     master menu


Enter choice: 1
```

(b) **Selecting a submenu choice. Here, the user decides to create a new menu or edit an existing one.**

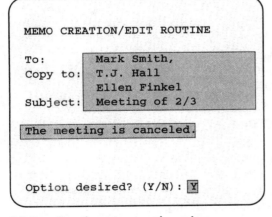

(c) **Creating the memo and naming recipients.**

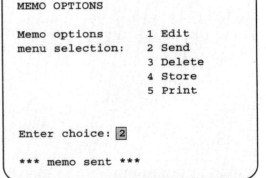

(d) **Sending the memo.**

Figure 12.9   Using an electronic mailbox system. Employees in an increasing number of organizations have access to electronic mailboxes that are managed by a mainframe, midrange computer, local area network, or an external information service such as CompuServe. Mailbox systems are often included as standard components in integrated office packages. In the panels illustrated above, user input is highlighted.

played back, sent along to one or more other members of the organization, saved, or deleted. As it is sent along from person to person, a message can usually be voice-annotated by anyone handling it.

With voice mail, one person calls a voice mailbox rather than a personal phone number. In stand-alone voice systems, the message is simply stored, awaiting pick-up by the person receiving the message; in integrated voice

E-MAIL SYSTEMS	
Product	**Vendor**
AT&T Mail	AT&T
Tymnet, OnTyme	British Telecom
InfoPlex	CompuServe
+Mail	Dialcom
Quick-Comm, GEnie	GE Information Services
MCI Mail	MCI
Telemail	Telenet/US Sprint
EasyLink	Western Union

Figure 12.10 Examples of publicly available electronic mail systems.

mail/PBX, the message receiver has the option of picking up the phone. People can usually access their voice mailboxes from any telephone (both inside and outside the organization). The telephone keypad is used to listen to messages in the mailbox, save them, delete them, or send them to others. This permits field representatives or traveling executives to maintain contact with the home office and to keep up with their messages. Salespeople can use these systems to enter orders over the telephone from the customer's office. Some universities are using voice mail systems to enable students to register for classes. All of these applications can provide organizations with a competitive edge.

Teleconferencing Applications

In addition to message-handling applications such as electronic mail and voice mail, an increasing number of organizations provide their employees with other electronic means of communication—especially when they must communicate over long distances. In this section, we will focus on three such systems: teleconferencing, in-house television, and telecommuting.

Types of Teleconferencing

The term **teleconferencing** refers to electronic meetings that involve people who are at physically different sites. Telecommunication technology systems allow meeting participants to interact with one another without traveling to the same location. Three major types of teleconferencing exist: video teleconferencing, computer conferencing, and audio teleconferencing. Wide area group decision support systems (GDSS), such as those described in Chapter 10, often involve some type of teleconferencing.

With video teleconferencing, participants can both see and hear each other. These systems combine voice and television images that allow two or more

Figure 12.11 Participants in a video teleconference.

groups to interact with one another. Video teleconferencing was first widely demonstrated in 1964 at New York's World Fair when AT&T introduced its picturephone, which dazzled onlookers and gave them a glimpse of what is now fairly common. In the early 1990s, approximately 10–15% of the Fortune 500 companies routinely use video teleconferencing for business meetings. According to Carolyn Brown, in 1990, video teleconferencing was approximately a $60 million market and an application area that should increase at an annual rate of 33.4 percent over the next several years.

Generally, video teleconferencing participants gather in relatively expensive, specially equipped rooms that can handle the complexities of simultaneous video and audio transmission (see Figure 12.11). Anyone who watches the TV program "Nightline," hosted by Ted Koppel, has probably seen an example of video teleconferencing. For instance, resident experts from Miami, New York, and Los Angeles might teleconference to discuss a controversial issue with the host and with each other. During Operation Desert Storm in 1991, all the major television networks—and even the military—widely used teleconferencing to overcome the coordination challenges presented by distance and time zone differences.

In business applications, video teleconferencing can be particularly effective because interaction between people is usually different when they can see each other. A few large hotel chains have invested in video teleconferencing facilities in order to woo their corporate clientele. AT&T, U.S. Sprint, and MCI all have videoconferencing service divisions to assist organizations in the implementation and operation of video teleconferencing systems; many other vendors also provide video teleconferencing services. Advances in teleconferencing technologies and the advent of ISDN should dramatically increase the use of video teleconferencing.

Computer conferencing involves computer terminals and E-mail or electronic bulletin boards. Conference participants broadcast messages to each other (or post them on a common electronic bulletin board); participants do not have to be present to receive messages. The messages are keyed in and then displayed on computer screens; hence, the "conversations" that take place are electronic. Computer conferencing can be particularly useful in project management and job-shop manufacturing situations. As critical pieces of a project are finished—possibly at numerous geographically dispersed sites—this information is recorded in the public electronic mailboxes of each project manager so that he or she has a real-time update on both costs and progress. The project managers can also communicate with each other through the mailboxes regarding any unusual events or any other important matters. Many vendors offer specialized computer conferencing software that coordinates and manages these electronic meetings.

Audio teleconferencing (conference phone calls) enables participants to hear each other only. A speakerphone may be used at one or more locations to allow groups to participate in the meeting. When portions of this book were in preparation, for instance, the publisher arranged an audio teleconference among marketing personnel, the authors, and several specialists in the MIS field. Although the most limited of the teleconferencing procedures discussed here, audio teleconferencing is by far the least expensive. According to Carolyn Brown, about 60 percent of the Fortune 500 companies use audio conferencing every day.

Facsimile devices and other specialized equipment are often used in conjunction with electronic meetings. For example, *electronic blackboards* are now more widely used; these allow participants at one location to write on an "electronic chalkboard" and then transmit the written images to television screens, computer screens, or other electronic blackboards at other locations.

Teleconferencing can save substantial traveling costs and time. Its disadvantages are that it can be expensive and, sometimes, it really cannot be substituted for meeting physically with people—especially in conflict-resolution matters. For instance, the most effective way to show an angry client that the company still cares might be to sacrifice a salesperson's time, have someone physically get onto a plane, and meet with the client at his or her site. A variety of federal, state, and local laws affect the recording of teleconferences. For example, participants must have proven prior knowledge that it is occurring and the room must clearly indicate that a recording is taking place.

In-House Television

One of the newest tools in business, and one that is a beneficial office systems application, is **in-house television**. With this technology, an organization invests in a studio, a period of time on a satellite, and a satellite transmitter for broadcasting. Company sites—or even customers—are given satellite dishes so that they can view the broadcast. Scramblers inhibit competitors from gaining access to the transmission.

The list of companies now using in-house television is impressive. Ford, Merrill Lynch, IBM, Eastman Kodak, JC Penney, and Federal Express are among the current users. Many others are considering it. The following list describes the variey of applications for which in-house TV is currently being used:

- Previously, buyers at local JC Penney outlets had to travel to headquarters to select merchandise for their stores. Now, they can use a TV to tune into a JC Penney channel, whose programming resembles a home shopping network that features JC Penney goods exclusively. The system not only cuts travel costs, but it provides a longer lead time for placing orders and enables buyers to take advantage of any late-breaking consumer trends.

- During the October 1987 stock market crash, Merrill Lynch used in-house TV to broadcast daily briefings from top executives and to field calls from concerned employees. The televised events, which also featured the chairman of the firm, helped to bring some order to the fear and confusion resulting from the chaos.

- Ever want to see yourself on TV? Domino's Pizza thinks many of its employees do and it is currently using in-house TV as an incentive tool. Any Domino's outlet with great ideas that other outlets should use will get a visit from the company's video team—which stages an on-site show.

In-house TV is relatively new and its creative uses are just beginning. As demonstrated here, it has already shown potential in the areas of competitive advantage, cost cutting, and employee motivation.

Telecommuting

With **telecommuting**, people use communications technology to work at home or in a remote city—and to avoid the usual physical commute to work. Using a remote communications terminal or a microcomputer workstation, for instance, a programmer can do his or her work at home instead of at the office. Or, using the same types of technologies, a Chicago-based lawyer who works alone most of the time might actually live in Sun Valley, Idaho.

Like other office system applications, telecommuting has its pros and cons. Advantages include eliminating the time spent traveling and having to deal directly with office politics, which can be very stressful. Organizations can also bypass the expense of establishing physical office space. And they can often retain a valuable employee that they might otherwise lose. According to Meghan O'Leary, advocates of telecommuting claim that it offers "concrete proof of productivity gains, cost savings, improved morale, and more effective work group communication." However, skeptics argue that there is no substitute for dealing with people face to face, since office politics often determine power structures within the organization. Also, the organization loses some control over an employee who telecommutes. In addition, many jobs are not conducive to telecommuting and some employees just do not have the self-discipline required to work productively on their own. Both the positive and negative aspects of telecommuting should be considered carefully by organizations when deciding whether to use this employment option.

Office Support Systems

So far in this chapter, we have discussed some of the major technologies for managing documents, exchanging messages, and holding meetings. In addition to these systems, numerous other applications help to coordinate and manage the activities of work groups. These are collectively called office support systems and include groupware and desktop organizers.

Groupware

As noted in Chapter 10, groupware consists of software packages designed to support the collaborative efforts of a group of coworkers. Such packages often provide integrated support for many of the typical activities of work groups previously identified, including:

- Word-processing services, including the ability for multiple users to work concurrently on the same document.
- Electronic mail services.
- Voice mail services.
- Computer conferencing services.
- Fax services.
- Access to on-line databases and telecommunication services such as CompuServe.

Groupware packages may also provide group members with other services, such as:

- Project management services.
- Shared "to-do" lists and phone number lists.
- Group calendaring and scheduling services.
- Bulletin board services.
- Personal desktop organizers (discussed in the next section).

Bulletin board services enable users to post information of interest to the other members in the work group. Project management services help ensure that the various activities needed to complete a group project are properly coordinated (project management software will be discussed more fully in Chapter 16). Group calendaring and shared to-do lists are similar to the individual calendaring and to-do list modules found in many desktop organizers.

Desktop Organizers

Like electronic mail systems, desktop organizers are generally found at a user's workstation or microcomputer. **Desktop organizers** are software packages that provide users with the electronic equivalent of the organizing and coordinating tools found on a typical office desk.

The features in a desktop organizer are often invoked through windows that pop up on the screen when the user presses a certain combination or sequence of keys while working with another application software package. For instance, the desktop organizer could be configured such that when the ALT and F4 keys are simultaneously depressed, an electronic calendar may pop up on the screen. If, instead, the ALT and F2 keys are simultaneously depressed, an electronic notepad may appear. After the user works with the summoned feature, another combination of keys returns the user to the exact place in the application program where he or she was. Of course, in the popular operating environments that use graphical user interfaces (such as Windows, OS/2, and Macintosh System 7), a mouse can often point and click on the icon for the desired organizer function.

Desktop organizers vary regarding the types of features they offer, but many of them offer the following tools, each of which is called a *desk accessory*:

- *Calendar*   Electronic calendars often consist of a series of routines that enable users to make up appointment calendars by the day, week, month, or year. Sophisticated calendar routines on multiuser systems allow users to establish access privileges that enable other authorized users to see their schedules—and, perhaps, schedule appointments into certain time slots. *To-do list* generation and modification are coordinated with the calendaring routines in many desktop organizers.

- *Card file*   With a card file feature, the user establishes a type of electronic Rolodex system. For instance, a list of client phone numbers and addresses can be stored. Some packages also provide automatic dialing features so that after a name is selected from this type of file, the modem can dial the number on the record.

- *Notepad*   The notepad feature facilitates the writing of notes as soon as ideas occur to the operator when using an application program. Some packages also allow these notes to be transported back to the resident application program.

- *Clock*   The clock feature enables the operator to keep track of the date and time. In some cases, an alarm feature works in conjunction with the clock,

GROUPWARE	
Product	**Vendor**
BrainStorm	Mustang Software, Inc.
Copy Flow	North Atlantic Publishing System
Document Management Systems	Odesta Corporation
For Comment	Broderbund Software
Lotus Notes	Lotus Development Corporation
Notepad	Notepad Systems International, Inc.
Office Works	Data Access Corporation
Participate	Evertures
Rhapsody	AT&T
Synchrony	Finalsoft Corporation

Figure 12.12 Examples of groupware software packages.

activating an audio unit at the workstation when an important event is about to happen.

- *Calculator* A calculator facility enables calculations to be done during the course of an application program. Some packages allow these computational results to be imported into the resident application program.

On mainframes and minicomputer systems, desk accessories are often an adjunct feature found in an integrated office system (discussed later in the chapter). On microcomputer systems, desk accessories are usually sold as separate packages (such as Borland International's SideKick—one of the best known and most widely used desktop organizer packages) or they are bundled as an additional feature in a window-based operating environment (such as Windows, OS/2, and Macintosh System 7). Figures 12.12 and 12.13 list many popular groupware and desktop organizer packages for microcomputers.

Other Office Support Applications

As mentioned earlier, a significant overlap often exists between the DSS and office systems areas. Therefore, a number of the DSS tools that were covered in Chapter 10—including database management systems, spreadsheets, modeling packages, and graphics generators—are also appropriate for office environments. These technologies can help users to analyze data, retrieve information, and prepare graphs and charts for presentations. Group decision support systems (GDSS)—also discussed in Chapter 10—are increasingly used in office settings.

Another technology that is frequently used in office environments is computer-aided design (CAD). CAD refers to computer systems that enable designers to work with a display-screen interface and specifications database to

DESKTOP ORGANIZERS	
Product	**Vendor**
Action Tracker	Information Research Corporation
Home Base	Brown Bag Software
HQ	TEK Microsystems, Inc.
In Control	Attain Corporation
Integrated Work Station	XYZT Computer Dimensions Inc.
Metro	Lotus Development Corporation
MORE	Symantec Corporation
Partner-PC	Time Works Inc.
PC-Desk	Software Studios Inc.
PC-Deskteam	Alternative Decision Software
PolyWindows Desk Plus	PolyTron Corporation
Pop-Up DeskSet Plus	Popular Programs, Inc.
Primetime Personal	Primetime Software, Inc.
SideKick	Borland Corporation
WordPerfect Library	WordPerfect Corporation

Figure 12.13 Examples of desktop organizer software packages.

design various products. CAD is widely found in engineering environments, but is also used in many office settings; for instance, in an architect's office, where floor plans and building designs can be summoned to the display screen and modified.

IMPLEMENTING OFFICE SYSTEMS

In this section, we will look at some of the ways in which office systems applications were successfully implemented in several industries. We will also consider a few of the problems encountered in some unsuccessful OA applications, plus several general concerns about OA.

Examples of Office Systems Applications

Many success stories are linked to the implementation of office systems. Here are a few of them:

- The U.S. Forest Service (USFS) performed before and after studies of its efforts to automate and electronically link its 900 offices. The postimplementation studies reveal that environmental impact statements now take 39 percent less time to prepare and timber contracts take 27 percent less time. As a result of these savings, the USFS trimmed 30 percent off the time it takes to do work and cut its staff by 25 percent.

Using Information Technology to Tame the Health Care Cost Monster

If a serious illness or injury puts you in the hospital, you will probably feel that no price is too high for the highly skilled doctors and high-tech medical equipment needed to help you recover. However, the medical bills must eventually be paid and businesses, employees, and insurance companies have covered most of them. During the last two decades, annual health care cost increases have exceeded the inflation rate—in most years by more than a 2 to 1 ratio. Understandably, bringing these rising costs under control is a widespread concern.

Information technology is being used by doctors and hospitals in an increasing number of ways to provide high-quality patient care. However, industry experts feel that billions of dollars could be saved each year if hospitals and doctors were also using information technology for the following:

- Electronic management and transmission of patient data—including systems that alert physicians to possible allergic reactions that they might have overlooked.

- Electronic submission and processing of health care claims—including systems that spot irregularities in patient bills.

"DURING THE LAST TWO DECADES, ANNUAL HEALTH CARE COST INCREASES HAVE EXCEEDED THE INFLATION RATE . . ."

- Electronic inventory management systems for hospital supplies.
- The use of videoconferencing for both professional training and remote medical consultations—patients would be able to "visit" specialists on-line from specially equipped offices.

These and many more cost-cutting applications are expected in the years ahead—and this is good news for everyone.

Adapted from Margolis and Booker (1992).

- At Beneficial Corporation, a large financial services company, a video terminal-based electronic mail system connects 1,200 managers, including the firm's CEO. According to William Bowen, the CEO claims: "I can communicate with or yank figures from any manager, anywhere. We can make a decision now in a quarter to half the time it took before." Eventually, he predicts, the system will change Beneficial's management structure, enabling it to operate with fewer levels of management.

- For several months, an account representative for Metropolitan Life Insurance Company called without results on the pension fund manager of a Chicago firm, attempting to sell him an annuity package that allows clients to tailor investments in a portfolio of six different funds. Then one day, the account representative brought in a laptop computer and a spreadsheet package. He and the client ran a few what-if analyses. What would happen to the client's total return, for example, if one portfolio were tried instead of another? Thus the account representative answered questions immediately, and a few weeks later, successfully closed the sell.

- In 1986, Hewlett-Packard Company (HP) began a pilot project that equipped 135 of its 1,700 sales representatives with laptop computers to assist them with various time-consuming tasks. Among these tasks were tracking the status of orders on mainframes and retrieving account histories. Six months after the project began, HP found that the laptops reduced time spent at meetings by 46 percent and decreased travel time to customers by 13 percent. Consequently, time spent with customers increased 27 percent and sales rose 10 percent. Claimed one HP executive, "We changed the way people communicate with their boss and peers." HP is currently equipping all of its sales representatives with laptops and expects benefits to exceed costs by five to ten times in just the first year of implementation.

- At Ace Hardware, outside Chicago, in-house desktop publishing has become the most cost-effective solution to continuing production of Ace's 4,000-page, 45,000-item catalog for its 13 regional warehouses. Each of these catalogs is tailored to specific regions (it is difficult to sell snow shovels in Miami, for instance). With the new system, claims Ace's office systems manager, "One operator in half a day of keyboarding does what dozens of operators and clerks used to do full time." The system saves Ace hundreds of thousands of dollars each year. As an additional benefit, the system created some new marketing tools that are used for competitive advantage; for instance, a catalog without prices, which dealers can distribute to their commercial and industrial accounts.

Challenges and Issues

As with applications in the DSS area, many office systems applications are difficult to justify to management by traditional cost-benefit formulas that require reducing benefits to quantifiable terms. A study at Harvard Business School of 40 corporations showed, in fact, that buyers often do not even bother calculating the bottom-line effects of many low-cost end-user systems. Claims James L. McKenney of Harvard, "Most of them did no cost justification at all."

Because little cost justification or analysis is made on many office information systems—either before or after purchase—some people wonder if OA really pays off. Although few people question that word processors can produce a finished document from a handwritten draft much more quickly than a conventional typewriter can, many critics claim that the ease of revision afforded by word processing is often used to overperfect documents. Sometimes, so many drafts of a document are churned out by computer-driven printers that the concept of a paperless office seems unattainable. Similarly, electronic mail systems are criticized as contributing to both a preponderance of trivial messages and an overbroadcasting of messages in general (that is, sending messages to everyone on a list when only a few people really need to see them), thereby using E-mail ineffectively.

Governmental studies report that, even as corporate spending on computers moves upward (almost 40 percent of U.S. capital spending—almost $100 billion per year—now goes to information systems), white collar productivity has not increased since the early 1970s. An economist in a leading U.S. investment bank underscores these statistics: "There has been virtually no relationship between spending on information systems and productivity."

Unfortunately, the statistics—reflecting many other sources of computer spending in addition to OIS—don't recognize that it may take more effort today, or a redistribution of effort into the office area, just to compete. For instance, increases in government-required paperwork and greater monitoring of the external environment by companies are responsible for many office systems-related expenses. Also, most companies will not send out ordinary letters done on inexpensive office equipment when their competitors use state-of-the-art equipment that produces professional-looking correspondence. The statistics on MIS spending and office productivity also don't recognize the learning curve that exists with new office technologies: it clearly takes time to become proficient with them.

Despite these statistics, companies clearly will not drop word-processing systems and spreadsheet packages and return to electric typewriters and adding machines. As *Business Week* reported, "Haphazard application of office technology. . . produces poor results. But what pacesetters are finding is that if the right technology is used where it can do the most good . . . and if the organization's work structure is adjusted to take advantage of the benefits . . . gains will result." Adds William Bowen in *Fortune*, "The large payoffs come not from increasing the efficiency with which people perform their old jobs, but from changing the way work is done." The bottom line is that the right technology in the right hands will produce favorable—even astonishingly good—results.

The companies that are most productive with their office systems are usually the ones that relate OIS to clear goals; for example, to make sales representatives productive to the point at which they spend 10 percent more time with customers. Typically, they are also the companies that are willing to sufficiently invest in training to ensure that users will make the best use of the office system technologies. As one technology consultant adds, "Winners use their systems in a highly focused way, targeting them at a person or a group and a `business deliverable' such as closing more sales."

THE INTEGRATED OFFICE

In the previous sections, we covered several application areas for computer- and communications-related office technologies. A firm can separately acquire the necessary hardware, software, or services required to implement any of these applications—or it can integrate several of them. Two such integration options are to acquire an integrated office software package and to build a completely integrated office.

Integrated Office Packages

Integrated office packages can be purchased or leased from many software vendors. Typically, an integrated office package features word processing, elec-

INTEGRATED OFFICE PACKAGES	
Product	**Vendor**
All-in-one	Digital Equipment Corporation
Comprehensive Electronic Office (CEO)	Data General Corporation
Enable OA	The Software Group
Office	Wang Laboratories, Inc.
Office Suite	Lotus Development Corporation
Personal Productivity Center	Hewlett-Packard Company
Professional Office System (PROFS)	IBM
Sperrylink	Unisys

Figure 12.14 Examples of integrated office packages.

tronic mail, and several desktop organizing routines (such as electronic calendaring). Most of these integrated packages are targeted to large, general-purpose computer systems: mainframes and minis; however, LAN-based integrated packages (such as Enable OA) are also available. The advantages and disadvantages of acquiring an integrated office package are virtually the same as those discussed in Chapter 6 for any other type of integrated software packages.

The Office of the Future

An integrated office package combines a number of OA-related software functions on a general-purpose computer system; an integrated office (sometimes referred to as the **office of the future**) networks together numerous diverse, OIS-related hardware and software activities. An example of an integrated office is provided in Figure 12.15. This might entail integrating any of the following sets of heterogeneous elements:

- The hardware and software products of several vendors.
- Various communications protocols.
- Text, graphics, voice, and video data, some of which will use the same communications lines.
- Several different types of computer networks and network elements; for instance, local area networks (LAN), wide area networks (WAN), private branch exchanges (PBX), intelligent copier systems, and gateways to large mainframes and/or remote commercial databases.

At this point, the computer and communications industries are still at the first stages of developing an office system that satisfactorily performs all of these tasks. Many organizations still accomplish such tasks with standalone devices or with several less powerful networks. However, ongoing

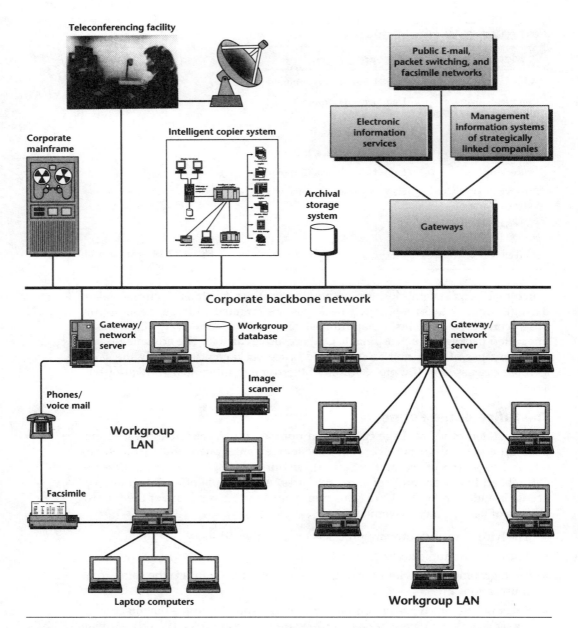

Figure 12.15 An integrated office. The office of the future is designed to integrate numerous separate office functions into a single network.

developments in communications and information technologies continue to bring the office of the future closer to becoming a reality.

Summary

Office automation (OA) refers to the movement toward automating office tasks. Perhaps more than any other area under the MIS umbrella, office information systems (OIS) are composed of technologies that are divergent instead of integrated.

An office is a place where white collar workers perform administrative tasks. Five types of workers are found in most offices: managers, staff professionals, and line professionals (the knowledge workers); and secretaries and clerical personnel (who perform support tasks).

The management and administrative tasks performed in an office fall into five general categories of activities: decision making, data manipulation, document handling, communications, and storage.

Many office systems technology areas have evolved. Among these are systems for document management, message handling, teleconferencing, and office support. Document management systems include word processing, desktop publishing, reprographics, image processing, and archival storage applications. Message-handling systems include facsimile systems, electronic mail, and voice mail systems. Teleconferencing systems include video teleconferencing, audio teleconferencing, computer conferencing, in-house television, and telecommuting. Office support systems include groupware and desktop organizers.

By far the best known OIS area is word processing. Word processing involves hardware and software tools that allow the computer to become much more than a typewriting device. Shared word-processing systems have increased in popularity as computer networks have become more prevalent in organizations. Desktop publishing involves the use of desktop microcomputer systems equipped with special features to produce documents that look professionally printed. Such systems combine text, art, and a variety of fonts. Advances in reprographics technologies, particularly the development of intelligent copiers, have made it easier to link microcomputers and copiers. Image-processing systems allow documents to be scanned and stored in image-oriented databases. Most of these systems involve the use of optical storage technologies; LAN-based systems are becoming quite common. Many claim that these are helping organizations make significant strides toward the paperless office. Archival storage refers to off-line storage used for historical and backup materials. Four common technologies for storing archival materials are magnetic tape, computer output microfilm (COM), optical disks, and diskettes.

Facsimile (fax) systems enable hardcopy images to be transmitted between locations. Electronic mail (E-mail) refers to technologies used to send messages or documents from one electronic workstation to another. Electronic mailboxes enable messages to be placed in personal storage areas until they can be accessed by the recipient. Voice mail enables voice messages to be sent via phone lines, digitally stored at the receiving end, and converted back to voice form when accessed.

Another OIS application is teleconferencing: holding meetings among people who are at physically different sites. Three main types of teleconferencing are video, computer, and audio. With in-house television, a relatively new OA area, an organization invests in a studio, time on a satellite, and a satellite transmitter. Restricted broadcasts are then prepared by company personnel and shown to employees or authorized outsiders. Telecommuting allows people, through communications technology, to work at home or at remote sites—thus avoiding the physical commute to work. Although this application saves time and money, the organization loses some control over employees who telecommute.

Groupware packages provide support for work group activities. They provide work groups with a variety of support functions, including the ones summarized earlier. Desktop organizers are software packages that provide users with electronic equivalents of the organizing and coordinating tools found on a typical office desk; for example, a calendar, card file, notepad, clock, and calculator.

Office information systems are successfully implemented in many ways. Most problems with implementation stem from a lack of clear goals for office systems. Success, on the other hand, is more likely when the organization implements new office technologies after a careful strategy is planned.

Individual OA applications can be implemented through integrated office software packages or through a more comprehensive integrated office strategy. The ideal of the latter approach is to someday achieve full integration: the office of the future.

REVIEW

KEY TERMS

Desktop organizer	Knowledge worker
Desktop publishing (DTP)	Office
Electronic mail (E-mail)	Office of the future
Electronic mailbox	Reprographics
Facsimile (fax)	Telecommuting
Image-processing system	Teleconferencing
In-house television	Voice mail
Integrated office package	Word processing
Intelligent copier system	

REVIEW QUESTIONS

1. How are office systems related to end-user computing?
2. What exactly is an office?
3. What distinguishes a knowledge worker from other types of workers?

4. What types of work are performed in offices?

5. What are the characteristics of the major types of office technologies?

6. How have word-processing systems changed over time? What are the characteristics of word-processing packages on the market today?

7. Identify the characteristics of desktop publishing systems.

8. What are the characteristics of reprographic and intelligent copier systems?

9. What are the characteristics and potential advantages of image-processing and document management systems?

10. Identify some media used for archival storage and give an example of a situation in which each type of medium is appropriate.

11. What are the characteristics and potential advantages of facsimile systems?

12. What are the characteristics of electronic mail systems? How are E-mail and voice mail systems different?

13. What is teleconferencing? How do video teleconferencing, audio conferencing, and computer conferencing differ?

14. How do video conferencing, in-house television, and telecommuting differ?

15. What is groupware? What functions may be found in groupware packages?

16. What types of features might be found in a desktop organizer?

17. Describe the office of the future.

DISCUSSION QUESTIONS

1. Many people know that various "islands of automation" currently exist within organizations—that is, many different technologies are developing into separate clusters of applications. They also point out that these applications do not communicate with each other. How does OA enter into such a discussion—and, perhaps, even more than other areas under the MIS umbrella (TPS, MRS, and DSS)?

2. Does office systems technology seem capable of someday producing the paperless office? Explain why or why not.

3. In what ways, do you feel, will desktop publishing result in both problems and opportunities in the publishing and typesetting industries?

4. Which new technologies do you feel are likely to have the biggest impacts on office work in the years ahead? Justify your arguments.

Global Positioning Systems: Spawning New Commercial Applications

Since 1978, the United States Department of Defense has spent more than $3 billion dollars developing its Navstar Global Positioning System. The system incorporates a string of 24 satellites orbiting 11,000 miles above the earth. Each of the system's satellites contains four atomic clocks that send out a steady stream of time and location signals. These transmissions identify the satellite and its path. Receivers linked to computers in moving vehicles on the ground compare the satellite's signals with their own clocks and use this comparison to calculate the distance between them and the satellite. By locking onto the signals from four satellites, the receiver can determine its location on the earth's surface to within 17.5 yards. By factoring in data from a second stationary receiver on the ground, the location of the moving vehicle can be calculated within one-half inch.

So what's the big deal? Well, during the Gulf War, soldiers were able to pinpoint their exact positions in an otherwise trackless desert. They did so by taking readings from the satellites, using receivers the size of paperback books. Also, the accuracy of such systems has a wide range of potential business applications that may increase operating efficiency and provide organizations with a competitive edge.

One company that is already taking advantage of the Navstar Global Positioning System is the Minute Man Delivery service in Gardena, California. It is using the global positioning system (GPS) to dispatch its fleet of 40 trucks more efficiently. In the past, dispatchers had to remember each driver's route and were constantly squawking over two-way radios in order to track their progress. Now, using the GPS, dispatchers are able to instantly pinpoint each truck's location. This makes it easy to alter routes throughout the day—for example, to add last-minute pick-ups—and relative to the old system, trucks can now be dispatched in half the time. This translates into reduced costs, more efficient operations, and improved customer service.

Northwest Airlines is one of several airlines that wants to adapt the GPS for widespread civilian use. By using GPS data, pilots, air traffic controllers, and regional Federal Aviation Administration (FAA) centers can know where every aircraft is at all times. This should make it easier and safer to place planes closer together for landings and takeoffs at crowded airports. Northwest is also working with the FAA to create safer, more efficient flight paths. Both of these applications are likely to reduce jet fuel consumption. Officials at the FAA feel that GPS may make it possible for automated landings and takeoffs in even the densest fog.

Geologists also expect to make good use of the GPS. They should be able to use such systems to monitor subtle changes in the earth's surface—changes that indicate whether an earthquake or volcanic eruption is imminent. Such an application has the potential to save many lives.

Combining GPS signals with other data may open up a number of other interesting applications. For example, the integration of GPS data and digitized land maps could lead to the development of sophisticated, intelligent vehicle-tracking systems. Small computer screens mounted on the dashboard of a car could show drivers how to avoid a traffic jam or where the nearest gas station, hospital, or automatic teller machine is located. Experts feel that satellite and GPS-oriented intelligent vehicle systems will be superior to ground-based systems such as that in Orlando, Florida.

More than a dozen companies are profiting from the GPS in another way—by manufacturing and marketing receivers for non-military applications. Sales of such receivers increased tenfold—to more than $600 million—from 1990 to 1993. During this time, Sony released a GPS receiver for hikers. More GPS applications will pop up as the cost of GPS receiver chips drops during the 1990s.

When the Navstar system is fully operational, the Department of Defense intends to continue to artificially degrade the signals from the satellites in order to prevent a potential enemy from using the system to launch missiles to knock out the satellites. By degrading the signals by a few nanoseconds, the satellite (and ground) locations calculated by receivers may be off by 110 yards. While the Department of Defense expects to provide classified equipment and codes that compensate for signal degradation for commercial applications, these compensating mechanisms will drive up the costs associated with non-military GPS applications.

Adapted from Eng and Borrus (1992).

DISCUSSION

1. Describe at least three other types of commercial applications of global positioning systems that are not mentioned in the case. Describe how each of your examples would make the user organization more efficient and effective.

2. What drawbacks (negatives) are associated with GPS applications? Why should organizations be careful about jumping into GPS applications too quickly?

3. Do you feel that the Department of Defense's decision to artificially degrade satellite signals will inhibit the development of commercial applications? Why or why not?

4. If you were attempting to convince your superiors to invest money in a GPS application for your company, what arguments would you use? How would you justify your recommendation?

Chapter 13

MIS in the Functional Areas of Business

After completing this chapter, you will be able to:

Explain what is meant by a functional area of business

Describe the major decision activities of the finance function and how technology can support them

Identify sources of information needed to make financial decisions

Describe the major decision activities of the marketing function and how technology can support them

Identify sources of information needed to make marketing decisions

Describe the role and major decision activities of the manufacturing function and how technology can support this function

Distinguish among computer-aided design (CAD), computer-aided manufacturing (CAM), computer-integrated manufacturing (CIM), flexible manufacturing system (FMS), materials resources planning (MRP II), and just-in-time (JIT) production

Identify sources of information needed to make manufacturing decisions

Describe the information systems that support the research and development (R&D) and human resource management (HRM) functions

So far, we have examined MIS from a number of different perspectives. First, we looked at the technological perspective: the software and hardware systems that serve different MIS needs. Then, we considered MIS from an application perspective, breaking MIS down into four specific activity areas: transaction processing systems (TPS), management reporting systems (MRS), decision support systems (DSS), and office information systems (OIS). During the process of covering transaction processing systems, the source of most internal information, we also looked at several data flow diagrams that enabled us to consider MIS from a data perspective. Finally, the decision-making support provided by management reporting, decision support, and executive information systems was addressed from an information perspective.

In this chapter, we consider MIS from yet another perspective: the functional area. After a brief introduction to the main functional areas of business, we look at information systems in three key functional areas: finance, marketing, and manufacturing. We will also examine research and development (R&D), information systems, and human resource information systems (HRIS). Information technology plays a key role in each of these areas and the importance of its role is steadily increasing. Figure 13.1 depicts some of the computerized activities in each of these areas.

THE FUNCTIONAL AREAS OF BUSINESS: AN OVERVIEW

Virtually every business consists of several well-defined functions. Often, these functions are organized into areas or departments. These areas are known as the **functional areas** of business; in each functional area, a well-defined business function is performed. For example, the area within a business organization responsible for pricing, coordinating consumer advertising efforts, and distributing the firm's products or services is known as the marketing function. The marketing function is usually performed by the marketing department. Similarly, the area within a firm responsible for making the product—if a product is indeed made—is the manufacturing department.

In this chapter, we will cover three of the functional areas believed to be the most critical in business: finance, marketing, and manufacturing. Overviews of other functional areas—such as research and development, engineering, and personnel—are also included. However, we have omitted coverage of industry-specific functional areas (such as the checking, loan, and portfolio-management functional areas found in the banking industry), concentrating instead on general areas that will interest most students.

Functional Area	Examples of Computerized Tasks
Finance/accounting	Accounts payable
	Accounts receivable
	Budgeting
	Financial statement compilation
	Fixed assets control
	Payroll
	Portfolio analysis
Marketing	Market analysis
	Order entry
	Sales tracking
Production	Computer-aided manufacturing (CAM)
	Inventory control
	Manufacturing scheduling
	Materials resources planning (MRP II)
Research and development	Computer-aided design (CAD)
	Patent searches
	Specialized engineering functions
Personnel/human resources management	Employee evaluation
	Employee tracking
	Government report generation
	Recruiting

Figure 13.1   Examples of computerized tasks in various functional areas of business.

As we cover each of the functional areas, remember that, ideally, data should be a resource belonging to the entire firm, and not just to particular individuals or departments. So, for instance, such resources as marketing data should be available to people in other functional areas who need them to do their jobs. In practice, this ideal is not always followed. After all, information represents power, and power is something that people do not easily relinquish.

The types of decisions made in each of the functional areas are generally far less structured than the types of data-handling activities required in the transaction processing systems covered in Chapter 9. For example, as you saw in Chapter 9, preparing an invoice requires a very predictable set of data inputs: a customer name and address, product descriptions, product prices, amounts ordered of each product, and a total. Preparing a sales forecast for a product, however, may require historical data (from the transaction processing system), marketing research data about consumer demand patterns, marketing intelligence data about competitive products, internal financial data (which might suggest limitations of funds available for promoting the product), and so on. In the final analysis, a sales forecast, like so many other decision-making outputs, depends on each person's judgment. If ten people prepared a sales forecast, each of them would probably use different sources of data and weigh the data from each source in their own ways.

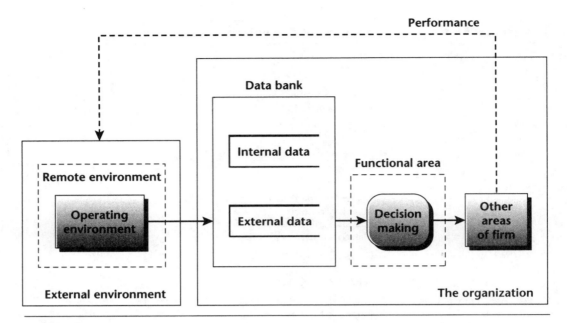

Figure 13.2   Data flow diagram for decision making.

In each of the functional areas, a data flow model portrays the local decision-making environment. Figure 13.2 shows the basic form of this model, which consists of the following components:

- ■ *External environment* The external environment consists of all important entities outside the firm that interacts with it. The external environment contains two components: the operating environment, which consists of consumers, suppliers, competitors, distributors, and the labor supply; and the remote environment, which consists of economic, social, political, technological, and industry concerns. All of these environmental sources generate key external information that flows into the firm, sometimes very informally.

- ■ *Data bank* An organization's bank of data (some or all of which may be available to a functional area) consists of "internal data"—such as those generated from the firm's transaction processing system or from internal forecasts—and "external data", which are those data collected from monitoring the external environment. Both types of data have information potential.
  The term "data bank" is used generically to describe the general storage of data. It should not be confused with the term "database", which refers to a specific logical and physical representation of data. A data bank, as used here, can include data existing in filing cabinets, in computer databases, or even in a copy of the *Wall Street Journal* sitting on a manager's desk.

- ■ *Decision making* Decision making is the heart of each functional data flow model. This process consists of selecting those data needed to make a decision and then making the decision. In the data flow diagram dedicated to each of the functional areas, we will look at the key decisions that take place in those areas.

- **Other areas of the firm**   This box indicates that information produced by decision making in one functional area is often data to another. For example, the sales forecast prepared by the marketing department is used as data by the finance department to produce the overall financial plan for the company.

- **Feedback mechanism**   The dotted feedback arrow indicates that decisions made by the firm ultimately affect its performance in the marketplace. The firm's performance, in turn, generates other data that are used by elements in the environment. The firm's performance is often important to the competitors, consumers, and suppliers in its operating environment, whereas the remote environment is generally not affected. Only a radical change coming from within a huge organization such as the federal government, a state (or provincial) government, or a corporate giant like IBM would cause noticeable change in the remote environment.

FINANCIAL INFORMATION SYSTEMS

The *finance* area is the functional arm of the firm that is responsible for overall financial planning and raising capital. Because the finance area controls the cash flow of the organization and because we are living in a merger-and-acquisition era in which financial deals can make or break a company, finance is often one of the fastest tracks to the top of an organization.

The ways in which firms organize to carry out the finance function differ widely. In many enterprises, an accounting/finance department is run by a person called a **chief financial officer (CFO)**. A *controller,* who is basically the chief accounting officer of the firm, often reports to a CFO. One of the tasks of the controller is to oversee the firm's transaction processing systems. As noted before, transaction processing systems are the backbone of a company's financial health because they account for virtually all of the money coming into and going out of a firm.

Since we have already covered transaction processing systems, we will now consider other aspects of the finance/accounting function—those related to decision-making activities. Specifically, we will look at financial planning and control—the systems involved with the organization's financial needs.

Types of Decisions

Three important decision activities comprise the finance area: forecasting, funds management, and auditing overall financial performance (see Figure 13.3). The first two activities are important to managerial planning, especially strategic planning; the third area, auditing, is primarily oriented toward managerial control.

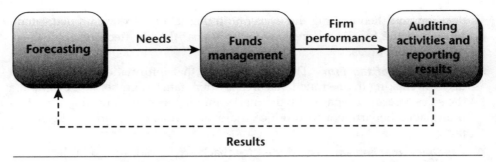

Figure 13.3 The finance function.

Forecasting

Based on forecasts submitted by each of the functional areas and on key external environment data, a **financial forecast** is prepared. The forecast normally shows sources (and amounts) of money coming into the firm and uses (and amounts) of money going out. Often, these forecasts cover a relatively long period of time, perhaps ten years or more. The forecast shows when the firm is likely to have a cash surplus and when a cash deficit may exist. Cash is a major financial concern because employees, creditors, stockholders, and bondholders all require cash payments at prespecified times; an I.O.U. normally will not suffice. The organization must constantly be concerned that it has the necessary cash available to meet current obligations.

Financial models that reflect inflows and outflows of cash are often called **cash flow models**. Many computerized tools can assist in the mathematical modeling of cash flow and in the preparation of forecasts. Financial modeling packages that facilitate simulation and what-if analyses are especially valuable in determining which source and use areas are particularly sensitive to future events. These types of tools were covered earlier (see Chapters 3 and 10).

The financial forecasting software available today is impressive—and constantly improving. Users can choose, or have the software choose, from among a variety of statistical forecasting techniques such as *exponential smoothing* (a procedure that takes weighted sums of past data in order to smooth or forecast a time series), *decomposition methods* (techniques that separate trend, seasonal, cyclical, and random components from data), or the *Box-Jenkins method* (a relatively complex, moving-average procedure used for short-term forecasting). Many of the commercially available forecasting packages also allow for some type of *intervention analysis* so that a modeler can eliminate the effects of components that might distort the data. Often, results can be output in both tabular and graphical formats.

Funds Management

Once a forecast is prepared that show when revenues will be collected and payments disbursed, the next step in financial planning is to determine whether any external financing is necessary. If the company is unable to meet its obligations at any time, the finance area must decide how to raise needed funds. Some possible sources are getting a loan, issuing bonds (called debt financing), issuing stock (called equity financing), merging with a company, and becoming acquired by another organization. The master schedule that combines the financial forecast with the income and disbursements related to external financing sources is often called the *financial plan*.

One type of high-tech tool that is especially useful for preparing such a schedule is Monte Carlo simulation, summarized in Chapter 3, which uses probabilities to represent uncertainty and risk. Often, some type of simulation tool (Monte Carlo or otherwise) is used to model alternatives for external financing under a variety of economic scenarios. Each simulation should show how the master financial plan is impacted under certain funding options and economic assumptions. A what-if simulation tool, for instance, could answer such questions as the following: What if a 10,000-share common stock issue is floated in 1995 at a $10 par? What if 100 bonds are issued in 1997 with a face value of $1,000 and an interest rate of 7 percent? What if a depression starts next year? And so on. Hundreds of realistic possible sources for external financing may exist, and simulation is a good technique for quickly assessing the relative efficacy of financing strategies. In fact, the number of financing options is reaching such staggering proportions today that modeling and simulation are almost mandatory tools for financial forecasters.

Whether or not a company chooses to borrow money depends in part on the leverage it gains through tax breaks and the strength of its current financial portfolio. Many companies have liquid assets to meet short-term obligations, as well as stocks and bonds in other organizations. A major responsibility of the finance area is managing this portfolio in a manner consistent with the goals of the organization. An abundance of computer software is available to assist in portfolio management. Organizations with large portfolios that must be monitored continuously find programs that automatically trigger buy and sell orders to be especially useful. However, these programs, which are used widely by large institutional investors, are also severely criticized for causing wild stock market swings.

Auditing

Another important responsibility in the finance/accounting area is **auditing**. An audit is an inspection that determines whether something is working according to organizational guidelines, or in the way that individuals or departments claim it is working. There are two types of audits: internal audits and external audits.

■ *Internal audits*   Virtually every large company has an internal auditing staff. The tasks of an internal audit vary. A *financial audit*, for example, verifies the accuracy of the company's financial accounting records. If the records show $10,000 in phone expenses, phone billings must be individually checked or sampled to ensure (or at least be reasonably certain) that the sum of the individual bills matches the records. The results of the financial audit can also verify how close portions of the forecast came to what actually happened. An *operational audit*, on the other hand, verifies whether a procedure works as claimed. For example, if a bank computer program is supposed to calculate interest in a certain way, the audit should verify that it does. Many firms use a person known as an *EDP (electronic data processing) auditor* to assist with audits related to computer and technology systems.

- **External audits**   External audits are financial audits performed by independent certified public accountants (CPA). External audits are a periodic necessity because creditors and investors require an unbiased testament that the wealth, revenues, and expenses claimed by the firm are legitimate. The principal outputs of the external audit are a *balance sheet*, showing the firm's assets and equities, and an *income statement*, reporting revenues and expenses. Frequently, both the balance sheet and the income statement—along with flattering accounts of the company's recent activities—are packaged into an impressive-looking annual report, which is sent to stockholders, creditors, investment firms, and other interested parties. In addition, large firms often produce quarterly reports. For any of these reports, the independent CPA normally also prepares a signed statement testifying that the balance sheet and income statement were prepared using either "generally accepted accounting principles" or, by necessity, some other approach.

Sources of Financial Information

Figure 13.4 shows a number of important data sources for information needed to make financial decisions. These sources are examined next.

- **Transaction processing data**   Transaction processing data are most useful for control and audit purposes. These data include the revenues for the firm as a whole and the expenses incurred in each of the functional areas. Transaction processing data are also especially helpful in updating the financial plan.

- **Internal forecast data**   For planning purposes, the company needs estimates of expected expenses from each of the functional areas, as well as sales and revenue projections from the marketing department. These types of planning data can be used later by the firm and by each functional area, for control purposes, to determine how actual results differed from projected results.

- **Funding data**   Funding data provide information on specific sources of funds, as well as on the availability and the terms that are associated with alternative funding packages. Included among the funding data are financial obligations: dividends to stockholders, bond interest payments, redemption payments, and loans.

- **Portfolio data**   Portfolio data show the current portfolio of securities held by the organization, as well as the prices of securities in the financial marketplace.

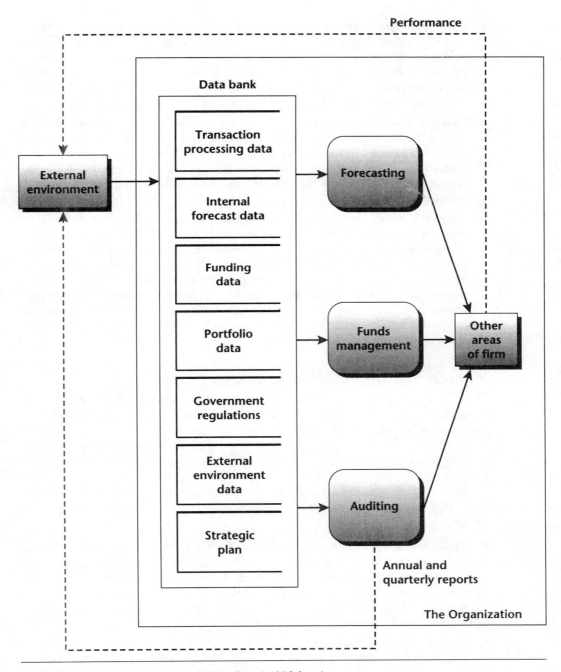

Figure 13.4 Data flow representation of the financial MIS function.

- **Government regulations** Government regulations are important sources of financial information. For instance, numerous government regulations dictate what firms can and cannot do as they raise money. Also, as evidenced by recent scandals on Wall Street, several rules regulate the trading of insider investment information. Additionally, the government regulates disclosure of certain financial data in both the private and public sectors.

- **External environment data** A critical part of the finance function relates to future events happening in the external environment. For example, if long-term interest rates are expected to rise, now might be a good time to create a bond issue. Thus, predictive data are needed regarding the economy, potential actions of the federal reserve, and the activities of other government entities.

- **Strategic plan** The strategic plan, because it charts the future of the company, is also a vital component of the financial plan. For example, if an organization's strategic plan calls for a 20 percent increase in profitability, that goal must be appropriately reflected in the financial plan. Also, specific instructions in the mission and scope statement may restrict certain sources of financing. Some firms, for instance, do not want to further dilute equity ownership by issuing more stock; others are wary of certain types and amounts of debt financing (for example, a firm might prohibit investments in certain countries).

Accounting Information Systems

Closely related to financial information systems are accounting information systems. Figure 13.5 illustrates the major components of an accounting system. These include the order processing system, the accounts receivable system, the accounts payable system, the inventory processing and control system, the purchasing system, the general ledger system, and the payroll system. Each of these components was described in Chapter 9.

According to a recent article in *Computerworld,* many enhancements have occurred in accounting software over the past few years. These are some of the major changes:

- **Consolidation packages** Accounting products now commonly incorporate high-quality consolidation packages. These make it possible to quickly consolidate the division-level results of multiple divisions on the parent company's accounting system(s). This enables top-level managers to compare the performances of the company's various divisions, and also gives them a picture of the company's overall performance.

- **Executive information systems (EIS)** In order to add a friendlier interface and to enable users to create more complicated, customized reports, many of the accounting software products now on the market incorporate EIS modules. The general characteristics of executive information systems were discussed in Chapter 10.

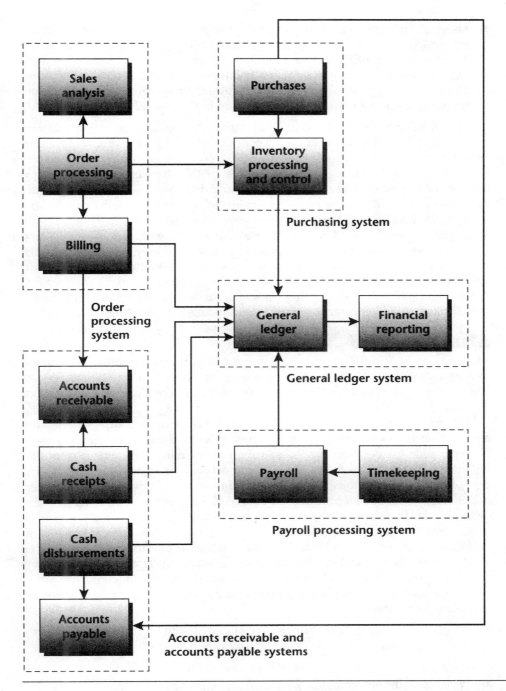

Figure 13.5 The major components of an accounting information system. Accounting information systems blend transaction processing and financial reporting systems. One possible relationship between a TPS and an organization's financial reporting functions is illustrated in this figure.

- **Imaging capabilities** One of the newest enhancements incorporates integrated imaging capabilities with accounting systems. While a limited number of accounting software vendors currently have products with these capabilities, accounting systems with integrated image processing features should become more common in the future. Image-processing and document management systems were discussed in Chapter 12.

The development of microcomputer- and LAN-based accounting software has sparked further interest in downsizing. Downsizing—moving applications from larger mainframe-based platforms to LAN- and microcomputer-based systems—is one of the emerging trends of the 1990s. The capacities and performances of the newest versions of LAN- and PC-based accounting software packages are rivaling those of mainframe-based packages; downsizing is now an option for all but the very largest corporations. According to Howard Millman, Davis Wess—a CPA and partner at Pollan, Mauner, and Wess in Scarsdale, NY (an accounting and financial systems consulting firm)—states that now "you may need a mainframe only if you have absolutely staggering storage needs." Because downsizing should pick up momentum over the next few years, Figure 13.6 lists accounting packages for both large (mainframe-based) systems and smaller (typically microcomputer-based) computing platforms.

MARKETING MIS

Marketing is the functional area of an organization that is responsible for determining the identity of the actual goods and services offered to consumers, as well as the methods needed to effectively price, promote, and distribute those goods and services.

Whereas such decisions as "this firm will produce microcomputer systems" are made at the executive (strategic-planning) level, the marketing department is responsible for determining the specific type of microcomputer system that will meet customer needs—such as a microcomputer system targeted to the entry-level desktop publishing market. The marketing department also determines the price of such a product, the distribution channels (such as retail stores or mail-order firms) necessary to get the product to consumers, and the promotional strategies (for example, television, periodicals, in-store promotional campaigns, and contests) necessary to communicate to consumers the product's value. As mentioned earlier, the marketing department is also responsible for forecasting both the demand for the product and its expected income.

Four important decision areas in marketing are products, prices, promotion, and place. For instance:

- Which *products* (goods or services) should be offered?
- At what *price* should the products be offered?
- Which strategies are most appropriate to *promote* the product?
- Which distribution channels (or *places*) are appropriate?

These four decision areas are often referred to as the **marketing mix** or as the "four Ps."

ACCOUNTING PACKAGES	
Large-System Packages	**Vendor**
Masterpiece	Computer Associates International
M&D	Dun & Bradstreet
Global Software	Global Software, Inc.
MSA	Dun & Bradstreet
Small-System Packages	**Vendor**
Platinum	Advanced Business Microsystems, Inc.
Accpac Plus	Computer Associates International
Professional Accounting Series	CYMA Systems, Inc.
Accounting Series	Great Plains Software
Macola Accounting Software	Macola, Inc.
Open Systems Accounting Software	Open Systems, Inc.
Realworld Series	Realworld Corporation
SBT Series	SBT Corporation
Solomon III	Solomon Software
MAS 90	State of the Art, Inc.

Figure 13.6 Some of the most popular accounting software packages for both large and PC-based systems. (Adapted from Crane)

Many firms consider marketing to be one of their most critical activities. In order for any firm to succeed, it must sell products or services that consumers will buy. Often, in companies in which marketing is extremely critical, executives refer to their firms as "marketing-oriented." In other words, these executives concede that most of their important decisions relate to satisfying consumer needs. According to Derek Slater, CSC Index, Inc., recently conducted a survey of senior MIS executives and found that four of the top six areas for technology investment for 1992 relate to customer service. These include order processing, postsale customer service, presale customer service, and product delivery.

The success of IBM is largely attributable to an emphasis on marketing. For example, in the mid-1950s, when Univac (then the largest producer of computers in the world) sent engineers to help business customers with their needs, IBM sent marketing representatives to perform the same functions. IBM emphasized that they were selling solutions to business problems, not merely computers. The strategy paid off; by 1960, IBM passed Univac as the world's largest computer maker, a position it still holds.

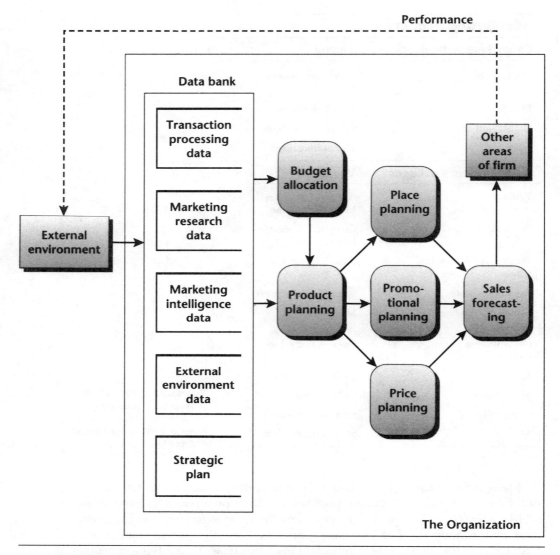

Figure 13.7   Data flow representation of the marketing MIS area.

Marketing Decisions

The principal decision areas in marketing are planning areas corresponding to the "four Ps" (marketing mix). Fifth and sixth decision-making areas are budgeting (allocating funds among the four Ps) and preparing a sales forecast (that is, predicting the product demand that the chosen fund allocation is expected to create in the marketplace). Figure 13.7 represents these six decision areas.

Product Planning

Place, promotion, and price decisions cannot be made until the company decides which products should be produced. Product planning is often a very complicated, unstructured decision. For example, if a past product showed poor performance in the marketplace, was it because the product was fundamentally poor, or because it was priced incorrectly? Or was it given an image that consumers found displeasing? Or was the sales force too small? Dozens of factors—and combinations of factors—contribute to a product's success or failure. Complicating these product planning decisions are the facts that the tastes of consumers constantly change and that competitors always develop new products that must be studied carefully.

Most products follow a *product growth cycle*, as Figure 13.8 shows. Growth cycles apply also to computer systems, organizations, and many other phenomena; one such growth cycle was discussed in Chapter 4. Product growth cycles have four stages: (1) the period when the product is being introduced, (2) the period when the product is becoming established, (3) the period when the product is experiencing its best performance, and (4) the period of the product's maturity. When the product is mature, it is often replaced by an improved product, and the growth cycle starts again.

As mentioned earlier, the product's stage in its growth cycle is an important consideration in decision making. At the beginning of the cycle, when whether or not to produce a product is decided, decision making is most unstructured. Such external environment data as consumer trends, the economic outlook, and competitor offerings are collected and evaluated. Here, the greatest benefits that technology provides are systems that monitor the external environment and that spot trends leading to product-introduction opportunities. Once a product is actually on the market and sales data are available, virtually the only product-related decisions are whether to refine the product or to discontinue it (most of the other marketing decisions at this point relate to price, promotion, and place). Here, technology is most useful by providing fast access to and analysis of sales data. For instance, according to Larry Stevens, the Wal-Mart chain uses point-of-sale (POS) terminals to collect sales data in each of its outlets, and it polls every one of its stores across the United States each night. The system thus enables central management to assess market performance daily. POS terminals are increasingly used to collect customer demographics and other important market research data.

Place Planning

Place planning concerns decisions about how the product is distributed. For example, firms such as JC Penney and Sears sell goods exclusively in their own stores or from their own catalogs. When the IBM PC was first introduced, IBM had to decide if it was going to sell the machines in its own retail outlets, in retail chains such as Computerland and MicroAge, through mail-order firms, or

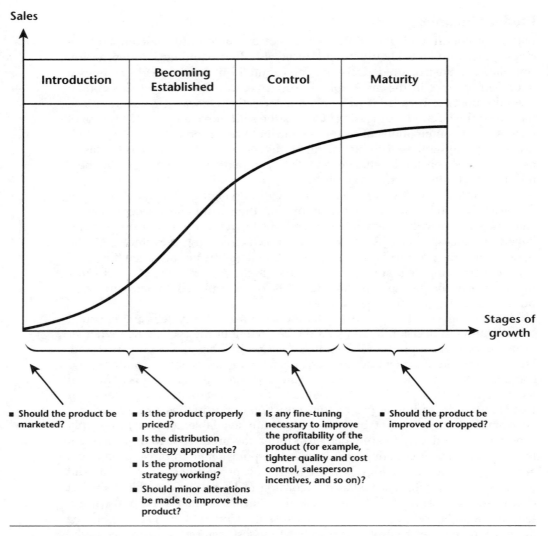

Figure 13.8 The product growth cycle and related decisions.

through a combination of these *distribution channels*. In some cases, such as the gas you buy at the service station, a chain of distributors is involved. For example, Texaco typically sells gasoline to a distributor in a geographical area. This distributor then sells the gas to service stations. When such a distribution chain is involved, removing the company from its ultimate consumer, it becomes more difficult to determine market penetration in a specific geographical area.

One of the most significant impacts that technology has in the distribution area is regarding the interorganizational and electronic data interchange (EDI) systems that tie firms more closely to their customers. For instance, Singer is one of many companies that put computer terminals in customer locations.

Customers can use the system to check prices and availabilities, order merchandise, arrange for shipment, and check the status of their orders. By establishing a direct link from the firm to the customer, a new marketing channel opens that enables customers to buy goods. As with any other channel, it can be enhanced; in this case, with such features as free software services for customers and increased ordering conveniences.

Information technology has also established the telemarketing center as a useful distribution channel. Ben Bencievenqa writes that by putting customer data at the fingertips of telemarketing salespeople, telemarketing firms are better able to target potential buyers. Recipients of the often bothersome calls of telemarketers are usually amazed at how much knowledge these marketers have about their recent purchases, tastes, and so on.

An information technology-based method that some firms use to review their distribution strategy is the computer-generated sales map. Such a map shows the geographical areas in which sales have taken place. One common distribution strategy is to concentrate distribution efforts in the areas of highest demand. The flipside of this strategy, which makes sense for different reasons, is to concentrate new distribution efforts on unexploited areas.

Besides deciding the specific channels for distribution, firms must establish procedures for determining the effectiveness of its distribution channels.

Promotion

Promotion is composed of two principal areas: personal selling and advertising.

Personal selling involves selling a product with a sales force. For years, virtually the only assistance given to sales managers by computers was a hardcopy sales report—generated by management reporting systems as a by-product of transaction processing—that showed sales made by divisions or by various salespeople. Usually, sales were also cross-classified with respect to product and region. Although such systems are useful for formal performance appraisal and for assessing the success of product strategies, the data obtained from them are of limited use for short-range planning purposes.

Today, decisions must be made much faster. As reflected in the comments of a Toro manager, employees no longer have the luxury of sitting back and waiting. Flexibility is mandatory; if something is not working according to plan, management must know about it immediately.

Technology is vital to the selling effort in several ways. For instance, technology ties customers and suppliers more closely to the selling effort through computers and communications, provides tools that give the salesperson more time to sell, supplies tools that make the salesperson more effective at the client site, helps uncover important selling opportunities, and makes salespeople more efficient. The following are some examples:

■ *Tying in customers and suppliers* Expanding a transaction processing system to include on-line communication with customers and suppliers—known as an interorganizational or an EDI system—has been covered extensively in this book. Such systems have several benefits. In the selling

Using Bank Debit Cards in the Supermarket

Automatic teller machines (ATM) are one of the most visible and successful aspects of the banking industry. With an ATM card, a bank customer can walk up to a kiosk, often mounted on an outside wall of the bank, and withdraw money whenever needed—7 days a week, 24 hours a day.

". . . THE FUNDS ARE ELECTRONICALLY SUBTRACTED FROM THE CUSTOMER'S ACCOUNT AND ADDED TO THE SUPERMARKET'S VIA A COMMUNICATIONS NETWORK."

Now, ATM debit cards issued by banks are providing shoppers with another way to pay for groceries. Here's how one system works: While the card is inserted into a small slot on the side of the point-of-sale (POS) register by the checkout clerk, the customer uses a shielded keypad to enter his or her secret personal identification number (PIN). If the payment is approved, the funds are electronically subtracted from the customer's account and added to the supermarket's via a communications network.

Advocates of such systems claim that the average value of a shopper's purchase is higher when the ATM cards are used, because the shopper is not limited by the amount of money in his or her physical possession. These systems can also help reduce clerical labor and back-office accounting costs.

Supermarkets are not the only types of businesses who see the benefits of such systems. ATM check-out systems have also been installed in department stores such as Wal-Mart and should become increasingly common during the 1990s.

Adapted from Garry (1992).

---

area, the most prominent benefit is cutting information float along the customer-firm-supplier chain.

Thus, instead of discovering such events as product shortages long after they occur, or learning that a product is not selling well weeks after the information first surfaced, with the right technology, management can have up-to-the-minute knowledge about selling activities and inventories. This keeps the salespeople maximally useful, focusing their attention on the hottest products and having the inventory available for them to close important sales.

■ *Increasing selling time*   Salespeople are often besieged with numerous routine questions that can take up a lot of time: Are these products in stock? How much do these products cost? When can I expect shipment? Some companies, such as Singer, set up interorganizational computing systems that free the sales force from many such questions by providing customers with on-line information-retrieval privileges that allow them to answer most of their own questions. Companies such as General Tire, on the other hand, set up telemarketing centers that customers can call to get a telemarketer's responses to these questions. General Tire also has the telemarketing center handle marginally profitable accounts—those that cannot be profitably serviced by the sales force. During the first month of operation, the telemarketing staff sold more to these accounts than the field sales force had sold to them over the entire previous year.

- ■ *Increasing effectiveness at the client site*   In the service area, Pitney-Bowes uses information technology to make its field engineering effort more effective. Customers call an 800 number if they have a problem with Pitney-Bowes equipment. The problem is then fed to a computerized diagnostic system to see if it can be solved over the phone. If the problem requires a visit by a field engineer, a computerized database is checked to determine the nearest engineer who can both handle the problem and service it at the lowest possible cost. Before the new system went into effect, Pitney-Bowes had to train every field engineer to solve a wide range of repair problems, resulting in high training costs and little opportunity to specialize.

  Some companies use technology to make their salespeople more effective at the client site by arming them with laptop or notebook computers (often including modems and fax boards), or with pen-based computers capable of immediately transmitting customer orders to the home office over wireless networks. We already mentioned two examples of these uses of information technology. In Chapter 1, we discussed the McKesson salesperson who, armed with a laptop computer at the client site, convinced the client not to switch to a competitive product after dialing into an FDA databank and discovering that the competitive product had not met certain effectiveness standards. The second case involved an account representative for an insurance company who sold a client on an investment package by running several what-if investment scenarios with a spreadsheet package while in the client's office.

  Nabisco outfitted its sales reps with handheld terminals tied into its mainframe-based Value-Added Selling Techniques (VAST) system. These terminals allow their sales force to enter and access store-by-store information about products' shelf movement, prices, and weekly promotions. The data can help sales reps make recommendations for more effective use of shelf space and marketing dollars. Elisabeth Horwitt writes that according to Don Castle, Jr. (director of sales technology and administration for Nabisco), once sales reps establish a connection to the mainframe, "VAST walks you through . . . you look up the numbers, push a few buttons, and out pops a graph." VAST even helps Nabisco's sales reps battle rivals who offer stores up-front money (a cash incentive) to put in a product display. In this case, Nabisco's sales rep first accesses VAST's "combatting up-front money" application to prove to the store's buyer that more profit could be brought in with a Nabisco display (without an up-front incentive) than with a rival's display (including the up-front incentive). According to Nabisco, VAST improves the sales force's productivity by more than $50 million per year.

- **Identifying selling opportunities** According to Jim Wallerstedt, a tickler system operated by a sales manager consists of a database of customers, word processing and data management software, and a calendaring system. Using this system, the manager quickly sees which customers need to be contacted in a specific time frame, sends timely letters to both present customers and new leads (to both maintain and initiate contact), and manages time better. The system also enables the manager to identify and address target markets and submarkets. The manager comments, "Where in the past we might have made a direct mail or telemarketing campaign that would shotgun across a group, we are now able to break into several more specific campaigns based on demographic fields and carry out these without increased manpower. The net result is performance that is only possible with computer support."

    At Hewlett-Packard, an electronic mail system ties sales representatives to the marketing department. When a lead is given to the salesperson by the marketing department, an electronic form automatically pops up in the salesperson's electronic mailbox. The form requires the rep to respond as to whether the client business was won or lost and why. The company uses these results to position and price products, as well as to design future product features. *Business Week* cites one HP marketing vice-president as claiming, "There is not a marketing executive around who wouldn't give his [or her] left hand to get that kind of information."

    At Grand Union Co., a large eastern supermarket chain, a software package called Spaceman II helps decide what to stock and where to stock it. The program suggests which shelf and floor layouts provide the best balance between profit and product movement, while maintaining acceptable stock levels. Spaceman II prints out graphically oriented "plan-o-grams" at a PC in corporate headquarters, and the outputs are distributed to the local stores. According to a vice-president at Grand Union, the average store holds about 7,000 items—and with about 7,000 new products appearing each year, automated planning tools are greatly needed. Grand Union firmly believes in the results delivered by Spaceman II; a store manager's performance is evaluated regarding both his or her results and how well the advice in the plan-o-grams was followed.

- **Making salespeople more efficient** As *Datamation* relates, a partner in a New York City-based package design firm states, "Our client requested some design changes that meant we had to redo ten [package designs]. This was at noon. We made the changes on the [computer] system that afternoon, photographed the new [designs] on a drugstore shelf that evening, and had a slide show ready for senior management at nine o'clock the next morning. Without the computer, we never would have been able to do that." The executive referred to a package design system called Contex Design System, which allows designers to use computer graphic techniques to create a package, color it, and duplicate it several times. This process produces an image that simulates the package standing on a shelf next to other products—thus providing marketing managers with a true feel for the package's design.

When planning advertising campaigns, which involves a lot of creativity, the computer now plays an increasingly important role. For example, approaches that take advantage of services such as single-source data are quite effective. *Single-source data* works by monitoring both the purchases of households and their television habits. By determining which types of purchasers watch which shows, advertising campaigns can be quickly changed. Subsequently, shifts in product sales levels by specific consumers can be measured to determine the effectiveness of such decisions. These approaches are becoming more sophisticated each year.

Computers are also now more widely used directly in the production of television advertisements. The same types of technologies used for producing TV ads are used in movie production, such as in the making of *The Last Starfighter*. We will elaborate on this later because it represents a case in which technology was used to "manufacture" a new product.

Price

Determining the price at which products are offered is an extremely important marketing decision. However, the computer was not historically very helpful in this area. Some attempts were made to develop computerized pricing models that simulate the possible results of pricing decisions but, to date, little success is reported. However, this area is considered ripe for applying pattern recognition systems such as neural networks.

Among the most successful applications of technology to pricing support are commercial database services. All a user really needs are a terminal or personal computer, a modem, access to a phone line, and a subscription to a service that specializes in information that is of interest. Using such services as Dow Jones News, for instance, managers can look over industry, competitor, and consumer statistics that may potentially impact pricing decisions. Additionally, the rapid feedback now obtainable through computer and communications networks enables firms to determine much more quickly the results of pricing decisions on demand. This facilitates more aggressive pricing strategies.

Budget Allocations and Sales Forecasting

In addition to the four Ps, two other important decision-making areas in marketing are the allocation of the marketing budget and sales forecasting.

Marketing, like any other functional area, does not have an unlimited source of funds. Thus, a budget must limit the overall size of expenditures. The marketing vice-president or manager must determine what portion of the budget is allocated to each of the marketing efforts. Some computerized allocation models can estimate desirable mixes in this area, but success is limited. This decision is still made largely through manual means and personal judgment.

The sales forecast reflects estimates by the marketing staff on future product sales. Because product sales are the main source of company revenue, the sales forecast is an important part of the financial plan. Sales forecasting models are widely used; many of them employ some type of regression analysis approach. Numerous technology tools used in sales forecasting are similar to those used in financial forecasting.

Sources of Marketing Information

Information used for marketing decisions comes from a variety of data sources, the most important of which were shown in Figure 13.7 (page 362).

- **Transaction processing data** Transaction processing data show the sales that result from specific mixes of the four Ps. Thus, they provide feedback on the effectiveness of past marketing strategies. They are also useful for appraising performance and controlling marketing expenditures.

- **Marketing research data** Marketing research is the marketing area responsible for gathering consumer-related data that can be used to support marketing decisions; for example, personal interviews, phone interviews, and mail surveys. Statistical packages are often used by the marketing research staff to analyze these data and to provide useful facts about a product that could not otherwise be obtained from analyzing raw sales figures. Often, tests determine if the research findings are statistically significant or if they should be attributed, instead, to chance.

- **Marketing intelligence data** Marketing intelligence refers to information about the strategies of competitors. The term "intelligence" is a carryover from the military, which uses the term to describe data gathered about enemy activities. Most marketing intelligence information is collected in an unstructured or semistructured manner: through word-of-mouth interaction or through observing statistics available in the media and commercial database services.

- **External environment data** In marketing, success is largely attributable to what will happen in the future external environment. For example, when a new car is introduced, the firm never knows exactly how consumers will react to it. Maybe a prototype was built, and the marketing research staff found that, perhaps, 98 out of 135 people who tested the prototype loved it and said they would buy it. But whether they actually do buy the car, in fact, depends on numerous other factors in the external environment. For instance, the economy may be in recession when the car comes out. Or the government may change its policy on imported cars. Or a change in the price of gas may change the way people react to the car.

- **Strategic plan** The strategic plan is really the starting point of all marketing decisions. It contains the types of products that the firm plans to supply to the consumer marketplace. These broad guidelines define the direction of the marketing effort. The tactical marketing plan addresses what, how, when, and where questions that are appropriate to the implementation of the strategic plan.

MANUFACTURING MIS

Manufacturing is the functional area of the organization that is responsible for producing goods from raw materials. Recently, manufacturing firms have received increasing attention because rapidly shifting consumer tastes and heightened global pressures now necessitate shorter product design cycles and more responsive manufacturing facilities. Pressures from abroad also led to an increasing emphasis on quality in the United States. The TQM (Total Quality Management) movement, which is picking up momentum in most industries and even in public sector organizations, reflects the increased importance of quality. Not every company selling goods, of course, is involved in manufacturing activities. As described in Chapter 2, companies that buy ready-made goods and resell them are known as merchandising firms.

Manufacturing Decisions

Figure 13.9 shows the primary decisions made in the manufacturing area. These include product design, production, facility design, and quality control.

Product Design

Product design (or *product engineering*) is the starting point of the manufacturing process. It is the step in which the design and technical specifications for the product are finalized. Increasingly, product design and engineering are becoming more computerized through approaches such as computer-aided design (CAD) and computer-aided engineering (CAE).

With **computer-aided design (CAD)** and computer-aided engineering (CAE), product designers or engineers use technology to design a product and, before it goes into production, to thoroughly test it for such concerns as safety, durability, and ease of producibility. The initial design can be input to the CAD system in various ways, including drawing sketches on a digitizing tablet, using an image scanner or a digitizing camera to create a digital image from sketches or photographs, or using solid-modeling software to build a series of equations that represent the surface contours of the product. After the product is digitally represented, it can be tested—by referencing specifications databases or by simulating its performance under real-world conditions—to make sure that it meets a set of standards. As changes are suggested, the original design is edited—similar to editing a letter on a word processor. Increasingly, artificial intelligence techniques are applied to CAD systems to analyze and appraise functional characteristics of a design and to help simulate product performance under various conditions, thus reducing the expenses associated with physical prototypes.

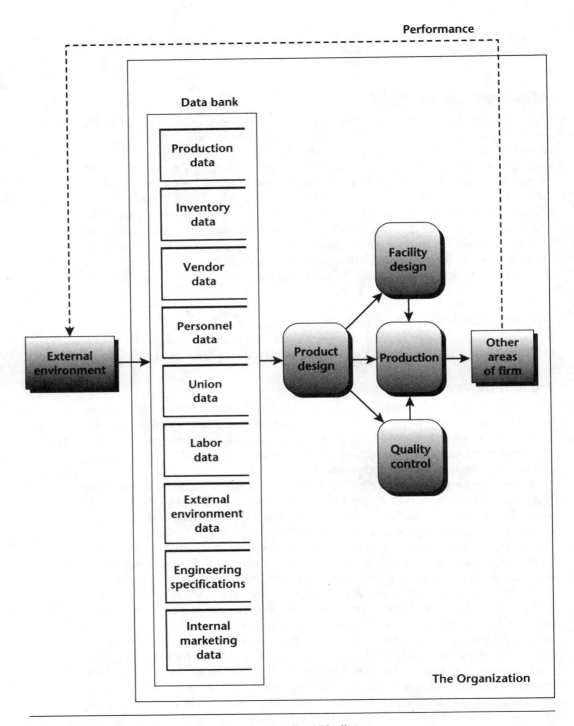

Figure 13.9 Data flow representation of the manufacturing MIS effort.

For companies that rely heavily on automation, product designs must also be fairly easy to produce. Designing products for easy assembly is critical because assembly often accounts for over half of the total manufacturing costs. For example, when Northern Telecom redesigned its phones by reducing the number of components in them from 325 to 156, it also drastically cut manual assembly times and manufacturing costs. Companies such as IBM, Xerox, Hewlett-Packard, and General Electric are among the many other firms whose product designs reflect production considerations. Ease of producibility is a major consideration in the development of flexible manufacturing systems (FMS), which we'll discuss later in this chapter.

CAD and CAE are especially helpful when designing such products as automobiles, aircraft, ships, buildings, electric circuits (including computer chips), and even running shoes. Besides playing an important decision support role in the design and engineering of durable goods, CAD is also very useful in such fields as art, advertising, and movie production. In the latter examples, CAD is used as a tool to produce a marketable product.

For example, for *The Last Starfighter*, Digital Productions of Los Angeles created approximately 30 minutes of digitally simulated scenes. The scenes were "manufactured" on a Cray X/MP-48 supercomputer, which modeled realistic-looking objects by combining and recombining thousands of polygons at ultra-fast speeds (the Cray X/MP-48 is capable of about a billion calculations per second). The simulated scenes were interspliced with live action throughout the film. Such types of high-tech special effects are also, of course, used by the television industry to create flashy graphics that impart impressive images for stations or shows. Increasingly, television commercials are also taking advantage of special effects in order to hold the viewer's attention.

Facility Design

After a product is designed, the facilities to manufacture it must be planned. This decision may be as simple as changing a few manufacturing stations on the production floor or as complex as designing an entirely new plant.

The computer can also model plant layout. Many of the layout algorithms proposed in the operations management literature use either an improvement or a construction approach (or both). *Improvement algorithms* require the user to specify an initial layout and the relationships among the elements within the layout. A combinatorial-based procedure is then applied to improve upon the initial layout. Often, this is done by using either brute-force or intelligent-search techniques to try thousands or even millions of promising layout alterations; for instance, the effect on the layout of switching the location of machine A with that of machine F. *Construction algorithms*, on the other hand, build one or more layout solutions from scratch, with or without initial suggestions from the user. Realistically, though, virtually all improvement and construction layout techniques require numerous stringent mathematical constraints that hamper their usefulness.

Monte Carlo simulation on computers has been used since the 1950s to address certain facility layout problems—sometimes with substantial success.

Simulation, for instance, was tried by one group of engineers at an Ingersoll-Rand consulting subsidiary when they designed a complicated assembly line for a client who made ball bearings. Originally, the engineers estimated that they would need 77 different machine tools, performing 16 different processes. However, when they simulated the line on the computer, they eliminated four machines and consequently the client saved $750,000.

Production

Production, or manufacturing, is the process of making new products from raw materials. Generally, the production process consists of many interrelated activities. Here, we will look at three of them: production scheduling (deciding which goods should be produced in a given span of time and in what lot sizes), the physical act of producing the goods, and the determination of inventory levels (raw materials and goods-in-process).

There are two basic types of production methods: job shop and process. In **job-shop production**, each order taken by the firm is considered to be a job and each job is identified with a specific customer. As the job progresses, costs related to the job are identified and tagged to it. Two examples of job shops are a shoe repair business and an aircraft builder.

Most production, however, is of the process type. In **process production**, goods are mass-produced for general consumption. The name for this approach derives from the facilities layout (called a process layout) used for assembly-line manufacturing. Process production should not be confused with continuous process operations—such as oil refineries and some chemical plants—that run 24 hours a day. In process production, the costs associated with the production processes are applied, uniformly, to all of the goods produced by those processes. For example, if the packaging process for a certain type of cereal costs the firm $10,000, and 20,000 boxes are made, a 50¢ packaging cost is applied to each unit.

Many computerized approaches are used by firms to model the production process as an integrated system. One particularly successful process production approach, which has been a staple in the automated factory since the early 1980s, is called **manufacturing resources planning (MRP II)**. In an MRP II system, the sales forecast is first used to identify the number of products that must be available for shipment at certain points in time. From this forecast, a production schedule is prepared to establish production goals to meet the projected demand. The production schedule is prepared by MRP II in such a way that it will not exceed physical (shop-floor and warehouse space) or time capacities. Next, a *bill of materials* is prepared on each product to be made (see Figure 13.10). The bill of materials shows all of the raw materials going into the product and their amounts. The bill of materials is then "exploded" (Figure 13.11) to arrive at total raw material requirements. These requirements are next checked against stock on hand (Figure 13.12) to determine order requirements. Often, orders reflect mathematically determined optimal order quantities—amounts that will help the firm minimize total ordering and inventory-carrying costs. The order requirements are also determined so that they do not exceed warehousing

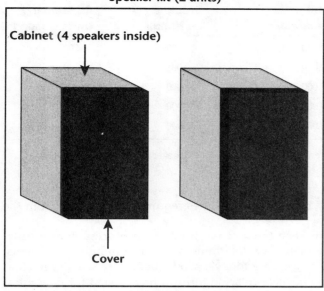

Speaker kit (2 units)

Cabinet (4 speakers inside)

Cover

Bill of materials for speaker kit	
Components	**Quantity**
Cabinet	2
Speakers	8
Cover	2
Screws	32
Packing carton	1

Figure 13.10 A stereo speaker kit and its accompanying bill of materials.

Component	Quantity per Kit	Number of Units to Produce	Total Requirement
Cabinet	2	10,000	20,000
Speakers	8	10,000	80,000
Cover	2	10,000	20,000
Screws	32	10,000	320,000
Packing carton	1	10,000	10,000

Figure 13.11 An exploded bill of materials for the speaker kit shown in Figure 13.10.

Component	Total Requirement	Stock on Hand	Additional Units Needed
Cabinet	20,000	10,000	10,000
Speakers	80,000	60,000	20,000
Cover	20,000	15,000	5,000
Screws	320,000	600,000	0
Packing carton	10,000	40,000	0

Figure 13.12 Raw materials inventory requirements for the speaker kit and bill of materials illustrated in Figures 13.10 and 13.11.

capacity. In addition, they reflect the lead times required for delivery from the vendor.

The MRP II system can keep track of the production process dynamically: checking the production schedule to determine daily, upcoming requirements; accepting new input data concerning today's production, purchase orders, and raw material receipts; allowing workplace figures to be adjusted for new numbers of people assigned to jobs and new work rates; monitoring progress regarding the schedule; and so on. An MRP II system can also be used to produce various management reports on the status of the production process. A complete MRP II system is shown in Figure 13.13.

MRP II and similar integrated production systems often contain 12 or more separate modules. These modules represent such processes as inventory, bill of materials, scheduling, costing, capacity requirements planning, purchasing management, and shop-floor control. Today, over 200 MRP II packages are available. Many of these packages are targeted to specialized manufacturing environments—and to microcomputers as well. Recently, electronic data interchange (EDI) modules were added to many systems to facilitate the generation of accurate sales forecasts and to place orders electronically with suppliers.

MRP II has its greatest support among discrete manufacturers, where components are assembled into a final product such as a car or freezer. According to Advanced Manufacturing Research, Inc., 75–80 percent of all discrete manufacturers use MRP II, while only 15 percent of continuous-process manufacturers (companies that mix fluids, solids, and gases to produce products such as paint, soup, or medicine) have MRP II systems.

Most MRP II systems support the traditional push philosophy of manufacturing by developing production schedules and monitoring production against those schedules. In *push* systems, products are made in large batches. As each batch is finished by one production area (for example, the cutting area), it is "pushed" along to the next production area (for example the assembly area). Many manufacturers in the United States and Canada have used the push method for years. In Japan, however, manufacturing is traditionally done by using the pull, or just-in-time (JIT) production, approach.

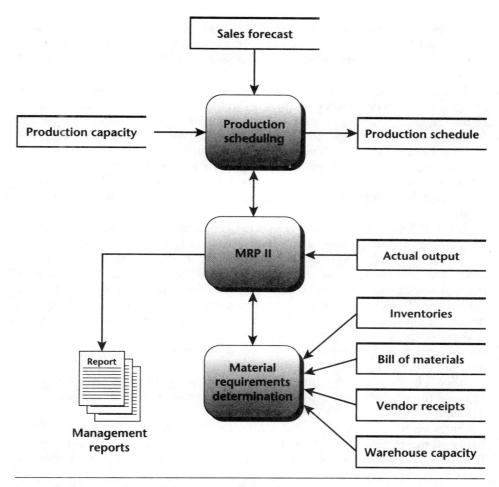

Figure 13.13 MRP II. In MRP II systems, sales forecasts and bills of material are used to generate the production schedules and material inventory requirements needed to meet the forecast demand for the product(s) being manufactured. EDI is increasingly used in conjunction with these computerized systems to develop accurate sales forecasts and to electronically place orders with suppliers.

In *pull* production, individual parts are "pulled" along to the next production process as soon as they are ready. Raw material inventory arrives "just in time" to be used by the plant; in-process inventories are completed by one process just in time to be used by the next process. There is minimal or no batching or stockpiling. Although pull production methods greatly reduce inventory holding costs in some manufacturing situations, they require almost perfect timing and cooperation from suppliers. Because inventory arrives just in time to the plant and to each production process, any shortages may result in either a shutdown or having to create special orders. This makes pull systems like JIT vulnerable to unexpected labor problems such as sit-down and wildcat strikes, both in the main production facility or in those that affect the operations of suppliers. Because pull methods require a complete reorganization of a push shop floor, they also require a considerable setup expense for organizations that want to use them.

Nonetheless, numerous organizations have proven that JIT methods can pay off handsomely. For instance, some firms in the auto industry, which have a lot of buying clout with suppliers, have tied suppliers into interorganizational information systems (such as EDI systems) that facilitate just-in-time buying. Suppliers either commit to certain inventory-holding policies or they are dropped and, therefore, lose a lot of business. Because JIT approaches are so information intensive—that is, suppliers must know how much is needed when—some companies have forced suppliers to establish interorganizational computer links.

MRP II may not be well suited to JIT environments. Kenneth Phelps, director of manufacturing and release systems for Marion Merrell Dow, Inc., feels that MRP II systems are ill-suited for the factory floor of the 1990s. MRP II is helpful for raw material inventories by effectively tracking production schedules. However, when customers demand just-in-time deliveries, MRP II production schedules may not consider customer delivery deadlines. Because more customers now demand JIT deliveries, Phelps expects MRP II systems to be replaced with systems such as *customer-oriented manufacturing management systems (COMMS)* and product-oriented *manufacturing execution systems (MES)*. Unlike MRP II, COMMS tracks schedules built around ("pulled") by customer deadlines; MES oversees the plant-floor steps necessary to make the product (and meet customer requirements) as it is pulled through the factory.

Early versions of COMMS and MES software are already available and virtually all major vendors in this market (including Andersen Consulting, Dun & Bradstreet, IBM, Oracle Corporation, and SAP America, Inc.) plan to produce sophisticated packages by 1994.

Computer-Aided Manufacturing (CAM)

MRP II, JIT, and similar manufacturing technologies represent only a few examples of computer-aided manufacturing applications. **Computer-aided manufacturing (CAM)** is an umbrella term that includes almost any use of computers in manufacturing operations. In addition to the manufacturing operations discussed already, CAM includes the following:

- **Monitoring** An example is the use of computers to open and shut valves at an oil refinery when a certain temperature is reached in a tank or when a prespecified amount of time elapses.

- **Numeric control** Numeric control refers to controlling manufacturing processes by computer. An example is the precision shaping of manufactured parts according to a sequence of operations that were coded into a computer program. A special type of numeric control is robotics.

Wait 'Til You Hear About the Book I Scrolled!

Before long, you may be able to get all bestselling books in one of three ways: hardcover, softcover, and CD-ROM. Electronic books are here, and in many cases, they add remarkable features to the familiar book format. For example, an electronic reference book makes it possible for readers to call up footnotes, illustrations, music, and whatever else they want at any spot in their reading. And, researchers and students appreciate the ease with which they can navigate through massive volumes of information.

During the 1990s, more electronic than bound encyclopedias have been purchased by school libraries; multimedia versions are especially popular. By typing in key words, students can use the electronic version of the *Encyclopaedia Britannica* to instantly browse through articles, illustrations, photos, and even brief animations of the subject they choose.

Electronic books are also entering classrooms. McGraw-Hill, Inc. released a CD-ROM containing interactive lessons in anatomy. Electronic foreign language textbooks with interactive drill-and-practice routines and electronic history books are also available.

"RESEARCHERS AND STUDENTS APPRECIATE THE EASE WITH WHICH THEY CAN NAVIGATE THROUGH MASSIVE VOLUMES OF INFORMATION."

Dozens of other types of electronic books have been developed, including medical references, technical manuals, film guides, and children's stories. The marriage of software and text has definitely captured the interest of publishers—and many of them think that electronic publishing is one of the hottest high-tech opportunities of the 1990s.

_____

Adapted from Schwartz (1992).

- **Robotics**   As discussed in Chapter 11, robotics is the use of computer-controlled machines to perform motor activities previously done by humans: welding a joint, painting, fitting parts together, and so on. Robots are successfully used in various manufacturing operations, notably automobile production.

- **Optimization**   A lot of manufacturing activities involve finding the "best," or optimum, way to allocate resources. Some examples include finding the cheapest way to mix crude oils to achieve a finished gasoline that meets certain restrictions and determining the best way to allocate and/or schedule workers on an assembly line to minimize production costs. These problems are commonly solved by mathematical techniques such as those mentioned in Chapter 3.

Emerging Application Areas

In addition to the trend toward providing computer support for pull manufacturing systems such as JIT, more sophisticated computer support is also emerging in a number of other manufacturing areas. These include computer-integrated manufacturing (CIM), flexible manufacturing systems (FMS), and quality control.

Computer-Integrated Manufacturing (CIM)

Some companies are trying to integrate CAD, CAM, and other manufacturing activities—a concept known as **computer-integrated manufacturing (CIM)**. Ideally, with CIM, all manufacturing processes concerned with information processing, storage, collection, and distribution are related in a way that optimizes performance of the total enterprise. Integration allows organizations to efficiently manage (and control) manufacturing and engineering information by eliminating barriers across departments and functions—possibly even across organizations. CIM increases a company's capability for planning, productivity, responsiveness, control, and innovation.

CIM can provide a major competitive advantage. For instance, the earlier examples of designing a product with producibility is only one example of the CIM movement: linking CAD and CAM. Another example involves a large aerospace company, Lockheed, that requires its major suppliers to acquire CAD equipment that ties into its own CAD system. The company claims that this move toward manufacturing integration sharply reduces total cost and time of design changes, parts acquisition, and inventory, making it more competitive. General Motors (GM) has its CAD/CAM and order-entry systems linked to some of its suppliers' production systems. This allows suppliers to know exactly what GM needs to fill its orders.

Computer-controlled manufacturing works best when products are designed to be manufactured automatically. The IBM team that developed the ProPrinter studied existing printers and found an average of 150 separate parts. They reduced this number to 62 and designed the ProPrinter in layers so that it can be assembled by robots from the bottom up; in the process, the team eliminated screws, springs, pulleys, and other items that required human adjustment. Without these design changes, the printers could not be produced by using robotics and automated manufacturing techniques.

As CIM continues to develop and integrates more manufacturing functions, factories may use such tools as simulation software and expert systems to design both the products to be produced and the facilities used to produce them. These tools might also be used for troubleshooting purposes after the product and facilities are in place. For instance, when monitoring software senses that something is wrong in a production process, data may be fed into an expert system and analyzed. As the expert system deduces possible solutions, they are fed to Monte Carlo simulation software to determine the ramifications. Within seconds or minutes, a course of action is output for consideration by the production supervisor.

Although some organizations have made great strides toward CIM, we are still a long way from realizing its full potential. Several studies indicate that CIM can lead to considerable cost savings (including engineering design, personnel, and inventory costs), improvements in productivity (including engineering, operational, and equipment), improvements in product quality, and more flexible responses to customers. In spite of these potential benefits, a survey of manufacturing executives performed by KPMG Peat Marwick indicates that many companies still feel that CIM is too expensive and too complex.

Flexible Manufacturing Systems (FMS)

As mentioned earlier, such factors as changing consumer tastes and increasing worldwide competition make it necessary for many companies to consider shorter product design cycles and responsive manufacturing facilities; that is, facilities that can be switched easily from making one product to making another. Such considerations have introduced the **flexible manufacturing system (FMS)**.

A manufacturer of metal products, for example, adopted an FMS when it recently shifted from a strategy of making a broad range of products to producing only a limited line. The products in the new line have comparable geometric shapes and similar manufacturing methods, both of which enable fewer product-line changeovers and greater worker familiarity with both the products and with the methods of making them. The company almost doubled its return on sales and increased its profitability by 30 percent after the change was made. Another example is Mitsubishi's VCR factory in Okayama, Japan—a facility whose efficiency is largely because only a few, very similar, basic models are produced. Thus, product-line changeovers are minimized.

Although CIM and FMS are two different concepts, they are related in that manufacturing flexibility is enhanced by integration. For example, if a firm's systems are integrated so that marketing and R&D data pass quickly to manufacturing, and design and production are integrated so that marketing feedback is quickly incorporated into designs that are immediately manufactured on the factory floor, the ultimate FMS is achieved. In other words, the higher the level of integration at every interface, the shorter the delay involved with detection, changeover, and production. A *flexible computer-integrated manufacturing (FCIM)* model that integrates FMS and CIM concepts has been developed; Figure 13.14 illustrates this.

Quality Control

Quality control relates to activities that ensure that the final product is of satisfactory quality. The quality control function is concerned with detecting existing quality deficiencies, as well as with preventing future product quality problems. Often, when the number of units produced is small and the final product is expensive, all produced units are inspected for quality before they leave the plant. The units of goods produced in large volumes, such as diskettes or clothespins, are usually statistically sampled to ensure that the defect rate does not exceed a certain percentage.

Quality control is both an important area of expense and an important area of opportunity. Regarding expense, a typical factory spends about a quarter of its production budget just fixing and finding mistakes. And this cost does not

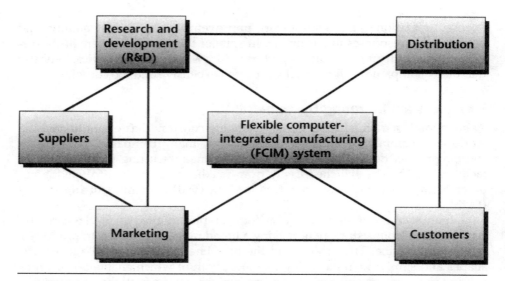

Figure 13.14 A flexible computer-integrated manufacturing (FCIM) system. FCIM combines CIM and flexible manufacturing system (FMS) concepts. FCIM systems demand electronic links among manufacturing, R&D, and marketing/distribution systems of the organization. (Adapted from Merrifield)

reflect losses due to flawed products that leave the factory and are purchased by a consumer. Receiving flawed products is often resented by the customer. The customer may return what is sent and/or may not place future orders. Regarding quality as an opportunity area, consider the Japanese auto industry. U.S. automakers discovered over 10 years ago that the quality of Japanese cars was superior to the autos produced here and that this had become a key factor, along with price, for U.S. car buyers. What makes the success of the Japanese automakers even more stunning is that, before 1960, Japanese cars were rarely seen in North America.

Tom Peters, in his book *Thriving on Chaos*, comments on the importance of quality as it relates to at least one U.S. auto manufacturer, Ford: "Quality really has become Job One at Ford. The once all-powerful finance function has assumed a less dominant role, and manufacturing, the prime source of quality, is no longer low in the organizational pecking order."

One group of computerized quality control techniques that has helped in manufacturing operations is known as *statistical process control (SPC)*. As described in Chapter 3, the objective of SPC is to closely monitor production units at various stages of the production process, identifying potential problems before they result in defects and adjusting the production process accordingly through such observations. Because many products today are highly complex and may involve hundreds of operations, only sophisticated statistical analyses—obtainable with a computer—can sift through the complex maze of variable relationships to pinpoint those that may lead to quality problems.

One joint venture between an American and a Japanese company used SPC successfully and found, when comparing performance figures to those of a decade earlier, that manufacturing costs dropped 42 percent, product defects dropped 79 percent, market share increased 193 percent, and profits increased 244 percent. In addition, applying SPC to research and development (R&D) processes can cut the time it takes to bring new products into the market by a third.

Another promising role for the computer in quality control is in the area of vision inspection systems, where robotic "eyes" replace humans in the quality-control inspection process. For example, today's vision systems find defects in integrated circuit (memory and processor) chips. As each chip is mounted for inspection, it is compared with the correct chip design, which is stored in computer memory. The vision system can detect subtle defects that are not even detectable by human operators looking at the chip under a microscope. Furthermore, the process is performed at automated speeds.

Sources of Manufacturing Information

Information needed for manufacturing decisions comes from a variety of data sources, many of which were shown in Figure 13.9 (page 572) and are described as follows:

- **Production data** By using terminals around the production floor, data on production processes can be quickly gathered and processed. These data are used for billing and in almost every aspect of production control.

- **Inventory data** Inventory data include inventories of raw materials, goods-in-process, and finished goods. Accurate raw material data are especially important in a manufacturing situation because running out of certain items at critical times can shut down production lines, leaving workers (who are still getting paid) idle.

- **Vendor data** Vendor data show sources and prices for raw materials. Often, vendor data are maintained by the purchasing department, although sometimes the manufacturing area will personally buy certain items. In any case, manufacturing personnel must be constantly aware of the origination of their raw materials, what new types of products are offered by vendors, and current prices.

- **Personnel data** Personnel data show various statistics on current manufacturing personnel. Often, in the course of production, people switch assignments, so personnel skills must be reviewed to fit the right person for the right job.

- **Union data** Many types of labor today are unionized. Unionized production shops usually have strict regulations regarding such items as pay scales, hiring and firing, promotion, and working conditions.

- **Labor data** Raw materials and people are at the core of manufacturing a product. While vendors are the source of raw materials, the labor market is the source of people. Data must be kept regarding where new personnel may be obtained as labor shortages occur in the firm.

- **External environment data** To manufacturing managers, the most pressing information need in the area of external environment data is the outlook for raw material prices and labor availability. For example, if certain raw material prices will skyrocket next month, it may be wise to pad inventories now. Or if labor threatens to strike, manufacturing managers should immediately make decisions regarding how to produce goods in a degraded mode.

- **Engineering specifications** Engineering specifications data indicate whether something can be built and how. Engineering specifications contain such facts as sizes of screws; whether a certain drill bit is suitable for wood, metal, or masonry; how to build a subassembly of a certain type; and so on. Massive libraries of such specifications are often assembled on magnetic media for retrieval by database management systems. Such technology applications as CD-ROM, hypertext, multimedia, object-oriented databases, and screen publishing (published materials in screen form) have great potential in this area.

- **Internal marketing data** Marketing ends where manufacturing begins, so marketing output is manufacturing input. Marketing specifies the number of units of goods that must be produced in each time period in order to meet consumer demand. Marketing data are also useful to production personnel as part of the engineering design process. Lee Iacocca relates an interesting point in his autobiography, which illustrates this idea: When the popular Ford Mustang was built, marketing decided that the car had to be small, hold four passengers, weigh 2,500 pounds or less, and sell for no more than $2,500. This is where the product design forces of manufacturing begin their work.

MIS IN OTHER BUSINESS AREAS

So far in this text, we have considered information systems in three primary business areas: finance, marketing, and production. We have also discussed accounting information systems. Advances in information technology have also spawned specialized information systems in many other business areas. Two areas that are receiving considerable attention are R&D and human resource management (personnel administration). The characteristics of the R&D information systems and human resources management information systems (HRIS) are outlined in this section.

Research and Development Information Systems

Like most areas of business, advances in information technology have made a significant impact on R&D activities. R&D has long been recognized as an information-intensive activity that is usually responsible for churning out a steady stream of new products and production process innovations for the organiza-

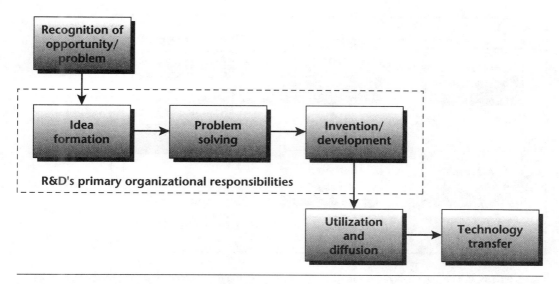

Figure 13.15 The primary responsibilities of research and development (R&D). (Adapted from Case and Pickett, 1991)

tion. Figure 13.15 illustrates the primary responsibilities of the R&D subsystem. As this figure indicates, R&D is responsible for creating and developing new products or services in order to capitalize on recognized opportunities. R&D may also be responsible for overcoming recognized weaknesses in current organizational production and operation processes in order to make them more efficient, cost-effective, and competitive. Because of this mandate and the potential of R&D to provide the organization with competitive advantage, many researchers suggest that R&D information systems should be considered to be strategic information systems.

Like many other organizational systems, R&D is an open system that has important information and communications exchanges with the external environment and other organizational subunits. Figure 13.16 depicts the major information flows crucial for R&D effectiveness. This figure suggests that strong linkages should exist between R&D and the external environment; it also suggests that solid links should exist between R&D and the marketing/production subsystems of the organization.

Thomas Case and John Pickett (1991) report that—in most organizations—the proportion of spending on information technology for R&D is increasing and that integrated laboratory information management systems (LIMS) are gaining in popularity. The productivity of R&D professionals has increased because of these changes, resulting in reduced product development times (the time it takes to progress from the idea formulation stage to the utilization and diffusion stage—see Figure 13.15). Case and Pickett also report that access to external databases (for example, to perform patent or library searches) and to

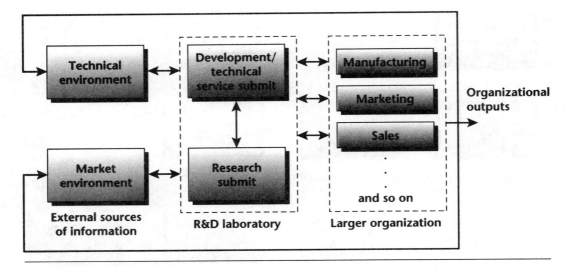

Figure 13.16 Critical information flows in R&D. To be effective, the R&D function must obtain appropriate information from both internal and external sources. (Adapted from Case and Pickett, 1991)

other sources of external information has increased dramatically over the past few years.

Despite these positive changes, the information linkages between R&D and other organizational subunits seem to be slower in developing. Thomas Case and John Pickett (1992) report very little change from 1987 to 1991 in the percentage of R&D subunits that have on-line access to marketing or production databases. Hence, it seems that progress to full-scale implementation of Merrifield's FCIM model (refer back to Figure 13.14) has been slow.

Human Resource Information Systems (HRIS)

In most organizations, the human resource/personnel management area is a staff function that supports the activities of the firm's line subunits. The functions carried out by personnel administrators and other human resource managers usually impact all of the other functional areas of an organization.

Today, most organizations recognize their employees as their most important (and often most expensive) resource. Because of the changing social structures in the U.S., the internationalization of many businesses, and an increasing preponderance of federal, state, and local laws and regulations, the management of human resources is now much more complex than it was in the past.

Human resource managers or personnel administrators are typically responsible for human resource planning, staffing (recruiting, hiring, and placement), training and development, performance appraisal, and termination (for exam-

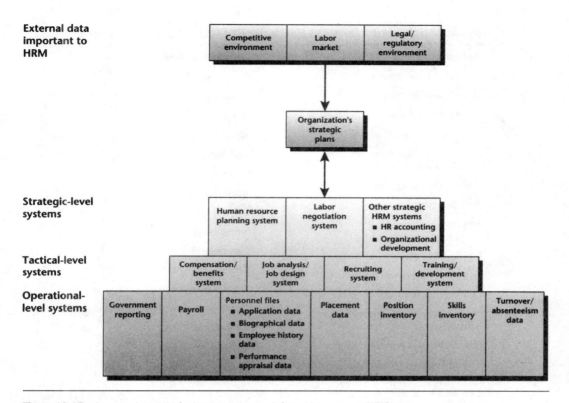

External data important to HRM

| Competitive environment | Labor market | Legal/ regulatory environment |

Organization's strategic plans

Strategic-level systems

| Human resource planning system | Labor negotiation system | Other strategic HRM systems ■ HR accounting ■ Organizational development |

Tactical-level systems

| Compensation/ benefits system | Job analysis/ job design system | Recruiting system | Training/ development system |

Operational-level systems

| Government reporting | Payroll | Personnel files ■ Application data ■ Biographical data ■ Employee history data ■ Performance appraisal data | Placement data | Position inventory | Skills inventory | Turnover/ absenteeism data |

Figure 13.17 A general model of a human resource information system (HRIS).

ple, firing and outplacement) activities. They may also be responsible for developing the salary structure and benefit package for the organization, negotiating contracts with unions, and ensuring compliance with EEO/AA (Equal Employment Opportunity/Affirmative Action) and OSHA (Occupational Safety and Health Administration) laws and regulations. Figure 13.17 provides a general model of a human resource information system (HRIS).

Figure 13.18 gives examples of the variety of human resource management (HRM) activities that may be supported by human resource information systems. Commercially available software packages support many of the activities listed in Figure 13.18—and the range of HRM activities that can be supported by such software is steadily increasing. HRM professionals can also take advantage of the information available through on-line databases such as Executive Telecom Systems Inc.'s Human Resource Information Network (HRIN).

A computer-based HRIS can help personnel/human resource management departments become more effective in keeping employee records and in producing reports. It can also help organizations plan for the future by enabling them to develop staffing estimates and human resource plans that support the

Types of Software Available to Support HRM Activities	
Applicant tracking	Immigration reform
Attendance management	Job analysis
Benefits administration	Job description
Career development	Payroll
Compensation administration	Pension and profit-sharing administration
Compliance with Americans with Disabilities Act	Performance improvement/planning
	Performance monitoring
Computer-based training	Relocation software
Data and survey analysis	Safety
Employee Assistance Administration Program	Stress management
	Substance abuse
Employee communications services	Succession planning
Employee manuals and handbooks	Temporary services management
Employment/recruitment and assessment	Training administration and management
Equal Employment Opportunity/ Affirmative Action	Turnover analysis
Flexible benefits administration	Wellness programs
Human resources forecasting/planning	

Figure 13.18 Examples of human resources management (HRM) functions supported by human resources information systems (HRIS).

organization's strategic initiatives and tactical plans. Because of this, continual enhancements in available software support and external databases are likely.

SUMMARY

Almost every business consists of numerous well-defined functions—finance, marketing, and manufacturing, for instance. These functions are commonly performed by distinct areas in the firm called functional areas.

The finance function is responsible for overall financial planning and for raising capital. This function is usually run by a chief financial officer (CFO). Three major decision activities in the finance area are forecasting, funds management, and auditing.

Forecasting involves using forecasts of each functional area—as well as key external environment data—to prepare a financial forecast that shows sources of money coming into the firm and uses of money going out. Financial forecasts that reflect cash inflows and outflows are often called cash flow models.

Funds management involves determining whether outside financing will be required to meet obligations. A number of techniques, including Monte Carlo simulation and what-if analysis, can help to plan in this area.

Auditing is another important finance responsibility. An audit is an inspection that determines whether something is working according to plan or in the way that organizations or departments claim it is. Audits can be internal or external.

Important data sources for information needed to make financial decisions include transaction processing data, internal forecasting data, funding data, portfolio data, data on government regulations, data on the external environment, and the organization's strategic plan.

Related to financial management are accounting information systems. Accounting information systems (AIS) include the general ledger system, the inventory control system, accounts receivable, accounts payable, order processing, and the payroll system. Chapter 10 described these in detail.

Marketing is the functional area that determines which specific goods and services will be offered to consumers, as well as the prices, promotion, and distribution channels appropriate for these products. These responsibility areas—products, prices, promotion, and place—are often called the "four Ps," or the marketing mix. The four Ps, allocating funds, and preparing sales forecasts constitute the primary decision-making areas in marketing.

Technology plays a major role in the marketing effort by helping to tie customers more closely to the firm, increasing selling time, increasing selling effectiveness at the client site, helping to identify selling opportunities, creating new selling opportunities, monitoring households through single-source data techniques and related methods, and providing information on competitors and the external environment in remote databases.

Information for marketing decisions comes from various data sources, including transaction processing data, marketing research data, marketing intelligence data, external environment data, and the firm's strategic plan. Marketing research is responsible for gathering consumer-related data. Marketing intelligence refers to gathering information about the strategies of competitors.

Manufacturing is the functional area responsible for producing goods from raw materials. Key areas of decision making are product design, facility design, production, and quality control.

Product design, or product engineering, is the manufacturing-related area in which technical specifications and design decisions for products must be determined. Increasingly, design and engineering are becoming computerized through computer-aided design (CAD). Decisions also must be made regarding the design of manufacturing facilities.

Another area of decision making is production, the process of making new products from raw materials. Two basic types of production are job-shop production and process production. Many firms use computerized approaches to model the production process as a system. One of these methods is manufacturing resources planning (MRP II), in which a production schedule is prepared and inventories of needed raw materials are carefully determined. Most MRP II systems support the traditional "push" philosophy of manufacturing, in which products are made in large batches. The "pull" philosophy—or just-in-time (JIT) production approach—is gaining supporters, however, in certain types of production situations. MRP II systems may not be well suited to JIT environments; software that may provide better support for these environments is now appearing on the market.

Computer-aided manufacturing (CAM) is an umbrella term that includes numerous computer-related manufacturing operations. Monitoring, numeric control, robotics, and production optimization fall under the CAM category. So, too, do computer-integrated manufacturing (CIM) and flexible manufacturing systems (FMS). Flexible computer-integrated manufacturing (FCIM) systems are a blend of CIM and FMS.

Quality control relates to activities ensuring that the manufactured product is of satisfactory quality. Computerized quality control techniques such as statistical process control (SPC) help in manufacturing operations.

Data sources for the information needed to make manufacturing decisions include production, inventory, vendor, personnel, union, labor, external environment, and internal marketing data, plus engineering specifications.

Specialized information systems that support other organizational subunits are also becoming quite common. Advances in information technology make it possible to develop research and development (R&D) information systems that improve the productivity of R&D professionals and shorten the time to develop innovative products, services, and production processes. Human resource information systems help improve the productivity of human resource managers and personnel administrators. The availability of software and external databases that support the human resource management function is increasing.

REVIEW

Key Terms

Auditing

Cash flow model

Chief financial officer (CFO)

Computer-aided design (CAD)

Computer-aided manufacturing (CAM)

Computer-integrated manufacturing (CIM)

Financial forecast

Flexible manufacturing system (FMS)

Functional areas

Job-shop production

Marketing intelligence

Marketing mix

Marketing research

Materials resources planning (MRP II)

Numeric control

Process production

Production

Quality control

REVIEW QUESTIONS

1. What is a cash flow model?
2. How does an internal audit differ from an external audit?
3. What types of information technology tools are most useful in the finance area?
4. What are the major components of accounting information systems? What changes have occurred in commercially available software packages over the last few years?
5. What functions does the marketing subsystem of an organization perform?
6. How is information technology useful in sales promotions?
7. What is meant by the term "single-source data"?
8. How may information technology be useful in the design of products?
9. How do MRP II and JIT systems differ?
10. What is computer-integrated manufacturing (CIM)?
11. What is the difference between process production and job-shop production?
12. What are the characteristics of flexible manufacturing systems?
13. What is CAM? How does it differ or relate to MRP II, JIT, FMS, CAD, CIM?
14. What are the characteristics of R&D information systems? What impacts do these have on the productivity of R&D professionals and on the competitiveness of the firm?
15. What types of decisions are supported by an HRIS? What types of software and external databases are available to assist human resource management decisions?

DISCUSSION QUESTIONS

1. In what way is Monte Carlo simulation especially useful in solving either strategic-level or ordinary, day-to-day operations problems in finance, marketing, and manufacturing? Provide several examples and classify each as either strategic or ordinary.
2. Explain how CIM might be implemented by one of the large auto manufacturers. Describe the role that EDI may play in the system you describe.
3. Is the finance area—more than either marketing or production—appropriate for strategic-level decision making? Why or why not? Should the most important strategic-level functions receive the greatest MIS support?
4. In what ways are the Japanese creating a competitive advantage by applying technology to production?

CASE STUDY

Network Allows Small Manufacturers to go Big Time

A partnership of industries, universities, and government agencies has established a network linking South Carolina manufacturing firms with technical experts at state colleges and universities. The partnership plans to expand the network to other southeastern states to form Semnet (Southeast Manufacturing Network). Eventually, they want to expand Semnet nationwide to form a manufacturing information infrastructure that allows small- and medium-sized firms to compete in national markets.

According to Paul Huray—vice-president for research at the University of South Carolina and director of the High Performance Manufacturing Consortium—many of the nation's 355,000 small manufacturers are isolated and lack ways to exchange technical information with suppliers, customers, and technical experts. "They market to the city they're in and that's it," says Huray.

However, interest in networks is not limited to small manufacturers. There are still a lot of large manufacturing firms that lack manufacturing telecommunication systems. Huray notes that many are struggling to implement basic electronic data interchange (EDI) and that most of their intracompany networks are dominated by finan- cial applications. As a result, they often don't have the technological capability to tap into the national pool of qualified parts suppliers.

Semnet will bring technological expertise and customers to the manufacturers that hook up. The network will be used to convey manufacturers' capabilities and bids to potential buyers around the nation.

An "electronic bidding board" is also being developed. Buyers will be able to use this to post requests for bids. Semnet users will be able to download the associated specifications and drawings from the bidding board in order to determine if they want to go after the business.

Larger customers may be able to use the network to aggregate capacity for larger jobs. The system may encourage smaller suppliers to band together to make a bid on a large job. Semnet is also expected to be used for the coordination of production schedules, to support electronic just-in-time (JIT), and for reducing factory set-up times.

Eventually, the network wants to support voice, data, and video exchanges. This will allow manufacturers to electronically exchange product design specifications—including three-dimensional images—and to have low-cost, interactive, multimedia communications capabilities with companies around the U.S.

Whether the potential benefits of Semnet will be realized remains to be seen. However, the concept is sound and the network just might give smaller manufacturers the economic boost they need to stay alive in our increasingly competitive domestic and international markets.

Adapted from Anthes (1992).

1. How will Semnet enhance the competitiveness of both large and small manufacturers?

2. How will the electronic bidding board improve the efficiency of the bidding process?

3. How do networks such as Semnet enhance economic development and the expansion of small manufacturers?

4. Explain how the network could be used to promote the development of a just-in-time relationship between a supplier and a manufacturer.

Part FIVE

Building Management Information Systems

Chapter

14 Requirements Analysis

After completing this chapter, you will be able to:

Describe the systems development life cycle (SDLC)

Compare the traditional, prototyping, and end-user approaches to systems development

Discuss the roles played by managers, users, and MIS professionals in the systems development process

Describe the activities that take place during the preliminary investigation and requirements analysis stages of systems development

Explain the importance of documentation in systems development

Every organization needs systems in order to run smoothly: systems for handling routine transaction processing as well as systems for getting information into the hands of the people who need it. The process of putting systems into place—and continuing to maintain or enhance them—is referred to as **systems development**.

Systems development can be subdivided into five activities:

Activity 1: Preliminary investigation

Activity 2: Requirements analysis

Activity 3: System design

Activity 4: System acquisition

Activity 5: System implementation and maintenance

Not every development effort will involve performing all of these activities, or even performing any of these activities in exactly this order. Large transaction processing systems are often developed by performing each of these steps in strict sequence. Often, an activity will not begin until the activity preceding it is completely done. On the other hand, many decision support, expert, and office systems are developed much differently. In fact, the distinction among the development activities often becomes blurred as these types of systems are being built.

Because systems development is a comprehensive and central topic for computer-based information systems (CBIS), we devote four chapters to it. This chapter opens by defining systems development and discussing the three major development approaches: the traditional approach, prototyping, and end-user development. Then, the chapter covers activities 1 (preliminary investigation) and 2 (requirements analysis). Chapters 15 and 16 examine the remaining three activities: system design, system acquisition, and system implementation and maintenance. Chapter 17 discusses the management of end-user computing and systems development.

THE NATURE OF SYSTEMS DEVELOPMENT

Most organizations—from the time they first open their doors for business—need systems to get their work done: a payroll system to process checks, an order-entry system to handle incoming customer orders, systems to inform managers of the activities within their departments, and so on. As needs, business conditions, and technologies change, so do existing systems. New systems must be developed for the organization to remain effective and competitive. For instance, changes in government regulations (especially tax codes) sometimes require changes to payroll processing systems. New technologies such as electronic data interchange (EDI), pen-based order-entry systems, and image-processing systems made improved levels of customer service possible and have changed the way many order-entry systems function. The availability of on-line financial database services for executives has created entirely new systems. Thus, systems development may be viewed as a process that explores both the modification of old systems and the creation of new ones—from the discovery of a problem or opportunity to the implementation of a final product.

The Role of Managers and Users in Systems Development

Managers and users play critical roles in all of the systems development activities just listed. In fact, they trigger the start of most systems development projects when they submit formal requests for new systems to MIS professionals. Because systems development activities enable managers and users to shape their computing destinies, they should take such activities seriously and work closely with MIS professionals when systems development projects are underway.

Systems development projects give managers and users the opportunity to tell MIS professionals: (1) which of their current data and information needs are not being met, (2) what they don't like about existing systems, and (3) what new features should be included in future systems. Since it is the responsibility of MIS professionals involved in such projects to develop systems that best satisfy users' computing needs, it is very important for users to have an active role in the systems development process. In fact, numerous research investigations indicate that the success of systems development projects is often directly related to the extent to which users actively participate in them; the greater the amount of user involvement, the greater the chances that the new systems will satisfy their data and information requirements.

As noted in Chapters 1 and 2, during systems development projects, managers and users interact most frequently with systems analysts. It is the systems analyst's job to determine user information and data requirements and to implement new systems that satisfy these requirements. As systems development projects unfold, systems analysts interview users and collect important information from them. To perform these tasks effectively, the systems analyst needs users and managers to clearly articulate their information and processing needs. Good communication between users and the analyst is extremely important.

At various points in the systems development process, users and managers should review and provide feedback on the work done by the systems analyst and other MIS professionals involved in the project. This activity must also be taken seriously by managers and users. They should ensure that their needs are understood by the systems developers and that important inaccuracies or omissions are rectified. Without negative feedback, the analyst and other MIS professionals working on the project will assume that their work is acceptable and proceed to the next set of activities. If they discover later that their work at this stage was unacceptable, their future work may, unfortunately, also be incorrect.

As we continue our discussion of systems development, we will point out numerous other roles that managers and users play in these important processes. However, you should keep in mind why these processes are important to managers and why active user involvement is a key to successful systems development efforts.

The Systems Development Life Cycle (SDLC)

Systems development consists of five activities, all or any of which may pertain to the development of a given system. These activities, which form a cycle, are described as follows.

- **Preliminary investigation** A preliminary investigation is undertaken when users note a problem or opportunity and submit a formal request for a new system to the MIS department. The investigation is brief, and numerous options concerning how to solve or take advantage of the situation are proposed to management so that it can decide how to proceed.

- **Requirements analysis** If, after studying the results of the preliminary investigation, management decides to continue the development process, user needs are studied. Then, systems requirements that must be met to satisfy the new or changed user applications environment are produced. This step is called requirements analysis (sometimes it is referred to as systems analysis).

- **System design** During system design, the user requirements that arose from analyzing the user applications environment are incorporated into a new system's design.

- **System acquisition** After the system design details are resolved, such resource needs as specific types of hardware, software, and services are determined. Subsequently, choices are made regarding which products to buy or lease from which vendors. These activities are part of system acquisition.

- **System implementation and maintenance** During system implementation, the system is set up and run, and any necessary adjustments are continually made. Users are then trained on the new system and eventually work on it alone. After the system is in place, the results of the development effort are reviewed to ensure that the new system satisfies user requirements. After implementation, the system is maintained; it is modified to adapt to changing user and business needs so that the system can be useful to the organization for as long as possible.

The **systems development life cycle (SDLC)** is so named because, for many applications, systems development is a process that never ends. Thus, even when a system is completely specified, designed, purchased, and running, it is continually being enhanced or maintained.

Enhancement and maintenance may require returning to one of the earlier stages of the systems development process. For instance, consider the evolution of order-entry systems. In the 1960s, when some firms first used computers for their order-entry operations, many of them went through the five stages of systems development to justify batch-oriented systems to management. These systems used mostly punched cards and magnetic tape. Subsequently, each time a new technology or business condition made it economically worthwhile to reconsider these systems, computer professionals had to undergo the systems development process again. For example, when disk technology made direct access possible, many order-entry systems were re-developed to take advantage of this. Such technology products as on-line terminals, sophisticated communications systems, and database processing often initiated further redevelopment. Thus, the evolution of the order-entry application conforms to a cyclical pattern in which each period of the cycle represents a new or modified order-entry system that was created by re-applying systems development practices.

Changing business conditions can play just as great a role as changing technologies in creating the need for systems to be maintained or enhanced. For example, a lot of companies look at their order-entry systems as competitive weapons, which means that many of these systems are being re-developed to accommodate on-line terminals at customer sites. On Wall Street, several investment firms built new on-line trading systems in the early 1980s that were then re-developed to handle such new business-related complexities as global markets and options trading. In 1992, pen-based computers were first introduced in some parts of the Chicago stock market, enabling traders to make complete transactions in the trading pits themselves. Similarly, airline deregulation caused the airline industry to have additional information needs, and many reservations systems were expanded to add new, strategic-oriented applications.

Potential Problems with Existing Systems

Before focusing on systems development processes, note that many systems development initiatives result from what managers and users perceive to be the inadequacies of existing systems. Some of the reasons why users and MIS professionals consider an existing system to be inadequate are because the system:

- Does not support business strategies and objectives.
- Does not satisfy user requirements and needs.
- Has inadequate systems controls.
- Has software that is unstructured and difficult to maintain.
- Consists of incompatible or inadequate technologies.
- Contains various design flaws and errors.
- Is poorly documented.
- Is difficult to use.

Numerous management problems result from poorly designed systems, including low levels of user productivity, poor customer service, and management decisions that are based on inaccurate or untimely information.

Successful Systems Development: Essential Elements

Many of the causes of system inadequacy can be minimized by using appropriate systems development methodologies, modeling tools, and techniques. These methods enable workers to build information systems that not only satisfy user requirements, but also are delivered on time and within budget. Systems development professionals know that the systems they build are more likely to be successful when:

- High levels of user involvement are present throughout the systems development process.
- Project management techniques are used to implement systems plans.
- Alternative systems designs are developed and critically evaluated prior to committing to final design, technology, and software development.
- System designs are used to guide software design, coding, and testing.
- Structured program design and coding is used.
- Clear, complete, and accurate documentation for the new system is generated throughout the systems development process.
- System implementation and user training are carefully planned and coordinated.
- Postimplementation reviews are conducted to ensure that user and management needs were met.
- The system is designed for easy maintenance.

While no system is guaranteed of success when these guidelines are followed, the chance that users and managers will be happy with the new system should increase.

APPROACHES TO SYSTEMS DEVELOPMENT

Since organizations vary significantly in the way that they automate their business procedures, and since each new type of system usually differs from any others, several different systems development approaches are often used within an organization. There are two ways to classify such approaches. The first is by the general manner in which the five systems development activities are implemented. In this classification, three approaches to systems development exist: the traditional approach, prototyping approaches, and the approach taken by end-users doing their own systems development (see Figure 14.1). These approaches are not mutually exclusive; for instance, it is possible to perform some prototyping while applying the traditional approach. The second way to classify systems development efforts is by whether the development follows a top-down or bottom-up approach, or some combination of these styles.

Approach	Description
▨ Traditional	An approach to systems development whereby the system under study is professionally developed in stages, each of which must be relatively complete before the next stage begins
▨ Prototyping	A set of different approaches to systems development, all of which are characterized by building small models of some system elements and gradually expanding them from user experiences
▨ End-user development	A set of different approaches to systems development, all of which are characterized by having the end-user take the primary initiative in the development process

Figure 14.1 Approaches to systems development. The three major approaches are the traditional approach, prototyping, and end-user development. Depending on the problem, either one or a combination of these approaches may be appropriate.

No single approach works in every situation, and no approach even works in all situations of a given type. The approach used depends on the complex combination of many variables. Therefore, in the following discussion, we will examine some of the factors to consider when deciding what approaches or combination of approaches to use.

In this text, systems development is discussed from an in-house point of view, although you should know that some companies hire firms called **systems integrators** to perform their development work for them on a contract basis.

Outsourcing is another trend that affects systems development efforts. Many organizations contract with external firms to perform their application processing activities; some even turn over application development activities to outsiders such as contract programming firms. Many people feel that systems integrators and outsourcing represent waves of the future, and that in-house systems developers will eventually become rare. It is still too early to tell whether this will happen, but managers should recognize that outsourcing, contract programming, and systems integrators represent alternative ways to acquire needed applications. These trends have emerged as important management issues of the 1990s. Because of this, we will discuss them in more detail in Chapter 18.

The Traditional Approach

In the **traditional approach** (see Figure 14.2), all five systems development activities are done in sequence. Figure 14.3 shows examples of the tasks performed during each phase of the traditional approach. Managers and users are most likely to interact with systems analysts, systems designers, and application programmers when the traditional approach is used. During the preliminary investigation and requirements analysis phases—in which user information needs are identified—systems development activities are usually lead by a systems analyst. The systems analyst may play a lesser role during the design,

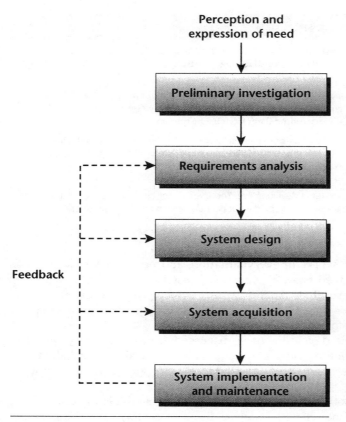

Perception and
expression of need

Preliminary investigation

Requirements analysis

System design

Feedback

System acquisition

System implementation
and maintenance

Figure 14.2 The traditional approach to systems development. In the traditional approach, each step is performed in this sequence. Generally, any problems, inaccuracies, or omissions uncovered during later steps necessitate returning to previous steps.

acquisition and implementation/maintenance stages. During these later stages, they may turn over the project to system designers. If new programs must be written (or if existing programs must be modified), application programmers become involved during the acquisition and implementation stages.

When the traditional development process is strictly applied, an activity is undertaken only when the prior step is fully completed. Typically, managers and users consider and review the work performed by the MIS professionals during each step of process before proceeding to the next step. Managers will probably review diagrams, explanations, checklists, charts, and so on, in order to ensure that the work is accurate and complete. If the work is satisfactory, managers and users formally sign off, or accept, the work and allow the systems development team to proceed to the next step. Because this sign-off represents formal acceptance of the completed work, managers and users should thoroughly review the work before granting their permission to start the next phase.

The traditional approach is historically applied to the development of larger computer-based information systems (CBIS) such as transaction processing systems. Because the processing requirements of these systems are typically well

Activity (Phase)	Tasks Performed
▨ Preliminary investigation	Determine nature of problem and scope of project
	Determine possible solutions
	Assess project feasibility
	Report to management
▨ Requirements analysis	Collect facts
	Analyze facts
	Report to management
▨ System design	Review requirements
	Design logical system
	Design physical system
	Finalize benefits and costs
	Report to management
▨ System acquisition	Review design
	Prepare specifications for vendors
	Evaluate and select vendors
	Report to management
▨ System implementation and maintenance	Schedule implementation tasks
	Code, debug, and test programs
	Train personnel
	Convert to new system
	Conduct postimplementation review
	Perform maintenance on system

Figure 14.3 Systems development activities undertaken during each phase of the traditional approach. Although not shown, documentation is an ongoing activity that happens as each development activity occurs.

understood, the risks of users and systems analysts misperceiving the target system are typically lower than for other types of systems. As noted in Chapter 9, transaction processing environments are usually quite structured regarding data and information requirements. Producing predictable, data-oriented types of outputs (such as customer statements and bills) is emphasized, rather than semistructured or unstructured outputs such as that produced by decision support systems (DSS), group descision support systems (GDSS), and executive information systems (EIS). Smaller computer-based information systems—ones that support a specialized set of users, such as decision support systems, group decision support systems, executive information systems, expert systems, and neural networks—are usually developed using a prototyping approach (discussed in detail later).

In recent years, the traditional approach has been heavily criticized. First, the systems to which this approach is applied may take years to analyze, design, and implement. This contributes to application backlog problems—both visible and invisible—mentioned in earlier chapters of this book. Also, because usually the business environment changes while the system is under development, the finished system might not meet the most pressing needs anymore. With the traditional approach, it is relatively difficult to respond to new needs after users have signed off on the requirements analysis—and, later, on the design for the new system.

Second, the system under development may not be the right one. Users often have a hard time clearly articulating what types of information they really need to perform their jobs. A study on development projects by A. M. Jenkins, J. D. Naumann, and J. C. Wetherbe found that in about three-fourths of the projects, requirements analysis had to be repeated because additional requirements were discovered or because users changed their minds as the development process unfolded. Frequently, people don't discover their real needs until they've worked with a system for awhile. Because the traditional approach doesn't allow users to really see and work with the new system until it is installed, they can't determine whether or not the new system fully satisfies their needs until the development process ends. Furthermore, during the traditional development process, users are often asked to sign off on system designs that are presented to them as a set of diagrams and specifications; because of this, many users have difficulty visualizing the actual system.

Many business managers are unexcited about the state of traditional systems development in their organizations—not because the systems that ultimately emerge are bad; many of them are, in fact, very successful. However, the process of completing them can be long, fraught with disappointing delays and unpleasant surprises. Systems developers are notoriously optimistic when estimating how long it will take to develop a new system. Deadlines are set and missed; then re-set and often missed again. Frequently, the new systems require more resources than originally planned, causing costs to climb over budget. Projects may be canceled as costs exceed benefits and the probability of ever finishing them within a reasonable span of time becomes increasingly remote. Projects may also be abandoned before completion because new technologies that came on the market while the system was developed convince management that their system will be obsolete before it is installed. Problems of miscommunication, omissions, and human error further complicate the process. These are just some of the reasons why managers become disenchanted by the traditional approach and develop an interest in alternative systems development approaches such as prototyping and end-user development.

Prototyping Approaches

In order to avoid potentially expensive surprises, organizations increasingly use prototyping techniques to develop smaller systems such as decision support systems, executive information systems, and expert systems. Prototyping approaches are also used more widely during the requirements analysis and design stages of the traditional approach in order to shorten the time needed to complete these steps. The goal of **prototyping** approaches is to develop a small or pilot version—called a prototype—of part or all of a system. A prototype is a usable system or system component that is built inexpensively, quickly, and with the intention of being modified or replaced by a full-scale fully operational system. As users work with the prototype, they make suggestions about ways to improve it. These suggestions are then incorporated into another prototype, which is also used and evaluated. And so on. Finally, when a prototype is developed that satisfies users, either it is refined and turned into the final system or it is scrapped. If it is scrapped, the knowledge gained from building the prototype is used to develop the real system.

For example, the first version of a prototype for a new order-entry system might consist of a set of mock screens, including menus and other graphical user interfaces (GUI), data-entry templates, report screens, and display-retrieval screens. These screens might be created with a 4GL-based prototyping package (such as FOCUS) by a software specialist who assists a systems analyst. The screens may not be connected to a database, but they typically enable users to understand what types of data they can access, how information will be formatted on-screen, and how to navigate from one screen to another. After the users experiment with the prototype for awhile—making suggestions about what they like, don't like, and what else they need—the prototype is refined by the software specialist and returned to users to try again. After this part of the prototype is completed to everyone's satisfaction, the analyst and software specialist might try to expand the prototype by constructing a dummy database and experimenting with some data retrievals and computations. Again, users experiment with the prototype—this time, using the more advanced version. After several feedback sessions and subsequent refinements, managers and developers should feel confident that the basic system will satisfy user needs. At this point, work on the final version begins. The final version of the system will typically have such features as editing routines, security procedures, and, if necessary, an audit trail, plus all of the prototype's desirable features. Figure 14.4 summarizes the steps typically taken in prototype development.

In one sense, prototyping combines the traditional approach's requirements analysis and system design processes into one step. By doing so, many of the problems associated with the traditional approach may be avoided. For example, users who are unable to clearly articulate their requirements can work with a prototype and then inform the systems developers whether or not it meets their needs. Experimenting with the prototype helps users to identify additional requirements and needs that they overlooked or forgot to mention. In addition, with prototyping, users have a clearer visual picture of what the final version will be like and they do not have to sign off on a system presented to them in the form of diagrams and specification lists.

Because decision support systems (DSS) are characterized by semistructured or unstructured management decision environments, they are ideal for the experimentation and trial-and-error development associated with prototyping. The managers requesting such systems often are not completely sure of their information needs or of the information technologies that may be most useful to them. As the prototyping process continues, their needs and the capabilities of information technology to satisfy their needs are clarified. The final result is

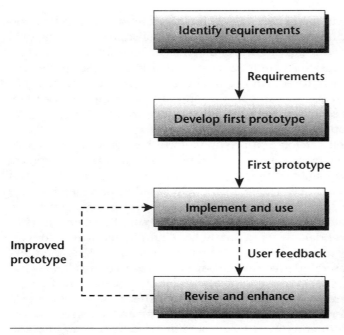

Figure 14.4 Prototyping. With prototyping, a small or pilot version of the system is initially developed and refined through active user involvement.

usually a DSS that is truly useful—and, more importantly, used. Expert systems are other ideal candidates for prototyping approaches because expert knowledge usually requires continual refinement.

Often, a DSS or expert system prototype is gradually expanded into the final system. However, the finished prototype is not always kept in active use. Some decision support systems are used for one-shot applications; for instance, a DSS may be specially created to help a manager in company A decide whether it is worthwhile to merge with company B. In such a case, the system often is discarded after its purpose is served. In other cases, the prototype is not scrapped in order to develop a functionally equivalent COBOL (or other language) program.

A key factor in throwaway versus evolutionary prototyping decisions is the trade-off between development time and execution efficiency. When it's important to get the system up and running quickly and when hardware costs are not important, evolutionary prototyping—which leaves most of the system coded in fourth-generation languages and may include potentially inefficient tools—is usually the better choice. When the system is intended for widespread use and hardware costs are important—such as a transaction processing system—re-implementation using a more efficient 3GL is often wisest.

Prototyping can also be successfully used in the development of transaction processing systems, management reporting systems, and other large systems that are usually developed using the traditional approach. With transaction processing systems, prototyping approaches are most commonly used during the system design stage; for instance, to develop the mock screens described in

System Type	Prototype
▪ TPS, MRS	Pilot versions developed of large-scale system
	CASE-type tools used to investigate several system alternatives during design stage
	Screen painters used to develop input/output screens in design stage
	Report generators used to develop hardcopy reports in design stage
	Simulation and modeling tools used to model system performance in acquisition stage
	Action diagrams used to develop program code in implementation stage
▪ DSS	4GL tools* used to develop templates or worksheets
	4GL tools used to develop hardcopy reports
	4GL tools used to create database
	4GL tools used to try out various forms of mathematical models
	Alternative hardware/software configurations tested at information center before selecting system

*Spreadsheets, database management systems, modeling packages, and so on

Figure 14.5 Examples of the prototyping approach. The list provides examples of how prototypes can be used to build various types of information systems.

the order-entry example given earlier. Prototyping approaches can also help develop reports generated by management reporting systems. Since the information handled by a management reporting system (MRS) is typically less structured than transaction processing system (TPS) data but more structured than decision support system (DSS) information, an MRS may be developed either like a TPS or like a DSS, depending on the situation.

Prototyping has both advantages and disadvantages. Because users have an active role in the development process, prototyping often leads to greater user satisfaction with the final system. Also, because users gain experience during development in working with the system, they are better equipped to work with the final system. A disadvantage is that users may be reluctant to give up the prototype if they like it. In addition, prototyping can also create unrealistic schedule expectations for the finished product. Users often do not realize that the prototype is just a small part of the final system. The missing parts—incorporating input validation, handling exception cases, putting in complete error messages, and so on—can amount to 80 percent or more of the time it takes to complete the operational system.

No single prototyping approach exists; rather, a variety of such approaches may be appropriate at any time during systems development. Prototyping represents a philosophy of problem solving. Figure 14.5 shows numerous situations in which prototypes are useful. Figure 14.6 gives a comparison of the conditions favoring the traditional approach, prototyping, and end-user development approach (discussed next).

End-User Development

With the increasing availability of low-cost technology, **end-user development** is now evident in many organizations. In end-user development, it is the

Circumstances Favoring Traditional Development

- Users have significant experience with the type of system to be designed
- Many important system features can be readily identified before development begins
- Data requirements can be identified in advance
- Management requires a comprehensive "picture" of the new system before giving approval
- The development staff is not experienced with 4GL or prototyping tools

Circumstances Favoring Prototyping

- Users do not have a feel for the information or system capabilities they require
- User needs are changing rapidly
- Users have little experience with the type of system under development
- The risk associated with delivering the wrong system is high
- The way users will react to the new system is an important development variable
- Many alternative design strategies must be tested
- The system must be developed quickly and at the lowest possible cost

Circumstances Favoring End-User Development

- The system under development is local rather than enterprisewide
- The system under development is inexpensive
- A suitable environment of end-user development tools and professional expertise is available
- Standards exist to minimize divergent efforts by the end-users and other dangers to the organization
- High levels of security are not necessary for the system being developed
- The system under development involves numerous customized queries and reports
- The system under development can easily be built and supported by the end-user
- The system under development does not involve high-volume transaction processing
- The development time is short and cannot be accommodated by the MIS department (possibly because of a huge application backlog)
- The user must be heavily involved in the development process

Figure 14.6 Circumstances favoring the traditional, prototyping, and end-user development approaches.

end-user—not the computer professional—who is responsible for systems development activities. Many different kinds of organizations allow end-users to develop systems. For example, whenever a department or manager acquires their own, relatively inexpensive microcomputing or office information system, end-user development is often taking place.

The number and nature of systems development activities followed by the end-user often differ from those found in more formal approaches (such as the traditional approach). Next, we will look at three ways in which end-user

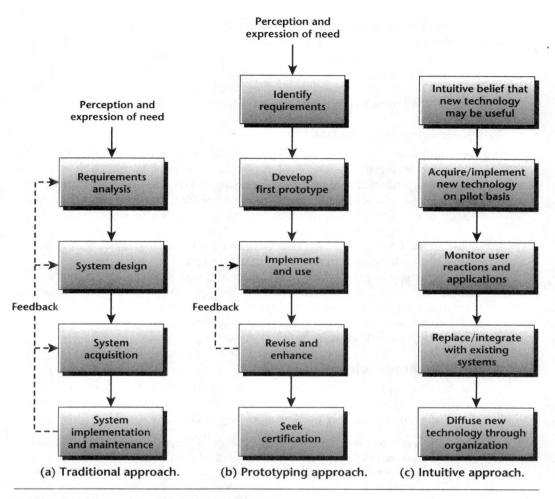

Perception and
expression of need

**Identify
requirements**

**Intuitive belief that
new technology
may be useful**

Perception and
expression of need

**Requirements
analysis**

**Develop
first prototype**

**Acquire/implement
new technology
on pilot basis**

System design

**Implement
and use**

**Monitor user
reactions and
applications**

Feedback

Feedback

**System
acquisition**

**Revise and
enhance**

**Replace/integrate
with existing
systems**

**System
implementation
and maintenance**

**Seek
certification**

**Diffuse new
technology through
organization**

(a) Traditional approach.   **(b) Prototyping approach.**   **(c) Intuitive approach.**

Figure 14.7   Three possible paths for end-user development.

development might be implemented: a traditional approach, a prototyping approach, and an intuitive approach.

A Traditional Approach

Figure 14.7(a) shows the activities that might be involved with end-user development patterned after the traditional approach. The systems development activities take place in a complete-one-step-before-starting-another process. They often begin with the user spending several days making lists of application needs and, later, lists of hardware and software alternatives to meet those needs. These activities do not have to be written. Either approach may be appropriate, depending on the situation.

The sequential, traditional type of development approach suggested by Figure 14.7(a) is especially suitable for managers and users who have reasonably good product knowledge and know what they want in a system. These users do not have to experiment a lot before selecting a system. The decisions made usually involve specific, technical needs, such as "Will I shortly need all the power and capacity an IBM PS/2 Model 90 can give me, or should I get just a plain IBM PS/2?" rather than something general, such as "What do spreadsheets do?" or "Do I need a spreadsheet or a modeling package?"

Prototyping Approaches

Many end-users try to develop systems by using some form of prototyping approach, as in Figure 14.7(b). Prototyping is especially appropriate when the end-user is undecided regarding processing needs and, perhaps, unsophisticated about high-technology products. For instance, the user might not know exactly how a spreadsheet or modeling package works, or understand the difference between the two, but does realize that such tools may be helpful in his or her work. Or the user might be technologically sophisticated, but have little product knowledge in a particular application area.

In any case, in prototyping, experimenting and learning are part of the development process. Users with such needs might investigate the corporate information center (a subunit that assists users in selecting commercially available technology) and experiment with numerous off-the-shelf software packages and hardware configurations before settling on a system.

Intuitive Approach

The intuitive approach to end-user development involves no formal development whatsoever, as Figure 14.7(c) shows. Daniel Isenberg relates an example of a CEO who successfully used such an approach:

> Rather than conducting an extensive needs analysis, [the] CEO simply bought a dozen PCs and distributed them casually throughout the office. A few staff members received computer training and began experimenting with potential applications; within weeks, the computers were fully employed. The CEO's approach did lead to some confusion at first, but it gave the company the experience it needed to take a more systematic approach later in introducing personal computers in other parts of the operation.

Intuitive, "let's try it out" approaches are effective when the technology or applications are new—especially when these new technologies or applications are likely to be better than what is currently in place.

End-user approaches are the most widely used in organizations, but prototyping and the traditional approach are also common. Figure 14.8 provides a comparison of these three systems development approaches and a summary of the differences among them.

Other Alternatives to the Traditional Approach

Different organizations use different systems development methodologies called by different names, but many of these approaches strongly resemble the

Characteristic	Traditional Approach	Prototyping Approach	End-User Development Approach
Requirements analysis	Requirements identified before design begins	Requirements identified in steps, along with design, through user experiences with working prototypes	May follow a pattern similar to traditional or prototyping; alternatively, no requirements analysis may be done
Role of analysts and users	Analysts assume full responsibility for development; user involvement is limited	Analysts and users interact extensively to improve and refine prototype	Users assume full responsibility for systems development; analysts perform advisor role
Application characteristics	Transaction processing systems and other systems with relatively predictable requirements	Decision support systems and other systems with relatively unpredictable requirements	Local decision support systems and personal applications
Software development tools	Third- and fourth-generation languages	Fourth-generation languages	User-oriented fourth-generation languages
Cost of systems development	Most expensive	If coordinated by MIS department, significantly less than traditional development, but usually more expensive than end-user development	Least expensive
Amount of time required to develop system	Longest	If coordinated by MIS department, significantly less than traditional development, but usually longer than end-user development	Shortest

Figure 14.8 A comparison of the three major systems development approaches.

traditional approach. For example, the *information engineering life cycle (IELC)* is divided into the following phases: information systems planning, business analysis, business systems design, technical design, construction, transition, and production. While the last five steps of the IELC translate readily into the final stages of the traditional approach, the first two stages illustrate that this approach may be driven (to a greater extent than the traditional approach) by MIS's strategic plans. Another systems development methodology is the *information engineering methodology (IEM)*. It includes four phases: systems planning, systems analysis, systems design, and systems construction and implementation. As you can see, the phases of an IEM are very similar to those of the traditional approach.

Fast food franchises have made fast service possible by keeping things simple—and simple is what they want in their information systems as well. During the 1990s, they are increasingly interested in information technology applications that help their employees work faster and more efficiently.

Because a very high turnover rate exists in the fast food industry, easy-to-learn and use systems are needed. Systems with long user learning curves don't have a place in fast food operations.

"SOME LOCATIONS HAVE . . . SET-UPS THAT ALLOW CUSTOMERS TO PUNCH IN AND VERIFY THEIR OWN ORDERS."

The fast food stores are automating everything they can—including their point-of-sale (POS) systems, inventory, payroll, labor scheduling, and accounting. Corporate headquarters for most of the big chains have also been gorging themselves on a broad range of software, including geographic information systems, building design, construction management, purchasing, shipping, and just-in-time inventory management.

During the 1990s, the hardware platform of choice is the microcomputer. Sbarro installed PC-based information systems at its 500 Italian restaurant franchises. Hardee's installed personal computers—with integrated POS equipment tied into corporate mainframes—in its 1,300 company-owned stores.

Some locations have POS set-ups that allow customers to punch in and verify their own orders. The PC arrangements have also enabled customers to pay with credit and bank debit cards at a growing number of locations.

Adapted from King (1992).

Joint Application Development (JAD)

Joint application development (JAD) is a technique developed by James Martin and Associates. In JAD, users and MIS professionals work together to analyze and design the system. The main goal of this approach is to maximize user involvement in the development process. JAD sessions can be used throughout the systems development process, but are particularly helpful during systems planning, requirements analysis, and systems design.

Figure 14.9 depicts a typical JAD session layout. Martin and Associates recommend seating participants at a U-shaped table; end-users, managers, and systems professionals are the usual participants. The session is conducted by a facilitator who is located at a separate table; additional tables are provided for observers and the scribe (who takes notes and develops mock-ups of screens, diagrams, and so on based on information provided by users). White boards and flip charts are used to capture and record participant dialogue. The scribe's workstation comes with computer-assisted software engineering (CASE) tools, which make it possible to capture user specifications and to display prototypes on the screen.

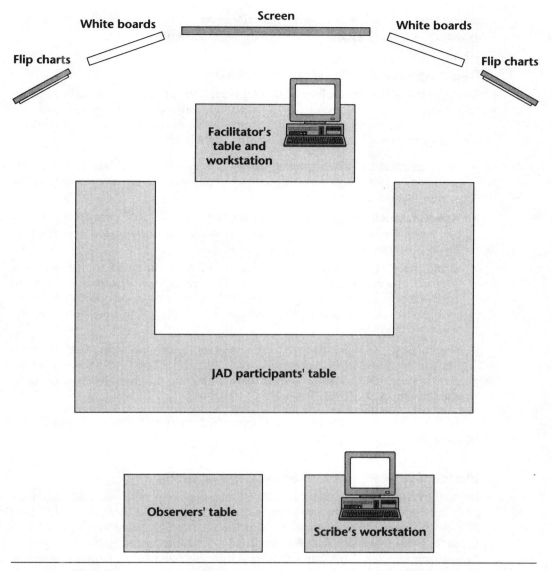

Figure 14.9 Joint application development (JAD). JAD is an alternative to the traditional approach; it attempts to maximize user involvement in the systems development process. This figure illustrates the typical layout of a JAD session room.

JAD sessions encourage strong user involvement throughout the systems development process. They help users develop a sense of ownership of the system; this often motivates them to work with the final product. This approach also helps deal with user resistance to change and helps ensure that user interfaces are truly user-friendly. Systems professionals can learn a lot about users' jobs and what managers and users really want or need from a new system.

Rapid Application Development (RAD)

Rapid application development (RAD) is another approach that James Martin and Associates have popularized. It incorporates numerous state-of-the-art approaches in order to speed up the systems development process and to deliver new systems faster. The four key elements of RAD are

- *Joint application development (JAD)* As noted in the last section, JAD users and systems professionals work together to analyze and design the system in specially equipped rooms.

- *Specialists with advanced tools (SWAT) teams* In RAD, the SWAT teams are generally composed of three or four skilled and motivated systems professionals armed with CASE tools.

- *CASE tools* CASE tools are used by SWAT team members to increase their productivity and work quality, as well as to minimize systems development time. Ideally, the use of appropriate CASE tools can add discipline to the systems development activities, reduce design errors and omissions, and reduce systems re-work.

- *Prototyping* In RAD, prototyping works hand-in-hand with JAD. Users are shown what they will receive and can react to it. The CASE tools facilitate prototyping by enabling SWAT team members to create screen designs, models, and so on while interacting with users.

In RAD, the evolving prototype becomes an integral part of the final systems design.

Systems Development in Small Organizations

In smaller organizations, fewer MIS professionals are employed and they may have such a variety of responsibilities that they have little time to develop new systems for users. In very small organizations, no MIS professionals may be on the staff. Does this mean that it is impossible for them to develop new systems? No—many smaller firms have developed good systems by using a systematic approach. This systematic approach is generally composed of the following approaches: (1) identify requirements, (2) locate, evaluate, and secure suitable software, (3) locate, evaluate, and select suitable hardware on which the software can be run, and (4) implement the system. As you can see, in the systematic approach, after information processing requirements are determined, a search for suitable software becomes the primary focus. After this is located, hardware is selected, and the system is put together and used. Note that managers in organizations employing large numbers of MIS professionals may also use a systematic approach such as this to develop the office information systems used in their own immediate work areas.

Top-Down Versus Bottom-Up Approaches

Top-down systems development is an approach in which the organization's needs are viewed from a strategic perspective and a system is developed to best meet that perspective. In this approach, systems that support the strategic activities of top-level managers are designed first, and other systems in the organization would be upgraded or re-designed after the strategic systems are in place.

This approach is appropriate in certain situations. For example, suppose that a firm has a mainframe, but that none of the top-level executives has desktop workstations that hook into this system. Furthermore, assume that the firm wants to install an executive information system (EIS). In designing the EIS, the computer professionals should look carefully at the executive decisions that will impact the company most. The EIS is designed around those particular decisions. Thus, the EIS might ultimately consist of individual microcomputer workstations—with spreadsheeting and communications capabilities tailored to the needs of each executive. After implementing the EIS, systems developers would turn their attention to other organizational systems.

Bottom-up systems development looks at existing organizational systems and attempts to meet new system needs based on them. Unlike the top-down approach (in which strategic needs trigger the development of new systems without concern about what is already in place), the bottom-up approach focuses on upgrading and/or expanding existing systems to meet new needs. For example, if all of the executives in the previous scenario had terminal workstations on their desks that hooked into the mainframe, that fact might deter the system designers from selecting desktop personal computers as an alternative to meeting any further needs these executives may have. Thus, if several executives need spreadsheeting capabilities, the system designers using a bottom-up approach are likely to consider mainframe-based spreadsheet packages. As another example, since many lower- and middle-level managers use data that come from transaction processing systems in their jobs, computer professionals using a bottom-up approach are likely to design systems to meet new needs by tapping (if possible) the vast data resources of the transaction processing systems that are already established.

In most cases, a combination of these development approaches is used, since a pure top-down or bottom-up approach may not be practical or desirable. With respect to top-down systems development, you should realize that new computer systems must work in an atmosphere in which certain resource commitments were already made. Thus, new decisions often depend upon what is already in place. Since money is limited in most organizations, managers often must make tough decisions that require MIS professionals to temper the ideal system with the resources currently available and ready for use. The pure bottom-up philosophy, on the other hand, might over-emphasize the use of existing organizational systems. Old data and old systems may be totally inappropriate to new information needs.

Does an Ideal Systems Development Methodology Exist?

As you can see, organizations may develop systems in many ways. One single, ideal systems development methodology will not work best in all situations. For example, some approaches are better suited for developing small systems than large ones. However, good systems development approaches share several basic goals, including:

- High levels of interaction with users and user involvement throughout the development process.
- Conscientious attempts to minimize development time and costs.
- The use of a rigorous and disciplined approach to systems development.
- A sincere concern with improving systems quality.
- The production of complete and accurate design specifications and documentation.
- The implementation of a system that satisfies user requirements and is easy to maintain.

If all the individuals involved with a systems development project work to ensure that it reaches these goals, the project is likely to succeed.

THE SYSTEMS DEVELOPMENT TEAM

Several different people in organizations are responsible for systems development. Figure 14.10 lists some of the roles played by various individuals and groups in the development of both large and small (end-user-developed) systems. Figure 14.11 gives an example of possible reporting relationships among the MIS professionals involved in systems development programs. Figure 14.12 provides an example of how systems development teams may fit into the overall scheme of an organization's MIS area.

In large systems, the worthiness of a particular project is typically decided by a top-management-level *steering committee*. This committee usually consists of a group of key MIS services users that acts as a review or overseeing body for MIS plans and application development. Steering committees help to formalize the concept of user involvement in MIS activities and to ensure that ongoing systems development activities are consistently aimed at satisfying the information requirements of managers and users within the organization. If the project appears worthwhile to the steering committee, the responsibility for successfully developing it becomes the MIS department's. Often, to coordinate development activities, a project management team—generally consisting of both

LARGE ENTERPRISE-LEVEL SYSTEMS	
Group	**Role**
Steering committee	Decides which projects will be undertaken
MIS management	Coordinates the planning of projects for development
Project managers	Manage specific projects
Systems analysts	Perform the actual work required in requirements analysis, system design, implementing systems, and so on
Programmers	Perform any programming-related tasks required
Information center personal	May assist the systems analysts and programmers in building prototypes and end-user systems
Users/general managers	Provide requirements information and feedback to the analyst during the preliminary investigation, requirements analysis, and design of a system
End-User-Developed (Small) Systems	
End-users	Have primary responsibility for successful systems development
Information center personnel	Assist end-users in developing systems; certify end-user systems; provide continuing support to end-user systems

Figure 14.10 Organizational personnel with systems development responsibilities.

computer professionals and key users—is appointed. Typically, systems analysts are subsequently assigned to determine user requirements, design the system, and assist in acquisition and implementation activities; however, in many systems organizations, system designers will take on a leading role during the design, acquisition, and implementation stages. If the project involves such systems development packages as prototyping fourth-generation languages or CASE tools, the analyst might ask a software specialist—possibly from the organization's information center—for assistance. Figure 14.13 summarizes some of the likely key players during each phase of the traditional systems development approach. As Figure 14.13 illustrates, the key roles shift as the project progresses from one stage to the next. Managers and users play particularly important roles during the early and later phases of the project. However, during the middle phases, MIS professionals tend to have key roles.

In end-user-developed systems, the end-user is ultimately responsible for the system. Generally, the end-user or end-user department seeks guidance from information center personnel when developing the system. Some organizations require the information center to certify the final system as a quality assurance measure.

In the rest of this chapter, and in Chapters 15 and 16, we will discuss the development of larger systems. Because larger systems are usually developed through the traditional approach, we will use it as the framework for our discussion. Chapter 17 will cover end-user development more fully.

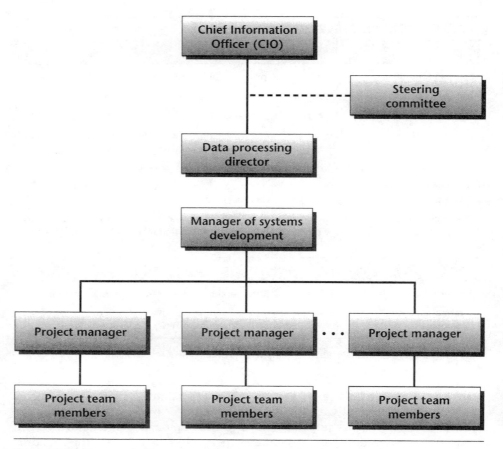

Figure 14.11 An example of reporting relationships among MIS professionals involved in systems development projects.

THE PRELIMINARY INVESTIGATION

Systems development usually begins when a problem or opportunity is identified by managers and users. For instance, personnel in a functional area may feel that an existing system is outdated. Or a manager might want access to specific, new information that he or she claims will lead to better decisions. Whatever the reason, managers and users may feel compelled to submit a request for a new system to the MIS department, and—if the need seems real—a systems analyst is assigned to make a **preliminary investigation**. This investigation should provide answers to the following questions:

- What is the problem or opportunity?
- What is the size of the systems development effort involved?
- What possible options exist as solutions?
- What types of costs and benefits are involved with each of the options?

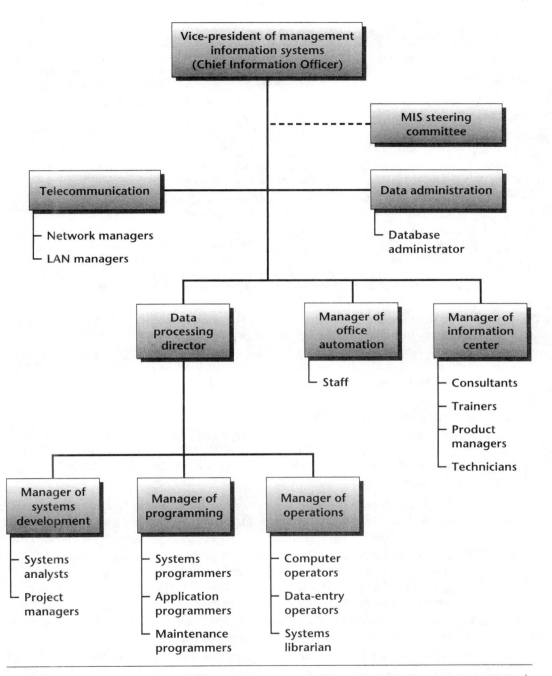

Figure 14.12 An example of how an MIS area may be organized within a firm. In this figure, systems development project managers report to the manager of systems development. Programmers needed on the project team would be assigned by the manager of programming. For end-user development projects, personnel from the information center will probably play key roles.

Development Phase	Key Roles
▪ System planning	The steering committee, CIO, and various MIS managers play a dominant role in this phase. A project team is formed after a proposed systems project is cleared for development.
▪ Requirements analysis	Managers, users, and systems analysts who are especially knowledgeable about business operations in the areas in which the systems will be used play major roles during this phase.
▪ System design	Systems analysts and technical support people are needed here.
▪ System acquisition	The same types of people needed for system design are needed here. Accounting support may also be needed.
▪ System implementaion	A number of systems analysts, programmers, trainers, and special technicians are needed in this phase.
▪ Post-implementation review	General managers play the predominant role during this phase, ensuring that the new system satisfies requirements.

Figure 14.13 A summary of the MIS professionals and managers who are likely to play key roles during each stage of the traditional approach to systems development.

In this section, we will look at how the analyst might approach each of these concerns and share his or her findings with the users who requested the new system. Remember that no universal formula will work best in every case. Nonetheless, a number of development principles, when carried out skillfully, will enhance the chances of the system's success.

Feasibility Assessment

In some situations, the preliminary investigation is called a *feasibility study* because its aim is to determine whether or not work on a new or modified system is capable of being accomplished (feasible). Generally, the feasibility study addresses four key feasibility types:

- **Technical feasibility** Can the system be built? Is the technology currently available to build such a system? If the technology is available, at what stage of the product life cycle is it?

- **Operational feasibility** If this system is built, will it be used? Will it operate in the way that users want? User input is critical in determining operational feasibility. The analyst must listen carefully to what users really want and to what types of systems they are likely to use.

- **Economic feasibility** Can the proposed system be cost justified? Will it pay for itself? Do anticipated benefits outweigh expected costs?

- **Schedule feasibility** Can the system be completed in the needed time frame?

If the preliminary investigation provides favorable answers to these feasibility questions, the chances increase that the organization will proceed with the proposed systems development project. Because non-MIS managers (especially those on the steering committee) are involved in making the "go-ahead" decision, and because the decision to develop a new system—especially a large system—can require a lot of staff time and money, the economic feasibility of the proposed system will probably be studied carefully.

Note that in many proposed systems, these feasibility factors are often interrelated. For example, a system that runs under Microsoft Windows' operating system may be proposed for users' microcomputers. When assessing the technical feasibility of this application, it may be determined that the application would run too slowly, even on the fastest personal computers. To solve this technical feasibility problem, it may be determined that the application would run faster if it were coded in assembly language. However, systems development time would be greatly increased if assembly language were used and this could create a schedule feasibility issue. The performance of the system might also be improved by replacing Windows and its graphical user interface with MS-DOS, but this option could be operationally infeasible if most of the users have never worked with MS-DOS. The speed problem might also be overcome by replacing the users' existing personal computers with $15,000 Sun workstations, but that could destroy the economic feasibility of the proposed system. As this example illustrates, in practice, it may be difficult (if not impossible) to meet all of these feasibility issues: compromises must often be made.

Strategic Factors

Besides being feasible, a proposed information system should also support an organization's strategic initiatives. The following are three potential strategic considerations:

- **Productivity** Will the proposed system increase the productivity of the organization and its workers? Is the system capable of reducing or eliminating costs?

- **Differentiation** By implementing the proposed system, can the organization offer products and/or services that are different from those offered by competitors? Will significant improvements occur in quality, variety, exception handling, service, price, cost, and so on?

- **Management** Will managers be able to carry out their tasks more effectively? Will managerial planning, decision-making, and controlling activities be positively impacted by the new system?

As you might guess, proposed information systems that are feasible and have substantial strategic value to the firm are viewed more favorably by managers and by the MIS steering committee.

Articulating Problems and Opportunities

Often, users identify a problem or an opportunity to the analyst in vague terms such as "We have a problem accounting for our receivables" or "The purchasing department needs better information." These statements alone offer little insight regarding what must be done in terms of systems development. Thus, in order to better understand the problem or opportunity, the analyst often must interact extensively with the users and managers in this area of the organization—and perhaps with personnel in other areas as well. When describing the problem or opportunity, the analyst must be concerned with matters such as those given in the following sections.

Symptoms Versus Problems

Because managers and users frequently communicate their problems in vague terms, systems analysts are frequently faced with the challenge of distinguishing *symptoms* from *problems*. For instance, if a marketing manager complains about not getting the "right information" about product sales, he or she may only be discussing a symptom of an underlying problem. In this instance, two possible underlying problems might be (1) sales data aren't being entered into the computer promptly or (2) the manager's staff doesn't know what information the manager requires. These two underlying problems have the potential to damage the organization because (1) service to customers may be sacrificed due to missing information and (2) costly mistakes may be made because information is not available to the manager at the right time. In this case and others, the analyst may need to talk at length with the manager to determine what to do about the real, underlying problems. Of course, to help analysts untangle symptoms and problems, users and managers should try to clearly describe their needs.

Documentation

Wherever possible, problems and opportunities should be carefully documented to ensure their authenticity. For instance, if a key user claims that the main computer system is "always down" or that response time is "unacceptable," the analyst should examine the systems log in the operations center to verify the accuracy and importance of the claim. As noted in Chapter 2, people occasionally exaggerate matters and sometimes have biases unrelated to the problem. Whenever possible, the analyst should define the problems identified by users in dollar terms. That is the easiest way for management and the steering committee to perceive the extent of a problem and to determine whether it is significant enough to try to solve.

Solvability

Not every problem is completely solvable. For instance, if users claim they are not getting the right types of information from an MIS, it might be that the type of information they want is impossible to obtain. A complaint frequently voiced by users is that certain systems are incapable of communicating with each other. Just because certain data are in the computer system does not always mean they are readily available to everyone who wants them. Today, many end-users discover this as they futilely attempt to have a recently purchased spreadsheet package or microcomputer system communicate with the corporate mainframe. In many organizations, when the analyst encounters such situations, he or she is directed to say, "Good luck—you're on your own" to users who have not adopted enterprise-recommended microcomputing products.

When performing the preliminary investigation, the analyst should know that he or she cannot always eliminate every user problem. The goal, instead, should be to minimize its impact. So, for instance, users should not expect a new credit authorization system to completely eliminate bad debts.

Opportunities

When studying problems, the analyst should look for possible opportunities that users didn't notice. For instance, when companies first started installing communications terminals at customer sites, it was often just to streamline their order-entry systems. What many of them did not realize was that this solution also contained an opportunity to lock in customers. Many companies missed the chance to design additional "hooks" into their systems to sustain competitive advantage.

Opportunities are usually more difficult to recognize than problems. Because problems interfere with preconceived plans, many of them can be anticipated. Opportunities are harder to find and tend to present themselves at random or unexpected times.

Perspective

Every problem or opportunity needs to be examined in perspective with other problems and opportunities. Numerous important problems and opportunities warrant consideration at any one time, for example, but usually limited resources are available to solve them. Because of this, problems and systems development projects typically have to be prioritized and attention may be devoted only to high-priority problems and projects. Steering committees are usually charged with keeping an eye on "the big picture."

Determining the Scale of the Development Effort

After a problem or opportunity is described by users, the analyst must next decide on the level of commitment involved. During the preliminary investigation, the analyst must determine the scale of response needed to respond to the user requests for a new system, as well as the approximate amount of time and money that will be required in the effort.

For instance, a marketing manager may want to have more timely information on sales in a company's retail outlets and most employees within the company may agree that this project should be developed. However, only $20,000 might remain in the budget for the current fiscal year. Thus, instead of recommending ambitious, expensive solutions (such as equipping all retail outlets with data-collection and transmission capabilities so they can send data nightly to a central site), the analyst might set up a small information system (perhaps one that enables a few key stores to send data semiweekly to the central site). The results obtained through these pilot stores may show whether other stores should be set up in the same way after more money is available for wider scale implementation.

Because many problems in an organization are interrelated, analysts and the steering committee must be very careful to determine which ones to change and which ones to leave alone. For instance, when trying to cut the time it takes to distribute up-to-date inventory data to warehouse personnel, the analyst might feel that the entire inventory system should be overhauled. However, this type of change could be beyond the scope of the analyst's assignment. While most people prefer top-down system development—tearing an existing system down and starting all over—this is rarely possible. For various reasons, both organizations and system analysts often have to keep what works and fix what doesn't.

Identifying Viable Options

After problems or opportunities are defined, and the analyst determines just how much management wants to spend or change, possible solutions are examined. Not every solution involves either computers or new information. Sometimes, just a simple procedural change is necessary; often, an inelegant, manual technique solves the problem. In our current information age, users and managers often mistakenly believe that technology is the answer to every problem. However, as scholars acknowledge, technology can easily make matters worse, not better.

When studying alternative solutions, the analyst sometimes considers the full spectrum of solution options—from inexpensive, makeshift solutions to expensive, top-of-the-line technology. Because of the myriad possibilities involved in most business situations, every problem is different, and may require a solution different from that used in the past. Common sense and intuition are key ingredients in the solution development process.

Estimating Costs and Benefits

After possible solution options are identified, the analyst should make a preliminary estimate of each solution's costs and benefits. Generally, the two cost components to any system are (1) the cost of initially developing the system and (2) ongoing operational costs.

Regarding the cost of developing the system, L. L. Gremillion and P. Pyburn comment that

> Development projects have a common cost pattern. Typically about a quarter of the cost is incurred during the definition phase, in which the basic functions of the system and its costs and benefits are identified. At least one-half goes into the design phase, in which programs and procedures are written, tested, and documented. The remainder of the cost is incurred during implementation, in training users, switching over to the new system, and doing a postaudit of the project.

These cost patterns are probably different when fourth-generation languages are used to develop applications. As noted previously, such languages have the potential to enhance programmer productivity and reduce application development time. Although determining the cost of a new system is a relatively straightforward process, it can also be a woefully inaccurate one. Tales of massive project cost overruns and gross underestimates abound among MIS professionals and non-MIS managers. In addition, determining benefits—and placing dollar values on them—can be tricky.

Ongoing operational costs for systems, because they involve people-related expenses, are often much greater than development costs. Although these costs fluctuate from system to system, such costs as program maintenance can run up to ten times the cost of initial development.

Reporting Results to Management

After the analyst articulates the problem and its scope, provides one or more solution alternatives, and estimates the costs and benefits of each alternative, he or she reports these results to management. The report should be accompanied by a short cover letter that summarizes the results and makes a recommendation regarding further procedures. From the analyst's report, management should determine what to do next, such as proceed with the systems development, implement a quick solution to the problem and start the next project, or abandon the system completely.

REQUIREMENTS ANALYSIS

If management decides to continue developing the system after reading the analyst's report, the requirements analysis phase of development begins. During the **requirements analysis** phase of the traditional approach, the focus is on determining user needs, studying the application area in depth, assessing the strengths and weaknesses of the present work method, and reporting results to management.

As Figure 14.8 (page 613) illustrated, the traditional and prototyping approaches differ regarding the way requirements analysis is performed. In the traditional approach, the full requirements analysis is performed before system design begins. Users typically sign a document at the end of the requirements analysis phase, confirming that the requirements identified by the systems analyst are correct.

Prototyping, by contrast, has the requirements and design phases proceed in tandem and in small increments. So, for example, user needs are determined at any time only to the degree that they are needed to design the next iteration of the prototype. While the user is experimenting with the prototype, the systems analyst observes the user and puts these observations into perspective in order to determine how the prototype should be further refined. Figure 14.8 also shows how the traditional and prototyping approaches differ in several other respects, and we will highlight these during subsequent discussions of systems development.

How thoroughly the current system is studied depends on the situation. To determine if the current system needs just a few adjustments instead of a complete overhaul, the system should be studied in depth. By doing this, the analyst may discover that the current system still works rather well and that the benefits of an entirely new system are not worth its cost. However, if management is determined to replace the current system, the analyst would probably just waste time by studying it thoroughly. In this case, time is better spent determining exactly what management desires in a new system.

For example, if the major objective of the application is to provide customers with better service, and it is clear that the current system does not and never will provide the level of service desired, then learning how this system functions is probably not important. In this case, the current system's outputs may be the only significant item. However, the new system may change those outputs anyway. For instance, in moving from a hardcopy, report-based environment to a screen-display environment, new types of information, in different formats, are required. Also, opportunities to use technology to create new, information-based products for the customer may appear.

Assessing Needs

Every system is built to meet some set of needs—for example, the need of the organization for lower operational costs, the need of managers for better information, the need of users for smoother operations, or the need of customers for better levels of service. To assess needs, the analyst often must interact extensively with the people who will benefit from the system in order to determine what they really require.

How the analyst determines needs depends on the problem studied and the development approach taken. In both the traditional and prototyping approaches, four useful sources of information for determining needs are

- Documents
- Questionnaires
- Interviews
- Personal observation

Each of these sources is useful, as well, for determining how the current system works.

In many prototyping projects, questionnaires are not used as extensively as the other approaches—and may not be used at all. Personal observation is by far the most important of the sources because creating a successful prototype requires that developers carefully observe users' experiences with prototype models at each iteration in the development process.

Documents

Documents include manuals, input forms, output forms, diagrams of how the current system works (including data flow diagrams and system flowcharts), organization charts showing hierarchies of user and manager responsibilities, job descriptions for the people who currently work with the current system, procedure manuals, program code for the applications associated with the current system, and so on. Documents are an especially good source of information about user needs and the current system because they are generally easy to collect, convey a lot of helpful information, and provide relatively objective data.

The documents collected by the analyst should be current. Managers and users are often asked to help collect documents and they should ensure that they locate the most accurate and up-to-date information possible. The analyst must have current data so that he or she can thoroughly understand the user environment necessary to design a system that better satisfies information needs. For example, if an aspect of the new system is an electronic mail network that automatically copies important memos to a worker's superiors, the analyst should use an up-to-date organizational chart. If provided with an outdated organizational chart, initial designs for the E-mail system will have to be reworked.

Questionnaires

Users and managers are often asked to complete *questionnaires* about the information system when the traditional systems development approach is chosen. The main strength of questionnaires is that large amounts of data can be collected from many users quickly. In addition, data can be collected over a wide geographical area without incurring travel expenses, the respondents to questionnaires can remain anonymous, and questionnaires are relatively inexpensive as a data-collection device. Also, if the questionnaire is skillfully crafted, responses can be analyzed rapidly by computer.

Although useful in many situations, questionnaires do present potential pitfalls to the unwary. For instance, results can be biased if questions are poorly worded or if the only people who respond to the questionnaire represent a specific viewpoint. Some examples of poorly worded questions include the *loaded question* ("Should you continue to be provided with the high level of service you've received in the past?"), the *leading question* ("We shouldn't be providing this type of service to you, should we?"), the *self-answering question* ("How much time does it take you to do this job? The current standard calls for one hour."), and the *ambiguous question* ("Is the documentation nice?"). An example of biasing a survey (whether intentional or not) is passing out a questionnaire about attitudes toward robotics when union workers are at a meeting and cannot respond.

Interviews

Users and managers may also be interviewed as part of the traditional systems development approach. *Interviews* are designed to capture the same type of data from users as questionnaires, but they are more in depth. Because conducting interviews is relatively expensive, a smaller number of managers and users is contacted. However, the data gathered in this way often provide systems developers with a fuller picture of the problems and opportunities. Interviews also give analysts the opportunity to note user reactions firsthand and to probe for further information. For example, if a user's response to a question puzzles the interviewer, he or she can follow it with a question that clarifies or digs deeper into the subject. This gives the interview a dynamic quality not found in more impersonal questionnaires.

Because interviews are time consuming and take users away from their work, an analyst should coordinate interview schedules with the managers of the workers that he or she wants to interview. This helps managers develop work schedules that accommodate the time needed to complete the interviews and helps to minimize potential disruptions to normal work routines.

As with designing questionnaires, interviewing is an important skill. Some interviewers establish rapport with users and obtain information easily, whereas others intimidate users, causing them to provide as little data as possible. When interviewing users, analysts should be especially careful to keep the conversation level as non-technical as possible. People who use a lot of computer jargon are sometimes considered arrogant, and this often makes users uncommunicative. Also, the interviewer should have a goal for the interview.

Therefore, sending the respondent a letter before the interview often helps. Not only is this courteous, but the user or manager can better prepare for the interview and provide the interviewer with more informative data. Finally, perhaps the most important skill in interviewing is listening. After all, the goal of most interviews is to encourage users to talk, not to impart the interviewer's own particular point of view.

Observation

In prototyping approaches, *observation* plays a central role in requirements analysis. Only by observing how users react to prototypes of a new system, for instance, can the system be successfully developed. In the traditional approach, observation is not always mandatory (as it is in prototyping), but it is still desirable in most instances. Because a new system is not yet in place, the analyst can only observe workers performing their jobs with the current system. This can help the analyst verify the existence (and extent) of expressed shortcomings of the existing system and may help him or her uncover other, possibly unvoiced, problems.

Generally, the analyst following either the traditional or some prototyping approach should visit the user site to watch work taking place. If managers are notified of upcoming visits in advance, they can often identify times when representative systems will be in use; they can also tell analysts not to come at times when their presence would be a distraction or a nuisance. The analyst should be at the workplace long enough for people to adjust to his or her presence, and then settle back into their normal work routines.

The value of observational visits by analysts can be great. Often, what the analyst hears from managers or reads in documents about the system is different from what he or she observes when watching people at work. Such a visit often helps the analyst get a clear picture of the user environment and why a request for a new system was submitted.

William Bowen relates an interesting story about how important observation can be in the development of systems. Analysts were observing a warehouse system in which telephone-switching equipment was packed in boxes. The boxes were sealed and passed on to the shipping department, which opened the boxes so they could be quality-control-inspected. Then the boxes were re-sealed for shipment. Sound bizarre? The analysts quickly observed that the inspectors were doing their work at the wrong stage of the operation. Before the analysts arrived, no one bothered to look across departmental lines at the whole process.

Analysis

After users provide the analyst with the information he or she needs about the application, it needs to be analyzed. In prototyping, analysis typically involves thinking about user experiences with the current prototype and determining how this feedback might be used to improve subsequent prototypes. It also often involves deciding how to expand the prototype; for instance, deciding whether mock data-entry screens should be enhanced with a dummy database at the next prototype iteration.

In the traditional approach, the analysis step often requires analysts to review their work with managers and users. This may include looking at diagrams of both the current and proposed systems, assessing the strategic impact of the system, and refining the estimates of benefits and costs. We will cover the first two items in this section; the determination of benefits and costs is examined in Chapter 18. This chapter also discusses the role of CASE tools in systems development. These tools help automate the work performed during requirements analysis and are also useful in other phases of the development process.

Diagrams

When systems development projects are underway, managers and users are often asked to review diagrams developed by the systems analyst or other members of the project team. Diagrams of both the existing system and proposed systems can be valuable in the analysis process. A major benefit of diagrams is that they quickly convey to both users and the analyst how a system works. Diagrams can be especially critical in the traditional approach because no working models of the system exist for the user to see or operate. The major limitations of documents are that they are time-consuming to prepare and users frequently cannot fully visualize how a system actually works simply by looking at a diagram.

Many types of diagrams may be developed by project team members to illustrate how a system is laid out and what it does. These diagrams are typically shared with managers and users, who are asked to comment on or approve the accuracy and completeness of their content. Two types of diagrams that managers and users will probably encounter are data flow diagrams and system flowcharts.

- **■ *Data flow diagrams*** Chapter 3 covered **data flow diagrams (DFD)**, and numerous examples of them were presented throughout the book. Data flow diagrams show graphically how data move within an organization. In most instances, data flow diagrams show logical descriptions of system elements; that is, they do not depict any physical hardware, such as printers or display devices. By not making hardware commitments, the data flow diagram enables users and the analyst to view a system more abstractly. This can uncover new possibilities that would not have occurred to the analyst if specific devices were named.

  Data flow diagrams can be specified on a general level (in *context diagrams*)—showing only the most critical data flows in a system—or on a detailed level. Figure 14.14 shows (a) a context diagram and (b) a top-level data flow diagram of a textbook order-processing system. The term **structured analysis** is commonly used to refer to the preparation of data flow diagrams.

(a) Context diagram.

(b) Top-level data flow diagram.

Figure 14.14 A context diagram (a) and a top-level data flow diagram (b) of a textbook order-processing system for a college or university bookstore. As orders for textbooks are received from faculty, they are batched and used to place orders with publishers.

- *System flowcharts* **System flowcharts** are graphical tools used for modeling systems in physical terms. Physical descriptions depict how specific types of hardware elements of a system fit together. Figure 14.15 shows some of the symbols used in drawing system flowcharts. When this type of flowchart is constructed, these symbols are used to represent identifiable components of the system. Figure 14.16 shows a system flowchart representation for 1.0 (Process faculty orders), originally shown in Figure 14.14(b).

CASE Tools

Today, the data flow diagrams and system flowcharts that users review are commonly generated (and revised) by systems developers using the on-screen drawing modules found in CASE software packages. **Computer-aided software**

Symbol	Description	Explanation
 ▢	Process	An event that changes the value or location of data; examples include a program and a clerical procedure
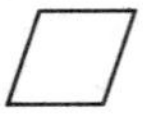 ▱	Input/output	A device-independent symbol for input, ouput, or both
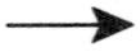 →	Flowline	A symbol that links other symbols and shows both sequence and flow direction
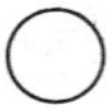 ○	Connector	An entry from or an exit to another part of the flowchart on the same page
 ▽	Off-page connector	An entry from or an exit to another page of the flowchart
 ⬭	Magnetic disk	A symbol showing magnetic disk input, output, or storage
◗	Magnetic tape	A symbol showing magnetic tape input, output, or storage
 ⊃	On-line storage	A symbol for on-line storage of any type
▽	Off-line storage	A symbol for any type of off-line storage, such as archival tapes
 ⬚	Printed output	A symbol used for any type of printed report or document
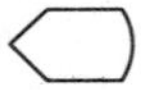 ⬠	Display	A symbol showing input or output using a display workstation
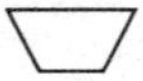 ⏢	Manual operation	An event performed by manual means
▢	Auxiliary operation	An off-line hardware operation
 ⟋	Communications	Telecommunication of data

Figure 14.15 System flowchart symbols and what they mean.

engineering (CASE) refers to the automation of anything that humans do to develop systems. Most of the earliest CASE products, introduced in the 1980s, enabled systems analysts and programmers to create flowcharts and data flow diagrams on a minicomputer or microcomputer workstation. Today, CASE products can support virtually all phases of the traditional systems development process. For example, several packages allow systems developers at a workstation to create complete and internally consistent requirements specifications with graphics generators and specification languages. Packages that sup-

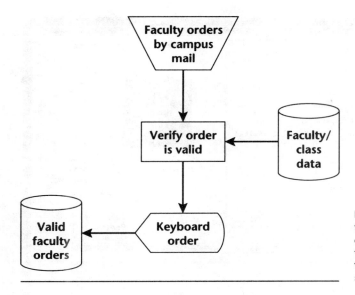

Figure 14.16 A system flowchart. This flowchart depicts the 1.0 (Process faculty orders) portion of the textbook-ordering process shown in Figure 14.14(b).

port the later stages of the systems development process often include code generators as part of the CASE toolkit. These can be applied directly to the specifications for the new system to produce structured program code. Many CASE products also include a comprehensive data dictionary facility that manages the entire process and helps to ensure that everything done by systems developers meets rigorous standards and is internally consistent with what is already in place (see Figure 14.17). Figure 14.18 gives a summary of the potential benefits of CASE products, as well as some of their limitations.

Most vendors would probably acknowledge that no company has yet created a complete CASE package—one that assists the systems development team all the way from requirements analysis through maintenance. Hence, what may be needed to facilitate systems development is not a single CASE tool, but an appropriate set of CASE tools. When considering CASE products, ask the following questions: What type of tool is it? Where does it fit in the development life cycle? What evidence is there that it reduces application development time?

CASE products are still relatively new and evolving. Nonetheless, numerous organizations already report great success with them. According to David Stamps, after using Cortex Corporation's Application Factory, DuPont realized impressive savings in cost, time, and labor. One application—a finishing area system for the production of nylon stretch-wrap—was originally estimated at $268,000. Using the CASE tool, it cost only $30,000. Although it was scheduled to take nine months and three full-time people, the application was finished in "record time," according to DuPont's manager of information engineering. For this job, Application Factory generated 90 percent of the code directly from design specifications. DuPont later installed the product at 11 sites and reported a 600 percent productivity increase.

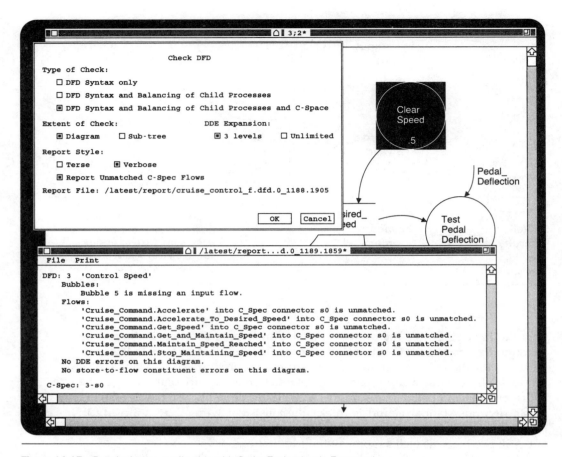

Figure 14.17 Developing an application with Cadre Technology's Teamwork.

David Stamps also mentions Arbitron Ratings Co., which installed Nastec Corporation's DesignAid CASE product, resulting in impressive productivity improvements. In the words of Arbitron's MIS director, "The increase is realized primarily in the requirements and design phases. Documentation is kept as current as possible, and the graphics and content of that documentation facilitates communication between designers and users . . . [Also] it is much easier to go back and make changes—which frees designers from having to erase and draw new lines. They can concentrate on design."

Figure 14.19 provides a list of selected CASE products. Not all of these products perform the same functions or cover the same phases of the systems development cycle.

Assessing Strategic Impact

Another resource that can be particularly helpful in requirements analysis is an analysis of the strategic impact of the application. Here, how the applications fit

ADVANTAGES AND DISADVANTAGES OF CASE TOOLS

Advantages

- Structured development standards are enforced
- The application is developed in an internally consistent fashion
- Development time is shortened
- Relatively bug-free code can be automatically generated from the system specification
- Documentation is automatically generated
- Trying several design alternatives is facilitated because any changes made to the specification will be reflected automatically in design, coding, and documentation
- A complete data dictionary is automatically produced
- Error-handling, system auditability, and security issues can be incorporated early, as part of the design
- Maintenance is easier because of the structured code and forced standards

Disadvantages

- No CASE tool can support the full systems development cycle.
- Many CASE products cannot interface effectively with databases and fourth-generation languages
- Many CASE products cannot support multiple types of diagrams
- Many CASE products are weak in the system maintenance area
- The CASE area lacks sufficient standards
- Many CASE products are relatively expensive
- CASE is not a remedy for every development problem

Figure 14.18 A summary of the advantages and disadvantages of CASE tools. These tools can potentially provide an automated, integrated approach to the entire systems development process.

into the strategic plans of the organization should be considered. Sometimes, during the requirements analysis, the analyst may get wrapped up in the details and lose sight of the original goal. Thus, it is often useful to ensure that the development effort is not veering off course. The project team should be especially concerned about the following areas:

- **Application importance** How critical is this application to the company?
- **Needs** What particular needs or goals should be met by this application? For example, an accounts payable system should provide payments to vendors at the proper time, inform the payables department whether or not to take advantage of vendor discounts for early payments, and help the treasurer manage cash. A sales support system should help identify fast- and slow-moving products, key selling sites, and the success or failure of promotional campaigns.

Product	Vendor	Description
Aims Plus	Aims Plus Inc.	Workstation-based automated development for Wang equipment
Application Factory	Cortex Corporation	Integrated application development and maintenance for DEC VAX
DesignAid	Nastec Corporation	Workstation-based automated development system
Design Machine	Ken Orr & Associates	Workstation-based automated development system
Excelerator	Intersolv	PC-based for workbench systems analysis, design, and documentation
CASEworks	CASEworks, Inc.	Windows-based package that generates program code from specifications in a variety of languages
Foundation	Arthur Andersen Consulting	PC-based workbench for analysis, design, and documentation
PC Prism	Intersolv	PC-based workbench for strategic-planning applications
Application Developer Workbench	KnowledgeWare	A family of CASE tools that supports planning analysis, design, documentation, maintenance, and RAD
Information Engineering Workbench	KnowledgeWare	AI-based expert development system
Life Cycle Manager	Nastec Corporation	Project manager workbench and analysis toolkit
Maestro	Softlab Inc.	Software engineering tools
MicroCICS	Unicorn Systems Corporation	Creates and tests CICS programs on an IBM PC
Teamwork/SA	Cadre Technologies Inc.	Automated development system for Apollo, DEC, and IBM

Figure 14.19 Selected CASE products. Intersolv's Excelerator has the largest installed base of any CASE product worldwide.

- **Information and system support capabilities** What types of information or system support capabilities are required to meet the needs of users? For example, what information is needed by the treasurer to manage cash? What types of technical decision support capabilities does a marketing or sales manager need to be more effective at postioning the company's sales force?

- **Roles of current and proposed systems** How well does the present system meet user needs? What specific weaknesses in the current system will a new system correct? Would a new system provide significant benefits to the organization relative to the cost of developing and operating it?

These questions and the answers to them should be addressed in a top-down way. That is, the analyst first assesses the application's importance, then determines user needs, and finally looks at the information and capabilities required to satisfy those needs. The strategic planning and critical success factors (CSF) models, discussed in Chapter 3, are particularly useful for structuring such questions. Chapter 18 covers a number of potentially useful procedures for determining strategic impact of the entire application portfolio.

Reporting to Management

In the traditional approach to systems development, after the data are collected and analyzed and users sign off on the requirements recommendations (thereby accepting them), the project manager reports findings to management. This report addresses many of the same issues covered in the preliminary investigation report, but goes into greater depth. Also, it may update management on some of the findings uncovered during the preliminary investigation—perhaps reporting that an initially promising alternative is infeasible or listing additional benefits and costs. The requirements analysis report should include:

- A statement of the problem or opportunity the system is addressing.
- A list of alternative solutions.
- A recommendation from the list of alternatives.
- A quantitative assessment of the benefits and costs of the new system.
- A timetable and schedule showing when and how the new system will be designed, acquired, and implemented.

In the prototyping approach, both requirements analysis and design proceed together, in iterative steps. If the project is large, management may require the analyst to prepare a progress report at each major milestone or at the completion of each iteration of the prototype. Depending on the size of the cash outlays and the time required to go from iteration to iteration in the prototype, the analyst may or may not need the approval of management at each iteration to proceed further.

DOCUMENTATION

Documentation describes all types of written instructions associated with using, operating, or developing a computer system. It is important for managers and users to have good documentation so that they will understand and use the system in the best possible manner. Typical documentation developed during requirements analysis includes system and program flowcharts, data flow diagrams, user manuals, system manuals, and sample input and output forms. When possible, documentation should be prepared by the analyst during each phase of development as the system is taking shape.

Unfortunately, some analysts treat documentation casually and wait until the entire system is almost finished to begin preparing it. As a result, documentation preparation is often rushed, and the analyst can easily forget how certain parts of the system work. Poor documentation can delay the implementation of a new system and can make it difficult for users to take full advantage of the new system. Three important types of documentation are project documentation, system documentation, and program documentation.

Project Documentation

Project documentation chronicles the systems development effort from preliminary investigation until the system is put into place. Project documentation is the input to the postimplementation review, which is the step in systems development that examines if the system really performs as expected. The original expectations placed on the system, all assumptions, and some of the practical problems encountered in meeting requirements objectives should be evident in the project documentation.

Documenting the project serves many purposes. For instance, if an enhancement is suggested for the completed system, the analyst assigned to this task should first look at the project documentation to see if that alternative was previously explored. Or if a serious complaint—perhaps even a legal issue—is later raised, it helps management to justify, through written documentation, why a certain course of action was chosen.

Types of materials that are typically included among the project documentation are the initial systems request from the functional areas involved, reports made to management, detailed computations of benefits and costs, written approvals, minutes from meetings, and analyses of important alternatives.

System Documentation

System documentation includes all of the materials that show how a particular system operates. This includes systems requirements, systems specifications, diagrams (such as data flow diagrams or system flowcharts), written narratives of job descriptions, and so on. Certain parts of this documentation package are especially useful to programmers, who need to study how the system works in order to code programs for it.

Program Documentation

Generally, *program documentation* includes manuals, program listings, or programming tools (such as program flowcharts and pseudocode, which are described in the next chapter) that help users, programmers, or operations personnel work with programs.

User documentation often consists of a written or computerized tutorial and a reference manual. The tutorial helps the user work with a package and, possibly, solve problems and diagnose errors. The reference manual provides more detail on each step of the program. If the user cannot figure out how a command works, he or she should consult the reference manual.

Programmer documentation exists for the benefit of the maintenance programmer: the person in charge of modifying programs and correcting program errors. Thus, any tools of possible benefit to the maintenance programmer are part of the documentation package. In a study conducted by Tor Giumaraes, maintenance programmers cited the following documentation package items as most important to them:

- A listing of the program.
- An English narrative describing what the program and program modules are supposed to do.
- Structured programming.
- Layout forms of inputs and outputs.
- A system flowchart depicting the programs, files, and so on, involved in the system.

Operator documentation consists mainly of written manuals that explain to operations personnel what procedures should be followed when running certain programs, mounting and dismounting tapes and disks, using input and output equipment, maintaining physical security, performing backup activities, and so on. If, for instance, the system crashes in the middle of processing data, the operator documentation should explain re-start procedures. Or if a terminal is out of order, operator documentation should provide the procedure to follow when getting it repaired.

Because documentation is important to many types of people in the organization, it is essential for managers and users to ensure that documentation is not overlooked by the project team. Like the other work performed by the project team, users and managers should scrutinize documentation to ensure that it adequately meets their needs.

SUMMARY

The process of putting into place the systems that organizations need to run smoothly is called systems development. The systems development life cycle (SDLC) is often subdivided into five activities: preliminary investigation, requirements analysis, system design, system acquisition, and system implementation. Some companies hire systems integrators to perform systems development for them.

Approaches to systems development are often classified according to how the five systems development activities are carried out or whether the development efforts are top-down or bottom-up. The first of these classifications organizes systems development into three basic approaches: the traditional approach, prototyping approaches, and end-user development.

In the traditional approach, developmental activities are followed in strict sequence, one after the other. This approach is criticized because it is often difficult for users to formulate their needs in advance.

With prototyping approaches, a small or pilot version of the system—called a prototype—is developed. Users work with the prototype, and feedback provided to the systems analyst leads to further prototype refinements or enhancements. This process of gradually improving the prototype through iterative user feedback continues until a final, acceptable system is developed.

With end-user development, the end-user is responsible for developing the system. The end-user may select a traditional type of approach, a prototyping approach, or an intuitive approach.

Top-down systems development views the organization's needs from a strategic perspective, and a new system is developed to meet that perspective. Bottom-up systems development looks at the existing organizational systems and tries to meet new systems needs within the constraints posed by those existing systems. In most cases, a combination of top-down and bottom-up approaches is used.

The preliminary investigation is the first step in systems development. After a user need or opportunity is identified, a systems analyst determines if a new or modified system is necessary. He or she also determines the scale of the development effort, indicates viable options, and assesses the benefits and costs of each proposed option. When the assessment is complete, the analyst reports these findings to management.

The requirements analysis activity involves studying the application area and user needs in depth. In the traditional approach, requirements are specified before the system design takes place. With prototyping approaches, however, the requirements analysis and design phases proceed together. In the traditional approach, four potential sources of information for determining user needs are documents, questionnaires, interviews, and personal observation. In prototyping approaches, personal observation is the most useful source of information about user needs.

Two useful diagram-based approaches that can assist in both systems analysis and system design are data flow diagrams (DFD) and system flowcharts. Data flow diagrams show logically how data move in an organization. The use of such diagrams in development is often referred to as structured analysis. System flowcharts are graphical tools used for modeling systems in physical terms.

Computer-aided software engineering (CASE) pertains to the automation of anything that humans do to develop systems. CASE products allow computer professionals to create complete and internally consistent requirements specifications at a display workstation.

The last step of requirements analysis is to report findings to management. This includes a recommendation from the list of alternative solutions; an assessment of costs and benefits; and a schedule covering future system design, acquisition, and implementation activities.

Documentation refers to the written instructions concerning the use, operation, and development of a computer system. Project documentation describes the entire systems development effort. System documentation describes how a particular system works. Program documentation describes how programs are used, coded, and operated.

KEY TERMS

Bottom-up systems development	Requirements analysis
Computer-aided software engineering (CASE)	Structured analysis
	System flowchart
Data flow diagram (DFD)	Systems development
Documentation	Systems development life cycle (SDLC)
End-user development	
Joint application development (JAD)	Systems integrator
Preliminary investigation	Top-down systems development
Prototyping	Traditional approach (to systems development)
Rapid application development (RAD)	

REVIEW QUESTIONS

1. What activities are part of the systems development life cycle (SDLC)?

2. What types of problems have been encountered when developing systems using the traditional approach?

3. In what respect can we say that many prototyping approaches exist, not just one?

4. What types of systems are best for development by the traditional approach? What types by prototyping approaches? What types by end-user development?

5. Identify the various types of end-user development approaches.

6. Differentiate between the top-down and bottom-up approaches to systems development.

7. How do joint application development (JAD) and rapid application development (RAD) differ from traditional systems development approaches?

8. How is systems development handled in smaller organizations?

9. What is the purpose of a preliminary investigation? What different types of feasibility may be assessed during the preliminary investigation?

10. What is the difference between a problem and a problem symptom?

11. In what ways may data about the information system be collected from managers and users?

12. How do system flowcharts differ from data flow diagrams?

13. In what ways are CASE tools useful in systems development?

14. When, during systems development, should documentation take place? Identify the different types of system documentation that can be developed.

15. What do project team members report to managers after determining the requirements for a new system?

DISCUSSION QUESTIONS

1. Many writers cite problems associated with system documentation. Patrick Brown makes the following claim, "Documentation . . . is becoming a major burden. It is not uncommon for projects to produce design documents thousands of pages long. Producing such documents costs far more than any value they may have to anybody. . . The cost of maintaining a current version of the document is simply too large to make it feasible . . . Should a person read a 1,200-page design document to find the format of a single interface? . . . Another significant problem . . . is that documents are rarely compatible with one another." Do you feel that all of these are indeed problems? Make a list of the benefits and problems you see associated with each type of documentation covered in the chapter.

2. What are the advantages and disadvantages to using a systems integrator? Why is outsourcing becoming a more popular application development option?

3. What types of implementation problems are likely to be encountered by using CASE tools during the systems development process?

CASE STUDY

Big Projects Bring Big Headaches for Uncle Sam

Understandably, the information systems needed to support the branches and agencies of the federal government are large and complex. Over the years, the Feds have learned—often the hard way—that upgrading existing systems and developing replacement systems can be problem-prone endeavors. And, because the systems are big, so are the problems associated with them.

The Farmers Home Administration (FHA) is one of several federal agencies that have run into major difficulties during large systems development projects. The FHA spent more than $26 million on two aborted efforts to overhaul its computer systems. The U.S. General Accounting Office (GAO) feels that the FHA's third attempt may be headed for disaster as well because the agency has not resolved the planning and oversight problems that haunted its earlier projects. In a report issued by the GAO, the FHA's current half-billion dollar project presents "an unacceptable risk that systems . . . may not meet users' needs."

After collecting data over a 32-month period, a GAO report identified ten problem areas that have plagued federal agencies systems development efforts:

1. **Inadequate management of the MIS life cycle** For example, in 1990, the GAO cited poor capacity planning as the main reason why the Federal Aviation Administration's new computers might not be able to handle the workload in the Los Angeles area.

2. **Ineffective oversight of information resources management** Because of faulty procedures, the U.S. Department of Education gave $109 million in new student loans to students who had defaulted on earlier loans.

3. **Security, integrity, and reliability problems** For example, inadequate access controls at a sensitive data center meant that security safeguards could be easily bypassed and the security of highly classified data at the U.S. Department of Justice (such as the names of informants and undercover agents) could not be ensured.

4. **Inability of systems to work in tandem** In one case, because key systems at the Veteran's Administration could not exchange data, the processing of client claims was unnecessarily long.

5. **Inadequate resources to accomplish goals** For example, the U.S. Navy awarded a time-sensitive contract for a submarine target detection system to a firm with an insufficient number of experienced Ada programmers and an inadequate Ada training program.

6. **Cost overruns** The GAO uncovered a whopping $7 billion in cost overruns, including an $800 million increase in the IRS's cost estimate for automating tax return examination.

7. **Schedule delays** By 1994, the Navy will have spent 17 years developing a system to automate the preparation and editing of payroll and personnel

documents. The system was originally scheduled for completion in 1984.

8. **Systems not performing as intended**
   For example, during 1988, the IRS experienced problems with an imaging system. This forced workers to use stopgap measures with paper copies of returns.

9. **Inaccurate or incomplete data**
   NASA had incomplete or missing data from many important space missions; no data from one Apollo mission could be found.

10. **Difficult access to data**   The U.S. Coast Guard's major law enforcement system was so difficult to use that it was essentially ignored.

Adapted from Anthes (1992).

DISCUSSION

1. Which of the problems cited in this Case Study would you consider to be the one(s) that should be corrected immediately? Explain your choices.

2. Based on what you have learned about systems development, what are likely to be the underlying reasons why the federal government is encountering such problems?

3. Based on what you have read in this chapter, what steps should be taken to minimize the occurrence of these problems in future systems development projects?

Chapter 15

System Design

After completing this chapter, you will be able to:

Define system design

Describe the difference between logical and physical system design

List and describe important activities and concerns associated with design of output, input, processing, storage, procedure, and personnel specification

Contrast the advantages and disadvantages resulting from acquiring application packages as opposed to developing in-house software

Describe several program design tools and approaches, both traditional and emerging

Descrbe the various types of procedures and controls that must be developed for new systems

After the requirements analysis for a system is completed in full (as in the traditional approach) or in part (as in many prototyping approaches), system design takes place. The **system design** phase usually consists of three activities:

- Reviewing the system's informational and functional requirements.
- Developing a model of the new system, including the logical and physical specification of output, input, processing, storage, procedures, and personnel.
- Reporting results to management.

In this chapter, we will look at each of these activities. First, we consider the advantages of reviewing the results of the requirements analysis. Then, we examine the six main areas in system design: output, input, processing, storage, procedures, and personnel. Finally, we consider reporting results to management.

In the traditional approach, these activities normally take place in the sequence described. That is, requirements are reviewed first, then a design model is constructed, and finally, a report to management is made that presents all important design-related findings and suggestions. As with requirements analysis, managers and users play crucial roles during each of these activities.

In prototyping approaches, these three design phase activities usually take place unevenly. System requirements are reviewed whenever necessary. The model of the system—which is usually a physical prototype on which users experiment—is revised at each prototype iteration. Thus, the analyst and users generally switch back and forth between determining system requirements and incorporating any new ideas into the design model. The last activity, reporting to management, normally takes place before the next major commitment of time and money must be made to develop the system further. In the case of a throwaway prototype, this is generally when the prototype has proven satisfactory and it's time to develop the actual system.

REVIEWING SYSTEMS REQUIREMENTS

The system's design must conform to the purpose, scale, and general concept of the system that management approved during the requirements analysis phase. Therefore, users and the analyst should review each of these matters again before starting the design because they establish both the direction and the constraints that the system developers must follow.

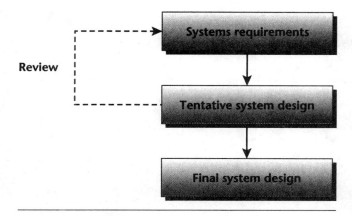

Figure 15.1 Review of systems requirements.

If, for instance, the recommendation approved by management at the end of the requirements phase was for a system that (1) supported order-entry operations, (2) was extremely easy for new employees to learn and use, (3) tied into the company's mainframe, and (4) cost less than $200,000 to develop and implement, these guidelines must be remembered during system design. That means not only reviewing these matters carefully at the outset of the design phase, but continually asking if these goals and restraints are met as the design unfolds. Will this design provide users with the necessary friendly interface? What factors must be anticipated so the spending limit is not exceeded? Systems developers must ponder these matters many times. Figure 15.1 shows the requirements review process.

DEVELOPING A MODEL FOR A NEW SYSTEM

When designing a system, the analyst and systems development team determine how both manual and software/hardware components will be realized at logical and physical levels in each of the following areas:

- Output
- Input
- Processing
- Storage
- Procedures
- Personnel

Figure 15.2 shows these considerations.

Logical and Physical Dimensions

The system model must address both the logical and physical dimensions of the proposed system. For example, suppose the systems developers are considering

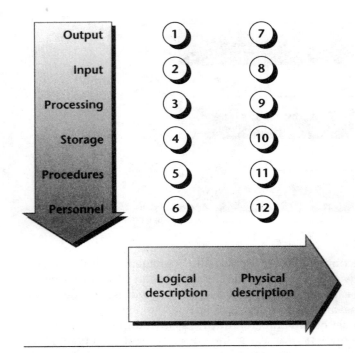

Figure 15.2 Considerations in MIS design. Many new systems are created by looking at design matters in the order suggested by the arrows and numbers, especially when the traditional approach is used. For instance, output is designed first; logical system design is undertaken before physical design.

the type of information inputs a mortgage loan manager needs during his or her dealings with a loan client. An input specification such as "Credit report" conveys a **logical description** of information that must be obtained. If bank policy will accept "written, oral, and electronically generated credit reports," then we have a **physical description** of the input. As Figure 15.2 indicates, the logical input description of the design element is usually specified first; then, the physical description.

The level of detail required in the design specification often depends on the application. In the credit report example, the design specification might include the identity of the loan applicant, the applicant's address and phone number, credit references, assets and liabilities, salary, and so forth. The systems developers must be careful not to overspecify or underspecify the design. Underspecification may result in the design's ultimate failure. The ideas in the design may be sketchy, giving people the wrong impression of the system—or they may be underdeveloped and just not workable. Overspecification (excessive detail), on the other hand, may result in a costly waste of time. Also, overspecification can cause intimidation or information overload when users review the project team's design work.

The system components shown on the left side of Figure 15.2 are also usually considered in the order given. For example, outputs are considered first because nothing makes much sense until the developers know what the system is supposed to produce. The nature and quality of the outputs desired by users determine what inputs are needed, what types of hardware and software are required, and so on. Similarly, storage needs cannot be fully determined until output, input, and processing requirements are established. If, for instance, users want an image-processing system, then appropriate scanning, optical storage, and laser printing equipment are needed. Also, personnel needs are difficult to estimate until every other requirement is specified and the developers can see how much work will be involved.

The numbers 1–12 in the middle part of Figure 15.2 indicate the overall order in which design elements should usually be considered. Note that all of the logical system design elements are considered first; then, the physical design elements.

Finally, you may wonder how software and hardware fit into all of this. Specific types of software and hardware are generally physical design matters that cut across all areas in Figure 15.2. An application software package, for example, will often include output, input, processing, or storage features. For instance, a database management system allows users to design reports (output), prepare templates (input), and create different views of the database (processing). It may also contain utilities that allow computer professionals to place data efficiently onto disks (storage). Hardware, however, is normally acquired for a single function; for instance, a printer for output, a keyboard for input, or a computer for processing. Some devices, such as display terminals, perform two or more functions (such as display terminals that are used for both output and input). Procedures and personnel are required to operate the software and hardware.

DESIGNING SYSTEM OUTPUTS

Six important factors should be considered when designing user outputs: content, form, volume, timeliness, media, and format. Figure 15.3 shows these output matters, plus concerns in other design areas that we will cover in subsequent sections of this chapter.

Content

Content refers to the actual pieces of data included among the outputs provided to users. For example, the content of a monthly VISA statement consists of such data as total charges due, total charges for this month, total unpaid charges accumulated in previous months, special charges or adjustments (such as finance charges or credits), and an itemized list of purchases for the month. The content of a weekly report to a sales manager might consist of salesperson names, sales calls made by each salesperson during the week, and the amount of each product sold by each salesperson to each major client category.

System designers generally put too much content into managerial reports instead of too little. Too much content can cause managers to waste time by making them isolate the information that they need; it also diminishes the impact of truly important information.

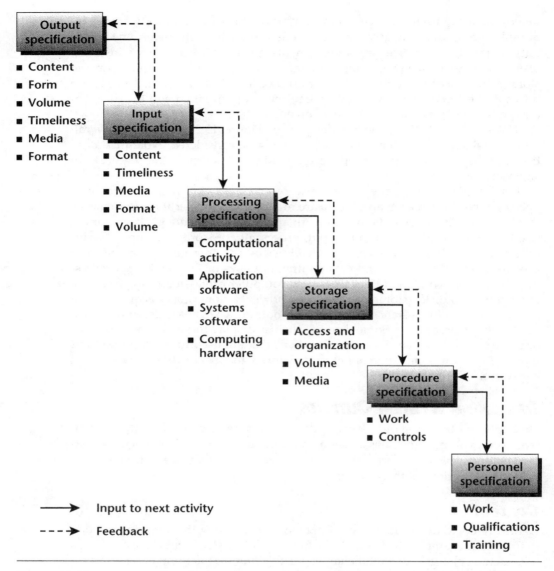

Output specification

- Content
- Form
- Volume
- Timeliness
- Media
- Format

Input specification

- Content
- Timeliness
- Media
- Format
- Volume

Processing specification

- Computational activity
- Application software
- Systems software
- Computing hardware

Storage specification

- Access and organization
- Volume
- Media

Procedure specification

- Work
- Controls

Personnel specification

- Work
- Qualifications
- Training

→ Input to next activity

- - -→ Feedback

Figure 15.3 Steps in the system design process. Also depicts the major factors considered during each step.

Form

Form refers to the way that content is presented to users. Content can be presented in various forms: quantitative, non-quantitative, text, graphics, audio, and video. For example, information on distribution channels may be more understandable to managers if it is presented in the form of a map, with dots representing individual outlets or stores. Managers prefer many types of both summary and detailed information in relative rather than absolute form, or per-

Freshmen	2000
Sophomores	1500
Juniors	1000
Seniors	500
	5000

(a) Absolute form (text, quantitative).

Freshmen	40%
Sophomores	30%
Juniors	20%
Seniors	10%
	100%

(b) Relative form (text, quantitative).

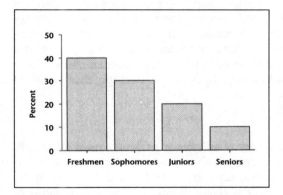

(c) Bar chart form (graphics, quantitative).

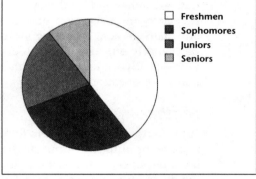

(d) Pie chart form (graphics, non-quantitative).

Figure 15.4 Identical information content presented in four different forms. These show the distribution of students at a moderate-sized college.

haps in chart form—such as a pie chart, line chart, or bar chart (see Figure 15.4). When data are in an absolute form, actual values are provided; for example, in Figure 15.4(a), the total number of students in each class is provided. However, converting absolute values to relative values—such as the percentages shown in Figure 15.4(b)—often helps managers comprehend the data and make better decisions. As noted in Chapter 3, color, graphics, and other formats can highlight and focus manager attention on particular parts of the content.

Output Volume

The term **volume** is commonly used in technology to measure the amount of activity taking place at a given time. The amount of data output required at any one time is known as *output volume*. Heavy volume often suggests a fast, frequently used output device, such as a high-speed printer or a rapid-retrieval display unit. Unusually heavy output volumes normally cause concern about paper costs—which are rising rapidly in many corporations—and environmental impacts.

Timeliness

Timeliness refers to when users need outputs. Some outputs are required on a regular, periodic basis—perhaps daily, weekly, monthly, at the end of a quarter, or annually. Other types of outputs are needed upon demand. A sales manager, for example, might be satisfied with a weekly sales report. Other users, such as airline agents, require both real-time information and rapid response times as they compete for clients. Hence, systems developers might require that display information be provided to the airline agents within five seconds at least 95 percent of the time.

Communications-oriented and real-time systems are often the solution to the problem of how to collapse information float (the time elapsing from when data are generated until they are received). Such systems are remarkably useful, especially in transaction processing environments. In decision support system and management reporting system environments, user-oriented 4GL tools are particularly effective. These tools provide both users and programmers with a time-sensitive alternative to the mounting application backlog that troubles many organizations.

Media

Input/output medium refers to the physical substance or device used for input, storage, or output. Output media choices are abundant in the marketplace and include paper, video display, microfilm, tape, disk, and voice. Many of these media are available in different forms. Paper, for example, can be purchased in a variety of sizes, with or without sprocket holes, in special formats, in cut-form or continuous-form, and so on.

The two most widely used media are paper and display. According to Janet Mann, some sources claim that paper is the medium for 90–95 percent or more of the information that flows into and around corporations. Paper, of course, usually involves printer or plotter hardware, whereas display suggests a monitor or display terminal.

The increasing use of paper is a concern in MIS, which once predicted widespread paperless offices. As Cathy Dingman and Steven Kriendler, OIS consultants, state, "Advances in printer technology have made it easy for corporations to forget the dream of replacing paper with electronic devices. Thanks to these advances, individual workstation users now have access to cheaper, better, and faster printers. Every improvement in printer technology strikes a blow at efforts to reduce paper use in offices."

Format

The manner in which data are physically arranged is referred to as **format**. This arrangement is called output format when referring to data output on a printed

```
       0          10          20          30          40          50          60          70          80
   1234567890 1234567890 1234567890 1234567890 1234567890 1234567890 1234567890 1234567890 1234567890
 1
 2                                              SOFTWARE DIVISION
 3  DATE: XX/XX/XX                                 SALES REPORT                                  PAGE 999
 4                                                JANUARY, 1993
 5
 6  PRODUCT                                                    SALES          UNIT              SALES
 7   CODE                 PRODUCT DESCRIPTION                 IN UNITS        PRICE           IN DOLLARS
 8
 9  XXXX        XXXXXXXXXXXXXXXXXXXXXXXX                       9,999          $99.99           $999,999
10  XXXX        XXXXXXXXXXXXXXXXXXXXXXXX                       9,999          $99.99           $999,999
11  XXXX        XXXXXXXXXXXXXXXXXXXXXXXX                       9,999          $99.99           $999,999
```

Figure 15.5 Partial printer spacing chart. This traditional formatting tool enables systems developers to describe the format of printed reports needed by managers or users.

report or on a display screen. Traditionally, when formatting a printed report for managers or users, a design tool called a *printer spacing chart* is used (see Figure 15.5). On the chart, titles, headings, columns of data, and other types of report elements are set up in the manner desired by users and managers. As the figure shows, a cell corresponds to every printable space on the page. Titles, dollar signs, commas, and so on are filled in as they will appear on the printed page; Xs are substituted for character fields and 9s for numeric fields.

Many prototyping fourth-generation languages available with application generators enable the printer spacing chart task to be performed automatically at a display workstation. A **prototyping 4GL** develops report prototypes quickly. For instance, in dBASE IV, as the operator fills in report-formatting choices on a series of pull-down menus, a mock-up of the report appears on the bottom half of the screen (Figure 15.6). Besides the time saved in finalizing formats, a major advantage to using an automated application generator is that once the mock-up is complete, the programming code can be generated automatically.

If display output is required by users, it may be formatted in a similar way. Many display devices can output in a variety of text modes—for instance, 25 lines of 80 regular-sized characters—and the mode will be an important factor for the analyst when designing display formats. Systems developers should consult users when determining which of several alternative screen formats is preferable. Display formats, like report formats, can be generated with the screen-painting software available with prototyping software and CASE tools (see Figure 15.7). Such software enables the developer to create mock-ups for the user—showing the format of output screens (such as information-retrieval screens and on-screen reports) and also input screens (such as on-screen menus and data-entry templates). In addition, with such software, developers and users can often choose which areas of the screen to color and highlight, plus when to invoke such features as blinking.

DESIGNING SYSTEM INPUTS

After the outputs are designed, user inputs should be designed next. Among the input issues to consider are content, timeliness, media, format, and volume. Many of the issues and concerns involved are similar to those of output.

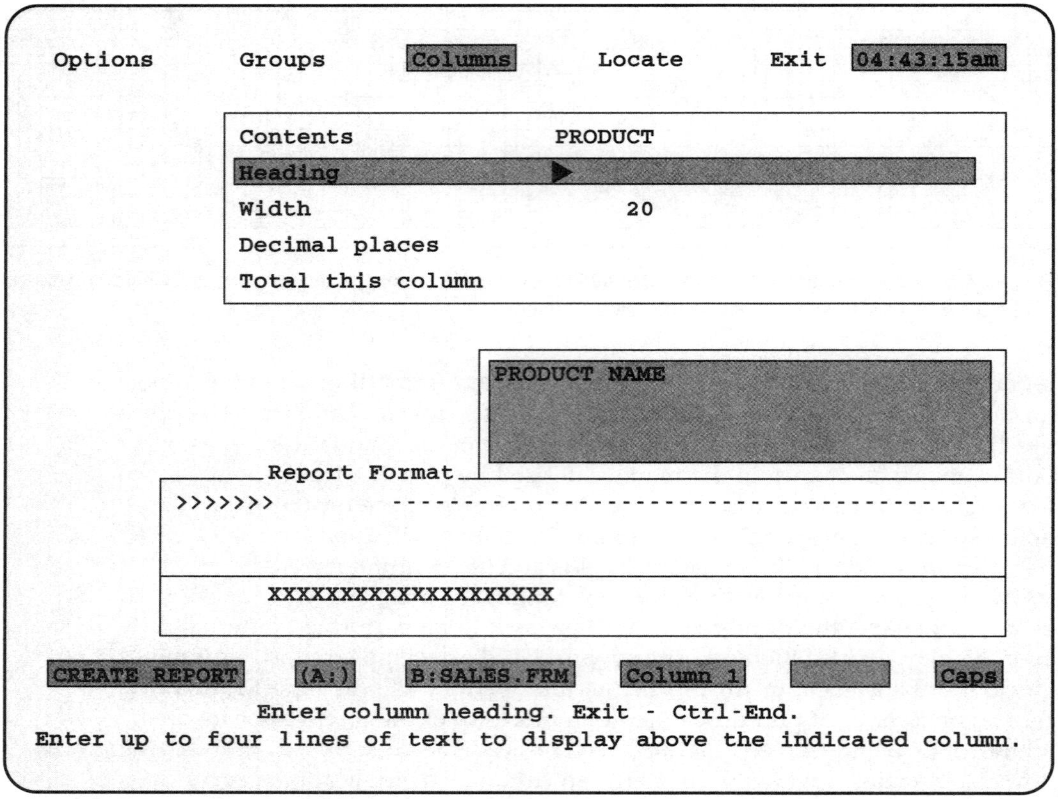

```
   Options          Groups        Columns          Locate         Exit    04:43:15am

              ┌─────────────────────────────────────────────────────────────┐
              │   Contents              PRODUCT                               │
              │   Heading                        ▶                           │
              │   Width                         20                           │
              │   Decimal places                                             │
              │   Total this column                                          │
              └─────────────────────────────────────────────────────────────┘

                               ┌─────────────────────────────────────┐
                               │ PRODUCT NAME                         │
                               │                                      │
                               │                                      │
                               └─────────────────────────────────────┘
           ┌───Report Format──────────────────────────────────────────────┐
           │ >>>>>>>             -------------------------------------------│
           │                                                               │
           │                                                               │
           │        XXXXXXXXXXXXXXXXXXXXXX                                  │
           └───────────────────────────────────────────────────────────────┘
    CREATE REPORT      (A:)      B:SALES.FRM      Column 1                Caps
                   Enter column heading. Exit - Ctrl-End.
     Enter up to four lines of text to display above the indicated column.
```

Figure 15.6   Creating a report mock-up with dBASE. The report format shown in the bottom part of the screen is developed by making successive choices from the menu/template in the top part of the screen.

Content

First, the analyst should consider the types of data that need to be gathered to generate user outputs. This can be complicated because new systems often mean new information, and new information often requires new sources of data, which can be expensive. Sometimes, the data needed for a new system are not available within the organization—but a close substitute might be. For example, cost data can sometimes be cleverly manipulated into useful substitute information. In other cases, this bottom-up approach might not be either possible or appropriate.

Timeliness

Exactly when inputs must enter the system is critical because outputs cannot be produced until certain inputs are available. Hence, a plan must be established

```
001      --010---+---+---+---030---+---+---+---050---+---+---+---070---+---
(MMMMMMMM                      ***ORDER PROCESSING***                  (MMMMM
CUSTOMER NUMBER:)99999999
CUSTOMER NAME:   :(XXXXXXXXXXXXXXXXXXXX

------------------------------------------------------------------------------
ART-NO        ART-QT     AV   ART-DESCRIPTION          ART-PRICE   ART-AMOUNT
------------------------------------------------------------------------------
)99999999     )999999    (XX  (XXXXXXXXXXXXXXXXXXX     (99999999   (99999999999
)99999999     )999999    (XX  (XXXXXXXXXXXXXXXXXXX     (99999999   (99999999999
)99999999     )999999    (XX  (XXXXXXXXXXXXXXXXXXX     (99999999   (99999999999
)99999999     )999999    (XX  (XXXXXXXXXXXXXXXXXXX     (99999999   (99999999999
)99999999     )999999    (XX  (XXXXXXXXXXXXXXXXXXX     (99999999   (99999999999
)99999999     )999999    (XX  (XXXXXXXXXXXXXXXXXXX     (99999999   (99999999999
)99999999     )999999    (XX  (XXXXXXXXXXXXXXXXXXX     (99999999   (99999999999
)99999999     )999999    (XX  (XXXXXXXXXXXXXXXXXXX     (99999999   (99999999999
)99999999     )999999    (XX  (XXXXXXXXXXXXXXXXXXX     (99999999   (99999999999
)99999999     )999999    (XX  (XXXXXXXXXXXXXXXXXXX     (99999999   (99999999999
)99999999     )999999    (XX  (XXXXXXXXXXXXXXXXXXX     (99999999   (99999999999
)99999999     )999999    (XX  (XXXXXXXXXXXXXXXXXXX     (99999999   (99999999999
)99999999     )999999    (XX  (XXXXXXXXXXXXXXXXXXX     (99999999   (99999999999
)99999999     )999999    (XX  (XXXXXXXXXXXXXXXXXXX     (99999999   (99999999999
)99999999     )999999    (XX  (XXXXXXXXXXXXXXXXXXX     (99999999   (99999999999
----PF1=CLOSE OFF ORDER;   PF2=CANCEL ORDER;   PF3=LEAVE ORDER SYSTEM----
```

Figure 15.7 Using a prototyping 4GL (Software AG's Natural) for screen design. Like many products, Natural can create both input and output screens for users.

regarding when different types of inputs will enter the system. For instance, banks must have customer withdrawals input to their systems immediately, but the timing for recording deposits is not as critical.

Timing logistics are usually most complex in transaction processing and information reporting systems. In many of these systems, the people needing output are not the same people who input most of the data. However, in a DSS, output and input operations are often performed by the same person, sometimes only seconds apart.

A trend in system input is to have users working at terminals collect data at the point of origin, rather than to rely on centralized data-entry departments. This movement, which some people claim provides more accurate data entry, is also influenced by management's need to cut costs and to have data available immediately for analysis. Mary Esparza, a staff analyst at one company that moved in this direction, states, "We no longer have a data-entry department . . . You reduce errors by having users control data entry. The farther down the line you get, the closer you get to people who know what the information means." This does not imply, however, that data-entry departments will disappear soon, or even within our lifetimes. A lot of future work will still require batched data entry.

Media

Another important input consideration includes the choice of input media and, subsequently, the devices on which to enter the data. Such user input alternatives include display workstations, magnetic tapes, magnetic disks, keyboards, optical character recognition (OCR), pen-based computers, and voice, to name a few.

Format

After the data content and the media requirements are determined, input formats are considered. When specifying record formats, for instance, the type and length of each data field, as well as any other special characteristics, must be defined. Figure 15.8 shows how this process can be performed with an application generator. First, in Figure 15.8(a), the name of each input field and its properties are described. For instance, CUSTOMER is defined as a three-byte character-data field in a file of customer records. After the fields of the record are fully described, the application generator automatically prepares a file template so that individual records can be created—Figure 15.8(b). In Figure 15.8(c), the first record is created by the user. When the template is filled in, the record is saved and a new template appears on-screen for the next record.

In this example, a user can easily create the input format. However, designing input formats in mainframe and minicomputer database environments often requires the assistance of a professional programmer or data administrator.

Input Volume

Input volume relates to the amount of data that must be entered in the computer system at any one time. In some decision support systems and many real-time transaction processing systems, input volume is light. In batch-oriented transaction processing systems, input volume can be heavy, involving thousands of records that are handled by a centralized data-entry department.

DETERMINING PROCESSING REQUIREMENTS

After user output and input requirements are established, the nature of the processing tasks must be assessed. This determination helps the project team decide which types of application software products are needed and, consequently, of the degree of processing the system needs to handle. This leads the systems developers to decisions regarding the systems software and computer hardware that will most effectively get outputs to users.

Application Software: Make or Buy?

The analysis of output and input needs usually suggests numerous processing requirements for application software. These requirements normally address such issues as the basic functions and capabilities that the software must

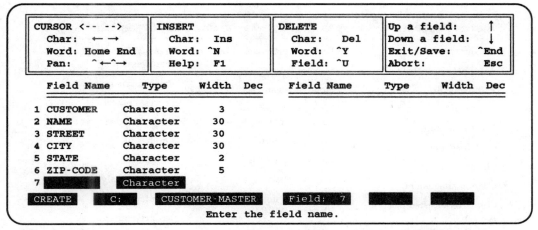

(a) Defining fields widths for records in a file. From this seven-field data definition, the applications generator produces the template in (b).

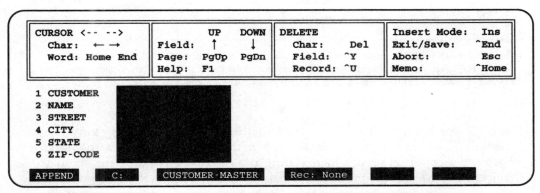

(b) A blank template. The user creates records by typing data into the shaded areas.

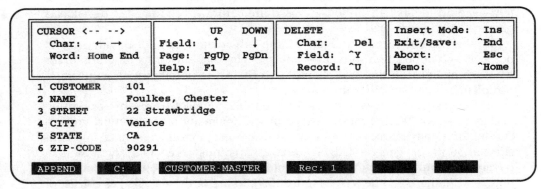

(c) A filled-in template for the first record. When the last data field (ZIP-CODE) is supplied data, the record is automatically saved and a new template appears on-screen.

Figure 15.8 Creating input formats with dBASE.

Types of Application Packages That Can Be Purchased by Organizations

- Accounts payable
- Accounts receivable
- Arithmetic drill
- Automobile rentals
- Benefits accounting
- Cash flow analysis
- Check processing
- Client management
- Computer-assisted design (CAD)
- Desktop publishing
- Econometric modeling
- EEO reporting and compliance

- Financial planning
- General ledger
- Hotel reservations
- Human resources/ personnel management
- Inventory control
- Life insurance
- Mailing labels
- Manufacturing resources planning (MRP II)
- Modeling
- Mortgage account calculation
- Payroll

- Personal finances management
- Presentation graphics
- Process control
- Property management
- Purchasing
- Simulation
- Statistical analysis
- Tax planning
- Tax preparation
- Videotape rental and tracking
- Word processing

Figure 15.9 Examples of commercial software packages. The increasing variety and quality of commercially available software packages have led numerous organizations to buy applications needed by users, rather than having programmers develop new programs in-house.

possess. For instance, it may be found that the application under study is a medium-sized information-retrieval system that requires about a thousand complex user retrievals per hour during peak periods. These retrievals may concern inquiries about products, prices, and stock availabilities. Given these and other considerations, the systems developers must determine whether the application software—or perhaps even the complete hardware/software system—should be created in-house or acquired from a vendor. This decision is often called the *make-or-buy decision*.

In this section, we will look at the advantages and disadvantages of prepackaged application software—and see why this is a compelling option for many companies. In the next chapter, we cover the possibility of acquiring a complete turnkey system from a vendor.

In the past several years, prepackaged application software—or application packages—have become increasingly popular for many business functions, including human resources accounting (for example, payroll, personnel, and benefits accounting), general ledger (such as accounts receivable and accounts payable), manufacturing (MRP II, inventory control, and so on), financial planning, and numerous others (see Figure 15.9). Many of these packages consist of several programs and a complete set of documentation tools; often, vendors even provide training about how to use the software to its full potential.

ADVANTAGES AND DISADVANTAGES TO USING APPLICATION PACKAGES

Advantages

- Packaged software may be appropriate when the application must be implemented rapidly
- In-house development risks are avoided
- Better quality software and documentation are usually provided
- Overall cost is generally lower
- The vendor is constantly enhancing the package
- The cost and quality of the software are known in advance
- Training costs may be lower if users are already familiar with the product
- A widely used package may help when recruiting and retaining computer professionals
- A user group may be available to share experiences; the vendor may even publish a regular newsletter or magazine about the product
- An organization heavily invested in application packages often needs fewer analysts and programmers

Disadvantages

- No appropriate package may be available for the application under development
- The package may not interface well with existing applications
- The package may match user needs closely, but not exactly
- It may be difficult to customize the package to match user needs
- The package may require hardware or systems software changes
- The user has little or no direct control over the evolution of the software

Figure 15.10 Advantages and disadvantages of acquiring application packages to satisfy user requirements. Advantages generally outweigh disadvantages; most industry experts expect interest in application packages to grow.

Advantages of Application Packages

Figure 15.10 summarizes the advantages and disadvantages of application packages. Perhaps the four most compelling advantages are rapid implementation, relatively low levels of risk, quality, and cost.

- **Rapid implementation** Application packages are practically ready to implement after they are purchased. In contrast, software developed in-house, from the beginning, may take months or years until it is ready to implement—especially in companies troubled by substantial application backlogs.

- **Low levels of risk** Because the application package is finished, the organization knows what it is getting for the price that it pays. With in-house developed software, the long and uncertain development time—during which almost anything can go wrong—makes both the quality of the final product and its final cost very risky.

- **Quality** The firms selling application packages are typically specialists in their products' niche areas. Generally, they have a lot of experience in their specialized application fields. In contrast, in-house programmers often have to work over a wide range of application areas.

- **Cost** Firms can leverage the cost of developing a product by selling the product to several other firms, thereby realizing a lower cost per application. Thus, an application package generally costs less than an in-house-developed package. In addition, many hidden costs are faced by organizations that want to develop applications in-house. For instance, it is hard to find and retain programmers who will risk their careers by working on a package that other companies will never use. Also, when running into problems, a firm may be unable to find outside experts who can solve the problem inexpensively. Plus, training costs are usually greater when fewer specialists know the package and fewer end-users are familiar with it.

Disadvantages of Application Packages

Although the advantages of application packages are compelling, these packages will not solve every problem in an organization. For instance, no quality application packages may exist in the area under study. If the vendors serving the area have a small base of expertise and if the application package the company is considering differs in many important respects from existing company applications, in-house development may be the only alternative. Also—and this is critical—some application packages do not use computer resources as efficiently as in-house programs developed in languages such as COBOL. In addition, modifying the package to perform customized tasks is sometimes very difficult. Notice some of the disadvantages of purchasing commercially available software packages in Figure 15.10.

John Dearden is one of a majority of MIS scholars who are optimistic about the prospects for application packages and pessimistic regarding those for traditional, in-house programs. Claims Dearden, "It is difficult to conceive of a more inefficient method for developing software than the one used for the past twenty-five years. Literally hundreds of companies have developed systems and written programs for the same types of applications. The duplication of effort has been enormous, and the quality and cost of the software has varied widely."

What may becoming normal procedure is that MIS organizations on the cutting edge of certain application areas—such as marketing, planning, financial forecasting, logistics, and others—will leverage their developmental investments in software products in these areas by adapting them for general use. Well-known firms in such industry sectors as financial services, insurance, airlines, and manufacturing—companies that already have large, experienced MIS staffs—have already sprouted software-producing subsidiaries. Some examples are Travelers Insurance, Citicorp, Celanese, JC Penney, and the "Big Six" accounting firms. Observes John Dearden about the packaged-software trend, "As this process develops, a user will be able to acquire a software package that includes state-of-the-art developments in the particular type of system [needed] . . . Consequently, purchased or leased software will not only be dramatically less expensive than internally generated software—even more important, it will also be dramatically better."

In-House Application Software Development

If the decision is made that all of the software for the application under consideration is best developed in-house, then the organization must expend a considerable effort on program design—and, subsequently, on program coding, testing, and documentation. In the case of purchased application packages, the customer buys a finished product in which virtually all of these activities are completed. Although organizations buying packaged application software do their own testing, possibly write some of their own documentation, and may do some customization that requires additional designing and coding, most of the work in program development was already performed by the packaged-software vendor.

In-house development of application software is generally a painstaking process. Computers must be told how to do everything, precisely, without error, and in the correct sequence. A major transaction processing subsystem might require a half million lines of programming code—the equivalent of expecting a writer to produce a 10,000-page book without any ambiguous phrases, misspelled words, or inconsistencies.

The Software Development Life Cycle

In many cases, the development of application software follows a life cycle similar to the one used to develop entire systems. The in-house creation of programs commonly involves six stages:

- ■ *Establishing software requirements* Identifying and defining the user and business requirements that the program will satisfy.
- ■ *Program design* Planning how the program will work.
- ■ *Program coding* Writing the program.
- ■ *Program debugging* Detecting and correcting program errors.
- ■ *Program testing* Running tests to ensure that the program works as planned.
- ■ *Program maintenance* Altering the program to address changing user and business needs.

Figure 15.11 shows these stages as following from the general systems requirements. Collectively, the six stages are known as the **program development life cycle** (or **program life cycle**). Managers are usually involved with this process during the first (establishing requirements), second (design), and sixth (maintenance) stages. Systems developers should find out exactly what users

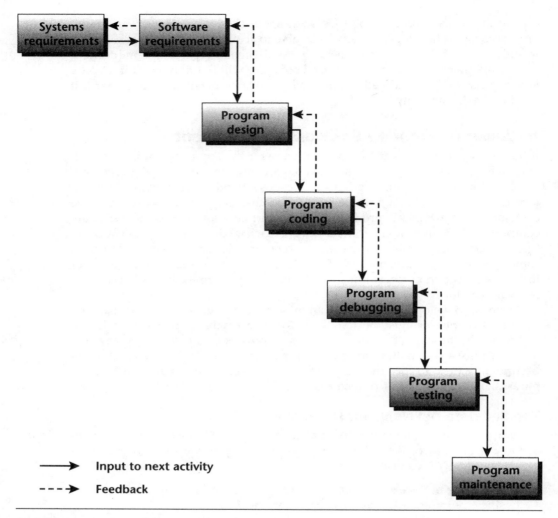

Figure 15.11   The program development life cycle.

want, and users should try to clearly communicate their software needs. As user needs change, these also must be communicated to the MIS department so that appropriate changes in the software can be made. As each change is realized in new or modified software, the next period of the cycle begins. Managers and users can also provide crucial input during the testing and debugging stages. Often, they can help identify appropriate test data (for example, invalid inputs) and tricky exceptions to normal procedures that the system must handle.

Program documentation—the writing of narrative procedures and instructions for people who will use the software—is done throughout the cycle.

Managers and users should carefully review the documentation in order to ensure that the software and system behave as the documentation indicates that they should. If they do not, the documentation should be revised. User documentation should also be reviewed for understandability; that is, the documentation should be stated in terms that users can understand, not in jargon that only sophisticated MIS professionals comprehend.

Not all of the software development life cycle's stages are handled during the design stage of the systems development life cycle. For instance, program coding, debugging, and testing are usually completed after the rest of the system is acquired and installed.

In many organizations, systems analysts (or systems designers) and programmers are responsible for application software development. Systems analysts work most closely with managers and users to determine their needs and to establish application software requirements. From these needs evolve a program design and a set of technical design specifications that include:

- A brief English narrative description of what the program should do.

- A description of the outputs, inputs, and processing to be performed by the program.
- A deadline for finishing the program.
- The identity of the programming language to use and the coding standards to follow.
- A description of the system environment into which the program should fit.
- A description of the testing required to certify the program for use.
- A description of documentation that must be generated for users, maintenance programmers, and operations personnel.

A number of these specifications will reflect the standard operating procedures (SOP) used at the organization, such as using COBOL for transaction processing and following certain coding and testing standards.

The technical design specifications are then given to a programmer, who uses them to design an approach to organizing the problem and developing the logic. To handle these types of design tasks, programmers may use such program design tools as pseudocode, structure charts, fourth-generation languages, and object-oriented development tools; all of these are discussed later. When the program design is complete, it is then translated into program code (actual programming language statements) by the programmer. One or more levels of such code may exist; for example, a prototyping software package or CASE tool may be used to initially develop the application and COBOL may be used to implement the completed program. After the application is running, maintenance programmers ensure that, as both technology and user/business needs change, the programs are modified accordingly.

Program Design

The better the program is designed, the less time it will take later to code, test, and maintain it. This is important because many large MIS departments spend 80 percent or more of their software budgets just maintaining existing programs. An error or design glitch that might cost a few dollars to repair as the program is designed might cost a few thousand dollars to repair at a later stage. The cost to the organization could be enormous if a program with bugs is released for general use. So it is important for managers and users to clearly communicate to systems developers what the program should do, and to review the work performed by the project team to ensure that the program design meets their needs.

Because good program design practices can potentially reduce coding, testing, and maintenance time, they also help organizations reduce substantial application backlogs. As noted in Chapter 7, the visible backlog of user requests for new programs and/or systems may consist of two to four years of work; the invisible backlog of unsubmitted requests (because users are intimidated by the visible backlog) may be twice as large.

Good program design practices do not just happen. In most firms, developing good design practices stretches over several years—and still continues. The need for good design became evident during the early days of computing, when few rules existed regarding how applications were developed. For instance, one programmer might use COBOL; another, FORTRAN or BASIC. The use of multiple languages makes it difficult to integrate applications and to effectively manage the programming environment; hence, many MIS organizations have standardized on a single language (or a small number of languages). Likewise, each programmer has his or her own style of coding. What seems logical to one programmer might appear haphazard to another. Furthermore, many programmers began coding without a plan about what the final program should look like—the equivalent of building a house without a floor plan. All of these factors contributed to the development of programs containing hard-to-follow, tortuous program code. This made programs harder and more costly to maintain, and also contributed to the build-up of application backlogs.

In many organizations, only the original programmer understood fully how certain applications worked. Some applications were patched so many times, with new pieces of code grafted onto old code, that the organization wouldn't let any more people than necessary work on the application, for fear of adding yet another style to the program. Also, training new people to learn a cryptic program is costly and maintenance programming is usually an undesirable task. As organizations began to spend more on program maintenance and application backlogs increased, it became clear that something had to be done.

Over the years, numerous solutions have been proposed to improve the initial development and maintainability of programs. One solution is to separate program design from program coding. This led to the evolution of techniques that apply to a wide variety of program design problems. It also led to the development of numerous tools that can be used directly to improve program coding. Both design and coding concerns are reflected in a group of techniques that are known as structured techniques. **Structured design** pertains to structured program design practices, whereas **structured programming** refers to creating program code that has structure. Two shared goals of structured design and structured programming are to shorten program development time and to decrease the cost of ongoing program maintenance.

Program Design Tools

In this section, we will briefly cover several program design tools that are consistent with structured programming and design techniques. Many other tools are available. The ones we will discuss here are structured program flowcharts, pseudocode, structure charts, fourth-generation languages, and object-oriented programming tools.

Program design tools are graphic models—diagrams, charts, and tables—that outline the organization of program tasks and/or the steps the program will follow. Examples of these tools include:

- ■ *Program flowcharts* Program flowcharts are among the most common program design tools that managers and users will encounter when reviewing the design work of the systems development project team. **Program**

flowcharts combine geometric symbols and mathematical symbols (see Figure 15.12)—along with the familiar numeric and alphanumeric symbols used to build instructions and represent data—to depict the logical steps through which a computer program must proceed when solving a problem. At one time, program flowcharts were considered the premier program design tool. Although still widely used, they are sometimes difficult for programmers to translate directly into structured code.

Figure 15.12 gives you an example of how a flowchart for determining regular and overtime pay might look. Each record contains a worker's name, identification, hours worked for the week, and rate of pay. Workers are paid at their regular rate for the first 40 hours of a week. They recieve time-and-a-half (that is, 150 percent of their regular pay rate) for every hour exceeding 40. As each record in the file is read, the regular and overtime pay are calculated for each employee and totaled. Then, the worker name, identification number, rate, hours worked, regular pay, overtime pay, and total pay are printed. This process continues until the last record is printed.

Program flowcharting symbols are especially useful for demonstrating several principles of structured programming. For instance, structured programs can be created by using only three simple *program-control structures*: sequence, selection, and looping. A *sequence* structure consists of a group of tasks that follow each other in a specific order. For example, in Figure 15.12, regular pay is always calculated before total pay. The *selection (if-then-else)* structure consists of a question and, depending on the answer, one of two logic paths is followed. The diamonds in Figure 15.12 illustrate selection; if the answer to the question is "Yes," one type of action is taken—if "No," another action is taken. A *looping (iteration)* structure involves repeating a series of tasks until a certain condition is either met or not met. In Figure 15.12, the arrow exiting "Read another employee record" and re-entering the program at the connector above "Any more records?" represents looping.

Program flowcharts depict the logical processing steps followed by a program quite well. However, unlike some of the other program design tools discussed in this chapter, they often do not provide a broad view of how the program is organized.

- **Pseudocode** When reviewing the work done by program designers, users may also need to review narrative descriptions of program logic. **Pseudocode**, like flowcharts, represents program logic. But instead of using graphical symbols and flowlines, pseudocode captures program logic in English-like statements. Pseudocode is frequently preferred by programmers over flowcharts because it more closely represents program code. Many users also find pseudocode more understandable than program flowcharts. Figure 15.13 shows the pseudocode form of the overtime pay problem that Figure 15.12 solved by using a flowchart.

Pseudocode is used in a variety of ways. For instance, many fourth-generation languages use pseudocode-like statements. Often, these statements can be translated directly into 3GL program code, such as COBOL.

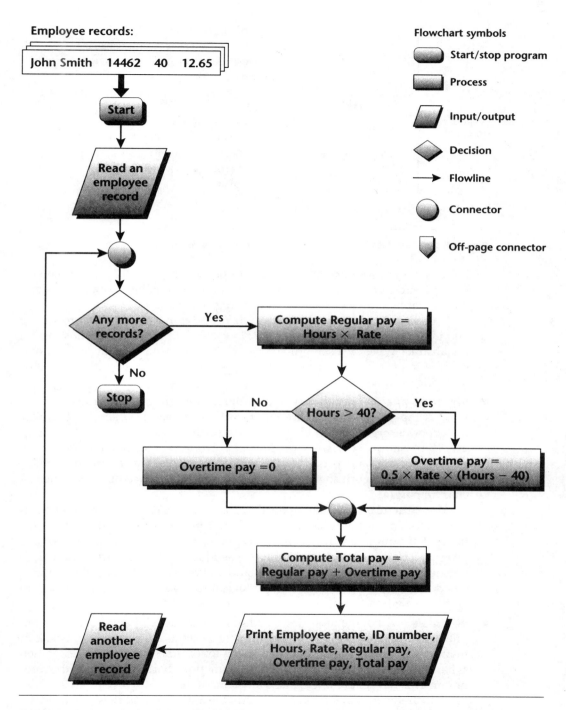

Employee records:

John Smith   14462   40   12.65

Flowchart symbols

- Start/stop program
- Process
- Input/output
- Decision
- Flowline
- Connector
- Off-page connector

Start

Read an employee record

Any more records?

Yes → Compute Regular pay = Hours × Rate

No → Stop

Hours > 40?

No → Overtime pay = 0

Yes → Overtime pay = 0.5 × Rate × (Hours − 40)

Compute Total pay = Regular pay + Overtime pay

Print Employee name, ID number, Hours, Rate, Regular pay, Overtime pay, Total pay

Read another employee record

Figure 15.12 Program flowchart showing employee records being processed. In this flowchart, after each employee record is read, regular and overtime pay are calculated and added together to determine total pay.

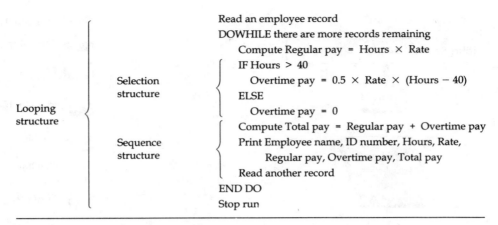

```
                              Read an employee record
                              DOWHILE there are more records remaining
                                  Compute Regular pay = Hours × Rate
              Selection       ⎧  IF Hours > 40
              structure       ⎨     Overtime pay = 0.5 × Rate × (Hours − 40)
                              ⎩  ELSE
Looping                            Overtime pay = 0
structure                    ⎧  Compute Total pay = Regular pay + Overtime pay
              Sequence       ⎨  Print Employee name, ID number, Hours, Rate,
              structure              Regular pay, Overtime pay, Total pay
                             ⎩  Read another record
                              END DO
                              Stop run
```

Figure 15.13   Pseudocode for the same program depicted in Figure 15.12.

Besides using pseudocode to design program code in a 3GL, it can be embedded into a completed 3GL program as non-executable "comment" statements that help to document what the program is doing.

Pseudocode is especially useful when designing transaction processing and information-retrieval programs. Flowcharts, in contrast, are most useful for abstract types of user problems—where the visual appeal of the flowchart is important—and in user problems involving many mathematical or scientific formulas.

■ **Structure charts**   Another type of program design tool that users may review is the program structure chart. **Structure charts**, which look similar to corporate organization charts, are useful for organizing programs. Figure 15.14 shows how the overtime pay problem, represented previously with flowcharts and pseudocode, can be organized into a structure chart. Part (b) of this figure shows the program output produced by the structure chart in part (a).

The structure chart hierarchically organizes each of the program tasks into well-defined **modules**. The higher-level modules represent control portions of the program; the lowest-level modules do the actual tasks of the program. Unlike either flowcharts or pseudocode, the structure chart does not detail the actual program logic and the order in which tasks are executed. Instead, it shows how all the logical functions of the program fit together as a whole.

■ **4GL tools**   All of the tools described so far were developed as manually applied methods for designing programs or systems. The main drawback of manually applied tools is that they take a lot of time to prepare. Also, when a hand-drawn structure chart or program flowchart is finished, the programmer is never sure if it is internally consistent.

Fourth-generation languages can provide a way around these obstacles by automating many of these manual tasks. They can also help ensure that the work done with them is consistent with the other work performed by the

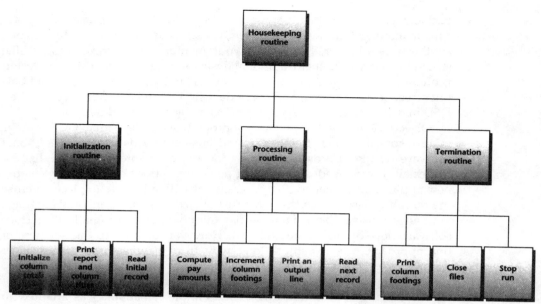

(a) Structure chart of program.

Payroll report 2/25/93						
Employee name	ID number	Rate	Hours	Regular pay	OT pay	Total pay
Zavali	42115	6.80	40	272	0	272
Martin	42119	8.20	40	328	0	328
Kashiva	42121	7.10	30	213	0	213
Larsen	42122	6.90	50	276	103.5	379.5
Rodriguez	42129	7.00	45	280	52.5	332.5
Totals				1369	156	1525

(b) Output.

Figure 15.14 A structure chart and corresponding program output for the overtime pay program depicted in Figure 15.12.

project team. The automation of manual tasks and internal consistency checks are two reasons why productivity gains often result from using 4GL tools.

■ ***Object-oriented programming and design tools*** As noted previously, object-oriented programming (OOP) is hailed as one of the most promising means of enhancing programmer productivity and of reducing the application backlogs common in many organizations. *Object-oriented software design* results in a model that describes objects, classes, and their relationships to one another (see Chapter 7 to refresh your memory about these terms). Like structure charts and other traditional design tools, the object-oriented design is often taken from a data flow diagram (DFD). In fact, every input and output screen, every process, and every data store found a in fully decomposed DFD may be a candidate for an object in an object-oriented design.

Object-oriented software design proponents believe that OOP can be more responsive to changing user and business needs than are traditional software design approaches. Ideally, an object-oriented database that includes all objects needed to support new applications can be built. When a new application is needed, the programmer will only have to piece together the reusable objects from the database. Hence, the use of an OOP language with an extensive object database has the potential to dramatically reduce software development time and cost. However, because of the newness of this approach, we are still a long way from having large databases of reusable objects that can be used to develop new business applications.

OOP language and development tool vendors provide a wide variety of *object-oriented development toolkits*. For example, Smalltalk was adapted to work with Microsoft's Windows and windowing standards; Borland's Turbo C++ also offers an exceptional development environment. Groups like the Object Management Group (OMG) are developing standards for OOP tools, including standards for Microsoft's Windows-based development systems and mouse-driven point-and-click graphical user interfaces. For instance, Microsoft's Application Factory provides an integrated OOP development system that includes (1) tools for creating and manipulating objects and for object-library browsing, (2) a *visual programming* environment for constructing object and application interfaces, and (3) a shell that supports either OOP or traditional structured programming.

Many OOP tools speed development time by allowing designers and programmers to break away from the traditional edit-link-compile cycle discussed in Chapter 7. Also, some vendors blend their OOP tools with expert systems, hypertext, and multimedia features. With mouse-driven, GUI development tools, programmers can do part of their work by incorporating pretested, reusable objects from the object database; they can complete tasks faster because less code is written. Also, with fewer lines of new code to write, there are fewer places for bugs to appear. Thus, OOP programs can potentially be highly reliable and require low maintenance. These are just a few reasons why many organizations are moving toward OOP environments and why non-MIS managers often encourage the MIS department to consider moving in this direction.

Organizations differ in their use of design tools. For instance, in some firms, a tool such as structure charts—which are used mostly for program organization and documentation purposes—might be used primarily by systems analysts or systems designers. The resultant designs (charts) are then handed to the programmer, who uses pseudocode or flowcharts to design the finer details of the program logic. On some projects, the systems analyst may construct only the higher-level structure charts and let the programmer design those showing the relationships between the more detailed lower-level modules. Some people claim that structured programming techniques applied to 3GL programs do not always result in the big productivity gains realized through structured 4GL programs and object-oriented programming (OOP). Still, structured 3GL programs are usually more beneficial to the organization than unstructured 3GL programs. 4GL application development time and programmer productivity improvements often occur because many fourth-generation languages encourage the development of structured program code; the structured-coding capabilities inherent in many fourth-generation languages are one reason why they are so easy to use. The use of re-usable program modules helps increase programmer productivity in OOP is environments. These are reasons why fourth-generation languages and OOP systems are often mentioned as ways in which organizations can decrease their application backlogs.

Other Processing Concerns

In addition to determining if the application software that users need will be purchased from an outside vendor or developed in-house, several other processing requirements are addressed during systems design. These include the systems software, computing hardware, computational environment, user volumes, and throughput that users require to be effective in their jobs.

Systems Software and Computing Hardware

As the design of application software takes shape, the impact of systems software and computing hardware in the design must be addressed. Application software cannot be planned alone—many types of application programs will not work unless certain types of systems software and computing hardware are available. As noted in Chapter 6, commercially available application software is designed under a specific operating system (for example, MS-DOS) and on particular types of hardware platforms (for example, on microcomputers with a 486 processor). If the application software needed by users runs only on powerful personal computers using GUI-oriented operating systems, new hardware and appropriate systems software may need to be acquired also.

Computational Environment

Computational requirements imposed by application software can be classified in various ways. Each computational requirement provides some insight into the appropriate computational environment required by the computer system's users in order to get work done. In most instances, systems developers rely on users to provide them with information about what type of computational environment will be needed. Hence, users and managers will probably be asked to provide information about processing volumes, frequency and types of data access, needed input controls, and so on.

Multimedia: Behind the Scenes

During the 1990s, managers will be seeing and hearing increasingly more about multimedia. Multimedia systems will be especially prevalent in education and training applications, and sales presentations. Software is available that makes it possible to develop multimedia applications on microcomputers and is expected to become as widely used as desktop publishing packages. Because of the surge in multimedia utilization, managers will be hearing more about the underlying technologies that make multimedia systems work. A thumbnail sketch of some of the more important ones includes:

- **Digital video processors** These are chips that mix graphics, text, and video for use in multimedia presentations and video-conferencing.

- **Graphics controllers** These controllers help create or alter an image being displayed on a monitor. These make it possible to spin a displayed object on an axis in three-dimensional space.

- **Image compression chips** These chips delete all but the most essential data from a picture so that the image takes up less space in computer memory; they also decompress the image for display.

- **Video random access memory chips (VRAM)** These store and retrieve segments of complete images. These are used in workstations, video games, and high definition television (HDTV).

"SOFTWARE IS AVAILABLE THAT MAKES IT POSSIBLE TO DEVELOP MULTIMEDIA APPLICATIONS ON MICROCOMPUTERS . . ."

Keeping up with these technologies will be challenging. Experts predict that the current generation of video chips will be replaced in five years.

Adapted from Gross (1992).

One of the most important ways to classify computational requirements is with respect to the processing tasks involved. For example, do users need only retrieval capability, or must users both retrieve and update data? Updating requires such extra processing burdens as input verification and tight security. Or do users need to do any types of modeling capabilities and, if so, which ones? Because some modeling tools, such as Monte Carlo simulation, can be computationally burdensome, more powerful computers may be needed.

Another important way to classify computational requirements is whether the tasks involved are input/output-oriented or computation-oriented. Transaction processing tasks tend to be input/output-oriented. That is, most of the time spent by the computer system is for inputting and outputting records—comparatively little time is spent on computation. Traditionally, such tasks were handled most efficiently on mainframes or midrange systems; however, a LAN environment is an increasingly attractive option for such processing activities.

Tasks such as scientific research, on the other hand, are computation-oriented, generally involving lots of computation and relatively little input and output. If processing needs are scientific, a system unit that is especially geared to this type of computing must be acquired. For example, for large amounts of computing, a supercomputer would normally be sought; for modest amounts of computing, a scientifically oriented mainframe (such as those produced by Control Data Corporation), a minicomputer, or a RISC-based microcomputer might be sufficient.

A third way to classify computation is regarding the general type of operating environment required. Do users need on-line capability? Real-time capability? Multitasking? Are users concurrently (simultaneously) attempting to access the same data? Is a telecommunication environment necessary? On-line, real-time, and concurrent-access environments need special operating systems and hardware devices. If communications are involved, the type of network architecture to adopt must also be decided. This may put further constraints on hardware and systems software choices.

User Volume

User volume relates to the number of users who are likely to be on the system at any one time. A large number of concurrent users suggests LAN-based, midrange, or mainframe computer hardware. If the users are at different locations, telecommunication options will have to be evaluated.

Throughput

Throughput relates to how much work the computer system can do in a given amount of time. Based on input and output volumes—as well as timing constraints—throughput requirements can be determined. Among the data used to determine throughput requirements are the number of certain types of documents that must be processed in a given time period and how many hours a day the system should be available to handle anticipated user workloads.

DETERMINING STORAGE REQUIREMENTS

In the specification of storage requirements, accessing and organizing data are considered. In addition, needed storage capacity and physical storage media options are identified.

Access and Organization

In Chapter 7, we covered file and database processing, noting that we generally must first determine in what ways users will need to access stored data—sequentially, directly, or both. User access requirements then help determine appropriate data and file organization methods. Some applications, such as batch-oriented billing, may require only sequential access. Others, such as real-time information retrieval (for example, airline reservation systems), demand extremely fast forms of direct access.

Most business data are organized logically into records. When physically organizing data, we also typically combine related data into records and files or, alternatively, into structures specified by database models. Concerning the physical placement of data, in both file-oriented and database processing methods, data can be organized sequentially, directly, or as indexed-sequential structures. Also, indexes and secondary keys can usually be established to provide users with rapid access and alternative retrieval paths to these data.

Storage Volume

Storage volume relates to the number of data aggregates—records, segments, sets, or whatever—that must be accessible to users at any one time. Generally, after systems developers determine the total bytes required for the number of records expected to be stored, that byte requirement is doubled or tripled to arrive at total secondary storage requirements. This is done because of such considerations as disk overhead (disk directories, indexes, and so on), uncontrollable wasted space, and anticipated file/database growth.

Media

Finally, physical media choices are made; for example, choices among secondary storage media alternatives and also among particular types of storage devices. The most appropriate medium—diskette, hard disk, tape, optical disk, or perhaps some combination of these—depends on the type of access and file organization specified earlier. For example, if a large image database is needed, optical disks will probably be the only feasible media. The choice of medium, in turn, narrows the range of appropriate secondary storage hardware. For example, if optical disks are the medium of choice, the analyst must select an appropriate optical disk unit or jukebox.

DEVELOPING PROCEDURES FOR USING THE SYSTEM

The design of a system is incomplete until procedures for using the system are finished. A procedure is a set of rules. Procedures fall into two major categories: work and control.

Work Procedures

This text has already covered several procedures that document how a firm's work should be performed. These are called *work procedures*. A work procedure for personnel in the purchasing department might state, "A copy of every purchase order created during a business day will be submitted to the purchasing director by 5:00 P.M. on that day."

We looked at several such procedures in Chapter 9. Many work procedures are outlined in writing so that the responsibilities of each person in the system are clear. Graphical MIS tools such as data flow diagrams and system flowcharts are widely used for documenting work procedures.

Control Procedures

Control procedures specify how something should be controlled. In computer systems, numerous controls must be implemented to ensure the security, accuracy, and privacy of data and other CBIS resources. Managers, users, and accountants generally know best what types of controls are needed.

■ **Security controls** Security controls try to reduce the risks associated with such events as unauthorized use of CBIS resources (by hackers, for example) and intentional or unintentional destruction of computer resources. Types of security controls are policies regarding the handling of data, locks and fire protection mechanisms, secret passwords that provide access to sensitive resources, audit trails that allow the reconstruction of original transactions, frequent audits of CBIS resources, and so on. We will more fully address data security in Chapter 19.

■ **Accuracy controls** Organizations can succeed or fail because of the accuracy of their data. If, for example, an invoicing system bills customers for incorrect amounts or a manager makes a poor decision based on inaccurate data, the organization has a problem. Today, with so many people capable of accessing their company's mainframe systems with microcomputers, employers have new concerns about data accuracy.

Many types of accuracy controls can ensure the correctness of data. For instance, when payroll checks are issued, controls are used to ensure that the correct number of checks are cut and that the amounts for which the checks are issued are within reason. Also, as clerks type transactions into the computers, control software checks to see that the information is both within reason and complete. Figure 15.15 lists numerous controls used to check on the accuracy of data.

The types of controls employed depend largely on whether the system is batch or real-time. For example, in batch processing, a validation procedure known as *batch totaling* is used to sum up all values in a particular field of the batch and to compare that total against one that was independently computed. A *sequence check* is often used to ensure that all records are in a certain sequence with respect to a specified key field. In real-time processing, however, special controls must be built into each application program to verify the integrity and completeness of each piece of incoming data. For example, if a customer makes a $1,000 purchase on a credit card, the control system should immediately check the validity of the account number and the customer's credit limit before the transaction enters the system.

Another set of control procedures used to ensure accuracy in computer systems is audit-related. Audits are used to certify both the correctness of account balances and adherence to a set of procedures or standards. For instance, the same types of audit trails used to ensure that no one is stealing from the company can be used to check the correctness of a customer

Input

Check digits   For some fields, it may be possible to use check digits, a particularly useful technique for on-line data input. A check digit is an extra digit attached to the field; it equals the results of a calculation performed on the other digits.

Control totals   On input, there should be control totals where appropriate, both for batch and on-line data entry; there should also be totals for rejected transactions so that runs can be balanced.

Duplicate data entry   Programs should check to be sure that the same data are not entered twice. For example, there should not be two identical records in a master file.

Edit checks   Checks should be done on input; for example, checks for incorrect characters in fields, illegal codes, and incomplete data (items missing).

Log of source documents   When source documents are transmitted from one area to another, they should be logged.

Reasonableness tests   These checks determine if input values are within reasonable ranges.

Transaction logs   In an on-line system, all input transactions should be logged for control and backup purposes.

Processing

Audit trail   It should be possible to reconstruct a transaction from input through processing and final output.

Encryption   It may be necessary to encrypt (scramble) critical information, especially where there is any form of data transmission.

Labels   Internal and external labels should be used on files; internal labels should be checked by programs to be sure that the right file for the right date is being accessed.

Limited access   On-line systems should recognize terminals and operators; certain terminals and operators may be limited to performing certain functions on the system.

Passwords   On-line systems should use some type of password to be certain that the operator is authorized to use the system.

Run totals   Where there is a sequence of runs, run-to-run totals should be produced and checked.

Sequence checks   Where a sequence is required for processing, programs should perform sequence checks to be certain that the sequence has been maintained in prior processing steps.

Output

Extra output   In an on-line system, extra identification data may be provided to verify that an inquiry response is correct.

Totals   Batch systems often provide control totals to check output fields.

General

Backup   Control is enhanced with adequate backup, including off-site file storage, arrangements for alternative processing sites, and so on.

Documentation   Adequate documentation can be one of the best controls associated with a system.

Figure 15.15   Examples of control techniques used in computer-based information systems (CBIS).

balance. Audit trails are used to trace computer system outputs back to original source documents.

Also, because many businesses need investors to survive, and because investors want assurance that the company's records are correct before parting with their money, an independent audit by a certified public accounting firm is often required. Thus, control procedures are necessary to show that the company has correctly accounted for its computerized transactions. In large companies, a trained professional known as an **EDP** (for Electronic Data Processing) **auditor** sees that audit standards are properly established and maintained for CBIS resources.

■ *Privacy controls*   Regarding technology, privacy controls ensure the protection of people's rights regarding how information about them is suppressed or used. Most of the privacy legislation in the United States applies to federal government agencies and the organizations to which they supply information. In Europe, privacy legislation is widespread—applying to agencies, citizens, and aliens—in both the public and private sectors.

DETERMINING PERSONNEL REQUIREMENTS

Personnel constitute one of the costliest aspects of most systems' operations. Specifications for personnel involve work descriptions for jobs, personnel qualifications, security, and training. Here, we will discuss each of these areas except security; Chapter 19 will cover that.

Work Description

Perhaps the most critical personnel-related specification involves the work that people perform. Here, a total business operation should be divided into well-defined tasks; then, those tasks should be combined into jobs. Each job must be both feasible from the firm's viewpoint and reasonable from the standpoint of the individual. Such matters as mental limitations, physical capabilities, and intergroup behavior—discussed previously in Chapter 2—are especially important.

Qualifications

After jobs are defined, qualifications must be specified for the individuals who will fill those jobs. Are keyboarding skills necessary? Should a certain minimum level of education be mandatory? Is familiarity with particular types of modeling packages required? When defining user tasks, managers must also remember that the more qualified the personnel, the scarcer and more expensive they are in the labor marketplace. Thus, designing the system in a way that requires lower skill levels may result in lower operational costs. For instance, many user interfaces are designed today so that operators do not need to know how to type—the ability to use a mouse or touch screen may be enough. By designing such user interfaces into a system, people without keyboarding skills can also use it—people who are often less expensive and easier to find.

Training

Training personnel is a major, ongoing system cost that should be considered when the system is being designed. As new software and hardware become available, users must be retrained—resulting in both the training expense and the costs for the loss of productive time while the user is trained. We will cover training in more detail in the next chapter when we look at system implementation.

REPORTING TO MANAGEMENT

After the system design is finished, users have indicated their satisfaction with the design, and the system's benefits and costs are revised to reflect any major changes, the project team reports the results of these activities to management. Typically, the report starts with a summary of the development project and a synopsis of the major recommendations. The report should include:

- A description of the application and user concerns that led to the project.
- A summary of the results of the requirements analysis.
- Design recommendations.
- Any changes in the costs and benefits of the new system.
- A plan for the remaining systems development activities.

Management will either approve of the design and ask that development proceed, request an alternative design, or cancel the project.

The generation of management reports throughout the systems development processes is greatly facilitated by the development of CASE systems. As already noted, providing application developers with appropriate CASE tools can also reduce application development time and enhance programmer productivity. Figure 15.16 depicts a full-featured CASE system, consisting of a set of CASE products that are useful throughout most of the traditional development approach. Such a system would incorporate a variety of program design, modeling, application development, and screen painting tools. It would also include software maintenance and project management tools, which are discussed more fully in the next chapter. Figure 15.17 shows in more detail some of the contents of the central repository of a full-featured CASE system.

Ensuring that systems developers have a well-stocked CASE repository is an important management concern.

SUMMARY

System design consists, generally, of three activities: reviewing informational and functional requirements, developing a model of the new system, and reporting the results to management. Developing a model of the new system comprises the bulk of system design.

When developing a new system, systems developers determine, at both the logical and physical levels, the components of the system in the areas of output, input, processing, storage, procedures, and personnel. A logical description of

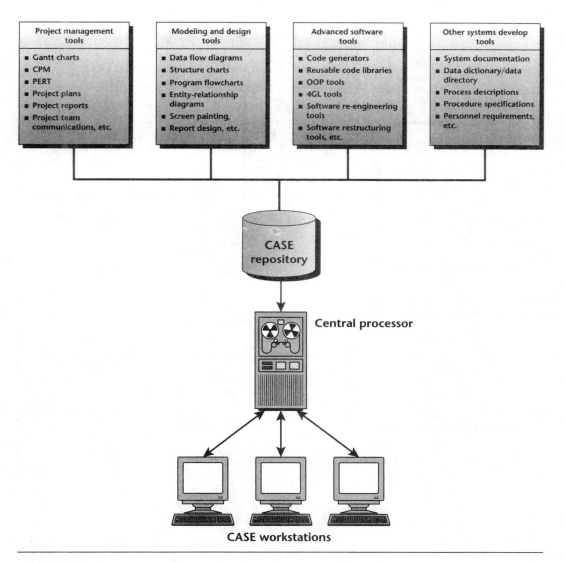

Project management tools	Modeling and design tools	Advanced software tools	Other systems develop tools
■ Gantt charts ■ CPM ■ PERT ■ Project plans ■ Project reports ■ Project team communications, etc.	■ Data flow diagrams ■ Structure charts ■ Program flowcharts ■ Entity-relationship diagrams ■ Screen painting, ■ Report design, etc.	■ Code generators ■ Reusable code libraries ■ OOP tools ■ 4GL tools ■ Software re-engineering tools ■ Software restructuring tools, etc.	■ System documentation ■ Data dictionary/data directory ■ Process descriptions ■ Procedure specifications ■ Personnel requirements, etc.

CASE repository

Central processor

CASE workstations

Figure 15.16 Using a CASE repository to provide application developers with support throughout the systems development process.

information describes how elements of the system relate to each other—without mention, perhaps, of specific hardware devices or software packages. A physical description, in contrast, identifies specific devices or products.

Six concerns in the output specification are content, form, volume, timeliness, media, and format. Content refers to the types of data included among the output. Form refers to the way content is presented to users; for example, in text form or in a graphical form such as a bar chart. Volume, in technology disciplines, is a measure of the activity taking place at a given time. Timeliness refers

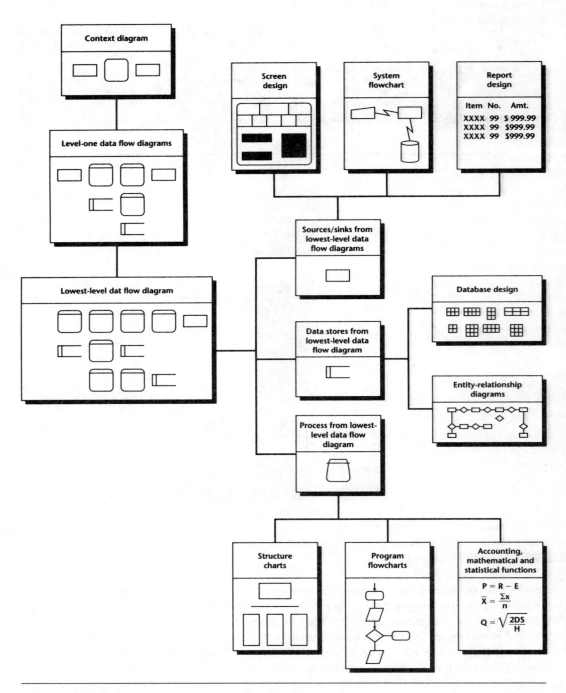

Figure 15.17 Examples of the contents of a CASE repository.

to when outputs are needed. Input/output medium is a physical design dimension referring to the substance or device used for input, storage, or output. Format refers to the manner in which data are physically arranged. Prototyping packages and CASE tools with screen-painting components are especially useful for creating and refining formats at a display workstation.

Input concerns include content, timeliness, media, format, and volume. These are similar to output concerns.

After output and input, the nature of the processing tasks involved must be considered. An important problem in this area is whether to make or buy application software. Application packages are designed for firms that want to buy their application software prepackaged. Such packages are characterized by rapid implementation, relatively low risk, high quality, and reasonable expense—especially in contrast to in-house-developed software. On the other hand, application packages may not suit every organizational need.

When software is created in-house, it follows a cycle similar to that of systems. In this case, however, the process is called the program development life cycle. Numerous solutions were proposed to improve the development and maintainability of programs, including separating design from coding. This led to a group of methods, known as structured techniques, which include structured design (structured program design practices) and structured programming (creation of structured program code). Fourth-generation languages (4GL) are also widely used in in-house program development. Object-oriented programming (OOP) is a popular approach for speeding up the in-house application development process.

Numerous program design tools embody structured programming and design techniques. One tool is the program flowchart, which uses geometric symbols to depict the logical steps through which a computer program must proceed when solving a problem.

Pseudocode also represents program logic, but does so with English-like statements. Pseudocode is preferred over flowcharts for business applications because it more closely represents program code; also, it is more difficult to construct poorly designed programs with pseudocode.

Structure charts are useful for organizing programs. They structure program tasks into well-defined, hierarchically related modules.

Fourth-generation language tools are also used in the program design process. Object-oriented programming tools, like fourth-generation languages, have the potential to improve programmer productivity and to reduce application development times.

The impact of systems software and computing hardware must also be assessed in the design process. Some issues to consider are the types of computations involved, whether or not telecommunication or real-time processing is necessary, and throughput (which relates to how much work a given computer system can do in a given amount of time).

Regarding storage specifications, systems developers must consider how data will be accessed and organized, what storage volumes are involved, and what the physical storage media should be.

Also, as part of design, an analyst must spell out the procedures to follow on the job. Procedures fall into two major categories: work and control. Work procedures describe how a job is to be done. Control procedures include security controls, accuracy controls, and privacy controls. Audit trails are accuracy controls that trace computer system outputs back to original source documents. EDP auditors are trained professionals retained by organizations to ensure that output, input, processing, storage, procedure, and personnel standards in a CBIS are properly established and maintained.

Systems developers also need to identify the personnel requirements for new systems. Personnel specifications include work descriptions, worker qualifications, and training requirements.

After system design activities are complete, they are reviewed by users and reported to management. Full-featured CASE products and CASE repositories can facilitate the development of such reports. If management is satisfied with the work, systems developers will proceed to the next phase of the systems development process.

REVIEW

KEY TERMS

EDP auditor	Prototyping 4GL
Format	Pseudocode
Input/output medium	Structure chart
Logical description	Structured design
Module	Structured programming
Physical description	System design
Program development life cycle (program life cycle)	Throughput
	Volume
Program flowchart	

REVIEW QUESTIONS

1. What types of activities make up system design?
2. Distinguish between the logical and physical design of a system.
3. Define output volume.
4. In what ways are prototyping packages and CASE tools useful in both output and input design?
5. What are the advantages and disadvantages of application packages?
6. What is accomplished during each step of the program development life cycle?
7. What types of technical design specifications could the systems analyst communicate to the programmer?
8. Describe several types of program design tools that managers and users may be asked to review.

9. In what ways is pseudocode different from a structure chart? In what ways are the two similar?

10. What is the difference between structured programming and structured design?

11. Describe the benefits of structured programming and structured design approaches.

12. Identify several types of computational environments that exist in practice and the special burdens that they place on the computer and its systems software.

13. Identify several types of controls that are used to ensure the accuracy of data.

14. Describe the various types of personnel specifications needed for a new system.

15. What are CASE repositories and why are they important?

DISCUSSION QUESTIONS

1. With application packages having so many compelling advantages, is it likely that any software will be developed in-house in the future? Why or why not?

2. What types of firms are most likely to sell application software as a sideline business?

3. In what ways are prototyping approaches useful in the system design process?

4. Many people, fascinated by the potential of fourth-generation languages, have played down the importance of structured programming. Is structured programming still a worthy pursuit for study, or is it just another body of knowledge that was important in its day and is now on the way out?

CASE STUDY

Software Leasing Becomes More Popular

The "make versus buy" decision that managers and MIS professionals must address during system acquisition may soon have a new dimension—at least for software acquisitions. For an increasing number of organizations, the decision is now "make versus buy versus lease."

The software leasing concept has been around since the 1980s and essentially allows a customer to purchase expensive software by borrowing money from a third-party lessor. It is gaining popularity as an alternative financing scheme for funding software purchases.

One of the biggest names in the software leasing business is the Software Leasing Corporation headquartered in Beverly Hills, California. Software Leasing has a client base of more than 100 firms, including well-known firms such as Wells Fargo, The New York Times Co., and Citibank, NA.

LaMode Incorporated, an apparel manufacturer in Los Angeles, has leased software through Software Leasing for over five years. According to Sherwood Sterling, executive vice-president at LaMode, "We were much smaller when we began leasing. It allowed us to use money other than our internal operating funds." According to another Software Leasing customer, leasing "gave me flexibility around corporate red tape. To purchase software, I would have to have it approved, and that process can take up to three months. By using leasing, I can stay within an approved budget, get the software I need quickly, and speed up the whole process."

Howard Smith, president and CEO of Software Leasing, has witnessed his company's revenue grow by at least 300 percent in each of the last several years. Besides having a growing number of businesses that are securing financing through his company, Software Leasing is also representing an increasing number of software vendors. During the early years of its operation, Software Leasing worked with only one software vendor: Atlanta-based Management Science America Corporation. Now, it represents more than 30 software vendors, including BMC Software Inc., Candle Corp., and Sterling Software, Inc.

How does Smith get software vendors interested? He says, "I basically go to the software company and show their sales force how to use this as a tool to close sales."

While the real impact of software leasing will probably not be felt until the mid-1990s, most industry experts agree that it's likely to be a high growth area. The number of leasing agencies is predicted to increase and software vendors will probably start adding their own leasing/financing packages.

Adapted from Ambrosio (1992).

DISCUSSION

1. What advantages does software leasing have over software purchases and in-house development?

2. Why may some companies prefer purchasing or in-house development over software leasing?

3. What types of problems may result if leased software does not perform as expected by the company leasing it? What should the organizations involved in leasing contracts do to avoid such problems?

Chapter

16

System Acquisition, Implementation, and Maintenance

After completing this chapter, you will be able to:

Identify some of the leading computing products vendors in each of several important market segments of the computer industry

Describe the process by which organizations deal with vendors when acquiring technology products and systems

Name and describe the steps that comprise system implementation

Differentiate among CPM, PERT, and Gantt charts

Describe several strategies used to make programmers more productive

Discuss why user training is an important aspect of implementation and describe some of the approaches that are implemented to train users

Identify several approaches that firms can use to convert from one system to another

Describe some of the activities that take place during the postimplementation review

Explain the importance of system maintenance and identify different types of system maintenance

After a system is designed, either partially or fully, the next phase of systems development starts: the acquisition of hardware, software, and services. At this point, computer resources that can best meet the specifications established during system design are selected. Then, after the go-ahead is given by management, the chosen system is acquired and put into working order. Just having the components does not mean that they will work together smoothly or that users will adapt to the new procedures immediately. Developing new programs, converting old facilities, and training personnel to use the new system are all part of the final phase of development: implementation. Finally, after the system is up and running, the success or failure of the systems development process is assessed. Also, the system must be maintained.

In this chapter, we look at each of these development areas. First, we cover vendor evaluation and selection. Next, system implementation is discussed, including such topics as scheduling; program coding, debugging, and testing; training; and system conversion. Finally, we address the postimplementation review and system maintenance.

ACQUIRING SYSTEM COMPONENTS FROM VENDORS

At the end of the design phase, the firm has a reasonably good idea of the types of hardware, software, and services it needs for the system being developed. These physical items are identified after the logical design of the system model is finished.

Organizations discover new hardware and software developments in various ways. Most MIS managers keep up-to-date about current hardware and software through published materials. Most large MIS shops subscribe to at least one directory (such as McGraw-Hill's *Datapro Reports* or *Faulkner Information Services*); smaller organizations can find these directories in libraries with good reference sections. Many large MIS departments subscribe to industry analyst services and assign at least one person to keep current on the computer industry.

Despite having readily available comparative data, vendors are not formally evaluated and selected until after the design is completed and management makes some firm commitments. At this point, the systems development team often approaches vendors with a statement of specific needs. Vendors, in turn, respond with specific systems and prices. After vendor alternatives are known, one or more alternative methods may be used by the firm to select specific resources.

Company	International Ranking
IBM	1
Fujitsu Ltd.	2
NEC	3
Digital Equipment Corp.	4
Hewlett-Packard Co.	5
Hitachi	6
AT&T	7
Unisys	8
Siemens/Nixdorf	9
Apple	10
Olivetti	11
Groupe Bull	12
Toshiba	13
Matsushita	14
Canon	15
EDS	16
Sun	17
ICL	18
Compaq	19
Xerox	20

Figure 16.1 The computer industry's global top 20 firms. (Adapted from Marion)

In this section, we will explore how this process—known as system acquisition—takes place. But first, we will look at the vendor marketplace and observe the types of goods and services currently offered.

The Vendor Marketplace

In the 1960s, a company needing a computer system usually chose one of a handful of vendors to meet all of its hardware and software needs. Today, thousands of technology-related vendors exist, and a single organization might buy from hundreds of companies before meeting its full set of processing needs. The technology industry can be broken down into three primary market segments: hardware, software, and services. Figure 16.1 shows the top 20 firms in the worldwide computer industry, regardless of market segment.

Hardware

The hardware segment of the computer industry consists of firms that make computer units (that is, system units), peripheral devices, and/or

Ranking	Microcomputers	Midrange	Large Scale
1	IBM	IBM	IBM
2	Apple	Digital	Fujitsu
3	NEC	Fujitsu	Hitachi
4	Compaq	NEC	NEC
5	Fujitsu	Toshiba	Amdahl
6	Toshiba	Unisys	Nikon Unisys
7	Olivetti	Siemans/Nixdorf	Siemans/Nixdorf
8	Unisys	Hewlett-Packard	Unisys
9	Intel	Tandem	Groupe Bull
10	Commodore	AT&T	Cray
11	AT&T	Hitachi	ICL
12	Groupe Bull	Mitsubishi	Control Data
13	Hitachi	Olivetti	Comparex
14	AST Resource	Stratus	AT&T
15	Tandy	Groupe Bull	Mitsubishi

Figure 16.2 The top 15 worldwide companies in the microcomputer, midrange, and large-scale computer industries. (Adapted from *Datamation*)

communications devices. Some firms primarily produce mainframes; others, minis; and still others, micros. Some firms have products in all three markets, and many make peripherals as well as computer units. Several of these firms produce software, as well. Figure 16.2 lists the leading worldwide firms in the microcomputer, minicomputer, and mainframe marketplaces.

It is possible to lease computing hardware (enter a contract with a vendor to possess and use a computer system over a specified time period for a specified payment) or to buy it. The larger the computer hardware system, the more likely that equipment will be leased. Both leasing and buying are often done through a third-party firm, rather than through the manufacturer. A market for used hardware also exists, but the demand for used equipment is comparatively small—especially if it is not made by IBM, DEC, or Apple.

Software

Figure 16.3 shows some of the leading firms in the worldwide software marketplace. With some notable exceptions such as Lotus and Microsoft (which produce software for microcomputer systems), most of the firms listed are also dominant in the hardware segment of the market—primarily in mainframe and minicomputer hardware.

Ranking	Company
1	IBM
2	Fujitsu
3	Microsoft
4	NEC
5	Computer Associates
6	Oracle
7	Siemans/Nixdorf
8	Hitachi
9	Lotus Development
10	Digital
11	Sema Group
12	Novell
13	Olivetti
14	ICL
15	Finsiel

Figure 16.3 Some of the leading worldwide firms in the software segment of the computer industry. (Adapted from *Datamation*)

As many firms in the hardware industry specialize in niches, so do software firms. For instance, Microsoft Corporation specializes in microcomputer-based systems and application software; Lotus Development Corporation in microcomputer-based application software; Computer Associates and Oracle in database products; and so on. Many small companies in the software segment feature only a single product.

Today, many large companies that traditionally were not considered software firms—such as JC Penney (retailing), Arthur Andersen Consulting (accounting), Martin Marietta (aircraft systems), Celanese (chemicals), Travelers (insurance), and Citicorp (banking)—have spun off parts of their MIS staffs into special units or subsidiaries to produce and market software. For years, these firms invested so much time and money into their own in-house software systems that they reached the same conclusion: Why not sell this software?

Unlike hardware, software is usually licensed (rather than leased or purchased). Its use may be licensed on a single-payment basis—as is the standard practice for microcomputer software—or on a monthly basis, which is common for mainframe software. Such licensing agreements give the organization the right to use the software. Licensing agreements may cover only a single copy of the software for a single user or multiple copies (up to a specified total) for multiple users. Agreements that cover multiple users are often called *site licenses*. With the increasing prevalence of local area networks, site licenses are becoming more common. Also, as illustrated in the case study on page 685, interest in software leasing has been on the upswing.

Services

Many firms in the computer industry supply services, including providing software and hardware maintenance, creating and maintaining banks of financial data that other companies can access, providing capacity on a communications network, allowing remote access to computing facilities, performing data processing and systems integration (systems development), giving advice, developing programs or applications, educating, and so on. The availability of such services has given many companies the option of outsourcing their information processing activities; that is, contracting with another firm to provide the information processing services that were previously provided in-house.

One type of services firm is the **service bureau**. Service bureaus generally perform some type of data processing for other firms. Many of them will use a standard mainframe application package—for example, GL:Millenium—for their accounting work. They can leverage the investment in the package by using it on a large number of client companies. The services company helps its clients organize their data so that these data are consistent with the software that the service company uses. Service bureaus are popular today for transaction processing work for both small and large firms, despite the availability of easy-to-use and inexpensive microcomputer systems. A large firm, for instance, might need extra mainframe-level capacity or need to have a job done faster than in-house services can provide. Service bureaus are also widely used for state-of-the-art presentation graphics and publishing applications.

Packaged Systems: The Turnkey Vendor

A firm that's considering a prepackaged application might do better than just acquire an application package. It might acquire the entire hardware/software system, ready to use, with a service contract, and from a single vendor. Such products are commonly called **turnkey systems**; they are produced by firms called turnkey or value-added vendors. These organizations, which buy hardware and software components from a variety of manufacturers and use these components to manufacture systems of their own, are sometimes called *original equipment manufacturers (OEM)*. The word "turnkey" reflects the fact that these systems should be easy to use. The user presumably just "turns the key" and the system is ready to go. The term "value-added" means that an OEM adds value to the product beyond what is offered by the original vendor.

If a firm decides to buy a turnkey system, it will often select the system during the acquisition stage of the systems development process; that is, after it decides what is needed.

The Request for Proposal (RFP)

Firms may approach vendors to acquire hardware, software, or services in various ways. One method is to send vendors a document called a **request for**

Hardware Requirements

- 100 IBM PS/2 units, each with four megabytes of RAM, one 3½-inch diskette drive, one 120-megabyte hard disk drive, and an enhanced keyboard

- 90 IBM ProPrinters, with attaching cables

- 3 IBM laser printers with necessary interfacing

- 100 SVGA color monitors

Software Requirements

- MS-DOS, OS/2, and Microsoft Windows operating systems licensing for all 100 systems (latest available versions)

Other Details to be Included in the Bid

- Purchase price for each item if bought in single units or in specified quantity

- Warranty period and terms

- Nature of support offered

- Shipping and installation charges

- Delivery terms (all systems must be delivered by March 1, 1993)

All bids must be postmarked by midnight, January 14, 1993, and sent to Unit-X Supervisor: Eshrom Associates; 33 Calle de Las Vegas; Albuquerque, NM 87155.

Figure 16.4 Example of the information supplied to vendors in a request for quotation (RFQ).

proposal **(RFP)**. This document outlines the firm's system needs and requests that interested vendors submit a formal proposal detailing how they will satisfy such needs. An RFP may range in length from a few pages to hundreds, depending on the size and complexity of the project. The RFP might be handled by the buyer in numerous ways, including the following.

Specific or Flexible Needs

An RFP for a specific system—sometimes called a **request for quotation (RFQ)**—tells vendors exactly what specific types of hardware, software, and services are required. Virtually everything is spelled out for the vendor; it only requires a quotation and a commitment to meet the buyer's terms. An RFQ for the purchase of 100 microcomputers, for instance, would probably include items such as those in Figure 16.4. Requests for quotations might be sent to computer manufacturers, distributors, wholesalers, mail-order suppliers, and/or retail stores.

A flexibly based RFP gives the vendor more freedom. Generally, copies of the system design alternatives and a list of constraints and objectives that must be met are submitted to vendors. The list addresses performance objectives rather than specific types of hardware, software, and services. Figure 16.5

- Diagrams of alternative system designs and guidelines for evaluating them.

- Price and budget constraints.

- General systems requirements, including expected growth, reliability requirements, the implementation timetable, desired levels of flexibility, desired levels of application integration, database and communications requirements, maintenance requirements, service requirements, and security and backup requirements.

- Processing requirements, including input, output, processing, and storage volumes; the application mix and the computational burdens entailed by it; response-time requirements; printing speeds; and output quality.

- A list of issues and considerations that must be addressed before the proposal is considered. A blank copy of the vendor's "standard contract" should be included among the requested items.

- Explicit instructions regarding to whom, where, and by when the proposal should be submitted.

- Criteria that will be used when selecting among vendor proposals.

Figure 16.5 Examples of information supplied to vendors in a flexibly based request for proposal. When responding to a flexibly based RFP, vendors often have considerable freedom in suggesting hardware, software, or service options that meet price, performance, and use requirements.

provides an example of such a list. The vendors then prepare a proposal that satisfies the terms in the list.

In both approaches, vendors are often encouraged to phone or visit the organizations prior to preparing their bids to improve the quality of their proposals. The advantage of the RFQ approach is that vendors can respond much more quickly because the guesswork is taken out of the request. The advantage to the flexible approach is that vendors have more freedom to compete and may uncover an attractive solution that the buyer did not anticipate. For instance, a distributor might suggest to an organization thinking about acquiring 100 IBM PS/2s that it should instead buy 100 Compaq Deskpro 486s or Apple Macintoshes because of speed or software considerations.

Not every new system involves selecting and acquiring new hardware. In fact, many do not. Today, most companies already have computers, and they are most interested in what new software systems can run on them. Also, when hardware upgrades are needed in companies with large multiuser systems, some firms may be most interested in upgrading to a larger model of the installed product line. Other firms may be more interested in downsizing to a smaller model or to a specific local area network hardware platform. Such constraints mean that the flexible RFQ process described prviously cannot be followed—something similar to an RFP may be needed. This flexible RFP process is, however, appropriate when requirements cannot be handled by existing platforms.

Selection Criterion	Weight	Vendor A Score	Vendor B Score
Functionality	10	7	8
Ease of learning use	10	5	10
Speed	7	8	6
Capacities	7	8	5
Cost	4	4	7
Support	5	3	7
Documentation	5	5	7
Total Score		288	355

Figure 16.6 An example of a weighted-criterion approach for evaluating competing software products. In this example, the maximum weight per criterion is 10 (with higher weights reflecting greater importance). Total scores for each vendor are calculated by summing the products found by multiplying the criterion weight and vendor criterion score on each selection criterion.

One Vendor or Several?

The other major consideration when acquiring resources is whether to contact one vendor or several. Contacting one vendor is simpler; the buyer does not need to spend as much effort in preparing a formal RFP and the task of evaluating several, possibly diverse, proposals is avoided. As noted previously, this may be the only feasible approach when upgrading to a larger model of the installed product line is anticipated. However, when comparison bids are possible, it makes vendors more competitive. Also, it makes the buyer more informed about various options. Therefore, a better system is usually obtained if a buyer looks at several vendors instead of just one. Typically, the greater the outlay of time, money, and other resources on the system, the better it is to involve several vendors in the RFP process.

Evaluating Vendor Proposals

After vendors submit their proposals or bids, they are evaluated and a selection is made. Two useful procedures to aid in this process are the vendor rating system and the benchmark test.

Vendor Rating Systems

A widely used tool for evaluating vendors is the **vendor rating system**. A vendor rating system is a system in which vendors are quantitatively scored with respect to how well their systems stack up against a specific set of criteria.

Figure 16.6 illustrates how a vendor rating system might be used in the adoption of a large application software package. The criterion and weighting scheme used to rate vendor products should ideally represent the consensus opinion of managers, users, and MIS professionals—that is, the input of each of these sources should be considered when developing the criteria to be used and the weights assigned to each criterion. As you can see in Figure 16.6, each criterion deemed important in the selection process is given a relative weight; in this example, the weights may range from one to ten. Criteria assigned higher weights are considered to be more important. Vendor products (or proposals) are then rated on each criterion (in this example, the weight that a vendor could receive on a particular criterion may range from a low of 1 to a high of 10). Next, the rating that the vendor receives on each criterion is multiplied by the respective criterion weight (for example, for vendor A, on functionality, vendor A's rating of 7 would be multiplied by the predetermined weight of 10, then vendor A's rating of 5 on ease of learning/use would be multiplied by 10, the criterion weight for ease of learning/use; this would continue for all selection criteria). Finally, these products are summed to produce a total score for each vendor. The vendor receiving the highest total would appear to be the most desirable. In this example, Vendor B would seem to be the more desirable.

Whether or not the vendor with the highest total score will be the one selected is another issue. Sometimes, an ad hoc committee of managers, users, and MIS professionals (assembled specifically to develop the vendor weighting scheme and to carry out the actual evaluation) will make a selection through the process just described, only to see it vetoed by the company president or the MIS steering committee. For instance, if a new company president had good experiences with IBM mainframe shops, an IBM mainframe may be the only realistic alternative in his or her eyes, regardless of what the rating system selection uncovers. Also, if two or more vendors are close in the final ratings, the selection committee might consider the results to be essentially even, and look for additional reasons to justify one vendor or another. In the private sector, the objective of the rating system is not necessarily to be fair; rather, it is to help select the best vendor. In the public sector, where equality is a prime consideration and decisions often must be objectively justified, the results of a vendor rating system may, in fact, largely determine the vendor.

Rating systems are relatively simple to use and they impart some objectivity to the vendor selection process. They also provide a mechanism for including users and managers in the vendor selection process. In addition, if someone on the committee is biased toward a particular vendor, it is more difficult to reflect that bias through a rating system that forces the vendor to be evaluated across various criteria. But whatever their advantages, vendor rating systems are basically crude mathematical models, and the best vendor will not always have the highest score.

Benchmark Tests

Suppose that, based on the results of a vendor rating system, one or two vendors emerge as the best options. What then? Many companies, before committing themselves fully, make a final decision based on the results of a benchmark test.

A **benchmark test** is a test in which one or more programs (or sets of data) are prepared by the potential buyer and then processed under the hardware or software of the vendors being considered. The collection of programs and data submitted by the potential buyer is called a *benchmark*. The benchmark should reflect the type of work that the vendor's hardware and software will actually perform, thereby providing a realistic indication of how well that hardware will do when used for real applications. For example, in the purchase of an order-entry system, the benchmark may consist of a set of sample transactions that provide an indication of processing throughput, error handling, and ease of use. When a computer is purchased for scientific use, on the other hand, the benchmark might consist of numerous tests that assess rounding accuracy, how quickly a matrix can be inverted, and similar functions.

Benchmark testing is expensive and not always accurate. It is expensive because the potential buyer must take the time to prepare a suitable benchmark, may require a visit to the vendor's benchmarking site, and (possibly) pay the vendor to perform the benchmarking on its equipment. Benchmark tests are not always accurate because they cannot check many real-life situations; for instance, how will the system perform when 2,500 users concurrently want service? Also, the results of the benchmark test are highly dependent on the quality of the individual tests that comprise the benchmark. Despite their authors' best intentions, many benchmark tests are biased toward products already in use. For example, a DB2 programmer who develops a benchmark test may subconsciously adopt a database organization scheme for the benchmark that optimizes DB2 performance. When used with a competing product (for example, Oracle), this database organization scheme may yield poorer performance than DB2. This may cause the organization to stay with DB2. Hence, rather than looking at the benchmark as a tool that eliminates the risk of a bad decision, management should see it as a tool that—like marketing research or prototyping methods—only reduces such a risk.

Contracting with Vendors

After a vendor is chosen, a contract is signed. A contract is a document, enforceable in a court of law, that defines such items as what the basic agreement is; who the parties to the agreement are; what goods, services, and monies are exchanged; what type of continuing expectations should be met; and what course of action will be taken if either of the parties signing the contract fails to live up to expectations. A good contract makes the terms of the agreement clear to everyone.

Although most people sign contracts with good intentions, many things can go wrong when dealing with a vendor and both parties could end up in litigation. For instance, the vendor may claim that a system can deliver a level of performance when, realistically, it does not come close to achieving this. Or the vendor may deliver a system with a critical bug that causes the buyer to suffer a severe financial loss. Or a system that is promised to be in place by mid-November is not installed until late January. Problems have thousands of possible causes. A good contract puts all important intentions into writing and specifies a suitable recourse when the vendor fails to meet such intentions.

Many firms retain lawyers—with special expertise in technology matters—to help them prepare or review contracts. When substantial sums of money can be lost, having a specialized computer lawyer is usually the best solution. The layperson's interpretation of right and wrong is often completely different from the legal interpretation, which bases its judgments on complicated federal, state, and local statutes, and on matters of precedent. Also, lawyers are familiar with the types of wording that have legal impact.

During the creation of a contract, the buyer should visualize as many scenarios as possible about how the future might evolve with a vendor and make sure that each of these scenarios is described in concrete, quantifiable terms in the contract. This means putting such vague phrases as "excellent throughput," "fast response time," or "little downtime" into objective, measurable terms, plus making a list of everything that could possibly go wrong and determining how the most important of these situations should be resolved.

SYSTEM IMPLEMENTATION

After vendors are chosen to provide the hardware, software, and services necessary to operate the system, the **system implementation** phase of development begins. Implementation consists of such activities as:

- Scheduling
- Program coding, debugging, and testing
- Training
- Conversion

We will discuss each of these tasks, in detail, in the next few sections.

Many activities associated with implementation start early in the systems development process. For example, some of the scheduling for the implementation is often worked out prior to this phase because the selection of vendors depends upon whether or not they can meet some broad delivery targets. In addition, numerous software development activities may start early if system approval seems imminent and the project has a tight deadline. Program coding, for example, might start during the system design phase—especially if software prototypes are developed that can be refined into the final system. Because such software development tasks may start before implementation, MIS professionals sometimes consider them to be part of the system design phase. However, in this text, they are discussed as part of the system implementation stage.

Scheduling

To ensure that the system will work by a certain date, the analyst must prepare an implementation timetable. Such a timetable shows when certain activities related to implementation must start and finish. A detailed implementation timetable is often essential to develop management's confidence in the installation plan and to ensure uninterrupted operation during the implementation period. In some cases, the installation period may be lengthy. For example, for an on-line teller network, one bank needed a three-year installation period to manage its transition from 140 on-line terminals to more than 1,600.

Three scheduling tools that can be used to establish an implementation timetable are CPM, PERT, and Gantt charts. These tools are flexible enough to be used in a wide range of scheduling applications. Companies use one or more of them for scheduling both the entire systems development effort and the implementation phase.

CPM

The acronym **CPM** stands for **critical path method**. The following example illustrates how CPM works.

A small company in the electronics industry normally shuts down for a three-week period during the Christmas holidays. During this break, the company wants to convert its present office system—which consists of several stand-alone electronic typewriters and two personal computers that are incompatible with each other—into a integrated office system. The new system will consist of a small local area network with a file server, a print server, and 12 workstations. The company has already committed several vendors and contractors to a tentative implementation schedule and, on this basis, it prepared a list of tasks that must be done in order to finish the conversion on time. A schedule of these tasks appears in Figure 16.7. Also shown in the figure are the times required to perform each task and all the preceding task relationships involved. The figure shows, for example, that task F (prepare acoustics) cannot be started until tasks D (enlarge work facility) and E (remove existing equipment) are both done.

In Figure 16.8, the schedule is modeled as a network. Each task is represented by an arrow, and both the task identity and the time required for the task are labeled on the arrows. Each numbered circle at the ends of the arrows represents a *milestone* (a point in time that designates the start or completion of a task or set of tasks). For example, milestone 3 represents the accomplishment of task B, as well as the beginning of tasks L, I, and D. The milestones are numbered for reference purposes. Note also the dotted arrows between milestones 5 and 6 and between milestones 8 and 9. These dotted arrows represent dummy tasks. Dummy tasks are not real activities; they are required in a CPM network representation of a project in order to maintain predecessor relationships.

In Figure 16.8, we chose to represent tasks on the arrows and milestones at the nodes (circles). This is just one of two ways in which CPM networks can be depicted. The other method, which you may encounter in operations management or management science courses, depicts tasks at the nodes. Neither approach is superior to the other; the determination of the critical path is the same in each approach.

The critical path of the network is the sequence of activities that will take the maximum amount of time to complete. The longest path in the network is

Task	Description	Expected Time in Days	Immediate Predecessors
A	Prepare specifications	6	None
B	Secure bids and award contracts	5	A
C	Sell existing equipment	2	A
D	Enlarge work facility	3	B
E	Remove existing equipment	3	C
F	Prepare acoustics	3	D, E
G	Electrical preparations	2	D, E
H	Cleaning and painting	4	E
I	Purchase equipment/await delivery	4	B
J	Assemble equipment	4	I
K	Install equipment	3	J, F, G
L	Conversion and training	4	B
M	Testing	2	K, L
N	Final preparations	1	M

Figure 16.7 Project tasks.

important to identify because, paradoxically, that is the minimum amount of time it will take to complete the entire project. Of course, if any task along the critical path takes longer than expected, the project will take longer to complete.

Several mathematical procedures are used to identify the critical path quickly. We will not discuss those procedures here; you can consult a book on management science or operations research techniques to see how they are done. The possible paths through the network in Figure 16.8 are

Path	Total Time (Days)
A-B-L-M-N	18
A-B-I-J-K-M-N	25
A-B-D-F-K-M-N	23
A-B-D-G-Y-K-M-N	22
A-C-E-X-F-K-M-N	20
A-C-E-X-G-Y-K-M-N	19
A-C-E-H	15

The critical path is A-B-I-J-K-M-N, with a time of 25 days. This means that the project cannot be completed within the company's three-week break unless some other steps are taken. In this case, because A and B are on the critical path

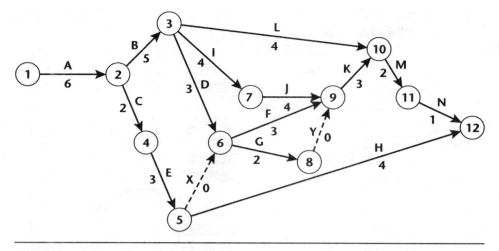

Figure 16.8 Network representation of the project tasks listed in Figure 16.7.

and represent events that can, perhaps, be started early, management should consider those alternatives. If the specification and bidding tasks are started before the break, management can trim 11 days off the critical path. This would allow the project to be completed at a comfortable pace, allowing slack for slip-ups.

PERT

Project evaluation and review technique (PERT) is a project scheduling procedure that works like CPM. The primary difference is that factors of time uncertainty are considered. The expected time of a task is computed by taking a weighted average of the most pessimistic time, most likely time, and most optimistic time it would take to complete the task. Also, a measure of the overall risk involved in meeting a scheduled completion date can be computed.

Gantt Charts

Gantt charts are project modeling tools that use a bar chart representation of project tasks. They are conceptually much easier to construct and to understand than CPM or PERT, but they capture and generate much less information. Figure 16.9 shows a Gantt chart for the project described in Figure 16.7.

Many graphics packages used for presentation graphics applications are equipped to produce Gantt charts. Project management software and some CASE packages also produce Gantt charts and project networks (such as the one depicted in Figure 16.8). Such packages enable users to develop project schedules and coordinate systems development project activities.

Program Coding

In the traditional approach to systems development, after new hardware is selected, program coding begins in earnest. **Coding** is the process of writing

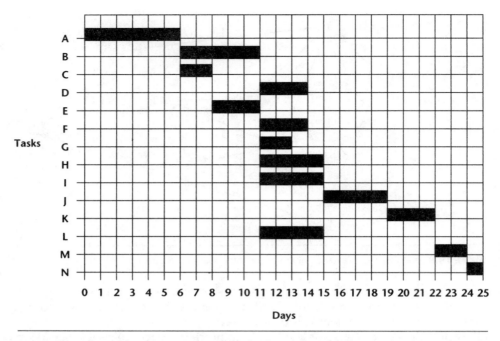

Figure 16.9 Gantt chart. In this figure, the project tasks listed in Figure 16.7 are represented as a Gantt chart. Many presentation graphics, CASE tools, and project management software packages allow data to be output in Gantt chart or project network form such as the one shown in Figure 16.8.

instructions that can be run on computer hardware. If the firm starts this task before reaching the acquisition phase of systems development, it may be taking a considerable risk. If hardware vendor plans change, for instance, any programs that were coded early may need to be modified to work on the new hardware.

Programming is very labor-intensive, which poses several dangers to the organization. For instance, anything that requires a lot of labor is usually expensive. Also, labor-intensive projects normally involve long time periods. This means that opportunities available today cannot be exploited until much later. In addition, the user requirements that the program is supposed to satisfy may change by the time the program is ready. As calculated by a partner at Arthur Andersen Consulting (an acknowledged authority in the systems development area), business software packages designed to run on mainframes and other large systems take an average of 32,000 workdays to finish—a task that would take a team of 36 programmers almost three years to finish.

Because of the present coding environment, the topic of programmer productivity has become crucial in many MIS departments. Once a relatively minor consideration, the speed at which programmers can get applications up and running is now a major strategic concern. In fact, some experts predict that if U.S. programmers do not become more productive, their work will be given to

Foreign Competitors Turn Up the Heat on U.S. PC Makers

The microcomputer has become a global commodity. During the early 1990s, more than 400 companies were manufacturing personal computers in Taiwan alone. These, plus Japanese PC makers (such as NEC) and Korean manufacturers (such as Leading Edge) are among the major international competitors that have heated up PC price wars in the U.S., where microcomputer prices have dropped by as much as 40 percent a year. This means that U.S. PC manufacturers are no longer able to set their pricing strategies without considering what foreign competitors are likely to ask for the models that they market in American stores.

Such price drops were welcomed by customers, who were able to use the reductions to stretch their information technology investment dollars. However, the price wars have forced microcomputer manufacturers— whose profit margins have been substantially eroded—to scramble for more cost-efficient operations and manufacturing strategies. In many cases, this meant turning to contractors around the world who can live on small profit margins. Taiwan has a number of such contractors and, as a result, it has become the world's leading supplier of notebook computers, providing more than 40 percent of the world's output.

"UNDERSTANDABLY . . . PRICE WARS ARE DRIVING A LOT OF MANUFACTURERS OUT OF BUSINESS."

Understandably, the price wars are driving a lot of manufacturers out of business. In Taiwan, only 12 or so major players are expected to still be manufacturing computers by the mid-1990s. Similar shakeouts have occurred around the globe, including the United States.

Adapted from Engardio (1992).

---

programmers in other parts of the world; programmers in Manila, Singapore, Brazil, and India typically earn five to six times less than their U.S. counterparts. For example, in June 1990, a Hong Kong newspaper ad solicited applications for a $180-a-month programmer position that required a college degree and two years of experience in UNIX and C. In the U.S., an applicant with such qualifications could expect to earn $3,000 to $5,000 a month.

Most industry experts agree that unless U.S. programmers make substantial gains in productivity and software quality in the next few years, U.S. companies will increasingly turn to cheaper foreign labor to perform programming tasks. A growing number of corporations feel that it is cost prohibitive not to do so.

As noted several times in this text, many people feel that CASE and object-oriented programming tools will substantially change the way that programs are designed and coded. However, the adoption and use of these productivity-enhancing approaches is not as rapid as it could be and may not be fast enough to keep software companies in the U.S. at a world-class level.

These cutting-edge approaches are not the only strategies that make programmers more productive. We will also examine coding and design tools, coding conventions, automated management tools, walkthroughs, and programmer teams. Collectively, the purpose of these techniques is to speed up the coding process, make program maintenance easier, and ensure that the program is relatively free of errors.

Coding and Design Tools

As discussed in Chapter 15, the three program design/coding tools that are most widely recognized as potentially making programmers more productive are structured programming techniques, fourth-generation languages (4GL), and, lately, object-oriented programming approaches. *Structured programming techniques*—a set of program design and coding tools developed throughout the 1970s—provide programmers with a well-defined and familiar set of control structures. These structures—sequence, selection, and looping—are the only ones allowed in a structured program. Using structured techniques, programs can be written in a systematic, standard style—thereby reducing development time and errors, plus making programs more maintainable. Principles of structured program design were also a guiding force in the development of fourth-generation languages.

During the 1980s, fourth-generation languages targeted to programmer-productivity applications began to see wide use. For instance, a technique that many programmers now use to write programs is to develop a quickly coded version of the program in a 4GL and then either refine this program or—after experience is gained with the application—recode the program in a 3GL. The quickly coded 4GL program is called a *software prototype*; the 4GL product that facilitates creation of software prototypes is an application generator.

Application generators and software prototypes are useful when the users are not exactly sure what they want, when gaining quick insight into user needs is critical, and when time is a limiting factor in software development. Additionally, software prototypes help provide some overall direction to the software development process, and advocates claim that the finished system is often better as a result. To give even greater levels of productivity, many application generators are packaged with code generators, which provide automatic translation of the 4GL into a language of another type. Thus, with a code generator, the user can translate a quickly coded 4GL program directly into COBOL, C, or another 3GL.

During the 1990s, another major approach for enhancing programmer productivity blossomed: object-oriented programming (OOP). As mentioned in Chapter 15, underlying this group of techniques is the concept of reusable code. What many people now envision as the solution to programming problems is the development of off-the-shelf, standardized modules that are customized to fit together into programs. Thus, instead of building a program from scratch, an organization buys the modules it needs—called **reusable code** because the code is designed to be used many times, as required—and has its programming staff quickly patch them together into a program.

Such a solution to programmer productivity is indeed compelling, but still far from realization. First, standards must be set so that such generalized modules are useful to a large number of organizations. As shown by the slow speed of developing suitable telecommunication standards, this will probably be difficult. Second, a gigantic inventory of COBOL and other 3GL programs is still in use and an army of programmers is proficient in 3GL coding. Many of these programmers will not suddenly change their techniques, and both OOP programmers and OOP packages with outstanding track records are scarce. However, steady improvements are underway in this area and the potential for this approach to redefine programming is substantial.

One set of techniques that ties together structured programming fourth-generation languages and OOP approaches to application development is the CASE approach, discussed in Chapters 14 and 15. Many of these tools allow programmers to generate structured code automatically through data flow diagrams, code generators, and by using other tools such as reusable code libraries. Many people expect CASE approaches to completely revolutionize systems development someday by providing an integrated approach to system design, program design, program coding, and maintenance. However great that potential, it is still far from realization.

Coordination Tools

Commercial programs often entail a large number of statements. Thus, methods are required to help manage and coordinate all of this code. Two widely used productivity tools are automated data dictionaries and automated documentation methods.

As discussed in Chapter 7, data dictionaries keep track of types of data, the programs in which the data are used, and the ways in which the data are used. Many CASE tools contain features that enable parts of the dictionary to be created automatically, as the application is developed. So, if a programmer is using data or a block of code incorrectly, the dictionary feature—which is monitoring the code as it is typed—will warn the programmer immediately, before development proceeds further and the error becomes more entrenched and harder to find.

Many of these CASE tools provide some type of *automated documentation* as the application is developed. Included in this type of documentation are the data dictionary, a log of program changes, data flow diagrams, and pseudocode.

Walkthroughs

A *walkthrough* (or review), which can be conducted at virtually any point during the systems development process, is a peer evaluation of a systems analyst's or a programmer's work. For instance, a programmer might submit a completed program module to five peers, who evaluate it and meet with the programmer to discuss its merits and shortcomings. Does the program exhibit a structure that makes it maintainable throughout the years? Were established naming conventions used? These are questions that the peers attempt to answer.

The object of a walkthrough is to provide constructive feedback about the program—not to assist in formal performance evaluation of the programmer. In fact, it is advisable not to have the programmer's boss present at the walkthrough. When a program is evaluated, the term *egoless programming* is used to describe the walkthrough: it should be used constructively to improve the program and should not be taken personally or as a criticism of the programmer.

Programmer Teams

A *programmer team* is often used on large programming projects. In such projects, the work is divided into logical modules; design and coding of these modules are assigned to members of the programming team. This approach often helps reduce program development time, especially when programmers communicate well and their tasks are coordinated effectively.

Program Debugging and Testing

Debugging refers to the process of ridding a program of errors—usually called **bugs** or "glitches." **Program testing**, on the other hand, is the process used to certify that a program is free of errors. Because a bug in a program can cause a lot of damage—such as paying someone $10,000 instead of $10, or causing a major transaction processing system at a corporation to grind to a halt—a great deal of development time is spent debugging and testing programs. These two activities alone can consume over half of the program development budget.

Classifying Bugs

Almost all computer programs contain bugs while they are developed. Most commercial programs, in fact, still have bugs in them after they are released. Program bugs can be grouped into three classifications: syntax errors, run-time errors, and logic errors.

A *syntax error* violates the grammatical rules of a programming language. For example, the syntax of COBOL's MULTIPLY-GIVING statement is

```
MULTIPLY x BY y GIVING z
```

Thus, a statement such as

```
MULTIPLY HOURS TIMES RATE GIVING PAY
```

produces a syntax error (that is, the word "BY" should be used instead of "TIMES"). Syntax errors are one of the easiest bugs to remove from a program. Some systems software packages use on-line syntax checkers that catch errors as soon as they are typed, while others catch and pinpoint them when attempts are made to compile or run the program.

Another type of bug is the *run-time error*—an error that causes the program to terminate abnormally. For instance, suppose the statement

```
DIVIDE PAY BY HOURS GIVING RATE
```

appears in a program. If HOURS is equal to zero when this division is performed, it will cause the program to stop. Division by zero is disallowed in most programming languages because the result of doing so is meaningless. Like syntax errors, run-time errors are relatively easy to spot.

Ironically, the potentially most devastating error is the one that does not cause the program to halt, but instead lets it continue to produce wrong results. This type of error is called a *logic error*. For instance, writing the previously mentioned pay-rate relationship as

MULTIPLY HOURS BY HOURS GIVING PAY

is a logic error (while multiplying hours by hours will yield a number that could be used in later calculations, the appropriate calculation for determining pay is to multiply hours by rate). The only way to uncover logic errors is through testing, which we will discuss next. Logic errors are especially troublesome in environments where departmental microcomputers are used because many end-users are not as skilled in checking computer-produced results as professionals are. Many non-MIS professionals, for instance, are so relieved when their programs run that they do not check carefully to ensure that the outputs produced are totally correct.

Program Testing

Program testing consists of running a new or modified program, which appears to be working correctly, with sample data. The sample data should be comprehensive enough so that they cover all the conditions the program will encounter in its foreseeable future. Managers and users should play a key role in the development of test data because—by working closely with the system—they should know what types of erroneous data and data-entry errors are most likely to happen. The development of test data and actual program testing, of course, is often more difficult and time-consuming—but it should generally be required, even of the most experienced programmers. For sensitive applications such as payroll, the people responsible for testing should not include the original programmer. This reduces the risk of programmer bias during the testing process, and reduces the possibility of a crime being committed.

As mentioned previously, virtually every commercial program has bugs of some type in it. It is almost impossible to find every bug in a commercial-level program. Thus, organizations must trade the thoroughness of testing against the cost of finding certain types of bugs. If found early, some bugs may cost very little to fix; if found after a program is released, those bugs may cost thousands of dollars to repair. They could even put a company out of business.

An integrated software testing approach usually consists of several stages, including module testing, program testing, systems testing, and acceptance testing.

Module testing is the process of testing the individual modules that make up the whole program. After all the individual modules are tested and assessed as working properly, they are combined so that *program testing* can begin. This often consists of ensuring that the interfaces between modules work as they should and that these individual modules do not have an adverse effect on one another. *Systems testing* ensures that all the programs that make up the new system work together as they should. User interfaces, the system's security features, the ability to deal with abnormal processing volumes (sometimes called stress testing), and the ability to recover from software failure are tested. *Acceptance testing* evaluates the extent to which the new system meets user requirements under normal operating conditions; this is often the last chance to test and re-think the program before the software is converted from development to operations. Of course, managers and users should be heavily involved in acceptance testing.

User Training

With the burst of activity in end-user computing and the appearance of new tools for computer professionals, training is becoming a major component of implementation. When a new system is acquired—which often involves new hardware and software—both users and computer professionals generally need some type of training. Often, this is through classes given by vendors and through hands-on learning techniques.

Training can be a significant system cost. Some experts estimate that more than $800 million a year is spent on end-user training, and these in-house estimates may not reveal the total costs. For instance, thousands of dollars in training costs may be covered by vendors supplying hardware and/or software for a new system. If the vendor says that the training is at no charge, this often means that the price of the "free" classes is added on to the hardware and software costs—usually with a profit tacked on. In any case, employees attending training classes usually miss work, making them less productive and unavailable during that time. Training also can be considered an ongoing cost because new vendor releases of the system and in-house system enhancements mean more training for people at some point. In addition, staff turnover makes this an ongoing activity; new users must also be trained.

Too often, training is viewed only as a cost item. Because of this, during periods of declining profits, some firms reduce or eliminate training activities. In addition, many firms overlook the costs of not training users. For example, they don't try to determine the costs of errors, below-average performance, improper system usage, or lost business because of poor customer service. However, an increasing number of firms recognize that training is critical to new system effectiveness and to the long-term effectiveness of the organization. These firms understand that well-trained users are generally more productive, happier with their jobs, and better prepared to provide high-quality customer service. For example, the Texas Department of Highways and Public Transportation estimates a savings of $5 million from its PC training program—primarily from increased user productivity.

Training is often seen as a necessary evil by managers. While recognizing its importance, many managers resent having to release employees from their regular job activities so that they can be trained. When managers are actively involved in determining training needs, they are usually more supportive of training efforts. It is generally also wise to have managers directly involved in evaluating the effectiveness of training activities because training deficiencies can translate into reduced user productivity levels.

Developing User Training Programs

When developing user training programs, several steps should be followed:

- **Determine user job requirements** The starting point for any training program should be the determination of exactly what trainees will be expected to do and how they will use the new system to perform their jobs. For example, the trainer should know how many invoices order-entry personnel will be expected to process per hour when using the new system.

- **Determine specific training needs** This step involves determining what trainees must know in order to use the new system to perform their jobs. For example, for the order-entry personnel just described, the activities that must be carried out by users in order to complete each invoice must be specified. This could include: (1) entering the customer's account number, (2) entering the order-detail line (product number, quantity, and price) for the first item, (3) entering the order-detail line for the remaining items on the invoice, and (4) visually verifying the reasonableness of the totals and other calculations performed on the data that was entered. As another example, when designing a word-processing training program for secretaries, it is important to know the types and contents of the documents that they will have to develop.

- **Evaluate training resources** During this step, the resources needed to provide adequate user training programs are evaluated. Questions such as, "Do we have needed trainers, adequate training facilities, training equipment, and training materials?" are addressed. If the answers to these questions are "No," external trainers and facilities may be needed.

- **Develop the training program** This step involves putting together all the resources needed to provide the training, such as equipment, facilities, training materials, and trainers. The contents of specific training sessions or activities are developed at this time. The schedule of specific training sessions is also developed and distributed to managers and users involved in the training program.

  Part of the training program development program should include its testing with a small group of trainees before training all users of the new system. This enables trainers to see potential problems with the training process, get candid reactions from users to the program and training materials, and discover from participants themselves how the program could be improved. Such tests can provide invaluable input about what is good—and bad—about the training program.

- **Implement the training program** During this step, the actual training sessions and activities take place. Paying attention to user reactions and suggestions can help trainers improve the program while it's underway.

■ ***Evaluate training outcomes*** This step enables the organization to determine if training is effective. Can users utilize the system as needed? Were the activities needed to use the system most effectively mastered by training participants? In general, training should be carefully evaluated to determine if it enhances user productivity and on-the-job performance. Increases in performance, work quality, and customer service should be documented and reported to management.

Trainee Considerations

In Chapter 2, we discussed some of the personal factors that should be considered by systems developers and why different types of interfaces may be needed by different types of users. Just as different types of interfaces may be needed, different types of training may be needed for different types of trainees. For example, an unskilled worker who has never used a computer may be afraid of them. Another person might be reluctant to learn new tools after old ones are mastered. Other workers, with computer experience, may be eager learners who are highly motivated. The first (unskilled) worker may require one-on-one instruction, repeated explanations, and extensive encouragement. The last worker, with computer experience, may become impatient with long explanations. This worker may need only a brief introduction and demonstration, self-instruction materials, and help only when major problems are encountered.

Because of these differences, several training guidelines should be followed:

■ Use different training activities for different users, depending on their prior experience with computers and their job duties. Because trainees learn at different speeds, different sets of training materials may be required: some that appeal to slower learners and others to use with faster or more computer-knowledgeable users.

■ Minimize trainee frustration and anxiety with the new system. Early training activities should be those that can be mastered by just about everyone; save the complex and difficult activities for later. Provide positive feedback when trainees reach important training milestones. Remember that some employees feel that their job security is threatened if they aren't successful in the training program.

■ Continually emphasize the personal benefits of the training—how the skills and concepts learned will help the trainee be a more effective and productive worker.

■ Encourage interaction between trainers and trainees. Users should be encouraged to ask questions. Trainers should ask questions of users to ensure that they are learning what they need to know. For example, a trainer could ask trainees to explain the exact keystrokes/commands sequence to perform a specific task.

Training Approaches

Two main categories of end-user training approaches exist: instructor-led training and self-study methods. Many different methods can be used with each approach.

- **Instructor-led methods**   Many experts feel that instructor-led training is the most effective approach because trainees can learn faster and more effectively when they interact with a good instructor. The most common instructor-led approach is the lecture, but this is seldom used by itself in end-user training. Discussion is often used along with lecture. Demonstration is also commonly used with lecture, especially when training users how to work with new software. After the instructor demonstrates the task, users practice it on their own. One-on-one training, or coaching, is often used for on-the-job training and may involve a combination of lecture, discussion, and demonstration. In many instances, new employees are taught by skilled users through one-on-one training.

- **Self-study methods**   In recent years, increasingly more user training programs have incorporated self-study methods as part of the training process. Computer-based training, tutorials, and multimedia training systems are three examples of self-study methods. *Computer-based training (CBT)* usually includes a combination of diskettes and manuals. Sometimes, audio and video tapes are also used. Most of these programs are prepared by vendors, professional training firms, or consulting firms. The main objective of these programs is to have the user interact directly with the computer as he or she is trained; this often involves multiple senses (such as sight, sound, and touch). For example, while learning the keystrokes (touch) needed to perform a job-related task, the trainee may read (sight) part of a manual, view (sight) a video segment, and/or listen (sound) to part of an audio tape.

   Tutorials are used extensively to train users in how to operate software packages and certain types of computer hardware. Typically, a tutorial is on a diskette and contains introductory lessons about how to use the software or hardware. Many popular software programs include tutorials covering basic operations; instructions appear on the screen and show the user which steps to follow.

   Multimedia training systems comprise the hottest area of the computer-based training technologies. Typically, optical disk technology is used to combine audio, video, tutorial, and even instructor-led methods into a single training tool. This approach makes it possible to integrate various training approaches and to appeal to multiple senses through one piece of training equipment: the microcomputer. Trainees can listen to and watch a demonstration, then practice what they have observed.

- **Other training methods**   Other training assistance is also available. Some vendors (including IBM) offer hotline assistance and technical support that allow users to call specialists to get questions answered. As you will see in Chapter 17, technical support and hotline assistance may also be available in-house through the information center. Some vendors—and even some companies—have set up electronic bulletin board systems that allow users to ask questions, share tips, and so on. In addition, many organizations use in-house television, video teleconferencing, and other distance learning approaches for training purposes.

Training Approaches in Action

Companies provide training in many different ways. The Traveler's Insurance Companies treat each division as a separate business unit; each has its own training group that provides specialized, totally customized end-user training. Pitney Bowes uses a combination of internal and external trainers. The Polaroid Corporation outsources all of the training activities previously carried out by the MIS staff.

Training methods also show considerable variation in practice. For example, the Hartford Insurance Group begins its microcomputer training with a short instructor-led approach. Trainees then complete numerous self-instructional sessions on their own; the instructor stays close by to help as needed. Manpower, a temporary help agency, provides its trainees with tailor-made instructional materials, including their own concise, non-technical reference manuals (rather than the ones that come from software vendors). The Traveler's Companies, mentioned previously, are moving toward multimedia training systems as quickly as possible.

Conversion Options

The process of switching from one system to another is called **system conversion**. At the point of conversion, users and computer operations personnel should be trained in their new duties, application software for the new system should be available and ready to use, the necessary data conversions should be completed, and hardware should be in place. Conversions are often accompanied by adjustment problems because users may be resistant to change. Potential conversion problems should be anticipated; contingency plans should be developed in case major problems are encountered.

A new system can be brought up to speed in many ways. Four popular methods are direct conversion, parallel conversion, phased conversion, and pilot studies. The method chosen depends on the particular situation.

In a *direct conversion*, the system that is currently being used is replaced, all at once, by a new system. This is equivalent to turning the old system off and turning the new system on. In some cases, the old system may be physically removed to make room for the new system. Turnkey systems—discussed earlier in the chapter—are often implemented by using this approach. Direct conversion is risky because if the new system fails, the company has nothing else to use. Thus, this conversion procedure requires much more careful planning than the other conversion methods we will discuss. The advantage of the direct approach is that, except for some possible chaos during changeover, the new system is put into place rapidly.

In a *parallel conversion*, both the old and the replacement system run together for a period of time. If the new system fails, the old one is available for backup. This is not possible in all cases, however, because the old and new systems may be entirely different. The main disadvantages of this approach are that it can be expensive and time-consuming to simultaneously operate two systems that do essentially the same thing. Today, this approach is rarely used, especially with on-line systems. It is usually impractical to enter transactions twice (once for each system), even though their output can then be compared.

In a *phased conversion*, the new system is phased in slowly, piece by piece. After one part of the system works well, the next piece is made operational. This approach avoids the problems associated with introducing too many changes too soon. A phased approach, however, usually takes longer to fully establish the new system. Also, the need to exchange data between those parts of the overall system that are still operating with the old software and those that use the new software can create major problems.

A *pilot study* is when a new system is tried in a specific area of the organization. If successful there, it is brought into other areas. For instance, an oil company looking at a new control system for managing crude oil inventories might try the system at one of its many refineries. If, after a year's operation, an audit proves the system successful, it could then be implemented at other refineries. The advantages and disadvantages to pilot studies are essentially the same as those for phased conversions.

Although many system conversions take place with few problems, the opposite can also occur:

- The Internal Revenue Service's 1985 tax processing season was plagued by computer processing difficulties that resulted in substantial taxpayer refund delays. According to outside auditors, the problems resulted from the IRS's mishandling a cutover to new mainframes and new COBOL software.

- A $600 million system conversion at a large insurance company in the early 1980s fared even worse. The new system caused serious problems for policy holders. Claims were either not paid at all or were substantially overpaid. The company lost $28 million in 1985 and nearly as much in 1986. It also lost over 20,000 policy holders before fixing the system.

- A large West Coast bank wanted to replace the outdated computer system used to manage $34 billion in institutional trust accounts. The firm they contracted to produce the new system's software couldn't get its programs to perform properly on the bank's hardware. During the shaky conversion period, the bank decided to play it safe and pay employees to work double shifts, processing data on both the new and old systems. When the cutover was finally made to the new system, it crashed. The bank lost pension fund accounts amounting to $1.5 million and statements to clients ran a month

Software Re-Engineering Products are Extending Old Program Lives

Some companies are doing a makeover on their aging programs, rather than scrapping or replacing them. To do so, they are implementing software re-engineering initiatives.

". . . WORKERS CAN CONTINUE TO USE THE OLD TRIED-AND-TRUE PROGRAMS THEY KNOW— BUT ON THE NEW HARDWARE SYSTEMS."

Software re-engineering efforts involve essentially a two-step process. First, reverse-engineering products analyze the program and product data flow diagrams and entity-relationship diagrams that depict cause and effect patterns between tasks performed by chunks of the program's code. Next, re-engineering products are used to rework and streamline the application.

Organizations are investing in software re-engineering products because they want to save on software maintenance costs or because they want to move the application to a different hardware platform as part of their down-sizing plans.

Numerous vendors market re-engineering products, including Bachman Information Systems, Inc., CGI Systems, Inc., Intersolv, Inc., KnowledgeWare, Inc., Texas Instruments, Inc./Price Waterhouse, and Viasoft, Inc.

During the 1990s, software re-engineering is expected to gain in popularity as increasingly more companies move their traditionally mainframe-based applications to minicomputer and LAN-based computing platforms. By re-engineering, workers can continue to use the old tried-and-true programs they know—but on the new hardware systems. This can make user transitions to new platforms less stressful.

Adapted from Nash (1992).

---

late. Three years into the project, the executive vice-presidents in charge of the technology and trust divisions resigned. A few months later, after more than 2.5 million lines of program code were written for the project, the bank finally abandoned the system.

POSTIMPLEMENTATION REVIEW

After the new system is installed and people feel comfortable using it, the system should be evaluated.

Systems are expensive to develop and their impacts within the organization are often far-reaching. It does not make sense for the organization to spend a lot of money on a system and then not do any follow-up. Such a follow-up evaluation is called a **postimplementation review**. It has two purposes: (1) to quickly correct any glitches that have arisen in the new system and (2) to provide feedback on the entire systems development process so that organizational skills in this area can improve. Virtually every aspect of the postimplementation review

Postimplementation Review Issues

- Is the system meeting its intended goals?

- Is the system providing the benefits outlined in the requirements analysis?

- Was the cost of developing, acquiring, and implementing the system within expectations?

- Are the ongoing system costs within expectations?

- Are users satisfied with the system?

- Is the system running optimally or do some aspects need fine-tuning?

- Are all the outputs to the system being used as expected?

Figure 16.10 Examples of postimplementation review issues.

is directed toward some measure of quality assurance; that is, ascertaining that the resulting system and the system-building process are meeting certain standards of acceptability.

Figure 16.10 gives a sample of some of the specific questions that the postimplementation review must address. The main focus of these questions is to discover if the system is delivering the benefits—both operational and strategic—expected at the anticipated costs. The answers to these questions can be determined in numerous ways. Three commonly used methods are a formal impact study, regular audits, and performance monitors.

Formal Impact Study

A *formal impact study* is a special investigation to evaluate the system and to determine if it is working as expected. This study generally takes place after the system is fully installed and employees have had enough experience with it to provide useful feedback.

During the impact study, systems developers gather objective data on system performance, observe how outputs are used, determine if any unanticipated problems have arisen, and evaluate costs. The opinions of users about the system are sought, usually through interviews and questionnaires. For example, if the system was supposed to cut the time to process customer orders by 50 percent, the impact study should objectively determine if this productivity gain is being realized. Or if a new software package was advertised by its vendor as very user-friendly, employees should be questioned to see if that is true.

The people supervising the impact study should check the original project documentation to determine the goals and objectives set for the system—and to determine if these are being met. Usually, the two most important areas of any impact study are performance and cost. Is the system providing the benefits for which it was designed? Are system costs running at the expected levels?

Regular Audit

The purpose of auditing a system is to ensure that it is functioning the way it should. A *regular audit* assures management that the system is processing data efficiently or providing information effectively, thus meeting the needs of users and the organization. An audit can be conducted by systems professionals, by the internal auditing staff, or—preferably—by the EDP auditor, who is skilled in both auditing and technology concepts.

A regular audit provides advantages beyond those of a one-time impact study. For instance, because business needs change over time, a system that may be working well a year after it is installed may not be as effective three years later. Continually assessing whether the needs of users are being met is one way of determining whether the system is still effective.

Also, changes in the technology environment could impact the effectiveness of a system. For example, the proliferation of microcomputer systems and local area networks has made some mainframe packages unnecessary. Many additional reasons for ongoing audits exist. The cost of paper may rise sharply, making paper-based parts of the system less cost-effective. Or a critical system bug, discovered a few years after the system was installed, might be causing some problems that an audit would uncover. Or, after a few years of studying the system, a person might decide to commit a computer crime. In many instances, computer crimes are uncovered during an audit.

Performance Monitors

Performance monitors are software packages that measure how efficiently resources are being used by a computer system. They also show the operations staff what the system is doing at all times. Monitors enable operations personnel to pinpoint critical performance weaknesses early so that these weaknesses can be corrected before they have a chance to materially degrade system throughput.

When evaluating the performance of a system, the monitor can be very useful in providing facts such as the following:

- The percentage of downtime (non-operational time) on the system.

- A log of all problems encountered by the system and a description of how each problem was handled.

- Throughput statistics, such as the number of transactions processed in a period or the average number of transactions processed over several periods.

- Statistics showing which programs or data files were used—plus when and how often.

- Statistics on users—for instance, how many users were on the system Tuesday or the profile of off-hours utilization.

- Usage statistics for individual hardware and software resources.

- The average time taken to access primary or secondary storage.

Theoretically, the monitor is capable of recording every event happening on the system and providing summary measures of events. When looking for a performance monitor, the user should determine the types of information that are needed to continually assess the system's performance and make sure that the monitor selected can provide such information.

Performance monitors are also available for local area and other computer networks. These provide many of the same statistics as performance monitors for mainframe- and minicomputer-based systems along with data regarding which circuits are used most frequently. The latter data can be very important in developing long-range plans for network growth.

SYSTEM MAINTENANCE

System **maintenance** involves making changes to a system over the course of its useful life. System maintenance can mean maintaining hardware, which may wear out or fail for physical reasons. For example, a real-time transaction processing system might require a new communications controller to manage terminals. However, most commonly, system maintenance refers to maintaining software that, until it is modified, behaves in the same manner as when it was first installed (unless damaged/altered by a virus or system failure). For example, a COBOL program might need a new routine to accommodate a change in government reporting requirements. Occasionally, system maintenance refers to a combination of hardware and software changes; for example, a DSS might be enhanced by a new macros feature and some hardware-acceleration features or add-on boards.

A study performed by researchers at MIT suggests that for every $1 invested in new systems development, an additional $9 will be spent on maintenance during the rest of the system's useful life. Furthermore, industry experts contend that more than $30 billion is spent annually worldwide on maintenance—with more than a third of that spent in the United States.

Ongoing maintenance is important to any system. If the system was designed well, it should be flexible enough to accommodate changes over a reasonable period of time with minimal disruption. If, at some point in the maturation phase of the system, however, a major change becomes necessary, another system will be required. At this point, the systems development cycle—from preliminary investigation to implementation—begins all over again.

In practice, firms often have different philosophies regarding maintenance. At one end of the maintenance spectrum, some firms employ the "if it's not broken, don't fix it" philosophy, hastily patching over elements that are not functioning properly. It is not until the system is noticeably cost-ineffective that a major overhaul takes place. Such a philosophy is likely to deter an organization from using MIS strategically as a competitive weapon. At the other end of the spectrum are firms that prefer regular ongoing maintenance—constantly modernizing the system to keep it functioning smoothly. These firms are often in a good position to change the system as business needs change and to use MIS for strategic advantage.

Four general approaches are used to maintain systems and programs. These are corrective maintenance, adaptive maintenance, perfective maintenance, and preventive maintenance.

Corrective maintenance may be the least noble and most burdensome type of maintenance because it corrects design, coding, and implementation errors that should never have occurred. The need for corrective maintenance can often be traced back to poor application (or non-use) of systems development and structured programming approaches.

Adaptive maintenance is performed in response to changes in processing, data, or user requirements. For example, a new tax law may require a change in the calculation of net pay, the generation of a new report, or the switch to a new accounting method before the end of the fiscal period. Because the business environment is dynamic, adaptive maintenance is continually needed to respond to changing user requirements.

Perfective maintenance enhances the performance or maintainability of the system or program. When successful, perfective maintenance results in the system's satisfying user requirements better. Or the changes may enhance processing efficiency and system throughput.

Preventive maintenance consists of periodic inspection and review of the system and its programs to uncover and anticipate problems. If potential problems are uncovered early, steps can be taken to ensure that they don't evolve into major ones.

Software Maintenance

The biggest single component in any organization's maintenance bill is generally software. In fact, over the last several years, about half of the MIS budget in a typical organization is spent on software maintenance; in some firms, software maintenance accounts for 75 percent or more of the total MIS budget. In addition, in the typical firm, approximately 50–80 percent of all available programmer time is allocated to software maintenance functions.

Maintenance programmers are responsible for maintaining the organization's library of existing programs. As *Computerworld* reports, one MIS manager at a large Midwestern phone company notes, "We spend millions of dollars every year not increasing the direct benefit to the business—not bringing in some new development that is going to bring in new revenue to the business— just enhancing the software that is already [in use]."

The heavy expense associated with program and system maintenance is one reason why organizations have developed an appreciation for structured systems development methodologies and structured programming approaches. Research indicates that structured systems and programs tend to be easier and less costly to maintain. Thus, it is not surprising that many organizations require their MIS professionals to use these structured techniques.

In many organizations, most of the software maintenance effort is focused on COBOL-based transaction processing programs. Of the many solutions proposed to reduce a firm's maintenance costs, perhaps the three most important are restructuring engines (sometimes called code regenerators), code generators, and reusable-code libraries.

- **Restructuring engines** A **restructuring engine**, or code regenerator, is a program that takes unstructured (or poorly structured) program code and converts it into easier-to-read and easier-to-maintain structured code. For example, KPMG Peat Marwick's Structured Retrofit cleans up poorly structured COBOL programs and re-packages them into a program with a much clearer hierarchical structure. One spokesperson for KPMG Peat Marwick observes that this is the equivalent of turning "spaghetti code"—a term often used in reference to tangled unstructured programs—into better structured and more maintainable "lasagna code."

  Restructuring engines are relatively new. A user still cannot feed a program into them and get, in a single pass, perfect code coming out. Some additional programming time is needed to finish the restructuring job, but not nearly what would be needed to completely rewrite the program in a structured form. Nonetheless, these programs are well-received in industry and can be customized to meet a wide variety of MIS shop standards.

- **Code generators** Most code generators found in maintenance shops work with fourth-generation languages that are designed to produce error-free, easily maintainable 3GL programs, especially COBOL. We mentioned the existence of such programs earlier, both in Chapter 6 and in an earlier section of this chapter. The programmer codes the application, using a 4GL available with the code generator. This step usually takes much less time and many fewer lines of code than would writing a comparable program or subprogram in COBOL (or other third-generation languages). The 4GL program is then fed to a precompiler, which translates the 4GL code into error-free 3GL code. Often, the programmer still has to do some fine-tuning beyond the output of the code generator. However, the generator might produce 70 percent or more of the code needed for the entire application.

  Naturally, code generators do not guarantee an error-free program. Although the generator may translate from the 4GL to the 3GL without syntax errors, the original 4GL may contain a run-time or logic error that the code generator did not detect. Also, programmers can introduce errors into the program during the customization stage after the generator delivers error-free code. Nonetheless, code generators are useful for software maintenance because they force programmers into a standard methodology and make results easier to verify.

  Program documentation can also be produced by most code generators, furthering more standardization and future ease in understanding the application. Because most code generators can produce fast software prototypes, they can potentially elicit more precise specifications of what users really want.

- ■ *Reusable-code libraries*   Whereas restructuring engines and code generators refer to programs, reusable-code libraries refer to data. Many reusable-code libraries employed today for software maintenance consist of blocks of code saved from existing application programs. These blocks can be used to create new software—in fact, according to some industry experts, they can provide up to 80 percent of many new applications. As noted several times, reusable-code libraries are closely associated with object-oriented programming (OOP) approaches. Although the application of reusable code is limited today, many industry observers expect it to play an increasingly important role in future software development and maintenance.

Restructuring engines are most useful for existing programs that need repair, whereas code generators are used to produce entirely new programs. Reusable-code libraries can supplement the activities of either restructuring engines or code generators.

SUMMARY

After the design phase of the systems development life cycle, the organization starts acquiring the hardware, software, and services it needs for the new system. This process is known as system acquisition.

Today, thousands of vendors of technology-related products collectively sell a rich variety of hardware, software, and services. The largest firms in the technology marketplace are the hardware and software vendors—with such firms as IBM, Unisys, DEC, Fujitsu, and NEC at the top of the list. One common type of services firm is the service bureau, which performs information processing for other firms. Turnkey, or value-added, vendors often put together entire hardware/software service packages in the form of a complete, ready-to-use system.

Organizations can approach hardware, software, or services vendors in numerous ways when planning to buy or lease products. One way is to send the vendor a request for proposal (RFP). This document outlines the organization's system needs and asks that vendors submit written proposals explaining how they will fulfill such needs. A request for quotation (RFQ) names specific products and requests a price quotation. A more flexibly based RFP does not name specific products, thereby giving the vendor more freedom when responding to the organization.

Bids are often evaluated through vendor rating systems and through the use of benchmark tests. In a vendor rating system, vendors are quantitatively scored under various criteria. A benchmark test is a test in which programs or data are prepared by the potential buyer and then processed by the vendor's hardware or software—thereby giving the buyer an idea of how well the vendor's products might do with real applications. After the vendor is chosen, a contract is written and signed.

The next phase of development is system implementation, which consists of such activities as scheduling; program coding, debugging, and testing; training; and conversion.

Three scheduling tools that might be used to set up an implementation timetable are CPM, PERT, and Gantt charts. With the critical path method (CPM), the schedule of all necessary implementation tasks is modeled as a network, and the sequence of activities that will take the maximum amount of time—known as the critical path—is found. PERT (project evaluation and review technique) works like CPM, except that factors of uncertainty regarding time are considered. Gantt charts are project modeling tools that use a bar chart representation of project tasks.

In the traditional approach, program coding—the process of writing instructions that the computer system can execute directly—begins next. Programs are broadly designed by a systems analyst and created in detail by a programmer. Numerous strategies can make programmers more productive at this stage. These include: the use of coding and design tools, coding conventions, automated coordination tools, walkthroughs, and programmer teams. Coding and design tools include structured techniques, fourth-generation languages (4GL), and object-oriented programming (OOP) tools. Coding conventions involve coding standards set up within companies. Automated coordination tools—such as data dictionaries and documentation tools—help manage and coordinate code. A walkthrough is an evaluation of the work of a systems analyst, programmer, or the entire systems development team. With programmer teams, code development is divided among a number of people.

Debugging is the process of getting rid of program errors (bugs). Bugs can be classified as syntax errors, run-time errors, or logic errors. Program testing is the process of determining that a program is free of errors.

User training is one of the most critical aspects of system implementation. After training needs are determined, numerous training approaches may be used. Instructor-led approaches include lecture, discussion, and demonstration. Self-study approaches may be computer-based; tutorials, programmed instruction, and multimedia systems may also be used.

The process of switching from one system to another is called system conversion. Four popular methods of conversion are direct conversion, parallel conversion, phased conversion, and pilot studies. Direct conversion is the quickest, but riskiest, conversion approach; in this approach, the old system is turned off when the new one is turned on. In the parallel approach, the old and new systems are run concurrently until management is assured that the new system is functioning properly. In the phased approach, applications are gradually and systematically moved from the old to the new system. With a pilot study, the new system is tried out in one location before being implemented throughout the organization.

A postimplementation review is a follow-up evaluation of a system that was implemented. Three popular methods by which this can be carried out are a formal impact study, regular audits, and performance monitoring. The impact study is a one-time investigation to see that the system is working as expected.

REVIEW

Regular audits assure management of a system's continuing effectiveness. Performance monitors are software packages that measure how efficiently a computer system is using its resources.

System maintenance refers to the ongoing monitoring of a system throughout its lifetime, with personnel making modest changes as needed. Software maintenance is the largest part of the maintenance effort. Maintenance programmers are the people in charge of maintaining existing software.

Three important ways of reducing the high cost of maintenance are restructuring engines, code generators, and reusable code libraries. A restructuring engine is a program that turns hard-to-read code into easier-to-read structured program code. Most code generators found in maintenance shops work with fourth-generation languages that are designed to produce error-free, easily maintained 3GL programs, especially COBOL. Reusable-code libraries are blocks of program code that can be reused to create new software.

KEY TERMS

Benchmark test

Bug

Coding

Critical path method (CPM)

Debugging

Gantt chart

Maintenance

Performance monitor

Postimplementation review

Program testing

Project evaluation and review technique (PERT)

Request for proposal (RFP)

Request for quotation (RFQ)

Restructuring engine

Reusable code

Service bureau

System conversion

System implementation

Turnkey system

Vendor rating system

REVIEW QUESTIONS

1. Describe the approaches that organizations may use to keep up with changes in the marketplace.
2. What types of activities are performed by a service bureau?
3. What is meant by the term "turnkey system"?
4. Identify the types of issues that should be addressed in a request for proposal (RFP). How does an RFQ differ from an RFP?
5. What are vendor rating systems and how are they used in systems development programs?
6. What is the purpose of a benchmark test?

7. Describe the types of activities that make up the system implementation phase of development.

8. What is the difference between CPM and PERT?

9. Identify several different types of program bugs and describe the differences among them.

10. What types of program and system testing are used during the systems development process?

11. Why is user training important? What types of training methods may be used to familiarize users with a new system?

12. In what different ways could system conversion take place?

13. What types of activities are performed during the postimplementation review?

14. What is a performance monitor?

15. What is the function of a restructuring engine?

16. What types of benefits are provided by reusable code?

DISCUSSION QUESTIONS

1. Suppose you are hired by an organization that has built up an inventory of $1 million in COBOL programs over the past 20 years. The organization is upset with the mounting maintenance expense of these programs and is looking to you for a solution. What alternatives are open to such a company? What opportunities and problems can you identify with each of these alternatives?

2. In the vendor selection process, what control measures can an organization take to ensure that the vendor chosen will truly supply a system that best meets the organization's needs? What types of events can happen to make the "wrong" vendor the one that is chosen?

3. What types of standards or guidelines must be established in a programming shop to ensure that programming takes place in the most effective or efficient manner?

CASE STUDY

The Competitive Edge of Bug-Free Computer Code

Growing user unrest with applications backlogs has increased pressure on MIS departments and programmers to get new systems in the hands of users as quickly as possible. Programmers used to respond to such demands with "Do you want it quick, or do you want it good?" These days, users and management are demanding both good and quick—in addition, they want it bug-free.

As noted many times in this text, companies are increasingly turning to fourth-generation languages (4GL), computer-aided software engineering (CASE) tools, and object-oriented programming (OOP) to reduce application development time. In many instances, impressive programmer productivity gains have been noted.

However, OOP-developed programs also seem to be a fertile new breeding ground for software bugs. OOP program bugs accounted for a hefty percentage of the estimated 150 million bugs produced by American programmers in 1990. And, all too often, bugs are found in mission-critical applications.

At worst, computer bugs can kill you. Several years ago, three people were permanently injured and another one died from overexposure to X-rays. Their assailant was a software bug in diagnostic medical equipment.

If they don't kill you, bugs can permanently maim your company's public image. For example, the Ashton-Tate Corporation never recovered from releasing a disastrously buggy version of its dBASE IV product. The demise predicted by many experts was averted when Borland International acquired Ashton-Tate.

And even if you aren't killed or maimed, bugs can end up costing you a bundle. According to Gregory Pope, director of validation technology at Tiburon Systems, Inc., "A bug that may take a half-day to fix in the creation process may take a week or more once the application is out in the field."

To help software vendors and organizations develop bug-free code the first time around, automated software testing tool-kits—which use advanced tools and technologies to eliminate code errors—have been developed. The market's reaction to these products is generally positive.

Other companies have found other ways to develop bug-free software. In many, this involves sharing applications with as many users and departments as possible. According to Frederick Gault, vice-president at The San Francisco Canyon Company (a software development shop), "The best bug detector we've ever found is lots of hands-on end-users . . . and that doesn't mean only programmers, who are often so ingrained with preconceived notions of what the program can do that they overlook the obvious. Instead, get people who are unfamiliar with the program to put it through the paces."

Some organizations have developed "useability labs" to test out programs that were developed in-house. Many of the labs videotape end-users as they work with the new software. This is done not only to help the developers ferret out bugs, but also to determine whether users will actually use the new programs.

Commercial vendors often get numerous end-users involved in finding bugs in their products during alpha and beta testing. However, many general and MIS managers concur that this luxury cannot always be feasibly incorporated with in-house development projects.

Still, many users feel that no expense should be spared when weeding out software bugs. As noted by Clem Hergenhan, president of CSF Corporation (a Somerville, N.J.-based telecommunication consulting firm), "If you put a buggy piece of software out in the field, there's a good chance that it's going to blow up in your face."

Adapted from Daly (1992).

DISCUSSION

1. In the long run, how can bug-free software save money for an organization?

2. Do you think it is a good idea to get end-users directly involved in testing new programs? Why or why not?

3. Which do you think is better? Encouraging programmers to cut back on program testing and debugging efforts so that they can deliver applications more quickly—or accepting lengthy applications backlogs? Explain your reasoning.

Chapter

17

End-User Computing and Development

After completing this chapter, you will be able to:

Describe what is meant by end-user computing

List several of the areas into which end-user applications fall

Discuss the benefits and problems of end-user computing

Name and describe the three principal approaches to end-user computing

Describe the types of services provided by information centers

Discuss the characteristics of effective information center management

Chapter 17 focuses on the computing and development activities performed by end-users. With the widespread availability of inexpensive microcomputer systems and the introduction of easy-to-use software, end-users (such as, executives, line managers, staff professionals, and support personnel) are more than ever before planning and acquiring computer systems to meet their own personal business needs. Many industry observers see the state of today's end-user computing and development as the start of a major change, rather than as just another passing fad. Consequently, it has become a top MIS priority in many organizations and an area that most MIS students will encounter as their careers unfold.

The chapter opens with a general discussion of today's end-user computing environment and how it evolved. Next, we cover the types of end-user computing needs commonly found in practice and the products that vendors have developed in response to those needs. These topics are followed by a discussion of the benefits and problems arising from end-user computing. Finally, we address some approaches to managing end-user activities and examine the current and future roles of the corporate information center—the facility many firms use in order to systematically respond to the growing need for end-user computing tools.

PERSPECTIVES ON END-USER COMPUTING

Before we discuss end-user computing, it is important to define some significant terms. We will also briefly explore how end-user computing has evolved to its current state.

The End-User Environment

An end-user, or user, is a person who needs the outputs produced by application software to perform his or her job. A company president reading a specialized report of quarterly profits generated by the organization's management reporting system (MRS), a secretary typing a memo on a word processor, and an accountant using a spreadsheet are all examples of end-users. **End-user computing (EUC)** is the involvement of end-users (including employees, managers, and executives) in the development and use of information systems. As the field of end-user computing evolves, more end-users are becoming directly involved in satisfying their data and information needs.

When we focus on the computer skills they possess, three categories of end-users may be observed: nonskilled, semiskilled, and skilled. *Nonskilled end-users* can, at best, perform only simple data-entry and selection tasks, such as filling data into templates or choosing among options presented on a screen. These end-users are not computer literate and must be heavily directed by the computer system (for example, by templates, graphical user interfaces with pointing devices, and easy-to-understand menus) to perform tasks that involve a lot of keyboard work or choice selection and that are low in computer-knowledge content. *Semiskilled end-users* can work with nonprocedurally oriented software tools that require a minimum level of computer knowledge—for instance, tools such as word processors, spreadsheets, and the fourth-generation languages available with many database management systems. *Skilled end-users* can write their own programs, as well as do all of the tasks that can be performed by semiskilled and unskilled users.

Computer professionals may sometimes be considered end-users, but most often, they are not. For example, an MIS manager using a spreadsheet to perform planning and budgeting tasks for the MIS department is an end-user while in this role. If the same manager later uses a 4GL to help the director of marketing prepare a report, the MIS manager will not be in an end-user role (but the director of marketing will). New products such as CASE workbenches, discussed in Chapters 14 and 15, are examples of software tools that are targeted to systems analysts and programmers operating in end-user roles as MIS professionals.

Strictly speaking, end-user computing is when the end-user actually uses a computer system in a hands-on way in order to get useful outputs from it. Some examples are an airline agent interacting at a terminal with a real-time reservations system, a manager using a 4GL to key in a report specification, and an executive using an electronic spreadsheet to prepare a budget.

When an end-user or a department of end-users takes the initiative to develop its own information systems—independent of formal MIS initiatives, approval, and financing—this process is known as end-user development. In many instances, the end-user may be assisted by MIS professionals when selecting and using information systems resources. Usually, however, the role of the MIS professional is to act as an advisor; normally, the responsibility for successful development is completely in the user's hands.

Although end-user computing and end-user development can be considered as two different concepts, they are interchangeable to most people. Today, many end-users perform development tasks as they do their computing. For instance, a dBASE user may often both set up his or her databases (a development activity) and use those databases to update information (a computing activity). Thus, in this text, we use the term "end-user computing (EUC)" to refer to both the computing and development activities performed by users.

A comparison of end-user computing and other approaches to systems development was provided in Chapter 14 (Figure 14.8, page 613). Particular application conditions that favor end-user development were summarized in Figure 14.6 (page 610). Before proceeding further, you may want to review these figures and our introductory comments on EUC in Chapter 14. Doing so should help clarify how EUC is different from the other systems development approaches we discussed in Chapters 14, 15, and 16.

Evolution of End-User Computing

During the early days of computing, end-users rarely interacted with computer systems at all. These were the days before interactive displays, friendly programming languages, graphical user interfaces, and easy-to-understand computer systems were widespread. A large corporation generally had one or two mainframes, an orientation toward punched-card input, and a heavy emphasis on third-generation and low-level languages. Because this computing environment was not open to users, if they wanted any output, it had to be provided by programmers who would interpret their needs and translate those needs into a program. Before managers had on-line access to reports, only hardcopy, report-type (MRS) output was available. In some organizations, on-line access to MRS-generated reports is still not available.

The direct involvement of end-users in computing activities began in the early 1970s with the introduction of departmental minicomputers. These machines were purchased by individual departments—such as accounting or engineering—specifically to handle either the transaction processing or information needs of those departments. Departmental minis accommodated faster and more convenient access to data, better local control, and shorter application development cycles. Although they were an improvement over past ways of meeting user needs, departmental minis represented only the initial spark in the blaze of end-user computing to follow.

The development of microminiaturized logic and memory chips throughout the 1970s started the big push toward end-user computing. These hardware elements made interactive display devices possible—and, more importantly, complete microcomputer systems. The development of complete systems soon gave way to an explosion in the development and availability of end-user software. The spreadsheet, for instance, which many managers today find invaluable, was first developed as a microcomputer tool. In fact, many people credit the spreadsheet as the first microcomputing product that made business people really notice that the microcomputer could be an extremely valuable organizational tool.

When IBM moved into the microcomputer market in 1981, the microcomputing movement was suddenly legitimatized for many people who wondered whether it would ever be a serious business machine. During the years that followed this movement, mainframe-type applications that were traditionally not in the realm of the end-user were successfully developed for both midrange systems and microcomputers. Even today, as software firms in the microcomputer area rush to meet new user demands, people want most of the same creative, user-friendly types of interfaces found in microcomputer packages to be incorporated into mainframe software. Many maintenance software vendors are responding to these requests.

After microcomputers became popular, even more useful software became available, as did gateways for communicating with corporate mainframes. Information about microcomputers popped up everywhere: in *Fortune*, *Time*, *Newsweek*, local newspapers, and even television. For example, during major televised sporting events, expensive advertisements targeted to managers discussed downloading data, local area networks, and desktop publishing—a sign that microcomputing had made its mark in business. Today, such advertising continues, but the products include imaging systems, multimedia systems, and GUI operating systems/environments such as OS/2 and Microsoft Windows.

The growing demand for application development has also fueled the movement in end-user computing. For several years, an ever-increasing need to apply the computer to various sorts of work has existed. This had overwhelmed the programming staff available in many organizations and has resulted in a waiting list for applications. Users might wait months, or even years, for a re-quested new program to be developed. In many large companies, in fact, this **applications backlog** is 2–4 years, and it is estimated to be growing at a rate of 25 percent per year. As we discussed previously, this is only the visible backlog. Many users sense that their needs will never be met, so they never submit re-quests for new applications—even though they feel such applications are needed. This creates an invisible backlog that MIT researchers estimate to aver-age 176 percent of the visible backlog.

Such applications backlogs and slow responses to user needs make many end-users resentful toward their MIS departments and toward MIS policies. In addition, an arrogance still exists among some MIS professionals that makes them more likely to tell users what they will provide instead of asking what users need. Obviously, such arrogance fuels user dissatisfaction with the MIS department in many organizations. Some experts feel that the failure of MIS to fully support legitimate end-user needs is a major force behind the end-user revolution. Many users are tired of the lack of responsiveness of MIS to their needs and would rather do it themselves. Increasing computer knowledge and sophistication among end-users has also enhanced their confi-dence, and many feel that they are capable of controlling their own computing destinies. The formal response of many organizations is to recognize the legiti-macy of their gripes and involve users directly with the computer as much as possible.

What began then, and is still evolving, might be called the end-user involve-ment era in computer history; it is changing the face of MIS drastically. Indeed, the percentage of end-users directly involved in processing and development activities has continually increased and should further expand in the years ahead (see Figure 17.1).

END-USER APPLICATIONS

A complete list of the applications that motivate end-users to employ comput-ing resources or to acquire their own computing resources—if such a list could be prepared—would be extensive. Thus, we will not attempt to enumerate these applications. Here, we will look at a few important application areas and at the types of software products that cater to them. All of these applications can be accomplished entirely on many microcomputer systems. Certain applica-tions, such as reporting and display retrieval, are often also mainframe-based, requiring either a display terminal or a micro-mainframe interface.

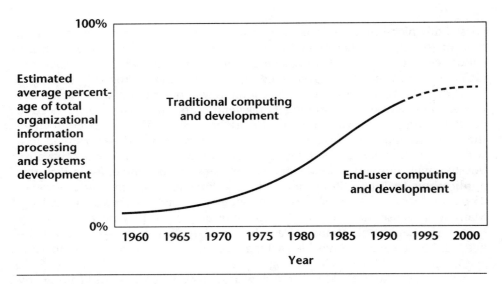

100%

Estimated
average percent-
age of total
organizational
information
processing
and systems
development

**Traditional computing
and development**

**End-user computing
and development**

0%

| 1960 | 1965 | 1970 | 1975 | 1980 | 1985 | 1990 | 1995 | 2000 |

Year

Figure 17.1   Past and projected growth in end-user computing.

Application Areas

Many end-user applications fall into one or more of eight areas: data entry, document processing, data management, extract reports, display retrieval, schedules and lists, analysis, and presentation. Each of these will be discussed briefly.

Data Entry

Data entry refers to entering data into the computer system. For example, unskilled and semiskilled end-users will often interface with templates and menu prompts to enter data into large databases. In some applications, such users may also be allowed to modify or delete data. Data entry is also commonly an added operation to most other forms of end-user computing.

Many data-entry operations are part of transaction processing operations. In this case, the entire application was probably developed by computer professionals and not by end-users.

Document Processing

Document processing includes such activities as the preparation of memos, letters, and other types of correspondence, as well as such tasks as electronic document management and routing. Most document preparation and document management activities can be performed with a relatively simple word processor. Document routing is often performed by electronic mail and image processing systems. An office or department may even have an integrated office system that ties together word processing, electronic mail, and imaging applications. As you may recall, such document management systems were discussed in Chapter 12.

Data Management

Data management refers to the set of computing and development activities involved with maintaining large, computerized banks of data; for example, records on employees, customers, students, or products. The types of activities that comprise data management, and the file and database management software used to implement these activities, were discussed in Chapter 7.

On stand-alone microcomputer systems, the end-user often creates, manages, and uses an application's file or database. Potential problems are associated with allowing users to do this; some of these will be discussed later in this chapter. When end-users employ workstations or microcomputer systems connected to mainframes to perform job-related duties, they were probably not involved in the original creation of the file and probably are not directly involved in managing it.

Extract Reports

Extract reports are business reports that use data extracted from files or databases. For instance, end-users can create a company phone book with a 4GL by extracting the employee name and phone extension fields from all records of an employee file. A user could, of course, create reports that consist only of selected records from a file. A user can also do arithmetic on report records and sort records in various ways quite easily. Many of the fourth-generation languages that are included in file and database management software packages have comprehensive report-writer features to carry out such tasks; some also perform data validation and file updating. The range of data management features available with mainframe- and minicomputer-based packages is likely to be considerably greater than those available with microcomputer-based packages.

Display Retrieval

Preparing extract reports normally involves permanent hardcopy output (often with an abundance of information), formatting information into a report style, and a completeness normally attributed to a report. Display retrieval, on the other hand, generally involves temporarily summoning only a few pieces of output to the display screen. For instance, a sales manager may want to know the suppliers of products B1655 and B1656. A few seconds later, the manager may need to know how many units of product F1633 are in inventory and, next, the size and date of the next scheduled delivery of that product. Retrieval of this type—in which queries span across several logical files—are often best done with the aid of a database management system and query products.

Schedules and Lists

Schedules and lists consist of such outputs as budgets, profit-and-loss statements, and annuity and depreciation schedules. These types of outputs are often created entirely by the user. That is, the user enters the data needed for the application and creates the formulas used to manipulate the data in the desired way. Most of these types of application needs can be satisfied by electronic spreadsheets and can be performed by semiskilled end-users.

Analysis

Analysis involves drawing conclusions from a set of data. Analysis can be performed by end-users in numerous ways; for example, what-if and why types of analyses, sensitivity analysis, statistical analysis, and mathematical modeling. Chapter 10 covered these types of analyses when we discussed decision support systems. Depending on the level of sophistication of the analysis required and the software in use, some analysis tasks can be performed by semiskilled or unskilled users.

Presentation

Many end-users, especially managers, need to put information into a highly presentable form. For example, presentations made at meetings often require that information be shown in an easily understood (and visually impressive) graphical format, such as a pie chart or a bar chart—both of which can be generated using presentation graphics and spreadsheet packages. As another example, reports going to superiors and important clients often have greater impact if they are printed using attractive fonts, such as those available with desktop publishing software and the latest versions of word-processing packages—especially those that run under GUI operating environments or systems, such as Microsoft Windows or Macintosh System 7.

BENEFITS AND CHALLENGES OF END-USER COMPUTING

Although end-user computing provides numerous benefits to the organization, it also creates many hazards. Here, we will look at some of the benefits and management challenges arising from end-user computing. Later, we will explore some approaches and guidelines to the management of end-user computing.

Benefits

End-user computing gives both users and the organization many distinct benefits, which are summarized in Figure 17.2 and discussed in the following subsections.

Increased Individual Performance

Perhaps the single most important benefit of EUC is increased individual performance—from the viewpoint of both effectiveness and efficiency. Most people agree that decision support system (DSS) tools in the hands of informed managers usually make those managers much more effective. For example, a sales manager using a communications package to retrieve market information available from a commercial database or information service might effectively

▪ Increased individual performance	▪ Increased competitive advantage
▪ Easier and more direct implementation	▪ Reduced applications backlog
▪ Enhanced computer and technological literacy	

Figure 17.2 Potential benefits from end-user computing. The rapid growth of end-user computing in organizations has contributed to growth in several information technology areas, including personal computing, decision support systems, and office information systems.

monitor more variables than he or she could do otherwise. Better decisions could then result. Or, instead of better decisions, that same manager might make decisions faster. Consequently, he or she will have more time to be effective in other ways.

Unfortunately, increased effectiveness—while potentially the most important benefit to the organization—is usually the hardest to cost-justify. Fortunately, however, many types of end-user tools that help a manager become more effective—such as 4GL software and such hardware as microcomputer systems, display terminals, and communications devices—are now inexpensive enough to warrant bypassing formal cost-justification procedures.

End-user tools such as word processors, desktop publishing systems, and calendaring software enable work to be done more efficiently. For instance, the use of word processors allows letters and other documents to be prepared at a lower cost with greater speed and accuracy (that is, cheaper, faster, and better). Many of these efficiency-oriented tools can also result in increased effectiveness. For example, word processors make it easy to create clear, persuasive documents—and polished documents often influence recipients favorably.

Easier and More Direct Implementation

In Chapters 14–16, we noted that one of the problems that may trouble the traditional systems development approach is an insufficient level of end-user involvement. This can lead to serious implementation problems. For example, the system might not be what end-users expected; worse, it might not satisfy their data and information needs. Or the end-user might feel removed from or intimidated by the final system. With end-user development, it is more likely that the final system will be exactly what the end-user wants and expects.

Technological Literacy

As users become more sophisticated with end-user tools, it is likely that benefits will accrue that management never expected. When new tools become available in the marketplace, word-of-mouth often propels them into appropriate end-user areas. As workers become more knowledgeable about information technology, they should be better able to assimilate new technologies into the organization and thus help the company take early advantage of any benefits that may occur. Consequently, an increased level of computer and information literacy might enable the organization to gain a competitive edge just by being there first.

Competitive Advantage

In earlier chapters, we covered numerous examples in which companies employed end-user technologies to establish a competitive advantage. For instance, establishing interorganizational systems (IOS) by putting terminals at customer or supplier sites are illustrations of providing end-user services of some type. Organizations that engage in such practices may benefit by locking customers in and locking competitors out. In interorganizational systems that reach out to customers, the end-users (customers) work outside the organization that owns the terminals. When interorganizational systems are established that lock in suppliers, the end-users are within the organization (for example, the purchasing staff, which scans supplier databases for prices and places orders). In these instances, benefits to the organization may include shifting inventory carrying costs to the supplier, greater control over suppliers, increased ordering efficiency, enhanced quality of incoming supplies, and easier shopping for the best price.

Reducing the Applications Backlog

Theoretically, as end-users become capable of meeting their own computing needs, both the visible and invisible applications backlogs may reduce. How much of the visible backlog will disappear is anyone's guess. According to one study of 21 St. Louis information center managers, the effect of EUC on the existing visible backlog is slight. Often, the application queue that makes up the visible backlog consists of large, complex systems end-users are incapable of developing on their own. However, the effect on the invisible backlog appears to be significant; many applications—that traditionally would become part of the invisible backlog—are now developed and implemented by end-users.

Challenges and Problems

From a management perspective, three of the most critical challenges associated with end-user computing and development concern cost control, product control, and data control. The emphasis given to computing activities is another potential problem area.

Cost Control

Because end-user computing is usually initiated through separate departments and supported by their own budgets—not the MIS department's budget—many organizations do not really know the total amount that they are spending on information technology and applications. Because end-users often buy such tools as microcomputers, spreadsheets, and database management systems from within their own budgets (without going through formal cost-justification procedures), many individual and group purchases are not made as cost-effectively as possible. For instance, the same software package may be purchased repeatedly, each time by a different group within the firm; as a result, greater savings through quantity discounts or multiuser licenses are not obtained. Also, in many organizations, the minimum purchase requiring formal cost-justification reviews has increased; this means that more users and departments are acquiring software and hardware without first securing the formal approval from upper-level managers or from the MIS department. Furthermore, because end-users often make their decisions independently, they generally do not consider whether the total organizational effort in end-user computing is being optimized.

In many organizations, EUC-related expenses are substantial. By some estimates, end-user computing now accounts for about a third of the total computing budget among the top firms—and that percentage is increasing rapidly. A survey of large organizations estimates that end-user computing accounted for approximately 40–50 percent of all organizational computing costs; at Xerox, it is estimated that EUC will plateau at about 75 percent of the total computing budget. Phillip Pyburn relates how end-user costs can sneak up on organizations: "Occasionally several hundred (or thousand) machines have been purchased at once by a central authority, but more often they have simply accumulated 1 or 2 at a time as separate purchases by many managers. With their low unit cost ($3,000–$7,000), one often hears managers dismiss such purchases as insignificant. In the aggregate, however, the investment in this computing technology can be large."

Product Control

Because end-users often make their own decisions on products, it is common to find many different products in a firm (for example, four different microcomputer-based database management systems) performing the same function. While having different products that do the same tasks is not necessarily a problem, difficulties may develop if these products are incompatible. Incompatible product proliferation is especially problematic when data cannot be transferred among applications. In addition, an unusual burden is placed on workers if they must be trained to use several packages that essentially perform the same functions.

The misuse of computer tools is another related concern. As satisfied users leave the information center with their products, they may start solving the wrong problems, solving the right problems with the wrong tool, or using the right tool with the wrong model. A gap often exists between the job knowledge of the end-user and the technical expertise of the information center staff. Often, too, little follow-up is done by the information center to see if users are employing EUC tools in an acceptable and effective manner.

Data Control

Data control involves all issues relating to the accuracy, integrity, security, and privacy of data. One of the most serious problems facing organizations today is deciding how far to let users go when creating their own microcomputer systems. End-users are, for the most part, not professional model builders or model testers. Also, because end-users are often not aware of efficient input techniques, data that could be entered automatically (with greater accuracy) are often entered manually instead. One MIT study, for instance, reported that less than 10 percent of the data used by microcomputer-based end-users was obtained directly from transaction processing systems, whereas more than half of the data were keyed in directly from computer-generated reports. Furthermore, issues such as security, audit trails, checks and balances, documentation, and backup are often not matters of high priority to end-users. Even if they were, it is doubtful that many end-users could (or would take the time to) handle them as completely as their organizations would like.

Although the information center may exert some control over how end-user systems are initially developed, unsupervised data could later find its way into critical decision-making processes that should be part of a larger, more formal system. If the user's microcomputer needs are seen as potentially disruptive to the organization in this regard, analysts or consultants at the information center may recommend that the user's problem should be handled as part of a formal systems development effort.

Emphasis

Some people argue that non-computer professionals can spend too much time developing computer applications and, later, using computers to the detriment of their primary job responsibilities. Phillip Pyburn writes that a senior partner in an investment firm echoed these sentiments and expressed concern over the appropriateness of highly paid money managers spending their work time programming by stating, "We pay these people a great deal of money to make good investment decisions, not write programs in Lotus."

Figure 17.3 summarizes a number of the problems associated with EUC.

MANAGING END-USER COMPUTING

According to Thomas Gerrity and John Rockart, three principal approaches to the management of end-user computing exist: monopolist, laissez-faire, and information center.

Monopolist Approach

End-user development is often perceived as a threat to the power of many MIS departments. As end-users acquire their own systems, they depend less on the resources of the MIS department to meet their needs.

In some companies, the MIS department has, at least temporarily, thwarted the onrush of end-user computing by convincing management that computer professionals should control all information processing. Thomas Gerrity and John Rockart cite an interesting example in which the MIS department of a consumer products company convinced management that it should adopt a cautious attitude toward EUC. According to the researchers, "Not only did the firm choose as the company standard a complex programming language, which is

Problems Arising From EUC

- The cost of EUC often cannot be effectively measured

- Many end-user-related costs are not formally justified in any way

- Some end-user computing costs are not optimized at the enterprise level

- End-users often buy products that are incompatible with those bought by other end-users, with whom someday they might have to integrate applications

- End-users often solve the wrong problems or apply the wrong tools and models

- The information center staff often does not follow up properly after initial end-user needs appear to be satisfied

- End-users typically do not apply rigorous data integrity or accuracy controls, making the results they get from their systems less reliable than those obtained from formal systems

- End-users typically have little security or backup on their systems

- Some end-users get carried away with their computer systems, using them inefficiently or ineffectively, to the detriment of their main job functions

- End-users are typically deficient at documentation and setting up audit trails

- End-users often fail to upgrade their systems

Figure 17.3 Potential problems that can arise from end-user computing. Despite the indisputable benefits of EUC, some problems may arise. Most of these problems revolve around two key areas: (1) overall management of EUC and (2) the dangers involved when non-MIS professionals perform systems development tasks.

inaccessible to all but the best-trained users, but it also created a set of policies that actively discourages managers from utilizing computer resources." In this firm, each microcomputer system must be carefully cost-justified and corporate databases are inaccessible to microcomputer users.

While this monopolist approach was once a viable strategy for MIS departments attempting to retain their power, it is now less popular for various reasons, including:

- The visible and invisible backlogs—and the user resentment toward MIS that these can cause—are putting pressure on management to allow end-users to create their own systems.

- The prices of computing resources are dropping.

- End-users and managers are becoming more knowledgeable about computers and about the benefits of end-user computing.

In some organizations that have tried to quash computer purchases, users have bootlegged systems by hiding computer-related acquisitions in other figures when they write proposals. For example, in one company, a user seeking a microcomputer system allegedly claimed that it was a "control instrument" in a laboratory process and buried the reference to it among other expenditures. The monopolistic approach is most likely to encourage users to "go around" or otherwise "beat" the control procedures put in place by the MIS group.

Is Your Keyboard a Health Hazard?

Monitor emissions may not be the only health threats to workers whose jobs demand long hours of work at a terminal, workstation, or personal computer. Repetitive motion injuries have increased at an alarming rate among computer keyboard users. These have resulted in a plethora of product liability lawsuits against such industry heavyweights as Apple Computer, Inc., IBM, NCR Corporation, and Northern Telecom, Inc.

"REPETITIVE MOTION INJURIES HAVE INCREASED AT AN ALARMING RATE AMONG KEYBOARD USERS."

In the past, the highest incidence of repetitive motion injuries were among blue-collar assembly-line workers whose jobs involve repetitive finger, hand, wrist, and/or arm motions. Tendinitis and carpal tunnel syndrome—which cause pain or numbness in the hands, wrists, and arms—are the most common ailments. However, over the past few years, the number of such injuries among office workers who spend most of the day working at a keyboard has dramatically increased.

Most lawsuits filed by office workers have focused on keyboard design and the lack of warnings from vendors about possible harmful effects. Juries now must decide whether the angle of the keyboard and the layout of the keys is appropriate, and if keyboards provide sufficient wrist support. The courts are also deciding if vendors should be required to put warning labels on keyboards, indicating that they could be dangerous unless regular rest breaks are taken. These lawsuits have prompted vendors to take a hard look at keyboard ergonomics and may result in significant design changes in the years ahead.

Adapted from Betts (1992).

Laissez-Faire Approach

The *laissez-faire approach* (French for "allow [them] to do") is in direct contrast to the monopolist approach. The organization's position with this approach is that end-user computing should be left completely to the discretion of the end-users themselves. Unfortunately, this approach can easily lead to chaos. End-user computing costs, which may already be substantial, can zoom out of control. As each user group does what it wants, the proliferation of technologies can make systems integration a nightmare. Small islands of technological expertise develop, so that the economies of scale usually obtained through centralized purchasing or shared knowledge are impossible to realize. Having a lot of diverse, maverick efforts can make it more difficult for the MIS department to provide any effective support.

Despite its numerous drawbacks, the laissez-faire approach might be reasonable during the early stages of EUC in an organization. In Chapter 4, we noted that the early stages of system growth are usually characterized by experimentation and free use. Hence, it might be unwise for an organization to attempt to control EUC at this point, especially if EUC expenditures are not large enough to warrant control.

Information Center Approach

The newest, and often the most sensible, approach to the management of EUC is the information center, which we will describe in detail in the next section. This approach enables users to retain the authority to care for their own needs (most end-users operate under normal budgetary constraints and are motivated to spend funds wisely) but, if properly managed, provides some control over the unbridled proliferation of end-user systems. The information center approach is usually most appropriate for organizations that have at least reached the control stage in the system growth cycle.

In practice, the best approach to take is not always clear. The essence of this problem is reflected in the comments of an MIS director of an investment firm. According to Phillip Pyburn, the director was asked by the president to get control over the influx of microcomputers: "I don't know whether I should take the lead with a strong personal computer strategy, follow the users' personal computer purchases with enough support to keep them out of trouble, or just get out of their way and simply monitor what's going on."

THE INFORMATION CENTER

The information center (IC) is relatively new to most MIS departments. It evolved from the need to help end-users and end-user departments learn about and take advantage of decision support resources. Among such resources are microcomputer systems, spreadsheet and database packages, communications packages, and fourth-generation languages. Also, with the use of microcomputing resources growing uncontrollably, a goal of many information centers is to bring about order from chaos and to serve as a clearinghouse for end-user activities. In many companies, the IC has the major responsibility for coordinating, developing, and supporting end-user activities.

The typical applications serviced by the information center—for example, advising a manager on spreadsheet packages or helping the purchasing department acquire a microcomputer system and database management software for it—do not usually require a traditional systems development process. Chapter 14 summarized the way that most end-user applications are developed in an organization.

Staffing

An information center may be staffed in many ways; Figure 17.4 shows one method.

Directing the IC is the *information center manager* or *director*. In many instances, the manager of the IC reports directly to the chief information officer

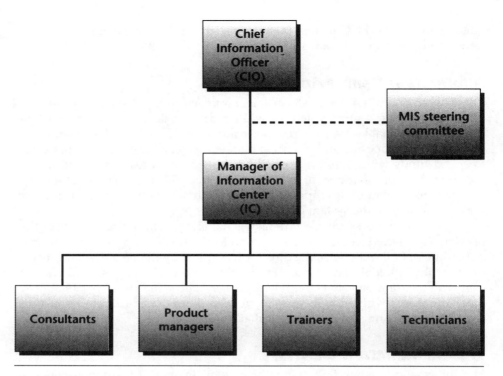

Figure 17.4 An organizational chart for an information center. Actual reporting relationships may vary among organizations, depending on the services that are provided to end-users. Figure 14.12 (page 621) illustrated one possible placement of the information center relative to other subunits within the MIS area.

(CIO) or the highest ranking MIS executive. Normally, the IC manager is an experienced systems analyst—a person with exceptional user-communications skills and a broad understanding of end-user technology areas (including microcomputer, 4GL, DSS, and database management system knowledge).

When end-users initially contact the information center for assistance, they often talk first with a person called a *consultant* or *information analyst* (an information center-based systems analyst). The job of the consultant is to diagnose end-user needs and either personally provide the help they want or put them in touch with other members of the IC staff who can help—such as product managers or trainers.

Product managers (sometimes called *specialists*) are staff personnel who specialize in specific types of end-user products. For example, one product manager may be particularly knowledgeable about IBM PC-compatible hardware. A second manager might specialize in center-supported microcomputer software products such as WordPerfect, Lotus 1-2-3, Excel, or dBASE. And a third manager might specialize in all end-user applications requiring mainframe connectivity. Whatever their specialties, product managers are responsible for seeing that users are matched with the right products. Some product managers may also have training responsibilities.

Information Center Services and Activities

Assistance in developing end-user communications interfaces	Information clearinghouse
	Installation and testing of new software/hardware
Assistance in setting up local area networks	Marketing of IC services
	Newsletter
Assistance with capacity and/or usage planning	Personal computer support
Computer literacy education	Project management for user-developed systems
Consulting services	Prototype development
Data management	Purchasing end-user hardware/software
Debugging and troubleshooting assistance	Quality assurance for user-written software
	Recommendations on hardware/software acquisitions
Documentation support for user applications, including customized documentation	Requirements analysis for end-user systems
	Security for end-user systems
End-user bulletin board systems	Support for standard products
End-user system maintenance	Technical and operational support
Hardware and software evaluation	Training for newly hired end-users
Hardware and software standards	Training users on new software/hardware
Help center with hotline service	

Figure 17.5 Examples of the types of services that information centers may provide.

Trainers work with users to teach them how to use computer technology and center-supported products. As just mentioned, many companies use product managers for training purposes. If the product manager is not qualified to provide the type of training involved, some firms will hire outside consultants to provide the training that end-users need.

Technicians support the center staff in maintaining end-user computing equipment. For example, technicians may help end-users establish communications with remote mainframes and set up local area networks.

IC Services

Figure 17.5 provides a list of the services typically provided by information centers. Many of these services involve giving advice and training. Also, because most information centers only support a finite number of products, they provide the organization with some control over the unbridled growth of end-user products.

Advice

The information center concept is still evolving. Many are set up like a typical computer store. First, a user talks to the center consultant about computing needs. Then, the user and consultant might sit down at a system and experiment with some hardware and software that seem appropriate to the user's job needs. A product manager may also be involved if the hardware or software requirements of the user go beyond the consultant's expertise.

Because the user or department will often acquire the computing resources from its own budget (not the MIS department's budget), the center has little control over the final choices made by the user. However, the user must understand that the center can, realistically, support only a finite number of products. If the center supports only Brand X spreadsheets and the user wants Brand Y, the user may have to bear complete responsibility for training, advising, and dealing with any problems that later arise.

Many information centers run a hotline service to help end-users with problems after an application is in use. Also, some centers audit end-user applications on a regular basis to ensure that they are working the way they should.

Training

Today, with so many end-users needing knowledge about computer technology to do their jobs more effectively, training has become a top priority—and a major expense. As we noted in Chapter 16, the amount that U.S. firms annually spend on end-user training is estimated at more than $800 million. Information center training can be provided on an individual, department-wide, or company-wide basis. Training may be directed to a specific need or a specific application, such as training the purchasing department to use dBASE or RBase to store and access purchasing records. It can also be aimed at increasing overall company literacy in a general or specific area of computing, such as instructing managers in the variety of end-user tools available in today's marketplace.

One common training objective is to concentrate efforts on identifying and teaching functional support personnel—enthusiastic and computer-literate end-users who can later assist other end-users. These people are sometimes referred to as **power users**. A few years ago, the average information center staff spent a lot of its time providing beginning microcomputer training and answering elementary support questions. Today, in many firms, power users have assumed that burden within user departments, making it unnecessary for users to contact the IC to answer every question or to solve every problem. Some experts feel that most IC activities will eventually be decentralized to functional departments, each of which will have its own resident power user who assists others with their application needs.

There is no substitute for good training. If the organization is truly serious about providing support for end-user computing, it is important for the IC to devote time to training users in areas other than purely technical ones. For example, a user who is trained in the problems that can surface when building a cheap, maverick computer system might resist the urge to buy a discounted (but inadequate) microcomputer system. Also, a user trained about the need for requirements analysis will be less likely to purchase a certain computer system or software package just because everyone else in the company has it. Training is invaluable for communicating potential problems or issues such as data integrity, technological versus functional obsolescence, compatibility among products and technologies, proper care of microcomputer systems, and security.

Effective Information Center Management

Unfortunately, most of the end-user management problems we identified earlier do not have a single, simple solution. In the following subsections, we will look at numerous solutions that might be collectively applied to manage these problems. We will also examine some general rules for effective information center management.

Develop Standards

Many times, it is useful for end-users to do the same tasks in the same way. For instance, we mentioned earlier that it is often a wise, company-wide policy to allow end-users to choose only the hardware and software products that are on an approved list. This should ensure some uniform buying standards. Furthermore, many organizations have standards in other areas, particularly with respect to the downloading and uploading of data.

Downloading refers to situations in which data are brought "down" from a large computer system to a smaller one. Downloading data manually from a mainframe or minicomputer database onto a microcomputer system often involves users re-typing the data from a printout or screen display. Thus, the data that are entered might be outdated, the user might make an error in retyping, or the user might take a shortcut and re-enter only a non-representative subset of these data. Any of these actions, of course, leads to inaccurate data. If, instead, the user has a direct micro-to-mainframe link, data can be downloaded quickly and automatically, virtually without error. Of course, this approach has some disadvantages: such links are expensive, involve extra security precautions, and require extra user training.

Uploading involves end-users creating data at a display terminal or microcomputer workstation and sending them "up" to a mainframe or mini, where they can be accessed by others. In on-line transaction processing operations, where data-entry clerks are involved, uploading is necessary; numerous built-in controls are established to ensure that only accurate and complete data are uploaded. However, a manager who creates his or her own decision-making data is different. Built-in validation controls may not be necessary in such cases, but controlling or prohibiting a manager's uploading capability might be. Standards can also be usefully applied in the areas of creating documentation, establishing audit trails, and securing individual workstations from malicious intent.

Audit End-User Activities

Performing regular audits is the only way to consistently discover what end-users are spending on hardware and software, what types of products they are using to meet their needs, and whether or not they are using their microcomputer systems productively. Depending on the technical nature of

The Boss's New Assistant is Digital

Personal Digital Assistants (PDA) are the newest, and smallest, types of personal computers. They most commonly perform datebook, Rolodex, notepad, and fax functions that busy executives need to help them do their jobs. They are available from an increasing number of vendors, but Apple's Newton is one of the most popular models.

"ALMOST ALL OF THE PERSONAL DIGITAL ASSISTANTS ON THE MARKET HAVE HANDWRITING RECOGNITION CAPABILITIES . . ."

Newton measures 6-by-8" and allows its owner to perform calculations, list phone numbers, and maintain schedules and to-do lists. It also contains the communications technology needed to send and receive faxes and to retrieve data from computers back at the office. Newton's software is user-friendly—all a user normally needs to do is to write a plain English command on the screen. For example, after composing a message, writing the command "Fax to Fred" causes Newton to look up Fred's fax number and send the message. Newton does not have a keyboard.

Almost all of the personal digital assistants on the market have handwriting recognition capabilities, but most new models are differentiating themselves from one another. For example, an IBM PDA uses cellular-phone networks to pick up stock quotes, news, and other data. Other vendors have developed digital assistants that include travel guides (containing maps), restaurant guides, and foreign language translations. While these more specialized digital assistants appeal to a limited set of managers, they indicate that we should not think of a PDA as only offering office assistance. Indeed, in the future, it may not be uncommon for a manager to have several digital assistants.

Adapted from Rebello, Brandt, Cox and Lewyn (1992).

---

the tasks involved, responsibilities in these areas can be shared by the internal auditing staff and the information center.

Provide for Follow-Up

The information center should follow up on both successful and unsuccessful encounters with end-users. If an application was successfully installed, the center should determine if the users are following through with their original plans and if they are using their systems correctly. This feedback is also valuable for getting ideas about other products or services that the center might need to offer in the future. Of course, it is also a way for the center to really observe how well their advice worked.

Train Users to Solve Problems

Many information centers train end-users in tools and techniques, then let them try to pinpoint and solve their own problems. A better technique is to train end-users to proceed in a manner similar to formal systems development. In other words, users should be trained to first study the decision-making environment to find out what and where the real problems are that might be solvable with information processing tools. Then, the tools and techniques that may be most helpful should be identified. Studying the problem area in this way can help uncover shortcuts or lead to the identification of add-on packages that could immeasurably benefit the user. By implementing such a training approach, the information center can help to make the user as independent as possible, so that he or she can eventually solve and troubleshoot problems alone.

Strategic IC Management

In many cases, the information center can be seen as an organization within an organization. The product it markets is service. The consumers of that product are end-users. Thus, the information center can benefit from the same type of strategic planning that a CIO might use. Some techniques for effectively managing the information center in this way include:

- Moving the information center in the same strategic direction as the host organization.

- Aggressively developing new products for users, rather than just reacting with routine answers (in other words, managing proactively rather than reactively).

- Honing the skills of the IC staff through ongoing training programs.

- Keeping end-users informed about ongoing activities—such as new products, services, and educational resources—on a regular basis.

- Establishing the information center as a central source of information about all types of end-user tools.

As we have just discovered, information centers can play a valuable role in providing support for end-user computing. Experts predict that they will continue to evolve and play important roles in the years ahead. Figure 17.6 summarizes many of the points that we made about information centers and the potential benefits they provide. Currently, the information center is probably the MIS segment that most needs the whole-hearted support of managers and end-users.

Summary

An end-user (or user) is the person who needs the outputs produced by application software to perform his or her job. End-users may be skilled, semiskilled, or nonskilled. When end-users develop their own systems—independent of a formal development approach—this process is known as end-user development. Although computing and development by end-users may be considered as separate activities, in practice they are difficult to separate and the term "end-user computing (EUC)" is used to include both.

End-user computing has evolved for numerous reasons. Fueling the trend toward end-user computing are advances in hardware technology (which led to inexpensive display devices and microcomputer systems); the development of

Potential Benefits of Information Centers

The services of the IC can contribute to supporting the competitive position of the organization

The IC can be a focal point for the implementation of corporate information plans relative to end-user computing

User-developed systems can help alleviate MIS development backlogs

End-user productivity can be enhanced

An IC can provide first-line support for end-users

An IC can be a clearinghouse to share solutions and applications among users

End-users often find the IC less intimidating and more understanding of their needs than the MIS department as a whole

End-users can be educated about the long-run implications of information system acquisitions

Compatibility among systems can be encouraged or enforced

The IC can usually obtain stronger vendor support and better hardware/software pricing than single end-users

Advice can be given regarding the benefits of developing systems on microcomputers versus mainframes

Users can be educated about standards for developing end-user systems

Individualized, flexible training can be provided on an as-needed basis

Users can be educated regarding data backup, data integrity, and security precautions, plus organizational standards in these areas

Users can be educated about uploading/downloading procedures and standards

Figure 17.6   Some of the potential advantages of information centers.

user-friendly software for microcomputers; and the applications backlog, both visible and invisible, in large companies.

End-user applications generally fall into the areas of data entry, document processing, data management, extract reports, schedules and lists, and analysis and presentation. Typically, data entry can be performed by the most unsophisticated types of end-users. Document processing refers to the application of such computer technologies as word processing and desktop publishing. Data management concerns activities involved with managing banks of data. Extract reports use data extracted from files or databases. Schedules and lists involve the development of outputs such as budgets, profit-and-loss statements, and depreciation schedules. Analysis involves drawing conclusions from data, often with the use of models. With presentation applications, users can prepare information in an easy-to-understand format.

End-user computing has both benefits and problems. The benefits include: increased individual performance, easier and more direct implementation of applications, technological literacy for more people, competitive advantage for the organization, and a reduction in the applications backlog. The problem areas include cost and product proliferation, applying end-user tools inappropriately or incorrectly, lack of follow-up, poor control of data, inadequate security, and wasting time on marginal applications.

Three principal approaches to managing end-user computing have developed. The monopolist approach is followed by MIS departments that try to limit end-user computing and to retain for themselves all information processing control. The laissez-faire approach advocates end-users meeting their own needs, with minimal organizational interference. The information center approach (the most common one) strikes a balance between the other two approaches; that is, it allows users to care for their own needs, but it provides some control over the unbridled development of systems.

The information center (IC) evolved from the need to help end-users learn about and take advantage of information systems. An information center staff typically consists of a manager, who runs the center; consultants (information analysts), who help diagnose user needs; product managers, who specialize in specific end-user products; trainers, who teach users how to use computer technology and center-supported products; and technicians, who maintain end-user-related equipment.

The main role of most information centers is to provide advice and training to users. One common training objective is to identify and educate enthusiastic, computer-literate end-users—known as power users—who might be able to help other end-users.

Numerous solutions can be applied to the problems of managing end-user computing. These include developing standards for users to follow, auditing end-user activities, providing for follow-up, training users to solve problems, and managing the IC strategically.

KEY TERMS

Applications backlog

End-user computing (EUC)

Power user

REVIEW QUESTIONS

1. What is an end-user? What are the differences among the various types of end-users?

2. What, precisely, is meant by the terms "end-user computing" and "end-user development"?

3. Explain the difference between the visible and invisible applications backlogs. How are each of these related to and affected by end-user computing?

4. Identify the major application areas of end-user computing.

5. Describe the benefits and management challenges associated with end-user computing.

6. Provide several examples showing how end-user computing can result in competitive advantage.

7. What approaches have organizations followed in the managing of end-user computing? Describe the differences among these approaches.

8. Describe the various specialists found in the information center and explain what each of them does.

9. What types of services are provided by the information center?

10. Are mainframe data downloading and uploading managed differently in end-user computing environments? Why or why not?

11. Describe the major issues and activities associated with the effective management of the information center.

12. Identify the types of activities performed in the proactive (strategic) management of the information center.

DISCUSSION QUESTIONS

1. Power users can present both opportunities and problems to an organization. Identify some of each.

2. Standards are a big issue in end-user computing and development. What specific topics should end-user standards cover? How does the stages-of-growth model discussed in Chapter 4 relate to the concern for setting end-user computing standards?

3. In what ways are end-user computing, office systems, and decision support systems related?

4. Is the information center approach always the best alternative to managing end-user computing? Why or why not?

CASE STUDY

When It Comes to Downsizing, NCR Speaks from Experience

NCR Corporation is one of the major vendors that is peddling distributed and co-operative computing solutions to the market. As noted throughout this book, the move toward distributed systems in most organizations almost always translates into downsizing—the offloading of large-system (mainframe or minicomputer) applications onto networks that support desktop computers and servers. Most organizations do this to reduce costs, and this was one of NCR's primary motivations to downsize.

Many companies are reluctant to share trade secrets about how they are cutting costs and implementing competitive applications. NCR found that it is possible to do both these things simultaneously. It also found it advantageous to tell others about its accomplishments. NCR's credibility with customers is increased by its willingness to reveal the downsizing techniques it has learned—in some cases, the hard way—while moving from mainframe to client/server platforms.

In the mid-1980s, NCR realized that it had to make substantial changes in the way it managed MIS. One of its first actions was to adopt a 4GL for program development. It also began distributing its databases to client/server local area networks. By 1990, it had developed considerable expertise in implementing client/server applications.

The payoffs from these actions are significant. The company pulled the plug on four of the eight mainframes that used to be supported at NCR headquarters. Programmer productivity improved by more than 180 percent since 1987 and the time it takes to develop new applications was reduced by a factor of five. These benefits are attributed to a combination of factors, including the use of fourth-generation languages, CASE tools, and client/server architectures.

NCR realizes that it can never go back to its old mainframe-based computing paradigm. Luckily, it has no inclination to do so. Insiders estimate that if they stay on the course they chose, they will experience a similar jump in productivity improvement between 1993 and 1997.

These changes have energized everyone in the organization. They want to share what they have learned about making the transition from centralized to distributed systems with customers—both the good and the bad.

Not all of it is good. Some of the negatives about downsizing that NCR shares with customers include:

- Programmers who are used to developing applications on mainframes can have a tough time adapting to the new tools, procedures, and methods needed to develop applications for client/server local area networks.

- There is rarely enough training (or training money) available for end-users or for LAN network staff personnel.

- Managing all the disparate parts of a distributed network is a complex, often awkward, process. In many organizations, network management means supporting several operating systems, many different types of hardware and peripherals, and dozens of communications protocols. It is often analogous to being an air traffic controller in wartime.

- Implementing dispersed applications at various domestic and international sites can turn out to be a logistical nightmare—especially when vendor support and communications regulations vary across geographies.

- Consultants and external help are often essential for the successful de-

velopment of the first few client/server applications.

Despite these drawbacks, customers find the downsizing and distributed computing seminars sponsored and taught by NCR to be inspiring. NCR's success with downsizing also lets prospects know that there is light at the end of the tunnel. Its willingness to share what it learned from its transition to client/server systems may provide NCR with a competitive edge in its industry during the 1990s.

Adapted from Gantz (1992).

DISCUSSION

1. Why do you think companies are reluctant to publicize how they are using informaion technology to reduce costs and to be more competitive in their industry?

2. In the long run, do you think it will be beneficial for NCR to share its downsizing experiences with customers? Why or why not?

3. Describe how each of the following can help companies reduce costs or enhance productivity: downsizing, using fourth-generation languages for application development, and using CASE tools.

Part SIX

MIS Management

Chapter 18
Information Resource Management

Chapter 19
Selected Issues in MIS Management

Chapter

18

Information Resource Management

After completing this chapter, you will be able to:

Describe the responsibilities and roles of the chief information officer (CIO)

Appreciate the role of strategic planning in the management of information systems

Identify, discuss, and compare various MIS cost-justification methods

Describe the role of risk in selecting MIS projects

Explain several methods used to price MIS services

Identify several approaches used to develop MIS budgets

Explain how the MIS function can be evaluated

Explain why downsizing and outsourcing are becoming more prevalent

The previous chapters addressed a number of the more technical issues associated with the building of information systems. In those chapters, we considered such topics as alternative approaches to systems development, design tools used to develop new systems, project and implementation schedules, and so on. In this chapter and the next, we address management issues related to information systems. This topic area is sometimes referred to as information resource management.

Like any other functional business area, MIS involves a management process that consists of planning, organizing, control, and appraisal. The outputs of an MIS are the data and information resources (many of which are intangible) provided by them to managers and users throughout the rest of the organization. The quality of MIS outputs depends on several factors, including: (1) the beginning mix of MIS resources (the products and services already in place), (2) the MIS budget as allocated by the organization, and (3) the effective management of MIS resources and budget allocations by the CIO and MIS staff. The various components of this performance model, illustrated in Figure 18.1, are the subject of this chapter. As this model shows, the success of MIS is also determined by the organizational environment in which it functions.

We start the chapter by briefly reviewing how MIS may be organized and by looking at the role of the CIO and the MIS strategic-planning function. Next, we turn to MIS outputs—meeting organizational and interorganizational transaction processing, management reporting, decision support, and office information system needs. We also discuss setting up a separate group to create and market information processing products and services to outside clients. Thus, we consider all types of MIS outputs—those that have an internal operations focus, an internal decision-making focus, and an external customer focus. Then, we look at project selection, pricing MIS products, and the MIS budget. Finally, we cover some approaches to evaluating MIS performance as well as two of the major issues impacting MIS plans and budgets for the 1990s: downsizing and outsourcing.

THE MIS ORGANIZATION

The MIS function in businesses can be organized in several ways. In many firms, the MIS area is organized in a centralized manner similar to that shown in Chapter 14 (Figure 14.12, page 621). When such centralized structures are used, key areas are often broken out as separate subunits. In Figure 14.12, five principal areas are identified: the information center, office automation, systems development, programming, and operations. This figure also shows two staff

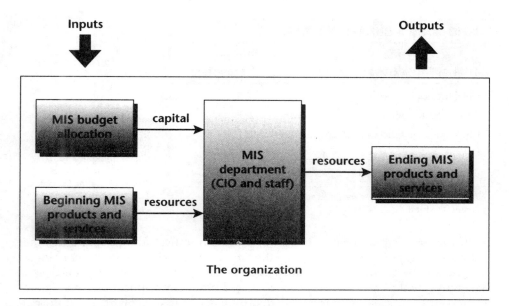

Inputs

Outputs

MIS budget allocation → capital → MIS department (CIO and staff) → resources → Ending MIS products and services

Beginning MIS products and services → resources →

The organization

Figure 18.1 A performance model for MIS.

functions that often cut across the line areas: telecommunication management and data administration.

It is important to note that the centralized structure illustrated in Figure 14.12 is only one of many alternative ways to organize the MIS area. Many firms, such as Manufacturers Hanover, find that a combination of centralized corporate structures and decentralized business functions is very effective.

Generally, the MIS area should be organized in a manner that enables it to achieve its (and the larger organization's) strategic objectives. As Alfred D. Chandler, Jr.—a noted business strategy scholar—states, "structure follows strategy," and the MIS area should, like all other functional areas of an organization, follow this principle. If the existing structure for MIS is not well suited to assist the organization in achieving its strategic goals, it should be reorganized. In some cases, entire organizations may be reorganized in order to adopt structures that are more in line with strategic initiatives. For example, in 1991 IBM underwent a major reorganization in order to shift its focus to strategic business units (SBU) that could be more responsive to particular types of customers. In 1992, Apple reorganized in order to capitalize on computer and communications-related technology areas that it wanted to enter.

For many other organizations, the MIS infrastructure is currently in the middle of what Richard Nolan describes as a period of "technological discontinuity"—that is, a transition period from a centralized, mainframe-oriented, transaction processing environment to one in which end-user concerns play an increasingly larger role. Such transitions often have an impact on the distribution of power within the MIS area. Traditionally, MIS line managers, especially data processing managers, had all of the attention. Now, they have to share it

WHO DOES A CIO REPORT TO?	
Title of CIO's Boss	**Approximate Percentage**
Chief financial officer (CFO)	33%
Chief executive officer (CEO) or chairman	23%
Chief operation officer (COO) or president	12%
Vice-president	30%
Other	4%

Figure 18.2 Common reporting relationships for the highest-ranking MIS executives in major companies. (Adapted from *The Computerworld IS Pocket Guide for Success*)

Note: Because percentages were rounded to the nearest whole percent, the total exceeds 100%.

with the information center, telecommunication, office automation, and other MIS areas responsible for helping the organization absorb new technologies and satisfy the changing data information needs of management and end-users. The movement of transaction processing and other key applications from mainframes to local area networks and distributed processing platforms (information systems designed to meet the computing needs of particular subunits) has also eroded the traditional power base of data processing managers. Additionally, the increased importance of networking has elevated the power of business telecommunication managers in many organizations.

MIS Management

At the top of the computer hierarchy in many organizations are the vice-president (or director) of information systems and the data processing director. The precise titles used to describe these jobs varies among organizations. The vice-president or director of information systems is often referred to as the chief information officer (CIO). In the rest of this chapter, when we use the acronym "CIO," we are referring to the highest-ranking MIS executive in the organization—regardless of his or her actual job title. However, you should remember that the highest-ranking MIS executive in an organization does not always have the title of CIO.

In firms that see information technologies as playing a key role in their future, the CIO slot is often at a vice-presidential level. Thus, the CIO actively participates in enterprise-level, strategic-planning processes. In firms that have transaction processing as almost all of the MIS effort, the CIO is often just a director, generally at the middle-management level. As Figure 18.2 shows, in practice, a variety of reporting relationships exist for the highest ranking MIS executives in organizations. As this figure suggests, in a majority of companies, the MIS executive of greatest rank does not report directly to the chief executive officer (CEO) or chief operations officer (COO). Rather, he or she is more likely to report to the chief financial officer (CFO) or a vice-president within the organization. In these cases, the MIS executive's input into the strategic-planning process is through that vice-president or CFO.

THE CHIEF INFORMATION OFFICER (CIO)

As we just discussed, the head of many MIS departments is the chief information officer (CIO). The CIO oversees all MIS-related activities, including transaction processing—which traditionally accounts for the largest share of the information processing budget—as well as telecommunication, data administration, and end-user support. Whether valid or not, the MIS department's successes or failures are usually attributed to the person at the top. Thus, if a systems analyst makes a serious mistake or an irate programmer destroys key data, the CIO is ultimately responsible.

Because technology in the world of information processing constantly changes, and because information processing involves an intimate knowledge of many business areas, the CIO's job is difficult and demanding. In many firms, it is a high turnover position.

Responsibilities of the CIO

Among the most important responsibilities of the CIO are the following tasks:

- Proactively participating in enterprise-level strategic planning.

- Developing a strategic plan for the MIS area and seeing that both plan and policy are effectively carried out.

- Allocating limited budget resources among a potentially large number of competing computer products and services functions—including systems development projects.

- Leading effectively—a person who can both convince management of the increasing importance of MIS and can motivate MIS personnel.

- Personally overseeing all security-related matters—especially monitoring those with potential disaster-level impacts.

- Managing such MIS employee-related matters as salary levels, hiring, firing, promotion, training, task assignments, and the work environment.

- Maintaining strong relationships with members of the steering and executive committees, and responding to their needs and concerns.

- Monitoring all new technological developments that could potentially benefit the organization.

The Role of the CIO

As mentioned earlier, the role of the CIO varies among organizations. In firms in which transaction processing is the entire MIS effort, the CIO may be just a glorified data processing manager. In firms that view information systems as a competitive weapon, the CIO position will probably be at a vice-presidential level. Three important determinants of the role of MIS in the organization are the industry in which the organization competes, corporate culture, and leadership within the CIO position.

Regarding the *industry* component, companies that produce information-intensive products—such as those found in the banking, financial services, and insurance sectors—are the types of firms that are most likely to have MIS executives at the vice-presidential level. Unless such firms view information as a strategic weapon with which to position themselves, they will be in a poor position to survive the 1990s.

In regard to *corporate culture*, the vision of the person at the top (that is, the CEO level) can exert a lot of influence on the impact of MIS within the firm. For example, chief executive officers who view MIS strictly as a cost area (a view that was common in the 1980s) may miss seeing it as an opportunity—an investment in strategic information weapons (a view that is crucial in the 1990s).

Finally, *leadership* within the CIO position can influence the role of MIS within the firm. As Warren Bennis and Bert Nanus skillfully point out, the difference between managers and leaders is "the difference between routine problem solvers and problem finders." The CIO who only manages responds reactively to pressures within the organization. The CIO who leads responds proactively by creating a vision of the appropriate role of MIS within the firm and then establishing a strategy for turning that vision into reality.

PLANNING AND MIS

One of the most critical activities performed by the CIO is planning. In recent years, MIS planning has become increasingly important. For instance:

- In many industries, MIS has emerged as a key competitive weapon. For example, consumers often differentiate firms in the banking, insurance, and financial services industries based on the convenience of their systems, the services they can package together, and the quality and timeliness of the information they provide. Often, these services are only possible through advanced computer and communications technologies. In the auto industry, the responsiveness provided by information technologies is seen as a key competitive weapon in eliminating the advantage currently held by Japanese automakers.

- So many tasks at all levels in organizations are now performed by using computer and communications technologies that planning for enterprise-level coordination and integration among them—to achieve even greater performance—has become increasingly complex. This problem is especially exacerbated by the ever-changing, ever-shifting technology base.

- The spending level on MIS-related tasks is growing, thus increasing the importance of planning expenditures carefully. Although the level of spending has increased, the ease in cost-justifying many MIS-related purchases has not.

Figure 18.3 lists some of these and other trends which have contributed to the increased importance of MIS planning.

Trend	Planning Ramifications
Rapid technology change	Forecasting key technological trends
	Minimizing costs due to technology obsolescence
	Taking advantage of integration possibilities as technologies merge
Increase in MIS expenditures	Coordinating and controlling MIS expenditures
	Increasing importance of strategic planning for MIS
	Elevating MIS to a level in the organization commensurate with its importance
	Using excess in-house MIS capacity to develop products for outside the firm
Enterprise-wide impact activities	Coordinating MIS expenditures
	Increasing importance of strategic planning for MIS
	Increasing awareness of MIS throughout the firm
Competitive advantage gained through MIS	Using MIS to develop new products or to differentiate current products
	Using MIS to lower prices or costs
	Using MIS to alter the competitive environment
	Using MIS to improve customer service

Figure 18.3 MIS-related trends and their impacts on planning.

STRATEGIC CHALLENGES AND MIS

As mentioned in Chapter 3, strategic planning is a top-level management activity in which the long-range course for an organization or strategic business unit is charted. Strategic planning is where all other planning efforts in organizations start. Most executives see it as a highly important activity. According to Daniel Gray, a CEO at one diversified manufacturing company states: "I can't conceive of doing business without a strategy and a plan. Every company has to do it. Either you get to be good at it or you do it poorly and suffer the consequences." Adds Remington CEO Victor Kiam: "If I had come into Remington without a plan, you wouldn't be seeing any of those commercials about how one entrepreneur liked the electric shaver so much, he bought the company."

In this section, we consider the MIS area as an organization, or strategic business unit, in its own right; that is, an entity capable of doing its own strategic planning. As we pointed out in Chapter 1, strategic planning has consistently ranked near the top of the list of critical issues facing MIS executives.

Two Views of MIS

One modern view of the MIS department is as a business within a business. At the top of the MIS business is their own "board of directors"—a steering committee of top-level executives and representatives from key user areas—that both approves a long-term plan for MIS development and votes on the undertaking of critical projects. The "CEO" of this MIS business is often the CIO.

Another modern perspective is to view this MIS business as a marketing firm. An example of a market-oriented MIS firm is provided in Figure 18.4. In

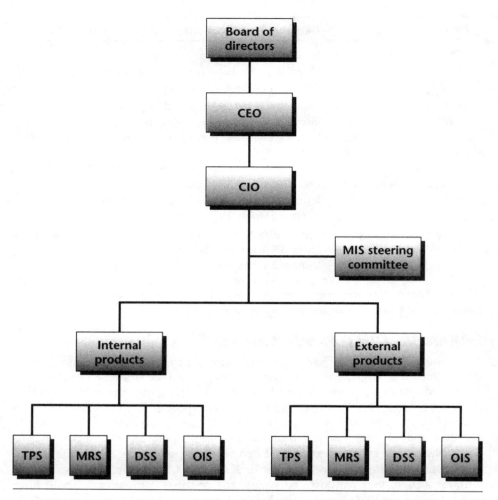

Figure 18.4 The MIS department as a marketing organization. In recent years, many of the products of MIS–systems and services—have become packageable items that can be useful both inside or outside the organization. Many MIS departments have become more competitive externally by leveraging investments in MIS products and marketing them to outside firms.

this figure, the MIS department is depicted as a marketing firm with clients inside and outside the parent organization. The viewpoint taken in this figure is that any product—or skill—developed internally is a candidate for external marketing efforts. This situation often occurs because firms can then optimize their investments in MIS expertise developed internally. The outputs of such a firm can be grouped into three categories.

1. Internally targeted outputs:

- ***Transaction processing and office systems that result in lower operating costs*** This class of data-oriented outputs provides for efficient internal operations at the lower levels of the organization. Includes payroll, accounts receivable and payable, and word-processing systems.

- **Decision support, information reporting, and office systems that result in improved decision making or productivity** This class of information-oriented outputs increases effectiveness at the middle and upper levels of the organization. Includes executive support and electronic mail systems.

- **CAD/CAM/CIM systems** These systems are frequently turnkey products purchased by the MIS departments from outside vendors. They are targeted to manufacturing goods of higher quality, with greater flexibility, and in more cost-effective and differentiated ways. As noted in Chapter 13, computer-integrated manufacturing (CIM) systems are designed to tie all manufacturing-related systems together, including computer-aided design (CAD), computer-aided manufacturing (CAM), robotics, just-in-time (JIT), manufacturing resources planning (MRP II), process control, quality control, and so on.

2. Externally targeted outputs:

- **Mainstream products and services to clients** Among this class of outputs are (1) products and services that, through information technology, are enhanced in the eyes of clients and (2) interorganizational systems that lock in customers and lock out competitors. Examples of enhanced products and services are an automobile manufacturer that adds a computerized dashboard to a car and a brokerage house that creates a new fund for its clients. An example of a system that locks in customers is a distributor that provides terminals at customer sites so they can order goods directly from the distributor's warehouse—plus check on prices, availabilities, and the statuses of previous orders.

- **Non-mainstream products and services to clients** A growing number of firms—including Traveler's Insurance, Celanese Corporation, Citicorp, JC Penney, Boeing, McDonnell Douglas, and the Big Six accounting firms (all best known for products and services other than high-tech ones)—have set up either separate departments or subsidiaries to produce software or provide information services for clients. These "organizations within organizations" generally operate as independent profit centers that have a different set of clients than that of the parent firm.

- **Supplier systems** Among this class of outputs are interorganizational systems that tie in suppliers, thus providing lower inventory holding costs and better response time and availability.

3. Mixed outputs:

- **All products and services that represent any combination of these categories** An example is a firm that has an interorganizational order-entry system that it uses both as a vehicle to provide efficient internal operations and as an externally targeted competitive weapon. Often, such systems provide better information for internal decision support as well.

This MIS business may function both as a merchandiser (by distributing to end-users some of the products it buys outside) and a manufacturer (by doing some of its own in-house programming and systems development).

STRATEGIC PLANNING AND MIS

Actually, two levels of strategic planning must be considered by the CIO. The first is the strategic plan for the parent organization. The second, in keeping with the view of the MIS function as a business within a business, is the strategic plan for the MIS area. Linking these two strategic plans is one of the major challenges faced by chief information officers.

The Corporate Strategic Plan

In organizations that consider information to be a critical resource, the CIO is probably included in the executive group that makes up the long-range strategic plan for the organization. As we discussed in Chapter 3, the strategic-planning process starts with consideration of the mission and scope statement of the organization, an analysis of the organization's current profile (which usually results in a list of strengths and weaknesses), and an analysis of the present and future external environment (which consists of competitors, consumers, suppliers, and numerous other entities that impact the organization). After that, a general strategy in dealing with the future is developed and, subsequently, measurable objectives for achieving that strategy. The objectives lead to specific plans and policies that are implemented at given times or places.

The CIO and other high-ranking MIS managers should review the organization's strategic plan—if such a plan exists—on a regular basis because the direction charted by the MIS department should be compatible with the general direction in which the company is moving. Often, key elements of this plan contain information of vital importance to MIS development and growth. For example, if the firm is a bank and its mission statement emphasizes a phrase such as "will be recognized as a national leader in client services," the MIS department should be aggressive in this area and take some risks in providing new services to its customers. The risk-taking in this area is often because: (1) the actual benefit to be realized in supplying new services is usually measurable only after the fact and (2) the condition of new services often involves being a pioneer and creating something that has no precedent.

It is imperative that the CIO study the strategic plan of the firm for many other reasons. For instance, if the profile of the firm reveals that it is disproportionately large in the middle management area and cost-cutting is imminent, the timing is probably not good for the CIO to launch projects dependent on middle management's current structure. Also, if the company feels its success is due to its innovative marketing of products, then the opportunity to provide outstanding information to the marketing area should draw the CIO's attention.

The bottom line is that the MIS department is like a boat in the current established by the organization's overall strategic plan. If the boat goes against the current, it must take responsibility for the consequences.

The MIS Strategic Plan

Figure 18.5 shows a strategic-planning model for the MIS department. This model is similar to the one presented in Chapter 3 (Figure 3.12, page 99) for the parent organization. As mentioned earlier, the strategic MIS plan is developed within the context of the strategic plan for the parent organization. Some examples of specific issues that this plan must address are listed next.

Mission and Scope   A possible issue is: Should the MIS department be involved with providing information processing products and services to outside clients?

Current Profile   Some likely concerns in this area include: Is MIS perceived by the parent management as a key activity? How much is the company spending on MIS? What are the current MIS outputs and how is spending distributed among those outputs? How much money for information technology and services is spent outside of the MIS budget by the parent organization (for example, by end-user departments)? How old is the base of hardware and software products now in use? Realistically, is the current budget adequate given the resource limitations of the organization? What is the skills profile of the current MIS staff? What are the general strengths and weaknesses of the MIS area?

External Environment   The external environment of MIS consists of users within the organization, plus outside clients, vendors of high-technology products, MIS professionals in the labor market, and such remote forces as the government (which has strict rules about the reporting and distributing of data), the economy (which determines general price levels), and so on. Some possible questions to ask include: Who are, or who could be, the clients served by MIS? Are current clients satisfied with the services they are receiving? How does the pricing of MIS services affect the demand for them? How are new services communicated to users? What new technologies might change the way business takes place in the future? What are MIS departments in competitive firms doing? What does the supply and demand of computer professionals look like now and in the future? What types of reporting are expected by the government currently and in a few years?

Strategies   Some possible questions regarding MIS strategies include: How well do the plans for the MIS area align with the future plans of the organization? Should the MIS department make any major changes? How should the soaring impact of end-user computing be handled? How can MIS best integrate various "islands of technology" that have developed throughout the firm?

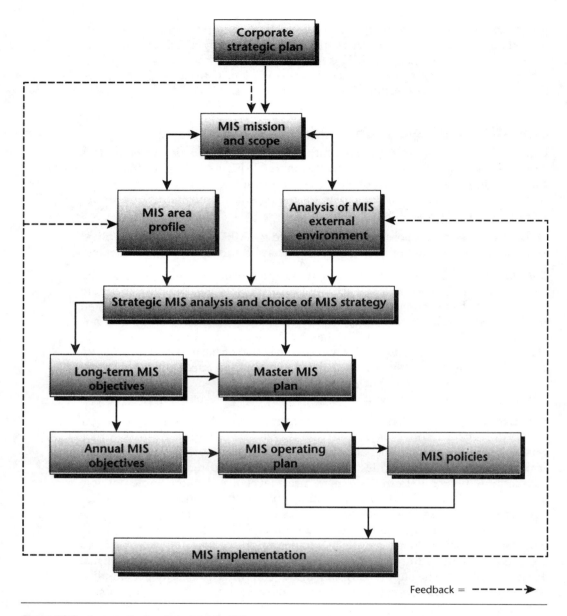

Figure 18.5 A strategic-planning model for MIS.

Some possible strategies include: (1) concentrating MIS development efforts on the organization's executives and (2) creating and marketing software outside the organization.

Long-Term Objectives In general, the long-term objectives of MIS must be ones that support the corporate strategy. Objectives should be clear statements regarding what must be done. Often, the use of quantitative and physical descriptions are needed to achieve the necessary clarity. Some possible long-term MIS objectives include: Software maintenance costs will be cut in half over the next five years. All current transaction processing operations will be moved into an integrated Oracle relational database environment within the next three years.

Annual Objectives   Some possible annual objectives include: Program maintenance costs will be cut by 20 percent during the coming year. Interactive response time for clerks handling telephone orders will be cut by 50 percent before January 1, 1995.

Master Plan   Some possible questions addressed by the master plan include: What dollar amounts should be budgeted for hardware, software, services, and personnel for each of the next five years? What new systems will be developed over the next five years—and what are their exact due dates?

Operating Plan   Some possible questions addressed by the operating plan include: What specific pieces of hardware and software should be purchased next year? What new systems will be developed next year? Who should be hired or terminated next year?

Policies   Some possible policies include: Only authorized personnel are allowed in the room containing the main computer. Backup will be done daily. Backup tapes will be sent to a backup site (located away from the main computer site) daily. No information center support will be given to end-user hardware and software products that are not on the approved list.

Like objectives, policies should be specific. For instance, in the previous examples, titles of authorized personnel should be specifically named. Also, the names of tapes to back up and and by whom should be identified.

Strategic-Planning Tools

Due to the importance and difficulty of strategic planning for MIS, the CIO and other MIS personnel responsible for developing long-range MIS plans should have a method for guiding the planning process. Over the years, numerous approaches were created to help MIS managers do a better job of developing the different aspects of the MIS strategic plan. The approaches discussed next take different views of MIS planning and often provide more assistance at some steps of the planning process than at others. For example, some focus on the assimilation of information technology in organizations, others help define information needs, and still others are concerned with categorizing MIS applications. Collectively, the approaches discussed next provide MIS planners with a set of tools that can be used to develop strategic plans for the MIS while retaining reasonably strong linkages to corporate strategies.

Parallel Plan Development   In order to ensure a congruence of strategies and objectives between the host organization and the MIS department, a parallel method is often used, as demonstrated in Figure 18.6. For each organizational

	Parent Organization (Publishing Company)	MIS Area
▪ Strategy	Produce high-quality books for fiction and nonfiction markets	Develop an information bank to help executives identify promising sources for new titles and areas in which to publish
		Develop support systems that help executives identify new ways to produce and market books
▪ Objectives	Have ten books that sell 100,000 or more copies by year's end	Develop a sales and marketing support system that provides sales and distribution information quickly enough to re-allocate resources when necessary
	Cut costs by 10 percent	Develop information that enables managers to identify the largest cost areas
		Develop a system that helps managers to quickly pinpoint any cost troubles

Figure 18.6 Development of an MIS strategy in response to organizational strategy. Elements of the strategic plan for the MIS department are developed alongside corresponding elements in the organizational strategic plan.

strategy and objective, corresponding ones for MIS are derived from the organization's strategic plan.

Role Assessment To assess the role of MIS within the organization, the CIO might want to determine where the firm's MIS is positioned within the matrix shown in Figure 18.7. This matrix—originally proposed by F. Warren McFarlan, James McKenney, and Philip Pyburn—rates the strategic importance of MIS along two dimensions: existing systems (leftmost margin of Figure 18.7) and planned systems (topmost margin).

Firms in the *support* category do not see information technology as critically important to their current operations or strategic success. Professional service firms with large MIS budgets and MIS activities that involve hundreds of employees would fall in this category. In such firms, MIS is seen almost strictly in its cost-effectiveness role, and the CIO might not be part of upper management. Ten years ago, the retailing industry fell in this category. Few competitors paid attention to Wal-Mart. Now, most competitors are playing catch-up to Wal-Mart and information technology has emerged as a strategic force in the industry.

At the other end of the scale is the *strategic* category, represented by such firms as banks and insurance companies. These firms already have a high commitment to information technology, and information technology is perceived as a critical competitive tool for future success. F. Warren McFarlan, James McKenney, and Philip Plyburn note how the CEO of a large financial institution succinctly captures this view of MIS: "It's clear that information systems are critical to our survival and success. In our business, the resources that determine our marketing and our operating performance are people and systems."

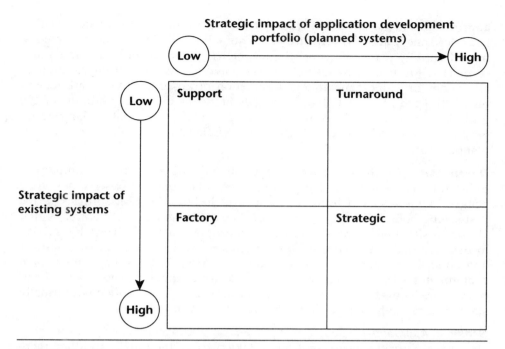

Figure 18.7 Role assessment matrix. (Adapted from McFarlan, McKenney, and Pyburn)

The *factory* category contains companies that depend heavily on MIS support for their existing, day-to-day operations. A firm that falls into this grid quadrant is not necessarily a manufacturing firm and does not have to be a traditional factory. Instead, this category name indicates that MIS operations in such firms are viewed as supporting day-to-day activities in a factory-like way. The project portfolios and applications under development in these firms suggest that they do not currently view information technology as a competitive weapon that will materially impact their ability to compete in the near future. A firm with an overly large percentage of system maintenance projects relative to new applications falls into this category.

The *turnaround* category contains firms that do not see MIS as critically important to their current operations. However, the applications under development are vital for achieving the company's strategic plan. A firm in the turnaround quadrant is not necessarily in a turnaround situation (for example, trying to reverse a decrease in business. In this context, the term "turnaround" is simply a quadrant label for firms that are beginning to realize the strategic potential of MIS. A manufacturing firm experiencing rapid growth and/or planning to expand internationally falls into this catagory.

The main point of McFarlan, McKenney, and Pyburn's work is not simply to place a firm in a quadrant on a grid. Their real point is that, after a firm is placed in the appropriate quadrant, managers can draw conclusions about appropriate and inappropriate ways to treat the corporate MIS function. McFarlan, McKenney, and Pyburn further identified six linking strategies, ranging from "centrally planned" (consisting of intense involvement by informed and supportive top management) to "necessary evil" (in which minimum resource allocations to support mandatory transaction processing activities are recommended). Each of these linking strategies fits firms in some quadrants of the grids, but not in others. By combining their grid with appropriate linking strategies, McFarlan, McKenney, and Pyburn have developed a valuable corporate planning tool.

Observation   An important way to determine the direction of the company is to listen to the people who have a key role in planning and observe how they behave. A view shared by many people, including Mark McCormack in his best-selling book *What They Don't Teach You at Harvard Business School*, is that "business situations always come down to people situations." The CIO is likely to discover that many strategy implementation issues often consist of power and politics, key attitudes, timing, and so on. Also, whereas the strategic plan contains important written statements, top management's vision of the company's direction—the force that drives the strategic plan—is often not formally stated and can only be discovered through shrewd observation.

Scenario Approaches   People using **scenario approaches** attempt to identify important, plausible events that might take place in the future, and then mentally simulate how they and others might react if such events did take place. Regarding MIS strategic planning, it is usually helpful to construct scenarios about future technologies, corporate policies, economic conditions, threats of global competition, availability of key resources, and so on. By determining which variables have the greatest impact—as well as which of these variables can be controlled—the CIO can gain more insight into the viability of certain strategies.

For example, suppose a project under consideration is developing an executive information system (EIS) for key executives. Suppose also that the current CEO, a heavy supporter of the EIS, is rumored to be quitting soon. A scenario worth consideration is what might happen to the EIS if the present CEO leaves after considerable time and effort were spent developing the EIS, but before it is fully installed. If the person who succeeds the current CEO is relatively hostile to the MIS cause, some serious implementation problems might arise. Consequently, the entire effort may fail and be blamed on the MIS area. If the EIS can be postponed, the CIO might want to stall its development until the new CEO arrives.

Scenarios are often developed for the most likely, most optimistic (best case), and most pessimistic (worst case) futures. The assumptions about the environment will differ for each scenario as, of course, will the actions to take.

The manner in which scenarios are developed can range from strictly manual methods to highly automated ones. Barbara C. McNurlin and Ralph H. Sprague, Jr., describe these scenario development approaches in their IRM book, *Information Systems Management in Practice*.

APPLICATION AREAS						
	Development	**Manufacturing**	**Marketing**	**Finance**	**Support**	**Totals**
Transaction processing		0.1	0.1	0.4	0.3	0.9
Professional support systems	0.1	0.2	0.1	0.1	0.1	0.6
Physical automation		0.2				0.2
Outside services (for example, IOS)				0.1		0.1
Technology infrastructure*		0.2	0.1	0.1	0.1	0.5
Totals	0.1	0.7	0.3	0.7	0.5	2.3

*(for example, communications, database)
Note: All numbers in the matrix are reported as a percentage of sales.

Figure 18.8 Investment analysis matrix. Investment analysis is a procedure in which MIS expenditures are broken down by specific categories and analyzed with respect to such items as planned targets, industry averages, and trends.

Investment Analysis **Investment analysis** approaches attempt to measure how funds are currently spent. A grid such as the one in Figure 18.8 is often used for this purpose. Once determined, the percentage of funds spent in each functional or application area might be compared against both intuition and industry averages, or against internally set targets. This, in turn, might give the firm a feel for whether it is underspending or overspending in critical areas.

Critical Success Factors (CSF) Approach The critical success factors (CSF) approach, first covered in Chapter 3, attempts to identify those activities that must take place for success to be realized. One way of implementing the CSF approach in the strategic-planning area is to look at the organization's critical success factors and then determine which information systems or MIS strategies are most pivotal to accomplishing them. For example, if the organization is in an industry in which success depends on staying ahead of foreign competition, then the CIO should determine how MIS can assist in meeting that challenge. Several U.S. suppliers in the textile industry, for instance, banded together to establish a just-in-time inventory-ordering approach to tie in huge retailers, thereby gaining a competitive advantage over inexpensive Asian imports. Critical success factors can also be established for the industry and for the external environment. Some software packages, such as Intersolv's PC Prism, contain routines to facilitate developing critical success factors (see Figure 18.9).

Value Chain Model Michael Porter and Victor Millar's **value chain model**, illustrated in Figure 18.10, attempts to identify the most urgent needs in the orga-

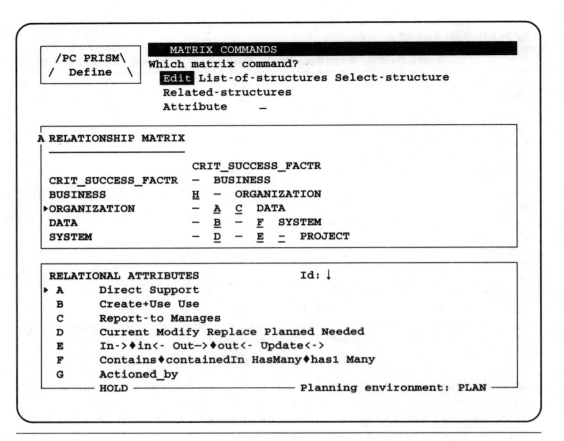

```
 /PC PRISM\          MATRIX COMMANDS
/  Define  \      Which matrix command?
                     Edit  List-of-structures Select-structure
                     Related-structures
                     Attribute      —

A RELATIONSHIP MATRIX


                       CRIT_SUCCESS_FACTR
 CRIT_SUCCESS_FACTR  —  BUSINESS
 BUSINESS            H  —  ORGANIZATION
▶ORGANIZATION        —  A  C  DATA
 DATA                —  B  —  F  SYSTEM
 SYSTEM              —  D  —  E  —  PROJECT


 RELATIONAL ATTRIBUTES                  Id: ↓
▶ A      Direct Support
  B      Create+Use Use
  C      Report-to Manages
  D      Current Modify Replace Planned Needed
  E      In->◆in<- Out—>◆out<- Update<->
  F      Contains◆containedIn HasMany◆has1 Many
  G      Actioned_by
 ———— HOLD ———————————————— Planning environment: PLAN ————
```

Figure 18.9 Developing critical success factors with Intersolv's PC Prism. Using a common framework, everyone concerned with building or managing information systems shares the same set of assumptions about the corporate mission and the relationship of each business segment to overall goals.

nization for information. The basis of this model is that each organization consists of an interconnected chain of primary activities—such as those involved with producing, selling, and servicing products—and support activities—such as purchased inputs, human resources, technology development, and enterprise-wide infrastructures (for instance, general management, and accounting)—that pull the entire firm together. As products are created, value is added throughout the chain. To do better than its rivals, an organization must perform the activities in the matrix at either a lower cost or in such a way that product values are enhanced. Thus, competitive opportunity for MIS exists at every cell in Figure 18.10's matrix. Strategic planners can use such a matrix either by determining in which cells current systems are located—and, therefore, in which cells gaps exist—or by successively considering the opportunity potential in each cell.

Competitive Forces Model The **competitive forces model** (Figure 18.11) encourages the planner to consider the external environment forces that will be

	Inbound logistics	Operations	Outbound logistics	Marketing and sales	Service
Firm infrastructure	X	X	X	X	X
Human resources	X	X	X	X	X
Technology development	X	X	X	X	X
Purchased inputs	X	X	X	X	X

Support activities (Firm infrastructure, Human resources, Technology development, Purchased inputs)

Primary activities (Inbound logistics, Operations, Outbound logistics, Marketing and sales, Service)

Figure 18.10 Value chain model. (Adapted from Porter and Millar)

sources of either opportunities or problems. When studying this model, the planner should consider how information technology might be used to handle each competitive force—both separately and jointly. For instance, can information technology be used to produce such advantages as creating barriers to entry? Generating new products? Changing relationships with suppliers? Changing the basis for competition?

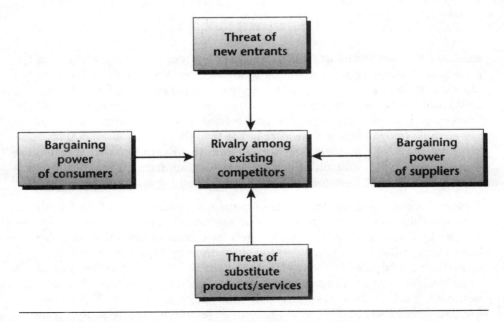

Figure 18.11 Competitive forces model. (Adapted from Porter and Millar)

NREN: The Data Highway of the Future

A fiber-optic public-access data highway is under development. It is called the National Research and Education Network (NREN) and it will revolutionize almost every facet of business, commerce, and communication in the United States. NREN will replace Internet, the computer web that connects more than 35 countries and is used by more than 2 million users each day. NREN will be able to transmit more than 1 billion bits per second (one gigabit)—capacity enough to send an entire 20-volume encyclopedia from coast to coast in less than one second.

NREN will have a broad range of impacts. With just a few keystrokes, customers at home will be able to custom order news, information services, and eventually, even their television programming. Medical doctors will be able to form gigantic consulting groups and ship X-rays, CAT scans, and other test results to specialists for their expert assessments. NREN will also enable local schools to scan any book in university libraries and copy any page, photo, or chart it contains—all in a matter of seconds. And, from the familiar surroundings of their own labs, researchers will be able to use distant supercomputers to help them perform complex experiments.

". . . FROM THE FAMILIAR SURROUNDINGS OF THEIR OWN LABS, RESEARCHERS WILL BE ABLE TO USE DISTANT SUPERCOMPUTERS TO HELP THEM PERFORM COMPLEX EXPERIMENTS."

The development of NREN will enable the U.S. to leapfrog Germany and Japan, who are working on comparable networks. It will also be a key component of the information infrastructure that America will need to be competitive in the 21st century.

Adapted from Schwartz (1992).

Business System Planning (BSP) **Business System Planning (BSP)** is an approach to strategic systems planning that was developed by IBM. The idea behind BSP is to form an enterprise-level view of business data; for instance, that all data created or used within the firm are organizational resources and should be managed comprehensively. The goal behind this way of thinking is to identify a stable information architecture in the firm. BSP advocates feel that if stable processes can be identified throughout the firm, a stable information framework can be built on which to develop long-term information system strategies. A general term for Business System Planning is *enterprise analysis*.

Project Portfolio Approaches Project **portfolio approaches** attempt to determine a sensible mix of new projects by balancing risks against potential returns. For example, executive information systems are risky because their benefits are hard to quantify; however, they offer an extremely high potential return because they are targeted to those who most materially impact the direction of the firm. Maintenance on transaction processing systems, by contrast, is a safer investment, but the potential return is often not as great as for the EIS. Generally, the CIO should seek a diversified project development portfolio that contains some high-risk/high-return projects as well as some low-risk/low-return ones. The proportion of each type of these projects should reflect an overall target risk level. We will discuss portfolio approaches to project development in greater detail in the next section of this chapter.

As our review of the strategic-planning approaches used in MIS indicates, various frameworks and methodologies may be used to develop MIS strategic plans that are linked to corporate strategies. No single method is best or most widely used in practice. In fact, many companies choose a combination of these approaches because they deal with different aspects of the MIS long-range planning process depicted previously in Figure 18.5 (page 768).

PROJECT PORTFOLIO MANAGEMENT

Many different aspects to project selection and project portfolio management exist. Here, we consider three: assessing the benefits and costs of an individual project, balancing project portfolios, and identifying those people ultimately responsible for selecting projects for development.

Analysis of Benefits and Costs

Before management will give its go-ahead for any large computer system, an appraisal of the benefits and costs of the system should be made. In the traditional and prototyping approaches to systems development, costs and benefits are most carefully scrutinized at the end of the design phase because it is almost impossible to make major changes after that point.

Among the cost items taken into consideration are hardware, software, personnel, and the establishment of new procedures and representations of data. The benefits divide into tangible benefits and intangible benefits. *Tangible benefits* are those that are most readily translated into costs; for instance, saving labor, cutting raw material costs, trimming inventory levels, and so on. *Intangible benefits*, on the other hand, are difficult to quantify. Some examples of intangible benefits are providing a better level of service to customers and establishing a system that enables managers to make better decisions. Figure 18.12 gives other examples of intangible benefits. Because managers who approve systems are held accountable for the results, and intangible benefits entail greater risks, tangible benefits are often given the greatest weight in assessing the total set of benefits.

Cost-Justification Approaches

Some of the methods that organizations use to analyze benefits and costs are described in the following subsections. Historically, the methods used to measure tangible benefits are most useful for justifying transaction processing systems, which normally have a relatively high proportion of such benefits. Information systems in the decision support and office automation areas—whose benefits may be largely intangible—are often not justified using tradi-

Intangible MIS Benefits
Enhanced strategic advantage
Improved customer service
Better responsiveness/adaptability to environmental changes
Better public image of organization
Increased organizational flexibility
Better utilization of organizational assets
Improved control over important organizational resources
Streamlined operations
Enhanced coordination of organizational activities
Higher-quality information
Higher-quality decision making
Improved planning
Increased user satisfaction with MIS
Improved morale among users
Improved work environment
Enhanced organizational climate
Modification of organizational culture

Figure 18.12 Examples of intangible benefits of management information systems.

tional cost-benefit methods. After discussing this, we will consider the growing role of risk in corporate cost-justification decisions.

Cost Justification—Tangible Benefits

Numerous approaches were developed to measure the value of a proposed project to an organization. Three of the most widely used methods are the payback approach, the present value approach, and the internal rate of return approach. We will discuss each of these methods briefly. Figure 18.13 provides an example showing how each method can be used to calculate benefits for a given project.

In the examples that follow, the effect of income taxes are ignored to keep them simple. When making real cost-justification decisions, taxes should be considered; most organizations make their decision on an after-tax basis.

■ *Payback approach* The **payback** approach is a crude cost-justification model that is regarded with disdain by many academic theorists. Nonetheless, it is relatively simple to apply and is one of the most widely used MIS investment decision models.

The payback approach attempts to measure the time it will take to recoup the original investment in benefits. One way to apply the payback

System will take 16 months to develop

System, once developed, will be used for 5 years

Costs and benefits:

Costs ▶	Year 1	$100,000	Benefits ▶	Year 1	$ 0
	Year 2	50,000		Year 2	30,000
	Total	$150,000		Year 3	70,000
				Year 4	120,000
				Year 5	120,000
				Year 6	120,000
				Year 7	80,000
				Total	$540,000

Computations

A. *Payback approach*:
- Average annual benefits = $540,000 ÷ 7 = $77,143/year
- Total cost = $150,000
- Years to pay off = 150,000 ÷ 77,143 = 1.94 years

B. *Net present value approach*:
- Assume a 15% cost of capital
- Present value of costs = $100,000 + ($50,000 × .870)

  = $143,500

- Present value of benefits: 0 + (30,000 × 0.870) = $ 26,100
  + (70,000 × 0.756) = $ 52,920
  + (120,000 × 0.658) = $ 78,960
  + (120,000 × 0.572) = $ 68,640
  + (120,000 × 0.497) = $ 59,640
  + (80,000 × 0.432) = $ 34,560

  Total $320,820

- Net present value = $320,820 − $143,500 = $177,320
- Benefit-cost (B/C) ratio = $320,820 ÷ $143,500 = 2.24

C. *Internal rate of return approach*:
- 100,000 (PVF) + 50,000 (PVF) = 30,000 (PVF) + 70,000 (PVF)
  + 120,000 (PVF) + 120,000 (PVF)
  + 120,000 (PVF) + 80,000 (PVF)

  PVF = present value factor based on discounting rate of 47%

Figure 18.13   Computation of traditional cost-justification approaches.

method is shown in part A of Figure 18.13. A person computes the average annual benefits of the system and divides these into the total cost. The calculations show that it will take 1.94 years for benefits to equal costs. Many organizations use a hurdle or goal of two years (that is, they will not consider a system that will not pay for itself in less than two years) for some projects and would find this payback desirable.

A criticism of the payback approach is that it ignores the time value of money (for example, because of inflation and other economic changes, the value of $1 decreases over time); thus, it does not fully measure profitability. Spreadsheet packages generally have easy-to-use functions that enable more sophisticated types of financial analysis, so the simplicity edge of the payback method is not as sharp as it once was.

- **Present value approach** The **present value** approach attempts to value future dollars in terms of their value today; in other words, unlike the payback approach, the present value approach considers the time value of money. For example, if money can be invested for an annual return of 10 percent, $100 today will be worth $110 one year from now and $121 two years from now. Viewed another way, $121 two years from now is worth only $100 today. That is, it has a present value of $100.

  The way present value analysis works is to deflate all future dollars by a present value factor that is based on a given interest rate and the number of years the amount must be discounted. Often, the interest rate chosen for the analysis is the organization's cost of capital; that is, the rate that funds would earn if they were invested in the capital markets or in project alternatives with the same degree of risk. Many organizations use a standard cost of capital that is determined by their finance departments. Present value factors for a variety of interest rates are widely published; often, they can be found in the appendices accompanying introductory cost accounting and finance textbooks.

  The calculations in part B of Figure 18.13 depict costs and benefits multiplied by present value factors representing a cost of capital of 15 percent. After the present values of the costs and benefits are separately calculated, they may be combined in various ways. For instance, the present value of the costs can be subtracted from the present value of the benefits, yielding a net present value. Or, the two present values can be divided—benefits by costs—to yield a benefit-cost (B/C) ratio. The B/C ratio is generally more useful; many organizations will compute a project's B/C ratio and then compare it against a standard hurdle ratio. If the project's B/C ratio exceeds the hurdle ratio, the project is considered seriously.

- **Internal rate of return approach** The **internal rate of return** approach is used to calculate the rate of return on the project investment. For example, a simple $100 investment today that would yield $121 two years from now has an internal rate of return of 10 percent. For more complicated cash flows, a person attempts to find the interest rate whose present value factors will make the cost stream equal to the benefit stream, as shown in part C of Figure 18.13. After this is known, management is in a better position to determine if it is more worthwhile to invest in the project than in other types of investment options. For example, if the comparable interest rate is 10 percent, the firm's external investment options would have to exceed 10 percent before it would choose them over investing in the project. Computations of internal rate of return can be relatively complicated, but many spreadsheet packages have routines that will compute internal rates of return automatically if given all of the cash flows involved in each year of the project.

Cost Justification—Intangible Benefits

The methods described in the preceding section—payback, present value, and internal rate of return—are useful for determining the attractiveness of projects with measurable benefits. However, numerous projects—especially those in the decision support systems (DSS) and office information systems (OIS) areas—have benefits that are largely intangible. Unfortunately, many firms find that the absence of a solid, quantifiable payoff makes it hard to justify investments.

For example, how can a value be put on the increase in effectiveness that might be possible by using a spreadsheet package? How can a person even demonstrate, in fact, that a spreadsheet package will produce better decisions in a given situation? Other types of technology products whose benefits are particularly hard to quantify include electronic mail, teleconferencing, expert systems, decision support systems, computer-aided design (CAD), computer-integrated manufacturing (CIM), and computer-aided software engineering (CASE). Lee Gremillion and Philip Pyburn cite an MIS director who claims, "I have to compete for my budget against other managers who can show hard dollar benefits within the next year or two. With many of these 'management support' type systems, the real payoff does not occur until nearly everyone is hooked up, which means a big long-term investment for both IS and user groups. Everyone is all for the intangible benefits these systems provide, but when money is tight, it is pretty clear where the investment will be made."

DSS and office information systems often provide two types of benefits. First, they may either shorten the time needed to accomplish a given task or allow more of a given task to be done in the same amount of time. That is, they may increase efficiency. Second, they often promote new ways to do old jobs. Thus, managers can spend more time performing important high-level activities and less time on clerical work. In other words, they can make managers more effective. Although this second benefit often has the greatest potential monetary return to a company, it is the most difficult to incorporate into traditional benefit-cost approaches.

Over the years, numerous methods have been suggested to justify projects with difficult-to-quantify benefits. One way is to combine these benefits with those that are more easily reduced to numbers. In this way, the combined size of the most measurable benefits can be estimated. These benefits might include labor displacement, inventory reduction, a reduced sales force, and so on. If, at this point, traditional cost-justification measures (payback, present value, or internal rate of return) show that the project is worthwhile, no further work needs to be done. Because the project can now be justified through measurable benefits, it is not really necessary to account for the intangible ones. If, on the other hand, the measurable benefits are not sufficient to carry the project over the required hurdle, then it becomes necessary to determine the exact amount that annual cash flows must increase in order for the project to clear the hurdle. Thus, rather than trying to quantify benefits that are difficult to put into monetary values, the process can be reversed to first estimate how sizable these benefits must be in order to justify the proposed project.

For example, suppose that after measuring both costs and quantifiable benefits, a person finds that an additional $20,000 per year in benefits is required to move a project over a benefit-cost (B/C) ratio hurdle of 2.5. Suppose also that two of the intangible benefits are a faster response to problems and better service. The next question is: Would the firm be willing to pay an extra $20,000 per year for these benefits? If the average client of the firm is worth $10,000 per year in business, the firm might also want to consider if the project will result in at least two extra clients (or in avoiding the loss of two clients). When viewed in these terms, intangible benefits become easier to understand.

When the costs of a project are relatively small, many firms do no cost justification. This might happen, for example, when a manager buys a spreadsheet package or even (in a large department) a complete microcomputer system. On an individual level, doing no cost justification often makes sense. However, with some firms spending 30 percent or more of their MIS-related costs on microcomputer systems, the combined costs can add up quickly unless some controls are established.

Project Selection

At any particular time, an organization has a specific mix of information systems products up in operation. It may now have, for instance, an IBM ES/9000 mainframe, with many important transaction processing applications in COBOL and IMS (DL/1); 600 microcomputers of various types, which collectively contain about 200 different software products that represent both DSS and OIS applications; an electronic mail system implemented on an Ethernet LAN; several computer applications on the factory floor and in engineering and design labs; a sales support system implemented by laptop computers and modems that tie into a central database; and so on. Also, the MIS department probably is planning a desired product mix for a future target date. For example, it may want to network many of the microcomputers to the mainframe; downsize to an IBM AS/400; do extensive maintenance work on part of the transaction processing system to accommodate some major changes in business conditions; or educate the finance staff on DSS modeling tools. To achieve the desired product mix, the projects that must be developed between now and the target date will be the MIS department's project portfolio (see Figure 18.14). Special care must be taken to ensure that the portfolio does not involve an undesirable amount of risk. As discussed in Chapter 4, risk is the degree of exposure to uncertain outcomes.

Project Risk

Project risk is the degree of exposure in a project to such events as not meeting implementation schedules, spending more money than anticipated, and achieving fewer benefits than planned. In fact, a proposed new system may not even

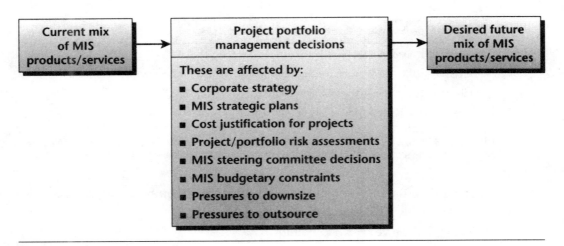

Figure 18.14 Project portfolio.

work. Three dimensions to a project that affect the amount of risk associated with it are project size, project structure, and project-related experience.

- **_Project size_**   A $3 million, five-year project that involves re-assigning 450 workers at six different sites obviously entails more risk than a $25,000, one-week project involving one department. If either of these projects fails to meet expectations in any way, the larger project will probably have the greater organizational impact.

- **_Project structure_**   Transaction processing projects and some of those involving OIS technologies are very structured (that is, their outputs are reasonably well defined and predictable). Decision-oriented management reporting system (MRS) and DSS projects may be among the least structured. The less structure, the greater the chance of having to return to earlier stages of systems development for refinement and the greater the chance of failing to properly identify the right needs. The less structure, generally the greater the risk involved.

- **_Project-related experience_**   In some cases, a prepackaged solution—such as an application package or turnkey system—exists for a problem, which greatly reduces the amount of risk that must be undertaken. In other cases, one or more members of the MIS staff may have experience with the project hardware, software, or problem area—which, again, lowers the risk. If neither of these situations pertains, risk increases.

The riskiness of a project may be quantitatively assessed in various ways. One approach is to prepare a set of questions and a set of point values that should apply to each question's response and then add up the points to assess the total relative risk for the project. For instance, one question might relate to

Project-Independent Factors Influencing Risk
▪ Recent work history of MIS systems development group
▪ Perceived quality of MIS systems development group by steering committee
▪ Stability of MIS systems development group
▪ General experience level and ability of MIS systems development group

Figure 18.15   Project–independent factors influencing risk. Generally, such items as time pressures and the criticalness of the project impact the amount of risk that management will tolerate.

the total time the project will take. Weights might then be applied to possible responses as follows:

Less than one year   5 points
One to two years   10 points
More than two years   20 points

Another risk-related question might inquire about the experience of the project team on projects of this type. The responses and weights could be:

A lot   0 points
Some   3 points
None   6 points

Points assigned to responses should reflect the overall importance of the question. In this example, the question about the time it takes to complete the project is of greater concern than the one about project-related experience. Using this approach, the higher the point score, the greater the risk. Figure 18.15 provides a list of other, project-independent factors that also influence the risk involved in undertaking a project.

Portfolio Risk

The total risk for the project portfolio—the **portfolio risk**—is proportional to the sum of the risks of the individual projects in the portfolio. What constitutes an acceptable level of portfolio risk depends on both the organizational and situational factors. For example, as we discussed in Chapter 2, decision makers differ in the level of risk that they find tolerable. Also, organizations such as banks and insurance companies, whose existences depend on the level of service afforded by information technologies, must assume a greater amount of risk than most other firms—greater, for instance, than those in the support category of the matrix shown previously in Figure 18.7 (page 771).

Beyond Portfolio Risk

Underlying conventional types of project risk and portfolio risk is a new type of risk—the risk that the organization may not be using technology strategically or really addressing the way technologically caused environmental changes will impact the entire corporate landscape. As Paul Tate notes,

> The traditional equation of costs and benefits is no longer enough to justify a corporate IS strategy . . . The issues that lie behind corporate vulnerability . . . [now include] a broad landscape of corporate concerns; the integrity, volume, and flow of information; the resulting organizational weaknesses; deficiencies in management skills; mutually dependent systems; and the pitfalls of the changing business markets around the world. . . . There is now a growing consensus among management theorists, social observers, and academicians that the traditional methods and structures of businesses are breaking down. Call it what you like, the management of change, of uncertainty, of risk, of crisis, or even of chaos—the bottom line is simply the management of complexity.

Responsibility for Project Portfolio Management

As noted in Chapter 14, responsibilities for systems development are often shared by several people. The CIO is the person with the heaviest burden of responsibility. As the highest-ranking manager of technology, the CIO should provide leadership in technology-related areas and take the blame when anything major goes wrong. To effectively carry out the business of MIS, the CIO must delegate parts of his or her workload to other people.

As the firm's leading technology officer, the CIO is responsible for identifying the systems within the organization that require the greatest amount of attention, then seeing that these systems are maintained, improved, re-engineered, or—if they are not yet developed—created. Because technology affects virtually every functional area of business, many firms use steering committees to oversee technology development. A technology **steering committee** usually consists of high-ranking officers within the various functional areas—as well as key personnel from the executive ranks—who collectively determine which systems are most needed by the organization. The committee generally establishes the priorities of the organization regarding technology and approves or disapproves projects having a major impact. The committee is usually not involved in the technical details of systems development, however; these details are left to the MIS department.

A study conducted by D. H. Drury, for instance, showed that corporate steering committees in Canadian companies had significant authority over establishing priorities for information processing, reviewing requests for information system resources, and resolving conflicts arising out of competing user needs. These committees had minor authority in such matters as monitoring the progress of specific projects, allocating money for computer resources, approving software purchases, and evaluating interfunctional applications. Eighty-five percent of the firms surveyed by R. L. Nolan in the early 1980s had executive steering committees, a sharp rise from the 50 percent reported in the mid-1970s.

Pricing MIS Products

During the early days of computers, which were heavily oriented toward transaction processing applications, little thought was given to pricing information systems products. Transaction processing systems cut across the entire organization and most employees seemed to benefit from them. Today, as information-intensive services targeted to specific users assume greater role, "free" computer use is not as prevalent as before. Therefore, organizations have developed various schemes to price MIS products.

Cost and Profit Approaches

Two major approaches are used to account for MIS services. One is the cost-center approach and the second is the profit-center approach.

The *cost-center approach* looks at MIS services as a cost. This cost is either left unallocated and is absorbed as an overhead expense by the organization, or it is allocated to various departments or functional areas by usage or some other method. Allocation procedures are often referred to as *chargeout* (or *chargeback*) methods. The number of different chargeout methods available is probably similar to the number of companies using them. Some firms have utility programs on their mainframes that monitor usage, assemble a list of services provided to each user, and allocate costs to users by a charge procedure determined by the MIS department. Other organizations—typically universities and research firms—use a chargeout method that apprises users of computing costs, but does not actually charge them. In order for chargeout to work as a costing method, it must be fair, consistent, and understandable to whoever is charged. For instance, problems will arise if a manager perceives that a service will cost only a few dollars and receives, instead, a bill for $200. The chargeout scheme should help users to make intelligent decisions about computer resources.

The *profit-center approach* operates the MIS department so that products are not necessarily priced at cost. Theoretically, the MIS group is allowed to charge functional areas within the company whatever the group thinks is appropriate. Likewise, the functional areas can purchase products or services outside the company if they want. In practice, numerous limitations should be established before this approach will work because, realistically, in-house consumers often cannot choose to use an outside service. The MIS department should not need to become a service bureau, with outside clients, in order to operate as a profit center.

Figure 18.16 shows these cost and profit approaches, along with their advantages and disadvantages. Traditionally, computing is considered to be a cost by many firms, and the cost-center approach was favored. In a firm where MIS is dominated by transaction processing, which benefits the entire enterprise, this might be expected. Recently, with many MIS departments developing products for individual internal departments and outside clients, and with MIS being viewed in strategic terms, the profit-center approach is becoming popular.

During the early phases of the system growth cycle, giving employees free use of computer facilities is often recommended. This encourages users to ex-

Approach	Advantage	Disadvantage
▪ Cost (unallocated)	Encourages experimentation No user hostility	Encourages waste Discourages MIS competitiveness
▪ Cost (allocated)	Discourages waste	Discourages experimentation Discourages MIS competitiveness
▪ Profit	Discourages waste Encourages MIS competitiveness	Discourages experimentation Can create user hostility May not be appropriate if MIS holds a monopoly

Figure 18.16 Approaches to pricing MIS services.

periment with the system, and the system is often improved as a consequence. In this sense, the system might be viewed as a prototype on which the MIS department is collecting further requirements data. Or the service provided for free might be looked upon as a giveaway, needed to collect valuable marketing research data. This approach can help get users excited about the new system. When users get enthusiastic, their managers are likely to become enthusiastic also. This is likely to translate into the perception that the investment in the new system is worthwhile.

Valuation Methods

When either the cost-center or the profit-center approach is implemented, one of three different methods can be used to establish a value for an MIS product. The methods include using a cost-based value, using a market-based value, and establishing a value through negotiation.

- **Cost-based value** To establish a cost-based value, a product is priced at the cost incurred by the MIS group. This cost is often determined through break-even rates, with end-of-period adjustments made to user accounts to ensure that the main computer facility pays for itself by year's end, or by standard rates that are set so the main computer facility theoretically breaks even. In the latter case, individual user accounts are not adjusted; any cost surplus simply falls into a general overhead account. Using cost-based value, of course, is not valid for products that are sold outside the firm. Cost-based value is the approach most commonly used with a cost-center philosophy.

- **Market-based value** To establish a market-based value, products are priced at market value—the price at which they should be profitable if sold outside of the company. This method is helpful when a profit-center philosophy is used.

- **Negotiated value** A negotiated value is a price that the buyer and seller jointly determine. It is most beneficial to use this approach when introducing new services or when phasing out old ones. Product values are commonly subject to negotiation when an individual or group is responsible for the cost of obtaining the product.

Unit Pricing

Traditionally, users were charged in such units as CPU hours, number of tape and disk accesses, lines or pages printed, and terminal connect hours. W. Synnot and W. Gruber, among others, suggest that prices be stated in units that are more understandable to users—for instance, cost per printed report, cost per check processed, cost per query or retrieval, and so on. Such a cost-per-transaction basis allows users to budget computing expenses better and to associate the value of information with its cost. If the costs reflect utility, such transaction pricing can better help users plan for future facilities.

BUDGETING FOR THE MIS FUNCTION

Budgeting is usually the final phase of the planning process. During this phase, managers develop a specific budget that shows how they intend to carry out their plans. Budgets are important because they express plans in specific, measurable terms and because they provide benchmarks against which actual managerial performance can be compared and controlled. The budget for the MIS area is generally used both to support the MIS staff and to buy or lease hardware, software, and services for the organization.

Figure 18.17 shows an example of an MIS budget. Because they are a major planning tool, budgets are usually prepared for both the long and short term. A long-term budget might show spending levels in various categories over several years. These spending levels should, of course, be consistent with the master plan developed out of the strategic-planning process depicted in Figure 18.5 (page 768). A short-term operational budget, such as the one in Figure 18.17, should be consistent with the operating plan (shown as part of the strategic plan in Figure 18.5). Once prepared, the budget also becomes part of the strategic plan.

Budgets serve various control purposes as well. For example, after the budget in Figure 18.17 is a year old, a variance analysis is often performed on it. A *variance analysis* shows how far actual spending in each budget category differs from planned spending.

Budgeting in corporations is performed in various ways. Three widely used approaches are top-down budgeting, bottom-up budgeting, and zero-based budgeting. The top-down and bottom-up budgeting methods are appropriate for projects; zero-based budgeting is used for both projects and for ongoing organizational activities.

Top-Down Budgeting

Top-down budgeting is based on the judgments of top and middle managers, as well as on data about past projects that are similar to the one under study. The managers estimate both total project costs and the costs of the major project

Staff salaries:

A1	Management	$230,000	
A2	Programmers and analysts	300,000	
A3	Information center	150,000	
A4	Secretarial	80,000	
	Total salaries		$760,000

Hardware:

B1	Equipment purchases	$250,000	
B2	Leases	100,000	
B3	Maintenance	50,000	
	Total hardware		400,000

Software:*

C1	Software purchases	$110,000	
C2	Leases	150,000	
	Total software		260,000

Services and supplies:

D1	ABC service bureau	$ 90,000	
D2	Supplies	20,000	
	Total services and supplies		110,000
	Total budget requirements		$1,530,000

Figure 18.17 An MIS operating budget.

*Program maintenance is included in programmer salaries

activities. The activity costs are then passed down to lower-level managers, who continue breaking down each activity into subactivities and identifying budgets for each subactivity. The breakdowns proceed to the lowest level.

An advantage to this approach is that higher-level budgets are usually acceptable, although some of the lower-level budgets might need adjustments. A disadvantage is that, if higher-level budgets are too tight, lower-level managers may make undesirable changes in order to complete the work within budget.

Bottom-Up Budgeting

Bottom-up budgeting is the reverse of the top-down approach. First, lower-level managers estimate their budgetary needs. Then, these budgets are combined into the total direct cost for the project. If necessary, the project leader and functional managers meet to resolve any disagreements. The project leader adds any overhead or contingency reserve to the final total.

An advantage to bottom-up budgets is that work modules might be budgeted more accurately. A disadvantage is possible abuse: Lower-level managers may overstate their resource needs because they fear that higher-level managers will cut budgets by some percentage no matter what they report.

Zero-Based Budgeting

Theoretically, in *zero-based budgeting*, the person creating the budget starts with no restrictions and carefully justifies in writing every item put on the budget. In practice, developing a budget this way is often time-consuming. Generally, such a budget is actually prepared by starting with a base amount, calculated by multiplying last year's budget by some percentage (for example, 80 percent). Any expenditures that exceed the base amount must then be justified in writing. Budget excesses are usually prioritized so that it is easier for executive management to choose where it wants to limit the budget.

Today, many end-user-related computing purchases are made outside of the MIS budget. Some industry observers feel that the end-user movement is just starting and that, at some point, the MIS budget will only cover transaction processing types of applications and a small staff of MIS professionals.

Evaluating the MIS Function

Periodically, the performance and worth of the MIS function must be assessed. Typically, such a review is done by the steering committee; the main focus of the review is on the performance of the chief information officer. The review covers such matters as the following:

- **Periodic performance reports** Periodic performance reports show how well the MIS area performed with respect to staying within planned spending limits. Because overspending may not be the CIO's fault, such reports are also often accompanied by a statement of controllable and uncontrollable expenses.

- **User surveys** User surveys (such as questionnaires or interviews) help to determine how satisfied users are with MIS performance. These surveys are designed to obtain subjective responses to questions such as the following: Are the systems that are supposed to be working really working? How responsive are MIS personnel to user needs? What should MIS be doing that it currently is not doing?

  Traditionally, MIS responsiveness to user needs is a problem. According to Leilani Allen, "Top managers routinely rate their computer departments dead last among staff functions. Not only is MIS slow and inefficient, they complain, but it is also expensive and unresponsive to inside customers."

- **System performance** Included under system performance are objective (and, often, quantifiable) measures concerning how well computer systems are performing. These are some examples of questions that need to be addressed in this area: How well are batch schedules met? Is on-line response time satisfactory? Is system downtime a problem? Is throughput satisfactory? Is the system error rate at an acceptable level?

- **Early warning signals** Included in the category of early warning signals are such matters as MIS staff turnover and changes in the user complaint level. These issues may or may not cause serious concern. Nonetheless, any of them might be an indication that something is seriously wrong.

IBM Restructures to Become More Competitive for the 1990s

n December 1991, IBM decided to eliminate stifling bureaucracy and plodding decision making by breaking its monolithic structure into a confederation of 13 smaller companies. Nine of the new businesses design and make IBM products. The rest are marketing units for different parts of the globe.

If the manufacturing and development businesses cannot provide what they need, the marketing units can buy (and sell) products from non-IBM suppliers. Personal computers made by another company have already been sold under this arrangement.

The 13 development and manufacturing units can market their products through non-IBM channels. For example, its semiconductor business has been doing a brisk business selling its memory chips to other computer manufacturers. This division also entered a long-range international research and development venture with Japan's NEC and the European Community's Siemans-Nixdorf to develop high-capacity memory chips.

Each unit is held accountable for its financial performance. If unit managers exceed revenue, profit, and operating goals, their pay is boosted and excess profits are reinvested in the unit. If goals are not achieved, the manager's pay is cut, along with the division's spending plans.

"THE 13 DEVELOPMENT AND MANUFACTURING UNITS CAN MARKET THEIR PRODUCTS THROUGH NON-IBM CHANNELS."

Whether these changes enhance IBM's competitiveness during the 1990s remains to be seen. However, Big Blue has transformed into the Baby Blues.

Adapted from Ziegler (1992).

- **Overall effectiveness** The bottom line in MIS performance is usually effectiveness. That is, did the MIS department function well and was it successful at what it did? If the MIS area set up an annual plan, and operated according to the guidelines of that plan (after the plan was approved by higher management), then it probably performed appropriately, assuming that the MIS department did not react poorly to any unanticipated events. How successful MIS was at meeting the plan can be determined by comparing planned operational objectives with actual performance. Such a comparison is possible, of course, if a strategic MIS plan was prepared.

KEY IRM ISSUES FOR THE 1990s

This textbook has discussed many important trends and issues facing MIS. As noted at several times, advances in information technology present continual challenges for MIS. Imaging technology, EDI, multimedia systems, and increasingly sophisticated knowledge-based systems are among the newer technologies that most experts think are especially likely to have a major impact on MIS plans and activities in the future. In addition, chief information officers often

1. Operating within budget constraints

2. Adapting to changing needs of internal customers

3. Overcoming resistance to change

4. Securing and maintaining senior management commitment

5. Overcoming deficiencies in internal customer involvement

6. Effectively dealing with corporate bureaucracy

7. Adapting to the effects of mergers/acquisitions

8. Overcoming the lack of cutting-edge MIS tools and techniques

9. Improving MIS staff development programs

10. Overcoming the inability to attract quality staff

Figure 18.18 Some of the major challenges impacting MIS services commonly reported by chief executive officers. (Adapted from *The Computerworld IS Pocket Guide for Success*)

Note: Responses are based on the most frequently stated answers.

mention numerous other MIS management challenges, such as those listed in Figure 18.18. However, two particular issues are currently the driving forces in MIS long-range planning and decision making: downsizing and outsourcing.

Downsizing

Among general management positions, **downsizing** usually refers to reducing the number of managers and professional staff members in an organization. This sometimes results in the elimination of selected middle management positions and levels. The rationale behind this type of downsizing is to reduce the distance between top-level managers and lower-level workers (which should improve communications between these levels), to further empower lower-level workers by having them assume tasks that their superiors traditionally performed and, of course, to reduce labor and managerial overhead costs. Such flattening of the organizational structure has, in many cases, resulted in leaner and more cost-effective operations. Hence, competitive advantage may result from downsizing efforts.

Like any other subunit, MIS has to handle the effects of downsizing personnel. However, in MIS, the term "downsizing" has a second meaning—the movement of applications that were traditionally run on mainframes (and large systems) to midrange systems, local area networks, and high-end workstations—often RISC-based. Many organizations realize that they can equal or surpass the computing power of their existing mainframes by moving to clustered or networked minicomputers and other distributed computing platforms. IBM's family of AS/400 minicomputers (which can be clustered like DEC VAX machines) are so successful that if the AS/400 division separated from IBM, it would be the second largest computer company in the world—second only to IBM itself, and still bigger than DEC.

The increasing availability of networkable minicomputers and workstations is causing most organizations to reassess their need for mainframes and other large systems. Some experts maintain that only the world's largest companies still need mainframes. High-end RISC-based workstations now rival low-end supercomputers in FLOPS, MIPS and other measures of throughput. Several experts predict that 80 percent of the new applications developed between now and the year 2000 will be for client-server local area networks. Hardware platform changes seem inevitable and these will undoubtedly impact MIS activities and staffing patterns.

Both definitions of downsizing suggest major changes in the internal mix of MIS personnel. As applications move from mainframes to minicomputers, fewer computer operators may be needed. The migration of applications from mainframes to other platforms will probably result in department-level and end-user development. This means that information center staff must develop and maintain expertise in LAN-based applications, LAN management, and applications for RISC-based workstations. In organizations moving toward distributing computing, even the CIO's job may be in danger; chief executive officers may wonder if chief information officers are needed in distributed environments. In sum, downsizing can potentially result in smaller MIS departments and a refocusing of MIS tasks and activities.

Outsourcing

Increasingly, organizations are looking outside for MIS services; doing so is called **outsourcing**. Outsourcing basically means turning over selected information systems functions to a third-party contractor. The functions outsourced can range from simple data entry to full systems development. Tracing its roots to the timesharing and professional services available during the 1960s, outsourcing has become an option in most MIS areas. When Kodak announced the development of partnership alliances with IBM (for managing its data centers and SNA network), Digital (for managing voice and data telecommunication), and Businessland (for microcomputer procurement and support), corporate America started to seriously consider outsourcing. Many saw the potential benefits of outsourcing, including cost cutting, gaining critically needed MIS skills, accelerating systems development, and relieving the firm of developing or operating non-strategic information systems.

Outsourcing is an umbrella term that covers many services. The following is a list of services that are available in the marketplace to an *outsourcer*—the firm interested in outsourcing some or all of its MIS functions:

- **Application development** Several studies indicate that application development is the most frequently outsourced MIS function. These activities may be outsourced to contract programmers or to systems integrators. *Contract programming* firms perform software development and maintenance activities, including systems analysis, design, programming, testing, implementation, conversion, and maintenance. The contract is typically on a one-time basis to meet a particular systems development or maintenance need that

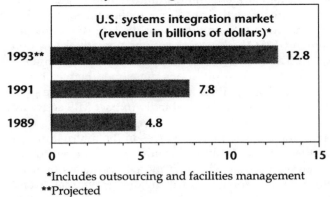

Systems Integration in the U.S.

**U.S. systems integration market
(revenue in billions of dollars)***

1993** 12.8

1991 7.8

1989 4.8

| 0 | 5 | 10 | 15 |

*Includes outsourcing and facilities management
**Projected

Figure 18.19 The systems integration market in the U.S. The revenues shown include both facilities management and outsourcing. (Adapted from *The Computerworld IS Pocket Guide for Success*)

cannot be adequately met by the outsourcer's MIS staff. Outsourcing to offshore systems development firms in countries with lower labor rates, such as the Philippines and India, are also increasing.

Systems integrators are firms that develop and install turnkey systems for a particular application. They may also perform other services, which may range from running the corporate data center to developing a strategic MIS plan for an organization. When developing turnkey systems, integrators combine (integrate) hardware and software from various vendors, as well as from its own development efforts. Using an integrator to develop a system may make it unnecessary for an organization to have an extensive array of highly qualified MIS personnel on its staff. In some cases, an integrator may be used to develop a system that would otherwise become part of the organization's visible backlog—thus freeing up the organization's MIS staff to concentrate on other needed applications, especially those identified during MIS planning as critical to its mission. As Figure 18.19 shows, the systems integration market in the United States has more than doubled since 1989, and continued growth is expected.

■ *Facilities management* An increasing number of organizations find it cost-effective to hire an outsourcing service provider to take over their data center operations. The outsourcing firm becomes responsible for operating and maintaining the outsourcer's data center equipment and applications (often, these are transaction processing systems).

This may be implemented in several ways. In some instances, the existing data center staff members become employees of the outsourcing firm. They continue to do their jobs, but their paychecks are issued by the outsourcing firm. In other cases, existing data center staff are replaced by employees of the outsourcing firm; the existing workers may be laid off or reassigned to other duties. In still other cases, the existing data center operations may be moved to the outsourcing service provider's location; MIS staff members from the original company may or may not also be moved.

Electronic Data Systems (EDS) is a well-known U.S. provider of such services. It was the first firm to exceed $1 billion in outsourcing contracts and is still the largest provider of these services. Ross Perot, whose bid to be president of the United States was unsuccessful, was the CEO of EDS for several years and contributed to making the company the force it is today. Perot now heads Perot Systems, another major outsourcing contractor.

- **Support operations** Support operations for maintenance, service, and disaster recovery are sometimes included in facilities management contracts, but these are usually considered to be specialty operations that are outsourced to firms specializing in these activities. Contracts for telephone hotline support centers are also included in this category.

- **Data entry and simple processing** These types of tasks can be outsourced easily because they are well defined, routine, and labor intensive. Because of this, high levels of interaction between the outsourcer and the firm providing these services are usually not necessary.

As you can see, outsourcing covers a lot of MIS activities. It ranges from leasing a whole MIS department to just having a programmer develop a simple application—whatever the organization needs to do outside of its normal routine.

Why Do Organizations Outsource?

Numerous factors contribute to the growing incidence of outsourcing. These include the inability of MIS departments to hire and keep suitable MIS professionals, plus the need for increased flexibility and access to international markets. Several other contributing factors are discussed next.

Cost Reduction and Containment During the 1980s, when organizations realized the competitive and strategic advantages of information systems, rapid MIS budget growth was normal. The recessionary times of the early 1990s resulted in flat or declining MIS budgets in most organizations. Today, mounting cost pressure is probably the most significant factor driving corporate interest in outsourcing. Personnel costs can be decreased by outsourcing application development and data center operations; also, problems with inexperienced personnel may be avoided. Even when the cost of outsourcing is not smaller, MIS costs may be more predictable; for example, in the case of application development, the burden for cost overruns can be contractually placed on the outsourcing service provider. With outsourcing, the need for in-house MIS staff is less—which can be a significant benefit because of the growing shortage of skilled MIS professionals. In addition, MIS staffing needs become more predictable and short-notice hiring to overcome an application development crisis may be needed less often.

Access to Cutting-Edge Technology and Knowledge Outsourcing MIS functions to an appropriate vendor can provide immediate access to the latest technology and expertise that would otherwise be beyond the reach of the outsourcer. For example, even if the in-house staff is not proficient in using

LARGE OUTSOURCING CONTRACTS		
Outsourcer	Outsourcing Service Provider	Contract Value
General Dynamics	Computer Sciences Corporation	$3 billion
Continental Airlines	EDS	$2.1 billion
Enron Corporation	EDS	$750 million
Continental Bank	EDS	$700 million
First City Bankcorp	IBM	$600 million
Eastman Kodak Company	IBM	$500 million
National Car Rental	EDS	$500 million

Figure 18.20 Some of the largest outsourcing contracts in effect during the 1990s. The magnitude of these contracts indicates that outsourcing will be a major issue for organizational computing in the future. (Adapted from *The Computerworld IS Pocket Guide for Success*)

object-oriented programming (OOP) and CASE tools, the appropriate outsourcer can apply them to an application development problem for the organization.

Improved Focus on the Strategic Use of Information Technology   Even for organizations whose MIS departments are filled with experienced and highly proficient development professionals, outsourcing may still be an attractive alternative. By outsourcing the routine maintenance and operations of transaction processing systems, available MIS talent can be used to promote competitiveness and strategic advantage. This may also increase flexibility and responsiveness in meeting market needs.

Increased Availability of Outsourcing Services   Recently, the number of outsourcing service providers has increased dramatically. Besides the traditional outsourcing service providers such as EDS, Computer Sciences Corporation, Perot Systems, Andersen Consulting (and the other five of the Big Six accounting firms), numerous other businesses from different industries now offer these services, including IBM, DEC, AT&T, Bechtel, Boeing, and the Mellon Bank. In 1989, the size of the U.S. outsourcing market was estimated at $26 billion; the market is projected to grow annually at about 15 percent, reaching $50 billion by 1994. Figure 18.20 lists some of the largest outsourcing contracts that exist. With increased competition, the prices for outsourcing services are falling, making outsourcing an even more attractive option to organizations.

In sum, outsourcing offers an organization various ways to leverage its resources, manage its costs, and increase its potential to achieve strategic objectives.

Despite arguments in favor of outsourcing, chief information officers and other MIS executives often resist its use. One source of dissatisfaction with outsourcing is the view that it reduces the CIO's control over the work performed on application development projects because the work is not being performed by his or her own subordinates. Many other MIS executives see outsourcing as a direct threat to the job security and career prospects of themselves and their subordinates. Having to address outsourcing-produced personnel displacement problems such as layoffs, retraining, and the absorption of displaced personnel by the outsourcing vendor can be difficult for both outsourcers and outsourcing contractors. For example, in February 1992, disgruntled workers transferred from Kodak to DEC filed a $5 million suit, claiming that both companies co-erced and misled them about benefits at DEC. EDS also faces legal action for laying off 92 of the 570 MIS workers it inherited in its $800 million outsourcing contract with Blue Cross/Blue Shield of Massachusetts; when bidding for the contract, EDS publicly announced that "no major" layoffs would occur—the affected workers claim that they were deliberately misled by EDS in order to gain their support.

Global Outsourcing

Global outsourcing is a recent trend that also interests an increasing number of companies. As noted previously, computer professionals can often be hired for much lower salaries in other parts of the world. For example, it is estimated that the "true" average annual cost of an MIS professional in the United States is about $100,000 when salary, benefits, computer usage, and other related over-head costs are included. The equivalent cost for the average MIS professional in India or the Philippines is only about $35,000. Software developers and contract programming firms in these countries see outsourcing as a profitable target market for their MIS services and recognize the pricing advantage that they have. Hence, it is not surprising that global outsourcing is a rapidly growing segment of the total outsourcing market.

Several U.S. corporations have used global outsourcing. Unisys outsourced numerous application development projects to programmers in Singapore and India. Citibank outsourced to firms in India and the Philippines; Merrill Lynch contracted with an Irish firm. Even such U.S. hardware vendors as DEC, Texas Instruments, and Tandem have entered into global outsourcing contracts.

Data entry and contract programming are the most commonly outsourced MIS services. Pacific Data Services has contracted data-entry services from China since 1961. Some vendors formed data-entry partnerships that employ data-entry personnel from numerous countries. For example, Mead Data Central has citizens of Jamaica, Haiti, and Barbados entering information for large databases such as Nexis.

In some cases, semi-skilled jobs are also globally outsourced. New York Life Insurance, for example, contracted with an Irish firm for claims processing. In still other cases, fairly sophisticated systems development tasks are outsourced. For example, Techna International in Calcutta, India, is developing an intelligent workstation for Internet Corporation, a Chicago-based company that develops banking software packages.

In sum, the range of globally outsourced MIS services has expanded re-cently—primarily due to the lower labor costs available in other countries. However, outsourcers may also increase their global visibility, helping them to gain a foothold in new foreign markets. Still, global outsourcing can present potential communications and coordination challenges to outsourcers and may open the door to other problems. (For example, Taiwan and Brazil have no real software copyright laws; contracting with firms in these areas may increase the chances of software specifications being copied or shared with an outsourcer's competitors.)

Both downsizing and outsourcing are becoming more important factors in the development of MIS's long-range plans. In some instances, they may both play a role in an organization's efforts to restructure its MIS operations. For example, Revlon, Inc., signed a transitional outsourcing contract with Andersen Consulting to handle its data processing, network management, and application maintenance tasks while it downsizes from its IBM mainframes and minicomputers to a distributed client-server architecture. About 100 Revlon MIS employees were moved from New York to Andersen's Dallas data center and are continuing the daily data processing operations. By outsourcing these tasks, the remaining MIS personnel at Revlon are free to focus on making the transition to a new platform and MIS culture with minimal disruption to the company's business. As the popularity of downsizing spreads, an increasing number of organizations will probably enter into transitional outsourcing contracts with vendors.

SUMMARY

In many organizations, the executive who heads up the MIS department has the title of chief information officer (CIO). CIO responsibilities often include: participating in organizational strategic planning, developing MIS strategic plans, allocating budget resources, effectively leading the MIS area, overseeing security, managing MIS personnel, maintaining relationships with other executives, and monitoring technological developments. The role of the CIO is determined by the role of MIS in the organization. MIS's role is determined by such factors as the organization's industry and corporate culture.

Strategic planning is a top-level management activity in which the long-range course for an organization or business unit is charted. It is a critical issue for MIS executives. For strategic-planning purposes, it is often useful to consider the MIS department as a business within a business and, possibly, as a "marketing firm" that is in the business of meeting consumer needs.

The CIO must consider two levels of strategic planning: for both the parent organization and for the MIS department. The parent organization's strategic plan is important because the direction of the MIS department must be compatible with that of the company itself. The MIS department's strategic plan must address many specific issues, including the mission and scope of the MIS function; the current profile of the MIS department within the organization; the MIS external environment; MIS strategies in relation to organizational strategies; long-term MIS objectives; annual MIS objectives; the master and operating MIS plans; and specific policies for the MIS department.

Numerous frameworks and methodologies can help the CIO to develop a strategic plan. These include: parallel plan development, which ensures compatibility between the strategic plan of the parent organization and that of the MIS department; role assessment, which assesses the role of MIS within the organization; observation, which assists in determining the apparent direction of the company; scenario approaches, which are used to hypothesize future events and plan reactions to them; investment analysis, which attempts to measure how funds are spent; the critical success factors (CSF) approach, which tries to identify the activities required for success; the value chain model, which attempts to identify the organization's most urgent needs for information; the competitive forces model, which encourages the planner to consider external environment factors that may pose problems or provide opportunities; Business System Planning (BSP), which approaches strategic planning by looking for stable infrastructures within the organization; and portfolio approaches, which try to determine a sensible mix of new projects.

One of the most important aspects of project selection is analyzing project benefits and costs. Cost-justification methods can be categorized according to whether the benefits derived are tangible or intangible. Three methods used to measure tangible benefits are the payback approach, the present value approach, and the internal rate of return approach. The payback approach attempts to measure the time it will take to recoup in benefits the money that was invested. The present value approach attempts to value future dollars in terms of their value today. The internal rate of return approach is used to calculate the rate of return on project investment by finding the interest rate that makes the project's cost stream equal its benefit stream.

Intangible benefits are difficult to cost justify. One method, however, is to combine tangible and intangible benefits, determine the value of the tangible benefits, and then estimate how sizable the intangible benefits must be to justify the proposed project.

Many organizations follow a portfolio approach to selecting projects, taking care to limit risk (the degree of exposure to uncertain outcomes). Sources of project risk are not meeting implementation schedules, spending more money than anticipated, and achieving fewer benefits than planned. Project size, project structure, and project-related experience all influence project risk. Portfolio risk is proportional to the sum of the risks of each project in the portfolio.

Responsibilities for project portfolio management are shared by the CIO, systems developers, and often by a steering committee of high-ranking officers from key user areas. These people collectively determine which systems are needed by the organization.

MIS services are priced according to either a cost-center approach or a profit-center approach. The cost-center approach views the services provided as a cost that must be recovered. Often, such costs are allocated to personnel according to their resource usage. These allocated costs become the price charged by the MIS department—which works on a breakeven basis—for its services. The profit-center approach prices products at a rate designed to generate a profit—for example, by a market-based value or a negotiated value.

The MIS department must follow a budget to encourage controlled and orderly spending. Three widely used approaches to budgeting are top-down budgeting, bottom-up budgeting, and zero-based budgeting. Top-down budgeting essentially allocates funds in a manner which is consistent with the organization's hierarchy of goals. Bottom-up budgeting filters management needs up through the hierarchy until an organization-wide budget is developed. Zero-based budgeting requires managers to justify each budgetary request and show how it contributes to achieving strategic goals.

The MIS function should be periodically assessed by upper management. Such an evaluation should include reviews of regular performance reports prepared by the MIS department, user surveys, and system performance statistics. Upper management should also look for early warning signals, such as high staff turnover. The ultimate consideration in the evaluation should be assessing the overall effectiveness of the MIS department.

The increasing popularity of downsizing and outsourcing have significantly impacted MIS plans and operations. The movement of applications from mainframes to minicomputers and local area networks (downsizing) caused many organizations to refocus their application development efforts. Outsourcing (contracting with another firm to provide MIS services) is also increasingly popular. An organization may outsource for many reasons, including cost reduction and containment, plus access to state-of-the art technology and expertise that would otherwise be unattainable. An increasing number of firms are providing outsourcing services. By outsourcing some of its MIS tasks, an organization can also concentrate on enhancing strategically important information systems. Global outsourcing is growing in popularity, largely because of lower MIS labor costs in other countries.

Both downsizing and outsourcing can result in the displacement of MIS personnel and even threaten the job security of chief information officers. Hence, MIS executives often resist these approaches. Still, both downsizing and outsourcing will probably become more common during the 1990s.

KEY TERMS

Budgeting	Payback
Business System Planning (BSP)	Portfolio approach
Competitive forces model	Portfolio risk
Downsizing	Present value
Global outsourcing	Project risk
Internal rate of return	Scenario approach
Investment analysis	Steering committee
Outsourcing	Value chain model

REVIEW QUESTIONS

1. Describe the responsibilities of the CIO.
2. What characteristics should chief information officers possess?

3. Why is strategic planning a vital activity for the MIS department?

4. What issues must the MIS department consider when addressing its mission and scope?

5. What issues must the MIS department consider when addressing the impact of its external environment?

6. Provide some examples of MIS policies. Which type(s) of people should policies cover?

7. Explain the purpose of the role-assessment matrix in Figure 18.7 (page 771).

8. How are scenario approaches useful as strategic-planning tools?

9. Why would an organization use the competitive forces model?

10. What methods are available to analyze the costs and benefits of a project?

11. What factors contribute to the riskiness of a particular project?

12. What types of activities are performed by a steering committee?

13. Discuss the various methods used to price MIS outputs.

14. In what ways can the MIS function be evaluated?

15. What is downsizing and why is it used in an increasing number of organizations?

16. What is outsourcing?

17. Why do organizations outsource?

18. Why may chief information officers resist outsourcing?

19. Why is global outsourcing increasing in popularity?

DISCUSSION QUESTIONS

1. The CIO position is typically characterized as a high-turnover slot in organizations. What factors contribute to this? Why are CIO positions threatened in many organizations?

2. What types of alternatives are open to an MIS department that wants to sell MIS products and services outside of the parent organization?

3. In what ways does risk enter into MIS management?

Using Critical Success Factors to Integrate MIS and Corporate Strategies at Boeing

The increasingly global and dynamic business environment of the 1990s has elevated the importance of strategic planning in many organizations. The importance of consistency between MIS's long-range plans and the strategic objectives of the rest of the organization is becoming more significant. Boeing is one of many organizations to discover that the critical success factor (CSF) approach can be effectively used to connect MIS plans with organizational plans.

The critical success factor approach is based on the idea that managers should focus their attention on a few things that are most crucial to their organization's success and survival. As A. C. Boynton and R. W. Zmud note: "Critical success factors are those few things that must go well to ensure success for a manager or an organization, and therefore, they represent those managerial or enterprise areas that must be given special and continual attention to bring high performance. CSFs include issues vital to an organization's current operating activities and to its future success."

In short, critical success factors are the managerial elements that can help an organization gain a competitive edge in its industry.

Since the late 1970s, numerous organizations have used the CSF approach as a planning tool for designing management information systems. The Boeing Military Airplanes Support Division (BMA Support Division) of Boeing Computer Services (BCS) has used this approach since 1983 and its experience provides insight into why the CSF concept is gaining in popularity.

BCS was established in the early 1970s as an operating company under the Boeing umbrella. Its purpose is to develop and provide the computing and telecommunication resources and expertise needed to meet The Boeing Company's business objectives. BMA Support Division's mission is to directly contribute to Boeing's success; to do so, it provides a broad range of computing services, including database management, engineering graphics, integrated logistics systems, and traditional MIS systems.

Before 1983, BMA Support Division used an MBO (management-by-objectives) approach to planning. This process resulted in a detailed set of objectives for the upcoming 12-month period. An action plan was developed for each objective—as well as the criteria used to measure the extent to which the objective was achieved. With this approach, operating managers collectively identified 15–20 objectives that provided them with a sense of direction and a set of performance targets. However, as Boeing's business volumes increased, it became clear that the MBO approach did not provide the BMA Support Division with the strategic focus that it needed.

After considering various alternative approaches for better connecting BMA Support Division's plans with corporate plans, they decided to adopt the CSF approach. Management felt that this approach would provide Boeing with a systematic thought process that would force them to think about the business they were in and to develop a set of strategies for action that would positively impact performance.

BMA Support Division's CSF approach evolved into a six-step process: (1) reassessing the mission of the firm in the context of the dynamic environment, (2) identifying critical success factors, (3) analyzing the firm's strengths and weaknesses related to each CSF, (4) developing specific action plans for overcoming weaknesses and achieving each CSF, (5) implementing the action plans, and (6) reviewing actual performance after action plan implementation.

BMA Support Division has used this approach since 1984 and has no plans to abandon it. Many managers feel positively about the way it handles issues and indicate that the CSF approach promotes a team atmosphere, effective communication, and a common understanding of the organization and its strategic direction.

The Boeing Company's annual assessments of BCS and the BMA Support Division have shown steady improvement since the CSF approach began. While the performance increases are not solely due to the CSF approach, many feel that it has been a major contributor. The entire BCS area is now using the CSF approach and its use is spreading to other parts of The Boeing Company.

Adapted from Chung and Friesen (1991) and Boynton and Zmud (1984).

DISCUSSION

1. In addition to the CSF approach, several other MIS strategic planning tools are described in this chapter, including parallel plan development, observation, scenario approaches, the value chain model, and the competitive forces model. Based on the information provided in the case, if the BMA Support Division had not chosen the CSF approach, which approach do you think they would have selected? Explain your reasoning and justify your choice.

2. What seem to be the major advantages of the CSF approach?

3. What problems may organizations encounter when they try to implement the CSF approach; that is, what weaknesses do you see in this approach?

4. Some experts feel that the CSF approach works best with managers at high levels in the organization, rather than with managers at lower levels. What do you think accounts for this?

Chapter 19

Selected Issues in MIS Management

After completing this chapter, you will be able to:

Explain the importance of security to computer-based information systems

Name and describe several types of computer crimes

Identify and describe several computer-related ethical issues

Describe several ways in which MIS careers can be developed

List some of the multinational issues that must be considered when building information systems that span across two or more countries

Identify some of the unfolding trends that are likely to impact MIS in the future

In the last several chapters, we discussed several topics related to information systems development and management. Chapters 14–17 addressed both formal and informal types of approaches to the technical planning and development of information systems, while Chapter 18 covered the more strategic components of MIS planning and development. In this chapter, we cover several other areas that can have a bearing on both the development and management of information systems.

We begin by looking at concerns that were raised regarding the security of data in information systems environments. Security concerns normally require that the MIS department establish some type of policy. Like security, ethical issues related to information issues are also a major concern. We will explore these topics before turning to training in the information systems area, plus some possible MIS career tracks. Then, we turn to international aspects of managing information systems. As we noted throughout this textbook, businesses are increasingly turning to foreign sites for competitive advantage. This is a movement that poses both problems and opportunities for MIS. Finally, we end this last chapter with some of the unfolding trends that will probably have a major impact on information systems—and on their use in the years ahead.

SECURITY

An important concern that accompanies the planning of most information systems is security. **Security** refers to the protection of computer-based resources—hardware, software, data, procedures, and people—against alteration, destruction, or unauthorized use.

Once, security was relatively straightforward—only a centralized mainframe needed guarding. The continual development of communications networks compounded security problems as people learned how to access centralized data from various sites—including international locations. Within the last several years, numerous other security threats have appeared. The rise in microcomputer-based processing, for example, has distributed electronic data to scores of local sites, many of which have very limited, if any, security controls. Plus, interorganizational systems (such as EDI and other systems that hook a company to supplier or client companies) have resulted in many firms using someone else's computer system at the firm's location—and the company often has little or no control over the system. Also, the surge in computer literacy and end-user computing enables increasingly more people to use computer systems for their own purposes. Figure 19.1 illustrates the vulnerable points in a firm's data communications network for which security may be necessary.

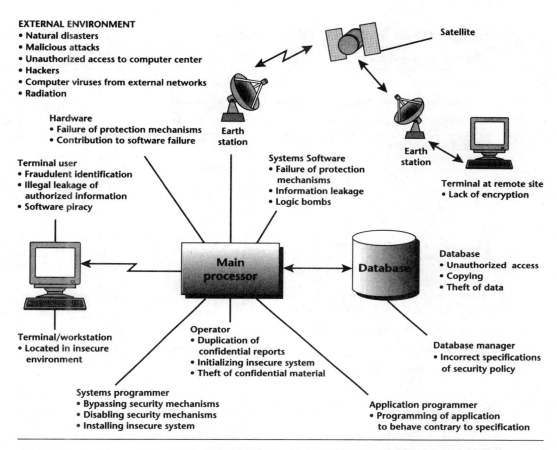

EXTERNAL ENVIRONMENT
- **Natural disasters**
- **Malicious attacks**
- **Unauthorized access to computer center**
- **Hackers**
- **Computer viruses from external networks**
- **Radiation**

Hardware
- **Failure of protection mechanisms**
- **Contribution to software failure**

Earth station

Satellite

Earth station

Systems Software
- **Failure of protection mechanisms**
- **Information leakage**
- **Logic bombs**

Terminal at remote site
- **Lack of encryption**

Terminal user
- **Fraudulent identification**
- **Illegal leakage of authorized information**
- **Software piracy**

Main processor

Database

Database
- **Unauthorized access**
- **Copying**
- **Theft of data**

Terminal/workstation
- **Located in insecure environment**

Operator
- **Duplication of confidential reports**
- **Initializing insecure system**
- **Theft of confidential material**

Database manager
- **Incorrect specifications of security policy**

Systems programmer
- **Bypassing security mechanisms**
- **Disabling security mechanisms**
- **Installing insecure system**

Application programmer
- **Programming of application to behave contrary to specification**

Figure 19.1 A summary of the major security threats in computer–based information systems. The development of distributive processing systems and the increased availability to various external databases and information services have added to the security challenges that MIS professionals face.

Figure 19.2 shows numerous security-related concerns. In Chapter 15, we identified several validation controls that can be built into individual computer systems to ensure against certain forms of human carelessness. Also discussed in that chapter were computer-based information systems (CBIS) concerns about protecting the privacy of individuals. Here, we will look at other, broader security-related issues. Specifically, we will examine ways of protecting against crime, natural disaster, and certain types of hardware and software failures.

The responsibility for security divides into two distinct areas: the design of security procedures (which is usually the responsibility of systems analysts and designers) and the day-to-day execution of security procedures (which increasingly is the job of the *corporate information security officer*, or *CISO*, on the computer operations staff). Of course, overall responsibility for security lies with an organization's top MIS executives. Chief information officers should know how vulnerable their organizations are to security problems and should assess

MAJOR TYPES OF MIS SECURITY PROBLEMS

Human Carelessness

- Keying or inputting error
- Computer operator error
- Wrong version of program used
- Program damaged during development or use
- Misplaced file or volume
- Physical damage of I/O media

Computer Crime

- System sabotage
- Espionage
- Using computer systems to steal money or products
- Sensitive data changed in an unauthorized way
- Program or data copied and used for unauthorized purposes

Natural or Political Disasters

- Earthquakes, fire, flood, or wind damage
- Rioting or war

Hardware and Software Failures

- Equipment malfunctions
- Power outages
- Damage caused by undetected viruses
- Data damaged by hardware or software failures
- Undetected data transmission errors

Figure 19.2 Some of the major sources of information systems security problems. Although security measures are increasingly more sophisticated, the spread of new technology products, the increased reliance on communications systems, the trend toward distributive computing, and the end-user computing revolution have all increased security-related risks.

the risk they are willing to tolerate. It is virtually impossible, and certainly impractical, to make any system 100 percent secure. However, as we will discuss a little later in this chapter, it is possible to take measures to protect an organization from losing data as a result of security breaches.

Computer Crime

Computer crime refers to using computer resources to engage in unauthorized or illegal acts. Computer crime includes such activities as stealing money by using the computer to electronically divert funds, using CBIS resources to falsify electronic data, copying or using programs or data without authorization, and invading networks not intended for that person's use. Today, with information technologies creating many changes in corporate life, what constitutes a computer crime is not well defined—its boundaries change with the evolving uses of technology.

Although almost every state has laws pertaining to such events as theft by means of a computer, very few computer crime cases go to trial. According to

Types of Computer Crimes	
▓ Data diddling	▓ Scavenging techniques
▓ Trojan Horse technique	▓ Leakage
▓ Salami technique	▓ Eavesdropping
▓ Superzap programs	▓ Wiretapping
▓ Trapdoor routines	▓ Software piracy
▓ Logic bombs	▓ Hacking
▓ Computer viruses	

Figure 19.3 Types of computer crimes. Studies show that most computer crimes involve employees.

statistics compiled by the National Center for Computer Crime Data in Los Angeles, most of the cases tried are insider jobs involving employees. However, a lot of computer crime cases go unreported because victim organizations would suffer adverse publicity if people knew that their computer security systems were vulnerable.

Because the full extent of computer crime is unknown—and unreported—the exact cost of computer crime to organizations is difficult to assess. By some estimates, it is billions of dollars. According to Patricia Keefe, in a survey conducted by Ernst & Whinney, more than half of the 562 respondents said they had experienced financial losses due to computer system tampering. Twelve percent estimated the losses as somewhere between $50,000 and $500,000.

Types of Computer Crimes

The range of computer crimes is extensive, with much of it involving programmers, data input clerks, bank tellers, insider-outsider teams, and students. High on the list of victims, according to the National Center for Computer Crime Data, are banks and telecommunication companies. The following is a list of several forms of computer crimes (see Figure 19.3 also).

■ *Data diddling* Data diddling involves performing unauthorized modifications to data stored within the computer system. For instance, in one case, an employee at an academic computing center used his privileged access to falsify his academic record. The employee was subsequently discharged, without facing criminal charges, to avoid embarrassment to the victimized institution. Another common data-diddling crime is, for example, when a clerk changes the destination addresses for shipments of goods, diverting them to accomplices. Still another is when someone working for a state agency deletes parking or speeding tickets from a computer database.

■ *The Trojan Horse technique* In Greek mythology, the Trojan Horse was a large wooden horse left by the Greeks upon their pretended retreat of the siege of Troy. The Trojans, thinking it was a sacrifice to Athena, let the horse into the city gates. At night, Greek soldiers hidden within the horse opened the gates to the Greek army, which conquered the city. Today's electronic-age counterpart to that myth is a block of criminal computer code, buried within an authorized program, that performs unauthorized acts—such as transferring money to a criminal's bank account.

- **The salami technique** The salami technique works under the assumption that, if small quantities of money are shaved from a lot of balances that are not closely checked, and these shavings are combined in a central account, that account will swell to a large amount over time. The finance sector is particularly vulnerable to the salami shaver. Interest posted to bank or security accounts is often not checked by its owners down to the nearest penny. A criminal with access to an interest payment program could divert into his or her account all hundredths of a cent in interest that should be credited to the real owners' accounts. Because the records of the bank remain in balance after the shaving is done, they may not realize what happened.

- **Superzap programs** A superzap program can bypass regular system controls when a malfunction or a significant error in the computer system exists. Superzap programs are intended as last resorts; for example, when a vital update program crashes and certain account balances—which can normally be updated only when that program is operative—must be reconstructed by other methods. Because superzap programs allow their users privileged operations, only certain key personnel are authorized to use them. In the hands of the wrong person, they could be used to perform various criminal acts.

- **Trapdoor routines** Trapdoors are routines used in program development to allow developers access to various parts of the computer system in order to see that the program is performing correctly. For instance, a trapdoor might be used in a systems program to view various sections of RAM, as a check that the program is storing data correctly. Although trapdoors are supposed to be removed before the program is put into general use, occasionally they aren't. In one reported case, criminals accessed passwords through a trapdoor that was not removed, and later used the passwords to break into the system.

- **Logic bombs** A logic bomb is a routine that causes parts of the computer system to become inoperative or to malfunction as soon as the routine is executed. Most malicious logic bombs are written by disgruntled programmers—who are, often, on the verge of being fired—to erase key files or programs, or to cause programs to halt or process data incorrectly. Other logic bombs are purposely incorporated into programs by software vendors—usually to disable a software package after a certain time period (for example, after a 30-day demonstration period). Most purposeful logic bombs of this type don't raise ethical issues, but undocumented ones can. For instance, in late 1991, Revlon made trade press headlines when parts of its data suddenly became inaccessible during a payment dispute with a software vendor. A bomb had stopped one of its programs; the vendor had never informed Revlon of its existence. Revlon successfully sued the vendor.

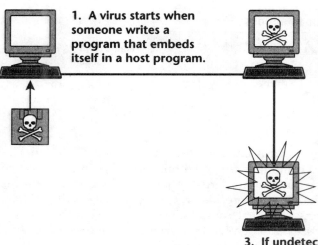

1. A virus starts when someone writes a program that embeds itself in a host program.

2. The virus attaches itself to the host program or data and travels anywhere that the host program or piece of data travels. Transmission can occur on floppy disk, over data communications networks, or through electronic bulletin boards.

3. If undetected by virus scanning and eradication software, the virus is set off by either a time limit or some set of circumstances—possibly a simple sequence of computer operations by the user. Then it does whatever the virus programmer intended, whether it is to print phrases such as "Beat the Vikings," erase data, or damage the system in the other ways described in the text.

Figure 19.4 How a computer virus can spread. Just as a biological virus causes disease by disrupting the normal operations of living cells in an organism, a computer virus invades the inner workings of computers and disrupts their normal operations.

■ *Computer viruses* Sometimes the term *computer virus* is used to describe a logic bomb in which a piece of unauthorized code acts as a parasite that attaches itself to a host program during a copy operation. Like their biological counterparts, computer viruses reproduce and spread; copy commands are embedded in the virus code to make it reproduce, and transmit commands may be inserted to spread the virus from one computer to others on its network. Virus code is often implanted by using the Trojan Horse technique discussed earlier. Once implanted, the manner in which a computer virus may spread is illustrated in Figure 19.4.

Viruses can cause various organizational problems. For example, in November 1988, Robert Morris—a computer science student at Cornell University—inserted a virus in a service linking several nationwide networks, bringing thousands of systems to a halt and impacting more than 6,000 users. The virus worked by filling up the RAM of each infected system; in effect, locking out all applications. Morris later became the first person convicted of the federal Computer Virus Eradication Act. A later scare

Problems Caused by Virus Infections

Loss of productivity	Corrupted files
Screen messages and lockup	Lost data
Unreliable applications	System crashes
Loss of user confidence	

Figure 19.5 A summary of the most commonly reported impacts of computer viruses. These are listed in order of occurrence from most to least.

involving the Michelangelo virus impacted users worldwide. In 1992, the internal clocks of infected computers triggered this virus. When they reached March 6—the birthday of sculptor/artist Michelangelo Buonarroti—the virus struck. During the week before March 6, even CNN Headline News publicized precautionary steps that could be taken to prevent the damage that the virus could cause. Apparently, the warnings were heeded because the virus's impact was minor—especially in the U.S.

Figure 19.5 provides a summary of the most commonly reported impacts of virus infections. Loss of productivity results from most virus infections. Screen messages and screen lockup (for example, as characters fall off the screen or start bouncing off the sides of the screen) are also common occurences. Corrupted files and/or lost data occur in approximately one-third of the cases. The remaining impacts listed in Figure 19.5 occur in approximately one-fifth to one-quarter of the reported incidents.

Some of the recent strains of viruses are encrypted (encoded) so that they defy detection by commercially available virus detection/eradication software packages such as Central Point Antivirus, Viruscan, ViruCide, Flu_Shot Plus, and Dr. Solomon's Anti-Virus Toolkit. Virus detection/eradication software packages are becoming standard fixtures in most offices; they are even packaged with microcomputer systems for home users. Apparently, the war between virus developers and virus detection/eradication package vendors continues. New virus strains are regularly found and the number of viruses that the detection/eradication packages can discover and eliminate is growing steadily.

Unfortunately, viruses are common in today's computer systems and the potential problems they may cause must be addressed. In 1992, the potential problems became even worse. Professional computer virus fighters were outraged by the publication of a book that contained the source code needed to create potentially destructive viruses, plus coupons for floppy disks containing executable virus programs. The publication of this book provided disgruntled employees and would-be hackers with the information needed to disable organizational computing systems. Now, more than ever, managers and users must stay alert for viruses and should take precautions in order to minimize the chance of infection. Figure 19.6 provides some precautionary steps to protect information systems from viruses.

■ **Scavenging techniques** Scavenging is a technique in which someone browses through garbage for information that can be used to perform a

Virus Prevention and Protection Guidelines

- Check public domain software and any other new software by using a virus-detection program before running it on your system.

- Keep original application disks safely tucked away so they can't be infected.

- Make frequent backups of important files and data.

- Limit the exchange of disks containing executable code (such as .EXE files).

- Put write-protect tabs on all of your floppy disks.

- Never boot a hard-disk system from any floppy disk except the original, write-protected system disk.

- Make virus security an extension of your overall system security. Do not deal with it as a separate issue.

- Don't assume a computer problem is virus-related. Human error is the cause of most problems.

- Education and awareness of the problem are among the best ways to deal with virus concerns.

Figure 19.6 Some of the precautionary steps that managers and users should employ to thwart the potential of computer virus infections.

criminal activity. In one famous case, a scavenger looked through trash cans containing computer output and illegally ordered thousands of dollars worth of communications equipment before being caught. Departmental microcomputers have provided a new target for scavengers.

- **Leakage** Leakage results when important data, programs, or computer resources—which are normally safeguarded—leave a site without authorization. For instance, sensitive data can be transported to a 3½" diskette, which can be put in an employee's pocket and never noticed when he or she leaves work. On a more sophisticated scale, mathematical algorithms can be used to hash programs or data so that they look like garbage and are allowed to leave the company undetected.

- **Eavesdropping** Eavesdropping allows a person to observe transmissions intended for other people. Micro-to-mainframe telecommunication links and local area networks are particularly vulnerable to eavesdroppers; however, their security features are improving over time. The primary targets of the eavesdropper are protected passwords and account numbers.

- **Wiretapping** Wiretapping, a special case of eavesdropping, consists of setting up a special transmission path to divert the flow of data. For instance, a wire or cable can be illegally attached into a network to perform various unauthorized acts, such as espionage, stealing programs, altering data, and so on. Satellite facilities are especially vulnerable to wiretapping. Fiber optic cable, on the other hand, is relatively safe from wiretaps because cutting the cable in any way deflects the transmitted light beams and garbles data completely.

- **Software piracy** **Software piracy** refers to the unauthorized copying or use of programs. The most familiar form of software piracy is when people make unauthorized copies of such programs as Lotus 1-2-3 or dBASE for their own use. In fact, several lawsuits have evolved from such abuses. The most costly form of software piracy to organizations, however, is when professional thieves make thousands of copies of a software program and sell them illegally. Several companies—including Microsoft and Autodesk—have had well-publicized software piracy problems abroad. In Brazil, for instance, pirated copies of Microsoft's MS-DOS and Autodesk's AutoCad caused the executive branch of the U.S. government to initiate sanctions against that country.

- **Hacking** The term "hacker" originally referred to computer professionals who solved complex computer problems. Today, the term "hacker" (or "cracker"—a term used in computer crime circles) has a much more negative meaning. Hacking is a computer crime in which the criminal breaks into a computer system just for the challenge of doing so. Perhaps the most publicized case of hacking is that of the high school hackers in a Milwaukee computer club who broke into computers at the Sloan-Kettering Cancer Institute and at the Los Alamos National Laboratory.

  In April 1992, Equifax, Inc.—one of the largest credit bureaus in the U.S.—reported that hackers had invaded their system and stolen numerous individuals' credit history records—containing, among other information, account numbers for credit cards. Equifax learned of the security breach from the FBI after police found printouts of 13 Equifax credit histories in the possession of a teenage hacker. Police fear that information from Equifax files was shared with an extensive network of hackers and that thousands of dollars' worth of illegal charges resulted from the theft of this data. After learning of the break-in from the FBI, Equifax immediately began a review of its security procedures and took steps to better protect this sensitive data. Despite the wide publicity that hacking receives, however, it constitutes a relatively small percentage of computer crime.

Preventing Computer Crime

Organizations have used various methods to prevent computer crime. Some of them are discussed here and listed in Figure 19.7.

- **Hire carefully** Because most computer crimes are committed by employees, one of the most logical ways to prevent them is to hire trustworthy people. Of course, this can be difficult because would-be criminals are not easily spotted. Some steps that an organization might take to ensure the trustworthiness of its employees are to check references and—for people required to work in sensitive environments—conduct background checks. Increasingly, and against public opinion, organizations are becoming interested in such matters as drug, alcohol, and gambling habits—all of which can either lead to a crime or make an employee oblivious to crimes being committed.

Preventing Computer Crime		

▧ Hire carefully	▧ Encrypt data and programs
▧ Beware of malcontents	▧ Monitor system transactions
▧ Separate employee functions	▧ Conduct frequent audits
▧ Restrict system use	▧ Educate people in security measures
▧ Protect resources with passwords or access cards	

Figure 19.7 A summary of the general solutions to computer crime. Solutions to stopping computer crime usually involve either establishing a security system or minimizing the potential for employees to commit the crimes.

- **Beware of malcontents** A particularly troublesome problem area—and one that many crime experts put at the top of their lists—is the disgruntled employee. For example, in a case described by M. Buss and Lynn Salerno, a data processing supervisor who was passed over for promotion used his after-hours access to a computer installation to locate and steal disks containing his company's most important financial records. In another case, an editor for *Encyclopedia Britannica* sought revenge for dismissal by substituting names of Britannica employees for historical figures and Allah for Jesus in numerous passages of that company's electronic storage banks.

- **Separate employee functions** Crimes are harder to commit when people have to collaborate. Many companies take advantage of this fact by separating sensitive business functions in such a way that it is difficult for a person acting alone to commit a crime. For instance, the person who issues paychecks in a corporation should not be permitted to update payroll data. Many companies employ a procedure that incorporates distinct check "makers," "checkers," and "signers" to prevent abuses in this area. As another example, someone with update privileges to financial data should not be permitted to audit the system.

  Many companies either force employees to take vacations or rotate workers away from critical positions. Data tampering can be uncovered when an employee, temporarily away from his or her normal job, can't generate fake transactions anymore.

- **Restrict system use** People should be allowed to use and have knowledge about only the computer resources they need to do their jobs. Although it may be difficult to always know who should be allowed access to what, organizations can adopt several procedures that follow this rule. For instance, people who need only access capability to information should be denied update capabilities. Certain software programs and hardware devices should be controlled very carefully regarding who uses them. Computer operations personnel should be given only instructions to load, start, stop, and unload programs—and not told what the programs do. Sensitive outputs should be shredded to eliminate any further use. Only authorized personnel should be allowed in certain areas. After-hours and off-premises activity should be carefully restricted and monitored. Depending on the type of company and its data, other methods of restricting use may also be effective.

- **Protect resources with passwords or other user authorization checks** A **password** is a group of characters that—when input to a computer system— allows access to certain hardware, software, or data. For instance, to gain entry into most mainframe systems or computer networks, an employee must successfully enter one or more passwords. These passwords can be changed regularly to further minimize criminal exposure. **Access cards** go a step beyond passwords. To gain access to a resource, a potential user must possess the card—as well as know the passwords. The most familiar type of access card is the one most people use to get money from automatic teller machines; however, they are also very useful as tools for in-house security systems. Biometric systems (see related box, page 825) are also being increasingly utilized for user authorization and verification.

  Managing important accesses and transactions originating from remote locations often involves using *callback screening devices.* For instance, if a user wants to log into a computer system at a remote location, many systems will hang up and immediately call the user back at the phone number that he or she should be using, in order to verify access.

- **Encrypt data and programs** **Encryption** is the process of disguising data or programs in coded form so they cannot be recognized. Encryption used to be a technique reserved for classified intelligence information, but—with faster computers, improved methods of encryption, and greater vulnerability than ever before—increasingly more ordinary transaction-based data are encrypted. In 1988, an encryption method developed through the National Bureau of Standards became mandatory for banks doing business with the U.S. Department of the Treasury.

- **Monitor system transactions** Many computer systems contain performance monitor programs that keep a journal of all computer system transactions. This includes such data as: Who logged on to and off of the computer system, where, and when? What files did these people access? What data were added, deleted, or updated? Such events as downtime should also be recorded.

- **Conduct frequent audits** Many computer crimes are revealed by accident—sometimes a long time after the crime was committed. For example, in a case cited by M. Buss and Lynn Salerno, a man used his personal computer to access credit card numbers from a credit bureau, eventually charging $50,000 of goods. He was caught when a United Parcel Service deliveryman became suspicious when he delivered so many packages addressed to different people at the same location. In another case discussed by Patricia Keefe, a California-based bank lost $7 million when someone illegally tapped into its electronic funds transfer system. It did not discover the loss until the bank notified the FBI that it had a problem. In still another case, employees of a European auto manufacturer data diddled the company books to cover up $259 million in trading losses on foreign currencies. The books were manipulated in 1984; the loss was finally discovered in 1987.

Audit Guidelines

Are administrative security procedures documented?

Are administrative procedures for hard disk and diskette backup documented?

Are administrative procedures for off-site backup and storage documented?

Does a written policy state when the user-based system is to be signed on and off—and by whom?

Are there written procedures to control the use of sensitive documents?

Are there written departmental policies and procedures stating how and what to document for in-house-developed applications?

Are eating, drinking, and smoking prohibited in the immediate computer area?

Is there a procedure for informing employees that corporate policy forbids the copying of copyrighted software, except for backup purposes?

Is there a written policy in place regarding the removal of hardware and/or software from bank premises?

Is there a written policy regarding the reformatting of the hard disk on leased or rented computers when that computer is returned to the lessor?

Figure 19.8 Microcomputer security objectives. The above audit guidelines for microcomputer security are used by EDP auditors at Banc One Corporation in Columbus, Ohio.

As cases such as these illustrate, many computer installations could benefit from regular audits—procedures that certify authenticity. EDP auditors at the Columbus, Ohio-based Banc One Corporation use the audit guidelines in Figure 19.8 to assess that company's microcomputer security systems.

■ **_Educate people in security measures_**   Employees should know about important security issues. For instance, if users are aware that disgruntled employees are potential threats to security, they are more likely to be on guard when, for example, a volatile employee who was passed over for promotion has access to vital records and starts asking security-related questions that are none of his or her business.

No matter how sophisticated the technology to protect hardware, software, and data resources, security is only as reliable as the people responsible for it. As Buck Bloombecker writes, "Interviews with several companies . . . reveal that rather than using sophisticated electronic security systems, the most common method of security is reliance on employee integrity." Perhaps here is where the benefits of technology can clash with corporate culture. Bloombecker further states that to one corporate security manager at a high-technology company, "Trusting employees is central to our way of doing business. . . . It leads to a lot of innovation when they have freedom."

At a societal level, vigorous enforcement of the laws that define and deter computer crime may be the only truly effective way to minimize its occurrence.

To date, relatively few cases have been prosecuted and the sentences for convicted law-breakers are not consistently severe.

Disaster Recovery

The term **disaster recovery** describes the contingency measures that organizations have adopted at key computing sites to recover from, or to prevent, any monumentally bad event or disaster. A disaster may result from natural causes (refer back to Figures 19.1 and 19.2, pages 807–808), or from some other source—such as a violent takeover, willful or accidental destruction of equipment, or any other act of such catastrophic proportions that the organization could be ruined. The two main strategies for disaster prevention and recovery are physical security and adequate backup.

Physical Security

Physical security includes protecting computer and MIS resources with such devices as locked doors, badge readers, access cards, biometric verification systems (see related box, page 825), theft-proof safes and vaults, fire detectors, fire-resistant containers, fire extinguishers, sprinklers, burglar alarms, closed-circuit television, and guards. Physical security also includes numerous methods for minimizing the impact of a disaster—such as positioning hardware resources in a certain way, following housekeeping policies that minimize exposure of data and input or output (I/O) media, and meeting with key personnel to clarify security policies.

The most critical areas for physical protection usually are the computer room, the data library (where important data are stored), and communications lines over which important data travel. In any given computer system, however, other key areas usually exist also. For example, the office of an employee who receives sensitive data might be considered a critical security area. With the proliferation of microcomputers throughout organizations, security devices such as locks on doors and limited-access computer rooms are not as effective as they once were. The microcomputers are, in many instances, "keys" that permit entry to systems in otherwise physically secure sites.

Backup

Organizations, no matter how physically secure their systems, are always vulnerable to disaster. Thus, a key issue is **backup**. Most large organizations have a backup plan for data, software, and hardware resources. Data and software backup involves creating duplicate copies of important data and software. Often, the originals are stored at a site that is physically distant from the site where the duplicate copies are used. Hardware backup involves establishing a contingency plan that will be enacted if a major problem befalls some key hardware element. One solution is to keep duplicate hardware available for backup purposes. However, for hardware other than microcomputers, low-cost peripherals, and dumb terminals, this alternative may be prohibitively expensive. More commonly, arrangements are made with another party, such as a firm specializing in disaster recovery—for hardware backup support. As noted in the last chapter, disaster recovery is increasingly outsourced.

Two prominent firms in the disaster recovery sector of the computer industry are SunGuard Recovery Systems and Comdisco Disaster Recovery Services. Each of these firms operates a handful of "hot sites" equipped with standby mainframes, telecommunication equipment, and other hardware resources in order to serve the needs of its clients. Depending on the extent of their needs, clients may pay from $2,000 to $100,000 monthly to ensure that they will be backed up during a disaster. These sums do not even include the extra charges that are added if a disaster does, in fact, occur.

ETHICAL CONSIDERATIONS

Ethics refer to standards of moral conduct. Unless people know the difference between right and wrong, it is unrealistic to expect them to be ethical. As Buck Bloombecker writes, one ethical awareness program conducted in Quebec found that employees were selling data maintained by the company because they were not aware of its confidential nature. "Employees saw no reason to protect data," explained the coordinator.

Computer ethics refer to standards of moral conduct demonstrated in computer-related matters. It is important to remember that unethical acts are not necessarily illegal. Let's look at several examples to illustrate this point:

■ People tend to use computer resources casually in ways that, while not necessarily criminal, are ethically questionable. For example, some people regularly use a software package that they don't own, often claiming that they are "just trying it out" before deciding whether to purchase their own copy. While most vendors encourage experimentation with their products, they dislike it when someone uses an unauthorized copy of the package.

■ A student may casually look at a university mainframe system or data that are not intended for his or her use. While this might not be a security breach or crime, the act may still be unethical.

■ Badly needed new software is promised by developers on a specific date. The project is late, incomplete, and the software is not fully tested. Should it be installed on the specified date with less functionality than promised or with bugs? If the developers install an incomplete version, should they tell the users?

These examples illustrate the sticky nature of ethical decisions related to computers. Such decisions face all types of computer users and often must be confronted daily. Unethical computer use can take many forms. Unethical acts may be performed by people both inside and outside organizations and may involve any type of computer system, large or small, networked or stand-alone. Networked computers are especially vulnerable to ethical activity and many of the publicized accounts of hacking are examples of unethical computer—even when laws were not broken. However, like computer crime, most unethical computer acts are performed by insiders—often by disgruntled employees.

Managing computer ethics is not easy for either the individual or the organization. Don Parker of SRI International claims, "The application of ethics in information science, technology, and business is more difficult than in other disciplines." Some of the reasons for this include:

- The use of computers and data communications alters relationships between people. Personal contact is reduced and the speed of communications may not give participants time to reflect upon the ethical implications of their actions.

- Information in electronic form is more fragile (easily changed, vulnerable to unauthorized access, and so on) than when it is in hardcopy form. This raises questions about property rights, privacy, plagiarism, and piracy.

- Efforts to protect information integrity, confidentiality, and availability often conflict with the competitive benefits that may be derived from information sharing.

Because of these problems, many organizations have taken a special interest in ethical education for users and computer professionals. To help them understand the ethical dilemmas that may arise, many businesses and professional organizations formulated general guidelines or codes of ethics.

Computer-Related Ethical Issues

The major issues that people face when working with information systems generally fall into four main categories: privacy, accuracy, property, and access. These are also summarized in Figure 19.9.

Privacy

Privacy concerns collection and the use (or misuse) of data about individuals, which are collected and stored in a computer system. Most Americans feel that they should not be monitored without consent, that they should not have to divulge personal information, and that personal information should be treated confidentially. In Japan, where the culture emphasizes the group rather than the individual, there is much less concern about privacy.

The information technology available today makes it quite easy to monitor individual behaviors with or without the user's awareness. In 1990, XTree (a California-based software company) announced a package that allows network managers to search any hard disk on the network without the user's permission or knowledge. While such software may help ensure that workers are using appropriate versions of software packages or performing required backups, users fear that the system could be used to snoop on personal documents or résumés. Many companies have developed computerized productivity and performance evaluation approaches that monitor and record how employees use computers to perform their jobs. Some companies use "smart" badges along with computerized surveillance equipment to track and record worker movements on company premises; the location of a worker can be instantly determined. The

MAJOR COMPUTER ETHICAL AND LEGAL ISSUES	
Ethical Issues	**Examples**
▪ Privacy	Electronic surveillance of employee behaviors; capturing customer demographics at the point of sale without buyer knowledge or approval.
▪ Accuracy	Credit denial because of inaccurate data in credit history files. Denial of employment or university admission because of inaccurate employment data or police records.
▪ Property	Intellectual property rights for software; imitating the "look and feel" of a successful software vendor's product; software piracy.
▪ Access	Adequacy of security of sensitive or confidential information about individuals stored in computer databases; degree of accommodation needed to allow handicapped workers access to information to technology.

Figure 19.9 A summary of the major categories of computer-related ethical issues.

digital PBX systems used in many larger companies capture and record information on phone calls; in some cases, both incoming and outgoing. While this information is helpful for billing purposes, many people fear that it can be used in other ways as well. While all of these monitoring systems may be beneficial for the organization, many employees feel that having a computer monitor them is unfair, unnecessary, and in some cases, unethical.

Information technology can also be used to pry into the personal lives of customers and employees. New POS systems implemented in many retail operations can capture buyer demographics at the point of transaction—usually without the customer's knowledge. Data can be collected whenever anyone uses a credit card, boards an airplane, or rents a video. By combining customer information obtained through the use of a credit card with product information captured by POS devices, customer and product profiles can be developed. Even bar-coded coupons received through the mail can be used to determine the buying habits and lifestyles of the people who redeem them; the bar codes they contain may be individualized.

The data collected are often sold to other companies, again without individual awareness. Mailing lists of customers or clients are commonly bought and sold. Thus, we are often the targets of computer-generated "personalized" letters or phone calls from telemarketers. For example, Marketplace (from Lotus Development Corporation) is a detailed database containing customer information. This product provides small- and medium-sized companies with a wealth of information on potential buyers, clients, and customers. Information can be obtained on 5,000 potential customers for as little as $500. After a public outcry, Lotus offered to remove the name of anyone who requested them to do so—which amounted to over 30,000 consumers.

Numerous publicly accessible databases contain information about financial transactions, media preferences, political affiliations, insurance claims, and so on. The five top credit bureaus in the U.S. have records on more than 150 million Americans; a credit summary sheet about any one of these can be obtained by merchants and financial institutions all over the country in just moments. A serious concern about the security of these and other publicly available databases also exists. For example, to exact revenge against a magazine columnist who wrote an article blasting hackers, a hacker broke into one of the credit databases and posted the columnist's credit card number on a national bulletin board so that other hackers could use it to make illegal charges. Incidents such as this raise questions about how much and which information about individuals should be available through a computerized information service—and also about the security of this data.

The federal government may be the largest collector of data on U.S. citizens. About four billion records on individuals have been collected by about 100 different agencies. Other collectors include state and local governments, plus nonprofit organizations of all types and sizes. With all of this information available and more being collected all the time—often without the individual's awareness—it is not surprising that people are concerned about the misuse of personal data, both illegal and unethical.

Accuracy

As organizations rely more on information in computerized databases and monitoring/control systems, the potential for individuals to be harmed by inaccurate data increases. Horror stories are told about individuals who were victimized because of inaccurate data in databases. Incorrect data in credit history files have caused many people to be denied credit and the procedures used to get credit history data corrected can be complicated. In some cases, people were denied admission to school or employment because of inaccurate data. In one study, researchers found that 25 percent of their sample of California citizens who checked their police records found inaccuracies. Another study found thousands of incorrect FBI files, which could have resulted in false arrests.

Much of the legislation passed since 1970 (see Figure 19.10) to protect the privacy of the data stored on individuals in databases also addresses accuracy. For example, the Fair Credit Reporting Act of 1970 stipulates that individuals have the right to inspect their own credit records; if inaccuracies are found, the law requires the credit bureau to investigate them. Also, the Privacy Act of 1974 states that individuals must be allowed to learn what information is stored about them and how it is used. This act also gives individuals the opportunity to correct or remove erroneous or trivial data.

The Fair Credit Reporting Act of 1970 regulates the operation of credit bureaus. This law specifies how credit bureaus are to collect, store, distribute, and use credit information.

The Freedom of Information Act of 1970 allows individuals to have access to data on them that are contained in federal agency files.

The Privacy Act of 1974 states that individuals have the right to know what data about them are being stored and how they are being used. This act also gives individuls the right to correct or remove erroneous or unimportant data.

The Tax Reform Act of 1976 restricts the IRS in obtaining and using certain types of personal information.

The Right to Financial Privacy Act of 1978 places restrictions on the government concerning access to certain records held by financial institutions.

The Electronic Funds Transfer Act outlines the responsibilities of companies using electronic funds transfer systems. This act also covers consumer rights and stipulates customer liability for bank cards. It went into effect in 1979 and 1980.

The Computer Matching and Privacy Act of 1988 regulates the matching of federal computer files in different agencies to verify information. This act helps the federal government determine if people are eligible for certain federal programs.

Figure 19.10 Some of the most important federal legislation passed since 1970 that is related to individual privacy and computer ethics.

Property

The widespread existence of electronic information on different media makes property rights for information and software a difficult legal and ethical question. Intellectual property law is now a specialty in the legal profession because intellectual property (such as a programmer's design or code for a new application) is different from other forms of property. For objects such as homes or automobiles, the issues of ownership and disposal are quite clear. However, when examining information and knowledge, the issues are often much vaguer. It is much harder to prove that information or knowledge was stolen or unlawfully used.

In the United States, intellectual property was traditionally protected by copyright, patent, and trade secret laws. Both patent and copyright laws require public disclosure of the intellectual property that is under protection; however, trade secrets are protected by contracts designed to ensure confidentiality and do not require public disclosure of the intellectual property. Because public disclosure opens the door to imitation, many software vendors prefer to consider the key parts of their systems to be trade secrets instead.

In addition to these legal considerations, numerous ethical issues are associated with information, knowledge, and intellectual property. For example, in high-tech industries such as semiconductors, much of the value of the new products emerging from R&D reside in the ideas and understanding that went into the development of the product. Employees involved in such R&D projects who decide to leave for jobs with competing organizations take some of that understanding with them. Such individuals may have to face ethical decisions about whether it is right to use this understanding to help their new employers develop a competing system.

The development of software with the look and feel of another package led to several well-known lawsuits. For example, during the 1980s, Lotus Development Corporation successfully sued Mosaic Software Inc. because Mosaic's Twin package had the same look and feel as the Lotus 1-2-3 spreadsheet. However, more recently, the judicial tide flowed in the opposite direction. For example, Apple's suit against Microsoft, Inc.—based on the argument that Microsoft's Windows had the "look and feel" of the systems software for the Macintosh—was unsuccessful. In this case, Apple's arguments were dismissed because—despite obvious similarities in the graphical user interfaces for the competing systems—substantial differences in the underlying program code existed. In addition, Microsoft presented evidence that Apple may have violated intellectual property rights by basing its operating system design on pre-existing program code that it did not have permission to use. In what could become a landmark decision affecting the entire software industry, a federal appeals court ruled in June 1992 (Computer Associates International, Inc. versus Altai, Inc.) that the behavior of a computer program is not protected under copyright law; in essence, that the creativity behind a software program could not be the subject of copyright protection. This decision should have a major impact on other "look-and-feel" litigation going through the judicial system.

The work and expense of developing new software are primary reasons why vendors worry about software piracy and the illegal reproduction of their packages. As we noted in the beginning of this section, the casual use of unauthorized copies of packages are considered unethical in some cases.

Access

The issue of access concerns the ability of individuals to gain entry to information systems and the information that they hold. It involves the extent of access individuals should have to information stored about them in databases, as well as the extent to which appropriate safeguards are available to prevent unwarranted access to personal or confidential data. For example, if a company has a credit history database on past customers, who should have access and modification privileges? A related question concerns whether individuals should pay to obtain information about themselves in a credit bureau's database (many credit bureaus impose such charges). Also, is it right for a company to sell data about customers to another firm when the selling company knows that the buying firm uses obnoxious hard-sell tactics?

Another set of issues concerns the extent to which handicapped and developmentally disabled individuals should be able to use information technology to perform their jobs to the same extent as mainstream workers. While the Americans with Disabilities Act (ADA) answered this question with a degree of

Information Technology and Biometrics Combine for New Levels of Security

Computer hackers can break into secure computer systems by obtaining passwords and other special access information that they are not supposed to have. Once in, they can steal or destroy data, insert viruses, or commit various computer crimes and unethical acts. To combat security breaches, more companies are turning to such biometric security devices as:

- Fingerprint readers, which identify people by the shape and number of the "lines" on a particular fingertip.

- Hand geometry, which uses light to construct a three-dimensional image of the hand—including thickness, finger length, and width.

- Voice verification, which constructs a mathematical model of spoken words in order to identify voice patterns.

- Signature recognition, which uses technology that learns both what a signature looks like and how it is written.

- Retinal scanners, which scan the pattern of blood vessels in the retina of the eye.

"HACKERS DON'T GET IN BECAUSE THEIR UNIQUE BIOLOGICAL CHARACTERISTICS ARE IMPOSSIBLE TO COPY."

Such systems work by "reading" the characteristics of users requesting access and comparing the reading to patterns stored in an authorized user database. Hackers don't get in because their unique biological characteristics are impossible to copy.

In addition to computer security, these systems are used to grant access to secure areas of plants, plus government or military installations. Some of these systems can be installed for less than $2,000, making them affordable by many smaller organizations.

Adapted from Daly (1992).

finality (by making equal access a requirement), numerous ethical and legal questions still must be addressed. For example, how hard should an organization try to ensure "equivalent" access to work-related information technology for disabled workers or customers? Questions like this don't have clear-cut answers yet.

General Guidelines for Resolving Ethical Dilemmas

Many of these computer-related ethical issues will never have well-defined solutions. Still, users and computer professionals should be aware of the issues and be prepared to confront them. The following are several guidelines that may be useful to individuals who are facing an ethical dilemma:

- Do the actions that I am contemplating violate the Golden Rule? (Will I be treating others as I would want them to treat me?)

- How many people will benefit from the action? Will the "greatest good for the greatest number" result, or will only a minority benefit? Will I be the only beneficiary of the action?

- Is the act consistent with corporate policy (either explicitly or implicitly)? Many corporate policies help identify right from wrong actions; for example, a policy against accepting gifts from vendors.

- Does the act violate corporate or professional codes of ethics? Figure 19.11 includes two such codes: one for members of the Data Processing Management Association (DPMA), and one developed by the Software Publishers Association (SPA).

By answering these questions and paying attention to the guidelines outlined in available ethical codes, an individual may have a better idea about how to behave in the situation that he or she currently faces—as well as what to do in similar future situations.

Although many people feel that MIS employees have certain ethical responsibilities, others feel that it is the job of the corporation to provide some type of ethics education for its employees. Ethics, after all, involves such general matters as conflict of interest and, furthermore, ethics in organizational life goes far beyond the issues related to information technology and should be a constant concern. These are issues for which all members of the organization are responsible.

MIS CAREERS

Perhaps never before in the history of technology have more opportunities for MIS-related careers existed. Although the chaos imparted by rapidly changing technology and business conditions resulted in new problems for MIS professionals, these changes also resulted in numerous opportunities. Basically, as organizations depend more on technology to play a key strategic role, who is in a better position to profit than the MIS professional—and, better yet, a professional with both a strong technology and business background?

In this section, we consider both traditional MIS careers and non-traditional careers, plus the educational paths that support them. *Traditional* jobs in firms include such positions as programmer, systems analyst, and technology manager. Many career paths, in organizations that have such opportunities, have been available for years and will probably continue being available. *Non-traditional* career paths involve both entrepreneurial and intrapraneurial (creating new "business" or strategic business units within an organization) opportunities—for example, as an independent consultant on desktop publishing or, perhaps, as an in-house company consultant. According to Alan Radding, one ex-IBM employee (who is now a successful independent consultant running her own training firm) offers the following advice to people who are not afraid to choose less traditional paths: "You must go beyond your job. You must create opportunities."

Certainly, those choosing non-traditional career paths take risks. Sacrifices are often made, and success is not guaranteed. However, joining a firm and choosing a traditional career path can also be risky. For instance, a programmer assigned to work on several programs in 3GL languages over ten years might later discover that the skills being learned, although good for the company, are

CODE OF ETHICS

I acknowledge:

That I have an obligation to management; therefore, I shall promote the understanding of information processing methods and procedures to management, using every resource at my command.

That I have an obligation to my fellow members; therefore, I shall uphold the high ideals of DPMA as outlined in its International Bylaws. Further, I shall cooperate with my fellow members and treat them with honesty and respect at all times.

That I have an obligation to society and will participate to the best of my ability in the dissemination of knowledge pertaining to the general development and understanding of information processing. Further, I shall not use knowledge of a confidential nature to further my personal interest, nor shall I violate the privacy and confidentiality of information entrusted to me or to which I may gain access.

That I have an obligation to my employer whose trust I hold; therefore, I shall endeavor to discharge this obligation to the best of my ability, to guard my employer's interests, and to advise him or her wisely and honestly.

That I have an obligation as a personal responsibility and as a member of this association. I shall actively discharge these obligations and I dedicate myself to that end.

(a) Data Processing Management Association (DPMA).

SOFTWARE PUBLISHERS ASSOCIATION
SOFTWARE CODE OF ETHICS

The purpose of this code of ethics is to state our organization's policy concerning software duplication. All employees shall use software only in accordance with the license agreement.

Any duplication of licensed software except for backup and archival purposes is a violation of the law. Any unauthorized duplication of copyrighted computer software violates the law and is contrary to the organization's standards of conduct.

The following points are to be followed in order to comply with software license agreements.

1. We will use all software in accordance with our license agreements.

2. Legitimate software will promptly be provided to all employees who need it. No employee of the company will make any unauthorized copies of any software under any circumstances. Anyone found copying software other than for backup purposes is subject to termination.

3. We will not tolerate the use of any unauthorized copies of software in our company. Any person illegally reproducing software can be subject to civil and criminal penalties, including fines and imprisonment. We do not condone illegal copying of software under any circumstances and anyone who makes, uses, or otherwise acquires unauthorized software shall be appropriately disciplined.

4. No employee shall give software to any outsider (including clients, customers, and others).

5. Any employee who determines that there may be a misuse of software within the company shall notify their department manager or legal counsel.

6. All software used by the organization on company computers will be properly purchased through appropriate procedures. I have read the company's software code of ethics. I am fully aware of our software policies and agree to abide by those policies.

(b) Software Publishers Association (SPA).

Figure 19.11 Examples of computer-related ethical codes.

becoming obsolete in the marketplace. Working with them is not in his or her best interest. Worse, the programmer's company might decide to outsource application development to another firm, resulting in layoffs and forcing workers to look for new jobs. These workers may have limited opportunities if they have only a limited knowledge of fourth-generation languages, OOP, and CASE tools.

As mentioned in Chapter 18, outsourcing and downsizing have changed the job security and career options available to many MIS professionals. Organizations that downsize or outsource often reduce the size of their MIS staffs. For example, downsizing has reduced the demand for programmers in mainframe environments. From 1990–1992, the number of mainframe programmers in the U.S. declined by approximately 10 percent—roughly equivalent to the decline in the number of mainframes used in U.S. companies. Outsourcing has also displaced many MIS professionals. Fortunately, many of the displaced workers become employed by the outsourcing service provider. As might be expected, organizations that outsource or downsize also typically reduce their need for entry-level MIS professionals. However, outsourcing generally creates a need for additional workers in the firms providing outsourcing services. New university graduates often find entry-level positions with firms that provide outsourcing services.

Despite the increased prevalence of downsizing and outsourcing, a heavy demand for computer professionals still exists. A quality graduate in a high-tech field such as computer information systems or computer science can usually acquire several job offers and a respectable starting salary. In fact, average salaries of MIS professionals continue to rise. From 1990–1991, the average weekly earnings of MIS professionals rose from $744 to $792 (up $48/ week). To be competitive and to continue bringing a steady stream of new MIS talent into the organization, management must be prepared to offer attractive salaries and other benefits.

Career Options

The MIS field has several different career options. Here, we look at some of them.

Career Path

A work option frequently chosen by people is the *career path*. This involves looking at an organization in terms of advancement opportunities and considering how an MIS professional would move from his or her present position up to a desired level in the firm. For instance, a possible career path in some firms is to move from programmer to systems analyst to manager to CIO.

No two companies are the same regarding career paths; exceptions to every rule can occur. Some firms, for instance, may follow the practice of promoting top-level MIS executives from within. However, if sales suddenly slump, people may be hired from the outside for high-level positions. Thus, the career path—considered a relatively safe form of employment and advancement for many years—is now riskier for MIS professionals. With the nature of technology and business changing rapidly, firms cannot guarantee that a current career path will exist for ten years (in some cases, even less) into the future.

Niche Expertise

Developing a career around a particular *niche* area has become popular in recent years. With this option, the MIS professional becomes an expert in some well-defined area; for instance, a particular database product, desktop publishing on the Apple Macintosh, local area networks, electronic data interchange (EDI) applications, imaging systems, bank-based decision support systems for IBM PS/2 computers, and so on. Some MIS professionals develop niche careers on their own (as entrepreneurs) or within the companies that employ them (as intrapreneurs). If an MIS professional is terminated by a company or decides to leave, a saleable niche skill is a valuable commodity that can put him or her back in business right away.

The chaos caused by sweeping changes in technology and the business environment has made niche careers more popular among MIS professionals. Not only has it become more difficult to learn every facet of MIS, but niche opportunities created by new products and technologies are appearing with greater frequency. Increasingly, more organizations find it beneficial to promote the development of niche expertise by their MIS professionals.

Lifestyle

Another option used to building an MIS career is to mold that career around a preferred *lifestyle*. For instance, with computer networking technologies creating more opportunities for telecommuting, a career option that many computer professionals are selecting involves finding the places where they want to live and setting up careers that enable them to live there. On an individual level, this type of strategy is often implemented by developing a niche—one that is both portable and in great enough demand that the person can exert some control over the workplace. Programming and documentation writing are two areas that are particularly conducive to people who consider lifestyle to be a major factor in the career decision.

Additional Training

Virtually everyone working in a fast-paced high-tech area must constantly retrain. New technologies and new products continually enter the market. Business systems are often altered entirely or fitted with new enhancements. All of this makes training, retraining, and continuing education a requirement, rather than a luxury.

MIS professionals can retool themselves in many ways, including taking classes, attending seminars or exhibitions, reading, and joining a professional association or club. Managers and users—especially in organizations that emphasize end-user computing—may also find these approaches effective for staying on top of changes.

Classes

A wide variety of options exist for people who want to take classes in an MIS-related area. Many companies, for instance, hold classes on information technology for their employees (both users and MIS professionals). Often, these classes are coordinated through the corporate information center, which serves as a clearinghouse for training information. Classes can also be taken at a university, college, or community college, on either a degree-seeking or continuing-education basis.

Seminars

Attending seminars provides an excellent opportunity for managers and MIS professionals to keep informed of the latest technologies, especially in niche areas. Whereas courses taken at a university or a college are likely to be broad (and sometimes limited by the equipment available), a seminar can provide a quick, in-depth look at a specific technology—perhaps one that is so new that it is not fully integrated into the academic curricula yet. Often, people can discover which seminars are being given in their areas by reading trade publications, checking with local hotels, or getting on the mailing list of a company—such as James Martin and Associates—that gives seminars around the country.

Exhibitions

Exhibitions, or shows, are events in which vendors exhibit their latest products or services. Some shows, such as COMDEX (Computer Dealer Expo), involve a wide variety of vendors and are given at different locations throughout the country several times a year. Other types of shows involve specialty areas. For instance, a show covering graphic arts would attract exhibitors featuring such products as commercial art systems, desktop publishing packages, laser printers, plotters, and film recorders. Sending managers and MIS professionals to related trade shows can benefit organizations that want their employees to stay on top of technological developments.

Reading

Reading is one of the easiest ways to learn about new technologies. It is also one of the least expensive. Many organizations have extensive in-house MIS libraries, but even if they don't, it is wise to encourage MIS professionals to keep up with the literature in this rapidly changing area. Many options are available to those who want to read, including those listed here:

- **Books** The latest books, especially those in the microcomputer area, can usually be found in bookstore chains such as B. Dalton and Waldenbooks. Many privately owned bookstores also carry a good selection of computer books, and some stores specialize only in high-tech titles. For learning general computer or communications concepts, the best source is usually a local college or university library.

- **Periodicals and journals** Books usually take several months to get into print, and some of the information in them will probably be dated by the time they become available. Thus, some of the freshest sources of information about technology are the daily, weekly, monthly, and quarterly periodicals and journals that are widely available. Figure 19.12 lists numerous useful MIS publications. Some of these periodicals are targeted to wide audiences (for example, to all computer professionals), whereas others are targeted to narrow audience segments (for example, to all IBM-compatible microcomputer users).

- **Topical reports** In the securities business, brokers and investors depend on up-to-date industry reports to get opinions on certain companies, industries, or products. A counterpart to these types of reports exists for computer and communications professionals. Such companies as Faulkner and DataPro regularly produce reports, which may cover a hardware or software product; a group of related products; a tutorial on a technology, a system, or an MIS management practice; and so on. Professionals subscribe to these sources although—compared to other sources of computer information—they are relatively expensive because they are so current and so specialized.

- **Electronic media** A lot of technological information is obtainable from videotapes, video disks, diskettes, and so on. For instance, one of the most familiar ways to learn how to use a software package is to work through the tutorial (demonstration) diskette that a software vendor typically provides.

- **Vendor literature** One of the most straightforward ways to learn about a product is to look at the literature that the vendor provides. Unfortunately, this literature is usually biased to show the vendor's product very favorably, but it is frequently both free and helpful. Also, this literature often contains a toll-free phone number where more (and frequently, less biased) information can be obtained.

Professional Associations

People sharing common goals often join professional associations, clubs, or user groups in order to share knowledge and experiences. Some associations that handle MIS-related issues are the Association for Computing Machinery (ACM), the Association for Systems Management (ASM), the Data Processing Management Association (DPMA), the Society for Information Management (SIM), and the EDP Auditor's Association. Most of these associations hold annual conferences or shows in which professional papers or demonstrations are presented. At these conferences, technology vendors often set up booths to feature some of their latest products or services. Management should encourage the MIS professionals in their companies to participate in these organizations and conferences. Such participation promotes communication among professionals and should help the organization keep aware of important developments in the MIS area.

Area	Title	Frequency
Executive management	*The Executive*	Monthly
	Harvard Business Review	Bi-monthly
General management	*Sloan Management Review*	Quarterly
	Business Horizons	Quarterly
	California Business Review	Quarterly
General business	*Business Week*	Weekly
	Fortune	Bi-weekly
	Forbes	Bi-weekly
Management information systems	*Journal of Management Information Systems*	Quarterly
	MIS Quarterly	Quarterly
	Journal of Systems Management	Monthly
	InformationWeek	Weekly
	CIO	Monthly
	Corporate Computing	Monthly
	Infosystems	Monthly
General computing	*Data Management*	Monthly
	Datamation	Monthly
	Computerworld	Weekly
	Communications of the ACM	Monthly
IBM-compatible microcomputing	*PC Magazine*	Monthly
	PC World	Monthly
	PC Week	Weekly
	PC Tech Journal	Monthly
	PC Publishing	Monthly
Macintosh microcomputing	*MacWeek*	Weekly
	MacWorld	Monthly
	MacUser	Monthly
Small business	*Digital News*	Bi-monthly
	Infoworld	Weekly
	Systems Integration Age	Monthly
	Byte	Monthly
	UNIX Review	Monthly
Office automation	*Office Systems*	Monthly
	Modern Office Technology	Monthly
	Mobile Office	Monthly
Telecommunication	*Data Communications*	Monthly
	Communications Week	Weekly
	Network World	Weekly
	LAN Technology	Monthly
	Telecommunications	Monthly

Figure 19.12 Some of the leading periodicals that publish MIS-related articles.

MULTINATIONAL ISSUES

Business is becoming increasingly multinational. Many of the products we use are made in other countries. Some of our largest companies have branches in foreign countries and many of the largest foreign companies have U.S. branches. Today's businesspeople must look beyond national borders to invest capital in the best markets, manufacture goods at the lowest cost, and sell both goods and services where the demand is strongest. In a sense, the movement toward a multinational economy was inevitable—just as it was probably inevitable to the local farmer in Batavia, New York, when the auto was first invented, that milk could be sold more effectively from a large dairy cooperative operating out of Buffalo.

Along with the potential benefits that an organization may realize, the multinational dimension creates numerous MIS problems. A basic problem is that multinational expansion causes a further distribution of resources and decision making with, generally, greater levels of risk. The increased risks are associated with the numerous differences encountered in other countries. Among the sources of these differences are language, culture, the political climate, laws and customs, equipment standards, nationalism, the economic situation, staffing, and workday differences. These are discussed in the following sections and are summarized in Figure 19.13.

Language

Often, a multinational business has subsidiaries in countries whose native languages are not English. Although English is the unofficial language of international business, domestic managers who know only one language may be at a disadvantage; they can only communicate their own needs and learn of the needs of these subsidiaries through multilingual foreign managers or hired translators. Subtle word choices or changes in tone may, therefore, go unnoticed.

Culture

Every culture has its own way of operating and its own set of priorities. In fast-paced cultures, meeting a critical deadline in 24 hours might be a major management crisis, and an elaborate contingency plan might be constructed in case something goes wrong. In slower-paced cultures, where managers are not as concerned with time, the response to such an event might be completely different. In countries where immediacy is not a high priority, schedules and commitments are often unreliable, but people understand and tolerate this.

Political Climate

In locations where large amounts of time and money are spent, considerable thought must be given to the stability of the political environment. A subsidiary facility could be taken over by a hostile government or irate students could destroy critical records in protest of some policy. Even worse, lives might be in danger. In particularly volatile environments, such issues as backup and disaster planning assume higher priority.

MIS CHALLENGES OF MULTINATIONAL FIRMS

Potential Problems	Examples	Possible Remedies
▪ Language difficulties	Inability to fully communicate information and data requirements	Language training; hiring skilled translators; hiring native managers and MIS professionals
▪ Cultural differences	Differences in MIS priorities, implementation schedules, and issues	Enhanced cultural awareness, personnel exchanges; training aimed at reducing culture shock for managers assigned to foreign venues
▪ Political climate	Level of political support for organizational activities and MIS initiatives; volatility of general political climate	Enhanced sensitivity to political climates; increased concern for MIS security and backup; increased emphasis on contingency planning
▪ Laws and customs	Differences in transborder data flow laws/regulations; protectionist policies for native computer firms	In-house international legal expertise; hiring native firms most familiar with developing an MIS within national legal guidelines
▪ Standards	Incompatible hardware, electronic, and communications standards that make it difficult to develop networks spanning two or more countries	Lobbying for adoption of international computing and communications standards; hiring experts capable of overcoming compatibility barriers
▪ Nationalism	Foreign-owned firms importing MIS workers rather than hiring locally; important MIS decisions made outside of the country	Importing workers sparingly, if at all; decentralizing decision making so that MIS decisions are made at the local level
▪ Economic differences	Movement of MIS operations or activities to nations with low wage rates	Ensuring wage equity throughout organization, regardless of where work is done
▪ Staffing	Finding a pool of qualified labor in MIS niche areas may be problematic in some countries	Enhancing MIS training and development opportunities in niche and state-of-the-art areas within countries in which shortages exist
▪ Workday differences	Differences in business hours and work habits among countries can have an impact on international business transactions	Using information and communications technology to monitor changes and extend the business day

Figure 19.13 Examples of some of the major problem areas that face organizations with international MIS operations. Some possible steps to remedy such problems are also listed.

Laws and Customs

Every country has a different set of laws. Not all countries, for instance, allow the same types of data to be exported from their borders. Some, in fact, do not allow data export at all. This problem, known as *transborder data flow*, is a particularly difficult one for international MIS development. As information assumes an even greater strategic resource role, more countries will probably set up protectionist policies—just as they do for such tangible commodities as automobiles—to keep their domestic information industries competitive.

The concern of the Germans about transborder data flow was evident during the mid-1980s when a leading European bank wanted to centralize a portion of its information processing activities in France. From France, the bank planned to service clients in Germany. However, German officials would not permit this and the bank was forced to open a center in Germany to process German clients. Canada has similar laws; the 1980 Canadian Banking Act requires banks doing business in Canada to process its Canadian customer records there.

As Martin Buss notes, a problem with transborder data flow was also experienced by a multinational firm headquartered in New York. The firm had to hold up its plans to build a skills database on key overseas employees because of the uncertainties involved in transferring this personal information from Europe to the United States.

According to a study performed by Russell Briner and Sidney Ewer, the country with the most obstacles to transborder data flow is Brazil, with Canada and Germany second and third. The transborder data flow problem is most acute for organizations that already have international telecommunication networks in place because critical changes in laws might require an entire system to be re-designed. The most vulnerable of these systems are those that are tightly centralized; any changes in existing laws might require duplicating an entire system in a foreign country in order to do business there.

Laws regarding taxes and tariffs also differ, as do customs regarding the unions that supply labor to the workplace. France, for instance, proposed taxing data the same as it taxes tangible resources. In several European countries—including England, Germany, and France—computer personnel belong to trade unions that sometimes strike. When this happens, the impact can be dramatic. As Martin Buss writes, a computer executive for a $2 billion corporation with computer installations in countries having trade unions commented, "Data processing unions have a great hold over our operation. I'm planning to build new computer centers in Switzerland, where the strike risks are, today at least, negligible and to transfer the work there. I know my ongoing costs will be higher. But my board believes the risk of a strike paralyzing our entire European operation warrants the expense."

Standards

Communications standards differ around the world, and the presence of specific hardware and software manufacturers varies also. Large problems can therefore result when the parent and subsidiary companies have incompatible hardware systems with incompatible communications protocols, and no foreseeable hope of integration.

Martin Buss relates the woes of an international consumer products company, headquartered in New Jersey, that regularly missed management

The Wheels of Justice are Eroding Software Copyright Protection

Software vendors are in a quandary. Little by little, the traditional court rulings that have protected their copyrights and research and development investments in mass market products are being overturned.

In one of the landmark cases of the 1980s—*Whelan* vs. *Jarlow*—the U.S. Court of Appeals (Third Circuit) ruled that the basic structure of a computer program cannot be copied. However, in 1992, the Whelan ruling was overturned in a Second Circuit case, *Computer Associates* vs. *Altai*. In this later case, the U.S. Court of Appeals ruled that the basic structure of a program is not copyrightable.

Another reversal occurred in two venues of the U.S. District Court. In the 1990 case *Lotus* vs. *Paperback*, the federal judge in Boston ruled that software makers can't copy screen layouts, menu sequences, and command organization. However, in 1992, the federal judge in San Francisco ruled that only

> " . . . THE U.S. COURT OF APPEALS RULED THAT THE BASIC STRUCTURE OF A PROGRAM IS NOT COPYRIGHTABLE."

specific screen elements are copyrightable, not the overall "look and feel" of the program (*Apple* vs. *Microsoft and Hewlett-Packard*).

Experts agree that in the future, vendors will probably have narrower copyright protection than they have now. This has sent many software vendors scurrying to patent their products, rather than to copyright them, because patents offer more absolute protection than copyrights. Until the inconsistencies in lower court rulings are resolved by the U.S. Supreme Court, this seems to be the vendors' safest strategy.

Adapted from Brandt, Schwartz, and Galen (1992).

reporting deadlines as it tried to pull together telexed performance data from around the globe:

> After repeatedly observing missed deadlines, the head of the international division finally intervened. After some digging, he discovered that his staff's inability to deliver was the fault of the company's international information processing capabilities, which woefully lagged behind its needs. Although the division's financial requirements were uniform throughout the world, nearly every regional office approached information processing differently. There were no corporate standards for international data processing. Computers, programming languages, operating systems software, and telecommunication equipment varied greatly among the affiliates.

Often, for completely valid reasons, foreign affiliates of a multinational company need to use different information systems—which can create problems in enforcing standards. For instance, different products and markets in each country may require different types of systems. Or a brand of hardware or software available in one country may not be available in another. Also, the foreign affiliates may be at different growth cycles in their computer systems, so that systems used in one country may not be economically justifiable in another.

Nationalism

In many countries, workers resent having foreigners brought in to perform work that they can do themselves. Many firms realize this and usually employ nationals. However, a related problem that often arises is that nationals may resent centralized decisions that were made outside of their country. This may pose a severe problem for centrally managed companies, which may have to distribute both considerable amounts of data and decision-making power to foreign subsidiaries in order to do business in some countries. Martin Buss cites, in still another example of nationalism, how the Brazilian Special Informatics Agency did not permit Chase Manhattan Bank to import a computer from a United States vendor because the computer was not manufactured locally.

Economic Differences

Both a problem and an opportunity to many multinational organizations are the differences among and the volatility of exchange rates. For example, although favorable and stable exchange rates once made certain countries economically competitive for manufacturing activities, because of shifts in rate behavior, some of those countries are now unable to compete.

For many U.S. companies, manufacturing in Mexico has become an increasingly attractive advantage in the battle against overseas competitors. Mexican cities such as Tijuana, Ciudad Juárez, and Matamoros are only a few miles from their respective northern U.S. neighbors: San Diego, CA; El Paso, TX; and Brownsville, TX. In late 1986, Brian O'Reilly wrote that the average wage rate for unskilled Mexican labor was one-sixth that of Japan and about half that of Singapore, South Korea, Hong Kong, and Taiwan—and the peso's value has not improved considerably since then. Using technology to take advantage of manufacturing economies made possible by favorable exchange rates, one large U.S. computer manufacturer set up a factory in Juárez, which it links by satellite to its technical staff in Dallas.

Communications costs can also differ greatly among countries, especially if communications penetrate national borders. Martin Buss mentions one international manager in Spain who reported that his lines to Germany cost six times more than a comparable setup in the United States. *Business Week* tells of an entrepreneur in Hackensack, NJ, who developed a business around the fact that calls to Europe (and other parts of the world) that originate in the United States are substantially cheaper than calls to the U.S. that originate in Europe. He put together a system in which a caller in Europe dials the switch in Hackensack and provides it with the number that the caller wants to reach. After the information is received, the switch breaks the connection and calls both the originator and the desired destination—thereby establishing a connection between them. The caller saves money by being switched through Hackensack and the entrepreneur's service charges give him a profit. Several European telecommunication companies are upset about the system and threaten to lobby for international laws that would outlaw such practices.

Staffing

It is not always possible to find a large pool of qualified professionals everywhere in the world. In some countries, nationals may not be trained well in certain MIS areas, and foreign professionals may be hired, generally at great expense. As Connie Winkler notes, technical professionals are especially needed in the Middle East and in developing countries, whereas less demand for them exists in Australia, Japan, and Europe. In numerous countries, such as Saudi Arabia, housing and meals are provided, enabling foreigners to save almost everything they make.

Workday Differences

All over the world, workday differences exist, such as differences in the time of day (for example, the three hours between New York and Los Angeles times), differences in working hours, and differences in what non-working holidays are celebrated. These differences can be both advantageous and disadvantageous. In many industries, workers can still conduct transactions with other countries after many local businesses close (often after 5:00 P.M.). However, these time differences can greatly extend an employee's working day if, for example, a person in New York must frequently contact people in both London (several hours ahead) and Los Angeles (several hours behind).

Workday differences are perhaps most evident in the financial markets, where important transactions take place that influence decisions in other parts of the globe virtually every hour of each day. Because a financial analyst cannot stay awake 24 hours every day to monitor these transactions, information systems technologies are critical for tracking ongoing happenings so that the analyst can learn immediately of important, recent events taking place worldwide.

Barriers to the Development of Global Networks

Today, more than ever, the decision to expand internationally is often tied to an organization's ability to develop the global telecommunication network that it needs to support international operations. The advent of the 1992 European Community (EC) resulted in a growing number of U.S. firms that are exploring the possibility of European expansion; a study performed by KPMG Peat Marwick indicates that the number of U.S. companies planning to expand into Europe rose sharply after 1990. Some businesses want to open European plants and offices. Others plan to acquire European companies, participate in mergers, or initiate joint ventures. Regardless of the approach, information systems will play a key role and senior MIS managers are already spearheading many projects—including enhancing or expanding existing networks, building new MIS teams and telecommunication centers, and integrating new subsidiaries' systems with that of the parent company.

Challenges Faced in the Development of Global Telecommunication Networks

■ Inconsistent and unreliable telecommunication services and installation schedules

■ Inconsistent or incompatible communications protocols and hardware standards

■ Government-controlled communications carriers with limited services and equipment

■ Substantial differences in telecommunication laws/regulations and taxes among countries

■ A confusing array of relationships between governments and telecommunication hardware/service vendors

Figure 19.14 A summary of some of the major difficulties that organizations developing global information networks must handle.

As Alice LaPlante and Joseph Maglitta note, Alamo Rent-a-Car, Inc., is one of the U.S. companies that decided in 1992 to expand to Europe. Like many other companies, Alamo has encountered several difficulties (such as those listed in Figure 19.14) in this endeavor. In the words of Thomas Loane—vice-president of computers and communications for Alamo—"This is not going to be simple. . . . We need to be able to begin designing and engineering the network as soon as the ink is dry." Loane's comments reflect the fact that numerous obstacles must be overcome when building or expanding networks in the EC and other parts of the world, including:

■ Unreliable and inconsistent telecommunication services between individual countries and cities.

■ Conflicting standards for everything from electronic data interchange (EDI) to modems.

■ Monopolistic, government-controlled communications carriers that limit vendor service and equipment options.

■ Unpredictable installation and service target dates.

■ Widely varying government regulations and tariff structures.

■ A bewildering proliferation of alliances, coalitions, joint ventures, and projects among vendors and government services.

Despite these obstacles, since the EC's advent, expanding to Europe is not as bad as it once was. Numerous reforms are sweeping Europe and relaxed regulations should encourage more open markets, better service quality, and an environment that is increasingly conducive to building sophisticated networks. By 1996, basic and primary access to Integrated Services Digital Network (ISDN) is expected to be readily available to commercial customers throughout Europe; virtual private networks (VPN)—which are based on public packet-switching networks—are also expected to become widespread.

Many U.S. companies are discovering that outsourcing international networks is a cost-effective way to maneuver through the obstacles of global networking. By outsourcing network services or network development to firms who already know the region, international expansion can often be accomplished more rapidly; the outsourcer can also avoid tackling the intricacies of building its own international networks. For example, the overseas branch of Hyatt Hotels, Inc., outsourced its European telecommunication operations five years ago. BT North America, Inc., also recently received outsourcing contracts; it signed contracts with J.P. Morgan and Co. and Gillette to handle its international networking needs. Outsourcing network services will probably remain popular until many of the obstacles to global networking (discussed previously) are removed.

After global networks are working, companies still must face the other previously discussed international factors (such as language barriers, differing business practices, changes in currencies, and so on). Hence, challenges are always associated with the decision to expand globally. The changes underway in Eastern Europe and the former Soviet Union also created both unprecedented opportunities and unparalleled expansion problems. Since the fall of the Berlin Wall in 1989, the number of companies initiating efforts to expand to Eastern Europe has grown dramatically. Experts agree that it will take billions of dollars to bring Eastern Europe's telecommunication infrastructure up to that of the rest of the continent. However, most people feel that this will be accomplished rapidly despite the fact that the tremendous investment required means that companies won't realize the benefits of these business moves for many years.

THE FUTURE OF INFORMATION TECHNOLOGY

Of course, no one can predict the future. Technology predictions are especially risky because the predictor must view the future with eyes that are used to today's world. In the 1940s, for instance, the director of the Harvard Computational Laboratory predicted that the computer industry would never amount to much because about six machines (such as the one used at Harvard at the time) could handle the world's demand. Fifty years later, millions of microcomputers that sell for several hundred dollars are widely available—and these tiny machines have more power than that gargantuan Harvard computer. The telephone, too, was at one time seen as a device that would receive limited use because there could never be enough telephone operators to handle widespread demand.

Each of us has favorite indicators that help us make intelligent guesses about the future. For example, in baseball, we can predict how well a team will do in a season on the basis of the relative strength of its starting lineup, pitching staff, and bench; key injuries; and how sharp the team looked in spring training. Each of these interdependent variables is carefully assessed and weighed according to some formal or informal model. Then, a prediction is made. Sometimes, the prediction proves to be right; sometimes (no matter how qualified the prophesier), the prediction is completely wrong.

When considering the future of information technology, two important variables that have a bearing on upcoming, technology-related products are user needs and technological breakthroughs. These variables intermix in somewhat random, unpredictable ways to bring successful products into the marketplace. Such products are evaluated by people in organizations and acquired by them. Products that make material differences in the way work is done may cause management to take certain actions. The way consumers and management react to products is reflected (as feedback) in shaping new needs.

Needs

Businesses have always needed technology products that cut costs, provide better service, make people more productive, improve managerial decision making, and can be used for competitive advantage. In the marketplace, the most successful products are usually the ones that satisfy these needs. Such products generally possess one or more of the following properties:

- **Functionality** The first question asked of any product should be: Is the product potentially useful? If this question is answered affirmatively, the features of the product are next explored. Fast processing speed, large memory or data-handling capacity, flexibility, wide breadth of tasks performed, and a logical problem-solving approach are usually included on people's checklists of desirable product features. For instance, a database system capable of preparing a report that relates data on 10,000 clients and 3,000 products in 30 seconds is potentially more useful than, perhaps, one that requires five hours to perform the same job.

    An important associated issue here is functionality as it relates to raw processing power. Raw power often means little to a manager who uses a microcomputer system for an hour or so each day, or to a secretary who cannot convert more computer power into increased typing speed. More power is usually significant only if it is accompanied by greater functionality. What the manager really needs are better decision-making software tools; what the secretary really needs is a word processor that accepts voice input. And by better, this usually means much better—perhaps revolutionary. As one manager in the financial services sector noted, "My people have been using Lotus [1-2-3] for two years and they're not ready to switch unless the new product is an order of magnitude better."

    A question that usually arises regarding power is "Why do we need faster, more powerful computers?" In other words, does the user really need supercomputer-level power on a desktop? The answer: As technology products become faster and more powerful, we can build more intelligence into them, enabling them to be increasingly more functional. Putting some types of human-like intelligence into machines requires computing power greater than that on today's best supercomputers. Thus, the quest for greater power will probably have its largest impact in the functionality area. That a computer can calculate a spreadsheet in half a second—rather than five seconds—may not be very important.

- **Low relative cost** Cost is always a bottom-line consideration in the marketplace. For a product to be successful, it not only must work well, but it also must be competitively priced. This is not to indicate that the product must be cheaply priced to be successful; a product costing $1,000 but saving the organization $3,000 through its efficiency is a much better bargain than one priced at $99 that saves nothing. When determining the true cost of a product, a customer must look at its asking price and add to that potential costs associated with conversion and the risk that the product may fail.

Many people underestimate the force that risk plays in determining the perceived cost of a product. They look at products such as the IBM PS/2 and Lotus 1-2-3 and ask why anyone would buy name-brand products when a compatible clone is available at a much lower price. The answer involves risk. Can anyone prove that the clone is fully compatible? Will upper management think less of the purchaser if the clone fails at a critical task? Fortunately for the clonemakers, as standard-setting products mature in the marketplace and information on how users employ them is better known, they become easier to clone. For instance, when the IBM PC first became a target for imitation, some clonemakers copied the wrong features. Consequently, many of these machines could not run some of the new IBM PC software products that subsequently entered the marketplace. Second-generation PC-clone products were, on the other hand, much more successful.

■ **Simplicity** In most fields—and perhaps technology fields top the list—things should be kept simple. If the customer finds a product and its support documentation hard to use, the product will probably not sell well. One of the greatest software successes of the 1980s was Lotus 1-2-3, for instance—a product so easy to use that customers barely needed any instructions to start working effectively.

■ **Compatibility** Setting universally acceptable standards is an old problem with technology-related products. Machines often cannot communicate with each other, and one software package often cannot read the data of another. This incompatibility has, over the years, caused much frustration for users, many of whom cannot understand why a common interface does not exist.

■ **Autonomy** Over the years, users have demonstrated a strong desire to have their own computer systems. This fact first became evident when minicomputers made it possible to distribute computing down to the divisional and departmental levels. The movement toward microcomputers and local area networks has only strengthened end-users' desires to control their own information needs.

An old joke says that it is no fun being a pioneer; you wind up with arrows in your back. When selecting technology, people with buying power traditionally fear taking risks—a fact that gives established brand names a strong competitive edge. Thus, unless a new product is truly remarkable, it will probably have to be a low-priced, low-risk clone of an established brand name in order to meet the needs just discussed and to be successful.

Breakthroughs

Throughout the history of technology, computer and communications products have become more powerful while also becoming less expensive and smaller in size. For example, the Mark I computer, completed in 1944, occupied an entire room, contained 500 miles of wire and three million electrical connections, and cost $500,000 to build. It could compute an ordinary multiplication problem in about three seconds and a division problem in about 12 seconds. Today, customers can purchase a desktop microcomputer system for less than $1,000 that is thousands of times faster and much easier to use and maintain than the Mark I.

Regarding hardware, the future should bring breakthroughs with respect to speed, memory capacity, size, and cost. Speed will be enhanced by putting circuitry even closer together and by coming up with new ways to store and move data, such as parallel processing (discussed in Chapter 5). Memory capacity is improving because new methods are continually found to store more data in less space on both magnetic and other types of media. Also, because computer and memory modules are becoming dense with data, their cost—as well as their size—is shrinking.

To show the magnitude of these changes, let's compare today's microcomputers to one of the largest commercially available computers in 1955—the IBM 604. Today's microcomputers are housed in a unit that is 1,000 times smaller than the 604 and available RAM has increased two million times. The average secondary storage available with today's personal computers is 32,000 times larger than that associated with the IBM 604. By the end of the century, terabyte (trillion-byte) storage systems for microcomputers are expected to be readily available. Such capacity would enable a user to store more information than he or she will probably produce in a lifetime—more than 400 million pages of text (at 300 words per page).

The RISC-based machines sold today have speeds up to 50 MIPS; by the year 2000, speeds in excess of 200 MIPS are likely. These continued hardware improvements will probably enable users to have articulate language translators, database management systems that feature instantaneous data storage and retrieval, and easy-to-use multimedia systems.

Networking is expected to continue. Connecting local area networks to wide area networks will be one of the major challenges. The development of global networks and gigabit data highways will continue. Charles Lecht predicts that network cooperatives spanning state and national boundaries will form. Wireless communications—both LAN and WAN—should be common by the year 2000, and ISDN services should be available in most parts of the world in a few years. EDI and other interorganizational systems—which are already showing explosive growth—will continue to change the way that organizations conduct business.

Imaging and document management systems should become common aspects of office systems and transaction processing systems by the year 2000.

Existing and Emerging MIS Technologies

Bar-code processing systems

CASE and other software productivity tools

Client/server network architectures

Database tools and database management systems (DBMS)

Electronic data interchange (EDI) and other interorganizational information systems (IOS)

Electronic mail systems

Expert systems

Fuzzy-logic applications

Graphical user interfaces (GUI) and windowing software

Imaging systems/document management systems

Integrated Services Digital Network (ISDN)

Laptop computer applications

Local area networks (LAN)

Multimedia systems

Neural networks and other knowledge-based systems

Object-oriented databases and reusable code libraries

Object-oriented programming (OOP)

Optical disk technologies

Parallel processing

Pen-based computers

Redundant arrays of independent disks (RAID) technologies

Relational databases

RISC-based workstations

Wireless networks

Figure 19.15 Information technologies expected to have a major impact on organizational computing during the 1990s. (Adapted from *The Computerworld IS Pocket Guide for Success*)

Pen-based computers are expected to improve in performance and to account for nearly 50 percent of all PC sales by 1997.

Regarding software, many developers want to make programs completely independent of their data. In addition, most future programs will probably contain several artificial intelligence (AI) components, thus enabling computer systems to process at a near-human level of complexity. Embedded AI routines could be to the future software industry what embedded (specialized) processors are to today's hardware industry.

Software packages will probably become more user-friendly in the future. Graphical user interfaces are likely to proliferate; this has already occurred in operating systems such as Windows NT, OS/2, and UNIX. Figure 19.15 provides a list of information technology areas that are expected to have a major impact on organizations during the 1990s.

Products, People, and Management

User needs and breakthroughs in technology eventually result in new products and in new ways of producing and marketing old products. These changes, in turn, affect changes in the way people work. Many of these changes also motivate management action (such as control over end-user computing and development). The following list contains some of the developments in these areas and the impacts that they will probably have:

- **Merging of technologies**   Some formerly distinct technologies are already merging. For example, the lines between word processing and desktop publishing are blurring, and many current printers are also plotters and image scanners. Some communications systems have so many computing devices that a communications system is often referred to as a computer system. Furthermore, as technologies in areas such as DSS and office systems merge with transaction processing systems, new ways must be found to manage them.

- **Prepackaged systems**   The continuing shortage of qualified computer professionals, accompanied by great demand for computer products, will fuel the production of prepackaged, end-user-oriented computer systems. This means that users will see even more high-quality application packages and specialized hardware systems—and fewer software systems developed in-house.

- **Distributed trends**   Expect to see more products made abroad, in order to take advantage of favorable labor markets. Also, as complete systems become cheaper and easier to operate, expect end-users to do work that was once performed only by computer professionals. Eventually, the MIS department may be responsible only for maintaining critical enterprise-wide hardware, software, and data; end-users may meet all other computing needs on their own.

- **Conflicting communications standards**   If history, progress, and today's situation can be used to draw a conclusion about communications standards, then it seems probable that a common interface will remain elusive. In the foreseeable future, we will still have many machines, software, and communications products that cannot talk to each other. The movement toward global communications will probably add to this problem. An example is the ongoing EDI protocol battle between X.12 (more popular in the United States) and EDIFACT (more popular in Europe).

SUMMARY

Security, with respect to information systems, refers to the protection of hardware, software, data, procedure, and people resources against such events as alteration, destruction, or unauthorized use. With the rise of communications networks and microcomputer-based processing—as well as with the general rise in computer literacy—security has become more difficult to manage effectively.

Computer crime is the use of computer resources to engage in unauthorized or illegal acts. Numerous types of computer crime exist, including data diddling (performing unauthorized modifications to data), the Trojan Horse technique (burying criminal code within authorized programs), the salami technique (shaving small quantities of money from client balances), unauthorized use of superzap programs (which allow the person to bypass regular system controls), unauthorized use of trapdoor routines (which allow access to various parts of the computer system), logic bombs (routines that cause a system to become inoperative or to malfunction), scavenging techniques (browsing through computer garbage for sensitive information), leakage (allowing data, programs, or computer resources to leave a site without authorization), eavesdropping (observing transmissions intended for others), wiretapping (diverting a transmission flow), software piracy (copying or using programs without authorization), and hacking (breaking into a computer system just for the challenge of doing so).

Recently, computer viruses have received a lot of publicity because of their ability to reproduce, spread, and cause productivity losses, data destruction, and system crashes. Today, virus detection and eradication software are standard components of most organizations' software libraries. However, the potential damage that viruses can cause may be eliminated by taking appropriate precautions.

Organizations can use various methods to prevent computer crime, including: hiring carefully, monitoring malcontents, separating employee functions, restricting system use, protecting resources with passwords or access cards, disguising data or programs in coded form through encryption, monitoring system transactions, conducting frequent audits, and educating people in security measures and considerations of ethics (standards of moral conduct).

Disaster recovery refers to the contingency plans of an organization to recover from a monumentally bad occurrence. The two main strategies for disaster recovery are physical security (such as locked doors and fire extinguishers) and backup. Backup plans for data and software involve creating duplicate copies and storing them at a remote site. Hardware backup involves buying duplicate hardware or using the facilities of another organization.

Ethical issues are a major MIS concern. Today's information technology enables people to capture and distribute personal data—often without the individual's knowledge or permission. Numerous organizations—both public and private—have assembled vast databases on U.S. citizens. Both legal and ethical questions must be raised about the privacy and accuracy of the data that are collected and stored about individuals. Intellectual property rights is also an issue that has both ethical and legal implications. To combat potential problems in this area, numerous companies and professional organizations developed computer-related ethics codes. General guidelines for addressing potential ethical dilemmas have also been developed.

Today, as computer and communications technology become increasingly more strategically important to organizations, more opportunities for MIS-related careers exist than ever before. Career options are also greater. MIS professionals can follow a career path within an organization—that is, try to advance within a company—or they can develop careers around particular niche areas or particular lifestyles. Today's MIS professional would benefit by looking at a career as a business and developing a strategic plan for success. Such a plan should include seeking additional training by taking classes, attending seminars or exhibitions, reading, and joining professional associations.

Business is becoming increasingly multinational necessitating the development of global networks. This multinational dimension causes numerous MIS problems. For example, multinational expansion causes further distribution of resources and decision making; it also increases risk. The risk arises from the numerous differences that exist among countries. These include language, culture, political climate, laws and customs, communications standards, nationalism, economic, staffing, and workday differences.

Numerous changes will occur in information technology in the future. The trend toward distributive processing and networking should continue and major challenges are expected in the development of global networks. Many significant changes should occur in both computer hardware and software; such changes will affect the way in which work is done by future managers and users.

KEY TERMS

Access card	Encryption
Backup	Ethics
Computer crime	Password
Computer ethics	Security
Disaster recovery	Software piracy

REVIEW

REVIEW QUESTIONS

1. What is "data diddling"? Provide three examples.
2. Identify the various forms that computer crime can take.
3. What approaches may be used to prevent or minimize computer crime?
4. In what ways should system use be restricted so that criminal activity is prevented?
5. What does encryption do?
6. How are ethics connected to computer crime?

7. Describe and provide examples of the major categories of computer-related ethical issues.

8. What guidelines should managers and users follow to effectively address computer-related ethical dilemmas?

9. Why is backup and disaster recovery important? Identify some of the procedures that may be used to avert disaster.

10. What advantages does niching have as an alternative for an MIS career path?

11. What alternatives are available for continuing MIS education?

12. Which journals are particularly slanted toward MIS-related issues?

13. Identify some of the areas that pose challenges for multinational corporations.

14. What challenges must be surmounted in the development of global networks?

15. What are some of the future trends that are likely to have a major impact on MIS in the years ahead?

DISCUSSION QUESTIONS

1. Why, do you think, are most computer crimes committed by employees?

2. Computer crime is an area that the legal system has found particularly difficult to handle. Why do you feel that this happens?

3. Organizations frequently claim to want chief information officers who think like businesspeople, yet these companies often seek technically oriented computer science graduates to fill entry-level slots. Is this a contradiction? Explain your answer.

4. In what ways can countries use data and information technologies as competitive weapons?

5. Should ethics have any other place in MIS besides in the area of computer crime?

CASE STUDY

The New Role of MIS Executives

Louis B. Hughes is the vice-president of information technology at the Greenwich, Connecticut-based Maxwell Macmillan Publishing Company. He is sometimes described as a next-generation MIS executive. Hughes is responsible not only for developing the company's information systems infrastructure, but is also accountable for generating new product ideas to join Macmillan products with emerging technologies.

As Hughes notes, "My role is [that of] an advocate for exploiting new technology for our business, to contribute to individual business plans and strategies." Because Macmillan is essentially an information distribution company that publishes books and travel guides (as well as providing data on CD-ROM), its top executives are often receptive to Hughes's ideas. Says Hughes, "We are invited to the table" to help brainstorm new technology-based business opportunities.

Hughes also gets together regularly with the top Macmillan executives to hear where the various business units are headed and to see how he and the MIS group can help the business units meld emerging technologies with their business plans. According to Hughes, "There are specific things I can do to foster this, like expose the senior business leaders to what the new technology looks like. I've arranged some high-level briefings and demos for selective execs."

Hughes feels that several things are needed for him to succeed in this role. Says Hughes, "The first is to understand the trends and have a clear scenario in terms of technology evolution." The second "is to visualize what the new products and services will look like using the technology that isn't here yet." The final step is the development of business plans and strategies that translate the ideas into tangible products.

In order to get the marriage of technology and product development beyond the honeymoon stage, Hughes developed a corporate data center in Oakbrook, Illinois, which serves as a centralized resource for most of the Macmillan companies. According to Hughes, Macmillan needs "an efficient, effective information processing center that houses a repository used to deliver new products and services and as a research and development engine for new product development."

Hughes, who's spent over 30 years in the computer industry, enjoys his new job. He finds that combining trade and analytics is "exciting and interesting. There is a great transition taking place with technology that will transform the business. It's an opportunity that few of us get."

Adapted from Ambrosio (1992).

1. What types of information do you suppose Hughes will need in order to formulate strategic MIS plans for Macmillan? Explain your reasoning. What are some of the possible sources for the information he would need?

2. Why is it important for Hughes to work closely with managers of Macmillan's other business units? In addition to what the Case Study describes, what else could Hughes do to help facilitate technological planning and the integration of information technology in Macmillan's business units?

3. Do you think that Hughes's role is unique—or do you feel that MIS executives in most major companies will assume roles similar to the one that Hughes is filling at Macmillan? Explain your reasoning.

REFERENCES

CHAPTER 1

Ackoff, Russell E. "Management Misinformation Systems." *Management Science*, December 1967, pp. 147–156.

Bakos, J. Yannis. "Information Links and Electronic Marketplaces: The Role of Interorganizational Information Systems in Vertical Markets." *Journal of Management Information Systems*, Fall 1991, pp. 25–47.

Ball, L., and R. Harris. "SMIS Members: A Membership Analysis." *MIS Quarterly*, March 1982, pp. 19–38.

Betts, Mitch. "House Bill Would Restrict Air Reservation Systems." *Computerworks*, August 17, 1992, pp. 1, 16.

Brancheau, James C., and James C. Wetherbe. "Key Issues in Information Systems Management." *MIS Quarterly*, March 1987, pp. 23–35.

Budney, James N. "Competing in the Global Community." *Telecommunications*, November 1991, pp. 55–58.

Bullers, William I., Jr., and Richard A. Reid. "Information System Capabilities and Organizational Applications: An Evolutionary Perspective." In Edward Szewcak, Coral Snodgrass, and Mehdi Khosrowpour (eds.), *Management Impacts of Information Technology: Perspectives on Organizational Change and Growth*. Harrisburg, PA: Idea Group, 1991, pp. 1–24.

Burkan, Wayne C. *Executive Information Systems*. New York: Van Nostrand Reinhold, 1991.

Burn, Janice, and Eveline Caldwell. *Management of Information Systems Technology*. New York: Van Nostrand Reinhold, 1990.

Business Week. "Foremost-McKesson: The Computer Moves Distribution to Center Stage." December 7, 1981, pp. 115–122.

Business Week. "How Arthur Andersen Became a High-Tech Hotshot." April 25, 1988, p. 125.

Case, Thomas L., and John R. Pickett. "Information Technology in R&D: Enhancing Organizational Competitiveness via R&D Information Systems." In Edward Szewcak, Coral Snodgrass, and Mehdi Khosrowpour (eds.), *Management Impacts of Information Technology: Perspectives on Organizational Change and Growth*. Harrisburg, PA: Idea Group, 1991, pp. 438–457.

Cash, James I., Jr., F. Warren McFarlan, James L. McKenney, and Lynda M. Applegate. *Corporate Information Systems Management: Text and Cases* (3rd Ed.). Homewood, IL: Irwin, 1992.

Christoff, Kurt A. *Managing the Information Center*. Glenview, IL: Scott, Foresman/Little, Brown Higher Education, 1990.

Copeland, Duncan G. "So You Want to Build the Next SABRE System." *Business Quarterly (Canada)*, Winter 1991, pp. 56–60.

Dickson, G. W., R. L. Leitheiser, J. C. Wetherbe, and M. Nechis. "Key Information Systems Issues for the 1980's." *MIS Quarterly*, September 1984, pp. 135–159.

Evans, Michael K., and R. D. Norton. "Flat Manufacturing Employment for the 1990s," *Industry Week*, October 2, 1989, pp. 34–36.

Feigenbaum, Edward, Pamela McCorduck, and H. Penny Nii. *The Rise of the Expert Company*. New York: Vintage Books, 1988.

Freedman, David. "Harvard MBAs Could be Hazardous to IS Managers." *Infosystems*, September 1986, pp. 26–28.

Frenzel, Carrol. *Management of Information Technology*. Boston, MA: Boyd & Fraser, 1992.

Gray, Paul, William R. King, Ephraim R. McLean, and Hugh J. Watson (eds.). *MoIS: Management of Information Systems*. Chicago, IL: The Dryden Press, 1989.

Hale, David P., William D. Huseman, and Frank Groom. "Integrating Islands of Automation." *MIS Quarterly*, December 1989, pp. 433–445.

Hartog, Curt, and Martin Herbert. "1985 Opinion Survey of MIS Managers: Key Issues." *MIS Quarterly*, December 1986, pp. 351–361.

Hershey, Gerald L., and Donna L. Kizzer. *Planning and Implementing End-User Information Systems*. Cincinnati, OH: South-Western, 1992.

Hopper, Max. D. "Rattling SABRE—New Ways to Compete on Information." *Harvard Business Review*, May-June 1990, pp. 118–120.

Ives, B., and G. P. Learmouth. "The Information System as a Competitive Weapon." *Communications of the ACM*, December 1984, pp. 1193-1201.

Johnson, H. Russell, and Michael R. Vitale. "Creating Competitive Advantage with Interorganizational Information Systems." *MIS Quarterly*, June 1988, pp. 153–165.

Kanter, Jerome. *Managing with Information* (4th Ed.). Englewood Cliffs, NJ: Prentice-Hall, 1992.

Kelley, Robert E. "Connectivity Reshapes the Corporate Landscape." *PC Week Connectivity*, April 12, 1988, p. C/7.

LaPlante, Alice. "For the Truly Brave Try Eastern Europe." *Computerworld*, April 13, 1992, p. 81.

LaPlante, Alice. "U.S. Companies Find Outsourcing a Sensible Way to Go International." *Computerworld*, April 13, 1992, p. 79.

LaPlante, Alice, and Joseph Maglitta. "Europe Ho!" *Computerworld*, April 13, 1992, pp. 77–78.

Lawrence, Jennifer. "Airlines See Ad $s in Reservations Systems." *Advertising Age*, June 15, 1992, p. 42.

Magnusson, Paul. "The High-Tech Brawl Over Free Trade." *Business Week*, April 6, 1992, p. 22.

Mallach, Efrem G. "The Organizational Impact of Strategic Systems." In Edward Szewczak, Coral Snodgrass, and Mehdi Khosrowpour (eds.), *Management Impacts of Information Technology: Perspectives on Organizational Change and Growth*. Harrisburg, PA: Idea Group, 1991, pp. 408–420.

Mayer, Martin. "Merrill Lynch Quacks Like a Bank." *Fortune*. October 20, 1980, pp. 135–139.

McConnell, Vicki C., and Karl W. Koch. *Computerizing the Corporation: The Intimate Link between People and Machines*. New York: Van Nostrand Reinhold, 1990.

McFarlan, F. Warren. "Information Technology Changes the Way You Compete." *Harvard Business Review*, May–June 1984, pp. 98–103.

McNurlin, Barbara C., and Ralph H. Sprague, Jr. *Information Systems Management in Practice* (2nd Ed.). Englewood Cliffs, NJ: Prentice-Hall, 1989.

Mensching, James R., and Dennis A. Adams. *Managing an Information System*. Englewood Cliffs, NJ: Prentice-Hall, 1991.

Naisbitt, John. *Megatrends 2000*. New York: Warner Books, 1990.

Neiderman, Fred, James C. Brancheau, and James C. Wetherbe. "Information Systems Management Issues for the 1990s." *MIS Quarterly*, December 1991, pp. 475–499.

Owen, Darrel E. "Information Systems Organizations—Keeping Pace with Pressure." *Sloan Management Review*, Spring 1986, pp. 59–68.

Parsons, G. L. "Information Technology: New Competitive Weapon." *Sloan Management Review*, Spring 1985, pp. 3–14.

Peters, Tom. *Thriving on Chaos*. New York: Knopf, 1987.

Pillsbury, Ann. "The Hard Selling Supplier to the Sick." *Fortune*, July 26, 1982, pp. 56–61.

Porat, M. U. *The Information Economy*. Washington, DC: U.S. Department of Commerce, Office of Telecommunications Policy, 1977.

Porter, Michael E. *Competitive Advantage*. New York: Free Press, 1985.

Porter, Michael E. *Competitive Strategy: Technology for Analyzing Industries and Competitors*. New York: Free Press, 1980.

Porter, Michael E., and Victor E. Millar. "How Information Gives You Competitive Advantage." *Harvard Business Review*, July–August 1985, pp. 149–160.

Schwartz, John. "The Next Revolution." *Newsweek*, April 6, 1992, pp. 42–48.

Slater, Derek. "IS at Your Service." *Computerworld*, January 20, 1992, pp. 71–72.

Spillman, Robert D., and Faye P. Teer. "Critical Information Systems Issues: Focus on the Future." *Proceedings of the International Academy for Information Management*, Minneapolis, Minnesota, November 30, 1988, pp. 156–165.

Toffler, Alvin. *Powershift*. New York: Bantam, 1990.

Wall Street Journal. "Big Board Curb on Electronic Trading Results in Halt at Stock-Index Markets." October 21, 1987, p. 3.

Winkler, Connie. "AMR Hones Sabre to Sharpen Competitive Edge." *Computerworld*, October 8, 1990, pp. 36–37.

Wiseman, C., and I. C. MacMillan. "Creating Competitive Weapons from Information Systems." *Journal of Business Strategy*, Fall 1984, pp. 42–49.

Wiseman, Charles. *Strategic Information Systems*. Homewood, IL: Irwin, 1988.

Wyman, John. "Technical Myopia—The Need to Think Strategically about Technology." *Sloan Management Review*, Summer 1985, pp. 59–64.

Wysocki, Robert K., and James Young. *Information Systems: Management Principles in Action*. New York: Wiley, 1990.

Yates, Joanne, and Robert I. Benjamin. "The Past and Present as a Window of the Future." In Michael S. Scott (ed.), *The Corporation of the 1990s: Information Technology and Organizational Transformation*. New York: Oxford University Press, 1991.

Zmud, Robert. *Information Systems in Organizations*. Glenview, IL: Scott, Foresman, 1983.

CHAPTER 2

Ahituv, Niv, and Seev Neumann. *Principles of Information Systems for Management* (3rd Ed.). Dubuque, IA: Wm. C. Brown, 1990.

Attewell, P. "Big Brother and the Sweatshop: Computer Surveillance in the Automated Office." *Sociological Theory*, Spring 1987, pp. 87–99.

Ballou, Melinda-Carol. "DEC Restructuring Takes Form." *Computerworld*, November 2, 1992, pp. 1, 20.

Benjamin, Robert I., Charles Dickinson, Jr., and John F. Rockart. "Changing Role of the Corporate Information Systems Officer." *MIS Quarterly*, September 1985, pp. 177–178.

Bird, Allan. "Information Technology in Japanese Organizations: A Report from the Field." In Edward Szewczak, Coral Snodgrass, and Mehdi Khosrowpour (eds.), *Management Impacts of Information Technology: Perspectives on Organizational Change and Growth*. Harrisburg, PA: Idea Group, 1991, pp. 330–369.

Brancheau, James C., and James C. Wetherbe. "The Adoption of Spreadsheet Software: Testing Innovation Diffusion Theory in the Context of End-User Computing." *Information Systems Research*, June 1990, pp. 115–143.

Cartwright, D., and A. Zander. *Group Dynamics: Research and Theory.* New York: Harper & Row, 1968.

Clemmons, Eric K., and Michael C. Row. "Sustaining IT Advantage: The Role of Structural Differences." *MIS Quarterly*, September 1991, pp. 275–292.

Chandler, Alfred. *Strategy and Structure.* Cambridge, MA: MIT Press, 1962.

Cole, Robert E. "Target Information for Competitive Performance." *Harvard Business Review*, May-June 1985, pp. 100–109.

Couger, J. Daniel, and Robert Zawacki. "What Motivates DP Professionals." *Datamation*, September 1978, pp. 116–123.

Dannon, S. *Stories of Mistrust and Manipulation: The Electronic Monitoring of the American Workforce.* Cleveland, OH: 9 to 5 Working Women Education Fund, 1990.

Davenport, Thomas H., and James E. Short. "The New Industrial Engineering: Information Technology and Business Process Redesign." *Sloan Management Review*, Summer 1990, pp. 11–27.

Davis, F. D. "Perceived Usefulness, Perceived Ease of Use, and End-User Acceptance of Information Technology." *MIS Quarterly*, September (1989), pp. 318–339.

Deal, E., and A. A. Kennedy. *Corporate Cultures.* Reading, MA: Addison-Wesley, 1982.

Eckerson, Wayne. "EDI's Future in the Automotive Industry." *Network World*, May 20, 1992, pp. 27–28, 50.

Er, Meng C. "The Impact of Information Technology on Organizations." *Journal of Systems Management*, April 1987, pp. 32–36.

Ferrat, Thomas W., and Larry E. Short. "Are Information Systems People Different? An Investigation of How They Are and Should Be Managed." *MIS Quarterly*, September 1988, pp. 427–444.

Forsyth, Donnelson R. *Group Dynamics* (2nd Ed.). Pacific Grove, CA: Brooks/Cole, 1990.

French, Wendell L., and Cecil H. Bell, Jr. *Organization Development: Behavioral Science Interventions for Organization Improvement* (4th Ed.). Englewood Cliffs, NJ: Prentice-Hall, 1990.

Gillette, Jonathan, and Marion McCollum. *Groups in Context: A New Perspective on Group Dynamics.* Reading, MA: Addison-Wesley, 1990.

Grant, R., C. Higgins, and R. Irving. "Computerized Monitoring Systems: Are They Costing You Customers?" *Sloan Management Review*, Vol. 29, No. 3 (1988), pp. 39–45.

Grant, Rebecca A., and Chris A. Higgins. "The Impact of Computerized Performance Monitoring on Service Work: Testing a Causal Model." *Information Systems Research*, June 1991, pp. 116–142.

Gray, Paul, William R. King, Ephraim R. McLean, and Hugh J. Watson (eds.). *MoIS: Management of Information Systems.* Chicago, IL: The Dryden Press, 1989.

Hershey, Gerald L., and Donna L. Kizzer. *Planning and Implementing End-User Information Systems.* Cincinnati, OH: South-Western, 1992.

Horwitt, Elisabeth. "High-Tech Heroes: Wilderness Society." *Computerworld*, June 15, 1992, p. 91.

Kaltnekar, Zdravko. "Information Technology and the Humanization of Work." In Edward Szewczak, Coral Snodgrass, and Mehdi Khosrowpour (eds.), *Management Impacts of Information Technology: Perspectives on Organizational Change and Growth.* Harrisburg, PA: Idea Group, 1991, pp. 493–533.

Katz, Ralph. *Managing Professionals in Innovative Organizations.* New York: HarperBusiness, 1988.

Koppes, Laura L., Wanda A. Trahan, E. Alan Hartman, Baron Perlman, and David J. Nelson. "Researching the Impact of Computer Technology in the Workplace: A Psychological Perspective." In Edward Szewczak, Coral Snodgrass, and Mehdi Khosrowpour (eds.), *Management Impacts of Information Technology: Perspectives on Organizational Change and Growth.* Harrisburg, PA: Idea Group, 1991, pp. 135–164.

Lederer, Albert L., and Jayosh Prasad. "Putting Estimates on Track." *Computerworld*, August 24, 1992, pp. 85–87.

Lee, Soonchul, and P. J. Guinan. "The Impact of Information Technology on Work Group Innovation and Control." In Edward Szewczak, Coral Snodgrass, and Mehdi Khosrowpour (eds.), *Management Impacts of Information Technology: Perspectives on Organizational Change and Growth.* Harrisburg, PA: Idea Group, 1991, pp. 241–272.

Lucas, H. "Organizational Power and the Information Services Department." *Communications of the ACM*, January 1984, pp. 58–65.

Mallach, Efrem. "The Organizational Impact of Strategic Systems." In Edward Szewczak, Coral Snodgrass, and Mehdi Khosrowpour (eds.), *Management Impacts of Information Technology: Perspectives on Organizational Change and Growth.* Harrisburg, PA: Idea Group, 1991, pp. 408–420.

Markus, M. Lynne. "Power, Politics, and MIS Implementation." *Communications of the ACM*, June 1983, pp. 430–444.

Maslow, Abraham. "A Theory of Human Motivation." *Psychological Review*, July 1943, pp. 370–396.

Matherly, Timothy A., and Lee P. Stepina. "Public Sector Personnel Policies May Threaten DP Operations." *Journal of Systems Management*, December 1985, pp. 20–25.

Mathieson, Kieran. "Predicting User Intentions: Comparing the Technology Acceptance Model with the Theory of Planned Behavior." *Information Systems Research*, September 1991, pp. 173–191.

McConnell, Vicki C., and Karl W. Koch. *Computerizing the Corporation: The Intimate Link between People and Machines.* New York: Van Nostrand Reinhold, 1990.

Miller, George A. "The Magical Number Seven, Plus or Minus Two: Some Limits on Our Capability for Processing Information." *The Psychological Review*,

Processing Information." *The Psychological Review*, March 1956, pp. 81–97.

Moore, Gary C., and Izak Benbasat. "Development of an Instrument to Measure the Perceptions of Adopting an Information Technology Innovation." *Information Systems Research*, September 1991, pp. 192–221.

Newell, Allen, and Herbert A. Simon. *Human Problem Solving*. Englewood Cliffs, NJ: Prentice-Hall, 1972.

Nolan, Richard L. "Managing the Crises in Data Processing." *Harvard Business Review*, March-April 1979, pp. 115–126.

Orilkowski, Wanda J., and Daniel Robey. "Information Technology and the Structuring of Organizations." *Information Systems Research*, June 1991, pp. 143–169.

O'Riordan, P. Declan. "The Emerging Role of the Chief Information Officer." *Information Strategy: The Executive's Journal*, Winter 1986.

Ott, J. Steven. *The Organizational Culture Perspective*. Chicago: The Dorsey Press, 1989.

Owens, Elizabeth L. "Federal Government Lags Behind Private Sector in Computer Modernization." *Data Management*, July 1987, p. 13.

Peters, Tom. *Thriving on Chaos*. New York: Alfred A. Knopf, 1987.

Rebello, Kathy. "Apple's Daring Leap into the All-Digital Future." *Business Week*, May 25, 1992, pp. 120–123.

Reiss, Levi, and Edwin G. Dolan. "Using Computers: Managing Change." Cincinnati, OH: South-Western, 1989.

Robey, Daniel, Dana L. Farrow, and Charles S. Franz. "Group Process and Conflict in Systems Development." *Management Science*, October 1989, pp. 1172–1191.

Robey, Daniel, and William Taggert. "Human Information Processing in Information and Decision Support Systems." *MIS Quarterly*, June 1982, pp. 61–73.

Ross, Lee, Mark Lepper, and Michael Hubbard. "Perseverance in Self-Perception: Biased Attributional Processes in the Debriefing Paradigm." *Journal of Personality and Social Psychology*, May 1975, pp. 880–892.

Shimada, Tatsumi. "The Impact of Information Technology on Organizations in Japanese Companies." In Edward Szewczak, Coral Snodgrass, and Mehdi Khosrowpour (eds.), *Management Impacts of Information Technology: Perspectives on Organizational Change and Growth*. Harrisburg, PA: Idea Group, 1991, pp. 298–329.

Stahl, Bob. "The Trouble With Applications Generators." *Datamation*, April 1, 1986, pp. 93–94.

Stephens, John M., and Robert P. McGowan. *Information Systems and Public Management*. New York: Praeger, 1985.

Swanson, E. B., and M. E. Treacy. *Information System Implementation: Bridging the Gap between Design and Utilization*. Homewood, IL: Irwin, 1988.

Szewcak, Edward. "Evaluating the Impacts of Information Technology in Organizational Systems." In Edward Szewczak, Coral Snodgrass, and Mehdi Khosrowpour (eds.), *Management Impacts of Information Technology: Perspectives on Organizational Change and Growth*. Harrisburg, PA: Idea Group, 1991, pp. 25–47.

Tom, Paul L. *Managing Information as a Corporate Resource* (2nd Ed.). New York: HarperCollins, 1991.

Tversky, A., and D. Kahneman. "The Framing of Decisions and the Psychology of Choice." *Science*, January 1981, pp. 453–458.

Williams, Joseph. "Negative Consequences of Information Technology." In Edward Szewczak, Coral Snodgrass, and Mehdi Khosrowpour (eds.), *Management Impacts of Information Technology: Perspectives on Organizational Change and Growth*. Harrisburg, PA: Idea Group, 1991, pp. 48–75.

CHAPTER 3

Ahituv, Niv, and Seev Neumann. *Principles of Information Systems for Management* (3rd Ed.). Dubuque, IA: Wm. C. Brown, 1990.

Anthony, R. N. *Planning and Control Systems: A Framework for Analysis*. Cambridge, MA: Harvard University Press, 1965.

Baldo, Anthony H. "Barrier Breakers." *Financial World*, April 18, 1989, pp. 70–71.

Besterfield, Dale H. *Quality Control*. Englewood Cliffs, NJ: Prentice-Hall, 1990.

Boulding, Kenneth. "General Systems Theory—The Skeleton of Science." *Management Science*, April 1956, pp. 197–208.

Burn, Janice, and Eveline Caldwell. *Management of Information Systems Technology*. New York: Van Nostrand Reinhold, 1990.

Cash, James I., Jr., F. Warren McFarlan, James L. McKenney, and Lynda M. Applegate. *Corporate Information Systems Management: Text and Cases* (3rd Ed.). Homewood, IL: Irwin, 1992.

Clemons, Eric K., and F. Warren McFarlan. "Chief Executives Define Their Own Needs." *Harvard Business Review*, July-August 1986, pp. 91–97.

Davenport, Thomas H., Michael Hammer, and Tauno J. Metsisto. "How Executives Can Shape Their Company's Information Systems." *Harvard Business Review*, March-April 1989, pp. 130–134.

Er, M. C. "Matching Information Systems with Corporate Information Needs." *Information and Software Technology*, Vol. 29, No. 2 (1987), pp. 66-68.

Frenzel, Carrol W. *Management of Information Technology*. Boston: Boyd & Fraser, 1992.

Goold, Michael. "Strategic Control in the Decentralized Firm." *Sloan Management Review*, Winter 1991, pp. 69–81.

Gray, Daniel H. "Uses and Misuses of Strategic Planning." *Harvard Business Review*, January-February 1986, pp. 89–97.

Gray, Paul, William R. King, Ephraim R. McLean, and Hugh J. Watson (eds.). *MoIS: Management of In-*

formation Systems. Chicago, IL: The Dryden Press, 1989.

Hershey, Gerald L., and Donna L. Kizzer. *Planning and Implementing End-User Information Systems.* Cincinnati, OH: South-Western, 1992.

Hodge, Bartow, and Robert N. Hodgson. *Management and the Computer in Information and Control Systems.* New York: McGraw-Hill, 1969.

Holsapple, Clyde W., Linda Ellis Johnson, and Ramakrishnan Pakath. "Model Management: Concepts, Challenges, and Opportunities." In Edward Szewczak, Coral Snodgrass, and Mehdi Khosrowpour (eds.), *Management Impacts of Information Technology: Perspectives on Organizational Change and Growth.* Harrisburg, PA: Idea Group, 1991, pp. 76–99.

Isenberg, Daniel J. "The Tactics of Strategic Opportunism." *Harvard Business Review,* March-April 1987, pp. 92–97.

King, W. R. "Strategic Planning for Management Information Systems." *MIS Quarterly,* March 1978, pp. 22–37.

Kolcum, Edward H. "Gulfstream Chairman Seeks to Boost Productivity and Entrepreneurial Focus." *Aviation Week and Space Technology,* April 2, 1990, p. 50.

Leavitt, Theodore. "Marketing Myopia." *Harvard Business Review,* November-December 1960, pp. 466–475.

Lemmers, Teri. "The Effective and Indispensible Mission Statement." *Inc. Magazine,* August 1992, pp. 75–77.

Lederer, Albert L., and Aubrey L. Mendelow. "Coordination of Information System Plans with Business Plans." *Journal of Management Information Systems,* Fall 1989, pp. 5–19.

Marcus, Lynne. *Systems in Organizations.* Boston: Pitman, 1984.

Martin, E. Wainright, Daniel W. DeHayes, Jeffrey A. Hoffer, and William C. Perkins. *Managing Information Technology: What Managers Need to Know.* New York: Macmillan, 1991.

McFarlan, F. Warren, James L. McKenney, and Philip Pyburn. "The Information Archipelago–Plotting a Course." *Harvard Business Review,* January-February 1983, pp. 145–156.

McLean, Ephraim R., and John V. Soden. *Strategic Planning for MIS.* New York: John Wiley, 1977.

Pearce, J. A., II, and F. R. David. "Corporate Mission Statements: The Bottom Line." *Academy of Management Executive,* May 1987, pp. 109–116.

Quinn, James Brian. "Managing Innovation: Controlled Chaos." *Harvard Business Review,* May-June 1985, pp. 73–84.

Radding, Alan, and Joseph Maglitta. "Buyer Beware." *Computerworld,* February 17, 1992, pp. 61–63.

Rasheed, Abdul M. A., and Deepak K. Datta. "Online Databases in Environmental Scanning: Usage and Organizational Impact." In Edward Szewczak,

Coral Snodgrass, and Mehdi Khosrowpour (eds.), *Management Impacts of Information Technology: Perspectives on Organizational Change and Growth.* Harrisburg, PA: Idea Group, 1991, pp. 389–407.

Rockart, John. "Chief Executives Define Their Own Needs." *Harvard Business Review,* March-April 1979, pp. 81–93.

Sass, C. J., and T. A. Keefe. "MIS for Strategic Planning and a Competitive Edge." *Journal of Systems Management,* June 1988, pp. 14–17.

Shank, M. E., A. C. Boynton, and R. W. Zmud. "CSF Analysis as a Methodology for MIS Planning." *MIS Quarterly,* Vol. 9, No. 2 (1985), pp. 121–129.

Tom, Paul L. *Managing Information as a Corporate Resource* (2nd Ed.). New York: HarperCollins, 1991.

von Bertalanffy, Ludwig. *General Systems Theory: Foundations, Development, Applications.* New York: George Braziller, 1968.

Ward, John, Pat Griffiths, and Paul Whitmore. *Strategic Planning for Information Systems.* New York: John Wiley & Sons, 1990.

CHAPTER 4

Adams, Walter, and James W. Brock. *The Bigness Complex: Industry, Labor, and Government in the American Economy.* New York: Pantheon, 1986.

Agor, Weston. "How Top Executives Use Their Intuition to Make Important Decisions." *Business Horizons,* January-February 1986, pp. 49-53.

Anthony, R. N. *Planning and Control Systems: A Framework for Analysis.* Cambridge, MA: Harvard University Press, 1965.

Bennis, Warren, and Burt Nanus. *Leaders.* New York: Harper & Row, 1985.

Bird, Allan. "Information Technology in Japanese Organizations: A Report from the Field." In Edward Szewczak, Coral Snodgrass, and Mehdi Khosrowpour (eds.), *Management Impacts of Information Technology: Perspectives on Organizational Change and Growth.* Harrisburg, PA: Idea Group, 1991, pp. 330–369.

Budney, James N. "Competing in the Global Community." *Telecommunications,* November 1991, pp. 55–58.

Bullers, William I., Jr., and Richard A. Reid. "Information System Capabilities and Organizational Applications: An Evolutionary Perspective." In Edward Szewcak, Coral Snodgrass, and Mehdi Khosrowpour (eds.), *Management Impacts of Information Technology: Perspectives on Organizational Change and Growth.* Harrisburg, PA: Idea Group, 1991, pp. 1–24.

Burkan, Wayne C. *Executive Information Systems.* New York: Van Nostrand Reinhold, 1991.

Cash, James I., Jr., F. Warren McFarlan, James L. McKenney, and Lynda M. Applegate. *Corporate Information Systems Management: Text and Cases* (3rd Ed.). Homewood, IL: Irwin, 1992.

Cole, Robert E. "Target Information for Competitive Performance." *Harvard Business Review*, May-June 1985, pp. 100-109.

Evans, James R. *Creative Thinking in the Decision and Management Sciences*, Cincinnati, OH: South-Western Publishing, 1991.

Fox, Bruce. "CAD Makes a Difference." *Chain Store Executive*, October 1991, pp. 47–50.

Frenzel, Carrol. *Management of Information Technology*. Boston, MA: Boyd & Fraser, 1992.

Gerrity, Thomas P., and John F. Rockart. "Are You a Leader or a Laggard?" *Sloan Management Review*, Summer 1986, pp. 25-34.

Gibson, C. F., and R. L. Nolan. "Managing the Four Stages of EDP Growth." *Harvard Business Review*, March-April 1974, pp. 72-88.

Gorry, G. A., and M. S. Scott Morton. "A Framework for Management Information Systems." *Sloan Management Review*, Spring 1989, pp. 49-72.

Gremillion, Lee L., and Philip J. Pyburn. "Justifying Decision Support and Office Administration Systems." *Journal of Management Information Systems*, Summer 1985, pp. 5-17.

House, R. J. "A Path-Goal Theory of Leadership Effectiveness." *Administrative Science Quarterly*, Vol. 16, No. 3 (1971), pp. 321–338.

Iacocca, Lee (with William Novak). *Iacocca: An Autobiography*. New York: Bantam, 1984.

Isenberg, Daniel J. "How Senior Managers Think." *Harvard Business Review*, November-December 1984, pp. 92–97.

Kanter, Jerome. *Managing with Information* (4th Ed.). Englewood Cliffs, NJ: Prentice-Hall, 1992.

Lindblom, C. E. "The Science of Muddling Through." *Public Administration Review*, Vol. 19 (1959), pp. 79-88.

Mallach, Efrem. "The Organizational Impact of Strategic Systems." In Edward Szewczak, Coral Snodgrass, and Mehdi Khosrowpour (eds.), *Management Impacts of Information Technology: Perspectives on Organizational Change and Growth*. Harrisburg, PA: Idea Group, 1991, pp. 408–420.

March, James G., and Herbert A. Simon. *Organizations*. New York: John Wiley & Sons, 1958.

McCormack, Mark H. *What They Don't Teach You at Harvard Business School*. New York: Bantam, 1984.

Mensching, James R., and Dennis A. Adams. *Managing an Information System*. Englewood Cliffs, NJ: Prentice-Hall, 1991.

Mintzberg, Henry. "The Manager's Job: Folklore and Fact." *Harvard Business Review*, July-August 1975, pp. 49-61.

Mintzberg, Henry. *The Nature of Managerial Work*. New York: Harper & Row, 1971.

Nolan, R. L. "Managing the Crisis in Data Processing." *Harvard Business Review*, March-April 1979, pp. 115–126.

Peters, Thomas J., and Robert H. Waterman. *In Search of Excellence*. New York: Harper & Row, 1982.

Rockart, John F. "Chief Executives Define Their Own Data Needs." *Harvard Business Review*, March-April 1979, p. 81.

Shimada, Tatsumi. "The Impact of Information Technology on Organizations in Japanese Companies." In Edward Szewcak, Coral Snodgrass, and Mehdi Khosrowpour (eds.), *Management Impacts of Information Technology: Perspectives on Organizational Change and Growth*. Harrisburg, PA: Idea Group, 1991, pp. 298–329.

Simon, Herbert A. *The New Science of Management Decision*. New York: Harper & Row, 1960.

Stasiowski, Frank A. "Is CAD Worth the Cost?" *CAE*, May 1989, pp. 60–64.

Stovicek, Donald R. "Rapid Prototyping Slices Time-to-Market." *Automation*, September 1991, pp. 20–24.

Tversky, A., and D. Kahneman. "The Framing of Decisions and the Psychology of Choice." *Science*, January 1981, pp. 453-458.

Wilder, Clinton. "Virtual Reality Seeks Practicality." *Computerworld*, April 27, 1992, p. 26.

Wrapp, H. Edward. "Good Managers Don't Make Policy Decisions." *Harvard Business Review*, July-August 1984, pp. 8-21.

Wysocki, Robert K., and James Young. *Information Systems: Management Principles in Action*. New York: Wiley, 1990.

Yates, Joanne, and Robert I. Benjamin. "The Past and Present as a Window of the Future." In Michael S. Scott (ed.), *The Corporation of the 1990s: Information Technology and Organizational Transformation*. New York: Oxford University Press, 1991.

Zaleznik, Abraham. "Managers and Leaders: Are They Different?" *Harvard Business Review*, May-June 1977, pp. 67-78.

CHAPTER 5

Alexander, Michael. "Intelligent Computer May Be Reality by 2001." *Computerworld*, January 20, 1992, p. 20.

Alexander, Michael. "Smart Cards the Better Way to Pay?" *Computerworld*, February 3, 1992, p. 20.

Alsup, Mike, and Mitch Shults. "Documents Perform with Imaging." *LAN Technology*, January 1992, pp. 44-58.

Ambrosio, Johanna. "BASF Tape Exchange Receives Mixed Reviews." *Computerworld*, January 20, 1992, p. 1ff.

Ambrosio, Johanna. "Host Plans Reveal Wider Options." *Computerworld*, January 6, 1992, p. 1ff.

Andrews, David, Janet Puistonen, and Dennis Godsill. "The AS/400 in an Open World." *The ADM Consulting Update*, January 1992, pp. 2–48.

Arend, Mark. "New Automated 'Experts' Ready for Lenders." *Banking Journal*, January 1992, pp. 61-62.

Batcha, Becky. "Three Vendors Give Cray a Chase." *Computerworld*, October 12, 1987, pp. 99–106.

Bermar, Amy. "Designing Fabric with Custom CAD Program." *PC Week*, December 15, 1987, pp. 48–50.

Bock, Martin. "RAID: The Disk Strategy for the Masses?" *Computer Technology Review*, May 1991, pp. 23–32.

Booker, Ellis. "Filenet Imaging Stays Ahead of Pack." *Computerworld*, January 27, 1992, pp. 109–110.

Booker, Ellis. "Unisys Brings Large Systems Features to Midrange Line." *Computerworld*, February 17, 1992, p. 12.

Bozman, Jean S. "Fujitsu Points Super CPU at U.S." *Computerworld*, March 9, 1992, p. 8.

Bozman, Jean S. "Storage Tek Eyes Small Tape Library Sites." *Computerworld*, January 27, 1992, pp. 29–32.

Bradsher, Keith. "Computers, Having Learned to Talk, Are Becoming More Eloquent." *New York Times*, January 2, 1991, p. C6.

Brown, Jim. "Banking: Sterling Service." *Network World*, June 5, 1989, pp. 29-35, 50.

Buell, Barbara. "The Pen: Computing's Next Big Leap." *Business Week*, May 14, 1990, pp. 128–129.

Buckler, Grant. "Data Imaging: A Picture is Worth a Thousand Records." *Oracle*, Winter 1991, pp. 43-46.

Business Week. "Power Computing on the Go." February 10, 1992, pp. 134–135.

Business Week. "Videos are Starring in More and More Training Programs." September 7, 1987, pp. 108–110.

Carey, John, and Robert D. Hof. "Meet Silicon Valley's New Screen Hopeful." *Business Week*, February 3, 1992, p. 32.

The Computerworld IS Pocket Guide for Success. Framingham, MA: CW Publishing/Inc., 1992.

Cusak, Sally. "DEC Firms Strategy for RAID Storage." *Computerworld*, February 27, 1992, p. 37.

Defler, Frank J., Jr. "486/33 File Servers." *PC Magazine*, March 17, 1992, pp. 187–284.

Eliasion, Alan. *Online Business Computer Applications* (3rd Ed.). New York: Macmillan, 1991.

Engardio, Pete. "Quick, Name Five Taiwanese PC Makers." *Business Week*, May 18, 1992, pp. 128–129.

Essex, David. "Pen Potables Prove Puzzling." *Portable Office*, October 1991, pp. 23–32.

Fitzgerald, Michael. "Hyundai Hits Road with Laptops." *Computerworld*, January 6, 1992, pp. 37–44.

Fitzgerald, Michael. "IBM PC Future Rides on System Advancements." *Computerworld*, February 24, 1992, p. 1ff.

Fitzgerald, Michael. "Itching to Put Pen to Computer." *Computerworld*, January 20, 1992, p. 8.

Fitzgerald, Michael. "Notebook Prices: How Low Can They Go?" *Computerworld*, February 17, 1992, pp. 35–39.

Fitzgerald, Michael. "Utility to Save $1.6M with Pen Computing Plan." *Computerworld*, May 25, 1992, p. 35.

Freedman, David H. "Breaking the Quantum Barrier." *Discover*, February 1992, pp. 72–77.

Gullo, Karen. "Supercomputing in the Real World." *Datamation*, October 10, 1986, pp. 70–74.

Hamilton, Rosemary. "Mission-Critical Tools Aim at Desktops." *Computerworld*, February 3, 1992, p. 37ff.

Henderson, Tom, and Ken Miller. "Does RAID Fly?" *LAN: The Local Area Network Magazine*, June 1992, pp. 164–174.

Hildebrand, Carol, and Michael Fitzgerald. "I486: The New Deal in Desktop Design." *Computerworld*, January 20, 1992, p. 1ff.

Hof, Robert D. "Inside Intel." *Business Week*, June 1, 1992, pp. 86–94.

Hof, Robert D. "Suddenly, Hewlett-Packard is Doing Everything Right." *Business Week*, March 23, 1992, pp. 88–89.

Howard, Bill. "High-End Notebook PCs." *PC Magazine*, April 14, 1992, pp. 113–181.

Inc. "*Inc.*'s Buyer's Guide to Office Equipment and Technology." October 1991, pp. 61–133.

Janus, Susan. "Optical Disk Technology Could Help Put a Stop to Paper Chase." *PC Week*, February 2, 1988, p. 79.

Johnson, Maryfran. "Clustering to Turbocharge RS/6000." *Computerworld*, May 4, 1992, p. 1ff.

Johnson, Maryfran. "IBM RS/6000 to Break $10,000 Mark." *Computerworld*, January 20, 1992, p. 4.

Jones, Mitt. "Nine Desktop Scanners That Do It All." *PC Magazine*, April 14, 1992, pp. 247–297.

Juneau, Lucie. "Pen and Inc." *CIO*, December, 1992, pp. 46–50.

LAN: The Local Area Network Magazine. "Tape Backup Hardware." June 1992, pp. 113–123.

Lecht, Charles P. "Future Considerations." *Computerworld*, March 16, 1992, pp. 77–81.

Lindquist, Christopher. "County Thinks Small, Dumps 4381 for LANs." *Computerworld*, April 6, 1992, p. 1ff.

Mantel, Kimberly. "Go Figure with a Pen." *Datamation*, May 1, 1992, pp. 91–92.

Marion, Larry. "The Hot Applications of 1992." *Datamation*, May 1, 1992, pp. 35–54.

Nash, Jim. "RAID Technology Steps Softly But May Be Making Big Strides." *Computerworld*, February 17, 1992, pp. 41–43.

Nash, Kim S. "Bank Enlists Neural Net to Fight Fraud." *Computerworld*, January 2, 1992, pp. 53, 55.

O'Heney, Sheila. "Bank's High Hopes for High-Tech Check Processing." *Bankers Monthly*, August 1991, pp. 16–19.

PC Week Supplement. "Printers: The Next Generation," September 1, 1987, pp. S/1–S/46.

Prince, E. Ted, and David R. Knielel. "What's the Object(ive)?" *Computerworld*, October 5, 1992, pp. 81–82.

Quain, John. "486/50: The New Performance Leader." *PC Magazine*, June 16, 1992, pp. 113–192.

Radding, Alan. "RISC Desktop Machines: PCs in Disguise?" *Computerworld*, March 23, 1992, pp. 85–97.

Radding, Alan, and Joseph Maglitta. "Buyer, Be Aware." *Computerworld*, February 17, 1992, pp. 61–63.

Rifkin, Glenn. "Technology in Banking: Who is Cashing In?" *Computerworld*, March 9, 1987, pp. 65ff.

Rosch, Winn L. "Minicartridge Tape Backup." *PC Magazine*, April 14, 1992, pp. 185–244.

Rosch, Winn L. "Voice Recognition: Understanding the Master's Voice." *PC Magazine*, October 27, 1987, pp. 261–308.

Sharp, Kevin R. "Big Bad Bar Code." *Computerworld*, May 25, 1992, pp. 81–83.

Steinberg, Don. "Retailers Replacing Cash with ATM Cards to Lure Customers." *PC Week Connectivity*, December 1, 1987a, p. C/1ff.

The Computerworld IS Pocket Guide for Success. Framingham, MA: CW Publishing/Inc., 1992.

Valigra, Lori. "New-Generation Screens are a Tough Nut to Crack." *Computerworld*, May 25, 1992, p. 28.

Verity, John W. "IBM's Major Triumph in Minis." *Business Week*, March 16, 1992, p. 111.

Verity, John W. "Rethinking the Computer: With Superchips, the Network is the Computer." *Business Week*, November 26, 1990, pp. 116–124.

Viskovich, Fred. "What Threatens Mainframe Computing?" *Computerworld*, October 19, 1987, pp. 75–84.

Ward, Bernie. "The New Art of 'Penputing.'" *Sky Magazine*, December 1991, pp. 73–80.

Wilder, Clinton, and Johanna Ambrosio. "Battered Banks Reappraising Their IS Investments." *Computerworld*, April 12, 1991, pp. 1, 103.

CHAPTER 6

Alexander, Michael. "Multimedia Focus Turns to Training." *Computerworld*, January 13, 1992, p. 18.

Appleby, Doris. "COBOL: Continued Use of Common Business Oriented Language Programming." *Byte*, October 1991, p. 129ff.

Bender, Eric. "Desktop Multimedia: You Ain't Seen Nothing Yet." *PC World*, November 1990, pp. 191–196.

Campbell, George. "Windows Word Processors." *PC World*, April 1992, pp. 147–166.

Cobb, Richard. "In Praise of 4GLs." *Datamation*, July 15, 1985, pp. 90-104.

Daly, James. "Windows for Pen Launched." *Computerworld*, April 13, 1992, p. 17.

Dyson, Esther. "Why Groupware is Gaining Ground." *Datamation*, March 1, 1990, pp. 52–56.

Eliot, Lance B. "Strategic Case is Best." *CASE Trends*, May 1992, pp. 46ff.

Fitzgerald, Michael. "GUI Revs PCs at Big Six Firm." *Computerworld*, January 13, 1992, p. 1ff.

Fitzgerald, Michael. "Users Leery of Multiprocessing." *Computerworld*, June 1, 1992, p. 10.

Garfunkel, Jerome. "COBOL—The Next Stage: It's Time to Modernize Old Faithful by Adding Object Orientation." *Computerworld*, July 23, 1990, p. 87–88.

Green, Jesse. "Productivity in the Fourth Generation." *Journal of Management Information Systems*, Winter 1984-85, pp. 53-62.

Gross, Neil. "A Japanese 'Flop' that Became a Launching Pad." *Business Week*, June 8, 1992, p. 103.

Harel, Elie C., and Ephraim R. McLean. "The Effects of Using a Nonprocedural Computer Language on Programmer Productivity." *MIS Quarterly*, June 1985, pp. 109-120.

Heintz, Timothy J. "An Object-Oriented Approach to Planning and Managing Software Development Projects." *Information & Management*, April 1991, pp. 281–293.

Hildebrand, J. D. "A Competitive Edge." *UNIX Review*, July 1991, pp. 22–25.

Inc. "*Inc.*'s Buyer's Guide to Office Equipment and Technology." October 1991, pp. 61–134.

Jones, Mary C., and Kirk P. Arnett. "CASE Use is Growing, But in Surprising Ways." *Datamation*, May 1, 1992, pp. 108–109.

Keyes, Jessica. "Languages: The New Generation." *Computerworld*, August 27, 1990, p. 96.

Lansman, Gary. "Avoid Buyer Remorse: Purchasing CASE tools." *Computerworld*, January 13, 1992, pp. 77--79.

Mann, Richard O. "How to Choose the Best Spreadsheet Program." *Compute!*, February-March 1992, pp. S2–S6.

Margolis, Nell. "Outsourcing Boom Over? You Ain't Seen Nothing." *Computerworld*, January 13, 1992, p. 8.

Marshall, Patrick. "Road Scholars Have All the Answers." *Portable Office*, October 1991, pp. 34–38.

Martin, James. *Applications Development Without Programmers*. Englewood Cliffs, NJ: Prentice-Hall, 1982.

Martin, James. *Fourth-Generation Languages: Vol. I*. Englewood Cliffs, NJ: Prentice-Hall, 1985a.

Martin, James. *Fourth-Generation Languages: Vol. II*. Englewood Cliffs, NJ: Prentice-Hall, 1985b.

Martin, James. *Fourth-Generation Languages: Vol. III*. Englewood Cliffs, NJ: Prentice-Hall, 1985c.

McClatchy, Will. "Multimedia for the Masses." *Information Week*, November 12, 1990, p. 88.

McClatchy, Will. "Windows, OS/2 Sales Jump." *Information Week*, November 12, 1990, pp. 88–89.

Mendelson, Edward. "Windows Word Processors." *PC Magazine*, February 25, 1992, pp. 113–184.

Miller, Rock. "To Inform and Convince: Ten Presentation Graphics Programs." *PC Magazine*, March 17, 1992, pp. 113–186.

Millman, Howard. "There's Something for All in Applications Generators." *Computerworld*, January 13, 1992, p. 68ff.

Moad, Jeff. "Smalltalk Grows Up." *Datamation*, July 15, 1991, pp. 64–66.

Morrison, John S. "Programming Perestroika." *Computerworld*, August 3, 1992, pp. 89–92.

Myers, Kara. "Training the End Users." *Information Week*, November 12, 1990, p. 46.

Nash, Jim. "Autoclerk PC Kiosks Enlisted as LA's Very Own 'Robocop' Team." *Computerworld*, January 27, 1992, p. 53.

Nelson, Robin. "Windows Opens Wide: The Managers Perspective." *Information Week*, November 12, 1990, pp. 36–37.

Petzold, Charles. "The Visual Development Environment: More Than Just a Pretty Face." *PC Magazine*, June 16, 1992, pp. 195–244.

Rebello, Kathy, and Evan I. Schwartz. "Microsoft: Bill Gates's Baby is on Top of the World. Can It Stay There?" *Business Week*, February 24, 1992, pp. 60–65.

Reinhardt, Andy. "Momenta Points to the Future." *Byte*, November 1991, pp. 48–49.

Rhodes, Wayne L., Jr. "The Applications Backlog." *Infosystems*, November 1986, p. 8.

Robins, Gary. "Off-the-Shelf PC: Retailers List Software Choices." *Stores*, January 1992, pp. 105–110.

Rogers, Michael. "Windows of Opportunity: Is 'Gooey' Software Worth the Trouble?" *Business Week*, April 27, 1992, p. 63.

Salemi, Joe, Greg Pastrick, and Stephen Walton. "Database Power Without the Programming." *PC Magazine*, December 1991, pp. 111–132.

Schnaidt, Patricia, and Dave Brambert. "The Netware Express." *LAN: The Local Area Network Magazine*, June 1992, pp. 36–40.

Stinson, Craig, and Bruce Brown. "Spreadsheets Begin to Put the User First." *PC Magazine*, December 31, 1991, pp. 241–266.

Verity, John W. "The OOPS Revolution." *Datamation*, May 1, 1987, pp. 73–78.

Verity, John W., and Evan I. Schwartz. "Software Made Simple: Will Object-Oriented Programming Transform the Computer Industry?" *Business Week*, September 30, 1991, pp. 92–100.

Ward, Bernie. "The New Art of 'Penputing.' " *Sky Magazine*, December 1991, pp. 73–80.

Yourdon, Edward. *Decline and Fall of the American Programmer*. Englewood Cliffs, NJ: Prentice-Hall, 1992.

Yourdon, Edward. "Kiss U.S. Coders Good-Bye." *Computerworld*, April 6, 1992, pp. 111–113.

CHAPTER 7

Alexander, Michael. "Multimedia Focus Turns to Training." *Computerworld*, January 13, 1992, p. 18.

Anthes, Gary H. "Cutting-Edge Software the Key to Food Distributor's Savings." *Computerworld*, February 3, 1992, p. 29.

Anthes, Gary H. "High-Tech Heroes: National Institutes of Health." *Computerworld*, June 15, 1992, p. 97.

Atwood, Thomas M. "The Case for Object-Oriented Databases." *IEEE Spectrum*, February 1991, pp. 44–47.

Balfour, A., and C. Britton. "InfoExec: Object-Oriented/Semantic Database Implementation." *Information and Software Technology*, May 1990, pp. 290–296.

Betts, Mitch. "Big Things Come in Small Buttons." *Computerworld*, August 3, 1992, p. 30.

Bhalla, Neelam. "Object-Oriented Data Models: A Perspective and Comparative Review." *Journal of Information Science Principles & Practices*. Vol. 17, No. 3 (1991), pp. 145–150.

Bieber, Michael P., and Steven O. Kimbrough. "On the Concept of Hypertext." *MIS Quarterly*, March 1992, pp. 77–93.

Booker, Ellis, and Alan J. Ryan. "Image Processing Systems: Between Now and Ideal." *Computerworld*, November 8, 1990, pp. 103–104.

Borzo, Jeanette, "Multimedia Uses Expected to Grow." *Infoworld*, February 10, 1992, pp. 19, 28.

Bozman, Jean S. "A New Approach to Data Management Catches On." *Computerworld*, October 26, 1992, p. 28.

Bozman, Jean S. "Coke Plans to Add Life with Relational Database Move." *Computerworld*, January 13, 1992, p. 35.

Brown, D. H. "Product Information Management: The Great Orchestrator." *CAE*, May 1991, pp. 60–66.

Buckler, Grant. "Data Imaging." *Oracle*, Winter 1991, pp. 43–46.

Carlyle, Ralph Emmett. "DB2: Dressed for Success." *Datamation*, March 1, 1987, pp. 59–62.

Chin, Roger S., and Samuel T. Chanson. "Distributed Object-Based Programming Systems." *ACM Computer Surveys*, March 1991, pp. 91–124.

Cohen, Howard. "The Electronic Database." *Bank Marketing*, January 1991, pp. 29–31.

Consumer Guide Magazine. "Database Software." November 27, 1991, pp. 189–201.

Curtice, Robert M., and Paul E. Jones, Jr. "Database: The Bedrock of Business." *Datamation*, June 15, 1984, p. 163ff.

Dalton, Michelle. "Multimedia: Full Speed Ahead." *Dealerscope Merchandising*, June 1991, pp. 86, 88.

Date, C. J. *An Introduction to Database Systems* (5th Ed.). Reading, MA: Addison-Wesley, 1990.

Date, C. J. "Twelve Rules for a Distributed Data Base." *Computerworld*, June 8, 1987, pp. 75–81.

Duncan, Ray. "Managing Random Access Files." *PC Magazine*, March 28, 1989, pp. 291–302.

Edelstein, Herb. "Distributed DBMS." *Computerworld*, November 4, 1991, pp. 77–79.

Edelstein, Herbert A. "Database World Targets Next-Generation Problems." *Software Magazine*, May 1991, pp. 79–86.

Gane, Chris. *Developing Business Systems in SQL*. New York: Rapid Systems Development Corp., 1987.

Goodhue, Dale, Judith Quillard, and John Rockart. "Managing Data Resources: A Contingency Perspective." *MIS Quarterly*, September 1988, pp. 373–391.

Goodhue, Dale L., Laurie J. Kirsch, Judith A. Quillard, and Michael D. Wybo. "Strategic Data Planning: Lessons from the Field." *MIS Quarterly*, March 1992, pp. 11–34.

Haight, Timothy. "Networked Multimedia." *Network Computing*, April 1992, pp. 70–81.

Harrington, Jan L. *Relational Database Management for Microcomputers: Design and Implementation.* New York: Holt, Rinehart & Winston, 1987.

Havened, Robert. "Hypertext: The Smart Tool for Information Overload." *Technology Review,* November-December 1990, pp. 43–50.

Hazzah, Ali. "Objects Are Taking Shape in Flat Relational World." *Software,* June 1990, pp. 32–42.

Heintz, Timothy J. "Object-Oriented Databases and Their Impact on Future Business Database Applications." *Information and Management,* February 1991, pp. 95–103.

Honkanen, Pentti A. "The Integrity Problem, and What Can Be Done About It Using Today's DBMSs." *Data Base,* Fall 1989, pp. 21–27.

Horwitt, Elisabeth. "Bank Builds Own Distributed Data Base." *Computerworld,* April 20, 1987.

Howell, Martin, and Bob Johnstone. "Technology in Japan: Multimedia Mania: The Mundane to the Magical." *Far Eastern Economic Review,* December 19, 1991, pp. 37–41.

I/S Analyzer. "The Emerging World of Multimedia." March 1991, pp. 1–12.

Jackson, M. S. "Tutorial on Object-Oriented Databases." *Information & Software Technology,* January-February 1991, pp. 4–12.

Kendall, Robert. "MIDI Goes Mainstream." *PC Magazine,* March 31, 1992, pp. 181–222.

Khoshafian, S. "Insight into Object-Oriented Databases." *Information and Software Technology,* May 1990, pp. 274–289.

Kim, Won. *Introduction to Object-Oriented Databases.* Cambridge, MA: MIT Press, 1990.

King, Julia. "Distributed Systems: Tough to Take Root." *Computerworld,* October 12, 1992, pp. 101–104.

Knight, Bob. "The Data Pollution Problem." *Computerworld,* September 28, 1992, pp. 81, 83.

Knowles, Steve. "Strategy for Opening Mainframes Needed." *Computer Technology Review,* November 1991, p. 8.

Lazos, James N. "Unleashing the Power of Your Marketing Database." *The Banker's Magazine,* March-April 1991, pp. 22–28.

Livingston, Dennis. "Here Come Object-Oriented Databases!" *Systems Integration,* July 1990, pp. 50–58.

LoPinto, Marie. "Integrated Imaging: Plugging into the Corporate Database." *Office Technology Management,* September-October 1991, pp. 78–82.

Lunin, Lois F. "Image Databases: Some Today, More Tomorrow." *Bulletin of ASIS,* February-March 1990, pp. 34–35.

Martin, James. *Managing the Data Base Environment.* Englewood Cliffs, NJ: Prentice-Hall, 1983.

McCleod, Dennis. "Perspectives on Object Databases." *Information and Software Technology,* January-February 1991, pp. 13–21.

McFadden, Fred R., and Jeffrey A. Hoffer. *Data Base Management* (2nd Ed.). Menlo Park, CA: Benjamin/Cummings, 1988.

Miller, Michael. "Multimedia." *PC Magazine,* March 31, 1992, pp. 112–123.

Myers, Edith. "Distributed DBMSs: In Search of the Wonder Glue." *Datamation,* February 1, 1987, pp. 41–48.

Nolan, Richard L. "Data Administration." In Richard L. Nolan (ed.), *Managing the Data Resource.* St. Paul, MN: West, 1982, pp. 282–296.

Oz, Effy. "Toward a Document Based Management System." *Information Executive,* Winter 1990, pp. 19–23.

Pastrick, Greg, and Stephen Walton. "Database Power Without Programming." *PC Magazine,* December 17, 1991, pp. 111–132.

Patton, N. W., and O. Diaz. "Object-Oriented Databases and Frame-Based Systems: A Comparison." *Information & Software Technology,* June 1991, pp. 357–365.

Pierce, Richard. "Hyperscribe." *Bulletin of ASIS,* December 1989-January 1990, pp. 15–17.

Pratt, Philip J., and Joseph J. Adamski. *Database Systems: Management and Design* (2nd Ed.). Boston, MA: Boyd & Fraser, 1991.

Prietula, Michael J., and Salvatore T. March. "Form and Substance in Physical Database Design." *Information Systems Research,* December 1991, pp. 287–314.

Rao, Pal V., and Laura M. Rao. "An Overview of Information Utilities." *Information Executive,* Winter 1991, pp. 12–14.

Rasheed, Abdul M. A., and Deepak K. Datta. "Online Databases in Environmental Scanning." In Edward Szewcak, Coral Snodgrass, and Mehdi Khosrowpour (eds.), *Management Impacts of Information Technology.* Harrisburg, PA: Idea Group, 1991, pp. 389–407.

Rose, Frank. "Now, Quality Means Service Too." *Fortune,* April 22, 1991, pp. 97–111.

Schneiderman, Ben, and Greg Kearsley. *Hypertext Hands-On.* Reading, MA: Addison-Wesley, 1989.

Schwartz, Evan I. "Multimedia is Here, and It's Amazing." *Business Week,* December 16, 1991, pp. 130–131.

Schwartz, Evan I. "The Lucie Show: Shaking up a Stody IBM." *Business Week,* April 6, 1992, pp. 64–65.

Sehr, Barbara. "Hierarchical Model Keeps Loyal Following." *Computerworld,* March 14, 1988, p. 53.

Slater, Derek. "Adabas Stays One Step Ahead." *Computerworld,* August 17, 1992, pp. 66–67.

Smith, Ted, and Alan Radding. "Images of the Future." *Bank Management,* November 1991, pp. 12–19.

Stoll, Marilyn. "Brewery Keeps Its Memorabilia on Tap." *PC Week,* January 5, 1988, pp. 39ff.

Sullivan, Robert K. "Image Management: The Ascent of the Imaging Industry." *Today's Office,* May 1991, pp. 45–49.

Taylor, David A. "ODBMS: Next Generation in Database Management." *Computer Technology Review,* October 1990, p. 8ff.

Tenopir, Carol. "The Most Popular Databases." *Library Journal*, April 1, 1991, pp. 96–97.

Todd, Daniel. "Multimedia Musters Support." *Information Week*, November 26, 1990, p. 40.

Trivette, Don. "Managing Your Money Via Modem: On-Line Services Help You Prosper." *PC Magazine*, October 29, 1991, pp. 496–500.

Trowbridge, Dave. "Evaluating ODBMS is a Tricky Business." *Computer Technology Review*, November 1991, p. 6.

Venditto, Gus. "Nine Multiuser Databases: Robust and Ready to Share." *PC Magazine*, March 31, 1992, pp. 289–335.

CHAPTER 8

Barrett, Amy. "Showdown." *Financial World*, April 14, 1992, pp. 20–25.

Becker, Pat. "LANs Around the World." *LAN Magazine*, April 1992, pp. 36–44.

Berg, Lynn. "The Scoop on Client/Server Costs." *Computerworld*, November 16, 1992, pp. 169–176.

Bing, George. "Slow but Steady: Building Low-Cost Wide Area Networks." *Networking Management*, September 1991, pp. 72–77.

Bolles, Gary. "Gearing Up for EDI: A Primer on Electronic Data Management." *Networking Management*, September 1991, pp. 88–91.

Booker, Ellis. "Earth to Laptop: Network Access from the Air." *Computerworld*, June 1, 1992, p. 28.

Booker, Ellis. "Motorola Builds on Wireless MAN." *Computerworld*, January 27, 1992, p. 10.

Booker, Ellis. "Pizza Hut: Making It Great with Imaging, EDI." *Computerworld*, January 27, 1992, p. 67ff.

Booker, Ellis. "Wireless LANs, WANs Draw New Attention." *Computerworld*, May 18, 1992, p. 80.

Brown, Ron. "High-Performance WANs: Threads that Link the World." *Networking Management*, April 1992, pp. 56–61.

Brown, Ron. "The Wireless Office Untethers Workers." *Networking Management*, June 1992, pp. 42–49.

Burns, Nina, and Kimberly Maxwell. "Peering at NOS Costs." *LAN Magazine*, May 1992, pp. 69–76.

Business Week. "Who Knows Where You Are? The Satellite Knows." February 10, 1992, pp. 120–121.

Camillus, John C., and Albert J. Lederer. "Corporate Strategy and the Design of Computerized Information Systems." *Sloan Management Review*, Spring 1985, pp. 35–42.

Cash, James I., Jr., and Benn R. Konsynski. "IS Redraws Competitive Boundaries." *Harvard Business Review*, March-April 1985, pp. 134–142.

Chen, Richard. "Distributed Data Processing Considerations." *Journal of Systems Management*, June 1986, pp. 10–13.

Clemons, Eric K., and F. Warren McFarlan. "Telecom: Hook Up or Lose Out." *Harvard Business Review*, July-August 1986, pp. 91–97.

Coy, Peter. "IBM Needs a New Network—But Not Too New." *Business Week*, April 20, 1992, pp. 95–96.

Coy, Peter. "The New Realism in Office Systems." *Business Week*, June 15, 1992, pp. 128–133.

Derfler, Frank J. "Modem Communications Software: Too Hard to Use?" *PC Magazine*, June 30, 1992, pp. 221–296.

Dortch, Michael. "Hospital Updates Network." *Communications Week*, January 27, 1992, p. 12ff.

Fitzgerald, Jerry. *Data Communications: Basic Concepts, Security, and Design* (3rd Ed.). New York: John Wiley & Sons, 1990.

Foley, John. "Bells Release ISDN Schedules, Start Hot Line." *Communications Week*, January 27, 1992, p. 39.

Frank, Alan. "Networking Without Wires." *LAN Technology*, March 1992, pp. 51–65.

Gantz, John. "A Practical Guide to Cutting Network Costs." *Networking Management*, May 1991, pp. 32–43.

Gantz, John. "The Public/Private Tug of War." *Networking Management*, January 1992, pp. 24–35.

Gilder, George. "Into the Telecosm." *Harvard Business Review*, March-April 1991, pp. 150–161.

Gold, Elliot. "Telcos Make Their Presence Felt in Video Markets." *Networking Management*, May 1991, pp. 52–55.

Greenstein, Irwin. "Pulling the Plug on LANs." *Networking Management*, June 1991, pp. 20–29.

Hammer, Michael, and Glenn E. Mangurian. "The Changing Value of Communications Technology." *Sloan Management Review*, Winter 1987, pp. 65–71.

Holland, Royce J. "Competitive Local Communications: The New Landscape." *Telecommunications*, February 1992, pp. 23–25.

Hopper, Max D. "Rattling SABRE—New Ways to Compete on Information." *Harvard Business Review*, May-June 1990, pp. 118–125.

Hudson, Heather. *Satellite Communications*. New York: Free Press, 1990.

Huntington-Lee, Jill. "The Latest in Frame Relay." *Computerworld*, August 31, 1992, pp. 87–91.

Janssens, Gerrit K., and Ludo Cuyvers. "EDI—A Strategic Weapon in International Trade." *Long Range Planning*, Vol. 24, No. 3 (1991), pp. 46–53.

Janusaitis, Bob. "LAN Management." *Computerworld*, January 27, 1992, pp. 91–93.

Johnson, William B. "Networking: A Strategic Advantage in Today's Global Marketplace." *Telecommunications*, February 1992, pp. 27–28.

Keen, Peter G. W. *Competing in Time: Using Telecommunications for Competitive Advantage*. Cambridge, MA: Ballinger, 1988.

Kennedy, Michael. D. "Improving Customer Service Through Advanced Networking Capabilities." *Telecommunications*, November 1992, pp. 19–22.

Kerr, Susan. "The Applications Wave Behind ISDN." *Datamation*, February 1, 1990, pp. 64–66.

Kerr, Susan. "One Last Chance for ISDN." *Datamation*, May 1, 1992, pp. 65–68.

Kindal, Sharon. "Networks that Work." *Financial World*, April 28, 1992, pp. 65–67.

Kobielus, James. "EFT and POS Networks Merge in Retail Industry." *Network World*, August 29, 1988, p. 1ff.

Kozel, Edward R. "Commercializing Internet: Impact on Corporate Users." *Telecommunications*, January 1992, pp. 11–14.

Lusa, John M. "Weaving an Imperfect Tapestry." *Networking Management*, April 1992, pp. 30–33.

McGovern, David. "The Origin of the Server Species." *LAN Technology*, June 1992, pp. 59–70.

Mier, Edwin. "SNMP, From Counters to Clocks." *Communications Week*, January 27, 1992, p. 57ff.

Molta, Dave. "Network Standards: Setting and Enforcing the Rules of the Road." *Network Computing*, February 1992, pp. 62–69.

Panchak, Patricia L. "Network Alternatives: Making the Right Choice." *Modern Office Technology*, March 1992, pp. 22–26.

Porter, Michael E. *The Competitive Advantage of Nations*. New York: Free Press, 1990.

Reddy, Shyamala. "Serving the Masses." *LAN Magazine*, October 1989, pp. 50–60.

Rymer, John R. "Welcome to the Brave New World of Global Networking." *Network World*, August 24, 1992, p. 37.

Schnaidt, Patricia, and Dave Brambert. "NetWare Express." *LAN Magazine*, June 1992, pp. 36–42.

Schwartz, Jeffrey. "WAN Switches Take Next Step." *Communications Week*, January 27, 1992, p. 1ff.

Schwartz, John. "The Highway to the Future." *Newsweek*, January 13, 1992, pp. 56–57.

Snell, Ned. "What's Holding Back Distributed Computing?" *Datamation*, April 1, 1992, pp. 54–58.

Stallings, William. *Local Networks: An Introduction*. NY: Macmillan, 1984.

Steinbart, Paul John, and Ravinder Nath. "Problems and Issues in the Management of International Data Networks: The Experience of American Companies." *MIS Quarterly*, March 1992, pp. 55–76.

Sullivan, Cornelius H., Jr., and John R. Smart. "Planning for Information Networks." *Sloan Management Review*, Winter 1987, pp. 39–44.

Therrien, Lois, and Chuck Hawkins. "Wireless Nets Aren't Just for Big Fish Anymore." *Business Week*, March 9, 1992, pp. 84–85.

Titch, Steven. "Weaving a Seamless National Packet Network." *Communications Week*, October 17, 1988, p. C7ff.

Volvino, Judd. "LAN Operating Systems." *Computerworld*, December 2, 1991, pp. 75–76.

CHAPTER 9

Ackoff, Russell E. "Management Misinformation Systems." *Management Science*, December 1967, pp. 147–156.

Adams, Eric J. "What is EDI?" *World Trade*, June-July 1991, pp. 46–48.

Alexander, Michael. "Smart Cards the Better Way to Pay." *Computerworld*, February 3, 1992, p. 20.

Anthes, Gary H. "Cutting Edge Software the Key to Food Distributor's Savings." *Computerworld*, February 3, 1992, p. 29.

Anthes, Gary H. "Food Stamp Program Soon to be Electronic." *Computerworld*, January 13, 1992, p. 51ff.

Booker, Ellis. "Bills: Going, Going, Gone Electronic." *Computerworld*, June 15, 1992, p. 56.

Booker, Ellis. "Pizza Hut: Making It Great with Imaging, EDI." *Computerworld*, January 27, 1992, p. 67ff.

Booker, Ellis. "Sears Selects Compuadd for $53M POS Project." *Computerworld*, January 13, 1992, p. 7.

Bryan, Shawn. "Numbers Gain New Meaning." *Computerworld*, July 20, 1987, pp. S1–S9.

Business Week. "EDI in Action." March 31, 1992, pp. 81–92.

Business Week. "Power Retailers." December 21, 1987, pp. 86–92.

Business Week. "Sabre Rattling." June 22, 1992, p. 5.

Cashin, Jerry. "Business Transactions Take Electronic Route." *Software Magazine*, December 1991, pp. 81–84, 86.

Cathay, Jack M. "What a Controller Should Know: Implementing EDI Can Be Both a Challenge and an Opportunity." *Management Accounting*, November 1991, pp. 47–51.

Coy, Peter. "The New Realism In Office Systems." *Business Week*, June 15, 1992, pp. 128–133.

Cusack, Sally. "Retailers Seek High-Tech Profit Boost." *Computerworld*, January 27, 1992, p. 33.

Dearden, John. "Will the Computer Change the Job of Top Management?" *Sloan Management Review*, Fall 1983, pp. 57–60.

Eliason, Alan L. *Online Business Computer Applications* (3rd Ed.). New York: Macmillan, 1991.

Greene, Alice. "MRP II: Out with the Old. . . ." *Computerworld*, June 8, 1992, pp. 73–77.

Horwitt, Elisabeth. "Telecommuting Project Keeps HP Execs In-House." *Computerworld*, January 20, 1992, p. 59.

Imaging Magazine. "Why Insurance Companies Take the Risk on Document Imaging." March 1992, pp. 48–51.

Industry Week. "Presidential Report on EDI." November 4, 1991, pp. EDI1–EDI17.

Jacobs, Paula. "EDI, Imaging Exploding." *Computerworld*, January 20, 1992, p. 80.

Janssens, Gerrit K., and Ludo Cuyvers. "EDI—A Strategic Weapon in International Trade." *Long Range Planning*, Vol. 24, No. 3 (1991), pp. 46–53.

Kay, Emily. "Relief for Your Order-Entry Headaches." *Datamation*, July 1, 1991, pp. 51–52.

King, Julia. "Best Market Research Prospects are in POS." *Computerworld*, January 6, 1992, p. 77.

Litsikas, Mary. "EDI Keeps Baby-Product Sales in the Pink." *Systems 3X/400*, August 1991, pp. 69–72.

Margolis, Nell. "Venerable Insurer Rides New Wave in Imaging." *Computerworld*, April 27, 1992, pp. 37–38.

McFarlan, F. Warren, James L. McKenney, and Philip Pyburn. "The Information Archipelago: Plotting a Course." *Harvard Business Review*, January-February 1983, pp. 145–156.

McWilliams, Gary. "Allied Stores Centralizes IS Amid Major Upheaval in Firm." *Datamation*, April 1, 1988, pp. 17–19.

Mehler, Mark. "Industrial and Automotive Products: New Spirit of Conservatism." *Computerworld*, September 14, 1992, pp. 21–25.

Mossberg, Walter S. "Things That You Really Need to Know About Staying Plugged in on the Road." *Wall Street Journal*, January 30, 1992, p. B2.

Mules, Glen R. J. "Beyond Paying the Bills: New Applications of EDI." *Chief Information Officer Journal*, Fall 1991, pp. 60–63.

Nash, Jim. "Autoclerk PC Kiosks enlisted as LA's Very Own 'Robocop' Team." *Computerworld*, January 27, 1992, p. 53.

Ogilvie, Heather. "Electronic Ties that Bind: Marks & Spencer's Pan-European JIT Inventory Management System." *The Journal of European Business*, September-October 1991, pp. 48–50.

Pompili, Tony. "Travel Firm Looks to Offshore Data-Entry for New Profits." *PC Week Connectivity*, June 30, 1987, p. C/4.

"Presidential Report on EDI." *Industry Week*, November 1, 1991, pp. EDI1–EDI19.

Senn, James A. "Electronic Data Interchange: The Elements of Implementation." *Information Systems Management*, Winter 1992, pp. 45–53.

Tracy, John J., Jr. "Why You Can't Afford to Ignore EDI." *Corporate Controller*, March-April 1991, pp. 33–36.

Trowbridge, Dave. "EDI for the People." *Computer Technology Review*, February 1992, pp. 4, 40.

Vanderlee, Peter. "JIT through EDI and Systems Integration." *Manufacturing Systems*, August 1991, pp. 48–49.

Verity, John W., and Gary McWilliams. "Is It Time to Junk the Way You Use Computers?" *Business Week*, July 1991, pp. 66–69.

Wilder, Clinton. "Codex Goes Paperless with EDI." *Computerworld*, January 13, 1992, p. 6.

Wilkinson, Joseph W. *Accounting and Information Systems*. (2nd Ed.). New York: John Wiley & Sons, 1986.

Zimmerman, Kim. "Banks Squeeze the Most Out of Imaging." *Imaging*, April 1992, pp. 20–21.

CHAPTER 10

Agor, Weston H. "How Top Managers Use Intuition to Make Important Decisions." *Business Horizons*, January-February 1986, pp. 49–53.

Alavi, Maryam. "Group Decision Support Systems: A Key to Business Team Productivity." *Journal of Information Systems Management*, Summer 1991, pp. 36–41.

Alexander, David J. "Planning and Building a DSS." *Datamation*, March 15, 1986, pp. 115–121.

Alter, Steven. *Decision Support Systems: Current Practices and Continuing Challenges*. Reading, MA: Addison-Wesley, 1980.

Ambrosio, Elisabeth. "The Almost Paperless Office." *Computerworld*, August 3, 1992, pp. 71–74.

Amirrezvanir, Anita. "Fidelity Investments Builds EIS to Simplify Access to Financial Data." *Computerworld*, April 6, 1992, p. 95.

Azine, Bay. "A Contingency Model of DSS Development Methodology." *Journal of Management Information Systems*, Summer 1991, pp. 149–156.

Betts, Kellyn S. "Executive Support Systems: The Electronic Facilitator for Better Decision Making." *Modern Office Technology*, June 1990, pp. 88–89.

Bieber, Michael P., and Steven O. Kimbrough. "On Generalizing the Concept of Hypertext." *MIS Quarterly*, March 1992, pp. 77–93.

Brandell, Mary. "Executive Information Systems." *Computerworld*, July 22, 1991, pp. 67–76.

Brinker, Scott J. "Corporate Bulletin Board Systems: Customer Support and More in the 1990s." *Telecommunications*, November 1991, pp. 33–36.

Brown, Ross. "EIS: Plenty of Questions, Plenty of Answers." *Systems 3X/400*, February 1992, pp. 30–38.

Brown, Ross. "The Evolution of Executive Information Systems." *Systems 3X/400*, March 1991, pp. 26–34.

Bucknall, Christopher. "A Manager's Guide to Executive Information Systems." *Industrial Management and Data Systems*, Vol. 91, No. 3 (1991), pp. 6–7.

Burkan, Wayne C. *Executive Information Systems: From Proposal Through Implementation*. New York: Van Nostrand Reinhold, 1991.

Burkan, Wayne C. "The New Role for 'Executive' Information Systems: EIS in a High-Leverage Role." *I/S Analyzer*, January 1992, pp. 1–14.

DeSanctis, Gerardine, and R. Brent Gallupe. "A Foundation for the Study of Group Decision Support Systems." *Management Science*, May 1987, pp. 589–609.

Earle, Donald V. "EIS: Unlocking the Computer's Strategic Potential." *Computers in Healthcare*, July 1991, pp. 47–49.

Ellis, C. A., S. J. Gibbs, and G. L. Rein. "Groupware: Some Issues and Experiences." *Communications of the ACM*, January 1991, pp. 38–58.

Eom, Hyuan B., and Sang M. Lee. "A Survey of Decision Support System Applications." *Interfaces*, May-June 1990, pp. 65–80.

Finley, Michael. "The New Meaning of Meetings." *IBAC Communication World*, March 1991, pp. 25–27.

Forgionne, Guisseppi A. "Decision Technology Systems: A Step Toward Complete Decision Support." *Journal of Information Systems Management*, Fall 1991, pp. 34–43.

Gauthier, Michael R. "Executives Go High Tech." *Business Month*, July 1989, pp. 44–47.

Ghoshal, Suantra, and Seok Ki Kim. "Building Effective Intelligence Systems for Competitive

Advantage." *Sloan Management Review*, Fall 1986, pp. 49–58.

Gorry, G. A., and M. S. Scott Morton. "A Framework for Management Information Systems." *Sloan Management Review*, Fall 1971, pp. 55–70.

Gray, Paul, and Lorne Olfman. "The User Interface in Group Decision Support Systems." *Decision Support Systems*, June 1989, pp. 119 -137.

Gremillion, Lee L., and Philip J. Pyburn. "Justifying Decision Support Systems and Office Administration Systems." *Journal of Management Information Systems*, Summer 1985, pp. 5–17.

Jacob, Varghese S., and Hasan Pirkul. "A Framework for Supporting Distributed Group Decision-Making." *Decision Support Systems*, January 1992, pp. 17–28.

Jones, Kirk. "Executive Support Systems Come of Age." *Modern Office Technology*, October 1989, pp. 78–80.

Keen, P. G. W., and M. S. Scott Morton. *Decision Support Systems: An Organizational Perspective*. Reading, MA: Addison-Wesley, 1982.

Kinlan, Jim. "EIS Moves to the Desktop." *Byte*, June 1992, pp. 206–214.

Kling, Rob. "Cooperation, Coordination, and Control in Computer Supported Work." *Communications of the ACM*, December 1991, pp. 83–87.

Kraemer, Kenneth L., and John Leslie King. "Computer-Based Systems for Cooperative Work and Group Decision Making." *ACM Computing Surveys*, June 1988, pp. 115–146.

Kyle, Albert S., and Terry A. Marsh. "Computers and the Crash: Is Technology the Problem or the Solution?" *Institutional Investor*, June 1988, pp. 6–10.

Le Blanc, Louis A., and Kenneth A. Kozar. "An Empirical Investigation of the Relationship Between DSS Usage and System Performance: A Case Study of a Navigation Support System." *MIS Quarterly*, September 1990, pp. 263–277.

Main, Jeremy. "At Last, Software That CEOs Can Use." *Fortune*, March 13, 1989, pp. 77–83.

McCullough, Charles, and Bob Wooton. "Education, Exposure Help Top Executives Accept Computers." *Data Management*, September 1986, pp. 38–40.

McKenney, J. L., and P. G. W. Keen. "How Managers' Minds Work." *Harvard Business Review*, July-August 1975, pp. 49–61.

Minear, Michael N. "Implementing an Executive Information System." *Computers in Healthcare*, July 1991, pp. 34–40.

Mohan, Lakshmi, William K. Holstein, and Robert B. Adams. "EIS: It Can Work in the Public Sector." *MIS Quarterly*, December 1990, pp. 435–448.

Nunamaker, J. F., Alan R. Dennis, Joseph S. Valacich, Douglas R. Vogel, and Joey F. George. "Electronic Meeting Systems to Support Group Work." *Communications of the ACM*, July 1991, pp. 40–61.

Regan-Cirincione, Patricia, Sandor Schuman, George P. Richardson, and Stanley A. Dorf. "Decision Modeling: Tools for Strategic Thinking." *Interfaces*, November-December 1991, pp. 52–65.

Reimann, Bernard C. "Decision Support Systems: Strategic Management Tools for the Eighties." *Business Horizons*, September-October 1985, pp. 71–77.

Rockart, John F. "Chief Executives Define Their Own Data Needs." *Harvard Business Review*, March-April 1979, pp. 81–93.

Rockart, John F., and David W. De Long. *Executive Support Systems: The Emergence of Top Management Computer Use*. Homewood, IL: Dow-Jones-Irwin, 1988.

Rockart, John F., and David W. De Long. "Moments of Executive Enlightenment." *Information Strategy: The Executive's Journal*, Fall 1988, pp. 21–27.

Rockart, John F., and Michael E. Treacy. "The CEO Goes On Line." *Harvard Business Review*, January-February 1982, pp. 82–88.

Schwartz, John. "The Next Revolution." *Newsweek*, April 6, 1992, pp. 42–48.

Silver, Mark S. "Decision Support Systems: Directed and Nondirected Change." *Information Systems Research*, March 1990, pp. 47–70.

Sprague, R. H., and E. D. Carlson. *Building Effective Decision Support Systems*. Englewood Cliffs, NJ: Prentice-Hall, 1982.

Sprague, Ralph H., Jr. "A Framework for the Development of Decision Support Systems." *MIS Quarterly*, December 1980, pp. 1–26.

Sprague, Ralph H., and Hugh J. Watson (ed.). *Decision Support Systems: Putting Theory into Practice*. Englewood Cliffs, NJ: Prentice-Hall, 1986.

Straub, Detmar, and Renee A. Beauclair. "Current and Future Uses of Group Decision Support System Technology: Report on a Recent Empirical Study." *Journal of Management Information Systems*, Summer 1988, pp. 101–116.

Turban, Efraim. *Decision Support and Expert Systems* (2nd Ed.). New York: Macmillan, 1990.

Turban, Efraim, and Paul R. Watkins. "Integrating Expert Systems and Decision Support Systems." *MIS Quarterly*, June 1986, pp. 121–136.

VanGundy, Arthur B. "Idea Collection Methods: Blending Old and New Technology." *Applied Marketing Research*, Spring 1987, pp. 14–19.

Volvino, Linda, and Watson, Hugh J. "The Strategic Business Objectives Method for Guiding Executive Information Systems Development." *Journal of Management Information Systems*, Winter 1990-1991, pp. 27–39.

Watson, Hugh. "Executive Information Systems: Expensive to Implement, Costly to Develop and Maintain." *Computerworld*, July 22, 1991, p. 70.

Watson, Hugh J., and Mark Frolick. "Executive Information Systems: Determining Information Requirements." *Information Systems Management*, Spring 1992, pp. 37–43.

Watson, Hugh J., and R. Kelley Rainer, Jr. "A Manager's Guide to Executive Support Systems." *Business Horizons*, March-April 1991, pp. 44–50.

Watson, Hugh J., R. Kelley Rainer, and Chang E. Loh. "Executive Information Systems: A Framework for Development and a Survey of Current Practices." *MIS Quarterly*, March 1991, pp. 13–30.

Wilkinson, Stephanie. "Changing Corporate Culture: The PC in the Executive Ranks." *PC Week*, September 15, 1987, p. 53ff.

CHAPTER 11

Alexander, Michael. "An Inside View of Neural Technology." *Computerworld*, January 21, 1991, p. 17.

Alexander, Michael. "Intelligent Computer May Be Reality by 2001." *Computerworld*, January 20, 1992, p. 20.

Alper, Alan. "Expert System Vs. Credit Fraud." *Computerworld*, April 13, 1987, p. 25ff.

Armstrong, Larry. "Software That Can Dethrone 'Computer Tyranny.'" *Business Week*, April 6, 1992, pp. 90–91.

Brody, Herb. "The Neural Computer." *Technology Review*, August-September 1990, pp. 43–49.

Business Week. "Office Automation: Making It Pay Off." October 12, 1987, p. 134ff.

Chase, Michael D., and Jae K. Shim. "Artificial Intelligence and Big Six Accounting—A Survey of the Current Uses of Expert Systems in the Modern Accounting Environment." *Computers and Industrial Engineering*, Vol. 21, 1991, pp. 205–209.

Cox, Earl, and Martin Goetz. "Fuzzy Logic Clarified." *Computerworld*, March 11, 1991, pp. 69–70.

Daly, James. "DOS Interface Understands Plain English." *Computerworld*, May 20, 1991, p. 20.

Deschamps, Paul B. "Standards for Expert System Tools: Reporting the Technology's Integration." *Information Systems Management*, Winter 1992, pp. 8–14.

Feigenbaum, Edward, Pamela McCorduck, and H. Penny Nii. *The Rise of the Expert Company*. New York: Times Books, 1988.

Freedman, Roy S. "AI on Wall Street." *IEEE Expert*, April 1991, pp. 3–9.

Gallagher, John P. *Knowledge Systems for Business: Integrating Expert Systems and MIS*. Englewood Cliffs, NJ: Prentice-Hall, 1988.

Higgins, Kevin T. "No Requiem for this Heavyweight." *Credit Card Management*, May 1992, pp. 34–36.

Holsapple, Clyde W., and Andrew B. Whinston. *Business Expert Systems*. Homewood, IL: Irwin, 1987.

Jablonowski, Mark. "Fuzzy Logic and Insurance Decisions." *CPCU Journal*, September 1991, pp. 181–187.

Jain, Sanjay, and David H. Osterfield. "Applying Expert Systems in Automated and Traditional Environments." *Manufacturing Systems*, August 1991, pp. 24–31.

Johnson, R. Colin. "Logic: That Fuzzy Feeling." *Datamation*, July 15, 1989, pp. 39–43.

Kader, Victoria. "Japanese Companies are Incorporating 'Fuzzy Logic' in a Growing Number of Products and Services." *Business America*, September 24, 1990, p. 7.

Keyes, Jessica. "Artificial Financial Accounting." *Financial and Accounting Systems*, Fall 1991, pp. 12–15.

Leonard-Barton, Dorothy, and John J. Sviokla. "Putting Expert Systems to Work." *Harvard Business Review*, March-April 1988, pp. 91–98.

Liebowitz, Jay. *Introduction to Expert Systems*. Santa Cruz, CA: Mitchell Publishing, 1988.

Lin, Engming. "Expert Systems for Business Applications: Potentials and Limitations." *Journal of Systems Management*, July 1986, pp. 18–21.

Loofbourrow, Tod Hayes. "The Payoff of Expert Systems." *Best's Review*, May 1991, pp. 56–64.

Magee, John F. "What Information Technology Has in Store for Managers." *Sloan Management Review*, Winter 1985, pp. 45–49.

Manufacturing Engineering. "Tomorrow's Manufacturing Technologies." January 1992, pp. 76–88.

Mason, Janet. "Next Wave of AI Tools Could Reach Market Next Year." *PC Week*, August 4, 1987, p. 59ff.

Martin, James, and Steven Oxman. *Building Expert Systems*. Englewood Cliffs, NJ: Prentice-Hall, 1988.

Martorelli, William P. "PC-Based Expert Systems Arrive." *Datamation*, April 1, 1988, pp. 56–66.

McGraw, Karen L., and Karan Harbison-Briggs. *Knowledge Acquisition: Principles and Guidelines*. Englewood Cliffs, NJ: Prentice-Hall, 1989.

Meyer, Marc H., and Kathleen Foley Curley. "An Applied Framework for Classifying the Complexity of Knowledge-Based Systems." *MIS Quarterly*, December 1991, pp. 455–472.

Meyer, Marc H., and Kathleen F. Curley. "Putting Expert System Technology to Work." *Sloan Management Review*, Winter 1991, pp. 21–31.

Mockler, Robert J. *Knowledge-Based Systems for Management Decisions*. Englewood Cliffs, NJ: Prentice-Hall, 1989.

Mockler, Robert J. *Knowledge-Based Systems for Strategic Planning*. Englewood Cliffs, NJ: Prentice-Hall, 1989.

Morrison, David. "Artificial Intelligence-Based Systems Target Complexities of Tax Accounting." *PC Week*, August 25, 1987, p. 135.

Nash, Jim. "The Many Tongues of Computers." *Computerworld*, February 18, 1991, p. 20.

Newquist, Harvey P., III. "Nearly Everything You Want to Know About AI." *Computerworld*, March 18, 1991, pp. 75–76.

Newquist, Harvey P., III. "The Other Side of AI." *AI Expert*, March 1992, pp. 50–51.

Nuten, Celestine A. "A Step-By-Step Procedure Provides a Beginning in Developing an Expert System." *Industrial Engineering*, October 1991, pp. 33–36.

O'Reilly, David. "Computers That Think Like People." *Fortune*, February 22, 1989, pp. 90–93.

Pearson, George W. "Robotics: A Future View of Workplace Safety." *Risk Management*, October 1990, pp. 42–46.

Pigford, D. V., and Greg Baur. *Expert Systems for Business: Concepts and Applications*. Boston: Boyd & Fraser, 1990.

Prerau, David S. *Developing and Managing Expert Systems*. Reading, MA: Addison-Wesley, 1990.

Rich, Elaine, and Kevin Knight. *Artificial Intelligence* (2nd Ed.). New York: McGraw-Hill, 1991.

Schwartz, Evan I., and James B. Treece. "Smart Programs Go to Work." *Business Week*, March 2, 1992, pp. 97–102.

Seligmann, Jean, and Chris Sulavik. "Software for Hard Issues." *Business Week*, April 27, 1992, p. 55.

Shapiro, Stuart (ed.). *Encyclopedia of Artificial Intelligence* (2nd Ed.). New York: John Wiley & Sons, 1992.

Sheil, Beau. "Thinking About Artificial Intelligence." *Harvard Business Review*, July-August 1987, pp. 91–97.

Shpilberg, David, and Lynford E. Graham. "Developing ExpertTAX: An Expert System for Corporate Tax Accrual and Planning." *Auditing: A Journal of Practice and Theory*, Fall 1986, pp. 75–94.

Stewart, John. "Can Neurocomputing Live Up to Its Promise?" *Credit Card Management*, September 1991, pp. 74–79.

Stix, Gary. "No Tipping Please." *Scientific American*, January 1992, p. 141.

Studt, Tim. "Neural Networks: Computer Toolbox for the '90s." *R&D*, September 1991, pp. 36–42.

Sviokla, J. J. "An Examination of the Impact of Expert Systems on the Firm: The Case of XCON." *MIS Quarterly*, June 1990, pp. 127–140.

Tanzer, Andrew. "Why Fuzzy Logic is Good for Business." *Forbes*, May 13, 1991, pp. 120, 122.

Trippi, Robert, and Efraim Turban. "The Impact of Parallel and Neural Computing on Managerial Decision Making." *Journal of Management Information Systems*, Winter 1989-1990, pp. 85–98.

Turban, Efraim. *Decision Support and Expert Systems: Management Support Systems* (2nd Ed.). New York: Macmillan, 1990.

Turban, Efraim, and Paul R. Watkins. "Integrating Expert Systems and Decision Support Systems." *MIS Quarterly*, June 1986, pp. 121–136.

VanLehn, Kurt (ed.). *Architectures for Intelligence*. Hillside, NJ: Lawrence Erlbaum Associates, 1991.

White, George M. "Natural Language Understanding and Speech Recognition." *Communications of the ACM*, August 1990, pp. 72–82.

Zadeh, Fatemeh. "An Introduction to Neural Networks and a Comparision with Artificial Intelligence and Expert Systems." *Interfaces*, March-April 1991, pp. 25–38.

Zadeh, Lofti A. "The Calculus of Fuzzy If/Then Rules." *AI Expert*, March 1992, pp. 23–27.

CHAPTER 12

Ashton, Kristin B. "Perfect Solution: All in the Name: Document Management Systems Get High Marks." *LAN Times*, May 1990, pp. 143–146.

Barcomb, David. *Office Automation: A Survey of Tools and Technology*. Boston: Digital Press, 1988.

Baronas, Jean. "A Guide to Quality Scanning." *Datamation*, April 15, 1990, pp. 96–97.

Bermar, Amy. "Sears Video-Conferencing Network Will Encompass Offices, 800 Stores," *PC Week Connectivity*, April 5, 1988, p. C/18.

Bernstein, Aaron. "Quality is Becoming Job One in the Office, Too." *Business Week*, April 29, 1991, pp. 52–56.

Booker, Ellis. "FileNet Imaging Stays Ahead of the Pack." *Computerworld*, January 27, 1992, pp. 109–110.

Bowen, William. "The Puny Payoff from Office Computers." *Fortune*, May 26, 1986, pp. 20–24.

Brinker, Scott J. "Corporate Bulletin Board Systems: Customer Support and More in the 1990s." *Telecommunications*, November 1991, pp. 33–36.

Brown, Carolyn M. "Next Best Thing to Being There." *Black Enterprise*, February 5, 1992, pp. 53–54.

Burns, Nina. "E-Mail Software." *Computerworld*, February 10, 1992, pp. 83–92.

Casey, Richard G., and David R. Ferguson. "Intelligent Forms Processing." *IBM Systems Journal*, Vol. 29, No. 3 (1990), pp. 435–450.

Cody, Angela. "Riding the Wave of Business Forms and Paper." *Office Technology Management*, December 1991, pp. 59, 64–-65.

Cullen, Scott W. "Multifunction Systems are New on the Scene." *The Office*, April 1991, pp. 20, 22.

Daly, James. "Insurer Sees Future in Imaging Strategy." *Computerworld*, January 6, 1992, p. 41.

Dennis, Alan R., Jay F. Nunamaker, Jr., and David Paranka. "Supporting the Search for Competitive Advantage." *Journal of Management Information Systems*, Summer 1991, pp. 5–36.

Eng, Paul M., and Amy Borrus. "Who Knows Where You Are? The Satellite Knows." *Business Week*, February 10, 1992, pp. 120–121.

Ford, Robert C. "Is Your Organization Ready for Telecommuting?" *SAM Advanced Management Journal*, Autumn 1991, pp. 19–23, 33.

Gold, Elliot, M. "Unified Systems Integrate Voice, Data, and Images." *Network Management*, December 1990, pp. 29–32.

Gremillion, Lee L., and Philip J. Pyburn. "Justifying Decision Support Systems and Office Administration Systems." *Journal of Management Information Systems*, Summer 1985, pp. 5–17.

Hall, P. A. V., and S. Papadopoulos. "Hypertext Systems and Applications." *Information and Software Technology*, September 1990, pp. 477–90.

Hamilten, Rosemary. "Electronic Meetings: No More ZZZ's." *Computerworld*, September 14, 1992, pp. 109, 113.

Henkoff, Ronald. "Make Your Office More Productive." *Fortune*, February 25, 1991, pp. 72–84.

Hershey, Gerald L., and Donna L. Kizzier. *Planning and Implementing End-User Information Systems: Of-*

fice and End-User Systems Management. Cincinnati, OH: South-Western, 1992.

I/S Analyzer. "The Emerging World of Multimedia." March 1991, pp. 1–12.

Johansen, Robert. Groupware: Computer Support for Business Teams New York: Free Press, 1988.

Jones, Virginia A. "The Latest Trends in Micrographics." Office Systems '90, April 1990, pp. 32–34.

Kingman, Lauren C., Robert E. Lambert, and Robert P. Steen. "Operational Image Systems." IBM Systems Journal, Vol. 29, No. 3 (1990), pp. 304–312.

Kobielus, James. "Multimedia Arrives at the Networked Desktop." Network World, August 1990, pp. 30–31.

Konstadt, Paul. "The Sharper Image." CIO, April 1991, pp. 32–40.

LaPlante, Alice. "Group(ware) Therapy." Computerworld, July 27, 1992, pp. 71–73.

Lauriston, Robert. "Work-Group Software Worth Waiting For." Software Magazine, February 1990, pp. 66–69.

Lee, Soonchul. "Impact of Office Information Systems on Potential Power and Influence." Journal of Management Information Systems, Fall 1991, pp. 135–152.

Mann, Janet. "An Image of Document Management." Datamation, November 15, 1991, pp. 81–82.

Margolis, Nell, and Ellis Booker. "Taming the Health Care Cost Monster." Computerworld, August 3, 1992, p. 1ff.

May, Thornton. "Justifying the Image." Datamation, April 15, 1990, pp. 82–84.

McCusker, Tom. "The Message is Integration." Datamation, August 15, 1991, pp. 31–32.

Mendelson, Edward. "Seven Windows Word Processors: What You See is What You'll Want." PC Magazine, February 25, 1992, pp. 113–189.

Miller, Rock. "To Inform and Convince: Ten Presentation Graphics Packages." PC Magazine, March 17, 1992, pp. 113–186.

Nash, Jim. "Imaging May Increase Productivity by 50%." Computerworld, February 10, 1991, p. 45.

Nash, Jim. "Industry Giants Agree on E-Mail Standard." Computerworld, February 10, 1992, p. 6.

Network Management. "Videoconferencing and Teleconferencing Directory." Mid-January 1991, pp. 6–59.

Newsweek. "Broadcast News, Inc." January 4, 1988, pp. 34–35.

O'Leary, Meghan. "Home Sweet Office." CIO, July 1991, pp. 30–40.

Popiul, Jacklyn. "How Good is Your Image." Computerworld, November 5, 1990, p. 117.

Rapaport, Matthew. "Groupware Vs. CCS: Comparing Benefits and Functionality." Telecommunications, November 1991, pp. 37–40.

Robbins, Marc. The Voice Mail Reference Manual and Buyer's Guide. Riverdale, NY: Robbins Press, 1989.

Rothschild, Edward S. "An Eye on Optical Disks." Datamation, March 1, 1986, pp. 73–74.

Sassone, Peter G., and A. Perry Schwartz. "Cost-Justifying OA." Datamation, February 15, 1986, pp. 83–88.

Sheridan, David. "Off the Road Again: Training Through Teleconferencing." Training, February 1992, pp. 63–69.

Sivula, Chris. "The White-Collar Productivity Push." Datamation, January 15, 1990, pp. 52–56.

Sox, Charlene W. Introduction to Office Automation. Englewood Cliffs, NJ: Prentice-Hall, 1990.

Stevens, Johanna M. "Combining Bar Coding and Image Processing for Document Management," Chief Information Officer Journal, Fall 1991, pp. 23–31.

Thuston, Francine. "Video Teleconferencing: The State of the Art." Telecommunications, January 1992, pp. 63–64.

Wallace, Scott. "Image Archiving." Corporate Computing, October 1992, pp. 74–82.

Williams, Daniel. "New Technologies for Coordinating Work." Datamation, May 15, 1990, pp. 92–96.

Young, J. A. "The Advantages of Telecommuting." Management Review, July 1991, pp. 19–21.

Zulke, Michael. "ISDN Applications in France." Telecommunications, March 1990, pp. 45–48.

CHAPTER 13

Alexander, Michael. "Group Finds Way to Speed Widgets to Market." Computerworld, March 9, 1992, p. 28.

Amirrezvani, Anita. "Fidelity Investments Builds EIS to Simplify Access to Financial Data." Computerworld, April 6, 1992, p. 95.

Anthes, Gary H. "Small Firms Unite Through Net." Computerworld, January 20, 1992, pp. 59, 62.

August, Raymond A. "Low-Cost Accounting Software: Big Gains for Small Business." PC Magazine, May 12, 1992, pp. 223–254.

Baer, Tony, and Bruce Richardson. "Flexible Manufacturing: How to Schedule in Unexpected Events." Computerworld, February 11, 1991, pp. 59–65.

Bakos, J. Yannis. "A Strategic Analysis of Electronic Marketplaces." MIS Quarterly, September 1991, pp. 295–310.

Bencievenqa, Ben. "Want to Clone Your Best Customers?" Target Marketing, August 1991, pp. 12–14.

Bennet, Earl D., Sarah A. Reed, and Ted Simmons. "Learning from the CIM Experience." Management Accounting, July 1991, pp. 28–33.

Besterfield, Dale H. Quality Control. Homewood, IL: Irwin, 1990.

Bourke, Richard W., and Eddy D. Miller. "Product Data Management Systems—A New Technology (Part 1)." Production & Inventory Management Review, February 1991, pp. 45–47.

Broderick, Renae, and John W. Boudreau. "Human Resource Management, Information Technology and the Competitive Edge." The Executive, May 1992, pp. 7–17.

Burns, O. Maxie, David Turnipseed, and Walter E. Riggs. "Critical Success Factors in Manufacturing

Resources Planning." *International Journal of Operations & Production Management*, Vol. 11, No. 4, 1991, pp. 5–19.

Business Week. "Office Automation: Making It Pay Off." October 12, 1987, pp. 134–146.

Caldwell, Bruce. "Factoring in the Future." *Information Week*, December 23, 1991, pp. 29–30.

Case, Thomas L., and John R. Pickett. "Enhancing R&D's Strategic Potential Via Information Technology: Electronic Linkages with Corporate Strategy and Other Subunits." *Proceedings of the Annual Meeting of the Southeastern Decision Sciences Institute*, 1992, pp. 269–272.

Case, Thomas L., and John R. Pickett. "Information Technology in R&D: Enhancing Organizational Competitiveness via R&D Information Systems." In Edward Szewczak, Coral Snodgrass, and Mehdi Khosrowpour (eds.), *Management Impacts of Information Technology: Perspectives on Organizational Change and Growth.* Harrisburg, PA: Idea Publishing, 1991, pp. 438–467.

Chaudhry, Anil. "From Art to Part." *Computerworld*, November 9, 1992, pp. 77–78.

Crane, Robert. "Accounting Systems." *Computerworld*, February 24, 1992, pp. 73–86.

Crosby, Philip B. *Quality Is Free: The Art of Making Certain.* New York: McGraw-Hill, 1979.

Datamation. "Industry by Industry Technology Forecast." January 15, 1988, pp. 58–92.

Davis, Sheila. "Retailers Go Shopping for EDI." *Datamation*, March 1, 1989, pp. 53–56.

Davis, Stanley, and Bill Davidson. "How Information Technology can Revitalize Mature Businesses." *Planning Review*, January-February 1992, pp. 10–14, 47.

Deming, W. Edwards. *Quality, Productivity, and Competitive Position.* Cambridge, MA: Center for Advanced Engineering Study, MIT, 1982.

Garry, Michael. "The Plot Thickens." *Progressive Grocer*, July 1992, pp. 103–106.

Granger, Ralph E. "Computer-Based Training Improves Job Performance." *Personnel Journal*, June 1989, pp. 116–123.

Greene, Alice. "MRP II: Out with the Old. . . ." *Computerworld*, June 8, 1992, pp. 73–77.

Hansell, Saul. "Getting to Know You." *Institutional Investor*, June 1991, pp. 71–80.

Higby, Mary A., and Badie N. Farah. "The Status of Marketing Information Systems, Decision Support Systems, and Expert Systems in the Marketing Function of U.S. Firms." *Information & Management*, January 1991, pp. 29–35.

Higgins, Lexis F., Scott C. McIntyre, and Cynthia G. Raine. "Design of Global Marketing Information Systems." *Journal of Business & Industrial Marketing*, Summer-Fall 1991, pp. 49–58.

Horwitt, Elisabeth. "High-Tech Keeps Nabisco No. 1." *Computerworld*, March 2, 1992, p. 12.

Howery, C. Kenneth, Earl D. Bennet, and Sarah Reed. "How Lockheed Implemented CIM." *Management Accounting (USA)*, December 1991, pp. 22–28.

Iacocca, Lee (with William Novak). *Iacocca: An Autobiography.* New York: Bantam, 1984.

Industry Week. "Presidential Report on EDI." November 4, 1991, pp. EDI1–EDI19.

Inman, R. Anthony. "Flexible Manufacturing Systems: Issues and Implementation." *Industrial Management*, July-August 1991, pp. 7–11.

Johnson, Maryfran. "CAD/CAM Users Seek Better Software Integration." *Computerworld*, March 9, 1992, p. 15.

Kakati, M., and U. R. Dhar. "Investment Justification in Flexible Manufacturing Systems." *Engineering Costs & Production Economics*, July 1991, pp. 203–209.

Kim, Ku Sim, and Suh S. Yoon. "Ranking of Accounting Information Systems for Management Control." *Journal of Accounting Research*, Autumn 1991, pp. 386–396.

King, Julia. "Life in the Slow Lane." *Computerworld*, February 3, 1992, pp. 67–71.

Louis, Raymond S. "MRP III: Material Acquisition System." *Production & Inventory Management*, July 1991, p. 26ff.

Malone, T. W., J. Yates, and R. I. Benjamin. "Electronic Markets and Electronic Hierarchies: Effects of Information Technology and Market Structure and Corporate Strategies." *Communications of the ACM*, June 1987, pp. 484–497.

Mayros, Van, and Dennis J. Dolan. "Hefting the Data Load: How to Design the MkIS That Works for You." *Business Marketing*, March 1988, pp. 47–69.

Merrifield, B. "The Overriding Importance of R&D as It Relates to Industrial Competitiveness." *Journal of Engineering and Technology Management*, Vol. 6 (1989), pp. 71–80.

Millman, Howard. "PC-Based Accounting Software Sparks Interest in Downsizing." *Computerworld*, February 24, 1992, pp. 76–77.

Ogilvie, Heather. "Electronic Ties That Bind: Marks & Spenser's Pan-European JIT Inventory System." *The Journal of European Business*, September-October 1991, pp. 48–50.

Parenti, Mark. "Expert Systems Move Manufacturing Software into the 1990s." *Automation*, February 1991, pp. 40–41.

Peters, Tom. *Thriving on Chaos.* New York: Knopf, 1987.

Popper, Walter J. "Finance 101 for the IS Pro: Real-Time Cost Accounting Poses a Definite Challenge for Systems People." *Computerworld*, March 5, 1990, p. 98.

Ptak, Carol A. "MRP, MRP II, OPT, JIT, and CIM—Succession, Evolution, or Necessary Combination." *Production and Inventory Management Journal*, Second Quarter 1991, pp. 7–11.

Sarkis, Joseph. "Production and Inventory Control Issues in Advanced Manufacturing Systems." *Pro-*

duction and Inventory Control Journal, First Quarter 1991, pp. 76–82.

Scheier, Robert L. "How to Cost-Justify Sales Force Automation." PC Week, April 23, 1990, pp. 115–116.

Schwartz, Evan I. "Scrolled Any Good Books Lately?" Business Week, September 7, 1992, p. 61.

Schwartz, Evan I., and James B. Treece. "Smart Systems Go to Work." Business Week, March 2, 1992, pp. 97–105.

Sheridan, John H. "The CIM Evolution." Industry Week, April 20, 1992, pp. 29–51.

Sisodia, Rajendra S. "Marketing Information and Decision Support Systems for Services." Journal of Services Marketing, Winter 1992, pp. 51–64.

Slater, Derek. "IS at Your Service." Computerworld, January 20, 1992, pp. 71–80.

Slater, Robert Bruce. "Marketing Magicians Turn Information Into Profits." Credit Card Management, July 1991, pp. 5A–7A.

Sperder, Robert M. "System Links MIS with Process Control." Food Processing, July 1991, pp. 56–58.

Stamps, David. "Human Resources: A Strategic Partner or an IS Burden." Datamation, June 1, 1990, pp. 47–52.

Stevens, Larry. "Front-Line Systems." Computerworld, March 2, 1992, pp. 61–63.

Sullivan, Deidre. "Due-Diligence Service Available to Lenders." American Banker, February 25, 1992, p. 3.

Sullivan, Deidre. "Prentice-Hall Data Base Enhances Credit Checks." American Banker, February 14, 1992, p. 3.

Takanaka, Hideo. "Critical Success Factors in Factory Automation." Long Range Planning, August 1991, pp. 29–35.

Taylor, Thayer C. "Strategic Information Systems for Marketing." Sales and Marketing Management, July 1990, pp. 90–91.

Tracy, John J. "Why You Can't Afford to Ignore EDI." Corporate Controller, March-April 1991, pp. 33–36.

Tremblay, Gary W. "MRP II—Quantifying the Benefits." Michigan CPA, Fall 1991, pp. 24–26.

Vanderlee, Peter. "JIT Through EDI and Systems Integration." Manufacturing Systems, August 1991, pp. 48–49.

Wallerstedt, Jim. "Emerging Sales Software Shows Bottom-Line Promise." Computerworld, March 16, 1987, pp. 71–78.

White, James R. "Computer-Aided Design." Info-World, May 28, 1990, pp. 51–61.

CHAPTER 14

Anthes, Gary H. "Why Uncle Sam Can't Compute." Computerworld, May 18, 1992, pp. 1, 20.

Arthur, Lowell J. "Quick & Dirty." Computerworld, December 14, 1992, pp. 109–110.

August, Judy. Joint Application Development: The Group Session Approach to System Design. Englewood Cliffs, NJ: Yourdan Press/Prentice-Hall, 1991.

Avison, David, and David Wilson. "Controls for Effective Prototyping." Journal of Management Information Systems, Vol. 3, No. 1 (1991), pp. 41–53.

Banker, Rajiv D., and Robert J. Kauffman. "Reuse and Productivity in Computer-Aided Software Design: An Empirical Study." MIS Quarterly, September 1991, pp. 375–401.

Bergeron, Francois, Suzanne Rivard, and Lyne De Serre. "Investigating the Support Role of the Information Center." MIS Quarterly, September 1990, pp. 247–262.

Bowen, William. "The Puny Payoff from Office Computers." Fortune, May 26, 1986, pp. 20–24.

Brown, Patrick. "Managing Software Development." Computerworld, April 15, 1985, pp. 133–136.

Burch, John G. Systems Analysis, Design, and Implementation. Boston: Boyd & Fraser, 1992.

Cerveny, Robert P., Edward J. Garrity, and G. Lawrence Sanders. "A Problem-Solving Perspective on Systems Development." Journal of Management Information Systems, Spring 1990, pp. 103–122.

Christensen, Dawn M. "The Gap Between Systems Developers and Users." Journal of Information Systems Management, Fall 1991, pp. 73–75.

Cooprider, Jay G., and John C. Henderson. "Technology-Process Fit: Perspectives on Achieving Prototyping Effectiveness." Journal of Management Information Systems, Winter 1990-1991, pp. 67–87.

Delligatta, Ann. "System Reengineering and the User." Information Systems Management, Winter 1992, pp. 76–77.

DeLone William H., and Ephraim R. McLean. "Information Systems Success: The Quest for the Dependent Variable." Information Systems Research, March 1992, pp. 60–95.

Desmond, John. "Mapping the Ideal, Comparing to Real: NASD Pursues Top-Down Development to Save Time, Money." Software Magazine, January 1992, pp. 46–47.

Ewusi-Mensah, Kweku, and Zbigniew H. Przasnyski. "On Information Systems Project Abandonment: An Exploratory Study of Organizational Practices." MIS Quarterly, March 1991, pp. 67–85.

Finkelstein, Clive. "Together at Last." Computerworld, December 15, 1991, pp. 91–94.

Flatten, Per O., Donald J. McCubbrey, P. Declan O'Riordan, and Keith Burgess. Foundations of Business Systems (2nd Ed.). Chicago: The Dryden Press, 1992.

Freedman, David. "What Do Users Really Want?" CIO, September 1, 1991, pp. 24–28.

Gane, Chris, and Trish Sarson. Structured Systems Analysis: Tools and Techniques. Englewood Cliffs, NJ: Prentice-Hall, 1979.

Gifford, Robert. "CASE Culture Shock." Computerworld, September 16, 1991, pp. 103–104.

Gremillion, L. L., and P. Pyburn. "Breaking the Systems Development Bottleneck." Harvard Business Review, March-April 1983, pp. 130–137.

Grudin, Jonathan. "Interactive Systems: Bridging the Gaps Between Developers and Users." *Computer*, April 1991, pp. 59–69.

Guimaraes, Tor. "A Study of Applications Program Development Techniques." *Communications of the ACM*, May 1985, pp. 494–499.

Guimaraes, Tor, and Jayant V. Saraph. "The Role of Prototyping in Executive Decision Systems." *Information & Management*, December 1991, pp. 257–267.

Hershey, Gerald L., and Donna L. Kizzer. *Planning and Implementing End-User Information Systems*. Cincinnati, OH: South-Western, 1992.

Hoffman, Gerald M. "Generating Ideas for Strategic Information Systems." *Management Forum*, August 1989, p. 3.

Isenberg, Daniel J. "The Tactics of Strategic Opportunism." *Harvard Business Review*, March-April 1987, pp. 92–97.

Jain, Hermant K., Moran R. Tanniru, and Bijan Fazlollahi. "MCMD Approach for Generating and Evaluating Alternative in Requirements Analysis." *Information Systems Research*, September 1991, pp. 223–239.

Jenkins, A. M., J. D. Naumann, and J. C. Wetherbe. "Empirical Investigation of Systems Development Practices." *Information and Management*, April 1984, pp. 73–82.

Jordon, Eleanor W., and Jerry J. Machesky. *Systems Development: Requirements, Evaluation, Design, and Implementation*. Boston: PWS-Kent, 1990.

Joyce, Edward J. "Innovative In-House Development." *Datamation*, October 15, 1988, pp. 81–83.

Kay, Sherryl. "Poor Communication Equals Vaporware." *Computerworld*, January 13, 1992, pp. 81–82.

Kendall, Kenneth E. "Behavioral Implications for Systems Analysis and Design: Prospects for the Nineties." *Journal of Management Information Systems*, Vol. 3, No. 1 (1991), pp. 1–4.

Kendall, Kenneth E., and Julie E. Kendall. *Systems Analysis and Design* (2nd Ed.). Englewood Cliffs, NJ: Prentice-Hall, 1992.

Kerr, James D. "Systems Design: Users in the Hot Seat." *Computerworld*, February 27, 1989, pp. 87–96.

King, Julia. "Fast Food Develops Appetite for PCs." *Computerworld*, June 1, 1992, p. 85.

Lansman, Gary. "Avoiding Buyer Remorse." *Computerworld*, January 13, 1992, pp. 77–79.

LaPlante, Alice. "MBA Improves Prospects but Not Pay." *Computerworld*, January 6, 1992, p. 74.

Lederer, Albert L., Rajesh Mirani, Boon Siong Neo, Carol Pollard, Jayesh Prasad, and K. Ramamurthy. "Information System Cost Estimating: A Management Perspective." *MIS Quarterly*, June 1990, pp. 159–176.

Lederer, Albert L., and Raghu Nath. "Managing Organizational Issues in Information Systems Development." *Journal of Systems Management*, November 1991, pp. 23–27, 39.

Lederer, Albert L. and Jayesh Prasad. "Putting Estimates on Track." *Computerworld*, August 24, 1992, pp. 85–87.

Litsikas, Mary. "CASE: Love It or Leave It." *Systems 3X/400*, November 1991, pp. 34–48.

Lucas, H.C., Jr. *The Analysis, Design, and Implementation of Information Systems* (4th Ed.). New York: Mitchell McGraw-Hill, 1992.

Martin, James. "SWAT Teams Will Play a Pivotal Role in '90s Development." *PC Week*, March 15, 1990.

Mathieson, Kieran. "Predicting User Intentions: Comparing the Technology Acceptance Model with the Theory of Planned Behavior." *Information Systems Research*, September 1991, pp. 173–191.

Menendez, Douglas A. "The Impact of CASE." *Internal Auditor*, December 1991, pp. 48–53.

Naumann, J. D., and A. M. Jenkins. "Prototyping: The New Paradigm for Systems Development." *MIS Quarterly*, September 1982, pp. 29–44.

Nolan, Richard L. "Managing Information Systems by Committee." *Harvard Business Review*, July-August 1982, pp. 72–79.

O'Sullivan, Brendan, and Brian Keith Whitehead. "Minting New Opportunities from Old Information." *Banking Software Review*, Autumn 1991, pp. 14–18.

Pinella, Paul. "The Race for Client/Server CASE." *Datamation*, March 1, 1992, pp. 51–54.

Ray, Howard N., and John E. Oliver. "Enhancing System Analysis and Design Through Value Training." *Journal of Information Technology Management*, Vol. 1, No. 1 (1990), pp. 29–32.

Richmond, Ken. "Information Engineering, The James Martin Way." *Information Strategy: The Executive's Journal*, Winter 1992, pp. 18–28.

Saffo, Paul. "Human-Centered Computing Requires Cooperative Systems." *InfoWorld*, November 25, 1991, p. 54.

Senn, James A. "User Involvement as a Factor in Information Systems Success: Key Questions for Research." *Journal of Management Information Systems*, Vol. 3, No. 1 (1991), pp. 31–40.

Shelton, Jim. "A Well-Oiled Methodology at Global." *Software Magazine*, January 1992, pp. 49–50.

Snodgrass, Coral R., and Edward J. Szewczak. "A Societal Culture Perspective on Systems Analysis and Design." *Journal of Management Information Systems*, Vol. 3, No. 1 (1991), pp. 69–78.

Stamps, David. "CASE: Cranking Out Productivity." *Datamation*, July 1, 1987, pp. 55–58.

The, Lee. "Bridging the CASE/OOP Gap." *Datamation*, March 1, 1992, pp. 63–64.

Vail, Simon. "Managing Information Technology: Happiness is a Fault-Free System." *Management Today*, November 1991, pp. 115–116.

Vanvick, Dennis. "Getting to Know U(sers)." *Computerworld*, January 27, 1992, pp. 103–107.

Vaughan, Merlyn. "Is RAD 'RAD'?" *Software Magazine*, February 1991, p. 9.

Walton, Richard E. *Up and Running: Integrating Information Technology and the Organization*. Homewood, IL: Irwin, 1988.

Yourdon, Edward. *Managing the Systems Life Cycle*. Englewood Cliffs, NJ: Yourdon Press, 1988.

Yourdon, Edward. *Modern Structured Analysis*. Englewood Cliffs, NJ: Yourdon Press/Prentice-Hall, 1989.

Yuval, Asher, and Dror Chevion. "Build Me a System." *Computerworld*, February 10, 1992, pp. 93–95.

CHAPTER 15

Abtan, Patrick. "Creative Programmers Still Alive and Kicking." *Computing Canada*, November 21, 1991, p. 15.

Ambrosio, Johanna. "Software Leasing Catching On." *Computerworld*, June 29, 1992, pp. 74–75.

Banker, Rajiv D., and Robert J. Kauffman. "Reuse and Productivity in Computer-Aided Software Design: An Empirical Study." *MIS Quarterly*, September 1991, pp. 375–401.

Belkin, N. J., P. G. Marchetti, M. Albrecht, L. Fusco, S. Skogvold, H. Stokke, and G. Troina. "User Interfaces for Information Systems." *Journal of Information Science Principles & Practices*, Vol. 17, No. 5 (1991), pp. 327–344.

Bermant, Charles. "The Jury is Still Out on Visual Programming." *Computerworld*, April 6, 1992, p. 97.

Booch, Grady. *Object Oriented Design*. Redwood City, CA: Benjamin/Cummings, 1991.

Burch, John G. *Systems Analysis, Design, and Implementation*. Boston: Boyd & Fraser, 1992.

Couger, J. Daniel, Scott C. McIntyre, Lexis F. Higgins, and Terry A. Snow. "Using a Bottom-Up Approach to Creativity Improvement in IS Development." *Journal of Systems Management*, September 1991, pp. 23–27, 36.

Crabb, Don. "OOP Tools Ease Windows' Developers' Pains." *Infoworld*, February 25, 1991, p. 52.

Daly, James. "Cooking Up Short-Order Software." *Computerworld*, December 16, 1991, pp. 73, 75.

Davis, Dwight. "Safe Deposit for Enterprise Data." *Datamation*, March 1, 1992, pp. 67–70.

Dearden, John. "The Withering Away of the IS Organization." *Sloan Management Review*, Summer 1987, pp. 87–91.

Deffenbaugh, Greg. "What CASE Delivers: Casing the Joint." *UNIX Review*, December 1991, pp. 24–30.

Dingman, Cathy, and Steven Kriendler. "Good-Bye Paperless Dreams." *Computer & Communication Decisions*, September 1987, p. 67.

Eliot, Lance B. "Strategic CASE is Best." *CASE Trends*, May 1992, pp. 46–47, 74.

Esparza, Mary S. "Out of the Back Room." *Infosystems*, May 1987, pp. 58–60.

Foss, W. Burry. "Software Piecework." *Computerworld*, September 23, 1991, pp. 69–70, 74.

Fox, Bruce A. "A Buyer's Guide to Custom Software." *Small Business Reports*, February 1992, pp. 45–49.

Gifford, Robert. "CASE Culture Shock." *Computerworld*, September 16, 1991, pp. 103–104.

Goldberg, Cheryl. "Notebook Computers." *Computerworld*, June 22, 1992, pp. 111–113.

Gould, John D., Stephen J. Boies, and Lewis Clayton. "Making Usable, Useful, Productivity-Enhancing Computer Applications." *Communications of the ACM*, January 1991, pp. 74–85.

Gremillion, Lee L., and Philip J. Pyburn. "Justifying Decision Support Systems and Office Administration Systems." *Journal of Management Information Systems*, Summer 1985, pp. 5–17.

Gross, Neil, "The Blazing Business in Video Chips." *Business Week*, August 24, 1992, pp. 74–75.

Gugini, Umberto. "The Problem of User Interface in Geometric Modelling." *Computers in Industry*, December 1991, pp. 335–339.

Guimaraes, Tor. "A Study of Application Program Development Techniques." *Communications of the ACM*, May 1985, pp. 494–499.

Kelley, Richard. "Build v. Buy: When the Going Gets Tough, Do the Tough Go Shopping. . . . Or Building?" *Insurance & Technology*, January 1992, pp. 28–32.

Kendall, Kenneth E., and Julie E. Kendall. *Systems Analysis and Design* (2nd Ed.). Englewood Cliffs, NJ: Prentice-Hall, 1992.

Keyes, Jessica. "How Software is Developed Undergoing Basic Changes." *Software Magazine*, January 1992, pp. 38–47, 55–56.

Knight, Robert. "Methodologies a Must: CASE Will Fail Without Proper Use of Tools." *Software Magazine*, January 1992, pp. 20–21.

Lansman, Gary. "Avoiding Buyer Remorse." *Computerworld*, January 13, 1992, pp. 77–79.

Larsen, Tor J., and Justus D. Naumann. "An Experimental Comparison of Abstract and Concrete Representations in Systems Analysis." *Information & Management*, January 1992, pp. 29–40.

Lattamore, F. Benton, and John Bush. "Lots of Tunnel, a Little Light." *Computer & Communication Decisions*. September 1987, pp. 58–68.

Lehner, Franz. "Software Life Cycle Management Based on a Phase Distinction Approach." *Microprocessing & Microprogramming*, August 1991, pp. 603–608.

Litsikas, Mary. "CASE: Love It or Leave It." *Systems 3X/400*, November 1991, pp. 34–48.

Lucas, H.C., Jr. *The Analysis, Design, and Implementation of Information Systems* (4th Ed.). New York: Mitchell MCGRAW-HILL, 1992.

Mann, Janet. "An Image of Document Management." *Datamation*, November 15, 1991, pp. 81–82.

Martin, James. *Information Engineering: Volumes 1–3.* Englewood Cliffs, NJ: Prentice-Hall, 1990.

Pastore, Richard. "Proving the Case." *CIO*, October 1, 1991, pp. 28–38.

Rambaugh, James, Michael Blaha, William Premerlani, Frederick Eddy, and William Lorensen. *Object-Oriented Modeling and Design.* Englewood Cliffs, NJ: Prentice-Hall, 1991.

Ryan, Hugh W. "Systems Development: The Human Metaphor." *Information Systems Management*, Winter 1992, pp. 72–75.

Sheridan, Shawn. "Quality Software is Worth the Strain." *Canadian Datasystems*, November 1991, pp. 40, 42.

Short, Keith W. "Methodology Integration: Evolution of Information Engineering." *Information & Software Technology*, November 1991, pp. 720–723.

Snell, Ned. "Quality Tools for Quality Software." *Datamation*, January 1, 1992, pp. 53–54.

Sorensen, H., T. A. Delaney, W. P. Kenneally, S. J. M. Murphy, F. B. O'Flaherty, A. B. Mahony, and D. M. J. Power. "Towards a Development Environment for Fifth Generation Systems." *Microprocessing and Microprogramming*, August 1991, pp. 489–496.

Sumner, Mary, and Jerry Sitek. "Are Structured Methods for Systems Analysis Being Used?" *Journal of Systems Management*, June 1986, pp. 18–23.

The, Lee. "Bridging the CASE/OOP Gap." *Datamation*, March 1, 1992, pp. 63–64.

Vail, Simon. "Managing Information Technology: Happiness is a Fault-Free System." *Management Today*, November 1991, pp. 115–116.

Wallmuller, Ernest. "Software Quality Management." *Microprocessing & Microprogramming*, August 1991, pp. 609–616.

Whitten, Jeffrey L., Lonnie D. Bentley, and Victor M. Barlow. *Systems Analysis and Design* (2nd Ed.). Homewood, IL: Irwin, 1989.

Wright, Janice. "The Evolution of Development Tools." *Datamation*, December 1, 1991, pp. 78–79.

Yourdon, Edward. *Decline and Fall of the American Programmer.* Englewood Cliffs, NJ: Prentice-Hall, 1992.

Yourdon, Edward. "Kiss U.S. Coders Good-Bye." *Computerworld*, April 6, 1992, pp. 111–113.

Yourdon, Edward, and Larry Constantine. *Structured Design* (2nd Ed.). Englewood Cliffs, NJ: Yourdon Press/Prentice-Hall, 1989.

CHAPTER 16

Alexander, Michael. "Multimedia Focus Turns to Training." *Computerworld*, January 13, 1992, p. 18.

Araki, Keijiro, Zengo Furukawa, and Jingde Cheng. "A General Framework for Debugging." *IEEE Software*, May 1991, pp. 14–20.

August, Judy. *Joint Application Design: The Group Approach to System Design.* Englewood Cliffs, NJ: Yourdon Press/Prentice-Hall, 1991.

Banker, Rajiv D., and Robert J. Kauffman. "Reuse and Productivity in Computer-Aided Software Design: An Empirical Study." *MIS Quarterly*, September 1991, pp. 375–401.

Bucken, Mike. "Throwing Your Hat in the Multivendor Ring." *Software Magazine*, November 1991, pp. 66–67.

Burch, John G. *Systems Analysis, Design, and Implementation.* Boston: Boyd & Fraser, 1992.

Burger, Katheline. "The Systems, They Are a Changing." *Insurance & Technology*, October 1991, pp. 68–69.

Computerworld. "Those Maintenance Blues." June 29, 1987, pp. 51–64.

Daly, James. "Bug-Free Code: The Competitive Edge." *Computerworld*, February 17, 1992, p. 55.

Datamation. "Global Leaders." June 15, 1992, pp. 26–27.

Davis, Steve. "PC Training Lays the Groundwork for Successful Computing." *Today's Office*, May 1990, pp. 17, 21–22.

Delone, William H., and Ephraim R. McLean. "Information Systems Success: The Quest for the Dependent Variable." *Information Systems Research*, March 1992, pp. 60–95.

Dysart, Joe. "Is Your Software About to Drop Dead?" *Restaurant Hospitality*, February 1992, p. 65.

Eliason, Alan L. *Systems Development: Analysis, Design, and Implementation* (2nd Ed.). Glenview, IL: Scott, Foresman/Little, Brown, 1990.

Engardio, Pete. "Quick, Name Five Taiwanese PC Makers." *Business Week*, May 18, 1992, pp. 128–129.

Feuche, Mike. "Marketing of Training Requires Corporate Credibility." *MIS Week*, May 14, 1990, pp. 26–27.

Finkelstein, Clive. "Together at Last." *Computerworld*, December 16, 1991, pp. 91–94.

Fox, Bruce A. "A Buyer's Guide to Custom Software." *Small Business Reports*, February 1992, pp. 45–49.

Freedman, David. "What Do Users Really Want?" *CIO*, September 1, 1991, pp. 24–28.

Gallegos, Frederick, Dana R. Richardson, and Faye A. Bortnick. *Audit and Control of Information Systems.* Cincinnati: South-Western, 1987.

Ginzberg, Michael J. "Key Recurrent Issues in the MIS Implementation Process." *MIS Quarterly*, June 1981, pp. 47–60.

Gould, John D., Stephen J. Boies, and Clayton Lewis. "Making Usable, Useful, Productivity-Enhancing Computer Applications." *Communications of the ACM*, January 1991, pp. 74–85.

Grudin, Jonathan. "Interactive Systems: Bridging the Gaps Between Developers and Users." *Computer*, April 1991, pp. 59–69.

Grupe, Fritz H., and Dorothy F. Clevenger. "Using Function Point Analysis as a Software Development Tool." *Journal of Systems Management*, December 1991, pp. 23–26.

Harding, Elizabeth U. "As World Grows Smaller, U.S. Users Worry About Support." *Software Magazine*, November 1991, pp. 31–34.

Hershey, Gerald L., and Donna L. Kizzer. *Planning and Implementing End-User Information Systems*. Cincinnati, OH: South-Western, 1992.

Hildebrand, J. D. "Optimizing the Process." *UNIX Review*, November 1991, pp. 30–33.

Jaakola, John. "Beware of 'Object-Oriented' Vendors." *Computing Canada*, January 20, 1992, p. 32.

Kador, John. "Study: Companies Need to Change Concepts of Training." *MIS Week*, November 27, 1989, pp. 33, 35.

Keen, Peter. *Shaping the Future: Business Design Through Information Technology*. Boston: Harvard Business School Press, 1991.

Kelley, Joseph. "World IT Sales Grow 8.9% to $278.5B: North America Hits $184.7B." *Datamation*, June 15, 1991, pp. 10–29.

Kelley, Richard. "Build v. Buy: When the Going Gets Tough, Do the Tough Go Shopping. . . . Or Building?" *Insurance & Technology*, January 1992, pp. 28–32.

Kendall, Kenneth E., and Julie E. Kendall. *Systems Analysis and Design* (2nd Ed.). Englewood Cliffs, NJ: Prentice-Hall, 1992.

Keyes, Jessica. "How Software is Being Developed Undergoing Basic Changes." *Software Magazine*, January 1992, pp. 38–47, 55–56.

Kumar, Kuldeep. "Post Implementation Evaluations of Computer-Based Information Systems: Current Practices." *Communications of the ACM*, February 1990, pp. 203–212.

Lattamore, G. Berton, and Joseph Maglitta. "Riding the Software Pricing Skyrocket." *Computerworld*, November 2, 1992, pp. 99–100.

Lehner, Franz. "Software Life Cycle Management Based on a Phase Distinction Approach." *Microprocessing & Microprogramming*, August 1991, pp. 603–608.

Lucas, H.C., Jr. *The Analysis, Design, and Implementation of Information Systems* (4th Ed.). New York: Mitchell McGraw-Hill, 1992.

Marion, Larry. "The DATAMATION 100." *Datamation*, June 15, 1992, pp. 13–22.

Martin, James. *Information Engineering: Volumes 1–3*. Englewood Cliffs, NJ: Prentice-Hall, 1990.

Martin, James. "Restructuring Code is a Sound Investment for the Future." *PC Week*, May 7, 1990.

Melymuka, Kathleen. "Managing Maintenance: The 4,000-Pound Gorilla." *CIO*, March 1991, pp. 74–82.

Nash, Kim S. "Whipping Worn-Out Code Into New Shape." *Computerworld*, August 17, 1992, pp. 69–70.

O'Leary, Meghan. "The Object of Their Affection." *CIO*, December 1992, pp. 28–32.

O'Sullivan, Brendan, and Brian Keith Whitehead. "Minting New Opportunities from Old Information." *Banking Software Review*, Autumn 1991, pp. 14–18.

Parker, Rachel. "Try It, You'll Like It: Microsoft Usability Lab Tests Human Factors." *Infoworld*, December 16, 1991, pp. 61–62.

Pinella, Paul. "The PC Big 50." *Datamation*, December 1, 1991, pp. 42–44.

Pitman, Ben. "A Systems Analysis Approach to Reviewing Completed Projects." *Journal of Systems Management*, December 1991, pp. 6–9, 37.

Portik, Stephen W. "The Accountant's Role in Systems Development." *Ohio CPA Journal*, November-December 1991, pp. 45–46.

Prasse, Michael J. "Achieving Better Systems Development Through Usability Testing." *Journal of Systems Management*, September 1991, pp. 10–12.

Rettig, Marc. "Software Teams." *Communications of the ACM*, October 1990, pp. 23–27.

Rettig, Marc. "Testing Made Palatable." *Communications of the ACM*, May 1991, pp. 15–19.

Rivard, Suzanne, and Sid L. Huff. "Factors for Success of End-User Computing." *Communications of the ACM*, May 1988, pp. 552 -561.

Senn, James A. "User Involvement as a Factor in Information Systems Success: Key Questions for Research." *Journal of Management Systems*, Vol. 3, No. 1 (1991), pp. 31–40.

Singleton, John P., Ephraim R. McLean, and Edward N. Altman. "Measuring Information Systems Performance." *MIS Quarterly*, June 1988, pp. 325–336.

Slater, Derek. "Mainframe Firms Feel Downsizing Heat." *Computerworld*, October 19, 1992, p. 153.

Swanson, E. Burton. *Information System Implementation: Bridging the Gap Between Design and Utilization*. Homewood, IL: Irwin, 1988.

The, Lee. "Bridging the CASE/OOP Gap." *Datamation*, March 1, 1992, pp. 63–64.

Vail, Simon. "Managing Information Technology: Happiness is a Fault-Free System." *Management Today*, November 1991, pp. 115–116.

Wallmuller, Earnest. "Software Quality Management." *Microprocessing and Microprogramming*, August 1991, pp. 609–616.

Walton, Richard E. *Up and Running: Integrating Information Technology and the Organization*. Boston: Harvard Business School Press, 1989.

Ware, Robb. "MIS Managers Are Often Responsible for Training Horror Stories." *MIS Week*, May 21, 1990, p. 36.

Weber, Ron. *EDP Auditing: Conceptual Foundations and Practice* (2nd Ed.). New York: McGraw-Hill, 1988.

Whitten, Jeffrey L., Lonnie D. Bentley, and Victor M. Barlow. *Systems Analysis and Design* (2nd Ed.). Homewood, IL: Irwin, 1989.

Wohl, Amy D. "Illuminating the Operating Systems Market." *Office Technology Management*, November 1991, pp. 22–28.

Yahdav, Daniel. "Project Management Gets Easier." *Computerworld*, October 19, 1992, pp. 97–101.

Yourdon, Edward. *Decline and Fall of the American Programmer*. Englewood Cliffs, NJ: Prentice-Hall, 1992.

Yourdon, Edward. "Kiss U.S. Coders Good-Bye." *Computerworld*, April 6, 1992, pp. 111–113.

Yourdon, Edward. *Structured Walkthroughs* (4th Ed.). Englewood Cliffs, NJ: Yourdon Press/Prentice-Hall, 1989.

CHAPTER 17

Alavi, Maryam, Nelson R. Ryan, and Ira R. Weiss. "Strategies for End-User Computing: An Integrative Framework." *Journal of Management Information Systems*, Winter 1987, pp. 28–49.

Alavi, Maryam, and Ira R. Weiss. "Managing the Risks Associated With End-User Computing." *Journal of Management Information Systems*, Winter 1985, pp. 5–20.

Armoso, Donald L., and Paul H. Cheney. "Testing a Causal Model of End-User Application Effectiveness." *Journal of Management Information Systems*, Summer 1991, pp. 63–89.

Barr, Aaron. "Transforming Support at the Help Desk." *Information Center Quarterly*, Summer 1991, pp. 20–27.

Bergeron, Francois, Suzanne Rivard, and Lyne De Serre. "Investigating the Support Role of the Information Center." *MIS Quarterly*, September 1990, pp. 247–262.

Betts, Mitch. "Keyboard Injuries Provoke Lawsuits." *Computerworld*, June 15, 1992, p. 24.

Braverman, Barbara, and Carol Hartwig. "Users Helping Users." *Computerworld*, April 23, 1990, pp. 99–104.

Carr, Houston H. *Managing End-User Computing.* Englewood Cliffs, NJ: Prentice-Hall, 1988.

Carr, Houston H. "When It's Time to Build Up the Info Center." *Information Center Quarterly*, Summer 1991, pp. 28–31.

Christoff, Kurt A. *Managing the Information Center.* Glenview, IL: Scott Foresman/Little, Brown, 1990.

Coburn, Edward J. *Business Graphics: Concepts and Applications.* Boston, MA: Boyd & Fraser, 1991.

Cotterman, William W., and Kuldeep Kumar. "User Cube: A Taxonomy of End Users." *Communications of the ACM*, November 1989, pp. 25–34.

Cougar, J. Daniel. "E Pluribus Computum." *Harvard Business Review*, October 1986, p. 87ff.

Crawford, Sally. "From Denial to Productivity." *Information Center*, July 1990, pp. 18–25.

Cronan, Timothy P., and David P. Douglas. "End-User Training and Computing Effectiveness in Public Agencies: An Empirical Study." *Journal of Management Information Systems*, Spring 1990, pp. 21–39.

Gallagher, Francis J. "Application Development and the User Partnership." *Information Center*, August 1990, pp. 24–28.

Gantz, John. "The Cooperative Computing Fire Ignites." *Networking Management*, June 1992, p. 74ff.

Gerlach, J. H., and F. Y. Kuo. "Understanding Human-Computer Interaction for Information Systems Design." *MIS Quarterly*, December 1991, pp. 527–549.

Gerrity, Thomas P., and John F. Rockart. "End-User Computing: Are You a Leader or a Laggard?" *Sloan Management Review*, Summer 1986, pp. 25–34.

Gremillion, Lee. "End-User Computing in the LAN Environment." *Datapro Information Services: Managing LANs*, January 1992, pp. 1–6.

Grey, Gloria. "What is Electronic Performance Support?" *Information Center Quarterly*, Summer 1991, pp. 36–39.

Henderson, John C., and Micheal C. Treacy. "Managing End-User Computing for Competitive Advantage." *Sloan Management Review*, Winter 1986, pp. 3–14.

Hershey, Gerald L., and Donna L. Kizzer. *Planning and Implementing End-User Information Systems.* Cincinnati, OH: South-Western, 1992.

Huff, Sid L., Malcolm C. Munro, and Barbara H. Martin. "Growth Stages of End User Computing." *Communications of the ACM*, May 1988, pp. 542–550.

Kador, John. "Help Desks Take the Initiative." *Information Center Quarterly*, Summer 1991, pp. 29–34.

Karten, Naomi. *Mind Your Business: Strategies for Managing End-User Computing.* Wellesley, MA: QED Information Sciences, 1990.

Lourtie, Kathryn. "Delivering Business-Driven Support Services." *Information Center Quarterly*, Summer 1991, pp. 32–35.

MacLean, Lisa. "A Refresher Course on System Design." *Information Center*, August 1990, pp. 17–18.

McNaught, Jay. "Thirty-Seven More Ways to Improve Training." *Information Center*, August 1990, pp. 19–23.

Mueller, Nancy S. "Microcomputer Software Selection Research Tools." *Information Center*, May 1990, pp. 24–29.

Munro, Malcolm C., Sid L. Huff, and Gary Moore. "Expansion and Control of End-User Computing." *Journal of Management Information Systems*, Winter 1987-1988, pp. 5–27.

Nelson, R. Ryan (ed.), *End-User Computing: Concepts, Issues, and Applications.* New York: John Wiley & Sons, 1989.

Nelson, R. R., and P. H. Cheney. "Training End-Users: An Exploratory Study." *MIS Quarterly*, December 1987, pp. 547–559.

Pyburn, Phillip J. "Managing Personal Computer Use: The Role of Corporate Management Information Systems." *Journal of Management Information Systems*, Winter 1986-1987, pp. 83–86.

Rebello, Kathy, Richard Brandt, Peter Cox, and Mark Lewyn. "Your Digital Future." *Business Week*, September 17, 1992, pp. 56–64.

Rivard, Suzanne, and Sid L. Huff. "Factors of Success for End-User Computing." *Communications of the ACM*, May 1988, pp. 552–561.

Rudner, Leonard. "Client-Centered Training." *Information Center*, May 1990, pp. 13–19.

Runge, Larry D. "New Tool for a New Era." *Information Center Quarterly*, Summer 1991, pp. 24–28.

Sipor, J. C., and G. L. Sanders. "Definitional Distinctions and Implications for Managing End User Computing." *Information and Management*, March 1989, pp. 115–123.

Sumner, M. R., and R. Klepper. "The Impact of Information Systems Strategy on End-User Computing." *Journal of Systems Management*, October 1987, pp. 12–17.

Trauth, Eileen M. "The Organizational Interface: A Method for Supporting End Users of Packaged Software." *MIS Quarterly*, March 1992, pp. 35–53.

White, C. E., and D. P. Christy. "The Information Center Concept: A Normative Model and a Study of Six Installations." *MIS Quarterly*, December 1987, pp. 451–458.

Whittle, Doug D. "Six Steps to the Strategic IC." *Information Center Quarterly*, Summer 1991, pp. 15–23.

CHAPTER 18

Ahituv, Niv, and Seev Neumann. *Principles of Information Systems for Management* (3rd Ed.). Dubuque, IA: Wm. C. Brown, 1990.

Alanis, Macedonio. "Controlling the Introduction of Strategic Systems." In Edward Szewczak, Coral Snodgrass, and Mehdi Khosrowpour (eds.), *Management Impacts of Information Technology: Perspectives on Organizational Change and Growth.* Harrisburg, PA: Idea Group, 1991, pp. 421–437.

Allen, Leilani. "How Companies Plan." *Computerworld*, September 21, 1987, pp. 97–105.

Ambrosio, Johanna. "Downsizing Spurs IBM, CA Pricing Review." *Computerworld*, March 2, 1992, p. 1ff.

Ambrosio, Johanna, and Kim S. Nash. "Development Centers Shift Focus to PCs." *Computerworld*, March 16, 1992, pp. 65–66.

Anthes, Gary H. "EDS to Reap $508M from FAA Corn Deal." *Computerworld*, February 10, 1992, p. 12.

Anthes, Gary H. "GAO Report Red Flags Bank Outsourcing." *Computerworld*, February 10, 1992, p. 12.

Applegate, Lynda M., James I. Cash, Jr., and D. Quinn Mills. "Information Technology and Tomorrow's Manager." *Harvard Business Review*, November-December 1988, pp. 128–136.

Ball, L., and R. Harris. "SMIS Members: A Membership Analysis." *MIS Quarterly*, March 1982, pp. 19–38.

Ballou, Melinda–Carol. "DEC Restructuring Takes Form." *Computerworld*, November 2, 1992, pp. 1, 20.

Barry, Curt. "Systems Strategies." *Catalog Age.* November 1991, pp. 115–118.

Beath, Cynthia Mathis. "Supporting the Information Technology Champion." *MIS Quarterly*, September 1991, pp. 355–372.

Bennis, Warren, and Bert Nanus. *Leaders.* New York: Harper & Row, 1985.

Booker, Ellis. "IS Managers Admit Downsizing Fears." *Computerworld*, March 23, 1992, pp. 59–60.

Booker, Ellis. "The Buck Stops Where?" *Computerworld*, October 5, 1992, pp. 83, 89.

Booker, Ellis. "United Takes Distributed Approach." *Computerworld*, March 30, 1992, p. 1ff.

Boynton, A. C., and R. W. Zmud. "An Assessment of Critical Success Factors," *Sloan Management Review*, Summer 1984, pp. 17–28.

Brancheau, James C., and James C. Wetherbe. "Key Issues in Information Systems Management." *MIS Quarterly*, March 1987, pp. 23–35.

Burn, Janice, and Eveline Caldwell. *Management of Information Systems Technology.* New York: Van Nostrand Reinhold, 1990.

Calhoun, Kenneth J., and Albert L. Lederer. "From Strategic Business Planning to Strategic Information Systems Planning: The Missing Link." *Journal of Information Technology Management*, Vol. 1, No. 1 (1990), pp. 1–6.

Carlson, Walter M., and Barbara C. McNurlin. "Do You Measure Up?" *Computerworld*, December 17, 1992, pp. 95–98.

Cash, James I., Jr., F. Warren McFarlan, James L. McKenney, and Lynda M. Applegate. *Corporate Information Systems Management: Text and Cases* (3rd Ed.). Homewood, IL: Irwin, 1992.

Chandler, Alfred D., Jr. *Strategy and Structure.* Garden City, NY: Doubleday, 1962.

Chung, Kae H., and Michael E. Friesen. "The Critical-Success-Factor Approach at Boeing," *Journal of Management Systems*, Vol. 3, No. 2 (1991), pp. 53–63.

Clemons, Eric K. "Evaluation of Strategic Investments in Information Technology." *Communications of the ACM*, January 1991, pp. 22–36.

The Computerworld Pocket Guide for Success. Framingham, MA: CW Publishing, 1992.

Cusack, Sally. "Downsizing Brings Unexpected Bonus." *Computerworld*, January 6, 1992, p. 31.

Davenport, Thomas H., Michael Hammer, and Tauno J. Metsisto. "How Executives Can Shape Their Company's Information Systems." *Harvard Business Review*, March-April 1989, pp. 130–134.

DeLone, William H., and Ephraim R. McClean. "Information Systems Success: The Quest for the Dependent Variable." *Information Systems Research*, March 1992, pp. 60–95.

Dickson, G. W., R. L. Leitheiser, M. Nechis, and J. C. Wetherbe. "Key Information Systems Issues for the 1980s." *MIS Quarterly*, September 1984, pp. 135–148.

Drury, D. H. "An Evaluation of Data Processing Steering Committees." *MIS Quarterly*, December 1984, pp. 257–266.

Elofson, Gregg, and Benn R. Konsynski. "Delegation Technologies: Environmental Scanning with Intelligent Agents." *Journal of Management Information Systems*, Summer 1991, pp. 69–81.

Fosdick, Howard. "How to Avoid the Pitfalls of Downsizing." *Datamation*, May 1, 1992, pp. 77–80.

Frenzel, Carrol. *Management of Information Technology*. Boston, MA: Boyd & Fraser, 1992.

Fried, Louis, and Richard Johnson. "Gaining the Technology Advantage: Planning for the Competitive use of IT." *Journal of Information Systems Management*, Fall 1991, pp. 7–15.

Gee, Trevor J. "Managing Computer Risk: What Could Go Wrong." *Financial Manager's Statement*, November-December 1991, pp. 6–9.

Goodhue, Dale L., Laurie J. Kirsch, Judith A. Quillard, and Michael Wybo. "Strategic Data Planning: Lessons from the Field." *MIS Quarterly*, March 1992, pp. 11–34.

Goold, Michael. "Strategic Control in the Decentralized Firm." *Sloan Management Review*, Winter 1991, pp. 69–81.

Gray, Daniel H. "Uses and Misuses of Strategic Planning." *Harvard Business Review*, January-February 1986, pp. 89–97.

Gray, Paul, William R. King, Ephraim R. McLean, and Hugh J. Watson (eds.). *MoIS: Management of Information Systems*. Chicago, IL: The Dryden Press, 1989.

Gremillion, Lee. "End-User Computing in the LAN Environment." *Datapro*, Report No. 1425, January 1992.

Gremillion, Lee L., and Philip J. Pyburn. "Justifying Decision Support Systems and Office Administration Systems." *Journal of Management Information Systems*, Summer 1985, pp. 5–17.

Hamel, Gary, and C. K. Prahalad. "Strategic Intent." *Harvard Business Review*, May-June 1989, pp. 63–76.

Hartog, C., and M. Herbert. "1985 Opinion Survey of MIS Managers: Key Issues." *MIS Quarterly*, December 1986, pp. 351–361.

Hopper, Max D. "Rattling SABRE—New Ways to Compete on Information." *Harvard Business Review*, May-June 1990, pp. 118–127.

Kanter, Jerome. *Managing with Information* (4th Ed.). Englewood Cliffs, NJ: Prentice-Hall, 1992.

Keen, Peter. *Shaping the Future: Business Design Through Information Technology*. Boston: Harvard Business School Press, 1991.

Kemerer, Chris F., and G. L. Sosa. "Systems Development Risks in Strategic Information Systems." *Information and Software Technology*, April 1991, pp. 212–223.

Kiam, Victor. *Going For It*. Signet: New York, 1986.

King, Julia. "It's C.Y.A. Time." *Computerworld*, March 30, 1992, pp. 85–86.

King, Julia. "Negotiating Your Company to Safety." *Computerworld*, March 30, 1992, p. 90.

King, Julia. "The New Spin-Offs." *Computerworld*, August 24, 1992, pp. 81–84.

LaPlante, Alice. "U.S. Companies Find Outsourcing a Sensible Way to Go International." *Computerworld*, April 13, 1992, p. 79.

Lederer, A. I., and A. L. Mendelow. "Convincing Top Management of the Strategic Potential of Information Systems." *MIS Quarterly*, December 1988, pp. 525–536.

Lederer, Albert I,. and Aubrey L. Mendelow. "Coordination of Information Systems Plans with Business Plans." *Journal of Management Information Systems*, Fall 1989, pp. 5–19.

Leinfuss, Emily. "Outsourcers Have Limited Liability." *Computerworld*, March 30, 1992, p. 88.

Lindquist, Christopher. "County Thinks Small, Dumps 4381 for LANs." *Computerworld*, April 6, 1992, p. 1ff.

Mallach, Efrem G. "The Organizational Impact of Strategic Systems." In Edward Szewczak, Coral Snodgrass, and Mehdi Khosrowpour (eds.), *Management Impacts of Information Technology: Perspectives on Organizational Change and Growth*. Harrisburg, PA: Idea Group, 1991, pp. 408–420.

Margolis, Nell. "Marching Orders." *Computerworld*, October 19, 1992, p. 108.

Margolis, Nell. "Mass. Blue Cross Tries EDS Rx." *Computerworld*, January 27, 1992, p. 1ff.

Margolis, Nell. "Revlon Makes Over IS Unit." *Computerworld*, February 10, 1992, p. 1ff.

Martin, E. Wainright, Daniel W. DeHayes, Jeffrey A. Hoffer, and William C. Perkins. *Managing Information Technology: What Managers Need to Know*. New York: Macmillan, 1991.

Martin, James, and Joe Leben. *Strategic Information Planning Methodologies*. Englewood Cliffs, NJ: Prentice-Hall, 1989.

McConnell, Vicki C., and Karl Wm. Koch. *Computerizing the Corporation: The Intimate Link Between People and Machines*. New York: Van Nostrand Reinhold, 1990.

McCormack, Mark H. *What They Don't Teach You at Harvard Business School*. New York: Bantam, 1984.

McFarlan, F. W. "Portfolio Approach to Information Systems." *Harvard Business Review*, September-October 1981, pp. 142–150.

McFarlan, F. Warren, James L. McKenney, and Philip Pyburn. "The Information Archipelago: Plotting a Course." *Harvard Business Review*, January-February 1983, pp. 145–156.

McNurlin, Barbara C., and Ralph H. Sprague. *Information Systems Management in Practice* (2nd Ed.). Englewood Cliffs, NJ: Prentice-Hall, 1989.

Mensching, James R., and Dennis A. Adams, *Managing an Information System*. Englewood Cliffs, NJ: Prentice-Hall, 1991.

Moad, Jeff. "Budget Growth Skids to 3.4%." *Datamation*, April 15, 1991, pp. 44–47.

Neiderman, Fred, James C. Brancheau, and James C. Wetherbe. "Information Systems Management Issues for the 1990s." *MIS Quarterly*, December 1991, pp. 475–499.

Nolan, R. L. "Managing Information Systems By Committee." *Harvard Business Review*, July-August 1982, pp. 72–79.

Porter, Michael E. *Competitive Advantage*. New York: Free Press, 1985.

Porter, Michael E., and Victor E. Millar. "How Information Gives You Competitive Advantage." *Harvard Business Review*, July-August 1985, pp. 149–160.

Radding, Alan. "Downsizing Without the Fuss." *Computerworld*, November 30, 1992, pp. 81–83.

Schulman, Richard E. "Technology and the Art of Developing a Strategic Plan." *Supermarket Business*, August 1991, pp. 19–20.

Schwartz, John. "The Highway to the Future." *Business Week*, September 7, 1992, pp. 56–57.

Slater, Derek. "IS at Your Service." *Computerworld*, January 20, 1992, pp. 71–73.

Symonds, William C. "Putting PCs where Mainframes Used to Reign." *Business Week*, April 27, 1992, p. 106.

Synnot, W., and W. Gruber. *Information Resource Management*. New York: John Wiley & Sons, 1981.

Szewczak, Edward. "Evaluating the Impacts of Information Technology in Organizational Systems." In Edward Szewczak, Coral Snodgrass, and Mehdi Khosrowpour (eds.), *Management Impacts of Information Technology: Perspectives on Organizational Change and Growth*. Harrisburg, PA: Idea Group, 1991, pp. 25–47.

Tate, Paul. "Risk! The Third Factor." *Datamation*, April 15, 1988, pp. 58–64.

Tom, Paul L. *Managing Information as a Corporate Resource* (2nd Ed.). New York: HarperCollins, 1991.

Wilder, Clinton. "CIOs Not Up to Snuff as Active Business Leaders." *Computerworld*, March 16, 1992, p. 6.

Wilder, Clinton. "Transferred Employees Sue Kodak, DEC." *Computerworld*, March 30, 1992, p. 24.

Wilder, Clinton. "Value Judgment." *Computerworld*, March 2, 1992, pp. 69–70.

Wilder, Clinton. "When the CIO Becomes Expendable." *Computerworld*, February 17, 1992, p. 16ff.

Wiseman, Charles. *Strategic Information Systems*. Homewood, IL: Irwin, 1988.

Wysocki, Robert K., and James Young. *Information Systems: Management Principles in Action*. New York: John Wiley & Sons, 1990.

Yates, Joanne, and Robert I. Benjamin. "The Past and Present as a Window of the Future." In Michael S. Scott (ed.), *The Corporation of the 1990s: Information Technology and Organizational Transformation*. New York: Oxford University Press, 1991.

Ziegler, Bart."IBM Finding Monolithic Structure has been a Drawback." *Savannah News-Press*, September 6, 1992, p. 88.

CHAPTER 19

Ajami, R. "Global Transborder Data Flows: Concerns and Options: *International Journal of Technology Management*, Vol. 9, No. 5 (1991), pp. 589–604.

Alexander, Michael. "Morris Case Impact Slight." *Computerworld*, January 21, 1991, p. 1ff.

Alexander, Michael. "Taking Five Top Technologies into the Future." *Computerworld*, September 30, 1991, p. 20.

Alter, Allen E. "International Affairs." *CIO*, December 1992, pp. 34–42.

Ambrosio, Johanna. "Doing IS By the Books." *Computerworld*, June 29, 1992, pp. 87–88.

Anderson, Julia. "How Technology Brings Blind People into the Workplace." *Harvard Business Review*, March-April 1989, pp. 36 -40.

Barnathan, Joyce, Bruce Einhorn, and Laxmi Nakami. "Asia's High-Tech Quest." *Business Week*, December 7, 1992, pp. 126–135.

Betts, Mitch. "A Mixed Bag for U.S. High Tech." *Computerworld*, September 30, 1990, p. 88.

Betts, Mitch. "Public: Computers Invade Privacy." *Computerworld*, November 23, 1992, p. 12.

Bloombecker, Buck. "Computer Ethics for Cynics." *Computerworld*, February 29, 1988, pp. 17–18.

Booker, Ellis. "IS Roundtable: Technologies of the Future." *Computerworld*, October 19, 1992, p. 28.

Brandt, Richard, Evan I. Schwartz, and Michele Galen. "Bit by Bit, Software Protection is Eroding." *Business Week*, July 20, 1992, pp. 86–87.

Briner, Russell F., and Sidney R. Ewer. "Financial Information Flow and Transborder Restrictions." *Journal of Systems Management*, August 1987, pp. 32–35.

Budney, James N. "Competing in the Global Community." *Telecommunications*, November 1991, pp. 55–58.

Business Week, "Where the Jobs Are," April 27, 1992, pp. 30-32.

Buss, Martin D. J. "Legislative Threat to Transborder Data Flow." *Harvard Business Review*, May-June 1984, pp. 111–118.

Buss, Martin D. J. "Managing International Information Systems." *Harvard Business Review*, May-June 1982, pp. 111–113.

Buss, M., and Lynn M. Salerno. "Common Sense and Computer Security." *Harvard Business Review*, March-April 1984, pp. 112–121.

Byrne, John A. "The Best-Laid Ethics Programs. . . ." *Business Week*, March 9, 1992, pp. 67–68.

Byrne, John A. "Can Ethics be Taught: Harvard Gives It the Old College Try." *Business Week*, April 6, 1992, p. 34.

Caldwell, Bruce. "Factoring in the Future." *InformationWeek*, December 23, 1991, pp. 29–31.

Carlyle, R. E. "The Tomorrow Organization." *Datamation*, February 1, 1990, pp. 22–29.

Carper, William. "Transborder Data Flows in the Information Age: Implications for International Management." *International Journal of Management*, December 1989, pp. 418–425.

Cash, James I., Jr., F. Warren McFarlan, James L. McKenney, and Lynda M. Applegate. *Corporate Information Systems Management: Text and Cases* (3rd Ed.). Homewood, IL: Irwin, 1992.

Clarke, Roger A. "Information Technology and Dataveillance." *Communications of the ACM*, May 1988, pp. 498–512.

The Computerworld IS Pocket Guide for Success. Framingham, MA: CW Publishing, 1992.

Daly, James. "Fingerprinting a Computer Security Code." *Computerworld*, July 27, 1992, p. 25.

Daly, James."Laptop Thefts Spur Security Efforts." *Computerworld*, October 12, 1992, pp. 1, 12.

Daly, James. "Virus Fighters Fume Over Little Black Book." *Computerworld*, June 29, 1992, p. 4.

Davis, Liselotte H. "Business As (Un)Usual." *Computerworld*, December 21, 1992, pp. 55–58.

Deans, P. Candace, and Michael J. Kane. *International Dimensions of Information Systems and Technology*. Boston: PWS-Kent, 1992.

Dejoie, R., G. Fowler, and D. Paradice, *Ethical Issues in Information Systems*. Boston: Boyd & Fraser, 1991.

Dwyer, Kelly E. "The Buck Stops Here." *Computerworld*, September 7, 1992, pp. 85–89.

Ellison, Carol. "On Guard: 20 Utilities that Battle the Virus Threat." *PC Magazine*, October 29, 1991, pp. 199–225.

Frenzel, Carrol. *Management of Information Technology*. Boston: Boyd & Fraser, 1992.

Freund, Mark. "Networking with an Accent." *LAN Technology*, January 1992, pp. 27–30.

Gantz, John. "Cooperative Processing and the Enterprise Network." *Network Management*, January 1991, pp. 25–40.

Gray, Paul, William R. King, Ephraim R. McLean, and Hugh J. Watson (eds.). *MoIS: Management of Information Systems*. Chicago, IL: The Dryden Press, 1989.

Hoffman, Thomas, and Johanna Ambrosio. "Copyright Grip on Source Code Weakened." *Computerworld*, June 29, 1992, p. 1ff.

Janssens, Gerrit K., and Ludo Guyvers. "EDI—A Strategic Weapon in International Trade." *Long Range Planning*, Vol. 24, No. 3 (1991), pp. 46–53.

Kallman, Earnest A., and Sanford Sherizen. "Private Matters." *Computerworld*, November 23, 1992, pp. 85–87.

Kanter, Jerome. *Managing with Information* (4th Ed.). Englewood Cliffs, NJ: Prentice-Hall, 1992.

Keefe, Patricia. "Lessons Learned the Hard Way." *Computerworld Focus*, April 6, 1988, p. 15.

King, Julia. "Lessons from Hell." *Computerworld*, June 29, 1992, pp. 77–80.

Korseniowski, Paul. "How to Avoid Disaster with a Recovery Plan." *Software*, February 1990, pp. 46–55.

LaPlante, Alice. "For the Truly Brave Try Eastern Europe." *Computerworld*, April 13, 1992, p. 81.

LaPlante, Alice. "Is Big Brother Watching?" *InfoWorld*, October 1990.

LaPlante, Alice. "U.S. Companies Find Outsourcing a Sensible Way to Go International." *Computerworld*, April 13, 1992, p. 79.

LaPlante, Alice, and Joseph Maglitta. "Europe Ho!" *Computerworld*, April 13, 1992, pp. 77–78.

Lecht, Charles P. "Future Considerations." *Computerworld*, March 16, 1992, pp. 77–81.

Lewis, Bryan. "Microcomputer Transmitted Disease." *CPA Journal*, January 1992, pp. 75–79.

Lewis, Geoff. "The Coming Sizzle in Computer Stocks." *Business Week*, October 16, 1989, pp. 110–111.

Longworth, R. C. "There's an Economic War Going On and We're Losing It." *Savannah News-Press*, May 31, 1992, pp. 1B, 9B.

Luczak, Mark. "Dramatic Changes in the Network Environment." *Telecommunications*, November 1991, pp. 47–50.

Maglitta, Joseph, and John P. Mello Jr. "The Enemy Within." *Computerworld*, December 7, 1992, pp. 87–89.

Marion, Larry. "The Hot Applications of 1992." *Datamation*, May 1, 1992, pp. 35–54.

Mason, Richard. "Four Ethical Issues of the Information Age." *MIS Quarterly*, March 1986, pp. 5–12.

Mensching, James R., and Dennis A. Adams, *Managing An Information System*. Englewood Cliffs, NJ: Prentice-Hall, 1991.

Minasi, Mark. "Computer Viruses From A to Z." *Compute*, October 1991, pp. 45–49.

Moslehi, Farid. "Reflections on Fault Tolerance." *LAN Technology*, January 1992, pp. 35–42.

Mula, Rose. "Employers Want MIS Degrees." *Computerworld*, March 16, 1987, p. 105.

Naisbitt, John, and Patricia Aburdene. *Ten Directions for the 1990s: Megatrends 2000*. New York: William Morrow & Company, 1990.

Nelson, R. Ryan. "Educational Needs as Perceived by IS and End-User Personnel: A Survey of Knowledge and Skill Requirements." *MIS Quarterly*, December 1991, pp. 503–525.

Neo, Boon Siong. "Information Technology and Global Competition: A Framework for Analysis." *Information and Management*, Spring 1991, pp. 151–160.

Ogilvie, Heather. "Electronic Ties That Bind: Marks & Spencer's Pan-European JIT Inventory System." *The Journal of European Business*, September-October 1991, pp. 48–50.

O'Reilly, Brian. "Business Makes a Run for the Border." *Fortune*, August 18, 1986.

Parker, D., S. Swope and B. Baker. *Ethical Conflicts in Information and Computer Science, Technology, and Business*. Wellesley, MA: QED Information Sciences, Inc., 1990.

Quinn, James Brian, and Penny C. Pacquette. " Technology in Services: Organizational Revolutions." *Sloan Management Review*, Winter 1990, pp. 67–78.

Radding, Alan. "Are You a Corporate Officer or a Consultant?" *Computerworld*, April 13, 1987, pp. 75–77.

Radding, Alan. "The Education of an Expert." *Computerworld*, May 2, 1988, p. 74.

Rebello, Kathy, Michele Galen, and Evan I. Schwartz. "It Looks and Feels as if Apple Lost." *Business Week*, April 27, 1992, p. 36.

Reed, Sandra R. "Technologies for the 90s." *Personal Computing*, January 1990, pp. 66–69.

Runyan, Linda. "40 Years on the Frontier." *Datamation*, March 15, 1991, pp. 34–43.

Runyan, Linda. "Global IS Strategies." *Datamation*, December 1, 1989, pp. 71–78.

Schultz, Ellen. "Worried About Your Financial Life Being Shared?" *The Wall Street Journal*, April 25, 1991, p. 1ff.

Schwartz, Evan I., and Michele Galen. "The Coming Showdown Over Software Patents." *Business Week*, May 13, 1991, pp. 104–106.

Schwartz, John. "The Highway to the Future." *Newsweek*, January 13, 1992, pp. 56–57.

Schwartz, John. "The Next Revolution." *Newsweek*, April 6, 1992, pp. 42–48.

Software Publishers Association. *White Paper: Software Piracy*. Framingham, MA: CW Publishing, 1992.

Steinbart, Paul John, and Ravinder Nath. "Problems and Issues in the Management of International Data Networks: The Experience of American Companies." *MIS Quarterly*, March 1992, pp. 55–76.

Straub, Detmar W. "Effective IS Security: An Empirical Study." *Information Systems Research*, September 1990, pp. 255–276.

Turner, Geoff. "I Spy." *Computerworld*, October 26, 1992, pp. 129–130.

Verity, John W. "Deconstructing the Computer Industry." *Business Week*, November 23, 1992, pp. 90–100.

Wagner, Jennifer L. "Ethical Issues in MIS." *Proceedings of the Association of Management Annual Conference*, Orlando, FL, August 6–12, 1990.

Watson, Richard T., and James C. Brancheau. "Key Issues in Information Systems Management: An International Perspective." *Information and Management*, Spring 1991, pp. 213–223.

Wilde, Candee. "After the Network is Up the Fun Has Just Begun." *Computerworld*, April 13, 1992, p. 81.

Williamson, Mickey. "People Who Need People." *CIO*, November 15, 1992, pp. 48–56.

Winkler, Connie. *Careers in High Tech*. Englewood Cliffs, NJ: Prentice-Hall, 1987.

INDEX

Roles (*continued*)
executive, 464–66
executive information system,
468–70
in groups, 75
management, 127–32
systems development, 599–600
Routers, 369
Rule-based expert systems,
486–*87*
Rules, 486

Salami technique, 810
Sales forecasting, 569–70
Satellite communications, 349
Scale of development, 625–26
Scavenging techniques, 812–13
Scenario approaches, 150, 772
Scheduled reports, 423
Scheduling, 700–703, 735–36
Secondary keys, 299–301
Secondary storage, 22, 194–206
Security, 315–16, 347, 677–79,
806–19, 825
Self-study training, 713
Seminars, 830
Semistructured decisions, 143–44,
433–34
Sequential access, 194–95, 291
Sequential organization, 293–94
Serial organization, 291–92
Serial transmission, 354–56
Service bureaus, 694
Shipping systems, 411–12
Signals, media, 351–57
Site licensing agreements, 269
Skills, 42–45
Smart card systems, 174–76, 187
Software, 20, 22, 150
application (*see* Application
software; Programs)
bug-free, 726–27
copyright protection, 836
decision support, 438–39
engineering, 264
file management, 23, 247, 282,
289–90
groupware, 480, 527, 534–35
integrated office, 540–43
leasing, 686–87
local area network, 372–73
maintenance, 720–22
management issues, 266–69
office support, 534–37

piracy, 814
programming languages,
249–66
re-engineering, 716
system design issues, 658–75
systems, 226–44, 673
vendors, 692–94
wide area network, 369
Software development life cycle,
663–66
Software piracy, 814
Solid-font printers, 211
Solution evaluation/choice,
150–51
Solvability, 624–25
Sort utilities, 242
Source data automation, 172
Span of control, 73
Specialists with advanced tools
(SWAT) teams, 616
Specific DSS, 451
Specific models, 86
Spooling software, 242–44
Spreadsheets, 246–47, 454
Staff positions, 62–64, 513
Stages-of-growth (SOG) curves,
123–26
Standard operating procedures
(SOP), 102
Standards, 346, 747, 835–37
Star networks, 359
Statistical process control (SPC),
109–11
Statistical quality control (SQC),
109–11
Statistical tools, 444–46
Steering committees, 785
Storage
archival, 514, 524–25
devices, 22, 194–206
requirements, 675–76
volume, 676
Strategic alliances, 341–43
Strategic impact, 623, 636–39
Strategic planning, 8–9, 25–26,
464, 469, 558, 570–71. *See also*
Competitive advantage
information centers, 749
MIS, 104–5, 763–77
models, 97–105
telecommunications, 336–43
upper-level management and,
119–20
Strategies, 101–2

Structure, organizational, 56–59
Structure charts, 88–90, 670, *671*
Structured analysis, 632
Structured decisions, 143–44, 433
Structured design, 667
Structured programming, 667
Structured Query Language
(SQL), 312–14
Styles, management, 126–27,
134–37, 148
Supercomputers, 191
Supermicrocomputers, 187–88
Superzap programs, 810
Suppliers, 94, 690–700
Switching, 360–62
Symptoms versus problems, 624
Synchronous transmission,
356–57
System clock, 179
System conversion, 714–16
System design
processing requirements,
658–75
reports to management, 680
requirements review, 648–49
storage requirements, 675–76
system inputs, 655–58
system models, 649–51
system outputs, 651–55
system personnel requirements,
679–80
system procedures, 676–79
System elements, 82
System implementation, 700–16
System Network Architecture
(SNA), 365
Systems, 82–86
development (*see* Systems
development)
documentation, 640
flowcharts, 633, *634*, *635*
integration, 55–56
models of, 86–94, 649–51
organizational (*see*
Organizations)
Systems analysts, 21, 67, 94
Systems development
approaches to, 602–18
decision support systems,
449–57
documentation, 639–41
end-user, 71, 609–12, 731 (*see
also* End-user computing (EUC))
expert systems, 493–96